THE WESTERN HERITAGE

EIGHTH EDITION

SINCE 1300

Donald Kagan
Yale University

Steven Ozment
Harvard University

Frank M. Turner
Yale University

PEARSON

Prentice
Hall

Upper Saddle River, New Jersey 07458

Library of Congress Cataloging-in-Publication Data

Kagan, Donald
    The Western Heritage / Donald Kagan, Steven Ozment, Frank M. Turner.—
    8th ed.
        p. cm.
    "Combined volume."
    Includes bibliographical references and index.
    ISBN 0-13-182839-8
    1. Civilization, Western. I. Ozment, Steven E. II. Turner, Frank M. (Frank Miller), 1944-III. Title.
  CB245.K28 2003
  909'.09821-dc21   2002044567

Editorial Director: Charlyce Jones Owen
Senior Acquisitions Editor: Charles Cavaliere
Associate Editor: Emsal Hasan
Editor-in-Chief, Development: Rochelle Diogenes
Development Editors: David Chodoff
  and Gerald Lombardi
Director of Production and Manufacturing:
  Barbara Kittle
Production Editor: Louise Rothman
Prepress and Manufacturing Manager:
  Nick Sklitsis
Prepress and Manufacturing Buyer: Sherry Lewis

Creative Design Director: Leslie Osher
Art Director: Kathryn Foot
Interior and Cover Designer: Jill Lehan
Manager: Production, Formatting and Art:
  Guy Ruggiero
Cartographer: CartoGraphics
Electronic Artist: Maria Piper
Director, Image Resource Center: Melinda Reo
Interior Image Specialist: Beth Boyd Brenzel
Cover Image Specialist: Karen Sanatar
Image Permission Coordinator: Charles Morris
Photo Researcher: Diana Gongora

Cover Art: Jan van Eyck (c. 1390-1441), *The Portrait of Giovanni Arnolfini and his Wife Giovanna
Cenami*. The Arnolfini Marriage, 1434 (oil on panel). National Gallery, London, UK/
Bridgeman Art Library

This book was set in 10/12 Trump Mediaeval by Lithokraft
and was printed and bound by RR Donnelley—Willard.
The cover was printed by Phoenix Color Corp.

TIME LINE PHOTO CREDITS:

Time Line 1: page 0, (left) Gary Cralle/The Image Bank; (right) Winfield I. Parks Jr./National Geographic Image Collection; page 1, The Granger Collection; page 2, Battle of Alexander the Great at Issus. Roman mosaic. Museo Archeologico Nazionale, Naples, Italy. Scala/ Art Resource; p. 3, Robert Frerck/Woodfin Camp & Associates.

Time Line 2: page 192, Marvin Trachtenberg; page 193, Bayeus, Musée de l'Eveche. "With special authorization of the City of Bayeaux." Giraudon/Art Resource.

Time Line 3: page 288, Elizabeth I, Armada Portrait, c. 1588 (oil on panel) by George Gower (1540-96) (attr. to). Woburn Abbey, Bedfordshire, UK/Bridgeman Art Library, London/New York; p. 289, The Granger Collection.

Time Line 4: page 586, Philosopher, dramatist, poet, historian, and populizer of scientific ideas, Voltaire (1694-1778). Bildarchiv Preussischer Kulterbesitz; page 587, By Permission of Musée de la Legion d'Honneur.

Time Line 5: page 778, Corbis; page 779, The Bridgeman Art Library International.

Time Line 6: page 994, (left) Hulton Getty/Archive Photos; (right) Franklin D. Roosevelt Library; page 995, (left) Corbis Sygma Photo News; (right, top) John Launois/Black Star; (right, bottom) Reuters/Natalie Behring/Archive Photos

BRIEF CONTENTS

CONTENTS

PART 2   THE MIDDLE AGES, 476–1300 — 192

PART 5   TOWARD THE MODERN WORLD   778

Documents

Maps

Encountering the Past

Art & the West

The West & the World

PREFACE

The heritage of Western civilization is a major point of departure for understanding the twenty-first century. The unprecedented globalization of daily life that is a hallmark of our era has occurred in large measure through the spread of Western technological, economic, and political influences. From the sixteenth century onwards, the West has exerted vast influences throughout the globe for both good and ill, and today's global citizens live in the wake of that impact. It is the goal of this book to introduce its readers to the Western heritage, so that they may be better informed and more culturally sensitive citizens of the emerging global age.

The attacks upon the mainland of the United States on September 11, 2001 and the events that have succeeded those attacks have concentrated the attention of teachers, students, and informed citizens upon the heritage and future of Western civilization as have no other events since the end of World War II. Whereas previously commentary about global civilization involved analysis of the spread of Western economic, technological, and political influences, such commentary now requires us to explain how the West has defined itself over many centuries and to think about how the West will articulate its core values as it confronts new and daunting challenges.

Twenty years ago, the West defined itself mainly in terms of the East-West tensions associated with the Cold War. The West is now in the process of defining itself in terms of global rivalries arising from conflict with political groups that are not identical with nation states and that define themselves in terms of opposition to what they understand the West to be. We have thus entered a new era in which citizens of the West need to understand how their culture, values, economy, and political outlooks have emerged. They cannot leave it to those who would attack the West to define Western civilization or to articulate its values.

Since *The Western Heritage* first appeared, we have sought to provide our readers with a work that does justice to the richness and variety of Western civilization. We hope that such an understanding of the West will foster lively debate about its character, values, institutions, and global influence. Indeed, we believe such a critical outlook on their own culture has characterized the peoples of the West since its earliest history. Through such debates we define ourselves and the values of our culture. Consequently, we welcome the debate and hope that *The Western Heritage*, eighth edition, can help foster a genuinely informed discussion through its overview of Western civilization, the West's strengths and weaknesses, and the controversies surrounding Western history.

Human beings make, experience, and record their history. In this edition as in past editions, our goal has been to present Western civilization fairly, accurately, and in a way that does justice to its great variety of human enterprise. History has many facets, no one of which alone can account for the others. Any attempt to tell the story of the West from a single overarching perspective, no matter how timely, is bound to neglect or suppress some important parts of that story. Like all authors of introductory texts, we have had to make choices, but we have attempted to provide the broadest possible introduction to Western civilization. To that end we hope that the many documents included in this book will allow the widest possible spectrum of people to give personal voice to their experiences over the centuries and will enable our readers to share that experience.

We also believe that any book addressing the experience of the West must also look beyond its historical European borders. Students reading this book come from a wide variety of cultures and experiences. They live in a world of highly interconnected economies and instant communication between cultures. In this emerging multicultural society it seems both appropriate and necessary to recognize how Western civilization has throughout its history interacted with other cultures, both influencing and being influenced by them. Examples of this two-way interaction, such as that with Islam, appear throughout the text. To further highlight the theme of cultural interaction, *The Western Heritage* includes a series of comparative essays, The West & the World. (For a fuller description, see below.)

Goals of the Text

Our primary goal has been to present a strong, clear, narrative account of the central developments in Western history. We have also sought to call attention to certain critical themes:

- The capacity of Western civilization from the time of the Greeks to the present to transform itself through self-criticism.
- The development in the West of political freedom, constitutional government, and concern for the rule of law and individual rights.
- The shifting relations among religion, society, and the state.
- The development of science and technology and their expanding impact on Western thought, social institutions, and everyday life.
- The major religious and intellectual currents that have shaped Western culture.

We believe that these themes have been fundamental in Western civilization, shaping the past and exerting a continuing influence on the present.

Flexible Presentation *The Western Heritage,* eighth edition, is designed to accommodate a variety of approaches to a course in Western civilization, allowing teachers to stress what is most important to them. Some teachers will ask students to read all the chapters. Others will select among them to reinforce assigned readings and lectures.

Integrated Social, Cultural, and Political History *The Western Heritage* provides one of the richest accounts of the social history of the West available today, with strong coverage of family life, the changing roles of women, and the place of the family in relation to broader economic, political, and social developments. This coverage reflects the explosive growth in social historical research in the past three decades, which has enriched virtually all areas of historical study. In this edition we have again expanded both the breadth and depth of our coverage of social history through revisions of existing chapters, the addition of major new material and a new feature, Encountering the Past (see following), and the inclusion of new documents.

While strongly believing in the study of the social experience of the West, we also share the conviction that internal and external political events have shaped the Western experience in fundamental and powerful ways. The experiences of Europeans in the twentieth century under fascism, national socialism, and communism demonstrate that influence, as has, more recently, the collapse of communism in the former Soviet Union and eastern Europe. We have also been told repeatedly by teachers that no matter what their own historical specialization, they believe that a political narrative gives students an effective tool to begin to understand the past. Consequently, we have

sought to integrate the political with the social, cultural, and intellectual.

No other survey text presents so full an account of the religious and intellectual development of the West. People may be political and social beings, but they are also reasoning and spiritual beings. What they think and believe are among the most important things we can know about them. Their ideas about God, society, law, gender, human nature, and the physical world have changed over the centuries and continue to change. We cannot fully grasp our own approach to the world without understanding the intellectual currents of the past and how they influenced our thoughts and conceptual categories.

Clarity and Accessibility Good narrative history requires clear, vigorous prose. As in earlier editions, we have paid careful attention to our writing, subjecting every paragraph to critical scrutiny. Our goal was to make the history of the West accessible to students without compromising vocabulary or conceptual level. We hope this effort will benefit both teachers and students.

The Eighth Edition

Encountering the Past As an important new feature of the eighth edition, each chapter now includes an essay on a significant issue of everyday life or popular culture. These essays explore a variety of subjects from ancient athletics and religious festivals to medieval games and diets to attitudes toward bathing and smoking in early modern Europe to the politics of rock music in the late twentieth century. These thirty-one essays, each of which includes an illustration and study questions, expand *The Western Heritage's* rich coverage of social history. (See p. xxiii for a complete list of the Encountering the Past essays.)

Art & The West In every chapter we highlight a work of art or architecture and discuss how it illuminates and reflects the artistic heritage of the West and the period in which the work was created. In Chapter 5, for example, a portrait of a young woman on the wall of a house in Pompeii and the accompanying essay provide a glimpse into the life of well-to-do women in the Roman Empire (p. 185). In Chapter 11, the discussion of Lucas Cranach's wedding portraits of Martin Luther and his wife Katherine von Bora sheds light on a remarkable marriage in the age of the Reformation (p. 387). In Chapter 16, paintings by Jean Baptiste Chardin and Elizabeth Vigée-Lebrun illustrate domestic life and gender roles in eighteenth-century

France (p. 548). In Chapters 30 and 31, paintings by the Soviet realist Tatjiana Yablonskaya and Jackson Pollock (pp. 1082–1083) and contemporary works by the British sculptor Rachel Whiteread (p. 1114) offer starkly contrasting comments on twentieth-century culture. Each essay includes questions for study and discussion. (See p. xxiv for a complete list of Art & The West essays.)

The West & The World In this feature, we focus on six subjects that compare Western institutions with those of other parts of the world, or discuss how developments in the West have influenced other cultures. In the eighth edition, the essays are:

Part 1: Ancient Warfare (p. 186)
Part 2: The Invention of Printing in China and Europe (p. 284)
Part 3: The Columbian Exchange (p. 582)
Part 4: The Abolition of Slavery in the Transatlantic Economy (p. 736)
Part 5: Imperialism: Ancient and Modern (p. 926)
Part 6: Energy and the Modern World (p. 1116)

Recent Scholarship As in previous editions, changes in this edition reflect our determination to incorporate the most recent developments in historical scholarship and the concerns of professional historians. Of particular interest are expanded discussions of:

- **Women in the history of the West**. Adding to our longstanding commitment to including the experience of women in Western civilization, this edition emphasizes new scholarship on women in the ancient world and the Middle Ages, during the scientific and industrial revolutions, and under the authoritarian governments of the twentieth century. (See, especially, Chapters 3, 4, 5, 7, 14, 24, 27, and 28.) The eighth edition also gives new prominence to women's contribution to the arts. The Art & the West essays in Chapters 12 (Artemisia Gentileschi), 15 (Rachel Ruysch), 16 (Elizabeth Vigee-Lebrun), 24 (Elizabeth Thompson, Lady Butler), 30 (Tatiana Yablonskaya), and 31 (Rachel Whiteread) discuss work by women artists whose paintings and sculpture have enriched Western culture and illuminated the role of women in it.
- **Islam and the West**. Among the most important and extensive new features of the eighth edition are a series of new sections on the interactions between the Islamic world and the West. Beginning with the discussion of the rise of Islam, this edition includes sections on the history of the Ottoman Empire, Islam and the European Enlightenment, Islam and the Romantic Movement, Islam in late nineteenth-century European thought, French decolonization in Algeria, Islamic immigration in twentieth-century Europe, and the rise of political Islamism in the contemporary world. Taken together these sections provide significant coverage of the Islamic world's relationship with the West.
- **Africa and the transatlantic economy**. An extensive section in Chapter 17 explores the relationship of Africa to the transatlantic economy of the sixteenth through eighteenth centuries. We examine the role of African society and politics in the slave trade, the experience of Africans forcibly transported to the Americas, and the incorporation of elements of African culture into the New World.
- **Russia under Peter the Great**. The section in Chapter 15 on the entry of Russia into European affairs and the role of Peter the Great has been substantially revised.
- **The Crimean War**. The discussion of this important conflict in Chapter 23 has been reshaped to highlight its impact on the Ottoman Empire and the rivalries of the European Great Powers in the Middle East.
- **The twentieth century**. We have made significant, clarifying organizational changes in the chapters on the twentieth century to help instructors teach this complicated era and to make the topic easier for their students to understand. Instructors will now be able to teach both the social and political histories of the twentieth century within the same chapters. The sections on the experiences of women under Communism, Fascism, and Nazism are now incorporated in the discussions of those political movements in Chapters 27 and 28. Chapter 27 now also includes the social history of the Soviet Union under Stalin. The entire coverage of the Holocaust and the destruction of Polish Jewry has been placed in Chapter 29, so that their relationship to World War II and Nazi ideology and foreign policy is clear.

CHAPTER-BY-CHAPTER REVISIONS

Chapter 15 contains a significant account of the rise and decline of the Ottoman Empire and of why the empire failed to counter Western military, technological, and economic power. The chapter also includes a revised account based on recent scholarship of the growth of Russian power under Peter the Great.

Chapter 18 discusses European thinking about the Islamic world in the seventeenth and eighteenth centuries and Islam's influence on the European Enlightenment.

Chapter 20 adds a section on Islam to its discussion of the Romantic Movement.

Chapter 22 expands the coverage of the Crimean War to discuss its effects on the Ottoman Empire, including the empire's attempts to reform itself along Western lines, and Western involvement in the Near East.

Chapter 25 discusses the challenges that modern Western thought presented to the Islamic world and how Islamic thinkers reacted to those ideas.

Chapter 26 has a new section on the end of the Ottoman Empire and more material on the extent of the casualties suffered by the belligerents during World War I.

Chapter 27 has been reorganized to include Soviet social history under Stalin and the experiences of women under Communism and Italian Fascism.

Chapter 28 now includes a discussion of the lives of women in Nazi Germany.

Chapter 29 incorporates the entire discussion of the Holocaust and the destruction of Polish Jewry in World War II.

Chapter 30 includes a major section on France's withdrawal from its colonial empire and the end of French rule in Algeria as well as new material on Gandhi and decolonization in India.

Chapter 31 has been thoroughly revised to focus on European social history during the last fifty years. It includes major new sections on the effects of Islamic immigration to Western Europe and on how the growth of anti-Western attitudes among Islamic populations in Europe and the Near East has presented the West with new challenges.

Maps and Illustrations To help students understand the relationship between geography and history, approximately one-half of the maps include relief features. New to the eighth edition, up to two maps in each chapter feature interactive exercises on the Companion Website that accompanies the text. All 93 maps have been carefully edited for accuracy. The text also contains close to 500 color and black and white illustrations, approximately half of which are new to the eighth edition.

Pedagogical Features This edition retains the pedagogical features of the previous edition, including part-opening comparative timelines, a list of key topics at the beginning of each chapter, chapter review questions, and questions accompanying the

more than 200 source documents in the text. It also adds two new pedagogical aids: the Art & the West essays now include questions, and there are 36 Map Explorations that appear in interactive form on the book's Companion Website. Each of these features is designed to make the text more accessible to students and to reinforce key concepts.

- **Illustrated timelines** open each of the six parts of the book summarizing, side-by-side, the major events in politics and government, society and economy, and religion and culture.
- **Primary-source documents**, more than one third new to this edition, acquaint students with the raw material of history and provide intimate contact with the people of the past and their concerns. Questions accompanying the source documents direct students toward important, thought-provoking issues and help them relate the documents to the material in the text. They can be used to stimulate class discussion or as topics for essays and study groups. In addition, over 200 primary-source documents, with accompanying questions, are found on the Documents in Western Civilization CD-ROM included with all new copies of the text.
- Each chapter includes an **outline**, a list of **key topics**, and an **introduction**. Together these features provide a succinct overview of each chapter.
- **Chronologies** follow each major section in a chapter, listing significant events and their dates.
- **In Perspective** sections summarize the major themes of each chapter and provide a bridge to the next chapter.
- **Chapter review questions** help students review the material in a chapter and relate it to broader themes. They too can be used for class discussion and essay topics.
- **Suggested readings lists** following each chapter have been updated with new titles reflecting recent scholarship.
- **Map Explorations,** new to the eighth edition, prompt students to engage with maps in an interactive fashion. Each Map Exploration is found on the Companion Website for the text.

A Note on Dates and Transliterations This edition of *The Western Heritage* continues the practice of using B.C.E. (before the common era) and C.E. (common era) instead of B.C. (before Christ) and A.D. (anno domini, the year of the Lord) to designate dates. We also follow the most accurate currently accepted English transliterations of Arabic words. For example, today Koran is being replaced by the more accurate Qur'an; similarly Muhammad is preferable to Mohammed and Muslim to Moslem.

Ancillary Instructional Materials

The ancillary instructional materials that accompany *The Western Heritage* include print and multimedia supplements that are designed to reinforce and enliven the richness of the past and inspire students with the excitement of studying the history of Western civilization.

PRINT SUPPLEMENTS FOR THE INSTRUCTOR

Instructor's Manual The Instructor's Manual contains chapter summaries, key points and vital concepts, and information on audio-visual resources that can be used in developing and preparing lecture presentations.

Test-Item File The Test-Item File includes 1500 multiple-choice, identification, map, and essay test questions.

Prentice Hall Custom Test This commercial-quality computerized test management program, for Windows and Macintosh environments, allows users to create their own tests using items from the printed Test Item File. The program allows users to edit the items in the Test Item File and to add their own questions. Online testing is also available.

Transparency Package This collection of full-color transparency acetates provides the maps, charts, and graphs from the text for use in classroom presentations.

Administrative Handbook by Jay Boggis provides instructors with resources for using *The Western Heritage* with the Annenberg/CPB telecourse, The Western Tradition.

PRINT SUPPLEMENTS FOR THE STUDENT

Practice Tests, Volumes I and II The Practice Tests include commentaries, definitions, and a variety of exercises designed to reinforce the concepts in the chapter. Practice Tests are free when packed with *The Western Heritage.*

Documents Set, Volumes I and II This carefully selected and edited set of documents provides over 200 additional primary source readings. Each document includes a brief introduction as well as

questions to encourage critical analysis of the reading and to relate it to the content of the text.

Lives and Legacies: Biographies in Western Civilization This new, two-volume collection provides brief, focused biographies of 60 people, both celebrated and uncelebrated, whose lives provide insight into the heritage of Western Civilization. Each biography includes an introduction, pre-reading questions, and suggested readings. Free when bundled with the text.

 Penguin Classics Prentice Hall is pleased to provide students significant discounts when copies of *The Western Heritage* are purchased together with titles from the acclaimed Penguin Classics series in Western civilization. Contact your Prentice Hall representative for details.

MapNotes This brief workbook gives students the opportunity to increase their knowledge of geography through identification and other map exercises. It is available free to students when shrink-wrapped with the text.

Historical Atlas of the World This four-color historical atlas provides additional map resources to reinforce concepts in the text

Understanding and Answering Essay Questions This brief guide suggests helpful study techniques as well as specific analytical tools for understanding different types of essay questions and provides precise guidelines for preparing well-crafted essay answers. This guide is available free to students when shrink-wrapped with the text.

Reading Critically about History: A Guide to Active Reading This guide focuses on the skills needed to learn the essential information presented in college history textbooks. Material covered includes vocabulary skills, recognizing organizational patterns, critical thinking skills, understanding visual aids, and practice sections. This guide is available free to students when shrink-wrapped with the text.

Telecourse Study Guide, Volumes I and II by Jay Boggis correlates *The Western Heritage* with the Annenberg/CPB telecourse, The Western Tradition.

MULTIMEDIA SUPPLEMENTS

 Companion Website™ A powerful study tool. The Companion Website™ for *The Western Heritage* is organized by the main subtopics in each chapter of the text. It includes study questions, map labeling exercises, interactive maps, related links, and document-based exercises. A faculty module provides material from the Instructor's Manual and the maps and charts from the text in Powerpoint™ format.

Documents in Western Civilization CD-ROM
Included with every new copy of *The Western Heritage*, the new Documents in Western Civilization CD-ROM offers over 200 primary sources central to the history of Western Civilization in easy-to-navigate PDF files. Students can address the problems raised in each document by answering analytical questions located at the end of each primary source and e-mailing their responses directly to their instructors. The end of each chapter in *The Western Heritage* includes a list of pertinent documents from the CD-ROM.

Evaluating Online Resources, 2003 Edition This brief guide focuses on developing the critical thinking skills necessary to evaluate and use online sources. It provides a brief introduction to navigating the Internet with comprehensive references to History web sites. It also provides an access code and instruction on using Research Navigator, a powerful research tool that streamlines and simplifies the research process by providing three exclusive databases of reliable source material: ContentSelect Academic Journal Database, *The New York Times* Search by Subject Archive, and Link Library. This supplementary book is free to students with the purchase of the textbook.

Course Management Systems For instructors interested in distance learning, Prentice Hall offers fully customizable, online courses with enhanced content, online testing, and many other course management features using the best available course management systems available, including WebCT, Blackboard, and CourseCompass. Contact your local Prentice Hall representative or visit our special Demonstration Central Website at http://www.prenhall.com/demo for more information.

Acknowledgments

We are grateful to the scholars and teachers whose thoughtful and often detailed comments helped shape this revision:

Magnus T. Bernhardsson, Hofstra University
Patricia Conroy, Torrington High School
Miriam Levy, Central Connecticut State University
Gary Johnson, University of Southern Maine
Kenneth Margerison, Southwestern Texas State University
David B. Mock, Tallahassee Community College
Jonathan S. Perry, University of Central Florida
Norman G. Raiford, Greenville Technical College
Larissa Taylor, Colby College
William B. Whisenhunt, College of DuPage
Andrew Wilson, Keene State College
Jonathan W. Zophy, University of Houston, Clear Lake

Steven Ozment would like to acknowledge the help of Adam Beaver and Elizabeth Russell. Frank Turner would like to acknowledge the aid of Magnus T. Bernhardsson. Finally, we would like to thank the dedicated people who helped produce this revision. Our acquisitions editor, Charles Cavaliere; our development editors, David Chodoff and Gerald Lombardi; Robert Lombardi for his help with the questions for the Art and the West features; our production editor, Louise Rothman; Jill Lehan, who created the handsome new design of this edition; Sherry Lewis, our manufacturing buyer; and Diana Gongora, photo researcher.

D.K.
S.O.
F.M.T.

About the Authors

DONALD KAGAN is Sterling Professor of History and Classics at Yale University, where he has taught since 1969. He received the A.B. degree in history from Brooklyn College, the M.A. in classics from Brown University, and the Ph.D. in history from Ohio State University. During 1958–1959 he studied at the American School of Classical Studies as a Fulbright Scholar. He has received three awards for undergraduate teaching at Cornell and Yale. He is the author of a history of Greek political thought, *The Great Dialogue* (1965); a four-volume history of the Peloponnesian war, *The Origins of the Peloponnesian War* (1969); *The Archidamian War* (1974); *The Peace of Nicias and the Sicilian Expedition* (1981); *The Fall of the Athenian Empire* (1987); and a biography of Pericles, *Pericles of Athens and the Birth of Democracy* (1991); *On the Origins of War* (1995), and *The Peloponnesian War* (2003). He is coauthor, with Frederick W. Kagan, of *While America Sleeps* (2000). With Brian Tierney and L. Pearce Williams, he is the editor of *Great Issues in Western Civilization*, a collection of readings. He was awarded the National Humanities Medal for 2002.

STEVEN OZMENT is McLean Professor of Ancient and Modern History at Harvard University. He has taught Western Civilization at Yale, Stanford, and Harvard. He is the author of nine books. *The Age of Reform, 1250-1550* (1980) won the Schaff Prize and was nominated for the 1981 National Book Award. Five of his books have been selections of the History Book Club: *Magdalena and Balthasar: An Intimate Portrait of Life in Sixteenth Century Europe* (1986), *Three Behaim Boys: Growing Up in Early Modern Germany* (1990), *Protestants: The Birth of a Revolution* (1992), *The Burgermeister's Daughter: Scandal in a Sixteenth Century German Town* (1996), and *Flesh and Spirit: Private Life in Early Modern Germany* (1999). His most recent book is *Ancestors: The Loving Family of Old Europe* (2001). A history of Germany, *A Mighty Fortress: A New History of the German People*, will be published in January 2004.

FRANK M. TURNER is John Hay Whitney Professor of History at Yale University, where he served as University Provost from 1988 to 1992. He received his B.A. degree at the College of William and Mary and his Ph.D. from Yale. He has received the Yale College Award for Distinguished Undergraduate Teaching. He has directed a National Endowment for the Humanities Summer Institute. His scholarly research has received the support of fellowships from the National Endowment for the Humanities and the Guggenheim Foundation and the Woodrow Wilson Center. He is the author of *Between Science and Religion: The Reaction to Scientific Naturalism in Late Victorian England* (1974), *The Greek Heritage in Victorian Britain* (1981), which received the British Council Prize of the Conference on British Studies and the Yale Press Governors Award, *Contesting Cultural Authority: Essays in Victorian Intellectual Life* (1993), and *John Henry Newman: The Challenge to Evangelical Religion* (2002). He has also contributed numerous articles to journals and has served on the editorial advisory boards of *The Journal of Modern History, Isis,* and *Victorian Studies.* He edited *The Idea of a University,* by John Henry Newman (1996). Since 1996 he has served as a Trustee of Connecticut College.

This limestone statue depicts the head of Queen Nefertiti (about 1348–1345 B.C.E.), wife of the rebel pharaoh Akhenaten of the Eighteenth Egyptian Dynasty in the period of the New Kingdom. It was discovered at the modern site called Tell el-Amarna, the ancient city of Akhetaten founded by the pharaoh as his new capital and the center of the new worship of Aten, the disc of the sun. The queen appears to have had unusual importance, serving, along with the pharaoh, as one of the only mediators between the god and the people.   Gary Cralle/The Image Bank

THE WEST BEFORE 1300

*H*ISTORY, *IN ITS TWO SENSES—as the events of the past that make up the human experience on earth and as the written record of those events—is a subject of both interest and importance. We naturally want to know how we came to be who we are and how the world we live in came to be what it is. But beyond its intrinsic interest, history provides crucial insight into present human behavior. To understand who we are now, we need to know the record of the past and to try to understand the people and forces that shaped it.*

For hundreds of thousands of years after the human species emerged, people lived by hunting, fishing, and collecting wild plants. Only some 10,000 years ago did they learn to cultivate plants, herd animals, and make airtight pottery for storage. These discoveries transformed them from gatherers to producers and allowed them to grow in number and to lead a settled life. About 5,000 years ago humans learned how to control the waters of great river valleys, making possible much richer harvests and supporting a further increase in population. The peoples of these river valley societies created the earliest civilizations. They invented writing, which, among other things, enabled them to keep inventories of food and other resources. They discovered the secret of smelting metal to make tools and weapons of bronze far superior to the stone implements of earlier times. They came together in towns and cities, where industry and commerce flourished. Complex religions took form, and social divisions increased. Kings—considered to be representatives of the gods or to be themselves divine—emerged as rulers, assisted by priests and defended by well-organized armies.

Early Humans and Their Culture

**Early Civilizations
to about 1000 B.C.E.**

The Greeks

Rome

**Europe Enters
the Middle Ages**

**Church and State
in the High Middle Ages**

In Perspective

KEY TOPICS

- The earliest history of humanity, including the beginnings of human culture in the Paleolithic Age, the agricultural revolution and the shift from food gathering to food production, and the emergence of civilization in the great river valleys of the Near East and Asia
- The ancient civilizations of Mesopotamia and Egypt
- The great Near Eastern empires, 1500–539 B.C.E.
- The emergence of Judaism
- The difference in outlook between ancient Near Eastern civilization and ancient Greek civilization

Early Humans and Their Culture

Scientists estimate that the earth may be as many as six billion years old and that creatures very much like humans may have appeared three to five million years ago. Our own species, **Homo sapiens,** probably emerged some 200,000 years ago, and the earliest remains of fully modern humans date to about 90,000 years ago.

Humans, unlike other animals, are cultural beings. **Culture** may be defined as the ways of living built up by a group and passed on from one generation to another. It includes behavior, material things, ideas, institutions, and beliefs.

THE PALEOLITHIC AGE

During the earliest period in human experience, the Paleolithic (from Greek, "old stone") Age, which lasted from the earliest use of stone tools some 1,000,000 years ago to about 10,000 B.C.E., people were hunters, fishers, and gatherers, but not producers, of food. They learned to make and use increasingly sophisticated tools of stone and of perishable materials like wood; they learned to make and control fire; and they acquired language and the ability to use it to pass on what they learned. Evidence of Paleolithic culture has been found in Europe, Asia, and Africa.

Evidence suggests human life in the Paleolithic Age was probably characterized by a division of labor by sex. The men engaged in hunting, fishing, making tools and weapons, and fighting against other families, clans, and tribes. The women, less mobile because of childbearing, gathered nuts, berries, and wild grains, wove baskets, and made clothing. Women gathering food probably discovered how to plant and care for seeds. This knowledge eventually made possible the coming of the Age of Agriculture—the Neolithic revolution.

THE NEOLITHIC AGE

Some 10,000 years ago, parts of what we now call the Middle East began to shift from a hunter-gatherer culture to a settled agricultural one. Because the shift to agriculture coincided with advances in stone tool technology, this period is called the Neolithic (from Greek, "new stone") Age. The important invention of pottery made it possible to store surplus liquid and dry foods. Cloth came to be made from flax and wool.

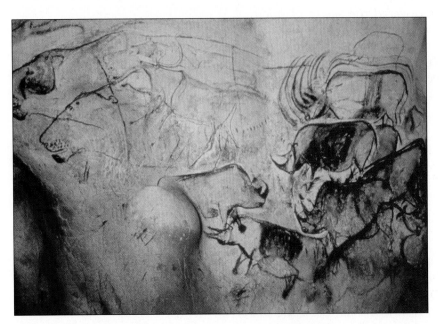

In Chauvet cave, near Avignon, France, Paleolithic artists decorated the walls with exquisite drawings of animals. Jean Clottes/Corbis Sygma Photo News

Crops required constant care from planting to harvest, and so the Neolithic people built permanent buildings, usually in clusters near the best fields.

Neolithic agricultural villages and herding cultures gradually replaced Paleolithic culture in much of the world. Then, beginning first about 4,000 years before the Christian era in the valley of the Tigris and Euphrates rivers in the region called Mesopotamia (modern Iraq), later in the valley of the Nile River in Egypt, and somewhat later still in the Indus Valley in India and the Yellow River basin in China, another major shift occurred. This shift was marked by the appearance of urban centers, the mastery of smelting and with it the techniques for making metal tools and weapons, and the invention of writing. These traits—urbanism, metallurgy, and writing—are defining characteristics of the form of human culture called *civilization*. At about the time the earliest civilizations were emerging, someone discovered how to smelt tin and copper to make a stronger and more useful material—bronze. The importance of this technological development is reflected in the term **Bronze Age.**

Early Civilizations to about 1000 B.C.E.

MESOPOTAMIAN CIVILIZATION

The first civilization appears to have arisen in the valley of the Tigris and Euphrates rivers, the area the Greeks and the Romans called Mesopotamia, where the rich alluvial plains made possible the production of unprecedented food surpluses (see Map I–1). Its founders, the Sumerians, controlled the southern part of the valley (Sumer) close to the head of the Persian Gulf by the dawn of history, around

This statue of Gudea, city ruler of Lagash after the fall of the Akkadian empire, shows him as a pious Sumerian ruler. It was carved of very hard imported black stone. A brief historical inscription is visible on his cloak. Gudea built a major temple to a local deity at Lagash, Ningirsu, and describes the work, step by step, in one of the longest Sumerian poems known today.
Gudea. Statue from Telloh. 2140 B.C.E. Iraq Museum. Baghdad, Iraq. Copyright Scala/Art Resource, NY

Key Events and People in Mesopotamian History	
ca. 3500 B.C.E.	Development of Sumerian cities, especially Uruk
ca. 2800–2370 B.C.E.	Early Dynastic period of Sumerian city-states
ca. 2370 B.C.E.	Sargon establishes Akkadian dynasty and empire
ca. 2125–2027 B.C.E.	Third Dynasty of Ur
ca. 2000–1800 B.C.E.	Establishment of Amorites in Mesopotamia
ca. 1792–1750 B.C.E.	Reign of Hammurabi
ca. 1550 B.C.E.	Establishment of Kassite Dynasty at Babylon

3000 B.C.E. While the Sumerians were fighting with their neighbors and among themselves for supremacy in the south, immediately upstream from them a people speaking a Semitic language (that is, a language in the same family as Arabic and Hebrew) established themselves. Making their capital at Akkad, near a later city known to us as Babylon, they soon absorbed Sumerian culture.

Despite a brief Sumerian resurgence about 2100 B.C.E., internal dissensions and an invasion by a Semitic people called the Amorites put an end to the Sumerians as an identifiable group. About 1900 B.C.E., the Amorites gained control of the region, establishing their capital at Babylon. Toward 1600 B.C.E., the Babylonian kingdom fell apart under the impact of invasions from the north and east by the Hittites and the Kassites. The Hittites were only a raiding party

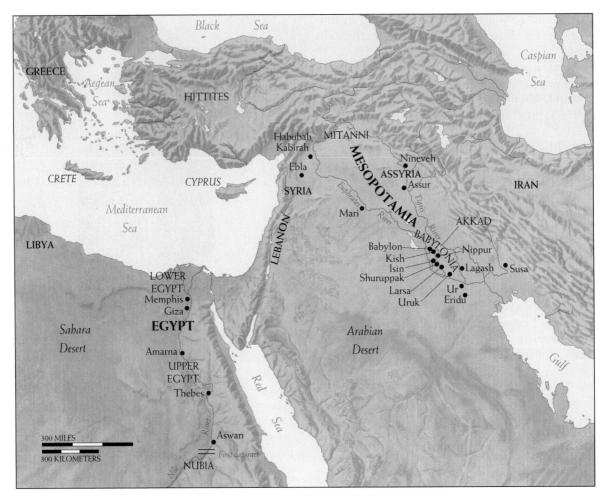

MAP I–1 THE ANCIENT NEAR EAST *There were two ancient river valley civilizations. While Egypt was united into a single state, Mesopotamia was long divided into a number of city-states.*

who plundered what they could and then withdrew to their home in Asia Minor. The Kassites stayed and ruled Mesopotamia for five centuries.

EGYPTIAN CIVILIZATION

While a great civilization arose in the valley of the Tigris and Euphrates, another, no less important, emerged in Egypt. The center of Egyptian civilization was the Nile River. The Nile alone made life possible in the almost rainless desert that surrounded it. Each year the river flooded and covered the land, and when it receded, it left a fertile mud that could produce two crops a year. The construction and maintenance of irrigation ditches to preserve the river's water, with careful planning and organization of planting and harvesting, produced agricultural prosperity unmatched in the ancient world. The Nile also served as a highway connecting the long, narrow country and encouraging its unification. Nature helped protect and isolate the ancient

Egyptians from outsiders. The cataracts, the sea, and the desert made it difficult for foreigners to reach Egypt for either friendly or hostile purposes.

The more-than-3,000-year span of ancient Egyptian history is traditionally divided into thirty-one royal dynasties. The first was founded by Menes, the unifier of Upper and Lower Egypt; the last was established by Alexander the Great, who conquered Egypt in 332 B.C.E. The unification of Egypt was vital because, even more than in Mesopotamia, the entire river valley required the central control of irrigation.

In the Old Kingdom (2700–2200 B.C.E.), royal power was absolute. The pharaoh, as he was later called (the term originally meant "great house" or "palace"), governed his kingdom through his family and appointed officials removable at his pleasure. The peasants were carefully regulated, their movement was limited, and they were taxed heavily, perhaps as much as one-fifth of what they produced. Luxury accompanied the king in life and death, and he was raised to a remote and exalted level by his

The three largest pyramids of Egypt, located at Giza, near Cairo, are the colossal tombs of pharaohs of the Fourth Dynasty (ca. 2640–2510 B.C.E.): Khufu (right), Chafre (center), and Menkaure (left). The small pyramids and tombs at their bases were those of the pharaohs' queens and officials. Pictor/Uniphoto Picture Agency

people. Such power and eminence cannot be long sustained by force alone. The Egyptians worked for the king and obeyed him because he was a living god on whom their lives, safety, and prosperity depended. He was the direct source of law and justice, and so no law codes were needed. In such a world, government was merely one aspect of religion, and religion dominated Egyptian life.

By the time of the Third Dynasty (ca. 2125–2027 B.C.E.), the pharaohs had achieved full supremacy over all of Egypt, imposing internal peace and order and overseeing a period of great prosperity. The capital was at Memphis in Upper Egypt, just above the delta. The king was regarded not as a mere representative of the gods but as a god himself. The land was his own personal possession, and the people were his servants.

The power of the kings of the Old Kingdom waned as priests and nobles gained more independence and influence. The governors of the regions of Egypt (called nomes) gained hereditary claim to their offices, and their families acquired large estates. About 2200 B.C.E., the Old Kingdom collapsed and gave way to the decentralization and disorder of the First Intermediate Period (ca. 2200–2052 B.C.E.). Finally, the nomarchs (governors) of Thebes in Upper Egypt gained control of the country and established the Middle Kingdom about 2052 B.C.E. The rulers of the Twelfth Dynasty restored the pharaoh's power over the whole of Egypt, though they did not completely control the nobles who ruled the nomes. Still, they brought order, peace, and prosperity to a troubled land. They encouraged trade and extended Egyptian power and influence northward toward Palestine and southward toward Ethiopia.

The Middle Kingdom disintegrated in the Thirteenth Dynasty, giving way, with the resurgence of the power of the local nobility, to the Second Intermediate Period. About 1700 B.C.E., Egypt suffered an invasion. Tradition speaks of a people called the Hyksos who came from the east and conquered the Nile Delta. They seem to have been a collection of Semitic peoples from the area of Palestine and Syria at the eastern end of the Mediterranean. Egyptian nationalism reasserted itself about 1575 B.C.E., when a dynasty from Thebes drove out the Hyksos and reunited Egypt, beginning the New Kingdom (or Empire) Period.

In reaction to the humiliation of the Second Intermediate Period, the pharaohs of the Eighteenth Dynasty created an absolute government based on a powerful army and an Egyptian empire extending far beyond the Nile Valley. They pushed the southern frontier back a long way and extended Egyptian power into Palestine and Syria and beyond the upper Euphrates River. They were not checked until they came into conflict with the powerful Hittite empire of Asia Minor. In the struggle that ensued between 1400 and 1200 B.C.E., both powers were weakened. Although Egypt survived, it again became the victim of foreign invasion and rule, falling under the sway of one foreign empire after another.

Major Periods in Ancient Egyptian History (Dynasties in Roman Numerals)	
3100–2700 B.C.E.	Early Dynastic Period (I–II)
2700–2200 B.C.E.	Old Kingdom (III–VI)
2200–2052 B.C.E.	First Intermediate Period (VII–XI)
2052–1630 B.C.E.	Middle Kingdom (XII–XIII)
1630–1550 B.C.E.	Second Intermediate Period (XIV–XVII)
1550–1075 B.C.E.	New Kingdom (XVIII–XX)

PALESTINE AND THE RELIGION OF THE ISRAELITES

None of the powerful kingdoms we have described has had as much influence on the future of Western civilization as the small stretch of land on the eastern shore of the Mediterranean between Syria and Egypt, the land called Palestine for much of its history (see Map I–2). The three great religions of the modern world outside the Far East—Judaism, Christianity, and Islam—trace their origins, at least in part, to the people who arrived there a little before 1200 B.C.E. and to the book that recounts their experiences, the Hebrew Bible.

The history of the Israelites must be pieced together from various sources. They are mentioned only rarely in the records of their neighbors, and so we must rely chiefly on their own account, the Bible. This is not a history in our sense, but a complicated

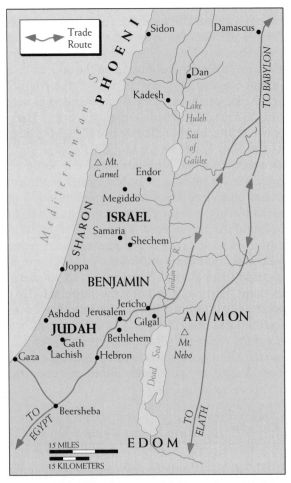

MAP I–2 ANCIENT PALESTINE *The Hebrews established a unified kingdom in Palestine under Kings David and Solomon in the tenth century* B.C.E.. *After the death of Solomon, however, the kingdom was divided into two parts—Israel in the north and Judah, with its capital, Jerusalem, in the south. Along the coast, especially to the north, were the great commercial cities of the Phoenicians, such as Sidon and Tyre.*

collection of historical narrative, wisdom literature, poetry, law, and religious witness. Scholars of an earlier time tended to discard it as a historical source, but the most recent trend is to take it seriously while using it with caution.

According to tradition, the patriarch Abraham came from Ur in Mesopotamia about 1900 B.C.E. and wandered west to tend his flocks in the land of the Canaanites. Some of his people settled there and others wandered into Egypt, perhaps with the Hyksos. By the thirteenth century B.C.E., led by Moses, they had left Egypt and wandered in the desert until they reached Canaan. They established a united kingdom that reached its peak under David and Solomon in the tenth century B.C.E. The sons of Solomon did not maintain the unity of the kingdom, and it split into two parts: Israel in the north and Judah, with its capital at Jerusalem, in the south.

The rise of great empires to the east brought disaster to the Israelites. The northern kingdom fell to the Assyrians in 722 B.C.E., and its people—the ten lost tribes of tradition—were scattered and lost forever. Only the kingdom of Judah remained, and hereafter we may call the Israelites Jews. In 586 B.C.E., Judah was defeated by the Babylonian king Nebuchadnezzar II. He destroyed the great temple built by Solomon and took thousands of hostages to Babylon. When the Persians defeated Babylonia, they ended this Babylonian Captivity of the Jews and allowed them to return to their homeland. After that the area of the old kingdom of the Jews in Palestine was dominated by foreign peoples for some 2,500 years until the establishment of the state of Israel in C.E. 1948.

The fate of this small nation would be of little interest were it not for its unique religious achievement. The great contribution of the Jews is the idea of monotheism, the existence of one universal God, the creator and ruler of the universe. Some scholars believe that a form of monotheism may have originated with the Egyptian pharaoh Akhenaton (r. 1367–1350 B.C.E.), although too little is known about his ideas and practices to be certain. Only in the Old Testament do we find the first unquestioned proof of monotheistic belief. This idea may be as old as Moses, as the Jewish tradition asserts, and it certainly dates as far back as the prophets of the eighth century B.C.E.

The Jewish God is neither a natural force nor like human beings or any other creatures. He is so elevated that those who believe in him are forbidden to picture him in any form. The faith of the Jews derives special strength from their belief that God made a covenant with Abraham, an agreement that Abraham's progeny would be a chosen people who would be rewarded for following his commandments and the law he revealed to Moses.

THE SECOND ISAIAH DEFINES HEBREW MONOTHEISM

The strongest statement of Hebrew monotheism is found in these words of the anonymous prophet whom we call the Second Isaiah. He wrote during the Hebrew exile in Babylonia, 597–539 B.C.E.

■ *How is the deity in this passage different from the deities of the Mesopotamian and Egyptian societies? Are there any similarities? Many peoples have claimed that a single god was the greatest and the ruler over all others. What is there in this selection that claims a different status for the Hebrew deity?*

42

⁵Thus says God, the Lord
who created the heavens and stretched them out,
who spread forth the earth and what comes
    from it,
who gives breath to the people upon it and spirit
to those who walk in it:
⁶I am the Lord, I have called you in righteousness,
I have taken you by the hand and kept you;
I have given you as a covenant to the people, a
    light to the nations,
⁷to open the eyes that are blind,
to bring out the prisoners from the dungeon,
from the prison those who sit in darkness.
⁸I am the Lord, that is my name;
my glory I give to no other,
nor my praise to graven images.
⁹Behold, the former things have come to pass,
    and new things I now declare;
before they spring forth I tell you of them."

44

⁶Thus says the Lord, the King of Israel and his
    Redeemer, the Lord of hosts:
"I am the first and I am the last; besides me
    there is no god.
⁷Who is like me? Let him proclaim it,
let him declare and set it forth before me.
Who has announced of old the things to come?
Let them tell us what is yet to be.
⁸Fear not, nor be afraid;
have I not told you from of old and declared it?

And you are my witnesses!
Is there a God besides me?
There is no Rock; I know not any."

49

²²Thus says the Lord God:
"Behold, I will lift up my hand to the nations,
and raise my signal to the peoples;
and they shall bring your sons in their bosom,
and your daughters shall be carried on their
    shoulders
²³Kings shall be your foster fathers,
and their queens your nursing mothers.
With their faces to the ground they shall bow
    down to you,
and lick the dust of your feet.
Then you will know that I am the Lord;
those who wait for me shall not be put to
    shame."
²⁴Can the prey be taken from the mighty, or the
    captives of a tyrant be rescued?
²⁵Surely, thus says the Lord:
"Even the captives of the mighty shall be taken,
and the prey of the tyrant be rescued,
for I will contend with those who contend
    with you
and I will save your children.
²⁶I will make your oppressors eat their own flesh,
and they shall be drunk with their own blood as
    with wine.
Then all flesh shall know
that I am the Lord your Savior,
and your Redeemer, the Mighty One of Jacob."

Bible, Revised Standard Version (New York: Division of Christian Education, National Council of Churches, 1952).

An essential ingredient of Jewish religious thought is the powerful ethical element it introduces. God is a severe but just judge. Ritual and sacrifice are not enough to achieve his approval. People must be righteous, and God himself appears to be bound to act righteously. The Jewish prophetic tradition was a powerful ethical force. The prophets constantly criticized any falling away from the law and the path of righteousness. The prophets placed God in history, blaming the misfortunes of the Jews on God's righteous and necessary intervention to punish them for their misdeeds, but the prophets also promised the redemption of the Jews if they repented. The prophetic tradition expected the redemption to come in the form of a Messiah (deliverer). Christianity, emerging from this tradition, maintains that Jesus of Nazareth was that Messiah.

Jewish religious ideas influenced the future development of the West, both directly and indirectly. The Jews' belief in an all-powerful creator, righteous himself and demanding righteousness and obedience from humankind, a universal God who is the father and ruler of all peoples, is a critical part of the Western heritage. (See "The Second Isaiah Defines Hebrew Monotheism.")

The Greeks

Western civilization as a distinct culture began with the Greeks. Greek-speaking people from the north settled the lands surrounding the Aegean Sea in the second millennium B.C.E. They established a style of life and formed ideas, values, and institutions that spread far beyond the Aegean corner of the Mediterranean Sea. They later influenced and

MAP I–3   THE AEGEAN AREA IN THE BRONZE AGE   *The Bronze Age in the Aegean area lasted from about 1900 to about 1100 B.C.E. Its culture on Crete is called Minoan and was at its height about 1900–1400 B.C.E. Bronze Age Helladic culture on the mainland flourished from about 1600–1200 B.C.E.*

shaped Roman society. Preserved and adapted by the Romans, Greek culture powerfully influenced the society of western Europe in the High Middle Ages and dominated the Byzantine Empire in the same period.

The Greeks of the Classical Age (500–400 B.C.E.) inherited and adapted many important elements of their culture from earlier civilizations (see Map I–3). The Minoan civilization (ca. 2900–1150 B.C.E.), with its center on the island of Crete, was literate. Its records reveal a palace-centered organization ruled by a king who was served by an extensive bureaucracy that kept remarkably detailed records. This sort of organization is typical of what we find in the Near East but is nothing like what is found among the Greeks. The Minoans powerfully influenced the Mycenaeans, a Greek-speaking people who dominated the mainland of Greece and the islands of the Aegean in the latter part of the Bronze Age (ca. 1600–1150 B.C.E.). Mycenaean civilization collapsed and gave way to a period often called the Greek Dark Ages (ca. 1150–750 B.C.E.). During this time, a new Hellenic culture, influenced by the Mycenaean world, but essentially independent of it, took shape. (See "Husband and Wife in Homer's Troy.")

At some time in their history, the Greeks of the ancient world founded cities on every shore of the Mediterranean Sea. Pushing through the Dardanelles, they placed many settlements on the coasts of the Black Sea in southern Russia and as far east as the approaches to the Caucasus Mountains. The center of Greek life, however, was always the Aegean Sea and the lands in and around

HUSBAND AND WIFE IN HOMER'S TROY

Homer's poems provide a picture of early Greek ideas and institutions. In the Iliad, *the poet tells of the return from the battle of the Trojan hero Hector. He is greeted by his loving, "warm, generous wife," Andromache, who is carrying their baby son. Hector reaches for the boy, who is frightened to tears by the plume on his father's helmet. The father removes the helmet and prays that his son will grow up to be called "a better man than his father . . . a joy to his mother's heart." The rest of the scene reveals the character of their marriage and the division of responsibility between men and women in their world.*

■ *How does Homer depict the feelings of husband and wife toward one another? What are the tasks of the aristocratic woman revealed in this passage? What can be learned about the attitude towards death and duty?*

So Hector prayed
and placed his son in the arms of his loving wife.
Andromache pressed the child to her scented breast,
smiling through her tears. Her husband noticed,
and filled with pity now, Hector stroked her gently,
trying to reassure her, repeating her name:
    "Andromache,
dear one; why so desperate? Why so much grief
    for me?
No man will hurl me down to Death, against
    my fate.
And fate? No one alive has ever escaped it,
neither brave man nor coward, I tell you—
it's born with us the day that we are born.
So please go home and tend to your own tasks,
the distaff and the loom, and keep the women
working hard as well. As for the fighting,
men will see to that, all who were born in Troy
but I most of all."
Hector aflash in arms
took up his horsehair-crested helmet once again.
And his loving wife went home, turning, glancing
back again and again and weeping live warm tears.
She quickly reached the sturdy house of Hector,
man-killing Hector, and found her women gathered
    there inside
and stirred them all to a high pitch of mourning.
So in his house they raised the dirges for the dead,
for Hector still alive, his people were so convinced
that never again would he come home from battle,
never escape the Argives' rage and bloody hands.

From *The Iliad by Homer*, translated by Robert Fagles, copyright © 1990 by Robert Fagles. Used by permission of Viking Penguin, a division of Penguin Putnam Inc.

it. This location at the eastern end of the Mediterranean very early put the Greeks in touch with the more advanced civilizations of the Near East.

THE POLIS

The characteristic Greek institution was the ***polis*** (plural, *poleis*). The common translation of that word as "city-state" is misleading, for it says both too much and too little. All Greek *poleis* began as little more than agricultural villages or towns and many stayed that way, and so the word *city* is inappropriate. All of them were states, in the sense of being independent political units, but they were much more than that. The *polis* was thought of as a community of relatives. All its citizens, who were theoretically descended from a common ancestor, belonged to subgroups, such as fighting brotherhoods (phratries), clans, and tribes, and worshiped the gods in common ceremonies.

The "Trojan Horse," depicted on a seventh-century B.C.E. *Greek vase. According to legend, the Greeks finally defeated Troy by pretending to abandon their siege of the city, leaving a giant wooden horse behind. Soldiers hidden in the horse opened the gates of the city to their compatriots after the Trojans had brought it within their walls. Note the wheels on the horse and the Greek soldiers holding weapons and armor who are hiding inside it.* Greek 10th-6th B.C.E. Trojan Horse and Greek Soldiers. Relief from neck of an earthenware amphora (640 B.C.E.) from Mykanos, overall ht. 120 cm. Archeological Museum, Mykonos, Greece. Art Resource, NY. © Photography by Erich Lessing

Originally, the word *polis* referred only to a citadel, an elevated, defensible rock to which the farmers of the neighboring area could retreat in case of attack. The Acropolis in Athens and the hill called Acrocorinth in Corinth are examples. For some time such high places and the adjacent farms comprised the *polis*. Availability of farmland and of a natural fortress determined its location. *Poleis* were placed either well inland or far enough away from the sea to avoid pirate raids. Only later and gradually did the agora appear. It grew to be not only a marketplace but also a civic center and the heart of the Greeks' remarkable social life, which was distinguished by conversation and argument carried on in the open air.

By the time the *polis* was in full flower, between ca. 750 and 700 B.C.E., true monarchy had disappeared in Greece. Kings survived in some places, but they were almost always ceremonial figures without power. The original form of the *polis* was an aristocratic republic dominated by the nobility through its council of nobles and its monopoly of the magistracies.

From the middle of the eighth century B.C.E. until well into the sixth, the Greeks vastly expanded their territory, their wealth, and their contacts with other peoples in a burst of colonizing activity that placed *poleis* from Spain to the Black Sea. A century earlier, a few Greeks had established trading posts in Syria. There they had learned new techniques in the arts and crafts and much more from the older civilizations of the Near East. About 750 B.C.E., they borrowed a writing system from one of the Semitic scripts and added vowels to create the first true alphabet. The new Greek alphabet was easier to learn than any earlier writing system and made possible the widely literate society of classical Greece. Furthermore, by confronting Greeks with the differences between themselves and the new peoples they met, colonization gave the Greeks a sense of cultural identity. It also fostered a Panhellenic ("all-Greek") spirit that led to the establishment of several common religious festivals.

Like most ancient peoples, the Greeks believed in many gods, and religion played an important part in their lives. A great part of Greek art and literature was closely connected with religion, as was the life of the *polis* in general. The Greek pantheon consisted of the twelve gods who lived on Mount Olympus and who therefore were known as Olympians. Each *polis* had one of the Olympians as its guardian deity and worshiped the god in its own special way; but all the gods were worshiped by all Greeks. In the eighth and seventh centuries B.C.E., common shrines were established at Olympia for the worship of Zeus, at Delphi for Apollo, at the Isthmus of

Corinth for Poseidon, and at Nemea once again for Zeus. Each *polis* held athletic contests in honor of its god, to which all Greeks were invited and for which a sacred truce was declared.

The somewhat cold religion of the Olympian gods did little to attend to human fears, hopes, and passions. For these needs, the Greeks turned to other deities and rites. Of these the most popular was Dionysus, a god of nature and fertility, of the grapevine and drunkenness, and of sexual abandon. In some of his rites, the god was followed by maenads, female devotees who cavorted by night, ate raw flesh, and were reputed to tear to pieces any creature they came across.

The heart of Greek life was the *polis*. Generalization about the *polis* becomes difficult not long after its appearance. Although the states had much in common, some of them developed in unique ways. Sparta and Athens, which became the two most powerful Greek states, had especially different characters.

Sparta About 725 B.C.E., Sparta conquered its western neighbor, Messenia, and reduced its population to the status of serfs, or helots. Almost a century later, the helots revolted. After the revolt had been put down, the Spartans were forced to reconsider their way of life. They could not expect to keep down the helots, who outnumbered them by perhaps ten to one, and still maintain the old free and easy habits typical of most Greeks. To maintain domination over the helots, the Spartans introduced fundamental reforms that turned their city permanently into a military academy and camp.

The Spartan reforms are attributed to the legendary figure Lycurgus. The new system that emerged late in the sixth century B.C.E. exerted direct control over each Spartan from birth until old age. Officials of the state decided which infants were physically fit to survive. At the age of seven, the Spartan boy was taken from his mother and turned over to young instructors who trained him in athletics and the military arts. At twenty, the Spartan youth was enrolled in the army and lived in barracks with his companions until the age of thirty. If married, he could visit his wife only infrequently and even then by stealth. At thirty, he became a full citizen. He took his simple meals at a public mess in the company of fifteen comrades. Military service was required until the age of sixty.

Women were also educated to subordinate themselves wholly to the ideal of service to Sparta. They were not given military training, but they were required to devote their children to the service of the *polis*. Nothing in Sparta was allowed to interfere with the only ambition permitted to a Spartan: to win glory and the respect of his peers by bravery in war.

The Spartan constitution was mixed, containing elements of monarchy, oligarchy, and democracy. There were two kings with very limited power. The oligarchic element was represented by a council of elders who had important judicial functions. The Spartan assembly consisted of all males over thirty. In addition, there was a board of five annually elected ephors who controlled foreign policy, oversaw the generalship of the kings on campaign, presided over the assembly, and guarded against rebellions by the helots. Most Greeks admired the Spartan state for its unmatched stability and also for its ability to mold its citizens into a single pattern, subordinated to an ideal.

Athens The life and politics of Athens developed in a direction very different from that of Sparta. In the seventh century B.C.E., Athens was a typical aristocratic *polis*. The aristocrats held the most and best land and dominated religious and political life. The state was governed by the Areopagus, a council of nobles deriving its name from the hill where it held its sessions. Toward the close of the century, economic hardship caused political conflict in Athens.

Tradition has it that in the year 594 B.C.E. the Athenians gave Solon extraordinary powers to

The Acropolis was both the religious and civic center of Athens. In its final form it is the work of Pericles and his successors in the late fifth century B.C.E. This photograph shows the Parthenon and to its left the Erechtheum. Meredith Pillon, Greek National Tourism Organization

legislate and revise the constitution. He carried out a series of economic reforms that restructured debts and credit. Solon also significantly changed the constitution. All male adults whose fathers were citizens were citizens, too, and to their number he added immigrant craftsmen. All citizens were divided into four classes according to wealth. He established a Council of Four Hundred, apparently to check the power of the Areopagus. Finally, he established a popular assembly. In 546 B.C.E., the constitution of Solon was overthrown by Pisistratus, who established his own rule. Despite this period of tyranny, however, the principle of a somewhat democratically governed *polis* had been established, and later leaders would build upon that foundation.

Hippias, the son of Pisistratus, was deposed in 510 B.C.E., and the government of Athens underwent another series of reforms. These were undertaken by Clisthenes, who may be regarded as the real founder of Athenian democracy. He made the **deme,** the equivalent of a small town in the country or a ward in the city, the basic unit of civic life. Henceforth, enrollment in the *deme* replaced enrollment in the phratry (clan brotherhood, where tradition and noble birth dominated) as evidence of

A Greek hoplite attacks a Persian soldier. The contrast between the Greek's metal body armor, large shield, and long spear and the Persian's cloth and leather garments indicates one reason the Greeks won. This Attic vase was found on Rhodes and dates from ca. 475 B.C.E.
The Metropolitan Museum of Art, Rogers Fund, 1906 (06.1021.117)
Photograph © 1986. The Metropolitan Museum of Art.

citizenship. He also further extended the classes of people who might become citizens. He established a Council of Five Hundred, which dealt with foreign policy and finances. Final authority in all things rested with the assembly composed of all adult male citizens. Debate was free and open. Any adult Athenian male could submit legislation, offer amendments, or argue the merits of any question. The reforms of Clisthenes nurtured strong patriotism among the Athenians. The freedom of their constitution also allowed them to achieve very considerable economic prosperity.

Whether a Greek citizen lived in Sparta, Athens, or another of the many *poleis*, he knew that his way of life was different from that of people who lived under the great monarchs of the East. The Greeks were determined to preserve the way of life of the *polis*. In 490 B.C.E., Darius, the king of Persia, (r. 521–485 B.C.E.) attempted to restore the tyrant Hippias in Athens. The Athenians, led by Miltiades, (ca. 550–487 B.C.E.) resisted and won a victory at Marathon (490 B.C.E.). This victory preserved Athenian freedom and instilled in the Athenians a sense of confidence and pride in their *polis*. In 480 B.C.E., the Persians under Xerxes (r. 485–465 B.C.E.) again attempted to conquer Greece. The Greek cities responded by forming a defensive league among themselves. Sparta as leader of the land forces held off the Persians at the Battle of Thermopylae. The Athenians led Greek naval forces to a great victory over Persia at Salamis.

In the half century after the defeat of the Persians, two important developments occurred among the Greeks. First, under the leadership of Pericles (ca. 494–429 B.C.E.), the constitution of Athens became even more democratic. Every decision of the state had to be approved by the popular assembly, a collection of the people themselves, not their representatives. Most officials were selected by lot without regard to class. There was no standing army, no police force, and no way to coerce the people. Yet even in democratic Athens, as in all the other Greek states, participation in government was denied to slaves, resident aliens, and women.

The Peloponnesian War The second development was the division of the Greek world into two spheres of influence, dominated by Sparta and Athens. Sparta led a relatively loose alliance, but the Athenian alliance quickly developed into an empire in which most of Athens' allies made financial payments in place of military service. The Athenians used the money not only for defense but for their own purposes as well. Increasingly, Athens controlled the policy of the alliance and used it to increase its own wealth, power, and glory. For many years, intense rivalry and occasional conflict occurred between the two cities and their respective allies. Then, in 431 B.C.E., a great conflict—the Peloponnesian War, recorded brilliantly in the history of Thucydides (ca. 460–400 B.C.E.)—began between them. This devastating conflict ended in 404 B.C.E. with the defeat of Athens. After this war, Greek prosperity and confidence were never again fully restored.

The long Peloponnesian War and the struggles accompanying the several attempts at hegemony brought results that undermined the foundations of the *polis*. By ravaging farmland, destroying crops and houses, interfering with commerce, and using up reserve funds, the warring armies and navies did severe and usually lasting damage to the economic well-being that made civic life possible. Civil strife and class conflict, encouraged by the pressure of want and disease as well as by the availability of help from foreign armies, were an even more terrible legacy than poverty. As time passed, people abandoned patriotism, morality, and even family to the interests of faction. The wars of the fourth century B.C.E. only intensified these developments. Democratic revolutions, accompanied by confiscations of property, executions, exiles, and even great atrocities, were answered with similar actions by victorious aristocratic oligarchs. Such upheavals left permanent scars and damaged the family feeling, the sense of community, and the commitment to the common good required for life in the *polis*.

GREEK POLITICAL PHILOSOPHY AND THE CRISIS OF THE *POLIS*

The decay of healthy political life in the *polis* gave rise to ideas in political philosophy that have influenced Western thought ever since. Probably the most complicated response to the crisis of the *polis* in the fourth century B.C.E. may be found in the life and teachings of Socrates (469–399 B.C.E.). He went into the Athenian marketplace and questioned and cross-examined people who were supposed to know something about politics. These included poets, craftsmen, and politicians. The result was always the same. Those he questioned might have technical information and skills, but they seldom had any substantial knowledge of the fundamental principles of human behavior. It is understandable that Athenians so exposed should be angry with their examiner, and it is not surprising that they thought Socrates was undermining the beliefs and values of the *polis*. Socrates' unconcealed contempt for democracy, which seemingly relied on ignorant amateurs to make important political decisions, created further hostility.

Yet despite this contempt, Socrates still believed that the *polis* had a legitimate claim on the loyalty and obedience of the citizen. He demonstrated this in the most convincing fashion. In 399 B.C.E., he was condemned to death by an Athenian jury on the charges of bringing new gods into the city and of corrupting the youth. He was given a chance to escape, but in the dialogue *Crito*, written by his disciple Plato, we are told of his refusal because of his veneration of the laws of the city. Socrates recognized the difficulties of political life in the *polis* and criticized its short-comings. He turned away from active political life, but he did not abandon the idea of the *polis*. He fought as a soldier in its defense, obeyed its laws, and sought to put its values on a sound foundation of reason.

Plato (429–347 B.C.E.) was by far the most important of Socrates' associates and is a perfect example of the pupil who becomes greater than his master. He was the first systematic philosopher and therefore the first to place political ideas in their full philosophical context. He presented his philosophy in the format of dialogues. In 386 B.C.E., he founded the Academy, a center of philosophical investigation. As a school for training statesmen and citizens, it had a powerful impact on Greek thought that lasted until it was closed by the Roman emperor Justinian in the sixth century. C.E.

Like Socrates, Plato believed in the *polis* and its values. Its virtues were order, harmony, and justice,

Marble head of Aristotle. Louvre, Dept. des Antiquities Grecques/Romaines, Paris, France. © Photograph by Erich Lessing/ Art Resource, NY

and one of its main objects was to produce good people. He accepted Socrates' doctrine of the identity of virtue and knowledge and made it plain what he regarded as genuine knowledge. It was *episteme*, science as a body of true and unchanging wisdom open to only a few philosophers, whose training, character, and intellect allowed them to see reality. Only such people were qualified to rule. They themselves would prefer the life of pure contemplation but would accept their political responsibility and take their turn as philosopher kings. The training of such rulers, which Plato outlined in the *Republic*, required a specialization of function and a subordination of the individual to the community even greater than that at Sparta.

For Plato, justice in society meant that each person should do only that one thing to which his nature is best suited. Plato saw quite clearly that the Athenian *polis* of his day suffered from terrible internal stress, class struggle, and factional divisions. For Plato, the way to harmony was to destroy the causes of that strife: private property, the family, or anything else that stood between the individual citizen and his complete loyalty and devotion to the *polis*. (See "Plato on the Role of Women in His Utopian Republic.")

Aristotle (384–322 B.C.E.) was a pupil of Plato and owed much to the thought of his master, but his very different experience and cast of mind led him in some new directions. In 336 B.C.E., he founded his own school in Athens, the Lyceum, or the Peripatos, as it was also called from the covered walk within it. The Lyceum was a very different place from the Academy. Its members took little interest in mathematics and were concerned with gathering, ordering, and analyzing all human knowledge. The range of subjects treated is astonishing, including logic, physics, astronomy, biology, ethics, rhetoric, literary criticism, and politics.

The Rise of Macedon

359–336 B.C.E.	Reign of Philip II
338 B.C.E.	Battle of Chaeronea; Philip conquers Greece
338 B.C.E.	Founding of League of Corinth
336–323 B.C.E.	Reign of Alexander III, the Great
334 B.C.E.	Alexander invades Asia
333 B.C.E.	Battle of Issus
331 B.C.E.	Battle of Gaugamela
330 B.C.E.	Fall of Persepolis
327 B.C.E.	Alexander reaches Indus Valley
323 B.C.E.	Death of Alexander

In each field, Aristotle's method was the same. He began with observation of the empirical evidence, which in some cases was physical and in others was common opinion. To this body of information he applied reason and discovered inconsistencies or difficulties. He then introduced metaphysical principles to explain the problems or to reconcile the inconsistencies. His view on all subjects, like Plato's, was teleological; that is, both philosophers recognized purposes apart from and greater than the will of the individual human being in nature and in social life. Plato's purposes, however, were contained in the Ideas or Forms—transcendental concepts outside the experience of most people. For Aristotle, the purposes of most things could be easily inferred by observation of their behavior in the world. Aristotle's most striking characteristics were his moderation and common sense. His theory of knowledge finds room for both reason and experience. His metaphysics gives meaning and reality to both mind and body. His ethics aims at the good life, which is the contemplative life, but recognizes the necessity for moderate wealth, comfort, and pleasure.

Characteristically, Aristotle was less interested in the best state—the Platonic utopia that required philosophers to rule it—than in the best state practically possible, one that would combine justice with stability. The constitution for that state he called *politeia*, not the best constitution, but the next best, the one most suited to and most possible for most states. Its quality was moderation, and it naturally gave power to neither the rich nor the poor but to the middle class, which must also be the most numerous. The middle class possessed many virtues. Because of its moderate wealth, it was free of the arrogance of the rich and the malice of the poor. Aristotle combined the practical analysis of political and economic realities with the moral and political purposes of the traditional defenders of the *polis*. The result was a passionate confidence in the virtues of moderation and of the middle class and the proposal of a constitution that would give them power. It is ironic that the ablest defense of the *polis* came toward its demise.

THE EMPIRE OF ALEXANDER THE GREAT

What finally brought the collapse of the independent political life of the Greek *poleis* was their conquest by the kingdom of Macedon in the middle of the fourth century B.C.E. The Macedonians inhabited the land to the north of Thessaly and until the fourth century B.C.E. played no great part in Greek affairs. Macedon possessed no *poleis* but was governed by a king chosen partly by descent and partly by the approval of the army. Under Philip II (r. 359–336 B.C.E.),

PLATO ON THE ROLE OF WOMEN IN HIS UTOPIAN REPUBLIC

The Greek invention of reasoned intellectual analysis of all things led the philosopher Plato to consider the problem of justice, which is the subject of his most famous dialogue, the Republic. *This leads him to sketch out a utopian state in which justice may be found and where the most radical arrangements may be necessary. These include the equality of the sexes and the destruction of the family in favor of the practice of men having wives and children in common. In the following excerpts, he argues for the fundamental equality of men and women and that women are no less appropriate as Guardians—leaders of the state—than men.*

■ *What are Plato's reasons for treating men and women the same? What objections could be raised to that practice? Would that policy, even if appropriate in Plato's utopia, also be suitable to conditions in the real world of classical Athens? In the world of today?*

"If, then, we use the women for the same things as the men, they must also be taught the same things."

"Yes."

"Now music and gymnastics were given to the men."

"Yes."

"Then these two arts, and what has to do with war, must be assigned to the women also, and they must be used in the same ways."

"On the basis of what you say," he said, "it's likely."

"Perhaps," I said, "compared to what is habitual, many of the things now being said would look ridiculous if they were to be done as is said."

"Indeed they would," he said.

"Well," I said, "since we've started to speak, we mustn't be afraid of all the jokes—of whatever kind—the wits might make if such a change took place in gymnastic, in music and, not the least, in the bearing of arms and the riding of horses."

"Then," I said, "if either the class of men or that of women show its superiority in some art or other practice, then we'll say that that art must be assigned to it. But if they look as though they differ in this alone, that the female bears and the male mounts, we'll assert that it has not thereby yet been proved that a woman differs from a man with respect to what we're talking about; rather, we'll still suppose that our guardians and their women must practice the same things."

"And rightly," he said.

"Therefore, my friend, there is no practice of a city's governors which belongs to woman because she's woman, or to man because he's man; but the natures are scattered alike among both animals; and woman participates according to nature in all practices, and man in all, but in all of them woman is weaker than man."

"Certainly."

"So, shall we assign all of them to men and none to women?"

"How could we?"

"For I suppose there is, as we shall assert, one woman apt at medicine and another not, one woman apt at music and another unmusical by nature."

"Of course."

"And isn't there then also one apt at gymnastic and at war, and another unwarlike and no lover of gymnastic?"

"I suppose so."

"And what about this? Is there a lover of wisdom and a hater of wisdom? And one who is spirited and another without spirit?"

"Yes, there are these too."

"There is, therefore one woman fit for guarding and another not, or wasn't it a nature of this sort we also selected for the men fit for guarding?"

"Certainly, that was it."

From *The Republic of Plato,* (2nd ed.) translated by Allan Bloom. Copyright © 1968 by Allan Bloom. Preface to paperback edition, © 1991 by Allan Bloom, pp. 130–134. Reprinted by permission of Basic Books, a member of Perseus Books, L.L.C.

the Macedonians developed a powerful army. Beginning about 355 B.C.E., Philip moved that army steadily against the various Greek cities. Years of fighting

and diplomatic maneuvering followed, but no Greek *polis,* including Athens, was able or willing to mount an effective resistance. Finally, in 338 B.C.E.,

This sculpture of Alexander the Great, king of Macedon and conqueror of the Persian Empire, was made in the second century B.C.E. and found at the ancient city of Magnesia in Asia Minor. Alexander's conquests spread Greek culture far from its homeland, laying the foundation of the Hellenistic world. Statue from Magnesia ad Sipylum. Archeological Museum, Istanbul, Turkey. Erich Lessing/Art Resource, N.Y.

at the Battle of Chaeronea the Macedonian monarchy defeated an alliance of Greek cities. This defeat ended Greek freedom and autonomy.

In 336 B.C.E., Philip II was assassinated. His successor, Alexander the Great (r. 336–323 B.C.E.), was one of the most extraordinary figures of antiquity. During the next ten years, Alexander led the army of Macedonia across Asia as far as the Indus River (see Map I–4). On the way, he conquered Asia Minor, Syria, Palestine, Egypt, Persia, and Mesopotamia. Alexander was filled with plans for the consolidation

and organization of his empire, for geographical exploration, and for building new cities, roads, and harbors. These plans were never carried out because in June of 323 B.C.E., he died of fever at the age of thirty-three. He left no real successor, and his generals fought over the lands he had conquered.

The conquests of Alexander and the establishment of successor kingdoms in Macedon, Mesopotamia, and Egypt put an end once and for all to the central role of the *polis* in Greek life. At the same time, his conquests spread Greek culture widely throughout the eastern Mediterranean, laying the foundation for the Hellenistic civilization that succeeded the civilization of classical Greece.

Deprived of control of their foreign affairs and with their important internal arrangements determined by a foreign monarchy, the postclassical Greek cities lost the kind of political freedom that was basic to the old outlook. As time passed, they changed from sovereign states to municipalities merged in military empires. It was not by the cities of Greece but by a city on the Italian peninsula that the future course of civilization in the West would be determined.

Rome

The political achievement of the Romans was one of the most remarkable in human history. The descendants of the inhabitants of a small village in central Italy governed the entire Italian peninsula and then the entire Mediterranean coastline. They conquered most of the Near East and finally much of continental Europe. They ruled this vast empire under a single government that provided peace and prosperity for centuries. Never before or since has that area been united, and rarely, if ever, has it enjoyed a stable peace.

THE REPUBLIC AND EXPANSION IN THE MEDITERRANEAN

From its foundation in 753 B.C.E. until 509 B.C.E., Rome was governed by kings (see Map I–5). In 509 B.C.E., tradition tells us, the republic replaced the monarchy after a revolution led by noble families incensed by the outrageous behavior of the last kings. The republican form of government, dominated by the institution of the aristocratic Senate, endured for almost five centuries.

By 265 B.C.E., the Romans had conquered most of central and southern Italy and had established a policy toward conquered peoples that would be repeated in many other areas. The Romans did not destroy any of the Latin cities or their people, nor did they

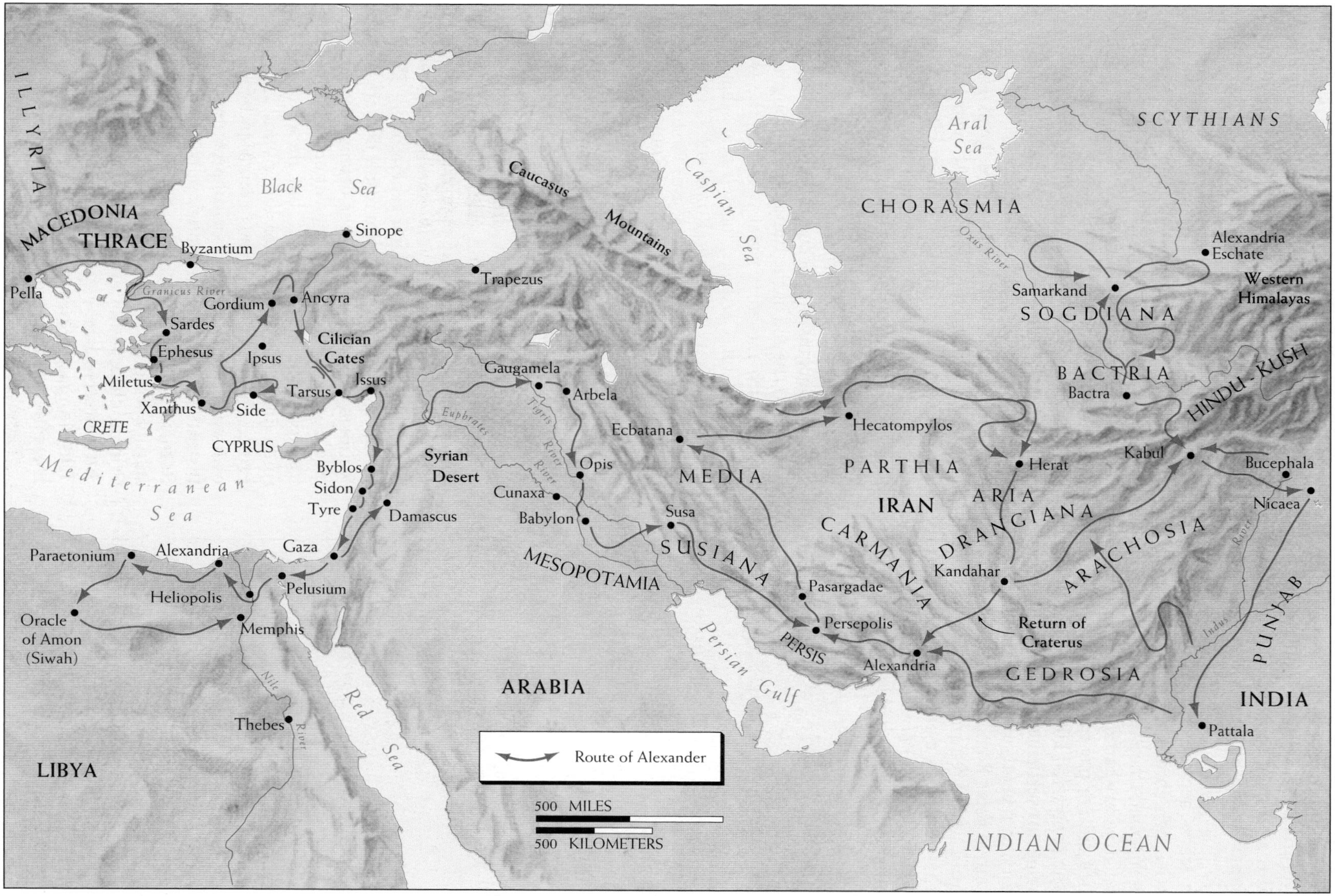

MAP I-4 ALEXANDER'S CAMPAIGNS *The route taken by Alexander the Great in his conquest of the Persian Empire, 334–323 B.C.E. Starting from the Macedonian capital at Pella, he reached the Indus Valley before being turned back by his own restive troops. He died of fever in Mesopotamia.*

SCYTHIANS
Alexandria Eschate
Western Himalayas
HINDU-KUSH
Bucephala
Nicaea
PUNJAB
INDIA
Pattala
SOGDIANA
Samarkand
BACTRIA
Bactra
Kabul
ARACHOSIA
ARIA
DRANGIANA
GEDROSIA
Herat
Return of Craterus
Kandahar
CHORASMIA
Aral Sea
Oxus River
IRAN
PARTHIA
Hecatompylos
CARMANIA
Alexandria
Pasargadae
Persepolis
PERSIS
Caspian Sea
MEDIA
Ecbatana
Susa
SUSIANA
INDIAN OCEAN
Caucasus Mountains
Arbela
Opis
Gaugamela
Tigris River
Euphrates River
Babylon
Cunaxa
MESOPOTAMIA
Persian Gulf
Trapezus
ARABIA
Black Sea
Sinope
Byzantium
Granicus River
Gordium
Ancyra
Cilician Gates
Issus
Tarsus
Ipsus
Side
Sardes
Ephesus
Miletus
Xanthus
CYPRUS
CRETE
Byblos
Sidon
Tyre
Damascus
Syrian Desert
Gaza
Pelusium
Memphis
Red Sea
Nile River
Thebes
Mediterranean Sea
Alexandria
Heliopolis
Paraetonium
Oracle of Amon (Siwah)
LIBYA
ILLYRIA
MACEDONIA
THRACE
Pella

→ Route of Alexander

500 MILES
500 KILOMETERS

treat them all alike. Some near Rome received full Roman citizenship; others farther away gained municipal status. Their citizens retained the rights of local self-government and could obtain full Roman citizenship if they moved to Rome. They followed Rome in foreign policy and provided soldiers to serve in the Roman legions.

Still other states became allies of Rome on the basis of treaties, which differed from city to city. All the allies supplied troops to the army, in which they fought in auxiliary battalions under Roman officers, but they did not pay taxes to Rome. Finally, on some of the conquered land the Romans placed colonies, permanent settlements of veteran soldiers in the territory of recently defeated enemies. The colonists retained their Roman citizenship and enjoyed home rule, and in return for the land they had been given they served as a permanent garrison to deter or suppress rebellion. The Romans did not regard the status given each newly conquered city

The Punic Wars	
264–241 B.C.E.	First Punic War
238 B.C.E.	Rome seizes Sardinia and Corsica
221 B.C.E.	Hannibal takes command of Punic army in Spain
218–202 B.C.E.	Second Punic War
216 B.C.E.	Battle of Cannae
209 B.C.E.	Scipio takes New Carthage
202 B.C.E.	Battle of Zama
149–146 B.C.E.	Third Punic War
146 B.C.E.	Destruction of Carthage

as permanent. They held out to loyal allies the prospect of improving their status, even of achieving the ultimate prize, full Roman citizenship. In doing so, the Romans gave their allies a stake in Rome's future and success. The result, in general, was that most of Rome's allies remained loyal even when put to the severest test.

Rome's acquisition of coastal territory and its expansion to the toe of the Italian boot brought it face to face with the great naval power of the western Mediterranean, Carthage, located near what is now the modern city of Tunis. Rome and Carthage engaged in two great conflicts, the First and Second Punic Wars (264–241 B.C.E. and 218–202 B.C.E.). At very considerable cost, Rome emerged victorious and thereafter ruled virtually all the western Mediterranean. After the defeat of Carthage, the attention of Rome moved toward the eastern Mediterranean and the successor kingdoms of Alexander's brief empire. By 168 B.C.E., after a series of military interventions in Macedon, the Romans effectively governed Greece as a kind of protectorate.

Roman expansion in Italy and overseas was accomplished without a grand general plan. The new territories were acquired as a result of wars that the Romans believed were either defensive or preventive. Foreign policy was aimed at providing security for Rome on Rome's terms, but these terms were often unacceptable to other nations and led to continued conflict. The various conquests of territory overseas presented new political problems to Rome. Instead of following the policy pursued in Italy, the Romans made Sicily, Spain, Sardinia, and Corsica into provinces. The new populations were neither Roman citizens nor allies; they were subjects who did not serve in the army but paid tribute instead. The old practice of extending citizenship and with it loyalty to Rome stopped at the borders of Italy.

These conquests changed both Roman political and cultural life. Roman expansion overseas brought about close and continued association with the

MAP I–5 ANCIENT ITALY *This map of ancient Italy and its neighbors before the expansion of Rome shows major cities and towns as well as several geographical regions and the locations of some of the Italic and non-Italic peoples.*

Ruins of the Roman Forum. From the earliest days of the city, the Forum was the center of Roman life. Augustus had it rebuilt, and it was frequently rebuilt and refurbished by his successors, so most of the surviving buildings date to the imperial period. © Michael S. Yamashita/Corbis

Greeks. Many Romans admired Greek art, literature, and philosophy but held Greek politics in contempt. Before long, the education of the Roman upper classes was bilingual. The Romans also often imitated the forms of Greek literature. Roman religion was influenced by the Greeks almost from the beginning because the Romans had early in their history identified their own gods with Greek equivalents and incorporated Greek mythology into their own. The Romans also drew heavily upon Greek philosophy. They always adapted Greek culture to their own particular needs. It was a commonplace in antiquity to think that while Rome had conquered Greece militarily, Greece had conquered Rome culturally.

FROM REPUBLIC TO EMPIRE

The political and economic problems raised by the overseas conquests eventually undermined the constitution of the republic. During the Punic Wars, much of the farmland in Italy was damaged and even more was bought up by wealthy nobles. Returning veterans found themselves without land and often settled in the city of Rome or other urban areas. The people of Rome became sharply divided into rich and poor, landed and landless, privileged and deprived. By 133 B.C.E. many Roman political leaders believed this issue had to be addressed, but there was no agreement on the method.

Between 133 and 121 B.C.E., two brothers, Tiberius and Gaius Gracchus, tried to carry out a program of limited land redistribution. The Gracchi met intense and violent opposition. Both were assassinated as the wealthy landowning classes moved to protect their interests. For a century after their deaths, political and military turmoil prevailed in the republic. The people who gained power were generals who had armies at their disposal and whose conquests made them popular. For example, Marius (ca. 157–86 B.C.E.)

The Fall of the Roman Republic

133 B.C.E.	Tribunate of Tiberius Gracchus
123–122 B.C.E.	Tribunate of Gaius Gracchus
111–105 B.C.E.	Jugurthine War
104–100 B.C.E.	Consecutive consulships of Marius
90–88 B.C.E.	War against the Italian allies
88 B.C.E.	Sulla's march on Rome
82 B.C.E.	Sulla assumes dictatorship
71 B.C.E.	Crassus crushes rebellion of Spartacus
71 B.C.E.	Pompey defeats Sertorius in Spain
70 B.C.E.	Consulship of Crassus and Pompey
60 B.C.E.	Formation of First Triumvirate
58–50 B.C.E.	Caesar in Gaul
53 B.C.E.	Crassus killed in Battle of Carrhae
49 B.C.E.	Caesar crosses Rubicon; civil war begins
48 B.C.E.	Pompey defeated at Pharsalus; killed in Egypt
46–44 B.C.E.	Caesar's dictatorship
45 B.C.E.	End of civil war
43 B.C.E.	Formation of Second Triumvirate
42 B.C.E.	Triumvirs defeat Brutus and Cassius at Philippi
31 B.C.E.	Octavian and Agrippa defeat Anthony at Actium

Lictors, pictured here, attended the chief Roman magistrates when they appeared in public. The axe carried by one of the lictors and the bound bundle of staffs carried by the others symbolize both the power of Roman magistrates to inflict corporal punishment on Roman citizens and the limits on that power. The bound staffs symbolize the right of citizens within the city of Rome not to be punished without a trial. The axe symbolizes the power of the magistrates, as commanders of the army, to put anyone to death without a trial outside the city walls. Alinari/Art Resource, N.Y.

defeated Roman enemies in North Africa and for a time dominated politics. Sulla (ca. 138–78 B.C.E.) established a dictatorship for a time after a series of military victories. The success of one general provided an example to other ambitious military figures. The unequal distribution of wealth and land meant there were always plenty of men willing to serve in the armies of ambitious generals. The Senate in Rome no longer really controlled Roman armies.

By the middle of the first century B.C.E., two generals were contending for domination, Gnaeus Pompey (106–48 B.C.E.) and Julius Caesar (100–44 B.C.E.). Pompey had won fame by ridding the Mediterranean of pirates. Somewhat later, Caesar conquered most of Gaul. For a time they tried to share political influence, but by 49 B.C.E. all cooperation had ceased. In that year Caesar, his career and life in jeopardy, defied the Roman Senate by leading his army out of his province across the Rubicon River (see Map I–6). In the civil war that followed, Caesar defeated the forces of Pompey and the Senate. Until his assassination in 44 B.C.E., Caesar virtually governed Rome alone. After his death, his nephew Octavian (63 B.C.E.—C.E. 14) rallied Caesar's forces. By 31 B.C.E., after years of ruthless civil war, Octavian emerged

victorious at the naval battle of Actium. At the age of thirty-two, Octavian stood as the absolute master of the Mediterranean world.

THE PRINCIPATE AND THE EMPIRE

Octavian was well aware of the fate of his uncle. He knew that it was dangerous to flaunt unprecedented powers and to disregard all republican tradition. He created a political structure that had republican trappings and the appearance of sharing power with the Senate and the people of Rome. Yet in reality the government of Octavian, like that of his successors, was a monarchy. Octavian was simply called by the un-official title of "first citizen," which in Latin is *princeps*. The Senate also heaped upon him other important political powers and honors. Among them was the semireligious title "Augustus," which carried implications of veneration, majesty, and holiness. From this time on, historians speak of Rome's first emperor as Augustus and of his regime as the Principate. The union of political and military power in the hands of the *princeps* made it possible for him to install rational, efficient, and stable government in the provinces for the first time.

The Augustan period was one of great prosperity. Augustus had brought in the wealth by the conquest of Egypt during the civil wars (see Map I–7). The great increase in commerce and industry made possible general peace and a vast program of public works. Finally, there was a strong return to successful small farming on the part of Augustus's resettled veterans.

The high point of Roman culture came in the last century of the republic and during the Principate of Augustus. The towering literary figure of the late republic was Cicero (106–43 B.C.E.); who delivered his famous orations in the law courts and in the Senate. Together with a considerable body of his private letters, these orations provide us with a clearer and fuller insight into his mind than into that of any other figure in antiquity. He also wrote treatises on rhetoric, ethics, and politics that put Greek philosophical ideas into Latin terminology and at the same time changed them to suit Roman conditions and values. He believed in a world governed by divine and natural law that human reason could perceive and human institutions reflect. His literary style, as well as his values and ideas, was an important legacy for the Middle Ages and, as reinterpreted, for the Renaissance.

Whereas Cicero was the last great voice of the republic, Vergil (70–19 B.C.E.) was the most important of the Augustan poets. Vergil's greatest work is the *Aeneid*, a long national epic. He glorified the civic greatness represented by Augustus and the peace and prosperity that he had brought to Rome.

MAP I–6   THE CIVIL WARS OF THE LATE ROMAN REPUBLIC   *This map shows the extent of the territory controlled by Rome at the time of Caesar's death and the sites of the major battles of the civil wars of the late republic.*

The central problem for Augustus's successors was the position of the ruler and his relationship to the ruled. Augustus tried to cloak the monarchical nature of his government, but his successors soon abandoned all pretense. The rulers came to be called ***imperator***—from which comes our word *emperor*—as well as *Caesar*. The latter title signified connection with the imperial house; the former indicated the military power on which everything was based. Because Augustus ostensibly was only the "first citizen" of a restored republic and his powers theoretically were voted him by the Senate and the people, he could not legally name his successor. He plainly designated his heirs, however, by lavishing favors on them and by giving them a share in the imperial power and responsibility.

The genius of the Augustan settlement lay in its capacity to enlist the active cooperation of the upper classes and their effective organ, the Senate. The election of magistrates was taken from the assemblies and given to the Senate, which became the major center for legislation and also exercised important judicial functions. Some emperors, like Vespasian, took pains to maintain, increase, and display the prestige and dignity of the Senate; others, like Caligula, Nero, and Domitian, degraded the Senate and paraded their own despotic power, but from the first the Senate's powers were illusory.

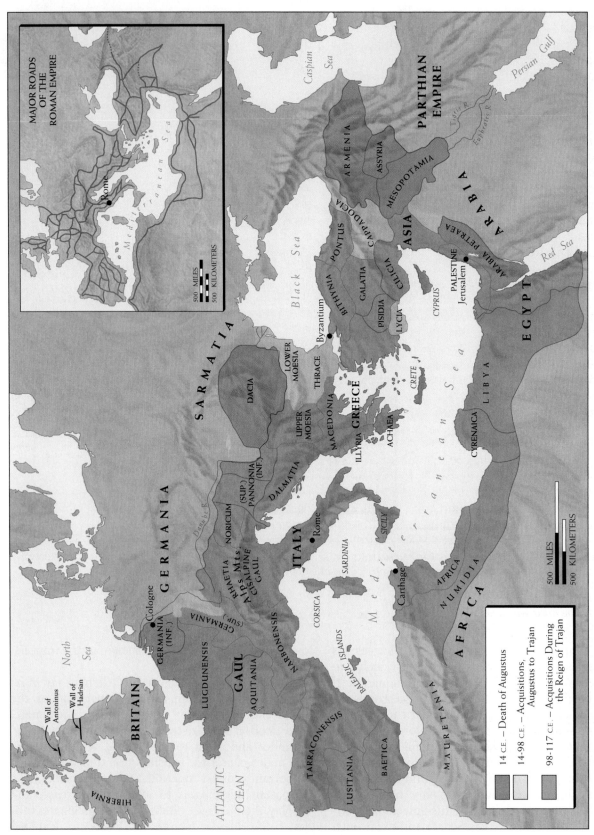

MAP I-7   PROVINCES OF THE ROMAN EMPIRE TO 117 C.E.   *The growth of the empire to its greatest extent is here shown in three stages—at the death of Augustus in 14 C.E., at the death of Nerva in 98, and at the death of Trajan in 117. The division into provinces is also shown. The insert shows the main roads that tied the far-flung empire together.*

Its true function was to be a legislative and administrative extension of the emperor's rule.

The provinces flourished economically and generally accepted Roman rule easily (see Map I–7). In the eastern provinces, the emperor was worshiped as a god, and even in Italy most emperors were deified after death as long as the imperial cult established by Augustus continued. Imperial policy was usually a happy combination of an attempt to unify the empire and its various peoples with a respect for local customs and differences. Roman citizenship was spread ever more widely, and by C.E. 212 almost every inhabitant of the empire was a citizen. Latin became the language of the western provinces. Although the east remained essentially Greek in language and culture, even it adopted many aspects of Roman life.

The army played an important role in the spread of Roman culture and the spiritual unification of the empire. The legionnaires married local women and frequently settled in the province of their service when their term was over.

From an administrative and cultural standpoint, the empire was a collection of cities and towns and had little to do with the countryside. Roman policy during the Principate was to raise urban centers to the status of Roman municipalities with the rights and privileges attached to them. A typical municipal charter left much responsibility in the hands of local councils and magistrates elected from the local aristocracy. Moreover, the holding of a magistracy, and later a seat on the council, carried Roman citizenship with it. Therefore, the Romans enlisted the upper classes of the provinces in their own government, spread Roman law and culture, and won the loyalty of the influential people.

Seen from the harsh perspective of human history, the first two centuries of the Roman Empire

A bust of Julius Caesar.   Museo Archeologico Nazionale, Naples, Italy. Copyright Scala/Art Resource, N.Y.

deserve their reputation as a "golden age." By the second century, however, troubles had arisen that foreshadowed the difficult times ahead. The literary efforts of the time reveal a flight from the present,

A panel from the Ara Pacis (Altar of Peace). The altar was dedicated in 9 B.C.E. It was part of a propaganda campaign—involving poetry, architecture, myth, and history— that Augustus undertook to promote himself as the savior of Rome and the restorer of peace. This panel shows the goddess Earth and her children with cattle, sheep, and other symbols of agricultural wealth.   Nimatallah/Art Resource, N.Y.

reality, and the public realm to the past, romance, and private pursuits. Some of the same aspects may be seen in everyday life, especially in the decline of vitality in local government. (See "Juvenal on Life in Rome.")

In the first century, members of the upper classes vied with one another for election to municipal office and for the honor of doing service to their communities. By the second century, much of their zeal had disappeared. It became necessary for the emperors to intervene to correct abuses in local affairs and even to force unwilling members of the ruling classes to accept public office. The reluctance to serve was caused largely by the imperial practice of holding magistrates and councilmen personally and collectively responsible for the revenues due. There were even some instances of magistrates fleeing to avoid their offices, a practice that became widespread in later centuries.

All of these difficulties reflected the presence of more basic problems. The prosperity brought by the end of civil war and the influx of wealth from the East, especially Egypt, could not sustain itself beyond the first half of the second century. There also appears to have been a decline in population for reasons that remain mysterious. The cost of government kept rising as the emperors were required (1) to maintain a costly standing army, (2) to keep the people in Rome happy with subsidized food and public entertainment ("bread and circuses"), (3) to pay an increasingly numerous bureaucracy, and (4) to wage expensive wars to defend the frontiers against dangerous and determined barbarian enemies. The ever-increasing need for money compelled the emperors to raise taxes, to press hard on their subjects, and to bring on inflation by debasing the coinage. These elements were to bring on the desperate crises that ultimately destroyed the empire.

JUVENAL ON LIFE IN ROME

The satirical poet Juvenal lived and worked in Rome in the late first and early second centuries C.E. His poems present a vivid picture of the material and cultural world of the Romans of his time. In the following passages, he tells of the discomforts and dangers of life in the city, both indoors and out.

■ *According to Juvenal, what dangers awaited pedestrians in the Rome of his day? Who had responsibility for the condition of Rome? If the situation was as bad as he says, why was nothing done about it? Why did people choose to live in Rome at all and especially in the conditions he describes?*

Who, in Praeneste's cool, or the wooded Volsinian
   uplands,
Who, on Tivoli's heights, or a small town like
   Gabii, say,
Fears the collapse of his house? But Rome is
   supported on pipestems,
Matchsticks; it's cheaper, so, for the landlord to
   shore up his ruins,
Patch up the old cracked walls, and notify all
   the tenants
They can sleep secure, though the beams are in
   ruins above them.
No, the place to live is out there, where no cry
   of *Fire!*
Sounds the alarm of the night, with a neighbor
   yelling for water,
Moving his chattels and goods, and the whole
   third story is smoking.

Look at other things, the various dangers
   of nighttime.
How high it is to the cornice that breaks, and a
   chunk beats my brains out,
Or some slob heaves a jar, broken or cracked,
   from a window.
Bang! It comes down with a crash and proves
   its weight on the sidewalk.
You are a thoughtless fool, unmindful of
   sudden disaster,
If you don't make your will before you go out to
   have dinner.
There are as many deaths in the night as there
   are open windows
Where you pass by; if you're wise, you will
   pray, in your wretched devotions,
People may be content with no more than
   emptying slop jars.

From Juvenal, *The Satires of Juvenal*, trans. by Rolfe Humphries (Bloomington, IN: Indiana University Press, 1958), pp. 40, 43.

CHRISTIANITY

The peace, stability, and prosperity of the first two centuries of the Roman Empire provided essential conditions for the rise of Christianity as one of the world's great religions and as the single most important cultural force in the future of Western civilization. Despite certain problems in regard to the historical character of the Gospels, there is no reason to doubt that Jesus was born in the province of Judaea in the time of Augustus and that he was a most effective teacher in the tradition of the Jewish prophets. Jesus had success and won a considerable following, especially among the poor. This success caused much suspicion among the upper classes. His message of love, charity, and humility, as seen in the Sermon on the Mount, and his criticism of the current Jewish religious practices provoked hostility within the religious establishment.

Jesus was put to death by Roman soldiers in Jerusalem probably in C.E. 30. His followers believed that he was resurrected on the third day after his death, and that belief became a critical element in the religion that they propagated throughout the Roman Empire and beyond. Through the early missionary work of Paul of Tarsus, the Christian faith was carried beyond the area of Palestine to virtually all the eastern Mediterranean world and to Rome itself. Christianity had its greatest success in the cities and among the poor and uneducated. (See "Mark Describes the Resurrection of Jesus.")

The future of Christianity depended on its communities finding an organization that would preserve unity within the group and help protect it against enemies outside. At first, the churches had little formal organization. By the second century C.E., however, the Christians of each city tended to accept the authority and leadership of a bishop. In time, bishops extended their authority over the Christian communities in outlying towns and the countryside. The power and authority of the bishops were soon enhanced by the doctrine of Apostolic Succession, which asserted that the powers that Jesus had given his original disciples were passed on from bishop to bishop by ordination.

The new faith soon incurred the distrust of the pagan world and of the imperial government, but in the first two centuries there was comparatively little official persecution. Division within the Christian church during these years was a greater threat. The great majority of Christians held to what even then were traditional, simple, conservative beliefs. This body of majority opinion and the Church that enshrined it came to be called **Catholic,** which means "universal." Its doctrines were deemed orthodox, whereas those holding contrary opinions were deemed heretics.

By the end of the second century, an orthodox canon had been shaped that included the Old Testament, the Gospels, and the Epistles of Paul, among other writings. The orthodox declared the Church itself to be the depository of Christian teaching and the bishops to be its receivers. They also drew up creeds, brief statements of faith to which true Christians should adhere.

By the end of the second century, an orthodox Christian—that is, a member of the Catholic church—was required to accept its creed, its canon of holy writings, and the authority of the bishops. During this same time, the Church in Rome and its bishop came to have special prominence; by C.E. 200, Rome was the most important center of Christianity.

DECLINE AND FALL OF THE ROMAN EMPIRE

By the time that the Christian religion had firmly established itself, the Roman Empire had entered a period of turmoil and instability known as the "crisis of the third century." There were massive external pressures on Rome's frontiers. The Persians pressed from the east and German tribes endangered the frontiers on the west and north. As the empire moved forces to fight one enemy, the frontier weakened in other areas.

The Roman army was no longer composed of citizens but rather of slaves, gladiators, barbarians, and brigands conscripted to fight. The emperors in this

A mosaic from Carthage illustrating aspects of life on the manorial estate of a certain Julian in the province of Africa. His housing, provisions, and entertainment appear to have been opulent. Social boundaries hardened in the late empire, and large fortified estates like this increasingly dominated social and economic life.
Musée Nationale du Bardo

MARK DESCRIBES THE RESURRECTION OF JESUS

Belief that Jesus rose from the dead after his Crucifixion (about 30 C.E.) was and is central to traditional Christian doctrine. The record of the Resurrection in the Gospel of Mark, *written a generation later (toward 70 C.E.), is the earliest we have. The significance to most Christian groups revolves about the assurance given them that death and the grave are not final and that, instead, salvation for a future life is possible. The appeal of these views was to be nearly universal in the West during the Middle Ages. The church was commonly thought to be the means of implementing the promise of salvation—hence the enormous importance of the church's sacramental system, its rules, and its clergy.*

■ *Why are the stories of miracles such as the one described here important for the growth of Christianity? What is special and important about this miracle? Why is it important in the story that days passed between the death of Jesus and the opening of the tomb? Why might the early Christians believe this story? Why was belief in the resurrection important for Christianity in the centuries immediately after the life of Jesus? Is it still important today?*

And when evening had come, since it was the day of Preparation, that is, the day before the sabbath, Joseph of Arimathea, a respected member of the council, who was also himself looking for the kingdom of God, took courage and went to Pilate, and asked for the body of Jesus. And Pilate wondered if he were already dead; and summoning the centurion, he asked him whether he was already dead. And when he learned from the centurion that he was dead, he granted the body to Joseph. And he brought a linen shroud, and taking him down, wrapped him in the linen shroud, and laid him in a tomb which had been hewn out of the rock; and he rolled a stone against the door of the tomb. Mary Magdalene and Mary the mother of Jesus saw where he was laid.

And when the sabbath was past, Mary Magdalene, and Mary the mother of James, and Salome, bought spices, so that they might go and anoint him. And very early on the first day of the week they went to the tomb when the sun had risen. And they were saying to one another, "Who will roll away the stone for us from the door of the tomb?" And looking up, they saw that the stone was rolled back; for it was very large. And entering the tomb, they saw a young man sitting on the right side, dressed in a white robe; and they were amazed. And he said to them, "Do not be amazed; you seek Jesus of Nazareth, who was crucified. He has risen, he is not here, see the place where they laid him. But go, tell his disciples and Peter that he is going before you to Galilee; there you will see him, as he told you." And they went out and fled from the tomb; for trembling and astonishment had come upon them; and they said nothing to any one, for they were afraid.

Gospel of Mark 15:42–47; 16:1–8, Revised Standard Version of the Bible *(New York: Thomas Nelson and Sons, 1946, 1952).*

century and later were almost wholly dependent on the army for their authority. The military expenses put great pressure on the economy. Because the empire was impoverished, with no system of credit financing, the emperors compelled the people to provide food, supplies, money, and labor. The upper classes in the cities were made to serve as administrators without pay and to meet deficits in revenue from their own pockets. The changes in the army, the tax system, and administrative procedures undermined both the authority and the morale of the traditional ruling classes in the empire.

Toward the end of the third century, the emperor Diocletian (r. C.E. 284–305) responded to these difficulties by dividing the empire into four separate administrative units, each with its own ruler and capital. This political reorganization did not prove to be particularly effective. The emperor Constantine (r. C.E. 306–337) re-united the empire, but only temporarily. In C.E. 330, he established his capital at Constantinople in the East. Fragmentation and the shifting of the capital meant that by the close of the fourth century the empire consisted of eastern and western halves virtually independent of each other.

Constantinople became the center of a vital and flourishing culture that we call *Byzantine* and that lasted until the fifteenth century.

Indeed, when we contemplate the decline and fall of the Roman Empire in the fourth and fifth centuries, we are speaking only of the West. There, life became increasingly rural as barbarian invasions continued and grew in intensity. The villa, a fortified country estate, became the basic unit of life. There, **coloni,** small landholders who were original settlers, gave their services to the local magnate in return for economic assistance and protection. Many cities shrank to no more than tiny walled fortresses ruled by military commanders and bishops. The failure of the central imperial authority to maintain the roads and the constant danger from robber bands sharply curtailed trade and communications. These circumstances forced greater self-reliance and a more primitive style of life. The only institution providing a high degree of unity was the Christian church.

The new central position of the Christian church was closely connected with the political and cultural turmoil of the third and fourth centuries. During these centuries, many people turned to various kinds of religions, Christianity among them, as traditional political institutions collapsed. Christianity offered converts a rich and attractive philosophy of life. It possessed a god who had suffered, died, and was resurrected, mystical and sacred rites, a moral code, a strong sense of community, the spiritual equality of male and female, rich and poor, a close, personal relationship with the deity, and the promise of immortality. The Church had an efficient organization. And its doctrines of love and the brotherhood of all humankind under a loving and forgiving God were deeply attractive.

Christianity prospered during the third century, but it also encountered new dangers. About the middle of the century, a brief official persecution occurred. In 303, Diocletian launched the most serious persecution the Church had yet experienced. In both cases, persecution backfired and created new sympathy for Christianity.

In 312, Constantine became a champion of the new faith in hopes that the Christian God would bring victory to his military forces. After he won the important Battle of the Milvian Bridge, his support of the Christian cause was unfailing. Although he did not outlaw pagan rituals or abolish the cult of emperor worship, Constantine did go far beyond simply tolerating Christianity by granting various official privileges to the Church. With one exception, the successors of Constantine in the fourth century favored Christianity. In 394, the emperor Theodosius (r. 379–395) forbade the celebration of pagan cults and abolished the pagan religious calendar. At the death of Theodosius, Christianity had become the official religion of the Roman Empire.

The establishment of Christianity as the state religion did not put an end to the troubles of Christians and their church. Instead, it created new ones and complicated some that were old. First, the favored position of the Church attracted converts for the wrong reasons. Second, the problem of the relationship between Church and state arose, presenting the possibility that Christianity would become completely subordinate to the state, as religion had been in the classical world and in earlier civilizations.

Empress Theodora and her attendants. The union of political and spiritual authority in the person of the empress is shown by the depiction on Theodora's mantle of three magi carrying gifts to the Virgin and Jesus. Early Christian Mosaic. San Vitale, Ravenna, Italy. Copyright Scala/Art Resource, N.Y.

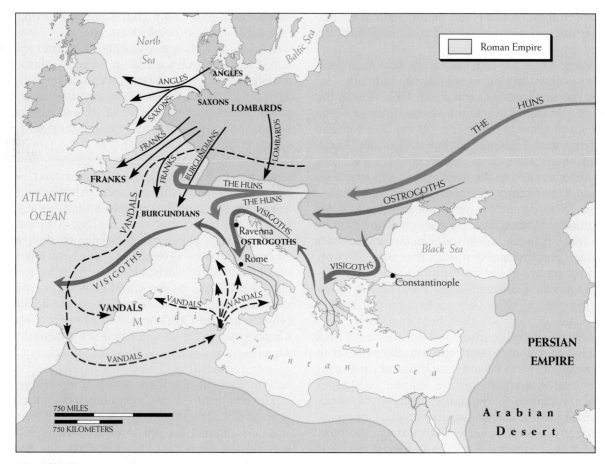

MAP I–8 BARBARIAN MIGRATIONS INTO THE WEST IN THE FOURTH AND FIFTH CENTURIES
The forceful intrusion of Germanic and non-Germanic barbarians into the Roman Empire from the last quarter of the fourth century through the fifth century made for a constantly changing pattern of movement and relations. The map shows the major routes taken by the usually unwelcome newcomers and the areas most deeply affected by main groups.

The position and the influence of the Christian church became strong during the very decades when the political structures of the Roman Empire began to crumble under waves of barbarian invasions from northern and eastern Europe (see Map I–8). In 378, German tribes handily defeated the Roman armies led by the emperor Valens (r. 364–378) at the Battle of Adrianople. Thereafter, the Romans passively permitted settlement after settlement of barbarians within the very heart of the Western empire. In 410 the Visigoths sacked Rome itself.

In 476, the traditional date for the fall of the Roman Empire, the Western emperor Romulus Augustulus (r. 475–476) was deposed and replaced by the barbarian Odoacer (ca. 434–493), who ruled as king of the Romans. By the end of the fifth century, power in western Europe had passed decisively from the hands of the Roman emperors to those of barbarian chieftains. The Ostrogoths settled in Italy, the Visigoths in Spain, the Franks in northern Gaul and Spain, the Vandals in Africa and the Mediterranean, and the Angles and Saxons in England.

Europe Enters the Middle Ages

Barbarians were now the Western masters, but they were masters who also were willing to learn from the people they had conquered. Although the barbarians were militarily superior, the Romans retained their cultural strength. This accommodation of cultures was assisted by the fact that the Visigoths, the Ostrogoths, and the Vandals had entered the West as people already partly Christianized by missionaries. All things considered, reconciliation and a gradual interpenetration of two strong cultures—a creative tension—marked the period of the Germanic invasions. The stronger culture was the Roman, and it became dominant in a later fusion.

The political collapse of western Europe, and with it the end of the political and economic unity between East and West that had characterized the Roman Empire, marked the beginning of the European Middle Ages. The early Middle Ages (476–1000) saw the birth of a distinctive western European culture. It was a period of recovery from the collapse of Roman civilization, a time of forced experimentation with new ideas and institutions. Western European culture, as we know it today, was born of a unique, inventive mix of surviving Graeco-Roman, new Germanic, and evolving Christian traditions. Experimentation was required because of the pressure of the invasions, the local political turmoil and economic stagnation, the replacement of paganism by Christianity, and the new problem posed to Europe from the Mediterranean world by the rise of a new, militant religion, Islam.

THE BYZANTINE EMPIRE

As western Europe succumbed to the Germanic invasions, imperial power shifted to the Byzantine Empire, that is, the eastern part of the Roman Empire, with its capital in Constantinople. Between 324 and 1453 the empire passed from an early period of expansion and splendor to a time of contraction and splintering, to final catastrophic defeat.

Between 324 and 632, the empire saw its greatest territorial expansion and its political and cultural golden age. Under Justinian (527–565); Roman law was collated and revised so that it could henceforth aid the growth of central government. Constantinople, with a population of 350,000, became the cultural crossroads of Asian and European civilization.

In the centuries after Justinian, however, Islamic armies progressively besieged the empire. Emperor Leo III (717–741) successfully repulsed them, but at the same time he created a new problem with western Christians by forbidding images to exist in eastern churches. The ensuing controversy contributed to a major schism between western (Roman Catholic) and eastern (Byzantine) Christianity.

In 1071, the Seljuk Turks overran the eastern provinces of the empire, and western Christians sacked Constantinople in 1204. These events sowed the seeds of the empire's demise, which came finally in the fifteenth century at the hands of the Ottoman Turks, who captured Constantinople in 1453.

THE RISE OF ISLAM

Muhammad (570–632), the founder of Islam, received his call to be "the Prophet" at age forty. The name of his religion, Islam, means "submission" (to Allah). Its adherents, called Muslims, which means "submissive" or "surrendering," obey the will of Allah as revealed in the Qur'an, a series of revelations received by Muhammad over a period of time and compiled by his successors. Islam recognizes Jesus Christ as a prophet sent by God, but not one so great as Muhammad and not God's son as the Christians believe. Islam is uncompromisingly monotheistic.

Among the things required of the faithful are prayer five times each day, generous almsgiving, and fasting during the daylight hours for one month each year. Another requirement is a pilgrimage to the holy city of Mecca, in what is now Saudi Arabia, at least once during one's lifetime. By its ability to forge a common Arab culture and its willingness to impose it by force, Islam became a spiritual force capable of uniting the Arab tribes in a true Arab empire.

By the middle of the eighth century, Muslims had conquered the southern and eastern Mediterranean coastline and occupied parts of Spain, which they controlled or strongly influenced until

Muslims are enjoined to live by the divine law, or Shari'a, *and have a right to have disputes settled by an arbiter of the* Shari'a. *Here we see a husband complaining about his wife before the state-appointed judge, or* qadi. *The wife, backed up by two other women, points an accusing finger at the husband. In such cases, the first duty of the* qadi, *who should be a learned person of faith, is to try to effect a reconciliation before the husband divorces his wife, or the wife herself seeks a divorce.* Cliche Bibliothèque Nationale de France, Paris

the fifteenth century (see Map I–9). In addition, their armies had pushed north and east through Mesopotamia and Persia and beyond.

Assaulted on both their eastern and their western frontiers, and everywhere challenged in the Mediterranean, Europeans developed a lasting fear and suspicion of Muslims. In 732, an army led by Charles Martel, (d. 741) the ruler of the Franks, defeated a raiding party of Arabs at Poitiers. This victory ended the threat of Arab expansion into western Europe by way of Spain. Nonetheless, from the end of the seventh century to the middle of the eleventh century, the Mediterranean remained something of a Muslim lake. Although trade was not entirely cut off during these centuries, it was significantly reduced and was carried on in keen awareness of Muslim dominance.

NEW IMPORTANCE OF THE CHRISTIAN CHURCH

When trade wanes, cities decline, and with them those cultural centers that enable a society to look and live beyond itself. The Arab invasions and domination of the Mediterranean during a crucial period of the early Middle Ages contributed to the conditions for the birth of western Europe as a distinctive cultural and social entity. As western shipping in the Mediterranean declined, so too did coastal urban centers. People who would otherwise have been engaged in trade-related work in the cities moved in large numbers to interior regions, where they worked on the farms of the great landholders. The domains of these landholders became the basic social and political units of society, and local barter economies sprang up within them.

The functions of the Christian church also became more important. Local bishops and cathedral chapters filled the vacuum of authority left by the removal of Roman governors. The local cathedral became the center of urban life, and the local bishop became the highest authority for those who remained in the cities. At this time, the Church alone possessed an effective hierarchical administration scattered throughout the old empire and staffed by the best-educated minds in Europe. The Church also strengthened itself through the institution of monasticism. Embracing the biblical "counsels of perfection" (chastity, poverty, and obedience), the monastic life became the purest form of Christian religious practice in the Middle Ages. The ideal of monasticism as the model for a superior Christian life eventually evolved into a belief in the general superiority of the clergy and the mission of the Church over the laity and the state.

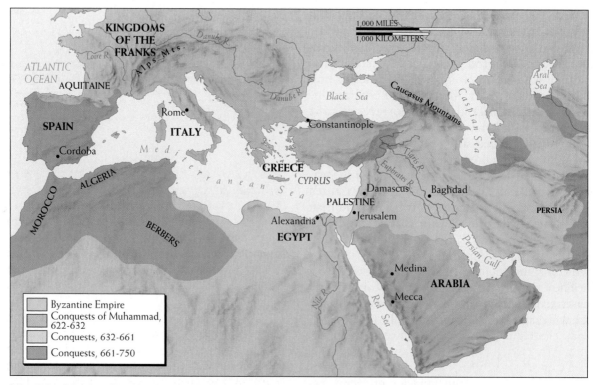

MAP I–9 MUSLIM CONQUESTS AND DOMINATION OF THE MEDITERRANEAN TO ABOUT 750 C.E. *The rapid spread of Islam (both as a religion and as a political-military power) is shown here. Within 125 years of Muhammad's rise, Muslims came to dominate Spain and all areas south and east of the Mediterranean.*

In addition to this distinctly moral and spiritual claim to superiority, the bishops of Rome made a separate claim to superiority within the Church; they had always opposed intervention by the secular state in Church matters. As early as the fifth and sixth centuries, they took advantage of imperial weakness and distraction to develop the doctrine of "papal primacy" for their own defense. This teaching in time raised the Roman pontiff to an unassailable supremacy within the Church when it came to defining orthodox Church doctrine and practice. It also put the pope in a position to make important secular claims that caused repeated conflicts between Church and state in the Middle Ages.

CHARLEMAGNE

The chief political characteristic of the Middle Ages was the absence of central political authority. The most persistent problem of medieval political history was the competing claims of the "one" and the "many"—on one hand, the king, who struggled for a centralized government in a particular area and transregional loyalty from his subjects, and on the other, powerful local magnates who strove to preserve their regional autonomy and purely local customs.

Between the sixth and eleventh centuries, only one figure achieved a significant degree of centralized political authority over a substantial region of Europe. This was the Frankish king Charlemagne (r. 768–814), whose kingdom loosely embraced modern France, Belgium, Holland, Switzerland, almost the whole of western Germany, much of Italy, a portion of Spain, and the island of Corsica (see Map I–10). Charlemagne carefully developed strong political ties with local nobles and with the Church, which regarded him as its protector. On Christmas Day, 800, Pope Leo III (r. 795–816) crowned Charlemagne emperor. With this papal act there came into being what would come to be known in the tenth century as the Holy Roman Empire, a revival, based in Germany, of the old Roman Empire in the West.

Charlemagne governed his kingdom through counts, of whom there were perhaps as many as 250. They were strategically located within the administrative districts into which the kingdom was divided. The counts often were local magnates who already possessed the arms and the self-interest to enforce the rule of a generous king. These counts served Charlemagne well, but they were never completely loyal and he never wholly controlled their political behavior.

Charlemagne accumulated great wealth in the form of loot and land from conquered tribes. He

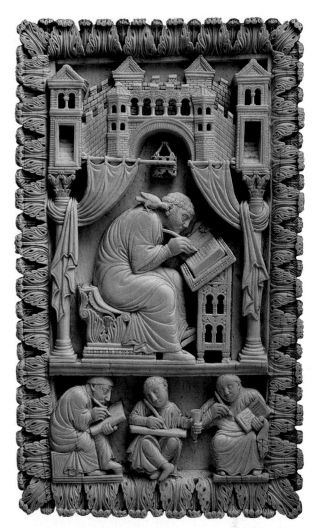

Saint Gregory the Great, shown in a monastic scriptorium, or study, receiving the divine word from a dove perched on his shoulder. Below him three monks are writing. The middle monk holds an inkwell in his left hand. Kunsthistorisches Museum, Vienna

used a large part of this booty to attract Europe's best scholars to his capital at Aachen (Aix-la-Chapelle). He intended them to use their learning in the classics and Christian writings to upgrade the administrative skills of the clerics and officials who staffed the royal bureaucracy. Through these efforts, a modest rebirth of antiquity occurred in the palace school as scholars collected, studied, and preserved ancient manuscripts.

Charlemagne's empire and the cultural revival it nurtured lasted for a relatively short time. After the death of his son and successor, Louis the Pious (r. 814–840), the kingdom was divided into three equal parts by the Treaty of Verdun (843): a middle section (Lotharingia, embracing roughly modern Holland, Belgium, Switzerland, Alsace-Lorraine, and Italy); a western part (roughly modern France); and

MAP I–10 THE EMPIRE OF CHARLEMAGNE TO 814 *Building on the successes of his prede-cessors, Charlemagne greatly increased the Frankish domains. Such traditional enemies as the Saxons and the Lombards fell under his sway.*

an eastern part (roughly modern Germany). Long-term loyalty to a single monarch by the nobles of various regions proved unattainable. Potential monarchs fought each other, and nobles looked out for their own interests. The papacy lost prestige as it cast its lot first with one monarch and then with another in an effort to preserve a major political role for itself.

On top of all these troubles, the late ninth and tenth centuries saw successive waves of attacks by the Vikings from Scandinavia, the Magyars from the eastern European plains, and the Muslims in the south. Local populations became more dependent than ever before on local strongmen to

protect them. This brute fact of life provided the essential precondition for the maturation of feudal society.

FEUDAL AND MANORIAL SOCIETY

The early Middle Ages were a time of fragmentation and decentralization, with the weaker seeking the protection of the stronger. The term **feudal society** refers to the social, political, military, and economic system that emerged in response to these conditions. A feudal society is one in which a regional prince or a local lord is dominant and the highest virtues are those of mutual trust and fidelity. In a feudal society what people most need is the firm assurance that others can be depended on in time of dire need.

The two chief institutions of feudal society were vassalage and the fief. *Vassalage* involved "fealty" to a lord. To swear fealty was to promise to refrain from any action that might in any way threaten the lord's well-being and to perform for him on his request personal services, the most important of which was military aid. In return, the lord agreed to protect the vassal from physical harm and to stand as his advocate in public court. After fealty was sworn, the lord provided for the vassal's physical maintenance by the bestowal of a fief. The *fief* was the physical or material wherewithal to meet the vassal's military and other obligations. It could take the form of liquid wealth or, more commonly, a grant of real property. Feudalism could lead to a very confused set of relationships, because often one person was the vassal of more than one lord. And as the centuries passed, personal loyalty and service became quite secondary to the acquisition of property.

The social and economic equivalents of the dependency relationships of feudalism on local levels were the manor and serfdom. It is important to realize, however, that the manorial system existed in many places where feudalism never became well developed. Village farms, normally owned by a local landlord, were called **manors.** Here peasants labored as farmers under a lord, who gave them small plots

of land and tenements in exchange for their services and a portion of their crops. Some of the peasants were free and owned certain lands themselves. They had specific legal rights even if they surrendered their land and services to a landlord in exchange for his support and protection. On the other hand, peasants who entered the service of a lord without any real property to bargain with ended up as unfree **serfs.** All serfs owed labor of several days a week to their lords and were also subject to socalled dues in kind: firewood for cutting the lord's wood, sheep for grazing their sheep on the lord's land, and the like. The discontent of many serfs is witnessed by the high number of recorded escapes.

An equestrian figure of Charlemagne (or possibly one of his sons) from the early ninth century. ³⁄₄ view. Louvre, Paris, France. Copyright Giraudon/Art Resource, N.Y.

Major Political and Religious Developments of the Early Middle Ages	
313	Emperor Constantine issues the *Edict of Milan*
325	Council of Nicaea defines Christian doctrine
410	Rome invaded by Visigoths under Alaric
413–426	Saint Augustine writes *City of God*
451	Council of Chalcedon further defines Christian doctrine
451–453	Europe invaded by the Huns under Attila
476	Barbarian Odoacer deposes Western emperor and rules as king of the Romans
489–493	Theodoric establishes kingdom of Ostrogoths in Italy
529	Saint Benedict founds monastery at Monte Cassino
533	Justinian codifies Roman law
622	Muhammad's flight from Mecca (*Hegira*)
732	Charles Martel defeats Muslims at Poitiers
754	Pope Stephen II and Pepin III ally

Church and State in the High Middle Ages

What are known as the High Middle Ages (ca. 1000–1300) mark a period of political expansion and consolidation and of intellectual flowering that followed Europe's deep difficulties during the ninth and tenth centuries. This period saw the borders of western Europe secured against foreign invaders. These centuries also saw the emergence of "national" monarchies in France, England, and Germany. Parliaments and popular assemblies, representing the interests of the landed nobility, the clergy, and townspeople, appeared at the same time to secure local rights and customs against the claims of the developing monarchies. During these centuries, there was also a great revival of trade and commerce, the growth of towns, and the emergence of a "new rich" merchant class, the ancestors of modern capitalists.

The High Middle Ages were also the time when the Western church, now centered on the pope in Rome, established itself as an authority independent of monarchical secular government. This occurred during the Investiture Struggle of the late eleventh and the twelfth centuries. The fortunes of both the empire and the papacy had begun to revive after the dark period of the late ninth and early tenth centuries. The Ottonians, successors to the Franks in Germany, now carried the title of Holy Roman emperor, and they produced some able leaders.

About the same time, the Church began to undergo a series of internal reforms sponsored by clerics influenced by the monastery of Cluny (founded 910) in France. The Cluny reformers demanded a higher moral standard from the clergy and asserted a sharp separation of Church and state. Previously, emperors and other political rulers often had controlled the appointment of bishops and other high Church officials.

Under Pope Gregory VII (r. 1073–1085), the papacy declared its independence from such lay control of Church offices. Henceforth, bishops were to be installed in their offices by high ecclesiastical authority as empowered by the pope and none other. For almost fifty years controversy raged, until the Concordat of Worms in 1122 provided that the pope or his representative would invest all bishops with the spiritual signs of their office and the emperor or his representative would invest them only with lands. Thereafter, the clergy were more independent of the state than ever before, and the papacy began to assert itself as an independent political power.

THE DIVISION OF CHRISTENDOM

Also in this period Christendom became firmly divided into Eastern and Western churches, the result of a long-developing conflict over Church practice and doctrine rooted in the early Middle Ages. From the start, there had been a difference in language (Greek in the East, Latin in the West) and culture. The Eastern patriarchs (rulers of the Church) also had a strong mystical orientation to the next world that caused them to submit more passively than Western popes to secular control of the Church (Caesaro-papism, "Caesar acting as pope"). Contrary to the evolving Western tradition of universal clerical celibacy, the Eastern church permitted the marriage of parish priests, while strictly forbidding bishops to marry. The Eastern church used leavened bread in the Eucharist, contrary to the Western custom of

Benedictine monks at choir. The reform movement that began at the Benedictine monastery at Cluny in northern France in the tenth century spread throughout the church and was ultimately responsible for the reassertion of papal authority. Courtesy of the Trustees of the British Library

THE CAROLINGIAN MANOR

A capitulary from the reign of Charlemagne known as "De Villis" itemizes what the king received from his royal manors or village estates. It is a testimony both to Carolingian administrative ability and domination over the countryside.

■ *What gave the lord the right to absolutely everything? (Has anything been overlooked?) How did the stewards and workers share in the manorial life? Was the arrangment a good deal for them as well as for the lord?*

That each steward shall make an annual statement of all our income: an account of our lands cultivated by the oxen which our ploughmen drive and of our lands which the tenants of farms ought to plough; an account of the pigs, of the rents, of the obligations and fines; of the game taken in our forests without our permission; of the various compositions; of the mills, of the forest, of the fields, of the bridges, and ships: of the free-men and the hundreds who are under obligations to our treasury; of markets, vineyards, and those who owe wine to us; of the hay, fire-wood, torches, planks, and other kinds of lumber; of the wastelands; of the vegetables, millet, panic; of the wool, flax, and hemp; of the fruits of the trees, of the nut trees, larger and smaller; of the grafted trees of all kinds; of the gardens; of the turnips; of the fishponds; of the hides, skins, and horns; of the honey, wax; of the fat, tallow and soap; of the mulberry wine, cooked wine, mead, vinegar; beer, wine new and old; of the new grain and the old; of the hens and eggs; of the geese; the number of fishermen, smiths [workers in metal], swordmakers, and shoemakers; of the bins and boxes; of the turners and saddlers; of the forges and mines, that is iron and other mines; of the lead mines; of the tributaries; of the colts and fillies; they shall make all these known to us, set forth separately and in order, at Christmas, in order that we may know what and how much of each thing we have.

In each of our estates our stewards are to have as many cow-houses, piggeries, sheep-folds, stables for goats, as possible, and they ought never to be without these.

They must provide with the greatest care that whatever is prepared or made with the hands, that is, lard, smoked meat, salt meat, partially salted meat, wine, vinegar, mulberry wine, cooked wine, garns, mustard, cheese, butter, malt beer, mead, honey, wax, flour, all should be prepared and made with the greatest cleanliness.

That each steward on each of our domains shall always have, for the sake of ornament, swans, peacocks, pheasants, ducks, pigeons, partridges, turtle-doves.

That in each of our estates, the chambers shall be provided with counterpanes, cushions, pillows, bed-clothes, coverings for the tables and benches; vessels of brass, lead, iron and wood; andirons, chains, pothooks, adzes, axes, augers, cutlasses and all other kinds of tools, so that it shall never be necessary to go elsewhere for them, or to borrow them. And the weapons, which are carried against the enemy, shall be well cared for, so as to keep them in good condition.

For our women's work they are to give at the proper time, as has been ordered, the materials, that is the linen, wool, woad, vermilion, madder, wool-combs, teasels, soap grease, vessels and the other objects which are necessary.

Of the food-products other than meat, two-thirds shall be sent each year for our own use, that is of the vegetables, fish, cheese, butter, honey, mustard, vinegar, millet, panic, dried and green herbs, radishes, and in addition of the wax, soap and other small products.

That each steward shall have in his district good workmen, namely, blacksmiths, goldsmiths, silversmiths, shoemakers, turners, carpenters, swordmakers, fishermen, foilers, soapmakers, men who know how to make beer cider, berry, and all the other kinds of beverages, bakers to make pastry for our table, net-makers who know how to make nets for hunting, fishing and fowling, and the other who are too numerous to be designated.

Translations and Reprints from the Original Sources of European History, Vol. 3 (Philadelphia: Department of History, University of Pennsylvania, 1909), pp. 2–4.

using unleavened bread. The Eastern church objected to the Western church's description of the Holy Spirit as proceeding from the Son as well as from the Father and opposed the Western church's use of icons and images in worship.

Beyond these issues was a major conflict over Church authority. The Eastern church put more stress on the authority of the Bible and of the ecumenical councils of the Church than on papal or Roman primacy. The Roman popes claimed a special primacy of authority on the basis of the apostle Peter's commission from Jesus in Matthew 16:18 ("Thou art Peter, and upon this rock I will build my church"). These claims were completely unacceptable to the East, where the independence and autonomy of national churches was preferred. This basic issue of authority in matters of faith lay behind the mutual excommunication of Pope Nicholas I and Patriarch Photius in the ninth century and that of Pope Leo IX and Patriarch Michael Cerularius in 1054.

THE RISE OF TOWNS

Western Europe had little international commerce and even less urban culture during the centuries following the collapse of the Roman Empire. By comparison with previous centuries, western Europe had become an isolated, agricultural society. This is one reason some historians refer to the centuries between 500 and 1000 as a comparative "dark age." By the late tenth century, thanks to improved climate, agricultural production, and the end of Viking invasions, the population had begun to grow rapidly. The increased numbers of people made possible the rebirth of the old Roman towns and the creation of many new ones. The great seaports of Italy had weathered the early Middle Ages better than any other western cities, maintaining vibrant urban cultures. Even in the darkest times, Venice, Pisa, and Genoa traded with Constantinople and the port cities of Palestine, Syria, and Egypt. The Venetians were especially successful merchants throughout the eastern world; their commercial success approached domination there after the First Crusade (1095) opened the Mediterranean to still greater western shipping.

The term **bourgeois,** or *burgher,* first appeared in the eleventh century as a negative description of the newly powerful townspeople. In the popular imagination, they were a new addition to the traditional social ranks of knight (or noble), cleric, and serf. Initially, the term designated the merchant groups who created the *bourgs,* or new market towns, as bases for their commercial operations in and around the old Roman towns. Because the burghers' sole business was trade and banking, the clergy condemned their work as usurious and immoral. The nobility also looked askance at their new wealth and mobility. Because the merchants departed from traditional ways of making money, that is, by owning and cultivating land, they seemed to pose a threat to political and social order.

The common people, by contrast, admired the merchants. They saw their commercial success as providing new economic opportunity for themselves. The new towns became magnets for ambitious and skilled peasants, who both gained their freedom from serfdom there and found new vocations. Lucky peasants experienced a heretofore unknown social mobility, and the diligent and successful among them even became gentlemen.

The merchants for their part resented the laws and customs of traditional society, which gave the nobility and the clergy special privileges. By allowing the nobility and the clergy to subject all others to their notions of morality and work, traditional law and custom impeded the new course of urban life and threatened its future development. Wherever merchants settled, they lobbied for the freedom necessary to pursue successful commerce. In doing so, they had the broad support of townspeople. They opposed tolls, tariffs, and other petty regulations that restricted trade and dampened commercial activity.

Many medieval towns, especially in northern Europe, were entirely enclosed by walls for protection. Here is the mid-fifteenth century walled city of Lüneburg in northern Germany.   Foto Makovec

Skilled workers were an integral component of the commerce of medieval towns. This scene shows the manufacture of cannons in a foundry in Florence. Scala/Art Resource, N.Y.

Whether they were wealthy merchants or struggling artisans, townspeople wanted a government in which traders and craftsmen determined policy. Policy made by secular and ecclesiastical overlords was calculated to control and exploit the towns rather than nurture and expand commerce. Such desire brought towns into conflict with the norms of static agricultural society. Merchant guilds and protective associations sprang up in the eleventh century, followed in the twelfth by guilds of craftsmen (drapers, haberdashers, furriers, hosiers, goldsmiths, and so on). These organizations worked to advance the business interest of both merchants and craftsmen as well as to enhance the personal well-being of their members.

During the High and later Middle Ages, towns also formed independent communes and allied with kings against the landed nobility. In this way, townspeople became a force in the breakup of traditional feudal society.

THE CRUSADES

If an index of popular piety and support for the pope in the High Middle Ages is needed, the Crusades amply provide it (see Map I–11). In 1095, Pope Urban II proclaimed the First Crusade at the Council of Clermont in France. Participants in this Crusade to liberate the Holy Land from Muslim control were promised a plenary indulgence should they die in battle, that is, a complete remission of the penance required of them for their mortal sins

and hence release from suffering for these sins in purgatory. To rescue Jerusalem, which had been in non-Christian hands since the seventh century, three great armies—tens of thousands of crusaders, gathered from France, Germany, and Italy—converged on the Middle East. Jerusalem fell to them on July 15, 1099. By the middle of the next century, however, Jerusalem had again fallen into Arab hands. Other Crusades attempted to duplicate the feat of the first but with little success.

The long-term achievement of the Crusades had little to do with their original purpose. The later Crusades became more important for the way they stimulated new trade between western Europe and the East than for regaining the Holy Land. The merchants of Venice, Pisa, and Genoa particularly benefited from them.

THE RISE OF NEW MONARCHIES

During the eleventh and twelfth centuries in England, France, and Germany, the central monarchies began to assert themselves with considerable success against the territorial influence of their respective nobilities. The latter remained very strong and influential. To a degree unknown for centuries, however, central political authority became established in matters of law, military affairs, and taxation. Different varieties and degrees of monarchical authority characterized each country.

England William, duke of Normandy (d. 1087), conquered England in 1066 by defeating the Anglo-Saxon

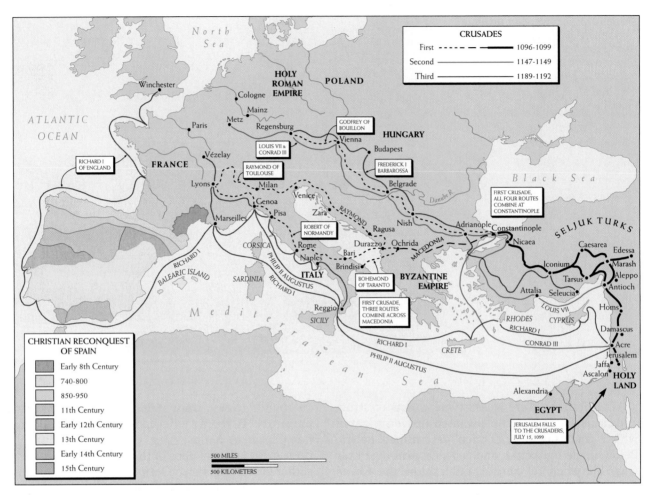

MAP I–11 THE EARLY CRUSADES *Routes and several leaders of the Crusades during the first century of the movement are shown. The names on this map do not exhaust the list of great nobles who went on the First Crusade. The even showier array of monarchs of the Second and Third Crusades still left the Crusades, on balance, ineffective in achieving their goals.*

army at Hastings. Within weeks of the invasion, William was crowned king of England both by right of a complex hereditary claim and by right of conquest. The new king of England remained, however, also the duke of Normandy, with extensive lands in France, the basis for later conflict between France and England. William organized his new English nation shrewdly. He subjected his noble vassals to the crown, yet he also consulted with them regularly about decisions of "state." The result was a unique blending of the "one" and the "many," a balance between monarchical and noble elements in the body politic.

William's successors tried to press their authority more boldly against the Church and the nobility. Henry II (r. 1165–1189) aroused the strong opposition of his one-time close friend Thomas à Becket (1118–1170), archbishop of Canterbury; eventually Henry's agents murdered Becket in his own cathedral. General moral and political opposition to the

act in the end weakened the king. English resistance to the monarchy became outright rebellion under Henry's successors, the brothers Richard the Lion-Hearted (r. 1189–1199) and John (r. 1199–1216). Richard's crusades to the Holy Land put a heavy burden of taxation on the nation. John's conflict with the pope led to his excommunication and the placement of England under a papal interdict, which cut off many essential Church services.

Unsuccessful military ventures finally led to a noble rebellion against John that resulted in his granting in 1215 of the Magna Carta ("Great Charter"). This monumental document was a victory of English noblemen, clergy, and towns over monarchical power. More important, it restored the internal political balance in the English state. The monarchy remained intact, and its legitimate powers and rights were duly recognized and preserved. (See "The English Nobility Imposes Restraints on King John.")

THE ENGLISH NOBILITY IMPOSES RESTRAINTS ON KING JOHN

The gradual building of a sound English constitutional monarchy in the Middle Ages required the king's willingness to share power. He had to be strong, but could not act as a despot or rule by fiat. The danger of despotism became acute in England under the rule of King John. In 1215, the English nobility forced him to recognize Magna Carta, which reaffirmed traditional rights and personal liberties that are still enshrined in English law.

■ *Does the Magna Carta protect basic rights or special privileges? Does this protection suggest that there was a sense of fairness in the past? Does the granting of such protection in any way weaken the king?*

A free man shall not be fined for a small offense, except in proportion to the gravity of the offense; and for a great offense he shall be fined in proportion to the magnitude of the offense, saving his freehold [property]; and a merchant in the same way, saving his merchandise; and the villein [a free serf, bound only to his lord] shall be fined in the same way, saving his wainage [wagon], if he shall be at [the king's] mercy. And none of the above fines shall be imposed except by the oaths of honest men of the neighborhood.. . .

No constable or other bailiff of [the king] shall take anyone's grain or other chattels without immediately paying for them in money, unless he is able to obtain a postponement at the good will of the seller.

No constable shall require any knight to give money in place of his ward of a castle [i.e., standing guard], if he is willing to furnish that ward in his own person, or through another honest man, if he himself is not able to do it for a reasonable cause; and if we shall lead or send him into the army, he shall be free from ward in proportion to the amount of time which he has been in the army through us.

No sheriff or bailiff of [the king], or any one else, shall take horses or wagons of any free man, for carrying purposes, except on the permission of that free man.

Neither we nor our bailiffs will take the wood of another man for castles, or for anything else which we are doing, except by the permission of him to whom the wood belongs. . . .

No free man shall be taken, or imprisoned, or dispossessed, or outlawed, or banished, or in any way injured, nor will we go upon him, nor send upon him, except by the legal judgment of his peers, or by the law of the land.

To no one will we sell, to no one will we deny or delay, right or justice.

From James Harvey Robinson, ed., *Readings in European History*, Vol. 1 (Boston: Athenaeum, 1904), pp. 236–237.

France The Norman conquest of England helped stir France to unity and make it possible for the Capetian dynasty, successor to the Franks in France, to establish a truly national monarchy. The duke of Normandy, who after 1066 had become master of the whole of England, was also among the vassals of the French king in Paris. French kings understandably viewed with alarm the new power of their Norman vassal. King Louis VI (r. 1108–1137) entered an alliance with Flanders, traditionally a Norman enemy. King Louis VII (r. 1137–1180) found allies in the great northern French cities and used their wealth to build a royal army.

Philip II Augustus (r. 1180–1223) inherited both financial resources and an administrative bureaucracy from his predecessors. He resisted the divisive French nobility and clergy and focused his attention on regaining French land from the control of the English king. Philip's armies occupied all the English territories on the French coast. At Bouvines on July 27, 1214, the first great European battle in history, the French handily defeated the English. This victory unified France around the monarchy and laid the foundation for French military and political ascendancy in the later Middle Ages.

Louis IX's (r. 1226–1270) reputation for piety and judicial fairness (he was declared a saint in the early fourteenth century) lent moral authority to the monarchy. The efficient French bureaucracy, which Louis's predecessors had used to exploit their subjects, now became an instrument of order and fair play in local government. The French people came

The crusaders capture the city of Antioch in 1098 during the First Crusade. From Le Miroir Historial *(fifteenth century) by Vincent de Beauvais.* Musée Conde Chantilly. E. T. Archive, London

to associate their king with justice—and national feeling, the glue of nationhood, grew very strong during his reign.

Holy Roman Empire The political experience of the Holy Roman Empire, which by the middle of the thirteenth century embraced Germany, Burgundy, and northern Italy, was very different (see Map I–12). There, two centuries of disunity and blood feuding left Germany fragmented until modern times.

Frederick I Barbarossa (r. 1152–1190) established the Hohenstaufen dynasty, which succeeded the Ottonians. He set out to reassert the power of the Holy Roman emperors after the setbacks suffered during the investiture controversy, a long conflict with the Church over the right of rulers to appoint high clergy to their offices. Frederick's efforts, however, led only to new and even fiercer disputes between the emperor and the pope.

In the thirteenth century, that conflict became a bitter, deadly feud. Popes excommunicated Emperor Frederick II (r. 1215–1250) no fewer than four times, and the emperor's reign ended in humiliation and defeat at the hands of the German princes. Thereafter, Germany was a politically primitive land by comparison with other major European countries. The victorious papacy now launched itself into European politics on a grand scale, particularly during the reign of Pope Innocent IV (r. 1243–1254). As a consequence, the papacy became vulnerable to new criticism from religious reformers and royal apologists alike, who did not believe such political self-aggrandizement was a proper mission for the Church.

The Emerging Contours of Europe By about 1300, then, the political contours of Europe as they would exist for the next two centuries were relatively clear. England and France had reasonably strong and stable central monarchies that competed economically and politically. The Holy Roman emperors presided rather than ruled over the other German princes, leaving the empire disunited. The papacy made and to some extent still enforced its own claims to what amounted to monarchical power. On the Italian peninsula, independent city-states composed of

William the Conqueror on horseback urging his troops into combat with the English at the Battle of Hastings (October 14, 1066). Detail from the Bayeux Tapestry, scene 51, about 1073–1083. Musée de la Tapisserie, Bayeux, France. Copyright Giraudon/Art Resource, N.Y.

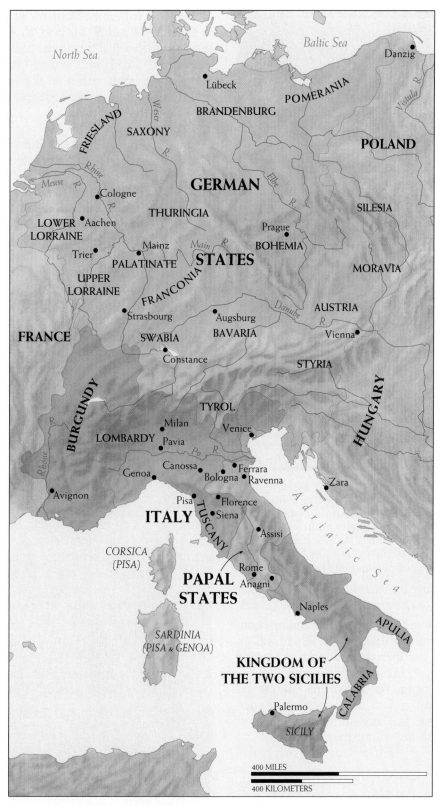

MAP I–12   GERMANY AND ITALY IN THE MIDDLE AGES   *Medieval Germany and Italy were divided lands. The Holy Roman Empire (Germany) embraced hundreds of independent territories that the emperor ruled only in name. The papacy controlled the Rome area and tried to enforce its will on Romagna. Under the Hohenstaufens (mid-twelfth to mid-thirteenth century), internal German divisions and papal conflict reached new heights; German rulers sought to extend their power to southern Italy and Sicily.*

of Roman law became available to Western scholars in the early twelfth century. Muslim scholars preserved these works, translated portions of the Greek tracts into Latin, and wrote extensive, thought-provoking commentaries on the ancient texts. This renaissance of ancient knowledge, in turn, led to the rise of universities in Europe.

The first important Western university was founded at Bologna in 1158 and specialized in law. The University of Paris, which specialized in theology, followed in 1200. Oxford, Cambridge, and, much later, Heidelberg were among Paris's imitators. All these universities required a foundation in the liberal arts for further study in the higher sciences of medicine, theology, and law. The arts program consisted of the *trivium* (grammar, rhetoric, and logic) and the *quadrivium* (arithmetic, geometry, astronomy, and music).

By the late twelfth century, enough of the works of Aristotle had penetrated Europe through Arab sources to influence European thought and education deeply. Logic and dialectic (the art of logical investigation), tools for bringing discipline to

A depiction of court and countryside in thirteenth-century Italy. The oldest of three parts of Castle Buonconsiglio in Trent, Italy was built in the mid-thirteenth century (1239–1255) between the city's north and east gates, through which workers can be seen hauling wood into the city by ox cart, while royals of both sexes ride out on horseback.   Scala/Art Resource, N.Y.

central urban areas and extensive surrounding countryside were the chief political units. There was an Arab presence on the Iberian Peninsula and strong Arab influence over Mediterranean trade. In the eastern Mediterranean, the Byzantine Empire remained intact. Europe had not experienced such widespread political stability since the demise of central Roman authority in the fourth century.

UNIVERSITIES AND SCHOLASTICISM

During the two centuries before 1300, an important intellectual flowering had occurred that complemented the achievements in trade, urbanization, and politics. Thanks largely to Spanish Muslim scholars, the logical works of Aristotle, the writings of Euclid and Ptolemy, the basic works of Greek physicians and Arab mathematicians, and the larger texts

In this engraving, a teacher at the University of Paris leads fellow scholars in a discussion. As shown here, all of the students wore the scholar's cap and gown.   Corbis

STUDENT LIFE AT THE UNIVERSITY OF PARIS

As the following account by Jacques de Vitry makes clear, not all students at the University of Paris in the thirteenth century were there to gain knowledge. Students fought constantly and subjected each other to ethnic insults and slurs.

■ *Why were students from different lands so prejudiced against one another? Does the rivalry of faculty members appear to have been as intense as that among students? What are the student criticisms of the faculty? Do they sound credible?*

Almost all the students at Paris, foreigners and natives, did absolutely nothing except learn or hear something new. Some studied merely to acquire knowledge, which is curiosity; others to acquire fame, which is vanity; others still for the sake of gain, which is cupidity and the vice of simony. Very few studied for their own edification, or that of others. They wrangled and disputed not merely about the various sects or about some discussions; but the differences between the countries also caused dissensions, hatreds and virulent animosities among them, and they impudently uttered all kinds of affronts and insults against one another.

They affirmed that the English were drunkards and had tails; the sons of France proud, effeminate and carefully adorned like women. They said that the Germans were furious and obscene at their feasts; the Normans, vain and boastful; the Poitevins, traitors and always adventurers. The Burgundians they considered vulgar and stupid. The Bretons were reputed to be fickle and changeable, and were often reproached for the death of Arthur. The Lombards were called avaricious, vicious and cowardly; the Romans, seditious, turbulent and slanderous; the Sicilians, tyrannical and cruel; the inhabitants of Brabant, men of blood, incendiaries, brigands and ravishers; the Flemish, fickle, prodigal, gluttonous, yielding as butter, and slothful. After such insults from words they often came to blows.

I will not speak of those logicians [professors of logic and dialectic] before whose eyes flitted constantly "the lice of Egypt," that is to say, all the sophistical subtleties, so that no one could comprehend their eloquent discourses in which, as says Isaiah, "there is no wisdom." As to the doctors of theology, "seated in Moses' seat," they were swollen with learning, but their charity was not edifying. Teaching and not practicing, they have "become as sounding brass or a tinkling cymbal," or like a canal of stone, always dry, which ought to carry water to "the bed of spices." They not only hated one another, but by their flatteries they enticed away the students of others; each one seeking his own glory, but caring not a whit about the welfare of souls.

Translations and Reprints from the Original Sources of European History, Vol. 2 (Philadelphia: Department of History, University of Pennsylvania, 1902), pp. 19–20.

knowledge and thought, rapidly triumphed in importance over the other liberal arts. Within the Scholastic program of study, the student read the traditional authorities in his field, formed short summaries of their teaching, elaborated arguments pro and con, and then drew his own modest conclusions.

Scholasticism had its critics even in the twelfth century. Some, anticipating the later Renaissance Humanists, believed Scholastics emphasized logic to the detriment of eloquence and relevance. Other critics feared that as theologians began to adopt the logic and metaphysics of Aristotle, a threat would arise to biblical and traditional theological authority with dire consequences for the Church.

In Perspective

The roots of Western civilization may be found in the experience and culture of the Greeks. Yet Greek civilization itself was richly nourished by older, magnificent civilizations to the south and east, especially in Mesopotamia and Egypt. In the valley of the Tigris and Euphrates rivers (Mesopotamia), and soon after in the valley of the Nile in Egypt, human beings moved from a life in agricultural villages, using tools of wood, bone, shell, and stone, into a much richer and more varied social organization that we call civilization.

The University of Bologna in central Italy was distinguished as the center for the revival of Roman law. This carving on the tomb of a Bologna professor of law shows students attending one of his lectures. Scala/Art Resource, N.Y.

Greek civilization arose after the destruction of the Bronze Age cultures on Crete and the Greek mainland before 1000 B.C.E. It took a turn sharply different from its predecessors in Egypt and western Asia. It was based on the independent existence of hundreds of city-states, called poleis, *which retained their autonomy for hundreds of years before being incorporated into larger units. These cities attained a degree of self-government, broad political participation, and individual freedom never achieved before that time. They also introduced a new way of thinking that looked on the world as the product of natural forces to be understood by the sense and human reason, unaided by reference to supernatural forces. The result was the invention of science and philosophy as we know them.*

Hellenistic culture was a mixture of Greek elements combined with some elements from the native peoples. It was without the particularism of the Hellenic world, and anyone speaking Greek could move comfortably from city to city and find a familiar and common culture. This was the world that succumbed to the Roman conquest in the last two centuries before the Christian era.

The Romans were tough farmers who began as inhabitants of a small town on the Tiber River in west-central Italy. After deposing their king in about 500 B.C.E., they invented a republican constitution and a code of law that provided a solid foundation for a stable and effective political order. From 264 until well into the first century

B.C.E., the Romans extended their conquests overseas until they had conquered the Carthaginians in the west and defeated all the great Hellenistic powers, dominating the shores of the Mediterranean and lands well beyond.

The Romans were fine engineers and road builders, but in art, literature, and philosophy they had barely made a start when they came into contact with the advanced Greek civilization of the Hellenistic world. In these areas, the Romans became eager students, and as the Roman poet Horace put it, "Captive Greece took Rome captive."

By the fifth century C.E., the Roman Empire in the West had collapsed and was shared out among different Germanic tribes, although the eastern portion of the empire, with its capital at Constantinople, survived for a thousand years more. Before Rome's fall, the empire had abandoned paganism and had adopted Christianity as its official religion. The heritage that the ancient world passed on to its medieval successor in western Europe was a combination of cultural traditions including those coming from Egypt, Mesopotamia, Israel, Greece, Rome, and the German tribes that destroyed the Roman Empire.

In western Europe, the centuries between 476 and 1300 saw both the decline of European classical civilization and the birth of a new European civilization. Beginning in the fifth century, barbarian invasions separated western Europe culturally from its classical past. Although some important works and concepts survived from antiquity, and the Christian church preserved major features of Roman government, the West would be recovering its classical heritage for centuries in "renaissances" that stretched into the sixteenth century. Out of the mixture of barbarian and surviving (or recovered) classical culture, a distinct Western culture was born. With the help of the Christian church, the Franks, under Charlemagne, created a new imperial tradition and shaped basic Western political and social institutions for centuries to come.

The Middle Ages also saw the lasting division of Christendom into Eastern and Western branches. As two different Christian churches evolved, bitter conflict ensued between popes and patriarchs. Constantinople far exceeded any city in the West in population and culture. Serving as both a buffer against Persian, Arab, and Turkish invasions of the West and as a major repository of classical learning and science for Western scholars, the Byzantine Empire did much to make the birth of western Europe possible. Another cultural and religious rival of the West, Islam, also saw its golden age during these same centuries. Like the Byzantine world, the Muslim world also proved a major conduit of ancient scholarship into the West, especially through Muslim Spain. Despite examples of coexistence and even friendship, however, Western and Arabic cultures were too different, their peoples too estranged and suspicious of one another, to coexist without hostility.

After 1000, the growth of Mediterranean trade revived old cities and occasioned the creation of new ones. The Crusades aided and abetted this development. One invaluable result of the new wealth of towns was a patronage of education and culture unseen since Roman times. Western Europe's first universities appeared in the eleventh century. Their numbers steadily expanded over the next four centuries: twenty universities by 1300 and seventy by 1500. Not only did Scholasticism flourish, but a new literature, art, and architecture developed as well, reflecting both a new human vitality and the reshaping of society and politics. For all this growth, western Europeans had no one to thank as much as the new class of merchants, whose greed, daring, and ambition had made it all possible.

REVIEW QUESTIONS

1. How was life during the Paleolithic Age different from that in the Neolithic Age? Present the broad outlines of the history of the earliest civilizations in Mesopotamia and Egypt. What was the significance of Hebrew monotheism for the future of Western civilization?

2. Define the concept of the *polis*. Compare the basic political, social, and economic institutions of Athens and Sparta around 500 B.C.E. Why did Sparta develop its unique form of government?

3. Discuss Rome's expansion to 265 B.C.E. What were some of the problems that plagued the republic in the last century? To what extent was the republic destroyed by ambitious generals who loved power more than Rome itself?

4. What solutions did Augustus provide for the problems that had plagued the Roman republic? How was the Roman Empire organized, and why did it function smoothly?

5. Trace the history of Christianity to the coronation of Charlemagne in 800. What distinctive features characterized the early Church? What role did the Church play in the world after the fall of the western Roman Empire?

6. What were some of the conditions that gave rise to feudal society? What are the essential characteristics of feudal society?

7. Trace the development of national monarchies in England and France in the High Middle Ages. How did the experience of those two countries differ from that of the Holy Roman Empire in the same period?

SUGGESTED READINGS

E. AMT (ED.), *Women's Lives in Medieval Europe: A Sourcebook* (1993). Outstanding collection of sources.

A. ANDREWES, *The Greeks* (1967). A thoughtful general survey.

E. BADIAN, *Roman Imperialism in the Late Republic*, 2nd ed. (1968).

G. BARRACLOUGH, *The Medieval Papacy* (1968). Brief, comprehensive, with pictures.

A. H. BERNSTEIN, *Tiberius Sempronius Gracchus: Tradition and Apostasy* (1978). A new interpretation of Tiberius's place in Roman politics.

P. BROWN, *Augustine of Hippo* (1967). Late antiquity seen through the biography of its greatest Christian thinker.

P. BROWN, *The World of Late Antiquity*, A.D. 150–750 (1971). A brilliant and readable essay.

G. CAWKWELL, *Philip of Macedon* (1978).

R. H. C. DAVIS, *A History of Medieval Europe: From Constantine to St. Louis* (1972). Unsurpassed in clarity.

E. R. DODDS, *The Greeks and the Irrational* (1955). An excellent account of the role of the supernatural in Greek life and thought.

R. DREWS, *The Coming of the Greeks* (1988). A fine study of the arrival of the Greeks as part of the movement of Indo-European peoples.

G. DUBY, *The Three Orders: Feudal Society Imagined*, trans. by A. Goldhammer (1981). Large, comprehensive, authoritative.

R. M. ERRINGTON, *The Dawn of Empire: Rome's Rise to Power* (1972). An account of Rome's conquest of the Mediterranean.

R. FAWTIER, *The Capetian Kings of France*, trans. by L. Butler and R. J. Adam (1972). Detailed standard account.

A. FERRILL, *Caligula: Emperor of Rome* (1991). A biography of the monstrous young emperor.

H. FICHTENAU, *The Carolingian Empire: The Age of Charlemagne*, trans. by P. Munz (1964). Strong on political history.

J. V. A. FINE, *The Early Medieval Balkans: Sixth to Twelfth Centuries* (1983). Insight into ethnic divisions.

M. I. FINLEY, *World of Odysseus*, rev. ed. (1965). A fascinating attempt to reconstruct Homeric society.

W. G. FORREST, *The Emergence of Greek Democracy* (1966). A lively interpretation of Greek social and political developments in the archaic period.

J. R. L. Fox, *Alexander the Great* (1973). An imaginative account that does more justice to the Persian side of the problem than is usual.

H. Frankfort et al., *Before Philosophy* (1949). A brilliant examination of the mind of ancient man from the Stone Age to the Greeks.

M. Grant, *The Fall of the Roman Empire* (1990). A lively, well-written account.

P. Green, *Xerxes at Salamis* (1970). A lively and stimulating history of the Persian wars.

E. S. Gruen, *The Last Generation of the Roman Republic* (1973). An interesting but controversial interpretation of the fall of the republic.

W. W. Hallo and W. K. Simpson, *The Ancient Near East: A History* (1971). A fine survey of Egyptian and Mesopotamian history.

V. D. Hanson, *The Western Way of War* (1989). A brilliant and lively discussion of the rise and character of the hoplite phalanx and its influence on Greek society.

C. H. Haskins, *The Rise of the Universities* (1972). A minor classic.

D. Herlihy, *Medieval Households* (1985). Survey of antiquity and the Middle Ages.

A. Hourani, *A History of the Arab People* (1991). Readable, comprehensive overview.

S. Isager and J. E. Skydsgaard, *Ancient Greek Agriculture. An Introduction* (1993). A new study of a fundamental subject.

D. Kagan (ed.), *The End of the Roman Empire: Decline or Transformation?* 3rd. ed. (1992). A collection of essays discussing the problem of the decline and fall of the Roman Empire.

D. Kagan, *The Great Dialogue: A History of Greek Political Thought from Homer to Polybius* (1965). A discussion of the relationship between the Greek historical experience and political theory.

D. Kagan, *The Outbreak of the Peloponnesian War* (1969). A study of the period from the foundation of the Delian League to the coming of the Peloponnesian War that argues that the war could have been avoided.

H. D. F. Kitto, *The Greeks* (1951). A personal and illuminating interpretation of Greek culture.

D. Knowles, *Christian Monasticism* (1969). Sweeping survey with helpful photographs.

J. Leclercq, *The Love of Learning and the Desire for God: A Study of Monastic Culture*, trans. by C. Misrahi (1962). Lucid, delightful, absorbing account of the ideals of monks.

K. Leyser, *Medieval Germany and Its Neighbors, 900–1250* (1982). Basic and authoritative.

R. MacMullen, *Soldier and Civilian in the Later Roman Empire* (1963). A study of the growing militarization of the whole society of the late empire.

R. MacMullen, *Corruption and the Decline of Rome* (1988). A study that examines the importance of changes in ethical ideas and behavior.

E. Mâle, *The Gothic Image: Religious Art in France in the Thirteenth Century* (1913). An enduring classic.

C. Mango, *Byzantium: The Empire of New Rome* (1982). Perhaps the most readable account.

P. B. Manville, *The Origins of Citizenship in Ancient Athens* (1990). An examination of the origins of the concept of citizenship in the time of Solon of Athens.

R. W. Mathison, *Roman Aristocrats in Barbarian Gaul: Strategies for Survival* (1993). An unusual slant on the late empire.

R. Meiggs, *The Athenian Empire* (1972). A fine study of the rise and fall of the empire, making excellent use of inscriptions.

J. B. Morrall, *Political Thought in Medieval Times* (1962). Readable and illuminating account.

P. Munz, *The Age of Charlemagne* (1971). Penetrating social history.

J. Oates, *Babylon*, revised edition (1986). An introduction to the history and archaeology of Babylonia revised to make use of newly discovered evidence.

H. M. Orlinsky, *Ancient Israel* (1960). Chiefly a political survey.

H. Pirenne, *Medieval Cities: Their Origins and the Revival of Trade*, trans. by F. D. Halsey (1970). A minor classic.

J. J. Pollitt, *Art and Experience in Classical Greece* (1972).

J. N. Postgate, *Early Mesopotamia* (1992). An excellent study of Mesopotamian economy and society from the earliest times to about 1500 B.C.E., helpfully illustrated with drawings, pictures, and translated documents.

S. Reynolds, *Kingdoms and Communities in Western Europe, 900–1300* (1984). For the medieval origins of Western political and cultural traditions.

V. Rudich, *Political Dissidence Under Nero, The Price of Dissimulation* (1993). A brilliant exposition of the lives and thoughts of political dissidents in the early empire.

S. Runciman, *Byzantine Civilization* (1970). Succinct, comprehensive account by a master.

H. H. Scullard, *A History of the Roman World from 753 to 146 B.C.*, 3rd ed. (1961). An unusually fine narrative history with useful critical notes.

J. Riley-Smith, *The Crusades: A Short History* (1987). Up-to-date, lucid, and readable.

R. W. Southern, *The Making of the Middle Ages* (1973). Originally published in 1953, but still a fresh account by an imaginative historian.

C. STEPHENSON, *Medieval Feudalism* (1969). Excellent short introduction.

B. STOCK, *The Implications of Literacy* (1983). How the ability to read changed medieval society.

R. SYME, *The Roman Revolution* (1960). A brilliant study of Augustus, his supporters, and their rise to power.

W. W. TARN AND G. T. GRIFFITH, *Hellenistic Civilization* (1961). A survey of Hellenistic history and culture.

L. R. TAYLOR, *Party Politics in the Age of Caesar* (1949). A fascinating analysis of Roman political theory.

B. TIERNEY, *The Crisis of Church and State 1050–1300* (1964). Very useful collection and interpretation of primary sources on key Church-state conflicts.

G. VERNADSKY, *A History of Russia, I–IV* (1946–1963). A graspable magisterial survey.

R. D. WEIGEL, *Lepidus: The Tarnished Triumvir* (1992). A biography of the less famous partner of Mark Antony and Augustus.

L. WHITE, JR., *Medieval Technology and Social Change* (1962). Often fascinating account of the way primitive technology changed life.

J. A. WILSON, *Culture of Ancient Egypt* (1956). A fascinating interpretation of the civilization of ancient Egypt.

PART 3
1300–1750

	POLITICS AND GOVERNMENT	SOCIETY AND ECONOMY	RELIGION AND CULTURE
1300–1400	1309-1377 Pope resides in Avignon 1337-1453 Hundred Years' War 1356 *Golden Bull* creates German electoral college	315-1317 Greatest famine of the Middle Ages 1347-1350 Black Death peaks 1358 *Jacquerie* shakes France 1378 Ciompi Revolt in Florence 1381 English peasants' revolt	1300-1325 Dante Alighierl writes *Divine Comedy* 1302 Boniface VIII issues bull *Unam Sanctam* 1350 Boccaccio, *Decameron* 1375-1527 The Renaissance in Italy 1378-1417 The Great Schism 1380-1395 Chaucer writes *Canterbury Tales* 1390-1430 Christine de Pisan writes in defense of women 1414-1417 The Council of Constance
1400–1500	1415-1433 Hussite revolt in Bohemia 1428-1519 Aztecs expand in central Mexico 1429 Joan of Arc leads French to victory in Orléans 1434 Medici rule begins in Florence 1455-1485 Wars of the Roses in England 1469 Marriage of Ferdinand and Isabella 1487 Henry Tudor creates Court of Star Chamber	1450 Johann Gutenberg invents printing with movable type 1492 Christopher Columbus encounters the Americas 1498 Vasco da Gama reaches India	1425-1450 Lorenzo Valla exposes the *Donation of Constantine* 1450 Thomas à Kempis, *Imitation of Christ* 1492 Expulsion of Jews from Spain
1500–1600	1519 Charles V crowned Holy Roman Emperor 1530 *Augsburg Confession* defines Lutheranism 1547 Ivan the Terrible becomes tsar of Russia 1555 *Peace of Augsburg* recognizes the legal principle, *cuius regio, eius religio* 1558-1603 Reign of Elizabeth I of England 1572 Saint Bartholomew's Day Massacre 1588 English defeat of Spanish Armada 1598 Edict of Nantes gives Huguenots religious and civil rights	1519 Hernan Cortes lands in Mexico 1519-1522 Ferdinand Magellan circumnavigates the Earth 1525 German Peasants' Revolt 1532-1533 Francisco Pizarro conquers the Incas 1540 Spanish open silver mines in Peru, Bolivia, and Mexico 1550-1600 The great witch panics	1513 Niccolo Machiavelli, *The Prince* 1516 Erasmus compiles a Greek New Testament 1516 Thomas More, *Utopia* 1517 Martin Luther's Ninety-five theses 1534 Henry VIII declared head of English Church 1540 Jesuit order founded 1541 John Calvin becomes Geneva's reformer 1543 Copernicus, *On the Revolutions of the Heavenly Spheres* 1545-1563 Council of Trent 1549 English *Book of Common Prayer*

Elizabeth I, The Armada Portrait

EUROPE IN TRANSITION

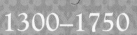

1300–1750

	POLITICS AND GOVERNMENT	SOCIETY AND ECONOMY	RELIGION AND CULTURE
1600–1700	1624–1642 **Era of Richelieu in France**	1600–1700 **Period of greatest Dutch economic prosperity**	1605 **Bacon, *The Advancement of Learning*; Shakespeare, *King Lear*, Cervantes, *Don Quixote***
	1629–1640 **Charles I's years of personal rule**	1600–early 1700s **Spain maintains commercial monopoly in Latin America**	
	1640 **Long Parliament convenes**	1607 **English settle Jamestown, Virginia**	1609 **Kepler, *The New Astronomy***
	1642 **Outbreak of civil war in England**	1608 **French settle Quebec**	1611 **King James Version of the English Bible**
	1643–1661 **Cardinal Mazarin regent for Louis XIV**	1618–1648 **Thirty Years' War devastates German economy**	1632 **Galileo, *Dialogue on the Two Chief Systems of the World***
	1648 **Peace of Westphalia**	1619 **African slaves first bought at Jamestown, Virginia**	1637 **Descartes, *Discourse on Method***
	1649–1652 **The *Fronde* in France**		1651 **Hobbes, *Leviathan***
	1649 **Charles I executed**	1650s–1670s **Commercial rivalry between Dutch and English**	
	1660 **Charles II restored to the English throne**		
	1661–1715 **Louis XIV's years of personal rule**	1661–1683 **Colbert seeks to stimulate French economic growth**	1687 **Newton, *Principia Mathematica***
	1682–1725 **Reign of Peter the Great**		1689 **English Toleration Act**
	1685 **James II becomes king of England**	1690 **Paris Foundling Hospital established**	1690 **Locke, *Essay Concerning Human Understanding***
		Louis XIV revokes Edict of Nantes		
	1688 **"Glorious Revolution" in Britain**		
1700–1789	1700–1721 **Great Northern War between Sweden and Russia**	1715–1763 **Era of major colonial rivalry in the Caribbean**	1739 **Wesley begins field preaching**
	1701–1714 **War of Spanish Succession**	1719 **Mississippi Bubble in France**	1748 **Montesquieu, *Spirit of the Laws***
	1713 **Treaty of Utrecht**	1733 **James Kay's flying shuttle**	1750 **Rousseau, *Discourse on the Moral Effects of the Arts and Sciences***
	1720–1740 **Age of Walpole in England and Fleury in France**	1750s **Agricultural Revolution in Britain**	
	1740 **Maria Theresa succeeds to the Habsburg throne**	1750–1840 **Growth of new cities**	1751 **First volume Diderot's *Encyclopedia***
	1740–1748 **War of the Austrian Succession**	1763 **Britain becomes dominant in India**	1762 **Rousseau, *Social Contract* and *Émile***
	1756–1763 **Seven Years' War**	1763–1789 **Enlightened absolutist rulers seek to spur economic growth**	1763 **Voltaire, Treatise on Tolerance**
	1767 **Legislative Commission in Russia**	1765 **James Hargreaves's spinning jenny**	
	1772 **First Partition of Poland**	1769 **Richard Arkwright's waterframe**	1774 **Goethe, *Sorrow of Young Werther***
	1776 **American Declaration of Independence**	1773–1775 **Pugachev's Rebellion**	1776 **Smith, *Wealth of Nations***
			1781 **Kant, *Critique of Pure Reason***
			Joseph II adopts policy of toleration in Austria
	Declaration of Independence		
	1778 **France aids the American colonies**		

The apparition of the Knight of Death, *an allegory of the plague approaching a city, whose defenses against it are all too unsure.*   From the *Très Riches Heures du Duc de Berry* (1284), Limbourg Brothers. Ms. 65/1284, fol. 90v. Musée Condé, Chantilly, France. Giraudon/Art Resource, N.Y.

CHAPTER 9

THE LATE MIDDLE AGES:

Social and Political Breakdown (1300–1527)

*T*HE LATE MIDDLE AGES SAW *almost unprecedented political, social, and ecclesiastical calamity. France and England grappled with each other in a bitter conflict known as the Hundred Years' War (1337–1453), an exercise in seemingly willful self-destruction that was made even more terrible in its later stages by the introduction of gunpowder and the invention of heavy artillery. Bubonic plague, known to contemporaries as the Black Death, swept over almost all of Europe, killing as much as one-third of the population in many regions between 1348 and 1350 and transforming many pious Christians into believers in the omnipotence of death. A schism emerged within the church, which lasted thirty-nine years (1378–1417) and led, by 1409, to the election of no fewer than three competing popes and colleges of cardinals. In 1453, the Turks marched seemingly invincibly through Constantinople and toward the West. As their political and religious institutions buckled, as disease, bandits, and wolves ravaged their cities in the wake of war, and as Islamic armies gathered at their borders, Europeans beheld what seemed to be the imminent total collapse of Western civilization.*

It was in this period that such scholars as Marsilius of Padua, William of Ockham, and Lorenzo Valla produced lasting criticisms of medieval assumptions about the nature of God, humankind, and society. Kings worked through parliaments and clergy through councils to place lasting limits on the pope's temporal power. The notion, derived from Roman law, that a secular ruler is accountable to the body he or she governs had already found expression in documents like the Magna Carta. It came increasingly to carry the force of accepted principle, and conciliarists (advocates of the judicial superiority of a church council over a pope) sought to extend it to establish papal accountability to the church.

But viewed in terms of their three great calamities—war, plague, and schism—the fourteenth and fifteenth centuries were years in which politics resisted wisdom, nature strained mercy, and the church was less than faithful to its mandate.

The Hundred Years' War and the Rise of National Sentiment

The Black Death

Ecclesiastical Breakdown and Revival: The Late Medieval Church

Medieval Russia

In Perspective

KEY TOPICS

- The Hundred Years' War between England and France
- The effects of the bubonic plague on population and society
- The growing power of secular rulers over the papacy
- Schism, heresy, and reform of the church

The Hundred Years' War and the Rise of National Sentiment

Medieval governments were by no means all-powerful and secure. The rivalry of petty lords kept localities in turmoil, and dynastic rivalries could plunge entire lands into war, especially when power was being transferred to a new ruler, and woe to the ruling dynasty that failed to produce a male heir.

To field the armies and collect the revenues that made their existence possible, late medieval rulers depended on carefully negotiated alliances among a wide range of lesser powers. Like kings and queens in earlier centuries, they, too, practiced the art of feudal government, but on a grander scale and with greater sophistication. To maintain the order they required, the Norman kings of England and the Capetian kings of France fine-tuned traditional feudal relationships, stressing the duties of lesser to higher power and the unquestioning loyalty noble vassals owed the king. The result was a degree of centralized royal power unseen before in these lands and a nascent almost national consciousness that equipped both France and England for international warfare.

THE CAUSES OF THE WAR

The conflict that came to be known as the Hundred Years' War began in May 1337 and lasted until October 1453. The English king Edward III (r. 1327–1377), the grandson of Philip the Fair of France (r. 1285–1314), may be said to have started the war by asserting a claim to the French throne when the French king Charles IV (r. 1322–1328), the last of Philip the Fair's surviving sons, died without a male heir. The French barons had no intention of placing the then fifteen-year-old Edward on the French throne, choosing instead the first cousin of Charles IV, Philip VI of Valois (r. 1328–1350), the first of a new French dynasty that ruled into the sixteenth century.

But there was more to the war than just an English king's assertion of a claim to the French throne. England and France were then emergent territorial powers in too close proximity to one another. Edward was actually a vassal of Philip's, holding several sizable French territories as fiefs from the king of France, a relationship that went back to the days of the Norman conquest. English possession of any French land was repugnant to the French because it threatened the royal policy of centralization. England and France also quarreled over control of Flanders, which, although a French fief, was subject to political influence from England because its principal industry, the manufacture of cloth, depended on supplies of imported English wool. Compounding these frictions was a long history of prejudice and animosity between the French and English people, who constantly confronted one

Edward III pays homage to his feudal lord Philip VI of France. Legally, Edward was a vassal of the king of France. Archives Snark International/ Art Resource, N.Y.

another on the high seas and in port towns. Taken together, these various factors made the Hundred Years' War a struggle for national identity as well as for control of territory.

French Weakness France had three times the population of England, was far the wealthier of the two countries, and fought on its own soil. Yet, for the greater part of the conflict, until after 1415, the major battles ended in often stunning English victories. (See Map 9–1.) The primary reason for these French failures was internal disunity caused by endemic social conflicts. Unlike England, France was still struggling in the fourteenth century to make the transition from a fragmented feudal society to a centralized "modern" state.

Desperate to raise money for the war, French kings resorted to such financial policies as depreciating the currency and borrowing heavily from Italian bankers, which aggravated internal conflicts. In 1355, in a bid to secure funds, the king convened a representative council of townspeople and nobles that came to be known as the **Estates General.** Although it levied taxes at the king's request, its members also used the king's plight to enhance their own regional rights and privileges, thereby deepening territorial divisions.

France's defeats also reflected English military superiority. The English infantry was more disciplined than the French, and English archers carried a formidable weapon, the longbow, capable of firing six arrows a minute with enough force to pierce an inch of wood or the armor of a knight at two hundred yards.

Finally, French weakness during the Hundred Years' War was due in no small degree to the comparative mediocrity of its royal leadership. English kings were far the shrewder.

PROGRESS OF THE WAR

The war had three major stages of development, each ending with a seemingly decisive victory by one or the other side.

The Conflict During the Reign of Edward III In the first stage of the war, Edward embargoed English wool to Flanders, sparking urban rebellions by merchants and the trade guilds. Inspired by a rich merchant, Jacob van Artevelde, the Flemish cities, led by Ghent, revolted against the French and in 1340 signed an alliance with England acknowledging Edward as king of France. On June 23 of that same year, in the first great battle of the war, Edward defeated the French fleet in the Bay of Sluys, but his subsequent effort to invade France by way of Flanders failed.

In 1346, Edward attacked Normandy and, after a series of easy victories that culminated at the Battle of Crécy, seized Calais. Exhaustion of both sides and the onset of the Black Death forced a truce in late 1347, and the war entered a brief lull. In 1356, near Poitiers, the English won their greatest victory, routing France's noble cavalry and taking the French king, John II the Good (r. 1350–1364), captive back to England. The defeat brought a complete breakdown of political order to France.

Power in France now lay with the Estates General. Led by the powerful merchants of Paris under Etienne Marcel, that body took advantage of royal weakness, demanding and receiving rights similar to those granted the English privileged classes in the Magna Carta. But unlike the English Parliament, which represented the interests of a comparatively unified English nobility, the French Estates General was too divided to be an instrument for effective government.

To secure their rights, the French privileged classes forced the peasantry to pay ever-increasing taxes and to repair their war-damaged properties without compensation. This bullying became more than the peasants could bear, and they rose up in several regions in a series of bloody rebellions known as the **Jacquerie** in 1358 (after the peasant revolutionary popularly known as Jacques Bonhomme, or "simple Jack"). The nobility quickly put down the revolt, matching the rebels atrocity for atrocity.

On May 9, 1360, another milestone of the war was reached when England forced the Peace of Brétigny on the French. This agreement declared an end to Edward's vassalage to the king of France and affirmed his sovereignty over English territories in France (including Gascony, Guyenne, Poitou, and Calais). France also agreed to pay a ransom of 3 million gold crowns to win King John the Good's release. In return, Edward simply renounced his claim to the French throne.

Such a partition of French territorial control was completely unrealistic, and sober observers on both sides knew it could not last long. France struck back in the late 1360s and by the time of Edward's death in 1377 had beaten the English back to coastal enclaves and the territory of Bordeaux.

French Defeat and the Treaty of Troyes After Edward's death the English war effort lessened, partly because of domestic problems within England. During the reign of Richard II (r. 1377–1399), England had its own version of the Jacquerie. In June 1381, long-oppressed peasants and artisans joined in a great revolt of the unprivileged classes under the leadership of John Ball, a secular priest, and Wat

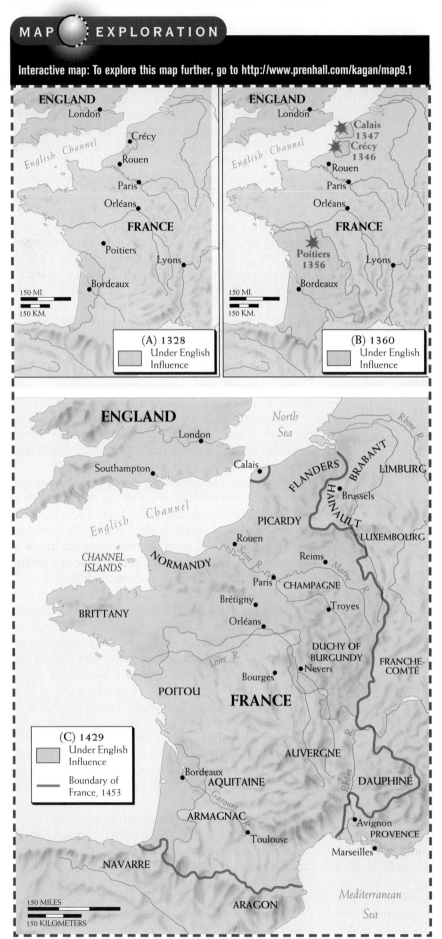

ENGLAND
London
Crécy
Rouen
Paris
Orléans
FRANCE
Poitiers
Lyons
Bordeaux
150 MI.
150 KM.

(A) 1328
Under English Influence

ENGLAND
London
Calais 1347
Crécy 1346
Rouen
Paris
Orléans
FRANCE
Poitiers 1356
Lyons
Bordeaux
150 MI.
150 KM.

(B) 1360
Under English Influence

ENGLAND
London
Southampton
Calais
North Sea
Rhine R.
FLANDERS
BRABANT
LIMBURG
HAINAULT
Brussels
PICARDY
LUXEMBOURG
English Channel
CHANNEL ISLANDS
NORMANDY
Rouen
Seine R.
Reims
Marne R.
Paris
CHAMPAGNE
Brétigny
Troyes
Orléans
BRITTANY
Loire R.
DUCHY OF BURGUNDY
Nevers
FRANCHE-COMTÉ
Bourges
POITOU
FRANCE
AUVERGNE
Rhône R.
DAUPHINÉ
Bordeaux
AQUITAINE
Garonne
ARMAGNAC
Avignon
PROVENCE
Toulouse
Marseilles
NAVARRE
Mediterranean Sea
ARAGON
150 MILES
150 KILOMETERS

(C) 1429
Under English Influence
Boundary of France, 1453

MAP 9–1   THE HUNDRED YEARS' WAR   *The Hundred Years' War went on intermittently from the late 1330s until 1453. These maps show the remarkable English territorial gains up to the sudden and decisive turning of the tide of battle in favor of the French by the forces of Joan of Arc in 1429.*

This miniature illustrates two scenes from the English peasant revolt of 1381. On the left, Wat Tyler, one of the leaders of the revolt, is executed in the presence of King Richard II. On the right, King Richard urges armed peasants to end their rebellion. Arthur Hacker, The Cloister of the World. The Bridgeman Art Library.

Tyler, a journeyman. As in France, the revolt was brutally crushed within the year, but it left the country divided for decades.

The war intensified under Henry V (r. 1413–1422), who took advantage of internal French turmoil created by the rise to power of the duchy of Burgundy. With France deeply divided, Henry V struck hard in Normandy. Happy to see the rest of France besieged, the Burgundians foolishly watched from the sidelines while Henry's army routed the opposition led by the count of Armagnac, who had picked up the royal banner at Agincourt on October 25, 1415. In the years thereafter, belatedly recognizing that the defeat of France would leave them easy prey for the English, the Burgundians closed ranks with French royal forces. The renewed French unity, loose as it was, promised to bring eventual victory over the English, but it was shattered in September 1419 when the duke of Burgundy was assassinated. In the aftermath of this shocking event, the duke's son and heir, determined to avenge his father's death, joined forces with the English.

France now became Henry V's for the taking—at least in the short run. The Treaty of Troyes in 1420 disinherited the legitimate heir to the French throne and proclaimed Henry V the successor to the French king, Charles VI. When Henry and Charles died within months of one another in 1422, the infant Henry VI of England was proclaimed in Paris to be king of both France and England. The dream of Edward III that had set the war in motion—to make

the ruler of England the ruler also of France—had been realized, at least for the moment.

The son of Charles VI went into retreat in Bourges, where, on the death of his father, he became Charles VII to most of the French people, who ignored the Treaty of Troyes. Displaying unprecedented national feeling inspired by the remarkable Joan of Arc, they soon rallied to his cause and came together in an ultimately victorious coalition.

The Hundred Years' War (1337–1453)

1340 English victory at Bay of Sluys

1346 English victory at Crécy and seizure of Calais

1347 Black Death strikes

1356 English victory at Poitiers

1358 Jacquerie disrupts France

1360 Peace of Brétigny recognizes English holdings in France

1381 English peasants revolt

1415 English victory at Agincourt

1422 Treaty of Troyes proclaims Henry VI ruler of both England and France

1429 Joan of Arc leads French to victory at Orléans

1431 Joan of Arc executed as a heretic

1453 War ends; English retain only coastal town of Calais

Joan of Arc and the War's Conclusion Joan of Arc (1412–1431), a peasant from Domrémy, presented herself to Charles VII in March 1429, declaring the King of Heaven had called her to deliver besieged Orléans from the English. The king was understandably skeptical, but being in retreat from what seemed to be a hopeless war, he was willing to try anything to reverse French fortunes. And the deliverance of Orléans, a city strategic to the control of the territory south of the Loire, would be a godsend. Charles's desperation overcame his skepticism, and he gave Joan his leave.

Circumstances worked perfectly to her advantage. The English force, already exhausted by a six-month siege of Orléans, was at the point of withdrawal when Joan arrived with fresh French troops. After repulsing the English from Orléans, the French enjoyed a succession of victories they popularly attributed to Joan. She deserved much of this credit, but not because she was a military genius. She provided the French with something military experts could not: inspiration and a sense of national identity and self-confidence. Within a few months of the liberation of Orléans, Charles VII received his crown in Rheims and ended the nine-year "disinheritance" prescribed by the Treaty of Troyes.

A contemporary portrait of Joan of Arc (1412–1431) in the National Archives in Paris. 15th c. Franco-Flemish miniature. Archives Nationales, Paris, France. © Giraudon/Art Resource, N.Y.

Charles forgot his liberator as quickly as he had embraced her. When the Burgundians captured Joan in May 1430, he was in a position to secure her release, but did little for her. The Burgundians and the English wanted her publicly discredited, believing this would also discredit Charles VII and demoralize French resistance. She was turned over to the Inquisition in English-held Rouen. The inquisitors broke the courageous "Maid of Orléans" after ten weeks of interrogation, and she was executed as a relapsed heretic on May 30, 1431. Twenty-five years later (1456), Charles reopened her trial, and she was declared innocent of all the charges. In 1920, the church declared her a saint.

In 1435, the duke of Burgundy made peace with Charles. France, now unified and at peace with Burgundy, continued progressively to force the English back. By 1453, the date of the war's end, the English held only their coastal enclave of Calais.

The Hundred Years' War, with sixty-eight years of at least nominal peace and forty-four of hot war, had lasting political and social consequences. It devastated France, but it also awakened French nationalism and hastened the transition there from a feudal monarchy to a centralized state. It saw Burgundy become a major European political power. And it encouraged the English, in response to the seesawing allegiance of the Netherlands throughout the conflict, to develop their own clothing industry and foreign markets. In both France and England the burden of the on-again, off-again war fell most heavily on the peasantry, who were forced to support it with taxes and services.

The Black Death

PRECONDITIONS AND CAUSES

In the late Middle Ages, nine-tenths of the population worked the land. The three-field system, in use in most areas since well before the fourteenth century, had increased the amount of arable land and thereby the food supply. The growth of cities and trade had also stimulated agricultural science and productivity. But as the food supply grew, so did the population. It is estimated that Europe's population doubled between the years 1000 and 1300 and by 1300 had begun to outstrip food production. There were now more people than there was food available to feed them or jobs to employ them, and the average European faced the probability of extreme hunger at least once during his or her expected thirty-five-year life span.

Between 1315 and 1317, crop failures produced the greatest famine of the Middle Ages. Densely populated urban areas such as the industrial towns of the

Netherlands experienced great suffering. Decades of overpopulation, economic depression, famine, and bad health progressively weakened Europe's population and made it highly vulnerable to a virulent bubonic plague that struck with full force in 1348.

This **Black Death,** so called by contemporaries because of the way it discolored the body, was probably introduced by seaborne rats from Black Sea areas and followed the trade routes from Asia into Europe. Appearing in Sicily in late 1347, it entered Europe through the port cities of Venice, Genoa, and Pisa in 1348, and from there it swept rapidly through Spain and southern France and into northern Europe. Areas that lay outside the major trade routes, like Bohemia, appear to have remained virtually unaffected.

Bubonic plague made numerous reappearances in succeeding decades. By the early fifteenth century, it is estimated that western Europe as a whole had lost as much as two-fifths of its population. A full recovery did not occur until the sixteenth century. (See Map 9–2.)

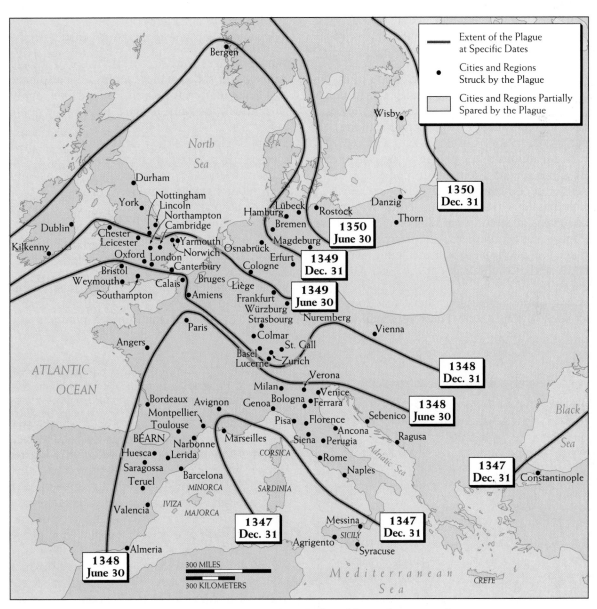

MAP 9–2   SPREAD OF THE BLACK DEATH   *Apparently introduced by seaborne rats from Black Sea areas where plague-infested rodents had long been known, the Black Death brought huge human, social, and economic consequences. One of the lower estimates of Europeans dying is 25 million. The map charts the plague's spread in the mid–fourteenth century. Generally following trade routes, the plague reached Scandinavia by 1350, and some believe it then went on to Iceland and even Greenland. Areas off the main trade routes were largely spared.*

POPULAR REMEDIES

The plague, transmitted by rat- or human-borne fleas, often reached a victim's lungs during the course of the disease. From the lungs, it could be spread from person to person by the victim's sneezing and wheezing. Contemporary physicians had no understanding of these processes, so even the most rudimentary prophylaxis against the disease was lacking. (See "Encountering the Past: Medieval Medicine.") To the people of the time, the Black Death was a catastrophe with no apparent explanation and against which there was no known defense. Throughout much of western Europe it inspired an obsession with death and dying and a deep pessimism that endured for decades after the plague years. (See "Art & the West: Images of Death," p. 314.)

Popular wisdom held that a corruption in the atmosphere caused the disease. Some blamed poisonous fumes released by earthquakes. Many adopted aromatic amulets as a remedy. According to the contemporary observations of Boccaccio, who recorded the varied reactions to the plague in the *Decameron* (1353), some sought a remedy in moderation and a temperate life; others gave themselves over entirely to their passions (sexual promiscuity within the stricken areas apparently ran high); and still others, "the most sound, perhaps, in judgment," chose flight and seclusion as the best medicine. (See "Boccaccio Describes the Ravages of the Black Death in Florence.")

Among the most extreme social reactions were processions of flagellants. These religious fanatics beat themselves in ritual penance until they bled, believing such action would bring divine intervention. The terror created by the flagellants (whose dirty bodies may actually have served to transport the disease) became so socially disruptive and threatening, even to established authority, that the church finally outlawed their processions.

Jews were cast as scapegoats for the plague. Centuries of Christian propaganda had bred hatred toward them, as had their role as society's moneylenders. **Pogroms** occurred in several cities, sometimes incited by the arrival of flagellants.

SOCIAL AND ECONOMIC CONSEQUENCES

Whole villages vanished in the wake of the plague. Among the social and economic consequences of this depopulation were a shrunken labor supply and a decline in the value of the estates of the nobility.

Farms Decline As the number of farm laborers decreased, their wages increased and those of skilled artisans soared. Many serfs now chose to commute their labor services by money payments or to abandon the farm altogether and pursue more interesting and rewarding jobs in skilled craft industries in the cities. Agricultural prices fell because of lowered demand, and the price of luxury and manufactured goods—the work of skilled artisans—rose. The noble landholders suffered the greatest decline in power from this new state of affairs. They were forced to pay more for finished products and for

This illustration from the Canon of Medicine *by the Iranian physician and philosopher Avicenna (980–1037), whose Arabic name was Ibn Sina, shows him visiting the homes of rich patients. In the High Middle ages, the* Canon of Medicine *was the standard medical textbook in the Middle East and Europe.* Scala/Art Resource, N.Y. Biblioteca Universitaria, Bologna, Italy.

Medieval Medicine

Marguerite Datini was an infertile gentle-woman who lived near Florence and wished to be a mother. In 1393 her sister suggested she have a local woman, renowned for magical remedies, prepare a poultice for her belly. Later, a physician sent Marguerite's husband a diet he believed would aid conception. Two years later (1395), when she had still not conceived, Marguerite's brother-in-law sent his own wife's solution: a belt inscribed with an incantation. Her sister-in-law instructed Marguerite to ask a young male virgin to gird the belt around her stomach as he prayed.

Such advice illustrates the state of medicine during the Middle Ages. Like Marguerite, medieval patients could choose from a broad spectrum of practices in which natural, religious, and magical remedies coexisted. They also had to take into account the power of celestial forces. Medieval people believed comets, stars, and planets constantly influenced their bodies and minds.

Because they presumed this intimate link between the individual and the universe, medical practitioners used astrological information to discover the causes of illness and to determine the right time to treat a patient.

Such desperate grasping for cures reflected the desperation of the age. In a world of high morbidity and infant mortality, the sick sought help from anyone who might provide it. University-trained physicians had the more prestigious clients, but their knowledge was not necessarily more authoritative than that of an illiterate healer whose magic worked. Patients sought any treatment they could afford from any healer who had a good reputation for effecting cures.

In this broad medical marketplace, university-trained physicians treated internal illnesses through diet and medication and apothecaries supplied doctors and patients with medicinal herbs. There were also university-trained surgeons and self-taught, or apprenticed, barber-surgeons.

At the base of all medical healing lay the ancient Greek idea that each bodily organism was composed of four elements (earth, air, water, and fire) and possessed four qualities (hot, cold, moist, and dry), whose mix determined a body's well-being. These elements and qualities accounted in turn for the condition of the four humors, or fluids (blood, black bile, yellow bile, and phlegm), that regulated the body's functions. Sickness resulted from an imbalance of humors within the body. The task of the healer was to restore balance by drawing off foul matter from the blood, or by directing good or bad humors to different parts of the body. The most frequent methods for revealing humoral imbalance were the examination of urine, blood, and the pulse. Like the stethoscope today, the urine flask, or uroscope, was the badge of the medieval physician.

■ *What kind of medical help was found in a medieval medical marketplace? How did the four humors determine illness or health?*

Nancy Siraisi, *Medieval and Early Renaissance Medicine: An Introduction to Knowledge and Practice* (University of Chicago Press, Chicago, 1990), ch. 2 and 6; Katharine Park, "Magic and Medicine: The Healing Arts," in *Gender and Society in Renaissance Italy*, ed. by Judith C. Brown and Robert C. Davis (Longman London, 1998).

A caricature of physicians (early sixteenth century). A physician carries a uroscope (for collecting and examining urine); discolored urine signaled an immediate need for bleeding. The physician/surgeon wears surgical shoes and his assistant carries a flail—a comment on the risks of medical services. Hacker Art Books Inc.

BOCCACCIO DESCRIBES THE RAVAGES OF THE BLACK DEATH IN FLORENCE

The Black Death provided an excuse to the poet, humanist, and storyteller Giovanni Boccaccio (1313–1375) to assemble his great collection of tales, the Decameron. *Ten congenial men and women flee Florence to escape the plague and pass the time telling stories. In one of the stories, Boccaccio embeds a fine clinical description of plague symptoms as seen in Florence in 1348 and of the powerlessness of physicians and the lack of remedies.*

■ *What did people do to escape the plague? Was any of it sound medical practice? What does the study of calamities like the Black Death tell us about the people of the past?*

In Florence, despite all that human wisdom and forethought could devise to avert it, even as the cleansing of the city from many impurities by officials appointed for the purpose, the refusal of entrance to all sick folk, and the adoption of many precautions for the preservation of health; despite also humble supplications addressed to God, and often repeated both in public procession and otherwise, by the devout; towards the beginning of the spring of the said year [1348] the doleful effects of the pestilence began to be horribly apparent by symptoms that [appeared] as if miraculous.

Not such were these symptoms as in the East, where an issue of blood from the nose was a manifest sign of inevitable death; but in men and women alike it first betrayed itself by the emergence of certain tumours in the groin or the armpits, some of which grew as large as a common apple, others as an egg, some more, some less, which the common folk called *gavoccioli*. From the two said parts of the body this deadly *gavoccioli* soon began to propagate and spread itself in all directions indifferently; after which the form of the malady began to change, spots black or livid making their appearance in many cases on the arm or the thigh or elsewhere, now few and large, now minute and numerous. And as the *gavoccioli* had been and still were an infallible token of approaching death, such also were these spots on whomsoever they shewed themselves. Which maladies seemed to set entirely at naught both the art of the physician and the virtues of physic; indeed, whether it was that the disorder was of a nature to defy such treatment, or that the physicians were at fault . . . and, being in ignorance of its source, failed to apply the proper remedies; in either case, not merely were those that recovered few, but almost all died within three days of the appearance of the said symptoms . . . and in most cases without any fever or other attendant malady.

From *The Decameron of Giovanni Boccaccio*, trans. by J. M. Rigg (London: J. M. Dent & Sons, 1930), p. 5.

farm labor, but received a smaller return on their agricultural produce. Everywhere their rents were in steady decline after the plague.

Peasants Revolt To recoup their losses, some landowners converted arable land to sheep pasture, substituting more profitable wool production for labor-intensive grain crops. Others abandoned the effort to farm their land and simply leased it to the highest bidder. Landowners also sought simply to reverse their misfortune—to close off the new economic opportunities opened for the peasantry by the demographic crisis—through repressive legislation that forced peasants to stay on their farms and froze their wages at low levels. In France the direct tax on the peasantry, the **taille,** was increased, and opposition to it was prominent among the grievances behind the Jacquerie. In 1351, the English Parliament passed a Statute of Laborers, which limited wages to preplague levels and restricted the ability of peasants to leave the land of their traditional masters. Opposition to such legislation was also a prominent factor in the English peasants' revolt in 1381.

Cities Rebound Although the plague hit urban populations especially hard, the cities and their skilled industries came, in time, to prosper from its effects. Cities had always been careful to protect their interests; as they grew, they passed legislation to regulate competition from rural areas and to control immigration. After the plague, the reach of such laws was progressively extended beyond the cities to include surrounding lands belonging to impoverished nobles and feudal landlords, many of whom were peacefully integrated into urban life.

The omnipresence of death whetted the appetite for goods that only skilled urban industries could produce. Expensive cloths and jewelry, furs from the north, and silks from the south were in great demand in the second half of the fourteenth century. Faced with life at its worst, people insisted on having the very best. Initially, this new demand could not be met. The basic unit of urban industry was the master and apprentices (usually one or two), whose numbers were purposely kept low and whose privileges were jealously guarded. The craft of the skilled artisan was passed from master to apprentice only very slowly. The first wave of plague transformed this already restricted supply of skilled artisans into a shortage almost overnight. As a result, the prices of manufactured and luxury items rose to new heights, and this in turn encouraged workers to migrate from the countryside to the city and learn the skills of artisans. Townspeople in effect profited coming and going from the forces that impoverished the landed nobility. As wealth poured into the cities and per capita income rose, the cost to urban dwellers of agricultural products from the countryside, now less in demand, declined.

There was also gain, as well as loss, for the church. Although it suffered losses as a great landholder and was politically weakened, it had received new revenues from the vastly increased demand for religious services for the dead and the dying and from the multiplication of gifts and bequests.

New Conflicts and Opportunities

By increasing the importance of skilled artisans, the plague contributed to new conflicts within the cities. The economic and political power of local artisans and trade guilds grew steadily in the late Middle Ages, along with the demand for their goods and services. The merchant and patrician classes found it increasingly difficult to maintain their traditional dominance and grudgingly gave guild masters a voice in city government. As the guilds won political power, they encouraged restrictive legislation to protect local industries. These restrictions, in turn, brought confrontations between master artisans, who wanted to keep their numbers low and expand their industries at a snail's pace, and the many journeymen, who were eager to rise to the rank of master. To the long-existing conflict between the guilds

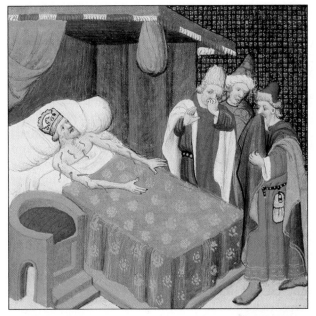

In this scene from an illustrated manuscript of Boccaccio's Decameron, *physicians apply leeches to an emperor. The text says he suffered from a disease that caused a terrible stench, which is why the physicians are holding their noses. Bleeding was the agreed-upon best way to prevent and cure illness and was practiced as late as the nineteenth century. Its popularity was rooted in the belief that a buildup of foul matter in the body caused illness by disrupting the body's four humors (blood, phlegm, yellow bile, and black bile). Bleeding released the foul matter and restored equilibrium among the humors, thus preserving good health by strengthening resistance to disease.* Jean-Loup Charmet/Science Photo Library

and the urban patriciate was now added a conflict within the guilds themselves.

After 1350, the two traditional "containers" of monarchy—the landed nobility and the church—were politically on the defensive, to no small degree as a consequence of the plague. Kings took full advantage of the new situation, drawing on growing national sentiment to centralize their governments and economies. As already noted, the plague reduced the economic power of the landed nobility. In the same period, the battles of the Hundred Years' War demonstrated the military superiority of paid professional armies over the traditional noble cavalry, thus bringing into question the role of the nobility. The plague also killed many members of the clergy—perhaps one-third of the German clergy fell victim to it as they dutifully ministered to the sick and dying. The reduction in clerical ranks occurred in the same century in which the residence of the pope in Avignon (1309–1377) and the Great Schism (1378–1417) were undermining much of the church's popular support.

Ecclesiastical Breakdown and Revival: The Late Medieval Church

At first glance, the popes may appear to have been in a favorable position in the latter half of the thirteenth century. Frederick II had been vanquished and imperial pressure on Rome had been removed. The French king, Louis IX, was an enthusiastic supporter of the church, as evidenced by his two disastrous Crusades, which won him sainthood. Although it lasted only seven years, a reunion of the Eastern church with Rome was proclaimed by the Council of Lyons in 1274, when the Western church took advantage of Byzantine emperor Michael Palaeologus's (r. 1261–1282) request for aid against the Turks. But despite these positive events, the church was not really in as favorable a position as it appeared.

THE THIRTEENTH-CENTURY PAPACY

As early as the reign of Pope Innocent III (r. 1198–1216), when papal power reached its height, there were ominous developments. Innocent had elaborated the doctrine of papal **plenitude of power** and on that authority had declared saints, disposed of *benefices*, and created a centralized papal monarchy with a clearly political mission. Innocent's transformation of the papacy into a great secular power weakened the church spiritually even as it strengthened it politically. Thereafter, the church as a papal monarchy and the church as the "body of the faithful" came increasingly to be differentiated. It was against the "papal church" and in the name of the "true Christian church" that both reformers and heretics raised their voices in protest until the Protestant Reformation.

What Innocent began, his successors perfected. Under Urban IV (r. 1261–1264), the papacy established its own law court, the *Rota Romana*, which tightened and centralized the church's legal proceedings. The latter half of the thirteenth century saw an elaboration of the system of clerical taxation; what had begun in the twelfth century as an emergency measure to raise funds for the Crusades became a fixed institution. In the same period, papal power to determine appointments to many major and minor church offices—the "reservation of *benefices*"—was greatly broadened. The thirteenth-century papacy became a powerful political institution governed by its own law and courts, serviced by an efficient international bureaucracy, and preoccupied with secular goals.

Papal centralization of the church undermined both diocesan authority and popular support. Rome's interests, not local needs, came to control church appointments, policies, and discipline. Discontented lower clergy appealed to the higher authority of Rome against the disciplinary measures of local bishops. In the second half of the thirteenth century, bishops and abbots protested such undercutting of their power. To its critics, the church in Rome was hardly more than a legalized, "fiscalized," bureaucratic institution. As early as the late twelfth century, heretical movements of Cathars and Waldensians had appealed to the biblical ideal of simplicity and separation from the world. Other reformers who were unquestionably loyal to the church, such as Saint Francis of Assisi, would also protest a perceived materialism in official religion.

Political Fragmentation The church of the thirteenth century was being undermined by more than internal religious disunity. The demise of imperial power meant the papacy in Rome was no longer the leader of anti-imperial (Guelf, or propapal) sentiment in Italy. Instead of being the center of Italian resistance to the emperor, popes now found themselves on the defensive against their old allies. That was the ironic price paid by the papacy to vanquish the Hohenstaufens.

Rulers with a stake in Italian politics now directed the intrigue formerly aimed at the emperor toward the College of Cardinals. For example, Charles of Anjou, king of Sicily, managed to create a French-Sicilian faction within the college. Such efforts to control the decisions of the college led Pope Gregory X (r. 1271–1276) to establish the practice of sequestering the cardinals immediately on the death of the pope. The purpose of this so-called conclave of cardinals was to minimize extraneous political influence on the election of new popes, but the college had become so politicized that it proved to be of little avail.

In 1294, such a conclave, in frustration after a deadlock of more than two years, chose a saintly, but inept, Calabrian hermit as Pope Celestine V. Celestine abdicated under suspicious circumstances after only a few weeks in office. He also died under suspicious circumstances; his successor's critics later argued that he had been murdered for political reasons by the powers behind the papal throne to ensure the survival of the papal office. His tragicomic reign shocked a majority of the College of Cardinals into unified action. He was quickly replaced by his very opposite, Pope Boniface VIII (r. 1294–1303), a nobleman and a skilled politician. His pontificate, however, would augur the beginning of the end of papal pretensions to great-power status.

BONIFACE VIII AND PHILIP THE FAIR

Boniface came to rule when England and France were maturing as nation-states. In England, a long tradition of consultation between the king and powerful members of English society evolved into formal parliaments during the reigns of Henry III (r. 1216–1272) and Edward I (r. 1272–1307), and these meetings helped create a unified kingdom. The reign of the French king Philip IV the Fair (r. 1285–1314) saw France become an efficient, centralized monarchy. Philip was no Saint Louis, but a ruthless politician. He was determined to end England's continental holdings, control wealthy Flanders, and establish French hegemony within the Holy Roman Empire.

Boniface had the further misfortune of bringing to the papal throne memories of the way earlier popes had brought kings and emperors to their knees. Very painfully he was to discover that the papal monarchy of the early thirteenth century was no match for the new political powers of the late thirteenth century.

The Royal Challenge to Papal Authority France and England were on the brink of all-out war when Boniface became pope in 1294. Only Edward I's preoccupation with rebellion in Scotland, which the French encouraged, prevented him from invading France and starting the Hundred Years' War a half century earlier than it did start. As both countries mobilized for war, they used the pretext of preparing for a Crusade to tax the clergy heavily. In 1215, Pope Innocent III had decreed that the clergy were to pay no taxes to rulers without prior papal consent. Viewing English and French taxation of the clergy as an assault on traditional clerical rights, Boniface took a strong stand against it. On February 5, 1296, he issued a bull, *Clericis laicos*, which forbade lay taxation of the clergy without prior papal approval and took back all previous papal dispensations in this regard.

In England, Edward I retaliated by denying the clergy the right to be heard in royal court, in effect removing from them the protection of the king. But it was Philip the Fair who struck back with a vengeance: In August 1296, he forbade the exportation of money from France to Rome, thereby denying the papacy the revenues it needed to operate. Boniface had no choice but to come quickly to terms with Philip. He conceded Philip the right to tax the French clergy "during an emergency," and,

Pope Boniface VIII (r. 1294–1303), depicted here, opposed the taxation of the clergy by the kings of France and England and issued one of the strongest declarations of papal authority over rulers, the bull Unam Sanctam. *This statue is in the Museo Civico, Bologna, Italy.* Scala/Art Resource, N.Y.

not coincidentally, he canonized Louis IX in the same year.

Boniface was then also under siege by powerful Italian enemies, whom Philip did not fail to patronize. A noble family (the Colonnas), rivals of Boniface's family (the Gaetani) and radical followers of

Saint Francis of Assisi (the Spiritual Franciscans), were at this time seeking to invalidate Boniface's election as pope on the grounds that Celestine V had resigned the office under coercion. Charges of heresy, simony, and even the murder of Celestine were hurled against Boniface.

Boniface's fortunes appeared to revive in 1300, a "Jubilee year." During such a year, all Catholics who visited Rome and fulfilled certain conditions had the penalties for their unrepented sins remitted. Tens of thousands of pilgrims flocked to Rome in that year, and Boniface, heady with this display of popular religiosity, reinserted himself into international politics. He championed Scottish resistance to England, for which he received a firm rebuke from an outraged Edward I and from Parliament.

But once again a confrontation with the king of France proved the more costly. Philip seemed to be eager for another fight with the pope. He arrested Boniface's Parisian legate, Bernard Saisset, the bishop of Pamiers and also a powerful secular lord, whose independence Philip had opposed. Accused of heresy and treason, Saisset was tried and convicted in the king's court. Thereafter, Philip demanded that Boniface recognize the process against Saisset, something Boniface could do only if he was prepared to surrender his jurisdiction over the French episcopate. This challenge could not be sidestepped, and Boniface acted swiftly to champion Saisset as a defender of clerical political independence within France. He demanded Saisset's unconditional release, revoked all previous agreements with Philip regarding clerical taxation, and ordered the French bishops to convene in Rome within a year. A bull, *Ausculta fili*, or "Listen, My Son," was sent to Philip in December 1301, pointedly informing him that "God has set popes over kings and kingdoms."

Unam Sanctam (1302) Philip unleashed a ruthless antipapal campaign. Two royal apologists, Pierre Dubois and John of Paris, refuted papal claims to the right to intervene in temporal matters. Increasingly placed on the defensive, Boniface made a last-ditch stand against state control of national churches. On November 18, 1302, he issued the bull *Unam Sanctam*. This famous statement of papal power declared that temporal authority was "subject" to the spiritual power of the church. On its face a bold assertion, *Unam Sanctam* was in truth the desperate act of a besieged papacy.

After *Unam Sanctam*, the French and the Colonnas moved against Boniface with force. Philip's chief minister, Guillaume de Nogaret, denounced Boniface to the French clergy as a common heretic and criminal. In mid-August 1303, his army surprised the pope at his retreat in Anagni, beat him up, and almost executed him before an aroused populace returned him safely to Rome. But the ordeal proved too much for him and he died a few months later, in October 1303.

Boniface's immediate successor, Benedict XI (r. 1303–1304), excommunicated Nogaret for his deed, but there was to be no lasting papal retaliation. Benedict's successor, Clement V (r. 1305–1314), was forced into French subservience. A former archbishop of Bordeaux, Clement declared that *Unam Sanctam* should not be understood as in any way diminishing French royal authority. He released Nogaret from excommunication and pliantly condemned the Knights Templars, whose treasure Philip thereafter seized.

In 1309, Clement moved the papal court to Avignon, an imperial city on the southeastern border of France. Situated on land that belonged to the pope, the city maintained its independence from the king. In 1311, Clement made it his permanent residence, to escape both a Rome ridden with strife after the confrontation between Boniface and Philip and further pressure from Philip. There the papacy was to remain until 1377.

After Boniface's humiliation, popes never again seriously threatened kings and emperors, despite continuing papal excommunications and political intrigue. In the future, the relation between church and state would tilt in favor of the state and the control of religion by powerful monarchies. Ecclesiastical authority would become subordinate to larger secular political purposes.

THE AVIGNON PAPACY (1309–1377)

The Avignon papacy was in appearance, although not always in fact, under strong French influence. During Clement V's pontificate the French came to dominate the College of Cardinals, testing the papacy's agility both politically and economically. Finding itself cut off from its Roman estates, the papacy had to innovate to get needed funds. Clement expanded papal taxes, especially the practice of collecting *annates*, the first year's revenue of a church office, or *benefice*, bestowed by the pope. Clement VI (r. 1342–1352) began the practice of selling *indulgences*, or pardons, for unrepented sins. To make the purchase of indulgences more compelling, church doctrine on purgatory—a place of punishment where souls would atone for venial sins—also developed during this period. By the fifteenth century, the church had extended indulgences to cover the souls of people already dead, allowing the living to buy a reduced sentence in purgatory for their deceased loved ones. Such practices contributed to the Avignon papacy's reputation for materialism and political scheming and gave reformers new ammunition.

Pope John XXII   Pope John XXII (r. 1316–1334), the most powerful Avignon pope, tried to restore papal independence and return to Italy. This goal led him into war with the Visconti, the powerful ruling family of Milan, and a costly contest with Emperor Louis IV (r. 1314–1347). John had challenged Louis's election as emperor in 1314 in favor of the rival Habsburg candidate. The result was a minor replay of the confrontation between Philip the Fair and Boniface VIII. When John obstinately and without legal justification refused to recognize Louis's election, the emperor retaliated by declaring John deposed and putting in his place an antipope. As Philip the Fair had also done, Louis enlisted the support of the Spiritual Franciscans, whose views on absolute poverty John had condemned as heretical. Two outstanding pamphleteers wrote lasting tracts for the royal cause: William of Ockham, whom John excommunicated in 1328, and Marsilius of Padua (ca. 1290–1342), whose teaching John declared heretical in 1327.

In his *Defender of Peace* (1324), Marsilius of Padua stressed the independent origins and autonomy of secular government. Clergy were subjected to the strictest apostolic ideals and confined to purely spiritual functions, and all power of coercive judgment was denied the pope. Marsilius argued that spiritual crimes must await an eternal punishment. Transgressions of divine law, over which the pope had jurisdiction, were to be punished in the next life, not in the present one, unless the secular ruler declared a divine law also a secular law. This assertion was a direct challenge to the power of the pope to excommunicate rulers and place countries under interdict. The *Defender of Peace* depicted the pope as a subordinate member of a society over which the emperor ruled supreme and in which temporal peace was the highest good. (See "Marsilius of Padua Denies Coercive Power to the Clergy.")

John XXII made the papacy a sophisticated international agency and adroitly adjusted it to the growing European money economy. The more the **Curia,** or papal court, mastered the latter, however, the more vulnerable it became to criticism. Under John's successor, Benedict XII (r. 1334–1342), the papacy became entrenched in Avignon. Seemingly forgetting Rome altogether, Benedict began construction of the great Palace of the Popes and attempted to reform both papal government and the religious life. His high-living French successor, Clement VI, placed papal policy in lockstep with the French. In this period the cardinals became

A book illustration of the Palace of the Popes in Avignon in 1409, the year in which Christendom found itself confronted by three duly elected popes. The "keys" to the kingdom of God, which the pope held on earth as the vicar of Christ, decorate the three turret flags of the palace. In the foreground, the French poet Pierre Salmon, then journeying via Avignon to Rome, commiserates with a monk over the sad state of the church and France, then at war with England.   Book illustration, French, 1409. Paris, Bibliotheque Nationale. AKG Photo.

barely more than lobbyists for policies favorable to their secular patrons.

National Opposition to the Avignon Papacy   As Avignon's fiscal tentacles probed new areas, monarchies took strong action to protect their interests. The latter half of the fourteenth century saw legislation restricting papal jurisdiction and taxation in France, England, and Germany. In England, where the Avignon papacy was identified with the French enemy after the outbreak of the Hundred Years' War, statutes that restricted payments and appeals to Rome and the pope's power to make high ecclesiastical appointments were passed by Parliament several times between 1351 and 1393.

In France, ecclesiastical appointments and taxation were regulated by the so-called Gallican liberties. These national rights over religion had long

MARSILIUS OF PADUA DENIES COERCIVE POWER TO THE CLERGY

According to Marsilius, the Bible gave the pope no right to pronounce and execute sentences on any person. The clergy held a strictly moral and spiritual rule, their judgments to be executed only in the afterlife, not in the present one. Here, on earth, they should be obedient to secular authority. Marsilius argued this point by appealing to the example of Jesus.

■ *Does Marsilius's argument, if accepted, destroy the worldly authority of the church? Why was his teaching condemned as heretical?*

We now wish . . . to adduce the truths of the holy Scripture . . . which explicitly command or counsel that neither the Roman bishop called pope, nor any other bishop or priest, or deacon, has or ought to have any rulership or coercive judgment or jurisdiction over any priest or nonpriest, ruler, community, group, or individual of whatever condition. . . . Christ himself came into the world not to dominate men, nor to judge them [coercively] . . . not to wield temporal rule, but rather to be subject as regards the . . . present life; and moreover, he wanted to and did exclude himself, his apostles and disciples, and their successors, the bishops or priests, from all coercive authority or worldly rule, both by his example and by his word of counsel or command. . . . When he was brought before Pontius Pilate . . . and accused of having called himself king of the Jews, and [Pilate] asked him whether he had said this . . . [his] reply included these words. . . . "My kingdom is not of this world," that is, I have not come to reign by temporal rule or dominion, in the way . . . worldly kings reign. . . . This, then, is the kingdom concerning which he came to teach and order, a kingdom which consists in the acts whereby the eternal kingdom is attained, that is, the acts of faith and the other theological virtues; not however, by coercing anyone thereto.

Excerpt from *Marsilius of Padua: The Defender of Peace*: The Defensor Pacis, trans. by Alan Gewirth. Copyright © 1967 by Columbia University Press, pp. 113–116. Reprinted by permission of the publisher.

been exercised in fact and were legally acknowledged by the church in the *Pragmatic Sanction of Bourges*, published by Charles VII (r. 1422–1461) in 1438. This agreement recognized the right of the French church to elect its own clergy without papal interference, prohibited the payment of annates to Rome, and limited the right of appeals from French courts to the Curia in Rome. In German and Swiss cities in the fourteenth and fifteenth centuries, local governments also took the initiative to limit and even to overturn traditional clerical privileges and immunities.

JOHN WYCLIFFE AND JOHN HUSS

The popular lay religious movements that most successfully assailed the late medieval church were the **Lollards** in England and the **Hussites** in Bohemia. The Lollards looked to the writings of John Wycliffe (d. 1384) to justify their demands, and both moderate and extreme Hussites to the writings of John Huss (d. 1415), although both Wycliffe and Huss would have disclaimed the extremists who revolted in their names.

Wycliffe was an Oxford theologian and a philosopher of high standing. His work initially served the anticlerical policies of the English government. He became within England what William of Ockham and Marsilius of Padua had been at the Bavarian court of Emperor Louis IV: a major intellectual spokesman for the rights of royalty against the secular pretensions of popes. After 1350, English kings greatly reduced the power of the Avignon papacy to make ecclesiastical appointments and collect taxes within England, a position that Wycliffe strongly supported. His views on clerical poverty followed original Franciscan ideals and, more by accident than by design, gave justification to government restriction and even confiscation of church properties within England. Wycliffe argued that the clergy "ought to be content with food and clothing."

Wycliffe also maintained that personal merit, not rank and office, was the only basis of religious authority. This was a dangerous teaching, because it raised allegedly pious laypeople above allegedly corrupt ecclesiastics, regardless of the latter's official stature. There was a threat in such teaching to secular as well as ecclesiastical dominion and jurisdiction. At his posthumous condemnation by the pope, Wycliffe was accused of the ancient heresy of **Donatism**—the teaching that the efficacy of the church's sacraments did not lie in their true performance, but also depended on the moral character of the clergy who administered them. Wycliffe also anticipated certain Protestant criticisms of the medieval church by challenging papal infallibility, the sale of indulgences, the authority of scripture, and the dogma of transubstantiation.

The Lollards, English advocates of Wycliffe's teaching, like the Waldensians, preached in the vernacular, disseminated translations of Holy Scripture, and championed clerical poverty. At first, they came from every social class. Lollards were especially prominent among the groups that had something tangible to gain from the confiscation of clerical properties (the nobility and the gentry) or that had suffered most under the current church system (the lower clergy and the poor people). After the English peasants' revolt in 1381, an uprising filled with egalitarian notions that could find support in Wycliffe's teaching, Lollardy was officially viewed as subversive. Opposed by an alliance of church and crown, it became a capital offense in England by 1401.

Heresy was not so easily brought to heel in Bohemia, where it coalesced with a strong national movement. The University of Prague, founded in 1348, became the center for both Czech nationalism and a native religious reform movement. The latter began within the bounds of orthodoxy. It was led by local intellectuals and preachers, the most famous of whom was John Huss, the rector of the university after 1403.

The Czech reformers supported vernacular translations of the Bible and were critical of traditional ceremonies and allegedly superstitious practices, particularly those relating to the sacrament of the Eucharist. They advocated lay communion with cup as well as bread, which was traditionally reserved only for the clergy as a sign of the clergy's spiritual superiority over the laity. Hussites taught that bread and wine remained bread and wine after priestly consecration, and they questioned the validity of sacraments performed by priests in mortal sin.

Wycliffe's teaching appears to have influenced the movement very early. Regular traffic between England and Bohemia had existed for decades, ever since the marriage in 1381 of Anne of Bohemia to King Richard II. Czech students studied at Oxford, and many returned with copies of Wycliffe's writings.

Huss became the leader of the pro-Wycliffe faction at the University of Prague. In 1410, his activities brought about his excommunication and the placement of Prague under papal interdict. In 1414, Huss won an audience with the newly assembled Council of Constance. He journeyed to the council eagerly, armed with a safe-conduct pass from Emperor Sigismund, naïvely believing he would convince his strongest critics of the truth of his teaching. Within weeks of his arrival in early November 1414, he was formally accused of heresy and imprisoned. He died at the stake on July 6, 1415, and was followed there less than a year later by his colleague Jerome of Prague.

The reaction in Bohemia to the execution of these national heroes was fierce revolt. Militant Hussites, the Taborites, set out to transform Bohemia by force into a religious and social paradise under the military leadership of John Ziska. After a decade of belligerent protest, the Hussites won significant religious reforms and control over the Bohemian church from the Council of Basel.

A portrayal of John Huss as he was led to the stake at Constance. After his execution, his bones and ashes were scattered in the Rhine River to prevent his followers from claiming them as relics. This pen-and-ink drawing is from Ulrich von Richenthal's Chronicle of the Council of Constance (ca. 1450). Corbis

Justice in the late Middle Ages. Depicted are the most common forms of corporal and capital punishment in Europe in the late Middle Ages and Renaissance. At top: burning, hanging, drowning. At center: blinding, quartering, the wheel, cutting of hair (a mark of great shame for a freeman). At bottom: thrashing, decapitation, amputation of hand (for thieves). Herzog August Bibliothek, Wolfenbuttel.

THE GREAT SCHISM (1378–1417) AND THE CONCILIAR MOVEMENT TO 1449

Pope Gregory XI (r. 1370–1378) reestablished the papacy in Rome in January 1377, ending what had come to be known as the "Babylonian Captivity" of the church in Avignon, a reference to the biblical bondage of the Israelites. The return to Rome proved to be short lived, however.

Urban VI and Clement VII On Gregory's death, the cardinals, in Rome, elected an Italian archbishop as Pope Urban VI (r. 1378–1389), who immediately announced his intention to reform the Curia. This was an unexpected challenge to the cardinals, most of whom were French, and they responded by calling for the return of the papacy to Avignon. The French king, Charles V, wanting to keep the papacy within the sphere of French influence, lent

his support to a schism, which came to be known as the **Great Schism.**

On September 20, 1378, five months after Urban's election, thirteen cardinals, all but one of whom was French, formed their own conclave and elected Pope Clement VII (r. 1378–1397), a cousin of the French king. They insisted they had voted for Urban in fear of their lives, surrounded by a Roman mob demanding the election of an Italian pope. Be that as it may, the papacy now became a "two-headed thing" and a scandal to Christendom. Allegiance to the two papal courts divided along political lines. England and its allies (the Holy Roman Empire, Hungary, Bohemia, and Poland) acknowledged Urban VI, whereas France and those in its orbit (Naples, Scotland, Castile, and Aragon) supported Clement VII. The Roman line of popes has, however, been recognized de facto in subsequent church history.

Two approaches were initially taken to end the schism. One tried to win the mutual cession of both popes, thereby clearing the way for the election of a new pope. The other sought to secure the resignation of the one in favor of the other. Both approaches proved completely fruitless. Each pope considered himself fully legitimate, and too much was at stake for a magnanimous concession on the part of either. One way remained: the forced deposition of both popes by a special council of the church.

Conciliar Theory of Church Government Legally, a church council could be convened only by a pope, but the competing popes were not inclined to summon a council they knew would depose them. Also, the deposition of a legitimate pope against his will by a council of the church was as serious a matter then as the forced deposition of a monarch by a representative assembly.

The correctness of a conciliar deposition of a pope was thus debated a full thirty years before any direct action was taken. Advocates of **conciliar theory** sought to fashion a church in which a representative council could effectively regulate the actions of the pope. The conciliarists defined the church as the whole body of the faithful, of which the elected head, the pope, was only one part. And the pope's sole purpose was to maintain the unity and wellbeing of the church—something the schismatic popes were far from doing. The conciliarists further argued that a council of the church acted with greater authority than the pope alone. In the eyes of the pope(s), such a concept of the church threatened both its political and its religious unity.

The Council of Pisa (1409–1410) On the basis of the arguments of the conciliarists, cardinals representing both popes convened a council on their own authority in Pisa in 1409, deposed both the Roman and the Avignon popes, and elected a new pope, Alexander V. To the council's consternation, neither pope accepted its action, and Christendom suddenly faced the spectacle of three contending popes. Although the vast majority of Latin Christendom accepted Alexander and his Pisan successor John XXIII (r. 1410–1415), the popes of Rome and Avignon refused to step down.

The Council of Constance (1414–1417)   The intolerable situation ended when Emperor Sigismund prevailed on John XXIII to summon a new council in Constance in 1414, which the Roman pope Gregory XII also recognized. In a famous declaration entitled Sacrosancta, the council asserted its supremacy and proceeded to elect a new pope, Martin V (r. 1417–1431), after the three contending popes had either resigned or been deposed. The council then made provisions for regular meetings of church councils, within five, then seven, and thereafter every ten years. (See "The Chronicler Calls the Roll at the Council of Constance.")

Despite the role of the Council of Constance in ending the Great Schism, in the official eyes of the church it was not a legitimate council. Nor have the schismatic popes of Avignon and Pisa been recognized as legitimate. (For this reason, another pope could take the name John XXIII in 1958.)

The Council of Basel (r. 1431–1449)   Conciliar government of the church peaked at the Council of Basel, when the council negotiated church doctrine with heretics. In 1432, the Hussites of Bohemia presented the Four Articles of Prague to the council as a basis for the negotiations. This document contained requests for (1) giving the laity the Eucharist with cup as well as bread; (2) free, itinerant preaching; (3) the exclusion of the clergy from holding secular offices and owning property; and (4) just punishment of clergy who commit mortal sins.

In November 1433, an agreement was reached between the emperor, the council, and the Hussites, giving the Bohemians jurisdiction over their church similar to that held by the French and the English. Three of the four Prague articles were conceded: communion with cup, free preaching by ordained clergy, and like punishment of clergy and laity for mortal sins.

The end of the Hussite wars and the reform legislation curtailing the papal power of appointment and taxation were the high points of the Council of Basel. The exercise of such power by a council did not please the pope, and in 1438, he gained the opportunity to upstage the Council of Basel by negotiating a reunion with the Eastern church. The agreement, signed in Florence in 1439, was short lived, but it restored papal prestige and signaled the demise of the conciliar movement. The Council of Basel collapsed in 1449. A decade later Pope Pius II (r. 1458–1464) issued the papal bull *Execrabilis* (1460) condemning appeals to councils as "erroneous and abominable" and "completely null and void."

Although many who had worked for reform now despaired of ever attaining it, the conciliar movement was not a total failure. It planted deep within the conscience of all Western peoples the conviction that the role of a leader of an institution is to provide for the well-being of its members, not just for that of the leader.

A second consequence of the conciliar movement was the devolving of religious responsibility onto the laity and secular government. Without papal leadership, secular control of national or territorial churches increased. Kings asserted power over the church in England and France. In German, Swiss, and Italian cities, magistrates and city councils reformed and regulated religious life. This development could not be reversed by the powerful popes of the High Renaissance. On the contrary, as the papacy became a limited territorial regime, national control of the church ran apace. Perceived as just one among several Italian states, the Papal States could now be opposed as much on the grounds of "national" policy as for religious reasons.

Medieval Russia

In the late tenth century, Prince Vladimir of Kiev (r. 980–1015), at that time Russia's dominant city, received delegations of Muslims, Roman Catholics, Jews, and Greek Orthodox Christians, each of which hoped to see Russians embrace their religion. Vladimir chose Greek Orthodoxy, which became the religion of Russia, adding strong cultural bonds to the close commercial ties that had long linked Russia to the Byzantine Empire.

POLITICS AND SOCIETY

Vladimir's successor, Yaroslav the Wise (r. 1016–1054), developed Kiev into a magnificent political and cultural center, with architecture rivaling that of Constantinople. He also sought contacts with the West in an unsuccessful effort to counter the political influence of the Byzantine emperors. After his death, rivalry among their princes slowly divided Russians into three cultural groups: the Great Russians, the White Russians, and the Little Russians

THE CHRONICLER CALLS THE ROLL AT THE COUNCIL OF CONSTANCE

The Council of Constance, in session for three years (1414–1417), not only drew many clergy and political representatives into its proceedings but also required a great variety of supporting personnel. Here is an inventory from the contemporary chronicle by Ulrich Richental.

■ *How "representative" of the church was this council? Why were foreign embassies in attendance? What does their presence suggest about the power of councils in the late Middle Ages?*

Pope John XXIII came with 600 men.
Pope Martin, who was elected pope at Constance, came with 30 men.
5 patriarchs, with 118 men.
33 cardinals, with 3,056 men.
47 archbishops, with 4,700 men.
145 bishops, with 6,000 men.
93 suffragan bishops, with 360 men.
Some 500 spiritual lords, with 4,000 men.
24 auditors and secretaries, with 300 men.
37 scholars from the universities of all nations, with 2,000 men.
217 doctors of theology from the five nations, who walked in the processions, with 2,600 men.
361 doctors of both laws, with 1,260 men.
171 doctors of medicine, with 1,600 men.
1,400 masters of arts and licentiates, with 3,000 men.
5,300 simple priests and scholars, some by threes, some by twos, some alone.
The apothecaries who lived in huts, with 300 men. (16 of them were masters.)
72 goldsmiths, who lived in huts.
Over 1,400 merchants, shopkeepers, furriers, smiths, shoemakers, innkeepers, and handworkers, who lived in huts and rented houses and huts, with their servants.

24 rightful heralds of the King, with their squires.
1,700 trumpeters, fifers, fiddlers, and players of all kinds.
Over 700 harlots in brothels came, who hired their own houses, and some who lay in stables and wherever they could, beside the private ones whom I could not count.
In the train of the Pope were 24 secretaries with 200 men, 16 doorkeepers, 12 beadles who carried silver rods, 60 other beadles for the cardinals, auditors and auditors of the camera, and many old women who washed and mended the clothes of the Roman lords in private and public.
132 abbots, all named, with 2,000 men.
155 priors, all recorded with their names, with 1,600 men.
Our lord King, two queens, and 5 princely ladies.
39 dukes, 32 princely lords and counts, 141 counts, 71 barons, more than 1,500 knights, more than 20,000 noble squires.
Embassies from 83 kings of Asia, Africa, and Europe, with full powers; envoys from other lords without number; for they rode in and out every day. There were easily 5,000.
472 envoys from imperial cities.
352 envoys from baronial cities.
72,460 persons.

Richental's *Chronicle of the Council, Constance*, in *The Council of Constance*, ed. by J. H. Mundy and K. M. Woodey, trans. by Louise R. Roomis (New York: Columbia University Press, 1961), pp. 189–190.

(Ukrainians). Autonomous principalities also challenged Kiev's dominance, and it became just one of several national centers. Government in the principalities combined monarchy (the prince), aristocracy (the prince's council of noblemen), and democracy (a popular assembly of all free adult males). The broadest social division was between freemen and slaves. Freemen included the clergy, army officers, **boyars** (wealthy landowners), townspeople, and peasants.

Slaves were mostly prisoners of war. Debtors working off their debts made up a large, semi-free, group.

MONGOL RULE (1243–1480)

In the thirteenth century, Mongol, or Tatar, armies swept over China, much of the Islamic world, and Russia. Ghengis Khan (1155–1227) invaded Russia in 1223, and Kiev fell to Batu Khan in 1240. Russian cities became dependent, tribute-paying principalities of the segment of the Mongol Empire called the *Golden Horde* (a phrase derived from the Tatar words for the color of Batu Khan's tent), which included the steppe region of what is now southern Russia and had its capital at Sarai, on the lower Volga. The Golden Horde stationed officials in all the principal Russian towns to oversee taxation and the conscription of soldiers into Tatar armies. Mongol rule created further cultural divisions between Russia and the West. The Mongols intermarried with the Russians and also created harems filled with Russian women. Russians who resisted were sold into slavery in foreign lands. Russian women—under the influence of Islam, which had become the religion of the Golden Horde—began to wear veils and to lead more secluded lives. The Mongols, however, left Russian political and religious institutions largely intact and, thanks to their far-flung trade, brought most Russians greater peace and prosperity than they had enjoyed before.

LIBERATION

The princes of Moscow cooperated with their overlords in the collection of tribute and grew wealthy under the Mongols. As Mongol rule weakened, the Moscow princes took control of the territory surrounding the city. In a process known as "the gathering of the Russian Land," they then gradually expanded the principality of Moscow through land purchases, colonization, and conquest. In 1380, Grand Duke Dimitri of Moscow (r. 1350–1389) defeated Tatar forces at Kulikov Meadow in a victory that marks the beginning of the decline of Mongol hegemony. Another century would pass before Ivan III, called Ivan the Great (d. 1505), would bring all of northern Russia under Moscow's control and end Mongol rule (1480). By the last quarter of the fourteenth century, however, Moscow had become the political and religious center of Russia, replacing Kiev. In Russian eyes, it became the "third Rome" after Constantinople fell to the Turks in 1453.

Genghis Khan holding an audience. This Persian miniature shows the great conqueror and founder of the Mongol empire with members of his army and entourage as well as an apparent supplicant (lower right). E.T. Archive

IN PERSPECTIVE

War, plague, and schism convulsed much of late medieval Europe throughout the fourteenth and into the fifteenth century. Two-fifths of the population, particularly along the major trade routes, died from plague in the fourteenth century. War and famine continued to take untold numbers after the plague had passed. The introduction of gunpowder and heavy artillery during the long years of warfare between England and France resulted in new forms of human destruction. Periodic revolts erupted in town and countryside as ordinary people attempted to defend their traditional communal rights and privileges against the new autocratic territorial regimes. Even God's house seemed to be in shambles in 1409, when no fewer than three popes came to rule simultaneously.

There is, however, another side to the late Middle Ages. By the end of the fifteenth century, the population losses were rapidly being made up. Between 1300 and 1500, education had become far more accessible, especially to laypeople. The number of universities increased 250 percent, from twenty to seventy, and the rise in the number of residential colleges was even more impressive, especially in France, where sixty-three were built. The fourteenth century saw the birth of humanism, and the fifteenth century gave us the printing press. Most impressive were the artistic and cultural achievements of the Italian Renaissance during the fifteenth century. The later Middle Ages were thus a period of growth and creativity, as well as one of waning and decline.

REVIEW QUESTIONS

1. What were the underlying and precipitating causes of the Hundred Years' War? What advantages did each side have? Why were the French finally able to drive the English almost entirely out of France?

2. What were the causes of the Black Death, and why did it spread so quickly throughout western Europe? Where was it most virulent? What were its effects on European society? How important do you think disease is in changing the course of history?

3. Discuss the struggle between Pope Boniface VIII and King Philip the Fair. Why was Boniface so impotent in the conflict? How had political conditions changed since the reign of Pope Innocent III in the late twelfth century, and what did that mean for the papacy?

4. Briefly trace the history of the church from 1200 to 1450. How did it respond to political threats from the growing power of monarchs? How great an influence did the church have on secular events?

5. What was the Avignon papacy, and why did it occur? What effect did it have on the state of the papacy? What relation does it have to the Great Schism? How did the church become divided and how was it reunited? Why was the conciliar movement a setback for the papacy?

6. Why were kings in the late thirteenth and early fourteenth centuries able to control the church more than the church could control the kings? How did kings attack the church during this period? Contrast these events with earlier ones in which the pope dominated rulers.

SUGGESTED READINGS

C. ALLMAND, *The Hundred Years' War: England and France at War, c. 1300–c. 1450* (1988). Good overview of the war's development and consequences.

P. ARIES, *The Hour of Our Death* (1983). People's familiarity with, and philosophy of, death in the Middle Ages.

P. R. BACKSCHEIDER ET AL. (Eds.). *A Journal of the Plague Year* (1992). Black death at ground level.

R. BARBER (ED.), *The Pastons: Letters of a Family in the War of the Roses* (1984). Rare revelations of English family life in an age of crisis.

P. S. BROOKS, *Beyond the Myth: The Story of Joan of Arc* (1990). What we really know about Joan of Arc.

E. H. GILLETT ET AL., *Life and Times of John Huss: The Bohemian Reformation of the Fifteenth Century* (2001). The latest biography.

J. HUIZINGA, *The Waning of the Middle Ages: A Study of the Forms of Life, Thought, and Art in France and the Netherlands in the Dawn of the Renaissance* (1924). A classic study of mentality at the end of the Middle Ages; exaggerated, but engrossing.

P. KAHN ET AL., *Secret History of the Mongols: The Origins of Chingis Kahn* (1998).

S. OZMENT, *The Age of Reform, 1250–1550* (1980). Highlights of late medieval intellectual and religious history.

E. Perroy, *The Hundred Years' War*, trans. by W. B. Wells (1965). Still the most comprehensive one-volume account.

C. Pratt, *King Death: The Black Death and Its Aftermath in Late-Medieval England* (1996). The peculiarities of the English plague.

Y. Renovard, *The Avignon Papacy, 1305–1403*, trans. by D. Bethell (1970). The standard narrative account.

M. Spinka, *John Huss's Concept of the Church* (1966). Lucid and authoritative account of Hussite theology.

W. R. Trask, (Ed./Trans.), *Joan of Arc in Her Own Words* (1996). Joan's interrogation and self-defense.

P. Ziegler, *The Black Death* (1969). Highly readable account.

DOCUMENTS CD-ROM

THE EARLY MIDDLE AGES

6.5 A Christian's Description of the Mongols

CHURCH AND STATE IN THE HIGH MIDDLE AGES

7.5 *Unam Sanctum*: Two Swords

THE LATE MIDDLE AGES

9.1 The Flagellants
9.2 Propositions of Wycliffe condemned at London, 1382, and at the Council of Constance, 1415
9.3 The Lollard Conclusions
9.4 Individual Heretics: Saints and Witches
9.5 How They Died
9.6 Workers Revolt: The Demands of the Ciompi

Images of Death
in the Late Middle Ages

The Prince of the World in the Church of St. Sebald, Nürnberg, 1320–1330.   Germnisches
Nationalmuseum, Nürnberg.

Throughout the Middle Ages, people perceived, and artists portrayed death both realistically and religiously: on the one hand, as a terrible, inescapable fate, and on the other, as the beginning of a new, eternal life, either in heaven or in hell. That life is death (transitory) and death is life (the afterlife) were two urgent and ironic teachings of the Christian church. Many laity, finding the present world undesirable and death no sure release into a better one, understandably resisted. Graphic and sermonic instruction in the "Art of Dying" became the church's response. Shown here, a sandstone sculpture, *The Prince of the World*, carries a vivid warning. When viewers looked behind this young, attractive prince, they discovered that beauty is only skin deep: His body, like everyone else's, is filled with worms and flesh-eating frogs. A serpent spirals up his left leg and enters his back—an allusion to the biblical teaching that the wages of sin are death. To drive home human mortality, the church instructed laity to think often about the inevitability of death by visiting dying relatives and friends, watching them die and being buried, and thereafter visiting their graves often. This, in turn, would move them to resist the devil's temptations, obey the church, avoid sin, and become eligible for heaven in the afterlife.

During the late Middle Ages, in both literature and art, the *Dance of Death* became a new reminder of human mortality and the need for Christian living and church instruction. (It was first painted in 1424, on the wall of the Church of the Holy Innocents in Paris.) Death appeared as a living skeleton in lively conversation with mortal representatives—from pope to friar in the religious world, from emperor to laborer in the secular—none of whom, no matter how mighty, can elude death's grasp. Even the Son of God, as an incarnate man, died a dreadful death. Although emerging in the late Middle Ages, the *Dance of Death* conveyed an old message, apparently urgently needed at the time because of the indiscipline and self-indulgence occasioned by the new horrors of the Black Death and the Hundred Years' War.

The church's last word on death, however, was resplendently positive: Mortal men and women of true faith, like the crucified Son of God, might look forward to eternal life as shown in *The Resurrection*, from the *Isenheim Altarpiece*, 1509/10–1515.

■ *What contrasting images of dearth were present in medieval art? How does* The Prince of the World *illustrate the importance people in the Middle Ages gave to the "art of dying"?*

Sources: Alberto Tenenti, "Death in History," in *Life and Death in Fifteenth Century Florence*, ed. by M. Tetel et al. (Durham, NC: Duke University Press, 1989); Donald Weinstein, "The Art of Dying Well and Popular Piety in the Preaching and Thought of Girolamo Savonarola," in ibid., 88–104; and James M. Clark, *The Dance of Death in the Middle Ages and the Renaissance* (Glasgow: Jackson, Son, and Col, 1950), pp. 1–4, 22–24, 106–110. Joseph L. Koerner, *The Moment of Self-Portraiture in German Renaissance Art* (Chicago, University of Chicago Press, 1993), pp. 199–200. H. W. Janson et al., *History of Art* (Upper Saddle River, NJ: Prentice Hall, 1997), p. 528.

Mathias Gruenwald (1460–1528), *The Resurrection.*
A panel from the Isenheim Altarpiece. Limewood (around 1515), 250 × 650 cm. Musée d'Unterlinden, Colmar, France. Copyright Erich Lessing/ Art Resource, N.Y.

The School of Athens *by Raphael (1483–1520). Painted in 1510–11 for the Vatican Palace in Rome, it attests the influence of the ancient world on the Renaissance. It depicts Greek philosophers whose works Humanists had recovered and printed. The model for the figure of Plato (center with upraised arm) was Leonardo da Vinci. Michelangelo is the model for an unidentified ancient thinker (center foreground with his head on his arm).* The Bridgeman Art Library International Ltd.

CHAPTER 10

RENAISSANCE AND DISCOVERY

*I*F THE LATE MIDDLE AGES saw unprecedented chaos, it also witnessed a rebirth that would continue into the seventeenth century. Two modern Dutch scholars have employed the same word (Herfsttij, or "harvesttide") with different connotations to describe the period. Johan Huizinga has used the word to mean a "waning" or "decline," and Heiko Oberman has used it to mean "harvest." If something was dying away, some ripe fruit was being gathered and seed grain was sown. The late Middle Ages was a time of creative fragmentation.

By the late fifteenth century, Europe was recovering well from two of the three crises of the late Middle Ages: the demographic and the political. The great losses in population were being recaptured, and increasingly able monarchs and rulers were imposing a new political order. A solution to the religious crisis, however, would have to await the Reformation and Counter-Reformation of the sixteenth century.

Although the opposite would be true in the sixteenth and seventeenth centuries, the city-states of Italy survived the century and a half between 1300 and 1450 better than the territorial states of northern Europe. This was due to Italy's strategic location between East and West and its lucrative Eurasian trade. Great wealth gave rulers and merchants the ability to work their will on both society and culture. They became patrons of government, education, and the arts, always as much for self-aggrandizement as out of benevolence, for whether a patron was a family, a firm, a government, or the church, their endowments enhanced their reputation and power. The result of such patronage was a cultural Renaissance in Italian cities unmatched elsewhere.

With the fall of Constantinople to the Turks in 1453, the shrinkage of Italy's once unlimited trading empire began. City-state soon turned against city-state, and by the 1490s, the armies of France invaded Italy. Within a quarter century, Italy's great Renaissance had peaked.

The fifteenth century also saw an unprecedented scholarly renaissance. Italian and northern humanists made a full recovery of classical knowledge and languages and set in motion educational reforms and cultural changes that would spread throughout Europe *in the fifteenth and sixteenth centuries. In the process the Italian humanists invented, for all practical purposes, critical historical scholarship and exploited a new fifteenth-century invention, the "divine art" of printing with movable type.*

In this period the vernacular—the local language—began to take its place alongside Latin, the international language, as a widely used literary and political means of communication. And European states progressively superseded the universal church as the community of highest allegiance, as patriotism and incipient nationalism seized hearts and minds as strongly as religion. Nations henceforth "transcended" themselves not by journeys to Rome, but by competitive voyages to the Far East and the Americas, as the age of global exploration opened.

For Europe, the late fifteenth and sixteenth centuries were a period of unprecedented territorial expansion and ideological experimentation. Permanent colonies were established within the Americas, and the exploitation of the New World's human and mineral resources was begun. Imported American gold and silver spurred scientific invention and a new weapons industry and touched off an inflationary spiral that produced an escalation in prices by the century's end. The new bullion also helped create an international traffic in African slaves as rival African tribes sold their captives to the Portuguese. These slaves were brought in ever-increasing numbers to work the mines and the plantations of the New World as replacements for American natives, whose population declined precipitously following the conquest. The period also saw social engineering and political planning on a large scale. Newly centralized governments began to put long-range economic policies into practice, a development that came to be known as mercantilism.

KEY TOPICS

- The politics, culture, and art of the Italian Renaissance
- Political struggle and foreign intervention in Italy
- The powerful new monarchies of northern Europe
- The thought and culture of the northern Renaissance

The Renaissance in Italy (1375–1527)

A historian has described the Renaissance as the "prototype of the modern world." In his *Civilization of the Renaissance in Italy* (1860), Jacob Burckhardt argued that in fourteenth—and fifteenth—century Italy, through the revival of ancient learning, new secular and scientific values began to supplant traditional religious beliefs. This was the period in which people began to adopt a rational, objective, and statistical approach to reality and to rediscover the importance of the individual and his or her artistic creativity. The result, in Burckhardt's words, was a release of the "full, whole nature of man."

Other scholars have found Burckhardt's description far too modernizing an interpretation of the Renaissance and have accused him of overlooking the continuity between the Middle Ages and the Renaissance. His critics especially stress the still strongly Christian character of Renaissance humanism. They point out that earlier "renaissances," especially that of the twelfth century, also saw the revival of the ancient classics, interest in the Latin language and Greek science, and an appreciation of the worth and creativity of individuals.

Despite the exaggeration and bias of Burckhardt's portrayal, most scholars agree that the **Renaissance** was a time of transition from the medieval to the modern world. Medieval Europe, especially before the twelfth century, had been a fragmented feudal society with an agricultural economy, and its thought and culture were largely dominated by the church. Renaissance Europe, especially after the fourteenth century, was characterized by growing national consciousness and political centralization, an urban economy based on organized commerce and capitalism, and ever-greater lay and secular control of thought and culture, including religion.

The distinctive features and achievements of the Renaissance are most strikingly revealed in Italy between 1375 and 1527, dates that bookend a century and a half of unprecedented cultural creativity. Two events coincide with the beginning of this period: the death in 1374 of Petrarch, considered the "father" of humanism, and the death in 1375 of Giovanni Boccaccio, author of the *Decameron*. Also in 1375, Coluccio Salutati succeeded to the Florentine chancellorship and leadership of the mature humanist movement. Thereafter, Florentine humanist culture spread throughout Italy and into northern Europe. (See "Art & the West: An Unprecedented Self-Portrait," p. 351.) This creative expansion, however, appeared to reach an abrupt end in 1527, when

Spanish-imperial soldiers looted and torched Rome much as Visigoths and Vandals had done in antiquity. At this time, French king Francis I and the Holy Roman Emperor Charles V were warring in Italy over their dynastic claims to Burgundy and Italian lands. Pope Clement VIII (r. 1523–1534) incurred the emperor's wrath by joining the French. The infamous sack of Rome in 1527 was less the result of a breach of papal loyalty, however, than the anger and boredom of Spanish-imperial soldiers who had not been properly paid and provisioned by the emperor. Their barbarous action, a seeming return to the savagery of earlier centuries, marked the end of the cultured Renaissance.

THE ITALIAN CITY-STATE

Renaissance society was no simple cultural transformation. It first took distinctive shape within the cities of late medieval Italy. Italy had always had a cultural advantage over the rest of Europe because its geography made it the natural gateway between East and West. Venice, Genoa, and Pisa traded uninterruptedly with the Near East throughout the Middle Ages and maintained vibrant urban societies. When commerce revived on a large scale in the eleventh century, Italian merchants quickly mastered the business skills of organization, bookkeeping, scouting new markets, and securing monopolies. During the thirteenth and fourteenth centuries, trade-rich cities expanded to become powerful city-states, dominating the political and economic life of the surrounding countryside. By the fifteenth century, the great Italian cities had become the bankers for much of Europe.

Growth of City-States The growth of Italian cities and urban culture was assisted by the endemic warfare between the emperor and the pope and the Guelf (propapal) and Ghibelline (proimperial) factions that this warfare had created. Either of these might have successfully challenged the cities had they permitted each other to concentrate on that. Instead, they chose to weaken one another and thus strengthened the merchant oligarchies of the cities. Unlike those of northern Europe, which tended to be dominated by kings and territorial princes, the great Italian cities were left free to expand. They became independent states, absorbing the surrounding countryside and assimilating the area's nobility in a unique urban meld of old and new rich. There were five such major, competitive states in Italy: the duchy of Milan; the republics of Florence and Venice; the Papal States; and the kingdom of Naples. (See Map 10–1.)

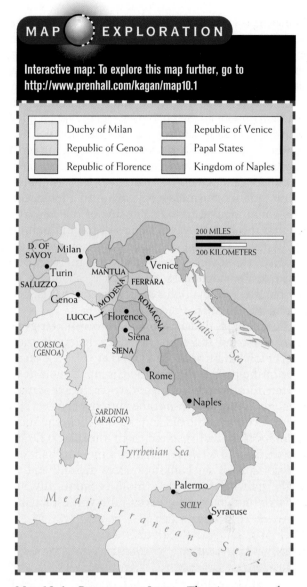

MAP 10–1   RENAISSANCE ITALY   *The city-states of Renaissance Italy were self-contained principalities whose internal strife was monitored by their despots and whose external aggression was long successfully controlled by treaty.*

Social strife and competition for political power were so intense within the cities that most had evolved into despotisms by the fifteenth century just to survive. Venice was a notable exception. It was ruled by a successful merchant oligarchy with power located in a patrician senate of three hundred members and a ruthless judicial body, the Council of Ten, which anticipated and suppressed rival groups. Elsewhere, the new social classes and divisions within society produced by rapid urban growth fueled chronic, near-anarchic conflict.

Social Class and Conflict Florence was the most striking example. There were four distinguishable social groups within the city. The first was the old rich, or *grandi*, the nobles and merchants who traditionally ruled the city. The second group was the emergent newly rich merchant class—capitalists and bankers known as the *popolo grosso*, or "fat people." They began to challenge the old rich for political power in the late thirteenth and early fourteenth centuries. Then there were the middle-burgher ranks of guild masters, shop owners, and professionals—those smaller businesspeople who, in Florence as elsewhere, tended to take the side of the new rich against the conservative policies of the old rich. Finally, there was the *popolo minuto*, or the "little people," the lower economic classes. In 1457, one-third of the population of Florence, about 30,000 people, were officially listed as paupers, that is, having no wealth at all.

These social divisions produced conflict at every level of society, to which was added the ever-present fear of foreign intrigue. In 1378, there was a great revolt of the poor known as the Ciompi Revolt. It resulted from a combination of three factors that made life unbearable for those at the bottom of society: the feuding between the old and the new rich; the social anarchy that had resulted from the Black Death, which cut the city's population almost in half; and the collapse of the banking houses of Bardi and Peruzzi, which left the poor more economically vulnerable than ever. The successful revolt established a chaotic four-year reign of power by the lower Florentine classes. True stability did not return to Florence until the ascent to power of Cosimo de' Medici (1389–1464) in 1434.

Despotism and Diplomacy The wealthiest Florentine, Cosimo de' Medici, was an astute statesman. He controlled the city internally from behind the scenes, skillfully manipulating the constitution and influencing elections. Florence was governed by a council, first of six and later of eight members, known as the *Signoria*. These men were chosen from the most powerful guilds—those representing the major clothing industries (cloth, wool, fur, and silk) and such other groups as bankers, judges, and doctors. Through his informal, cordial relations with the electoral committee, Cosimo was able to keep councillors loyal to him in the *Signoria*. As head of the Office of Public Debt, he was able to favor congenial factions. His grandson Lorenzo the Magnificent (1449–1492; r. 1478–1492) ruled Florence in almost totalitarian fashion during the last quarter of the fifteenth century. The assassination of his brother in 1478 by a rival family, the Pazzi, who plotted with the pope against Medici rule, made Lorenzo a cautious and determined ruler.

Despotism was less subtle elsewhere. To prevent internal social conflict and foreign intrigue from paralyzing their cities, the dominant groups cooperated to install a hired strongman. Known as a *podestà*, his purpose was to maintain law and order.

Florentine women doing needlework, spinning, and weaving. These activities took up much of a woman's time and contributed to the elegance of dress for which Florentine men and women were famed. Alinari/Art Resource

He was given executive, military, and judicial authority. His mandate was direct and simple: to permit, by whatever means required, the normal flow of business activity without which neither the old rich, the new rich, nor the poor of a city could long survive. Because these despots could not depend on the divided populace, they operated through mercenary armies, which they obtained through military brokers known as **condottieri.**

It was a hazardous job. Not only were despots subject to dismissal by the oligarchies that hired them, but they were also popular objects of assassination attempts. The spoils of success, however, were very great. In Milan, it was as despots that the Visconti family came to power in 1278 and the Sforza family in 1450. Both ruled without constitutional restraints or serious political competition. The latter produced one of Machiavelli's heroes, Ludovico il Moro.

Political turbulence and warfare gave birth to diplomacy. Consequently, the various city-states could stay abreast of foreign military developments and, if shrewd enough, gain power and advantage short of actually going to war. Most city-states established resident embassies in the fifteenth century. Their ambassadors not only represented them in ceremonies and as negotiators, but also became their watchful eyes and ears at rival courts.

Whether within the comparatively tranquil republic of Venice, the strong-arm democracy of Florence, or the undisguised despotism of Milan, the disciplined Italian city proved a most congenial climate for an unprecedented flowering of thought and culture. Italian Renaissance culture was promoted as vigorously by despots as by republicans and as enthusiastically by secularized popes as by the more spiritually minded. Such widespread support occurred because the main requirement for patronage of the arts and letters was the one thing that Italian cities of the High Renaissance had in abundance: great wealth.

HUMANISM

Several schools of thought exist on the meaning of the term *humanism*. There are those who see the Italian Renaissance as the birth of modernity, characterized by an un-Christian philosophy that stressed the dignity of humankind and championed individualism and secular values. (These are the followers of the nineteenth-century historian Jacob Burckhardt.) Others argue that humanists were the very champions of authentic Catholic Christianity, who opposed the pagan teaching of Aristotle and the ineloquent Scholasticism that his writings nurtured. Still others see humanism as a form of scholarship

Cosimo de' Medici (1389–1464), Florentine banker and statesman, in his lifetime the city's wealthiest man and most successful politician. This portrait is by Pontormo.
Erich Lessing, Art Resource, N.Y.

consciously designed to promote a sense of civic responsibility and political liberty.

An authoritative modern commentator on humanism, Paul O. Kristeller, has accused all these views of dealing more with the secondary effects than with the essence of humanism. Humanism, he believes, was no particular philosophy or value system, but simply an educational program that concentrated on rhetoric and sound scholarship for their own sake.

There is truth in each of these definitions. **Humanism** was the scholarly study of the Latin and Greek classics and of the ancient Church Fathers both for its own sake and in the hope of a rebirth of ancient norms and values. Humanists advocated the **studia humanitatis,** a liberal arts program of study that embraced grammar, rhetoric, poetry, history, politics, and moral philosophy. Not only were these subjects considered a joy in themselves, but they were also seen as celebrating the dignity of humankind and preparing people for a life of virtuous action. The Florentine Leonardo Bruni (ca. 1370–1444) first gave the name *humanitas,* or "humanity," to the learning

The Garden

In the Middle Ages and early Renaissance, few possessions were as prized, or as vital, as a garden. Within that enclosed space grew both ornamental and medicinal flowers and herbs. The more common kitchen garden existed in every manor, castle, monastery, guildhall, and small household. In addition to their large, elaborate gardens, the rich also had orchards and vineyards to grow the fruit from which they made sweet drinks and wine. Behind their shops and guildhalls, apothecaries and barber-surgeons cultivated the curative flowers and herbs from which they concocted the medicines of their trades. And beyond manor and guildhall walls, small householders and cottagers hoed the small, narrow plots behind their houses in which they grew the basic herbs and vegetables of their diet. Although the grandeur and variety of a garden reflected the prestige of its owner, every garden's main purpose was to serve the immediate needs of the household.

Versatility and pungency distinguished the most popular flowers and herbs. The violet was admired for its beauty, fragrance, and utility. Medieval people put violets in baths, oils, and syrups, prizing its soft scent and healing power as well as its ability to color, flavor, and garnish dishes. Nonetheless, subtlety and delicacy were not as important to the medieval palate as they are to ours. An herb or flower was only as good as its impact on the senses. Potent scents and flavors were loved for their ability to bring an otherwise starchy and lackluster meal to life. Fruit, although it was the main ingredient for sweet drinks, rarely appeared on a medieval plate, and vegetables were only slightly more common. Cabbage, lentils, peas, beans, onions, leeks, beets, and parsnips were the most often served vegetables at the medieval table, made palatable by heavy application of the sharpest and bitterest spices.

Beyond its practical function as a source of food and medicine, the medieval garden was a space of social and religious significance. In Christian history, gardens represented sacred places on earth. During the Middle Ages and early Renaissance, it was not the sprawling paradise of the Garden of Eden that captured the imagination, but rather the closed garden of the Bible's Song of Songs (4:12): "A garden enclosed is my sister, my spouse; a spring shut up, a fountain sealed." Such sensuous imagery symbolized the soul's union with God, Christ's union with the Catholic Church, and the bond of love between a man and a woman.

Gardens were enclosed behind walls, fences, or hedges to protect them as vital food sources, but they were also private places for dreamers and lovers. Pleasure gardens bloomed around the homes of the wealthy. There, amid grottoes and fountains, lovers breathed the warm scents of roses and lilies and pursued the romantic trysts made popular in court poetry. The stories of courtly love were cautionary as well as titillating, for as the catechism reminded every medieval Christian, the garden was also a place of temptation and lost innocence.

■ *What kinds of gardens existed in the Middle Ages and early Renaissance? How did religion give meaning to gardens?*

Teresa McClean, *Medieval English Gardens* (Viking Press New York, 1980), pp. 64, 133. Marilyn Stokstad and Jerry Stannard, *Gardens of the Middle Ages* (Spencer Museum, Lawrence, Kansas, 1983), pp. 19–21, 61.

A wealthy man oversees apple-picking at harvest time in a fifteenth-century French orchard. In the town below, individual house gardens can be seen. Protective fences, made of woven sticks, keep out predatory animals. In the right foreground, a boar can be seen overturning an apple barrel. The British Library

that resulted from such scholarly pursuits. Bruni was a student of Manuel Chrysoloras, a Byzantine scholar who opened the world of Greek scholarship to a generation of young Italian humanists when he taught at Florence between 1397 and 1403.

The first humanists were orators and poets. They wrote original literature in both the classical and the vernacular languages, inspired by and modeled on the newly discovered works of the ancients. They also taught rhetoric within the universities. When humanists were not employed as teachers of rhetoric, their talents were sought as secretaries, speechwriters, and diplomats in princely and papal courts.

The study of classical and Christian antiquity existed before the Italian Renaissance. There were recoveries of ancient civilization during the Carolingian renaissance of the ninth century, within the cathedral school of Chartres in the twelfth century, during the great Aristotelian revival in Paris in the thirteenth century, and among the Augustinians in the early fourteenth century. These precedents, however, only partially compare with the grand achievements of the Italian Renaissance of the late Middle Ages. The latter was far more secular and lay dominated, had much broader interests, was blessed with far more recovered manuscripts, and possessed far superior technical skills than had been the case in the earlier "rebirths" of antiquity.

Unlike their Scholastic rivals, humanists were less bound to recent tradition; they did not focus all their attention on summarizing and comparing the views of recognized authorities on a text or question, but went directly to the original sources themselves. And their most respected sources were classical and biblical, not the medieval philosophers and theologians. Avidly searching out manuscript collections, Italian humanists made the full sources of Greek and Latin antiquity available to scholars during the fourteenth and fifteenth centuries. Mastery of Latin and Greek was the surgeon's tool of the humanist. There is a kernel of truth—but only a kernel—in the humanists' arrogant assertion that the period between themselves and classical civilization was a "dark middle age."

Petrarch, Dante, and Boccaccio Francesco Petrarch (1304–1374) was the "father of humanism." He left the legal profession to pursue letters and poetry. Most of his life was spent in and around Avignon. He was involved in Cola di Rienzo's popular revolt and two-year reign (1347–1349) in Rome as "tribune" of the Roman people. Petrarch also served the Visconti family in Milan in his later years.

Petrarch celebrated ancient Rome in his *Letters to the Ancient Dead*, fancied personal letters to Cicero, Livy, Vergil, and Horace. He also wrote a Latin epic poem (*Africa*, a poetic historical tribute to the Roman general Scipio Africanus) and biographies of famous Roman men (*Lives of Illustrious Men*). Petrarch's most famous contemporary work was a collection of highly introspective love sonnets to a certain Laura, a married woman he admired romantically from a safe distance.

His critical textual studies, elitism, and contempt for the allegedly useless learning of the Scholastics were features that many later humanists also shared. Classical and Christian values coexist, not always harmoniously, in his work, an uneasy coexistence that is seen in many later humanists. Medieval Christian values can be seen in Petrarch's imagined dialogues with Saint Augustine and in tracts written to defend the personal immortality of the soul against the Aristotelians.

Petrarch was, however, far more secular in orientation than his famous near-contemporary Dante Alighieri (1265–1321), whose *Vita Nuova* and *Divine Comedy* form, with Petrarch's sonnets, the cornerstones of Italian vernacular literature. Petrarch's student and friend Giovanni Boccaccio (1313–1375) was also a pioneer of humanist studies. His *Decameron*—one hundred often bawdy tales told by three men and seven women in a country retreat from the plague that ravaged Florence in 1348—is both a stinging social commentary (especially in its exposé of sexual and economic misconduct) and a sympathetic look at human behavior. An avid collector of manuscripts, Boccaccio also assembled an encyclopedia of Greek and Roman mythology.

Educational Reforms and Goals Humanists were not bashful scholars. They delighted in going directly to primary sources and refused to be slaves to tradition. Such an attitude not only made them innovative educators, but also kept them constantly in search of new sources of information. Magnificent manuscript collections were assembled with great care, as if they were potent medicines for the ills of contemporary society.

The goal of humanist studies was to be wise and to speak eloquently, to know what is good, and to practice virtue. Learning was not to remain abstract and unpracticed. "It is better to will the good than to know the truth," Petrarch had taught, and this became a motto of many later humanists, who, like Petrarch, believed learning ennobled people. Pietro Paolo Vergerio (1349–1420), the author of the most influential Renaissance tract on education, *On the Morals That Befit a Free Man*, left a classic summary of the humanist concept of a liberal education:

We call those studies liberal which are worthy of a free man; those studies by which we attain and practice virtue and wisdom; that education which calls forth,

Dante Alighieri (1265–1321) portrayed with scenes of hell, purgatory, and paradise from the Divine Comedy, *his classic epic poem.* Scala/Art Resource, N.Y.

trains, and develops those highest gifts of body and mind which ennoble men and which are rightly judged to rank next in dignity to virtue only, for to a vulgar temper, gain and pleasure are the one aim of existence, to a lofty nature, moral worth and fame.[1]

The ideal of a useful education and well-rounded people inspired far-reaching reforms in traditional education. Quintilian's *Education of the Orator*, whose complete text was discovered in 1416, became the basic classical guide for the humanist revision of the traditional curriculum. Vittorino da Feltre (d. 1446) exemplified the ideals of humanist teaching. He not only had his students read the difficult works of Pliny, Ptolemy, Terence, Plautus, Livy, and Plutarch, but also subjected them to vigorous physical exercise and games. Another famous educator, Guarino da Verona (d. 1460), rector of the new University of Ferrara and a student of the age's most renowned Greek scholar, Manuel Chrysoloras, streamlined the study of classical languages and gave it systematic form.

Humanist learning was not confined to the classroom, as Baldassare Castiglione's (1478–1529) famous *Book of the Courtier* illustrates. Written as a practical guide for the nobility at the court of Urbino, it embodies the highest ideals of Italian humanism. It depicts the successful courtier as one who knew how to integrate knowledge of ancient languages and history with athletic, military, and musical skills while at the same time practicing good manners and exhibiting a high moral character.

Noblewomen also played a role at court in education and culture, among them none more so than Christine de Pisan (1363?–1434). The Italian-born daughter of the physician and astrologer of the French king Charles V, she received as fine an education at the French court as anyone could have. She became expert in classical, French, and Italian languages and literature. Married at fifteen and the widowed mother of three at twenty-seven, she turned to writing lyric poetry to support herself. She soon became a well-known woman of letters who was much read throughout the courts of Europe. Her most famous work, *The Treasure of the City of Ladies*, is a chronicle of the accomplishments of the great women of history. (See "Christine de Pisan Instructs Women on How to Handle Their Husbands.")

The Florentine "Academy" and the Revival of Platonism Of all the important recoveries of the past made during the Italian Renaissance, none stands out more than the revival of Greek studies, especially the works of Plato, in fifteenth-century Florence. Many factors combined to bring this revival about. An important foundation was laid in 1397 when the city invited Manuel Chrysoloras to come from Constantinople to promote Greek learning. A half century later (1439), the ecumenical Council of Ferrara-Florence, having convened to negotiate the reunion of the Eastern and Western churches, opened the door for many Greek scholars and manuscripts to enter the West. After the fall of Constantinople to the Turks in 1453, Greek scholars fled to Florence for refuge. This was the background against which the Florentine Platonic Academy evolved

---

[1]Cited by De Lamar Jensen, *Renaissance Europe: Age of Recovery and Reconciliation* (Lexington, MA: D.C. Health, 1981), p. 111.

CHRISTINE DE PISAN INSTRUCTS WOMEN ON HOW TO HANDLE THEIR HUSBANDS

Renowned Renaissance noblewoman Christine de Pisan has the modern reputation of being perhaps the first feminist, and her book, The Treasure of the City of Ladies *(also known as* The Book of Three Virtues*), has been described as the Renaissance woman's survival manual. Here she gives advice to the wives of artisans.*

■ *How does Christine de Pisan's image of husband and wife compare with other medieval views? Would the church take issue with her advice in any way? As a noblewoman commenting on the married life of artisans, does her high social standing influence her advice? Would she give similar advice to women of her own social class?*

All wives of artisans should be very painstaking and diligent if they wish to have the necessities of life. They should encourage their husbands or their workmen to get to work early in the morning and work until late. . . . [And] the wife herself should [also] be involved in the work to the extent that she knows all about it, so that she may know how to oversee his workers if her husband is absent, and to reprove them if they do not do well. . . . And when customers come to her husband and try to drive a hard bargain, she ought to warn him solicitously to take care that he does not make a bad deal. She should advise him to be chary of giving too much credit if he does not know precisely where and to whom it is going, for in this way many come to poverty. . . .

In addition, she ought to keep her husband's love as much as she can, to this end: that he will stay at home more willingly and that he may not have any reason to join the foolish crowds of other young men in taverns and indulge in unnecessary and extravagant expense, as many tradesmen do, especially in Paris. By treating him kindly she should protect him as well as she can from this. It is said that three things drive a man from his home: a quarrelsome wife, a smoking fireplace, and a leaking roof. She too ought to stay at home gladly and not go off every day traipsing hither and yon gossiping with the neighbours and visiting her chums to find out what everyone is doing. That is done by slovenly housewives roaming about the town in groups. Nor should she go off on these pilgrimages got up for no good reason and involving a lot of needless expense.

Excerpt from *The Treasure of the City of Ladies* by Christine de Pisan, trans. by Sarah Lawson (Penguin, 1985), pp. 167–168. Copyright © Sarah Lawson, 1985. Reproduced by permission of Penguin Books Ltd.

under the patronage of Cosimo de' Medici and the supervision of Marsilio Ficino (1433–1499) and Pico della Mirandola (1463–1494).

The thinkers of the Renaissance were interested in every variety of ancient wisdom. They were especially attracted, however, to the Platonic tradition and to those Church Fathers who tried to synthesize Platonic philosophy with Christian teaching. The so-called Florentine Academy was actually not a formal school, but an informal gathering of influential Florentine humanists devoted to the revival of the works of Plato and the Neoplatonists: Plotinus, Proclus, Porphyry, and Dionysius the Areopagite. To this end, Ficino edited and published the complete works of Plato.

The appeal of **Platonism** lay in its flattering view of human nature. It distinguished between an eternal sphere of being and the perishable world in which humans actually lived. Human reason was believed to belong to the former—indeed, to have preexisted in this pristine world and to continue to commune with it, to which the present knowledge of mathematical and moral truth bore witness.

Strong Platonic influence can be seen in Pico's *Oration on the Dignity of Man*, perhaps the most famous Renaissance statement on the nature of humankind. (See "Pico della Mirandola States the Renaissance Image of Man.") Pico wrote the *Oration* as an introduction to a pretentious collection of nine hundred theses. Published in Rome in

PICO DELLA MIRANDOLA STATES THE RENAISSANCE IMAGE OF MAN

One of the most eloquent descriptions of the Renaissance image of human beings comes from the Italian humanist Pico della Mirandola (1463–1494). In his famed Oration on the Dignity of Man *(ca. 1486), Pico describes humans as free to become whatever they choose.*

■ *How great, really, is the choice outlined here? Are the basic options limited? Do they differ from what the church thought life's possibilities were? Is the concept of freedom in this passage a modern one?*

The best of artisans [God] ordained that that creature (man) to whom He had been able to give nothing proper to himself should have joint possession of whatever had been peculiar to each of the different kinds of being. He therefore took man as a creature of indeterminate nature and, assigning him a place in the middle of the world, addressed him thus: "Neither a fixed abode nor a form that is thine alone nor any function peculiar to thyself have we given thee, Adam, to the end that according to thy longing and according to thy judgment thou mayest have and possess what abode, what form, and what functions thou thyself shalt desire. The nature of all other beings is limited and constrained within the bounds of laws prescribed by Us. Thou, constrained by no limits, in accordance with thine own free will, in whose hand We have placed thee, shall ordain for thyself the limits of thy nature. We have set thee at the world's center that thou mayest from thence more easily observe whatever is in the world. We have made thee neither of heaven nor of earth, neither mortal nor immortal, so that with freedom of choice and with honor, as though the maker and molder of thyself, thou mayest fashion thyself in whatever shape thou shalt prefer. Thou shalt have the power to degenerate into the lower forms of life, which are brutish. Thou shalt have the power, out of thy soul's judgment, to be reborn into the higher forms, which are divine." O supreme generosity of God the Father, O highest and most marvelous felicity of man! To him it is granted to have whatever he chooses, to be whatever he wills.

Giovanni Pico della Mirandola, *Oration on the Dignity of Man*, in *The Renaissance Philosophy of Man*, ed. by E. Cassirer et al. (Chicago: Phoenix Books, 1961), pp. 224–225.

December 1486, the theses were intended to serve as the basis for a public debate on all of life's important topics. The *Oration* drew on Platonic teaching to depict humans as the only creatures in the world who possessed the freedom to be whatever they chose, able at will to rise to the height of angels or to descend to the level of pigs.

Critical Work of the Humanists: Lorenzo Valla
Because they were guided by a scholarly ideal of philological accuracy and historical truthfulness, the humanists could become critics of tradition even when that was not their intention. Dispassionate critical scholarship shook long-standing foundations, not the least of which were those of the medieval church.

The work of Lorenzo Valla (1406–1457), author of the standard Renaissance text on Latin philology, the *Elegances of the Latin Language* (1444), reveals the explosive character of the new learning. Although a good Catholic, Valla became a hero to later Protestants. His popularity among Protestants stemmed from his defense of predestination against the advocates of free will, and especially from his exposé of the *Donation of Constantine*. (See Chapter 6.)

The fraudulent *Donation*, written in the eighth century, purported to be a grant of vast territories made by the fourth-century Roman emperor Constantine to the pope. Valla did not intend the exposé of the *Donation* to have the devastating force that Protestants later attributed to it. He only proved in a careful, scholarly way what others had long suspected. Using the most rudimentary textual analysis and historical logic, Valla demonstrated that the document was filled with such anachronistic terms as *fief* and contained material that could not be in a genuine fourth-century document. In the same dispassionate way, Valla also pointed out errors in the Latin Vulgate, still the authorized version of the Bible for the Western church.

Such discoveries did not make Valla any less loyal to the church, nor did they prevent his faithful fulfillment of the office of apostolic secretary in Rome under Pope Nicholas V. Nonetheless, historical criticism of this type served those less loyal to the medieval church. It was no accident that young humanists formed the first identifiable group of Martin Luther's supporters.

Civic Humanism Italian humanists were exponents of applied knowledge; their basic criticism of traditional education was that much of it was useless. Education, they believed, should promote individual virtue and public service. This ideal inspired what has been called **civic humanism,** by which is meant examples of humanist leadership of the political and cultural life. The most striking instance is to be found in Florence. There three humanists served as chancellors: Coluccio Salutati (1331–1406), Leonardo Bruni (ca. 1370–1444), and Poggio Bracciolini (1380–1459). Each used his rhetorical skills to rally the Florentines against the aggression of Naples and Milan. Bruni and Poggio also wrote adulatory histories of the city. Another accomplished humanist scholar, Leon Battista Alberti (1402–1472), was a noted architect and builder in the city. Whether it was humanism that accounted for such civic activity or just a desire to exercise great power remains a debated issue.

Many humanists, however, became cliquish and snobbish, an intellectual elite concerned only with pursuing narrow, antiquarian interests and writing pure, classical Latin in the quiet of their studies. It was in reaction to this elitist trend that the humanist historians Niccolò Machiavelli (1469–1527) and Francesco Guicciardini (1483–1540) adopted the vernacular and made contemporary history their primary source and subject matter.

RENAISSANCE ART

In Renaissance Italy, as in Reformation Europe, the values and interests of the laity were no longer subordinated to those of the clergy. In education, culture, and religion, the laity assumed a leading role and established models for the clergy to imitate. This was a development due in part to the church's loss of international power during the great crises of the late Middle Ages. It was also encouraged by the rise of national sentiment, the creation of competent national bureaucracies staffed by laymen rather than by clerics, and the rapid growth of lay education during the fourteenth and fifteenth centuries. Medieval Christian values were adjusting to a more this-worldly spirit. Men and women began again to appreciate and even glorify the secular world, secular learning, and purely human pursuits as ends in themselves.

This new perspective on life is prominent in the painting and sculpture of the High Renaissance—the late fifteenth and early sixteenth centuries, when Renaissance art reached its full maturity. Whereas medieval art tended to be abstract and formulaic, Renaissance art was emphatically concerned with the observation of the natural world and the communication of human emotions. Renaissance artists also tried to give their works a greater rational (chiefly mathematical) order—a symmetry and proportionality that reflected pictorially their deeply held belief in the harmony of the universe. The interest of Renaissance artists in ancient Roman art was closely allied to an independent interest in humanity and nature.

Renaissance artists had the advantage of new technical skills developed during the fifteenth century. In addition to the availability of oil paints, two special techniques were perfected: that of using shading to enhance naturalness (**chiaroscuro**) and that of adjusting the size of figures to give the viewer a feeling of continuity with the painting (*linear perspective*). These techniques permitted the artist to "rationalize" space and paint a more natural world. The result was that, compared to their flat Byzantine and Gothic counterparts, Renaissance paintings were filled with energy and life and stood out from the canvas in three dimensions.

The new direction was signaled by Giotto (1266–1336), the father of Renaissance painting. An admirer of Saint Francis of Assisi, whose love of nature he shared, Giotto painted a more natural world than his Byzantine and Gothic predecessors. Though still filled with religious seriousness, his work was no longer so abstract and unnatural a depiction of the world. The painter Masaccio (1401–1428) and the sculptor Donatello (1386–1466) continued to portray the world around them more literally and naturally. The heights were reached by the great masters of the High Renaissance: Leonardo da Vinci (1452–1519), Raphael (1483–1520), and Michelangelo Buonarroti (1475–1564).

Leonardo da Vinci More than any other person in the period, Leonardo exhibited the Renaissance ideal of the universal person. He was a true master of many skills. One of the greatest painters of all time, he was also a military engineer for Ludovico il Moro in Milan, Cesare Borgia in Romagna, and the French king Francis I. Leonardo advocated scientific experimentation, dissected corpses to learn anatomy, and was an accomplished, self-taught botanist. His inventive mind foresaw such modern machines as airplanes and submarines. Indeed, the variety of his interests was so great that it could shorten his attention span, so he was constantly moving from

Giotto's portrayal of the funeral of Saint Francis of Assisi. The saint is surrounded by his admiring brothers and a knight of Assisi (first on the right). Giotto's (1266–1336) work signals the evolution toward Renaissance art. The damaged areas on this fresco resulted from the removal of nineteenth-century restorations. Giottodi Bondone, "The Death of St. Francis of Assisi," S. Croce, Florence, Italy/Scala/Art Resource, N.Y.

one activity to another. His great skill in conveying inner moods through complex facial features can be seen in the most famous of his paintings, the *Mona Lisa*, as well as in his self-portrait.

Raphael A man of great sensitivity and kindness, Raphael was apparently loved by contemporaries as much for his person as for his work. His premature death at thirty-seven cut short his artistic career. He is famous for his tender madonnas, the best known of which graced the monastery of San Sisto in Piacenza and is now in Dresden. Art historians praise his fresco *The School of Athens*, a grandly conceived portrayal of the great masters of Western philosophy, as a virtually perfect example of Renaissance technique. Reproduced on the opening page of this chapter, it depicts Plato and Aristotle surrounded by the great philosophers and scientists of antiquity, who are portrayed with features of Raphael's famous contemporaries, including Leonardo and Michelangelo.

Michelangelo The melancholy genius Michelangelo also excelled in a variety of arts and crafts. His eighteen-foot godlike sculpture David, which long stood majestically in the great square of Florence, is a perfect example of the Renaissance artist's devotion to harmony, symmetry, and proportion, as well as the extreme glorification of the human form. Four different popes commissioned works by Michelangelo. The most famous of these works are the frescoes for the Sistine Chapel, painted during the pontificate of Pope Julius II (r. 1503–1513), who also set Michelangelo to work on the pope's own magnificent tomb. (See "Michaelangelo and Pope Julius II.") The Sistine frescoes originally covered 10,000 square feet and involved 343 figures, over

half of which exceeded 10 feet in height. But it is their originality and perfection as works of art that impress most. This labor of love and piety took four years to complete. A person of incredible energy and endurance who lived to be almost ninety, Michelangelo insisted on doing almost everything himself and permitted his assistants only a few of the many chores involved in his work.

His later works are more complex and suggest deep personal changes. They mark, artistically and philosophically, the passing of High Renaissance painting and the advent of a new style known as **mannerism,** which reached its peak in the late sixteenth and early seventeenth centuries. A reaction against the simplicity and symmetry of High Renaissance art (which also found expression in music and literature), mannerism made room for the strange and even the abnormal and gave freer reign to the subjectivity of the artist. Mannerism acquired its name because the artist was permitted to express his or her own individual perceptions and feelings, to paint, compose, or write in a "mannered," or "affected," way. Tintoretto (d. 1594) and especially El Greco (d. 1614) became mannerism's supreme representatives.

SLAVERY IN THE RENAISSANCE

Throughout Renaissance Italy, slavery flourished as extravagantly as art and culture. A thriving western slave market existed as early as the twelfth century, when the Spanish sold Muslim slaves captured in raids and war to wealthy Italians and other interested buyers. Contemporaries looked on such slavery as a merciful act, since these captives would otherwise have been killed. In addition to widespread

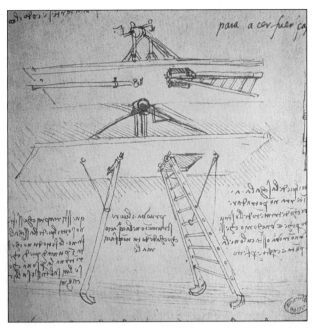

Aviation drawings by Leonardo da Vinci (1452–1519), who imagined a possible flying machine with a retractable ladder for boarding. David Forbert/SuperStock, Inc.

Donatello's youthful, sexy David stands awkwardly and seemingly puzzled on the head of the slain Goliath. Created in 1440, it is the earliest free-standing nude made in the West since Roman times. Art Resource, N.Y.

household or domestic slavery, collective plantation slavery, following East Asian models, also developed during the High Middle Ages in the eastern Mediterranean. In the savannas of Sudan and on Venetian estates on the islands of Cyprus and Crete, gangs of slaves worked sugarcane plantations, the model for later western Mediterranean and New World slavery.

After the Black Death (1348–1350) had reduced the supply of laborers everywhere in western Europe, the demand for slaves soared. Slaves now began to be imported from Africa, the Balkans, Constantinople, Cyprus, Crete, and the lands surrounding the Black Sea. Because slaves were taken randomly from conquered people, they consisted of many races: Tatars, Circassians, Greeks, Russians, Georgians, and Iranians as well as Asians and Africans. According to one source, "By the end of the fourteenth century, there was hardly a well-to-do household in Tuscany without at least one slave: brides brought them [to their marriages] as part of their dowry, doctors accepted them from their patients in lieu of fees—and it was not unusual to find them even in the service of a priest."[2]

Owners had complete dominion over their slaves; in Italian law, this meant the "[power] to

---

[2]Iris Origo, *The Merchant of Prato: Francesco di Marco Datini, 1335–1410* (New York: David Godine, 1986), pp. 90–91.

MICHELANGELO AND POPE JULIUS II

Vasari here describes how Pope Julius, the most fearsome and worldly of the Renaissance popes, forced Michelangelo to complete the Sistine Chapel before Michelangelo was ready to do so.

■ *Did Michelangelo hold his own with the pope? What does this interchange suggest about the relationship of patrons and artists in the Renaissance? Were great artists like Michelangelo so revered that they could do virtually as they pleased?*

[T]he pope was very anxious to see the decoration of the Sistine Chapel completed and constantly inquired when it would be finished.] On one occasion, therefore, Michelangelo replied, "It will be finished when I shall have done all that I believe is required to satisfy Art." "And we command," rejoined the pontiff, "that you satisfy our wish to have it done quickly," adding that if it were not at once completed, he would have Michelangelo thrown headlong from the scaffolding. Hearing this, our artist, who feared the fury of the pope, and with good cause, without taking time to add what was wanting, took down the remainder of the scaffolding to the great satisfaction of the whole city on All Saints' day, when Pope Julius went into that chapel to sing mass. But Michelangelo had much desired to retouch some portions of the work *a secco* [that is, after the damp plaster upon which the paint had been originally laid *al fresco* had

dried], as had been done by the older masters who had painted the stories on the walls. He would also have gladly added a little ultramarine to the draperies and gilded other parts, to the end that the whole might have a richer and more striking effect.

The pope, too, hearing that these things were still wanting, and finding that all who beheld the chapel praised it highly, would now fain have had the additions made. But as Michelangelo thought reconstructing the scaffold too long an affair, the pictures remained as they were, although the pope, who often saw Michelangelo, would sometimes say, "Let the chapel be enriched with bright colors and gold; it looks poor." When Michelangelo would reply familiarly, "Holy Father, the men of those days did not adorn themselves with gold; those who are painted here less than any, for they were none too rich; besides which they were holy men, and must have despised riches and ornaments."

From James Harvey Robinson, ed., *Readings in European History*, Vol. 1 (Boston: Athenaeum, 1904), pp. 538–539.

---

have, hold, sell, alienate, exchange, enjoy, rent or unrent, dispose of in [their] will[s], judge soul and body, and do with in perpetuity whatsoever may please [them] and [their] heirs and no man may gainsay [them]."[3] A strong, young, healthy slave cost the equivalent of the wages paid a free servant over several years. Considering the lifetime of free service thereafter, slaves could be well worth the cost.

The Tatars and Africans appear to have been the worst treated. But as in ancient Greece and Rome, slaves at this time were generally accepted as family members and were integrated into households. Not a few women slaves became mothers of their masters' children. Quite a few children of such unions were adopted and raised as legitimate heirs of their fathers. It was clearly in the interest of their owners to keep slaves healthy and happy; otherwise

they were of little use and could even become a threat. Still, slaves remained a foreign and suspected presence in Italian society; they were, as all knew, uprooted and resentful people.

Italy's Political Decline: The French Invasions (1494–1527)

THE TREATY OF LODI

As a land of autonomous city-states, Italy had always relied on internal cooperation for its peace and safety from foreign invasion—especially by the Turks. Such cooperation had been maintained during the latter half of the fifteenth century, thanks to a carefully constructed political alliance known as the Treaty of Lodi (1454–1455). The terms of the treaty brought Milan and Naples, long traditional enemies, into alliance with Florence. These three stood together for

[3]Ibid., p. 209.

Michelangelo's Last Judgment *covers the altar wall of the Sistine Chapel in the Vatican Palace.* Michelangelo Buonarroti, "Last Judgment," 1534–1541, fresco, Sistine Chapel, Vatican Apostolic Palace. Photo Vatican Museums, A. Bracchetti/P. Zigrossi, February 1995.

decades against Venice, which was frequently joined by the Papal States, to create an internal balance of power. When a foreign enemy threatened Italy, however, the five formed a united front.

Around 1490, following the rise to power of the Milanese despot Ludovico il Moro, hostilities between Milan and Naples resumed. The peace made possible by the Treaty of Lodi ended in 1494 when Naples, supported by Florence and the Borgia Pope Alexander VI (r. 1492–1503), prepared to attack Milan. Ludovico made what proved to be a fatal response in these new political alignments: He appealed for aid to the French. French kings had ruled Naples from 1266 to 1435, before they were driven out by Duke Alfonso of Sicily. Breaking a wise Italian rule, Ludovico invited the French to reenter Italy and revive their dynastic claim to Naples. In his haste to check his rival Naples, Ludovico did not recognize sufficiently that France also had dynastic claims to Milan. Nor did he foresee how insatiable the French appetite for Italian territory would become once French armies had crossed the Alps.

CHARLES VIII'S MARCH THROUGH ITALY

The French king Louis XI had resisted the temptation to invade Italy while nonetheless keeping French dynastic claims in Italy alive. His successor,

Charles VIII (r. 1483–1498), an eager youth in his twenties, responded to Ludovico's call with lightning speed. Within five months, he had crossed the Alps (August 1494) and raced as conqueror through Florence and the Papal States into Naples. As Charles approached Florence, the Florentine ruler, Piero de' Medici, who had allied with Naples against Milan, tried to placate the French king by handing over Pisa and other Florentine possessions. Such appeasement only brought about Piero's forced exile by a population that was revolutionized then by the radical Dominican preacher Girolamo Savonarola (1452–1498). Savonarola convinced most of the fearful Florentines that the French king's arrival was a long-delayed and fully justified divine vengeance on their immorality.

Charles entered Florence without resistance. Thanks to Savonarola's flattery and the payment of a large ransom, the city was spared a threatened destruction. Savonarola continued to exercise virtual rule over Florence for four years after Charles's departure. The Florentines proved, however, not to be the stuff theocracies are made of. Savonarola's moral rigor and antipapal policies made it impossible for him to survive indefinitely. This became especially true after the Italian cities reunited and the ouster of the French invader, whom Savonarola had praised as a godsend, became national policy. Savonarola was imprisoned and executed in May 1498.

Charles's lightning march through Italy also struck terror in non-Italian hearts. Ferdinand of Aragon, who hoped to expand his own possessions in Italy from his kingdom of Sicily, now found himself vulnerable to a French-Italian axis. He took the initiative to create a counteralliance—the League of Venice, formed in March 1495—in which he joined with Venice, the Papal States, and Emperor Maximilian I against the French. The alliance set the stage for a conflict between France and Spain that would not end until 1559.

Ludovico il Moro meanwhile recognized he had sown the wind; having desired a French invasion only so long as it weakened his enemies, he now saw Milan threatened by the whirlwind of events that he had himself created. In reaction, he joined the League of Venice, and this alliance was able to send Charles into retreat by May. Charles remained thereafter on the defensive until his death in April 1498.

POPE ALEXANDER VI AND THE BORGIA FAMILY

The French returned to Italy under Charles's successor, Louis XII (r. 1498–1515). This time they were assisted by a new Italian ally, the Borgia pope, Alexander VI. Alexander was probably the most

Major Political Events of the Italian Renaissance (1375–1527)

1378–1382	The Ciompi Revolt in Florence
1434	Medici rule in Florence established by Cosimo de' Medici
1454–1455	Treaty of Lodi allies Milan, Naples, and Florence (in effect until 1494)
1494	Charles VIII of France invades Italy
1494–1498	Savonarola controls Florence
1495	League of Venice unites Venice, Milan, the Papal States, the Holy Roman Empire, and Spain against France
1499	Louis XII invades Milan (the second French invasion of Italy)
1500	The Borgias conquer Romagna
1512–1513	The Holy League (Pope Julius II, Ferdinand of Aragon, Emperor Maximilian, and Venice) defeats the French
1513	Machiavelli writes *The Prince*
1515	Francis I leads the third French invasion of Italy
1516	Concordat of Bologna between France and the papacy
1527	Sack of Rome by imperial soldiers

corrupt pope who ever sat on the papal throne. He openly promoted the political careers of Cesare and Lucrezia Borgia, the children he had had before he became pope, and he placed papal policy in tandem with the efforts of his powerful family to secure a political base in Romagna.

In Romagna, several principalities had fallen away from the church during the Avignon papacy. And Venice, the pope's ally within the League of Venice, continued to contest the Papal States for their loyalty. Seeing that a French alliance could give him the opportunity to reestablish control over the region, Alexander took steps to secure French favor. He annulled Louis XII's marriage to Charles VIII's sister so Louis could marry Charles's widow, Anne of Brittany—a popular political move designed to keep Brittany French. The pope also bestowed a cardinal's hat on the archbishop of Rouen, Louis's favorite cleric. Most important, Alexander agreed to abandon the League of Venice; this withdrawal of support made the league too weak to resist a French reconquest of Milan. In exchange, Cesare Borgia received the sister of the king of Navarre, Charlotte d'Albret, in marriage, a union that greatly enhanced Borgia military strength. Cesare also received land grants from Louis XII and the promise of French military aid in Romagna.

All in all it was a scandalous trade-off, but one that made it possible for both the French king and the pope to realize their ambitions within Italy. Louis successfully invaded Milan in August 1499. Ludovico il Moro, who had originally opened the Pandora's box of French invasion, spent his last years languishing in a French prison. In 1500, Louis and Ferdinand of Aragon divided Naples between them, and the pope and Cesare Borgia conquered the cities of Romagna without opposition. Alexander awarded his victorious son the title "duke of Romagna."

POPE JULIUS II

Cardinal Giuliano della Rovere, a strong opponent of the Borgia family, succeeded Alexander VI as Pope Julius II (r. 1503–1513). He suppressed the Borgias and placed their newly conquered lands in Romagna under papal jurisdiction. Julius came to be known as the "warrior pope," because he brought the Renaissance papacy to a peak of military prowess and diplomatic intrigue. Shocked, as were other contemporaries, by this thoroughly secular papacy, the humanist Erasmus (1466?–1536), who had witnessed in disbelief a bullfight in the papal palace during a visit to Rome, wrote a popular anonymous satire entitled *Julius Excluded from Heaven.* This humorous account purported to describe the pope's unsuccessful efforts to convince Saint Peter he was worthy of admission to heaven.

Assisted by his powerful allies, Pope Julius succeeded in driving the Venetians out of Romagna in 1509. Thus, he ended Venetian claims in the region and fully secured the Papal States. Having realized this long-sought papal goal, Julius turned to the second major undertaking of his pontificate: ridding Italy of his former ally, the French invader. Julius, Ferdinand of Aragon, and Venice formed a second Holy League in October 1511, and within a short period Emperor Maximilian I and the Swiss joined them. By 1512, the league had the French in full retreat, and they were soundly defeated by the Swiss in 1513 at Novara.

The French were nothing if not persistent. They invaded Italy a third time under Louis's successor, Francis I (r. 1515–1547). French armies massacred Swiss soldiers of the Holy League at Marignano in September 1515, avenging the earlier defeat at Novara. The victory won the Concordat of Bologna from the people in August 1516. The agreement gave the French king control over the French clergy in exchange for French recognition of the pope's superiority over church councils and his right to collect annates in France. This was an important compromise that helped keep France Catholic after the outbreak of the Protestant Reformation. But the new French entry into Italy also led to the first of four major wars with Spain in the first half of the sixteenth century: the Habsburg-Valois wars, none of which France won.

NICCOLÒ MACHIAVELLI

The period of foreign invasions made a shambles of Italy. The same period that saw Italy's cultural peak in the work of Leonardo, Raphael, and Michelangelo also witnessed Italy's political tragedy. One who watched as French, Spanish, and German armies wreaked havoc on Italy was Niccolò Machiavelli (1469–1527). The more he saw, the more convinced he became that Italian political unity and independence were ends that justified any means.

A humanist and a careful student of ancient Rome, Machiavelli was impressed by the way Roman rulers and citizens had then defended their homeland. They possessed *virtù*, the ability to act decisively and heroically for the good of their country. Stories of ancient Roman patriotism and self-sacrifice were Machiavelli's favorites, and he lamented the absence of such traits among his compatriots. Such romanticizing of the Roman past caused some exaggeration of both ancient virtue and contemporary failings. His Florentine contemporary, Francesco Guicciardini, a more sober historian less given to idealizing antiquity, wrote truer chronicles of Florentine and Italian history.

Machiavelli also held deep republican ideals, which he did not want to see vanish from Italy. He believed a strong and determined people could struggle successfully with fortune. He scolded the Italian people for the self-destruction their own internal feuding was causing. He wanted an end to that behavior above all, so a reunited Italy could drive all foreign armies out.

But were his fellow citizens up to such a challenge? The juxtaposition of what Machiavelli believed the ancient Romans had been with the failure of his contemporaries to attain such high ideals made him the famous cynic whose name—in the epithet "Machiavellian"—has become synonymous with ruthless political expediency. Only a strongman, he concluded in the end, could impose order on so divided and selfish a people; the salvation of Italy required, for the present, a cunning dictator.

It has been argued that Machiavelli wrote *The Prince* in 1513 as a cynical satire on the way rulers actually did behave and not as a serious recommendation of unprincipled despotic rule. To take his advocacy of tyranny literally, it is argued, contradicts both his earlier works and his own strong family tradition of republican service. But Machiavelli seems to have been in earnest when he advised rulers to discover the advantages of fraud and brutality, at least as a temporary means to the higher end of a unified Italy. He apparently hoped to see a strong ruler emerge from the Medici family, which had captured the papacy in 1513 with the pontificate of Leo X (r. 1513–1521). At the same time, the Medici family retained control over the powerful territorial state of Florence. The situation was similar to that of Machiavelli's hero Cesare Borgia and his father Pope Alexander VI, who had earlier brought factious Romagna to heel by placing secular family goals and religious policy in tandem. *The Prince* was pointedly dedicated to Lorenzo de' Medici, duke of Urbino and grandson of Lorenzo the Magnificent.

Whatever Machiavelli's hopes may have been, the Medicis were not destined to be Italy's deliverers. The second Medici pope, Clement VII (r. 1523–1534), watched helplessly as Rome was sacked by the army of Emperor Charles V in 1527, also the year of Machiavelli's death.

Revival of Monarchy in Northern Europe

After 1450, there was a progressive shift from divided feudal to unified national monarchies as "sovereign" rulers emerged. This is not to say the dynastic and chivalric ideals of feudal monarchy vanished. Territorial princes did not pass from the scene; representative bodies persisted and in some areas even grew in influence. But in the late fifteenth and early sixteenth centuries, the old problem of the one and the many was decided in favor of the interests of monarchy.

The feudal monarchy of the High Middle Ages was characterized by the division of the basic powers of government between the king and his semi-autonomous vassals. The nobility and the towns had acted with varying degrees of unity and success through evolving representative assemblies such as the English Parliament, the French Estates General, and the Spanish *Cortés* to thwart the centralization of royal power. Because of the Hundred Years' War and the Great Schism in the church, the nobility and the clergy were in decline by the late Middle Ages and less able to contain expanding monarchies.

The increasingly important towns began to ally with the king. Loyal, business-wise townspeople, not the nobility and the clergy, increasingly staffed the royal offices and became the king's lawyers, bookkeepers, military tacticians, and foreign diplomats. This new alliance between king and town

Santi di Tito's portrait of Machiavelli, perhaps the most famous Italian political theorist, who advised Renaissance princes to practice artful deception and inspire fear in their subjects if they wished to be successful.
Art Resource, NY

broke the bonds of feudal society and made possible the rise of sovereign states.

In a sovereign state, the powers of taxation, war making, and law enforcement no longer belong to semiautonomous vassals, but are concentrated in the monarch and are exercised by his or her chosen agents. Taxes, wars, and laws become national, rather than merely regional, matters. Only as monarchs became able to act independently of the nobility and representative assemblies could they overcome the decentralization that had been the basic obstacle to nation building. Ferdinand and Isabella of Spain rarely called the *Cortés* into session. The French Estates General did not meet at all from 1484 to 1560. Henry VII (r. 1485–1509) of England managed to raise revenues without going begging to Parliament after Parliament voted him customs revenues for life in 1485. Monarchs were also assisted by brilliant theorists, from Marsilius of Padua in the fourteenth century to Machiavelli to Jean Bodin in the sixteenth, who eloquently argued the sovereign rights of monarchy.

The many were, of course, never totally subjugated to the one. But in the last half of the fifteenth century, rulers demonstrated that the law was their creature. They appointed civil servants whose vision was no longer merely local or regional. In Castile they were the *corregidores*, in England the justices of the peace, and in France bailiffs operating through well-drilled lieutenants. These royal ministers and agents could become closely attached to the localities they administered in the ruler's name. And regions were able to secure congenial royal appointments. Throughout England, for example, local magnates served as representatives of the Tudors. Nonetheless, these new executives remained royal executives, bureaucrats whose outlook was "national" and whose loyalty was to the "state."

Monarchies also began to create standing national armies in the fifteenth century. The noble cavalry receded as the infantry and the artillery became the backbone of royal armies. Mercenary soldiers were recruited from Switzerland and Germany to form the major part of the "king's army." Professional soldiers who fought for pay and booty proved far more efficient than feudal vassals who fought simply for honor's sake. Monarchs who failed to meet their payrolls, however, faced a new danger of mutiny and banditry on the part of foreign troops.

The growing cost of warfare in the fifteenth and sixteenth centuries increased the need of monarchs for new national sources of income, but their efforts to expand royal revenues were hampered by the stubborn belief among the highest classes that they were immune from government taxation. The nobility guarded their properties and traditional rights and despised taxation as an insult and a humiliation. Royal revenues accordingly grew at the expense of those least able to resist and least able to pay.

The monarchs had several options when it came to raising money. As feudal lords, they could collect rents from their royal domains. They could also levy national taxes on basic food and clothing, such as the salt tax (**gabelle**) in France and the 10 percent sales tax (*alcabala*) on commercial transactions, in Spain. The rulers could also levy direct taxes on the peasantry, which they did through agreeable representative assemblies of the privileged classes in which the peasantry did not sit. The *taille*, which the French kings independently determined from year to year after the Estates General was suspended in 1484, was such a tax. Innovative fund-raising devices in the fifteenth century included the sale of public offices and the issuance of high-interest government bonds. But rulers did not levy taxes on the powerful nobility. Rather, they borrowed from rich nobles and the great bankers of Italy and Germany. In money matters, the privileged classes remained as much the kings' creditors and competitors as their subjects.

FRANCE

Charles VII (r. 1422–1461) was a king made great by those who served him. His ministers created a permanent professional army, which—thanks initially to the inspiration of Joan of Arc—drove the English out of France. And largely because of the enterprise of an independent merchant banker named Jacques Coeur, the French also developed a strong economy, diplomatic corps, and national administration during Charles's reign. These were the sturdy tools with which Charles's son and successor, the ruthless Louis XI (r. 1461–1483), made France a great power.

There were two cornerstones of French nation building in the fifteenth century. The first was the collapse of the English Empire in France following the Hundred Years' War. The second was the defeat of Charles the Bold and his duchy of Burgundy. Perhaps Europe's strongest political power in the mid–fifteenth century, Burgundy aspired to dwarf both France and the Holy Roman Empire as the leader of a dominant middle kingdom. It might have done so had not the continental powers joined in opposition.

When Charles the Bold died in defeat in a battle at Nancy in 1477, the dream of Burgundian Empire died with him. Louis XI and Habsburg emperor Maximilian I divided the conquered Burgundian lands between them, with the treaty-wise Habsburgs getting the better part. The dissolution of Burgundy ended its constant intrigue against the French king and left Louis XI free to secure the monarchy. The newly acquired Burgundian lands and his own Angevin inheritance permitted the king to end his reign with a kingdom almost twice the size of that with which he had started. Louis successfully harnessed the nobility, expanded the trade and industry so carefully nurtured by Jacques Coeur, created a national postal system, and even established a lucrative silk industry at Lyons (later transferred to Tours).

A strong nation is a two-edged sword. Because Louis's successors inherited a secure and efficient government, they felt free to pursue what proved ultimately to be a debilitating foreign policy. Conquests in Italy in the 1490s and a long series of losing wars with the Habsburgs in the first half of the sixteenth century left France by the mid–sixteenth century again a defeated nation almost as divided internally as during the Hundred Years' War.

SPAIN

Spain, too, became a strong country in the late fifteenth century. Both Castile and Aragon had been poorly ruled and divided kingdoms in the mid–fifteenth century. The union of Isabella of Castile (r. 1474–1504) and Ferdinand of Aragon (r. 1479–1516) changed that situation. The two future sovereigns married in 1469, despite strong protests from neighboring Portugal and France, both of whom foresaw the formidable European power the marriage would create. Castile was by far the richer and more populous of the two, having an estimated 5 million inhabitants to Aragon's population of under 1 million. Castile was also distinguished by its lucrative sheep-farming industry, run by a government-backed organization called the *Mesta*, another example of a developing centralized economic planning. Although the marriage of Ferdinand and Isabella dynastically united the two kingdoms, they remained constitutionally separated. Each retained its respective government agencies—separate laws, armies, coinage, and taxation—and cultural traditions.

Ferdinand and Isabella could do together what neither was able to accomplish alone: subdue their realms, secure their borders, venture abroad militarily, and Christianize the whole of Spain. Between 1482 and 1492 they conquered the Moors in Granada. Naples became a Spanish possession in 1504. By 1512, Ferdinand had secured his northern borders by conquering the kingdom of Navarre. Internally, Ferdinand and Isabella won the allegiance of the *Hermandad*, a powerful league of cities and towns that served them against stubborn landowners. Townspeople allied themselves with the crown and progressively replaced the nobility within the royal administration. The crown also extended its authority over the wealthy chivalric orders, a further circumscription of the power of the nobility.

Spain had long been remarkable among European lands as a place where three religions—Islam, Judaism, and Christianity—coexisted with a certain degree of toleration. This toleration was to end dramatically under Ferdinand and Isabella, who made Spain the prime exemplar of state-controlled religion.

Ferdinand and Isabella exercised almost total control over the Spanish church as they placed religion in the service of national unity. They appointed the higher clergy and the officers of the Inquisition. The latter, run by Tomás de Torquemada (d. 1498), Isabella's confessor, was a key national agency established in 1479 to monitor the activity of converted Jews (*conversos*) and Muslims (*Moriscos*) in Spain. In 1492, the Jews were exiled and their properties were confiscated. In 1502, non-converting Moors in Granada were driven into exile by Cardinal Francisco Jiménez de Cisneros (1437–1517), under whom Spanish spiritual life remained largely uniform and successfully controlled. This was a major reason Spain remained a loyal Catholic country throughout the sixteenth century and provided a base of operation for the European Counter-Reformation.

Despite a certain internal narrowness, Ferdinand and Isabella were rulers with wide horizons. They contracted anti-French marriage alliances that came to determine a large part of European history in the sixteenth century. In 1496, their eldest daughter, Joanna, later known as "the Mad," married Archduke Philip, the son of Emperor Maximilian I. The fruit of this union, Charles I, was the first ruler over a united Spain; by his inheritance and election as emperor in 1519, he came to rule over a European kingdom almost equal in size to that of Charlemagne. A second daughter, Catherine of Aragon, wed Arthur, the son of the English king Henry VII. After Arthur's premature death, she was betrothed to his brother, the future King Henry VIII (r. 1509–1547), whom she married eight years later, in 1509. The failure of this marriage became the key factor in the emergence of the Anglican church and the English Reformation.

The new power of Spain was also revealed in Ferdinand and Isabella's promotion of overseas exploration. They sponsored the Genoese adventurer Christopher Columbus (1451–1506), who arrived at the islands of the Caribbean while sailing west in search of a shorter route to the spice markets of the Far East. This patronage led to the creation of the Spanish Empire in Mexico and Peru, whose gold and silver mines helped make Spain Europe's dominant power in the sixteenth century.

ENGLAND

The latter half of the fifteenth century was a period of especially difficult political trial for the English. Following the Hundred Years' War, a defeated England was subjected to internal warfare between two rival branches of the royal family: the House of York and the House of Lancaster. This conflict, known to us today as the Wars of the Roses (because York's symbol, according to legend, was a white rose and Lancaster's a red rose), kept England in turmoil from 1455 to 1485.

The Lancastrian monarchy of Henry VI (r. 1422–1461) was consistently challenged by the duke of York and his supporters in the prosperous southern towns. In 1461, Edward IV (r. 1461–1483), son of the duke of York, successfully seized power and instituted a strong-arm rule that lasted more than twenty years; it was only briefly interrupted, in 1470–1471, by Henry VI's short-lived restoration. Assisted by loyal and able ministers, Edward effectively increased the power and finances of the monarchy.

His brother, Richard III (r. 1483–1485), usurped the throne from Edward's son, and after Richard's death,

the new Tudor dynasty portrayed him as an unprincipled villain who had also murdered Edward's sons in the Tower of London to secure his hold on the throne. The best known version of this characterization—unjust according to some—is found in Shakespeare's *Richard III.* Be that as it may, Richard's reign saw the growth of support for the exiled Lancastrian Henry Tudor, who returned to England to defeat Richard on Bosworth Field in August 1485.

Henry Tudor ruled as Henry VII (r. 1485–1509), the first of the new Tudor dynasty that would dominate England throughout the sixteenth century. To bring the rival royal families together and to make the hereditary claim of his offspring to the throne uncontestable, Henry married Edward IV's daughter, Elizabeth of York. He succeeded in disciplining the English nobility through a special instrument of the royal will known as the Court of Star Chamber. Created with the sanction of Parliament in 1487, the court was intended to end the perversion of English justice by "over-mighty subjects," that is, powerful nobles who used intimidation and bribery to win favorable verdicts in court cases. In the Court of Star Chamber, the king's councillors sat as judges and were not swayed by such tactics. The result was a more equitable court system.

It was also a court more amenable to the royal will. Henry shrewdly construed legal precedents to the advantage of the crown, using English law to further the ends of monarchy. He managed to confiscate lands and fortunes of nobles with such success that he was able to govern without dependence on Parliament for royal funds, always a cornerstone of strong monarchy. In these ways, Henry began to shape a monarchy that would develop into one of early modern Europe's most exemplary governments during the reign of his granddaughter, Elizabeth I.

THE HOLY ROMAN EMPIRE

Germany and Italy were the striking exceptions to the steady development of politically centralized lands in the last half of the fifteenth century. Unlike England, France, and Spain, the Holy Roman Empire saw the many thoroughly repulse the one. In Germany, territorial rulers and cities resisted every effort at national consolidation and unity. As in Carolingian times, rulers continued to partition their kingdoms, however small, among their sons. By the late fifteenth century, Germany was hopelessly divided into some three hundred autonomous political entities.

The princes and the cities did work together to create the machinery of law and order, if not of union, within the divided empire. The emperor and the major German territorial rulers reached an agreement in 1356, the **Golden Bull.** It established a seven-member electoral college consisting of the archbishops of Mainz, Trier, and Cologne; the duke of Saxony; the margrave of Brandenburg; the count Palatine; and the king of Bohemia. This group also functioned as an administrative body. They elected the emperor and, in cooperation with him, provided what transregional unity and administration existed.

The figure of the emperor gave the empire a single ruler in law if not in fact. The conditions of his rule and the extent of his powers over his subjects, especially the seven electors, were renegotiated with every imperial election. Therefore, the rights of the many (the princes) were always balanced against the power of the one (the emperor).

In the fifteenth century, an effort was made to control incessant feuding by the creation of an imperial diet known as the *Reichstag*. This was a national assembly of the seven electors, the nonelectoral princes, and representatives from the sixty-five imperial free cities. The cities were the weakest of the three bodies represented in the diet. During such an assembly in Worms in 1495, the members won from Emperor Maximilian I (r. 1493–1519) an imperial ban on private warfare, the creation of a Supreme Court of Justice to enforce internal peace, and an imperial Council of Regency to coordinate imperial and internal German policy. The latter was only grudgingly conceded by the emperor because it gave the princes a share in executive power.

Although important, these reforms were still a poor substitute for true national unity. In the sixteenth and seventeenth centuries, the territorial princes became virtually sovereign rulers in their various domains. Such disunity aided religious dissent and conflict. It was in the cities and territories of still feudal, fractionalized, backward Germany that the Protestant Reformation broke out in the sixteenth century.

The Northern Renaissance

The scholarly works of northern humanists created a climate favorable to religious and educational reforms on the eve of the Reformation. Northern humanism was initially stimulated by the importation of Italian learning through such varied intermediaries as students who had studied in Italy, merchants who traded there, and the Brothers of the Common Life. This last was an influential lay religious movement that began in the Netherlands and permitted men and women to live a shared religious life without making formal vows of poverty, chastity, and obedience.

The northern humanists, however, developed their own distinctive culture. They tended to come

This portrait of Katharina, by Albrecht Dürer, provides evidence of African slavery in Europe during the sixteenth century. Katharina was in the service of one João Bradao, a Portuguese economic minister living in Antwerp, then the financial center of Europe. Dürer became friends with Bradao during his stay in the Low Countries in the winter of 1520–1521. Albrecht Dürer, Portrait of the Moorish Woman Katharina. Drawing. Uffizi Florence, Italy. Copyright Foto Marburg/Art Resource, N.Y.

from more diverse social backgrounds and to be more devoted to religious reforms than their Italian counterparts. They were also more willing to write for lay audiences as well as for a narrow intelligentsia. Thanks to the invention of printing with movable type, it became possible for humanists to convey their educational ideals to laypeople and clerics alike. Printing gave new power and influence to elites in both church and state, who now could popularize their viewpoints freely and widely.

THE PRINTING PRESS

A variety of forces converged in the fourteenth and fifteenth centuries to give rise to the invention of the printing press. Since the days of Charlemagne, kings and princes had encouraged schools and literacy, to help provide educated bureaucrats to staff the offices of their kingdoms. Without people who could read, think critically, and write reliable reports, no kingdom, large or small, could be properly governed. By the fifteenth century, a new literate lay public had been created, thanks to the enormous expansion of schools and universities during the late Middle Ages. (The number of universities more than tripled between 1300 and 1500, growing from twenty to seventy.)

The invention of a cheap way to manufacture paper also helped make books economical and broaden their content. Manuscript books had been inscribed on vellum, a cumbersome and expensive medium. (It required 170 calfskins or 300 sheepskins to make a single vellum Bible.) Single-sheet woodcuts had long been printed. This involved carving a block of wood, inking it, and then stamping out as many copies as possible before the wood deteriorated. The end product was much like a modern poster.

In response to the demand for books created by the expansion of lay literacy, Johann Gutenberg (d. 1468) invented printing with movable type in the mid–fifteenth century in the German city of Mainz, the center of printing for the whole of western Europe. Thereafter, books were rapidly and handsomely produced on topics both profound and practical and were intended for ordinary lay readers, scholars, and clerics alike. Especially popular in the early decades of print were books of piety and religion, calendars and almanacs, and how-to books (for example, on child rearing, making brandies and liquors, curing animals, and farming successfully).

The new technology proved enormously profitable to printers, whose numbers exploded. By 1500, within a scant fifty years of Gutenberg's press, printing presses operated in at least sixty German cities and in more than two hundred cities throughout Europe. The printing press was a boon to the careers of humanists, who now gained international audiences.

Literacy deeply affected people everywhere, nurturing self-esteem and a critical frame of mind. By standardizing texts, the print revolution made anyone who could read an instant authority. Rulers in church and state now had to deal with a less credulous and less docile laity. Print was a powerful tool for political and religious propaganda as well. Kings could now indoctrinate people as never before, and clergymen found themselves able to mass-produce both indulgences and pamphlets. (See "The West & the World: The Invention of Printing," p. 284.)

ERASMUS

The far-reaching influence of Desiderius Erasmus (1466?–1536), the most famous of the northern humanists and the "prince of the humanists," illustrates the impact of the printing press. Erasmus gained fame both as an educational and as a religious reformer. His life and work make clear that many loyal Catholics wanted major reforms long before the Reformation made them a reality.

Erasmus earned his living by tutoring when patrons were scarce. He prepared short Latin dialogues for his students that were intended to teach them how to speak and live well, inculcating good

The printing press made possible the diffusion of Renaissance learning. But no book stimulated thought more at this time than did the Bible. With Gutenberg's publication of a printed Bible in 1454, scholars gained access to a dependable, standardized text, so Scripture could be discussed and debated as never before. Reproduced by permission of The Huntington Library, San Marino, California

manners and language by encouraging them to imitate what they read.

These dialogues were published under the title *Colloquies*; they grew in number and length in consecutive editions, coming also to embrace anticlerical dialogues and satires on popular religious superstition. Erasmus collected ancient and contemporary proverbs as well, which he published under the title *Adages*. Beginning with about 800 examples, he increased his collection to more than 5,000 in the final edition of the work. Among the locutions that the *Adages* popularized are the common modern expression "to leave no stone unturned" and the saying "Where there is smoke, there is fire."

Erasmus aspired to unite the classical ideals of humanity and civic virtue with the Christian ideals of love and piety. He believed disciplined study of the classics and the Bible, if begun early enough, was the best way to reform both individuals and society. He summarized his own beliefs with the phrase *philosophia Christi*, a simple, ethical piety in imitation of Christ. He set this ideal in starkest contrast to what he believed to be the dogmatic, ceremonial, and factious religious practice of the later Middle Ages. What most offended him about the Scholastics, both those of the late Middle Ages and, increasingly, the new Lutheran ones, was their letting doctrine and disputation overshadow humble piety and Christian practice.

To promote his own religious beliefs, Erasmus labored to make the ancient Christian sources available in their original versions. He believed that only as people drank from the pure, unadulterated sources could moral and religious health result. He edited the works of the Church Fathers and produced a Greek edition of the New Testament (1516), which became the basis for his new, more accurate Latin translation (1519).

These various enterprises did not please church authorities. They were unhappy with both Erasmus's "improvements" on the Vulgate, Christendom's Bible for over a thousand years, and his popular anticlerical satires. At one point in the mid–sixteenth century, all of Erasmus's works were placed on the *Index of Forbidden Books.* Erasmus also received Luther's unqualified condemnation for his views on the freedom of human will. Still, Erasmus's works became basic tools of reform in the hands of both Protestant and Catholic reformers.

HUMANISM AND REFORM

In Germany, England, France, and Spain, humanism stirred both educational and religious reform.

Germany   Rudolf Agricola (1443–1485), the "father of German humanism," spent ten years in Italy and introduced Italian learning to Germany when he returned. Conrad Celtis (d. 1508), the first German poet laureate, and Ulrich von Hutten (1488–1523), a fiery knight, gave German humanism a nationalist coloring hostile to non-German cultures, particularly Roman culture. Von Hutten especially illustrates the union of humanism, German nationalism, and Luther's religious reform. A poet who admired Erasmus, he attacked indulgences and published an edition of Valla's exposé of the *Donation of Constantine*. He died in 1523, the victim of a hopeless knights' revolt against the princes.

The cause célèbre that brought von Hutten onto the historical stage and unified reform-minded German humanists was the Reuchlin affair. Johann Reuchlin (1455–1522) was Europe's foremost Christian authority on Hebrew and Jewish learning. He wrote the first reliable Hebrew grammar by a Christian scholar and was personally attracted to Jewish mysticism. Around 1506, supported by the Dominican order in Cologne, a Christian who had converted from Judaism began a movement to suppress Jewish writings. When this man, whose name was Pfefferkorn, attacked Reuchlin, many German humanists, in the name of academic freedom and good scholarship—not for any pro-Jewish sentiment—rushed to Reuchlin's defense. The controversy lasted several years and produced one of the great satires of the period, the *Letters of Obscure Men* (1515), a merciless satire of monks and Scholastics to which von Hutten contributed. When Martin Luther came under attack in 1517 for his famous ninety-five theses against indulgences, many German humanists saw a repetition of the Scholastic attack on Reuchlin and rushed to his side.

England   Italian learning came to England by way of English scholars and merchants and visiting Italian prelates. Lectures by William Grocyn (d. 1519) and Thomas Linacre (d. 1524) at Oxford and those of Erasmus at Cambridge marked the scholarly maturation of English humanism. John Colet (1467–1519), dean of Saint Paul's Cathedral, patronized humanist studies for the young and promoted religious reform as well.

Thomas More (1478–1535), a close friend of Erasmus, is the best known English humanist. His *Utopia* (1516), a conservative criticism of contemporary society, rivals the plays of Shakespeare as the most read sixteenth-century English work. *Utopia* depicted an imaginary society based on reason and tolerance that overcame social and political injustice by holding all property and goods in common and requiring everyone to earn their bread by their own work.

More became one of Henry VIII's most trusted diplomats. But his repudiation of the Act of Supremacy (1534), which made the king of England head of the English church in place of the pope (see Chapter 11), and his refusal to recognize the king's marriage to Anne Boleyn led to his execution in July 1535. Although More remained Catholic, humanism in England, as also in Germany, played an important role in preparing the way for the English Reformation.

France The French invasions of Italy made it possible for Italian learning to penetrate France, stirring both educational and religious reform. Guillaume Budé (1468–1540), an accomplished Greek scholar, and Jacques Lefèvre d'Etaples (1454–1536), a biblical authority, were the leaders of French humanism. Lefèvre's scholarly works exemplified the new critical scholarship and influenced Martin Luther. Guillaume Briçonnet (1470–1533), the bishop of Meaux, and Marguerite d'Angoulême (1492–1549), sister of King Francis I, the future queen of Navarre, and a successful spiritual writer in her own right, cultivated a generation of young reform-minded humanists. The future Protestant reformer John Calvin was a product of this native reform circle.

Spain Whereas in England, France, and Germany, humanism prepared the way for Protestant reforms, in Spain it entered the service of the Catholic Church. Here the key figure was Francisco Jiménez de Cisneros (1437–1517), a confessor to Queen Isabella and, after 1508, the "Grand Inquisitor"—a position that allowed him to enforce the strictest religious orthodoxy. Jiménez founded the University of Alcalá near Madrid in 1509, printed a Greek edition of the New Testament, and translated many religious tracts designed to reform clerical life and better direct lay piety. His great achievement, taking fifteen years to complete, was the *Complutensian Polyglot Bible*, a six-volume work that placed the Hebrew, Greek, and Latin versions of the Bible in parallel columns. Such scholarly projects and internal church reforms joined with the repressive measures of Ferdinand and Isabella to keep Spain strictly Catholic throughout the Age of Reformation.

Voyages of Discovery and the New Empire in the West

On the eve of the Reformation, the geographical as well as the intellectual horizons of Western people were changing. The fifteenth century saw the beginning of western Europe's global expansion and the transference of commercial supremacy from the Mediterranean and the Baltic to the Atlantic seaboard.

GOLD AND SPICES

Mercenary motives, reinforced by traditional missionary ideals, inspired the Portuguese prince Henry the Navigator (1394–1460) to sponsor the Portuguese exploration of the African coast. His main object was the gold trade, which Muslims had monopolized for centuries. By the last decades of the fifteenth century, gold from Guinea was entering Europe by way of Portuguese ships calling at the port cities of Lisbon and Antwerp, rather than by the traditional Arab land routes. Antwerp became the financial center of Europe, a commercial crossroads where the enterprise and derring-do of the Portuguese, the Spanish, and especially the Flemish met the capital funds of the German banking houses of Fugger and Welser.

The rush for gold quickly expanded into a rush for the spice markets of India. In the fifteenth century, the diet of most Europeans was a dull combination of bread and gruel, cabbage, turnips, peas, lentils, and onions, together with what meat became available during seasonal periods of slaughter. Spices, especially pepper and cloves, were in great demand, both to preserve and to enhance the taste of food.

Bartholomeu Dias (d. 1500) opened the Portuguese Empire in the East when he rounded the Cape of Good Hope at the tip of Africa in 1487. A decade later, in 1498, Vasco da Gama (d. 1524) reached the coast of India. When he returned to Portugal, he brought with him a cargo worth sixty times the cost of the voyage. Later, the Portuguese established themselves firmly on the Malabar Coast with colonies in Goa and Calcutta and successfully challenged the Arabs and the Venetians for control of the European spice trade.

While the Portuguese concentrated on the Indian Ocean, the Spanish set sail across the Atlantic. They did so in the hope of establishing a shorter route to the rich spice markets of the East Indies. But rather than beating the Portuguese at their own game, Christopher Columbus (1451–1506) came upon the Americas instead.

Amerigo Vespucci (1451–1512) and Ferdinand Magellan (1480–1521) showed that these new lands were not the outermost territory of the Far East, as Columbus died believing. Their travels proved the lands to be an entirely new continent that opened on the still greater Pacific Ocean. Magellan, in search of a westward route to the East Indies, died in the Philippines. (See Map 10–2.)

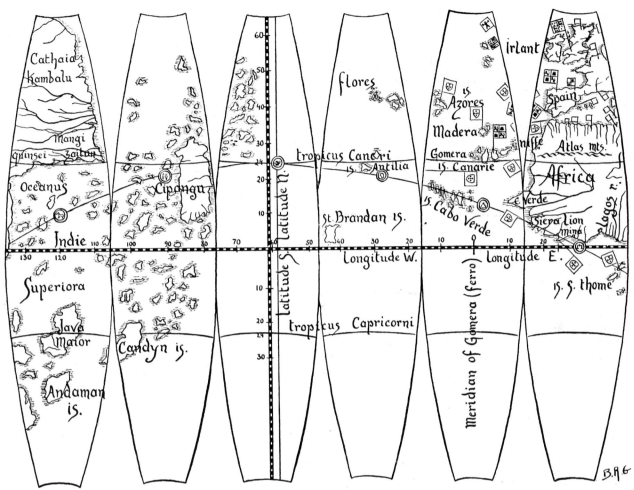

What Columbus knew of the world in 1492 was contained in this map by the Nuremberg geographer Martin Behaim, creator of the first spherical globe of the earth. The ocean section of Behaim's globe is reproduced here. Departing the Canary Islands (in the second section from the right), Columbus expected his first major landfall to be Japan (Cipangu, in the second section from the left). When he landed at San Salvador, he thought he was on the outer island of Japan. And when he arrived in Cuba, he thought he was in Japan.
Reprinted from *Admiral of the Ocean Sea* by Samuel Eliot Morison. Copyright 1942 by Samuel Eliot Morison; renewed 1970 by Samuel Eliot Morison. By permission of Little, Brown and Company, Boston, Massachusetts

THE SPANISH EMPIRE IN THE NEW WORLD

Columbus's voyage of 1492 marked, unknowingly to those who undertook and financed it, the beginning of more than three centuries of Spanish conquest, exploitation, and administration of a vast American empire. That imperial venture produced important results for the cultures of both the European and the American continents. The gold and silver extracted from its American possessions financed Spain's major role in the religious and political conflicts of the age and contributed to European inflation in the sixteenth century.

In large expanses of both South and North America, Spanish government set an imprint of Roman Catholicism, economic dependence, and hierarchical social structure that has endured to the present day. Such influence was already clear with Columbus. On October 12, 1492, after a thirty-three-day voyage from the Canary Islands, Columbus landed in San Salvador (Watlings Island) in the eastern Bahamas. He thought he was on an outer island of Japan (or what he called Cipangu); he had undertaken his journey in the mistaken notion that the island of Japan would be the first land mass he would reach as he sailed west. This belief was based on Marco Polo's accounts of his years in China in the thirteenth century and the first globe map of the world, by Martin Behaim. That map, published in 1492, showed only ocean between the west coast of Europe and the east coast of Asia. Not until his

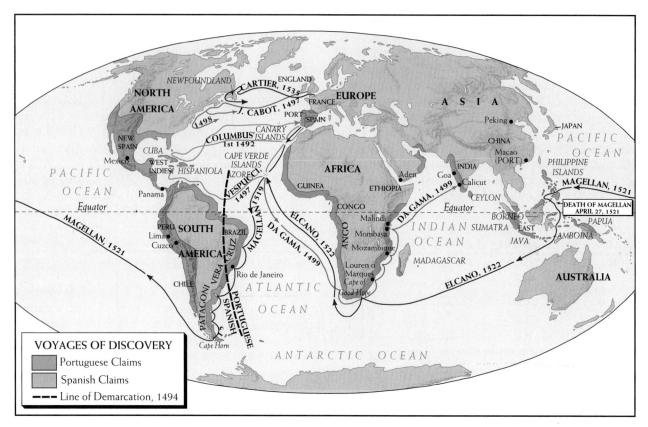

MAP 10–2   EUROPEAN VOYAGES OF DISCOVERY AND THE COLONIAL CLAIMS OF SPAIN AND
PORTUGAL IN THE FIFTEENTH AND SIXTEENTH CENTURIES   *The map dramatizes Europe's*
global expansion in the fifteenth and sixteenth centuries.

third voyage to the Caribbean did Columbus realize
that the island of Cuba was not Japan and the South
American continent beyond it was not China.

When Columbus landed in San Salvador, his
three ships were met on the beach by naked and extremely friendly natives. Like all the natives
Columbus met on his first voyage, they were Taino
Indians, who spoke a variant of a language known as
Arawak. From the start, the natives' generosity
amazed Columbus. They freely gave his men all the
corn and yams they desired and many sexual favors
as well. "They never say no," Columbus marveled.
At the same time Columbus observed how very easily they could be enslaved.

A CONQUERED WORLD

Mistaking the islands where he landed for the East
Indies, Columbus called the native peoples he encountered "Indians." That name persisted even
after it had become clear this was a new continent
and not the East Indies. These native peoples had
migrated across the Bering Straits from Asia onto
the American landmass many thousands of years
before the European voyages of discovery, creating

communities all the way from Alaska to South
America. The islands that Columbus mistakenly
believed to be the East Indies came to be known as
the West Indies.

Native Americans had established advanced civilizations going back to as early as the first millennium B.C.E. in two parts of what is today known as
Latin America: Mesoamerica, which stretches from
central Mexico into the Yucatán and Guatemala,
and the Andean region of South America, primarily
modern-day Peru and Bolivia. The earliest civilization in Mesoamerica, that of the Olmec, dates to
about 1200 B.C.E. By the early centuries of the first
millennium C.E., much of the region was dominated
by the powerful city of Teotihuacán, which at the
time was one of the largest urban centers in the
world. The first millennium C.E. saw the flowering
of the remarkable civilization of the Mayas in the
Yucatán region. The Mayans built large cities with
immense pyramids and achieved considerable skills
in mathematics and astronomy.

The first great interregional civilization in Andean South America, that of Chavín, emerged during
the first millennium B.C.E. Regional cultures of the
succeeding Early Intermediate Period (100–600 C.E.)

included the Nazca on the south coast of Peru and the Moche on the north coast. The Huari-Tiahuanco culture again imposed interregional conformity during the Middle Horizon (600–1000). In the Late Intermediate Period, the Chimu Empire (800–1400) dominated the valleys of the Peruvian north coast. These early Andean societies built major ceremonial centers throughout the Andes, constructed elaborate irrigation systems, canals, and highways, and created exquisite pottery, textiles, and metalwork.

At the time of the arrival of the first Spanish explorers, the Aztec Empire dominated Mesoamerica and the Inca Empire dominated Andean South America. (See Map 10–3.) Both were very rich, and their conquest promised the Spanish the possibility of acquiring large quantities of gold.

The Aztecs in Mexico   The forebears of the Aztecs had arrived in the Valley of Mexico early in the twelfth century, where they lived as a subservient people. In 1428, however, they began a period of rapid conquest and expansion. The Aztec capital, Tenochtitlán (modern-day Mexico City), was located on an island in the center of a lake. At the time of the Spanish conquest, the Aztec realm included almost all of central Mexico. The Aztecs demanded heavy tribute in goods and labor from their subjects and, believing the gods must literally be fed with human blood to guarantee continuing sunshine and fertility, they claimed thousands of captives each year for human sacrifice. These policies fed resentment and fear among subject peoples.

In 1519, Hernan Cortés (1485–1547) landed in Mexico with about five hundred men and a few horses. He opened communication with nearby communities and then with Moctezuma II (1466–1520), the Aztec emperor. Moctezuma may initially have believed Cortés to be the god Quetzalcoatl, who, according to legend, had been driven away centuries earlier but had promised to return. Whatever the reason, Moctezuma hesitated to confront Cortés, attempting at first to appease him with gifts of gold that only whetted Spanish appetites. Cortés succeeded in forging alliances with some subject peoples and, most importantly, with Tlaxcala, an independent state and traditional enemy of the Aztecs. His forces then marched on the Aztec capital of Tenochtitlán, where Moctezuma welcomed him. Cortés soon seized Moctezuma, making him a prisoner in his own capital. Moctezuma died in unexplained circumstances, and the Aztecs' wary acceptance of the Spaniards turned to open hostility. The Spaniards were driven from Tenochtitlán and nearly wiped out, but they ultimately returned and laid siege to the city. The Aztecs, under their last ruler, Cuauhtemoc (ca. 1495–1525), resisted fiercely, but were finally defeated in late 1521. Cortés razed Tenochtitlán, building his own capital over its ruins, and proclaimed the Aztec Empire to be New Spain.

The Incas in Peru   The second great Native American civilization conquered by the Spanish was that of the Incas, located in the highlands of Peru. The Incas began to expand rapidly in the fifteenth century and by the time of the Spanish conquest controlled an empire that rivaled that of China and the Ottoman Empire in size. Unlike the Aztecs, who extracted tribute from their subject peoples, the Incas relied on various forms of labor taxation, compelling local people to work for the state on a regular basis. Men also served in the army and on public works projects.

Armored Spanish soldiers, under the command of Pedro de Alvarado (d. 1541) and bearing crossbows, engage unprotected and crudely armed Aztecs, who are nonetheless portrayed as larger than life by Spanish artist Diego Duran (16th century).   Codex Duran: Pedro de Alvarado (c. 1485–1541), companion-at-arms of Hernando Cortes (1485–1547) besieged by Aztec warriors. Biblioteca Nacional, Madrid, Spain. The Bridgeman Art Library International Ltd.

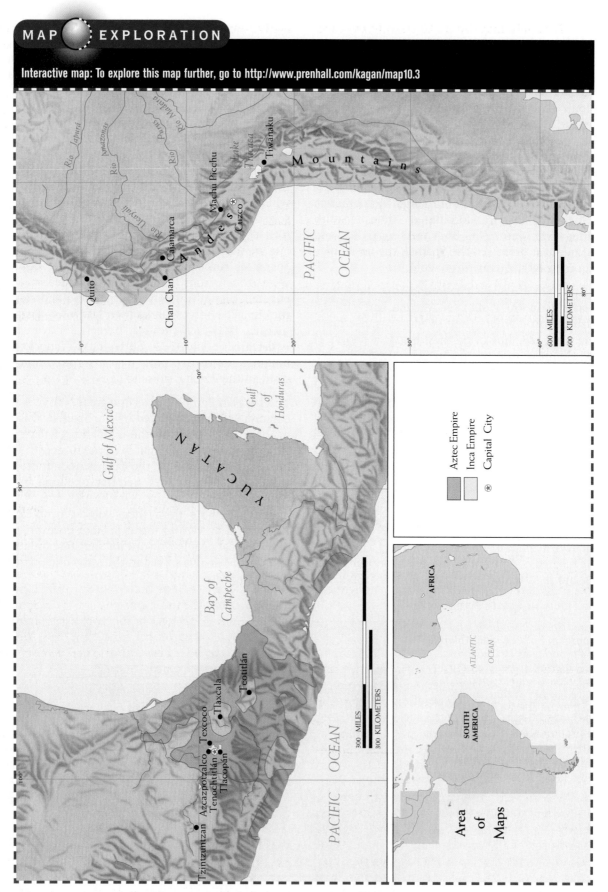

MAP 10–3 THE AZTEC AND INCA EMPIRES ON THE EVE OF THE SPANISH CONQUEST.

In 1532, largely inspired by Cortés's example in Mexico, Francisco Pizarro (c. 1478–1541) landed on the western coast of South America to take on the Inca Empire. His force included about two hundred men armed with guns, swords, and horses. Pizarro lured Atahualpa (ca. 1500–1533), the Inca ruler, into a conference, then seized him, killing hundreds of Atahualpa's followers in the process. The imprisoned Atahualpa tried to ransom himself with a hoard of gold. But instead of releasing him, Pizarro had him garroted in 1533. The Spaniards fought their way to Cuzco, the Inca capital, and captured it, effectively ending the Inca Empire. The Spanish faced insurrections, however, and fought among themselves for decades. Effective royal control was not established until the late 1560s.

The conquests of Mexico and Peru are among the most dramatic and brutal events in modern world history. Small military forces armed with advanced weapons subdued, in a remarkably brief time, two powerful peoples. The spread of European diseases, especially smallpox, among the Native Americans, also aided the conquest. The native populations had long lived in isolation, and many of them succumbed to the new diseases. But beyond the drama and bloodshed, these conquests, as well as those of other Native American peoples, marked a fundamental turning point. Whole civilizations with long histories and a record of enormous social, architectural, and technological achievement were effectively destroyed. Native American cultures endured, accommodating to European dominance, but there was never any doubt about which culture had the upper hand. In that sense, the Spanish conquests of the early sixteenth century marked the beginning of the process whereby South America was transformed into Latin America.

THE CHURCH IN SPANISH AMERICA

Roman Catholic priests had accompanied the earliest explorers and the conquerors of the Native Americans. Because of internal reforms within the Spanish church at the turn of the sixteenth century, these first clergy tended to be imbued with many of the social and religious ideals of Christian humanism. They believed they could foster Erasmus's concept of the "philosophy of Christ" in the New World. Consequently, these missionary priests were filled with zeal not only to convert the inhabitants to Christianity, but also to bring to them learning and civilization of a European kind.

Real tension, however, existed between the early Spanish conquerors and the mendicant friars who sought to minister to the Native Americans. Without conquest, the church could not convert the Native Americans, but the priests often deplored the harsh conditions imposed on the native peoples. By far the most effective and outspoken clerical critic of the Spanish conquerors was Bartolomé de Las Casas (1474–1566), a Dominican. He contended that conquest was not necessary for conversion. One result of his campaign was new royal regulations after 1550.

Another result of Las Casas's criticism was the emergence of the "Black Legend," according to which all Spanish treatment of the Native Americans was unprincipled and inhumane. (See "A Defense of American Natives.") Those who created this view of Spanish behavior drew heavily on Las Casas's writings. Although substantially true, the "Black Legend" nonetheless exaggerated the case against Spain. Certainly the rulers of the native empires—as the Aztec demands for sacrificial victims attest—had often themselves been exceedingly cruel to their subject peoples.

By the end of the sixteenth century, the church in Spanish America had become largely an institution upholding the colonial status quo. Although individual priests did defend the communal rights of Indian tribes, the colonial church prospered as the Spanish elite prospered through its exploitation of the resources and peoples of the New World. The church became a great landowner through crown grants and through bequests from Catholics who died in the New World. The monasteries took on an economic as well as a spiritual life of their own. Whatever its concern for the spiritual welfare of the Native Americans, the church remained one of the indications that Spanish America was a conquered world. Those who spoke for the church did not challenge Spanish domination or any but the most extreme modes of Spanish economic exploitation. By the end of the colonial era in the late eighteenth century, the Roman Catholic Church had become one of the most conservative forces in Latin America.

THE ECONOMY OF EXPLOITATION

From the beginning, both the native peoples of America and their lands were drawn into the Atlantic economy and the world of competitive European commercialism. For the Indians of Latin America and somewhat later, the blacks of Africa, that drive for gain meant various arrangements of forced labor.

There were three major components in the colonial economy of Latin America: mining, agriculture, and shipping. Each of them involved labor, servitude, or a relationship of dependence of the New World economy on that of Spain.

A DEFENSE OF AMERICAN NATIVES

Bartolomé de Las Casas (1474–1566), a Dominican missionary to the New World, describes the native people of the islands of the Caribbean and their systematic slaughter by the Spanish.

■ *Is Las Casas romanticizing the American natives? Does he truly respect their native culture and beliefs?*

This infinite multitude of people was so created by God that they were without fraud . . . or malice. . . . Toward the Spaniards whom they serve, patient, meek, and peaceful, [they] lay aside all contentious and tumultuous thoughts, and live without any hatred or desire of revenge. The people are most delicate and tender, enjoying such a feeble constitution of body as does not permit them to endure labour. . . . The[ir] nation [the West Indies] is very poor and indigent, possessing little, and by reason that they gape not after temporal goods, [being] neither proud nor ambitious. Their diet is such that the most holy hermit cannot feed more sparingly in the wildernesse. They go naked . . . and a poor shag mantle . . . is their greatest and their warmest covering. They lie upon mats; only those who have larger fortunes lie upon a kind of net which is tied at the four corners and so fasten'd to the roof, which the Indians in their natural language call *Hamecks* [hammocks]. They are of a very apprehensive and docile wit, and capable of all good learning, and very apt to receive our Religion, which when they have but once tasted [it], they are carried [off] with a very ardent and zealous desire to make further progress in it; so that I have heard divers Spaniards confess that they had nothing else to hinder them from enjoying heaven, but the ignorance of the true God.

To these quiet Lambs, endued with such blessed qualities, came the Spaniards like most cruel Tygres, Wolves, and Lions . . . for these forty years, minding nothing else but the slaughter of these unfortunate wretches . . . [whom] they have so cruelly and inhumanely butchered, [so] that of three millions of people which Hispaniola [modern Haiti and the Dominican Republic] itself did contain, there are left remaining alive scarce three hundred persons. And the island of Cuba . . . lies wholly desert, untilled and ruined. The islands of St. John and Jamaica lie waste and desolate. The Lycayan islands neighboring to the north upon Cuba and Hispaniola . . . are now totally unpeopled and destroyed; the inhabitants thereof amounting to above 500,000 souls, partly killed, and partly forced away to work in other places. . . . Other islands there were near the island of St. John more than thirty in number, which were totally made desert. All which islands . . . lie now altogether solitary without any people or inhabitant.

Bartolomé de Las Casas, *The Tears of the Indians*, trans. by John Phillips (1656), from reprint of original edition (Stanford, CA: Academic Reprints, n.d.), pp. 2–4.

Mining The early **conquistadores,** or "conquerors," were primarily interested in gold, but by the middle of the sixteenth century, silver mining provided the chief source of metallic wealth. The great mining centers were Potosí in Peru and somewhat smaller sites in northern Mexico. The Spanish crown was particularly interested in mining because it received one-fifth (the *quinto*) of all mining revenues. For this reason, the crown maintained a monopoly over the production and sale of mercury, required in the silver-mining process. Exploring for silver never lost predominance during the colonial era. Its production by forced labor for the benefit of Spaniards and the Spanish crown epitomized the wholly extractive economy that stood at the foundation of colonial life.

Agriculture The major rural and agricultural institution of the Spanish colonies was the **hacienda,** a large landed estate owned by persons originally born in Spain (*peninsulares*) or persons of Spanish descent born in America (*creoles*). Laborers on the hacienda usually stood in some relation of formal servitude to the owner and were rarely free to move from the services of one landowner to another.

The hacienda economy produced two major products: foodstuffs for mining areas and urban centers and leather goods used in mining machinery. Both farming and ranching were subordinate to the mining economy.

In the West Indies, the basic agricultural unit was the plantation. In Cuba, Hispaniola, Puerto Rico, and other islands, the labor of black slaves from Africa produced sugar to supply an almost insatiable demand for the product in Europe.

A final major area of economic activity in the Spanish colonies was urban service occupations, including government offices, the legal profession, and shipping. Practitioners of these occupations were either *peninsulares* or *creoles*, with the former dominating more often than not.

Labor Servitude All of this extractive and exploitive economic activity required labor, and the Spanish in the New World decided very early the native population would supply that labor. A series of social devices was used to draw them into the new economic life imposed by the Spanish.

The first of these was the ***encomienda,*** a formal grant of the right to the labor of a specific number of Indians, usually a few hundred, but sometimes thousands, for a particular period of time. The institution stood in decline by the middle of the sixteenth century because the Spanish monarchs feared the holders of *encomienda* might become a powerful independent nobility in the New World. They were also persuaded on humanitarian grounds against this particular kind of exploitation of the Indians.

The passing of the *encomienda* led to a new arrangement of labor servitude: the *repartimiento.* This device required adult male Indians to devote a certain number of days of labor annually to Spanish economic enterprises. In the mines of Peru, the *repartimiento* was known as the *mita,* the Inca term for their labor tax. *Repartimiento* service was often extremely harsh, and in some cases Indians did not survive their stint. The limitation on labor time led some Spanish managers to abuse their workers on the assumption that fresh workers would soon be appearing on the scene.

The eventual shortage of workers and the crown's pressure against extreme versions of forced labor led to the use of free labor. The freedom, however, was more in appearance than reality. Free Indian laborers were required to purchase goods from the landowner or mine owner, to whom they became forever indebted. This form of exploitation, known as *debt peonage,* continued in Latin America long after the nineteenth-century wars of liberation.

Black slavery was the final mode of forced or subservient labor in the New World. Both the Spanish and the Portuguese had earlier used African slaves in Europe. The sugar plantations of the West Indies now became the major center of black slavery.

The conquest, the forced labor of the economy of exploitation, and the introduction of European diseases had devastating demographic consequences for the Native American population. For centuries, Europeans had lived in a far more complex human and animal environment than Native Americans did. They had frequent contact with different ethnic and racial groups and with a variety of domestic animals. Such interaction helped them develop strong immune systems that enabled them to survive the ravages of measles, smallpox, and typhoid. Native Americans, by contrast, grew up in a simpler and more sterile environment and were completely defenseless against these diseases. Within a generation, the native population of New Spain (Mexico) was reduced to an estimated 8 percent of its numbers, from 25 million to 2 million.

THE IMPACT ON EUROPE

Among contemporary European intellectuals, Columbus's discovery increased skepticism about the wisdom of the ancients. If traditional knowledge about the world had been so wrong geographically, how could it be trusted on other matters? For many, Columbus's discovery demonstrated the folly of relying on any fixed body of presumed authoritative knowledge. Both in Europe and in the New World, there were those who condemned the explorers' treatment of American natives, as more was learned about their cruelty. (See "Montaigne on 'Cannibals' in Foreign Lands.") Three centuries later, however, on the third anniversary of Columbus's discovery (1792), the great thinkers of the age lionized Columbus for having opened up new possibilities for civilization and morality. By establishing new commercial contacts among different peoples of the world, Columbus was said to have made cooperation, civility, and peace among them indispensable. Enlightenment thinkers drew parallels between the discovery of America and the invention of the printing press—both portrayed as world-historical events opening new eras in communication and globalization, an early multicultural experiment.[4]

On the material side, the influx of spices and precious metals into Europe from the new Spanish Empire was a mixed blessing. It contributed to a steady rise in prices during the sixteenth century that created an inflation rate estimated at 2 percent

---

[4]Cf. Anthony Pagden, "The Impact of the New World on the Old: The History of an Idea," *Renaissance and Modern Studies* 30 (1986): 1–11.

MONTAIGNE ON "CANNIBALS" IN FOREIGN LANDS

The French philosopher Michel de Montaigne (1533–1592) had seen a Brazilian native in Rouen in 1562, an alleged cannibal brought to France by the explorer Villegagnon. The experience gave rise to an essay on the subject of what constitutes a "savage." Montaigne concluded that no people on earth were more barbarous than Europeans, who take natives of other lands captive.

■ *Is Montaigne romanticizing New World natives? Is he being too hard on Europeans? Had the Aztecs or Incas had the ability to discover and occupy Europe, would they have enslaved and exploited Europeans?*

Now, to return to my subject, I think there is nothing barbarous and savage in that nation [Brazil], from what I have been told. . . . Each man calls barbarism whatever is not his own practice; for indeed it seems we have no other test of truth and reason than the example and pattern of the opinions and customs of the country we live in. There [we] always [find] the perfect religion, the perfect government, the perfect and accomplished manners in all things. Those [foreign] people are wild, just as we call wild the fruits that Nature has produced by herself and in her normal course; where really it is those that we have changed artificially and led astray from the common order that we should rather call wild. The former retain alive and vigorous their genuine virtues and properties, which we have debased in the latter by adapting them to gratify our corrupted taste. And yet for all that, the savor and delicacy of some uncultivated fruits of those countries is quite as excellent, even to our taste, as that of our own. It is not reasonable that [our human] art should win the place of honor over our great and powerful mother Nature. We have so overloaded the beauty and richness of her works by our inventions that we have quite smothered her. Yet wherever her purity shines forth, she wonderfully puts to shame our vain and frivolous attempts: "Ivy comes readier without our care;/In lonely caves the arbutus grows more fair;/No art with artless bird song can compare."[1] All our efforts cannot even succeed in reproducing the nest of the tiniest little bird, its contexture, its beauty and convenience; or even the web of the puny spider. All things, says Plato,[2] are produced by nature, by fortune, or by art; the greatest and most beautiful by one or the other of the first two, the least and most imperfect by the last.

These nations, then, seem to me "barbarous" in this sense, that they have been fashioned very little by the human mind, and are still very close to their original naturalness. The laws of nature still rule them, very little corrupted by ours; and they are in such a state of purity that I am sometimes vexed that they were unknown earlier, in the days when there were men able to judge them better than we.

[1]Propertius, 1.11.10.
[2]Laws, 10.

From *The Complete Essays of Montaigne*, trans. by Donald M. Frame (Stanford: Stanford University Press, 1958), pp. 153–154.

a year. The new supply of bullion from the Americas joined with enlarged European production to increase greatly the amount of coinage in circulation, and this increase in turn fed inflation. Fortunately, the increase in prices was by and large spread over a long period and was not sudden. Prices doubled in Spain by midcentury, quadrupled by 1600. In Luther's Wittenberg, the cost of basic food and clothing increased almost 100 percent between 1519 and 1540. Generally, wages and rents remained well behind the rise in prices.

The new wealth enabled governments and private entrepreneurs to sponsor basic research and expansion in the printing, shipping, mining, textile, and weapons industries. There is also evidence of large-scale government planning in such ventures as the French silk industry and the Habsburg-Fugger development of mines in Austria and Hungary.

In the thirteenth and fourteenth centuries, capitalist institutions and practices had already begun to develop in the rich Italian cities. (We may point to the activities of the Florentine banking houses of

Bardi and Peruzzi.) Those who owned the means of production, either privately or corporately, were clearly distinguished from the workers who operated them. Wherever possible, entrepreneurs created monopolies in basic goods. High interest was charged on loans—actual, if not legal, usury. And the "capitalist" virtues of thrift, industry, and orderly planning were everywhere in evidence—all intended to permit the free and efficient accumulation of wealth.

The late fifteenth and the sixteenth centuries saw the maturation of this type of capitalism together with its attendant social problems. The Medicis of Florence grew very rich as bankers of the pope, as did the Fuggers of Augsburg, who bankrolled Habsburg rulers. The Fuggers lent Charles I of Spain more than 500,000 florins to buy his election as Holy Roman Emperor in 1519 and boasted they had created the emperor. The new wealth and industrial expansion also raised the expectations of the poor and the ambitious and heightened the reactionary tendencies of the wealthy. This effect, in turn, aggravated the traditional social divisions between the clergy and the laity, the urban patriciate and the guilds, and the landed nobility and the agrarian peasantry.

These divisions indirectly prepared the way for the Reformation as well, by making many people critical of traditional institutions and open to new ideas—especially those that seemed to promise greater freedom and a chance at a better life.

In Perspective

As it recovered from national wars during the late Middle Ages, Europe saw the establishment of permanent centralized states and regional governments. The foundations of modern France, Spain, England, Germany, and Italy were laid at this time. As rulers imposed their will on regions outside their immediate domains, the "one" progressively took control of the "many," and previously divided lands came together as nations.

Thanks to the work of Byzantine and Islamic scholars, ancient Greek science and scholarship found their way into the West in these centuries. Europeans had been separated from their classical cultural heritage for almost eight centuries. No other world civilization had experienced such a disjunction from its cultural past. The discovery of classical civilization occasioned a rebirth of intellectual and artistic activity in both southern and northern Europe. One result was the splendor of the Italian Renaissance, whose scholarship, painting, and sculpture remain among western Europe's most impressive achievements.

Ancient learning was not the only discovery of the era. New political unity spurred both royal greed and national ambition. By the late fifteenth century, Europeans were in a position to venture far away to the shores of Africa, the southern and eastern coasts of Asia, and the New World of the Americas. European discovery was not the only outcome of these voyages: The exploitation of the peoples and lands of the New World revealed a dark side of Western civilization. Some penalties were paid even then. The influx of New World gold and silver created new human and economic problems on the European mainland. In some circles, Europeans even began to question their civilization's traditional values.

REVIEW QUESTIONS

1. Discuss Jacob Burkhardt's interpretation of the Renaissance. What criticisms have been leveled against it? How would you define the term Renaissance in the context of fifteenth- and sixteenth-century Italy?

2. How would you define Renaissance humanism? In what ways was the Renaissance a break with the Middle Ages, and in what ways did it owe its existence to medieval civilization?

3. Who were some of the famous literary and artistic figures of the Italian Renaissance? What did they have in common that might be described as "the spirit of the Renaissance"?

4. Why did the French invade Italy in 1494? How did this event trigger Italy's political decline? How do the actions of Pope Julius II and the ideas of Niccolò Machiavelli signify a new era in Italian civilization?

5. A common assumption is that creative work proceeds best in periods of calm and peace. Given the combination of political instability and cultural productivity in Renaissance Italy, do you think this assumption is valid?

6. How did the Renaissance in the north differ from the Italian Renaissance? In what ways was Erasmus the embodiment of the northern Renaissance?

7. What factors led to the voyages of discovery? How did the Spanish establish their empire in the Americas? Why was the conquest so violent? What was the experience of native peoples during and after the conquest?

SUGGESTED READINGS

L. B. ALBERTI, *The Family in Renaissance Florence*, trans. by R. N. Watkins (1962). A contemporary humanist, who never married, explains how a family should behave.

K. ATCHITY (ED.), *The Renaissance Reader* (1996). The Renaissance in its own words.

H. BARON, *The Crisis of the Early Italian Renaissance*, vols. 1 and 2 (1966). A major work, setting forth the civic dimension of Italian humanism.

P. F. BROWN, *Life and Art in Renaissance Venice* (1997).

G. A. BRUCKER, *Giovanni and Lusanna: Love and Marriage in Renaissance Florence* (1986). Love in the Renaissance shown to be more Bergman than Fellini.

J. BURCKHARDT, *The Civilization of the Renaissance in Italy* (1958). Modern edition of an old nineteenth-century classic that still has as many defenders as detractors.

R. E. CONRAD, *Children of God's Fire: A Documentary History of Black Slavery in Brazil* (1983). Not for the squeamish.

E. L. EISENSTEIN, *The Printing Press as an Agent of Change: Communications and Cultural Transformations in Early Modern Europe*, 2 vols. (1979). Bold, stimulating account of the centrality of printing to all progress in the period.

F. GILBERT, *Machiavelli and Guicciardini* (1984). The two great Renaissance historians lucidly compared.

L. HANKE, *Bartholomé de Las Casas: An Interpretation of His Life and Writings* (1951). Biography of the great Dominican critic of Spanish exploitation of Native Americans.

J. HANKINS, *Plato in the Renaissance* (1992). A magisterial study of how Plato was read and interpreted by Renaissance scholars.

D. HERLIHY AND C. KLAPISCH-ZUBER, *Tuscans and Their Families* (1985). Important work based on unique demographic data that give the reader a new appreciation of quantitative history.

M. L. KING, *Women in the Renaissance* (1991). For comparison and contrast with Brucker and Klapisch-Zuber.

C. KLAPISCH-ZUBER, *Women, Family, and Ritual in Renaissance Italy* (1985). Provocative, wideranging essays documenting Renaissance Italy as very much a man's world.

P. O. KRISTELLER, *Renaissance Thought: The Classic, Scholastic, and Humanist Strains* (1961). A master shows the many sides of Renaissance thought.

L. MARTINES, *Power and Imagination: City States in Renaissance Italy* (1980). Stimulating account of cultural and political history.

S. E. MORRISON, *Admiral of the Ocean Sea: A Life of Christopher Columbus* (1946). Still the best Columbus read.

C. G. NAUERT, JR., *Humanism and the Culture of Renaissance Europe* (1995). Updated survey.

E. PANOFSKY, *Meaning in the Visual Arts* (1955). Eloquent treatment of Renaissance art.

J. H. PARRY, *The Age of Reconnaissance* (1964). A comprehensive account of exploration in the years 1450 to 1650.

I. A. RICHTER (ED.), *The Notebooks of Leonardo da Vinci* (1985). The master in his own words.

Q. SKINNER, *The Foundations of Modern Political Thought; I: The Renaissance* (1978). Broad survey, including absolutely every known political theorist, major and minor.

A. VEZZOSI, *Leonardo da Vinci, Renaissance Man* (1996). Updated biography.

A. WHEATCROFT, *The Habsburgs* (1995). The dynasty that ruled the center of late medieval and early modern Europe.

C. C. WILLARD, *Christine de Pizan* (1984). Demonstration of what an educated woman could accomplish in the Renaissance.

DOCUMENTS CD-ROM

THE RENAISSANCE

EUROPEAN EXPANSION

An Unprecedented Self-Portrait

Albrecht Dürer (1471–1528), the greatest German painter of the Renaissance, was the son of a Nuremberg goldsmith and the apprentice of the city's then most famous painter, Michael Wolgemut. Naturally gifted and trained from childhood, Dürer at thirteen could draw so lifelike a reflection of himself in a mirror, that senior artists already then recognized his genius. A dowry from his marriage at twenty-two (his wife, Agnes Frey, was nineteen) permitted him to travel to Venice, where he acquired the skills of the great Italian artists. His ability to paint realistically led contemporaries to compare him to the legendary ancient Greek painter Apelles and won him many humanistic and princely patrons. According to one story, his dog, passing by a just finished self-portrait of his master had put outside to dry, mistook the work for the master himself and gave it a loving lick, leaving a permanent mark on the painting that Dürer proudly pointed out.

The *Self-Portrait* of 1500 was one of perhaps thirty self-portraits over Dürer's lifetime. (No previous artist painted himself as often or as provocatively.) For some scholars this painting signals a change from the medieval toward a more modern worldview. The individual becomes the primary focus, supplanting God and king. Exalting the power of art and the artist, Dürer presents himself as Christ-like and full faced, a pose traditionally reserved for members of the Holy Trinity. His own autograph, placed at eye level, backs up the portrait's bold proclamation: "I, Albrecht Dürer, divinely inspired artist."

The portrait's powerful effect is achieved by strict adherence to the rules of geometric proportionality (a subject on which Dürer wrote a major book) and by painstaking attention to detail. It is a work of perfect symmetry, and each hair of his head—even the fur on his coat—seems to have been drawn individually with great care. What the viewer beholds is neither Christ nor Everyman, but the gifted individual as many Renaissance thinkers dreamed him to be: a divinely endowed person capable of great achievement.

■ *Why did his contemporaries compare Dürer to the ancient Greek painter Apelles? How does Dürer's self-portrait illustrate a change from the medieval worldview? What techniques did Dürer use to make this portrait more powerful?*

Albrecht Dürer (1471–1528). *Self-portrait at Age 28 with Fur Coat. 1500.* Oil on wood, 67 × 49 cm. Alte Pinakothek, Munich, Germany. Copyright Scala/Art Resource, N.Y.

Sources: Jane Campbell Hutchison, *Albrecht Dürer: A Biography* (Princeton: Princeton University Press, 1990); Joseph Leo Koerner, *The Moment of Self-Portraiture in German Renaissance Art* (Chicago, 1993), esp. pp. xviii, 8–9, 40–42.

A Catholic Portrayal of Martin Luther Tempting Christ *(1547). Reforma-tion propaganda often portrayed the pope as the Antichrist or the devil. Here Catholic propaganda turns the tables on the Protestant reformers by portraying a figure of Martin Luther as the devil (note the monstrous feet and tail under his academic robes). Recreating the biblical scene of Christ being tempted by the devil in the wilderness, the figure of Luther asks Christ to transform stone into bread, to which temptation Christ responds by saying that humans do not live by bread alone.* Versucung Christi, 1547, Gemälde, Bonn, Rheinisches Landesmuseum, Inv. Nr. 58.3.

CHAPTER 11

THE AGE OF REFORMATION

*I*N THE SECOND DECADE OF *the sixteenth century, a powerful religious movement began in Saxony in Germany and spread rapidly throughout northern Europe, deeply affecting society and politics, as well as the spiritual lives of men and women. Attacking what they believed to be burdensome superstitions that robbed people of both their money and their peace of mind, Protestant reformers led a broad revolt against the medieval church. In a short span of time, hundreds of thousands of people from all social classes set aside the beliefs of centuries and adopted a more simplified religious practice.*

The Protestant Reformation challenged aspects of the Renaissance, especially its tendency to follow classical sources in glorifying human nature and its loyalty to traditional religion. Protestants were more impressed by the human potential for evil than by the inclination to do good; they encouraged parents, teachers, and magistrates to be firm disciplinarians. But they also embraced many Renaissance values, especially in the sphere of educational reform and particularly with regard to training in ancient languages. Like the Italian humanists, the Protestant reformers prized the tools that allowed them to go directly to the original sources. For them, this meant the study of the Hebrew and Greek scriptures, enabling them to root their consequent challenges to traditional institutions in biblical authority.

KEY TOPICS

- The social and religious background of the Reformation
- Martin Luther's challenge to the church and the course of the Reformation in Germany
- The Reformation in Switzerland, France, and England
- Transitions in family life between medieval and modern times

Society and Religion

The Protestant **Reformation** occurred at a time of sharp conflict between the emerging nation-states of Europe, bent on conformity and centralization within their realms, and the self-governing small towns and regions, long accustomed to running their own affairs. Since the fourteenth century, the king's law and custom had progressively overridden local law and custom almost everywhere. Many towns and territories were keenly sensitive to the loss of traditional rights and freedoms. Many townspeople and village folk perceived in the religious revolt an ally in their struggle to remain politically free and independent. The Reformation came to be closely identified in the minds of its supporters with what we today might call states' rights or local control.

SOCIAL AND POLITICAL CONFLICT

The Reformation broke out first in the free imperial cities of Germany and Switzerland. There were about sixty-five such cities, and each was in a certain sense a little kingdom unto itself. The great majority had Protestant movements, but with mixed success and duration. Some quickly turned Protestant and remained so. Some were Protestant only for a short time. Others developed mixed confessions, frowning on sectarianism and aggressive proselytizing, and letting Catholics and Protestants live side by side with appropriate barriers.

What seemed a life-and-death struggle with higher princely or royal authority was not the only conflict cities were experiencing. They also suffered deep internal social and political divisions. Certain groups favored the Reformation more than others. In many places, guilds whose members were economically prospering and socially rising were in the forefront of the Reformation. The printers' guild is a prominent example. Its members were literate, sophisticated about the world, in a rapidly growing industry, and economically very ambitious. They also had an economic stake in fanning religious conflict with Protestant propaganda, which many, of course, also sincerely believed. Guilds with a history of opposition to reigning governmental authority also stand out among early Protestant supporters, regardless of whether their members were literate.

Evidence suggests that people who felt pushed around and bullied by either local or distant authority—a guild by an autocratic local government, an entire city or region by a powerful prince or king—often perceived an ally in the Protestant movement, at least initially.

Social and political experience thus coalesced with the larger religious issues in both town and countryside. A Protestant sermon or pamphlet seemed directly relevant, for example, to the townspeople of German and Swiss cities who faced incorporation into the territory of a powerful local prince, who looked on them as obedient subjects rather than as free citizens. When Martin Luther and his comrades wrote, preached, and sang about a priesthood of all believers, scorned the authority of ecclesiastical landlords, and ridiculed papal laws as arbitrary human inventions, they touched political as well as religious nerves. And this was as true in the villages as in the towns. Like city dwellers, the peasants on the land also heard in the Protestant sermon and pamphlet a promise of political liberation and even a degree of social betterment. More than the townspeople, the peasants found their traditional liberties—from fishing and hunting rights to representation at local diets—progressively being chipped away by the great secular and ecclesiastical landlords who ruled over them.

POPULAR RELIGIOUS MOVEMENTS AND CRITICISM OF THE CHURCH

The Protestant Reformation could also not have occurred without the monumental crises of the medieval church during the "exile" in Avignon, the Great Schism, the Conciliar period, and the Renaissance papacy. For increasing numbers of people, the medieval church had ceased to provide a viable foundation for religious piety. Many intellectuals and laypeople felt a sense of crisis about the traditional teaching and spiritual practice of the church. Between the secular pretensions of the papacy and the dry teaching of Scholastic theologians, laity and clerics alike began to seek a more heartfelt, idealistic, and—often, in the eyes of the pope—increasingly heretical religious piety. The late Middle Ages were marked by independent lay and clerical efforts to reform local religious practice and by widespread experimentation with new religious forms.

The Reformation broke out against a background of deep social and political divisions that bred resentment against authority. This early-sixteenth-century woodcut by Georg Pencz presents a warning against tyranny. It shows a world turned upside down, with the hunted becoming the hunters. The rabbits capture the hunters and their dogs and subject them to the same brutal treatment—skinning, butchering, and cooking—that the hunters and dogs routinely inflict on rabbits. The message: Tyranny eventually begets rebellion.   From Max Geisberg, *The German Single-Leaf Woodcut, 1500–1550*, edited by Walter L. Strauss. Hacker Art Books, 1974. Used by permission of Hacker Art Books, Inc.

A variety of factors contributed to the growth of lay criticism of the church. The laity in the cities were becoming increasingly knowledgeable about the world and those who controlled their lives. They traveled widely—as soldiers, pilgrims, explorers, and traders. New postal systems and the printing press increased the information at their disposal. The new age of books and libraries raised literacy and heightened curiosity. Laypeople were increasingly able to take the initiative in shaping the cultural life of their communities.

From the Albigensians, Waldensians, Beguines, and Beghards in the thirteenth century to the Lollards and Hussites in the fifteenth, lay religious movements shared a common goal of religious simplicity in imitation of Jesus. Almost without exception, they were inspired by an ideal of apostolic poverty in religion; that is, all wanted a religion of true self-sacrifice like that of Jesus and the first disciples. The laity sought a more egalitarian church, one that gave the members as well as the head of the church a voice, and a more spiritual church, one that lived manifestly according to its New Testament model.

The Modern Devotion   One of the most constructive lay religious movements in northern Europe on the eve of the Reformation was that of the Brothers of the Common Life, or what came to be known as the Modern Devotion. The brothers fostered religious life outside formal ecclesiastical offices and apart from formal religious vows. Established by Gerard Groote (1340–1384), the Modern Devotion was centered at Zwolle and Deventer in the Netherlands. The brother and (less numerous) sister houses

of the Modern Devotion, however, spread rapidly throughout northern Europe and influenced parts of southern Europe as well. In these houses clerics and laity came together to share a common life, stressing individual piety and practical religion. Lay members were not expected to take special religious vows or to wear special religious dress, nor did they abandon their ordinary secular vocations.

The brothers were also active in education. They worked as copyists, sponsored many religious and a few classical publications, ran hospices for poor students, and conducted schools for the young, especially boys preparing for the priesthood or a monastic vocation. As youths, Nicholas of Cusa, Johann Reuchlin, and Desiderius Erasmus were looked after by the brothers. Thomas à Kempis (d. 1471) summarized the philosophy of the brothers in what became the most popular religious book of the period, the *Imitation of Christ*. This semimystical guide to the inner life was intended primarily for monks and nuns, but was widely appropriated by laity who also wanted to pursue the ascetic life.

The Modern Devotion has been seen as the source of humanist, Protestant, and Catholic reform movements in the sixteenth century. Some scholars, however, believe it represented an individualistic approach to religion, indifferent and even harmful to the sacramental piety of the church. It was actually a very conservative movement. The brothers retained the old clerical doctrines and values while placing them within the new framework of an active common life. Their practices clearly met a need for a more personal piety and a more informed religious life. Their movement appeared at a time when the laity was demanding good preaching in the **vernacular** and was even taking the initiative to endow special preacherships to ensure it. The Modern Devotion permitted laypeople to practice a full religious life without surrendering their life in the world.

Lay Control over Religious Life   On the eve of the Reformation, Rome's international network of church offices, which had unified Europe religiously during the Middle Ages, began to fall apart in many areas. This collapse was hurried along by a growing sense of regional identity—incipient nationalism—and local secular administrative competence. The long-entrenched *benefice* system of the medieval church had permitted important ecclesiastical posts to be sold to the highest bidders and had left residency requirements in parishes unenforced. Such a system did not result in a vibrant local religious life. The substitutes hired by nonresident holders of *benefices* lived elsewhere, mostly in Rome. They milked the revenues of their offices, often performed their chores mechanically, and had neither firsthand knowledge of, nor much sympathy with, local needs and problems. Rare was the late medieval German town that did not have complaints about the maladministration, concubinage, or fiscalism of its clergy, especially the higher clergy (bishops, abbots, and prelates).

Communities had loudly protested the financial abuses of the medieval church long before Luther published his famous summary of economic grievances in 1520 in the *Address to the Christian Nobility of the German Nation*. The sale of indulgences in particular had been repeatedly attacked before Luther came on the scene. On the eve of the Reformation, this practice had expanded to permit people to buy release from time in purgatory for both themselves and their deceased loved ones. Rulers and magistrates had little objection to their sale and might even encourage it, so long as a generous portion of the income they generated remained in the local coffers. But when an indulgence was offered primarily for the benefit of distant interests, as with the Saint Peter's indulgence protested by Luther, resistance arose for strictly financial reasons, because their sale drained away local revenues.

The sale of indulgences would not end until rulers found new ways to profit from religion and the laity found a more effective popular remedy for religious anxiety. The Reformation provided the former by sanctioning the secular dissolution of monasteries and the confiscation of ecclesiastical properties. It held out the latter in its new theology of justification by faith.

City governments also undertook to improve local religious life on the eve of the Reformation by endowing preacherships. These positions, supported by *benefices*, provided for well-trained and dedicated pastors who could offer regular preaching and pastoral care that went beyond the routine performance of the mass and traditional religious functions. In many instances, these preacherships became platforms for Protestant preachers.

Magistrates also carefully restricted the growth of ecclesiastical properties and clerical privileges. During the Middle Ages, canon and civil law had come to recognize special clerical rights in both property and person. Because they were holy places, churches and monasteries had been exempted from the taxes and laws that affected others. They were treated as special places of "sacral peace" and asylum. It was considered inappropriate for holy persons (clergy) to be burdened with such "dirty jobs" as military service, compulsory labor, standing watch at city gates, and other obligations of citizenship. Nor was it thought right that the laity, of whatever rank, should sit in judgment on those who were their shepherds and intermediaries with God. The clergy, accordingly, came to enjoy an immunity of place (which exempted ecclesiastical properties from taxes and recognized their right of asylum) and an immunity of person (which exempted the clergy from the jurisdiction of civil courts).

On the eve of the Reformation, measures were passed to restrict these privileges and to end their abuses. Among them, we find efforts to regulate ecclesiastical acquisition of new property, to circumvent the right of asylum in churches and monasteries (a practice that posed a threat to the normal administration of justice), and to bring the clergy under the local tax code. Governments had understandably tired of ecclesiastical interference in what to them were strictly political spheres of competence and authority.

Martin Luther and German Reformation to 1525

Unlike France and England, late medieval Germany lacked the political unity to enforce "national" religious reforms during the late Middle Ages. There were no lasting Statutes of Provisors and Praemunire, as in England, nor a Pragmatic Sanction of Bourges, as in France, limiting papal jurisdiction and taxation on a national scale. What happened on a unified national level in England and France occurred only locally and piecemeal within German territories and towns. As popular resentment of clerical immunities and ecclesiastical abuses, especially over the selling of indulgences, spread among German cities and towns, an unorganized "national" opposition to Rome formed. German humanists had long given voice to such criticism, and by 1517 it was pervasive enough to provide a solid foundation for Martin Luther's reform.

Luther (1483–1546) was the son of a successful Thüringian miner. He was educated in Mansfeld, Magdeburg (where the Brothers of the Common Life were his teachers), and Eisenach. Between 1501 and 1505 he attended the University of Erfurt, where the nominalist teachings of William of Ockham and Gabriel Biel (d. 1495) prevailed. After receiving his master-of-arts degree in 1505, Luther registered with the law faculty, following his parents' wishes. But he never began the study of law. To the disappointment of his family, he instead entered the Order of the Hermits of Saint Augustine in Erfurt on July 17, 1505. This decision had apparently been building for some time and was resolved during a lightning storm in which Luther, terrified and crying out to Saint Anne for assistance (Saint Anne was the patron saint of travelers in distress), promised to enter a monastery if he escaped death.

Ordained in 1507, Luther pursued a traditional course of study. In 1510, he journeyed to Rome on the business of his order, finding there justification for the many criticisms of the church he had heard in Germany. In 1511, he moved to the Augustinian monastery in Wittenberg, where he earned his doctorate in theology in 1512. Thereafter, he became a leader within the monastery, the new university, and the spiritual life of the city.

JUSTIFICATION BY FAITH ALONE

Reformation theology grew out of a problem then common to many of the clergy and the laity: the failure of traditional medieval religion to provide either full personal or intellectual satisfaction. Luther was especially plagued by the disproportion between his own sense of sinfulness and the perfect righteousness that God required for salvation, according to medieval theology. Traditional church teaching and the sacrament of penance proved no consolation. Luther wrote that he came to despise the phrase "righteousness of God," for it seemed to demand of him a perfection he knew neither he nor any other human being could ever achieve. His insight into the meaning of "justification by faith alone" was a gradual process that extended between 1513 and 1518. The righteousness that God demands, he concluded, did not result from many religious works and ceremonies, but was given in full measure to those who believe and trust in Jesus Christ, who alone is the perfect righteousness satisfying to God. To believe in Christ meant to stand before God clothed in Christ's sure righteousness.

THE ATTACK ON INDULGENCES

An **indulgence** was a remission of the temporal penalty imposed by priests on penitents as a "work of satisfaction" for their mortal sins. According to medieval theology, after the priest absolved a penitent of guilt for the sins, the penitent remained under an eternal penalty, a punishment God justly imposed for sin. After absolution, however, this eternal penalty was said to be transformed into a temporal penalty, a manageable "work of satisfaction" that the penitent might perform here and now (for example, through prayers, fasting, almsgiving, retreats, and pilgrimages). Penitents who defaulted on such prescribed works of satisfaction could expect to suffer for them in purgatory.

At this point, indulgences, which had earlier been given to Crusaders who did not complete their penances because they had fallen in battle, became an aid to laity, made genuinely anxious by their belief in a future suffering in purgatory for neglected penances or unrepented sins. In 1343, Pope Clement VI (r. 1342–1352) had proclaimed the existence of a "treasury of merit," an infinite reservoir of good works in the church's possession that could be dispensed at the pope's discretion. On the basis of this declared treasury, the church sold "letters of indulgence," which covered the works of satisfaction owed by penitents. In 1476, Pope Sixtus IV (r. 1471–1484) extended indulgences also to cover purgatory.

Originally, indulgences had been given only for the true self-sacrifice of going on a Crusade to the Holy Land. By Luther's time, they were regularly dispensed for small cash payments (very modest sums that were regarded as a good work of almsgiving). They were presented to the laity as remitting not only their own future punishments, but also those of their dead relatives presumed to be suffering in purgatory.

In 1517, Pope Leo X (r. 1513–1521) revived a plenary Jubilee Indulgence that had first been issued by Pope Julius II (r. 1503–1513), whose proceeds were to be used to rebuild St. Peter's Basilica in Rome. Such an indulgence promised forgiveness of all outstanding unrepented sins upon the completion of certain acts. That kind of indulgence was subsequently preached on the borders of Saxony in the territories of the future Archbishop Albrecht of Mainz, who was much in need of revenues because of the large debts he had incurred in order to hold, contrary to church law, three ecclesiastical

A contemporary caricature depicts John Tetzel, the famous indulgence preacher. The last lines of the jingle read, "As soon as gold in the basin rings, right then the soul to Heaven springs." It was Tetzel's preaching that spurred Luther to publish his ninety-five theses. Courtesy Staatliche Lutherhalle

appointments. The selling of the indulgence was a joint venture by Albrecht, the Augsburg banking house of Fugger, and Pope Leo X, with half the proceeds going to the pope and half to Albrecht and his creditors. The famous indulgence preacher John Tetzel (d. 1519) was enlisted to preach the indulgence in Albrecht's territories because he was a seasoned professional who knew how to stir ordinary people to action. As he exhorted on one occasion:

Don't you hear the voices of your dead parents and other relatives crying out, "Have mercy on us, for we suffer great punishment and pain. From this you could release us with a few alms. . . . We have created you, fed you, cared for you, and left you our temporal goods. Why do you treat us so cruelly and leave us to suffer in the flames, when it takes only a little to save us?"[1]

When Luther, according to tradition, posted his ninety-five theses against indulgences on the door of Castle Church in Wittenberg, on October 31, 1517, he protested especially against the impression created by Tetzel that indulgences actually remitted sins and released the dead from punishment in purgatory. Luther believed these claims went far beyond the traditional practice and seemed to make salvation something that could be bought and sold.

[1]*Die Reformation in Augenzeugen berichten,* ed. by Helmar Junghaus (Düsseldorf: Karl Rauch Verlag, 1967), p. 44.

ELECTION OF CHARLES V

The ninety-five theses were embraced by humanists and other proponents of reform. The theses made Luther famous overnight and prompted official proceedings against him. In October, he was called before the general of the Dominican order in Augsburg. But as sanctions were being prepared against Luther, Emperor Maximilian I died (January 12, 1519), and this event, fortunate for the Reformation, turned attention away from heresy in Saxony to the contest for a new emperor.

The pope backed the French king, Francis I. However, Charles I of Spain, a youth of nineteen, succeeded his grandfather and became Emperor Charles V. (See Map 11–1.) Charles was assisted by both a long tradition of Habsburg imperial rule and a massive Fugger campaign chest, which secured the votes of the seven electors. The electors, who traditionally enhanced their power at every opportunity, wrung new concessions from Charles for their votes. The emperor agreed to a revival of the Imperial Supreme Court and the Council of Regency and promised to consult with a diet of the empire on all major domestic and foreign affairs that affected the empire. These measures also helped the development of the Reformation by preventing unilateral imperial action against the

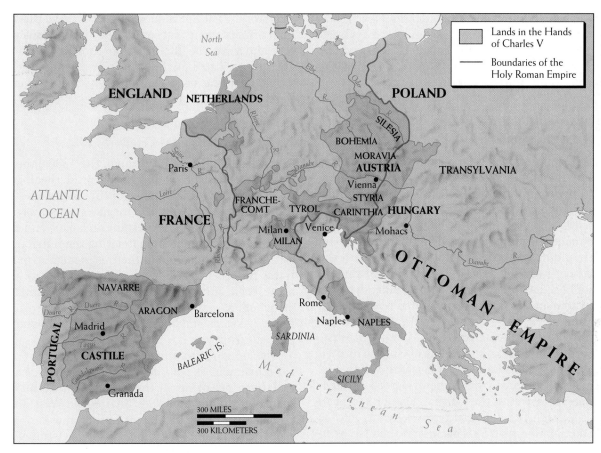

MAP 11–1 THE EMPIRE OF CHARLES V *Dynastic marriages and simple chance concentrated into Charles's hands rule over the lands shown here, plus Spain's overseas possessions. Crowns and titles rained down on him; his election in 1519 as emperor gave him new distractions and responsibilities.*

Germans, something Luther could be thankful for in the early years of the Reformation.

LUTHER'S EXCOMMUNICATION AND THE DIET OF WORMS

In the same month in which Charles was elected emperor, Luther entered a debate in Leipzig (June 27, 1519) with the Ingolstadt professor John Eck. During this contest, Luther challenged the infallibility of the pope and the inerrancy of church councils, appealing, for the first time, to the sovereign authority of Scripture alone. He burned all his bridges to the old church when he further defended certain teachings of John Huss that had been condemned by the Council of Constance.

In 1520, Luther signaled his new direction with three famous pamphlets. The *Address to the Christian Nobility of the German Nation* urged the German princes to force reforms on the Roman church, especially to curtail its political and economic power in Germany. The *Babylonian Captivity of the Church* attacked the traditional seven sacraments, arguing that only two, baptism and the Eucharist, were biblical, and exalted the authority of Scripture, church councils, and secular princes over that of the pope. The eloquent *Freedom of a Christian* summarized the new teaching of salvation by faith alone.

On June 15, 1520, Leo's papal bull *Exsurge Domine* condemned Luther for heresy and gave him sixty days to retract. The final bull of excommunication, *Decet Pontificem Romanum*, was issued on January 3, 1521.

In April 1521, Luther presented his views before the empire's Diet of Worms, over which the newly elected Emperor Charles V presided. Ordered to recant, Luther declared that to do so would be to act against Scripture, reason, and his own conscience. On May 26, 1521, he was placed under the imperial ban and thereafter became an "outlaw" to secular as well as religious authority. For his own protection, friends hid him in a secluded castle, where he spent almost a year, from April 1521 to March

1522. During his stay, he translated the New Testament into German, using Erasmus's new Greek text and Latin translation, and he attempted, by correspondence, to oversee the first stages of the Reformation in Wittenberg.

IMPERIAL DISTRACTIONS: FRANCE AND THE TURKS

The Reformation was greatly helped in these early years by the emperor's war with France and the advance of the Ottoman Turks into eastern Europe. Against both adversaries Charles V, who also remained a Spanish king with dynastic responsibilities outside the empire, needed German troops, and to that end he promoted friendly relations with the German princes. Between 1521 and 1559, Spain (the Habsburg dynasty) and France (the Valois dynasty) fought four major wars over disputed territories in Italy and along their borders. In 1526, the Turks overran Hungary at the Battle of Mohacs; in western Europe the French-led League of Cognac formed against Charles for the second Habsburg-Valois war.

Thus preoccupied, the emperor agreed through his representatives at the German Diet of Speyer in 1526 that each German territory was free to enforce the Edict of Worms (1521) against Luther "so as to be able to answer in good conscience to God and the

The Emperor Charles V at the Battle of Muhlberg.
© Gianni Dagli Orti/CORBIS

emperor." That concession, in effect, gave the German princes territorial sovereignty in religious matters and gave the Reformation time to put down deep roots. Later (in 1555), the Peace of Augsburg would enshrine such local princely control over religion in imperial law.

HOW THE REFORMATION SPREAD

In the late 1520s and on through the 1530s, the Reformation passed from the hands of the theologians and pamphleteers into those of the magistrates and princes. In many cities, the magistrates quickly followed the lead of the Protestant preachers and their sizable congregations in mandating the religious reforms they preached. In numerous instances, magistrates had themselves worked for decades to bring about basic church reforms and thus welcomed the preachers as new allies. Reform now ceased to be merely slogans and became laws that all townspeople had to obey.

The religious reform became a territorial political movement as well, led by the elector of Saxony and the prince of Hesse, the two most powerful German Protestant rulers. (See "Art & the West: Lucas Cranach's Portrait of Martin Luther and Katherine von Bora," p. 387.) Like the urban magistrates, the German princes quickly recognized the political and economic opportunities offered them by the demise of the Roman Catholic Church in their regions. Soon they, too, were pushing Protestant faith and politics onto their neighbors. By the 1530s, Protestant cities and lands formed powerful defensive alliances and prepared for war with the Catholic emperor.

THE PEASANTS' REVOLT

In its first decade, the Protestant movement suffered more from internal division than from imperial interference. By 1525, Luther had become as much an object of protest within Germany as was the pope. Original allies, sympathizers, and fellow travelers declared their independence from him.

Like the German humanists, the German peasantry also had at first believed Luther to be an ally. Since the late fifteenth century, the peasantry had been organized against efforts by territorial princes to override their traditional laws and customs and to subject them to new regulations and taxes. (See "German Peasants Protest Rising Feudal Exactions.") Peasant leaders, several of whom were convinced Lutherans, saw in Luther's teaching about Christian freedom and his criticism of monastic landowners a point of view close to their own. They openly solicited Luther's support of their political and economic rights, including their revolutionary request for release from serfdom.

Luther and his followers sympathized with the peasants. Indeed, for several years Lutheran pamphleteers made Karsthans, the burly, honest peasant who earned his bread by the sweat of his brow and sacrificed his own comfort and well-being for others, a symbol of the simple life that God desired all people to live. The Lutherans, however, were not social revolutionaries. When the peasants revolted against their masters in 1524–1525, Luther, not surprisingly, condemned them in the strongest possible terms as "un-Christian" and urged the princes to crush their revolt without mercy. Tens of thousands of peasants (estimates run between 70,000 and 100,000) died by the time the revolt was put down.

For Luther, the freedom of the Christian was to be found in an inner release from guilt and anxiety, not in a right to restructure society by violent revolution. Had Luther supported the peasants' revolt, he would not only have contradicted his own teaching, but probably would also have ended any chance of the survival of his reform beyond the 1520s. Still, many believe his decision ended the promise of the Reformation as a social revolution.

The punishment of a peasant leader in a village near Heilbronn. After the defeat of rebellious peasants in and around the city of Heilbronn, Jacob Rorbach, a well-to-do peasant leader from a nearby village, was tied to a stake and slowly roasted to death. © Badische Landesbibliothek

The Reformation Elsewhere

Although Luther's was the first, Switzerland and France had their own independent church reform movements almost simultaneously with Germany's. From these movements developed new churches as prominent and lasting as the Lutheran.

ZWINGLI AND THE SWISS REFORMATION

Switzerland was a loose confederacy of thirteen autonomous *cantons*, or states, and allied areas. (See Map 11–2.) Some cantons became Protestant, some remained Catholic, and a few other cantons and regions managed to effect a compromise. There were two main preconditions of the Swiss Reformation. First was the growth of national sentiment occasioned by popular opposition to foreign mercenary service. (Providing mercenaries for Europe's warring nations was a major source of Switzerland's livelihood.) Second was a desire for church reform that had persisted in Switzerland since the councils of Constance (1414–1417) and Basel (1431–1449).

The Reformation in Zurich Ulrich Zwingli (1484–1531), the leader of the Swiss Reformation, had been humanistically educated in Bern, Vienna, and Basel. He was strongly influenced by Erasmus, whom he

credited with having set him on the path to reform. He served as a chaplain with Swiss mercenaries during the disastrous Battle of Marignano in Italy in 1515 and thereafter became an eloquent critic of mercenary service. Zwingli believed this service threatened both the political sovereignty and the moral well-being of the Swiss confederacy. By 1518, Zwingli was also widely known for opposition to the sale of indulgences and to religious superstition.

In 1519, he entered the competition for the post of people's priest in the main church of Zurich. His candidacy was contested because of his acknowledged fornication with a barber's daughter, an affair he successfully minimized in a forcefully written self-defense. Actually, his conduct was less scandalous to his contemporaries, who sympathized with the plight of the celibate clergy, than it may be to the modern reader. One of Zwingli's first acts as a reformer was to petition for an end to clerical celibacy and for the right of all clergy to marry, a practice that quickly became accepted in all Protestant lands.

From his new position as people's priest in Zurich, Zwingli engineered the Swiss Reformation. In March 1522, he was party to the breaking of the Lenten fast—an act of protest analogous to burning one's national flag today. Zwingli's reform guideline was very simple and very effective: Whatever lacked

GERMAN PEASANTS PROTEST RISING FEUDAL EXACTIONS

In the late fifteenth and early sixteenth centuries, German feudal lords, both secular and ecclesiastical, tried to increase the earnings from their lands by raising demands on their peasant tenants. As the personal freedoms of peasants were restricted, their properties confiscated, and their traditional laws and customs overridden, massive revolts occurred in southern Germany in 1525. Some historians see this uprising and the social and economic conditions that gave rise to it as the major historical force in early modern history. The list that follows is the most representative and well-known statement of peasant grievances.

■ *Are the peasants' demands reasonable, given the circumstances of the sixteenth century? Are the peasants more interested in material than in spiritual freedom? Which of the demands are the most revolutionary?*

1. It is our humble petition and desire . . . that in the future . . . each community should choose and appoint a pastor, and that we should have the right to depose him should he conduct himself improperly. . . .

2. We are ready and willing to pay the fair tithe of grain. . . . The small tithes [of cattle], whether [to] ecclesiastical or lay lords, we will not pay at all, for the Lord God created cattle for the free use of man. . . .

3. We . . . take it for granted that you will release us from serfdom as true Christians, unless it should be shown us from the Gospel that we are serfs.

4. It has been the custom heretofore that no poor man should be allowed to catch venison or wildfowl or fish in flowing water, which seems to us quite unseemly and unbrotherly as well as selfish and not agreeable to the Word of God. . . .

5. We are aggrieved in the matter of woodcutting, for the noblemen have appropriated all the woods to themselves. . . .

6. In regard to the excessive services demanded of us which are increased from day to day, we ask that this matter be properly looked into so that we shall not continue to be oppressed in this way. . . .

7. We will not hereafter allow ourselves to be further oppressed by our lords, but will let them demand only what is just and proper according to the word of the agreement between the lord and the peasant. The lord should no longer try to force more services or other dues from the peasant without payment. . . .

8. We are greatly burdened because our holdings cannot support the rent exacted from them. . . . We ask that the lords may appoint persons of honor to inspect these holdings and fix a rent in accordance with justice. . . .

9. We are burdened with a great evil in the constant making of new laws. . . . In our opinion we should be judged according to the old written law. . . .

10. We are aggrieved by the appropriation . . . of meadows and fields which at one time belonged to a community as a whole. These we will take again into our own hands. . . .

11. We will entirely abolish the due called Todfall [that is, *heriot*, or death tax, by which the lord received the best horse, cow, or garment of a family upon the death of a serf] and will no longer endure it, nor allow widows and orphans to be thus shamefully robbed against God's will, and in violation of justice and right. . . .

12. It is our conclusion and final resolution, that if any one or more of the articles here set forth should not be in agreement with the Word of God, as we think they are, such article we will willingly retract.

From *Translations and Reprints from the Original Sources of European History*, Vol. 2 (Philadelphia: Department of History, University of Pennsylvania, 1897), p. 113.

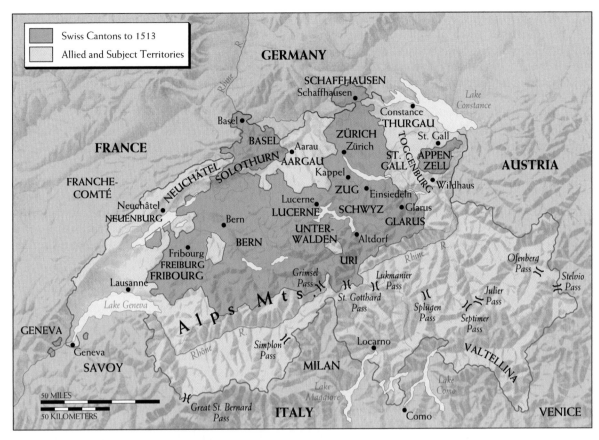

MAP 11–2   THE SWISS CONFEDERATION   *Although nominally still a part of the Holy Roman Empire, Switzerland grew from a loose defensive union of the central "forest cantons" in the thirteenth century into a fiercely independent association of regions with different languages, histories, and, finally, religions.*

literal support in Scripture was to be neither believed nor practiced. As had also happened with Luther, that test soon raised questions about such honored traditional teachings and practices as fasting, transubstantiation, the worship of saints, pilgrimages, purgatory, clerical celibacy, and certain sacraments. A disputation held on January 29, 1523, concluded with the city government granting its sanction to Zwingli's Scripture test. Thereafter Zurich became, to all intents and purposes, the center of the Swiss Reformation. The new regime imposed a harsh discipline that made the city one of the first examples of puritanical Protestantism.

The Marburg Colloquy   Landgrave Philip of Hesse (1504–1567) sought to unite Swiss and German Protestants in a mutual defense pact, a potentially significant political alliance. His efforts were spoiled, however, by theological disagreements between Luther and Zwingli over the nature of Christ's presence in the Eucharist. Zwingli maintained a symbolic interpretation of Christ's words, "This is my body"; Christ, he argued, was only spir-

itually, not bodily, present in the bread and wine of the Eucharist. Luther, to the contrary, insisted that Christ's human nature could share the properties of his divine nature; hence, where Christ was spiritually present, he could also be bodily present, for his was a special nature. Luther wanted no part of an abstract, spiritualized Christ. Zwingli, however, feared that Luther had not broken sufficiently with medieval sacramental theology.

Philip of Hesse brought the two Protestant leaders together in his castle in Marburg in early October 1529, but they were unable to work out their differences on this issue. Luther left thinking Zwingli a dangerous fanatic. Although cooperation between the two sides did not cease, the disagreement splintered the Protestant movement theologically and politically. Separate defense leagues formed, and semi-Zwinglian theological views came to be embodied in the *Tetrapolitan Confession*. This confession of faith was prepared by the Strasbourg reformers Martin Bucer and Caspar Hedio for presentation to the Diet of Augsburg (1530) as an alternative to the Lutheran *Augsburg Confession*.

Swiss Civil Wars As the Swiss cantons divided between Protestantism and Catholicism, civil wars began. There were two major battles, both at Kappel, one in June 1529 and a second in October 1531. The first ended in a Protestant victory, which forced the Catholic cantons to break their foreign alliances and to recognize the rights of Swiss Protestants. During the second battle Zwingli was found wounded on the battlefield and was unceremoniously executed, his remains scattered to the four winds so his followers would have no relics to console and inspire them. The subsequent treaty confirmed the right of each canton to determine its own religion. Heinrich Bullinger (1504–1575), who was Zwingli's protégé and later married his daughter, became the new leader of the Swiss Reformation and guided its development into an established religion.

ANABAPTISTS AND RADICAL PROTESTANTS

The moderate pace and seemingly low ethical results of the Lutheran and Zwinglian reformations discontented many people, among them some of the original followers of Luther and Zwingli. They desired a more rapid and thorough implementation of apostolic Christianity—that is, a more visible moral transformation—and accused the major reformers of going only halfway. The most important of these radical groups were the **Anabaptists,** the sixteenth-century ancestors of the modern Mennonites and Amish. The Anabaptists were especially distinguished by their rejection of infant baptism and their insistence on only adult baptism. (The term *Anabaptism* derives from the Greek word meaning "to rebaptize.") They believed that baptism performed on a consenting adult conformed to Scripture and was more respectful of human freedom.

Conrad Grebel and the Swiss Brethren Conrad Grebel (1498–1526), with whom Anabaptism originated, performed the first adult rebaptism in Zurich in January 1525. Initially a co-worker of Zwingli's and an even greater biblical literalist, Grebel broke openly with that reformer. In a religious disputation in October 1523, Zwingli supported the city government's plea for a very gradual removal of traditional religious practices.

The alternative of the Swiss Brethren, as Grebel's group came to be called, was embodied in the *Schleitheim Confession* of 1527. This document distinguished Anabaptists not only by their practice of adult baptism, but also by their refusal to go to war, to swear oaths, and to participate in the offices of secular government. Anabaptists physically separated from society to form a more perfect community in imitation of what they believed to be the example of the first Christians. Because of the close connection between religious and civic life in this period, the political authorities viewed such separatism as a threat to basic social bonds.

The Anabaptist Reign in Münster At first, Anabaptism drew its adherents from all social classes. But as Lutherans and Zwinglians joined with Catholics in opposition to the Anabaptists and persecuted them within the cities, a more rural, agrarian class came to make up the great majority. In 1529, rebaptism became a capital offense throughout the Holy Roman Empire. Estimates are that between 1525 and 1618 at least 1,000, and perhaps as many as 5,000, men and women were executed for rebaptizing themselves as adults. Brutal measures were universally applied against nonconformists after Anabaptist extremists came to power in the German city of Münster in 1534–1535.

Led by two Dutch emigrants, a baker, Jan Matthys of Haarlem, and a tailor, Jan Beukelsz of Leiden, the Anabaptist majority in Münster forced Lutherans and Catholics either to convert or to emigrate. The Lutherans and Catholics left, and the city was blockaded by besieging armies. Münster transformed itself into an Old Testament theocracy, replete with charismatic leaders and the practice of polygamy. The latter was undertaken as a measure of social control, because there were so many more women, recently widowed or deserted, than men in the city. Many women revolted against the practice and were allowed to leave the resented polygynous marriages.

The outside world was deeply shocked by such developments in Münster. Protestant and Catholic armies united to crush the radicals. The skeletons of their leaders long hung in public view as a warning to all who would so offend traditional Christian sensitivities. After this episode, moderate, pacifistic Anabaptism became the norm among most nonconformists. The moderate Anabaptist leader Menno Simons (1496–1561), the founder of the Mennonites, set the example for the future.

Spiritualists Another radical movement, that of the Spiritualists, was made up mostly of isolated individuals distinguished by their disdain of all traditions and institutions. They believed the only religious authority was God's spirit, which spoke here and now to every individual. Among them were several former Lutherans. Thomas Müntzer (d. 1525), who had close contacts with Anabaptist leaders in Germany and Switzerland, died as a leader of a peasants' revolt. Sebastian Franck (d. 1541), a freelance critic of all dogmatic religion, proclaimed the religious autonomy of every individual soul. Caspar Schwenckfeld (d. 1561) was a prolific writer and wanderer after whom the Schwenckfeldian Church is named.

Antitrinitarians A final group of radical Protestants was the Antitrinitarians, exponents of a common-sense, rational, and ethical religion. Chief among this group were the Spaniard Michael Servetus (1511–1553), executed in 1553 in Geneva for "blasphemies against the Holy Trinity," and the Italians Lelio (d. 1562) and Faustus Sozzini (d. 1604), the founders of Socinianism. These thinkers were the strongest opponents of Calvinism, especially its belief in original sin and predestination, and have a deserved reputation as defenders of religious toleration.

JOHN CALVIN AND THE GENEVAN REFORMATION

In the second half of the sixteenth century, Calvinism replaced Lutheranism as the dominant Protestant force in Europe. Calvinism was the religious ideology that inspired or accompanied massive political resistance in France, the Netherlands, and Scotland. It established itself within the geographical region of the Palatinate during the reign of Elector Frederick III (r. 1559–1576). Calvinists believed strongly in both divine predestination and the individual's responsibility to reorder society according to God's plan. They became zealous reformers determined to transform and order society so men and women would act externally as they believed, or should believe, internally and were presumably destined to live eternally.

In his famous study, *The Protestant Ethic and the Spirit of Capitalism* (1904), the German sociologist Max Weber argues that this peculiar combination of religious confidence and self-disciplined activism produced an ethic that stimulated and reinforced the spirit of emergent capitalism. According to Weber's argument, there was thus a close association between Calvinism and other later forms of Puritanism and the development of modern capitalist societies.

The founder of Calvinism, John Calvin (1509–1564), was born into a well-to-do family, the son of the secretary to the bishop of Noyon in Picardy. He received church *benefices* at age twelve, which financed the best possible education at Parisian colleges and a law degree at Orléans. In the 1520s, he associated with the indigenous French reform party. Although he would finally reject this group as ineffectual, its members contributed to his preparation as a religious reformer.

It was probably in the spring of 1534 that Calvin experienced that conversion to Protestantism by which he said his "long stubborn heart" was "made teachable" by God. His own experience became a personal model of reform that he would later apply to the recalcitrant citizenry of Geneva. His mature theology stressed the sovereignty of God over all creation and the necessity of humankind's conformity to his will. In May 1534, Calvin dramatically surrendered the *benefices* he had held for so long and at such profit and joined the Reformation.

Political Revolt and Religious Reform in Geneva Whereas in Saxony religious reform paved the way for a political revolution against the emperor, in Geneva a political revolution against the local prince-bishop laid the foundation for the religious change. Genevans successfully revolted against their resident prince-bishop in the late 1520s, and the city council assumed his legal and political powers in 1527.

In late 1533, the Protestant city of Bern dispatched two reformers to Geneva: Guillaume Farel (1489–1565) and Antoine Froment (1508–1581). In the summer of 1535, after much internal turmoil, the Protestants triumphed, and the traditional mass and other religious practices were removed. On May 21, 1536, the city voted officially to adopt the Reformation: "to live according to the Gospel

A portrait of the young John Calvin. Bibliothèque Publique et Universitaire, Geneva

and the Word of God . . . without . . . any more masses, statues, idols, or other papal abuses."

Calvin arrived in Geneva after these events, in July 1536. He was actually en route to a scholarly refuge in Strasbourg, in flight from the persecution of Protestants in France, when warring between France and Spain forced him to turn sharply south to Geneva. Farel successfully pleaded with him to stay in the city and assist the Reformation, threatening Calvin with divine vengeance if he turned away from this task.

Before a year had passed, Calvin had drawn up articles for the governance of the new church, as well as a catechism to guide and discipline the people. Both were presented for approval to the city councils in early 1537. Because of the strong measures they proposed to govern Geneva's moral life, many suspected the reformers were intent on creating a "new papacy." Opponents attacked Calvin and Farel, fearing they were going too far too fast. Geneva's powerful Protestant ally, Bern, which had adopted a more moderate Protestant reform, pressured Geneva's magistrates to restore traditional religious ceremonies and holidays that Calvin and Farel had abolished. When the reformers opposed these actions, they were exiled from the city.

Calvin went to Strasbourg, a model Protestant city, where he became pastor to French exiles and wrote biblical commentaries. He also produced a second edition of his masterful *Institutes of the Christian Religion*, which many consider the definitive theological statement of the Protestant faith. Most important, he learned from the Strasbourg reformer Martin Bucer how to achieve his goals.

Calvin's Geneva In 1540, Geneva elected syndics who were both favorable to Calvin and determined to establish full Genevan political and religious independence from Bern. They knew Calvin would be a valuable ally in this project and invited him to return. This he did in September 1540, never to leave the city again. Within months of his return, the city implemented new ecclesiastical ordinances that provided for cooperation between the magistrates and the clergy in matters of internal discipline.

Following the Strasbourg model, the Genevan Church was organized into four offices: (1) pastors, of whom there were five; (2) teachers or doctors to instruct the populace in, and to defend, true doctrine; (3) elders, a group of twelve laypeople chosen by and from the Genevan councils and empowered to "oversee the life of everybody"; and (4) deacons to dispense church goods and services to the poor and the sick.

Calvin and his followers were motivated above all by a desire to transform society morally. Faith, Calvin taught, did not sit idly in the mind, but conformed one's every action to God's law. The "elect" should live in a manifestly God-pleasing way if they were truly God's "elect." In the attempted realization of this goal, Calvin spared no effort. The consistory, or regulatory court, became his instrument of power. This body was composed of the elders and the pastors and was presided over by one of the four syndics. It enforced the strictest moral discipline.

Among the many personal conflicts in Geneva that gave Calvin his reputation as a stern moralist, none proved more damaging than his active role in the capture and execution of the Spanish physician and amateur theologian Michael Servetus in 1553. Earlier, Servetus had been condemned by the Inquisition. He died at the stake in Protestant Geneva for denying the doctrine of the Trinity, a subject on which he had written a scandalous book.

After 1555, the city's syndics were all devout Calvinists, greatly strengthening Calvin's position, and Geneva became home to thousands of exiled Protestants who had been driven out of France, England, and Scotland. Refugees (more than 5,000), most of them utterly loyal to Calvin, eventually made up more than one-third of the population of Geneva.

To the thousands of persecuted Protestants who flocked to Geneva in midcentury, the city was a beacon and a refuge, Europe's only free city. During Calvin's lifetime, Geneva also gained the reputation of being a "woman's paradise" because the laws there severely punished men who beat their wives.

Political Consolidation of the Lutheran Reformation

By 1530, the Reformation was in Europe to stay. It would, however, take several decades and major attempts to eradicate it, before all would recognize this fact. With the political triumph of Lutheranism in the empire by the 1550s, Protestant movements elsewhere gained a new lease on life.

THE DIET OF AUGSBURG

Emperor Charles V, who spent most of his time on politics and military maneuvers outside the empire, especially in Spain and Italy, returned to the empire in 1530 to direct the Diet of Augsburg. This meeting of Protestant and Catholic representatives assembled to impose a settlement of the religious divisions. With its terms dictated by the Catholic emperor, the diet adjourned with a blunt order to all Lutherans to revert to Catholicism.

The Reformation was by this time too firmly established for that to occur. In February 1531, the Lutherans responded with the formation of their own defensive alliance, the Schmalkaldic League. The league took as its banner the **Augsburg Confession,** a moderate statement of Protestant beliefs that had been spurned by the emperor at the Diet of Augsburg. In 1538, Luther drew up a more strongly worded Protestant confession known as the *Schmalkaldic Articles.* Under the leadership of Landgrave Philip of Hesse and Elector John Frederick of Saxony, the league achieved a stalemate with the emperor, who was again distracted by renewed war with France and the ever-resilient Turks.

THE EXPANSION OF THE REFORMATION

In the 1530s, German Lutherans formed regional consistories, judicial bodies composed of theologians and lawyers, which oversaw and administered the new Protestant churches. These consistories replaced the old Catholic episcopates. Philip Melanchthon, the "praeceptor of Germany," oversaw the enactment of educational reforms that provided for compulsory primary education, schools for girls, a humanist revision of the traditional curriculum, and catechetical instruction of the laity in the new religion.

The Reformation also entrenched itself elsewhere. Introduced into Denmark by Christian II (r. 1513–1523), Lutheranism thrived there under Frederick I (r. 1523–1533), who joined the Schmalkaldic League. Under Christian III (r. 1536–1559), Lutheranism became the official state religion.

In Sweden, King Gustavus Vasa (r. 1523–1560), supported by a Swedish nobility greedy for church lands, embraced Lutheranism, confiscated church property, and subjected the clergy to royal authority at the Diet of Vesteras (1527).

In politically splintered Poland, Lutherans, Anabaptists, Calvinists, and even Antitrinitarians found room to practice their beliefs. Primarily because of the absence of a central political authority, Poland became a model of religious pluralism and toleration in the second half of the sixteenth century.

REACTION AGAINST PROTESTANTS: THE INTERIM

Charles V made abortive efforts in 1540–1541 to enforce a compromise between Protestants and Catholics. As these and other conciliar efforts failed, he turned to a military solution. In 1547, imperial armies crushed the Protestant Schmalkaldic League, defeating John Frederick of Saxony in April and taking Philip of Hesse captive shortly thereafter.

The emperor established puppet rulers in Saxony and Hesse and issued as imperial law the Augsburg Interim, a new order mandating that Protestants everywhere readopt old Catholic beliefs and practices. Protestants were granted a few cosmetic concessions, for example, clerical marriage (with papal approval of individual cases) and communion in both kinds (that is, bread and wine). Although the Interim met only surface acceptance within Germany, it forced many Protestant leaders into exile. The Strasbourg reformer Martin Bucer, for example, departed to England, where he would play an important role in drafting the religious documents of the English Reformation during the reign of Edward VI. In Germany, the city of Magdeburg became a refuge for persecuted Protestants and the center of Lutheran resistance.

THE PEACE OF AUGSBURG

The Reformation was too entrenched by 1547 to be ended even by brute force. Maurice of Saxony, hand-picked by Charles V to rule Saxony, recognized the inevitable and shifted his allegiance to the Protestants. Confronted by fierce resistance and weary from three decades of war, the emperor was forced to relent. After suffering a defeat by Protestant armies in 1552, Charles reinstated the Protestant leaders and guaranteed Lutherans religious freedoms in the Peace of Passau (August 1552). With this declaration, he effectively surrendered his lifelong quest for European religious unity.

The Peace of Augsburg in September 1555 made the division of Christendom permanent. This agreement recognized in law what had already been well established in practice: *Cuius regio, eius religio,* meaning the ruler of a land would determine the religion of the land. Lutherans were permitted to retain all church lands forcibly seized before 1552. An "ecclesiastical reservation" was added, however, that was intended to prevent high Catholic prelates who converted to Protestantism from taking their lands, titles, and privileges with them. Those discontented with the religion of their region were permitted to migrate to another.

The Peace of Augsburg did not extend official recognition to Calvinism and Anabaptism as legal forms of Christian belief and practice. Anabaptists had long adjusted to such exclusion by forming their own separatist communities. Calvinists, however, were not separatists and could not choose that route. They remained determined not only to secure the right to worship publicly as they pleased, but also to shape society according to their own religious convictions. While Anabaptists retreated and Lutherans enjoyed the security of an established religion, Calvinists organized to lead national revolutions throughout northern Europe in the second half of the sixteenth century.

The English Reformation to 1553

Late medieval England had a well-earned reputation for maintaining the rights of the crown against the pope. Edward I (r. 1272–1307) had rejected efforts by Pope Boniface VIII to prevent secular taxation of the clergy. Parliament passed the first Statutes of Provisors and Praemunire in the mid–fourteenth century, curtailing payments and judicial appeals to Rome as well as papal appointments in England. Lollardy, humanism, and widespread anticlerical sentiment prepared the way religiously and intellectually for Protestant ideas, which entered England in the early sixteenth century.

THE PRECONDITIONS OF REFORM

In the early 1520s, future English reformers met at the White Horse Inn in Cambridge to discuss Lutheran writings smuggled into England by merchants and scholars. One of these future reformers was William Tyndale (ca. 1492–1536), who translated the New Testament into English in 1524–1525 while in Germany. Printed in Cologne and Worms, Tyndale's New Testament began to circulate in England in 1526.

Cardinal Thomas Wolsey (ca. 1475–1530), the chief minister of King Henry VIII (r. 1509–1547), and Sir Thomas More (1478–1535), Wolsey's successor, guided royal opposition to incipient English Protestantism. The king himself defended the seven sacraments against Luther, receiving as a reward the title "Defender of the Faith" from Pope Leo X. Following Luther's intemperate reply to Henry's amateur theological attack, More wrote a lengthy *Response to Luther* in 1523.

THE KING'S AFFAIR

Lollardy and humanism may be said to have provided the native seeds for religious reform, but it was Henry's unhappy marriage that broke the soil and allowed the seeds to take root. In 1509, Henry had married Catherine of Aragon (d. 1536), daughter of Ferdinand and Isabella of Spain and the aunt of Emperor Charles V. By 1527, the union had produced no male heir to the throne, and only one surviving child, a daughter, Mary. Henry was justifiably concerned about the political consequences of leaving only a female heir. In this period, people believed it unnatural for women to rule over men. At best a woman ruler meant a contested reign, at worst turmoil and revolution.

Henry even came to believe his union with Catherine, who had many miscarriages and stillbirths, had been cursed by God, because Catherine had first been the wife of his brother, Arthur. Henry's father, King Henry VII, had betrothed Catherine to Henry after Arthur's untimely death in order to keep the English alliance with Spain intact. They were officially married in 1509, a few days before Henry VIII received his crown. Because marriage to the wife of one's brother was prohibited by both canon and biblical law (see Leviticus 18:16, 20:21), the marriage had required a special dispensation from Pope Julius II.

By 1527, Henry was thoroughly enamored of Anne Boleyn, one of Catherine's ladies-in-waiting. He determined to put Catherine aside and take Anne as his wife. This he could not do in Catholic England, however, without papal annulment of the marriage to Catherine. And therein lay a special problem. The year 1527 was also the year when soldiers of the Holy Roman Empire mutinied and sacked Rome. The reigning Pope Clement VII was at the time a prisoner of Charles V, who happened also to be Catherine's nephew. Even if this had not been the case, it would have been virtually impossible for the pope to grant an annulment of a marriage that not only had survived for eighteen years, but had been made possible in the first place by a special papal dispensation.

Cardinal Wolsey, who aspired to become pope, was placed in charge of securing the royal annulment. Lord Chancellor since 1515 and papal legate-at-large since 1518, Wolsey had long been Henry's heavy and the object of much popular resentment. When he failed to secure the annulment through no fault of his own, he was dismissed in disgrace in 1529. Thomas Cranmer (1489–1556) and Thomas Cromwell (1485–1540), both of whom harbored Lutheran sympathies, thereafter became the king's closest advisers. Finding the way to a papal annulment closed, Henry's new advisers struck a different course: Why not simply declare the king supreme in English spiritual affairs as he was in English temporal affairs? Then the king could settle the king's affair himself.

THE "REFORMATION PARLIAMENT"

In 1529, Parliament convened for what would be a seven-year session that earned it the title the "Reformation Parliament." During this period, it passed a flood of legislation that harassed, and finally placed royal reins on, the clergy. In so doing, it established a precedent that would remain a feature of English government: Whenever fundamental changes are made in religion, the monarch must consult with and work through Parliament. In January 1531, the Convocation (a legislative assembly representing the English clergy) publicly recognized Henry as head of the church in England "as far as the law of Christ allows." In 1532, Parliament published official grievances against the church, ranging from alleged indifference to the needs of the laity to an excessive number of religious holidays. In the same year, Parliament passed the Submission of the Clergy, which effectively placed canon law under royal control and thereby the clergy under royal jurisdiction.

In January 1533, Henry wed the pregnant Anne Boleyn, with Thomas Cranmer officiating. In February 1533, Parliament made the king the highest court of appeal for all English subjects. In March 1533, Cranmer became archbishop of Canterbury and led the Convocation in invalidating the king's marriage to Catherine. In 1534, Parliament ended all payments by the English clergy and laity to Rome and gave Henry sole jurisdiction over high ecclesiastical appointments. The Act of Succession in the same year made Anne Boleyn's children legitimate heirs to the throne, and the **Act of Supremacy** declared Henry "the only supreme head in earth of the Church of England."

When Thomas More and John Fisher, bishop of Rochester, refused to recognize the Act of Succession and the Act of Supremacy, Henry had them executed, making clear his determination to have his way regardless of the cost. In 1536 and 1538, Parliament dissolved England's monasteries and nunneries.

WIVES OF HENRY VIII

Henry's domestic life lacked the consistency of his political life. In 1536, Anne Boleyn was executed for alleged treason and adultery, and her daughter, Elizabeth, was declared illegitimate. Henry had four further marriages. His third wife, Jane Seymour, died in 1537 shortly after giving birth to the future Edward VI. Henry wed Anne of Cleves sight unseen on the advice of Cromwell, the purpose being to create by the marriage an alliance with the Protestant princes. Neither the alliance nor the marriage proved worth the trouble; the marriage was annulled by Parliament, and Cromwell was dismissed and eventually executed. Catherine Howard, Henry's fifth wife, was beheaded for adultery in 1542. His last wife, Catherine Parr, a patron of humanists and reformers, for whom Henry was the third husband, survived him to marry still a fourth time—obviously she was a match for the English king.

THE KING'S RELIGIOUS CONSERVATISM

Henry's boldness in politics and his domestic affairs did not extend to religion. True, because of Henry's actions, the pope had ceased to be head of the English church and English Bibles were placed in English churches, but despite the break with Rome, Henry remained decidedly conservative in his religious beliefs. With the Ten Articles of 1536, he made only mild concessions to Protestant tenets, otherwise maintaining Catholic doctrine in a country

An allegorical depiction of the Tudor succession by the painter Lucas de Heere (1534–1584). On Henry VIII's right stands his Catholic daughter Mary (1533–1558) and her husband Philip II of Spain. They are accompanied by Mars, the god of war. Henry's son, Edward VI (r. 1547–1553), kneels at the king's left. Elizabeth I (1558–1603) is shown standing in the foreground attended by Peace and Plenty, allegorical figures of what her reign brought to England. Sudeley Castle National Museums & Galleries of Wales

filled with Protestant sentiment. Despite his many wives and amorous adventures, Henry absolutely forbade the English clergy to marry and threatened any clergy who were caught twice in concubinage with execution.

Angered by the growing popularity of Protestant views, even among his chief advisers, Henry struck directly at them in the Six Articles of 1539. These reaffirmed transubstantiation, denied the Eucharistic cup to the laity, declared celibate vows inviolable, provided for private masses, and ordered the continuation of oral confession. (Protestants referred to the articles as the "whip with six stings.") Although William Tyndale's English New Testament grew into the Coverdale Bible (1535) and the Great Bible (1539), and the latter was mandated for every English parish, England had to await Henry's death before it could become a genuinely Protestant country.

THE PROTESTANT REFORMATION UNDER EDWARD VI

When Henry died, his son and successor, Edward VI (r. 1547–1553), was only ten years old. Edward reigned under the successive regencies of Edward Seymour, who became the duke of Somerset

Main Events of the English Reformation	
1529	Reformation Parliament convenes
1532	Parliament passes the Submission of the Clergy
1533	Henry VIII weds Anne Boleyn; Convocation proclaims marriage to Catherine of Aragon invalid
1534	Act of Succession makes Anne Boleyn's children legitimate heirs to the English throne
1534	Act of Supremacy declares Henry VIII "the only supreme head of the Church of England"
1535	Thomas More executed for opposition to Acts of Succession and Supremacy
1535	Publication of Coverdale Bible
1539	Henry VIII imposes the Six Articles
1547	Edward VI succeeds to the throne under protectorships of Somerset and Northumberland
1549	First Act of Uniformity imposes *Book of Common Prayer* on English churches
1553–1558	Mary Tudor restores Catholic doctrine
1558–1603	Elizabeth I fashions an Anglican religious settlement

(1547–1550), and the earl of Warwick, who became known as the duke of Northumberland (1550–1553). During this time, England fully enacted the Protestant Reformation. The new king and Somerset corresponded directly with John Calvin. During Somerset's regency, Henry's Six Articles and laws against heresy were repealed, and clerical marriage and communion with cup were sanctioned.

In 1547, the chantries, places where endowed masses had traditionally been said for the dead, were dissolved. In 1549, the Act of Uniformity imposed Thomas Cranmer's *Book of Common Prayer* on all English churches. Images and altars were removed from the churches in 1550. After Charles V's victory over the German princes in 1547, German Protestant leaders had fled to England for refuge. Several of these refugees, with Martin Bucer prominent among them, now directly assisted the completion of the English Reformation.

The Second Act of Uniformity, passed in 1552, imposed a revised edition of the *Book of Common Prayer* on all English churches. A forty-two-article confession of faith, also written by Thomas Cranmer, was adopted, setting forth a moderate Protestant doctrine. It taught justification by faith and the supremacy of Holy Scripture, denied transubstantiation (although not real presence), and recognized only two sacraments.

All these changes were short lived, however. In 1553, Catherine of Aragon's daughter succeeded Edward (who had died in his teens) to the English throne as Mary I (r. 1553–1558) and proceeded to restore Catholic doctrine and practice with a single-mindedness rivaling that of her father. It was not until the reign of Anne Boleyn's daughter, Elizabeth I (r. 1558–1603), that a lasting religious settlement was worked out in England.

Catholic Reform and Counter-Reformation

The Protestant Reformation did not take the medieval church completely by surprise. There were many internal criticisms and efforts at reform before there was a Counter-Reformation in reaction to Protestant successes.

SOURCES OF CATHOLIC REFORM

Before the Reformation began, ambitious proposals had been made for church reform. But sixteenth-century popes, ever mindful of how the councils of Constance and Basel had stripped the pope of his traditional powers, quickly squelched such efforts to bring about basic changes in the laws and institutions of the church. They preferred the charge given to the Fifth Lateran Council (1513–1517) in the keynote address by the superior general of the Hermits of Saint Augustine: "Men are to be changed by, not to change, religion."

Despite such papal foot-dragging, the church was not without its reformers. Many new religious orders also sprang up in the sixteenth century to lead a broad revival of piety within the church. The first of these orders was the Theatines, founded in 1524 to groom devout and reform-minded leaders at the higher levels of the church hierarchy. One of the cofounders was Bishop Gian Pietro Carafa, who would be Pope Paul IV. Another new order, whose mission pointed in the opposite direction, was the Capuchins. Recognized by the pope in 1528, they sought to return to the original ascetic and charitable ideals of Saint Francis and became very popular among the ordinary people to whom they directed their ministry. The Somaschi, who became active in the mid-1520s, and the Barnabites, founded in 1530, directed their efforts at repairing the moral, spiritual, and physical damage done to people in wartorn areas of Italy.

For women, there was the new order of Ursulines, founded in 1535. It established convents in Italy and France for the religious education of girls from all social classes and became very influential. Another new religious order, the Oratorians, officially recognized in 1575, was an elite group of secular clerics who devoted themselves to the promotion of religious literature and church music. Among their members was the great Catholic hymnist and musician Giovanni Perluigi da Palestrina (1526–1594).

In addition to these lay and clerical movements, the mystical piety of medieval monasticism was revived and popularized by the Spanish mystics Saint Teresa of Avila (1515–1582) and Saint John of the Cross (1542–1591).

IGNATIUS OF LOYOLA AND THE JESUITS

Of the various reform groups, none was more instrumental in the success of the Counter-Reformation than the Society of Jesus, the new order of Jesuits. Organized by Ignatius of Loyola in the 1530s, it was officially recognized by the church in 1540. The society grew within the space of a century from its original 10 members to more than 15,000 members scattered throughout the world, with thriving missions in India, Japan, and the Americas.

The founder of the Jesuits, Ignatius of Loyola (1491–1556), was a heroic figure. A dashing courtier and *caballero* in his youth, he began his spiritual pilgrimage in 1521 after he had been seriously wounded in the legs during a battle with the French.

During a lengthy and painful convalescence, he passed the time by reading Christian classics. So impressed was he with the heroic self-sacrifice of the church's saints and their methods of overcoming mental anguish and pain that he underwent a profound religious conversion. Henceforth, he, too, would serve the church as a soldier of Christ.

After recuperating, Ignatius applied the lessons he had learned during his convalescence to a program of religious and moral self-discipline that came to be embodied in the *Spiritual Exercises*. (See "Ignatius of Loyola's 'Rules for Thinking with

Protestant Reformation and Catholic Reform on the Continent	
1513–1517	Fifth Lateran Council fails to bring about reform in the church
1517	Luther posts ninety-five theses against indulgences
1519	Charles I of Spain elected Holy Roman Emperor (as Charles V)
1519	Luther challenges authority of pope and inerrancy of church councils at Leipzig Debate
1521	Papal bull excommunicates Luther for heresy
1521	Diet of Worms condemns Luther
1521–1522	Luther translates the New Testament into German
1524–1525	Peasants' revolt in Germany
1527	The *Schleitheim Confession* of the Anabaptists
1529	Marburg Colloquy between Luther and Zwingli
1530	Diet of Augsburg fails to settle religious differences
1531	Formation of Protestant Schmalkaldic League
1534–1535	Anabaptists assume political power in city of Münster
1536	Calvin arrives in Geneva
1540	Jesuits, founded by Ignatius of Loyola, recognized as order by pope
1546	Luther dies
1547	Armies of Charles V crush Schmalkaldic League
1548	Augsburg Interim outlaws Protestant practices
1555	Peace of Augsburg recognizes rights of Lutherans to worship as they please
1545–1563	Council of Trent institutes reforms and responds to the Reformation

The Ecstasy of Saint Teresa of Avila *by Gianlorenzo Bernini (1598–1680). Mystics like Saint Teresa and Saint John of the Cross helped revive the traditional piety of medieval monasticism.* S. Maria della Vittoria, Rome. Copyright Scala/Art Resource, N.Y.

the Church.'") This psychologically perceptive devotional guide contained mental and emotional exercises designed to teach one absolute spiritual self-mastery over one's feelings. It taught that a person could shape his or her own behavior—even create a new religious self—through disciplined study and regular practice.

Whereas in Jesuit eyes Protestants had distinguished themselves by disobedience to church authority and by religious innovation, the exercises of Ignatius were intended to teach good Catholics to deny themselves and submit without question to higher church authority and spiritual direction. Perfect discipline and self-control were the essential conditions of such obedience. To these were added the enthusiasm of traditional spirituality and mysticism and uncompromising loyalty to the church's cause above all else. This was a potent combination that helped counter the Reformation and win many Protestants back to the Catholic

fold, especially in Austria and Bavaria and along the Rhine. (See Map 11–3).

THE COUNCIL OF TRENT (1545–1563)

The broad success of the Reformation and the insistence of the Emperor Charles V forced Pope Paul to call a general council of the church to reassert church doctrine. In anticipation, the pope appointed a reform commission, chaired by Caspar Contarini (1483–1542), a leading liberal theologian. His report, presented to the pope in February 1537, bluntly criticized the fiscal practices and simony of the papal Curia as the primary source of the church's loss of esteem. The report was so critical that Pope Paul attempted unsuccessfully to suppress its publication, and Protestants reprinted and circulated it as justification of their criticism.

The long-delayed council of the church met in 1545 in the imperial city of Trent in northern Italy. There were three sessions, spread over eighteen years, with long interruptions due to war, plague, and imperial and papal politics. The council met from 1545 to 1547, from 1551 to 1552, and from 1562 to 1563, a period that spanned the careers of four different popes.

Unlike the general councils of the fifteenth century, Trent was strictly under the pope's control, with high Italian prelates prominent in the proceedings. Initially four of the five attending archbishops and twenty-one of the twenty-three attending bishops were Italian. Even at its final session in 1562, more than three-quarters of the council fathers were Italians. Voting was limited to the high levels of the clergy; university theologians, the lower clergy, and the laity were not permitted to share in the council's decisions.

The council's most important reforms concerned internal church discipline. Steps were taken to curtail the selling of church offices and other religious goods. Many bishops who resided in Rome rather than within their dioceses were forced to move to their appointed seats of authority. Trent strengthened the authority of local bishops so they could effectively discipline popular religious practice. The bishops were also subjected to new rules that required them not only to reside in their dioceses, but also to be highly visible by preaching regularly and conducting annual visitations. Trent also sought to give the parish priest a brighter image by requiring him to be neatly dressed, better educated, strictly celibate, and active among his parishioners. To this end, Trent also called for the construction of a seminary in every diocese.

Not a single doctrinal concession was made to the Protestants, however. In the face of Protestant

IGNATIUS OF LOYOLA'S "RULES FOR THINKING WITH THE CHURCH"

As leaders of the Counter-Reformation, the Jesuits attempted to live by and instill in others the strictest obedience to church authority. The following are some of the eighteen rules included by Ignatius in his Spiritual Exercises *to give Catholics positive direction. These rules also indicate the Catholic reformers' refusal to compromise with Protestants.*

■ *Would Protestants find any of Ignatius's "rules" acceptable? Might any of them be controversial among Catholic laity as well as among Protestant laity?*

In order to have the proper attitude of mind in the Church Militant we should observe the following rules:

1. Putting aside all private judgment, we should keep our minds prepared and ready to obey promptly and in all things the true spouse of Christ our Lord, our Holy Mother, the hierarchical Church.
2. To praise sacramental confession and the reception of the Most Holy Sacrament once a year, and much better once a month, and better still every week. . . .
3. To praise the frequent hearing of Mass. . . .
4. To praise highly the religious life, virginity, and continence; and also matrimony, but not as highly. . . .
5. To praise the vows of religion, obedience, poverty, chastity, and other works of perfection and supererogation. . . .
6. To praise the relics of the saints . . . [and] the stations, pilgrimages, indulgences, jubilees, Crusade indulgences, and the lighting of candles in the churches.
7. To praise the precepts concerning fasts and abstinences . . . and acts of penance. . . .
8. To praise the adornments and buildings of churches as well as sacred images. . . .
9. To praise all the precepts of the church. . . .
10. To approve and praise the directions and recommendations of our superiors as well as their personal behaviour. . . .
11. To praise both the positive and scholastic theology. . . .
12. We must be on our guard against making comparisons between the living and those who have already gone to their reward, for it is no small error to say, for example: "This man knows more than St. Augustine"; "He is another Saint Francis, or even greater." . . .
13. If we wish to be sure that we are right in all things, we should always be ready to accept this principle: I will believe that the white that I see is black, if the hierarchical Church so defines it. For I believe that between . . . Christ our Lord and . . . His Church, there is but one spirit, which governs and directs us for the salvation of our souls.

From *The Spiritual Exercises of St. Ignatius*, trans. by Anthony Mottola. Copyright © 1964 by Doubleday, a division of Bantam, Doubleday, Dell Publishing Group, Inc., pp. 139–141. Used by permission of Doubleday, a division of Random House, Inc.

criticism, the Council of Trent gave a ringing reaffirmation to the traditional Scholastic education of the clergy; the role of good works in salvation; the authority of tradition; the seven sacraments; transubstantiation; the withholding of the Eucharistic cup from the laity; clerical celibacy; the reality of purgatory; the veneration of saints, relics, and sacred images; and the granting of letters of indulgence. The council resolved medieval Scholastic quarrels in favor of the theology of Saint Thomas Aquinas, further enhancing his authority within the church. Thereafter, the church offered its strongest resistance to groups like the Jansenists, who strongly endorsed the medieval Augustinian tradition, a source of alternative Catholic, as well as many Protestant, doctrines.

Rulers initially resisted Trent's reform decrees, fearing a revival of papal political power within their lands. But with the passage of time and the pope's assurances that religious reforms were his sole intent, the new legislation took hold, and parish life revived under the guidance of a devout and better trained clergy.

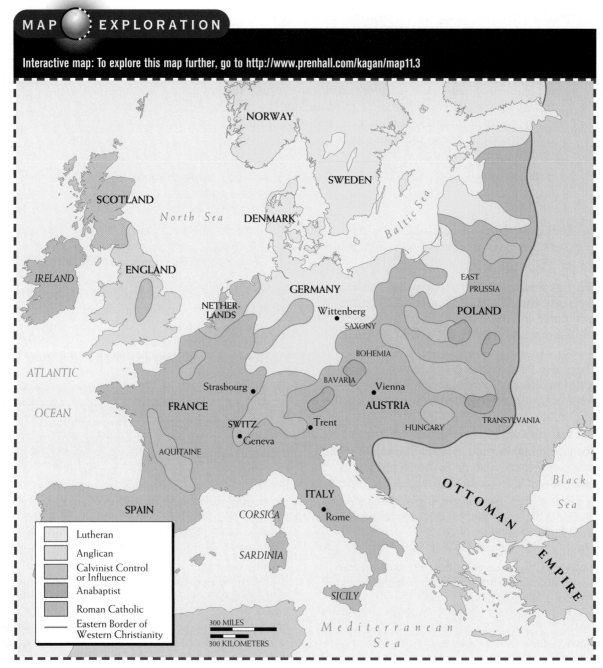

Interactive map: To explore this map further, go to http://www.prenhall.com/kagan/map11.3

MAP 11–3   THE RELIGIOUS SITUATION ABOUT 1560   *By 1560, Luther, Zwingli, and Loyola were dead, Calvin was near the end of his life, the English break from Rome was complete, and the last session of the Council of Trent was about to assemble. This map shows "religious geography" of western Europe at the time.*

The Social Significance of the Reformation in Western Europe

It was a common trait of the Lutheran, Zwinglian, and Calvinist reformers to work within the framework of reigning political power. Luther, Zwingli, and Calvin saw themselves and their followers as subject to definite civic responsibilities and obligations. Their conservatism in this regard has led scholars to characterize them as "magisterial reformers," meaning not only that they were the leaders of the major Protestant movements, but also that they succeeded by the force of the magistrate's sword. Some have argued that this willingness to resort to coercion led the reformers to compromise their principles. They themselves, however, never contemplated reform outside or against the societies of which they were members. They wanted it to take shape within the laws and institutions of the sixteenth century. To that end, they remained highly sensitive to what was politically and socially possible in their age. Some scholars believe the reformers were too conscious of the historically possible, that their reforms went forward with such caution they changed late medieval society very little and actually encouraged acceptance of the sociopolitical status quo.

The Revolution in Religious Practices and Institutions

The Reformation may have been politically conservative, but by the end of the sixteenth century it had brought about radical changes in traditional religious practices and institutions in those lands where it succeeded.

Religion in Fifteenth-Century Life In the fifteenth century, on the streets of the great cities of central Europe that later turned Protestant (for example, Zurich, Strasbourg, Nuremberg, and Geneva), the clergy and the religious were everywhere. They made up 6 to 8 percent of the total urban population, and they exercised considerable political as well as spiritual power. They legislated and taxed, they tried cases in special church courts, and they enforced their laws with threats of excommunication.

The church calendar regulated daily life. About one-third of the year was given over to some kind of religious observance or celebration. There were frequent periods of fasting. On almost a hundred days out of the year a pious Christian could not, without special dispensation, eat eggs, butter, fat, or meat.

Monasteries, and especially nunneries, were prominent and influential institutions. The children of society's most powerful citizens resided there. Local aristocrats were closely identified with particular churches and chapels, whose walls recorded their lineage and proclaimed their generosity. On the streets, friars from near and far begged alms from passersby. In the churches, the mass and liturgy were read entirely in Latin. Images of saints were regularly displayed, and on certain holidays their relics were paraded about and venerated.

Local religious shrines enjoyed a booming business. Pilgrims gathered there by the hundreds—even thousands—many sick and dying, all in search of a cure or a miracle, but also for diversion and entertainment. Several times during the year, special preachers arrived in the city to sell letters of indulgence.

Many clergy walked the streets with concubines and children, although they were sworn to celibacy and forbidden to marry. The church tolerated such relationships upon payment of penitential fines.

People everywhere could be heard complaining about the clergy's exemption from taxation and, in many instances, also from the civil criminal code. People also grumbled about having to support church offices whose occupants actually lived and worked elsewhere. Townspeople also expressed concern that the church had too much influence over education and culture.

Religion in Sixteenth-Century Life In these same cities, after the Reformation had firmly established itself, few changes in politics and society were evident. The same aristocratic families governed as before, and the rich generally got richer and the poor poorer. But overall numbers of clergy fell by two-thirds and religious holidays shrank by one-third. Cloisters were nearly gone, and many that remained were transformed into hospices for the sick and poor or into educational institutions, their endowments also turned over to these new purposes. A few cloisters remained for very devout old monks and nuns who could not be pensioned off or who lacked families and friends to care for them. But these remaining cloisters died out with their inhabitants.

In the churches, which had also been reduced in number by at least one-third, worship was conducted almost completely in the vernacular. In some, particularly those in Zwinglian cities, the walls were stripped bare and whitewashed to make sure the congregation meditated only on God's word. The laity observed no obligatory fasts. Indulgence preachers no longer appeared. Local shrines were closed down, and anyone found openly venerating saints, relics, and images was subject to fine and punishment.

Copies of Luther's translation of the New Testament or, more often, excerpts from it could be found in private homes, and meditation on them was encouraged by the new clergy. The clergy could marry, and most did. They paid taxes and were punished for their crimes in civil courts. Domestic moral life was regulated by committees composed of roughly equal numbers of laity and clergy, over whose decisions secular magistrates had the last word.

Not all Protestant clergy remained enthusiastic about this new lay authority in religion. And the laity themselves were also ambivalent about certain aspects of the Reformation. Over half of the original converts returned to the Catholic fold before the end of the sixteenth century. Whereas one-half of Europe could be counted in the Protestant camp in the mid–sixteenth century, only one-fifth would be there by the mid–seventeenth century.[2]

THE REFORMATION AND EDUCATION

Another important cultural achievement of the Reformation was its implementation of many of the educational reforms of humanism in the new Protestant schools and universities. Many Protestant reformers in Germany, France, and England were humanists. And even when their views on church doctrine and humankind separated them from the humanist movement, the Protestant reformers continued to share with the humanists a common opposition to Scholasticism and a belief in the unity of wisdom, eloquence, and action. The humanist program of studies, which provided the language skills to deal authoritatively with original sources, proved to be a more appropriate tool for the elaboration of Protestant doctrine than did scholastic dialectic, which remained ascendant in the Counter-Reformation.

The Catholic counterreformers recognized the close connections between humanism and the Reformation. Ignatius of Loyola observed the way in which the new learning had been embraced by and served the Protestant cause. In his *Spiritual Exercises*, he insisted that when the Bible and the Church Fathers were read directly, they be read under the guidance of the authoritative scholastic theologians: Peter Lombard, Bonaventure, and Thomas Aquinas. The last of these worthies, Ignatius argued, being "of more recent date," had the clearest understanding of what Scripture and the Fathers meant and therefore should guide the study of the past.

When, in August 1518, Philip Melanchthon (1497–1560), a young humanist and professor of Greek, arrived at the University of Wittenberg, his first act was to implement curricular reforms on the humanist model. In his inaugural address, entitled *On Improving the Studies of the Young*, Melanchthon presented himself as a defender of good letters and classical studies against "barbarians who practice barbarous arts." By the latter, he meant the Scholastic theologians of the later Middle Ages, whose methods of juxtaposing the views of conflicting authorities and seeking to reconcile them by disputation had, he believed, undermined

both good letters and sound biblical doctrine. Scholastic dominance in the universities was seen by Melanchthon as having bred contempt for the Greek language and learning and as having encouraged neglect of the study of mathematics, sacred studies, and the art of oratory. Melanchthon urged the careful study of history, poetry, and other humanist disciplines.

Together, Luther and Melanchthon restructured the University of Wittenberg's curriculum. Commentaries on Lombard's *Sentences* were dropped, as was canon law. Straightforward historical study replaced old Scholastic lectures on Aristotle. Students read primary sources directly, not by way of accepted Scholastic commentators. Candidates for theological degrees defended the new doctrine on the basis of their own exegesis of the Bible. New chairs of Greek and Hebrew were created. Luther and Melanchthon also pressed for universal compulsory education so both boys and girls could reach vernacular literacy in the Bible.

In Geneva, John Calvin and his successor, Theodore Beza, founded the Genevan Academy, which later evolved into the University of Geneva. That institution, created primarily for training Calvinist ministers, pursued ideals similar to those set forth by Luther and Melanchthon. Calvinist refugees trained in the academy carried Protestant educational reforms to France, Scotland, England, and the New World. Through such efforts, a working knowledge of Greek and Hebrew became commonplace in educated circles in the sixteenth and seventeenth centuries.

Some contemporaries decried what they saw as a narrowing of the original humanist program as Protestants took it over. Erasmus, for example, came to fear the Reformation as a threat to the liberal arts and good learning. Sebastian Franck pointed to parallels between Luther's and Zwingli's debates over Christ's presence in the Eucharist and such old Scholastic disputations as that over the Immaculate Conception of the Virgin.

Humanist culture and learning nonetheless remained indebted to the Reformation. The Protestant endorsement of the humanist program of studies remained as significant for the humanist movement as the latter had been for the Reformation. Protestant schools and universities consolidated and preserved for the modern world many of the basic pedagogical achievements of humanism. There, the *studia humanitatis*, although often as little more than a handmaiden to theological doctrine, found a permanent home, one that remained hospitable even in the heyday of conservative Protestantism.

[2]Geoffrey Parker, *Europe in Crisis, 1598–1648* (Ithaca, NY: Cornell University Press, 1979), p. 50.

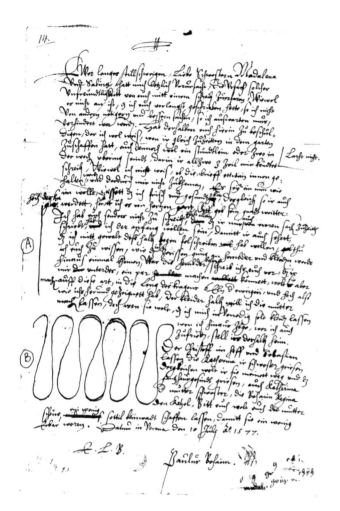

Brothers and sisters. While away from home at law school in Padua, Italy, nineteen-year-old Paul Behaim, Jr., wrote in July 1577 to his older sisters Magdalena (twenty-two) and Sabina (twenty-one) to complain about the infrequency of their writing to him. Typical of sibling relations in every age, the letter is affectionate and joking. The sisters were then at home with their widowed mother and busy with the many chores of the self-sufficient sixteenth-century domestic household—especially, at this time of the year, gardening. Because of their alleged neglect Paul teasingly tells them they must now do "penance" by making him two new shirts, as his were embarrassingly tattered. He indicated in the left margin the exact collar length (A) and style (B) he wishes the shirts to be. Sewing for the household was another regular domestic chore for burgher and patrician women not working in trades outside the home. But Magdalena and Sabina went even further to "cover" their brother: They also allowed him to receive income (to be repaid in the future) from their own paternal inheritances so he might finish his legal education, on the successful completion of which the whole family depended for its future success.   Geramnisches National Museum, Nuremberg, Germany, Behaim-Archiv Fasz. 106; Steven Ozment, *Flesh and Spirit: Private Life in* Early Modern Germany (New York: Viking/Penguin, 1999), pp. 174–176.

THE REFORMATION AND THE CHANGING ROLE OF WOMEN

The Protestant reformers took a positive stand on clerical marriage and strongly opposed monasticism and the celibate life. From this position, they challenged the medieval tendency alternately to degrade women as temptresses (following the model of Eve) and to exalt them as virgins (following the model of Mary). Protestants opposed the popular antiwoman and antimarriage literature of the Middle Ages. They praised woman in her own right, but especially in her biblical vocation as mother and housewife. Although from a modern perspective, women remained subject to men, new marriage laws gave them greater security and protection.

Relief of sexual frustration and a remedy for fornication were prominent in Protestant arguments for marriage. But the reformers also viewed their wives as indispensable companions in their work, and this not solely because they took domestic cares off their husbands' minds. Luther, who married in 1525 at the age of forty-two, wrote the following of women:

Imagine what it would be like without women. The home, cities, economic life, and government would virtually disappear. Men cannot do without women. Even if it were possible for men to beget and bear children, they still could not do without women.[3]

John Calvin wrote this at the death of his wife:

I have been bereaved of the best companion of my life, of one who, had it been so ordered, would not only have been the willing sharer of my indigence, but even of my death. During her life she was the faithful helper of my ministry.[4]

---

[3]*Luther's Works, Vol. 54: Table Talk*, ed. and trans. by Theodore G. Tappert (Philadelphia: Fortress Press, 1967), p. 161.

[4]*Letters of John Calvin*, Vol. 2, trans. by J. Bonnet (Edinburgh: T. Constable, 1858), p. 216.

Such tributes were intended in part to overcome Catholic criticism that marriage distracted the cleric from his ministry. They were primarily the expression of a new value placed on the estate of marriage and family life. In opposition to the celibate ideal of the Middle Ages, Protestants stressed as no religious movement before them the sacredness of home and family. This attitude contributed to a more respectful and sharing relationship between husbands and wives and between parents and children.

The ideal of the companionate marriage—that is, of husband and wife as co-workers in a special God-ordained community of the family, sharing authority equally within the household—led to an important expansion of the grounds for divorce in Protestant cities as early as the 1520s. Women now had an equal right with men to divorce and remarry in good conscience—unlike the situation in Catholicism, where only a separation from bed and table, not divorce and remarriage, was permitted a couple in a failed marriage. The reformers were actually more willing to permit divorce and remarriage on grounds of adultery and abandonment than were secular magistrates, who feared liberal divorce laws would lead to social upheaval.

Protestant doctrines were as attractive to women as they were to men. Renegade nuns wrote exposés of the nunnery in the name of Christian freedom and justification by faith, declaring the nunnery was no special woman's place at all and that supervisory male clergy (who alone could hear the nuns' confessions and administer sacraments to them) made their lives as unpleasant and burdensome as any abusive husband. Women in the higher classes, who enjoyed new social and political freedoms during the Renaissance, found in Protestant theology a religious complement to their greater independence in other walks of life. Some cloistered noblewomen, however, protested the closing of nunneries. They believed the cloister provided them a more interesting and independent way of life than they would have known in the secular world.

Because they wanted women to become pious housewives, Protestants encouraged the education of girls to literacy in the vernacular, with the expectation that they would thereafter model their lives on the Bible. During their studies, however, women found biblical passages which suggested they were equal to men in the presence of God. Education also gave some women a role as independent authors in the Reformation. From a modern perspective, these may seem like small advances, but they were significant, if indirect, steps in the direction of the emancipation of women.

Family Life in Early Modern Europe

Changes in the timing and duration of marriage, in family size, and in infant and child care suggest that family life was under a variety of social and economic pressures in the sixteenth and seventeenth centuries. The Reformation was a factor in these changes, but not the only or even the major one.

A family has a certain force and logic of its own, regardless of the time and place in which it exists. The routine of family life conspires with basic instincts to establish characteristic patterns of behavior, reinforcing natural feelings and building expectations among family members. Time, place, and culture, however, are important. A person raised in a twelfth-century family would be different from one raised in a twenty-first-century family, and growing up in Europe is not the same as growing up in China. But the differences do not lie in the ability of husbands and wives to love one another or of parents to make sacrifices for their children. They lie, rather, in the ways different cultures and religions infuse family life with values and influence the behavior of family members. (See "Encountering the Past: Table Manners.")

LATER MARRIAGES

Between 1500 and 1800, men and women in western Europe and England married at later ages than they had in previous centuries. Men tended to be in their mid- to late twenties rather than in their late teens and early twenties, and women in their early to mid-twenties rather than in their teens. The canonical, or church-sanctioned, age for marriage remained fourteen for men and twelve for women, and engagements might occur at these young ages, especially among royalty and nobility. As it had done throughout the High and late Middle Ages, the church also recognized as valid free, private exchanges of vows between a man and a woman at these minimal ages. However, after the Reformation, which condemned such clandestine unions, the church increasingly required both parental agreement and public vows in church before a marriage could be recognized as fully licit—procedures it had always actually preferred.

Late marriage in the West reflected the difficulty couples had supporting themselves independently. The difficulty arose because of the population growth that occurred during the late fifteenth and early sixteenth centuries, when western Europe recovered much of the population loss incurred during the Great Plague. Larger families meant more heirs and hence a greater division of resources. In Germanic and Scandinavian countries, the custom of fair sharing of inheritance among all male children worked to delay marriages, for divided inheritances often meant small incomes for the recipients. It simply took the average couple a longer time than previously to prepare themselves materially for marriage. In the sixteenth century, one in five women never married, and these, combined with the estimated 15 percent who were unmarried widows, constituted a sizable unmarried female population.

A later marriage meant a marriage of shorter duration, since couples who married in their thirties would not spend as much time together as couples who married in their twenties. Such marriages also contributed to more frequent remarriage for men because women who bore children for the first time at advanced ages had higher mortality rates than younger mothers. Moreover, as growing church condemnation and the rapid growth of orphanages and foundling homes between 1600 and 1800 confirm, delayed marriage increased premarital sex and raised the number of illegitimate children.

ARRANGED MARRIAGES

Marriage tended to be "arranged" in the sense that the parents customarily met and discussed the terms of the marriage before the prospective bride and bridegroom became party to the discussions. But the wealth and social standing of the bride and the bridegroom were not the only things considered when parents arranged a marriage. By the fifteenth century, it was not unusual for the two involved people to have known each other in advance and even to have had some prior relationship. Also, emotional feeling for one another was increasingly respected by parents. Parents did not force total strangers to live together, and children had a legal right to protest and resist an unwanted marriage. A forced marriage was by definition invalid, and parents understood that unwanted marriages could fail. The best marriage was one desired by both parties and supported by their families.

FAMILY SIZE

The western European family was conjugal, or nuclear; that is, it consisted of a father and a mother and two to four children who survived into adulthood. This nuclear family lived with a larger household, consisting of in-laws, servants, laborers, and boarders. The average husband and wife had seven or eight children—a birth about every two years. Of these, however, an estimated one-third died by age

The Subservient Husband *by Hans Schaufelein. In the sixteenth century, the husband who failed to rule his wife properly was thought to risk creating a shrew who would assume authority in the marriage. Note that in this woodcut the woman has the pocketbook and keys around her waist, for she has become the master of the house. Her husband has been forced to do "woman's work," which was considered a sure sign of a house no longer in order.* From Max Geisberg, *The German Single-Leaf Woodcut, 1500–1550*, edited by Walter L. Strauss. Hacker Art Books, 1974. Used by permission of Hacker Art Books, Inc.

five, and one-half by their teens. Rare is the family, at any social level, that did not experience infant mortality and child death.

BIRTH CONTROL

Artificial birth control has existed since antiquity. The ancient Egyptians used alligator dung and other acidic sperm killers, and sponges were also popular. In the West, the church's condemnation of coitus interruptus (male withdrawal before ejaculation) during the thirteenth and fourteenth centuries suggests that a contraceptive mentality—that is, a conscious and regular effort at birth control—may have been developing at this time. But early birth control measures, when applied, were not very effective, and for both historical and moral reasons the church firmly opposed them. During the eleventh century it suppressed an extreme ascetic sect, the Cathars, whom it accused of practicing birth control. The church also opposed (and still opposes) contraception on moral grounds. According to Saint Thomas

Table Manners

Pleasure at table in the sixteenth century was considered a matter of self-control. The well-dressed table taught the lessons of life as well as offered its bread. Neatness and order showed respect, respect ensured attentiveness, and attentiveness made for learning. The union of pleasure and discipline at mealtime was believed to inculcate in the young the traits that would keep them free and safe in an unforgiving world. Here is how Hans Sachs, a sixteenth-century father, expected children to behave:

Listen you children who are going to table.
Wash your hands and cut your nails.
Do not sit at the head of the table;
This is reserved for the father of the house.
Do not commence eating until a blessing has been
    said.
Dine in God's name
And permit the eldest to begin first.
Proceed in a disciplined manner.
Do not snort or smack like a pig.
Do not reach violently for bread,
Lest you may knock over a glass.
Do not cut bread on your chest,
Or conceal pieces of bread or pastry under your
    hands.
Do not tear pieces for your plate with your teeth.
Do not stir food around on your plate
Or linger over it.
Do not fill your spoon too full.
Rushing through your meal is bad manners.
Do not reach for more food
While your mouth is still full,
Nor talk with your mouth full.
Be moderate; do not fall upon your plate like an
    animal.
Be the last to cut your meat and break your fish.
Chew your food with your mouth closed.
Do not lick the corners of your mouth like a dog.
Do not hover greedily over your food.
Wipe your mouth before you drink,
So that you do not grease up your wine.
Drink politely and avoid coughing into your cup.
Do not belch or cry out.
With drink be most prudent.
Sit smartly, undisturbed, humble. . .
Do not stare at a person
    As if you were watching him eat.
Do not elbow the person sitting next to you.

Sit up straight; be a model of gracefulness.
Do not rock back and forth on the bench,
Lest you let loose a stink.
Do not kick your feet under the table.
Guard yourself against all shameful
Words, gossip, ridicule, and laughter. . .
If sexual play occurs at table,
Pretend you do not see it.
Never start a quarrel,
Quarreling at table is most despicable.
Say nothing that might offend another.
Do not blow your nose
Or do other shocking things.
Do not pick your nose.
If you must pick your teeth, be discreet about it.
Never scratch your head
(This goes for girls and women too);
Or fish out lice.
Let no one wipe his mouth on the table cloth,
Or lay his head in his hands.
Do not lean back against the wall
Until the meal is finished.
Silently praise and thank God
For the food he has graciously provided. . . .

■ *How do table manners prepare a child for life?*
Has table etiquette changed since the sixteenth
century?

Translation by S. Ozment, from S. Ozment, *When Fathers Ruled: Family Life in Reformation Europe* (Harvard University Press, Cambridge, MA, 1983), 142–43.

A Family Meal. In Max Geisberg, *The German Single-Leaf Woodcuts*, III: *1500–1550*, rev. and ed. by W. L. Strauss (New York, Hacker Art Books, 1974).

Aquinas, a moral act must always aid and abet, never frustrate, the natural end of the being or thing in question, and he believed the natural end of sex could be only the birth of children and their godly rearing within the bounds of holy matrimony and the community of the church.

WET NURSING

The church allied with the physicians of early modern Europe on another intimate family matter: the condemnation of women who hired nurses to suckle their newborn children, sometimes for as long as a year and a half. The practice was popular among upper-class women, who looked on it as a symbol of their high rank. Wet nurses were women who had recently had a baby or were suckling a child of their own, and who, for a fee, agreed also to suckle another child. The practice appears to have increased the risk of infant mortality, exposing infants to a strange and shared milk supply from women who were usually not as healthy as the infants' own mothers and who often lived under less sanitary conditions. But nursing an infant was a chore some upper-class women found distasteful, and their husbands also preferred that they not do it. Among women, vanity and convenience appear to have been motives for turning to wet nurses. For husbands, more was at stake in the practice. Because the church forbade sexual intercourse while a women was lactating, and sexual intercourse was also believed to spoil a lactating woman's milk (pregnancy, of course, eventually ended her milk supply), a nursing wife often became a reluctant lover. In addition, nursing had a contraceptive effect (about 75 percent effective). Some women prolonged nursing their children precisely to delay a new pregnancy, and some husbands understood and cooperated in this form of family planning. For other husbands, however, especially noblemen and royalty who desired an abundance of male heirs, nursing seemed to rob them of offspring and to jeopardize the patrimony—hence their support of wet nursing.

LOVING FAMILIES?

The traditional western European family had features that may seem cold and unloving. When children were between the ages of eight and thirteen, parents routinely sent them out of their homes into apprenticeships, off to school, or into employment in the homes and businesses of relatives, friends, and even strangers. In addition, the emotional ties between spouses seem to have been as tenuous as those between parents and children. Widowers and widows often married again within a few months of their spouses' deaths, and marriages with extreme disparity in age between partners also suggest limited affection.

In response to modern-day criticism, an early modern parent would surely have asked, "What greater love can parents have for their children than to equip them to make their way vocationally in the world?" An apprenticed child was a self-supporting child, and hence a child with a future. Considering primitive living conditions, contemporaries could also appreciate the purely utilitarian and humane side of marriage and understand when widowers and widows quickly married again. Marriages with extreme disparity in age, however, were no more the norm in early modern Europe than the practice of wet nursing, and they received just as much criticism and ridicule. (See "A Sixteenth-Century Father Describes His One-Year-Old Son.")

Literary Imagination in Transition

Alongside the political and cultural changes brought about by the new religious systems of the Reformation (Lutheranism, Calvinism, and Puritanism) and Catholic reform, medieval outlooks and religious values continued into the seventeenth century. Major literary figures of the post-Reformation period had elements of both the old and the new in their own new transitional works. Two who stand out are Miguel de Cervantes Saavedra (1547–1616), writing in still deeply Catholic Spain, and William Shakespeare (1564–1616), who wrote in newly Anglican England.

MIGUEL DE CERVANTES SAAVEDRA: REJECTION OF IDEALISM

Spanish literature of the sixteenth and seventeenth centuries reflects the peculiar religious and political history of Spain in this period. Traditional Catholic teaching was a major influence on all aspects of Spanish life. Since the joint reign of Ferdinand and Isabella (1479–1504), the church had received the unqualified support of the reigning political power. Although there was religious reform in Spain, and genuine Protestant groups were persecuted for "Lutheranism," a Protestant Reformation never occurred there, thanks largely to the entrenched power of the church and the Inquisition.

A second influence on Spanish literature was the aggressive piety of Spanish rulers. Their intertwining of Catholic piety and political power underlay

A SIXTEENTH-CENTURY FATHER DESCRIBES HIS ONE-YEAR-OLD SON

On the occasion of his son's first birthday, April 19, 1533, Christoph Scheurl, Nuremberg jurist and diplomat, wrote the following description of his eldest child, Georg. Thereafter on each boy's birthday, he described the salient features of his development, leaving a rare clinical record of sixteenth-century parenting and childhood.

■ *What conclusions may we draw from such a description? Is it a fair portrayal of parent-child relations in the past? What concerns the father most? Might the fact that the father was fifty-two, and Georg his first surviving son, intensify the loving tone? Is the description in any way surprising for the times?*

This Sunday, April 19, my dear son Georg is one year old. So far, he is hearty, and apart from an episode of colic has remained healthy. Presently, only his teeth, of which there are five and a half (the upper front two being great shovels) have caused him to run a temperature. [The milk of] his wet nurse has agreed with him throughout the year, and his physical growth and development have been good. He has a large, strong head, likes to laugh, and is a happy, high-spirited child. He can say "ka, ka" [meaning "da, da"] extend his little hand to Father, and point to birds in the bird house on the window. He also likes to go out into the open air. When he sees Father washing his hands, he must wash his too and splash about in the sink. He also takes after his father in liking horses.

There are about ten warts on his body, which our neighbor says is a sign of long life, as is also the soft spot that can still be felt on his head and is the size of a Mark. He is a fast eater and drinker. By no means will he sit or otherwise remain still in his chair, but he bends over double, as he struggles against it. Otherwise, he does not whine, nor is he willful. He freely allows the nurse to suckle him and points out the chair to her [when he is hungry]. He loves her very much, as she does him. And he goes happily to Father and loves him too. Moreover, he is Father's every joy, delight, and treasure . . .

Father will say to him: "Georg, be a bad one," and he then wrinkles up his nose and sneers. If Father coughs, he coughs too; and he can sit only beside Father. He can understand and duplicate an action [once it has been shown him]. In sum, Georg Scheurl, by his bearing, gestures, and role playing, presents himself at one year as a plucky, resolute child. He is learning to use his hands now and really likes to go through books, letters, and papers; he throws up his arms and shrieks with joy.

Reprinted from Steven Ozment, *Flesh & Spirit: Family Life in Early Modern Germany* (New York: Penguin, 1999), pp. 98–99.

a third influence: preoccupation with medieval chivalric virtues, in particular, questions of honor and loyalty. The novels and plays of the period almost invariably focus on a special test of character, bordering on the heroic, that threatens honor and reputation. In this regard, Spanish literature remained more Catholic and medieval than that of England and France, where major Protestant movements had occurred. Two of the most important Spanish writers of this period became priests (Lope de Vega and Pedro Calderón de la Barca). The one generally acknowledged to be the greatest Spanish writer of all time, Cervantes, was preoccupied in his work with the strengths and weaknesses of traditional religious idealism.

Cervantes (1547–1616) had only a smattering of formal education. He educated himself by wide reading in popular literature and immersion in the "school of life." As a young man, he worked in Rome for a Spanish cardinal. As a soldier, he was decorated for gallantry in the Battle of Lepanto (1571). He also spent five years as a slave in Algiers after his ship was pirated in 1575. Later, while working as a tax collector, he was imprisoned several times for padding his accounts, and it was in prison that he began, in 1603, to write his most famous work, *Don Quixote*.

The first part of *Don Quixote* appeared in 1605. The intent of this work seems to have been to satirize the chivalric romances then popular in Spain.

But Cervantes could not conceal his deep affection for the character he created as an object of ridicule. The work is satire only on the surface and has remained as much an object of study by philosophers and theologians as by students of Spanish literature. Cervantes presented Don Quixote as a none-too-stable middle-aged man. Driven mad by reading too many chivalric romances, he had come to believe he was an aspiring knight who had to prove his worthiness by brave deeds. To this end, he donned a rusty suit of armor and chose for his inspiration a quite unworthy peasant girl (Dulcinea), whom he fancied to be a noble lady to whom he could, with honor, dedicate his life.

Don Quixote's foil—Sancho Panza, a clever, worldly wise peasant who serves as Quixote's squire—watches with bemused skepticism as his lord does battle with a windmill (which he has mistaken for a dragon) and repeatedly makes a fool of himself as he gallops across the countryside. The story ends tragically with Don Quixote's humiliating defeat by a well-meaning friend who, disguised as a knight, bests Quixote in combat and forces him to renounce his quest for knighthood. The humiliated Don Quixote does not, however, come to his senses as a result. He returns sadly to his village to die a shamed and brokenhearted old man.

Throughout the novel, Cervantes juxtaposes the down-to-earth realism of Sancho Panza with the old-fashioned religious idealism of Don Quixote. The reader perceives that Cervantes admired the one as much as the other and meant to portray both as representing attitudes necessary for a happy life.

WILLIAM SHAKESPEARE: DRAMATIST OF THE AGE

There is much less factual knowledge about Shakespeare (1564–1616) than we would expect of the greatest playwright in the English language. He married at the early age of eighteen, in 1582, and he and his wife, Anne Hathaway, were the parents of three children (including twins) by 1585. He apparently worked as a schoolteacher for a time and in this capacity gained his broad knowledge of Renaissance learning and literature. His own reading and enthusiasm for the learning of his day are manifest in the many literary allusions that appear in his plays.

Shakespeare lived the life of a country gentleman. There is none of the Puritan distress over worldliness in his work. He took the new commercialism and the bawdy pleasures of the Elizabethan Age in stride and with amusement. He was a radical neither in politics nor religion. The few allusions in his works to the Puritans seem more critical than complimentary.

That Shakespeare was interested in politics is apparent from his historical plays and the references to contemporary political events that fill all his plays. He viewed government through the character of the individual ruler, whether Richard III or Elizabeth Tudor, not in terms of ideal systems or social goals. By modern standards, he was a political conservative, accepting the social rankings and the power structure of his day and demonstrating unquestioned patriotism.

Shakespeare knew the theater as one who participated in every phase of its life—as a playwright, an actor, and part owner of a theater. He was a member and principal writer of a famous company of actors known as the King's Men. Between 1590 and 1610, many of his plays were performed at court, where he moved with comfort and received both Queen Elizabeth's and King James's enthusiastic patronage.

Elizabethan drama was already a distinctive form when Shakespeare began writing. Unlike French drama of the seventeenth century, which was dominated by classical models, English drama developed in the sixteenth and seventeenth centuries as a blending of many forms: classical comedies and tragedies, medieval morality plays, and contemporary Italian short stories.

Two contemporaries, Thomas Kyd and Christopher Marlowe, influenced Shakespeare's tragedies. Kyd (1558–1594) wrote the first dramatic version of *Hamlet*. The tragedies of Marlowe (1564–1593) set a model for character, poetry, and style that only Shakespeare among the English playwrights of the period surpassed. Shakespeare synthesized the best past and current achievements. A keen student of human motivation and passion, he had a unique talent for getting into people's minds.

Shakespeare wrote histories, comedies, and tragedies. *Richard III* (1593), a very early play, stands out among the histories, although the picture it presents of Richard as an unprincipled villain is viewed by some scholars as "Tudor propaganda." Shakespeare's comedies, although not attaining the heights of his tragedies, surpass his history plays in originality.

Shakespeare's tragedies are considered his unique achievement. Four of these were written within a three-year period: *Hamlet* (1603), *Othello* (1604), *King Lear* (1605), and *Macbeth* (1606). The most original of the tragedies, *Romeo and Juliet* (1597), transformed an old popular story into a moving drama of "star-cross'd lovers." Both Romeo and Juliet, denied a marriage by their warring families, die tragic deaths. Romeo, believing Juliet to be dead when she has merely taken a sleeping potion, poisons himself. When Juliet awakes to find Romeo dead, she kills herself with his dagger.

Shakespeare's works struck universal human themes, many of which were deeply rooted in contemporary religious traditions. His plays were immensely popular with both the playgoers and the play readers of Elizabethan England. Still today, the works of no other dramatist from his age are performed in theaters or on film more regularly than his.

IN PERSPECTIVE

During the early Middle Ages, Christendom had been divided into Western and Eastern churches with irreconcilable theological differences. When, in 1517, Martin Luther posted ninety-five theses questioning the selling of indulgences and the traditional sacrament of penance that lay behind them, he created a division within Western Christendom itself—an internal division between Protestants and Catholics.

The Lutheran protest came at a time of political and social discontent with the church. Not only princes and magistrates, but many ordinary people as well, resented traditional clerical rights and privileges. In many instances the clergy were exempted from secular laws and taxes while remaining powerful landowners whose personal lifestyles were not all that different from those of the laity. Spiritual and secular protest combined to make the Protestant Reformation a successful assault on the old church. In town after town and region after region within Protestant lands, the major institutions and practices of traditional piety were significantly transformed.

It soon became clear, however, that the division would not stop with the Lutherans. Making Scripture the only arbiter in religion had opened a Pandora's box. People proved to have very different ideas about what Scripture taught. Indeed, there seemed to be as many points of view as there were readers. Rapidly, the Reformation created Lutheran, Zwinglian, Anabaptist, Spiritualist, Calvinist, and Anglican versions of biblical religion—a splintering of Protestantism that has endured until today.

Catholics had been pursuing reform before the Reformation broke out in Germany, although

without papal enthusiasm and certainly not along clear Protestant lines. When major reforms finally came in the Catholic Church around the mid–sixteenth century, they were doctrinally reactionary, but administratively and spiritually flexible. The church enforced strict obedience and conformity to its teaching, but it also provided the laity with a better educated and disciplined clergy. For laity who wanted a deeper and more individual piety, experimentation with proven spiritual practices was now permitted. By century's end, such measures had successfully countered, and in some areas even spectacularly reversed, Protestant gains.

After the Reformation, pluralism steadily became a fact of Western religious life. It did so at first only by sheer force, since no one religious body was then prepared to concede the validity of alternative Christian beliefs and practices. During the sixteenth and seventeenth centuries, only those groups that fought doggedly for their faith gained the right to practice it freely. Despite these struggles, religious pluralism endured. Never again would there be only a Catholic Christian Church in Europe.

REVIEW QUESTIONS

1. What were the main problems of the church that contributed to the Protestant Reformation? Why was the church unable to suppress dissent as it had earlier?

2. What were the basic similarities and differences between the ideas of Luther and Zwingli? Between Luther and Calvin? Did the differences tend to split the Protestant ranks and thereby lessen the effectiveness of the movement?

3. Why did the Reformation begin in Germany? What political factors contributed to the success of the Reformation there as opposed to France or Italy?

4. What was the Catholic Reformation, and what principal decisions and changes were instituted by the Council of Trent? Was the Protestant Reformation a healthy movement for the Catholic Church?

5. Why did Henry VIII finally break with the Catholic Church? Was the "new" religion he established really Protestant? What problems did his successors face as a result of Henry's move?

6. What impact did the Reformation have on women in the sixteenth and seventeenth

centuries? What new factors and pressures affected relations between men and women, family size, and child care during this period?

SUGGESTED READINGS

H. BLOOM, *Shakespeare: The Invention of the Human* (1998). A modern master's complete analysis of the greatest writer in the English language.

T. A. BRADY, JR. ED., *Handbook of European History: Late Middle Ages, Renaissance, Reformation* (1995). Essays summarizing recent research on aspects of the Reformation.

G. DONALDSON, *The Scottish Reformation* (1960). Dependable, comprehensive narrative.

E. DUFFY, *The Stripping of the Altars: Traditional Religion in England, 1400–1580* (1992). Strongest of recent arguments that popular piety survived the Reformation in England.

M. DURAN, *Cervantes* (1974). Detailed biography.

H. O. EVENNETT, *The Spirit of the Counter Reformation* (1968). Essay on the continuity of Catholic reform and its independence from the Protestant Reformation.

B. S. GREGORY, *Salvation at Stake: Christian Martyrdom in Early Modern Europe* (1999). Massive, can't-put-down study covering a wide spectrum.

R. HOULBROOKE, *English Family Life, 1450–1716. An Anthology from Diaries* (1988). A rich collection of documents illustrating family relationships.

J. C. HUTCHISON, *Albrecht Dürer: A Biography* (1990). An art historian chronicles both the life and work of the artist.

H. JEDIN, *A History of the Council of Trent*, vols. 1 and 2 (1957–1961). Comprehensive, detailed, and authoritative.

P. JOHNSTON AND R. W. SCRIBNER, *The Reformation in Germany and Switzerland* (1993). Reformation from the bottom up.

A. MACFARLANE, *The Family Life of Ralph Josselin: A Seventeenth Century Clergyman* (1970). A model study of Puritan family life!

S. MARSHALL (ED.), *Women in Reformation and Counter Reformation Europe: Private and Public Worlds* (1989). Lucid and authoritative presentations.

H. A. OBERMAN, *Luther: Man between God and the Devil* (1989). Perhaps the best account of Luther's life, by a Dutch master.

J. O'MALLEY, *The First Jesuits* (1993). Extremely detailed account of the creation of the Society of Jesus and its original purposes.

S. OZMENT, *The Age of Reform, 1250–1550: An Intellectual and Religious History of Late Medieval and Reformation Europe* (1980). A broad survey of major religious ideas and beliefs.

S. OZMENT, *Flesh and Spirit: Private Life in Early Modern Germany* (1999). Family life from courtship and marriage to the sending of a new generation into the world.

J. G. RIDLEY, *Thomas Cranmer* (1962). The basic biography.

B. ROBERTS, *Through the Keyhole: Dutch Child-Rearing Practices in the 17th and 18th Centuries* (1998). A study of three elite families.

Q. SKINNER, *The Foundations of Modern Political Thought II: The Age of Reformation* (1978). A comprehensive survey that treats every political thinker and tract.

D. STARKEY, *Elizabeth: The Struggle for the Throne* (2000).

D. STARKEY, *The Reign of Henry VIII* (1985). Portrayal of the king as in control of neither his life nor his court.

L. STONE, *The Family, Sex and Marriage in England 1500–1800* (1977). Controversial but enduring in many respects.

G. STRAUSS (ED. AND TRANS.), *Manifestations of Discontent in Germany on the Eve of the Reformation* (1971). Rich collection of sources of both rural and urban scenes.

M. TREU, *Katherine von Bora* (1995). Short biography of Martin Luther's wife.

F. WENDEL, *Calvin: The Origins and Development of His Religious Thought*, trans. by P. Mairet (1963). The best treatment of Calvin's theology.

G. H. WILLIAMS, *The Radical Reformation* (1962). Broad survey of the varieties of dissent within Protestantism.

J. WITTE, JR., *From Sacrament to Contract: Marriage, Religion and Law in the Western Tradition* (1997). Five major legal-religious systems elucidated and compared.

H. WUNDER, *He Is the Sun, She Is the Moon: A History of Women in Early Modern Germany* (1998). A model of gender history.

DOCUMENTS CD-ROM

CHURCH AND STATE IN THE HIGH MIDDLE AGES

THE REFORMATION

Lucas Cranach's Portrait of
Martin Luther and Katherine von Bora

On June 13, 1525, Martin Luther, aged forty-two, married the renegade nun Katherine von Bora, aged twenty-six. According to Luther, it was not a marriage of love, but one he entered out of obedience to his father, who had wanted him to marry, and in support of the Reformation's rejection of clerical celibacy as unnatural and unbiblical. Luther, however, had been instrumental in bringing Katherine to Wittenberg, where he was residing, from a Cistercian cloister in Saxony, where her noble but poor family had placed her as a nun.

Katherine arrived in Wittenberg on April 7, 1523, and settled into the household of Lucas Cranach (1472–1553). Cranach was Germany's most famous painter after Albrecht Dürer (d. 1528) and a friend of Luther, who, in 1520, stood as godfather to Cranach's son.

Between Katherine's arrival and their marriage, Luther attempted to find her a husband. That none of the candidates proved successful may not have been accidental. Catholic propaganda accused him of having a premarital relationship with Katherine.

After the two were married, they moved into a former monastery and filled it with students, visitors, and six children of their own. Katherine remodeled the building to accommodate up to thirty guests. She also expanded its garden, earning a reputation as an herbalist, and repaired its brewery, making a beer that was served at the court of the ruler of Saxony. Luther acknowledged her skills by referring to her as "Mr. Kathy." In further recognition of their power-sharing, he declined in his will to appoint the customary male guardian to help her oversee his estate. She would manage his modest property after his death as she had done during his lifetime.

Perhaps as early as 1526, Cranach painted the two in a "pair portrait." In it, he apparently spliced two separate paintings, one portraying Luther in his academic gown, the other Katherine in her finest dress. This portrait was also a propaganda piece popularizing the marriage of the leader of the Reformation with a renegade nun in defiance of church rules, and doing so with strong, attractive images of them both.[5]

■ *Why did Luther put unusual trust in his wife? Why is Cranach's wedding portrait of Luther and von Bora an example of propaganda for the Reformation?*

[5] E. G. Schwiebert, *Luther and His Times* (St. Louis, MO, Concordia, 1950), pp. 226–227, 266–268, 581–602; Steven Ozment, *Protestants: The Birth of a Revolution* (New York: Doubleday, 1992), pp. 17, 154, 159–162.

Martin Luther and Katherine von Bora, *ca. 1526/29, by Lucas Cranach.* Gemalde von Lucas Cranach d.A., 1529. Oil painting on book wood, 36 × 23 cm. Darmstadt, Hessisches Landesmuseum. Bildarchiv Preussisches Kulturbesitz.

The massacre of worshiping Protestants at Vassy, France (March 1, 1562), which began the French wars of religion. An engraving by an unidentified seventeenth-century artist. The Granger Collection

CHAPTER 12

THE AGE OF RELIGIOUS WARS

*T*HE LATE SIXTEENTH CENTURY AND *the first half of the seventeenth century are described as the Age of Religious Wars because of the bloody opposition of Protestants and Catholics across Europe. Both genuine religious conflict and bitter dynastic rivalries fueled the wars. In France, the Netherlands, England, and Scotland in the second half of the sixteenth century, Calvinists fought Catholic rulers for the right to govern their own territories and to practice their chosen religion openly. In the first half of the seventeenth century, Lutherans, Calvinists, and Catholics marched against one another in central and northern Europe during the Thirty Years' War. By the middle of the seventeenth century, English Puritans had successfully revolted against the Stuart monarchy and the Anglican Church.*

Renewed Religious Struggle

The French Wars of Religion (1562–1598)

Imperial Spain and the Reign of Philip II (r. 1556–1598)

England and Spain (1553–1603)

The Thirty Years' War (1618–1648)

In Perspective

KEY TOPICS

- The war between Calvinists and Catholics in France
- The Spanish occupation of the Netherlands
- The struggle for supremacy between England and Spain
- The devastation of central Europe during the Thirty Years' War

Renewed Religious Struggle

During the first half of the sixteenth century, religious conflict had been confined to central Europe and was primarily a struggle by Lutherans to secure rights and freedoms for themselves. In the second half of the sixteenth century, the focus shifted to western Europe—to France, the Netherlands, England, and Scotland—and became a struggle by Calvinists for recognition. After the Peace of Augsburg (1555) and, with it, acceptance of the principle that a region's ruler would determine its religion (*cuius regio, eius religio*), Lutheranism became a legal religion in the Holy Roman Empire. The Peace of Augsburg did not, however, extend recognition to non-Lutheran Protestants. Both Catholics and Lutherans scorned Anabaptists and other sectarians as anarchists, and Calvinists were not yet strong enough to demand legal standing.

Outside the empire, the struggle for Protestant religious rights had intensified in most countries by the mid–sixteenth century. After the Council of Trent adjourned in 1563, Catholics began a Jesuit-led international counteroffensive against Protestants. At the time of John Calvin's death in 1564, Geneva had become both a refuge for Europe's persecuted Protestants and an international school for Protestant resistance, producing leaders fully equal to the new Catholic challenge.

Genevan Calvinism and Catholicism as revived by the Council of Trent were two equally dogmatic, aggressive, and irreconcilable church systems. Calvinists may have looked like "new papists" to critics when they dominated cities like Geneva. Yet when, as minorities, they found their civil and religious rights denied, they became true firebrands and revolutionaries. Calvinism adopted a presbyterian organization that magnified regional and local religious authority. Boards of presbyters, or elders, representing the many individual congregations of Calvinists, directly shaped the policy of the church at large.

By contrast, the **Counter-Reformation** sponsored a centralized episcopal church system, hierarchically arranged from pope to parish priest, that stressed absolute obedience to the person at the top. The high clergy—the pope and his bishops—not the synods of local churches, ruled supreme. Calvinism proved attractive to proponents of political decentralization who opposed totalitarian rulers, whereas Catholicism remained congenial to proponents of absolute monarchy determined to maintain, in the words of Louis XIV, "one king, one law, one faith."

The opposition between the two religions can be seen even in the art and architecture that each came to embrace. The Catholic Counter-Reformation found the baroque style congenial. A successor to mannerism, **baroque** art is a grandiose, three-dimensional display of life and energy. Great baroque artists like Peter Paul Rubens (1571–1640) and Gianlorenzo Bernini (1598–1680) were Catholics. Protestants by contrast opted for a simpler and more restrained art and architecture, as can be seen in the English churches of Christopher Wren (1632–1723) and the gentle, searching portraits of the Dutch Mennonite, Rembrandt van Rijn (1606–1669).

As religious wars engulfed Europe, the intellectuals perceived the wisdom of religious pluralism and toleration more quickly than did the politicians. A new skepticism, relativism, and individualism in religion became respectable in the sixteenth and seventeenth centuries. (See Chapter 14.) Sebastian Castellio's (1515–1563) pithy censure of John Calvin for his role in the execution of the anti-Trinitarian Michael Servetus summarized a growing sentiment: "To kill a man is not to defend a doctrine, but to kill a man."[1] The French essayist Michel de Montaigne (1533–1592) asked in scorn of the dogmatic mind, "What do I know?" And the Lutheran Valentin Weigel (1533–1588), surveying a half century of religious strife in Germany, advised people to look within themselves for religious truth and no longer to churches and creeds.

Such skeptical views gained currency in larger political circles only at the cost of painful experience. Religious strife and civil war were best held in check where rulers tended to subordinate theological doctrine to political unity, urging tolerance, moderation, and compromise—even indifference—in religious matters. Rulers of this kind came to be known as ***politiques***, and the most successful among them was Elizabeth I of England. By contrast, such rulers as Mary I of England, Philip II of Spain, and Oliver Cromwell, who took their religion with the utmost seriousness and refused every compromise, did not in the long run achieve their political goals.

---

[1]*Contra libellum Calvini* (N.P., 1562), p. E2a.

As we shall see, the wars of religion were both internal national conflicts and truly international wars. Catholic and Protestant subjects struggled against one another for control of the crown of France, the Netherlands, and England. The Catholic governments of France and Spain conspired and finally sent armies against Protestant regimes in England and the Netherlands. The outbreak of the Thirty Years' War in 1618 made the international dimension of the religious conflict especially clear; before it ended in 1648, the war drew every major European nation directly or indirectly into its deadly net.

The French Wars of Religion (1562–1598)

ANTI-PROTESTANT MEASURES AND THE STRUGGLE FOR POLITICAL POWER

French Protestants are known as **Huguenots,** a term derived from Besançon Hugues, the leader of Geneva's political revolt against the House of Savoy in the 1520s, a prelude to that city's Calvinist Reformation. Huguenots were under surveillance in France already in the early 1520s when Lutheran writings and doctrines began to circulate in Paris. The capture of the French king Francis I by the forces of Emperor Charles V at the Battle of Pavia in 1525 provided a motive for the first wave of Protestant persecution in France. The French government hoped thereby to pacify their Habsburg conqueror, a fierce opponent of German Protestants, and to win their king's swift release.

A second major crackdown came a decade later. When Protestants plastered Paris and other cities with anti-Catholic placards on October 18, 1534, mass arrests of suspected Protestants followed. The government retaliation drove John Calvin and other members of the French reform party into exile. In 1540, the Edict of Fontainebleau subjected French Protestants to the Inquisition. Henry II (r. 1547–1559) established new measures against Protestants in the Edict of Chateaubriand in 1551. Save for a few brief interludes, the French monarchy remained a staunch foe of the Protestants until the ascension to the throne of Henry of Navarre in 1589.

The Habsburg-Valois wars (see Chapter 11) had ended with the Treaty of Cateau-Cambrésis in 1559, after which Europe experienced a moment of peace. But the same year marked the beginning of internal French conflict and a shift of the European balance of power away from France to Spain. The shift began with an accident. During a tournament held to celebrate the marriage of his thirteen-year-old daughter to Philip II, the son of Charles V and heir to the Spanish Habsburg lands, the French king,

Henry II, was mortally wounded when a lance pierced his visor. This unforeseen event brought to the throne his sickly fifteen-year-old son, Francis II, under the regency of the queen mother, Catherine de Médicis. With the monarchy so weakened by Henry's death, three powerful families saw their chance to control France and began to compete for the young king's ear: the Bourbons, whose power lay in the south and west; the Montmorency-Chatillons, who controlled the center of France; and the Guises, who were dominant in eastern France.

The Guises were by far the strongest and had little trouble establishing firm control over the young king. Francis, duke of Guise, had been Henry II's general, and his brothers, Charles and Louis, were cardinals of the church. Mary Stuart, Queen of Scots and wife of Francis II, was their niece. Throughout the latter half of the sixteenth century, the name "Guise" remained interchangeable with militant, reactionary Catholicism.

The Bourbon and Montmorency-Chatillon families, in contrast, developed strong Huguenot sympathies, largely for political reasons. The Bourbon Louis I, prince of Condé (d. 1569), and the Montmorency-Chatillon admiral Gaspard de Coligny (1519–1572) became the political leaders of the French Protestant resistance. They collaborated early in an abortive plot to kidnap Francis II from his Guise advisers in the Conspiracy of Amboise in 1560. This conspiracy was strongly condemned by John Calvin, who considered such tactics a disgrace to the Reformation.

APPEAL OF CALVINISM

Often for quite different reasons, ambitious aristocrats and discontented townspeople joined Calvinist churches in opposition to the Guise-dominated French monarchy. In 1561, more than 2,000 Huguenot congregations existed throughout France. Yet Huguenots were a majority of the population in only two regions: Dauphiné and Languedoc. Although they made up only about one-fifteenth of the population, Huguenots were in important geographic areas and were heavily represented among the more powerful segments of French society. More than two-fifths of the French aristocracy became Huguenots. Many apparently hoped to establish within France a principle of territorial sovereignty akin to that secured within the Holy Roman Empire by the Peace of Augsburg. In this way, Calvinism indirectly served the forces of political decentralization.

John Calvin and Theodore Beza consciously sought to advance their cause by currying favor with powerful aristocrats. Beza converted Jeanne d'Albert, the mother of the future Henry IV. The prince of Condé was apparently converted in 1558

Catherine de Médicis (1519–1589) exercised power in France during the reigns of her three sons Francis II (r. 1559–1560), Charles IX (r. 1560–1574), and Henry III (r. 1574–1589). Liaison Agency, Inc.

under the influence of his Calvinist wife. For many aristocrats—Condé probably among them—Calvinist religious convictions were attractive primarily as aids to long-sought political goals.

The military organization of Condé and Coligny progressively merged with the religious organization of the French Huguenot churches, creating a potent combination that benefited both political and religious dissidents. Calvinism gave political resistance justification and inspiration, and the forces of political resistance made Calvinism a viable religious alternative in Catholic France. Each side had much to gain from the other. The confluence of secular and religious motives, although beneficial to aristocratic resistance and the Calvinist religion alike, tended to cast suspicion on the religious appeal of Calvinism. Clearly, religious conviction was neither the only nor always the main reason for becoming a Calvinist in France in the second half of the sixteenth century.

CATHERINE DE MÉDICIS AND THE GUISES

Following Francis II's death in 1560, Catherine de Médicis continued as regent for her minor son, Charles IX (r. 1560–1574). At a colloquy in Poissy,

she tried unsuccessfully to reconcile the Protestant and Catholic factions. Fearing the power and guile of the Guises, Catherine, whose first concern was always to preserve the monarchy, sought allies among the Protestants. In 1562, after conversations with Beza and Coligny, she issued the January Edict, a measure that granted Protestants freedom to worship publicly outside towns—although only privately within them—and to hold synods. In March, this royal toleration came to an abrupt end when the duke of Guise surprised a Protestant congregation at Vassy in Champagne and proceeded to massacre several scores of worshipers. That event marked the beginning of the French wars of religion (March 1562).

Had Condé and the Huguenot armies rushed immediately to the queen's side after this attack, Protestants might well have secured an alliance with the crown. The queen mother's fear of Guise power was great at this time. But the hesitation of the Protestant leaders, due primarily to indecision on the part of Condé, placed the young king and the queen mother, against their deepest wishes, in firm Guise control. Cooperation with the Guises became the only alternative to capitulation to the Protestants.

The Peace of Saint-Germain-en-Laye During the first French war of religion, fought between April 1562 and March 1563, the duke of Guise was assassinated. It is a measure of the international character of the struggle in France that troops from Hesse and the palatinate fought alongside the Huguenots. A brief resumption of hostilities in 1567–1568 was followed by the bloodiest of all the conflicts, between September 1568 and August 1570. In this period, Condé was killed and Huguenot leadership passed to Coligny. This was actually a blessing in disguise for the Protestants, because Coligny was far the better military strategist. In the peace of Saint-Germain-en-Laye (1570), which ended the third war, the crown, acknowledging the power of the Protestant nobility, granted the Huguenots religious freedoms within their territories and the right to fortify their cities.

Perpetually caught between fanatical Huguenot and Guise extremes, Queen Catherine had always sought to balance one side against the other. Like the Guises, she wanted a Catholic France; she did not, however, desire a Guise-dominated monarchy. After the Peace of Saint-Germain-en-Laye the crown tilted manifestly toward the Bourbon faction and the Huguenots, and Coligny became Charles IX's most trusted adviser. Unknown to the king, Catherine began to plot with the Guises against the ascendant Protestants. As she had earlier sought Protestant support when Guise power threatened to subdue the monarchy, she now sought Guise support as Protestant influence grew.

There was reason for Catherine to fear Coligny's hold on the king. Louis of Nassau, the leader of Protestant resistance to Philip II in the Netherlands, had gained Coligny's ear. Coligny used his position of influence to win the king of France over to a planned French invasion of the Netherlands in support of the Dutch Protestants. Such a course of action would have placed France squarely on a collision course with mighty Spain. Catherine recognized far better than her son that France stood little chance in such a contest. She and her advisers had been much sobered in this regard by news of the stunning Spanish victory over the Turks at Lepanto in October 1571 (discussed later).

The Saint Bartholomew's Day Massacre When Catherine lent her support to the infamous Saint Bartholomew's Day Massacre of Protestants, she did so out of a far less reasoned judgment. Her decision appears to have been made in a state of near panic. On August 22, 1572, four days after the Huguenot Henry of Navarre had married the king's sister, Marguerite of Valois—still another sign of growing Protestant power—Coligny was struck down, although not killed, by an assassin's bullet. Catherine had apparently been party to this Guise plot to eliminate Coligny. After its failure, she feared both the king's reaction to her complicity with the Guises and the Huguenot response under a recovered Coligny. Catherine convinced Charles that a Huguenot coup was afoot, inspired by Coligny, and that only the swift execution of Protestant leaders could save the crown from a Protestant attack on Paris.

On Saint Bartholomew's Day, August 24, 1572, Coligny and 3,000 fellow Huguenots were butchered in Paris. Within three days an estimated 20,000 Huguenots were executed in coordinated attacks throughout France. It is a date that has ever since lived in infamy for Protestants.

Pope Gregory XIII and Philip II of Spain reportedly greeted the news of the Protestant massacre with special religious celebrations. Philip especially had good reason to rejoice. By throwing France into civil war, the massacre ended for the moment any planned French opposition to his efforts to subdue his rebellious subjects in the Netherlands. But the massacre of thousands of Protestants also gave the discerning Catholic world cause for new alarm. The event changed the nature of the struggle between Protestants and Catholics both within and beyond the borders of France. It was thereafter no longer an internal contest between Guise and Bourbon factions for French political influence, nor was it simply a Huguenot campaign to win basic religious freedoms. Henceforth, in Protestant eyes, it became an international struggle to the death for sheer survival against an adversary whose cruelty now justified any means of resistance.

Protestant Resistance Theory Only as Protestants faced suppression and sure defeat did they begin to sanction active political resistance. At first, they tried to practice the biblical precept of obedient subjection to worldly authority (Romans 13:1). Luther had only grudgingly approved resistance to the emperor after the Diet of Augsburg in 1530. In 1550, Lutherans in Magdeburg had published a highly influential defense of the right of lower authorities to oppose the emperor's order that all Lutherans return to the Catholic fold.

Calvin, who never faced the specter of total political defeat after his return to Geneva in September 1540, had always condemned willful disobedience and rebellion against lawfully constituted governments as un-Christian. But he also taught that lower magistrates, as part of the lawfully constituted government, had the right and duty to oppose tyrannical higher authority.

The exiled Scottish reformer John Knox, who had seen his cause crushed by Mary of Guise, the Regent of Scotland, and Mary I of England, laid the groundwork for later Calvinist resistance. In his famous *First Blast of the Trumpet against the Terrible Regiment of Women* (1558), he declared that the removal of a heathen tyrant was not only permissible, but a Christian duty. He had the Catholic queen of England in mind.

After the great massacre of French Protestants on Saint Bartholomew's Day, 1572, Calvinists everywhere came to appreciate the need for an active defense of their religious rights. Classical Huguenot theories of resistance appeared in three major works of the 1570s. The first was the *Franco-Gallia* of François Hotman (1573), a humanist argument that the representative Estates General of France historically held higher authority than the French king. The second was Theodore Beza's *On the Right of Magistrates over Their Subjects* (1574), which, going beyond Calvin's views, justified the correction and even the overthrow of tyrannical rulers by lower authorities. Finally, Philippe du Plessis Mornay's *Defense of Liberty against Tyrants* (1579) admonished princes, nobles, and magistrates beneath the king, as guardians of the rights of the body politic, to take up arms against tyranny in other lands.

THE RISE TO POWER OF HENRY OF NAVARRE

Henry III (r. 1574–1589) was the last of Henry II's sons to wear the French crown. He found the monarchy wedged between a radical Catholic

League, formed in 1576 by Henry of Guise, and vengeful Huguenots. Neither group would have been reluctant to assassinate a ruler they considered heretical and a tyrant. Like the queen mother, Henry sought to steer a middle course. In this effort, he received support from a growing body of neutral Catholics and Huguenots, who put the political survival of France above its religious unity. Such *politiques* were prepared to compromise religious creeds as might be required to save the nation.

The Peace of Beaulieu in May 1576 granted the Huguenots almost complete religious and civil freedom. France, however, was not ready then for such sweeping toleration. Within seven months of the Peace, the Catholic League forced Henry to return to the illusory quest for absolute religious unity in France. In October 1577, the king truncated the Peace of Beaulieu and once again circumscribed areas of permitted Huguenot worship. Thereafter, Huguenot and Catholic factions quickly returned to their accustomed anarchical military solutions. The Protestants were led by Henry of Navarre, now heir to the French throne by virtue of his marriage to Margaret of Valois, Henry III's sister.

In the mid-1580s, the Catholic League, supported by the Spanish, became completely dominant in Paris. In what came to be known as the Day of the Barricades, Henry III attempted to rout the league with a surprise attack in 1588. The effort failed badly, and the king had to flee Paris. Forced by his weakened position into unkingly guerrilla tactics, and also emboldened by news of the English victory over the Spanish Armada in 1588, Henry successfully plotted the assassinations of both the duke and the cardinal of Guise. These assassinations sent France reeling once again. Led by still another Guise brother, the Catholic League reacted with a fury that matched the earlier Huguenot response to the Massacre of Saint Bartholomew's Day. The king now had only one course of action: He struck an alliance with the Protestant Henry of Navarre in April 1589.

As the two Henrys prepared to attack the Guise stronghold of Paris, however, a fanatical Jacobin friar stabbed and killed Henry III. Thereupon, the Bourbon Huguenot Henry of Navarre succeeded the childless Valois king to the French throne as Henry IV (r. 1589–1610). Pope Sixtus V and Philip II stood aghast at the sudden prospect of a Protestant France. They had always wanted France to be religiously Catholic and politically weak, and they now acted to achieve that end. Spain rushed troops to support the besieged Catholic League. Philip II apparently even harbored hopes of placing his eldest daughter, Isabella, the granddaughter of Henry II and Catherine de Médicis, on the French throne.

Direct Spanish intervention in the affairs of France seemed only to strengthen Henry IV's grasp on the crown. The French people viewed his right to hereditary succession more seriously than his espoused Protestant confession. Henry was also widely liked. Notoriously informal in dress and manner—a factor that made him especially popular with the soldiers— Henry also had the wit and charm to neutralize the strongest enemy in a face-to-face confrontation. He came to the throne as a *politique*, long weary with religious strife and fully prepared to place political peace above absolute religious unity. He believed a royal policy of tolerant Catholicism would be the best way to achieve such peace. On July 25, 1593, he publicly abjured the Protestant faith and embraced the traditional and majority religion of his country. "Paris is worth a mass," he is reported to have said.

It was, in fact, a decision he had made only after a long period of personal agonizing. The Huguenots were understandably horrified by this turnabout, and Pope Clement VIII remained skeptical of Henry's sincerity. But most of the French church and people, having known internal strife too long, rallied to the king's side. By 1596, the Catholic League was dispersed, its ties with Spain were broken, and the wars of religion in France, to all intents, had ground to a close.

THE EDICT OF NANTES

On April 13, 1598, Henry IV's famous Edict of Nantes proclaimed a formal religious settlement. The following month, on May 2, 1598, the Treaty of Vervins ended hostilities between France and Spain.

In 1591, Henry IV had already assured the Huguenots of at least qualified religious freedoms. The Edict of Nantes made good that promise. It recognized and sanctioned minority religious rights within what was to remain an officially Catholic country. This religious truce—and it was never more than that—granted the Huguenots, who by this time numbered well over a million, freedom of public worship, the right of assembly, admission to public offices and universities, and permission to maintain fortified towns. Most of the new freedoms, however, were to be exercised within their own towns and territories. Concession of the right to fortify their towns reveals the continuing distrust between French Protestants and Catholics. As significant as it was, the edict only transformed a long hot war between irreconcilable enemies into a long cold war. To its critics, it had only created a state within a state. (See "Henry IV Recognizes Huguenot Religious Freedom.")

A Catholic fanatic assassinated Henry IV in May 1610. Although he is best remembered for the Edict of Nantes, Henry IV put in place political and

Main Events of French Wars of Religion

1559	Treaty of Cateau-Cambrésis ends Habsburg-Valois wars
1559	Francis II succeeds to French throne under regency of his mother, Catherine de Médicis
1560	Conspiracy of Amboise fails
1562	Protestant worshipers massacred at Vassy in Champagne by the duke of Guise
1572	The Saint Bartholomew's Day Massacre leaves thousands of Protestants dead
1589	Assassination of Henry III brings the Huguenot Henry of Navarre to throne as Henry IV
1593	Henry IV embraces Catholicism
1598	Henry IV grants Huguenots religious and civil freedoms in the Edict of Nantes
1610	Henry IV assassinated

economic policies that were equally important. They laid the foundations for the transformation of France into the absolute state it would become under Cardinal Richelieu and Louis XIV. Ironically, in pursuit of the political and religious unity that had escaped Henry IV, Louis XIV, calling for "one king, one law, one faith," would revoke the Edict of Nantes in 1685. (See Chapter 13.) This action would force France and Europe to learn again by bitter experience the hard lessons of the wars of religion. Rare is the politician who learns from the lessons of history rather than repeating its mistakes.

Imperial Spain and the Reign of Philip II (r. 1556–1598)

PILLARS OF SPANISH POWER

Until the English defeated the mighty Spanish Armada in 1588, no one person stood larger in the second half of the sixteenth century than Philip II of Spain. Philip was heir to the intensely Catholic and militarily supreme western Habsburg kingdom. The eastern Habsburg lands of Austria, Bohemia, and Hungary had been given over by his father, Charles V, to Philip's uncle, the emperor Ferdinand I. These lands, together with the imperial title, remained in the possession of the Austrian branch of the family.

New World Riches Populous and wealthy Castile gave Philip a solid home base. The regular arrival in Seville of bullion from the Spanish colonies in the New World provided additional wealth. In the 1540s, great silver mines had been opened in Potosí

in present-day Bolivia and in Zacatecas in Mexico. These gave Philip the great sums needed to pay his bankers and mercenaries. He nonetheless never managed to erase the debts left by his father or to finance his own foreign adventures fully. He later contributed to the bankruptcy of the Fuggers when, at the end of his life, he defaulted on his enormous debts.

Increased Population The new American wealth brought dramatic social change to the peoples of Europe during the second half of the sixteenth century. As Europe became richer, it was also becoming more populous. In the economically and politically active towns of France, England, and the Netherlands, populations had tripled and quadrupled by the early seventeenth century. Europe's population exceeded 70 million by 1600.

The combination of increased wealth and population triggered inflation. A steady 2-percent-a-year rise in prices in much of Europe had serious cumulative effects by midcentury. There were more people than before and greater coinage in circulation, but less food and fewer jobs; wages stagnated while prices doubled and tripled in much of Europe.

This was especially the case in Spain. Because the new wealth was concentrated in the hands of a few, the traditional gap between the haves—the propertied, privileged, and educated classes—and the have-nots greatly widened. Nowhere did the unprivileged suffer more than in Spain, where the Castilian peasantry, the backbone of Philip II's great empire, became the most heavily taxed people of Europe. Those whose labor contributed most to making possible Spanish hegemony in Europe in the second half of the sixteenth century prospered least from it.

Efficient Bureaucracy and Military A subjugated peasantry and wealth from the New World were not the only pillars of Spanish strength. Philip II shrewdly organized the lesser nobility into a loyal and efficient national bureaucracy. A reclusive man, he managed his kingdom by pen and paper rather than by personal presence. He was also a learned and pious Catholic, although some popes suspected he used religion as much for political as for devotional purposes. That he was a generous patron of the arts and culture is evident in his unique retreat outside Madrid, the Escorial, a combination palace, church, tomb, and monastery. Philip also knew personal sorrows: His mad and treacherous son, Don Carlos, died under suspicious circumstances in 1568—some contemporaries suspected that Philip had him quietly executed—only three months before the death of the queen.

Supremacy in the Mediterranean During the first half of Philip's reign, attention focused almost

HENRY IV RECOGNIZES HUGUENOT RELIGIOUS FREEDOM

By the Edict of Nantes (April 13, 1598), Henry IV recognized Huguenot religious freedoms and the rights of Protestants to participate in French public institutions. Here are some of its provisions.

■ *Are Huguenots given equal religious standing with Catholics? Are there limitations on their freedoms?*

We have by this perpetual and irrevocable Edict pronounced, declared, and ordained and we pronounce, declare, and ordain:

Art. I. Firstly, that the memory of everything done on both sides from the beginning of the month of March, 1585, until our accession to the Crown and during the other previous troubles, and at the outbreak of them, shall remain extinct and suppressed, as if it were something which had never occurred. . . .

Art. II. We forbid all our subjects, of whatever rank and quality they may be, to renew the memory of these matters, to attack, be hostile to, injure or provoke each other in revenge for the past, whatever may be the reason and pretext. . . . but let them restrain themselves and live peaceably together as brothers, friends, and fellow-citizens. . . .

Art. III. We ordain that the Catholic, Apostolic, and Roman religion shall be restored and reestablished in all places and districts of this our kingdom and the countries under our rule, where its practice has been interrupted. . . .

Art. VI. And we permit those of the so-called Reformed religion to live and dwell in all the towns and districts of this our kingdom and the countries under our rule, without being annoyed, disturbed, molested or constrained to do anything against their conscience, or for this cause to be sought out in their houses and districts where they wish to live, provided that they conduct themselves in other respects to the provisions of our present Edict. . . .

Art. XXI. Books dealing with the matters of the aforesaid so-called Reformed religion shall not be printed and sold publicly, except in the towns and districts where the public exercise of the said religion is allowed. . . .

Art. XXII. We ordain that there shall be no difference or distinction, because of the aforesaid religion, in the reception of students to be instructed in Universities, Colleges, and schools, or of the sick and poor into hospitals, infirmaries, and public charitable institutions. . . .

Art. XXVII. In order to reunite more effectively the wills of our subjects, as is our intention, and to remove all future complaints, we declare that all those who profess or shall profess the aforesaid so-called Reformed religion are capable of holding and exercising all public positions, honours, offices, and duties whatsoever . . . in the towns of our kingdom . . . notwithstanding all contrary oaths.

From *Church and State through the Centuries: A Collection of Historic Documents*, trans. and ed. by S. Z. Ehler and John B. Morrall (New York: Biblo and Tannen, 1967), pp. 185–187. Reprinted by permission of Biblo-Moser Book Publishers.

exclusively on the Mediterranean and the Turkish threat. By history, geography, and choice, Spain had traditionally been Catholic Europe's champion against Islam. During the 1560s, the Turks advanced deep into Austria, and their fleets dominated the Mediterranean. Between 1568 and 1570, armies under Philip's half brother, Don John of Austria, the illegitimate son of Charles V, suppressed and dispersed the moors in Granada.

In May 1571, a Holy League of Spain, Venice, and the pope, again under Don John's command, formed to check Turkish belligerence in the Mediterranean. In what was the largest naval battle of the sixteenth century, Don John's fleet engaged the Ottoman navy under Ali Pasha off Lepanto in the Gulf of Corinth on October 7, 1571. Before the engagement ended, over one-third of the Turkish fleet had been sunk or captured and 30,000 Turks had died. The Mediterranean for the moment belonged to Spain, and the Europeans were left to fight each other. Philip's armies also succeeded in putting down resistance in neighboring Portugal, which Spain annexed in 1580. The conquest of Portugal not only added to Spanish sea power, but also brought the magnificent Portuguese overseas empire in Africa, India, and the Americas into the Spanish orbit.

A view of the Escorial, Philip II's massive palace-monastery-mausoleum northwest of Madrid. Built between 1563 and 1584, it was a monument to the piety and power of the king. Philip vowed to build the complex after the Spanish defeated the French at Saint-Quentin on St. Lawrence's Day in 1577. The floor plan of the Escorial resembles a grill, the symbol of St. Lawrence (who, according to legend, was martyred by being roasted alive on a grill.) Getty Images, Inc.

THE REVOLT IN THE NETHERLANDS

The spectacular Spanish military success in southern Europe was not repeated in northern Europe. When Philip attempted to impose his will within the Netherlands and on England and France, he learned the lessons of defeat. The resistance of the Netherlands especially proved the undoing of Spanish dreams of world empire. (See Map 12–1.)

Cardinal Granvelle The Netherlands was the richest area not only of Philip's Hapsburg kingdom, but of Europe as well. In 1559, Philip had departed the Netherlands for Spain, never again to return. His half sister, Margaret of Parma, assisted by a special council of state, became regent in his absence. The council was headed by Philip's handpicked lieutenant, the extremely able Antoine Perrenot (1517–1586), known after 1561 as Cardinal Granvelle. Granvelle hoped to check Protestant gains by internal church reforms. He planned to break down the traditional local autonomy of the seventeen Netherlands provinces by stages and establish in its place a centralized royal government directed from Madrid. A politically docile and religiously uniform country was the goal.

The merchant towns of the Netherlands were, however, Europe's most independent; many, like magnificent Antwerp, were also Calvinist strongholds. By tradition and habit, the people of the Netherlands inclined far more toward variety and toleration than toward obeisant conformity and hierarchical order. Two members of the council of state formed a stubborn opposition to the Spanish overlords, who now sought to reimpose their traditional rule with a vengeance. They were the Count of Egmont (1522–1568) and William of Nassau, the Prince of Orange (1533–1584), known as "the Silent" because of his extremely small circle of confidants.

Like other successful rulers in this period, William of Orange placed the political autonomy and well-being of the Netherlands above religious creeds. He personally passed through successive Catholic, Lutheran, and Calvinist stages. In 1561, he married Anne of Saxony, the daughter of the Lutheran elector Maurice and the granddaughter of the late landgrave Philip of Hesse. He maintained his Catholic practices until 1567, when he turned Lutheran. After the Saint Bartholomew's Day Massacre (1572), Orange (as he was called) became an avowed Calvinist.

In 1561, Cardinal Granvelle proceeded with a planned ecclesiastical reorganization of the Netherlands. It was intended to tighten the control of the Catholic hierarchy over the country and to accelerate its consolidation as a Spanish ward. Orange and Egmont, organizing the Dutch nobility in opposition, succeeded in gaining Granvelle's removal from office in 1564. Aristocratic control of the country after Granvelle's departure, however, proved woefully inefficient. Popular unrest continued to grow, especially among urban artisans, who joined the congregations of radical Calvinist preachers in increasing numbers.

The Compromise The year 1564 also saw the first fusion of political and religious opposition to Regent Margaret's government. This opposition resulted from Philip II's unwise insistence that the decrees of the Council of Trent be enforced throughout the Netherlands. William of Orange's younger brother, Louis of Nassau, who had been raised a

MAP 12–1   THE NETHERLANDS DURING THE REFORMATION   *The northern and southern provinces of the Netherlands. The former, the United Provinces, were mostly Protestant in the second half of the sixteenth century; the southern Spanish Netherlands made peace with Spain and remained largely Catholic.*

Lutheran, led the opposition, and it received support from the Calvinist-inclined lesser nobility and townspeople. A national covenant called the *Compromise* was drawn up, a solemn pledge to resist the decrees of Trent and the Inquisition. Grievances were loudly and persistently voiced. When Regent Margaret's government spurned the protesters as "beggars" in 1566, Calvinists rioted through the country. Louis called on French Huguenots and German Lutherans to send aid to the Netherlands, and a full-scale rebellion against the Spanish regency appeared imminent.

The Duke of Alba   The rebellion failed to materialize, however, because the higher nobility of the Netherlands would not support it. Their shock at Calvinist iconoclasm and anarchy was as great as their resentment of Granvelle's more subtle repression. Philip, determined to make an example of the Protestant rebels, dispatched the duke of Alba to suppress the revolt. His army of 10,000 journeyed northward from Milan in 1567 in a show of combined Spanish and papal might. A special tribunal, known to the Spanish as the Council of Troubles and among the Netherlanders as the Council of Blood, reigned over the land. The counts of Egmont and Horn and several thousand suspected heretics were publicly executed before Alba's reign of terror ended.

The Spanish levied new taxes, forcing the Netherlands to pay for the suppression of its own revolt. One of these taxes, the "tenth penny," a 10 percent sales tax, met such resistance from merchants and artisans that it remained uncollectible in some areas even after a reduction to 3 percent. Combined persecution and taxation sent tens of thousands fleeing from the Netherlands during Alba's cruel six-year rule. Alba came to be more hated than Granvelle or the radical Calvinists had ever been.

Resistance and Unification   William of Orange was an exile in Germany during these turbulent years. He now emerged as the leader of a broad movement for the independence of the Netherlands from Spain. The northern, Calvinist-inclined provinces of Holland, Zeeland, and Utrecht, of which Orange was the *Stadholder*, or governor, became his base. As in France, political resistance in the Netherlands gained both organization and inspiration by merging with Calvinism.

The early victories of the resistance attest to the popular character of the revolt. A case in point is the capture of the port city of Brill by the "Sea Beggars," an international group of anti-Spanish exiles and criminals, among them many Englishmen. William of Orange did not hesitate to enlist their services. Their brazen piracy, however, had forced Queen

Elizabeth to disassociate herself from them and to bar their ships from English ports. In 1572, the Beggars captured Brill and other seaports in Zeeland and Holland. Mixing with the native population, they quickly sparked rebellions against Alba in town after town and spread the resistance southward. In 1574, the people of Leiden heroically resisted a long Spanish siege. The Dutch opened the dikes and flooded their country to repulse the hated Spanish. The faltering Alba had by that time ceded power to Don Luis de Requesens, who replaced him as commander of Spanish forces in the Netherlands in November 1573.

The Pacification of Ghent   The greatest atrocity of the war came after Requesens's death in 1576. Spanish mercenaries, leaderless and unpaid, ran amok in Antwerp on November 4, 1576, leaving 7,000 people dead in the streets. The event came to be known as the Spanish Fury.

These atrocities accomplished in four short days what neither religion nor patriotism had previously been able to do. The ten largely Catholic southern provinces (what is roughly modern Belgium) now came together with the seven largely Protestant northern provinces (what is roughly the modern Netherlands) in unified opposition to Spain. This union, known as the Pacification of Ghent, was accomplished on November 8, 1576. It declared internal regional sovereignty in matters of religion, a key clause that permitted political cooperation among the signatories, who were not agreed over religion. It was a Netherlands version of the territorial settlement of religious differences brought about in the Holy Roman Empire in 1555 by the Peace of Augsburg. Four provinces initially held out, but they soon made the resistance unanimous by joining the all-embracing Union of Brussels in January 1577. For the next two years, the Spanish faced a unified and determined Netherlands.

Don John, the victor over the Turks at Lepanto in 1571, had taken command of Spanish land forces in November 1576. He now experienced his first defeat. Confronted by unified Netherlandic resistance, he signed the humiliating Perpetual Edict in February 1577. This edict provided for the removal of all Spanish troops from the Netherlands within twenty days. The withdrawal of troops gave the country to William of Orange and effectively ended for the time being whatever plans Philip may have had for using the Netherlands as a staging area for an invasion of England.

The Union of Arras and the Union of Utrecht   The Spanish, however, were nothing if not persistent. Don John and Alessandro Farnese of Parma, the Regent Margaret's son, revived Spanish power in the southern provinces, where constant fear of Calvinist extremism had moved the leaders to break the union of Brussels. In January 1579, the southern provinces formed the Union of Arras, and within five months they made peace with Spain. These provinces later served the cause of the Counter-Reformation. The northern provinces responded with the formation of the Union of Utrecht.

The Milch Cow, a sixteenth-century satirical painting depicting the Netherlands as a cow in whom all the great powers of Europe have an interest. Elizabeth of England is feeding her (England had long-standing commercial ties with Flanders); Philip II of Spain is attempting to ride her (Spain was trying to reassert its control over the entire area); William of Orange is trying to milk her (he was the leader of the anti-Spanish rebellion); and the king of France holds her tail (France hoped to profit from the rebellion at Spain's expense).
Rijksmuseum, Amsterdam

Netherlands Independence Seizing what now appeared to be a last opportunity to break the back of Netherlandic resistance, Philip II declared William of Orange an outlaw and placed a bounty of 25,000 crowns on his head. (See "Phillip II Declares William of Orange an Outlaw.") The act predictably stiffened the resistance of the northern provinces. In a famous defiant speech to the Estates General of Holland in December 1580, known as the Apology, Orange publicly denounced Philip as a heathen tyrant whom the Netherlands need no longer obey.

On July 22, 1581, the member provinces of the Union of Utrecht met in The Hague and formally declared Philip no longer their ruler. They turned instead to the French duke of Alençon, the youngest son of Catherine de Médicis. The southern provinces had also earlier looked to him as a possible middle way between Spanish and Calvinist overlordship. All the northern provinces save Holland and Zeeland accepted Alençon as their "sovereign" (Holland and Zeeland distrusted him almost as much as they did Philip II), but with the understanding that he would be only a titular ruler. But Alençon, an ambitious failure, saw this as his one chance at greatness. When he rashly attempted to take actual control of the provinces in 1583, he was deposed and returned to France.

PHILLIP II DECLARES WILLIAM OF ORANGE AN OUTLAW

In the following proclamation the king of Spain accused William of Orange of being the "chief disturber of the public peace" and offered his captors, or assassins, generous rewards.

■ *What were the religious differences between Spain and the Netherlands? How did William undermine what Philip II believed to be true religion? Did the reward lead to William's capture, or execution?*

Philip, by the grace of God king of Castile, etc, to all to whom these presents may come, greeting:

It is well known to all how favorably the late emperor, Charles V, . . . treated William of Nassau. . . . Nevertheless, as everyone knows, we had scarcely turned our back on the Netherlands before the said William . . . (who had become . . . prince of Orange) began . . . by sinister arts, plots, and intrigues . . . to gain [control] over those whom he believed to be malcontents, or haters of justice, or anxious for innovations, and . . . above all, those who were suspected in the matter of religion. . . . With the knowledge, advice, and encouragement of the said Orange, the heretics commenced to destroy the images, altars, and churches. . . . So soon as the said Nassau was received into the government of the provinces, he began, through his agents and satellites, to introduce heretical preaching. . . . Then he introduced liberty of conscience . . . which soon brought it about that the Catholics were openly persecuted and driven out. . . . Moreover he obtained such a hold upon our poor subjects of Holland and Zeeland . . . that nearly all the towns, one after the other, have been besieged. . . .

Therefore, for all these just reasons, for his evil doings as chief disturber of the public peace . . . we outlaw him forever and forbid our subjects to associate with him . . . in public or in secret. We declare him an enemy of the human race, and in order the sooner to remove our people from his tyranny and oppression, we promise, on the word of a king and as God's servant, that if one of our subjects be found so generous of heart and so desirous of doing us a service and advantaging the public that he shall find the means of executing this decree and of ridding us of the said pest, either by delivering him to us dead or alive, or by depriving him at once of life, we will give him and his heirs landed estates or money, as he will, to the amount of twenty-five thousand gold crowns. If he has committed any crime, of any kind whatsoever, we will pardon him. If he be not noble, we will ennoble him for his valor; and should he require other persons to assist him, we will reward them according to the service rendered, pardon their crimes, and ennoble them too.

James Harvey Robinson (ed.), *Readings in European History*, Vol. 2 (Boston: Ginn and Co., 1906), pp. 174–177.

Spanish efforts to reconquer the Netherlands continued into the 1580s. William of Orange, assassinated in July 1584, was succeeded by his seventeen-year-old son, Maurice (1567–1625), who, with the assistance of England and France, continued Dutch resistance. Fortunately for the Netherlands, Philip II began now to meddle directly in French and English affairs. He signed a secret treaty with the Guises (the Treaty of Joinville in December 1584) and sent armies under Farnese into France in 1590. Hostilities with the English, who had openly aided the Dutch rebels, also increased. Gradually, they built toward a climax in 1588, when Philip's great Armada was defeated in the English Channel.

These new fronts overextended Spain's resources, strengthening the Netherlands. Spanish preoccupation with France and England permitted the northern provinces to drive out all Spanish soldiers by 1593. In 1596, France and England formally recognized the independence of these provinces. Peace was not, however, concluded with Spain until 1609, when the Twelve Years' Truce gave the northern provinces virtual independence. Full recognition came finally in the Peace of Westphalia in 1648.

England and Spain (1553–1603)

MARY I

Before Edward VI died in 1553, he agreed to a device to make Lady Jane Grey, the teenage daughter of a powerful Protestant nobleman and, more important, the granddaughter on her mother's side of Henry VIII's younger sister Mary, his successor in place of the Catholic Mary Tudor (r. 1553–1558). But popular support for the principle of hereditary monarchy was too strong to deprive Mary of her rightful rule. Popular uprisings in London and elsewhere led to Jane Grey's removal from the throne within days of her crowning, and she was eventually beheaded.

Once enthroned, Mary proceeded to act even beyond the worst fears of the Protestants. In 1554, she entered a highly unpopular political marriage with Prince Philip (later Philip II) of Spain, a symbol of militant Catholicism to English Protestants. At his direction, she pursued a foreign policy that in 1558 cost England its last enclave on the Continent, Calais.

Mary's domestic measures were equally shocking to the English people and even more divisive. During her reign, Parliament repealed the Protestant statutes of Edward and reverted to the Catholic religious practice of her father, Henry VIII. The great Protestant leaders of the Edwardian Age—John Hooper, Hugh Latimer, and Thomas Cranmer—were executed for heresy. Hundreds of Protestants either

Portrait of Mary I (r. 1553–1558), Queen of England. By Sir Anthony Mor (Antonio Moro) (1517/20–1576/7), Prado, Madrid. 1554 (panel). Prado, Madrid/Bridgeman Art Library, London/Index

joined them in martyrdom (287 were burned at the stake during Mary's reign) or took flight to the Continent. These "Marian exiles" settled in Germany and Switzerland, forming especially large communities in Frankfurt, Strasbourg, and Geneva. (John Knox, the future leader of the Reformation in Scotland, was prominent among them.) There they worshiped in their own congregations, wrote tracts justifying armed resistance, and waited for the time when a Protestant counteroffensive could be launched in their homelands. They were also exposed to religious beliefs more radical than any set forth during Edward VI's reign. Many of these exiles later held positions in the Church of England during Elizabeth I's reign.

ELIZABETH I

Mary's successor was her half sister, Elizabeth I (r. 1558–1603), the daughter of Henry VIII and Anne Boleyn. Elizabeth had remarkable and enduring successes in both domestic and foreign policy. Assisted by a shrewd adviser, Sir William Cecil (1520–1598), she built a true kingdom on the ruins of Mary's reign. Between 1559 and 1563, she and Cecil guided a religious settlement through Parliament that prevented England from being torn asunder by religious differences in the sixteenth century, as the Continent was. Another ruler who subordinated religious to political unity, Elizabeth merged a centralized episcopal system, which she firmly controlled, with broadly defined Protestant doctrine and traditional Catholic ritual. In the resulting Anglican Church, inflexible religious extremes were not permitted.

In 1559, an Act of Supremacy passed Parliament, repealing all the anti-Protestant legislation of Mary Tudor and asserting Elizabeth's right as "supreme governor" over both spiritual and temporal affairs. In the same year, the Act of Uniformity mandated a revised version of the second *Book of Common Prayer* (1552) for every English parish. In 1563, the issuance of the **Thirty-Nine Articles** on Religion, a revision of Thomas Cranmer's original forty-two, made a moderate Protestantism the official religion within the Church of England.

Elizabeth I (r. 1558–1603) standing on a map of England in 1592. An astute politician in both foreign and domestic policy, Elizabeth was perhaps the most succesful ruler of the sixteenth century. National Portrait Gallery, London

Catholic and Protestant Extremists   Elizabeth hoped to avoid both Catholic and Protestant extremism at the official level by pursuing a middle way. Her first archbishop of Canterbury, Matthew Parker (d. 1575), represented this ideal. But Elizabeth could not prevent the emergence of subversive Catholic and Protestant zealots. When she ascended the throne, Catholics were in the majority in England. The extremists among them, encouraged by the Jesuits, plotted against her. Catholic radicals were also encouraged and later directly assisted by the Spanish, who were piqued both by Elizabeth's Protestant sympathies and by her refusal to follow the example of her half sister Mary and take Philip II's hand in marriage. Elizabeth remained unmarried throughout her reign, using the possibility of a marriage as a political alliance very much to her diplomatic advantage.

Catholic extremists hoped eventually to replace Elizabeth with Mary Stuart, Queen of Scots. Unlike Elizabeth, who had been declared illegitimate during the reign of her father, Mary Stuart had an unblemished claim to the throne by way of her grandmother Margaret, the sister of Henry VIII. Elizabeth acted swiftly against Catholic assassination plots and rarely let emotion override her political instincts. Despite proven cases of Catholic treason and even attempted regicide, she executed fewer Catholics during her forty-five years on the throne than Mary Tudor had executed Protestants during her brief five-year reign. She showed little mercy, however, to separatists and others who threatened the unity of her rule.

Elizabeth dealt cautiously with the Puritans, who were Protestants working within the national church to "purify" it of every vestige of "popery" and to make its Protestant doctrine more precise. The Puritans had two special grievances:

1. the retention of Catholic ceremony and vestments within the Church of England, which made it appear to the casual observer that no Reformation had occurred, and
2. the continuation of the episcopal system of church governance, which conceived of the English church theologically as the true successor to Rome, while placing it politically under the firm hand of the queen and her compliant archbishop.

Sixteenth-century Puritans were not separatists. They enjoyed wide popular support and were led by widely respected men like Thomas Cartwright (d. 1603). They worked through Parliament to create an alternative national church of semiautonomous congregations governed by representative presbyteries (hence, **Presbyterians**), following the model of Calvin and Geneva. Elizabeth dealt firmly, but subtly, with this group, conceding absolutely nothing that lessened the hierarchical unity of the Church of England and her control over it.

The more extreme Puritans wanted every congregation to be autonomous, a law unto itself, with neither higher episcopal nor presbyterian control. They came to be known as **Congregationalists.** Elizabeth and her second archbishop of Canterbury, John Whitgift (d. 1604), refused to tolerate this group, whose views on independence they found patently subversive. The Conventicle Act of 1593 gave such separatists the option of either conforming to the practices of the Church of England or facing exile or death.

Deterioration of Relations with Spain A series of events led inexorably to war between England and Spain, despite the sincerest desires on the part of both Philip II and Elizabeth to avoid a confrontation. In 1567, the Spanish duke of Alba marched his mighty army into the Netherlands, which was, from the English point of view, simply a convenient staging area for a Spanish invasion of England. Pope Pius V (r. 1566–1572), who favored a military conquest of Protestant England, "excommunicated" Elizabeth for heresy in 1570. This mischievous act only encouraged both internal resistance and international intrigue against the queen. Two years later, as noted earlier, the piratical sea beggars, many of whom were Englishmen, occupied the port city of Brill in the Netherlands and aroused the surrounding countryside against the Spanish.

Following Don John's demonstration of Spain's awesome sea power at the famous naval battle of Lepanto in 1571, England signed a mutual defense pact with France. Also in the 1570s, Elizabeth's famous seamen John Hawkins (1532–1595) and Sir Francis Drake (1545?–1596) began to prey regularly on Spanish shipping in the Americas. Drake's circumnavigation of the globe between 1577 and 1580 was one in a series of dramatic demonstrations of English ascendancy on the high seas.

After the Saint Bartholomew's Day Massacre, Elizabeth was the only protector of Protestants in France and the Netherlands. In 1585, she signed the Treaty of Nonsuch, which provided English soldiers and cavalry to the Netherlands. Funds that had previously been funneled covertly to support Henry of Navarre's army in France now flowed openly.

Mary, Queen of Scots These events made a tinderbox of English–Spanish relations. The spark that finally touched it off was Elizabeth's execution of Mary, Queen of Scots (1542–1587).

Mary Stuart was the daughter of King James V of Scotland and Mary of Guise and had resided in France from the time she was six years old. This thoroughly French and Catholic queen had returned to Scotland after the death of her husband, the French king Francis II, in 1561. There she found a successful, fervent Protestant Reformation that had won legal sanction the year before in the Treaty of Edinburgh (1560). As hereditary heir to the throne of Scotland, Mary remained queen by divine and human right. She was not intimidated by the Protestants who controlled her realm. She established an international French court culture, the gaiety and sophistication of which impressed many Protestant nobles whose religion often made their lives exceedingly dour.

Mary was closely watched by the ever-vigilant Scottish reformer John Knox. He fumed publicly and always with effect against the queen's private mass and Catholic practices, which Scottish law made a capital offense for everyone else. Knox won support in his role of watchdog from Elizabeth and Cecil. Elizabeth personally despised Knox and never forgave him for writing the *First Blast of the Trumpet against the Terrible Regiment of Women*, a work aimed at provoking a revolt against Mary Tudor, but published in the year of Elizabeth's ascent to the throne. Elizabeth and Cecil tolerated Knox because he served their foreign policy, never permitting Scotland to succumb to the young Mary and her French and Catholic ways.

In 1568, a public scandal forced Mary's abdication and flight to her cousin Elizabeth in England. Mary's reputed lover, the earl of Bothwell, was, with cause, suspected of having killed her legal husband, Lord Darnley. When a packed court acquitted Bothwell, he subsequently married Mary. The outraged reaction from Protestant nobles forced Mary to surrender the throne to her one-year-old son, who became James VI of Scotland (and, later, Elizabeth's successor as King James I of England). Because of Mary's clear claim to the English throne, she remained an international symbol of a possible Catholic England, and she was consumed by the desire to be queen of England. Her presence in England, where she resided under house arrest for nineteen years, was a constant discomfort to Elizabeth.

In 1583, Elizabeth's vigilant secretary, Sir Francis Walsingham, uncovered a plot against Elizabeth involving the Spanish ambassador Bernardino de Mendoza. After Mendoza's deportation in January 1584, popular antipathy toward Spain and support for Protestant resistance in France and the Netherlands became massive throughout England.

In 1586, Walsingham uncovered still another plot against Elizabeth, the so-called Babington plot (after Anthony Babington, who was caught seeking Spanish support for an attempt on the queen's life). This time he had uncontestable proof of Mary's complicity. Elizabeth believed the execution of a sovereign, even a dethroned sovereign, weakened royalty everywhere. She was also aware of the outcry that Mary's execution would create throughout the Catholic world, and Elizabeth sincerely wanted peace with English Catholics. But she really had no choice in the matter and consented to Mary's execution, which took place on February 18, 1587. This event dashed all Catholic hopes for a bloodless reconversion of Protestant England. After the execution of the Catholic queen of Scotland, Pope Sixtus V (r. 1585–1590), who feared Spanish domination almost as much as he abhorred English Protestantism, could no longer withhold public support for a Spanish invasion of England. Philip II ordered his Armada to make ready.

The Armada Spain's war preparations were interrupted in the spring of 1587 by Sir Francis Drake's successful shelling of the port city of Cádiz, an attack that inflicted heavy damage on Spanish ships and stores. After "singeing the beard of Spain's king," as he put it, Drake raided the coast of Portugal, further incapacitating the Spanish. The success of these strikes forced the Spanish to postpone their planned invasion of England until the spring of 1588.

On May 30 of that year, a mighty fleet of 130 ships bearing 25,000 sailors and soldiers under the command of the duke of Medina-Sidonia set sail for England. In the end, however, the English won a stunning victory. The invasion barges that were to transport Spanish soldiers from the galleons onto English shores were prevented from leaving Calais and Dunkirk. The swifter English and Netherlandic ships, helped by what came to be known as an "English wind," dispersed the waiting Spanish fleet, over one-third of which never returned to Spain.

The news of the Armada's defeat gave heart to Protestant resistance everywhere. Although Spain continued to win impressive victories in the 1590s, it never fully recovered from that defeat. Spanish soldiers faced unified and inspired French, English, and Dutch armies. By the time of Philip's death on September 13, 1598, his forces had been successfully rebuffed on all fronts. His seventeenth-century successors were all inferior leaders who never knew responsibilities equal to his. Nor did Spain ever again know such imperial grandeur. The French soon dominated the Continent, and in the New World the Dutch and the English progressively whittled away Spain's once glorious overseas empire.

Elizabeth died on March 23, 1603, leaving behind her a strong nation poised to expand into a global empire. (See "An Unknown Contemporary Describes Queen Elizabeth" and "Encountering the Past: Going to the Theater in the Elizabethan Age.")

The Thirty Years' War (1618–1648)

The Thirty Years' War in the Holy Roman Empire was the last and most destructive of the wars of religion. Religious and political differences had long set Catholics against Protestants and Calvinists against

A portrayal of the execution of Mary, Queen of Scots and the apparent subsequent burning (left) of her body, so no relics might survive for her followers to revere. Unknown Dutch artist. National Galleries of Scotland

AN UNKNOWN CONTEMPORARY DESCRIBES QUEEN ELIZABETH

No sixteenth-century ruler governed more effectively than Elizabeth I of England (r. 1558–1603), who was both loved and feared by her subjects. An unknown contemporary has left the following description, revealing not only her intelligence and political cunning, but also something of her immense vanity.

■ *What qualities of Elizabeth impressed this observer? Why did the queen take such care with her appearance?*

I will proceed with the description of the queen's disposition and natural gifts of mind and body, wherein she either matched or exceeded all the princes of her time, as being of a great spirit yet tempered with moderation, in adversity never dejected, in prosperity rather joyful than proud; affable to her subjects, but always with due regard to the greatness of her estate, by reason whereof she was both loved and feared.

In her later time, when she showed herself in public, she was always magnificent in apparel; supposing haply thereby that the eyes of her people (being dazzled by the glittering aspect of her outward ornaments) would not so easily discern the marks of age and decay of natural beauty; and she came abroad the more seldom, to make her presence the more grateful and applauded by the multitude, to whom things rarely seen are in manner as new.

She suffered not, at any time, any suitor to depart discontented from her, and though ofttimes he obtained not that he desired, yet he held himself satisfied with her manner of speech, which gave hope of success in the second attempt. . . .

Latin, French, and Italian she could speak very elegantly, and she was able in all those languages to answer ambassadors on the sudden. . . . Of the Greek tongue she was also not altogether ignorant. She took pleasure in reading of the best and wisest histories, and some part of Tacitus's *Annals* she herself turned into English for her private exercise. She also translated Boethius's *On the Consolation of Philosophy* and a treatise of Plutarch, *On Curiosity*, with divers others. . . .

It is credibly reported that not long before her death, she had a great apprehension of her own age and declination by seeing her face (then lean and full of wrinkles) truly represented to her in a glass, which she a good while very earnestly beheld; perceiving thereby how often she had been abused by flatterers (whom she held in too great estimation) that had informed her the contrary.

From James Harvey Robinson, ed., *Readings in European History*, Vol. 2 (Boston: Ginn and Co., 1906), pp. 191–193.

Lutherans. What made the Thirty Years' War so devastating was the entrenched hatred of the various sides and their seeming determination to sacrifice all for their religious beliefs and extension of political power. As the conflicts multiplied, virtually every major European land became involved either directly or indirectly. When the hostilities ended in 1648, the peace terms shaped the map of northern Europe much as we know it today.

PRECONDITIONS FOR WAR

Fragmented Germany In the second half of the sixteenth century, Germany was an almost ungovernable land of about 360 autonomous political entities. (See Map 12–2.) There were independent secular principalities (duchies, landgraviates, and marches); ecclesiastical principalities (archbishoprics, bishoprics, and abbeys); numerous free cities; and castle regions dominated by knights. The Peace of Augsburg (1555) had given each a significant degree of sovereignty within its own borders. Each levied its own tolls and tariffs and coined its own money, practices that made land travel and trade between the various regions difficult and sometimes impossible. In addition, many of these little lands were filled with great-power pretensions. Political decentralization and fragmentation characterized Germany as the seventeenth century opened; it was not a unified nation like Spain, England, or even strife-filled France.

Because of its central location, Germany had always been Europe's highway for merchants and traders going north, south, east, and west. Europe's

Going to the Theater

The modern English stage play originated in the religious dramas that educated and entertained medieval Europeans for centuries before Shakespeare's birth in 1564. Teaching a lesson as well as telling a suspenseful story, these dramas were known as *morality plays* and typically presented in the countryside by roving bands of players under church supervision. The medieval theater usually consisted of a small circular field for the actors, ringed by earthen mounds for the spectators. The circular stage was divided into four quadrants, each with its own tent at the four points of the compass: heaven at the east, evil at the north, worldly rulers at the west, and good characters at the south.

Each player emerged from his tent in turn to speak his lines, then went back in to await his next appearance. This format was a way of shifting scenes and a forerunner of the custom in modern theaters of ending a scene by lowering a curtain.

In England in the fifteenth century, as the urban population grew, ambitious promoters moved their productions into the courtyards of inns. London, the seat of the royal court, became the center of English theatrical life.

This sheltered, urban setting gave theater companies several advantages. Audiences were larger, and the inns could be easily renovated to provide permanent stages and more complex sets. The enclosed courtyards also made it easier to keep out nonpaying crashers, the greatest enemies of the new showmen—capitalists who produced and often wrote the plays and had to make a living from them.

Several of London's more scrupulous clergymen decried another advantage of the combined inn and theater—the opportunity it gave for sexual license. By the sixteenth century, the allegorical moralizing of the medieval country theater had evolved into the ribald, worldly entertainment of the London stage. Going to the theater was now more like being part of a festival than listening to a sermon. The workmen and young women who comprised much of the audience found it convenient to hire rooms in which they might romance one another during or after the performance.

London's theater world reached full maturity in the late sixteenth and early seventeenth centuries. The Rose and The Globe theaters, where many of Shakespeare's plays were presented, were built in the 1590s on the south bank of the River Thames, reachable only by water taxis. During Shakespeare's heyday, some 40,000 waterboys were said to ferry customers to these theaters. Performances by troupes of adult males or boys (women were banned from the stage) were often rowdy affairs, the crowds egged on both by the witty repartee on stage and the food and beer sold in the pit.

■ *What were the basic elements and purpose of the medieval stage, and what was carried over from it to the Elizabethan theater?*

Sources: E. K. Chambers, *The Elizabethan Stage*, vols. I–IV (Oxford, 1923); Lawrence M. Clopper, *Drama, Play, and Game: English Festive Culture in the Medieval and Early Modern Period* (Chicago, 2001); F. E. Halliday, *Shakespeare in His Age* (New York, 1956).

A seventeenth-century sketch of the Swan Theatre, which stood near Shakespeare's Globe Theatre on the south bank of the Thames. The Bridgeman Art Library

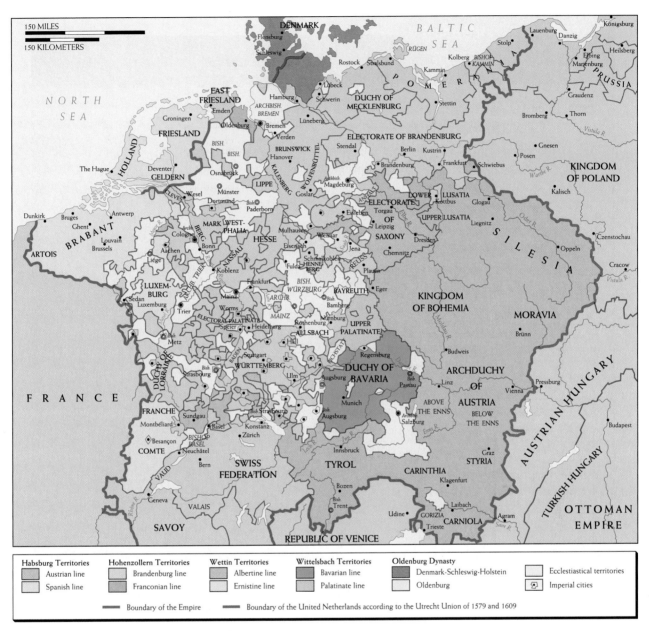

MAP 12–2   GERMANY IN 1547   *Mid-sixteenth-century Germany was an almost ungovernable land of about 360 autonomous political entities. Originally "Map of Germany Showing Its Great Division/Fragmentation in the 16th Century" from Majo Holborn,* A History of Germany: The Reformation, *Copyright (c) 1982 by Princeton University Press. Reprinted by permission of Princeton University Press.*

rulers pressed in on Germany both for reasons of trade and because some held lands or legal privileges within certain German principalities. German princes, in their turn, looked to import and export markets beyond German borders and opposed any efforts to consolidate the Holy Roman Empire, lest their territorial rights, confirmed by the Peace of Augsburg, be overturned. German princes were not loath to turn to Catholic France or to the kings of Denmark and Sweden for allies against the Habsburg emperor.

After the Council of Trent, Protestants in the empire suspected the existence of an imperial and papal conspiracy to recreate the Catholic Europe of pre-Reformation times. The imperial diet, which the German princes controlled, demanded strict observance of the constitutional rights of Germans, as set forth in agreements with the emperor since the mid–fourteenth century. In the late sixteenth century, the emperor ruled only to the degree to which he was prepared to use force of arms against his subjects.

MAP 12–3   RELIGIOUS DIVISIONS ABOUT 1600   *By 1600, few could seriously expect Christians to return to a uniform religious allegiance. In Spain and southern Italy, Catholicism remained relatively unchallenged, but note the existence elsewhere of large religious minorities, both Catholic and Protestant.*

Religious Division Religious conflict accentuated the international and internal political divisions. (See Map 12–3.) During this period, the population within the Holy Roman Empire was about equally divided between Catholics and Protestants, the latter having perhaps a slight numerical edge by 1600. The terms of the Peace of Augsburg had attempted to freeze the territorial holdings of the Lutherans and the Catholics (the so-called *ecclesiastical reservation*). In the intervening years, however, the Lutherans had gained and kept political control in some Catholic areas, as had the Catholics in a few previously Lutheran areas. Such territorial reversals, or the threat of them, only increased the suspicion and antipathy between the two sides.

The Lutherans had been far more successful in securing their rights to worship in Catholic lands than the Catholics had been in securing such rights in Lutheran lands. The Catholic rulers, who were in a weakened position after the Reformation, had made, but resented, concessions to Protestant communities within their territories. With the passage of time, they demanded that all ecclesiastical princes, electors, archbishops, bishops, and abbots who had deserted the Catholic for the Protestant side be immediately deprived of their religious offices and that their ecclesiastical holdings be promptly returned to Catholic control in accordance with the ecclesiastical reservation. However, the Lutherans and, especially, the Calvinists in the Palatinate ignored this stipulation at every opportunity.

There was also religious strife in the empire between liberal and conservative Lutherans and between Lutherans and the growing numbers of Calvinists. The last half of the sixteenth century was a time of warring Protestant factions within German universities. And in addition to the heightened religious strife, a new scientific and material culture was becoming ascendant in intellectual and political circles, increasing the anxiety of religious people of all persuasions.

Calvinism and the Palatinate As elsewhere in Europe, Calvinism was the political and religious leaven within the Holy Roman Empire on the eve of the Thirty Years' War. Unrecognized as a legal religion by the Peace of Augsburg, it gained a strong foothold within the empire when Frederick III (r. 1559–1576), a devout convert to Calvinism, became elector Palatine (ruler within the Palatinate; see Map 12–3) and made it the official religion of his domain. Heidelberg became a German Geneva in the 1560s: both a great intellectual center of Calvinism and a staging area for Calvinist penetration into the empire. By 1609, Palatine Calvinists headed a Protestant defensive alliance that received outside support from Spain's sixteenth-century enemies: England, France, and the Netherlands.

The Lutherans came to fear the Calvinists almost as much as they did the Catholics. Palatine Calvinists seemed to the Lutherans directly to threaten the Peace of Augsburg—and hence the legal foundation of the Lutheran states—by their bold missionary forays into the empire. Also, outspoken Calvinist criticism of the doctrine of Christ's real presence in the Eucharist shocked the more religiously conservative Lutherans. The elector Palatine once expressed his disbelief in transubstantiation by publicly shredding the host and mocking it as a "fine God." To Lutherans, such religious disrespect and aggressiveness disgraced the Reformation as well as the elector.

Maximilian of Bavaria and the Catholic League If the Calvinists were active within the Holy Roman Empire, so also were their Catholic counterparts, the Jesuits. Staunchly Catholic Bavaria, supported by Spain, became militarily and ideologically for the Counter-Reformation what the Palatinate was for Protestantism. From there, the Jesuits launched successful missions throughout the empire, winning such major cities as Strasbourg and Osnabrück back

to the Catholic fold by 1600. In 1609, Maximilian, duke of Bavaria, organized a Catholic league to counter a new Protestant alliance that had been formed in the same year under the leadership of the Calvinist elector Palatine, Frederick IV (r. 1583–1610). When the league fielded a great army under the command of Count Johann von Tilly, the stage was set, both internally and internationally, for the worst of the religious wars, the Thirty Years' War. (See Map 12–4.)

FOUR PERIODS OF WAR

The war went through four distinguishable periods. During its course, it drew in every major western European nation—at least diplomatically and financially if not by direct military involvement. The four periods were the Bohemian (1618–1625); the Danish (1625–1629); the Swedish (1630–1635); and the Swedish-French (1635–1648).

The Bohemian Period The war broke out in Bohemia after the ascent to the Bohemian throne in 1618 of the Habsburg Ferdinand, archduke of Styria, who was also in the line of succession to the imperial throne. Educated by the Jesuits and a fervent Catholic, Ferdinand was determined to restore the traditional faith to the eastern Habsburg lands (Austria, Bohemia, and Poland).

No sooner had Ferdinand become king of Bohemia than he revoked the religious freedoms of Bohemian Protestants. In force since 1575, these freedoms had even been recently broadened by Emperor Rudolf II (r. 1576–1612) in his Letter of Majesty in 1609. The Protestant nobility in Prague responded to Ferdinand's act in May 1618 by throwing his regents out the window. The event has ever since been known as the "defenestration of Prague." (The three officials fell fifty feet into a dry moat that, fortunately, was padded with manure, which cushioned their fall and spared their lives.) In the following year Ferdinand became Holy Roman Emperor as Ferdinand II, by the unanimous vote of the seven electors. The Bohemians, however, defiantly deposed him in Prague and declared the Calvinist elector Palatine, Frederick V (r. 1616–1623), their overlord.

What had begun as a revolt of the Protestant nobility against an unpopular king of Bohemia thereafter escalated into an international war. Spain sent troops to Ferdinand, who found more immediate allies in Maximilian of Bavaria and the opportunistic Lutheran elector John George I of Saxony (r. 1611–1656), who saw a sure route to territorial gain by joining in an easy victory over the weaker elector Palatine. This was not the only time politics and

MAP 12–4 THE HOLY ROMAN EMPIRE ABOUT 1618 *On the eve of the Thirty Years' War, the Holy Roman Empire was politically and religiously fragmented, as revealed by this somewhat simplified map. Lutherans dominated the north and Catholics the south; Calvinists controlled the United Provinces and the Palatinate and were important in Switzerland and Brandenburg.*

greed would overshadow religion during the long conflict, although Lutheran-Calvinist religious animosity also overrode a common Protestantism.

Ferdinand's army under Tilly routed Frederick V's troops at the Battle of White Mountain in 1620. By 1622, Ferdinand had managed not only to subdue and re-Catholicize Bohemia, but to conquer the Palatinate as well. Meanwhile, the duke of Bavaria pressed the conflict into northwestern Germany, laying claim to land as he went.

The Danish Period These events raised new fears that a reconquest and re-Catholicization of the empire now loomed, which was precisely Ferdinand II's design. The Lutheran king Christian IV (r. 1588–1648) of Denmark, who already held territory within the empire as the duke of Holstein, was eager to extend Danish influence over the coastal towns of the North Sea. Encouraged by the English, the French, and the Dutch, he picked up the Protestant banner of resistance, opening the Danish period of the conflict (1625–1629). Entering Germany with his army in 1626, he was, however, quickly humiliated by Maximilian and forced to retreat into Denmark.

As military success made Maximilian stronger and an untrustworthy ally, Emperor Ferdinand sought a more pliant tool for his policies in Albrecht of Wallenstein (1583–1634), a powerful mercenary. Another opportunistic Protestant, Wallenstein had gained a great deal of territory by joining Ferdinand during the conquest of Bohemia. A brilliant and ruthless military strategist, Wallenstein carried Ferdinand's campaign into Denmark. By 1628, he commanded a crack army of more than 100,000 and also became a law unto himself, completely outside the emperor's control.

Wallenstein, however, had broken Protestant resistance so successfully that Ferdinand could issue the Edict of Restitution in 1629, a proclamation that dramatically reasserted the Catholic safeguards of the Peace of Augsburg (1555). It reaffirmed the illegality of Calvinism—a completely unrealistic move by 1629—and ordered the return of all church lands acquired by the Lutherans since 1552, an equally unrealistic mandate despite its legal basis. Compliance would have involved the return of no less than sixteen bishoprics and twenty-eight cities and towns to Catholic allegiance. The new edict struck panic in the hearts of Protestants and Habsburg opponents everywhere.

The Swedish Period   Gustavus Adolphus of Sweden (r. 1611–1632), a deeply pious king of a unified Lutheran nation, became the new leader of Protestant forces within the empire, opening the Swedish period of the war (1630–1635). He was bankrolled by two very interested bystanders: the French minister Cardinal Richelieu, whose foreign policy was to protect French interests by keeping Habsburg armies tied down in Germany, and the Dutch, who had not forgotten Spanish Habsburg domination in the sixteenth century. In alliance with the electors of Brandenburg and Saxony, the Swedish king won a smashing victory at Breitenfeld in 1630, one that so dramatically reversed the course of the war that it has been regarded as the most decisive engagement of the long conflict.

One of the reasons for the overwhelming Swedish victory at Breitenfeld was the military genius of Gustavus Adolphus. The Swedish king brought a new mobility to warfare by having both his infantry and his cavalry employ fire-and-charge tactics. At six deep, his infantry squares were smaller than the traditional ones, and he filled them with equal numbers of musketeers and pikemen. His cavalry also alternated pistol shots with charges with the sword. His artillery was lighter and more mobile in battle. Each unit of his army—infantry, cavalry, and artillery—had both defensive and offensive capability and could quickly change from one to the other.

Gustavus Adolphus died at the hands of Wallenstein's forces during the Battle of Lützen (November 1632)—a very costly engagement for both sides that created a brief standstill. Ferdinand had long been resentful of Wallenstein's independence, although he was the major factor in imperial success. In 1634, Ferdinand had Wallenstein assassinated. By that time, not only had Wallenstein served his purpose for the emperor, but, ever opportunistic, he was even trying openly to strike bargains with the Protestants for his services. The Wallenstein episode is a telling commentary on this war without honor. Despite the deep religious motivations, greed and political gain were the real forces at work in the Thirty Years' War. Even allies that owed one another their success were not above treating each other as mortal enemies.

In the Peace of Prague in 1635, the German Protestant states, led by Saxony, reached a compromise with Ferdinand. The Swedes, however, received continued support from France and the Netherlands. Desiring to maximize their investment in the war, they refused to join the agreement. Their resistance to settlement plunged the war into its fourth and most devastating phase.

The Swedish-French Period   The French openly entered the war in 1635, sending men and munitions as well as financial subsidies. After their entrance, the war dragged on for thirteen years, with French, Swedish, and Spanish soldiers looting the length and breadth of Germany—warring, it seemed, simply for the sake of warfare itself. The Germans, long weary of the devastation, were too disunited to repulse the foreign armies; they simply watched and suffered. By the time peace talks began in the Westphalian cities of Münster and Osnabrück in 1644, an estimated one-third of the German population had died as a direct result of the war. It has been

A contemporary engraving portraying the assassination of the opportunistic mercenary Albrecht of Wallenstein.
Zeitgenossischer Kupferstich von C. Luyken. Bildarchiv Preussischer Kulturbesitz.

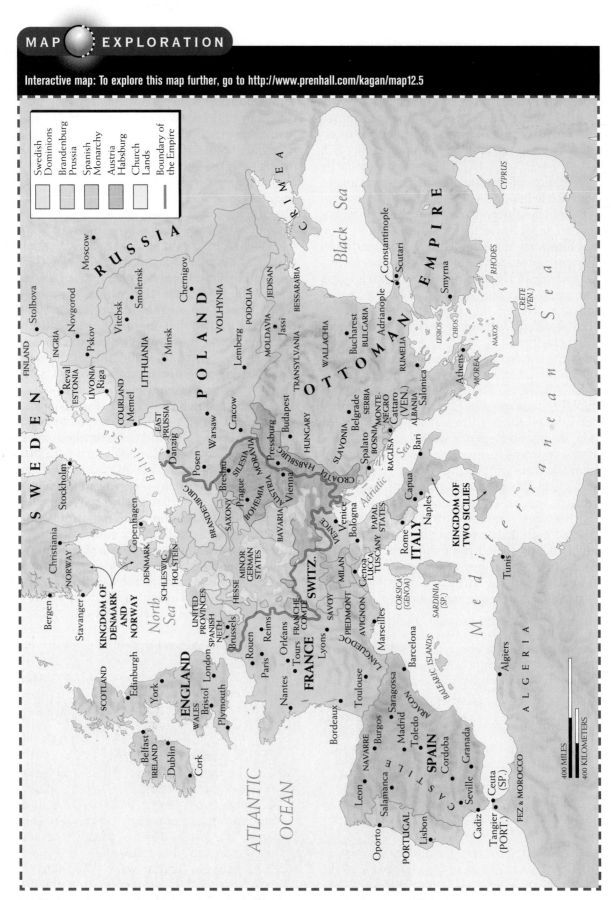

MAP 12–5 EUROPE IN 1648 *At the end of the Thirty Years' War, Spain still had extensive possessions. Austria and Brandenburg-Prussia were rising powers, the independence of the United Provinces and Switzerland was recognized, and Sweden had footholds in northern Germany.*

called the worst European catastrophe since the Black Death of the fourteenth century.

THE TREATY OF WESTPHALIA

The Treaty of Westphalia in 1648 brought all hostilities within the Holy Roman Empire to an end. (See Map 12–5.) It rescinded Ferdinand's Edict of Restitution and firmly reasserted the major feature of the religious settlement of the Peace of Augsburg, with the ruler of each land again permitted to determine the religion there. The treaty also gave the Calvinists their long-sought legal recognition. The independence of the Swiss Confederacy and the United Provinces of Holland, long recognized in fact, was now proclaimed in law. And the treaty elevated Bavaria to the rank of an elector state. The provisions of the treaty made the German princes supreme over their principalities. Yet, as guarantors of the treaty, Sweden and France found many occasions to meddle in German affairs until the century's end, France to considerable territorial gain. Brandenburg-Prussia emerged as the most powerful northern German state. Because the treaty broadened the legal status of Protestantism, the pope opposed it altogether, but he had no power to prevent it.

France and Spain remained at war outside the empire until 1659, when French victories forced the humiliating Treaty of the Pyrenees on the Spanish. Thereafter France became Europe's dominant power, and the once vast Habsburg kingdom waned.

By confirming the territorial sovereignty of Germany's many political entities, the Treaty of Westphalia perpetuated German division and political weakness into the modern period. Only two German states attained any international significance during the seventeenth century: Austria and Brandenburg-Prussia. The petty regionalism within the empire also reflected on a small scale the drift of larger European politics. In the seventeenth century, distinctive nation-states, each with its own political, cultural, and religious identity, reached maturity and firmly established the competitive nationalism of the modern world.

IN PERSPECTIVE

Both religion and politics played major roles in each of the great conflicts of the Age of Religious Wars—the internal struggle in France, Spain's unsuccessful effort to subdue the Netherlands, England's successful resistance of Spain, and the steady march of virtually every major European power through the hapless Holy Roman Empire during the first half of the seventeenth century. Parties and armies of different religious persuasions are visible in each conflict, and in each we also find a life-or-death political struggle.

The wars ended with the recognition of minority religious rights and a guarantee of the traditional boundaries of political sovereignty. In France, the Edict of Nantes (1598) brought peace by granting Huguenots basic religious and civil freedoms and by recognizing their towns and territories. With the departure of the Spanish, peace and sovereignty also came to the Netherlands, guaranteed initially by the Twelve Years' Truce (1609) and secured fully by the Peace of Westphalia (1648). The conflict between England and Spain ended with the removal of the Spanish threat to English sovereignty in politics and religion, which resulted from the execution of Mary, Queen of Scots (1587) and the English victory over the Armada (1588). In the Holy Roman Empire, peace came with the reaffirmation of the political principle of the Peace of Augsburg (1555), as the Peace of Westphalia brought the Thirty Years' War to an end by again recognizing the sovereignty of rulers within their lands and their right to determine the religious beliefs of their subjects. Europe at midcentury had real, if brief, peace.

REVIEW QUESTIONS

1. What part did politics play in the religious positions of the French leaders? How did the king (or his regent) decide which side to favor? What led to the infamous Saint Bartholomew's Day Massacre, and what did it achieve?
2. How did Spain achieve a position of dominance in the sixteenth century? What were its strengths and weaknesses as a nation? What were Philip II's goals? Which was he unable to achieve and why?
3. Henry of Navarre (Henry IV of France), Elizabeth I, and William of Orange were all *politiques*. Define the term and explain why it applies to these three rulers.
4. Discuss the background to the establishment of the Anglican Church in England. What were the politics of Mary I? What was Elizabeth I's settlement, and how difficult was it to impose on all of England? Who were her detractors and what were their criticisms?
5. Why was the Thirty Years' War fought? To what extent did politics determine the outcome of the war? Discuss the Treaty of Westphalia in 1648. Could matters have been resolved without war?

6. It has been said that the Thirty Years' War is the outstanding example in European history of meaningless conflict. Evaluate this statement and provide specific reasons for or against it.

SUGGESTED READINGS

F. BRAUDEL, *The Mediterranean and the Mediterranean World in the Age of Philip the Second*, vols. 1 and 2 (1976). Widely acclaimed work of a French master historian.

N. Z. DAVIS, *Society and Culture in Early Modern France* (1975). Essays on popular culture.

R. DUNN, *The Age of Religious Wars, 1559–1689* (1979). Excellent brief survey of every major conflict.

J. H. ELLIOTT, *Europe Divided 1559–1598* (1968). Direct, lucid narrative account.

J. H. FRANKLIN (ED. AND TRANS.), *Constitutionalism and Resistance in the Sixteenth Century: Three Treatises by Hotman, Beza, and Mornay* (1969). Three defenders of the right of people to resist tyranny.

P. GEYL, *The Revolt of the Netherlands, 1555–1609* (1958). The authoritative survey.

J. GUY, *Tudor England* (1990). The standard history and good synthesis of recent scholarship.

C. HAIGH, *Elizabeth* I (1988). Elizabeth portrayed as a magnificent politician and propagandist.

D. LOADES, *Mary Tudor* (1989). Authoritative and good storytelling.

G. MATTINGLY, *The Armada* (1959). A masterpiece and resembling a novel in style.

J. E. NEALE, *The Age of Catherine de Médicis* (1962). Short, concise summary.

A. SOMAN (ED.), *The Massacre of St. Bartholomew's Day: Reappraisals and Documents* (1974). Results of an international symposium on the anniversary of the massacre.

K. THOMAS, *Religion and the Decline of Magic* (1971). Provocative, much-acclaimed work focused on popular culture.

C. WEDGWOOD, *William the Silent* (1944). Excellent political biography of William of Orange.

J. WORMALD, *Mary, Queen of Scots: A Study in Failure* (1991). Mary portrayed as a queen who did not understand her country and was out of touch with the times.

DOCUMENTS CD-ROM

THE REFORMATION

11.5   The Edict of Nantes

SOCIETY AND POLITICS IN EARLY MODERN EUROPE

12.4   The Peace of Westphalia, 1648
12.5   Putting the Poor to Work

A Woman Paints Her Life and Times

Not until the baroque period (1550–1700) did some exceptional women painters take their place beside their great male counterparts. None was more impressive than Artemisia Gentileschi (1593–ca. 1635), who was trained by her accomplished artist-father Orazio (1563–1639). By age nineteen she was, in his opinion, without peer among contemporary artists.

Artemisia's early work focused on biblical and ancient women who had been sexually threatened (Susanna), raped (Lucretia), or had suffered irrevocable personal loss (Judith). These women were commonplace subjects of great Renaissance and baroque male artists, such as Paolo Veronese, Michelangelo Caravaggio (with whom Artemisia's father had studied), and Peter Paul Rubens. Artemisia, however, painted these historic figures with a difference that many believe stemmed from her own traumatic experience as a woman.

When Artemisia, at seventeen, painted her *Susanna and the Elders* (1610), she may have been, like Susanna, the object of unwanted sexual advances. The painting shows a frightened Susanna with two male elders, one of whom is possibly a likeness of her suitor and soon to be rapist, Agostino Tassi. According to well-documented charges brought against him in May 1611, Tassi, with an accomplice, raped Artemisia in her father's house. The violation remained her secret for almost a year before her father learned of it and accused Tassi. In the intervening period, Artemisia, desperate to save her reputation and evidently having feelings for Tassi, tried to hold him to the promise of marriage he made after the rape. Had he been willing to marry her, the details of the rape would have remained unknown to history, and there would have been no trial.

But Tassi had a wife, and with the help of his friends, he impugned Artemisia's character in the hope of avoiding any court action against himself. Because the evidence of a rape was overwhelming, his efforts failed, and he was sentenced to a five-year exile from Rome. However, in the end, he was allowed to remain in Rome, and his sentence was soon revoked. At this same time, Artemisia, now nineteen, married someone else and moved to Florence, where she continued her career.

These experiences may have left Artemisia, like other women who have experienced similar ordeals, with a jaundiced view of men. Some critics perceive such an outlook in Artemisia's portrayal (1612–1613) of the biblical heroine Judith's assassination of the Assyrian general Holofernes, who was threatening to massacre the Israelites. In the painting, Judith, with rolled-up sleeves and a businesslike demeanor, and her maid decapitate the surprised Assyrian as if they were slaughtering a pig or a goat for a roast.

■ *Did Artemisia depict women differently than male artists of the period painted women? Did Artemisia receive justice after she was raped?*n

Sources: R. Ward Bassell, *Artemisia Gentileschi and the Authority of Art* (University Park, PA: Pennsylvania State University Press, 1998), pp. 1-2, 8, 14-15, 17, 78; H.W. Janson and Anthony F. Janson, *History of Art*, 5th ed. (New York: Harry N. Abrams, 1995), p. 52.

Artemisia Gentileschi, *Judith Decapitating Holofernes*, ca. 1611–1612. Naples, Museo di Capodimonte. ©t Alinari/Art Resource, N.Y.

Versailles, as painted in 1668 by Pierre Patel the Elder (1605–1676). The central building is the hunting lodge built by Louis XIII earlier in the century. Louis XIV added the wings, the gardens, and the forecourt. Pierre Patel, *Perspective View of Versailles*, Chateau de Versailles et de Trianon, Versailles, France. Copyright Giraudon/Art Resource, N.Y.

CHAPTER 13

PATHS TO CONSTITUTIONALISM AND ABSOLUTISM:

England and France in the Seventeenth Century

*D*URING THE SEVENTEENTH CENTURY, ENGLAND and France moved in two different political directions. By the close of the century, after decades of fierce civil war and religious conflict that pitted Parliament against monarch, England had developed into a parliamentary monarchy with a policy of limited religious toleration. Parliament, composed of the House of Lords and the House of Commons, shared responsibility for government with the monarch. It met regularly, and the Commons, composed primarily of wealthy landed gentry, had to stand for election every three years. By contrast, France developed an absolutist, centralized form of government dominated by a monarchy that shared little power with any other national institutions. Its authority resided rather in a complex set of relationships with local nobility, guilds, and towns and in its ability to support the largest standing army in Europe. In the seventeenth century, France also abandoned Henry IV's policy of religious toleration and proscribed all but the Roman Catholic Church.

These English and French forms of government became models for other nations. The French model, termed absolutism *in the nineteenth century, would be imitated by other monarchies across the Continent during the eighteenth century. The English model would later inspire the political creed known in the nineteenth century as* liberalism. *Like all such political labels, these terms, although useful, can conceal considerable complexity. English "parliamentary monarchs" did not share all power with Parliament; they controlled the army, foreign policy, and much patronage. Likewise the "absolute monarchs" of France and their later imitators elsewhere in Europe were not truly absolute: Laws, traditions, and many local institutions and customs limited their power.*

Two Models of European Political Development

Constitutional Crisis and Settlement in Stuart England

Rise of Absolute Monarchy in France

The Years of Louis XIV's Personal Rule

In Perspective

Two Models of European Political Development

In the second half of the sixteenth century, changes in military organization, weapons, and tactics sharply increased the cost of warfare. Because traditional sources of revenue were inadequate to finance these growing costs—as well as the costs of government—monarchs sought new sources. Only monarchies that built a secure financial base which was not deeply dependent on the support of estates, diets, or assemblies of nobles achieved absolute rule. The French monarchy succeeded in this effort after midcentury, whereas the English monarchy failed. The paths to that success and failure led to the two models of government—**absolutism** in France and **parliamentary monarchy** in England—that shaped subsequent political development in Europe.

In their pursuit of adequate income, English monarchs of the seventeenth century threatened the local political interests and economic well-being of the country's nobility and others of great landed and commercial wealth. These politically active groups, invoking traditional English liberties in their defense, effectively resisted the monarchs' attempted intrusions throughout the century.

The experience of Louis XIV, the French king, was different. During the second half of the seventeenth century, he would make the French nobility dependent on his goodwill and patronage. In turn, he would support their local influence and their place in a firm social hierarchy. But even the French king's dominance of the nobility was not complete. Louis accepted the authority of the noble-dominated

Parlement of Paris to register royal decrees before they officially became law, and he permitted regional **parlements** to exercise considerable authority over local administration and taxation. Funds from taxes levied by the central monarchy found their way into many local pockets.

Religious factors also affected the political destinies of England and France. A strong Protestant religious movement known as Puritanism arose in England and actively opposed the Stuart monarchy. Puritanism represented a nonpolitical force that sought at first to limit and eventually to overturn the English monarchy. Louis XIV, in contrast, crushed the Protestant communities of France. He was generally supported in these efforts by Roman Catholics, who saw religious uniformity enforced by the monarchy working to their advantage.

There were also major institutional differences between the two countries. In Parliament, England possessed a political institution that had long bargained with the monarch over political issues. In the early seventeenth century, to be sure, Parliament did not meet regularly and was not the strong institution it would become by the close of the century. Nor was there anything certain or inevitable about the transformation it underwent over the course of the century. The institutional basis for it, however, was in place. Parliament was there and expected to be consulted from time to time. Its members—nobility and gentry—had experience organizing and speaking, writing legislation, and criticizing royal policies. Furthermore, the English had a legal and political tradition based on concepts of liberty to which members of Parliament and their supporters throughout the country could and did appeal in their conflict with the monarchy.

For all intents, France lacked a similarly strong tradition of broad liberties, representation, and bargaining between the monarchy and other national institutions. The Estates General had met from time to time to grant certain revenues to the monarch, but it played no role after the early seventeenth century. It met in 1614, but thereafter the monarchy was able to find other sources of income, and the Estates General was not called again until the eve of the French Revolution in 1789. Consequently, whatever political forces might have wished to oppose or limit the monarchy lacked both an institutional base from which to operate and a tradition of meetings during which the necessary political skills might have been developed.

Finally, personalities played an important role. During the first half of the century, France profited from the guidance of two of its most able statesmen: Cardinals Richelieu and Mazarin. Mazarin trained Louis XIV to be a hardworking, if not always wise, monarch. Louis drew strong and capable ministers about himself. The four Stuart monarchs of England, in contrast, had trouble simply making people trust them. They did not always keep their word. They acted on whim. They often displayed faulty judgment. In a political situation that demanded compromise, they rarely offered any. They offended significant groups of their subjects unnecessarily. In a nation that saw itself as strongly Protestant, they were suspected, sometimes accurately, of Catholic sympathies. Many of Charles's opponents in Parliament, of course, had flaws of their own, but the nature of the situation focused attention and criticism on the king.

In both England and France, the nobility and large landowners stood at the top of the social hierarchy and sought to protect their privileges and local interests. Important segments of the British nobility and landed classes came to distrust the Stuart monarchs, whom they believed sought to undermine their local political control and social standing. Parliamentary government was the result of the efforts of these English landed classes to protect their concerns and limit the power of the monarchy to interfere with life on the local level. The French nobility under Louis XIV, in contrast, eventually concluded that the best way to secure its own interests was to support his monarchy. He provided nobles with many forms of patronage, and he protected their tax exemptions, their wealth, and their local social standing.

The divergent developments of England and France in the seventeenth century would have surprised most people in 1600. It was not inevitable that the English monarchy would have to govern through Parliament or that the French monarchy would avoid dealing with national political institutions that could significantly limit its authority. The Stuart kings of England certainly aspired to the autocracy Louis XIV achieved, and some English political philosophers eloquently defended the divine right of kings and absolute rule. At the beginning of the seventeenth century, the English monarchy was strong. Queen Elizabeth, after a reign of almost forty-five years, was much revered. Parliament met only when called to provide financial support to the monarch. France, however, was emerging from the turmoil of its religious wars. The strife of that conflict had torn the society asunder. The monarchy was relatively weak. Henry IV, who had become king in 1589, pursued a policy of religious toleration. The French nobles had significant military forces at their disposal and in the middle of the seventeenth century confronted the king with rebellion. These conditions would change dramatically in both nations by the late seventeenth century.

This elegant painting portrays a very quiet London of the mid-1630s. During the next sixty years it would suffer wrenching political turmoil and the devastation of a great fire.
Claude de Jongh (fl. 1615–1663), *The Thames at Westminster Stairs*, signed and dated 163(?1 or 7). Oil on panel, 18-1/4 × 31-1/2 inches (46.4 × 80 cm). B1973.1.31. Yale Center for British Art, Paul Mellon Collection

Constitutional Crisis and Settlement in Stuart England

JAMES I

In 1603, without opposition or incident, James VI of Scotland (r. 1603–1625), the son of Mary Stuart, Queen of Scots, succeeded the childless Elizabeth as James I of England. His was a difficult situation. The elderly queen had been very popular and was totally identified with the nation. James was not well known, would never be popular, and, as a Scot, was an outsider. He inherited not only the crown, but also a large royal debt and a fiercely divided church—problems that his politically active subjects expected him to address. The new king strongly advocated the divine right of kings, a subject on which he had written a book—*A Trew Law of Free Monarchies*—in 1598. He expected to rule with a minimum of consultation beyond his own royal court.

James quickly managed to anger many of his new subjects, but he did not wholly alienate them. In this period, Parliament met only when the monarch summoned it, which James hoped to do rarely. Its chief business was to grant certain sources of income. The real value of these revenues, however, had been falling during the past half century, limiting their importance and thus the importance of Parliament to the king. To meet his needs, James developed other sources of income, largely by levying—solely on the authority of ill-defined privileges claimed to be attached to the office of king—new custom duties known as *impositions*. These were a version of the older customs duties known as *tonnage* and *poundage*. Members of Parliament resented these independent efforts to raise revenues as an affront to their authority over the royal purse, but they did not seek a serious confrontation. Rather, throughout James's reign, they wrangled and negotiated behind the scenes.

The religious problem also festered under James. **Puritans** within the Church of England had hoped that James's experience with the Scottish Presbyterian church and his own Protestant upbringing would incline him to favor their efforts to further the reformation of the English church. Since the days of Elizabeth, they had sought to eliminate elaborate religious ceremonies and replace the hierarchical episcopal system of church governance with a more representative Presbyterian form like that of the Calvinist churches on the Continent.

In January 1604, the Puritans had their first direct dealing with the new king. James responded in that month to a statement of Puritan grievances, the so-called Millenary Petition, at a special religious conference at Hampton Court. The political implications of the demands in this petition concerned him, and their tone offended him. To the dismay of the Puritans, he firmly declared his intention to maintain and even enhance the Anglican episcopacy. "A Scottish presbytery," he snorted, "agreeth as well with monarchy as God and the devil. No bishops, no king." James was not simply being arbitrary. Elizabeth also had not accommodated the Puritan demands. To have done so would have worsened the already existing strife within the Church of England.

Both sides left the conference with their suspicions of one another largely confirmed. The Hampton Court conference did, however, sow one fruitful seed: A commission was appointed to render a new translation of the Bible. That mission was fulfilled in 1611 with the publication of the eloquent authorized, or King James, version.

James also offended the Puritans with his opposition to their narrow view of human life and social activities. The Puritans believed that Sunday should be a day taken up largely with religious observances and little leisure or recreation. James believed that recreation and sports were innocent activities and good for his people. He also believed that Puritan narrowness discouraged Roman Catholics from converting to the Church of England. Consequently, in 1618, he issued the *Book of Sports*, which permitted games on Sunday for people who attended Church of England services. Many clergy refused to read his order from the pulpit, and he had to rescind it. (See "King James I Defends Popular Recreation against the Puritans" and "Encountering the Past: Early Controversy over Tobacco and Smoking.")

It was during James's reign that some religious dissenters began to leave England. In 1620, Puritan separatists founded Plymouth Colony in Cape Cod Bay in North America, preferring flight from England to Anglican conformity. Later in the 1620s, a larger, better financed group of Puritans left England to found the Massachusetts Bay Colony. In each case, the colonists believed that reformation would or could not go far enough in England and that only in America could they worship freely and organize a truly reformed church.

Although James inherited a difficult situation, he also created special problems for himself. His court became a center of scandal and corruption. He governed by favorites, with the most influential the duke of Buckingham, whom rumor made the king's homosexual lover. Buckingham controlled royal patronage and openly sold peerages and titles to the highest bidders—a practice that angered the nobility because it cheapened their rank. There had always

KING JAMES I DEFENDS POPULAR RECREATION AGAINST THE PURITANS

The English Puritans believed in strict observance of the Sabbath, disapproving any sports, games, or general social conviviality on Sunday. James I thought these strictures prevented many Roman Catholics from joining the Church of England. In 1618, he ordered the clergy of the Church of England to read the Book of Sports *from their pulpits. In this declaration, he permitted people to engage in certain sports and games after church services. His hope was to allow innocent recreations on Sunday while encouraging people to attend the Church of England. Despite the king's good intentions, the order offended the Puritans. The clergy resisted his order and he had to withdraw it.*

■ *What motives of state might have led James I to issue this declaration? How does he attempt to make it favorable to the Church of England? Why might so many clergy have refused to read this statement to their congregations?*

With our own ears we heard the general complaint of our people, that they were barred from all lawful recreation and exercise upon the Sunday's afternoon, after the ending of all divine service, which cannot but produce two evils: the one the hindering of the conversion of many [Roman Catholic subjects], whom their priests will take occasion hereby to vex, persuading them that no honest mirth or recreation is lawful or tolerable in our religion, which cannot but breed a great discontentment in our people's hearts, especially as such as are peradventure upon the point of turning [to the Church of England]: the other inconvenience is, that this prohibition barreth the common and meaner sort of people from using such exercises as may make their bodies more able for war, when we or our successors shall have occasion to use them; and in place thereof sets up filthy tipplings and drunkenness, and breeds a number of idle and discontented speeches in their ale-houses. For when shall the common people have leave to exercise, if not upon the Sundays and holy days, seeing they must apply their labor and win their living in all working days? . . .

[A]s for our good people's lawful recreation, our pleasure likewise is, that after the end of divine service our good people be not disturbed, . . . or discouraged from any lawful recreation, such as dancing, either men or women; archery for men, leaping, vaulting, or any other such harmless recreation, or from having of Hay-games, Whitsun-ales, and Morris-dances; and the setting up of May-poles and other sports therewith used; . . . but withal we do here account still as prohibited all unlawful games to be used upon Sundays only, as bear and bull-baitings . . . and at all times in the meaner sort of people by law prohibited, bowling.

And likewise we bar from this benefit and liberty all such known as recusants [Roman Catholics], either men or women, as will abstain from coming to church or divine service, being therefore unworthy of any lawful recreation after the said service, that will not first come to the church and serve God; prohibiting in like sort the said recreations to any that, though [they] conform in religion [i.e., members of the Church of England], are not present in the church at the service of God, before their going to the said recreations.

From Henry Bettenson, ed., *Documents of the Christian Church*, 2nd ed. (London: Oxford University Press, 1963), pp. 400–403. By permission of Oxford University Press.

---

been court favorites, but never before had a single person so controlled access to the monarch.

James's foreign policy also roused opposition. He regarded himself as a peacemaker. Peace reduced pressures on royal revenues and the need for larger debts. The less his demands for money, the less the king had to depend on the goodwill of Parliament.

In 1604, he concluded a much-needed peace with Spain, England's chief adversary during the second half of the sixteenth century. His subjects viewed this peace as a sign of pro-Catholic sentiment. James further increased suspicions when he tried unsuccessfully to relax the penal laws against Catholics. The English had not forgotten the brutal

ENCOUNTERING THE PAST

Early Controversy over Tobacco and Smoking

Smoking today is widely condemned throughout the West, but the controversy over tobacco goes back to the earliest European encounter with the plant, which was native to the Americas.

Christopher Columbus on his first voyage in 1492 saw Native Americans smoking tobacco. Later, the first Spanish missionaries associated smoking with pagan religious practices and tried to stop Native Americans from using tobacco. Once tobacco reached Europe in the late sixteenth century, more opposition to smoking arose (although—ironically—some physicians thought it might cure diseases of the lungs and internal organs). As early as 1610, Sir Francis Bacon (1561–1626) noted that smokers found it difficult to stop smoking. The Christian clergy throughout Europe denounced smoking as immoral, and Muslim clerics condemned the practice as contrary to Islam when it spread to the Ottoman Empire. Nonetheless, smoking tobacco in pipes became popular.

The chief British critic of the new practice was none other than King James I (r. 1603–1625). While he defended Sunday sports against Puritan critics who believed any amusements on the Sabbath were sinful, he detested smoking. In 1604, he published his *Counterblast to Tobacco* in which he declared, "Have you not reason then to be ashamed, and to forbear this filthy novelty . . .? In your abuse thereof sinning against God, harming yourselves in person . . . and taking thereby the marks . . . of vanity upon you. . . . A custom loathsome to the eye, hateful to the nose, harmful to the brain, dangerous to the lungs, and the black stinking fume thereof, nearest resembling the horrible Stygian smoke of the pit that is bottomless."[1]

To discourage smoking, James's government put a high tax on tobacco. But when a brisk trade in smuggled tobacco developed, the government decided to lower the tax to a level where people would not seek to evade it. In 1614, James created a royal monopoly to import tobacco into England, which created a steady government revenue that the increasingly unpopular king badly needed. James, like governments to the present day, may also have regarded this policy as a tax on sin. By 1619, James approved the incorporation of a company of clay pipe makers in London, and 40,000 pounds of tobacco arrived from Virginia the next year. Other European governments would also find tobacco a significant source of tax revenue. Often they would tax tobacco and at the same time attempt to regulate its use, especially among the young.

■ *Which groups in Europe in the sixteenth and seventeenth centuries opposed the habit of smoking tobacco? Why did the English government under King James I modify its opposition to tobacco?*

Practically from the moment of its introduction into Europe tobacco smoking was controversial. Here a court jester is portrayed as exhaling rabbits from a pipe as three pipe-smoking gentlemen look on. © Christel Gerstenberg/Corbis

[1]*A Counterblaste to Tobacco* (1604), reprinted by the Rodale Press, London, 1954, p. 36.

reign of Mary Tudor and the acts of treason by Catholics during Elizabeth's reign. In 1618, James hesitated, not unwisely, to rush English troops to the aid of Protestants in Germany at the outbreak of the Thirty Years' War. This hesitation caused some to question his loyalty to the Anglican church. These suspicions increased when he tried to arrange a marriage between his son Charles and the Spanish *Infanta* (the daughter of the king of Spain). In the king's last years, as his health failed and the reins of government passed increasingly to his son Charles and to Buckingham, parliamentary opposition and Protestant sentiment combined to undo his pro-Spanish foreign policy. In 1624, shortly before James's death, England entered a continental war against Spain largely in response to the pressures of members of Parliament.

CHARLES I

Parliament had favored the war with Spain, but would not adequately finance it because its members distrusted Buckingham. Unable to gain adequate funds from Parliament, Charles I (r. 1625–1649), like his father, resorted to extraparliamentary measures. He levied new tariffs and duties and attempted to collect discontinued taxes. He even subjected the English people to a so-called forced loan (a tax theoretically to be repaid), imprisoning those who refused to pay. The government quartered troops in transit to war zones in private homes. All these actions intruded on life at the local level and challenged the power of the local nobles and landowners to control their districts.

When Parliament met in 1628, its members were furious. Taxes were being illegally collected for a war that was going badly for England and that now, through royal blundering, involved France as well as Spain. Parliament expressed its displeasure by making the king's request for new funds conditional on his recognition of the Petition of Right. This important declaration of constitutional freedom required that henceforth there should be no forced loans or taxation without the consent of Parliament, that no freeman should be imprisoned without due cause, and that troops should not be billeted in private homes. It was thus an expression of resentment and resistance to the intrusion of the monarchy on the local level. Though Charles agreed to the petition, there was little confidence he would keep his word.

Years of Personal Rule In August 1628, Charles's chief minister, Buckingham, with whom Parliament had been in open dispute since 1626, was assassinated. His death, although sweet to many, did not resolve the hostility between the king and Parliament.

In January 1629, Parliament further underscored its resolve to limit royal prerogative. It declared that religious innovations leading to "popery"—the term used to condemn Charles's high-church policies—and the levying of taxes without parliamentary consent were acts of treason. By "popery," Parliament meant Charles's high-church policies that favored powerful bishops, elaborate liturgy, and personal religious observance and devotion rather than the preaching favored by the Puritans. Perceiving that things were getting out of hand, Charles promptly dissolved Parliament and did not call it again until 1640, when war with Scotland forced him to do so.

To conserve his limited resources, Charles made peace with France in 1629 and Spain in 1630. This policy again roused fears among some of his subjects that he was too friendly to Roman Catholic powers. The French and Roman Catholic background of Charles's wife furthered these suspicions. Part of her marriage contract permitted her to hear mass daily at the English court. Charles's attitude toward the Church of England also raised suspicions. He supported a group within the church, known as **Arminians,** who rejected many Puritan doctrines and favored elaborate high-church practices. The Puritans were convinced these practices would bring a return to Roman Catholicism.

To allow Charles to rule without renegotiating financial arrangements with Parliament, his chief minister, Thomas Wentworth (after 1640, earl of Strafford), instituted a policy known as *thorough*. This policy imposed strict efficiency and administrative centralization in government. Its goal was absolute royal control of England. Its success depended on the king's ability to operate independently of Parliament, which no law required him to summon.

Charles's ministers exploited every legal fund-raising device. They enforced previously neglected laws and extended existing taxes into new areas. For example, starting in 1634, they gradually extended inland to the whole of England a tax called *ship money*, normally levied only on coastal areas to pay for naval protection. A great landowner named John Hampden mounted a legal challenge to the extension of this tax. Although the king prevailed in what was a close legal contest, his victory was costly. It deepened the animosity toward him among the powerful landowners, who would elect and sit in Parliament should he need to summon it.

During these years of personal rule, Charles surrounded himself with an elaborate court and patronized some of the greatest artists of the day. Like his father, he sold noble titles and knighthoods, lessening their value and the social exclusiveness conferred on those who already possessed them. Nobles

and preach. In 1637, Charles and Laud, against the opposition of the English Puritans as well as the Scots, tried to impose on Scotland the English episcopal system and a prayer book almost identical to the Anglican *Book of Common Prayer*.

The Scots rebelled, and Charles, with insufficient resources for a war, was forced to call Parliament. The members of Parliament opposed his policies almost as much as they wanted to crush the rebellion. Led by John Pym (1584–1643), they refused even to consider funds for war until the king agreed to redress a long list of political and religious grievances. The king, in response, immediately dissolved Parliament—hence its name, the Short Parliament (April–May 1640). When the Presbyterian Scots invaded England and defeated an English army at the Battle of Newburn on the Tyne in the summer of 1640, Charles reconvened Parliament, this time on its terms, for a long and most fateful duration.

The Long Parliament The landowners and the merchant classes represented by Parliament had resented the king's financial measures and paternalistic rule for some time. The Puritans in Parliament resented his religious policies and deeply distrusted the influence of the Roman Catholic queen. What became known as Long Parliament (1640–1660) thus acted with widespread support and general unanimity when it convened in November 1640.

The House of Commons impeached both the earl of Strafford and Archbishop Laud. Disgraced and convicted by a parliamentary bill of attainder (a judgment of treason entailing loss of civil rights), Stafford was executed in 1641. Laud was imprisoned and also later executed (1645). Parliament abolished the Court of Star Chamber and the Court of High Commission, royal instruments of political and religious *thorough*, respectively. The levying of new taxes without the consent of Parliament and the inland extension of *ship money* now became illegal. Finally, Parliament resolved that no more than three years should elapse between its meetings and that it could not be dissolved without its own consent. Parliament was determined that neither Charles nor any future English king could again govern without consulting it.

Despite its cohesion on these initial actions, Parliament was divided over the precise direction to take on religious reform. Both moderate Puritans (the Presbyterians) and more extreme Puritans (the Independents) wanted the complete abolition of the episcopal system and the *Book of Common Prayer*. The majority of Presbyterians sought to reshape England religiously along Calvinist lines, with local congregations subject to higher representative

William Laud, the Archbishop of Canterbury, attempted in 1637, with the support of Charles I, to impose the English Book of Common Prayer on Scotland. In 1645, in the midst of the English Civil War, Laud was executed under parliamentary authority. © Stapleton Collection/Corbis

and great landowners feared that the growth of the court, the king's relentless pursuit of revenue, and the inflation of titles and honors would reduce their local influence and social standing. They also feared the monarch might actually succeed in governing without ever again calling Parliament into session.

Charles might very well have ruled indefinitely without Parliament had not his religious policies provoked war with Scotland. James I had allowed a wide variety of religious observances in England, Scotland, and Ireland. Charles, by contrast, hoped to impose religious conformity at least within England and Scotland. William Laud (1573–1645), who was first Charles's religious adviser and, after 1633, archbishop of Canterbury, held high-church views of Anglicanism. As a member of the Court of High Commission, Laud had already radicalized the English Puritans by denying them the right to publish

governing bodies (presbyteries). Independents wanted a much more fully decentralized church with every congregation as its own final authority. Finally, many conservatives in both houses of Parliament were determined to preserve the English church in its current form. Their numbers fell dramatically after 1642, however, when many of them left the House of Commons with the outbreak of civil war.

These divisions further intensified in October 1641, when a rebellion erupted in Ireland and Parliament was asked to raise funds for an army to suppress it. Pym and his followers, loudly reminding the House of Commons of the king's past behavior, argued that Charles could not be trusted with an army and that Parliament should become the commander-in-chief of English armed forces. Parliamentary conservatives, however, were appalled by such a bold departure from tradition.

Eruption of Civil War Charles saw the division within Parliament as a chance to reassert his power. On December 1, 1641, Parliament presented him with the "grand remonstrance," a more-than-200-article summary of popular and parliamentary grievances against the crown. In January 1642, he invaded Parliament with his soldiers. He intended to arrest Pym and the other leaders, but they had been forewarned and managed to escape. The king then withdrew from London and began to raise an army. Shocked by his action, a majority of the House of Commons passed the Militia Ordinance, which gave Parliament authority to raise an army of its own. The die was now cast. For the next four years (1642–1646), civil war engulfed England.

Charles assembled his forces at Nottingham, and the war began in August. It was fought over two main issues:

- Would an absolute monarchy or a parliamentary government rule England?
- Would English religion be controlled by the king's bishops and conform to high Anglican practice or adopt a decentralized, Presbyterian system of church governance?

Charles's royalist supporters, known as Cavaliers, were located in the northwestern half of England. The parliamentarian opposition, known as *Roundheads* because of their close-cropped hair, had its stronghold in the southeastern half of the country. Supporters of both sides included nobility, gentry, and townspeople. The chief factor distinguishing them was religion; the Puritans tended to favor Parliament.

OLIVER CROMWELL AND THE PURITAN REPUBLIC

Two factors led finally to Parliament's victory. The first was an alliance with Scotland consummated in 1643 when John Pym persuaded Parliament to accept the terms of the Solemn League and Covenant, an agreement that committed Parliament, with the Scots, to a Presbyterian system of church government. For the Scots, this policy meant they would never again be confronted with an attempt to impose the English prayer book on their religious services. The second factor was the reorganization of the parliamentary army under Oliver Cromwell (1599–1658), a middle-aged country squire of iron discipline and strong Independent

Oliver Cromwell's New Model Army defeated the royalists in the English Civil War. After the execution of Charles I in 1649, Cromwell dominated the short-lived English republic, conquered Ireland and Scotland, and ruled as lord protector from 1653 until his death in 1658. Stock Montage, Inc./Historical Pictures Collection

religious sentiment. Cromwell and his "godly men" favored neither the episcopal system of the king nor the pure Presbyterian system of the Solemn League and Covenant. They were willing to tolerate an established majority church, but only if it also permitted Protestant dissenters to worship outside it. (See "John Milton Defends Freedom to Print Books.")

The allies won the Battle of Marston Moor in 1644, the largest engagement of the war. In June 1645, Cromwell's newly reorganized forces, known as the New Model Army, fighting with disciplined fanaticism, won a decisive victory over the king at Naseby. (See Map 13–1.)

Defeated militarily, Charles tried again to take advantage of divisions within Parliament, this time seeking to win the Presbyterians and the Scots over to the royalist side. But Cromwell and his army foiled him. In December 1648, Colonel Thomas Pride physically barred the Presbyterians, who made up a majority of Parliament, from taking their seats. After "Pride's Purge," only a "rump" of fewer than fifty members remained. Though small in numbers, this Independent Rump Parliament did not hesitate to use its power. On January 30, 1649, after a trial by a special court, the Rump Parliament executed Charles as a public criminal and thereafter abolished the monarchy, the House of Lords, and the Anglican church. What had begun as a civil war had at this point become a revolution.

From 1649 to 1660, England became officially a Puritan republic, although for much of that time it was dominated by Cromwell. During this period, Cromwell's army conquered Ireland and Scotland, creating the single political entity of Great Britain. Cromwell, however, was a military man

JOHN MILTON DEFENDS FREEDOM TO PRINT BOOKS

Certain Puritans were as concerned about resisting potential tyranny from Parliament as from the monarchy. During the English Civil War, the Parliament passed a very strict censorship measure. In "Areopagitica" (1644), John Milton, later the author of Paradise Lost *(1667), attacked this law and contributed one of the major defenses of the freedom of the press in the history of Western culture. In the passage that follows, he compares the life of a book with the life of a human being.*

■ *Why does Milton think that it may be more dangerous and harmful to attack a book than to attack a person? Was life cheaper and intelligence rarer in his time? Does he have particular kinds of books in mind? What can a book do for society that people cannot?*

I deny not but that it is of greatest concern in the Church and Commonwealth to have a vigilant eye how books demean themselves as well as men; and thereafter to confine, imprison, and do sharpest justice on them as [if they were criminals]; for books are not absolutely dead things, but do contain a progeny of life in them to be as active as that soul was whose progeny they are; nay, they do preserve as in a vial the purest efficacy and extraction of that living intellect that bred them. . . . He who kills a man kills a reasonable creature, God's Image; but he who destroys a good book, kills reason itself, kills the Image of God, as it were. . . . Many a man lives [as] a burden to the Earth; but a good book is the precious life-blood of a master spirit, embalmed and treasured up on purpose to a life beyond life. It is true, no age can restore a life, whereof, perhaps there is no great loss; and revolutions of ages do not oft recover the loss of a rejected truth, for the want of which whole nations fare the worse. We should be wary, therefore, what persecution we raise against the living labours of public men, how we spill that seasoned life of man preserved and stored up in books; since we see a kind of homicide may be thus committed, sometimes a martyrdom, and if it extends to the whole impression, a kind of massacre, whereof the execution ends not in the slaying of an elemental life, but strikes at that ethereal . . . essence, the breath of reason itself; slays an immortality rather than a life.

From J. A. St. John, ed., *The Prose Works of John Milton* (London: H. G. Bohn, 1843–1853), 2:8–9.

and no politician. He was increasingly frustrated by what seemed to him to be pettiness and dawdling on the part of Parliament. When, in 1653, the House of Commons entertained a motion to disband his expensive army of 50,000, Cromwell responded by marching in and disbanding Parliament. He ruled thereafter as Lord Protector according to a written constitution known as the Instrument of Government.

This military dictatorship, however, proved no more effective than Charles's rule had been and became just as harsh and hated. Cromwell's great army and foreign adventures inflated his budget to three times that of Charles's. Near chaos reigned in many places, and commerce suffered throughout England. Cromwell was as intolerant of Anglicans as Charles had been of Puritans. People deeply resented his Puritan prohibitions of drunkenness, theatergoing, and dancing. Political liberty vanished in the name of religious liberty.

Cromwell's challenge had been to devise a political structure to replace that of monarch and Parliament. He tried various arrangements, none of which worked. He quarreled with the various Parliaments that were elected while he was Lord Protector. By the time of his death in 1658, most of the English were ready to end both the Puritan religious and the republican political experiments and return to their traditional institutions. Negotiations between leaders of the army and the exiled Charles II (r. 1660–1685), son of Charles I, led to the restoration of the Stuart monarchy in 1660.

CHARLES II AND THE RESTORATION OF THE MONARCHY

Charles II returned to England amid great rejoicing. A man of considerable charm and political skill, Charles set a refreshing new tone after eleven years of somber Puritanism. His restoration returned England to the status quo of 1642, with a hereditary monarch once again on the throne, no legal requirement that he summon Parliament regularly, and the Anglican church, with its bishops and prayer book, supreme in religion.

The king, however, had secret Catholic sympathies and favored a policy of religious toleration. He wanted to allow all those outside the Church of England, Catholics as well as Puritans, to worship freely so long as they remained loyal to the throne. But in Parliament, even the ultraroyalist Anglicans did not believe patriotism and religion could be separated. Between 1661 and 1665, through a series of laws known as the Clarendon Code, Parliament excluded Roman Catholics, Presbyterians, and Independents from the religious and political life of the

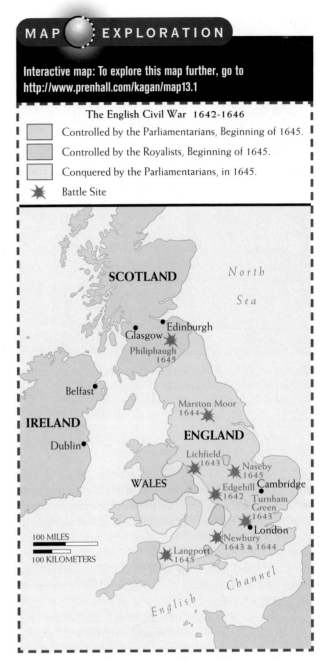

MAP 13–1   THE ENGLISH CIVIL WAR.   *This map shows the rapid deterioration of the royalist position in 1645.*

nation. These laws imposed penalties for attending non-Anglican worship services, required strict adherence to the *Book of Common Prayer* and the *Thirty-Nine Articles*, and demanded oaths of allegiance to the Church of England from all persons serving in local government.

At the time of the Restoration, England, again as under Cromwell in 1651, adopted navigation acts that required all imports to be carried either in English ships or in ships registered to the country from which the cargo originated. Dutch ships carried

The bleeding head of Charles I is exhibited to the crowd after his execution on a cold day in January 1649. The contemporary Dutch artist also professed to see the immediate ascension of Charles's soul to heaven. In fact, many saw the king as a martyr. An Eye-witness Representation of the Execution of King Charles I (1600–1649) of England, 1649 (oil on canvas) by Weesop (fl. 1641–1649). Private Collection/Bridgeman Art Library, London

cargo from many nations, and such laws struck directly at Dutch dominance in the shipping industry. A series of naval wars between England and Holland ensued. Charles also attempted to tighten his grasp on the rich English colonies in North America and the Caribbean, many of which had been settled and developed by separatists who desired independence from English rule.

Although Parliament strongly supported the monarchy, Charles, following the pattern of his predecessors, required greater revenues than Parliament appropriated. These he obtained in part by increased customs duties. Because England and France were both at war with Holland, he also received aid from France. In 1670, England and France formally allied against the Dutch in the Treaty of Dover. In a secret portion of this treaty, Charles pledged to announce his conversion to Catholicism as soon as conditions in England permitted. In return for this announcement (which was never made), Louis XIV of France promised to pay a substantial subsidy to England.

In an attempt to unite the English people behind the war with Holland, and as a sign of good faith to Louis XIV, Charles issued the Declaration of Indulgence in 1672. This document suspended all laws against Roman Catholics and Protestant noncon-

formists. But again, the conservative Parliament proved less generous than the king and refused to grant money for the war until Charles rescinded the measure. After he did, Parliament passed the Test Act, which required all officials of the crown, civil and military, to swear an oath against the doctrine of transubstantiation—a requirement that no loyal Roman Catholic could honestly meet.

Parliament had aimed the Test Act largely at the king's brother, James, duke of York, heir to the throne and a recent devout convert to Catholicism. In 1678, a notorious liar named Titus Oates swore before a magistrate that Charles's Catholic wife, through her physician, was plotting with Jesuits and Irishmen to kill the king so James could assume the throne. The matter was taken before Parliament, where Oates was believed. In the ensuing hysteria, known as the Popish Plot, several people were tried and executed. Riding the crest of anti-Catholic sentiment and led by the earl of Shaftesbury (1621–1683), opposition members of Parliament, called Whigs, made an impressive, but unsuccessful, effort to enact a bill excluding James from succession to the throne.

More suspicious than ever of Parliament, Charles II turned again to increased customs duties and the assistance of Louis XIV for extra income. By these means, he was able to rule from 1681 to 1685 without recalling Parliament. In those years, Charles suppressed much of his opposition. He drove the earl of Shaftesbury into exile, executed several Whig leaders for treason, and bullied local corporations into electing members of Parliament who were submissive to the royal will. When Charles died in 1685 (after a deathbed conversion to Catholicism), he left James the prospect of a Parliament filled with royal friends.

JAMES II AND RENEWED FEARS OF A CATHOLIC ENGLAND

James II (r. 1685–1688) did not know how to make the most of a good thing. He alienated Parliament by insisting on the repeal of the Test Act. When Parliament balked, he dissolved it and proceeded openly to appoint known Catholics to high positions in both his court and the army. In 1687, he issued the Declaration of Indulgence, which suspended all religious tests and permitted free worship. Local candidates for Parliament who opposed the declaration were removed from their offices by the king's soldiers and were replaced by Catholics. In June 1688, James went so far as to imprison seven Anglican bishops who had refused to publicize his suspension of laws against Catholics. Each of these actions represented a direct royal attack on the local power and authority of nobles, landowners, the church, and other corporate bodies whose members believed they possessed particular legal privileges. James was attacking English liberty and challenging all manner of social privileges and influence.

Under the guise of a policy of enlightened toleration, James was actually seeking to subject all English institutions to the power of the monarchy. His goal was absolutism, and even conservative, loyalist Tories, as the royal supporters were called, could not abide this policy. The English feared, with reason, that James planned to imitate the religious intolerance of Louis XIV, who had, in 1685, revoked the Edict of Nantes (which had protected French Protestants for almost a century) and imposed Catholicism on the entire nation, using his dragoons against those who protested or resisted.

James soon faced united opposition. When his Catholic second wife gave birth to a son and Catholic male heir to the throne on June 20, 1688, opposition turned to action. The English had hoped that James would die without a male heir so the throne would pass to Mary, his Protestant eldest daughter. Mary was the wife of William III of Orange, *stadtholder* of the Netherlands, great-grandson of William the Silent, and the leader of European opposition to Louis XIV's imperial designs. Within days of the birth of James's son, Whig and Tory members of Parliament formed a coalition and invited Orange to invade England to preserve "traditional liberties," that is, the Anglican church and parliamentary government.

THE "GLORIOUS REVOLUTION"

William of Orange arrived with his army in November 1688 and was received without opposition by the English people. In the face of sure defeat, James fled to France and the protection of Louis XIV. With James gone, Parliament declared the throne vacant and, on its own authority in 1689, proclaimed William and Mary the new monarchs, completing

England in the Seventeenth Century	
1603	James VI of Scotland becomes James I of England
1604	Hampton Court conference
1611	Publication of the authorized, or King James, version of the English Bible
1625	Charles I becomes English monarch
1628	Petition of Right
1629	Charles I dissolves Parliament and embarks on eleven years of personal rule
1640	April–May, Short Parliament November, Long Parliament convenes
1641	Grand Remonstrance
1642	Outbreak of the Civil War
1645	Charles I defeated at Naseby
1648	Pride's Purge
1649	Charles I executed
1649–1660	Various attempts at a Puritan Commonwealth
1660	Charles II restored to the English throne
1670	Secret Treaty of Dover between France and England
1672	Parliament passes the Test Act
1678	Popish Plot
1685	James II becomes king of England
1688	"Glorious Revolution"
1689	William and Mary proclaimed English monarchs
1701	Acts of Settlement provides for Hanoverian succession
1702–1714	Reign of Queen Anne, the last of the Stuarts

the successful bloodless **Glorious Revolution.** William and Mary, in turn, recognized a Bill of Rights that limited the powers of the monarchy and guaranteed the civil liberties of the English privileged classes. Henceforth, England's monarchs would be subject to law and would rule by the consent of Parliament, which was to be called into session every three years. The Bill of Rights also pointedly prohibited Roman Catholics from occupying the English throne. The Toleration Act of 1689 permitted worship by all Protestants but outlawed Roman Catholics and anti-Trinitarians (those who denied the Christian doctrine of the Trinity).

The measure closing this century of strife was the Act of Settlement in 1701. This bill provided for the English crown to go to the Protestant House of Hanover in Germany if none of the children of Queen Anne (r. 1702–1714), the second daughter of James II and the last of the Stuart monarchs, was alive at her death. She outlived all of her children, so in 1714, the elector of Hanover became King George I of England, the third foreign monarch to occupy the English throne in just over a century.

The Glorious Revolution of 1688 established a framework of government by and for the governed that seemed to bear out the arguments of John Locke's *Second Treatise of Government* (1690). In this work, which is discussed more fully in the next chapter, Locke described the relationship of a king and his people as a bilateral contract. If the king broke that contract, the people, by whom Locke meant the privileged and powerful, had the right to depose him. Locke had written the essay before the revolution, but it came to be read as a justification for it. Although neither in fact nor in theory a "popular" revolution such as would occur in America and France a hundred years later, the Glorious Revolution did establish in England a permanent check on monarchical power by the classes represented in Parliament. At the same time, as we see in Chapter 15, in its wake the English government had achieved a secure financial base that would allow it to pursue a century of warfare.

William and Mary became the monarchs of England in 1689. Their accession brought England's economic and military resources into the balance against the France of Louis XIV. Robert Harding Picture Library

Rise of Absolute Monarchy in France

Seventeenth-century France, in contrast to England, saw both discontent among the nobility and religious pluralism smothered by the absolute monarchy and the closed Catholic state of Louis XIV (r. 1643–1715). An aggressive ruler who sought glory (*la gloire*) in foreign wars, Louis XIV subjected his subjects at home to "one king, one law, one faith."

Historians once portrayed Louis XIV's reign as a time when the rising central monarchy exerted far-reaching, direct control of the nation at all levels. A somewhat different picture has now emerged. Louis's predecessors and their chief ministers, in the half century before his reign, had already tried to impose direct rule, arousing discontent and, at midcentury, a rebellion among the nobility. Louis's genius was to make the monarchy the most important and powerful political institution in France while also assuring the nobles and other wealthy groups of their social standing and political and social influence on the local level. Rather than destroying existing local social and political institutions, Louis largely worked through them. Once nobles understood that the king would support their local authority, they supported his central royal authority. In other words, the king and the nobles came to recognize that they needed each other. Nevertheless, Louis made it clear to all concerned that he was the senior partner in the relationship.

Louis's royal predecessors laid the foundations for absolute monarchy and also taught him to avoid certain practices. Just as the emergence of a strong Parliament was not inevitable in England, neither was the emergence of an absolute monarchy in France.

HENRY IV AND SULLY

Coming to the throne after the French wars of religion, Henry of Navarre who became Henry IV (r. 1589–1610; see Chapter 12) sought to curtail the privileges of the French nobility. His targets were the provincial governors and the regional *parlements*, especially the powerful *Parlement* of Paris, where a divisive spirit lived on. Here were to be found the old privileged groups, tax-exempt magnates who were preoccupied with protecting their self-interests. During the subsequent reign of Louis XIII (r. 1610–1643), royal civil servants known as **intendants** subjected these privileged groups to stricter supervision, implementing the king's will with some success in the provinces. An important function of the *intendants* was to prevent abuses from the sale of royal offices that conferred the right to collect revenues, sell licenses, or carry out other remunerative forms of administration. It was usually nobles who acquired these lucrative offices, which was one reason for their ongoing influence.

After decades of religious and civil war, an economy more amenable to governmental regulation emerged during Henry IV's reign. Henry and his finance minister, the duke of Sully (1560–1641), established government monopolies on gunpowder, mines, and salt, preparing the way for the mercantilist policies of Louis XIV and his minister, Colbert. They began a canal system to link the Atlantic and the Mediterranean by joining the Saône, the Loire, the Seine, and the Meuse Rivers. They introduced the royal **corvée,** a labor tax that created a national force of drafted workers who were employed to improve roads and facilitate internal travel. Sully even dreamed of organizing the whole of Europe politically and commercially into a kind of common market.

LOUIS XIII AND RICHELIEU

Henry IV was assassinated in 1610, and the following year Sully retired. Because Henry's son and successor, Louis XIII, was only nine years old at his father's death, the task of governing fell to the queen mother, Marie de Médicis (d. 1642). Finding herself in a vulnerable position, she sought security abroad by signing a ten-year mutual defense pact with France's arch rival Spain in the Treaty of Fontainebleau (1611). This alliance also arranged for marriages between Louis XIII and a Spanish princess and between the queen's daughter Elizabeth and the heir to the Spanish throne. The queen sought internal security against pressures from the French nobility by promoting the career of Cardinal Richelieu (1585–1642) as the king's chief adviser. Richelieu,

Cardinal Richelieu laid the foundations for the political ascendancy of the French monarchy. *Cardinal Richelieu* by Philippe de Champaigne. The National Gallery, London

loyal and shrewd, sought to make France the supreme European power. He, more than any other person, was responsible for French success in the first half of the seventeenth century.

An apparently devout Catholic who also believed the church best served both his own ambition and the welfare of France, Richelieu pursued a strongly anti-Habsburg policy. Although he supported the Spanish alliance of the queen and Catholic religious unity within France, he was determined to contain Spanish power and influence, even when that meant aiding and abetting Protestant Europe. It is an indication both of Richelieu's awkward political situation and of his diplomatic agility that he could, in 1631, pledge funds to the Protestant army of Gustavus Adolphus, the king of Sweden, while also insisting that Catholic Bavaria be spared from attack and that Catholics in conquered countries be permitted to practice their religion. One measure of the success of Richelieu's foreign policies can be seen in France's substantial gains in land and political influence when the Treaty of Westphalia (1648) ended hostilities in the Holy Roman Empire (see Chapter 12) and the Treaty of the Pyrenees (1659) sealed peace with Spain.

At home, Richelieu pursued centralizing policies utterly without qualm. Supported by the king, who let his chief minister make most decisions of state, Richelieu stepped up the campaign against separatist provincial governors and *parlements*. He made it clear that there was only one law, that of the king, and none could stand above it. When disobedient nobles defied his edicts, they were imprisoned and even executed. Such treatment of the nobility won Richelieu much enmity, even from the queen mother, who, unlike Richelieu, was not always willing to place the larger interests of the state above the pleasure of favorite nobles.

Richelieu started the campaign against the Huguenots that would end in 1685 with Louis XIV's revocation of the Edict of Nantes. Royal armies conquered major Huguenot cities in 1629. The subsequent Peace of Alais (1629) truncated the Edict of Nantes by denying Protestants the right to maintain garrisoned cities, separate political organizations, and independent law courts. Only Richelieu's foreign policy, which involved France in ties with Protestant powers, prevented the earlier implementation of the policy of extreme intolerance that marked the reign of Louis XIV. In the same year that Richelieu rescinded the independent political status of the Huguenots in the Peace of Alais, he also entered negotiations to make Gustavus Adolphus his counterweight to the expansion of Habsburg power within the Holy Roman Empire. By 1635, the Catholic soldiers of France were fighting openly with Swedish Lutherans against the emperor's army in the final phase of the Thirty Years' War. (See Chapter 12.)

Richelieu employed the arts and the printing press to defend his actions and to indoctrinate the French people in the meaning of **raison d'état** ("reason of state"). This also set a precedent for Louis XIV, who made elaborate use of royal propaganda and spectacle to assert and enhance his power.

YOUNG LOUIS XIV AND MAZARIN

Although Richelieu helped lay the foundations for a much expanded royal authority, his immediate legacy was strong resentment of the monarchy among the French nobility and wealthy commercial groups. The crown's steady multiplication of royal offices, its replacement of local authorities by "state" agents, and its reduction of local sources of patronage undermined the traditional position of the privileged groups in French society. Among those affected were officers of the crown in the law courts and other royal institutions.

When Louis XIII died in 1643, Louis XIV was only five years old. During his minority, the queen mother, Anne of Austria (d. 1666), placed the reins of government in the hands of Cardinal Mazarin (1602–1661), who continued Richelieu's determined policy of centralization. During Mazarin's regency, long-building resentment produced a backlash: Between 1649 and 1652, in a series of widespread rebellions known as the **Fronde** (after the slingshot used by street boys), segments of the nobility and townspeople sought to reverse the drift toward absolute monarchy and to preserve local autonomy.

The *Parlement* of Paris initiated the revolt in 1649, and the nobility at large soon followed. Urging them on were the influential wives of princes whom Mazarin had imprisoned for treason. The many (the nobility) briefly triumphed over the one (the monarchy) when Mazarin released the imprisoned princes in February 1651. He and Louis XIV thereafter went briefly into exile (Mazarin leaving France, Louis fleeing Paris). They returned in October 1652 after an interlude of nearly anarchic rule by the nobility. The *Fronde* convinced most French people that the rule of a strong king was preferable to that of many regional powers with competing and irreconcilable claims. At the same time, Louis XIV and his later advisers learned that heavy-handed policies like those of Richelieu and Mazarin could endanger the monarchy. Louis would ultimately concentrate unprecedented authority in the monarchy, but he would use more clever means than those of his predecessors.

The Years of Louis XIV's Personal Rule

On the death of Mazarin, Louis XIV assumed personal control of the government. Unlike his royal predecessors, he appointed no single chief minister. One result was to make revolt more difficult. Rebellious nobles would now be challenging the king directly; they could not claim to be resisting only a bad minister.

Mazarin prepared Louis XIV well to rule France. The turbulent events of his youth also made an indelible impression on the king. Louis wrote in his memoirs that the *Fronde* caused him to loathe "kings of straw," and he followed two strategies to assure that he would never become one.

First, Louis and his advisers became masters of propaganda and the creation of a political image. Indoctrinated with a strong sense of the grandeur of his crown, Louis never missed an opportunity to impress it on the French people. When the *dauphin* (the heir to the French throne) was born in 1662, for example, Louis appeared for the celebration dressed as a Roman emperor.

Second, Louis made sure the French nobles and other major social groups would benefit from the growth of his own authority. Although he maintained control over foreign affairs and limited the influence of noble institutions on the monarchy, he never tried to abolish those institutions or limit their authority at the local level. The crown, for example, usually conferred informally with regional *parlements* before making rulings that would affect them. Likewise, the crown would rarely enact economic regulations without consulting local opinion. Local *parlements* enjoyed considerable latitude in all regional matters. In an exception to this pattern, Louis did clash with the *Parlement* of Paris, with which he had to register laws, and eventually, in 1673, he curtailed much of its power. Many regional *parlements* and other regional authorities, however, had resented the power of that body.

Employing these strategies of propaganda and cooperation, Louis set out to anchor his rule in the principle of the divine right of kings, to domesticate the French nobility by binding them to the court rituals of Versailles, and to crush religious dissent. (See "Art & the West: Rigaud's Louis XIV: The State Portrait," p. 446.)

King by Divine Right

Reverence for the king and the personification of government in his person had been nurtured in France since Capetian times. It was a maxim of French law and popular opinion that "the king of France is emperor in his realm" and the king's wish the law of the land. Building on this reverence, Louis XIV defended absolute royal authority on the grounds of divine right.

An important source for Louis's concept of royal authority was his devout tutor, the political theorist Bishop Jacques-Bénigne Bossuet (1627–1704). An ardent champion of the Gallican liberties—the traditional rights of the French king and church against the pope in matters of ecclesiastical appointments and taxation—Bossuet defended what he called the **"divine right of kings."** In support of his claims, he cited examples of Old Testament rulers divinely appointed by, and answerable only to, God. As medieval popes had insisted that only God could judge a pope, so Bossuet argued that none save God could judge the king. Kings may have remained duty-bound to reflect God's will in their rule—in this sense, Bossuet considered them always subject to a higher authority. Yet as God's regents on earth, they could not be bound to the dictates of mere princes and parliaments. Such assumptions lay behind Louis XIV's alleged declaration, *"L'état, c'est moi"* ("I am the state").

This medallion shows Anne of Austria, the wife of Louis XIII, with her son, Louis XIV. She wisely placed political authority in the hands of Cardinal Mazarin, who prepared Louis to govern France. Giraudon/Art Resource, N.Y.

Versailles

More than any other monarch of the day, Louis XIV used the physical setting of his royal court to exert political control. The palace court at Versailles on the outskirts of Paris became Louis's permanent residence after 1682. It was a true temple to royalty, architecturally designed and artistically decorated to proclaim the glory of the Sun King, as Louis was known. A spectacular estate with magnificent fountains and acres of orange groves, it became home to thousands of the more important nobles, royal officials, and servants. Although its physical maintenance and new additions, which continued throughout Louis's lifetime, consumed over half his annual revenues, Versailles paid significant political dividends.

Because Louis ruled personally, he was the chief source of favors and patronage in France. To emphasize his prominence, he organized life at court around his own daily routine. He encouraged nobles to approach him directly, but required them to do so through elaborate court etiquette. Fawning nobles competed to be in attendance at especially favored moments. The king's rising and dressing in particular were times of rare intimacy, when nobles could whisper their special requests in his ear. Fortunate nobles held his night candle as they accompanied him to his bed.

Although only five feet four inches tall, the king had presence and was always engaging in conversation. He turned his own sexuality to political ends and encouraged the belief at court that it was an honor to lie with him. Married to the Spanish *Infanta* Marie Thérèse for political reasons in 1660, he kept many mistresses. After Marie's death in 1683, he settled down in a secret marriage to Madame de Maintenon and apparently became much less the philanderer.

Court life was a carefully planned and successfully executed effort to domesticate and trivialize the nobility. Barred by law from high government positions, the ritual and play kept them busy and dependent, so they had little time to plot revolt. Dress codes and high-stakes gambling contributed to their indebtedness and dependency on the king. Members of the court spent the afternoons hunting, riding, or strolling about the lush gardens of Versailles. Evenings were given over to planned entertainment in the large salons (plays, concerts, gambling, and the like), followed by supper at 10 P.M. Even the king's retirement was part of the day's spectacle.

Françoise d'Aubigne, Madame de Maintenon (1635–1719), a mistress to Louis XIV, secretly married him after his first wife's death. The deeply pious Maintenon influenced Louis's policy to make Roman Catholicism France's only religion. Pierre Mignard (1612–1695), "Portrait of Françoise d'Aubigne, marquise de Maintenon (1635–1719), mistress and second wife of Louis XIV," c. 1694. Oil on canvas, 128 × 97 cm. Inv.: MV 3637. Art Resource, N.Y.

Moments near the king were important to most court nobles because they were effectively excluded from the real business of government. Louis ruled through powerful councils that controlled foreign affairs, domestic relations, and economic regulations. Each day after morning mass, which Louis always attended, he spent hours with the chief ministers of these councils, whom he chose from families long in royal service or from among people just beginning to rise in the social structure. Unlike the nobles at court, they had no real or potential power bases in the provinces and depended solely on the king for their standing in both government and society.

Some nobles, of course, did not attend Versailles. Some tended to their local estates and cultivated their local influence. Many others were simply too poor to cut a figure at court. All the nobility understood, however, that Louis, unlike Richelieu and Mazarin, would not threaten their local social standing. Louis supported France's traditional social structure and the social privileges of the nobility.

SUPPRESSION OF THE JANSENISTS

Like Richelieu before him, Louis believed that political unity and stability required religious conformity. His first move to impose it, which came early in his personal reign, was against the Roman Catholic Jansenists.

The French crown and the French church had by long tradition—originating with the so-called Gallican liberties in the fourteenth century—jealously guarded their independence from Rome. A great influx of Catholic religious orders, the Jesuits prominent among them, followed Henry IV's conversion to Catholicism. Because of their leadership at the Council of Trent and their close connections to Spain, the Jesuits had been banned from France by Catherine de Médicis. Henry IV, however, lifted the ban in 1603, with certain conditions: He required members of the order to swear an oath of allegiance to the king, he limited the number of new colleges they could open, and he required them to have special licenses for public activities.

The Jesuits were not, however, easily harnessed. They rapidly monopolized the education of the upper classes, and their devout students promoted the religious reforms and doctrine of the Council of Trent throughout France. In a measure of their success, Jesuits served as confessors to Henry IV, Louis XIII, and Louis XIV.

Jansenism arose in the 1630s as part of the opposition among some Catholics to the theology and the political influence of the Jesuits. Jansenists adhered to the teachings of St. Augustine (354–430) that had also influenced many Protestant doctrines.

Serious and uncompromising, they particularly opposed Jesuit teachings about free will. They believed with Augustine that original sin had so corrupted humankind that individuals could do nothing good nor secure their own salvation without divine grace. The namesake of the movement, Cornelius Jansen (d. 1638), was a Flemish theologian and the bishop of Ypres. His posthumously published *Augustinus* (1640) assailed Jesuit teaching on grace and salvation.

A prominent Parisian family, the Arnaulds, became Jansenist allies, adding a political element to the Jansenists' theological objections to the Jesuits. Like many other French people, the Arnaulds believed the Jesuits had been behind the assassination of Henry IV in 1610.

The Arnaulds dominated Jansenist communities at Port-Royal and Paris during the 1640s. In 1643, Antoine Arnauld published a work entitled *On Frequent Communion* in which he criticized the Jesuits for confessional practices that permitted the easy redress of almost any sin. The Jesuits, in turn, condemned the Jansenists as "crypto-Calvinists."

On May 31, 1653, Pope Innocent X declared heretical five Jansenist theological propositions on grace and salvation. In 1656, the pope banned Jansen's *Augustinus* and the Sorbonne censured Antoine Arnauld. In the same year, Antoine's friend, Blaise Pascal (1623–1662), the most famous of Jansen's followers, published the first of his *Provincial Letters* in defense of Jansenism. A deeply religious man, Pascal tried to reconcile the "reasons of the heart" with growing seventeenth-century reverence for the clear and distinct ideas of the mind. (See Chapter 14.) He objected to Jesuit moral theology not only as being lax and shallow, but also because he felt its rationalism failed to do full justice to the religious experience.

In 1660, Louis permitted the papal bull *Ad Sacram Sedem* (1656) to be enforced in France, thus banning Jansenism. He also closed down the Port-Royal community. Thereafter, Jansenists either retracted their views or went underground. Much later, in 1710, Louis lent his support to a still more thorough purge of Jansenist sentiment.

Jansenism had offered the prospect of a Catholicism broad enough to appeal to France's Protestant Huguenots. By suppressing it, Louis also eliminated the best hope for bringing peaceful religious unity to his country.

GOVERNMENT GEARED FOR WARFARE

Louis's France was in many ways like much of the rest of contemporary Europe. It had a largely subsistence economy, and its cities enjoyed only limited commercial prosperity. It did not, in other words, achieve the economic strength of a modern industrial economy. By the 1660s, however, France was superior to any other European nation in administrative bureaucracy, armed forces, and national unity. Louis could afford to maintain a large and powerful army. His enemies and some later historians claimed that Louis wished to dominate all Europe, but it would appear his chief military and foreign policy goal was to achieve secure international boundaries for France. He was particularly concerned to secure its northern borders along the Spanish Netherlands, the Franche-Comté, Alsace, and Lorraine from which foreign armies could easily invade France. Louis was also determined to frustrate Habsburg ambitions that endangered France and, as part of that goal, sought to secure his southern borders toward Spain. Furthermore, events abroad, particularly problems raised by disputed succession to the throne in other states, led to war as often as Louis's own ambition did. Nonetheless, he saw himself as a warrior king and on more than one occasion personally accompanied his armies on their campaigns. Whether reacting to external events or pursuing his own ambitions, Louis's pursuit of French interests threatened and terrified neighboring states and led them to form coalitions against France.

Three remarkable French ministers established and supported Louis XIV's great war machine: Colbert, Louvois, and Vauban.

Colbert and the French Economy Jean-Baptiste Colbert (1619–1683), controller general of finances and Louis's most brilliant minister, created the economic base Louis needed to finance his wars. Colbert worked to centralize the French economy with the same rigor that Louis had worked to centralize the French government. Colbert tried, with modest success, to organize much economic activity under state supervision and, through tariffs, carefully regulated the flow of imports and exports. He sought to create new national industries and organized factories around a tight regimen of work and ideology. He simplified the administrative bureaucracy, abolished unnecessary positions, and reduced the number of tax-exempt nobles. He also increased the *taille*, a direct tax on the peasantry and a major source of royal income.

This kind of close government control of the economy came to be known as **mercantilism** (a term invented by later critics of the policy). Its aim was to maximize foreign exports and internal reserves of bullion, the gold and silver necessary for making war. Modern scholars argue that Colbert overcontrolled the French economy and cite his

Colbert was Louis XIV's most influential minister. He sought to expand the economic life of France and to associate the monarchy with the emerging new science from which he hoped might flow new inventions and productive technology. Here he is portrayed presenting members of the French Academy of Science to the monarch. On the founding of the French Academy, see chapter 14. Photo Gerard Blot. Chateau de Versailles et de Trianon, Versailles, France. Reunion des Musees Nationaux/Art Resource, N.Y.

"paternalism" as a major reason for the failure of French colonies in the New World. Be that as it may, his policies unquestionably transformed France into a major commercial power, with foreign bases in Africa, in India, and in the Americas, from Canada to the Caribbean.

Louvois, Vauban, and the French Military Louis's army, about a quarter of a million strong, was the creation of Michel Tellier and his more famous son, the marquis of Louvois (1641–1691). Louis's war minister from 1677 to 1691, Louvois was a superior military tactician.

Before Louvois, the French army had been an amalgam of local recruits and mercenaries, uncoordinated groups whose loyalty could not always be counted on. Without regular pay or a way to supply their everyday needs, troops often lived by pillage. Louvois instituted good salaries and improved discipline, making soldiering a respectable profession. He limited military commissions and introduced a system of promotion by merit, bringing dedicated fighters into the ranks. Enlistment was for four years and restricted to single men. *Intendants*, the king's ubiquitous civil servants, monitored conduct at all levels.

Because it was well disciplined, this new, large, and powerful standing army had considerable public support. Unlike its undisciplined predecessor, the new army no longer threatened the lives, homes, or well-being of the people it was supposed to protect. It thus provides an excellent example of the kinds of benefits many saw in the growing authority of the central monarchy.

What Louvois was to military organization, Sebastien Vauban (1633–1707) was to military engineering. He perfected the arts of fortifying and besieging towns. He also devised the system of trench warfare and developed the concept of defensive frontiers that remained basic to military tactics through World War I.

LOUIS'S EARLY WARS

The War of Devolution Louis's first great foreign adventure was the War of Devolution (1667–1668). It was fought, as would be the later and more devastating War of the Spanish Succession, over Louis's claim to the Spanish Belgian provinces through his wife, Marie-Thérèse (1638–1683). According to the terms of the treaty of the Pyrenees (1659), Marie had renounced her claim to the Spanish succession on condition that a 500,000-crown dowry be paid to Louis within eighteen months of the marriage, a condition that was not met. When Philip IV of Spain died in September 1665, he left all his lands to his sickly four-year-old son by a second marriage, Charles II (r. 1665–1700) and explicitly denied any lands to his daughter. Louis had always harbored the hope of turning the marriage to territorial gain and even before Philip's death had argued that Marie was entitled to a portion of the inheritance.

Louis had a legal argument on his side, which gave the war its name. He maintained that in certain regions of Brabant and Flanders, which were part of the Spanish inheritance, property "devolved" to the children of a first marriage rather than to those of a second. Therefore, Marie had a higher claim than Charles II to these regions. Although such regional laws could hardly bind the king of Spain, Louis was not deterred from sending his armies, under the viscount of Turenne, into Flanders and the Franche-Comté in 1667. In response to this aggression, England, Sweden, and the

United Provinces of Holland formed the Triple Alliance, a force sufficient to compel Louis to agree to peace under the terms in the Treaty of Aix-la-Chapelle (1668). The treaty gave him control of certain towns bordering the Spanish Netherlands. (See Map 13–2.)

Invasion of the Netherlands In 1670, with the signing of the Treaty of Dover, England and France became allies against the Dutch. Without the English, the Triple Alliance crumbled. This left Louis in a stronger position to invade the Netherlands for a second time, which he did in 1672. This time he aimed directly at Holland, which had organized the Triple Alliance in 1667, foiling French designs in Flanders. Dutch gloating after the Treaty of Aix-la-Chapelle had offended Louis. Such cartoons as one depicting the sun (Louis was called the "sun king") eclipsed by a great moon of Dutch cheese incensed him. Without neutralizing Holland, he knew he could never hope to acquire land in the Spanish Netherlands, much less fulfill his dreams of European hegemony.

Louis's invasion of the United Provinces in 1672 brought the downfall of the Dutch statesmen Jan and Cornelius De Witt. Replacing them was the twenty-seven-year-old Prince of Orange, destined after 1689 to become King William III of England. Orange was the great-grandson of William the Silent, who had repulsed Philip II and dashed Spanish hopes of dominating the Netherlands in the sixteenth century.

Orange, an unpretentious Calvinist who was in almost every way Louis's opposite, galvanized the seven provinces into a fierce fighting unit. In 1673, he united the Holy Roman Emperor, Spain, Lorraine, and Brandenburg in an alliance against Louis. His enemies now saw the French king as a "Christian Turk," a menace to the whole of western Europe, Catholic and Protestant alike. In the ensuing warfare, both sides experienced gains and losses. Louis lost his ablest generals, Turenne and Condé, in 1675, but a victory by Admiral Duquesne over the Dutch fleet in 1676 gave France control of the Mediterranean. The Peace of Nijmwegen, signed with different parties in successive years (1678 and 1679), ended the hostilities of this second war. There were various minor territorial adjustments, but no clear victor except the United Netherlands, which retained all of its territory.

REVOCATION OF THE EDICT OF NANTES

In the decade after his invasion of the Netherlands, Louis made his second major move to assure religious conformity. Following the proclamation of the Edict of Nantes in 1598, relations between the great Catholic majority (nine-tenths of the French population) and the Protestant minority remained hostile. There were still about 1.75 million Huguenots in France in the 1660s, but their numbers were declining. The French Catholic Church denounced Calvinists as heretical and treasonous and supported their persecution as both pious and patriotic.

Following the Peace of Nijmwegen in 1678–1679, which halted for the moment his aggression in Europe, Louis launched a methodical campaign against the Huguenots in a determined effort to unify France religiously. He hounded the Huguenots out of public life, banning them from government office and excluding them from such professions as printing and medicine. He used subsidies and selective taxation to encourage Huguenots to convert to Catholicism. And in 1681, he bullied them by quartering his troops in their towns. Finally, Louis revoked the Edict of Nantes in October 1685. As a result, Protestant churches and schools were closed, Protestant ministers exiled, Protestant laymen forced to be galley slaves, and Protestant children baptized by Catholic priests. (See "Louis XIV Revokes the Edict of Nantes.")

The revocation of the Edict of Nantes was a major blunder. Protestant countries saw Louis as a new Philip II, intent on a Catholic reconquest of the whole of Europe, who must be resisted at all costs. The revocation prompted the voluntary emigration of more than a quarter million French people, who joined the resistance to France in England, Germany, Holland, and the New World. Thousands of French Huguenots served in the army of Louis's arch foe, William of Orange. Many of those who remained in France became part of an uncompromising guerrilla resistance to the king. Despite the many domestic and foreign liabilities it brought him, Louis, to his death, considered the revocation to be his most pious act, one that placed God in his debt.

LOUIS'S LATER WARS

The League of Augsburg and the Nine Years' War After the treaty of Nijmwegen, Louis maintained his army at full strength and restlessly probed beyond his perimeters. In 1681, his forces conquered the free city of Strasbourg, prompting new defensive coalitions to form against him. One of these, the League of Augsburg, created in 1686 to resist

MAP EXPLORATION

Interactive map: To explore this map further, go to http://www.prenhall.com/kagan/map13.2

THE EARLY WARS OF LOUIS XIV, 1667–1697

Treaty of Aix-la-Chapelle, 1668
  To France

Treaty of Nijmwegen, 1678–1679
  To France
  To Spain

Treaty of Ryswick, 1697
  To France
  —— Boundary of France, 1648

MAP 13–2 THE WARS OF LOUIS XIV *This map shows the territorial changes resulting from Louis XIV's first three major wars. The War of the Spanish Succession was yet to come.*

French expansion into Germany, had grown by 1689 to include England, Spain, Sweden, the united provinces, and the electorates of Bavaria, Saxony, and the palatinate. It also had the support of the Austrian emperor Leopold. In 1688, Louis's armies invaded the palatinate, ostensibly to claim on very weak ground its succession for his sister-in-law Charlotte Elisabeth. A long, extraordinarily destructive war resulted. Between 1688 and 1697, the league and France battled each other in

LOUIS XIV REVOKES THE EDICT OF NANTES

Believing a country could not be under one king and one law unless it was also under one religious system, Louis XIV stunned much of Europe in October 1685 by revoking the Edict of Nantes, which had protected the religious freedoms and civil rights of French Protestants since 1598. Compare this document to the one in Chapter 15 in which the elector of Brandenburg welcomes displaced French Protestants into his domains.

■ *What specific actions does this declaration order against Protestants? Does it offer any incentives for Protestants to convert to Catholicism? How does this declaration compare with the English Test Act?*

Art. 1. Know that we . . . with our certain knowledge, full power and royal authority, have by this present, perpetual and irrevocable edict, suppressed and revoked the edict of the aforesaid king our grandfather, given at Nantes in the month of April, 1598, in all its extent . . . together with all the concessions made by [this] and other edicts, declarations, and decrees, to the people of the so-called Reformed religion, of whatever nature they be . . . and in consequence we desire . . . that all the temples of the people of the aforesaid so-called Reformed religion situated in our kingdom . . . should be demolished forthwith.

Art. 2. We forbid our subjects of the so-called Reformed religion to assemble any more for public worship of the above-mentioned religion. . . .

Art. 3. We likewise forbid all lords, of whatever rank they may be, to carry out heretical services in houses and fiefs . . . the penalty for . . . the said worship being confiscation of their body and possessions.

Art. 4. We order all ministers of the aforesaid so-called Reformed religion who do not wish to be converted and to embrace the Catholic, Apostolic, and Roman religion, to depart from our kingdom and the lands subject to us within fifteen days from the publication of our present edict . . . on pain of the galleys.

Art. 5. We desire that those among the said [Reformed] ministers who shall be converted [to the Catholic religion] shall continue to enjoy during their life, and their wives shall enjoy after their death as long as they remain widows, the same exemptions from taxation and billeting of soldiers, which they enjoyed while they fulfilled the function of ministers. . . .

Art. 8. With regard to children who shall be born to those of the aforesaid so-called Reformed religion, we desire that they be baptized by their parish priests. We command the fathers and mothers to send them to the churches for that purpose, on penalty of a fine of 500 livres or more if they fail to do so; and afterwards, the children shall be brought up in the Catholic, Apostolic, and Roman religion. . . .

Art. 10. All our subjects of the so-called Reformed religion, with their wives and children, are to be strongly and repeatedly prohibited from leaving our aforesaid kingdom . . . or of taking out . . . their possessions and effects. . . .

The members of the so-called Reformed religion, while awaiting God's pleasure to enlighten them like the others, can live in the towns and districts of our kingdom . . . and continue their occupation there, and enjoy their possessions . . . on condition . . . that they do not make public profession of [their religion].

S. Z. Ehler and John B. Morrall, ed. and trans., *Church and State Through the Centuries: A Collection of Historic Documents* (New York: Biblo and Tannen, 1967), pp. 209–213. Reprinted by permission of Biblo and Tannen Booksellers and Publishers.

the Nine Years' War. During the same period, England and France struggled for control of North America in what came to be known as King William's War.

The Nine Years' War ended when stalemate and exhaustion forced both sides to accept an interim settlement. The Peace of Ryswick, signed in September 1697, was a triumph for William of Orange, now William III of England, and Emperor Leopold. It secured Holland's borders and thwarted Louis's expansion into Germany. (See "Louis XIV's Sister-in-Law Grieves for Her Homeland.")

LOUIS XIV'S SISTER-IN-LAW GRIEVES FOR HER HOMELAND

Charlotte Elisabeth, Duchesse d'Orléans (1652–1722), who was married to the brother of Louis XIV of France, had been born the daughter of the elector of the palatinate. After her marriage in 1671, she moved to the French court and was never permitted to revisit her homeland. She did, however, carry out an extensive correspondence with friends and family in Germany throughout her life. In August 1688, Louis XIV invaded the palatinate under the guise of restoring it to his sister-in-law. He had no real purpose except the conquest of the German region. This invasion was important for two reasons. First, it opened a war that continued until 1697. Second, at the onset of the original invasion, the French forces committed enormous atrocities against the civilian population, killing many civilians and destroying their homes. In these letters to her aunt and foster mother, Charlotte Elisabeth recounts her sadness and anger over the plight of these civilians and the difficulty of her own situation in the French court.

■ *How do these letters reflect the plight of a woman who had been required to enter a dynastic marriage when war broke out? How does she report Louis XIV's using her name to further his own political and financial ends in the palatinate? What kind of destruction was Charlotte Elisabeth aware of in her homeland?*

MARCH 20, 1689

I had barely began to recover somewhat from poor Carllutz's death [her brother] when the horrendous and piteous calamity was visited upon the poor Palatinate, and what pains me most is that my name is being used to cast these poor people into utter misery. And when I cry about it, I am treated to great annoyance and sulking [by those in the French royal court at Versailles]. But to save my life I cannot stop lamenting and bemoaning the thought that I am as it were, my fatherland's ruin, especially when I see all of the Elector's, my late father's, hard work and care suddenly reduced to rubble in poor Mannheim. I am so horrified by all the destruction that has been wrought that every night when I have finally dozed off, I imagine that I am in Mannheim and Heidelberg amidst all the destruction, and then I wake up with a dreadful start and cannot go back to sleep for two whole hours. Then I see in my mind how everything was in my day and in what state it is now, indeed in what state I am myself, and then I cannot hold back a flood of tears. It also grieves me deeply that the King [Louis XIV] waited to inflict the ultimate devastation precisely until I had begged him to spare Mannheim and Heidelberg.

JUNE 5, 1689

Although I should be accustomed by now to the thought of my poor fatherland in flames, having heard nothing else for so long, I still cannot help being regretful and grieved every time I am told that yet another place has been put to the torch. . . . Recently Monsieur [her husband] told me something that annoys me to the depth of my soul and which I had not known before, namely that the King [Louis XIV] has all taxes in the Palatinate levied in my name; now these poor people must think that I am profiting from their misery and that I am the cause of it, and that makes me deeply sad.

OCTOBER 30, 1689

Yesterday I was told something that touched my heart very deeply, and I could not hear it without tears; namely that the poor people of Mannheim have all returned and are living in their cellars as if they were houses and even hold a daily market as if the town were still in its previous state.

From *Louis XIV's Sister-in-Law Grieves for Her Homeland,* Elborg Forster, ed., in Von der Pfalz, *A Woman's Life in the Court of the Sun King,* pp. 61, 64, 68, © 1984 The Johns Hopkins University Press. Reprinted by permission.

War of the Spanish Succession: Treaties of Utrecht and Rastatt After Ryswick, Louis, who seemed to thrive on partial success, made another attempt to secure and expand French interests against Habsburg influence. On November 1, 1700, Charles II of Spain, known as "the sufferer" because of his genetic deformities and lingering illnesses, died.

Both Louis and the Austrian emperor Leopold had claims to the Spanish inheritance through their grandsons, Louis through his marriage to Marie-Thérèse and Leopold through his marriage to her younger sister, Margaret Theresa. Although Louis's grandson, Philip of Anjou, had the better claim (because Marie-Thérèse was Margaret Theresa's older sister), Marie-Thérèse had renounced her right to the Spanish inheritance in the Treaty of the Pyrenees (1659), and the inheritance was expected to go to Leopold's grandson.

Louis nurtured fears that the Habsburgs would dominate Europe should they gain control of Spain as well as the Holy Roman Empire. Most of the nations of Europe, however, feared France more than the Habsburgs and determined to prevent a union of the French and Spanish crowns. As a result, before Charles II's death, negotiations began among the nations involved to partition his inheritance in a way that would preserve the existing balance of power.

Charles II upset these negotiations by leaving his entire inheritance to Philip of Anjou, Louis's grandson. At a stroke, Spain and its possessions had fallen to France. Although Louis had been party to the partition agreements that preceded Charles's death, he now saw God's hand in Charles's will; he chose to enforce its terms over those of the partition agreement. Philip of Anjou moved to Madrid and became Philip V of Spain. Louis, in what was interpreted as naked French aggression, sent his troops again into Flanders, this time to remove Dutch soldiers from Spanish territory in the name of the new French king of Spain. Louis also declared Spanish America open to French ships.

In September 1701, England, Holland, and the Holy Roman Empire formed the Grand Alliance to counter Louis. They sought to preserve the balance of power by securing Flanders as a neutral barrier between Holland and France and by gaining for the emperor his fair share of the Spanish inheritance. After the formation of the Grand Alliance, Louis increased the stakes of battle by recognizing the claim of James Edward, the son of James II of England, to the English throne.

In 1701, the thirteen-year War of the Spanish Succession (1701–1714) began, and once again total war enveloped western Europe. France, for the first

Philip of Anjou, grandson of Louis XIV, was bequeathed the Spanish monarchy by Charles II of Spain. He became Philip V of Spain in 1700, triggering the War of the Spanish Succession. Philip retained the Spanish throne, but the war cost both France and Spain and their respective monarchies much power and prestige. Hyacinthe Rigaud (1659–1743), French, "King Philip V of Spain 1700–46 with crown and Golden Fleece." The Art Archive/Museo del Prado Madrid/Album/Joseph Martin. The Picture Desk Kobal Collection.

time, went to war with inadequate finances, a poorly equipped army, and mediocre generals. The English, in contrast, had advanced weaponry (flintlock rifles, paper cartridges, and ring bayonets) and superior tactics (thin, maneuverable troop columns rather than the traditional deep ones). John Churchill, the duke of Marlborough, who succeeded William of Orange as military leader of the alliance, bested Louis's soldiers in every major engagement. He routed French armies at Blenheim in August 1704 and on the plain of Ramillies in 1706—two decisive battles of the war. In 1708–1709, famine, revolts, and uncollectible taxes tore France apart internally. Despair pervaded the French court. Louis wondered aloud how God could forsake one who had done so much for him.

Though ready to make peace in 1709, Louis could not bring himself to accept the stiff terms of the alliance. These included a demand that he transfer all Spanish possessions to the emperor's grandson Charles and remove Philip V from Madrid. Hostilities continued, and an indecisive clash at Malplaquet (September 1709) left carnage on the battlefield unsurpassed until modern times.

France finally signed an armistice with England at Utrecht in July 1713 and concluded hostilities with Holland and the emperor in the Treaty of Rastatt in March 1714. This agreement confirmed Philip V as king of Spain, but gave Gibraltar and the island of Minorca to England, making it a Mediterranean power. (See Map 13–3.) It also won Louis's recognition of the right of the House of Hanover to accede to the English throne.

Spanish power declined in the wake of the war. Philip should have tried to consolidate his internal power and protect Spanish overseas trade. However, his second wife, Elizabeth Farnese, used Spanish power to secure thrones for her two sons in Italy. Such diversions of government resources allowed the nobility and the provinces to continue to assert their privileges against the monarchy. Not until the reign of Charles III (r. 1759–1788) did Spain have a monarch concerned with efficient domestic and imperial administration and internal improvement. By the third quarter of the century, Spain was better governed, but it could no longer compete effectively in great-power politics.

The Reign of Louis XIV (1643–1715)	
1643	Louis ascends the French throne at the age of five
1643–1661	Cardinal Mazarin directs the French government
1648	Peace of Westphalia
1649–1652	The *Fronde* revolt
1653	The pope declares Jansenism a heresy
1659	Treaty of Pyrenees between France and Spain
1660	Papal ban on Jansenists enforced in France
1661	Louis commences personal rule
1667–1668	War of Devolution
1670	Secret Treaty of Dover between France and Great Britain
1672–1679	French war against the Netherlands
1685	Louis revokes the Edict of Nantes
1688–1697	War of the League of Augsburg
1701	Outbreak of the War of the Spanish Succession
1713	Treaty of Utrecht between France and Great Britain
1714	Treaty of Rastatt between France and Spain
1715	Death of Louis XIV

Politically, the eighteenth century would belong to England as the sixteenth had belonged to Spain and the seventeenth to France. Although France remained intact and strong, the realization of Louis XIV's territorial ambitions had to await the rise of Napoleon Bonaparte. On his deathbed on September 1, 1715, Louis fittingly warned his heir, the *dauphin*, not to imitate his love of buildings and his liking for war.

LOUIS XIV'S LEGACY

Louis XIV left France a mixed legacy. His wars had brought widespread death and destruction and had sapped many of the nation's resources. Only a long period of peace could permit full economic recovery. Yet the years of war had established among both the army and much of the nobility a self-image of life in pursuit of military glory. Mid-eighteenth-century wars initiated in part from that outlook would undermine the recovering royal finances and cause an ongoing financial crisis that the monarchy never solved. Louis's policies of centralization would later make it difficult for France to develop effective institutions of representation and self-government. The aristocracy, after its years of domestication at Versailles, would have difficulty providing the nation with effective leaders and ministers. Yet his reign had also laid the groundwork for a new French Empire by expanding trade into Asia and colonizing North America.

Despite his own ambitions for absolute rule and the association of the term *absolutism* with his mode of government, it is important to recognize that Louis's rule was not so absolute as to exert oppressive control over the daily lives of his subjects, as would be the case with police states of the nineteenth and twentieth centuries. His absolutism functioned primarily in the classic areas of European state action—the making of war and peace, the regulation of religion, and the oversight of economic activity. Even at the height of his power, local institutions, some controlled by townspeople and others by nobles, continued to exert administrative authority at the local level. The king and his ministers supported the high status and tax exemptions of these local elites. But in contrast to the Stuart kings of England, Louis firmly prevented them from capturing or significantly limiting his authority on the national level. Not until the French monarchy was so weakened by financial crisis at the end of the eighteenth century would it succumb to demands for a more representative form of government.

MAP 13–3   EUROPE IN 1714   *The War of the Spanish Succession ended in the year before the death of the aged Louis XIV. By then, France and Spain, although not united, were both ruled by members of the Bourbon family, and Spain had lost its non-Iberian possessions.*

IN PERSPECTIVE

In the seventeenth century, England and France developed divergent forms of government. England became the model for parliamentary monarchy, France for absolute monarchy.

The politically active English elite—the nobility, along with the wealthy landowning and commercial classes—struggled throughout the century to limit the authority of rulers—including Oliver

Cromwell as well as the Stuart monarchs—over local interests. In the process, they articulated a political philosophy that stressed the need to prevent the central concentration of political power. The Bill of Rights of 1689 and the Toleration Act following the Glorious Revolution of William and Mary seemed to achieve the goals of this philosophy. These acts brought neither democracy nor full religious freedom in a modern sense; the Bill of Rights protected only the privileged, not all the English people, and the Toleration Act outlawed Catholics and Unitarians. Still, they firmly established representative government in England and extended legal recognition, at least in principle, to a variety of religious beliefs. The Bill of Rights required the monarch to call Parliament regularly.

In France, by contrast, the monarchy remained supreme. Although the king had to mollify privileged local elites by considering the interests of the nobility and the traditional rights of towns and regions, France had no national institution like Parliament through which he had to govern. Louis XIV was able, on his own authority, to fund the largest army in Europe. He could and did crush religious dissent. His own propaganda and the fear of his adversaries may have led to an exaggerated view of Louis's power, but his reign nonetheless provided a model of effective centralized power that later continental rulers tried to follow.

REVIEW QUESTIONS

1. Why did England and France develop differently in the seventeenth century? How did the personalities of their rulers affect each nation's political institutions?

2. Why did the English king and Parliament quarrel in the 1640s? Was king or Parliament more to blame? What role did religion play in the conflict?

3. What was the Glorious Revolution and why did it take place? What kind of settlement emerged from the revolution?

4. How did absolutism develop in France? What policies of Henry IV and Louis XIII were essential in creating the absolute monarchy?

5. How did Louis XIV consolidate his monarchy? What limits were there on his authority? What was Louis's religious policy?

6. What were the aims of Louis XIV's foreign policy? Were they realistic? To what extent did he initiate wars and to what extent did he react to events outside France?

SUGGESTED READINGS

ROBERT ASHTON, *Counter-Revolution: The Second Civil War and Its Origins, 1646–1648* (1995). A major examination of the resumption of civil conflict in England that ended with the abolition of the monarchy, House of Lords, and established church.

W. BEIK, *Absolutism and Society in Seventeenth-Century France* (1985). An important study that questions the extent of royal power.

R. W. BERGER, *A Royal Passion: Louis XIV as Patron of Architecture* (1997). Follows the building of Versailles and other structures embodying royal absolutism.

R. BONNEY, *Political Change in France under Richelieu and Mazarin, 1624–1661* (1978). A careful examination of how these two cardinals laid the foundation for Louis XIV's absolutism.

P. BURKE, *The Fabrication of Louis XIV* (1992). Examines the manner in which the public image of Louis XIV was forged in art.

P. COLLINSON, *The Religion of Protestants: The Church in English Society, 1559–1625* (1982). The best introduction to Puritanism.

J. H. ELLIOTT AND L. BROCKLISS (EDS.), *The Age of the Favourite* (1999). Explores, in the European setting, the political impact of those figures who received extraordinary royal favor and patronage.

M. KISHLANSKY, *A Monarchy Transformed: Britain, 1603–1714* (1996). An important overview.

J. R. MAJOR, *From Renaissance Monarchy to Absolute Monarchy: French Kings, Nobles and Estates* (1994). A major study by a leading scholar exploring the complexities of the relationship of the monarchy to other political and social groups.

R. METTAM, *Power and Faction in Louis XIV's France* (1988). Examines the political intricacies of the reign and suggests the limits to absolutism.

P. K. MONOD, *The Power of Kings: Monarchy and Religion in Europe, 1589–1715* (1999). An important and innovative examination of the roots of royal authority as early modern Europe became modern Europe.

H. PHILLIPS, *Church and Culture in Seventeenth-Century France* (1997). A clear examination of the major religious issues confronting France and their relationship to the larger culture.

O. RANUM, *The Fronde: A French Revolution, 1648–1652* (1993). The best work on the subject.

C. RUSSELL, *The Fall of the English Monarchies, 1637–1642* (1991). A major revisionist account.

S. SCHAMA, *A History of Britain : The Wars of the British, 1603–1776* (2001). A highly accessible narrative originally designed for television that explores the major themes of British development during this period.

G. TREASURE, *Louis XIV* (2001). The best, most accessible recent study.

G. TREASURE, *Mazarin: The Crisis of Absolutism in France* (1996). An examination not only of Mazarin, but also of the larger national and international background.

R. D. TUMBLESON, *Catholicism in the English Protestant Imagination: Nationalism, Religion, and Literature, 1660–1745* (1998). Explores the impact of anti-Catholicism on English life during this critical period in the search for religious and political stability.

N. TYACKE, *Anti-Calvinists: The Rise of English Arminianism c. 1590–1640* (1987). The most important study of Archbishop Laud's policies and his predecessors.

D. UNDERDOWN, *A Freeborn People: Politics and the Nation in Seventeenth-Century England* (1996). A lively reply to C. Russell above.

DOCUMENTS CD-ROM

SOCIETY AND POLITICS IN EARLY MODERN EUROPE

THOUGHT AND CULTURE IN EARLY MODERN EUROPE

ABSOLUTISM

Rigaud's *Louis XIV:*
The State Portrait

Even if Louis XIV may never actually have said, "I am the state," the famous remark attributed to him, most of his subjects and the other crowned heads of Europe certainly saw him as such. Hyacinthe Rigaud painted Louis as the embodiment of official political power and authority, establishing the model for what became known for the rest of the century as "the state portrait."

Hyacinthe Rigaud, *Louis XIV*, 1701. Giraudon/Art Resource, N.Y.

Previously, most portraits or statues of Louis—and there were many—set him in an allegorical setting where he embodied qualities of mythical heroes or in a historical setting in which he resembled a Roman emperor. Rigaud's portrait (1701) is largely, though not entirely, a painting of royal majesty and royal symbols. A mature Louis appears in his coronation robes, decorated with fleurs-de-lis, which he would not have worn for decades. The robes, along with the crown and the throne which rests beside and behind him in the background, suggest that each day he is again crowned by his accomplishments, his justice, and his divine right to rule. He holds the scepter of state as a staff that steadies him, as he presumably saw himself steadying the French nation after the decades of turmoil that had preceded his reign. The sword of state hangs by his side partially covered, though he had led the nation in war through most of his reign and would do so throughout the next decade as well. On the base of the column at the rear of the painting in the shadows resides the figure of justice.

The Italian sculptor Bernini, who sculpted a bust of Louis taken from a portrait, once wrote, "The secret of portraits is to exaggerate what is fine, add a touch of grandeur, and diminish what is ugly or petty or even suppress it when this is possible without flattery."[1] Rigaud followed this advice in his portrait of Louis, which displays many ironies about which both Louis and the artist must have been aware. The full, long wig suggests a more youthful figure than the now aged king of sixty-three years. Furthermore, through disease early in his reign, Louis had lost much of his hair. By the time the portrait was

[1] Quoted in Peter Burke, *The Fabrication of Louis XIV* (New Haven, CT: Yale University Press, 1992), p. 23.

painted, he was often ill with gout and other diseases. The portrait hid these facts, but Rigaud, presumably with Louis's encouragement, did give his sitter a face reflecting maturity and perhaps a kind of worldly wisdom. Louis may have been comfortable with such a portrayal, because, from the middle of the 1680s, he had led a very restricted personal life after marrying his strictly devout mistress, Madame de Maintenon. The dancing monarch of the early years of the reign, suggested by the remarkably handsome athletic legs and red shoes, had given way to a more restrained person and one so rigorously devout, that in 1685 he had undertaken a policy of persecuting French Protestants.

This portrait is of a single person and carries the name of a single artist. The majesty of the lone Louis XIV concealed a multilayered network of royal ministers and bureaucrats working, negotiating, and compromising with hundreds of local officials, councils, and courts that really constituted the royal government, later termed *absolutism*. The attribution of the portrait to Rigaud alone concealed the fact that this painting, as was the custom with many other portraits and large paintings of the late seventeenth and eighteenth centuries, was completed in an artist's workshop. The master of the workshop, Rigaud in this case, would have personally painted the face and usually the hands. Different artists would have completed other elements of the picture, with, for example, some specializing in drapery and others in clothing. These workshops allowed the master artist to preside over a commercialized artistic business serving the expanding demand for the luxury good of a personal portrait on the part of aristocrats and members of the expanding commercial and professional classes. The business of art extended beyond these workshops into the world of engravers and printers, who could disperse commercially more inexpensive paper copies of important works of art for their own profit and, in the case of political portraits, for purposes of establishing a popular image of persons in public life.

Louis deeply admired this portrait. Originally, he had intended to send it to Philip V of Spain, the grandson he installed on the Spanish throne, thus provoking the greatest European war of his reign. But he decided to keep it for himself and had several copies made and distributed. When various councils or other ministerial bodies met at Versailles in his absence after 1701, the portrait was carried into the room to remind all those present of the monarch whom they served and whose policies they carried out.

■ *What qualities did Rigaud seek to invest Louis XIV with in this painting? Why was the king so pleased with the portrait? What were the parallels between the way Rigaud's workshop produced a painting and how Louis conducted the government of France?*

Peter Burke, *The Fabrication of Louis XIV* (New Haven, CT: Yale University Press, 1992); Daniel Roche, *France in the Age of the Enlightenment* (Cambridge, MA: Harvard University Press, 1998), pp. 273–277; Germain Bazin, *Baroque and Rococo Art* (New York: Praeger, 1966); Marilyn Stockstad, *Art History* (New York: Harry N. Abrams and Prentice Hall, 1999), pp. 750–751.

Queen Christina of Sweden (r. 1632–1654), shown here with the French philosopher and scientist René Descartes, was one of many women from the elite classes interested in the New Science. In 1649 she invited Descartes to live at her court in Stockholm, but he died a few months after moving to Sweden. Chateau de Versailles, France/Bridgeman Art Library

NEW DIRECTIONS IN THOUGHT AND CULTURE IN THE SIXTEENTH AND SEVENTEENTH CENTURIES

*T*HE SIXTEENTH AND SEVENTEENTH CENTURIES *witnessed a sweeping change in the scientific view of the universe. An earth-centered picture gave way to one in which the earth was only another planet orbiting about the sun. The sun itself became one of millions of stars. This transformation of humankind's perception of its place in the larger scheme of things led to a profound rethinking of moral and religious matters, as well as of scientific theory. Faith and reason needed new modes of reconciliation, as did faith and science. The new ideas and methods of science, usually termed* natural philosophy *at the time, challenged those modes of thought associated with late medieval times: Scholasticism and Aristotelian philosophy.*

The impact of the new science that explored the realm of the stars through the newly invented telescope and the world of microorganisms through the newly invented microscope must be viewed in the context of two other factors that simultaneously challenged traditional modes of European thought and culture in the sixteenth and seventeenth centuries. The first of these was the Reformation, which permanently divided the religious unity of central and western Europe and fostered decades of warfare and theological dispute. Although by no means a complete break with medieval thought, the theology of the Reformation did question many ideas associated with medieval Christianity and society. The second factor was the cultural impact of the encounter of Europe with the New World of the Americas. The interaction with the Americas meant that Europeans directly or indirectly acquired knowledge of new peoples, plants, and animals wholly different from their own and about which people in neither ancient nor medieval times had any information. Consequently, new uncertainties and unfamiliar vistas confronted many Europeans as they considered their souls, geographical knowledge, and physical nature.

Side by side with this new knowledge and science, however, came a new wave of superstition and persecution. The changing world of religion, politics, and knowledge also created profound fear and anxiety among both the simple and the learned, resulting in Europe's worst witch-hunts.

KEY TOPICS

- The astronomical theories of Copernicus, Brahe, Kepler, Galileo, and Newton and the emergence of the scientific worldview
- Impact of the new science on philosophy
- Social setting of early modern science
- Women and the scientific revolution
- Approaches to science and religion
- Witchcraft and witch-hunts

The Scientific Revolution

The process that established the new view of the universe is normally termed the **scientific revolution.** The revolution-in-science metaphor must be used carefully, however. Not everything associated with the "new" science was necessarily new. Sixteenth- and seventeenth-century natural philosophers were often reexamining and rethinking theories and data from the ancient world and the late Middle Ages. Moreover, the word *revolution* normally denotes rapid, collective political change involving large numbers of people. The scientific revolution was not rapid. It was a complex movement with many false starts and brilliant people suggesting wrong as well as useful ideas. Nor did it involve more than a few hundred people who labored in widely separated studies and crude laboratories located in Poland, Italy, Denmark, Bohemia, France, and Great Britain. Furthermore, the achievements of the new science were not simply the function of isolated brilliant scientific minds. The leading figures of the scientific revolution often drew on the aid of artisans and craftspeople to help them construct new instruments for experimentation and to carry out those experiments. Thus the scientific revolution involved a reappropriation of older knowledge as well as new discoveries. Additionally, because the practice of science involves social activity as well as knowledge, the revolution also saw the establishment of new social institutions to support the emerging scientific enterprise.

Science was only in the process of becoming science as we know it today during the era of the scientific revolution. In fact the word *scientist*, which was only coined in the 1830s, did not yet exist in the seventeenth century, nor did anything resembling the modern scientific career. Individuals devoted to natural philosophy might work in universities or in the court of a prince or even in their own homes and workshops. Only in the second half of the seventeenth century did formal societies and academies devoted to the pursuit of natural philosophy come into existence. Even then the entire process of the pursuit of natural knowledge was a largely informal one.

Yet by the close of the seventeenth century, the new scientific concepts and the methods of their construction were so impressive that they set the standard for assessing the validity of knowledge in the Western world. From the early seventeenth century through the end of the twentieth century, science achieved greater cultural authority in the Western world than any other form of intellectual activity, and the authority and application of scientific knowledge became one of the defining characteristics of modern Western civilization.

Although new knowledge emerged in many areas during the sixteenth and seventeenth centuries, including medicine, chemistry, and natural history, the scientific achievements that most captured the learned imagination and persuaded people of the cultural power of natural knowledge were those that occurred in astronomy.

NICOLAUS COPERNICUS REJECTS AN EARTH-CENTERED UNIVERSE

Nicolaus Copernicus (1473–1543) was a Polish astronomer who enjoyed a high reputation during his life. He had been educated first at the University of Cracow in Poland and later in Italy. He led a largely isolated intellectual career and was not known for strikingly original or unorthodox thought. In 1543, the year of his death, Copernicus published *On the Revolutions of the Heavenly Spheres*. Copernicus's book was "a revolution-making rather than a revolutionary text."[1] What Copernicus did was to provide an intellectual springboard for a complete criticism of the then-dominant view of the position of the earth in the universe.

The Ptolemaic System At the time of Copernicus, the standard explanation of the place of the earth in the heavens combined the mathematical astronomy of Ptolemy, contained in his work entitled the *Almagest* (150 C.E.), with the physical cosmology of Aristotle. Over the centuries, commentators on Ptolemy's work had developed several alternative **Ptolemaic systems,** on the basis of which they made mathematical calculations relating to astronomy. Most of these writers assumed the earth was the

---

[1]Thomas S. Kuhn, *The Copernican Revolution: Planetary Astronomy in the Development of Western Thought* (New York: Vintage, 1959), p. 135.

center of the universe, an outlook known as *geocentrism*. Drawing on Aristotle, these commentators assumed that above the earth lay a series of concentric spheres, probably fluid in character, one of which contained the moon, another the sun, and still others the planets and the stars. At the outer regions of these spheres lay the realm of God and the angels. The earth had to be the center because of its heaviness. The stars and the other heavenly bodies had to be enclosed in the spheres so they could move, since nothing could move unless something was actually moving it. The state of rest was presumed natural; motion required explanation. This was the astronomy found in such works as Dante's *Divine Comedy*.

Numerous problems were associated with the Ptolemaic model, and these had long been recognized. The most important was the observed motions of the planets. At certain times the planets actually appeared to be going backward. The Ptolemaic model accounted for these motions primarily through epicycles. The planet moved uniformly about a small circle (an *epicycle*), and the center of the epicycle moved uniformly about a larger circle (called a *deferent*), with the earth at or near its center. The combination of these two motions, as viewed from the earth, was meant to replicate the changing planetary positions among the fixed stars—and did so to a high degree of accuracy. The circles employed in Ptolemaic systems were not meant to represent the actual paths of anything; that is, they were not orbits. Rather, they were the components of purely mathematical models meant to predict planetary positions. Other intellectual, but nonobservational, difficulties related to the immense speed at which the spheres had to move around the earth. To say the least, the Ptolemaic

systems were cluttered. They were effective, however, as long as one assumed Aristotelian physics.

Copernicus's Universe Copernicus's *On the Revolutions of the Heavenly Spheres* challenged the Ptolemaic picture in the most conservative manner possible. (See "Copernicus Ascribes Movement to the Earth.") He adopted many elements of the Ptolemaic model, but transferred them to a heliocentric (sun-centered) model, which assumed the earth moved about the sun in a circle. Copernicus's model, which retained epicycles, was actually no more accurate than Ptolemy's. However, Copernicus could claim certain advantages over the ancient model. In particular, the epicycles were smaller. The retrograde motion of the planets was now explained as a result of an optical illusion that arose because people were observing the planets from earth, which was moving itself. Furthermore, Copernicus argued that the farther planets were from the sun, the longer they took to revolve around it. The length of these individual revolutions made it easier to determine the order of the planets, how they ranked in terms of distance from the sun.

The repositioning of the earth had not been Copernicus's goal. Rather, Copernicus appears to have set out to achieve new intelligibility and mathematical elegance to astronomy. The means of doing so was to reject Aristotle's cosmology and to remove the earth from the center of the universe. His system was no more accurate than the existing ones for predicting the location of the planets. He had used no new evidence. The major impact of his work was to provide another way of confronting some of the difficulties inherent in Ptolemaic astronomy. The Copernican system did not immediately replace the

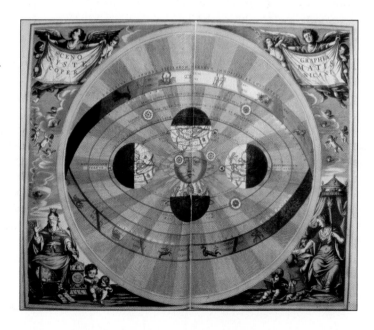

This 1543 map of the heavens based on the writings of Nicholas Copernicus shows the earth and the other planets moving about the sun. Until well into the 1600s, however, astronomers continued to debate whether the sun revolved around the earth. British Library, London. The Bridgeman Art Library International Ltd.

COPERNICUS ASCRIBES MOVEMENT TO THE EARTH

Copernicus published De Revolutionibus Orbium Caelestium *(On the Revolutions of the Heavenly Spheres) in 1543. In his preface, addressed to Pope Paul III, he explained what had led him to think that the earth moved around the sun and what he thought were some of the scientific consequences of the new theory.*

■ *How does Copernicus justify his argument to the pope? How important was historical precedent and tradition to the pope? Might Copernicus have thought that the pope would be especially susceptible to such an argument, even though what Copernicus proposed (the movement of the earth) contradicted the Bible?*

I may well presume, most Holy Father, that certain people, as soon as they hear that in this book about the Revolutions of the Spheres of the Universe I ascribe movement to the Earthly globe, will cry out that, holding such views, I should at once be hissed off the stage. . . .

So I should like your Holiness to know that I was induced to think of a method of computing the motions of the spheres by nothing else than the knowledge that the Mathematicians [who had previously considered the problem] are inconsistent in these investigations.

For, first, the mathematicians are so unsure of the movements of the Sun and Moon that they cannot even explain or observe the constant length of the seasonal year. Secondly, in determining the motions of these and of the other five planets, they use neither the same principles and hypotheses nor the same demonstrations of the apparent motions and revolutions. . . . Nor have they been able thereby to discern or deduce the principal thing—namely the shape of the Universe and the unchangeable symmetry of its parts. . . .

I pondered long upon this uncertainty of mathematical tradition in establishing the motions of the system of the spheres. At last I began to chafe that philosophers could by no means agree on any one certain theory of the mechanism of the Universe, wrought for us by a supremely good and orderly Creator. . . . I therefore took pains to read again the works of all the philosophers on whom I could lay hand to seek out whether any of them had ever supposed that the motions of the spheres were other than those demanded by the [Ptolemaic] mathematical schools. I found first in Cicero that Hicetas [of Syracuse, fifth century B.C.E.] had realized that the Earth moved. Afterwards I found in Plutarch that certain others had held the like opinion. . . .

Thus assuming motions, which in my work I ascribe to the Earth, by long and frequent observations I have at last discovered that, if the motions of the rest of the planets be brought into relation with the circulation of the Earth and be reckoned in proportion to the circles of each planet, not only do their phenomena presently ensue, but the orders and magnitudes of all stars and spheres, nay the heavens themselves, become so bound together that nothing in any part thereof could be moved from its place without producing confusion of all the other parts of the Universe as a whole.

As quoted in Thomas S. Kuhn, *The Copernican Revolution: Planetary Astronomy in the Development of Western Thought* (New York: Vintage Books, 1959), pp. 137–139, 141–142.

old astronomy, but it allowed other people who were also discontented with the Ptolemaic view to think in new directions. Indeed, for at least a century, the Copernican system was embraced by a distinct minority of natural philosophers and astronomers.

Tycho Brahe and Johannes Kepler Make New Scientific Observations

Tycho Brahe (1546–1601) took the next major step toward the conception of a sun-centered system.

He did not embrace Copernicus's view of the universe and actually spent most of his life advocating an earth-centered system. He suggested that the moon and the sun revolved around the earth and that the other planets revolved around the sun. In pursuit of his own theory, Brahe constructed scientific instruments with which he made more extensive naked-eye observations of the planets than anyone else had ever done. His labors produced a vast body of astronomical data from which his successors could work.

When Brahe died, these tables came into the possession of his assistant, Johannes Kepler (1571–1630), a German astronomer. Kepler was a convinced Copernican and a more consistently rigorous advocate of a heliocentric model than Copernicus himself. Deeply influenced by Renaissance Neoplatonism, which held the sun in special honor, Kepler was determined to find in Brahe's numbers mathematical harmonies that would support a sun-centered universe. After much work, Kepler discovered that to keep the sun at the center of things, he must abandon the circular components of Copernicus's model, particularly the epicycles. The mathematical relationships that emerged from his consideration of Brahe's observations suggested that the motions of the planets were elliptical. Then Kepler set forth the first astronomical model that actually portrayed motion—that is, the path of the planets—and those orbits were elliptical. Kepler published his findings in his 1609 book entitled *The New Astronomy*. He had solved the problem of planetary motion by using Copernicus's sun-centered universe and Brahe's empirical data.

Kepler had also defined a new problem. None of the available theories could explain why the planetary orbits were elliptical or, for that matter, why planetary motion was orbital at all rather than simply moving off along a tangent. That solution awaited the work of Sir Isaac Newton.

GALILEO GALILEI ARGUES FOR A UNIVERSE OF MATHEMATICAL LAWS

From Copernicus to Brahe to Kepler, there had been little new information about the heavens that might not have been known to Ptolemy. In 1609, however, the same year that Kepler published *The New Astronomy*, an Italian mathematician and natural philosopher named Galileo Galilei (1564–1642) first turned a telescope on the heavens. Using that recently invented Dutch instrument, he saw stars where none had been known to exist, mountains on the moon, spots moving across the sun, and moons orbiting Jupiter. The heavens were far more complex than anyone had suspected. These discoveries, with some work, could have been accommodated into the Ptolemaic model. Such accommodation would, however, have required a highly technical understanding of Ptolemaic astronomy. Galileo knew that few people who controlled patronage possessed such complex knowledge. Consequently, in the *Starry Messenger* (1610) and *Letters on Sunspots* (1613) he used his considerable rhetorical skills to argue that his newly observed physical evidence, particularly the phases of Venus, required a Copernican interpretation of the heavens.

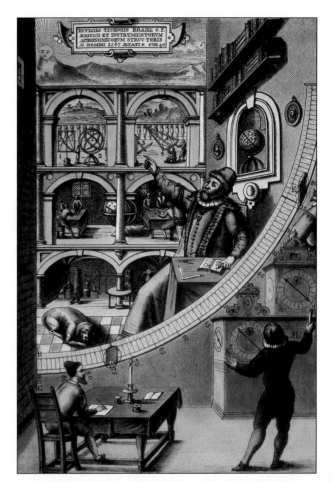

Tycho Brahe in the Uranienburg observatory on the Danish island of Hven (1587). Brahe made the most important observations of the stars since antiquity. Kepler used his data to solve the problem of planetary motion in a way that supported Copernicus's sun-centered view of the universe. Ironically, Brahe himself had opposed Copernicus's view. Bildarchiv Preussischer Kulturbesitz

Galileo's career illustrates that the forging of the new science involved more than just the presentation of arguments and evidence. In 1610, he had left the University of Padua for Florence, where he became the philosopher and mathematician to the Grand Duke of Tuscany, who was a Medici. Galileo was now pursuing natural philosophy in a princely court and had become dependent on princely patronage. To win such support for both his continued work and the theories he propounded, he named the moons of Jupiter after the Medicis. As a natural philosopher working with the new telescope, he had literally presented recently discovered heavenly bodies to his patron. By both his political skills and his excellent prose, he had transformed himself into a high-profile advocate of Copernicanism. Galileo's problems with the Roman Catholic Church, discussed later in the chapter, arose from both his ideas and his flair for self-advertisement.

Galileo not only popularized the Copernican system, but also articulated the concept of a universe subject to mathematical laws. More than any other writer of the century, he argued that nature displayed mathematical regularity in its most minute details:

Philosophy is written in that great book which ever lies before our eyes—I mean the universe—but we cannot understand it if we do not first learn the language and grasp the symbols in which it is written. This book is written in the mathematical language, and the symbols are triangles, circles, and other geometrical figures, without whose help it is impossible to comprehend a single word of it; without which one wanders through a dark labyrinth.[2]

The universe was rational; however, its rationality was not that of scholastic logic, but of mathematics. Copernicus had thought that the heavens conformed to mathematical regularity; Galileo saw this regularity throughout all physical nature.

A world of quantities was replacing one of qualities. All aspects of the world—including color, beauty, and taste—would increasingly be described in terms of the mathematical relationships among quantities. Mathematical models would eventually be applied even to social relations. The new natural philosophy portrayed nature as cold, rational, mathematical, and mechanistic. What was real and lasting was what was mathematically measurable. For many people, the power of the mathematical arguments that appeared irrefutable proved more persuasive than the new information from physical observation that produced so much controversy. Few intellectual shifts have wrought such momentous changes for Western civilization.

ISAAC NEWTON DISCOVERS THE LAWS OF GRAVITATION

The question that continued to perplex seventeenth-century scientists who accepted the theories of Copernicus, Kepler, and Galileo was how the planets and other heavenly bodies moved in an orderly fashion. The Ptolemaic and Aristotelian answer had been the spheres and a universe arranged in the order of the heaviness of its parts. Many unsatisfactory theories had been set forth to deal with the question. It was this issue of planetary motion that the Englishman Isaac Newton (1642–1727) addressed and, in so doing, established a basis for physics that endured for more than two centuries.

In 1687, Newton published *The Mathematical Principles of Natural Philosophy*, better known by its Latin title of *Principia Mathematica*. Much of the research and thinking for this great work had taken place more than fifteen years earlier. Galileo's mathematical bias permeated Newton's thought, as did his view that inertia applied to bodies both at rest and in motion. Newton reasoned that the planets and all other physical objects in the universe moved through mutual attraction, or gravity. Every object in the universe affected every other object through gravity. The attraction of gravity explained why the planets moved in an orderly, rather than a chaotic, manner. Newton had found that "the force of gravity towards the whole planet did arise from and was compounded of the forces of gravity towards all its parts, and towards every one part was in the inverse proportion of the squares of the distances from the part."[3] Newton demonstrated this relationship mathematically; he made no attempt to explain the nature of gravity itself.

Newton was a great mathematical genius, but he also upheld the importance of empirical data and observation. Like Francis Bacon (see later), he believed that one must observe phenomena before attempting to explain them. The final test of any theory or hypothesis for him was whether it described what was actually observed. Newton was a great opponent of the rationalism of the French philosopher Descartes (see later), which he believed included insufficient guards against error. Consequently, as Newton's own theory of universal gravitation became increasingly accepted, so, too, was Baconian empiricism.

Philosophy Responds to Changing Science

The revolution in scientific thought contributed directly to a major reexamination of Western philosophy. Several of the most important figures in the Scientific Revolution, such as Bacon and Descartes, were also philosophers discontented with the scholastic heritage. Bacon stressed the importance of empirical research. Descartes attempted to find certainty through the exploration of his own thinking processes. Newton's interests likewise extended to philosophy; he wrote broadly on many topics, including scientific method and theology.

If a single idea informed all of these philosophers, though in different ways, it was the idea of mechanism. The proponents of the new science sought to explain the world in terms of mechanical

---

[2]Quoted in E. A. Burtt, *The Metaphysical Foundations of Modern Physical Science* (Garden City, NY: Anchor-Doubleday, 1954), p. 75.

[3]Quoted in A. Rupert Hall, *From Galileo to Newton, 1630–1720* (London: Fontana, 1970), p. 300.

metaphors, or the language of machinery. The image to which many of them turned was that of the clock. Johannes Kepler once wrote, "I am much occupied with the investigation of the physical causes. My aim in this is to show that the machine of the universe is not similar to a divine animated being, but similar to a clock."[4] Nature conceived as machinery removed much of the mystery of the world and the previous assumption of the presence of divine purpose in nature. The qualities that seemed to inhere in matter came to be understood as the result of mechanical arrangement. Some writers came to understand God as a kind of divine watchmaker or mechanic who had arranged the world as a machine that would thereafter function automatically. The drive to a mechanical understanding of nature also meant that the language of science and of natural philosophy would become largely that of mathematics. The emphasis that Galileo had placed on mathematics spread to other areas of thought.

This new mode of thinking transformed physical nature from a realm in which Europeans looked for symbolic or sacramental meaning related to the divine into a realm where they looked for utility or usefulness. Previously, philosophers had often believed a correct understanding of the natural order would reveal divine mysteries or knowledge relating to sacred history. Henceforth, they would tend to see knowledge of nature as revealing nothing beyond itself—nothing about divine purposes for the life of humankind on earth. Natural knowledge became the path toward the physical improvement of human beings through their ability to command the processes of nature. Many people associated with the new science also believed such knowledge would strengthen the power of their monarchs.

FRANCIS BACON: THE EMPIRICAL METHOD

Bacon (1561–1626) was an Englishman of almost universal accomplishment. He was a lawyer, a high royal official, and the author of histories, moral essays, and philosophical discourses. Traditionally, he has been regarded as the father of **empiricism** and of experimentation in science. Much of this reputation was actually unearned. Bacon was not a natural philosopher, except in the most amateur fashion. His real accomplishment was setting an intellectual tone and helping create a climate conducive to scientific work.

Sir Isaac Newton's experiments dealing with light passing through a prism became a model for writers praising the experimental method. Corbis

In books such as *The Advancement of Learning* (1605), the *Novum Organum* (1620), and the *New Atlantis* (1627), Bacon attacked the scholastic belief that most truth had already been discovered and only required explanation, as well as the scholastic reverence for authority in intellectual life. (See "Bacon Attacks the Idols That Harm Human Understanding.") He believed scholastic thinkers paid too much attention to tradition and to the knowledge of the ancients. He urged contemporaries to strike out on their own in search of a new understanding of nature. He wanted seventeenth-century Europeans to have confidence in themselves and their own abilities rather than in the people and methods of the past. Bacon was one of the first major European writers to champion the desirability of innovation and change.

Bacon believed that human knowledge should produce useful results—deeds rather than words. In particular, knowledge of nature should be enlisted to improve the human condition. These goals required the modification or abandonment of scholastic modes of learning and thinking. Bacon contended, "The [scholastic] logic now in use serves more to fix and give stability to the errors which have their

[4]Quoted in Steven Shapin, *The Scientific Revolution* (Chicago: University of Chicago Press, 1996), p. 33.

Sir Francis Bacon (1561–1626), champion of the inductive method of gaining knowledge. By courtesy of the National Portrait Gallery, London

foundation in commonly received notions than to help the search after truth."[5] Scholastic philosophers could not escape from their syllogisms to examine the foundations of their thought and intellectual presuppositions. Bacon urged that philosophers and investigators of nature examine the evidence of their senses before constructing logical speculations. In a famous passage, he divided all philosophers into "men of experiment and men of dogmas" and then observed,

The men of experiment are like the ant, they only collect and use; the reasoners resemble spiders, who make cobwebs out of their own substance. But the bee takes a middle course: it gathers its material from the flowers of the garden and of the field, but transforms and digests it by a power of its own. Not unlike this is the true business of philosophy.[6]

---

[5]Quoted in Franklin Baumer, *Main Currents of Western Thought*, 4th ed. (New Haven, CT: Yale University Press, 1978), p. 281.
[6]Quoted in Baumer, p. 288.

By directing natural philosophy toward an examination of empirical evidence, Bacon hoped it would achieve new knowledge and thus new capabilities for humankind.

Bacon boldly compared himself with Columbus, plotting a new route to intellectual discovery. The comparison is significant, because it displays the consciousness of a changing world that appears so often in writers of the late sixteenth and early seventeenth centuries. They were rejecting the past not from simple contempt or overweening pride, but rather from a firm understanding that the world was much more complicated than their medieval forebears had thought. Neither Europe nor European thought could remain self-contained. Like the new worlds on the globe, new worlds of the mind were also emerging.

Most of the people in Bacon's day, including the intellectuals influenced by humanism, thought that the best era of human history lay in antiquity. Bacon dissented vigorously from that view. He looked to a future of material improvement achieved through the empirical examination of nature. His own theory of induction from empirical evidence was unsystematic, but his insistence on appealing to experience influenced others whose methods were more productive. He and others of his outlook received almost daily support from the reports not only of European explorers, but also of ordinary seamen who now sailed all over the world and could describe wondrous cultures, as well as plants and animals, unknown to the European ancients.

Bacon believed that science had a practical purpose and its goal was human improvement. Some scientific investigation does have this character. Much pure research does not. Bacon, however, linked science and material progress in the public mind. This was a powerful idea and has continued to influence Western civilization to the present day. It has made science and those who can appeal to the authority of science major forces for change and innovation. Thus, although not making any major scientific contribution himself, Bacon directed investigators of nature to a new method and a new purpose. As a person actively associated with politics, Bacon also believed the pursuit of new knowledge would increase the power of governments and monarchies. Again, his thought in this area opened the way for the eventual strong linkage between governments and the scientific enterprise.

RENÉ DESCARTES: THE METHOD OF RATIONAL DEDUCTION

Descartes (1596–1650) was a gifted mathematician who invented analytic geometry. His most important contribution, however, was to develop a scientific

BACON ATTACKS THE IDOLS THAT HARM HUMAN UNDERSTANDING

Francis Bacon wanted the men and women of his era to have the courage to change the way they thought about physical nature. In this famous passage from the Novum Organum *(1620), he attempted to explain why it is so difficult to ask new questions and seek new answers.*

■ *Is Bacon's view of human nature pessimistic? Are people hopelessly trapped in overlapping worlds of self-interest and fantasy imposed by their nature and cultural traditions? How did Bacon expect people to overcome such formidable barriers?*

The idols and false notions which are now in possession of the human understanding and have taken deep root therein. . . . so beset men's minds that truth can hardly find entrance. . . . There are four classes of Idols which beset men's minds. To these for distinction's sake I have assigned names—calling the first class Idols of the Tribe; the second, Idols of the Cave; the third, Idols of the Marketplace; the fourth, Idols of the Theatre.

The Idols of the Tribe have their foundation in human nature itself; and in the tribe or race of men. For it is a false assertion that the sense of man is the measure of things. On the contrary, all perceptions as well as the sense as of the mind are according to the measure of the universe. And the human understanding is like a false mirror, which, receiving rays irregularly, distorts and discolours the nature of things by mingling its own nature with it.

The Idols of the Cave are the idols of the individual man. For every one (besides the errors common to human nature in general) has a cave or den of his own, which refracts and discolours the light of nature; owing either to his own proper and peculiar nature; or to his education and conversation with others; or to the reading of books, and the authority of those whom he esteems and admires. . . .

There are also Idols formed by the intercourse and association of men with each other, which I call Idols of the Marketplace, on account of the commerce and consort of men there. For it is by discourse that men associate; and words are imposed according to the apprehension of the vulgar. And therefore the ill and unfit choice of words wonderfully obstructs the understanding. . . .

Lastly, there are Idols which have immigrated into men's minds from the various dogmas of philosophies, and also from wrong laws of demonstration. These I call Idols of the Theatre; because in my judgment all the received systems are but so many stage plays, representing worlds of their own creation after an unreal and scenic fashion.

From Francis Bacon, *Essays, Advancement of Learning, New Atlantis, and Other Pieces,* ed. by Richard Foster Jones (New York: Odyssey, 1937), pp. 278–280.

method that relied more on deduction than empirical observation and induction.

In 1637, he published his *Discourse on Method,* in which he rejected scholastic philosophy and education and advocated thought founded on a mathematical model. (See "Descartes Explores the Promise of Science.") The work appeared in French rather than in Latin because Descartes wanted it to have wide circulation and application. In the *Discourse,* he began by saying he would doubt everything except those propositions about which he could have clear and distinct ideas. This approach rejected all forms of intellectual authority, except the conviction of his own reason. Descartes

concluded that he could not doubt his own act of thinking and his own existence. From this base, he proceeded to deduce the existence of God. The presence of God was important to Descartes because God guaranteed the correctness of clear and distinct ideas. Since God was not a deceiver, the ideas of God-given reason could not be false.

On the basis of such an analysis, Descartes concluded that human reason could fully comprehend the world. He divided existing things into two basic categories: thinking things and things occupying space—mind and body, respectively. Thinking was the defining quality of the mind, and extension (the property by which things occupy space) was the

DESCARTES EXPLORES THE PROMISE OF SCIENCE

In 1637, Descartes published his Discourse on Method. *He wrote against what he believed to be the useless speculations of scholastic philosophy. He championed the careful investigation of physical nature on the grounds that it would expand the scope of human knowledge beyond anything previously achieved and in doing so make human beings the masters of nature. This passage contains much of the broad intellectual and cultural argument that led to the ever-growing influence and authority of science from the seventeenth century onward.*

■ *How does Descartes compare the usefulness of science with previous speculative philosophy? How does he portray science as an instrument whereby human beings may master nature? What, if any, limits does he place on the extension of scientific knowledge? Why does he place so much emphasis on the promise of science to improve human health?*

My speculations were indeed truly pleasing to me; but I recognize that other men have theirs, which perhaps please them even more. As soon, however, as I had acquired some general notions regarding physics, and on beginning to make trial of them in various special difficulties had observed how far they can carry us and how much they differ from the principles hitherto employed, I believed that I could not keep them hidden without grievously sinning against the law which lays us under obligation to promote, as far as in us lies, the general good of all mankind. For they led me to see that it is possible to obtain knowledge highly useful in life, and that in place of the speculative philosophy taught in the Schools we can have a practical philosophy, by means of which, knowing the force and the actions of fire, water, air, and of the stars, of the heavens, and of all the bodies that surround us—knowing them as distinctly as we know the various crafts of the artisans—we may in the same fashion employ them in all the uses for which they are suited, thus rendering ourselves the masters and possessors of nature. This is to be desired, not only with a view to the invention of an infinity of arts by which we would be enabled to enjoy without heavy labor the fruits of the earth and all its conveniences, but above all for the preservation of health, which is, without doubt, of all blessings in this life, the first of all goods and the foundation on which the others rest. For the mind is so dependent on the temper and disposition of the bodily organisms that if any means can ever be found to render men wiser and more capable than they have hitherto been, I believe that it is in the science of medicine that the means must be sought. . . . With no wish to depreciate it, I am yet sure there is no one, even of those engaged in the profession, who does not admit that all we know is almost nothing in comparison with what remains to be discovered; and that we could be freed from innumerable maladies, both of body and of mind, and even perhaps from the infirmities of age, if we had sufficient knowledge of their causes and of the remedies provided by nature.

From René Descartes, *Discourse on Method*, in Norman Kemp Smith, ed., *Descartes's Philosophical Writings* (New York: The Modern Library, 1958), pp. 130–131. Reprinted by permission of Macmillan Press Ltd.

defining quality of material bodies. Human reason could grasp and understand the world of extension, which became the realm of the natural philosopher. That world had no place for spirits, divinity, or anything nonmaterial. Descartes separated mind from body to banish nonmaterial matters from the realm of scientific speculation and analysis. Reason was to be applied only to the mechanical realm of matter or to the exploration of itself.

Descartes's emphasis on deduction, rational speculation, and internal reflection by the mind, all of which he explored more fully in his *Meditations* of 1641, have exercised broad influence among philosophers from his time to the present. His deductive methodology, however, eventually lost favor to **scientific induction,** whereby scientists draw generalizations derived from and test hypotheses against empirical observations.

Thomas Hobbes: Apologist for Absolute Government

Nowhere did the impact of the methods of the new science so deeply affect political thought as in the thought of Thomas Hobbes (1588–1679), the most original political philosopher of the seventeenth century. In his low view of human nature and his concept of a commonwealth based on a convenant between the community and an all-powerful sovereign, Hobbes's thought contained echoes of Calvinism. Yet Hobbes presented these arguments in a materialistic philosophical framework that led many of his contemporaries rightly or wrongly to regard him as an atheist.

An urbane and much-traveled man, Hobbes enthusiastically supported the new scientific movement. During the 1630s, he visited Paris, where he came to know Descartes, and he spent time with Galileo in Italy as well. He took special interest in the works of William Harvey (1578–1657), who was famous for his discovery of the circulation of blood through the body. Hobbes was also a superb classicist. His earliest published work was the first English translation of Thucydides' *History of the Peloponnesian War* and is still being reprinted today. Part of the darkness of Hobbes's view of human nature would appear to derive from Thucydides' historical analysis.

Hobbes had written works of political philosophy before the English civil war, but the turmoil of that struggle led him in 1651 to publish his *Leviathan*, a work of contemporaneous controversy and lasting influence. He was deeply concerned with the problem of how a strong central political authority might receive rigorous philosophical justification. In the *Leviathan*, Hobbes portrayed human beings and society in a thoroughly materialistic and mechanical way. He traced all psychological processes to bare sensation and regarded all human motivations as egoistical, intended to increase pleasure and minimize pain. According to his analysis, human reasoning penetrated to no deeper reality or wisdom than those physical sensations. Consequently, for Hobbes, unlike both previous Christian and ancient philosophers, human beings exist for no higher spiritual ends or larger moral purpose than those of meeting the needs of daily life. In his view, human beings could fulfill even those limited goals only within the confines of a sovereign commonwealth established by a contract that prevented the free exercise of the natural human pursuit of self-interest with all its attendant potential for conflict.

Much of the persuasive power of Hobbes's political philosophy lay in his brilliant myth or political fiction about the original state of humankind.

According to his account, human beings in their natural state are inclined to a "perpetual and restless desire" for power. Because all people want and, in their natural state, possess a natural right to everything, their equality breeds enmity, competition, diffidence, and perpetual quarreling—"a war of every man against every man." As Hobbes put it in a famous summary,

> In such condition there is no place for industry, because the fruit thereof is uncertain; and consequently no culture of the Earth; no navigation nor use of the commodities that may be imported by sea; no commodious building; no instruments of moving and removing such things as require much force; no knowledge of the face of the Earth; no account of time; no arts; no letters; no society; and, which is worst of all, continual fear and danger of violent death; and the life of man solitary, poor, nasty, brutish, and short.[7]

As seen in this passage, Hobbes, contrary to Aristotle and Christian thinkers like Thomas Aquinas, did not believe human beings were naturally sociable. Rather, they were self-centered creatures lacking a master. Whereas earlier and later philosophers saw the original human state as a paradise from which humankind had fallen, Hobbes saw it as a state of natural, inevitable conflict in which neither safety, security, nor any final authority existed. Human beings in this state of nature were constantly haunted by fear of destruction and death.

Human beings escaped this terrible state of nature, according to Hobbes, only by entering into a particular kind of political contract according to which they agreed to live in a commonwealth tightly ruled by a recognized sovereign. This contract obliged every person, for the sake of peace and self-defense, to agree to set aside personal rights to all things and to be content with as much liberty against others as he or she would allow others against himself or herself. All agreed to live according to a secularized version of the golden rule, "Do not that to another which you would not have done to yourself."[8]

Because, however, words and promises are insufficient to guarantee this agreement, the contract also established the coercive use of force by the sovereign to compel compliance. Believing the dangers of anarchy to be always greater than those of tyranny, Hobbes thought that rulers should be absolute and unlimited in their power, once established as authority. Hobbes's political philosophy has no room for protest in the name of individual conscience or for individual appeal to some other

---

[7]Thomas Hobbes, *Leviathan*, Parts I and II, ed. by H. W. Schneider (Indianapolis: Bobbs-Merrill, 1958), p. 86, 106–107.

[8]Hobbes, p. 130.

The famous title page illustration for Hobbes's Leviathan. *The ruler is pictured as absolute lord of his lands, but note that the ruler incorporates the mass of individuals whose self-interests are best served by their willing consent to accept him and cooperate with him.*   Rare Books Division, The New York Public Library. Astor, Lenox and Tilden Foundations.

legitimate authority beyond the sovereign. In a reply to critics of his position on sovereign authority, Hobbes pointed out the alternative:

The greatest [unhappiness] that in any form of government can possibly happen to the people in general is scarce sensible in respect of the miseries and horrible calamities that accompany a civil war or that dissolute condition of masterless men, without subjection to laws and a coercive power to tie their hands from rapine and revenge.[9]

The specific structure of this absolute government was not of enormous concern to Hobbes. He believed absolute authority might be lodged in either a monarch or a legislative body. But once that

person or body had been granted authority, there existed no argument for appeal. For all practical purposes, obedience to the Hobbesian sovereign was absolute.

Hobbes's argument for an absolute political authority that could assure order aroused sharp opposition. Monarchists objected to his willingness to assign sovereign authority to a legislature. Republicans rejected his willingness to accept a monarchical authority. Some religious writers, including those who supported the divine right of kings, furiously criticized his materialist arguments for an absolute political authority. Other religious writers attacked his refusal to recognize the authority of either God or the church as standing beside or above his secular sovereign. The influence of Hobbes's political analysis so severely criticized in his own day

[9]Hobbes, p. 152.

would grow over the next three centuries as political and religious authority in the West became increasingly separated.

JOHN LOCKE: DEFENDER OF MODERATE LIBERTY AND TOLERATION

Locke (1632–1704) proved to be the most influential philosophical and political thinker of the seventeenth century. Although he was less original than Hobbes, his political writings became a major source of criticism of absolutism and provided a foundation for later liberal political philosophy in both Europe and America. His philosophical works dealing with human knowledge became the most important work of psychology for the eighteenth century.

Locke's family had Puritan sympathies, and during the English civil war his father had fought for the parliamentary forces against the Stuart monarchy. Although a highly cerebral person who was well read in all the major seventeenth-century natural philosophers, Locke became deeply involved with the tumultuous politics of the English Restoration period. He was a close associate of Anthony Ashley Cooper, the earl of Shaftesbury, considered by his contemporaries to be a radical in both religion and politics. Shaftesbury organized an unsuccessful rebellion against Charles II in 1682, after which both he and Locke, who lived with him, were forced to flee to Holland.

During his years of association with Shaftesbury and the opposition to Charles II, Locke wrote two treatises on government, which were eventually published in 1690. In the first of these, he rejected arguments for absolute government that based political authority on the patriarchal model of fathers ruling over a family. After the publication of this treatise, no major political philosopher again appealed to the patriarchal model. In that regard, though not widely read today, Locke's *First Treatise of Government* proved enormously important by clearing the philosophical decks, so to speak, of a long-standing traditional argument that could not stand up to rigorous analysis.

In his *Second Treatise of Government*, Locke presented an extended argument for a government that must necessarily be both responsible for and responsive to the concerns of the governed. Locke portrayed the natural human state as one of perfect freedom and equality in which everyone enjoyed, in an unregulated fashion, the natural rights of life, liberty, and property. Locke, contrary to Hobbes, regarded human beings in their natural state as creatures of reason and basic goodwill rather than of

John Locke (1632–1704), defender of the rights of the people against rulers who think their power absolute.
By courtesy of the National Portrait Gallery, London

uncontrolled passion and selfishness. For Locke, human beings possess a strong capacity for dwelling more or less peacefully in society before they enter a political contract. What they experience in the state of nature is not a state of war, but a condition of competition and modest conflict that requires a political authority to sort out problems rather than to impose sovereign authority. They enter into the contract to form political society to secure and preserve the rights, liberty, and property that they already possess prior to the existence of political authority. In this respect, government exists to protect the best achievements and liberty of the state of nature, not to overcome them. Thus, by its very foundation, Locke's government is one of limited authority.

The conflict that Hobbes believed characterized the state of nature emerged for Locke only when rulers failed to preserve people's natural freedom and attempted to enslave them by absolute rule.

The relationship between rulers and the governed is that of trust, and if the rulers betray that trust, the governed have the right to replace them. In this regard, Locke's position resembled that of St. Thomas Aquinas, who also permitted rebellion against government when it violated laws of nature.

In his *Letter Concerning Toleration* (1689), Locke used the premises of the as yet unpublished *Second Treatise* to defend extensive religious toleration among Christians which he saw as an answer to the destructive religious conflict of the past two centuries. To make his case for toleration, Locke claimed that each individual stood charged with working out his or her own religious salvation and these efforts might lead various people to join different religious groups. For its part, government existed by its very nature to preserve property, not to make religious decisions for its citizens. Governments that attempted to impose religious uniformity thus misunderstood their real purpose. Moreover, government-imposed religious uniformity could not achieve real religious ends, because assent to religious truth must be freely given by the individual's conscience rather than by force. Consequently, Locke urged a wide degree of religious toleration among differing voluntary Christian groups. He did not, however, extend toleration to Roman Catholics, whom he believed to have given allegiance to a foreign prince (i.e., the pope), or to atheists, whom he believed could not be trusted to keep their word. Despite these limitations, Locke's *Letter Concerning Toleration* established a powerful foundation for the future extension of toleration, religious liberty, and the separation of church and state. His vision of such expansive toleration was partially realized in England after 1688 and most fully in the United States after the American Revolution.

Finally, just as Newton had set forth laws of astronomy and gravitation, Locke hoped to elucidate the basic structures of human thought. He did so in the most immediately influential of his books, his *Essay Concerning Human Understanding* (1690), which became the major work of European psychology during the eighteenth century. There, Locke portrayed a person's mind at birth as a blank tablet whose content would be determined by sense experience. His vision of the mind has been aptly compared to an early version of behaviorism. It was a reformer's psychology which believed that the human condition could be improved by changing the environment.

Locke's view of psychology rejected the Christian understanding of original sin, yet he believed his psychology had preserved religious knowledge. He thought such knowledge came through divine revelation in scripture and also from the conclusions that human reason could draw from observing nature. He hoped this interpretation of religious knowledge would prevent human beings from falling into what he regarded as fanaticism arising from the claims of alleged private revelations and irrationality arising from superstition. For Locke, reason and revelation were compatible and together could sustain a moderate religious faith that would avoid religious conflict.

The New Institutions of Expanding Natural Knowledge

One of the most fundamental features of the expansion of science was the emerging idea that *genuinely new knowledge* about nature and humankind could be discovered. In the late Middle Ages, the recovery of Aristotle and the rise of humanistic learning looked back to the ancients to rediscover the kind of knowledge that later Europeans needed. Luther and other Reformers had seen themselves as recovering a better understanding of the original Christian message. By contrast, the proponents of the new natural knowledge and the new philosophy sought to pursue what Bacon called the advancement of learning. New knowledge would be continuously created. This outlook required new institutions.

There were powerful social implications to the expansion of natural knowledge. Both the new science and the philosophical outlook associated with it opposed Scholasticism and Aristotelianism. These were not simply disembodied philosophical outlooks, but ways of approaching the world of

---

Major Works of the Scientific Revolution

1543	*On the Revolutions of the Heavenly Spheres* (Copernicus)
1605	*The Advancement of Learning* (Bacon)
1609	*The New Astronomy* (Kepler)
1610	*The Starry Messenger* (Galileo)
1620	*Novum Organum* (Bacon)
1632	*Dialogue on the Two Chief World Systems* (Galileo)
1637	*Discourse on Method* (Descartes)
1651	*Leviathan* (Hobbes)
1687	*Principia Mathematica* (Newton)
1689	*Letter Concerning Toleration* (Locke)
1690	*An Essay Concerning Human Understanding* (Locke)
1690	*Treatises of Government* (Locke)

knowledge still espoused by most scholars in the universities of the day. Such scholars had a clear vested interest in preserving those traditional outlooks. As they saw it, they were defending the ancients against the moderns. Not surprisingly, the advanced thinkers of the seventeenth century often criticized the universities. For example, in his *Discourse on Method*, Descartes was highly critical of the education he had received. Hobbes filled the *Leviathan* with caustic remarks about the kind of learning then dominating schools and universities, and Locke advocated educational reform.

Some of the criticism of universities was exaggerated. Medical faculties, on the whole, welcomed the advancement of learning in their fields of study. Most of the natural philosophers had themselves received their education at universities. Moreover, however slowly new ideas might penetrate universities, the expanding world of natural knowledge would be taught to future generations. And with that diffusion of science into the universities came new supporters of scientific knowledge beyond the small group of natural philosophers themselves. Universities also provided much of the physical and financial support for the teaching and investigation of natural philosophy and employed many scientists, the most important of whom was Newton himself. University support of science did, however, vary according to country, with the Italian universities being far more supportive than the French.

Yet because of the reluctance of universities to rapidly assimilate the new science, its pioneers quickly understood that they required a framework for cooperation and sharing of information that went beyond existing intellectual institutions. Consequently, they and their supporters established what have been termed "institutions of sharing" that allowed information and ideas associated with the new science to be gathered, exchanged, and debated.[10] The most famous of these institutions was the Royal Society of London, founded in 1660, whose members consciously saw themselves as following the path Bacon had laid out almost a half century earlier. The Royal Society had been preceded by the Academy of Experiments in Florence in 1657 and was followed by the French Academy of Science in 1666. Germany only slowly overcame the destruction of the Thirty Years' War, with the Berlin Academy of Science being founded in 1700. In addition to these major academies, there were many local societies and academies at which the new science was discussed and experiments were carried out.

These societies provided organizations that met regularly to hear papers and observe experiments. One of the reasons many early experiments achieved credibility was that they had been observed by persons of social respectability who belonged to one or more of the societies and who, because of their social standing, were presumed to be truthful witnesses of what they had observed. These groups also published information relating to natural philosophy and often organized libraries for their members. Perhaps most important, they attempted to separate the discussion and exploration of natural philosophy from the religious and political conflicts of the day. They intended science to exemplify an arena for the polite exchange of ideas and for civil disagreement and debate. This particular function of science as fostering civility became one of its major attractions.

The activities of the societies also constituted a kind of crossroads between their own members always drawn from the literate classes, and people outside the elite classes, whose skills and practical knowledge might be important for advancing the new science. The latter included craftspeople who could manufacture scientific instruments, sailors whose travels had taken them to foreign parts and who might report on the plants and animals they had seen there, and workers who had practical knowledge of problems in the countryside. In this respect, the expansion of the European economy and the drive toward empire contributed to the growth of the scientific endeavor by bringing back to Europe specimens and experiences that required classification, analysis, and observation.

In good Baconian fashion, the members of the societies presented science as an enterprise that could aid the goals of government and the growth of the economy. For example, mathematicians portrayed themselves as being useful for solving surveying and other engineering problems and for improving armaments. Furthermore, people who had ideas for improving production, navigation, or military artillery might seek the support of the associated societies. In the English context, these people became known as *projectors* and were often regarded as people simply eager to sell their often improbable ideas to the highest bidder. Nonetheless, their activities brought the new science and technology before a wider public.

The work, publications, and interaction of the scientific societies with both the government and private business established a distinct role and presence for scientific knowledge in European social life. By 1700, that presence was relatively modest, but it would grow steadily during the coming decades. The groups associated with the new science saw themselves as championing modern practical

[10]Lewis Pyenson and Susan Sheets-Pyenson, *Servants of Nature: A History of Scientific Institutions, Enterprises and Sensibilities* (New York: W. W. Norton, 1999), p. 75.

The sixteenth and seventeenth centuries saw Europeans expanding their knowledge into the ancient past, into the New World, and into the starry heavens. In this painting, The Sciences and the Arts, *the artist depicts recent paintings that connect contemporary culture with the ancient world and the Bible. In the same room, he sets globes depicting the New World and astronomical instruments used by natural philosophers exploring the heavens according to the theories of Copernicus, Kepler, and Galileo. Yet throughout all of the expansion of mind and geographical knowledge, women were generally excluded as they are in this painting. For example, only on the rarest occasion were women permitted to visit the Royal Society of London.*   Adriaen Stalbent (1589–1662), *The Sciences and the Arts.* Wood, 93 × 114 cm. Inv. 1405. Museo del Prado, Madrid, Spain. Copyright Erich Lessing/Art Resource, N.Y.

achievements of applied knowledge and urging religious toleration, mutual forbearance, and political liberty. Such people would form the social base for the eighteenth-century movement known as the **Enlightenment.**

Women in the World of the Scientific Revolution

The absence of women in the emergence of the new science of the seventeenth century has been a matter of much historical speculation. What characteristics of early modern European intellectual and cultural life worked against extensive contributions

by women? Why have we heard so little of the activity by women that did actually occur in regard to the new science?

The same factors that had long excluded women from participating in most intellectual life continued to exclude them from working in the emerging natural philosophy. Traditionally, the institutions of European intellectual life had all but excluded women. Both monasteries and universities had been institutions associated with celibate male clerical culture. Except for a few exceptions in Italy, women had not been admitted to either medieval or early modern European universities; they would continue to be excluded from them until the end of the nineteenth century. Women could and did exercise much influence over princely courts where natural philosophers, such as Galileo, sought patronage, but they usually did not determine those patronage decisions or benefit from them. Queen Christina of Sweden was an exception by engaging René Descartes to provide the regulations for a new science academy. When various scientific societies were founded, women were not admitted to membership. In that regard, there were virtually no social spaces that might have permitted women easily to pursue science.

Yet a few isolated women from two different social settings did manage to engage in the new scientific activity—noblewomen and women from the artisan class. In both cases, they could do so only through their husbands or other men in their families.

The social standing of certain noblewomen allowed them to command the attention of ambitious natural philosophers who were part of their husband's social circle. Margaret Cavendish (1623–1673) actually made significant contributions to the scientific literature of the day. After she had been privately tutored and become widely read, her marriage to the duke of Newcastle introduced her into a circle of natural philosophers. She understood the new science, quarreled with the ideas of Descartes and Hobbes, and criticized the Royal Society for being more interested in novel scientific instruments than in solving practical problems. Her most important works were *Observations upon Experimental Philosophy* (1666) and *Grounds of Natural Philosophy* (1668). She was the only woman in the seventeenth century to be allowed to visit a meeting of the Royal Society of London. (See "Margaret Cavendish Questions the Fascination with Scientific Instruments.")

Women associated with artisan crafts actually achieved greater freedom in pursuing the new sciences than did noblewomen. Traditionally, women had worked in artisan workshops, often with their husbands, and might take over the business when their spouse died. In Germany, much astronomy occurred in these settings, with women assisting their fathers or husbands. One such German female astronomer, Maria Cunitz, published a book on astronomy that many people thought her husband had written until he added a preface supporting her sole authorship. Elisabetha and Johannes Hevelius constituted a wife-and-husband astronomical team, as did Maria Winkelmann and her husband Gottfried Kirch. In each case, the wife served as the assistant to an artisan astronomer. Although Winkelmann discovered a comet in 1702, not until 1930 was the discovery ascribed to her rather than to her husband. Nonetheless, con-

Margaret Cavendish, who wrote widely on scientific subjects, was the most accomplished woman associated with the New Science in seventeenth-century England.
Mary Evans Picture Library Ltd.

temporary philosophers did recognize her abilities and understanding of astronomy. Winkelmann had worked jointly with her husband who was the official astronomer of the Berlin Academy of Sciences and was responsible for establishing an official calendar published by the academy. When her husband died in 1710, Winkelmann applied for permission to continue the work, basing her application for the post on the guild's tradition of allowing women to continue their husband's work, in this case the completion of observations required for creating an accurate calendar. After much debate, the academy formally rejected her application on the grounds of her gender, although its members knew of her ability and previous accomplishments. Years later, she returned to the Berlin Academy as an assistant to her son, who had been appointed astronomer. Again, the academy insisted that she leave, forcing her to abandon astronomy. She died in 1720.

Such policies of exclusion, however, did not altogether prevent women from acquiring knowledge about the scientific endeavors of the age. Margaret Cavendish had composed a *Description of a New World, Called the Blazing World* (1666) to introduce women to the new science. Other

MARGARET CAVENDISH QUESTIONS THE FASCINATION WITH SCIENTIFIC INSTRUMENTS

Margaret Cavendish, Duchess of Newcastle, was the most scientifically informed woman of seventeenth-century England. She read widely in natural philosophy and had many acquaintances who were involved in the new science. Although she was enthusiastic about the promise of science, she also frequently criticized some of its leading proponents, including Descartes and Hobbes. She was skeptical of the activities of the newly established Royal Society of London, which she was once permitted to visit. She believed some of its members had become overly enthusiastic about experimentation and new scientific instruments for their own sakes and had begun to ignore the practical questions that she thought science should address. In this respect, her criticism of the Royal Society and its experiments is a Baconian one. She thought the society had replaced scholastic speculation with experimental speculation and that both kinds of speculation ignored important problems of immediate utility.

■ *Why might Margaret Cavendish think that the experiments which were reported about new optical instruments dealt with superficial wonders? Why does she contrast experimental philosophy with the beneficial arts? Do you find a feminist perspective in her comparison of the men of the Royal Society with boys playing with bubbles?*

Art has intoxicated so many men's brains, and wholly imployed their thoughts and bodily actions about phaenomena, or the exterior figure of objects, as all better Arts and Studies are laid aside; . . . But though there be numerous Books written of the wonder of these [experimental optical] Glasses, yet I cannot perceive any such; at best, they are but superficial wonders, as I may call them. But could Experimental Philosophers find out more beneficial Arts then our Fore-fathers have done, either for the better increase of Vegetables and brute Animals to nourish our bodies, or better and commodious contrivances in the Art of Architecture to build us houses, or for the advancing of trade and traffick . . . it would not only be worth their labour, but of as much praise as could be given to them: But, as Boys that play with watry Bubbles . . . are worthy of reproof rather than praise, for wasting their time with useless sports; so those that addict themselves to unprofitable Arts, spend more time than they reap benefit thereby.

From Margaret Cavendish, *Observations Upon Experimental Philosophy; to which is added, The Description of a New Blazing World* (London, 1666), pp. 10–11, as quoted in Anna Battigelli, *Margaret Cavendish and the Exiles of the Mind* (Lexington: University of Kentucky Press, 1998), p. 94.

examples of scientific writings for a female audience were Bernard de Fontenelle's *Conversations on the Plurality of Worlds* and Francesco Algarotti's *Newtonianism for Ladies* (1737). During the 1730s, Emilie du Châtelet aided Voltaire in his composition of an important French popularization of Newton's science. Her knowledge of mathematics was more extensive than his and crucial to his completing his book.

Still, with only a few exceptions, women were barred from science and medicine until the late nineteenth century, and not until the twentieth century did they enter these fields in any significant numbers. Not only did the institutions of science exclude them, but also, the ideas associated with medical practice, philosophy, and biology suggested that women and their minds were essentially different from, and inferior to, men and theirs. By the early eighteenth century, despite isolated precedents of women pursuing natural knowledge, reading scientific literature, and engaging socially with natural philosophers, it had become a fundamental assumption of European intellectual life that the pursuit of natural knowledge was a male vocation.

The New Science and Religious Faith

In the minds of many contemporaries, the new science posed a potential challenge to religion. Three major issues were at stake. First, certain theories and discoveries did not agree with biblical statements about the heavens. Second, the question arose of whether church authorities or the natural philosophers would decide conflicts between religion and science. Finally, for many religious thinkers, the new science offered only a materialistic universe, replacing one of spiritual meaning and significance. Yet most of the natural philosophers genuinely saw their work as contributing to a deeper knowledge of the divine, thus supporting religious belief. Their efforts and those of their supporters to reconcile faith and the new science constituted a fundamental factor in the spread of science and its widespread acceptance in educated European circles. The process was not an easy one. (See "Art & the West: Vermeer's *The Geographer* and *The Astronomer*: Painting and the New Knowledge," p. 478.)

THE CASE OF GALILEO

The condemnation of Galileo by Roman Catholic authorities in 1633 is the single most famous incident of conflict between modern science and religious institutions. For centuries it was interpreted as exemplifying the forces of religion smothering scientific knowledge. More recent research has modified that picture.

The condemnation of Copernicanism and of Galileo occurred at a particularly difficult moment in the history of the Roman Catholic Church. In response to Protestant emphasis on private interpretation of scripture, the Council of Trent (1545–1563) had stated that only the church itself possessed the authority to interpret the Bible. Furthermore, after the Council, the Roman Catholic Church had adopted a more literalist mode of reading the Bible in response to the Protestant emphasis on the authority of scripture. Galileo's championing of Copernicanism took place in this particular climate of opinion and practice when the Roman Catholic Church, on the one hand, could not surrender the interpretation of the Bible to a layman and, on the other, had difficulty moving beyond a literal reading of the Bible for fear of being accused by the Protestants of abandoning scripture.

In a *Letter to the Grand Duchess Christina* (1615), Galileo, as a layman, had published his own views about how scripture should be interpreted to accommodate the new science. (See "Galileo Discusses the Relationship of Science to the Bible.") To certain Roman Catholic authorities, his actions resembled that of a Protestant who looked to himself rather than the church to understand the Bible. In 1615 and 1616, he visited Rome and discussed his views openly and aggressively. In early 1616, however, the Roman Catholic Inquisition formally censured Copernicus's views, placing *On the Revolutions of the Heavenly Spheres* on the Index of Prohibited Books. The ground for the condemnation was the disagreement of Copernicus with the literal word of the Bible and the biblical interpretations of the Church Fathers. It should be recalled that at the time there did not yet exist, even in Galileo's mind, fully satisfactory empirical evidence in support of Copernicus.

Galileo, who was not on trial in 1616, was formally informed of the condemnation of Copernicanism. It remains unclear exactly what agreement he and the Roman Catholic authorities reached as to what he would be permitted to write about Copernicanism. It appears that he agreed not to advocate the physical truthfulness of Copernican astronomy, but to suggest only its theoretical possibility.

In 1623, however, a Florentine acquaintance of Galileo's was elected as Pope Urban VIII. He gave Galileo permission to resume discussing the Copernican system, which he did in *Dialogue on the Two Chief World Systems* (1632). The book clearly was designed to defend the physical truthfulness of Copernicanism. Moreover, the voices in the dialogue favoring the older system appeared slow-witted, and those voices presented the views of Pope Urban. Feeling both humiliated and betrayed, the pope ordered an investigation of Galileo's book. The actual issue in Galileo's trial of 1633 was whether he had disobeyed the mandate of 1616, and it must have been clear to any observer that he had done so. Galileo was condemned, required to abjure his views, and placed under the equivalent of house arrest in his home near Florence for the last nine years of his life.

Although much more complicated than a simple case of a conflict between science and religion, the condemnation of Galileo cast a long and troubled shadow over the relationship of the emerging new science and the authority of the Roman Catholic Church. The controversy continued into the late twentieth century, when Pope John Paul II formally ordered the reassessment of the Galileo case. In 1992, the Roman Catholic Church admitted that errors had occurred, particularly in the biblical interpretation of Pope Urban VIII's advisers.

BLAISE PASCAL: REASON AND FAITH

One of the most influential efforts to reconcile faith and the new science was presented by Pascal (1623–1662), a French mathematician and a physical

GALILEO DISCUSSES THE RELATIONSHIP OF SCIENCE TO THE BIBLE

The religious authorities were often critical of the discoveries and theories of sixteenth- and seventeenth-century science. For years before his condemnation by the Roman Catholic Church in 1633, Galileo had contended that scientific theory and religious piety were compatible. In his Letter to the Grand Duchess Christiana (of Tuscany), *written in 1615, he argued that God had revealed truth in both the Bible and physical nature and that the truth of physical nature did not contradict the Bible if the latter were properly understood. Galileo encountered difficulties regarding this letter because it represented a layman telling church authorities how to read the Bible.*

■ *Is Galileo's argument based on science or theology? Did the church believe that nature was as much a revelation of God as the Bible was? As Galileo describes them, which is the surer revelation of God, nature or the Bible? Why might the pope reject Galileo's argument?*

The reason produced for condemning the opinion that the Earth moves and the sun stands still is that in many places in the Bible one may read that the sun moves and the Earth stands still. . . .

With regard to this argument, I think in the first place that it is very pious to say and prudent to affirm that the holy Bible can never speak untruth—whenever its true meaning is understood. But I believe nobody will deny that it is often very abstruse, and may say things which are quite different from what its bare words signify. . . .

This being granted, I think that in discussions of physical problems we ought to begin not from the authority of scriptural passages, but from sense-experiences and necessary demonstrations; for the holy Bible and the phenomena of nature proceed alike from the divine Word, the former as the dictate of the Holy Ghost and the latter as the observant executrix of God's commands. It is necessary for the Bible, in order to be accommodated to the understanding of every man, to speak many things which appear to differ from the absolute truth so far as the bare meaning of the words is concerned. But Nature, on the other hand, is inexorable and immutable; she never transgresses the laws imposed upon her, or cares a whit whether her abstruse reasons and methods of operation are understandable to men. For that reason it appears that nothing physical which sense-experience sets before our eyes, or which necessary demonstrations prove to us, ought to be called in question (much less condemned) upon the testimony of biblical passages which may have some different meaning beneath their words. For the Bible is not chained in every expression to conditions as strict as those which govern all physical effects; nor is God any less excellently revealed in Nature's actions than in the sacred statements of the Bible. . . .

From this I do not mean to infer that we need not have an extraordinary esteem for the passages of holy Scripture. On the contrary, having arrived at any certainties in physics, we ought to utilize these as the most appropriate aids in the true exposition of the Bible and in the investigation of those meanings which are necessarily contained therein for these must be concordant with demonstrated truths. I should judge the authority of the Bible was designed to persuade men of those articles and propositions which, surpassing all human reasoning, could not be made credible by science, or by any other means than through the very mouth of the Holy Spirit. . . .

But I do not feel obliged to believe that the same God who has endowed us with senses, reason, and intellect has intended to forgo their use and by some other means to give us knowledge which we can attain by them.

scientist who surrendered his wealth to pursue an austere, self-disciplined life. He aspired to write a work that would refute both dogmatism (which he saw epitomized by the Jesuits) and skepticism. Pascal considered the Jesuits' casuistry (i.e., arguments designed to minimize and excuse sinful acts) a distortion of Christian teaching. He rejected the skeptics of his age because they either denied religion altogether (atheists) or accepted it only as it conformed to reason (deists). He never produced a definitive refutation of the two sides. Rather, he formulated his views on these matters in piecemeal fashion in a provocative collection of reflections on humankind and religion published posthumously under the title *Pensées*. (See "Pascal Meditates on Human Beings as Thinking Creatures.")

Pascal allied himself with the Jansenists, seventeenth-century Catholic opponents of the Jesuits. (See Chapter 13.) His sister was a member of the Jansenist convent of Port-Royal, near Paris. The Jansenists shared with the Calvinists Saint Augustine's belief in human beings' total sinfulness, their eternal predestination to heaven or hell by God, and their complete dependence on faith and grace for knowledge of God and salvation.

Pascal believed that in matters of religion, only the reasons of the heart and a "leap of faith" could prevail. For him, religion was not the domain of reason and science. He saw two essential truths in the Christian religion: A loving God exists, and human beings, because they are corrupt by nature, are utterly unworthy of God. He believed the atheists and the deists of his age had overly estimated reason. To Pascal, reason itself was too weak to resolve the problems of human nature and destiny. Ultimately, reason should drive those who truly heeded it to faith in God and reliance on divine grace.

Pascal made a famous wager with the skeptics. It is a better bet, he argued, to believe God exists and to stake everything on his promised mercy than not to do so. This is because, if God does exist, the believer will gain everything, whereas, should God prove not to exist, comparatively little will have been lost by having believed in him.

Convinced that belief in God improved life psychologically and disciplined it morally (regardless of whether God proved in the end to exist), Pascal worked to strengthen traditional religious belief. He urged his contemporaries to seek self-understanding by "learned ignorance" and to discover humankind's greatness by recognizing its misery. He hoped thereby to counter what he believed to be the false optimism of the new rationalism and science.

THE ENGLISH APPROACH TO SCIENCE AND RELIGION

Francis Bacon established a key framework for reconciling science and religion that long influenced the English-speaking world. He had argued there were two books of divine revelation: the Bible and nature. In studying nature, the natural philosopher could achieve a deeper knowledge of things divine, just as could the theologian studying the Bible. Because both books of revelation shared the same author, they must be compatible. Whatever discord might first appear between science and religion must eventually be reconciled. Natural theology based on a scientific understanding of the natural order would thus support theology derived from scripture.

Later in the seventeenth century, with the work of Newton, the natural universe became a realm of law and regularity. Many scientists were devout people who saw in the new picture of physical nature a new picture of God. The Creator of this rational, lawful nature must also be rational. To study nature was to come to a better understanding of that Creator. Science and religious faith were not only compatible, but mutually supportive. As Newton wrote, "The main Business of Natural Philosophy is to argue from Phaenomena without feigning Hypothesis, and to deduce Causes from Effects, till we come to the very first Cause, which certainly is not mechanical."[11]

The religious thought associated with such deducing of religious conclusions from nature became known as *physico-theology*. This reconciliation of faith and science allowed the new physics and astronomy to spread rapidly. At the very time when Europeans were finally tiring of the wars of religion, the new science provided the basis for a view of God that might lead away from irrational disputes and wars over religious doctrine. Faith in a rational God encouraged faith in the rationality of human beings and in their capacity to improve their lot once liberated from the traditions of the past. The scientific revolution provided the great model for the desirability of change and of criticism of inherited views.

Finally, the new science and the technological and economic innovations associated with its culture came again, especially among English thinkers, to be interpreted as part of a divine plan. By the late seventeenth century, natural philosophy and its practical achievements had become associated in

---

[11]Quoted in Baumer, p. 323.

PASCAL MEDITATES ON HUMAN BEINGS AS THINKING CREATURES

Pascal was both a religious and a scientific writer. Unlike other scientific thinkers of the seventeenth century, he was not overly optimistic about the ability of science to improve the human condition. But science and philosophy might help human beings understand their situation better. In these passages from his Pensées *(Thoughts), he ponders the uniqueness of human beings as thinking creatures.*

■ *Is this an intellectual's view of human nature? Where does the idea that man is a rational creature come from, that human reason is more noble than the universe? Does Pascal ignore human will and emotion, selfishness, and destructiveness?*

339

I can well conceive a man without hands, feet, head (for it is only experience which teaches us that the head is more necessary than feet). But I cannot conceive man without thought; he would be a stone or a brute.

344

Reason commands us far more imperiously than a master; for in disobeying the one we are unfortunate, and in disobeying the other we are fools.

346

Thought constitutes the greatness of man.

347

Man is but a reed, the most feeble thing in nature; but he is a thinking reed. The entire universe need not arm itself to crush him. A vapour, a drop of water suffices to kill him. But, if the universe were to crush him, man would still be more noble than that which killed him, because he knows that he dies and the advantage which the universe has over him; the universe knows nothing of this.

All our dignity consists, then, in thought. By it we must elevate ourselves, and not by space and time which we cannot fill. Let us endeavour, then, to think well; this is the principle of morality.

348

A thinking reed—It is not from space that I must seek my dignity, but from the government of my thought. I shall have no more if I possess worlds. By space the universe encompasses and swallows me up like an atom; by thought I comprehend the world.

Blaise Pascal, *Pensées* and *The Provincial Letters* (New York: Modern Library, 1941), pp. 115–116.

the public mind with consumption and the market economy. Writers such as the Englishman John Ray in *The Wisdom of God Manifested in His Works of Creation* (1690) argued it was evident that God had placed human beings in the world in order to understand it and then, having understood it, to turn it to productive practical use through rationality. Scientific advance and economic enterprise came to be interpreted in the public mind as the fulfillment of God's plan: Human beings were meant to improve the world. This outlook provided a religious justification for the processes of economic improvement that would characterize much of eighteenth-century western Europe.

Continuing Superstition

Despite the great optimism among certain European thinkers associated with the new ideas in science and philosophy, traditional beliefs and fears long retained their hold on Western culture. During the sixteenth and seventeenth centuries, many Europeans remained preoccupied with sin, death, and the devil. Religious people, including many among the learned and many who were sympathetic to the emerging scientific ideas, continued to believe in the power of magic and the occult. Until the end of the seventeenth century, almost all Europeans in one way or another believed in the power of demons.

Pascal invented this adding machine, the ancestor of mechanical calculators, around 1644. It has eight wheels with ten cogs each, corresponding to the numbers 0 through 9. The wheels move forward for addition, backward for subtraction. Bildarchiv Preussischer Kulturbesitz

WITCH-HUNTS AND PANIC

Nowhere is the dark side of early modern thought and culture better seen than in the witch-hunts and panics that erupted in almost every Western land. Between 1400 and 1700, courts sentenced an estimated 70,000 to 100,000 people to death for harmful magic (*malificium*) and diabolical witchcraft. In addition to inflicting harm on their neighbors, these witches were said to attend mass meetings known as *sabbats*, to which they were believed to fly. They were also accused of indulging in sexual orgies with the devil, who appeared at such gatherings in animal form, most often as a he-goat. Still other charges against them were cannibalism (they were alleged to be especially fond of small Christian children) and ritual acts and practices designed to insult every Christian belief and value.

Why did the great witch panics occur in the second half of the sixteenth and early seventeenth centuries? The misfortune created by religious division and warfare were major factors. Some argue that the Reformation was responsible for the witch panics. Although the new theology portrayed demons and the devil as still powerful, it weakened the traditional religious protections against them. Subsequently, the argument goes, people felt compelled to protect themselves by executing those perceived as witches. The new levels of violence exacerbated fears and hatreds and encouraged scapegoating, but political motives also played a role. As governments expanded control in their realms, they, like the church, wanted to eliminate all competition for the loyalty of their subjects. Secular rulers, as well as the pope, could pronounce their competitors "devilish." In fact, however, beliefs in witches and witch-hunts had existed since the fifteenth century, well before the Reformation began.

Three witches charged with practicing harmful magic are burned alive in Baden in southwest Germany. On the left, two of them are feasting with demons at a sabbat.
Bildarchiv Preussischer Kulturbesitz

VILLAGE ORIGINS

The roots of the search for witches extended well beyond the world of the princes into both popular and elite cultures. In village societies, so-called cunning folk helped people cope with calamity. People turned to them when such natural disasters as plague and famine struck or when such physical disabilities as lameness or inability to conceive offspring befell either humans or animals. The cunning folk provided consolation and gave people hope that magic could avert or undo natural calamities. In this way, they provided an important service and helped village life to keep functioning.

Possession of magical powers, for good or ill, made one an important person within village society.

Not surprisingly, claims to such powers quite often were made by the people most in need of security and influence, namely, the old and the impoverished, especially single or widowed women. Belief in witches by village society may also have been a way of defying urban Christian society's attempts to impose its laws and institutions on the countryside. From this perspective, village satanism became a fanciful substitute for an impossible social revolt, a way of spurning the values of one's new masters. It is also possible, although unlikely, that beliefs in witches among the rural population had a foundation in local fertility cults, whose semipagan practices, designed to ensure good harvests, may have acquired the features of diabolical witchcraft under church persecution.

INFLUENCE OF THE CLERGY

Popular belief in magic was the essential foundation of the great witch-hunts of the sixteenth and seventeenth centuries. Had ordinary people not believed that certain gifted individuals could aid or harm others by magical means, and had they not been willing to make accusations, the hunts could never have occurred. Yet the contribution of learned society was equally great. The Christian clergy also practiced magic, that of the holy sacraments, and the exorcism of demons had been one of the clergy's traditional functions. Fear of demons and the devil, which the clergy actively encouraged, allowed clergymen to assert their moral authority over people and to enforce religious discipline and conformity.

In the late thirteenth century, the church declared that only its priests possessed legitimate magical power. Since such power was not human, theologians reasoned, it had to come either from God or from the devil. If it came from God, then it was properly confined to, and exercised only on behalf of, the church. Those who practiced magic outside the church evidently derived their power from the devil. From such reasoning grew accusations of "pacts" between non-Christian magicians and Satan. This made the witch-hunts a life-and-death struggle against Christian society's worst heretics and foes: those who had directly sworn allegiance to the devil himself.

The church based its intolerance of magic outside its walls on sincere belief in, and fear of, the devil. But attacking witches was also a way for established Christian society to extend its power and influence into new areas. To accuse, try, and execute witches was a declaration of moral and political authority over a village or territory. Because the cunning folk were local spiritual authorities, revered and feared by people, their removal became a major step in establishing a Christian beachhead in village society.

WHY WOMEN?

A good 80 percent of the victims of witch-hunts were women, most between forty-five and sixty years of age and single. This suggests to some that misogyny fueled the witch-hunts. Based on male hatred and sexual fear of women, and occurring at a time when women threatened to break out from under male control, witch-hunts, it is argued, were simply woman hunts. Older single women may, however, have been vulnerable for a more basic social reason: They were a largely dependent social group in need of public assistance and hence became natural targets for the peculiar "social engineering" of the witch-hunts. Some accused witches were women who sought to protect and empower themselves within their communities by claiming supernatural powers.

Gender, however, may have played a largely circumstantial role. Because of their economic straits, more women than men laid claim to the supernatural powers that made them influential in village society. For this reason, they found themselves on the front lines in disproportionate numbers when the church declared war against all who practiced magic without its blessing. Also, the involvement of many of these women in midwifery associated them with the deaths of beloved wives and infants and thus made them targets of local resentment and accusations. Both the church and midwives' neighbors were prepared to think and say the worst about these women. It was a deadly combination. (See "Why More Women Than Men Are Witches" and "Enountering the Past: Midwives.")

END OF THE WITCH-HUNTS

Why did the witch-hunts end in the seventeenth century? Many factors played a role. The emergence of a new, more scientific worldview made it difficult to believe in the powers of witches. When in the seventeenth century mind and matter came to be viewed as two independent realities, many people no longer believed that words and thoughts could affect the material world. A witch's curse was merely words. With advances in medicine and the beginning of insurance companies, people learned to rely on themselves when faced with natural calamity and physical affliction and no longer searched for supernatural causes and solutions. Witch-hunts also tended to get out of hand. Accused witches sometimes alleged that important townspeople had also attended *sabbats*; even the judges could be so accused. At that point, the trials ceased to serve the purposes of those who were conducting them. They not only became dysfunctional, but threatened anarchy.

Although Protestants, like Catholics, hunted witches, the Reformation may also have contributed to an attitude of mind that put the devil in a more manageable perspective. Protestants ridiculed the sacramental magic of the old church as superstition and directed their faith to a sovereign God absolutely supreme over time and eternity. Even the devil was believed to serve God's purposes and acted only with his permission. Ultimately, God was the only significant spiritual force in the universe. This belief made the devil a

WHY MORE WOMEN THAN MEN ARE WITCHES

A classic of misogyny, The Hammer of Witches *(1486), written by two Dominican monks, Heinrich Krämer and Jacob Sprenger, was sanctioned by Pope Innocent VIII as an official guide to the church's detection and punishment of witches. Here, Krämer and Sprenger explain why they believe most witches are women rather than men.*

■ *Why would two Dominican monks say such things about women? What are the biblical passages that they believe justify them? Do their descriptions have any basis in the actual behavior of women in that age? What is the rivalry between married and unmarried people that they refer to?*

Why are there more superstitious women than men? The first [reason] is that they are more credulous; and since the chief aim of the devil is to corrupt faith, therefore he rather attacks them. . . . The second reason is that women are naturally more impressionable and ready to receive the influence of a disembodied spirit. . . . The third reason is that they have slippery tongues and are unable to conceal from their fellow-women those things which by evil arts they know; and since they are weak, they find an easy and secret manner of vindicating themselves by witchcraft. . . . [Therefore] since women are feebler both in mind and body, it is not surprising that they should come more under the spell of witchcraft. For as regards intellect, or the understanding of spiritual things, they seem to be of a different nature from men, a fact which is vouched for by the logic of the authorities, backed by various examples from the Scriptures. . . .

But the natural reason [for woman's proclivity to witchcraft] is that she is more carnal than a man, as is clear from her many carnal abominations. And it should be noted that there was a defect in the formation of the first woman, since she was formed from a bent rib, that is, a rib of the breast, which is bent as it were in a contrary direction to a man. And since through this defect she is an imperfect animal, she always deceives. . . .

As to her other mental quality, her natural will, when she hates someone whom she formerly loved, then she seethes with anger and impatience in her whole soul, just as the tides of the sea are always heaving and boiling. . . .

Truly the most powerful cause which contributes to the increase of witches is the woeful rivalry between married folk and unmarried women and men. This [jealousy or rivalry exists] even among holy women, so what must it be among the others . . .?

Just as through the first defect in their intelligence women are more prone [than men] to abjure the faith, so through their second defect of inordinate affections and passions they search for, brood over, and inflict various vengeances, either by witchcraft or by some other means. Wherefore it is no wonder that so great a number of witches exist in this sex. . . . [Indeed, witchcraft] is better called the heresy of witches than of wizards, since the name is taken from the more powerful party [that is, the greater number, who are women]. Blessed be the Highest who has so far preserved the male sex from so great a crime.

From *Malleus Maleficarum,* trans. by Montague Summers (Bungay, Suffolk, U.K.: John Rodker, 1928), pp. 41–47. Reprinted by permission.

less fearsome creature. "One little word can slay him," Luther wrote of the devil in the great hymn of the Reformation, "A Mighty Fortress Is Our God."

Finally, the imaginative and philosophical literature of the sixteenth and seventeenth centuries, although continuing to display concern for religion and belief in the supernatural, also suggested that human beings have a significant degree of control over their own lives and need not be constantly fearing demons and resorting to supernatural aid.

Midwives

Although women in early modern Europe generally found themselves excluded from the world of the new science, midwives across Europe oversaw the delivery of children until well into the eighteenth century. Often known as *wise women* because of their knowledge and medical skills, midwives were among the few women who carried out independent economic and public roles.

Midwivery was a trade, often pursued by elderly or widowed women of the lower social classes, for which women apprenticed for several years. In the 1630s, the Hotel Dieu, a public hospital near Paris, set up a basic course for training midwives. Unlike other skilled workers and tradesmen, however, midwives were not allowed to organize guilds or associations to protect their trade, pass on their skills, and stabilize their incomes. Instead, civil or church authorities, who were invariably men, licensed midwives and often appointed upper-class women, known as honorable women, to supervise them.

Personal respectability and respect for the privacy of the women they attended were essential qualities for successful midwives. They were present at some of the most private moments in the lives of women and their families and were expected not to gossip about family secrets. Furthermore, women from all social classes feared that if their attending midwives were not of good character their own babies might be stillborn or imperfectly formed. Careless or incompetent midwives who injured mother or child could lose their license.

Midwives also performed important religious and civic functions at births. In emergencies they could baptize a frail newborn. They also often registered births and were officially required both to discourage abortion and infanticide and to report those activities when they occurred to the authorities. The respectability of midwives also gave them legal standing to testify to a child's legitimacy or illegitimacy.

Midwifery was one of numerous skills and occupations associated with women in early modern Europe that men took over during the eighteenth century. (See Chapter 16.) Male medical practitioners claimed to possess better training, which was available to them in medical schools, and more professional knowledge about delivering children. Over time, civil and medical authorities began to demand that people who delivered children be trained as doctors in medical schools, which women were not allowed to attend until well into the nineteenth century. In particular, the use of forceps by male surgeons to deliver a child involved a level of training unavailable to women. Yet even as medical professionalization became entrenched, midwives continued to provide their services to the poor and rural populations of Europe.

■ *What types of women became midwives in early modern Europe? How did the authorities regulate the practice of midwivery? Why did male professionals gradually replace midwives in delivering babies?*

Linda Schiebinger, *The Mind Has No Sex? Women in the Origins of Modern Science* (Cambridge, MA: Harvard University Press, 1989); Hilary Marland, ed., *The Art of Midwifery: Early Modern Midwives in Europe* (London: Routledge, 1993).

Until well into the eighteenth century, midwives oversaw the delivery of most children in Europe. Corbis

In Perspective

The scientific revolution and the thought of writers whose work was contemporaneous with it mark a major turning point in the history of Western culture and eventually had a worldwide impact. The scientific and political ideas of the late sixteenth and seventeenth centuries gradually overturned many of the most fundamental premises of the medieval worldview. The sun replaced the earth as the center of the solar system. The solar system itself came to be viewed as one of many possible systems in the universe. The new knowledge of the physical universe provided occasions for challenging the authority of the church and of scripture. Mathematics began to replace theology and metaphysics as the tool for understanding nature.

Parallel to these developments and sometimes related to them, political thought became much less concerned with religious issues. Hobbes generated a major theory of political obligation with virtually no reference to God. Locke theorized about politics with a recognition of God, but with little attention to scripture. He also championed greater freedom of religious and political expression. Locke produced a psychology that emphasized the influence of environment on human character and action. All of these new ideas gradually displaced or reshaped theological and religious modes of thought and placed humankind and life on earth at the center of Western thinking. Intellectuals in the West consequently developed greater self-confidence in their own capacity to shape the world and their own lives.

None of this change came easily, however. The new science and enlightenment were accompanied by new anxieties that were reflected in a growing preoccupation with sin, death, and the devil. The worst expression of this preoccupation was a succession of witch-hunts and trials that took the lives of as many as 100,000 people between 1400 and 1700.

REVIEW QUESTIONS

1. Discuss the contributions of Copernicus, Brahe, Kepler, Galileo, and Newton to the scientific revolution. Which do you think made the most important contributions and why? What did Francis Bacon contribute to the foundation of scientific thought?

2. How would you define the term scientific revolution? In what ways was the event truly revolutionary? Which is more enduring, a political revolution or an intellectual one?

3. Compare and contrast the political philosophies of Thomas Hobbes and John Locke. How did each view human nature? Would you rather live under a government designed by Hobbes or by Locke? Why?

4. What factors prevented women from fully participating in the new science? How did family relationships help some women become involved in the advance of natural philosophy?

5. What were the chief factors accounting for the condemnation of Galileo? How did Pascal seek to reconcile faith and reason? How did English natural theology support economic expansion?

6. How do you explain the phenomena of witchcraft and witch-hunts in an age of scientific enlightenment? Why did the witch panics occur in the late sixteenth and early seventeenth centuries? How might the Reformation have contributed to them?

SUGGESTED READINGS

R. Ashcraft, *Revolutionary Politics and Locke's Two Treatises of Government* (1986). A major study emphasizing the radical side of Locke's thought.

J. Barry, M. Hester, and G. Roberts (eds.), *Witchcraft in Early Modern Europe: Studies in Culture and Belief* (1998). A collection of recent essays.

M. Biagioli, *Galileo Courtier: The Practice of Science in the Culture of Absolutism* (1993). A major revisionist work that emphasizes the role of the political setting on Galileo's career and thought.

P. Dear, *Revolutionizing the Sciences: European Knowledge and Its Ambitions, 1500–1700* (2001). A broad-ranging study of both the ideas and institutions of the new science.

M. A. Finocchiaro, *The Galileo Affair: A Documentary History* (1989). A collection of all the relevant documents and introductory commentary.

S. Gaukroger, *Descartes: An Intellectual Biography* (1995). A major work that explores both the science and philosophy in Descartes's work.

S. Gaukroger, *Francis Bacon and the Transformation of Early-Modern Philosophy* (2001). An excellent, accessible introduction.

I. Harris, *The Mind of John Locke: A Study of Political Theory in Its Intellectual Setting* (1994). The most comprehensive recent treatment.

E. Harth, *Cartesian Women: Versions and Subversions of Rational Discourse in the Old Regime*

(1992). A pioneering work on the relationship of educated French women to the new science.

J. L. HEILBRON, *The Sun in the Church: Cathedrals as Solar Observatories* (2000). A remarkable study of the manner in which Roman Catholic cathedrals were used to make astsronomical observations and calculations.

L. JARDINE, *Ingenious Pursuits: Building the Scientific Revolution* (1999). A lively exploration of the interface of personalities, new knowledge, and English society.

T. S. KUHN, *The Copernican Revolution* (1957). Remains the leading work on the subject.

B. LEVACK, *The Witch Hunt in Early Modern Europe* (1986). Lucid survey.

P. MACHAMER (ED.), *The Cambridge Companion to Galileo* (1998). A wide-ranging collection of essays that aid the understanding of the entire spectrum of the new science.

D. NOBLE, *A World Without Women: The Christian Clerical Culture of Western Science* (1992). A controversial account.

M. OSLER, *Rethinking the Scientific Revolution* (2000). A collection of revisionist essays particuarly exploring issues of the interrelationship of the new science and religion.

R. POPKIN, *The History of Scepticism from Erasmus to Spinoza* (1979). A classic study of the fear of loss of intellectual certainty.

L. PYENSON AND S. SHEETS-PYENSON, *Servants of Nature: A History of Scientific Institutions, Enterprises, and Sensibilities* (1999). A history of the settings in which the creation and diffusion of scientific knowledge have occurred.

L. SCHIEBINGER, *The Mind Has No Sex? Women in the Origins of Modern Science* (1989). A major study of the subject.

S. SHAPIN, *The Scientific Revolution* (1996). A readable brief introduction.

Q. SKINNER, *Reason and Rhetoric in the Philosophy of Hobbes* (1996). A major study by one of the leading scholars of Hobbes and early modern political thought.

K. THOMAS, *Religion and the Decline of Magic* (1971). Provocative, much acclaimed work focused on popular culture.

R. TUCK, *Philosophy and Government 1572–1651* (1993). A continent-wide survey.

R. S. WESTFALL, *The Construction of Modern Science: Mechanisms and Mechanics* (1971). A classic work.

R. S. WESTFALL, *Never at Rest: A Biography of Isaac Newton* (1981). The major study.

P. ZAGORIN, *Francis Bacon* (1998). A comprehensive treatment.

DOCUMENTS CD-ROM

THOUGHT AND CULTURE IN EARLY MODERN EUROPE

13.1 Francis Bacon: from *First Book of Aphorisms*

13.4 Thomas Hobbes: Chapter XIII from *Leviathan*

13.5 Rejecting Aristotle: Galileo Defends the Heliocentric View

13.6 Rethinking the Bible: Galileo Confronts his Critics

Vermeer's *The Geographer* and *The Astronomer*: Painting and The New Knowledge

During the sixteenth and seventeenth centuries, just as the theories and observations published by Copernicus, Kepler, and Galileo led to a new understanding of the heavens, the encounter with the Americas and the opening of new shipping lanes to Asia flooded Europe with new information about areas of the world previously unknown to Europeans. The Netherlands stood at a crucial juncture in both enterprises. Dutch opticians and metalworkers produced scientific instruments of the highest quality. Their boatyards constructed advanced ships that transported goods throughout the world as the Dutch established the first far-flung commercial empire. Religious toleration in the Netherlands permitted an active and open intellectual life, as did the Dutch policy of welcoming immigrants from everywhere. Dutch freedom of the press allowed the Netherlands to become a center for the publication of books that carried the new knowledge of astronomy, optics, geography and other sciences across Europe.

Two paintings of the late 1660s by the Dutch artist Jan Vermeer (1632–1675) reflect these developments: *The Astronomer* (1668) and *The Geographer* (1668–1669). Sales records suggest that Vermeer painted them as pendants; that is, they were meant to hang beside each other and to give meaning to each other. Astronomy and geography would have been closely related in the minds of a seventeenth-century Dutch artist and his contemporaries because the improved knowledge of the heavens was important for both navigation and calendars.

The geographer is shown consulting maps, which, over the course of the past two centuries, had seen the additions of new continents, islands, and rivers never recorded by the ancients. Used by Dutch fleets, those maps had opened the way for a worldwide trade that enriched the nation and led it into conflict with both France and England. Consequently, the geographer could look out through the window onto a wider world filled with more different kinds of goods and natural wonders than any Europeans had ever known. By placing on a map the regions where those goods originated and those wonders lay, the geographer could make that expanding new world familiar to ordinary Europeans.

Vermeer's astronomer sits at his desk with his hand on a globe depicting the constellations of the night sky. On the side of the cabinet

Jan Vermeer van Delft, *The Geographer (1668–1669).* Oil on canvas. Staedelsches Kunstinstitute, Frankfurt am Main. The Granger Collection

in the back of the room hangs a chart containing other astronomical information, and on the table is an instrument for making observations of the heavens. The scene portrays the kind of setting in which much theorizing about astronomy occurred. Clearly, science involved thinking and working through tables of observations as much as it did peering into the night sky. Through such mathematical theorizing, Newton would achieve the culmination of the scientific revolution about twenty years later with his publication of *Principia Mathematica* (1687). But the cultural fascination with astronomy predated that publication.

The Astronomer also depicts an important theme relating to science and religion. On the wall to the right, as a painting within the painting, hangs the *Finding of Moses*, an image artists often used to symbolize God's providential purposes. Because the *Finding of Moses* is at the side of the painting and the astronomer's back is to it, Vermeer might be suggesting that those practicing the new science must look to the light of nature alone, which streams in through the window. But as a Roman Catholic well aware of the fate of Galileo, Vermeer is probably suggesting that the new natural knowledge, like the life of Moses, did fulfill divine purposes. The presence of the astronomer with both the biblical painting and the astronomical globe thus appears to indicate that devout faith and the pursuit of rigorous science are compatible and mutually reinforcing.

Vermeer's method of painting as well as his content displays his fascination with optics, a subject that also interested many natural philosophers. In these and other paintings, Vermeer portrayed light illuminating interiors. He is believed to have used a *camera obscura*, a darkened box with a pinhole through which light projected the outside scene in precise detail and vibrant color. As one contemporary wrote, "I am certain that vision from these reflections in the dark can give no small light to the sight of the young artists; because besides gaining knowledge of nature, so one sees

here what main or general [characteristics] should belong to a truly natural painting."[12] Vermeer's use of the *camera obscura* illustrates how the science and experiments of the new optics could influence the traditional craft of painting, expanding its capacity to portray the natural world.

■ *How do these paintings by Vermeer reflect the progress of the scientific revolution? Why were astronomy and geography important to the Dutch in the seventeenth century? What might Vermeer have been trying to suggest by putting* The Finding of Moses *in the background of the* The Astronomer?

Mariet Westermann, *A Worldly Art: The Dutch Republic 1585–1718* (New York: Prentice Hall/Abrams, 1996); Arthur K. Wheelock, Jr., *Vermeer and the Art of Painting* (New Haven: Yale University Press, 1995); J. M. Montias, *Vermeer and His Milieu: A Web of Social History* (Princeton: Princeton University Press, 1989); Arthur K. Wheelock, Jr., *Perspective, Optics, and Delft Artists Around 1650* (New York: Garland Press, 1977).

[12]Arthur K. Wheelock, Jr., *Vermeer and the Art of Painting* (New Haven, CT: Yale University Press, 1995), p. 18.

Jan Vermeer van Delft, *(1632–1675), The Astronomer (1668).* Oil on canvas 31.5 × 45.5 cm. Louvre, Dép. des Peintures, Paris, France. Copyright Erich Lessing, Art Resource, N.Y.

Peter the Great (r. 1682–1725), seeking to make Russia a military power, reorganized the country's political and economic structures. His reign saw Russia enter fully into European power politics. The Apotheosis of Tsar Peter the Great 1672–1725 by unknown artist, 1710.

Historical Museum, Moscow, Russia/E.T. Archive

CHAPTER 15

SUCCESSFUL AND UNSUCCESSFUL PATHS TO POWER (1686–1740)

*T*HE LATE SEVENTEENTH AND EARLY *eighteenth centuries witnessed significant shifts of power and influence among the states of Europe. Nations that had been strong lost their status as significant military and economic units. Other countries that in some cases had figured only marginally in international relations came to the fore. Great Britain, France, Austria, Russia, and Prussia emerged during this period as the powers that would dominate Europe until at least World War I. Their political and economic dominance occurred at the expense of Spain, the United Netherlands, Poland, Sweden, and the Ottoman Empire. Equally essential to their rise was the weakness of the Holy Roman Empire after the Treaty of Westphalia (1648), which ended the Thirty Years' War.*

The successful competitors for international power were those states that created strong central political authorities. Farsighted observers in the late seventeenth century already understood that in the future those domains that would become or remain great powers must imitate the political and military organization of Louis XIV's France. Strong monarchy alone could impose unity of purpose on the state. The turmoil of seventeenth-century civil wars and aristocratic revolts had impressed people with the value of a firm centralized monarch as the guarantor of minimum domestic tranquility.

Imitation of French absolutism involved more than belief in a strong centralized monarchy; it usually also required building a standing army, organizing an efficient tax structure to support the army, and establishing a bureaucracy to collect the taxes. Moreover, the political classes of the country—especially the nobles— had to be converted to a sense of duty and loyalty to the central government that was more intense than their loyalty to other competing political and social institutions.

The waning powers were those that failed to achieve such effective organization. They were unable to employ their political, economic, and human resources to resist external aggression or to overcome the forces of domestic dissolution. Internal and external failures were closely related. If a state did not maintain or establish a central political authority with sufficient power over the nobility, the cities, the guilds, and the church, it could not raise a strong army to defend its borders or its economic interests. More often than not, the key element leading to success or failure was the character, personality, and energy of the monarch.

The Maritime Powers

Central and Eastern Europe and the Ottoman Empire

Russia Enters the European Political Arena

In Perspective

KEY TOPICS

- The Dutch Golden Age
- French aristocratic resistance to the monarchy
- Early-eighteenth-century British political stability
- Power and decline of the Ottoman Empire
- The efforts of the Habsburgs to secure their holdings
- The emergence of Prussia as a major power under the Hohenzollerns
- The efforts of Peter the Great to transform Russia into a powerful centralized nation along Western lines

The Maritime Powers

In western Europe, Britain and France emerged as the dominant powers. This development represented a shift of influence away from Spain and the United Netherlands. Both of the latter countries had been powerful and important during the sixteenth and seventeenth centuries, but they became politically and militarily marginal during the eighteenth century. Neither, however, disappeared from the map, and both retained considerable economic vitality and influence. Spanish power declined after the War of the Spanish Succession. (See Chapter 13.) The case of the Netherlands was more complicated.

THE NETHERLANDS: GOLDEN AGE TO DECLINE

The seven provinces that became the United Provinces of the Netherlands were the single genuinely new state to appear on the European scene during the early modern period. They emerged as a nation after revolting against Spain in 1572. Spain acknowledged their autonomy only in a truce in 1609, though other European powers had recognized Dutch independence in the 1580s. The Netherlands won formal independence from Spain in the Treaty of Westphalia (1648). These eighty years of on-again, off-again warfare forged much of the national identity of the Netherlands. During the middle of the seventeenth century, the Dutch fought a series of naval wars with England. Then, in 1672, the armies of Louis XIV invaded the

Netherlands. William III, the *stadtholder* of Holland, the most important of the United Provinces, rallied the Dutch and eventually led the entire European coalition against France. As a part of that strategy, he answered the invitation of Protestant English aristocrats in 1688 to assume, along with his wife Mary who was the daughter of King James II, the English throne. (See Chapter 13.)

During both the seventeenth and eighteenth centuries, the political and economic life of the Netherlands differed from that of the rest of Europe. The other major nations pursued paths toward strong central government, generally under monarchies, as with France, or in the case of England, under a strong parliamentary system. By contrast, the Netherlands was formally a republic. Each of the provinces retained considerable authority, and the central government, embodied in the States General that met in the Hague, exercised its authority through a kind of ongoing negotiation with the provinces. Prosperous and populous Holland dominated the States General. The Dutch deeply distrusted monarchy and the ambitions of the House of Orange. Nonetheless, when confronted with major military challenges, the Dutch would permit the House of Orange and, most notably, William III to assume dominant leadership. These political arrangements proved highly resilient and allowed the republic to establish itself permanently in the European state system during the seventeenth century. When William died in 1702 and the wars with France ended in 1714, the Dutch reverted to their republican structures.

Although the provinces making up the Netherlands were traditionally identified with the Protestant cause in Europe during their revolt against Spain and the wars against Louis XIV, extensive toleration marked Dutch religious life. The Calvinist Reformed Church was the official church of the nation, and most of the political elite belonged to it, but it was not an established church. There were always a significant number of Roman Catholics and Protestants living in the Netherlands who did not belong to the Reformed Church. The country also became a haven for Jews driven out of other lands, particularly those who had been expelled from Spain. Consequently, while other European states attempted to impose a single religion on their people or tore themselves apart in religious conflict, in the Netherlands peoples of differing religious faiths lived together peacefully.

Urban Prosperity Beyond the climate of religious toleration, what most amazed seventeenth-century contemporaries about the Dutch Republic was its economic prosperity. While the rest of Europe fought over religion, the Dutch attained a high standard of living. Their remarkable economic achievement was built on the foundations of urbanization, transformed agriculture, extensive trade and finance, and an overseas commercial empire. (See "Art & the West: Rachel Ruyseh, *Flower Still Life*," p. 510.)

In the Netherlands, more people lived in cities than in any other area of Europe. By 1675, in Holland, the province where Amsterdam was located, at least 60 percent of the population were urban dwellers. Not until after the onset of industrialization in the late eighteenth century would such urbanization occur elsewhere, and then notably in England. Trade, manufacture, shipbuilding, and finance were the engine of Dutch urban prosperity.

This urban concentration had been made possible by key transformations in Dutch farming that served as the model for the rest of Europe. During the seventeenth century, the Dutch drained and reclaimed much land from the sea. The Dutch were able to use this reclaimed terrain for highly profitable farming because their shipping interests dominated the Baltic trade, which provided them with a steady supply of grain. The availability of this cheap grain meant that Dutch farmers could use their land to produce more profitable dairy products and beef. Dutch farmers also diversified into the cultivation of cash products such as tulip bulbs. So successful was tulip cultivation, that for a few years in the late 1630s, market speculation led to the sale of tulip bulbs at astounding prices.

The Baltic grain trade was just one example of the Dutch acting as the chief trading nation of Europe. Their fishermen dominated the market for herring and supplied much of the Continent's dried fish. The Dutch also supplied textiles to many parts of Europe. Dutch ships appeared in harbors all over the Continent, with their captains purchasing goods that they then transported and resold at a profit to other nations. Or such goods might be returned to the Netherlands, stored, and then sold later at more advantageous prices. Many of the handsome merchant houses lining the canals of Amsterdam had storage facilities on their upper floors. The overseas trades also supported a vast domestic industry of shipbuilding and ship supplies.

All of this trade, commerce, and manufacturing was supported by the most advanced financial system of the day. Capital could be more easily raised in Amsterdam than anyplace else in the seventeenth century. Shares traded easily and often speculatively in the Amsterdam bourse. Dutch capital financed economic life outside its own borders.

The final foundation of Dutch prosperity was the Dutch seaborne empire. During the late sixteenth and early seventeenth centuries, Dutch traders established a major presence in East Asia, particularly in spice-producing areas of Java, the Moluccas, and

In the mid–eighteenth century, when this picture of the Amsterdam Exchange was painted, Amsterdam had replaced the cities of Italy and south Germany as the leading banking center of Europe. Amsterdam retained this position until the late eighteenth century. Painting by Hiob A. Berckheyde, *The Amsterdam Exchange.* Canvas 85 × 105 cm. Coll. Museum Boijmans Van Beuningen, Rotterdam, The Netherlands, Inv. no. 1043

Sri Lanka. The vehicle for this penetration was the Dutch East Indies Company (chartered in 1602), shares of which traded on the Amsterdam bourse. The Dutch East Indies Company eventually displaced Portuguese dominance in the spice trade of East Asia and for many years prevented English traders from establishing a major presence there. Initially, the Dutch had only wanted commercial dominance of the spice trade, but in time, that goal led them to move toward producing the spices themselves, which required them to control many of the islands that today constitute Indonesia. The Netherlands remained the colonial master of this region until after World War II.

Economic Decline The decline in political influence of the United Provinces of the Netherlands occurred within the eighteenth century. After the death of William III of Britain in 1702, the various local provinces prevented the emergence of another strong *stadtholder*. Unified political leadership therefore vanished. During the earlier long wars with Louis XIV and Britain, naval supremacy had slowly but steadily passed to the British. The fishing industry declined, and the Dutch lost their technological superiority in shipbuilding. Countries between which Dutch ships had once carried goods now traded directly with each other. For example, the British began to use their own vessels in the Baltic traffic with Russia.

Similar stagnation overtook the Dutch domestic industries, such as textile finishing, papermaking, and glassblowing. The disunity of the provinces and the absence of vigorous leadership hastened this economic decline and prevented action that might have slowed or halted it.

What saved the United Provinces from becoming completely insignificant in European affairs was their continued financial dominance. Well past the middle of the eighteenth century, their banks continued to finance European trade. Moreover, the Amsterdam bourse remained an important financial institution because, as we see later in this chapter, both France and England experienced disastrously excessive and politically disruptive stock speculations in the early eighteenth century, which made them fearful to invest in shares.

FRANCE AFTER LOUIS XIV

Despite its military reverses in the War of the Spanish Succession, France remained a great power. It was less strong in 1715 than in 1680, but it still possessed the largest European population, an advanced, if troubled, economy, and the administrative structure bequeathed it by Louis XIV. Moreover, even if France and its resources had been drained by the last of Louis's wars, the other major states of Europe were similarly debilitated. What France required was economic recovery and consolidation, wiser political leadership, and a less ambitious foreign policy. It did enjoy a period of recovery, but its leadership was at best indifferent. Louis XIV was succeeded by his five-year-old

The impending collapse of John Law's bank triggered a financial panic throughout France. Desperate investors, such as those shown here in the city of Rennes, sought to exchange their paper currency for gold and silver before the banks' supply of precious metals was exhausted.
Collection Musée de Bretagne, Rennes

great-grandson Louis XV (r. 1715–1774). The young boy's uncle, the duke of Orléans, became regent and remained so until his death in 1720. The regency, marked by financial and moral scandals, further undermined the faltering prestige of the monarchy.

John Law and the Mississippi Bubble The duke of Orléans was a gambler, and for a time he turned over the financial management of the kingdom to John Law (1671–1729), a Scottish mathematician and fellow gambler. Law believed an increase in the paper-money supply would stimulate France's economic recovery. With the permission of the regent, he established a bank in Paris that issued paper money. Law then organized a monopoly, called the Mississippi Company, on trading privileges with the French colony of Louisiana in North America.

The Mississippi Company also took over the management of the French national debt. The company issued shares of its own stock in exchange for government bonds, which had fallen sharply in value. To redeem large quantities of bonds, Law encouraged speculation in Mississippi Company stock. In 1719, the price of the stock rose handsomely. Smart investors, however, took their profits by selling their stock in exchange for paper money from Law's bank, which they then sought to exchange for gold. The bank, however, lacked enough gold to redeem all the paper money brought to it.

In February 1720, all gold payments were halted in France. Soon thereafter, Law himself fled the country. The Mississippi Bubble, as the affair was called, had burst. The fiasco brought disgrace on the government that had sponsored Law. The Mississippi Company was later reorganized and functioned profitably, but fear of paper money and speculation marked French economic life for decades.

Renewed Authority of the *Parlements* The duke of Orléans made a second decision that also lessened the power of the monarchy: He attempted to draw the French nobility once again into the decision-making processes of the government. Louis XIV had filled his ministries and bureaucracies with persons from non-noble families. The regent, under pressure from the nobility, tried to restore a balance. He set up a system of councils on which nobles were to serve along with bureaucrats. The years of idle noble domestication at Versailles, however, had worked too well, and the nobility seemed to

Cardinal Fleury (1653–1743) was the tutor and chief minister of Louis XV from 1726 to 1743. Fleury gave France a period of peace and prosperity, but was unable to solve the state's long-term financial problems. This portrait is by Hyacinthe Rigaud. © Réunion des Musées Nationaux/Art Resource, N.Y.

lack both the talent and the desire to govern. The experiment failed.

Despite this failure, the great French nobles did not surrender their ancient ambition to assert their rights, privileges, and local influence over those of the monarchy. The chief feature of eighteenth-century French political life was the attempt of the nobility to use its authority to limit the power of the monarchy. The most effective instrument in this process was the *parlements*, or courts dominated by the nobility.

The French *parlements* were different from the English Parliament. These French courts, the most important of which was the *Parlement* of Paris, could not legislate. Rather, they had the power to recognize or not to recognize the legality of an act or law promulgated by the monarch. By long tradition, their formal approval had been required to make a royal law valid. Louis XIV had often restricted stubborn, uncooperative *parlements*. In another major political blunder, however, the duke of Orléans had formally approved the full reinstitution of the *parlements'* power to allow or disallow laws. Thereafter, the growing financial and moral weakness of the monarchy allowed these aristocratic judicial institutions to reassert their authority. This situation meant that until the revolution in 1789 the *parlements* became natural centers for aristocratic resistance to royal authority.

Administration of Cardinal Fleury In 1726, Cardinal Fleury (1653–1743) became the chief minister of the French court. He was the last of the great clerics who loyally and effectively served the French monarchy. Like his seventeenth-century predecessors, the cardinals Richelieu and Mazarin, Fleury was a realist. He understood the political ambition and incapacity of the nobility and worked quietly to block their undue influence. He was also aware of the precarious financial situation of the royal treasury. The cardinal, who was seventy-three years old when he came to office, was determined to give the country a period of peace. He surrounded himself with able assistants who tried

to solve France's financial problems. Part of the national debt was repudiated. New industries enjoying special privileges were established and roads and bridges built. On the whole, the nation prospered, but Fleury could never draw sufficient tax revenues from the nobles or the church to put the state on a stable financial footing.

Fleury died in 1743, having unsuccessfully attempted to prevent France from intervening in the war that was then raging between Austria and Prussia. The cost of this intervention was to undo all his financial pruning and planning.

Another failure must also be attributed to this elderly cleric. Despite his best efforts, he had not trained Louis XV to become an effective monarch. Louis XV possessed most of the vices and almost none of the virtues of his great-grandfather Louis XIV. He wanted to hold on to absolute power, but was unwilling to work the long hours required. He did not choose many wise advisers after Fleury. He was tossed about by the gossip and intrigues of the court. His personal life was scandalous. Louis XV was not an evil person, but a mediocre one. And in a monarch, mediocrity was unfortunately often a greater fault than vice. Consequently, it was not a lack of resources or military strength that plagued France, but the absence of political leadership to organize, direct, and inspire its people.

GREAT BRITAIN: THE AGE OF WALPOLE

In 1713, Britain had emerged as a victor over Louis XIV, but the nation required a period of recovery. As an institution, the British monarchy was not in the degraded state of the French monarchy, yet its stability was not certain.

The Hanoverian Dynasty In 1714, the Hanoverian dynasty, as designated by the Act of Settlement (1701), came to the throne. Almost immediately, George I (r. 1714–1727) faced a challenge to his new title. The Stuart pretender James Edward (1688–1766), the son of James II, landed in Scotland in December 1715. His forces marched southward, but met defeat less than two months later. Although militarily successful against the pretender, the new dynasty and its supporters saw the need for consolidation.

Whigs and Tories During the seventeenth century, England had been one of the most politically restive countries in Europe. The closing years of

Under Louis XV (r. 1715–1774) France suffered major defeats in Europe and around the world and lost most of its North American empire. Louis himself was an ineffective ruler, and during his reign, the monarchy encountered numerous challenges from the French aristocracy. Corbis

Queen Anne's reign (1702–1714) had seen sharp clashes between the political factions of Whigs and Tories over whether to end the war with France. The Tories had urged a rapid peace settlement and after 1710 had opened negotiations with France. During the same period, the Whigs were seeking favor from the elector of Hanover, the future George I, who would soon be their monarch. His concern for French threats to his domains in Hanover made him unsympathetic to the Tory peace policy. In the final months of Anne's reign, some Tories, fearing they would lose power under the waiting Hanoverian dynasty, opened channels of communication with the Stuart pretender; a few even rallied to his cause.

Under these circumstances, George I, on his arrival in Britain, clearly favored the Whigs. Previously, the differences between the Whigs and the Tories had been vaguely related to principle. The Tories emphasized a strong monarchy, low taxes for landowners, and firm support of the Anglican church. The Whigs supported monarchy, but wanted Parliament to retain final sovereignty. They favored urban commercial interests as well as the prosperity of the landowners. They encouraged a policy of religious toleration toward the Protestant nonconformists in England. Socially, both groups supported the status quo.

Neither group was organized like a modern political party. Outside Parliament, each party consisted of political networks based on local connections and economic influence. Each group acknowledged a few national spokesmen, who articulated positions and principles. After the Hanoverian accession and the eventual Whig success in achieving the firm confidence of George I, the chief difference between the Whigs and the Tories for almost forty years was that one group had access to public office and patronage and the other did not. This early Hanoverian proscription of Tories from public life was one of the most prominent features of the age.

The Leadership of Robert Walpole The political situation after 1715 remained in flux, until Robert Walpole (1676–1745) took over the helm of government. Though previously active in the House of Commons since the reign of Queen Anne and a cabinet minister, what gave Walpole special prominence under the new dynasty was a British financial scandal similar to the French Mississippi Bubble.

Management of the British national debt had been assigned to the South Sea Company, which exchanged government bonds for company stock. As in the French case, the price of the stock soared, only to crash in 1720 when prudent investors sold their holdings and took their speculative profits. Parliament intervened and, under Walpole's leadership, adopted measures to honor the national debt. To most contemporaries, Walpole had saved the financial integrity of the country and had thus proved himself a person of immense administrative capacity and political ability.

George I gave Walpole his full confidence. For this reason, Walpole has often been regarded as the first prime minister of Great Britain and the originator of the cabinet system of government. Walpole generally demanded that all the ministers in the cabinet agree on policy, but he could not prevent frequent public differences among them. Unlike a modern English prime minister, he was not chosen by the majority of the House of Commons. The real sources of his power were the personal support of the king, first George I and later George II (r. 1727–1760), his ability to handle the House of Commons, and his ironfisted control of government patronage, which bought support for himself and his policies from people who wanted jobs, appointments, favors, and government contracts. Such corruption supplied the glue of political loyalty.

Walpole's favorite slogan was *Quieta non movere* (roughly, "Let sleeping dogs lie"). To that end, he pursued peace abroad and supported the status quo at home. In this regard he much resembled Cardinal Fleury.

The Structure of Parliament The structure of the eighteenth-century British House of Commons aided Walpole in his pacific policies. It was neither a democratic nor a representative body. Each of the counties into which Britain was divided elected two members. (See "Lady Mary Wortley Montagu Advises Her Husband on Election to Parliament.") But if the more powerful landed families in a county agreed on the candidates, there was no contest. Most members, however, were elected from a variety of units called *boroughs*. A few boroughs were large enough for elections to be relatively democratic, but most had few electors. For example, a local municipal corporation or council of only a dozen members might have the right to elect a member of Parliament. In Old Sarum, one of the most famous corrupt, or "rotten," boroughs, the Pitt family simply bought up those pieces of property to which a vote was attached and thus in effect owned a seat in the House of Commons. Through proper electoral management, which involved favors to the electors, the House of Commons could be controlled.

Sir Robert Walpole (1676–1745), far left, is shown talking with the Speaker of the House of Commons. Walpole, who dominated British political life from 1721 to 1742, is considered the first prime minister of Britain. Mansell/Time Pix

The structure of Parliament and the manner in which the House of Commons was elected meant the owners of property, especially wealthy nobles, dominated the government of England. They did not pretend to represent people and districts or to be responsive to what would later be called public opinion. They regarded themselves as representing various economic and social interests, such as the West Indian interest, the merchant interest, and the landed interest. These owners of property were suspicious of an administrative bureaucracy controlled by the crown or its ministers. To diminish royal influence, they or their agents served as local government administrators, judges, militia commanders, and tax collectors. In this sense, the British nobility and large landowners actually did govern the nation. And because they regarded the Parliament as the political sovereign, there was no absence of central political authority and direction. Consequently, the supremacy of Parliament gave Britain the unity that strong central monarchy provided elsewhere in Europe.

These parliamentary structures also helped strengthen the financial position of the British government, which, under William III, had learned much about government finance from Dutch practices. The British monarch could not raise taxes the way his continental counterparts could, but the British government consisting of the monarch and Parliament could and did raise vast sums of tax revenue and loans to wage war throughout the eighteenth century. All Britons paid taxes; there were virtually no exemptions. The British credit market was secure through the regulation of the Bank of England, founded in 1693. This strong system of finance and tax collection was one of the cornerstones of eighteenth-century British power.

Freedom of Political Life   British political life was genuinely more free than that on the Continent. There were real limits on the power of Robert Walpole. Parliament could not wholly ignore popular

LADY MARY WORTLEY MONTAGU ADVISES HER HUSBAND ON ELECTION TO PARLIAMENT

In this letter of 1714, Lady Mary Wortley Montagu discussed with her husband the various paths that he might follow to gain election to the British House of Commons. Note her emphasis on knowing the right people and on having large amounts of money to spend on voters. Eventually, her husband was elected to Parliament in a borough that was controlled through government patronage.

■ *What are the various ways in which candidates and their supporters used money to campaign? What role did friendships play in the campaigning? How important do the political ideas or positions of the candidates seem to be? Women could not vote in eighteenth-century parliamentary elections. Was there some other influence they exerted?*

You seem not to have received my letters, or not to have understood them: you had been chose undoubtedly at York, if you had declared in time; but there is not any gentleman or tradesman disengaged at this time; they are treating every night. Lord Carlisle and the Thompsons have given their interest to Mr. Jenkins. I agree with you of the necessity of your standing this Parliament, which, perhaps, may be more considerable than any that are to follow it; but, as you proceed, 'tis my opinion, you will spend your money and not be chose. I believe there is hardly a borough unengaged. I expect every letter should tell me you are sure of some place; and, as far as I can perceive you are sure of none. As it has been managed, perhaps it will be the best way to deposit a certain sum in some friend's hands, and buy some little Cornish borough: it would, undoubtedly, look better to be chose for a considerable town; but I take it to be now too late. If you have any thoughts of Newark,

it will be absolutely necessary for you to enquire after Lord Lexington's interest; and your best way to apply yourself to Lord Holdernesse, who is both a Whig and an honest man. He is now in town, and you may enquire of him if Brigadier Sutton stands there; and if not, try to engage him for you. Lord Lexington is so ill at the Bath, that it is a doubt if he will live 'till the elections; and if he dies, one of his heiresses, and the whole interest of his estate, will probably fall on Lord Holdernesse.

'Tis a surprize to me, that you cannot make sure of some borough, when a number of your friends bring in so many Parliament-men without trouble or expense. 'Tis too late to mention it now, but you might have applied to Lady Winchester, as Sir Joseph Jekyl did last year, and by her interest the Duke of Bolton brought him in for nothing; I am sure she would be more zealous to serve me, than Lady Jekyl.

From Lord Wharncliffe, ed., *Letters and Works of Lady Mary Wortley Montagu*, 3rd ed., Vol. 1 (London: 1861), p. 211.

political pressure. Even with the extensive use of patronage, many members of Parliament maintained independent views. Newspapers and public debate flourished. There was freedom of speech and association. There was no large standing army. Those Tories barred from political office and the Whig enemies of Walpole could and did openly oppose his policies—which would have been far more difficult on the Continent.

For example, in 1733, Walpole presented a scheme to the House of Commons to expand the

scope of the excise tax, a tax that resembled a modern sales tax. The outcry in the press, on the public platforms, and in the streets was so great that he eventually withdrew the measure. What the British regarded as their traditional political rights raised a real and potent barrier to the power of the government. Again, in 1739, the public outcry over the alleged Spanish treatment of British merchants in the Caribbean pushed Britain into a war that Walpole opposed and deplored. He left office in 1742.

Lady Mary Wortley Montagu (1689–1762) was a famous writer of letters and an extremely well-traveled woman of the eighteenth century. As the document on p. 489 suggests, she was also a shrewd and tough-minded political adviser to her husband. By courtesy of the National Portrait Gallery, London

Central and Eastern Europe and the Ottoman Empire

The major factors in the shift of political influence among the maritime nations were naval strength, economic progress, foreign trade, and sound domestic administration. The conflicts among them occurred less in Europe than on the high seas and in their overseas empires. These nations existed in well-defined geographical areas with established borders. Their populations generally accepted the authority of the central government.

Central and eastern Europe were different. The entire region was economically much less advanced than western Europe. Except for the Baltic ports, the economy was agrarian. There were fewer cities and many more large estates populated by serfs. The states in this region did not possess overseas empires; nor did they engage in extensive overseas trade of any kind, except for the supply of grain to western Europe, grain more often than not carried on west European ships.

Changes in the power structure normally involved changes in borders or in the prince who ruled a particular area. Military conflicts took place at home rather than overseas. The political structure of this region, which lay largely east of the Elbe River, was very "soft." The almost constant warfare of the seventeenth century had led to a habit of temporary and shifting political loyalties. The princes and aristocracies of small states and principalities were unwilling to subordinate

This etching by Hogarth is the last of a series of four that satirizes the notoriously corrupt English electoral system. In the others, Hogarth shows the voters going to the polls after having been bribed and intoxicated with free gin. (Voting was then in public. The secret ballot was not introduced in England until 1872.) This fourth etching, Chairing the Member, *shows the triumphal procession of the victorious candidate, which is clearly turning into a brawl.* William Hogarth, "Chairing the Member." Etching. Metropolitan Museum of Art, Harris Brisbane Dick Fund, 1932. 32.35 (214).

themselves to a central monarchical authority. Consequently, the political life of the region and the kind of state that emerged there were different from those of western Europe.

During the last half of the seventeenth century, the region of central and eastern Europe began to assume the political and social contours that would characterize it for the next two centuries. After the Peace of Westphalia, the Austrian Habsburgs recognized the basic weakness of the position of the Holy Roman Emperor and started to consolidate their power outside Germany. At the same time, Prussia emerged as a factor in North German politics and as a major challenger to Habsburg domination of Germany. Most important, Russia at the opening of the eighteenth century became a military and naval power of the first order. These three states (Austria, Prussia, and Russia) achieved their new status largely as a result of the political decay or military defeat of Sweden, Poland, and the Ottoman Empire.

SWEDEN: THE AMBITIONS OF CHARLES XII

Under Gustavus Adolphus II (r. 1611–1632), Sweden had played an important role as a Protestant combatant in the Thirty Years' War. During the rest of the seventeenth century, Sweden had consolidated its control of the Baltic, thus preventing Russian possession of a Baltic port and permitting Polish and German access to the sea only on Swedish terms. The Swedes also possessed one of the better armies in Europe. Sweden's economy, however, based primarily on the export of iron, was not strong enough to ensure continued political success.

In 1697, Charles XII (r. 1697–1718) came to the throne. He was headstrong, to say the least, and

France and Great Britain in the Early Eighteenth Century	
1713	Treaty of Utrecht ends the War of the Spanish Succession
1714	George I becomes king of Great Britain and establishes the Hanoverian dynasty
1715	Louis XV becomes king of France
1715–1720	Regency of the duke of Orléans in France
1720	Mississippi Bubble bursts in France and South Sea Bubble bursts in Great Britain
1720–1742	Robert Walpole dominates British politics
1726–1743	Cardinal Fleury serves as Louis XV's chief minister
1727	George II becomes king of Great Britain
1733	Excise-tax crisis in Britain

perhaps insane. In 1700, Russia began a drive to the west against Swedish territory. The Russian goal was a foothold on the Baltic. In the resulting Great Northern War (1700–1721), Charles XII led a vigorous and often brilliant campaign, but one that eventually resulted in the defeat of Sweden. In 1700, he defeated the Russians at the Battle of Narva, but then he turned south to invade Poland. The conflict dragged on, and the Russians were able to strengthen their forces.

In 1708, the Swedish monarch began a major invasion of Russia, but became bogged down in the harsh Russian winter. The next year, his army was decisively defeated at the Battle of Poltava. Thereafter, the Swedes could maintain only a holding action against their enemies. Charles himself sought refuge in Turkey and did not return to Sweden until 1714. He was killed under uncertain circumstances four years later while fighting the Danes in Norway.

The Great Northern War came to a close in 1721. Sweden had exhausted its military and economic resources and had lost its monopoly on the Baltic coast. Russia had conquered a large section of the eastern Baltic, and Prussia had gained a part of Pomerania. Internally, after the death of Charles XII, the Swedish nobles were determined to reassert their power over the monarchy. They did so, but then quarreled among themselves. Sweden played a very minor role in European affairs thereafter.

The Ottoman Empire

Now that it no longer exists, it is difficult to realize the enormous importance and geographical magnitude of the Ottoman Empire. Governing a remarkably diverse collection of peoples that ranged from Baghdad across the Arabian peninsula, Anatolia, the Balkan peninsula, and North Africa from Egypt to Algiers, the **Ottoman Empire** was the largest and most stable political entity to arise in or near Europe after the collapse of the Roman Empire. It had achieved this power between the eleventh and early sixteenth centuries as Ottoman tribes migrated eastward from the steppes of Asia. In 1453, they conquered Constantinople, thus putting an end to the Byzantine Empire. By the early seventeenth century only cities in China were larger than the Ottoman capital and only the emperors of China governed a larger area than the Ottoman sultan supported by his administrative bureaucracy and army.

The Ottoman Empire was the dominant political power in the Muslim world, after 1516 administering the holy cities of Mecca and Medina as well as Jerusalem, and arranging the safety of Muslim pilgrimages to Mecca. Yet its population was exceedingly diverse ethnically, linguistically, and religiously with significant numbers of Orthodox and Roman Catholic Christians and after the late fifteenth century many thousands of Jews from Spain. The Ottomans extended considerable religious toleration to their subjects, indeed far more toleration than existed anywhere in Europe. The Ottoman sultans governed their empire through units, called **millets**, of officially recognized religious communities. Various laws and regulations applied to the persons who belonged to a particular millet rather than to a particular administrative territory. Non-Islamic persons in the empire, known as *dhimmis*, or followers of religions tolerated by law, could practice their religion and manage their internal community affairs through their own religious officials, but were second-class citizens generally unable to rise in the service of the empire. *Dhimmis* paid a special poll tax (*jizyah*), could not serve in the military, and were prohibited from wearing certain colors. Their residences and places of worship could not be as large as those of Muslims. Over the years, however, they often attained economic success because they possessed the highest level of commercial skills in the empire. Because the Ottomans discouraged their various peoples from interacting with each other, the Islamic population rarely acquired these and other skills from their non-Islamic neighbors. Thus, for example, when the Ottomans negotiated with European powers, their Greek subjects almost invariably served as the interpreters.

The Ottoman dynasty also kept itself separated from the most powerful families of the empire by recruiting military leaders and administrative officers from groups whom the sultans believed would be personally loyal to them. For example, through a practice known as the *devshirme*, the Ottomans until the end of the seventeenth century recruited their most elite troops from Christian communities usually in the Balkans. Christian boys so recruited were raised as Muslims and organized into elite military units, the most famous of which were infantry troops called *Janissaries*. It was thought these troops would be extremely loyal to the sultan and the state because they owed their life and status to the sultan. As a result of this policy, entry into the elite military organizations and advancement in the administrative structures of the empire remained generally closed to the native Islamic population and most especially to members of the most elite Islamic families. Instead, in addition to the army, thousands of persons usually from the outer regions of the empire who were technically slaves of the sultan filled government posts and achieved major political influence and status. Thus in contrast to the situation in Europe, few people from the socially leading families in the empire gained military, administrative, or political experience in the central institutions of the empire, but remained primarily linked to local government in provincial cities. Paradoxically, many people in the Ottoman Empire believed it was better to be a favored slave than a free subject.

Again in contrast to the long-standing tension between church and state in Europe, Islamic religious authorities played a significant and enduring role in the political, legal, and administrative life of the Ottoman Empire. The dynasty saw itself as one of the chief protectors of Islamic law (*Shari'a*) and the Sunni traditions of the Islamic faith as well as its holy places. Islamic scholars, or *Ulama*, dominated not only Ottoman religious institutions but also schools and courts of law. There essentially existed a trade-off between Ottoman political and religious authorities. Through what was known as "the circle of equity," the sultan and his administrative officials would consult these Islamic scholars for advice with regard to how their policies and the behavior of their subjects accorded with Islamic law and the Qur'an. In turn, the Ulama would support the Ottoman state while the latter deferred to their judgments. This situation would prove a key factor in the fate of

the Ottoman Empire. From the late seventeenth century onward, the Ulama urged Ottoman rulers to conform to traditional life even as the empire confronted a rapidly changing and modernizing Europe. At the same time the Janissaries also resisted any changes that might undermine their own privileged status.

From the fifteenth century onward, the Ottoman Empire had tried to push further westward into Europe. Even after its naval defeat in 1571 at the Battle of Lepanto, the empire retained control of the eastern Mediterranean and the lands bordering it. Still determined to move toward the west, the Ottomans made their deepest military invasion into Europe in 1683, when they unsuccessfully besieged Vienna (see Map 15–1). Although that defeat proved to be decisive, many observers at the time thought it the result only of an overreach of power by the Ottomans rather than as a symptom of a deeper decline, which was actually the case.

Gradually, from the seventeenth century onward, the authority of the grand vizier, the major political figure after the sultan, began to grow. This development meant that more and more authority lay with the administrative and military bureaucracy. Rivalries for power among army leaders and nobles, as well as their flagrant efforts to enrich themselves, weakened the effectiveness of the government. About the same time local elites in the various provincial cities of the empire began to assert their own influence. They did not so much reject imperial authority as quietly renegotiate its

In 1683 the Ottomans laid siege to Vienna. Only the arrival of Polish forces under King John III Sobieski (r. 1674–1696) saved the Habsburg capital. © Bettmann/Corbis

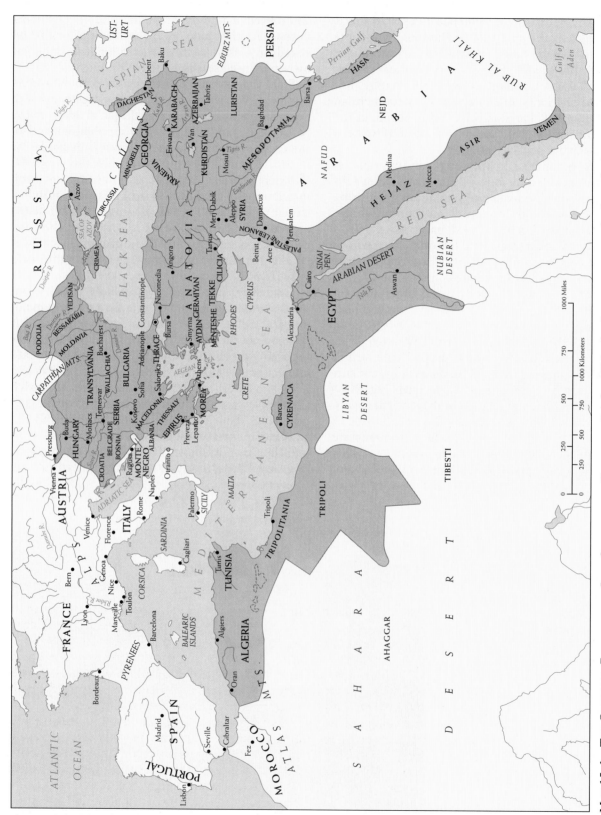

MAP 15–1 THE OTTOMAN EMPIRE IN THE LATE SEVENTEENTH CENTURY By the 1680s the Ottoman Empire had reached its maximum extent, but the Ottoman failure to capture Vienna in 1683 marked the beginning of a long and inexorable decline that ended with the empire's collapse after World War I.

conditions. For example, in the outer European provinces, such as Transylvania, Wallachia, and Moldavia (all parts of modern Romania), the empire depended on the goodwill of local rulers, who paid tribute, but never submitted fully to imperial authority. The same was true in Egypt, Algeria, Tunisia, and elsewhere.

External factors also accounted for both the blocking of Ottoman expansion in the late seventeenth century and then its slow decline thereafter. During the European Middle Ages the Islamic world had far outdistanced Europe in learning, science, and military prowess. From the fifteenth century onward, however, Europeans had begun to make rapid advances in technology, wealth, and scientific knowledge. For example, they designed ships for the difficult waters of the Atlantic and thus eventually opened trade routes to the East around Africa and reached the American continents. As trade expanded, Europeans achieved new commercial skills, founded trading posts in South Asia, established the plantation economies and precious metal mines of the Americas, and became much wealthier. By the seventeenth century, Europeans, particularly the Dutch and Portuguese, imported directly from Asia or America commodities such as spices, sugar, and coffee that they had previously acquired through the Ottoman Empire. By sailing around the Cape of Good Hope in Africa, the Europeans literally circumnavigated the Middle East, which could not match the quantity of raw goods and commodities available in South Asia. During the same decades Europeans developed greater military and naval power and new weapons.

The Ottoman defeats at Lepanto and Vienna had occurred at the outer limits of their expansion. Then, however, during the 1690s, the Ottomans unsuccessfully fought a league of European states including Austria, Venice, Malta, Poland, and Tuscany joined by Russia, which, as we see later in this chapter, was emerging as a new aggressive power to the north. In early 1699, the defeated Ottomans negotiated the Treaty of Carlowitz, which required them to surrender significant territory lying not at the edges but at the very heart of their empire in Europe, including most of Hungary, to the Habsburgs, Poland, and Venice. This treaty meant not only the loss of territory but also of the revenue the Ottomans had long drawn from those regions. From this time onward, Russia and the Ottomans would duel for control of regions around the Black Sea with Russia achieving ever greater success by the close of the eighteenth century.

Despite these defeats, the Ottomans remained deeply inward looking, continuing to regard themselves as superior to the once underdeveloped European West. Virtually no works of the new European science were translated into Arabic or Ottoman Turkish. Few Ottoman subjects traveled in Europe. The Ottoman leaders, isolated from both their own leading Muslim subjects and from Europe, failed to understand what was occurring far beyond their immediate borders, especially European advances in military technology. When during the eighteenth century the Ottoman Empire began to recognize the new situation, it tended to borrow European technology and import foreign advisers, thus failing to develop its own infrastructure. Moreover, the powerful influence of the Ulama worked against imitation of Christian Europe. Although traditionally opposed to significant interaction with non-Muslims, they did eventually allow non-Muslim teachers into the empire and approved alliances with non-Muslim powers. But the Ulama limited such relationships. For example, in the middle of the eighteenth century, the Ulama persuaded the sultan to close a school of technology and to abandon a printing press he had opened. This influence by Muslim religious teachers occurred just as governments, such as that of Peter the Great, and secular intellectuals across Europe through the influence of the Enlightenment (see Chapter 18) were increasingly diminishing the influence of the Christian churches in political and economic affairs. Consequently, intellectual circles in Europe began to view the once much-feared Ottoman Empire as a declining power and Islam as a backward-looking religion.

POLAND: ABSENCE OF STRONG CENTRAL AUTHORITY

In no other part of Europe was the failure to maintain a competitive political position so complete as in Poland. In 1683, King John III Sobieski (r. 1674–1696) had led a Polish army to rescue Vienna from the Turkish siege. Following that spectacular effort, however, Poland became a byword for the dangers of aristocratic independence.

The Polish monarchy was elective, but the deep distrust and divisions among the nobility prevented their electing a king from among themselves. Sobieski was a notable exception. Most of the Polish monarchs were foreigners and were the tools of foreign powers. The Polish nobles did have a central legislative body called the **Sejm**, or diet. It included only the nobles and specifically excluded representatives from corporate bodies, such as the towns. In the diet, however, there existed a practice known as the *liberum veto*, whereby the staunch opposition of any single member, who might have been bribed by a foreign power, could require the body to disband. Such opposition was termed "exploding the diet." This practice was most often the work of a group of dissatisfied nobles rather than of one person. Nonetheless, the requirement of unanimity was a major stumbling block to effective government. The price of this noble liberty would eventually be the disappearance of Poland from the map of Europe during the latter half of the eighteenth century.

THE HABSBURG EMPIRE AND THE PRAGMATIC SANCTION

The close of the Thirty Years' War with the Treaty of Westphalia marked a fundamental turning point in the history of the Austrian Habsburgs. Previously, allied with the Spanish branch of the family, they had hoped to dominate all of Germany and to return it to the Catholic fold. They did not achieve either goal, and the decline of Spanish power meant that in future diplomatic relations the Austrian Habsburgs were on their own.

After 1648, the Austrian Habsburgs retained the title of Holy Roman Emperor, but their political effectiveness depended less on force of arms than on the cooperation that the emperor could elicit from the over three hundred corporate political entities in the empire, including those that were Protestant, whose representatives met in the imperial diet that from 1663 until the empire was dissolved in 1806 sat at Regensburg.

Consolidation of Austrian Power While concentrating on their hereditary Austrian holdings among the German states, the Habsburgs also began to consolidate their power and influence within their other hereditary possessions. (See Map 15–2.) These included, first, the Crown of Saint Wenceslas, encompassing the kingdom of Bohemia (in the modern Czech Republic and Slovakia) and the duchies of Moravia and Silesia and, second, the Crown of Saint Stephen, which included Hungary, Croatia, and Transylvania. In the middle of the seventeenth century, much of Hungary remained occupied by the Ottoman Empire

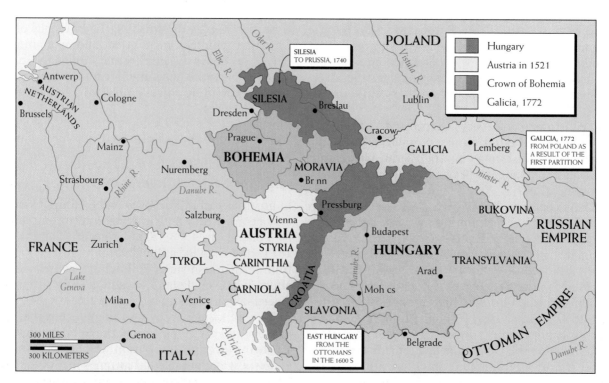

MAP 15–2   THE AUSTRIAN HABSBURG EMPIRE, 1521–1772   *The empire had three main units: Austria, Bohemia, and Hungary. Expansion was mainly eastward: East Hungary from the Ottomans (seventeenth century) and Galicia from Poland (1772). Meantime, Silesia was lost, but the Habsburgs retained German influences as Holy Roman emperors.*

and only came under Habsburg rule in 1699 through the Treaty of Carlowitz.

In the early eighteenth century, the Habsburgs extended their domains further, receiving the former Spanish (thereafter Austrian) Netherlands, Lombardy in northern Italy, and, briefly, the kingdom of Naples in southern Italy through the Treaty of Utrecht in 1713. During the eighteenth and nineteenth centuries, the Habsburgs' power and influence in Europe were based primarily on their territories outside Germany.

In the second half of the seventeenth century and later, the Habsburgs faced immense problems in these hereditary territories. In each, they ruled by virtue of a different title and had to gain the cooperation of the local nobility. There was almost no common basis for political unity among peoples of such diverse languages, customs, and geography. The Habsburgs established various central councils to chart common policies for their far-flung domains. Virtually all of these bodies dealt with only part of the Habsburgs' holdings. Repeatedly, the Habsburgs had to bargain with nobles in one part of their empire to maintain their position in another. The most difficult of these were the largely Calvinist **Magyar** nobility of Hungary.

Despite all these internal difficulties, Leopold I (r. 1658–1705) rallied his domains to resist the advances of the Ottomans and the aggression of Louis XIV, achieved Ottoman recognition of his sovereignty over Hungary in 1699, and began the suppression of a long Magyar rebellion that lasted from 1703 to 1711. He also conquered much of the Balkan Peninsula and western Romania. These southeastward extensions allowed the Habsburgs to hope to develop Mediterranean trade through the port of Trieste. Habsburg expansion at the cost of the Ottoman Empire helped them compensate for their loss of domination over the Holy Roman Empire. The new strength in the East gave them somewhat greater political leverage in Germany. Leopold I was succeeded by Joseph I (r. 1705–1711), who continued Leopold's policies.

The Habsburg Dynastic Problem   When Charles VI (r. 1711–1740) succeeded Joseph, he had no male heir, and there was only the weakest of precedents for a female ruler of the Habsburg domains. Charles feared that on his death the Austrian Habsburg lands might fall prey to the surrounding powers, as had those of the Spanish Habsburgs in 1700. He was determined to prevent that disaster and to provide his domains with the semblance of legal unity. To those ends, he devoted much of his energy throughout his reign to seeking the approval of his family, the estates of his realms, and the major foreign powers for a document called the **Pragmatic Sanction**.

This instrument provided the legal basis for a single line of inheritance within the Habsburg dynasty through Charles VI's daughter Maria Theresa (r. 1740–1780). Other members of the Habsburg family recognized her as the rightful heir. The nobles of the various Habsburg domains did likewise after extracting various concessions from Charles. So, when Charles VI died in October 1740, he believed he had secured legal unity for the Habsburg Empire and a safe succession for his daughter.

Charles VI had indeed established a permanent line of succession and the basis for future legal bonds within the Habsburg holdings. He had failed, however, to protect his daughter from foreign aggression, either through the Pragmatic Sanction or, more importantly, by leaving her a strong army and a full treasury. Less than two months after his death, the fragility of the foreign agreements became apparent. In December 1740, Frederick II of Prussia invaded the Habsburg province of Silesia. Maria Theresa had to fight to defend her inheritance.

PRUSSIA AND THE HOHENZOLLERNS

The Habsburg achievement had been to draw together into an uncertain legal unity a collection of domains possessed through separate feudal titles. The achievement of the Hohenzollerns of Brandenburg-Prussia was to acquire a similar collection of titular holdings and then to forge them into a centrally administered unit. They subordinated every social class and most economic pursuits to the strengthening of the single institution that united their far-flung realms: the army. They thus made the term *Prussian* synonymous with administrative rigor and military discipline.

A State of Disconnected Territories   The rise of Prussia is the story of the extraordinary Hohenzollern family, which had ruled the German territory of Brandenburg since 1417. (See Map 15–3.) Through inheritance, the family had acquired the duchy of Cleves and the counties of Mark and Ravensburg in 1609, the duchy of East Prussia in 1618, and the duchy of Pomerania in 1637. Except for Pomerania, none of these lands was contiguous with Brandenburg. East Prussia lay inside

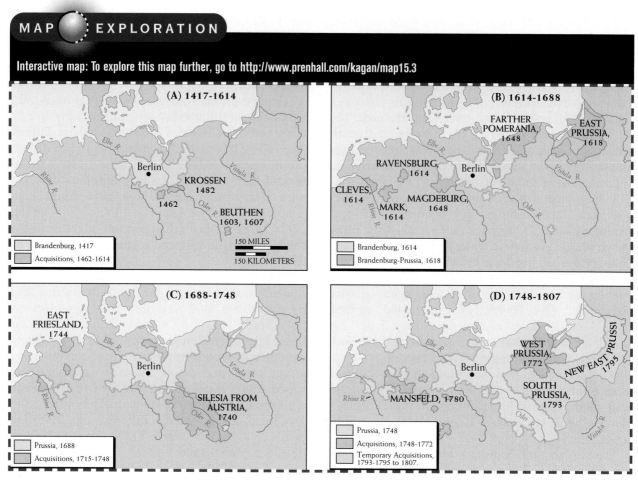

MAP 🔘 **EXPLORATION**

Interactive map: To explore this map further, go to http://www.prenhall.com/kagan/map15.3

MAP 15–3 EXPANSION OF BRANDENBURG-PRUSSIA *In the seventeenth century, Brandenburg-Prussia expanded mainly by acquiring dynastic titles in geographically separated lands. In the eighteenth century, it expanded through aggression to the east, seizing Silesia in 1740 and various parts of Poland in 1772, 1793, and 1795.*

Poland and outside the authority of the Holy Roman Emperor. All of the territories lacked good natural resources, and many of them were devastated during the Thirty Years' War. At Westphalia the Hohenzollerns lost part of Pomerania to Sweden, but were compensated by receiving three more bishoprics and the promise of the archbishopric of Magdeburg when it became vacant, as it did in 1680. By the late seventeenth century, the scattered Hohenzollern holdings represented a block of territory within the Holy Roman Empire second in size only to that of the Habsburgs.

Frederick William, the Great Elector The person who began to forge these separated regions and diverse nobles into a modern state was Frederick William (r. 1640–1688), who became known as the Great Elector. (The ruler of Brandenburg was called an *elector* because he was one of the princes who

elected the Holy Roman Emperor.) He established himself and his successors as the central uniting power by breaking the local noble estates, organizing a royal bureaucracy, and establishing a strong army. (See "The Great Elector Welcomes Protestant Refugees from France.")

Between 1655 and 1660, Sweden and Poland engaged in a war that endangered the Great Elector's holdings in Pomerania and East Prussia. Frederick William had neither the military nor the financial resources to confront this threat. In 1655, the Brandenburg estates1 refused to grant him new taxes; however, he proceeded to collect the required taxes by military force. In 1659, a different grant of taxes, originally made in 1653, elapsed; Frederick William continued to collect them, as well as those he had imposed by his own authority. He used the money to build up an army that allowed him to continue to enforce his will without

THE GREAT ELECTOR WELCOMES PROTESTANT REFUGEES FROM FRANCE

The Hohenzollern dynasty of Brandenburg-Prussia pursued a policy of religious toleration. The family itself was Calvinist, whereas most of its subjects were Lutherans. When Louis XIV of France revoked the Edict of Nantes in 1685, Frederick William, the Great Elector, seized the opportunity to invite French Protestants into his realms. As his proclamation indicates, he wanted to attract persons with productive skills who could aid the economic development of his domains.

■ *In reading this document, do you believe religious or economic concerns more nearly led the elector of Brandenburg to welcome the French Protestants? What specific privileges did the elector extend to them? To what extent were these privileges a welcoming measure, and to what extent were they inducements to emigrate to Brandenburg? In what kind of economic activity does the elector expect the French refugees to engage?*

We, Friedrich Wilhelm, by Grace of God Margrave of Brandenburg . . .

Do hereby proclaim and make known to all and sundry that since the cruel persecutions and rigorous ill-treatment in which Our co-religionists of the Evangelical-Reformed faith have for some time past been subjected in the Kingdom of France, have caused many families to remove themselves and to betake themselves out of the said Kingdom into other lands, We now . . . have been moved graciously to offer them through this Edict . . . a secure and free refuge in all Our Lands and Provinces. . . .

Since Our Lands are not only well and amply endowed with all things necessary to support life, but also very well-suited to the reestablishment of all kinds of manufactures and trade and traffic by land and water, We permit, indeed, to those settling therein free choice to establish themselves where it is most convenient for their profession and way of living. . . .

The personal property which they bring with them, including merchandise and other wares, is to be totally exempt from any taxes, customs dues, licenses, or other imposts of any description, and not detained in any way. . . .

As soon as these Our French co-religionists of the Evangelical-Reformed faith have settled in any town or village, they shall be admitted to the domiciliary rights and craft freedoms customary there, gratis and without payments of any fee; and shall be entitled to the benefits, rights, and privileges enjoyed by Our other, native, subjects, residing there. . . .

Not only are those who wish to establish manufacture of cloth, stuffs, hats, or other objects in which they are skilled to enjoy all necessary freedoms, privileges and facilities, but also provision is to be made for them to be assisted and helped as far as possible with money and anything else which they need to realize their intention. . . .

Those who settle in the country and wish to maintain themselves by agriculture are to be given a certain plot of land to bring under cultivation and provided with whatever they need to establish themselves initially. . . .

From C. A. Macartney, ed., *The Habsburg and Hohenzollern Dynasties in the Seventeenth and Eighteenth Centuries* (New York: Walker, 1970), pp. 270–273.

the approval of the nobility. Similar threats and coercion took place against the nobles in his other territories.

There did occur, however, an important political and social trade-off between the elector and his various nobles: In exchange for their obedience to the Hohenzollerns, the **Junkers** received the right to demand obedience from their serfs. Frederick William also tended to choose as the local administrators of the tax structure men who would normally have been members of the noble estates. He thus coopted potential opponents into his service.

Austria and Prussia in the Late Seventeenth and Early Eighteenth Centuries

1640–1688	Reign of Frederick William, the Great Elector
1658–1705	Leopold I rules Austria and resists the Turkish invasions
1683	Turkish siege of Vienna
1688–1713	Reign of Frederick I of Prussia
1699	Peace treaty between Turks and Habsburgs
1711–1740	Charles VI rules Austria and secures agreement to the Pragmatic Sanction
1713–1740	Frederick William I builds up the military power of Prussia
1740	Maria Theresa succeeds to the Habsburg throne
1740	Frederick II violates the Pragmatic Sanction by invading Silesia

His taxes fell most heavily on the backs of the peasants and the urban classes.

Frederick William I, King of Prussia Yet, even with the considerable accomplishments of the Great Elector, the house of Hohenzollern did not possess a crown. The achievement of a royal title was one of the few state-building accomplishments of Frederick I (r. 1688–1713). This son of the Great Elector was the least "Prussian" of his family during these crucial years. He built palaces, founded Halle University (1694), patronized the arts, and lived luxuriously. In 1701, however, at the outbreak of the War of the Spanish Succession, he put his valuable, well-trained army at the disposal of the Habsburg Holy Roman Emperor. In exchange for this loyal service, the emperor permitted Frederick to assume the title of "King in Prussia." Thereafter Frederick became Frederick I, and he passed the much-desired royal title to his son Frederick William I in 1713.

Frederick William I (r. 1713–1740) was both the most eccentric and one of the most effective Hohenzollerns. His political aims seem to have been the consolidation of an obedient, compliant bureaucracy and the establishment of a bigger army. He initiated a policy of *Kabinett* government, which meant that lower officials submitted all relevant documents to him in his office, or *Kabinett*. Then he alone examined the papers, made his decisions, and issued his orders. He thus skirted the influence of ministers and ruled alone.

Frederick William I organized the bureaucracy along military lines. He united all departments under the *General-Ober-Finanz-Kriegs-und-Domänen-Direktorium*, more happily known to us as the General Directory. He imposed taxes on the nobility and changed most remaining feudal dues into monetary payments. He sought to transform feudal and administrative loyalties into a sense of duty to the monarch as a political institution rather than as a person. He once described the perfect royal servant as an intelligent, assiduous, and alert person who after God values nothing higher than his king's pleasure and serves him out of love and for the sake of honor rather than money and who in his conduct solely seeks and constantly bears in mind his king's service and interests, who, moreover, abhors all intrigues and emotional deterrents.[1]

Service to the state and the monarch was to become impersonal, mechanical, and, in effect, unquestioning.

The Prussian Army During Frederick William's reign, the size of the army grew from about 39,000 in 1713 to more than 80,000 in 1740. It was the third or fourth largest army in Europe, whereas Prussia ranked thirteenth in population. Rather than using recruiters, the king made each canton or local district responsible for supplying a quota of soldiers.

After 1725, Frederick William I always wore an officer's uniform. He formed one regiment from the tallest soldiers he could find in Europe. Separate laws applied to the army and to civilians. Laws, customs, and royal attention made the officer corps the highest social class of the state. Military service attracted the sons of Junkers. Thus, the army, the Junker nobility, and the monarchy were forged into a single political entity. Military priorities and values dominated Prussian government, society, and daily life as in no other state of Europe. It has often been said that whereas other nations possessed armies, the Prussian army possessed its nation.

Although Frederick William I built the best army in Europe, he avoided conflict. He wanted to drill his soldiers, but not to order them into battle. The army was for him a symbol of Prussian power and unity, not an instrument to be used for foreign adventures or aggression.

---

[1]Quoted in Hans Rosenberg, *Bureaucracy, Aristocracy, and Autocracy* (Boston: Beacon Press, 1958), p. 93.

At his death in 1740, he passed to his son Frederick II, later known as "the Great" (r. 1740–1786), this superb military machine, but he could not also pass on the wisdom to refrain from using it. Almost immediately on coming to the throne, Frederick II upset the Pragmatic Sanction, invaded Silesia, and thus crystallized the Austrian-Prussian rivalry for control of Germany that would dominate central European affairs for over a century.

Russia Enters the European Political Arena

Though ripe with consequences for the future, the rise of Prussia and the new consolidation of the Austrian Habsburg domains seemed to many at the time only another shift in the long-troubled German scene. The emergence of Russia, however, as an active European power was a wholly new factor in European politics. Previously, Russia had been considered part of Europe only by courtesy, and before 1673 it did not send permanent ambassadors to western Europe, though it had sent various diplomatic missions since the fifteenth century. Geographically and politically, it lay on the periphery. Hemmed in by Sweden on the Baltic and by the Ottoman Empire on the Black Sea, Russia had no warm-water ports. Its chief outlet for trade to the west was Archangel on the White Sea, which was ice free for only part of the year. What Russia did possess was a vast reserve of largely undeveloped natural and human resources.

BIRTH OF THE ROMANOV DYNASTY

The reign of Ivan the Terrible, which had begun so well and closed so frighteningly, was followed by anarchy and civil war known as the "Time of Troubles." In 1613, hoping to restore stability, an assembly of nobles elected a seventeen-year-old boy named Michael Romanov (r. 1613–1654) as tsar. Thus began the dynasty that, despite palace revolutions, military conspiracies, assassinations, and family strife, ruled Russia until 1917.

Michael Romanov and his two successors, Aleksei (r. 1654–1676) and Theodore II (r. 1676–1682), brought stability and modest bureaucratic centralization to Russia. The country remained, however, weak and impoverished. After years of turmoil, the bureaucracy was still largely controlled by the *boyars*, the old nobility. This administrative apparatus could barely suppress a revolt of peasants and Cossacks (horsemen who lived on the steppe frontier) under Stepan Razin in 1670–1671. Furthermore, the government and the tsars faced the danger of mutiny from the *streltsy*, or guards of the Moscow garrison.

PETER THE GREAT

In 1682, another boy—ten years old at the time—ascended the fragile Russian throne as co-ruler with his half brother. His name was Peter (r. 1682–1725), and Russia would never be the same after him. He and the sickly Ivan V had come to power on the shoulders of the *streltsy*, who expected to be rewarded for their support. Much violence and bloodshed had surrounded the disputed succession. Matters became even more confused when the boys' sister, Sophia, was named regent. Peter's followers overthrew her in 1689. From that date onward, Peter ruled personally, although in theory he shared the crown until Ivan died in 1696. The dangers and turmoil of his youth convinced Peter of two things: first, the power of the tsar must be made secure from the jealousy of the *boyars* and the greed of the *streltsy*; second, the military power of Russia must be increased. In both respects, he self-consciously resembled Louis XIV of France, who had experienced the turmoil of the *Fronde* during his youth and resolved to establish a strong monarchy safe from the nobility and defended by a powerful army.

Northwestern Europe, particularly the military resources of the maritime powers, fascinated Peter I, who eventually became known as Peter the Great. In 1697, he made a famous visit in transparent disguise to western Europe. There he dined and talked with the great and the powerful, who considered this almost seven-foot-tall ruler crude. He spent his happiest moments on the trip inspecting shipyards, docks, and the manufacture of military hardware in England and the Netherlands. While Peter traveled in northwestern Europe, he had ordered other Russians to travel elsewhere on the Continent to learn languages and new commercial and military skills. An imitator of the first order, Peter returned to Moscow determined to copy what he had seen abroad, for he knew warfare would be necessary to make Russia a great power. But he understood his goal would require him to confront the long-standing power and traditions of the Russian nobles.

Rise of Russian Power	
1533–1584	Reign of Ivan the Terrible
1584–1613	"Time of Troubles"
1613	Michael Romanov becomes tsar
1682	Peter the Great, age ten, becomes tsar
1689	Peter assumes personal rule
1696	Russia captures Azov on the Black Sea from the Turks
1697	European tour of Peter the Great
1698	Peter returns to Russia to put down the revolt of the *streltsy*
1700	The Great Northern War opens between Russia and Sweden; Russia defeated at Narva by Swedish army of Charles XII
1703	St. Petersburg founded
1709	Russia defeats Sweden at the Battle of Poltava
1718	Charles XII of Sweden dies
1718	Son of Peter the Great dies in prison under mysterious circumstances
1721	Peace of Nystad ends the Great Northern War
1721	Peter establishes a synod for the Russian church
1722	Peter issues the Table of Ranks
1725	Peter dies, leaving an uncertain succession

Taming the *Streltsy* and *Boyars*

In 1698, prior to Peter's return from abroad, the *streltsy* had rebelled. On his return, Peter brutally suppressed the revolt with private tortures and public executions, in which Peter's own ministers took part. Approximately a thousand of the rebels were put to death, and their corpses remained on public display to discourage future disloyalty. (See "Encountering the Past: Public Executions.")

The new military establishment that Peter built would serve the tsar and not itself. He introduced effective and ruthless policies of conscription, drafting an unprecedented 130,000 soldiers during the first decade of the eighteenth century and almost 300,000 troops by the end of his reign. He had adopted policies for the officer corps and general military discipline patterned on those of west European armies.

Peter also determined to make a sustained attack on the *boyars* and their attachment to traditional Russian culture. After his European journey, he personally shaved the long beards of the court *boyars*

and sheared off the customary long hand-covering sleeves of their shirts and coats, which had made them the butt of jokes among other European courts. During the 1690s, Peter had gradually stopped granting *boyar* status to new individuals. Throughout his reign he made numerous major decisions in both foreign and domestic policy without consulting the *boyars*. Consequently, Peter faced considerable opposition from troublesome and potentially seditious factions of court nobility. Never able fully to dominate them, he became highly skilled at balancing one group off against another while never completely excluding any as he set about to organize Russian government and military forces along the lines of the more powerful European states.

Developing a Navy

When Peter came to the throne, Russia had no real navy. One historian has described the building of a Russian navy as "Peter the Great's most revolutionary innovation."[2] The creation of a navy was one part of Peter's strategy to secure warm-water ports that would allow Russia to trade with the West and to influence European affairs.

In the mid-1690s, he oversaw the construction of ships to protect his interests in the Black Sea against the Ottoman Empire. In 1695, he began a war with the Ottomans and captured Azov on the Black Sea in 1696.[3] Part of the reason for Peter's trip to western Europe in 1697 was to learn how to build still better warships, this time for combat on the Baltic. The construction of a Baltic fleet, largely constructed on the Finnish coast, was essential in the Great Northern War with Sweden, a struggle that over the years accounted for many of Peter's major steps toward westernizing his realm.

Russian Expansion in the Baltic: The Great Northern War

Following the end of the Thirty Years' War in 1648, Sweden had consolidated its control of the Baltic, thus preventing Russian possession of a port on that sea and permitting Polish and German access to the sea only on Swedish terms. The Swedes also had one of the better armies in Europe. Sweden's economy, however, based primarily on the export

---

[2]Simon Dixon, *The Modernization of Russia, 1676–1825* (Cambridge: Cambridge University Press, 1999), p. 35.

[3]Although Peter had to return Azov to the Ottomans in 1711, its recapture became a goal of Russian foreign policy. See Chapter 18.

Public Executions

Executions—the judicial taking of life—are the most stringent exercise of authority. In early modern Europe most executions were held in public before crowds of onlookers.

The ritual of the public execution changed little from the close of the Middle Ages through the end of the eighteenth century. Executions were carried out by professional executioners, a trade that was often passed from father to son. Hanging was the most common method, but the condemned could also be "broken on the wheel" (have their bones fractured and then be strangled), burned at the stake, beheaded, or buried alive with a stake driven through their heart (a penalty often reserved for women in central Europe). The condemned person was taken in a procession from prison to the place of execution. Normally a clergyman accompanied the prisoner—a sign that church and state agreed the death penalty was appropriate. The crowds before whom the judgment would be read and the condemned person permitted to speak expected the penalty to be carried out efficiently, without any more suffering than necessary. Careless or inept executioners could provoke a riot. Often, however, a carnival atmosphere surrounded the proceedings. Hawkers sold food and drink or pamphlets and woodcuts about the criminal. As a warning the bodies or heads of common criminals and political offenders were frequently left to rot in a public place after the execution.

For centuries most Europeans appear to have accepted the need for these executions and to have gained satisfaction, if not enjoyment, from watching them. Order had to be maintained and crime punished. Retribution was a valid social and religious norm, and although some of the common people may have resented the power of the state and the way local social elites enforced the law, it was ordinary people, then as now, who were most often the victims of crime. Moreover, most of those who were executed appear to have committed what their societies regarded as terrible crimes—murder, incest, rape, treason, banditry. In condemning these offenders to death, the courts thus upheld the law and the expectations of the local communities, both of which were harsh. The courts also understood, however, that too frequent imposition of the death penalty might lead to public disapproval and unrest.

From the early 1600s onward, the number of executions actually carried out declined across Europe. Hard service—rowing naval galleys, imprisonment, and, in Britain, being shipped to Australia—became substitutes for execution. Although some thinkers during the Enlightenment condemned capital punishment itself (see Chapter 18), public executions continued throughout Europe during the nineteenth century. From the late nineteenth century onward, however, executions in Europe increasingly occurred within prisons. The last public execution occurred in France in 1939. The law might still require execution for certain crimes, but the state no longer considered it edifying—or even decent—for the public to witness it. Executions were no longer a public spectacle.

After World War II, the nations of Western Europe began to do away with the death penalty in reaction to the Nazi Holocaust and as a result of campaigns for its abolition. Since 1998, no state can be a member of the European Union unless it abolishes the death penalty.

■ *Why did most Europeans support public executions in the early modern period? Why did support for capital punishment eventually weaken in Europe?*

Julius R. Ruff, *Violence in Early Modern Europe, 1500–1800* (Cambridge: Cambridge University Press, 2001); V. A. C. Gatrell, *The Hanging Tree: Execution and the English People, 1770–1868* (Oxford: Oxford University Press, 1994); Richard J. Evans, *Rituals of Retribution: Capital Punishment in Germany, 1600–1987* (Oxford: Oxford University Press, 1996)

The execution of Colonel Turner © Bettmann/Corbis

of iron, was not strong enough to ensure continued political success.

In 1697, Charles XII (r. 1697–1718) came to the throne. He was headstrong, to say the least, and perhaps insane. In 1700, Peter the Great began a drive to the west against Swedish territory to gain a foothold on the Baltic. In the resulting Great Northern War (1700–1721), Charles XII led a vigorous and often brilliant campaign defeating the Russians at the Battle of Narva (1700). As the conflict dragged on, however, Peter was able to strengthen his forces. By 1709, he decisively defeated the Swedes at the Battle of Poltava. Thereafter, the Swedes could maintain only a holding action against their enemies. Charles himself sought refuge in Turkey and did not return to Sweden until 1714. He was killed under uncertain circumstances four years later while fighting the Danes in Norway. When the Great Northern War came to a close in 1721, the Peace of Nystad confirmed the Russian conquest of Estonia, Livonia, and part of Finland. Henceforth, Russia possessed ice-free ports and a permanent influence on European affairs.

FOUNDING ST. PETERSBURG

At one point, the domestic and foreign policies of Peter the Great intersected. This was at the site on the Gulf of Finland where he founded his new capital city of St. Petersburg in 1703. There he built government structures and compelled the *boyars* to construct town houses. He thus imitated those European monarchs who had copied Louis XIV by constructing smaller versions of Versailles. The founding of St. Petersburg went beyond establishing a central imperial court, however; it symbolized a new Western orientation of Russia and Peter's determination to hold his position on the Baltic coast. He had begun the construction of the city and had moved the capital there even before his

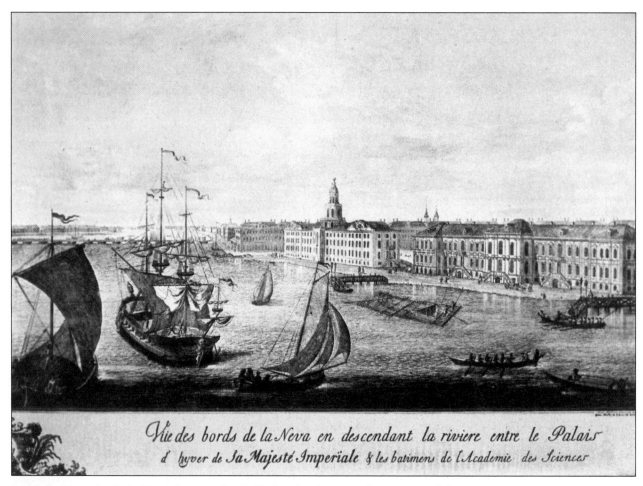

Peter the Great built St. Petersburg on the Gulf of Finland to provide Russia with better contact with western Europe. He moved Russia's capital there from Moscow in 1712. This is an eighteenth-century view of the city. The Granger Collection

victory over Sweden was assured. Moreover, he and his successors employed architects from western Europe for many of the most prominent buildings in and around the city. Consequently, St. Petersburg looked different from other Russian cities. Both in Peter's day and later, many Russians saw St. Petersburg as a kind of illegitimate west European growth on Russian culture that symbolized Peter's autocracy and rejection of traditional Russian life and government.

REORGANIZING DOMESTIC ADMINISTRATION

Hard upon his successes in the war against Sweden, Peter in 1711 created a Senate of nine members. The Senate, which replaced the former Privy Chancellery, was to direct virtually all aspects of government when the tsar was away with the army. The purpose of this and other more local administrative reforms was to establish a bureaucratic structure that could support an efficient military establishment.

The Senate was also intended to represent the authority of the tsar against intriguing court nobles. The membership of the Senate would shift as Peter's political favorites changed. Over time, however, the Senate itself would become a center for intrigue and possible opposition to Peter's policies. These would come to a head in a conspiracy involving Peter's son.

THE CASE OF PETER'S SON ALEKSEI

Peter's son Aleksei had been born to his first wife whom he had divorced in 1698. Peter was jealous of the young man, who had never demonstrated strong intelligence or ambition, and feared that Aleksei might undertake sedition by gathering court factions around him or by cooperating with foreign rulers. Over the years Peter had constantly quarreled with Alexsei, criticizing the young man's shortcomings as a future ruler. (See "Peter the Great Tells His Son to Acquire Military Skills.") By 1716, Peter was becoming convinced that his opponents looked to Aleksei as a focus for their possible sedition while Russia remained at war with Sweden.

Late that year Aleksei undertook a secret visit to Vienna where he appears to have entered into a vague military plot with the Habsburg emperor Charles VI against Peter's interests in the Great Northern War. There is evidence that Sweden itself was interested in furthering this conspiracy. Nothing actually came of these secret conversations, however, although Aleksei remained under the protection of Charles VI until late in 1717 when the emperor decided the whole affair was too dangerous. Much compromised, Alexsei then returned to Russia surrounded by rumors and suspicions.

Peter, who was investigating official corruption, realized his son might become a rallying point for those he accused. Early in 1718, when Aleksei reappeared in St. Petersburg, the tsar began to look into his son's relationships with Charles VI and with Russian nobles including members of the Senate opposed to Peter's policies. Peter discovered that although any actual conspiracy probably did not extend beyond Aleksei and Charles VI, had those two moved against him, numerous Russian nobles, administrators, and churchmen might have joined them. During this six-month investigation Peter personally interrogated Aleksei, who was eventually condemned to death and died under mysterious circumstances on June 26, 1718. The case of the tsar's son had enormous ramifications for the rest of Peter's reign.

REFORMS OF PETER THE GREAT'S FINAL YEARS

The difficulties between Peter and his son were much more than a tragic family quarrel. The interrogations surrounding Aleksei had revealed greater degrees of court opposition than Peter had suspected. Recognizing he could not eliminate his numerous opponents the way he had attacked the *streltsy* in 1698, Peter undertook radical administrative reforms designed to bring the nobility and the Russian Orthodox Church more closely under the authority of persons loyal to the tsar. As an historian has commented recently, "The case of Aleksei was the greatest spur to Peter's reform in the history of the reign, greater even than the Northern War."[4]

Administrative Colleges In December 1717, while his son was returning to Russia, Peter reorganized his domestic administration to sustain his own personal authority and to fight rampant corruption. To achieve this goal, Peter looked to Swedish institutions called *colleges*—bureaus of several persons operating according to written instructions rather than departments headed by a single minister. These colleges, eight of which he

---

[4]Peter Bushkovitch, *Peter the Great: The Search for Power, 1671–1725* (Cambridge: Cambridge University Press, 2001), p. 425.

PETER THE GREAT TELLS HIS SON TO ACQUIRE MILITARY SKILLS

Enormous hostility existed between Peter the Great and his son Aleksei. Peter believed his son was not prepared to inherit the throne. In October 1715, he composed a long letter to Aleksei in which he berated him for refusing to take military matters seriously. The letter indicates how an early-eighteenth-century ruler saw the conduct of warfare as a fundamental part of the role of a monarch. Peter also points to Louis XIV of France as a role model. Peter and Aleksei did not reach an agreement. Aleksei died under mysterious circumstances in 1718, with Peter possibly responsible for his death.

■ *How did Peter use the recent war with Sweden to argue for the necessity of his son acquiring military skills? What concept of leadership does Peter attempt to communicate to his son? Why did Peter see military prowess as the most important ability in a ruler?*

You cannot be ignorant of what is known to all the world, to what degree our people groaned under the oppression of the Swede before the beginning of the present war. . . . You know what it has cost us in the beginning of this war . . . to make ourselves experienced in the art of war, and to put a stop to those advantages which our implacable enemies obtained over us. . . .

But you even will not so much as hear warlike exercises mentioned: though it was by them that we broke through that obscurity in which we were involved, and that we make ourselves known to nations, whose esteem we share at present.

I do not exhort you to make war without lawful reasons: I only desire you to apply yourself to learn the art of it: for it is impossible well to govern without knowing the rules and discipline of it, was it for no other end than for the defense of the country. . . .

You mistake, if you think it is enough for a prince to have good generals to act under his order. Everyone looks upon the head; they study its inclinations and conform themselves to them: all the world own this. . . .

You have no inclination to learn war. You do not apply yourself to it, and consequently you will never learn it: And how then can you command others, and judge of the reward which those deserve who do their duty, or punish others who fail of it? You will do nothing, nor judge of anything but by the assent and help of others, like a young bird that holds up his bill to be fed. . . .

If you think there are some, whose affairs do not fail of success, though they do not go to war themselves; it is true: But if they do not go themselves, yet they have an inclination for it, and understand it.

For instance, the late King of France did not always take the field in person; but it is known to what degree he loved war, and what glorious exploits he performed in it, which make his campaigns to be called the theatre and school of the world. His inclinations were not confined solely to military affairs, he also loved mechanics, manufacture and other establishment, which rendered his kingdom more flourishing than any other whatsoever.

From Friedrich C. Weber, *The Present State of Russia* (London, 1722), 2:97–100; *The Global Experience*, 3/3rd ed., Vol. 2 by P. F. Riley, © 1998. Reprinted by permission of Prentice Hall, Inc., Upper Saddle River, NJ.

imposed on Russian administration, were to look after matters such as the collection of taxes, foreign relations, war, and economic affairs. Each college was to receive advice from a foreigner. Peter used his appointive power to balance the influence in these colleges between nobles and persons he was certain would be personally loyal to himself. The presence of the colleges to some degree balanced the influence of the Senate where Aleksei had sympathizers.

Table of Ranks Peter made another major administrative reform with important consequences when in 1722 he published a **Table of Ranks** intended to draw the nobility into state service. That table equated a person's social position and privileges with his rank in the bureaucracy or the military, rather than with his lineage among the traditional landed nobility, many of whom continued to resent the changes Peter had introduced into Russia. Peter thus made the social standing of individual *boyars* a function of their willingness to serve the central state. Earlier tsars had created some service nobles on the basis of merit, but none had envisioned drawing all nobles into state service. Unlike Prussian Junkers, however, the Russian nobility never became perfectly loyal to the state. They repeatedly sought to reassert their independence and their control of the Russian imperial court and to bargain with later tsars over local authority and the nobles' dominance of the serfs.

Achieving Secular Control of the Church Peter also moved to suppress the independence of the Russian Orthodox Church. Here Peter was confronting a problem that had arisen both in the turbulent decades preceding his reign and from the sympathy some church leaders had displayed toward Aleksei.

The history of the Russian Orthodox Church of this era is extremely complicated. In the mid–seventeenth century, a reformist movement led by Patriarch Nikon had introduced changes into church texts and ritual. A group of Russian Orthodox Christians, known as the **Old Believers**, strongly opposed these changes. Although condemned by the hierarchy, the Old Believers persisted in their opposition. Thousands committed suicide rather than submit to the new rituals. In response to this traditionalist opposition, church leaders began to advocate both popular preaching and a more Western form of clerical education, including the teaching of Latin. In that respect, like Peter, they were modernizers, but they moved too slowly to please the tsar. Consequently, by 1700 he had begun to appoint his own bishops, especially Ukrainians, many of whom had been trained in European schools. But both reform-minded Ukrainian and Russian-born bishops objected to Peter's heavy-handed influence on religious matters. Those objections lay behind their sympathy for the tsar's son.

After Aleksei's death, Peter set about curtailing the capacity of the Russian Orthodox Church to oppose his interference in its affairs and to meddle in politics. In 1721, he simply abolished the position of *patriarch*, the bishop who had been head of the church. In its place he established a government department called the *Holy Synod*, which consisted of several bishops headed by a layman, called the *procurator general*. This body would govern the church in accordance with the tsar's secular requirements. This ecclesiastical reorganization, which drew on German Lutheran models, was the most radical transformation of a traditional institution in Peter's reign. It produced further futile opposition from the Old Believers, who saw the tsar as leading the church into new heresy. Peter's policy toward the Russian church stood in sharp contrast to the Ottoman sultans' contemporary policy of deference to the Muslim Ulama.

For all the numerous decisive actions Peter had taken since 1718, he still had not settled on a successor. Consequently, when he died in 1725, there was no clear line of succession to the throne. For more than thirty years, soldiers and nobles again determined who ruled Russia. Peter had laid the foundations of a modern Russia, but not the foundations of a stable state.

In Perspective

By the second quarter of the eighteenth century, the major European powers were not nation-states in which the citizens felt themselves united by a shared sense of community, culture, language, and history. Rather, they were monarchies in which the personality of the ruler and the personal relationships of the great noble families exercised considerable influence over public affairs. The monarchs, except in Great Britain, had generally succeeded in making their power greater than the nobility's. The power of the aristocracy and its capacity to resist or obstruct the policies of the monarch were not destroyed, however.

In Britain, of course, the nobility had tamed the monarchy, but even there tension between nobles and monarchs would continue throughout the rest of the century.

In foreign affairs, the new arrangement of military and diplomatic power established early in the century prepared the way for two long conflicts. The first was a commercial rivalry for trade and overseas empire between France and Great Britain. During the reign of Louis XIV, these two nations had collided over the French bid for dominance in Europe. During the eighteenth century, they dueled for control of commerce on other continents. The second arena of warfare was in central Europe, where Austria and Prussia fought for the leadership of the German states.

Behind these international conflicts and the domestic rivalry of monarchs and nobles, however, the society of eighteenth-century Europe began to change. The character and the structures of the societies over which the monarchs ruled were beginning to take on some features associated with the modern age. These economic and social developments would eventually transform the life of Europe to a degree beside which the state building of the early-eighteenth-century monarchs paled.

REVIEW QUESTIONS

1. Why did Britain and France remain leading powers in western Europe while the United Netherlands declined?

2. How did the structure of British government change under the leadership of Robert Walpole?

3. Compare and contrast the weakening of the Ottoman Empire with the rise of Russia under Peter the Great.

4. How were the Hohenzollerns able to forge their diverse landholdings into the state of Prussia? How did the Habsburgs try to resolve their problems? Were the Habsburgs as successful as the Hohenzollerns?

5. Why did Sweden, the Ottoman Empire, and Poland decline?

6. How and why did Russia emerge as a great power? What were Russia's domestic problems before Peter the Great came to power? To what extent did his reforms succeed? What problems did his son cause? Compare and contrast Peter the Great with Louis XIV of France.

7. How did the problems and uncertainties of who would and could succeed to the thrones of the various states constitute one of the major political and diplomatic problems of European politics between approximately 1685 and 1740?

SUGGESTED READINGS

T. M. BARKER, *Army, Aristocracy, Monarchy: Essays in War, Society and Government in Austria, 1618–1780* (1982). Examines the intricate power relationships among these major institutions.

J. BLACK, *Eighteenth-Century Europe, 1700–1789* (1990). An excellent survey.

C. R. BOXER, *The Dutch Seaborne Empire* (1965). Remains the best treatment of the subject.

J. BREWER, *The Sinews of Power: War, Money and the English State, 1688–1783* (1989). An extremely important study of the financial basis of English power.

P. BUSHKOVITCH, *Peter the Great: The Struggle for Power, 1671–1725* (2001). Replaces all previous studies.

J. C. D. CLARK, *English Society: 1688–1832: Social Structure and Political Practice during the Ancien Régime* (1985). An important, controversial work that emphasizes the role of religion in English political life.

N. DAVIS, *God's Playground*, Vol. 1 (1991). Excellent on prepartition Poland.

J. DE VRIES AND A. VAN DER WOUDE, *The First Modern Economy* (1997). An account of Holland comparing it to other European nations.

W. DOYLE, *The Old European Order, 1660–1800* (1992). The most thoughtful treatment of the subject.

R. J. W. EVANS, *The Making of the Habsburg Monarchy, 1550–1700: An Interpretation* (1979). Places much emphasis on intellectual factors and the role of religion.

F. FORD, *Robe and Sword: The Regrouping of the French Aristocracy after Louis XIV* (1953). Remains important for political, social, and intellectual history.

C. J. INGRAO, *The Habsburg Monarchy, 1618–1815* (1994). The best recent survey.

J. I. ISRAEL, *The Dutch Republic, Its Rise, Greatness, and Fall, 1477–1806* (1995). The major survey of the subject.

R. A. KANN AND Z. V. DAVID, *The Peoples of the Eastern Habsburg Lands, 1526–1918* (1984). A helpful overview of the subject.

D. MCKAY, *The Great Elector: Frederick William of Brandenburg-Prussia* (2001). An account of the origins of Prussian power.

D. MCKAY AND H. M. SCOTT, *The Rise of the Great Powers, 1648–1815* (1983). Now a standard survey.

G. PARKER, *The Military Revolution: Military Innovation and the Rise of the West (1500–1800)* (1988). A major work.

S. SCHAMA, *An Embarrassment of Riches: An Interpretation of Dutch Culture in the Golden Age* (1987). Lively and controversial.

P. F. SUGAR, *Southeastern Europe under Ottoman Rule, 1354–1804* (1977). An extremely clear presentation.

DOCUMENTS CD-ROM

Absolutism

Rachel Ruysch, *Flower Still Life*: Flowers, Commerce, and Morality

Rachel Ruysch, Dutch, 1664–1750, *Flower Still Life (1956.57).* The Toledo Museum of Art, Toledo, Ohio; Purchased with funds from the Libbey Endowment, Gift of Edward Drummond Libbey

Paintings often are intended to convey more than first meets the eye. Such is more or less obvious in allegorical scenes in which themes appear in the guise of ancient gods or other mythological figures. But a painting of objects of everyday life arranged on tables, known as a still life, can also hold deep symbolic and cultural meaning. From the Middle Ages onward, particular flowers had religious meaning, but during the seventeenth century flowers took on more worldly associations.

Rachel Ruysch (1664–1750) was a Dutch woman artist living in Amsterdam who specialized in depicting elaborate arrangements of flowers. These paintings stand as very beautiful images, but they are also much more. The floral still life portrayed flowers usually raised from bulbs, a major Dutch commercial enterprise. Several decades before Ruysch completed this particular painting, *Flower Still Life* (after 1700), a financial mania had gripped Holland, with speculation in rare tulip bulbs reaching enormous extravagance before the bubble burst. Consequently, a painting such as this one from the early eighteenth century—and there were hundreds of such still-life floral works executed in seventeenth- and eighteenth-century Holland—would have recalled that event.

The flowers in this and other Dutch floral paintings represent work and commerce, not the natural bounty of the Dutch countryside. Commercial growers and traders brought such flowers to the Netherlands from its overseas empire and trading partners, and the flowers came to symbolize Dutch interaction with the most far-flung regions of the globe.

The variety of flowers in the bowl suggests wealth and abundance; these are valuable species, not humble objects of ordinary life. And never, except on canvas, would these flowers have bloomed at one time. Only the painter can gather them together in a single place at a single moment, in effect overcoming the cycle of nature.

Paintings such as this one have been called "a dialogue between this newly affluent society and its material possessions" and "an expression of how the phenomenon of plenty is to be viewed and understood."[5] These rich still-life paintings allowed the Calvinist Dutch to accommodate a morality that emphasized frugality and abstinence with life in the single wealthiest society in Europe. The melancholy surrounding the images conveys a lesson in the vanity and transience of earthly beauty and richness. All of these beautiful, valuable, rare natural objects, whether flowers or food, will soon decay. The flowers in this bowl, so stunning at the peak of their blossoming, will in a matter of days wilt and eventually rot. The insects buzzing about the flowers will also disappear. Even the empty snail shells on the table suggest that earthly life is only temporary. Similarly, the shadows in so many of the floral arrangements suggest the shadows that surround human life and the transience of both light and life. Yet, by owning a painting of an exquisite, diverse collection of flowers, one could possess an object of great beauty that would itself not decay.

The amazing attention to detail in Ruysch's work reflects the growth in botanical observation and knowledge during the previous century. Van Leeuwenhoek, the inventor of the microscope, hired artists to draw the organisms he could see through the instrument. That invention, as well as other Dutch optical achievements, such as the magnifying glass, led many artists to paint with enormous attention to detail.

Many of the most important illustrators of botanical manuals and other works of natural history were women. Among the leading figures was Anna Maria Sibylla Merian (1647–1717), a German woman who moved to the Netherlands and traveled to the Dutch colony of Surinam to study both plants and insects. Her work would have been enormously helpful to Ruysch, who would only rarely have worked from an actual bowl of real flowers.

■ *What does Ruysch's* Flower Still Life *tell us about the importance of flowers and commerce in seventeenth-century Holland? How does the painting indicate advances in botanical observations? How does the work deal with Calvinist morality and the richness and beauty of art?*

Sources: Norman Bryson, *Looking at the Overlooked: Four Essays on Still Life Painting* (Cambridge, MA: Harvard University Press, 1990); Mariët Westermann, *A Worldly Art: The Dutch Republic, 1585–1718* (Upper Saddle River, NJ, and New York: Prentice Hall and Harry N. Abrams, 1990); Marilyn Stokstad, *Art History*, rev. ed. (Upper Saddle River, NJ, and New York: Prentice Hall and Harry N. Abrams, 1999), pp. 798–801.

[5]Norman Bryson, *Looking at the Overlooked: Four Essays on Still Life Painting* (Cambridge, MA: Harvard University Press, 1990), p. 104.

This painting shows the pithead of an eighteenth-century coal mine in England. The machinery on the left includes a steam engine that powered equipment to bring mined coal to the surface or to pump water from the mine. Britain's rich veins of coal were one of the factors contributing to its early industrialization. *British School—A Pithead.* Board of Trustees of the National Museums and Galleries on Merseyside, Walker Art Galley, Liverpool

CHAPTER 16

SOCIETY AND ECONOMY UNDER THE OLD REGIME IN THE EIGHTEENTH CENTURY

*D*URING THE FRENCH REVOLUTION AND *the turmoil spawned by that upheaval, it became customary to refer to the patterns of social, political, and economic relationships that had existed in France before 1789 as the* ancien régime, *or the* **Old Regime.** *The term has come to be applied generally to the life and institutions of prerevolutionary Europe. Politically, it meant the rule of theoretically absolute monarchies with growing bureaucracies and aristocratically led armies. Economically, a scarcity of food, the predominance of agriculture, slow transport, a low level of iron production, comparatively unsophisticated financial institutions, and, in some cases, competitive commercial overseas empires characterized the Old Regime. Socially, men and women living during the period saw themselves less as individuals than as members of distinct corporate bodies that possessed certain privileges or rights as a group.*

Tradition, hierarchy, a corporate feeling, and privilege were the chief social characteristics of the Old Regime. Yet it was by no means a static society. Change and innovation were fermenting in its midst. Farming became more commercialized, and both food production and the size of the population increased. The early stages of the Industrial Revolution made more consumer goods available, and domestic consumption expanded throughout the century. The colonies in the Americas provided strong demand for European goods and manufactures. Merchants in seaports and other cities were expanding their businesses. By preparing their states for war, European governments put new demands on the resources and the economic organizations of their nations. The spirit of rationality that had been so important to the scientific revolution of the seventeenth century continued to manifest itself in the economic life of the eighteenth century. The Old Regime itself fostered the changes that eventually transformed it into a different kind of society.

KEY TOPICS

- The varied privileges and powers of Europe's aristocracies in the Old Regime and their efforts to increase their wealth
- The plight of rural peasants
- Family structure and family economy
- The transformation of Europe's economy by the Agricultural and Industrial Revolutions
- Urban growth and the social tensions that accompanied it
- The strains on the institutions of the Old Regime brought about by social change

Major Features of Life in the Old Regime

Socially, prerevolutionary Europe was based on (1) aristocratic elites possessing a wide variety of inherited legal privileges; (2) established churches intimately related to the state and the aristocracy; (3) an urban labor force usually organized into guilds; and (4) a rural peasantry subject to high taxes and feudal dues. Of course, the men and women living during this period did not know it was the Old Regime. Most of them earned their livelihoods and passed their lives as their forebears had done for generations before them and as they expected their children to do after them.

MAINTENANCE OF TRADITION

During the eighteenth century, the past weighed more heavily on people's minds than did the future. Few persons outside the government bureaucracies, the expanding merchant groups, and the movement for reform called the Enlightenment (see Chapter 18) considered change or innovation desirable. This was especially true of social relationships. Both nobles and peasants, for different reasons, repeatedly called for the restoration of traditional, or customary, rights. The nobles asserted what they considered their ancient rights against the intrusion of the expanding monarchical bureaucracies. The peasants, through petitions and revolts, called for the revival or the maintenance of the customary manorial rights that allowed them access to particular lands, courts, or grievance procedures.

Except for the early industrial development in Britain and the accompanying expansion of personal consumption, the eighteenth-century economy was also predominantly traditional. The quality and quantity of the grain harvest remained the most important fact of life for most of the population and the gravest concern for governments.

HIERARCHY AND PRIVILEGE

Closely related to this traditional social and economic outlook was the hierarchical structure of the society. The medieval sense of rank and degree not only persisted, but became more rigid during the century. In several continental cities, sumptuary laws regulating the dress of the different classes remained on the books. These laws forbade persons in one class or occupation from wearing clothes like those worn by their social superiors. The laws, which sought to make the social hierarchy easily visible, were largely ineffective by this time. What really enforced the hierarchy was the corporate nature of social relationships.

Each state or society was considered a community composed of numerous smaller communities. Eighteenth-century Europeans did not enjoy what Americans regard as "individual rights." Instead, a person enjoyed such rights and privileges as were guaranteed to the particular communities or groups of which she or he was a part. The "community" might include the village, the municipality, the nobility, the church, the guild, a university, or the parish. In turn, each of these bodies enjoyed certain privileges, some great and some small. The privileges might involve exemption from taxation or from some especially humiliating punishment, the right to practice a trade or craft, the right of one's children to pursue a particular occupation, or, for the church, the right to collect the tithe.

The Aristocracy

The eighteenth century was the great age of the aristocracy. The nobility constituted approximately 1 to 5 percent of the population of any given country. Yet in every country, the nobility was the single wealthiest sector of the population, had the widest degree of social, political, and economic power, and set the tone of polite society. In most countries, the nobility had their own separate house in the parliament, estates, or diet. Only nobles had any kind of representation in Hungary and Poland. Land continued to provide the aristocracy with its largest source of income, but aristocrats did not merely own estates: Their influence was felt throughout social and economic life. In much of Europe, however, it was felt that manual labor was regarded as beneath a noble. In Spain, it was assumed that even the poorer nobles would lead lives of idleness. In other nations, however, the nobility often fostered economic innovation and embraced the commercial spirit. Such willingness to change helped protect the nobility's wealth.

VARIETIES OF ARISTOCRATIC PRIVILEGE

To be an aristocrat was a matter of birth and legal privilege. This much the aristocracy had in common across the Continent. In almost every other respect, they differed markedly from country to country.

British Nobility The smallest, wealthiest, best defined, and most socially responsible aristocracy resided in Great Britain. It consisted of about four hundred families, and the eldest male members of each family sat in the House of Lords. Through the corruptions of the electoral system, these families also controlled many seats in the House of Commons. The estates of the British nobility ranged from a few thousand to fifty thousand acres, from which they received rents. The nobles owned about one-fourth of all the arable land in the country. Increasingly, the British aristocracy invested its wealth in commerce, canals, urban real estate, mines, and even industrial ventures. Because only the eldest son inherited the title and the land, younger sons moved into commerce, the army, the professions, and the church. British landowners in both houses of Parliament levied taxes and also paid them. They had few significant legal privileges, but their direct or indirect control of local government gave them immense political power and social influence. The aristocracy dominated the society and politics of the English counties. Their country houses, many of which were built in the eighteenth century, were centers for local society.

French Nobility The situation of the continental nobilities was less clear cut. In France, the approximately 400,000 nobles were divided between nobles "of the sword," or those whose nobility was derived from military service, and those "of the robe," or those who had acquired their titles either by serving in the bureaucracy or by having purchased them. The two groups had quarreled in the past, but often cooperated during the eighteenth century to defend their common privileges.

The foundation of aristocratic life was the possession of land. English aristocrats and large landowners controlled local government as well as the English Parliament. This painting of Robert Andrews and his wife by Thomas Gainsborough (1728–1788) shows an aristocratic couple on their estate. The gun and the hunting dog in this portrait suggest the importance landowners assigned to the virtually exclusive hunting privileges they enjoyed on their land. © National Gallery, London

The French nobles were also divided between those who held office or favor with the royal court at Versailles and those who did not. The court nobility reaped the immense wealth that could be gained from holding high office. The nobles' hold on such offices intensified during the century. By the late 1780s, appointments to the church, the army, and the bureaucracy, as well as other profitable positions, tended to go to the nobles already established in court circles. Whereas these well-connected aristocrats were rich, the provincial nobility, called *hobereaux*, were often little better off than wealthy peasants.

Despite differences in rank, origin, and wealth, certain hereditary privileges set all French aristocrats apart from the rest of society. They were exempt from many taxes. For example, most French nobles did not pay the *taille*, or land tax, the basic tax of the Old Regime. The nobles were technically liable for payment of the **vingtième,** or the "twentieth," which resembled an income tax, but they rarely had to pay it in full. The nobles were not liable for the royal *corvées*, or forced labor on public works, which fell on the peasants. In addition to these exemptions, French nobles could collect feudal dues from their tenants and enjoyed exclusive hunting and fishing privileges.

Eastern European Nobilities East of the Elbe River, the character of the nobility became even more complicated and repressive. Throughout the area, the military traditions of the aristocracy remained important. In Poland, there were thousands of nobles, or *szlachta*, who were entirely exempt from taxes after 1741. Until 1768, these Polish aristocrats possessed the right of life and death over their serfs. Most of the Polish nobility were relatively poor. A few rich nobles who had immense estates exercised political power in the fragile Polish state.

In Austria and Hungary, the nobility continued to possess broad judicial powers over the peasantry through their manorial courts. They also enjoyed various degrees of exemption from taxation. The wealthiest of them, Prince Esterhazy of Hungary, owned ten million acres of land.

In Prussia, after the accession of Frederick the Great in 1740, the position of the Junker nobles became much stronger. Frederick's various wars required their full support. He drew his officers almost wholly from the Junker class. Nobles also increasingly made up the bureaucracy. As in other parts of eastern Europe, the Prussian nobles had extensive judicial authority over the serfs.

In Russia, the eighteenth century saw what amounted to the creation of the nobility. Peter the Great's (r. 1682–1725) linking of state service and noble social status through the Table of Ranks (1722) established among Russian nobles a self-conscious class identity that had not previously existed. Thereafter, they were determined to resist compulsory state service. In 1736, Empress Anna (r. 1730–1740) reduced such service to twenty-five years. In 1762, Peter III (r. 1762) exempted the greatest nobles entirely from compulsory service. In 1785, in the Charter of the Nobility, Catherine the Great (r. 1762–1796) legally defined the rights and privileges of noble men and women in exchange for the assurance that the nobility would serve the state voluntarily. Noble privileges included the right of transmitting noble status to a nobleman's wife and children, the judicial protection of noble rights and property, considerable power over the serfs, and exemption from personal taxes.

ARISTOCRATIC RESURGENCE

The Russian Charter of the Nobility constituted one aspect of the broader European-wide development termed the **aristocratic resurgence.** This was the nobility's reaction to the threat to their social position and privileges that they felt from the expanding power of the monarchies. This resurgence took several forms in the eighteenth century. First, all nobilities tried to preserve their exclusiveness by making it more difficult to become a noble. Second, they pushed to reserve appointments to the officer corps of the armies, the bureaucracies, the government ministries, and the church exclusively for nobles. By doing this, they hoped to resist the encroaching power of the monarchies.

Third, the nobles attempted to use the authority of existing aristocratically controlled institutions against the power of the monarchies. These institutions included the British Parliament, the French courts, or *parlements*, and the local aristocratic estates and provincial diets in Germany and the Habsburg Empire.

Fourth, the nobility sought to improve its financial position by gaining further exemptions from taxation or by collecting higher rents or long-forgotten feudal dues from the peasantry. The nobility tried to shore up its position by various appeals to traditional and often ancient privileges that had lapsed over time. This aristocratic challenge to the monarchies was a fundamental political fact of the day and potentially a very disruptive one.

The Land and Its Tillers

Land was the economic basis of eighteenth-century life and the foundation of the status and power of the nobility. Well over three-fourths of all Europeans lived in the country, and few of them ever traveled more than a few miles from their birthplace. Except for the nobility and the wealthier nonaristocratic landowners, most people who dwelled on the land were poor—in many regions, desperately poor. They lived in various states of economic and social dependency, exploitation, and vulnerability.

PEASANTS AND SERFS

Rural social dependency related directly to the land. The nature of the dependency differed sharply for free peasants, such as English tenants and most French cultivators, and for the serfs of Germany, Austria, and Russia, who were legally bound to a particular plot of land and a particular lord. But everywhere, the class that owned most of the land also controlled the local government and the courts. For example, in Great Britain, all farmers and smaller tenants had the legal rights of English citizens. The justices of the peace, however, who presided over the county courts and who could call out the local militia, were always substantial landowners, as were the members of Parliament, who made the laws. In eastern Europe, the landowners presided over the manorial courts. On the Continent, the burden of taxation fell on the tillers of the soil.

Obligations of Peasants The power of the landlord increased as one moved across Europe from west to east. Most French peasants owned some land, but there were a few serfs in eastern France. Nearly all French peasants were subject to certain feudal dues, called *banalités*. These included the required use-for-payment of the lord's, or **seigneur's,** mill to grind grain and his oven to bake bread. The seigneur could also require a certain number of days each year of the peasant's labor. This practice of forced labor was termed the *corvée*. Because even landowning French peasants rarely possessed enough land to support their families, they had to rent more land from the

Eighteenth-century France had some of the best roads in the world, but they were often built with forced labor. French peasants were required to work part of each year on such projects. This system, called the **corvée,** *was not abolished until the French Revolution in 1789.*   Claude Joseph Vernet, *Construction of a Road*. Louvre, Paris, France. Giraudon/Art Resource, N.Y.

Emelyan Pugachev (1726–1775) led the largest peasant revolt in Russian history. In this contemporary propaganda picture he is shown in chains. An inscription in Russian and German was printed below the picture decrying the evils of revolution and insurrection.
Bildarchiv Preussischer Kulturbesitz

domain of the landlords was termed a *çift*. The landlord was often an absentee who managed the estate through an overseer. During the seventeenth and eighteenth centuries, these landlords, like those elsewhere in Europe, often became more commercially oriented and turned to the production of crops, such as cotton, vegetables, potatoes, and maize, that could be sold in the market.

A scarcity of labor rather than the recognition of their legal rights supported the independence of the southeastern European peasants. A peasant might migrate from one landlord to another. Because the second landlord needed the peasant's labor, he had no reason to return him to the original landlord. During the seventeenth and eighteenth centuries, however, disorder originating in the capital of Constantinople (now Istanbul) spilled over into the Balkan Peninsula. In this climate, landlords increased their authority by offering their peasants protection from bandits or rebels who might destroy peasant villages. As in medieval times, the manor house or armed enclosure of a local landlord became the peasants' refuge. These landlords also owned all the housing and tools required by the peasants and furnished their seed grain. Consequently, despite legal independence, Balkan peasants under the Ottoman Empire became largely dependent on the landlords, though never to the extent of serfs in eastern Europe or Russia.

seigneur and were also subject to feudal dues attached to those plots. In Prussia and Austria, despite attempts by the monarchies late in the century to improve the lot of the serfs, the landlords continued to exercise almost complete control over them. In many of the Habsburg lands, law and custom required the serfs to provide service, or **robot,** to the lords.

Serfs were worst off in Russia. There, nobles reckoned their wealth by the number of "souls," or male serfs, owned rather than by the acreage the landlord possessed. Russian landlords, in effect, regarded serfs merely as economic commodities. They could demand as many as six days a week of labor, known as *barshchina*, from the serfs. Like Prussian and Austrian landlords, they enjoyed the right to punish their serfs. On their own authority, Russian landlords could even exile a serf to Siberia. Serfs had no legal recourse against the orders and whims of their lords. There was little difference between Russian serfdom and slavery.

In southeastern Europe, where the Ottoman Empire held sway, peasants were free, though landlords tried to exert authority in every way. The

Peasant Rebellions The Russian monarchy itself contributed to the further degradation of the serfs. Peter the Great gave whole villages to favored nobles. Later in the century, Catherine the Great confirmed the authority of the nobles over their serfs in exchange for the landowners' political cooperation. Russia experienced vast peasant unrest, with well over fifty peasant revolts occurring between 1762 and 1769. These culminated in Pugachev's Rebellion between 1773 and 1775, when Emelyan Pugachev (1726–1775) promised the serfs land of their own and freedom from their lords. (See "Russian Serfs Lament Their Condition.") All of southern Russia was in turmoil until the government brutally suppressed the rebellion. Thereafter, any thought of liberalizing or improving the condition of the serfs was set aside for a generation.

Pugachev's was the largest peasant uprising of the eighteenth century, but smaller peasant revolts or disturbances took place in Bohemia in 1775, in Transylvania in 1784, in Moravia in 1786, and in Austria in 1789. There were almost no revolts in western Europe, but England experienced many rural riots. Rural rebellions were violent, but the peasants and serfs normally directed their wrath against property rather than persons. The rebels usually sought to reassert traditional or customary rights against practices that they perceived as innovations. Their targets were carefully chosen and included unfair pricing, onerous new or increased feudal dues, changes in methods of payment or land use, unjust officials, or extraordinarily brutal overseers and landlords. Peasant revolts were thus conservative in nature.

ARISTOCRATIC DOMINATION OF THE COUNTRYSIDE: THE ENGLISH GAME LAWS

One of the clearest examples of aristocratic domination of the countryside and of aristocratic manipulation of the law to its own advantage was English legislation on hunting.

Between 1671 and 1831, English landowners had the exclusive legal right to hunt game animals, including, in particular, hares, partridges, pheasants, and moor fowl. Similar legislation covered other animals such as deer, the killing of which by an unauthorized person became a capital offense in the eighteenth century. By law, only persons owning a particular amount of landed property could hunt these animals. Excluded from the right to hunt were all persons renting land, wealthy city merchants who did not own land, and poor people in cities, villages, and the countryside. The poor were excluded because the elite believed that allowing the poor to enjoy the sport of hunting would undermine their work habits. The city merchants were excluded because the landed gentry in Parliament wanted to demonstrate visibly and legally the superiority of landed wealth over commercial wealth. Thus the various game laws upheld the superior status of the aristocracy and the landed gentry.

The game laws represent a prime example of legislation related directly to economic and social status. The gentry who benefited from the laws and whose parliamentary representatives had passed them also served as the local justices of the peace who administered the laws and punished their violation. The justices of the peace could levy fines and even have poachers impressed into the army. Gentry could also take civil legal action against wealthier poachers, such as rich farmers who rented land, and thus saddle them with immense legal fees. The gentry also employed gamekeepers to protect game from poachers. The gamekeepers were known to kill the dogs belonging to people suspected of poaching. By the middle of the century, gamekeepers had devised guns to shoot poachers who tripped their hidden levers.

A small industry arose to circumvent the game laws, however. Many poor people living either on an estate or in a nearby village would kill game for food. They believed the game actually belonged to the community, and this poaching increased during hard times. Poaching was thus one way for the poor to find food.

Even more important was the black market in game animals sustained by the demand in the cities for this kind of luxury meat. This created the possibility of poaching for profit, and indeed, poaching technically meant the stealing or killing of game for sale. Local people from both the countryside and the villages would steal the game and then sell it to intermediaries called *higglers*. Later, coachmen took over this function. The higglers and the coachmen would smuggle the game into the cities, where poulterers would sell it at a premium price. Everyone involved made a bit of money along the way. During the second half of the century, English aristocrats began to construct large game preserves. The rural poor, who had lost their rights to communal land as a result of its enclosure by the large landowners, resented these preserves, which soon became hunting grounds to organized gangs of poachers.

Penalties against poaching increased in the 1790s after the outbreak of the French Revolution, but so did the amount of poaching as the economic hardships caused by Britain's participation in the wars of the era put a greater burden on poor people and as the demand for food in English cities grew along with their population. By the 1820s, both landowners and reformers called for a change in the law. In 1831, Parliament rewrote the game laws, retaining the landowners' possession of the game, but permitting them to allow other people to hunt it. Poaching continued, but the exclusive right of the landed classes to hunt game had ended.

Family Structures and the Family Economy

In preindustrial Europe, the household was the basic unit of production and consumption. Few productive establishments employed more than a handful of people not belonging to the family of the owner, and those rare exceptions were in cities. The overwhelming majority of Europeans, however, lived in rural areas. There, as well as in small

RUSSIAN SERFS LAMENT THEIR CONDITION

As with other illiterate groups in European history, it is difficult to recapture the voices of Russian serfs. The following verses from "The Slaves' Lament," a popular ballad from the era of the Pugachev Rebellion (1773–1775), indicate the serfs were aware of how the legislation of that era which favored the landowning classes affected their lives. The verses embody the resentment that Pugachev's Rebellion ignited. Note how the verses suggest that the tsar may be more favorable to serfs than their landowners are. Pugachev claimed to be Tsar Peter III, and many Russian serfs believed him and thus considered him a liberator from landlord tyranny. Throughout this ballad, serfs present themselves as slaves.

■ *What specific complaints about landlords are expressed in these verses? What charges indicate that serfs may believe their situation has worsened? What hope do they seem to place in the tsar? What idealized picture of the world do the serfs believe they would themselves create?*

O woe to us slaves living for the masters!
We do not know how to serve their ferocity!
Service is like a sharp scythe;
And kindness is like the morning dew.
* * * * *
Brothers, how annoying it is to us
And how shameful and insulting
That another who is not worthy to be equal
   with us
Has so many of us in his power.
* * * * *
And if we steal from the lord one half
   kopeck,
The law commands us to be killed like a
   louse.
And if the master steals ten thousand,
Nobody will judge who should be hanged.
The injustice of the Russian sheriffs has
   increased:
Whoever brings a present is right beyond
   argument.
They have stopped putting their trust in the
   Creator for authority,
And have become accustomed to own us like
   cattle.
All nations rebuke us and wonder at our
   stupidity,
That such stupid people are born in Russia.
And indeed, stupidity was rooted in us long ago,
   as each honour here has been given to vagrants.
The master can kill the servant like a gelding;
The denunciation by a slave cannot be believed.
Unjust judges have composed a decree

That we should be tyrannically whipped with a
   knout for that.
* * * * *
Better that we should agree to serve the tsar.
Better to live in dark woods
Than to be before the eyes of these tyrants;
They look on us cruelly with their eyes
And eat us as iron eats rye. No one wants to
   serve the tsar
But only to grind us down to the end.
And they try to collect unjust bribes,
And they are not frightened that people die cruelly.
* * * * *
Ah brothers, if we got our freedom,
We would not take the lands or the fields for
   ourselves.
We would go into service as soldiers, brothers,
And would be friendly among ourselves,
Would destroy all injustice
And remove the root of evil lords.
* * * * *
They [the landlords] sell all the good rye to
   the merchants,
And give us like pigs the bad.
The greedy lords eat meat at fast time,
And even when meat is allowed, the slaves
   must cook meatless cabbage soup.
O brothers, it is our misfortune
   always to have rye kasha.
The lords drink and make merry,
And do not allow the slaves even to burst
   out laughing.

From Paul Dukes, trans. and ed., *Russia under Catherine the Great: Select Documents on Government and Society* (Oriental Research Partners, 1978), pp. 115–117. Reprinted by permission of Oriental Research Partners.

towns and cities, the household mode of organization predominated on farms, in artisans' workshops, and in small merchants' shops. With that mode of economic organization, there developed what is known as the **family economy.** Its structure as described here had prevailed over most of Europe for centuries.

HOUSEHOLDS

What was a household in the preindustrial Europe of the Old Regime? There were two basic models, one characterizing northwestern Europe and the other eastern Europe.

Northwestern Europe In northwestern Europe, the household almost invariably consisted of a married couple, their children through their early teenage years, and their servants. Except for the few wealthy people, households were small, usually consisting of not more than five or six members. Furthermore, in these households, more than two generations of a family rarely lived under the same roof. High mortality and late marriage prevented formation of families of three generations. In other words, grandparents rarely lived in the same household as their grandchildren, and families consisted of parents and children. The family structure of northwestern Europe was thus nuclear rather than extended.

Prior to recent research into family structures, historians had assumed that before industrialization Europeans lived in extended familial settings, with several generations living together in a household. Demographic investigation has now sharply reversed this picture. Children lived with their parents only until their early teens. Then they normally left home, usually to enter the work force of young servants who lived and worked in another household. A child of a skilled artisan might remain with his or her parents to learn a valuable skill; but only rarely would more than one child do so, because children's labor was more remunerative outside the home.

During the eighteenth century, most goods were produced in small workshops, such as this iron forge painted by Joseph Wright of Derby (1734– 1797), or in the homes of artisans. Not until very late in the century, with the early stages of industrialization, did a few factories appear. In the small early workshops, it would not have been uncommon for the family of the owner to visit, as portrayed in this painting.
The Iron Forge, 1772 (oil on canvas) by Joseph Wright of Derby (1734–1797). Broadlands Trust, Hampshire, UK/Bridgeman Art Library, London.

Those young men and women who had left home would eventually marry and form an independent household of their own. This practice of moving away from home is known as *neolocalism*. These young people married relatively late. Men were usually over twenty-six, and women over twenty-three. The new couple usually had children as soon after marriage as possible. Frequently, the woman was already pregnant at marriage. Family and community pressure often compelled the man to marry her. In any case, premarital sexual relations were common, though illegitimate births were rare. The new couple would soon employ a servant, who, together with their growing children, would undertake whatever form of livelihood the household used to support itself.

The word *servant* in this context may be confusing. It does not refer to someone looking after the needs of wealthy people. Rather, in preindustrial Europe, a servant was a person—either male or female—who was hired, often under a clear contract, to work for the head of the household in exchange for room, board, and wages. The servant was usually young and by no means always socially inferior to his or her employer. Normally, the servant was an integral part of the household and ate with the family.

Young men and women became servants when their labor was no longer needed in their parents' household or when they could earn more money for their family outside the parental household. Being a servant for several years—often as many as eight or ten—allowed young people to acquire the productive skills and the monetary savings necessary to begin their own household. These years spent as servants largely account for the late age of marriage in northwestern Europe.

Eastern Europe As one moved eastward across the Continent, the structure of the household and the pattern of marriage changed. In eastern Europe, both men and women usually married before the age of twenty. Consequently, children were born to much younger parents. Often—especially among Russian serfs—wives were older than their husbands. Eastern European households were generally larger than those in the West. Frequently a rural Russian household consisted of more than nine, and possibly more than twenty, members, with three or perhaps even four generations of the same family living together. Early marriage made this situation more likely. In Russia, marrying involved not starting a new household, but remaining in and expanding one already established.

The landholding structure in eastern Europe accounts, at least in part, for these patterns of marriage and the family. The lords of the manor who owned land wanted to ensure it would be cultivated so they could receive their rents. Thus, in Poland, for example, landlords might forbid marriage between their own serfs and those from another estate. They might also require widows and widowers to remarry to assure adequate labor for a particular plot of land. Polish landlords also frowned on the hiring of free laborers—the equivalent of servants in the West—to help cultivate land. The landlords preferred to use other serfs. This practice inhibited the formation of independent households. In Russia, landlords ordered the families of young people in their villages to arrange marriages within a short set time. These lords discouraged single-generation family households because the death or serious illness of one person in such a household might mean the land assigned to it would go out of cultivation.

The Family Economy

Throughout Europe, most people worked within the family economy. That is to say, the household was the basic unit of production and consumption. Almost everyone lived within a household of some kind because it was virtually impossible for ordinary people to support themselves independently. Indeed, except for members of religious orders, people living outside a household were viewed with great suspicion. They were considered potentially criminal, disruptive, or at least dependent on the charity of others. Everywhere beggars met deep hostility.

Depending on their ages and skills, everyone in the household worked. The need to survive poor harvests or economic slumps meant that no one could be idle. Within this family economy, all goods and income produced went to the benefit of the household rather than to the individual family member. On a farm, much of the effort went directly into raising food or producing other agricultural goods that could be exchanged for food. Few western Europeans, however, had enough land to support their household from farming alone. Thus one or more family members might work elsewhere and send wages home. For example, the father and older children might work as harvesters or might fish or might engage in other labor, either in the neighborhood or farther from home. If the father was such a migrant worker, the burden of farmwork would fall on his wife and their younger children. This was not an uncommon pattern.

The family economy also dominated the life of skilled urban artisans. The father was usually the chief artisan. He normally employed one or more servants, but would expect his children to work in the enterprise also. His eldest child was usually trained in the trade. His wife often sold his wares or opened a small shop of her own. Wives of merchants also frequently ran their husbands' businesses, especially when the husband traveled to purchase new goods. In any case, everyone in the family was involved. If business was poor, family members would look for employment elsewhere—not to support themselves as individuals, but to ensure the survival of the family unit.

In western Europe, the death of a father often brought disaster to the economy of the household. The continuing economic life of the family usually depended on his land or skills. The widow might take on the farm or the business, or his children might do so. The widow usually sought to remarry quickly to restore the labor and skills of a male to the household and to prevent herself from becoming dependent on relatives or charity.

The high mortality rate of the time meant that many households were reconstituted second-family groups that included stepchildren. Because of the advanced age of the widow or economic hard times, however, some households might simply dissolve. The widow became dependent on charity or relatives. The children became similarly dependent or entered the work force of servants earlier than they would otherwise. In other cases, the situation could be so desperate that they would resort to crime or to begging. The personal, emotional, and economic vulnerability of the family cannot be overemphasized.

In eastern Europe, the family economy functioned in the context of serfdom and landlord domination. Peasants clearly thought in terms of their families and expanding the land available for cultivation. The village structure may have mitigated the pressures of the family economy, as did the multigenerational family. Dependence on the available land was the chief fact of life. There were many fewer artisan and merchant households, and there was far less geographical mobility than in western Europe.

WOMEN AND THE FAMILY ECONOMY

The family economy established many of the chief constraints on the lives and personal experiences of women in preindustrial society. Most of the historical research that has been undertaken on this subject relates to western Europe. There, a woman's life experience was largely the function of her capacity to establish and maintain a household. For women, marriage was an economic necessity, as well as an institution that fulfilled sexual and psychological needs. Outside a household, a woman's life was vulnerable and precarious. Some women succeeded in becoming economically independent. They were the exception. Normally, unless she were an aristocrat or a member of a religious order, a woman probably could not support herself solely by her own efforts. Consequently, a woman devoted much of her life first to maintaining her parents' household and then to devising some means of getting her own household to live in as an adult. Bearing and rearing children were usually subordinate to these goals.

By the age of seven, a girl would have begun to help with the household work. On a farm, this might mean looking after chickens, watering the animals, or carrying food to adults working the land. In an urban artisan's household, she would do light work, perhaps cleaning or carrying and later sewing or weaving. The girl would remain in her parents' home as long as she made a real contribution to the family enterprise or as long as her labor elsewhere was not more remunerative to the family.

An artisan's daughter might not leave home until marriage, because at home she could learn increasingly valuable skills associated with the trade. The situation was different for the much larger number of girls growing up on farms. Their parents and brothers could often do all the necessary farmwork, and a girl's labor at home quickly became of little value to her family. She would then leave home, usually between the ages of twelve and fourteen. She might take up residence on another farm, but more likely she would migrate to a nearby town or city. She would rarely travel more than thirty miles from her parents' household. She would then normally become a servant, once again living in a household, but this time in the household of an employer. (See "Art & the West: Two Scenes from Domestic Life in the Old Regime," p. 548.)

Having migrated from home, the young woman's chief goal was to accumulate enough capital for a dowry. Her savings would make her eligible for marriage, because they would allow her to make the necessary contribution to form a household with her husband. Marriage within the family economy was a joint economic undertaking, and the wife was expected to make an immediate contribution of capital for establishing the household. A young woman might well work for ten years or more to accumulate a dowry. This practice meant that marriage was usually postponed until her mid- to late twenties.

Within marriage, earning enough money or producing enough farm goods to ensure an adequate food supply dominated women's concerns. Domestic duties, childbearing, and child rearing were subordinate to economic pressures. Consequently, couples tried to limit the number of children they had, usually through the practice of coitus interruptus, the withdrawal of the male before ejaculation. Parents often placed young children with wet nurses so the mother could continue to make her economic contribution to the household. The wet nurse, in turn, contributed to the economic welfare of her own household. The child would be fully reintegrated into its own family when it was weaned and would then be expected to aid the family at an early age.

The work of married women differed markedly between city and country and was in many ways a function of their husbands' occupations. If the peasant household had enough land to support itself, the wife spent much of her time quite literally carrying things for her husband—water, food, seed, harvested grain, and the like. There were few such adequate landholdings, however. If the husband had to do work besides farming, such as fishing or migrant labor, the wife might actually be in charge of the farm and do the plowing, planting, and harvesting. In the city, the wife of an artisan or a merchant might well be in charge of the household finances and actively participate in managing the trade or manufacturing enterprise. When her husband died, she might take over the business and perhaps hire an artisan. Finally, if economic disaster struck the family, it was usually the wife who organized what Olwen Hufton has called the "economy of expedients,"[1] within which family members might be sent off to find work elsewhere or even to beg in the streets.

Despite all this economic activity, women found many occupations and professions closed to them because they were women. They labored with less education than men, because in such a society women at all levels of life consistently found fewer opportunities for education than men. They often received lower wages than men for the same work. As we discuss later in the chapter, all of these disabilities worsened as a result of the mechanization of agriculture and the textile industries.

CHILDREN AND THE WORLD OF THE FAMILY ECONOMY

For women of all social ranks, childbirth was a time of fear and personal vulnerability. Contagious diseases endangered both mother and child. Puerperal fever was frequent, as were other infections from unsterilized medical instruments. (See "An Edinburgh Physician Describes the Dangers of Childbirth.") Not all midwives were skillful practitioners. Furthermore, most mothers and children immediately encountered immense poverty and wretched housing. Assuming both mother and child survived, the mother might nurse the infant, but often the child would be sent to a wet nurse. Convenience may have led to this practice among the wealthy, but economic necessity dictated it for the poor. The structures and customs of the family economy did not permit a woman to devote herself entirely to rearing a child. The wet-nursing industry was well organized, with urban children being frequently transported to wet nurses in the country, where they would remain for months or even years.

Throughout Europe, the birth of a child was not always welcome. The child might represent another economic burden on an already hard-pressed household. Or it might be illegitimate. The number of illegitimate births seems to have increased during the eighteenth century, possibly because increased migration of the population led to fleeting romances.

Through at least the end of the seventeenth century, unwanted or illegitimate births could lead to infanticide, especially among the poor. The parents might smother the infant or expose it to the elements. These practices were one result of both the ignorance and the prejudice surrounding contraception.

The late seventeenth and the early eighteenth centuries saw a new interest in preserving the lives of abandoned children. Although foundling hospitals established to care for abandoned children had existed before, their size and number expanded during these years. Two of the most famous were the Paris Foundling Hospital (1670) and the London Foundling Hospital (1739). Such hospitals cared for thousands of European children, and the demand for their services increased during the eighteenth century. For example, early in the century, an average of 1,700 children a year were admitted to the Paris Foundling Hospital. In the peak year of 1772, however, that number rose to 7,676 children. Not all of those children came from Paris. Many had been brought to the city from the provinces, where local foundling homes and hospitals were

---

[1] Olwen Hufton, "Women and the Family Economy in Eighteenth-Century France," *French Historical Studies* 9 (1976): 19.

An eighteenth-century French governess with her pupil. During the eighteenth century, with their employment opportunities tightly restricted, many unmarried women and widows served as governesses to children of the aristocracy and other wealthy groups in Europe. At the other end of the spectrum, many children born out of wedlock or to very poor parents might be left at foundling hospitals where many of them died quite young. Jean-Baptiste-Siméon Chardin, (1699–1779, French) *The Governess,* © 1739. Oil on canvas, 46.7 × 37.5 cm. © National Gallery of Canada, Ottawa. Purchased 1956.

overburdened. The London Foundling Hospital lacked the income to deal with all the children brought to it. In the middle of the eighteenth century, the hospital found itself compelled to choose children for admission by a lottery system.

Sadness and tragedy surrounded abandoned children. Most of them were illegitimate infants from across the social spectrum. Many, however, were left with the foundling hospitals because their parents could not support them. There was a close relationship between rising food prices and increasing numbers of abandoned children in Paris. Parents would sometimes leave personal tokens or saints' medals on the abandoned baby in the vain hope they might one day be able to reclaim the child. Few children were reclaimed. Leaving a child at a foundling hospital did not guarantee its survival. In Paris, only about 10 percent of all abandoned children lived to the age of ten.

Despite all of these perils of early childhood, children did grow up and come of age across Europe. The world of the child may not have received the kind of attention it does today, but during the eighteenth century the seeds of that modern sensibility were sown. Particularly among the upper classes, new interest arose in the education of children. In most areas, education remained firmly in the hands of the churches. As economic skills became more demanding, literacy became more valuable, and literacy rates rose during the century. Yet most Europeans remained illiterate. Not until the late nineteenth century was the world of childhood inextricably linked to the process of education. Then children would be reared to become members of a national citizenry. In the Old Regime, they were reared to make their contribution to the economy of their parents' family and then to set up their own households.

AN EDINBURGH PHYSICIAN DESCRIBES THE DANGERS OF CHILDBIRTH

Death in childbirth was a common occurrence throughout Europe until the twentieth century. This brief letter from an Edinburgh physician illustrates how devastating infectious diseases could be to women at the time of childbirth.

■ *How does the passage illustrate a health danger that only women confronted? How might the likelihood of the death of oneself or a spouse in childbirth have affected one's attitudes toward children? How does the passage illustrate limitations on knowledge about disease in the eighteenth century?*

We had puerperal fever in the infirmary last winter. It began about the end of February, when almost every woman, as soon as she was delivered, or perhaps about twenty-four hours after, was seized with it; and all of them died, though every method was tried to cure the disorder. What was singular, the women were in good health before they were brought to bed, though some of them had been long in the hospital before delivery.

One woman had been dismissed from the ward before she was brought to bed; came into it some days after with her labor upon her; was easily delivered, and remained perfectly well for twenty-four hours, when she was seized with a shivering and the other symptoms of the fever. I caused her to be removed to another ward; yet notwithstanding all the care that was taken of her she died in the same manner as the others.

From a letter to Mr. White from a Dr. Young of Edinburgh, 21 November 1774, cited in C. White, *Treatise on the Management of Pregnant and Lying-In Women* (London, 1777), pp. 45–46, as quoted in Bridget Hill, ed., *Eighteenth-Century Women: An Anthology* (London: George Allen & Unwin, 1984), p. 102.

The Revolution in Agriculture

Thus far, this chapter has examined those groups that sought stability and that, except for certain members of the nobility, resisted change. Other groups, however, wished to pursue significant new directions in social and economic life. The remainder of the chapter considers those forces and developments that would transform European life during the next century. These developments first appeared in agriculture.

The main goal of traditional peasant society was a stability that would ensure the local food supply. Despite differences in rural customs throughout Europe, the tillers resisted changes that might endanger the sure supply of food, which they generally believed traditional cultivation would provide. The food supply was never certain, and the farther east one traveled, the more uncertain it became. Failure of the harvest meant not only hardship, but death from either outright starvation or protracted debility. Often, people living in the countryside had more difficulty finding food than did city dwellers, whose local government usually stored reserve supplies of grain.

Poor harvests also played havoc with prices. Smaller supplies or larger demand raised grain prices. Even small increases in the cost of food could exert heavy pressure on peasant or artisan families. If prices increased sharply, many of those families fell back on poor relief from their local municipality or county or the church.

Historians now believe that during the eighteenth century bread prices slowly but steadily rose, spurred largely by population growth. Since bread was their main food, this inflation put pressure on all of the poor. Prices rose faster than urban wages and brought no appreciable advantage to the small peasant producer. However, the rise in grain prices benefited landowners and those wealthier peasants who had surplus grain to sell.

The rising grain prices gave landlords an opportunity to improve their incomes and lifestyle. To achieve those ends, landlords in western Europe began a series of innovations in farm production that became known as the **Agricultural Revolution.**

Landlords commercialized agriculture and thereby challenged the traditional peasant ways of production. Peasant revolts and disturbances often resulted. The governments of Europe, hungry for new taxes and dependent on the goodwill of the nobility, used their armies and militias to smash peasants who defended the practices of the past.

New Crops and New Methods The drive to improve agricultural production began during the sixteenth and seventeenth centuries in the Low Countries, where the pressures of the growing population and the shortage of land required changes in cultivation. Dutch landlords and farmers devised better ways to build dikes and drain land, so they could farm more extensive areas. They also experimented with new crops, such as clover and turnips, that would increase the supply of animal fodder and restore the soil. These improvements became so famous that early in the seventeenth century English landlords hired Cornelius Vermuyden, a Dutch drainage engineer, to drain thousands of acres of land around Cambridge.

English landlords provided the most striking examples of eighteenth-century agricultural improvement. They originated almost no genuinely new farming methods, but they popularized ideas developed in the previous century either in the Low Countries or in England. Some of these landlords and agricultural innovators became famous. For example, Jethro Tull (1674–1741) was willing to conduct experiments himself and to finance the experiments of others. Many of his ideas, such as the rejection of manure as fertilizer, were wrong. Others, however, such as using iron plows to turn the earth more deeply and planting wheat by a drill rather than by casting, were excellent. His methods permitted land to be cultivated for longer periods without having to be left fallow.

Charles "Turnip" Townsend (1674–1738) encouraged other important innovations. He learned from the Dutch how to cultivate sandy soil with fertilizers. He also instituted crop rotation, using wheat, turnips, barley, and clover. This new system of rotation replaced the fallow field with one sown with a crop that both restored nutrients to the soil and supplied animal fodder. The additional fodder meant that more livestock could be raised. These fodders allowed animals to be fed during the winter and assured a year-round supply of meat. The larger number of animals increased the quantity of manure available as fertilizer for the grain crops. Consequently, in the long run, there was more food for both animals and human beings.

The English agricultural improver Jethro Tull devised this seed drill, which increased wheat crops by planting seed deep in the soil rather than just casting it randomly on the surface. Mary Evans Picture Library Ltd

A third British agricultural improver was Robert Bakewell (1725–1795), who pioneered new methods of animal breeding that produced more and better animals and more milk and meat.

These and other innovations received widespread discussion in the works of Arthur Young (1741–1820), who edited the *Annals of Agriculture*. In 1793, he became secretary of the British Board of Agriculture. Young traveled widely across Europe, and his books are among the most important documents of life during the second half of the eighteenth century.

Enclosure Replaces Open-Field Method Many of the agricultural innovations, which were adopted only slowly, were incompatible with the existing organization of land in England. Small cultivators who lived in village communities still farmed most of the soil. Each farmer tilled an assortment of unconnected strips. The two- or three-field systems of rotation left large portions of land fallow and unproductive each year. Animals grazed on the common land in the summer and on the stubble of the harvest in the winter. Until at least the middle of the eighteenth century, the decisions about what crops would be planted were made communally. The entire system discouraged improvement and favored the poorer farmers, who needed the common land and stubble fields for their animals. The village method precluded expanding pastureland to raise more animals that would, in turn, produce more manure, which could be used for fertilizer. Thus the methods of traditional production aimed at a steady, but not a growing, supply of food.

In 1700, approximately half the arable land in England was farmed by this open-field method. By the second half of the century, the rising price of wheat encouraged landlords to consolidate or enclose their lands to increase production. The **enclosures** were intended to use land more rationally and to achieve greater commercial profits. The process involved the fencing of common lands, the reclamation of previously untilled waste, and the transformation of strips into block fields. These procedures brought turmoil to the economic and social life of the countryside. Riots often ensued.

Because many English farmers either owned their strips or rented them in a manner that amounted to ownership, the larger landlords usually resorted to parliamentary acts to legalize the enclosure of the land, which they owned but rented to the farmers. Because the large landowners controlled Parliament, such measures passed easily. Between 1761 and 1792, almost 500,000 acres were enclosed through acts of Parliament, compared with 75,000 acres between 1727 and 1760. In 1801, a general enclosure act streamlined the process.

The enclosures were controversial at the time and have remained so among historians. They permitted the extension of both farming and innovation and thus increased food production on larger agricultural units. They also disrupted small traditional communities; they forced off the land independent farmers, who had needed the common pasturage, and poor cottage dwellers, who had lived on the reclaimed wasteland. The enclosures, however, did not depopulate the countryside. In some counties where the enclosures took place, the population increased. New soil had come into production, and services subsidiary to farming also expanded.

The enclosures did not create the labor force for the British Industrial Revolution. What the enclosures most conspicuously displayed was the introduction of the entrepreneurial or capitalistic attitude of the urban merchant into the countryside. This commercialization of agriculture, which spread from Britain slowly across the Continent during the next century, strained the paternal relationship between the governing and governed classes. Previously, landlords often had looked after the welfare of the lower orders through price controls or waivers of rent during depressed periods. As the landlords became increasingly concerned about profits, they began to leave the peasants to the mercy of the marketplace.

Limited Improvements in Eastern Europe Improving agriculture tended to characterize farm production west of the Elbe. Dutch farming was quite efficient. In France, despite the efforts of the government to improve agriculture, enclosures were restricted. Yet there was much discussion in France about improving agricultural methods. These new procedures benefited the ruling classes because better agriculture increased their incomes and assured a larger food supply, which discouraged social unrest.

In Prussia, Austria, Poland, and Russia, agricultural improvement was limited. Nothing in the relationship of the serfs to their lords encouraged innovation. In eastern Europe, the chief method of increasing production was to bring previously untilled lands under the plow. The landlords or their agents, and not the villages, normally directed farm management. By extending tillage, the great landlords sought to squeeze more labor from their serfs, rather than greater productivity from the soil. Eastern European landlords, like their western counterparts, sought to increase their profits, but they were much less ambitious and successful. The only significant nutritional gain achieved through their efforts was the introduction of maize and the potato. Livestock production did not increase significantly.

EXPANSION OF THE POPULATION

The population explosion with which the entire world must contend today had its origins in the eighteenth century. Before that time, Europe's population had experienced dramatic increases, but plagues, wars, or famine had redressed the balance. Beginning in the second quarter of the eighteenth century, the population began to increase steadily. The need to feed this population caused food prices to rise, which spurred agricultural innovation. The need to provide everyday consumer goods for the expanding numbers of people fueled the demand side of the Industrial Revolution.

Our best estimates are that in 1700 Europe's population, excluding the European provinces of the Ottoman Empire, was between 100 million and 120 million people. By 1800, the figures had risen to almost 190 million and by 1850, to 260 million. The population of England and Wales rose from 6 million in 1750 to more than 10 million in 1800. France grew from 18 million in 1715 to about 26 million in 1789. Russia's population increased from 19 million in 1722 to 29 million in 1766. Such extraordinary sustained growth put new demands on all resources and considerable pressure on the existing social organization.

The population expansion occurred across the Continent in both the country and the cities. Only a limited consensus exists among scholars about the causes of this growth. There was a clear decline in the death rate. There were fewer wars and somewhat fewer epidemics in the eighteenth century. Hygiene and sanitation also improved. Better medical knowledge and techniques were once thought to have contributed to the decline in deaths. This factor is now discounted, because the more important medical advances came after the initial population explosion or would not have contributed directly to it.

Rather, changes in the food supply itself may have allowed population growth to be sustained. Improved and expanding grain production made one contribution. Another and even more important change was the cultivation of the potato. This tuber was a product of the New World and came into widespread European production during the eighteenth century. (See "The West & The World," p. 582.) On a single acre, enough potatoes could be raised to feed one peasant's family for an entire year. This more certain food supply enabled more children to survive to adulthood and rear children of their own.

The impact of the population explosion can hardly be overestimated. It created new demands for food, goods, jobs, and services. It provided a new pool of labor. Traditional modes of production and living had to be revised. More people lived in the countryside than could find employment there. Migration increased. There were also more people who might become socially and politically discontented. And because the population growth fed on itself, these pressures and demands continued to increase. The society and the social practices of the Old Regime literally outgrew their traditional bounds.

The Industrial Revolution of the Eighteenth Century

The second half of the eighteenth century witnessed the beginning of the industrialization of the European economy. That achievement of sustained economic growth is termed the **Industrial Revolution.** Previously, the economy of a province or a country might grow, but growth soon reached a plateau. Since the late eighteenth century, however, the economy of Europe has managed to expand at an almost uninterrupted pace. Depressions and recessions have been temporary, and even during such economic downturns, the Western economy has continued to grow.

Flax, from which linen cloth was produced, was a labor-intensive crop in pre-industrial Europe. Here German peasants are shown cultivating flax in the fields while a young woman sits spinning it into thread by hand.
AKG London Ltd

At considerable social cost, industrialization made possible the production of more goods and services than ever before in human history. Industrialization in Europe eventually overcame the economy of scarcity. The new means of production demanded new kinds of skills, new discipline in work, and a large labor force. The goods produced met immediate consumer demand and also created new demands. In the long run, industrialization raised the standard of living and overcame the poverty that most Europeans, who lived during the eighteenth century and earlier, had taken for granted. It gave human beings greater control over the forces of nature than they had ever known before; yet by the middle of the nineteenth century, industrialism would also cause new and unanticipated problems with the environment.

During the eighteenth century, people did not call these economic developments a *revolution.* That term came to be applied to the British economic phenomena only after the French Revolution. Then continental writers observed that what had taken place in Britain was the economic equivalent of the political events in France, hence an Industrial Revolution. It was revolutionary less in its speed, which was on the whole rather slow, than in its implications for the future of European society.

A Revolution in Consumption

The most familiar side of the Industrial Revolution was the invention of new machinery, the establishment of factories, and the creation of a new kind of work force. Recent studies, however, have emphasized the demand side of the process and the vast increase in both the desire and the possibility of consuming goods and services that arose in the early eighteenth century.

The inventions of the Industrial Revolution increased the supply of consumer goods as never before in history. The supply of goods was only one side of the economic equation, however. The supply was created by an unprecedented demand for the humble goods of everyday life. Those goods included everyday consumer items such as clothing of all kinds, buttons, toys, china, furniture, rugs, kitchen utensils, candlesticks, brassware, silverware, pewterware, glassware, watches, jewelry, soap, beer, wines, and foodstuffs. It was the ever-increasing demand for these goods that sparked the ingenuity of designers and inventors. Furthermore, there seemed to be no limits to consumer demand.

Many social factors came into play to establish the markets for these consumer goods. During the seventeenth century, the Dutch had enjoyed enormous prosperity and had led the way in new forms of both everyday consumption and that of luxury goods. For reasons that are still not clear, during the eighteenth century, increasing numbers first of the English and then of people living on the Continent came to have more disposable income. This wealth may have resulted from the improvements in agriculture. Those incomes allowed people to buy consumer goods that previous generations had inherited or did not possess. What is key to this change in consumption is that it depended primarily on expanding the various domestic markets in Europe.

This revolution, if that is not too strong a term, in consumption was not automatic. People became persuaded that they needed or wanted new consumer goods. Often, entrepreneurs caused it to happen by developing new methods of marketing. An enterprising manufacturer such as the porcelain manufacturer Josiah Wedgwood (1730–1795) first attempted to find customers among the royal family and the aristocracy. Once he had gained their business with luxury goods, he would then produce a somewhat less expensive version of the chinaware for middle-class customers. He also used advertising. He opened showrooms in London and had salespeople traveling all over England with samples and catalogs of his wares. On the Continent, he equipped salespeople with bilingual catalogs. There seemed to be no limit to the markets for different kinds of consumer goods that could be stimulated by social emulation on the one hand and advertising on the other.

Furthermore, the process of change in style itself became institutionalized. New fashions and inventions were always better than old ones. If new kinds of goods could be produced, there usually was a market for them. If one product did not find a market, its failure provided a lesson for the development of a different new product.

This expansion of consumption quietly, but steadily, challenged the social assumptions of the day. Fashion publications made all levels of society aware of new styles. Clothing fashions could be copied. Servants could begin to dress well if not luxuriously. There were changes in the consumption of food and drink that also called forth demand for new kinds of dishware for the home. Tea and coffee became staples. The brewing industry became fully commercialized. Those developments entailed the need for new kinds of cups and mugs and many more of them.

There would always be critics of this consumer economy. The vision of luxury and comfort it offered contrasted with the asceticism of ancient Sparta and contemporary Christian ethics. Yet ever-increasing consumption and production of the goods of everyday life became a hallmark of modern Western society from the eighteenth century to our own day. It would be difficult to overestimate the importance of the desire for consumer goods and the increasing material standard of living that they made possible in Western history after the eighteenth century. The presence and accessibility of such goods became the hallmark of a nation's prosperity. It is perhaps relevant to note that it was the absence of such consumer goods, as well as of civil liberties, that during the 1980s led to such deep discontent with the communist regimes in Eastern Europe and the former Soviet Union.

Industrial Leadership of Great Britain

Great Britain was the home of the Industrial Revolution and, until the middle of the nineteenth century, maintained the industrial leadership of Europe. Several factors contributed to the early start in Britain.

Consumption of all forms of consumer goods increased greatly in the eighteenth century. This engraving illustrates a shop, probably in Paris. Here women, working apparently for a woman manager, are making dresses and hats to meet the demands of the fashion trade. As the document on page 538 demonstrates, some women writers urged more such employment opportunities for women. Bildarchiv Preussischer Kulturbesitz

Great Britain took the lead in the consumer revolution that expanded the demand for goods that could be efficiently supplied. London was by far the largest city in Europe. It was the center of a world of fashion and taste to which hundreds of thousands, if not millions, of British citizens were exposed each year. In London, these people learned to want the consumer goods they saw on visits for business and pleasure. Newspapers thrived in Britain during the eighteenth century, allowing for advertising that increased consumer wants. The social structure of Britain allowed and even encouraged people to imitate the lifestyles of their social superiors. It seems to have been in Britain that a world of fashion first developed that led people to want to accumulate goods. In addition to the domestic consumer demand, the British economy

benefited from demand from the colonies in North America.

Britain was also the single largest free-trade area in Europe. The British had good roads and waterways without internal tolls or other trade barriers. The country was endowed with rich deposits of coal and iron ore. Its political structure was stable, and property was absolutely secure. The sound systems of banking and public credit established a stable climate for investment. Taxation in Britain was heavy, but it was efficiently and fairly collected, largely from indirect taxes. Furthermore, British taxes received legal approval through Parliament, with all social classes and all regions of the nation paying the same taxes. In contrast to the Continent, there was no pattern of privileged tax exemptions.

Finally, British society was mobile by the standards of the time. Persons who had money or could earn money could rise socially. The British aristocracy would receive into its midst people who had amassed large fortunes. Even persons of wealth not admitted to the aristocracy could enjoy their riches, receive social prominence, and exert political influence. No one of these factors preordained the British advance toward industrialism. Together, however, when added to the progressive state of British agriculture, they provided the nation with the marginal advantage to create a new mode of economic production.

NEW METHODS OF TEXTILE PRODUCTION

The industry that pioneered the Industrial Revolution and met growing consumer demand was the production of textiles for clothing. This industry provides the key example of industrialism emerging to supply the demands of an ever-growing market for everyday goods. Furthermore, it illustrates the surprising fact that much of the earliest industrial change took place not in cities, but in the countryside.

Although the eighteenth-century economy was primarily agricultural, manufacturing also permeated rural areas. The peasant family living in a one- or two-room cottage, rather than the factory, was the basic unit of production. The same peasants

who tilled the land in spring and summer often spun thread or wove textiles in the winter.

Under what is termed the **domestic,** or putting-out, **system of textile production,** agents of urban textile merchants took wool or other unfinished fibers to the homes of peasants, who spun it into thread. The agent then transported the thread to other peasants, who wove it into the finished product. The merchant sold the wares. In thousands of peasant cottages from Ireland to Austria, there stood a spinning wheel or a hand loom. Sometimes the spinners or weavers owned their own equipment, but more often than not by the middle of the century, the merchant capitalist owned the machinery as well as the raw material.

The domestic system of textile production was a basic feature of this family economy and would continue to be so in Britain and on the Continent well into the nineteenth century. By the mid–eighteenth century, however, a series of production bottlenecks had developed within the domestic system. The demand for cotton textiles was growing more rapidly than production, especially in Great Britain, which had a large domestic and North American market for cotton textiles. Inventors devised some of the most famous machines of the early Industrial Revolution in response to this consumer demand for cotton textiles.

The Spinning Jenny Cotton textile weavers had the technical capacity to produce the quantity of fabric demanded. The spinners, however, did not have the equipment to produce as much thread as the weavers needed. John Kay's invention of the flying shuttle, which increased the productivity of the weavers, had created this imbalance during the 1730s. Thereafter, various groups of manufacturers and merchants offered prizes for the invention of a machine to eliminate this bottleneck.

About 1765, James Hargreaves (d. 1778) invented the **spinning jenny.** Initially, this machine allowed 16 spindles of thread to be spun, but by the close of the century its capacity had been increased to as many as 120 spindles.

The Water Frame The spinning jenny broke the bottleneck between the productive capacity of the spinners and the weavers, but it was still a piece of machinery used in the cottage. The invention that took cotton textile manufacture out of the home and put it into the factory was Richard Arkwright's (1732–1792) **water frame,** patented in 1769. This was a water-powered device designed to permit the production of a purely cotton fabric, rather than a cotton fabric containing linen fiber for durability. Eventually Arkwright lost his patent rights, and

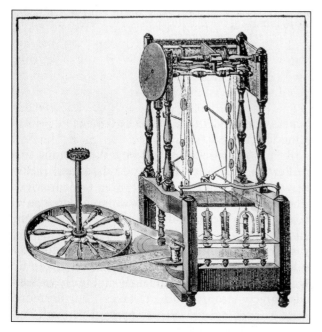

James Hargreave's Spinning Jenny permitted the spinning of numerous spindles of thread on a single machine. AKG London Ltd

other manufacturers could use his invention freely. As a result, many factories sprang up in the countryside near streams that provided the necessary water power. From the 1780s onward, the cotton industry could meet an ever-expanding demand. Cotton output increased by 800 percent between 1780 and 1800. By 1815, cotton composed 40 percent of the value of British domestic exports and by 1830, just over 50 percent.

The Industrial Revolution had commenced in earnest by the 1780s, but the full economic and social ramifications of this unleashing of human productive capacity were not really felt until the early nineteenth century. The expansion of industry and the incorporation of new inventions often occurred rather slowly. For example, Edmund Cartwright (1743–1822) invented the power loom for machine weaving in the late 1780s. Yet not until the 1830s were there more power-loom weavers than hand-loom weavers in Britain. Nor did all the social ramifications of industrialism appear immediately. The first cotton mills used water power, were located in the country, and rarely employed more than two dozen workers. Not until the late-century application of the steam engine, perfected by James Watt (1736–1819) in 1769, to the running of textile machinery could factories easily be located in or near existing urban centers. The steam engine not only vastly increased and regularized the available energy, but also made possible the combination of urbanization and industrialization.

THE STEAM ENGINE

More than any other invention, the steam engine permitted industrialization to grow on itself and to expand into one area of production after another. This machine provided for the first time in human history a steady and essentially unlimited source of inanimate power. Unlike engines powered by water or the wind, the steam engine, driven by the burning of coal, provided a portable source of industrial power that did not fail or falter as the seasons of the year changed. Unlike human or animal power, the steam engine depended on mineral energy that did not tire during a day. Finally, the steam engine could be applied to many industrial and, eventually, transportation uses.

The first practical engine using steam power had been the invention of Thomas Newcomen (1663–1729) in the early eighteenth century. The piston of this device was moved when the steam that had been induced into the cylinder condensed, causing the piston to fall. The Newcomen machine was large, inefficient in its use of energy because both the condenser and the cylinder were heated,

Major Inventions in the Textile-Manufacturing Revolution
1733   James Kay's flying shuttle
1765   James Hargreaves's spinning jenny (patented 1770)
1769   James Watt's steam engine patent
1769   Richard Arkwright's water frame patent
1787   Edmund Cartwright's power loom

and practically untransportable. Despite these problems, English mine operators used the Newcomen machines to pump water out of coal and tin mines. By the third quarter of the eighteenth century, almost a hundred Newcomen machines were operating in the mining districts of England.

During the 1760s, James Watt, a Scottish engineer and machine maker, began to experiment with a model of a Newcomen machine at the University of Glasgow. He gradually understood that separating the condenser from the piston and the cylinder would achieve much greater efficiency. In 1769, he patented his new invention, but transforming his idea into a practical application presented difficulties. His design required precise metalwork. Watt soon found a partner in Matthew Boulton (1728–1809), a successful toy and button manufacturer in Birmingham, the city with the most skilled metalworkers in Britain. Watt and Boulton, in turn, consulted with John Wilkinson (1728–1808), a cannon manufacturer, to find ways to drill the precise metal cylinders required by Watt's design. In 1776, the Watt steam engine found its first commercial application pumping water from mines in Cornwall.

The use of the steam engine spread slowly because until 1800 Watt retained the exclusive patent rights. He was also reluctant to make further changes in his invention that would permit the engine to operate more rapidly. Boulton eventually persuaded him to make modifications and improvements that allowed the engines to be used not only for pumping, but also for running cotton mills. By the early nineteenth century, the steam engine had become the prime mover for all industry. With its application to ships and then to wagons on iron rails, the steam engine also revolutionized transportation.

IRON PRODUCTION

The manufacture of high-quality iron has been basic to modern industrial development. (See "Frederick the Great Grants Special Privileges to

FREDERICK THE GREAT GRANTS SPECIAL PRIVILEGES TO AN IRONWORKS

To encourage investment in plant and equipment, some continental monarchies, like governments today, would give certain producers special privileges that relieved them from taxes and made working for them particularly attractive. Frederick the Great (r. 1740–1786), who was always concerned about armaments that required metal, granted such privileges to an ironworks.

■ *What kinds of taxes did Frederick use to raise revenues in his kingdom? What other practices did he follow to keep from spending money? What are the labor arrangements that might have made this ironworks a place where workers might have preferred to work? By looking at the special privileges given to the workers at this ironworks, what can you conclude about the situation of workers employed in factories, mines, or foundries that did not enjoy special privileges?*

[I]n order that the newly discovered iron stone in Pomerania . . . shall not be without benefit but be used for the good of his lands and loyal subjects in Pomerania . . . H. M. [His Majesty King Frederick] is graciously pleased . . . to grant the following liberties to their servants and workmen, or to those to be employed by them in the future.

(1) It is H. M. highest wish and command that each and every man and servant accepted by the said works or volunteering for them, shall be exempt together with all his family from all quartering of troops, . . . from all taxes and services, such as Contributions, Cavalry Tax, Land and Roof Tax, War contribution, Income Taxes, and all other burden, of whatever title, which have been enacted or may be enacted in the future, for now and for evermore as long as they remain employees of the furnaces. . . .

Further, the said servants and workmen employed about the furnaces shall remain subject to the laws of the land regarding prohibited goods and in other respects, and shall refrain from smuggling, on pain of incurring the usual penalties, provided that the searches which may become necessary in this regard about the furnaces shall be in the presence of the appropriate factor, so that disorders may be avoided and the factor be made responsible for the prevention of smuggling.

(2) The furnace servants and workmen are hereby given the right and the liberty to purchase all that they need for themselves and their families in the way of necessities, food, drink and otherwise, from anywhere in the King's dominions, either in the country or in the towns, wherever they can best be got.

(3) All the servants and workmen employed in the said iron furnaces and rolling mills, . . . as well as their families, shall be wholly exempt from impressment and recruitment.

(4) They shall be paid their wages promptly and in cash, and they shall in no manner be forced to accept against their will food or other truck in place of ready cash, as happens quite often at other furnaces, and whereby the poor workmen may be cheated of their hard-earned wage.

(5) All furnace servants and workmen receive free lodging and firing, but the latter is to consist of windfall twigs and branches only, gathered by members of their families.

(6) If one or other of the furnace servants or workmen should wish, after the expire of the term of his binding [i.e., expiration of his work contract], to remove to his home or elsewhere with his property, brought with him, acquired later or earned in the Royal dominions at work at the furnace, he shall be allowed to do so freely and without hindrance, and no deduction shall be demanded from his goods or money.

From *Privilegium für die Hütten-Bediente und Arbeiter bey den Königlichen Chur-Mäkschen, Pommerschen und Neumärckschen Eisen Hütten und Blech Werken* (Berlin, 1 November 1768), as quoted and translated in S. Pollard and C. Holmes, eds., *Documents of European Economic History*, Vol. I (London: Edward Arnold, 1968), pp. 71–72.

an Ironworks.") Iron is the chief element of all heavy industry and land or sea transport. It has also been the material out of which most productive machinery itself has been manufactured. During the early eighteenth century, British ironmakers produced somewhat less than 25,000 tons annually. Three factors held back the production of the metal. First, charcoal rather than coke was used to smelt the ore. Charcoal, derived from wood, was becoming scarce and does not burn at as high a temperature as coke, derived from coal. Second, until the perfection of the steam engine, insufficient blasts could be achieved in the furnaces. Finally, the demand for iron was limited. The elimination of the first two problems also eliminated the third.

Eventually, British ironmakers began to use coke, and the steam engine provided new power for the blast furnaces. Coke was an abundant fuel because of Britain's large coal deposits. The existence of the steam engine both improved iron production and increased the demand for iron.

In 1784, Henry Cort (1740–1800) introduced a new puddling process, that is, a new method for melting and stirring the molten ore. Cort's process allowed more slag (the impurities that bubbled to the top of the molten metal) to be removed and a purer iron to be produced. Cort also developed a rolling mill that continuously shaped the still-molten metal into bars, rails, or other forms. Previously, the metal had to be pounded into these forms.

All these innovations achieved a better, more versatile product at a lower cost. The demand for iron grew as its price became lower. By the early nineteenth century, the British produced over a million tons annually. The lower cost of iron, in turn, lowered the cost of steam engines and allowed them to be used more widely.

THE IMPACT OF THE AGRICULTURAL AND INDUSTRIAL REVOLUTIONS ON WORKING WOMEN

The transformation of agriculture and industry led to a series of seemingly modest changes that, taken collectively, diminished the importance and the role of those women already in the work force.

Women had been an important part of traditional European agriculture. They worked in the fields and often were permitted to glean the grain left over after the general harvest. Some women also managed industries like milking and cheese production. However, primarily in western Europe, increasing commercialization and mechanization eroded these traditional roles. Machinery operated by men displaced the work of women in the field and their industry skills in dairying and home industry, particularly in Britain. Even nonmechanized labor came to favor men. For example, during the late eighteenth century, heavy scythes wielded by men replaced the lighter sickles that women had used to harvest grain. Moreover, the drive to maximize profits led landlords to enclose lands and curtail customary rights like gleaning.

This transformation of farming constricted women's ability to earn their living from the land. Women in farming regions came to be viewed as opponents of agricultural improvement because of its negative impact on their economic life. As a result, proponents of the new agriculture often demeaned the role of women in farming and its related work. Indeed, the vast literature on agricultural improvement specifically advocated removing women from the agricultural work force.

A similar process took place in textile manufacturing, where mechanization deprived many women of one of their most traditional means of earning income. Before mechanization thousands of women worked at spinning wheels to produce thread that hand-loom weavers, who were often their husbands, then wove. The earlier, small spinning jennies did not immediately disrupt this situation because women could use them in the loft of a home, but the larger ones required a factory setting where men often ran the machinery. As a result, most women spinners were put out of work, and those women who did move into the factory labor force performed less skilled work than men. But in the long run, the mechanization of spinning left many other women without one of their most traditional means of earning income.

Many working women, displaced from spinning thread or from farming, slowly turned to cottage industries, such as knitting, button making, straw plaiting, bonnet making, or glove stitching, that invariably earned them less than their former occupations. In later generations, women who earlier would have been spinners or farm workers moved directly into cottage industries. The work and skills involved in these occupations were considered inferior; and because it paid so poorly, women who did this work might become prostitutes or engage in other criminal activity. Consequently, the reputations and social standing of many such working women suffered.

Among women who did not work in the cottage industries, thousands became domestic servants in the homes of landed or commercial families. During the nineteenth century, such domestic service became the largest area of female employment. It was far more respectable than the cottage

(a)

(b)

Francis Wheatley (1747–1801), an English artist, painted these and many other scenes of late eighteenth-century rural life. These four paintings portray a very idealized view of the farming family. Had Wheatley painted this family a half-century or more earlier, the women might have appeared with the father and husband in the fields, as workers or as gleaners picking up grain left by the harvesters.

After the mid-century changes in agricultural production, women worked in the home and men in the fields. Wheatley illustrates this division in the paintings shown here: Women work at home, or look after the needs of men and children. Men work in the fields and return home in the evening. During the early nineteenth century, much of the dairy work shown in the first painting would also have become mechanized, performed largely by male workers. Francis Wheatley (RA) (1747–1801) (a) *Morning,* (b) *Noon,* (c) *Evening,* (d) *Night,* signed and dated 1799, oil on canvas, each $17^1/_2 \times 21^1/_2$ in. (44.5 × 54.5 cm), Yale Center for British Art, Paul Mellon Collection B1977.14.120, B1977.14.119, B1977.14.118, B1977.14.121.

(c)

(d)

PRISCILLA WAKEFIELD DEMANDS MORE OCCUPATIONS FOR WOMEN

At the end of the eighteenth century, Priscilla Wakefield was one of several English women writers who began to demand a wider life for women. She was concerned that women found themselves able to pursue only occupations that paid poorly. Often, they were excluded from work on the grounds of their alleged physical weakness. She also believed women should receive equal wages for equal work. These issues reflected a narrowing of opportunities for women that had occurred in England during the second half of the eighteenth century. As a result of the mechanization of both agriculture and the textile industry, many women found traditional occupations closing to them. Wakefield is thus addressing a general question of opportunities available to women and more recent developments. Many of the issues she raised have yet to be adequately addressed on behalf of women.

■ *From reading this passage, what do you understand to have been the arguments at the end of the eighteenth century to limit the kinds of employment that women might enter? Why did women receive lower wages for work similar to or the same as that done by men? What occupations traditionally filled by men does Wakefield believe women might also pursue?*

Another heavy discouragement to the industry of women, is the inequality of the reward of their labor, compared with that of men; an injustice which pervades every species of employment performed by both sexes.

In employments which depend on bodily strength, the distinction is just; for it cannot be pretended that the generality of women can earn as much as men, when the produce of their labor is the result of corporeal exertion; but it is a subject of great regret, that this inequality should prevail even where an equal share of skill and application is exerted. Male stay-makers, mantua-makers, and hair-dressers, are better paid than female artists of the same professions; but surely it will never be urged as an apology for this disproportion, that women are not as capable of making stays, gowns, dressing hair, and similar arts, as men; if they are not superior to them, it can only be accounted for upon this principle, that the prices they receive for their labor are not sufficient to repay them for the expense of qualifying themselves for their business; and that they sink under the mortification of being regarded as artisans of inferior estimation. . . .

Besides these employments which are commonly performed by women, and those already shown to be suitable for such persons as are above the condition of hard labor, there are some professions and trades customarily in the hands of men, which might be conveniently exercised by either sex. Watchmaking requiring more ingenuity than strength, seems peculiarly adapted to women; as do many parts of the business of stationer, particularly, ruling account books or making pens. The compounding of medicines in an apothecary's shop, requires no other talents than care and exactness; and if opening a vein occasionally be an indispensable requisite, a woman may acquire the capacity of doing it, for those of her own sex at least, without any reasonable objection. . . . Pastry and confectionery appear particularly consonant to the habits of women, though generally performed by men; perhaps the heat of the ovens, and the strength requisite to fill and empty them, may render male assistants necessary; but certain women are most eligible to mix up the ingredients, and prepare the various kinds of cakes for baking. Light turnery and toy-making depend more upon dexterity and invention than force, and are therefore suitable work for women and children. . . .

Farming, as far as respects the theory, is commensurate with the powers of the female mind: nor is the practice of inspecting agricultural processes incompatible with the delicacy of their frames if their constitution be good.

Priscilla Wakefield, *Reflections on the Present Condition of the Female Sex* (1798) (London, 1817), pp. 125–127, as quoted in Bridget Hill, ed., *Eighteenth-Century Women: An Anthology* (London: George Allen & Unwin, 1984), pp. 227–228.

industries, but was separate from the technologically advanced world of factory manufacture or transport.

By the end of the eighteenth century, the work and workplaces of men and women were becoming increasingly separate and distinct. In this respect, many people, such as the English writer Priscilla Wakefield, believed the kinds of employment open to women had narrowed. Wakefield called for new occupations for women. (See "Priscilla Wakefield Demands More Occupations for Women.")

This shift in female employment, or what one historian has termed "this defamation of women workers,"[2] produced several long-term results. First, women's work, whether in cottage industries or domestic service, became associated with the home rather than with places where men worked. Second, the laboring life of most women was removed from the new technologies present in the new farming, transportation, and manufacturing. Woman's work thus appeared traditional, and people assumed women could do only such work. Third, during the nineteenth and early twentieth centuries, Europeans also assumed most women worked only to supplement a spouse's income. Finally, because the work women did was considered marginal and only as supplementing a male income, men were paid much more than women. Most people associate the Industrial Revolution with factories, but for many working women, the result of these revolutions was a life located more in homes than ever before. Indeed, in the nineteenth century, one, though only one, motive behind efforts to restrict the hours and improve the conditions of women in factories was the belief that it was bad for them to be there in the first place. We address the larger picture of the relationship of the new industrial workplace to family life in Chapter 21.

The Growth of Cities

Remarkable changes occurred in the pattern of city growth between 1500 and 1800. In 1500, within Europe (excluding Hungary and Russia) 156 cities had a population greater than 10,000. Only four of those cities—Paris, Milan, Venice, and Naples—had populations larger than 100,000. By 1800, 363 cities had 10,000 or more inhabitants, and 17 of them had populations larger than 100,000. The percentage of the European population living in

urban areas had risen from just over 5 percent to just over 9 percent. There had also occurred a major shift in urban concentration from southern, Mediterranean Europe to the north.

PATTERNS OF PREINDUSTRIAL URBANIZATION

The eighteenth century witnessed a considerable growth of towns, closely related to the tumult of the day and the revolutions with which the century closed. London grew from about 700,000 inhabitants in 1700 to almost 1 million in 1800. By the time of the French Revolution, Paris had more than 500,000 inhabitants. Berlin's population tripled during the century, reaching 170,000 in 1800. Warsaw had 30,000 inhabitants in 1730, but almost 120,000 in 1794. St. Petersburg, founded in 1703, numbered more than 250,000 inhabitants a century later. In addition to the growth of these capitals, the number of smaller cities of 20,000 to 50,000 people increased considerably. This urban growth must, however, be kept in perspective. Even in France and Great Britain, probably somewhat less than 20 percent of the population lived in cities. And the town of 10,000 inhabitants was much more common than the giant urban center.

These raw figures conceal significant changes that took place in how cities grew and how the population distributed itself. The major urban development of the sixteenth century had been followed by a leveling off, and even a decline, in the seventeenth. New growth began in the early eighteenth century and accelerated during the late eighteenth and the early nineteenth centuries.

Between 1500 and 1750, major urban expansion took place within already established and generally already large cities. After 1750, the pattern changed with the birth of new cities and the rapid growth of older smaller cities.

Growth of Capitals and Ports In particular, between 1600 and 1750, the cities that grew most vigorously were capitals and ports. This situation reflects the success of monarchical state building during those years and the consequent burgeoning of bureaucracies, armies, courts, and other groups who lived in the capitals. The growth of port cities, in turn, reflects the expansion of European overseas trade—most especially, that of the Atlantic routes. Except for Manchester in England and Lyons in France, the new urban conglomerates were nonindustrial cities.

Furthermore, between 1600 and 1750, cities with populations of fewer than 40,000 inhabitants declined. These included older landlocked trading

[2]Deborah Valenze, *The First Industrial Woman* (New York: Oxford University Press, 1995), p. 183.

centers, medieval industrial cities, and ecclesiastical centers. They contributed less to the new political regimes, and the expansion of the putting-out system transferred to the countryside much production that had once occurred in medieval cities. Rural labor was cheaper than urban labor, and cities with concentrations of labor declined as production was moved from the urban workshop into the country.

Emergence of New Cities and Growth of Small Towns In the middle of the eighteenth century, a new pattern emerged. The rate of growth of existing large cities declined, and new cities began to emerge and existing smaller cities began to grow. Several factors were at work in the process, which Jan De Vries has termed "an urban growth from below."[3] First, there was the general overall population increase. Second, the early stages of the Industrial Revolution, particularly in Britain, occurred in the countryside and fostered the growth of smaller towns and cities located near factories. Factory organization itself led to new concentrations of population.

Cities also grew as a result of the new prosperity of European agriculture, even where there was little industrialization. Improved agricultural production promoted the growth of nearby market towns and other urban centers that served agriculture or allowed more prosperous farmers to have access to the consumer goods and recreation they wanted. This new pattern of urban growth—new cities and the expansion of smaller existing ones—would continue into the nineteenth century.

Urban Classes

Social divisions were as marked in the cities of the eighteenth century as they were in the industrial centers of the nineteenth. Visible segregation often existed between the urban rich and the urban poor. The nobles and the upper middle class lived in fashionable town houses, often constructed around newly laid-out green squares. The poorest town dwellers usually congregated along the rivers. Small merchants and artisans lived above their shops. Whole families might live in a single room. Modern sanitary facilities were still unknown. There was little pure water. Cattle, pigs, goats, and other animals walked the streets with the people. All reports on the cities of Europe during this period emphasize both the striking grace and beauty of

the dwellings of the wealthy and the dirt, filth, and stench that filled the streets. (See "Encountering the Past: Water, Washing, and Bathing.")

Poverty was not just an urban problem; it was usually worse in the countryside. In the city, however, poverty was more visible in the form of crime, prostitution, vagrancy, begging, and alcoholism. Many a young man or woman from the countryside migrated to the nearest city to seek a better life, only to discover poor housing, little food, disease, degradation, and finally death. It did not require the Industrial Revolution and the urban factories to make the cities into hellholes for the poor and the dispossessed. The full darkness of London life during the midcentury "gin age," when consumption of that liquor blinded and killed many poor people, is evident in the engravings of William Hogarth (1697–1764).

Also contrasting with the serenity of the aristocratic and upper-commercial-class lifestyle were the public executions that took place all over Europe, the breaking of men and women on instruments of torture in Paris, and the public floggings in Russia. Brutality condoned and carried out by the ruling classes was simply a fact of everyday life.

The Upper Classes At the top of the urban social structure stood a generally small group of nobles, large merchants, bankers, financiers, clergy, and government officials. These upper-class men controlled the political and economic affairs of the town. Normally, they constituted a self-appointed and self-electing oligarchy that governed the city through its corporation or city council. These rights of self-government had usually been granted by some form of royal charter that gave the city corporation its authority and the power to select its own members. In a few cities on the Continent, artisan guilds controlled the corporations, but more generally, the councils were under the influence of the local nobility and the wealthiest commercial people.

The Middle Class Another group in the city was the prosperous, but not always immensely wealthy, merchants, tradespeople, bankers, and professional people. They were the most dynamic element of the urban population and constituted the persons traditionally regarded as the middle class, or bourgeoisie. The concept of the middle class was much less clear cut than that of the nobility. The middle class itself was and would remain diverse and divided, with persons employed in the professions often resentful of those who drew their incomes from commerce. Less wealthy members of the middle class of whatever occupation resented wealthier

---

[3]Jan De Vries, "Patterns of Urbanization in Pre-Industrial Europe, 1500–1800," in H. Schmal, ed., *Patterns of Urbanization since 1500* (London: Croom Helm, 1981), p. 103.

Water, Washing, and Bathing

Before the late nineteenth century, clean water was scarce in Europe. Except for the few households and institutions that had their own wells, all water had to be carried from a public fountain or public well. Drought in the summer and freezing in the winter could lead to shortages.

Governments made little effort to provide water. Everyone assumed that people required little water for their personal use—less than 7.5 liters per day, according to one eighteenth-century commentator. (In the year 2000, the average American used 210 liters per day.) Commerce and agriculture used much more water than individuals: to power mills, in the cloth and dye trades, and to quench the thirst of work animals and irrigate fields.

Attitudes toward personal appearance also determined the use of water. In the Middle Ages, public bathhouses were common. The appearance of the body—cleanliness—was believed to reflect the state of the soul, and most townspeople and aristocrats bathed fairly often. However, during the Renaissance and the Reformation, the quality and condition of clothing, not bodily cleanliness, were thought to mirror the soul. Clean clothes also revealed a person's social status—clothes made the man and the woman.

Moreover, from the late Middle Ages through the end of the eighteenth century, etiquette and medical manuals advised people to wash only those parts of their bodies that could be seen in public—the hands, the face, the neck, and the feet. And all forms of public bathing were associated with immoral behavior—public bathing meant public nudity, and prostitutes frequented bathhouses.

The switch from woolen to linen clothing accompanied the decline in bathing. By the sixteenth century, easily washable linen clothing had begun to replace woolen garments in much of western Europe. Clean linen shirts or blouses allowed persons who had not bathed to appear clean. Possession of large quantities of freshly laundered linens was a sign of high social status.

Appearance thus became more important than bodily hygiene. Medical opinion supported these practices. Physicians believed odors or *miasma* (bad air), such as might be found in soiled linens—along with lice, fleas, and other vermin—caused disease. One should therefore change one's shirt every few days but avoid baths, which might let the bad air enter the body through the open pores. Consequently, in an age in which there were practically no personal bathtubs, thousands of shirts were washed each week, almost always by female laundresses, in every city.

Attitudes toward bathing only began to change toward the middle of the eighteenth century when writers argued that frequent bathing might lead to greater health. Large public baths, such as had been known in the ancient world and were a fixture of the Ottoman Empire, would revive during the nineteenth century, and the germ theory of disease would lead health authorities to urge people to bathe often to rid their bodies of germs. The great water projects of the nineteenth century (see Chapter 24) would assure vast quantities of water for personal hygiene.

■ *Why did bathing become less frequent after the late Middle Ages? How did the use of linen clothing contribute to this change?*

Daniel Roche, *The Culture of Clothing: Dress and Fashion in the "Ancien Regime"* (Cambridge: Cambridge University Press, 1994); Georges Vigarello, *Concepts of Cleanliness: Changing Attitudes in France since the Middle Ages* (Cambridge: Cambridge University Press, 1988); Alain Corbin, *The Foul and the Fragrant: Odor and the French Social Imagination* (Cambridge, MA: Harvard University Press, 1988).

In the eighteenth century washing linen clothing by hand was a major task of women servants. J.B.S. Chardin, *The Washerwoman,* National Museum med Prins Eugens Waldemarsudde.

members who might be connected to the nobility through social or business relationships.

The middle class had less wealth than most nobles, but more than urban artisans. Middle-class people lived in the cities and towns, and their sources of income had little or nothing to do with the land. In one way or another, they all benefited from expanding trade and commerce, whether as merchants, as lawyers, or as small-factory owners. Theirs was a world in which the earning and saving of money allowed for rapid social mobility and change in lifestyle. They saw themselves as people willing to put their capital and energy to work, whereas they portrayed the nobility as idle. The members of the middle class tended to be economically aggressive and socially ambitious. People often made fun of them for these characteristics and were jealous of their success. The middle class normally supported reform, change, and economic growth. The bourgeoisie also wanted more rational regulations for trade and commerce, as did some of the more progressive aristocrats.

The middle class was made up of people whose lives fostered the revolution in consumption. On one hand, as owners of factories and of wholesale and retail businesses, they produced and sold goods for the expanding consumer market; on the other hand, members of the middle class were among the chief consumers. It was to their homes that the vast array of new consumer goods made their way. They were also the people whose social values clearly embraced the commercial spirit most fully. They might not enjoy the titles or privileges of the nobility, but they could enjoy considerable material comfort and prosperity. It was this style of life that less well-off people could still emulate as they sought to acquire consumer goods for themselves.

During the eighteenth century, the relationship between the middle class and the aristocracy was complicated. On one hand, the nobles, especially in England and France, increasingly embraced the commercial spirit associated with the middle class by improving their estates and investing in cities. On the other hand, wealthy members of the middle class often tried to imitate the lifestyle of the nobility by purchasing landed estates. The aspirations of the middle class for social mobility, however, conflicted with the determination of the nobles to maintain and reassert their own privileges and to protect their own wealth. The middle-class commercial figures—traders, bankers, manufacturers, and lawyers—often found their pursuit of both profit and prestige blocked by the privileges of the nobility and its social exclusiveness, by the inefficiency of monarchical bureaucracies dominated by

the nobility, or by aristocrats who controlled patronage and government contracts.

The bourgeoisie was not rising to challenge the nobility; rather, both were seeking to add new dimensions to their existing political power and social prestige. The tensions that arose between the nobles and the middle class during the eighteenth century normally involved issues of power sharing or access to political influence, rather than clashes over values or goals associated with class.

The middle class in the cities also feared the lower urban classes as much as they envied the nobility. The lower orders were a potentially violent element in society, a potential threat to property, and, in their poverty, a drain on national resources. The lower classes, however, were much more varied than either the city aristocracy or the middle class cared to admit.

Artisans Shopkeepers, artisans, and wage earners were the single largest group in any city. They were grocers, butchers, fishmongers, carpenters, cabinetmakers, smiths, printers, hand-loom weavers, and tailors, to give a few examples. They had their own culture, values, and institutions. Like the peasants of the countryside, they were in many respects conservative. Their economic position was highly vulnerable. If a poor harvest raised the price of food, their own businesses suffered. These urban classes also contributed to the revolution in consumption, however. They could buy more goods than ever before, and, to the extent their incomes permitted, many of them sought to copy the domestic consumption of the middle class.

The lives of these artisans and shopkeepers centered on their work and their neighborhoods. They usually lived near or at their place of employment. Most of them worked in shops with fewer than a half dozen other artisans. Their primary institution had historically been the guild, but by the eighteenth century, the guilds rarely exercised the influence of their predecessors in medieval or early modern Europe.

Nevertheless, the guilds were not to be ignored. They played a conservative role. Rather than seeking economic growth or innovation, they tried to preserve the jobs and skills of their members. In many countries, the guilds were still able to determine who could pursue a particular craft. To lessen competition, they attempted to prevent too many people from learning a particular skill.

The guilds also provided a framework for social and economic advancement. At an early age, a boy might become an apprentice to learn a craft or trade. After several years, he would be made a journeyman. Still later, if successful and sufficiently

This engraving illustrates a metalworking shop such as might have been found in almost any town of significance in Europe. Most of the people employed in the shop probably belonged to the same family. Note that two women are also working. The wife may very well have been the person in charge of keeping the accounts of the business. The two younger boys might be children of the owner or apprentices in the trade, or both.
Bildarchiv Preussischer Kulturbesitz

competent, he might become a master. The artisan could also receive certain social benefits from the guilds, including aid for his family during sickness or the promise of admission for his son. The guilds were the chief protection for artisans against the operation of the commercial market. They were particularly strong in central Europe.

THE URBAN RIOT

The artisan class, with its generally conservative outlook, maintained a rather fine sense of social and economic justice based largely on traditional practices. If the collective sense of what was economically "just" was offended, artisans frequently manifested their displeasure by rioting. The most sensitive area was the price of bread, the staple food of the poor. If a baker or a grain merchant announced a price that was considered unjustly high, a riot might well ensue. Artisan leaders would confiscate the bread or grain and sell it for what the urban crowd considered a "just price." They would then give the money paid for the grain or bread to the baker or merchant.

The potential for bread riots restrained the greed of merchants. Such disturbances represented a collective method of imposing the "just price"

in place of the price set by the commercial marketplace. Thus bread and food riots, which occurred throughout Europe, were not irrational acts of screaming, hungry people, but highly ritualized social phenomena of the Old Regime and its economy of scarcity.

Other kinds of riots also characterized eighteenth-century society and politics. The riot was a way in which people who were excluded in every other way from the political processes could make their will known. Sometimes urban rioters were incited by religious bigotry. For example, in 1753, London Protestant mobs compelled the government ministry to withdraw an act to legalize Jewish naturalization. In 1780, the same rabidly Protestant spirit manifested itself in the Gordon riots. Lord George Gordon (1751–1793) had raised the specter of an imaginary Catholic plot after the government relieved military recruits from having to take specifically anti-Catholic oaths.

In these riots and in food riots, violence was normally directed against property rather than against people. The rioters themselves were not disreputable people but usually small shopkeepers, freeholders, artisans, and wage earners. They usually wanted only to restore a traditional right or practice that seemed endangered. Nevertheless, considerable turmoil and destruction could result from their actions.

During the last half of the century, urban riots increasingly involved political ends. Though often simultaneous with economic disturbances, the political riot always had nonartisan leadership or instigators. In fact, the "crowd" of the eighteenth century was often the tool of the upper classes. In Paris, the aristocratic *Parlement* often urged crowd action in its disputes with the monarchy. In Geneva, middle-class citizens supported artisan riots against the local oligarchy. In Great Britain in 1792, the government incited mobs to attack English sympathizers of the French Revolution. Such outbursts indicate that the crowd or mob first entered the European political and social arena well before the revolution in France.

The Jewish Population: The Age of the Ghetto

Although the small Jewish communities of Amsterdam and other western European cities became famous for their intellectual life and financial institutions, the vast majority of European Jews lived in eastern Europe. In the eighteenth century and thereafter, the Jewish population of Europe was concentrated in Poland, Lithuania, and the Ukraine, where no fewer than 3 million Jews dwelled. There were perhaps as many as 150,000 Jews in the Habsburg lands, primarily Bohemia, around 1760. Fewer than 100,000 Jews lived in Germany. There were approximately 40,000 Jews in France. Much smaller Jewish populations resided in England and Holland, each of which had a Jewish population of fewer than 10,000. There were even smaller groups of Jews elsewhere.

In 1762, Catherine the Great of Russia specifically excluded Jews from a manifesto that welcomed foreigners to settle in Russia. She relaxed the exclusion a few years later, but Jews during her reign often felt they needed assurances of imperial protection for their livelihoods and religious practices against the ordinances of local officials. (See "Belorussian Jews Petition Catherine the Great.") After the first partition of Poland of 1772, discussed in Chapter 18, Russia included a large Jewish population. There were also larger Jewish communities in Prussia and under Austrian rule.

Jews dwelled in most nations without enjoying the rights and privileges of other subjects of the monarchs, unless such rights were specifically granted to them. They were regarded as a kind of resident alien whose residence might well be temporary or changed at the whim of local rulers or the monarchical government.

No matter where they dwelled, the Jews of Europe under the Old Regime lived apart in separate communities from non-Jewish Europeans. These communities might be distinct districts of cities known as **ghettos** or in primarily Jewish villages in the countryside. Jews were also treated as a distinct people religiously and legally. In Poland for much of the century, they were virtually self-governing. In other areas, they lived under the burden of discriminatory legislation. Except in England, Jews could not and did not mix in the mainstream of the societies in which they dwelled. This period, which really may be said to have begun with the expulsion of the Jews from Spain at the end of the fifteenth century, is known as the age of the ghetto, or separate community.

During the seventeenth century, a few Jews had helped finance the wars of major rulers. These financiers often became close to the rulers and were known as "court Jews." Perhaps the most famous was Samuel Oppenheimer (1630–1703), who helped the Habsburgs finance their struggle against the Turks and the defense of Vienna. Even these privileged Jews, including Oppenheimer, however, often failed to have their loans repaid. The court Jews and their financial abilities became famous. They tended to marry among themselves.

The overwhelming majority of the Jewish population of Europe, however, lived in poverty. They occupied the most undesirable sections of cities or poor rural villages. They pursued moneylending in some cases, but often worked at the lowest occupations. Their religious beliefs, rituals, and community set them apart. Virtually all laws and social institutions kept them apart from their Christian neighbors in situations of social inferiority.

Under the Old Regime, it is important to emphasize, all of this discrimination was based on religious separateness. Jews who converted to Christianity were welcomed, even if not always warmly, into the major political and social institutions of gentile European society. Until the last two decades of the eighteenth century, in every part of Europe, however, those Jews who remained loyal to their faith were subject to various religious, civil, and social disabilities. They could not pursue the professions freely, they often could not change residence freely, and they stood outside the political structures of the nations in which they lived. Jews could be expelled from the cities in which they resided, and their property could be confiscated. They were regarded as socially and religiously inferior. They could be required to listen

BELORUSSIAN JEWS PETITION CATHERINE THE GREAT

In the 1780s, through military expansion, Empress Catherine the Great of Russia (see Chapter 18) annexed Belorussia, bringing a new Jewish minority under her imperial government. In response to her decree, governing many aspects of the region's law and economy, Belorussian Jews petitioned the empress to protect certain of their traditional rights regarding distillation and sale of spirits. They also petitioned for protection in court and for the right to retain their own traditional practices and courts for matters relating to their own community. The petition indicates how in Russia, as elsewhere in Europe, Jews were treated as a people apart. It also illustrates how Jews, like other minorities in Old Regime Europe, sought both to receive the protection of monarchies against arbitrary local officials and to maintain the integrity of long-standing social practices. The document also illustrates the Jews' dependence on the goodwill of the surrounding non-Jewish community.

■ *In the first part of the petition, how do the petitioners attempt to appeal to long-standing custom to defend their interests? How do both parts of the petition suggest that Jewish law and practice distinct from the rest of the society governed Jewish social life? In the context of this petition, which non-Jewish authorities may actually or potentially influence Jewish life?*

. . . 2. According to an ancient custom, when the squires built a new village, they summoned the Jews to reside there and gave them certain privileges for several years and then permanent liberty to distill spirits, brew beer and mead, and sell these drinks. On this basis, the Jews built houses and distillation plants at considerable expense. . . . A new decree of Her Imperial Majesty . . . reserved [this right] to the squires. . . . But a decree of the governor-general of Belorussia has now forbidden the squires to farm out distillation in their villages to Jews, even if the squires want to do this. As a result, the poor Jews who built houses in small villages and promoted both this trade and distillation have been deprived of these and left completely impoverished. But until all the Jewish people are totally ruined, the Jewish merchants suffer restraints equally with the poor rural Jews, since their law obliges them to assist all who share their religious faith. They therefore request an imperial decree authorizing the squire, if he wishes, to farm out distillation to Jews in rural areas.

3. Although, with Her Imperial Majesty's permission, Jews may be elected as officials . . ., Jews are allotted fewer votes than other people and hence no Jew can ever attain office. Consequently, Jews have no one to defend them in courts and find themselves in a desperate situation—given their fear and ignorance of Russian—in case of misfortune, even if innocent. To consummate all the good already bestowed, Jews dare to petition that an equal number of electors be required from Jews as from others (or, at least, that in matters involving Jews and non-Jews, a representative from the Jewish community hold equal rights with non-Jews, be present to accompany Jews in court, and attend the interrogation of Jews). But cases involving only Jews (except for promissory notes and debts) should be handled solely in Jewish courts, because Jews assume obligations among themselves, make agreements and conclude all kinds of deals in the Jewish language and in accordance with Jewish rites and laws (which are not known to others). Moreover, those who transgress their laws and order should be judged in Jewish courts. Similarly, preserve intact all their customs and holidays in the spirit of their faith, as is mercifully assured in the imperial manifesto.

During the Old Regime, European Jews were separated from non-Jews, typically in districts known as ghettos. Relegated to the least desirable section of a city or to rural villages, most lived in poverty. This watercolor painting depicts a street in Kazimlesz, the Jewish quarter of Cracow, Poland. Judaica Collection, Max Berger, Vienna, Austria. Copyright Erich Lessing/Art Resource, N.Y.

to sermons that insulted their religion. Jews might find their children taken away from them and given Christian instruction. They knew their non-Jewish neighbors might suddenly turn against them and kill them.

As we will see in subsequent chapters, the end of the Old Regime brought major changes in the lives of these Jews and in their relationship to the larger culture.

In Perspective

Near the close of the eighteenth century, European society was on the brink of a new era. That society had remained traditional and corporate largely because of an economy of scarcity. Beginning in the eighteenth century, the commercial spirit and the values of the marketplace, although not new, were permitted fuller play than ever before in European history. The newly unleashed commercial spirit led increasingly to a conception of human beings as individuals rather than as members of communities. In particular, that spirit manifested itself in the Agricultural and Industrial Revolutions, as well as in the drive toward greater consumption. Together, those two vast changes in production overcame most of the scarcity that had haunted Europe and the West

generally. The accompanying changes in landholding and production would bring major changes to the European social structure.

The expansion of population provided a further stimulus for change. More people meant more labor, more energy, and more minds contributing to the creation and solution of social difficulties. Cities had to accommodate themselves to expanding populations. Corporate groups, such as the guilds, had to confront the existence of a larger labor force. New wealth meant that birth would eventually become less and less a determining factor in social relationships, except in regard to the social roles assigned to the two sexes. Class structure and social hierarchy remained, but the boundaries became somewhat blurred.

Finally, the conflicting ambitions of monarchs, the nobility, and the middle class generated innovation. In the pursuit of new revenues, the monarchs interfered with the privileges of the nobles. In the name of ancient rights, the nobles attempted to secure and expand their existing social privileges. The middle class, in all of its diversity, was growing wealthier from trade, commerce, and the practice of the professions. Its members wanted social prestige and influence equal to their wealth. They resented privileges, frowned on hierarchy, and rejected tradition.

All these factors meant the society of the eighteenth century stood at the close of one era in European history and at the opening of another.

REVIEW QUESTIONS

1. Describe the life of an English aristocrat at the beginning of the eighteenth century and toward its close. What kind of privileges separated European aristocrats from other social groups?
2. How would you define the term family economy? In what ways were the lives of women constrained by the family economy in preindustrial Europe?
3. What caused the Agricultural Revolution? To what extent did the English aristocracy contribute to the Agricultural Revolution? What were some of the reasons for peasant revolts in Europe in the eighteenth century?
4. What factors explain the increase in Europe's population in the eighteenth century? How did population growth contribute to changes in consumption?
5. What caused the Industrial Revolution of the eighteenth century? Why did Great Britain take the lead in the Industrial Revolution? How did the consumer contribute to the Industrial Revolution?
6. What changes had taken place in the distribution of population in cities and towns? Compare the lifestyle of the upper class with that of the middle and lower classes. What were some of the causes of urban riots?

SUGGESTED READINGS

J. BLUM, *Lord and Peasant in Russia from the Ninth to the Nineteenth Century* (1961). Remains a classic discussion.

J. BREWER AND R. PORTER, *Consumption and the World of Goods* (1993). A large, wide-ranging collection of essays.

A. CLARKE, *The Struggle for the Breeches: Gender and the Making of the British Working Class* (1995). A major, deeply researched exploration of the subject.

P. DEANE, *The First Industrial Revolution* (1999). A well-balanced and systematic treatment.

P. EARLE, *The Making of the English Middle Class: Business, Community, and Family Life in London, 1660–1730* (1989). The most careful study of the subject.

M. W. FLINN, *The European Demographic System, 1500–1820* (1981). Remains a major summary.

E. HOBSBAWM, *Industry and Empire: The Birth of the Industrial Revolution* (1999). A survey by a major historian of the subject.

K. HONEYMAN, *Women, Gender and Industrialization in England, 1700–1850* (2000). Emphasizes how certain work or economic roles became associated with either men or women.

O. H. HUFTON, *The Poor of Eighteenth-Century France, 1750–1789* (1975). A brilliant study of poverty and the family economy.

A. KAHAN, *The Plow, the Hammer, and the Knout: An Economic History of Eighteenth-Century Russia* (1985). An extensive and detailed treatment.

D. I. KERTZER AND M. BARBAGLI, *The History of the European Family: Family Life in Early Modern Times, 1500–1709* (2001). A series of broad-ranging essays covering the entire Continent.

S. KING AND G. TIMMONS, *Making Sense of the Industrial Revolution: English Economy and Society, 1700–1850* (2001). Examines the Industrial Revolution through the social institutions that brought it about and were changed by it.

D. LANDES, *The Wealth and Poverty of Nations: Why Some Are So Rich and Some So Poor* (1998). A lively, opinionated overview of economic development.

F. E. MANUEL, *The Broken Staff: Judaism Through Christian Eyes* (1992). An important discussion of Christian interpretations of Judaism.

M. OVERTON, *Agricultural Revolution in England: The Transformation of the Agrarian Economy, 1500–1850* (1996). A highly accessible treatment.

G. RUDE, *The Crowd in History, 1730–1848* (1964). A pioneering study.

P. STEARNS, *The Industrial Revolution in World History* (1998). An extremely broad interpretive account.

D. VALENZE, *The First Industrial Woman* (1995). An elegant, penetrating volume.

A. VICKERY, *The Gentleman's Daughter: Women's Lives in Georgian England* (1998). A richly documented study.

E. A. WRIGLEY, *Continuity, Chance and Change: The Character of the Industrial Revolution in England* (1994). A major conceptual reassessment.

DOCUMENTS CD-ROM

EIGHTEENTH-CENTURY SOCIETY

16.1 Tortured Execution vs. Prison Rules
16.2 Life in the Eighteenth Century: An Artisan's Journey
16.3 Instructions for a New Law Code
16.4 Jonathan Swift: *A Description of a City Shower*
16.5 The Creation of the Steam Loom
16.6 Protesting the Machines
16.7 G. M. Trevelyan: Chapter XIII from *English Social History*

Two Scenes of Domestic Life
in the Old Regime

Under the Old Regime and for long after, domestic life, housework, and child rearing were often regarded as the "woman's sphere." But that female domestic sphere, as these works by the French artists Jean-Baptiste-Siméon Chardin (1699–1779) and Elisabeth-Louise Vigée-Lebrun (1755–1842) reveal, was a complex world. The home might be the feminine empire, but it was an empire of many provinces. Moreover, as a female artist,

Vigée-Lebrun demonstrated that in rare instances women could lead lives outside the home.

Chardin's *The Return from the Market* (1738) presents what was often, at least in art, a hidden area within the domestic sphere: that of the servant. The woman in the painting is a servant in what appears to be a household of moderate means, perhaps that of a merchant. In this and other of his paintings, Chardin portrays a world of

Jean-Baptiste Chardin, 1699–1779. *The Return from the Market (La Pourvoyeuse)*. (1738). French. Musée du Louvre, Paris/SuperStock

domestic order and tranquility, set apart from the bustle of an eighteenth-century street. Most domestic servants in this age were women. Yet even among them, a clear social hierarchy existed. This woman would have held a lower status than that of a governess who looked after the family's children.

Chardin portrayed the work of servants with quiet dignity and warmth. Here the servant putting down the bread seems to be listening to a conversation in the other room. Chardin does not intrude on the scene, which assumes a timeless quality: Households have needed to secure bread from time immemorial. This return from market is simply the most recent example. Chardin described his painting as a craft rather than a work of inspiration. He seems to have seen it as similar to the dignified, everyday domestic work that he shows this woman performing.

On the surface, Elisabeth-Louise Vigée-Lebrun's self-portrait of 1789 with her daughter Julie presents another side of women's life in the domestic sphere, that of the devoted mother. The classical garb of mother and child, with its echoes of the ancient world, suggests the timelessness of this role no less than Chardin's servant returning to the household with bread. But because Vigée-Lebrun was a woman artist who had been encouraged to paint by a father who was also an artist, the self-portrait also undermines the concept of a timeless, unchanging domestic sphere for women. She was a wife and a mother, but she was also one of the most fashionable and successful portrait artists of her day who had begun her career when she was only six years older than her daughter is in the painting.

Vigée-Lebrun had married an art dealer whose business and social connections gave her access to aristocratic and royal clients, the most famous of whom was Queen Marie Antoinette. Vigée-Lebrun succeeded through her painting in making herself economically secure. No longer dependent on her husband for money, she had thus broken out of the traditional domestic female sphere, although she remained a devoted wife and mother. She was also one of the few women admitted to the prestigious French Royal Academy. Ironically, after the French Revolution, that academy closed its doors to women artists.

Her aristocratic and royal connections forced Vigée-Lebrun to flee France during the revolution. For over a decade she traveled across Europe, being admitted to one distinguished academy of art after another while painting portraits of rulers and fashionable people. She eventually came back to France in 1805 after more than two hundred artists petitioned Napoleon for her return. She continued to paint portraits until 1835 when she was eighty years old.

■ *How does the work of Chardin and Vigée-Lebrun reveal the complex world of women under the Old Regime? What aspects of domestic life does Chardin's painting illustrate? How did Vigée-Lebrun's portrait and her career undermine the traditional concept of women's domestic sphere?*

Albert Boime, *Art in an Age of Revolution, 1750–1800* (Chicago: University of Chicago Press, 1987); Norman Bryson, *Looking at the Overlooked: Four Essays on Still Life Painting* (Cambridge, MA: Harvard University Press, 1990); Richard Rand, *Intimate Encounters: Love and Domesticity in Eighteenth-Century France* (Princeton, NJ: Princeton University Press, 1997); S. Evans, *The Memoirs of Madame Vigée LeBrun* (Bloomington: Indiana University, 1989); Angelica Goodden, *The Sweetness of Life: A Biography of Elisabeth Vigée Le Brun* (London: 1997).

Elizabeth-Louise Vigée-Lebrun. *Self-portrait with Her Daughter Julie.* Louvre, Paris, France. Erich Lessing/Art Resource.

During the seventeenth and eighteenth centuries, European maritime nations established overseas empires and set up trading monopolies within them in an effort to magnify their economic strength. As this painting of the **Old Custom House Quay** *in London suggests, trade from these empires and the tariffs imposed on it were expected to generate revenue for the home country. But behind many of the goods carried in the great sailing ships in the harbor and landed on these docks lay the labor of African slaves working on the plantations of North and South America.* Samuel Scott *Old Custom House Quay* Collection. V & A Picture Library, The Victoria & Albert Museum

CHAPTER 17

THE TRANSATLANTIC ECONOMY, TRADE WARS, AND COLONIAL REBELLION

*T*HE MIDDLE OF THE EIGHTEENTH *century witnessed a renewal of European warfare on a worldwide scale. The conflict involved two separate, but interrelated, rivalries. Austria and Prussia fought for dominance in central Europe while Great Britain and France dueled for commercial and colonial supremacy. The wars were long, extensive, and costly in both effort and money. They resulted in a new balance of power on the Continent and on the high seas. Prussia emerged as a great power, and Great Britain gained a world empire.*

The expense of these wars led every major European government after the Peace of Paris of 1763 to reconstruct its policies of taxation and finance. The revised fiscal programs produced internal conditions for the monarchies of Europe that had significant effects lasting the rest of the century, including the American Revolution, enlightened absolutism on the Continent, a continuing financial crisis for the French monarchy, and reform of the Spanish Empire in South America.

KEY TOPICS

- Europe's mercantilist empires
- Spain's vast colonial empire in the Americas
- Africa, slavery, and the transatlantic plantation economies
- The wars of the mid–eighteenth century in Europe and the colonies
- The struggle for independence in Britain's North American colonies

Periods of European Overseas Empires

Since the Renaissance, European contacts with the rest of the world have gone through four distinct stages. The first was that of the European discovery, exploration, initial conquest, and settlement of the New World. This phase also witnessed the penetration of Southeast Asian markets by Portugal and the Netherlands, which established major imperial outposts and influence in the region. The period closed by the end of the seventeenth century.

The second era—that of the mercantile empires, which are largely the concern of this chapter—was one of colonial trade rivalry among Spain, France, and Great Britain. Although during the sixteenth and seventeenth centuries differing motives had led to the establishment of overseas European empires, by the eighteenth century they generally existed to foster trade and commerce. Those commerical goals, however, often led to intense rivalry and conflict in key imperial trouble spots. As a result, the various imperial ventures led to the creation of large navies and fostered a series of major naval wars at the midcentury—wars that in turn became linked to warfare on the European continent. The Anglo-French side of the contest has often been compared to a second Hundred Years' War, with theaters of conflict in Europe, the Americas, and India.

A fundamental element of these first two periods of European imperial ventures in the Americas was the presence of slavery. By the eighteenth century, the slave population of the New World consisted almost entirely of a black population either recently forcibly imported from Africa or born to slaves whose forebears had been forcibly imported from Africa. There existed no precedent in human history for so large a forced migration of peoples from one continent to another or for the mid-Atlantic plantation economies supported by such slave labor.

The creation in the Americas of this slave-based plantation economy led directly to over three centuries of extensive involvement in the slave trade by Europeans and white Americans with Africa—most particularly, the societies of West Africa. In turn, the slave trade created on the American continent extensive communities of Africans from the Chesapeake region of Maryland and Virginia south to Brazil. The Africans brought to the American experience not only their labor, but their languages, customs, and ethnic associations. The Atlantic economy and the societies that arose in the Americas were consequently very much the creation of both Europeans and Africans while, as a result of the Spanish conquest, native Americans were pressed toward the margins of those societies.

Finally, during the second period, both the British colonies of the North American seaboard and the Spanish colonies of Mexico and Central and South America emancipated themselves from European control. This era of independence, part of which is discussed in this chapter and part in Chapter 21, may be said to have closed during the 1820s.

The third stage of European contact with the non-European world occurred in the nineteenth century. During that period, European governments carved new formal empires involving the direct European administration of indigenous peoples in Africa and Asia. Those nineteenth-century empires also included new areas of European settlement, such as Australia, New Zealand, and South Africa. The bases of these empires were trade, national honor, Christian missionary enterprise, and military strategy.

The last period of European empire occurred during the mid- and late twentieth century, with the decolonization of peoples who had previously lived under European colonial rule.

During the four-and-one-half centuries before decolonization, Europeans exerted political dominance over much of the rest of the world that was far disproportional to the geographical size or population of Europe. Europeans frequently treated other peoples as social, intellectual, and economic inferiors. They ravaged existing cultures because of greed, religious zeal, or political ambition. These actions are major facts of both European and world history and remain significant factors in the contemporary relationship between Europe and its former colonies. What allowed the Europeans to exert such influence and domination for so long over so much of the world was not any innate cultural superiority, but a technological supremacy related to naval power and gunpowder. Ships and guns allowed the Europeans to exercise their will almost wherever they chose.

Mercantile Empires

Navies and merchant shipping were the keystones of the mercantile empires that were meant to bring profit to a nation rather than to provide areas for settlement. The Treaty of Utrecht (1713) established the boundaries of empire during the first half of the century.

Except for Brazil, which was governed by Portugal, Spain controlled all of mainland South America. In North America, it ruled Florida, Mexico, California, and the Southwest. The Spanish also governed Central America and the islands of Cuba, Puerto Rico, and half of Hispaniola.

The British Empire consisted of the colonies along the North Atlantic seaboard, Nova Scotia, Newfoundland, Jamaica, and Barbados. Britain also possessed a few trading stations on the Indian subcontinent.

The French domains covered the Saint Lawrence River valley and the Ohio and Mississippi River valleys. They included the West Indian islands of Saint Domingue (Hispaniola), Guadeloupe, and Martinique and also stations in India. To the French and British merchant communities, India appeared as a vast potential market for European goods, as well as the source of calicos and spices that were in much demand in Europe.

The Dutch controlled Surinam, or Dutch Guiana, in South America, and various trading stations in Ceylon and Bengal. Most important, they controlled the trade with Java in what is now Indonesia. The Dutch had opened these markets largely in the seventeenth century and had created a vast trading empire far larger in extent, wealth, and importance than the geographical size of the United Netherlands would have led one to expect. The Dutch had been daring sailors and made important technological innovations in sailing.

All of these powers also possessed numerous smaller islands in the Caribbean. So far as eighteenth-century developments were concerned, the major rivalries existed among the Spanish, the French, and the British.

MERCANTILIST GOALS

Where any formal economic theory lay behind the conduct of eighteenth-century empires, it was mercantilism, that practical creed of hard-headed businesspeople. The terms *mercantilism* and *mercantile system* were invented by later opponents and critics of the system whereby governments heavily regulated trade and commerce in hope of increasing national wealth. Economic writers believed it necessary for a nation to gain a favorable trade balance of gold and silver bullion. They regarded bullion as the measure of a country's wealth, and a nation was truly wealthy only if it amassed more bullion than its rivals.

The mercantilist statesmen and traders regarded the world as an arena of scarce resources and economic limitation. The attitudes associated with mercantilist thinking assumed very modest levels of economic growth. Such thinking predated the expansion of agricultural and later industrial productivity discussed in the previous chapter. Prior to the beginning of such sustained economic growth, the wealth of one nation was assumed to grow or to be increased largely at the direct cost of another nation. That is to say, the wealth of one state might expand only if its armies or navies conquered the domestic or colonial territory of another state and thus gained the productive capacity of that area, or

The technologically advanced fleet of the Dutch East India Company, shown here at anchor in Amsterdam, linked the Netherlands' economy with that of southeast Asia. Oil on copper. Johnny van Haeften Gallery, London, U.K. The Bridgeman Art Library.

if a state expanded its trading monopoly over new territory, or if, by smuggling, it could intrude on the trading monopoly of another state.

From beginning to end, the economic well-being of the home country was the primary concern of mercantilist writers. Colonies were to provide markets and natural resources for the industries of the home country. In turn, the home country was to furnish military security and political administration for the colonies. For decades, both sides assumed the colonies were the inferior partner in the relationship. The home country and its colonies were to trade exclusively with each other. To that end, they tried to forge trade-tight systems of national commerce through navigation laws, tariffs, bounties to encourage production, and prohibitions against trading with the subjects of other monarchs. National monopoly was the ruling principle.

Mercantilist ideas had always been neater on paper than in practice. By the early eighteenth century, mercantilist assumptions were far removed from the economic realities of the colonies. The colonial and home markets simply did not mesh. Spain could not produce enough goods for South America. Economic production in the British North American colonies challenged English manufacturing and led to British attempts to limit certain colonial industries, such as iron and hatmaking.

Colonists of different countries wished to trade with each other. English colonists could buy sugar more cheaply from the French West Indies than from English suppliers. The traders and merchants of one nation always hoped to break the monopoly of another. For all these reasons, the eighteenth century became what one historian many years ago termed the "golden age of smugglers."[1] The governments could not control the activities of all their subjects. Clashes among colonists could and did bring about conflict between governments.

FRENCH-BRITISH RIVALRY

Major flash points existed between France and Britain in North America. Their colonists quarreled endlessly with each other. Both groups of settlers coveted the lower Saint Lawrence River valley, upper New England, and, later, the Ohio River valley. There were other rivalries over fishing rights, the fur trade, and alliances with Native American tribes.

The heart of the eighteenth-century colonial rivalry in the Americas, however, lay in the West Indies. These islands, close to the American continents, were the jewels of empire. The West Indies raised

tobacco, cotton, indigo, coffee, and, above all, sugar, for which there existed strong markets in Europe. These commodities were becoming part of daily life, especially in western Europe. They represented one aspect of those major changes in consumption that marked eighteenth-century European culture. Sugar in particular had become a staple rather than a luxury. It was used in coffee, tea, and cocoa, for making candy and preserving fruits, and in the brewing industry. There seemed no limit to its uses, no limit to consumer demand for it, and, for a time, almost no limit to the riches it might bring to plantation owners. Only slave labor allowed the profitable cultivation of these products during the seventeenth and eighteenth centuries. (See "Encountering the Past: Sugar Enters the Western Diet.")

India was another area of French-British rivalry. On the Indian subcontinent, both France and Britain traded through privileged chartered companies that enjoyed a legal monopoly. The East India Company was the English institution; the French equivalent was the *Compagnie des Indes*. The trade of India and Asia figured only marginally in the economics of empire. Nevertheless, enterprising Europeans always hoped to develop profitable commerce with India. Others regarded India as a springboard into the even larger potential market of China. The original European footholds in India were trading posts called *factories*. They existed through privileges granted by various Indian governments.

Two circumstances in the middle of the eighteenth century changed this situation in India. First, the indigenous administration and government of several Indian states had decayed. Second, Joseph Dupleix (1697–1763) for the French and Robert Clive (1725–1774) for the British saw the developing power vacuum as opportunities for expanding the control of their respective companies. To maintain their own security and to expand their privileges, each of the two companies began in effect to take over the government of some regions. Each group of Europeans hoped to checkmate the other.

The Dutch maintained their extensive commercial empire futher to the east in what today is Indonesia. By the eighteenth century, the other European powers more or less acknowledged Dutch predominance in that region.

The Spanish Colonial System

Spanish control of its American Empire involved a system of government and a system of monopolistic trade regulation. Both were more rigid in appearance than in practice. Actual government was often informal, and the trade monopoly was frequently

[1]Walter Dorn, *Competition for Empire, 1740–1763* (New York: Harper, 1940), p. 266.

Sugar Enters the Western Diet

Before the European discovery of the Americas, sugar was a luxury product that only the wealthy could afford. Because it requires subtropical temperatures and heavy rainfall, sugarcane could not be grown in Europe. Sugar had to be imported, at great expense, from the Arab world or from Spanish and Portuguese islands off the coast of Africa, which were too arid for the plant to flourish.

The Caribbean, however, is ideal for sugarcane. Columbus carried it to the New World in 1493, and within about a decade sugar was being cultivated—by slaves—on Santo Domingo.

But sugar production did not begin to soar until Britain and France established themselves in the Caribbean in the seventeenth century and demand for sugar began to grow in Europe, first slowly and then insatiably. By the eighteenth century, the small British and French islands in the Caribbean where sugar was produced by African slave labor had become some of the most valuable real estate on earth.

Whereas the North American colonies imported Caribbean molasses to make rum, Europeans desired sugar to sweeten other foods. Sugar, the largest colonial import into Britain, embodied the mercantile policy of a closed economic system. It was raised in British colonies, paid for by British exports, shipped on British ships, insured by British firms, refined in British cities, and consumed on British tables.

The voracious demand for sugar as a sweetener was tied up with three other tropical products—coffee, tea, and chocolate—that European consumers began to drink in enormous quantities in the seventeenth and eighteenth centuries. Each of these beverages is a stimulant, which helps explain their popularity, but by themselves they taste bitter. Sugar made them palatable to European consumers. The demand for sugar and these drinks became mutually reinforcing. As the markets for coffee, chocolate, and especially tea grew in England and the English colonies, so did the demand for sugar.

As the production of sugar rose, its price fell. The cheaper sugar became, the more of it Europeans consumed. By the end of the eighteenth century, tea with sugar was cheaper than beer or milk, and it had become the most popular drink among the British poor (while remaining an elegant drink for the wealthy). Moreover, because sugar had originally been a luxury item, people felt they were improving their standard of living if they consumed more of it.

During the nineteenth century, sugar consumption continued to expand, and sugar became even cheaper when free-trade policies reduced protective import duties and when the French began to manufacture it from sugar beets, which could easily be grown in Europe. Nineteenth-century Westerners developed the custom of ending a meal with dessert, food usually sweetened with sugar.

Sidney Mintz, *Sweetness and Power: The Place of Sugar in Modern History* (New York: Penguin Books, 1985).

■ *How did the colonization of the Americas affect the European demand for sugar? Why did sugar consumption increase so rapidly in Europe during the eighteenth and nineteenth centuries?*

Sugar was both raised and processed on plantations such as this one in Brazil. Hulton/Corbis

breached. Until the middle of the eighteenth century, the primary purpose of the Spanish Empire was to supply Spain with the precious metals mined in the New World.

COLONIAL GOVERNMENT

Because Queen Isabella of Castile (r. 1474–1504) had commissioned Columbus, the technical legal link between the New World and Spain was the crown of Castile. Its powers both at home and in America were subject to few limitations. The Castilian monarch assigned the government of America to the Council of the Indies, which, with the monarch, nominated the viceroys of New Spain (Mexico) and Peru. These viceroys served as the chief executives in the New World and carried out the laws promulgated by the Council of the Indies.

Each of the viceroyalties was divided into several subordinate judicial councils, known as *audiencias*. There was also a variety of local officers, the most important of which were the *corregidores*, who presided over municipal councils. All of these officers provided the monarchy with a vast array of patronage, usually bestowed on persons born in Spain. Virtually all power flowed from the top of this political structure downward; in effect, local initiative or self-government scarcely existed.

The fortress of El Morro in the harbor of San Juan, Puerto Rico. This massive citadel protected the Spanish treasure fleets that carried gold and silver each year to Spain from the mines of Mexico and Peru. Comstock Images

TRADE REGULATION

The colonial political structures functioned largely to support Spanish commercial self-interest. The *Casa de Contratación* (House of Trade) in Seville regulated all trade with the New World. Cádiz was the only port authorized for use in the American trade. The *Casa* was the most influential institution of the Spanish Empire. Its members worked closely with the *Consulado* (Merchant Guild) of Seville and other groups involved with American commerce in Cádiz.

A complicated system of trade and bullion fleets administered from Seville was the key to maintaining Spain's trade monopoly. Each year, a fleet of commercial vessels (the *flota*) controlled by Seville merchants and escorted by warships carried merchandise from Spain to a few specified ports in America, including Portobello, Veracruz, and Cartagena on the Atlantic coast. (See "Visitors Describe the Portobello Fair.") There were no authorized ports on the Pacific Coast. Areas far to the south, such as Buenos Aires on the Rio de la Plata, received goods only after the shipments had been unloaded at one of the authorized ports. After selling their wares, the ships were loaded with silver and gold bullion, usually wintered in heavily fortified Caribbean ports, and then sailed back to Spain. The *flota* system always worked imperfectly, but trade outside it was illegal. Regulations prohibited the Spanish colonists within the American Empire from establishing direct trade with each other and from building their own shipping and commercial industry. Foreign merchants were also forbidden to breach the Spanish monopoly.

COLONIAL REFORM UNDER THE SPANISH BOURBON MONARCHS

A crucial change occurred in the Spanish colonial system in the early eighteenth century. The War of the Spanish Succession (1701–1714) and the Treaty of Utrecht (1713) replaced the Spanish Habsburgs with the Bourbons of France on the Spanish throne. Philip V (r. 1700–1746) and his successors tried to use French administrative skills to reassert the imperial trade monopoly, which had decayed under the last Spanish Habsburgs, and thus attempted to improve the domestic economy and revive Spanish power in European affairs.

Under Philip V, Spanish coastal patrol vessels tried to suppress smuggling in American waters. (See "Buccaneers Prowl the High Seas.") An incident arising from this policy (discussed later in the chapter) led to war with England in 1739, the year in which Philip established the viceroyalty of New

VISITORS DESCRIBE THE PORTOBELLO FAIR

• •

The Spanish tried to restrict all trade within their Latin American Empire to a few designated ports. Each year, a fair was held in certain of these ports. The most famous such port was Portobello on the Isthmus of Panama. In the 1730s, two visitors saw the event and described it. This fair was the chief means of facilitating trade between the western coast of South America and Spain.

■ *What products were sold at the fair? How does this passage illustrate the inefficiency of monopoly trade in the Spanish Empire and the many chances for smuggling?*

The town of Portobello, so thinly inhabited, by reason of its noxious air, the scarcity of provisions, and the soil, becomes, at the time of the [Spanish] galleons one of the most populous places in all South America. . . .

The ships are no sooner moored in the harbour, than the first work is, to erect, in the square, a tent made of the ship's sails, for receiving its cargo; at which the proprietors of the goods are present, in order to find their bales, by the marks which distinguish them. These bales are drawn on sledges, to their respective places by the crew of every ship, and the money given them is proportionally divided.

Whilst the seamen and European traders are thus employed, the land is covered with droves of mules from Panama, each drove consisting of above an hundred, loaded with chests of gold and silver, on account of the merchants of Peru. Some unload them at the exchange, others in the middle of the square; yet, amidst the hurry and confusion of such crowds, no theft, loss, or disturbance, is ever known. He who has seen this place during the *tiempo muerto*, or dead time, solitary, poor, and a perpetual silence reigning everywhere; the harbour quite empty, and every place wearing a melancholy aspect; must be filled with astonishment at the sudden change, to see the bustling multitudes,

every house crowded, the square and streets encumbered with bales and chests of gold and silver of all kinds; the harbour full of ships and vessels, some bringing by the way of Rio de Chape the goods of Peru, such as *cacao*, *quinquina*, or Jesuit's bark, Vicuña wool, and bezoar stones; others coming from Carthagena, loaded with provisions; and thus a spot, at all times detested for its deleterious qualities, becomes the staple of the riches of the old and new world, and the scene of one of the most considerable branches of commerce in the whole earth.

The ships being unloaded, and the merchants of Peru, together with the president of Panama, arrived, the fair comes under deliberation. And for this purpose the deputies of the several parties repair on board the commodore of the galleons, where, in the presence of the commodore, and the president of Panama, . . . the prices of the several kinds of merchandizes are settled. . . . The purchases and sales, as likewise the exchanges of money, are transacted by brokers, both from Spain and Peru. After this, every one begins to dispose of his goods; the Spanish brokers embarking their chests of money, and those of Peru sending away the goods they have purchased, in vessels called *chatas* and *bongos*, up the river Chagres. And thus the fair of Portobello ends.

From George Juan and Antonio de Ulloa, *A Voyage to South America*, Vol. 1 (London, 1772), pp. 103–110, as quoted in Benjamin Keen, ed., *Readings in Latin-American Civilization, 1492 to the Present* (New York: Houghton Mifflin, 1955), pp. 107–108.

Granada in the area that today includes Venezuela, Colombia, and Ecuador. The goal was to increase direct royal government in the area.

During the reign of Ferdinand VI (r. 1746–1759), the great midcentury wars exposed the vulnerability of the empire to naval attack and economic penetration. As an ally of France, Spain emerged as one

of the defeated powers in 1763. Government circles became convinced that further changes in the colonial system had to be undertaken.

Charles III (r. 1759–1788), the most important of the royal imperial reformers, attempted to reassert Spain's control of the empire. Like his two Bourbon predecessors, Charles emphasized royal ministers

BUCCANEERS PROWL THE HIGH SEAS

By no means did all of the trade in the Caribbean Sea occur at the Portobello fair described in the previous document. Piracy was a major problem for transatlantic trade. There was often a fine line between freewheeling buccaneering pirates operating for their own gain and privateers who in effect worked for various European governments that wanted to penetrate the commercial monopoly of the Spanish Empire. Alexander Exquemelin was a ship's surgeon who for a time plied his trade on board a pirate ship and then later settled in Holland. He wrote an account of those days in which he emphasizes the careful code of conduct among the pirates themselves and the harshness of their behavior toward both those on ships they captured and poor farmers and fishermen whom they robbed and virtually enslaved.

■ *How did the restrictive commercial policy of the Spanish Empire encourage piracy and privateering? Was there a code of honor among the pirates? What kinds of people may have suffered most from piracy? To what extent did pirates have any respect for individual freedom? How romantic was the real world of pirates?*

When a buccaneer is going to sea he sends word to all who wish to sail with him. When all are ready, they go on board, each bringing what he needs in the way of weapons, powder and shot.

On the ship, they first discuss where to go and get food supplies. . . . The meat is either [salted] pork or turtle. . . . Sometimes they go and plunder the Spaniards' *corrales*, which are pens where they keep perhaps a thousand head of tame hogs. The rovers . . . find the house of the farmer . . . [whom] unless he gives them as many hogs as they demand, they hang . . . without mercy. . . .

When a ship has been captured, the men decide whether the captain should keep it or not: if the prize is better than their own vessel, they take it and set fire to the other. When a ship is robbed, nobody must plunder and keep the loot to himself. Everything taken . . . must be shared . . ., without any man enjoying a penny more than his faire share. To prevent deceit, before the booty is distributed everyone has to swear an oath on the Bible that he has not kept for himself so much as the value of a sixpence. . . . And should any man be found to have made a false oath, he would be banished from the rovers, and never be allowed in their company. . . .

When they have captured a ship, the buccaneers set the prisoners on shore as soon as possible, apart from two or three whom they keep to do the cooking and other work they themselves do not care for, releasing these men after two or three years.

The rovers frequently put in for fresh supplies at some island or other, often . . . lying off the south coast of Cuba. . . . Everyone goes ashore and sets up his tent, and they take turns to go on marauding expeditions in their canoes. They take prisoner . . . poor men who catch and set turtles for a living, to provide for their wives and children. Once captured, these men have to catch turtle for the rovers as long as they remain on the island. Should the rovers intend to cruise along a coast where turtle abound, they take the fishermen along with them. The poor fellows may be compelled to stay away from their wives and families four or five years, with no news whether they are alive or dead.

Alexander O. Exquemelin, *The Buccaneers of America*, trans. by Alexis Brown, (Baltimore: Penguin Books, 1969), pp. 70–72.

rather than councils. Thus the role of both the Council of the Indies and the *Casa de Contratación* diminished. After 1765, Charles abolished the monopolies of Seville and Cádiz and permitted other Spanish cities to trade with America. He also opened more South American and Caribbean ports to trade and authorized some commerce between Spanish ports in America. In 1776, he organized a fourth viceroyalty in the region of Rio de la Plata, which included much of present-day Argentina, Uruguay, Paraguay, and Bolivia. (See Map 17–1.)

While relaxing Spanish trade with and in America, Charles III attempted to increase the efficiency of tax collection and to end bureaucratic corruption.

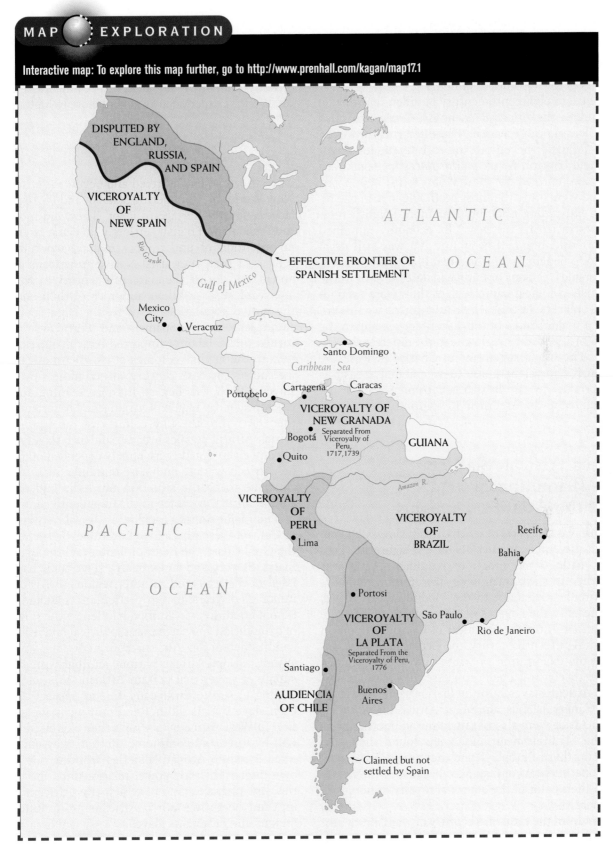

MAP EXPLORATION

Interactive map: To explore this map further, go to http://www.prenhall.com/kagan/map17.1

DISPUTED BY
ENGLAND,
RUSSIA,
AND SPAIN

VICEROYALTY
OF
NEW SPAIN

Rio Grande

EFFECTIVE FRONTIER OF
SPANISH SETTLEMENT

ATLANTIC

OCEAN

Gulf of Mexico

Mexico
City
Veracruz

Santo Domingo

Caribbean Sea

Portobelo
Cartagena
Caracas

VICEROYALTY OF
NEW GRANADA

Bogotá
Separated From
Viceroyalty of
Peru,
1717, 1739

GUIANA

Quito

Amazon R.

VICEROYALTY
OF
PERU

VICEROYALTY
OF
BRAZIL

Reeife

Lima

Bahia

PACIFIC

Portosi

OCEAN

São Paulo
Rio de Janeiro

VICEROYALTY
OF
LA PLATA

Separated From the
Viceroyalty of Peru,
1776

Santiago

Buenos
Aires

AUDIENCIA
OF CHILE

Claimed but not
settled by Spain

MAP 17–1   VICEROYALTIES IN LATIN AMERICA IN 1780   *The late-eighteenth-century
viceroyalties in Latin America display the effort of the Spanish Bourbon monarchy
to establish more direct control of the colonies. They sought this control through the introduction of more royal officials and by establishing more governmental districts.*

To achieve those ends, he introduced the institution of the *intendant* into the Spanish Empire. These loyal royal bureaucrats were patterned on the French *intendants* made so famous and effective as agents of the absolutism of Louis XIV.

The late-eighteenth-century Bourbon reforms did stimulate the imperial economy. Trade expanded and became more varied. These reforms, however, also brought the empire more fully under direct Spanish control. Many **peninsulares** (persons born in Spain) entered the New World to fill new posts, which were often the most profitable jobs in the region. Expanding trade brought more Spanish merchants to Latin America. The economy remained export oriented, and economic life was still organized to benefit Spain. As a result of these policies, the **creoles** (persons of European descent born in the Spanish colonies) came to feel they were second-class subjects. In time, their resentment would provide a major source of the discontent leading to the wars of independence in the early nineteenth century. The imperial reforms of Charles III were the Spanish equivalent of the new colonial measures undertaken by the British government after 1763, which led to the American Revolution.

Black African Slavery, the Plantation System, and the Atlantic Economy

Within various parts of Europe itself, slavery had existed since ancient times. Before the eighteenth century, little or no moral or religious stigma was attached to slave owning or slave trading. It had a continuous existence in the Mediterranean world, where only the sources of slaves changed over the centuries. After the conquest of Constantinople in the mid–fifteenth century, the Ottoman Empire forbade the exportation of white slaves from regions under its control. The Portuguese then began to import African slaves into the Iberian Peninsula from the Canary Islands and West Africa. Black slaves from Africa were also not uncommon in other parts of the Mediterranean, and a few found their way into northern Europe. There they might be used as personal servants or displayed because of the novelty of their color in the courts of royalty or homes of the wealthy.

But from the sixteenth century onward, first within the West Indies and the Spanish and Portuguese settlements in South America and then in the British colonies on the South Atlantic seaboard of North America, slave labor became a fundamental social and economic factor. The development of those plantation economies based on slave labor led to an unprecedented interaction between the peoples of Europe and Africa and between the European settlers in the Americas and Africa. It was from that point onward that Africa and Africans became drawn into the Western experience as never before in history.

THE AFRICAN PRESENCE IN THE AMERICAS

Once they had encountered and begun to settle the New World, the conquering Spanish and Portuguese faced a severe shortage of labor. They and most of the French and English settlers who came later had no intention of undertaking manual work themselves. At first, they used Native Americans as laborers, but during the sixteenth century as well as afterward, disease killed hundreds of thousands of the native population. As a result, labor soon became scarce. The Spanish and Portuguese then turned to the labor of imported African slaves. Settlers in the English colonies of North America during the seventeenth century turned more slowly to slavery, with the largest number coming to the Chesapeake Bay region of Virginia and Maryland and then later into the low country of the Carolinas. Which African peoples became sold into slavery during any given decade very largely depended on internal African warfare and state-building. Such would continue to be the situation until the end of the transatlantic slave trade in the nineteenth century.

The major sources for slaves were slave markets in Central West Africa in Senegambia, Sierra Leone, the Gold Coast, the Bight of Benin, and the Bight of Biafra. Slavery and an extensive slave trade had existed in these as well as other regions of Africa for hundreds of years. Just as particular social and economic conditions in Europe had led to the voyages of exploration and settlement, political and military conditions in the African continent and warfare among various African nations similiarly created a supply of slaves that certain African societies were willing to sell to Europeans. In that respect, European slave traders did not confront a passive situation in West Africa over which they exercised their will by force and commerce. Rather, they encountered dynamic African societies working out their own internal historic power relationships and rivalries, one characteristic of which was Africans selling and acquiring other Africans from different regions and nations as slaves.

The West Indies, Brazil, and Sugar   To grasp the full impact of the forced immigration of Africans on the Americas, we must take into account both continents and the entire picture of the transatlantic

This eighteenth-century print shows bound African captives being forced to a slaving port. It was largely African middlemen who captured slaves in the interior and marched them to the coast. North Wind Picture Archives

economy. Far more slaves were imported into the West Indies and Brazil than into North America. Although citizens of the United States mark the beginning of slavery in 1619 with the arrival of African slaves on a Dutch ship in Jamestown, Virginia, over a century of slave trading in the West Indies and South America had preceded that event. Indeed, by the late sixteenth century, Africans had become a major social presence on the islands of the West Indies and in the major cities of both Spanish and Portuguese South America. That presence and influence in those regions would grow over the centuries. African labor and African immigrant slave communities were the most prominent social feature of those regions, making the development of those economies and cultures what one historian has described as "a Euro-African phenomenon."[2] There, African slaves equaled or more generally surpassed the numbers of white European settlers in what soon constituted multiracial societies. Someone passing through the marketplace of those towns and cities would have heard a vast number of different African, as well as European, languages. Although Native American labor continued to be exploited on the South American continent, it was increasingly a marginal presence in the ever-expanding African slave-based plantation economy of the Atlantic seaboard, the Caribbean, and offshore islands.

Within much of Spanish South America, the numbers of slaves declined during the late seventeenth century, and slavery became somewhat less fundamental there than elsewhere. Slavery continued to expand its influence, however, in Brazil and in the Caribbean through the spreading cultivation of sugar to meet the demand of the European market. By the close of the seventeenth century, the Caribbean islands were the world center for the production of sugar and the chief supplier for the ever-growing consumer demand for the product. The opening of new areas of cultivation and other economic enterprises required additional slaves during the eighteenth century, a period of major slave importation. The growing prosperity of sugar islands that had begun to be exploited in the late seventeenth century, as well as new sugar, coffee, and tobacco regions of Brazil, where gold mining also required additional slaves, accounts for this increase in slave commerce and allowed higher prices to be paid for slaves. In Brazil, the West Indies, and the southern British colonies, prosperity and slavery went hand in hand.

A vast increase in the number of Africans brought as slaves to the Americas occurred during the eighteenth century, with the majority arriving in the Caribbean or Brazil. Early in the century, as many as 20,000 new Africans a year arrived in the West Indies as slaves. By 1725, it has been estimated, almost 90 percent of the population of Jamaica was black slaves. After the middle of the century, for some time the numbers were even larger. The influx of new Africans in most areas—even in the British colonies—meant the numbers of new forced immigrants outnumbered the slaves of African descent already present.

Newly imported African slaves were needed because the fertility rate of the earlier slave population was low and the death rate high from disease, overwork, and malnutrition. The West Indies proved a particularly difficult region in which to secure a stable, self-reproducing slave population. The conditions for slaves there simply led to very high rates of mortality with new slaves coming primarily

[2]John Thornton, *Africa and the Africans in the Making of the Atlantic World, 1400–1800*, 2nd ed. (Cambridge, UK: Cambridge University Press, 1998), p. 140.

from the ongoing slave trade. A similar situation prevailed in Brazil. Restocking through the slave trade meant the slave population of those areas consisted of African-born persons rather than of persons of African descent. Consequently, one of the key factors in the social life of many of the areas of American slavery during the eighteenth century was the presence of persons newly arrived from Africa, carrying with them African languages, religion, culture, and local African ethnic identities that they would infuse into the already existing slave communities. Thus the eighteenth century witnessed an enormous impact of a new African presence throughout the Americas.

SLAVERY AND THE TRANSATLANTIC ECONOMY

Different nations dominated the slave trade in different periods. During the sixteenth century, the Portuguese and the Spanish were most involved. The Dutch supplanted them during most of the seventeenth century. Thereafter, during the late seventeenth and eighteenth centuries, the English constituted the chief slave traders. French traders also participated.

Slavery touched most of the economy of the transatlantic world. Colonial trade followed roughly a geographic triangle. European goods—quite often guns—were carried to Africa to be exchanged for slaves, who were then taken to the West Indies, where they were traded for sugar and other tropical products, which were then shipped to Europe. Not all ships covered all three legs of the triangle. Another major trade pattern existed between New England and the West Indies with New England fish or ship stores being traded for sugar. At various moments, the prosperity of such cities as Amsterdam, Liverpool, England, and Nantes, France, rested very largely on the slave trade. Cities in the British North American colonies, such as Newport, Rhode Island, profited from slavery sometimes by trading in slaves, but more often by supplying other goods to the West Indian market. All the shippers who handled cotton, tobacco, and sugar depended on slavery, though they might not have had direct contact with the institution, as did all the manufacturers and merchants who produced the finished products for the consumer market. (See "Art & the West: A Dramatic Moment in the Transatlantic World," p. 580.)

As had been the case during previous centuries, eighteenth-century political turmoil in Africa, such as the Kongo civil wars, made possible the increasing supply of slaves during that period. These Kongo wars had originated in a dispute over succession in the late seventeenth century and continued into the eighteenth. In some cases, captives were simply sold to European slave traders calling at ports along the West African coast. In other cases, African leaders conducted slave raids so their captives could be sold to further finance the purchase of weapons for warfare. Similar political unrest and turmoil in the Gold Coast during the eighteenth century led to an increased supply of African captives to be sold into American slavery. Consequently, there existed a close relationship between warfare in West Africa, often far into the interior, and the economic development of the American Atlantic seaboard.

THE EXPERIENCE OF SLAVERY

The Portuguese, Spanish, Dutch, French, and English slave traders forcibly transported several million (perhaps more than 9 million, the exact numbers being in much dispute) Africans to the New World—the largest example of forced intercontinental migration in human history. During the first four centuries of settlement, far more black slaves came involuntarily to the New World than did free European settlers or European indentured servants. The conditions of slaves' passage across the Atlantic were wretched. (See "A Slave Trader Describes the Atlantic Passage.") Quarters were unspeakably cramped, food was bad, disease was rampant. Many Africans died during the crossing. There were always more African men than women transported, so it was difficult to keep any form of traditional African extended family structures in place. During the passage and later, many Africans attempted to recreate such structures among themselves, even if they were not actually related by direct family ties. (See "Olaudah Equiano Recalls His Experience at the Slave Market in Barbados.")

In the Americas, the slave population stood divided among new Africans recently arrived, old Africans who had lived there for some years, and creoles who were the descendants of earlier generations of African slaves. Plantation owners preferred the two latter groups, who were accustomed to the life of slavery. They sold for higher prices. The newly arrived Africans were subjected to a process known as *seasoning*, whereby they were prepared for the laborious discipline of slavery and made to understand they were no longer free. The process might involve receiving new names, acquiring new work skills, and learning, to an extent, the local European language. In some cases, newly arrived Africans would

A SLAVE TRADER DESCRIBES THE ATLANTIC PASSAGE

During 1693 and 1694, Captain Thomas Phillips carried slaves from Africa to Barbados on the ship Hannibal. *The financial backer of the voyage was the Royal African Company of London, which held an English crown monopoly on slave trading. Phillips sailed to the west coast of Africa, where he purchased the Africans who were sold into slavery by an African king. Then he set sail westward.*

■ *Who are the various people described in this document who in one way or another were involved in or profited from the slave trade? What dangers did the Africans face on the voyage? What contemporary attitudes could have led this ship captain to treat and think of his human cargo simply as goods to be transported? What are the grounds of his self-pity for the difficulties he met?*

Having bought my complement of 700 slaves, 480 men and 220 women, and finish'd all my business at Whidaw [on the Gold Coast of Africa], I took my leave of the old king and his *cappasheirs* [attendants], and parted, with many affectionate expressions on both sides, being forced to promise him that I would return again the next year, with several things he desired me to bring from England.... I set sail the 27th of July in the morning, accompany'd with the East-India Merchant, who had bought 650 slaves, for the Island of St. Thomas ... from which we took our departure on August 25th and set sail for Barbadoes.

We spent in our passage from St. Thomas to Barbadoes two months eleven days, from the 25th of August to the 4th of November following: in which time there happened such sickness and mortality among my poor men and Negroes. Of the first we buried 14, and of the last 320, which was a great detriment to our voyage, the Royal African Company losing ten pounds by every slave that died, and the owners of the ship ten pounds ten shillings, being the freight agreed on to be paid by the charter-party for every Negro delivered alive ashore to the African Company's agents at Barbadoes.... The loss in all amounted to near 6500 pounds sterling.

The distemper which my men as well as the blacks mostly died of was the white flux, which was so violent and inveterate that no medicine would in the least check it, so that when any of our men were seized with it, we esteemed him a dead man, as he generally proved....

The Negroes are so incident to the small-pox that few ships that carry them escape without it, and sometimes it makes vast havock and destruction among them. But tho' we had 100 at a time sick of it, and that it went thro' the ship, yet we lost not above a dozen by it. All the assistance we gave the diseased was only as much water as they desir'd to drink, and some palm-oil to annoint their sores, and they would generally recover without any other helps but what kind nature gave them....

But what the small pox spar'd, the flux swept off, to our great regret, after all our pains and care to give them their messes in due order and season, keeping their lodgings as clean and sweet as possible, and enduring so much misery and stench so long among a parcel of creatures nastier than swine, and after all our expectations to be defeated by their mortality....

No gold-finders can endure so much noisome slavery as they do who carry Negroes; for those have some respite and satisfaction, but we endure twice the misery; and yet by their mortality our voyages are ruin'd, and we pine and fret ourselves to death, and take so much pains to so little purpose.

From Thomas Phillips, "Journal," *A Collection of Voyages and Travels*, Vol. 6, ed. by Awnsham and John Churchill (London, 1746), as quoted in Thomas Howard, ed., *Black Voyage: Eyewitness Accounts of the Atlantic Slave Trade* (Boston: Little, Brown, 1971), pp. 85–87.

work in a kind of apprentice relationship to an older African slave of similar ethnic background. Other slaves were broken into slave labor through work on field gangs. Occasionally, plantation owners would prefer to buy younger Africans, whom they thought might be more easily acculturated to the labor conditions of the Americas. Generally, it was only such recently arrived Africans, seasoned in the West Indies, whom North American plantation owners were willing to purchase.

OLAUDAH EQUIANO RECALLS HIS EXPERIENCE AT THE SLAVE MARKET IN BARBADOS

Olaudah Equiano composed one of the most popular and influential slave narratives of the late eighteenth and early nineteenth centuries. He had led a remarkable life. Born in West Africa in what is today Nigeria, he spent his early life among the Ibo. He was captured and sold into slavery, making the dreaded Atlantic crossing described in the previous document. In the passage that follows, he recounts his arrival in Barbados and the experience of cultural disorientation, sale into slavery, and seeing Africans separated from their families. Equiano's life did not end in slavery, the most destructive aspects of which he also described in vivid detail. He achieved his freedom and then led an adventuresome life on various commercial and military ships plying the Caribbean, the Atlantic, and the Mediterranean. He also made a trip to the Arctic Ocean. Equiano's account consequently describes not only the life of a person taken from Africa and sold into American slavery, but also the life of a person who, once free, explored the entire transatlantic world. His autobiographical narrative, which first appeared in 1789 and displayed Equiano's wide reading, served two purposes for the antislavery campaign that commenced in the second half of the eighteenth century. (See "The West & the World," pp. 736–741.) First, it provided a firsthand report of the slave experience in crossing from Africa to America. Second, his powerful rhetoric and clear arguments demonstrated that, if free, Africans could achieve real personal independence. Many defenders of slavery had denied that Africans possessed the character and intelligence to be free persons.

■ *What were the fears of the Africans on the slave ship as they approached the port? How were older slaves in Barbados used to calm their fears? How did the sale of slaves proceed? What happened to African families in the process of the sale?*

Language and Culture The plantation to which the slaves eventually arrived always lay in a more or less isolated rural setting, but its inhabitants usually could visit their counterparts on other plantations or in nearby towns on market days. Within the sharply restricted confines of slavery, the recently arrived Africans were able at least for a time to sustain elements of their own culture and social structures. From the West Indies southward throughout the eighteenth century, there were more people whose first language was African rather than European. For example, Coromantee was the predominant language on Jamaica. In South Carolina and on St. Domingue, Kikongo was the language most commonly spoken among African slaves. It would take more than two generations for the colonial language to dominate, and even then what often resulted was a dialect combining an African and a European language.

Through these languages, Africans on plantation estates could organize themselves into nations with similar, though not necessarily identical, ethnic ties to regions of West Africa. The loyalty achieved through a shared African language in the American setting created a solidarity among African slaves that was wider than what in Africa had probably been a primary loyalty to a village. These nations organized and sustained by the plantation experience might also become the basis for a wide variety of religious communities among African slaves that might have some kind of roots in their African experience. In this manner, some Africans maintained a loyalty to the Islamic faith of their homeland.

Many of the African nations on plantations, such as those of Brazil, organized lay brotherhoods that carried out various kinds of charitable work within the slave communities. In the Americas,

At last, we came in sight . . . of Barbados, . . . and we soon anchored . . . off Bridgetown. Many merchants and planters now came on board. . . . They put us in separate parcels, and examined us attentively. They also made us jump, and pointed to the land, signifying we were to go there. We thought by this we should be eaten by these ugly men, as they appeared to us; and when, soon after we were all put down under the deck again, there was much dread and trembling among us, and nothing but bitter cries to be heard all the night from these apprehension, insomuch that at last the white people got some old slaves from the land to pacify us. They told us we were not to be eaten, but to work, and were soon to go on land, where we should see many of our country people. This report eased us much. . . . We were conducted immediately to the merchant's yard, where we were all pent up together like so many sheep in a fold, without regard to sex or age. As every object was new to me, everything filled me with surprise . . . and indeed I thought these people were full of nothing but magical arts. . . . We were not many days in the merchant's custody before we were sold after their usual manner which was this: On a signal given (as the beat of a drum), the buyers rush at once into the yard where the slaves are confined, and make choice of that parcel they like best. The noise and clamour with which this is attended, and the eagerness visible in the countenances of the buyers, serve not a little to increase the apprehension of the terrified Africans, who may well be supposed to consider them as the ministers of that destruction to which they think themselves devoted. In this manner, without scruple, relations and friends separate, most of them never to see each other again. I remember in the vessel in which I was brought over, in the men's apartment, there were several brothers who, in the sale, were sold in different lots; and it was very moving on this occasion to see and hear their cries at parting. . . . Surely this is a new refinement in cruelty, which, while it has no advantage to atone for it, thus aggravates distress, and adds fresh horrors even to the wretchedness of slavery.

From *The Interesting Narrative of the Life of Olaudah Equiano* or *Gustavus Vassa, The African, Written by Himself* (first published 1789), as quoted in Henry Louis Gates, Jr., and William L. Andrews, eds., *Pioneers of the Black Atlantic: Five Slave Narratives from the Enlightenment, 1772–1815* (Washington, DC: Counterpoint, 1998), pp. 221–223.

the various African nations would elect their own kings and queens, who might preside over gatherings of the members of the nation drawn from various plantations.

The shared language of a particular African nation in an American setting provided a means for exclusive communication among slaves on the occasions of revolts such as that in South Carolina in 1739, in Jamaica in the early 1760s, and, most successfully, during the Haitian Revolution of the 1790s. In the South Carolina revolt, the slave owners believed their slaves had communicated among themselves by playing African drums. In the aftermath of the revolt, the owners attempted to suppress the presence of such drum playing in the slave community.

Daily Life   The life conditions of plantation slaves differed from colony to colony. Black slaves living in Portuguese areas had the fewest legal protections. In the Spanish colonies, the church attempted to provide some protection for black slaves, but devoted more effort toward protecting the Native Americans. Slave codes were developed in the British and the French colonies during the seventeenth century, but they provided only the most limited protection to slaves while assuring dominance to owners. Virtually all slave owners feared a revolt, and legislation and other regulations were intended to prevent one. All slave laws favored the master rather than the slave. Slave masters were permitted to whip slaves and inflict other exceedingly harsh corporal punishment. Furthermore, slaves were often forbidden to gather in large groups lest they plan a revolt. In most of these slave societies, the marriages of slaves were not recognized by law. Legally, the children of slaves continued to be slaves and were owned by the owner of their parents.

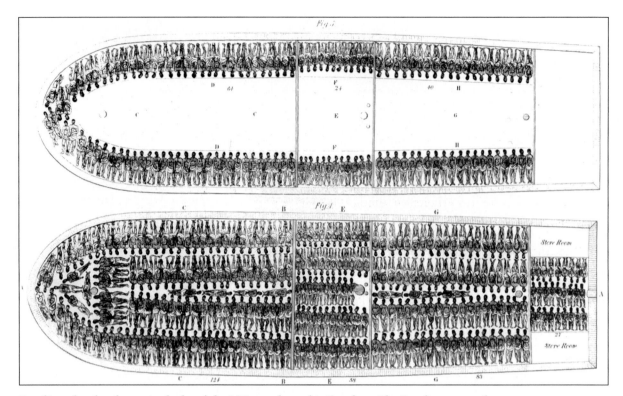

Loading plan for the main decks of the 320-ton slave ship Brookes. *The* Brookes *was only 25 feet wide and 100 feet long, but as many as 609 slaves were crammed on board for the nightmarish passage to the Americas. The average space allowed each person was only about 78 inches by 16 inches. The document from Thomas Phillips's journal describes the voyage across the Atlantic. (See "A Slave Trader Describes the Atlantic Passage.")*
Photographs and Prints Division, Schomburg Center for Research in Black Culture, The New York Public Library, Astor, Lenox and Tilden Foundations

The daily life of most slaves during these centuries was one of hard agricultural labor, poor diet, and inadequate housing. Slave families could be separated by the owner during his life or sold separately after his death. Their welfare and their lives were sacrificed to the continuing expansion of the sugar, rice, and tobacco plantations that made their owners wealthy and that produced goods for European consumers. Scholars have sometimes concluded that slaves in one area lived better than in another. Today, it is generally accepted that all the slaves in plantation societies led exposed and difficult lives with little variation among them.

Conversion to Christianity The African slaves who were transported to the Americas, were, like the Native Americans, eventually converted in most cases to Christianity. In the Spanish, French, and Portuguese domains, they became Roman Catholics, and in the English colonies they became Protestants of one denomination or another. Both forms of Christianity preached to slaves the acceptance of their situation and a natural social hierarchy with masters at the top.

Although African religion of a systematic character eventually disappeared, especially in the British colonies, some African religious practices survived in muted forms, gradually separated from African religious belief. These included an African understanding of nature and the cosmos and the belief in witches and other people with special spiritual powers, such as conjurers, healers, and practitioners of voodoo. Although slaves did manage to mix Christianity with their previous African religions, their conversion to Christianity was nonetheless another example, like that of the Native Americans, of the crushing of a set of non-European cultural values in the context of the New World economies and social structures.

European Racial Attitudes The European settlers in the Americas and the slave traders also carried with them prejudices against black Africans. Many Europeans considered Africans to be savages or less than civilized. Still others looked down on them simply because they were slaves. Both Christians and Muslims had shared these attitudes in the Mediterranean world, where slavery had for so long

Slaves on the plantations of the American South were the chattel property of their masters, and their lives were grim. Some artists sought to disguise this harsh reality by depicting the lighter moments of slave society as in this scene of slaves dancing. Getty Images Inc.— Hulton Archive Photos

existed. Furthermore, many European languages and cultures attached negative connotations to the idea and image of blackness. In virtually all these plantation societies, race was an important element in keeping black slaves in a position of marked subservience. Although racial thinking in regard to slavery became important primarily in the nineteenth century, the fact of slaves being differentiated from the rest of the population by race, as well as by their being chattel property, was fundamental to the system. All of these factors formed the racial prejudice that continues to plague society today in the former slave-owning regions.

The plantations that stretched from the middle Atlantic colonies of North America through the West Indies and into Brazil constituted a vast corridor of slave societies in which social and economic subordination was based on both involuntary servitude and race. These societies had not existed before the European discovery and exploitation of the resources of the Americas. In its extent and totality of dependence on slave labor and racial differences, this kind of society was novel in both European and world history. As already noted, its social and economic influence touched not only the plantation societies themselves, but West Africa, western Europe, and New England. It existed from the sixteenth century through the second half of the nineteenth century, when the emancipation of slaves had been completed through the slave revolt of Saint Domingue (1794), British outlawing of the slave trade (1807), the Latin American wars of independence, the Emancipation Proclamation of 1863 in the United States, and the Brazilian emancipation of 1888. To the present day, every society in

which plantation slavery once existed still contends with the long-term effects of that institution.

Mid-Eighteenth-Century Wars

From the standpoint of international relations, the state system of the middle of the eighteenth century was quite unstable and tended to lead the major states of Europe into periods of prolonged warfare. The statesmen of the period generally assumed that warfare could be used to further national interests. There were essentially no forces or powers who saw it in their interest to prevent war or to maintain peace. Because eighteenth-century wars before the French Revolution were fought by professional armies and navies, civilian populations were rarely drawn deeply into the conflicts. Wars were not associated with domestic political or social upheaval, and peace was not associated with the achievement of international stability. Consequently, periods of peace at the conclusion of a war were often viewed simply as times when a nation might become strong enough to recommence warfare at a later period for the purpose of seizing another nation's territory or of invading another empire's area of trading monopoly.

There were two fundamental areas of great power rivalry: the overseas empires and central and eastern Europe. Alliances and general strategic concerns repeatedly interrelated these regions of conflict.

THE WAR OF JENKINS'S EAR

In the middle of the eighteenth century, the West Indies had become a hotbed of trade rivalry. Spain attempted to tighten its monopoly, and English smugglers, shippers, and pirates attempted to pierce it. Matters came to a climax in the late 1730s.

The Treaty of Utrecht (1713) gave two special privileges to Great Britain in the Spanish Empire. The British received a thirty-year **asiento,** or contract, to furnish slaves to the Spanish. Britain also gained the right to send one ship each year to the trading fair at Portobello, a major Caribbean seaport on the Panamanian coast. These two privileges allowed British traders and smugglers potential inroads into the Spanish market. Little but friction arose from those rights. During the night, offshore, British ships often resupplied the annual legal Portobello ship with additional goods as it lay in port. Much to the chagrin of the British, the Spanish government took its own alleged trading monopoly seriously and maintained coastal patrols, which boarded and searched English vessels to look for contraband.

In 1731, during one such boarding operation, there was a fight, and the Spaniards cut off the ear of an English captain named Robert Jenkins. Thereafter he carried about his severed ear preserved in a jar of brandy. This incident was of little importance until 1738, when Jenkins appeared before the British Parliament, reportedly brandishing his ear as an example of Spanish atrocities to British merchants in the West Indies. The British merchant and West Indies interests put great pressure on Parliament to relieve Spanish intervention in their trade. Sir Robert Walpole (1676–1745), the British prime minister, could not resist these pressures. In late 1739, Great Britain went to war with Spain. This war might have been a relatively minor incident, but because of developments in continental European politics, it became the opening encounter to a series of European wars fought across the world until 1815.

THE WAR OF THE AUSTRIAN SUCCESSION (1740–1748)

In December 1740, after being king of Prussia for less than seven months, Frederick II seized the Austrian province of Silesia in eastern Germany. The invasion shattered the provisions of the Pragmatic Sanction (see Chapter 15) and upset the continental balance of power as established by the Treaty of Utrecht. The young king of Prussia had treated the House of Habsburg simply as another German state rather than as the leading power in the region. Silesia itself rounded out Prussia's possessions, and Frederick was determined to keep his ill-gotten prize.

Maria Theresa Preserves the Habsburg Empire The Prussian seizure of Silesia could have marked the

opening of a general hunting season on Habsburg holdings and the beginning of revolts by Habsburg subjects. Instead, it led to new political allegiances. Maria Theresa's great achievement was not the reconquest of Silesia, which eluded her, but the preservation of the Habsburg Empire as a major political power.

Maria Theresa was then only twenty-three and had succeeded to the Habsburg realms only two months before the invasion. She won loyalty and support from her various subjects not merely through her heroism, but, more specifically, by granting new privileges to the nobility. Most significant, the empress recognized Hungary as the most important of her crowns and promised the Magyars considerable local autonomy. She thus preserved the Habsburg state, but at considerable cost to the power of the central monarchy.

Hungary would continue to be, as it had been in the past, a particularly troublesome area in the Habsburg Empire. When the monarchy enjoyed periods of strength and security, guarantees made to Hungary could be ignored. At times of weakness or when the Magyars could stir enough opposition, the monarchy promised new concessions.

France Draws Great Britain into the War The war over the Austrian succession and the British-Spanish commercial conflict could have remained separate disputes. What quickly united them was the role of France. Just as British merchant interests had pushed Sir Robert Walpole into war, a group of aggressive court aristocrats compelled the elderly Cardinal Fleury (1653–1743), first minister of Louis XV, to abandon his planned naval attack on British trade and instead to support the Prussian aggression against Austria, the traditional enemy of France. This was among the more fateful decisions in French history.

In the first place, aid to Prussia consolidated a new and powerful state in Germany. That new power could, and indeed later did, endanger France. Second, the French move against Austria brought Great Britain into the continental war, as Britain sought to make sure the Low Countries remained in the friendly hands of Austria, not France. In 1744, the British-French conflict expanded beyond the Continent, as France decided to support Spain against Britain in the New World. As a result, French military and economic resources were badly divided. France could not bring sufficient strength to the colonial struggle. Having chosen to continue the old struggle with Austria, France lost the struggle for the future against Great Britain. The war ended in stalemate in 1748 with the Treaty of Aix-la-Chapelle. Prussia retained Silesia, and Spain

Maria Theresa of Austria provided the leadership that saved the Habsburg Empire from possible disintegration after the Prussian invasion of Silesia in 1740. Kunsthistorisches Museum, Vienna

renewed the *asiento* agreement with Great Britain. Most observers rightly thought the treaty was a truce rather than a permanent peace.

THE "DIPLOMATIC REVOLUTION" OF 1756

Before the rivalries again erupted into war, a dramatic shift of alliances took place. In January 1756, Prussia and Great Britain signed the Convention of Westminster, a defensive alliance aimed at preventing the entry of foreign troops into the Germanies. Frederick II feared invasions by both Russia and France. The convention meant that Great Britain, the ally of Austria since the wars of Louis XIV, had now joined forces with Austria's major eighteenth-century enemy.

Maria Theresa was despondent over this development. It delighted her foreign minister, Prince Wenzel Anton Kaunitz (1711–1794), however. He had long hoped for an alliance with France to help dismember Prussia. The Convention of Westmin-

ster made possible this alliance, which would have been unthinkable a few years earlier. France was agreeable because Frederick had not consulted with its ministers before coming to his understanding with Britain. So, later in May 1756, France and Austria signed a defensive alliance. Kaunitz had succeeded in completely reversing the direction that French foreign policy had followed since the sixteenth century. France would now fight to restore Austrian supremacy in central Europe.

THE SEVEN YEARS' WAR (1756–1763)

Although the Treaty of Aix-la-Chapelle had brought peace in Europe, France and Great Britain continued to struggle unofficially on the colonial front. There were constant clashes between their settlers in the Ohio River valley and in upper New England. These were the prelude to what is known in American history as the French and Indian War. Once again, however, Frederick II precipitated a European war that extended into a colonial theater.

Frederick the Great Opens Hostilities In August 1756, Frederick II opened what would become the Seven Years' War by invading Saxony. Frederick considered this to be a preemptive strike against a conspiracy by Saxony, Austria, and France to destroy Prussian power. He regarded the invasion as a continuation of the defensive strategy of the Convention of Westminster. The invasion itself, however, created the very destructive alliance that Frederick feared. In the spring of 1757, France and Austria made a new alliance dedicated to the destruction of Prussia. They were eventually joined by Sweden, Russia, and many of the smaller German states. (See "Frederick the Great Rallies His Officers for Battle.")

Two factors in addition to Frederick's stubborn leadership (it was after this war that he came to be called Frederick the Great) saved Prussia. First, Britain furnished considerable financial aid. Second, in 1762, Empress Elizabeth of Russia died. Her successor was Tsar Peter III (he was murdered the same year), whose admiration for Frederick was boundless. He immediately made peace with Prussia, thus relieving Frederick of one enemy and allowing him to hold off Austria and France. The Treaty of Hubertusburg of 1763 ended the continental conflict with no significant changes in prewar borders. Silesia remained Prussian, and Prussia clearly stood among the ranks of the great powers.

William Pitt's Strategy for Winning North America The survival of Prussia was less impressive to the rest of Europe than were the victories of Great Britain in every theater of conflict. The architect of these victories was William Pitt the Elder (1708–1778). Pitt was a person of colossal ego and administrative genius who had grown up in a commercial family.

Although he had previously criticized British involvement with the Continent, once he became secretary of state in charge of the war in 1757, he reversed himself and pumped huge financial subsidies into the coffers of Frederick the Great. He regarded the German conflict as a way to divert French resources and attention from the colonial struggle. He later boasted of having won America on the plains of Germany.

North America was the center of Pitt's real concern. Put quite simply, he wanted all of North America east of the Mississippi for Great Britain, and that was exactly what he won. He sent more than 40,000 regular English and colonial troops against the French in Canada. Never had so many soldiers been devoted to a field of colonial warfare. He achieved unprecedented cooperation with the American colonies, whose leaders realized they might finally defeat their French neighbors.

The French government was unwilling and unable to direct similar resources against the English in America. Their military administration was corrupt, the military and political commands in Canada were divided, and France could not adequately provision its North American forces. In September 1759, on the Plains of Abraham, overlooking the valley of the Saint Lawrence River at Quebec City, the British army under General James Wolfe defeated the French under Lieutenant General Louis Joseph de Montcalm. The French Empire in Canada was ending.

Pitt's colonial vision, however, extended beyond the Saint Lawrence valley and the Great Lakes basin. The major islands of the French West Indies fell to British fleets. Income from the sale of captured sugar helped finance the British war effort. British slave interests captured the bulk of the

General James Wolfe was mortally wounded during his victory over the French at Quebec in 1759. This painting by the American artist Benjamin West (1738–1820) became famous for portraying the dying Wolfe and the officers around him in poses modeled after classical statues. Getty Images Inc.—Hulton Archive Photos

FREDERICK THE GREAT RALLIES HIS OFFICERS FOR BATTLE

In December 1757, Frederick the Great of Prussia addressed his officers before the Battle of Leuthen with the Austrians. Although he had recently defeated the French at Rossbach, he remained in a difficult position with Berlin in the hands of enemy forces.

■ *How does Frederick appeal to patriotism and also to fear of humiliation on the part of his officers? How does he anticipate overcoming his numerical disadvantage? What evidence does this document provide about the kind of obedience and discipline Frederick expected?*

You are aware, gentlemen, that Prince Karl of Lorraine has succeeded in taking Schweidnitz, defeating the duke of Bevern and making himself master of Breslau, while I was engaged in checking the advance of the French and imperial forces. A part of Schleswig, my capital, and all the military stores it contained, are lost, and I should feel myself in dire straits indeed if it were not for my unbounded confidence in your courage, your constancy, and your love for the fatherland, which you have proved to me on so many occasions in the past. . . .

I should feel that I had accomplished nothing if Austria were left in possession of Schleswig. Let me tell you that I propose, in defiance of all the rule of the art of war, to attack the army of Prince Karl, three times as large as ours, wherever I find it. It is here no question of the numbers of the enemy nor of the importance of the positions they have occupied; all this I hope to overcome by the devotion of my troops and the careful carrying out of my plans.

I must take this step or all will be lost; we must defeat the enemy, else we shall all lie buried under his batteries. So I believe—so I shall act.

Communicate my decision to all the officers of the army; prepare the common soldier for the exertions that are to come, and tell him that I feel justified in expecting unquestioning obedience from him. Remember that you are Prussians and you cannot show yourselves unworthy of that distinction. . . .

The regiment of cavalry that does not immediately on the receipt of orders throw itself upon the enemy I will have unmounted immediately after the battle and make it a garrison regiment. The battalion of infantry that even begins to hesitate, no matter what the danger may be, shall lose its flags and its swords and have the gold lace stripped from its uniforms.

And now, gentlemen, farewell; erelong we shall either have defeated the enemy or we shall see each other no more.

James Harvey Robinson, ed., *Readings in European History*, Vol. 2 (New York: Ginn & Company, 1906), pp. 323–324.

French slave trade. Between 1755 and 1760, the value of the French colonial trade fell by more than 80 percent. In India, the British forces under the command of Robert Clive defeated the French in 1757 at the Battle of Plassey. This victory opened the way for the eventual conquest of Bengal in northeast India and later of all India by the British East India Company. Never had Great Britain or any other European power experienced such a complete worldwide military victory.

The Treaty of Paris of 1763 The Treaty of Paris of 1763 reflected somewhat less of a victory than Britain had won on the battlefield. Pitt was no longer in office. George III (r. 1760–1820) and Pitt

had quarreled over policy, and the minister had departed. His replacement was the earl of Bute (1713–1792), a favorite of the new monarch. Bute was responsible for the peace settlement. Britain received all of Canada, the Ohio River valley, and the eastern half of the Mississippi River valley. Britain returned Pondicherry and Chandernagore in India and the West Indian sugar islands of Guadeloupe and Martinique to the French.

The Seven Years' War had been a vast conflict. Tens of thousands of soldiers and sailors had been killed or wounded. Major battles had been fought around the globe. At great internal sacrifice, Prussia had permanently wrested Silesia from Austria and had turned the Holy Roman Empire into an empty

Conflicts of the Mid–Eighteenth Century

1713	Treaty of Utrecht
1739	Outbreak of War of Jenkins's Ear between England and Spain
1740	War of the Austrian Succession commences
1748	Treaty of Aix-la-Chapelle
1756	Convention of Westminster between England and Prussia
1756	Seven Years' War opens
1757	Battle of Plassey
1759	British forces capture Quebec
1763	Treaty of Hubertusburg
1763	Treaty of Paris

shell. Habsburg power now depended largely on the Hungarian domains. France, though still having sources of colonial income, was no longer a great colonial power. The Spanish Empire remained largely intact, but the British were still determined to penetrate its markets.

On the Indian subcontinent, the British East India Company was able to continue to impose its own authority on the decaying indigenous governments. The ramifications of that situation would extend until the middle of the twentieth century. In North America, the British government faced the task of organizing its new territories. From this time until World War II, Great Britain was a world power, not just a European one.

The quarter century of warfare also caused a long series of domestic crises among the European powers. The French defeat convinced many people in that nation of the necessity for political and administrative reform. The financial burdens of the wars had astounded all contemporaries. Every power had to begin to find ways to increase revenues to pay its war debt and to finance its preparation for the next combat. Nowhere did this search for revenue lead to more far-ranging consequences than in the British colonies in North America.

The American Revolution and Europe

The revolt of the British colonies in North America was an event in both transatlantic and European history. It erupted from problems of revenue collection common to all the major powers after the Seven Years' War. The War of the American Revolution also continued the conflict between France and Great Britain. The French support of the Americans deepened the existing financial and administrative difficulties of the French monarchy.

RESISTANCE TO THE IMPERIAL SEARCH FOR REVENUE

After the Treaty of Paris of 1763, the British government faced two imperial problems. The first was the sheer cost of empire, which the British felt they could no longer carry alone. The national debt had risen considerably, as had domestic taxation. Since the American colonies had been the chief beneficiaries of the conflict, the British felt it was rational for the colonies henceforth to bear part of the cost of their protection and administration. The second problem was the vast expanse of new territory in North America that the British had to organize. This included all the land from the mouth of the Saint Lawrence River to the Mississippi River, with its French settlers and, more importantly, its Native American possessors. (See Map 17–2.)

The British drive for revenue began in 1764 with the passage of the Sugar Act under the ministry of George Grenville (1712–1770). The measure attempted to produce more revenue from imports into the colonies by the rigorous collection of what was actually a lower tax. Smugglers who violated the law were to be tried in admiralty courts without juries. The next year, Parliament passed the Stamp Act, which put a tax on legal documents and certain other items such as newspapers. The British considered these taxes legal because the decision to collect them had been approved by Parliament. They regarded them as just because the money was to be spent in the colonies.

The Americans responded that they alone, through their assemblies, had the right to tax themselves and that they were not represented in Parliament. Furthermore, the expenditure in the colonies of the revenue levied by Parliament did not reassure the colonists. They feared that if colonial government was financed from outside, they would lose control over it. In October 1765, the Stamp Act Congress met in America and drew up a protest to the crown. There was much disorder in the colonies, particularly in Massachusetts, roused by groups known as the Sons of Liberty. The colonists agreed to refuse to import British goods. In 1766, Parliament repealed the Stamp Act, but through the Declaratory Act said it had the power to legislate for the colonies.

The Stamp Act crisis set the pattern for the next ten years. Parliament, under the leadership of a royal minister, would approve revenue or administrative legislation. The Americans would then resist by reasoned argument, economic pressure, and violence. Then the British would repeal the legislation, and the process would begin again. Each time, tempers on both sides became more frayed and positions more irreconcilable. With each clash, the Americans more fully developed their own thinking about political liberty.

THE CRISIS AND INDEPENDENCE

In 1767, Charles Townshend (1725–1767), as Chancellor of the Exchequer, the British finance minister, led Parliament to pass a series of revenue acts relating to colonial imports. The colonists again resisted. The ministry sent over its own customs agents to administer the laws. To protect these new officers, the British sent troops to Boston in 1768. The obvious tensions resulted. In March 1770, the Boston Massacre, in which British troops killed five citizens, took place. That same year, Parliament repealed all of the Townshend duties except the one on tea.

In May 1773, Parliament passed a new law relating to the sale of tea by the East India Company. The measure permitted the direct importation of tea into the American colonies. It actually lowered the price of tea while retaining the tax imposed without the colonists' consent. In some cities, the colonists refused to permit the unloading of the tea; in Boston, a shipload of tea was thrown into the harbor.

The British ministry of Lord North (1732–1792) was determined to assert the authority of Parliament over the resistant colonies. During 1774, Parliament passed a series of laws known in American history as the **Intolerable Acts.** These measures closed the port of Boston, reorganized the government of Massachusetts, allowed troops to be quartered in private homes, and removed the trials of royal customs officials to England. The same year, Parliament approved the Quebec Act for the future administration of Canada. It extended the boundaries of Quebec to include the Ohio River valley. The Americans regarded the Quebec Act as an attempt to prevent the extension of their mode of self-government westward beyond the Appalachian Mountains.

During these years, citizens critical of British policy had established committees of correspondence throughout the colonies. They made the various sections of the eastern seaboard aware of common problems and aided united action. In September 1774, these committees organized the gathering of the First Continental Congress in Philadelphia. This body hoped to persuade Parliament to restore self-government in the colonies and to abandon its attempt at direct supervision of

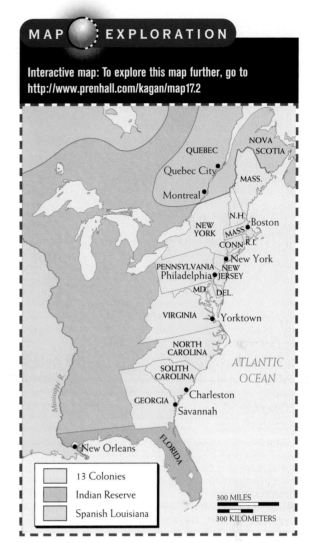

MAP EXPLORATION

Interactive map: To explore this map further, go to
http://www.prenhall.com/kagan/map17.2

MAP 17–2   NORTH AMERICA IN 1763   *In the year of the victory over France, the English colonies lay along the Atlantic seaboard. The difficulties of organizing authority over the previous French territory in Canada and west of the Appalachian Mountains would contribute to the coming of the American Revolution.*

colonial affairs. Conciliation, however, was not forthcoming. By April 1775, the Battles of Lexington and Concord had been fought. In June, the colonists suffered defeat at the Battle of Bunker Hill. Despite that defeat, the colonial assemblies soon began to meet under their own authority rather than under that of the king.

The Second Continental Congress gathered in May 1775. It still sought conciliation with Britain, but the pressure of events led it to begin to conduct the government of the colonies. By August 1775, George III had declared the colonies in rebellion. During the winter, Thomas Paine's (1737–1809) pamphlet *Common Sense* galvanized public opinion

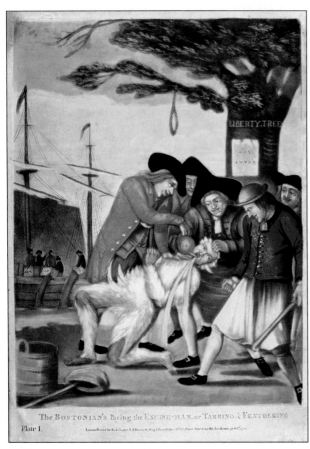

Many Americans fiercely objected to the British Parliament's attempts to tax the colonies. This print of a British tax collector being tarred and feathered warned officials of what could happen to them if they tried to collect these taxes. Joseph Zehavi/Art Resource, N.Y.

in favor of separation from Great Britain. A colonial army and navy were organized. In April 1776, the Continental Congress opened American ports to the trade of all nations. And on July 4, 1776, the Continental Congress adopted the Declaration of Independence. Thereafter, the War of the American Revolution continued until 1781, when the forces of George Washington defeated those of Lord Cornwallis at Yorktown. Early in 1778, however, the war had widened into a European conflict when Benjamin Franklin (1706–1790) persuaded the French government to support the rebellion. In 1779, the Spanish also came to the aid of the colonies. The 1783 Treaty of Paris concluded the conflict, and the thirteen American colonies had established their independence.

AMERICAN POLITICAL IDEAS

The political ideas of the American colonists had largely arisen out of the struggle of seventeenth-century English aristocrats and gentry against the absolutism of the Stuart monarchs. The American colonists looked to the English Revolution of 1688 as having established many of their own fundamental political liberties, as well as those of the English. The colonists claimed that, through the measures imposed from 1763 to 1776, George III and the British Parliament were attacking those liberties and dissolving the bonds of moral and political allegiance that had formerly united the two peoples. Consequently, the colonists employed a theory that had developed to justify an aristocratic rebellion to support their own popular revolution.

These Whig political ideas, largely derived from the writings of John Locke, were, however, only a part of the English ideological heritage that affected the Americans. Throughout the eighteenth century, they had become familiar with a series of British political writers called the Commonwealthmen, who held republican political ideas that had their intellectual roots in the most radical thought of the Puritan revolution. During the early eighteenth century, these writers, the most influential of whom were John Trenchard (1662–1723) and Thomas Gordon (d. 1750) in *Cato's Letters* (1720–1723), had relentlessly criticized the government patronage and parliamentary management of Sir Robert Walpole and his successors. They argued that such government was corrupt and undermined liberty. They regarded much parliamentary taxation as simply a means of financing political corruption. They also considered standing armies instruments of tyranny. In Great Britain, this republican political tradition had only a marginal impact. The writers were largely ignored because most British subjects regarded themselves as the freest people in the world. Three thousand miles away, however, colonists read the radical books and pamphlets and often accepted them at face value. The policy of Great Britain toward America following the Treaty of Paris of 1763 and certain political events in Britain had made many colonists believe the worst fears of the Commonwealthmen were coming true. All of these events coincided with the accession of George III to the throne.

EVENTS IN GREAT BRITAIN

George III (r. 1760–1820) believed a few powerful Whig families and the ministries they controlled had bullied and dominated his two immediate royal predecessors. George III also believed he should have ministers of his own choice and Parliament should function under royal rather than aristocratic management. When William Pitt resigned after a disagreement with George over war policy, the king appointed the earl of Bute as his first minister. In doing so, he ignored the great Whig families that

The surrender of Lord Cornwallis' British army at Yorktown, Virginia, in 1781 to American and French forces under George Washington ended Britain's hopes of suppressing the American Revolution. John Trumbull (American, 1756–1843), *Surrender of Lord Cornwallis at Yorktown, 19 October 1781*. Oil on canvas, 20⁷⁄₈ × 30⁵⁄₈ inches. Yale University Art Gallery, Trumbull Collection.

had run the country since 1715. The king sought the aid of politicians whom the Whigs hated. Moreover, he tried to use the same kind of patronage techniques developed by Walpole to achieve royal control of the House of Commons.

Between 1761 and 1770, George tried one minister after another, but each in turn failed to gain enough support from the various factions in the House of Commons. Finally, in 1770, he turned to Lord North, who remained the king's first minister until 1782. The Whig families and other political spokespersons claimed that George III was attempting to impose a tyranny. What they meant was that the king was attempting to curb the power of a particular group of the aristocracy. George III certainly was seeking to restore more royal influence to the government of Great Britain, but he was not attempting to make himself a tyrant.

The Challenge of John Wilkes Then, in 1763 began the affair of John Wilkes (1725–1797). This London political radical and member of Parliament published a newspaper called *The North Briton*. In issue number 45, Wilkes strongly criticized Lord Bute's handling of the peace negotiations with France. Wilkes was arrested under the authority of a general warrant issued by the secretary of state. He pleaded the privileges of a member of Parliament and was released. The courts also later ruled that the vague kind of general warrant by which he had been arrested was illegal. The House of Commons, however, ruled that issue number 45 of *The North Briton* constituted libel, and it expelled Wilkes. He soon fled the country and was outlawed.

Throughout these procedures there was widespread support for Wilkes, and many popular demonstrations were held in his cause.

In 1768, Wilkes returned to England and again stood for election to Parliament. He won the election, but the House of Commons, under the influence of George III's friends, refused to seat him. He was elected three more times. After the fourth election, the House of Commons simply ignored the results and seated the government-supported candidate. As had happened earlier in the decade, large, popular, unruly demonstrations of shopkeepers, artisans, and small-property owners supported Wilkes. He also received aid from some aristocratic politicians who wished to humiliate George III. Wilkes himself contended during all his troubles that his was the cause of English liberty. "Wilkes and Liberty" became the slogan of all political radicals and many noble opponents of the monarch. Wilkes was finally seated in 1774, after having become the lord mayor of London.

The American colonists followed these developments closely. Events in Britain confirmed their fears about a monarchical and parliamentary conspiracy against liberty. The king, as their Whig friends told them, was behaving like a tyrant. The Wilkes affair displayed the arbitrary power of the monarch, the corruption of the House of Commons, and the contempt of both for popular electors. That same monarch and Parliament were attempting to overturn the traditional relationship of Great Britain to its colonies by imposing parliamentary taxes. The same government had then landed troops in Boston, changed the government of Massachusetts, and

The Horse America throwing his Master, *an eighteenth-century cartoon (1779) mocking George III about the rebellion of the American colonies. Although he tried to reassert some of the monarchical influence on Britain's politics that had eroded under George I and George II, the first two Hanoverian kings, George III never sought to make himself a tyrant as his critics charged.* The Granger Collection

undermined the traditional right of jury trial. All of these events fulfilled too exactly the portrait of political tyranny that had developed over the years in the minds of articulate colonists.

Movement for Parliamentary Reform The political influences between America and Britain operated both ways. The colonial demand for no taxation without representation and the criticism of the adequacy of the British system of representation struck at the core of the eighteenth-century British political structure. British subjects at home who were no more directly represented in the House of Commons than were the Americans could adopt the colonial arguments. The colonial questioning of the tax-levying authority of the House of Commons was related to the protest of John Wilkes. Both the Americans and Wilkes were challenging the power of the monarch and the authority of Parliament. Moreover, both the colonial leaders and Wilkes

appealed over the head of legally constituted political authorities to popular opinion and popular demonstrations. Both were protesting the power of a largely self-selected aristocratic political body. The British ministry was fully aware of these broader political implications of the American troubles.

The American colonists also demonstrated to Europe how a politically restive people in the Old Regime could fight tyranny and protect political liberty. They established revolutionary, but orderly, political bodies that could function outside the existing political framework: the congress and the convention. These began with the Stamp Act Congress of 1765 and culminated in the Constitutional Convention of 1787. The legitimacy of those congresses and conventions lay not in existing law, but in the alleged consent of the governed. This approach represented a new way to found a government.

Toward the end of the War of the American Revolution, calls for parliamentary reform arose in

Britain itself. The method proposed for changing the system was the extralegal Association Movement.

The Yorkshire Association Movement By the close of the 1770s, many in Britain resented the mismanagement of the American war, the high taxes, and Lord North's ministry. In northern England in 1778, Christopher Wyvil (1740–1822), a landowner and retired clergyman, organized the Yorkshire Association Movement. Property owners, or freeholders, of Yorkshire met in a mass meeting to demand rather moderate changes in the corrupt system of parliamentary elections. They organized corresponding societies elsewhere. They intended that the association examine—and suggest reforms for—the entire government. The Association Movement was thus a popular attempt to establish an extralegal institution to reform the government.

The movement collapsed during the early 1780s because its supporters, unlike Wilkes and the American rebels, were not willing to appeal for broad popular support. Nonetheless, the agitation of the Association Movement provided many people with experience in political protest. Several of its younger figures lived to raise the issue of parliamentary reform after 1815.

Parliament was not insensitive to the demands of the Association Movement. In April 1780, the Commons passed a resolution that called for lessening the power of the crown. In 1782, Parliament adopted a measure for "economical" reform, which abolished some patronage at the disposal of the monarch. These actions, however, did not prevent George III from appointing a minister of his own choice. In 1783, shifts in Parliament obliged Lord North to form a ministry with Charles James Fox (1749–1806), a longtime critic of George III. The monarch was most unhappy with the arrangement.

In 1783, the king approached William Pitt the Younger (1759–1806), son of the victorious war minister, to manage the House of Commons. During the election of 1784, Pitt received immense patronage support from the crown and constructed a House of Commons favorable to the monarch. Thereafter, Pitt sought to formulate trade policies that would give his ministry broad popularity. In 1785, he attempted one measure of modest parliamentary reform. When it failed, the young prime minister, who had been only twenty-four at the time of his appointment, abandoned the cause of reform.

By the mid-1780s, George III had achieved a part of what he had sought since 1761. He had reasserted the influence of the monarchy in political affairs. It proved a temporary victory, because his own mental illness, which would eventually require a regency, weakened the royal power. The cost of his years of

Events in Britain and America Relating to the American Revolution	
1760	George III becomes king
1763	Treaty of Paris concludes the Seven Years' War
1763	John Wilkes publishes issue number 45 of *The North Briton*
1764	Sugar Act
1765	Stamp Act
1766	Stamp Act repealed and Declaratory Act passed
1767	Townshend Acts
1768	Parliament refuses to seat John Wilkes after his election
1770	Lord North becomes George III's chief minister
1770	Boston Massacre
1773	Boston Tea Party
1774	Intolerable Acts
1774	First Continental Congress
1775	Second Continental Congress
1776	Declaration of Independence
1778	France enters the war on the side of America
1778	Yorkshire Association Movement founded
1781	British forces surrender at Yorktown
1783	Treaty of Paris concludes War of the American Revolution

dominance had been high, however. On both sides of the Atlantic, the issue of popular sovereignty had been raised and widely discussed. The American colonies had been lost. Economically, this loss did not prove disastrous. British trade with America after independence actually increased.

BROADER IMPACT OF THE AMERICAN REVOLUTION

The Americans—through their state constitutions, the Articles of Confederation, and the federal Constitution adopted in 1788—had demonstrated to Europe the possibility of government without kings and hereditary nobilities. They had established the example of a nation in which written documents based on popular consent and popular sovereignty—rather than on divine law, natural law, tradition, or the will of kings—were the highest political and legal authority. The political novelty of these assertions should not be ignored.

As the crisis with Britain unfolded during the 1760s and 1770s, the American colonists had come to see themselves first as preserving traditional

English liberties against the tyrannical crown and corrupt Parliament and then as developing a whole new sense of liberty. By the mid-1770s, the colonists had rejected monarchical government and embraced republican political ideals. They would govern themselves through elected assemblies without any presence of a monarchical authority. Once a constitution was adopted, they would insist on a Bill of Rights specifically protecting a whole series of civil liberties. The Americans would reject the aristocratic social hierarchy that had existed in the colonies. They would embrace democratic ideals—even if the franchise remained limited. They would assert the equality of white male citizens not only before the law, but in ordinary social relations. They would reject social status based on birth and inheritance and assert the necessity of the liberty for all citizens to improve their social standing and economic lot by engaging in free commercial activity. They did not free their slaves, nor did they address issues of the rights of women or of Native Americans. Yet in making their revolution, the American colonists of the eighteenth century produced a society more free than any the world had seen and one that would eventually expand the circle of political and social liberty. In all these respects, the American Revolution was a genuinely radical movement, whose influence would widen as Americans moved across the continent and as other peoples began to question traditional modes of European government.

In Perspective

During the sixteenth and seventeenth centuries, the west European maritime powers established extensive commercial, mercantile empires in North and South America. The point of these empires was to extract wealth and to establish commercial advantage for the colonial power. The largest of these empires was that of Spain, but by the end of the seventeenth century Britain and France had also each established a major American presence. As a vast plantation economy emerged from the Chesapeake Bay through the southern North American Atlantic seaboard and the Caribbean south to Brazil, significant portions of these American empires became economically dependent on slave labor, drawn from the forced immigration of Africans. Through this large slave labor force, African linguistic, social, and religious influences became major cultural factors in these regions.

During the eighteenth century, the great European powers engaged in warfare over their American empires and over their power in India. These colonial wars became entangled in dynastic wars in central and eastern Europe and resulted in worldwide midcentury European conflict.

In the New World, Britain, France, and Spain battled for commercial dominance. France and Britain also clashed over their spheres of influence in India. By the third quarter of the century, Britain had succeeded in ousting France from most of its major holdings in North America and from any significant presence in India. Spain, though no longer a military power of the first order, had managed to maintain its vast colonial empire in Latin America and a large measure of its monopoly over the region's trade.

On the Continent, France, Austria, and Prussia collided over conflicting territorial and dynastic ambitions. Britain became involved to protect its continental interests and to use the continental wars to divert France from the colonial arena. With British aid, Prussia had emerged in 1763 as a major continental power. Austria had lost considerable territory to Prussia. France had accumulated a vast debt.

The midcentury conflicts in turn led to major changes in all the European states. Each of the monarchies needed more money and tried to govern itself more efficiently. This problem led Britain to attempt to tax the North American colonies, which led to a revolution and the colonies' independence. Already deeply in debt, the French monarchy aided the Americans, fell into a deeper financial crisis, and soon clashed sharply with the nobility as royal ministers tried to find new revenues. That clash eventually unleashed the French Revolution. Spain moved to administer its Latin American empire more efficiently, which increased revolutionary discontent in the early nineteenth century. In preparation for future wars, the rulers of Prussia, Austria, and Russia pursued a mode of activist government known as Enlightened Absolutism (see Chapter 18). In that regard, the mid-eighteenth-century wars set in motion most of the major political developments of the next half century.

REVIEW QUESTIONS

1. What were the fundamental ideas associated with mercantile theory? Did they work? Which European country was most successful in establishing a mercantile empire? Least successful? Why?

2. What were the main points of conflict between Britain and France in North America, the West Indies, and India? How did the triangles of

trade function between the Americas, Europe, and Africa?

3. How was the Spanish colonial empire in the Americas organized and managed? What changes did the Bourbon monarchs institute in the Spanish Empire?

4. What was the nature of slavery in the Americas? How was it linked to the economies of the Americas, Europe, and Africa? In what respects was the plantation system unprecedented? What was the plantation system, and how did it contribute to the inhumane treatment of slaves?

5. The Seven Years' War was a major conflict, with battles fought around the globe. What were the results of this war? Which countries emerged in a stronger position and why?

6. Discuss the American Revolution in the context of European history. To what extent were the colonists influenced by European ideas and political developments? To what extent did their actions in turn influence Europe?

SUGGESTED READINGS

B. BAILYN, *The Ideological Origins of the American Revolution* (1967). Remains an important work illustrating the role of English radical thought in the perceptions of the American colonists.

C. A. BAYLY, *Imperial Meridian: The British Empire and the World, 1780–1830* (1989). A major study of the empire after the loss of America.

I. BERLIN, *Many Thousands Gone: The First Two Centuries of Slavery in North America* (1998). The most extensive recent treatment emphasizing the differences in the slave economy during different decades.

L. BETHELL (ED.), *The Cambridge History of Latin America*, vols. 1 and 2 (1984). Excellent essays on the colonial era.

R. BLACKBURN, *The Making of New World Slavery from the Baroque to the Modern, 1492–1800* (1997). An extraordinary work.

D. BRADING, *The First Americans* (1991). A major study of colonial Latin America.

L. COLLEY, *Britons: Forging the Nation, 1707–1837* (1992). A major work with important discussions of the recovery from the loss of America.

P. CURTIN, *The Atlantic Slave Trade, a Census* (1969). Remains a major contribution.

D. B. DAVIS, *The Problem of Slavery in the Age of Revolution, 1770–1823* (1975). A major work on both European and American history.

D. B. DAVIS, *The Problem of Slavery in Western Culture* (1966). A classic far-ranging discussion.

R. DAVIS, *The Rise of the Atlantic Economies* (1973). A major synthesis.

W. DORN, *Competition for Empire, 1740–1763* (1940). Still one of the best accounts of the mid-century struggle.

R. HARMS, *The Diligent: A Voyage through the Worlds of the Slave Trade* (2002). A powerful narrative of the voyage of a French slave trader.

P. LANGFORD, *A Polite and Commercial People: England, 1717–1783* (1989). An excellent survey covering social history, politics, the overseas wars, and the American Revolution.

G. MACDONAGH, *Frederick the Great* (2001). Now the standard biography.

P. MAIER, *American Scripture: Making the Declaration of Independence* (1997). Replaces previous works on the subject.

J. R. MCNEIL, *Atlantic Empires of France and Spain: Louisbourg and Havana, 1700–1763* (1985). An examination of imperial policies for two key overseas outposts.

S. W. MINTZ, *Sweetness and Power: The Place of Sugar in Modern History* (1985). Traces the role of sugar in the world economy and how sugar has had an impact on world culture.

A. PAGDEN, *Lords of All the World: Ideologies of Empire in Spain, Britain, and France, 1492–1830* (1995). One of the few comparative studies of empire during this period.

G. RUDE, *Wilkes and Political Liberty* (1962). A close analysis of popular political behavior.

R. L. STEIN, *The French Sugar Business in the Eighteenth Century* (1988). A study that covers all aspects of the French sugar trade.

J. THORNTON, *Africa and the Africans in the Making of the Atlantic World, 1400–1800*, 2nd ed. (1998). A discussion of the role of Africans in the emergence of the transatlantic economy.

G. S. WOOD, *The Radicalism of the American Revolution* (1991). A major interpretation.

DOCUMENTS CD-ROM

EUROPE AND THE AMERICAS IN THE EIGHTEENTH CENTURY

17.1 Slaves in the City
17.2 Demands from a Slave Rebellion
17.3 The Stamp Act: "Unconstitutional and Unjust"
17.4 "Declaration of Sentiments": American Women Want Independence Too
17.6 Thomas Paine: from "Common Sense"
17.7 John Adams: *Thoughts on Government*

THE ENLIGHTENMENT

18.6 Medicine from Turkey: The Small Pox Vaccination

A Dramatic Moment
in the Transatlantic World:
Copley's *Watson and the Shark*

John Singleton Copley, American, 1738–1815. *Watson and the Shark*, 1778. Oil on canvas, 72 1/4 × 90 3/8 inches. Gift of Mrs. George von Lengerke Meyer. © 2003 Museum of Fine Arts, Boston.

Both the career of the North American born painter John Singleton Copley (1738–1815) and his monumental painting, *Watson and the Shark* (1778), illustrate the economic and cultural interconnections of the eighteenth-century transatlantic world. Copley was born in Massachusetts and became an accomplished portrait painter of the Boston elite. When hostilities erupted between Britain and the colonies, Copley moved to London in 1774, where his reputation had preceded him. He never returned to America.

In Britain, he undertook commissions for *history painting*, then considered the most prestigious subject for artists. Traditionally, history painting drew its subject matter from mythology, biblical narratives, or ancient history, but Copley was interested in portraying contemporary events. His figures were modern people, dressed in modern clothing but striking poses taken from classical and Renaissance art.

History painting claimed to convey a moral message usually of heroism, patriotism, or self-sacrifice. In 1778, Copley completed *Watson and the Shark*, recounting the experience of Brook Watson's rescue, as a boy of fourteen in 1749, from the jaws of a shark in the harbor of Havana, Cuba. Watson, who later became Lord Mayor of London, lost most of his leg in the attack, but regarded his rescue and subsequent success as a merchant as an inspiring example to others who had encountered adversity.

In portraying the terrifying moment just before Watson's rescue, Copley presents the event as a profound drama, which he invites the viewer to attend. By seeking to evoke a powerful emotional response from the viewer, Copley was working in the category of art known at the time as the *sublime*. Yet Copley also used his power as a portraitist to depict each man in the painting as a real person, not as some allegorical figure.

Watson and the Shark is also one of the first paintings to prominently depict an African American. The black man in the middle of the painting holds the rope that will soon be used to rescue Watson. His presence also places the action in the world of the plantation economy and transatlantic trade. It is not clear whether he is a slave or whether, like Olaudah Equiano in the document earlier in the chapter, a former slave now working as a sailor in the commercial shipping trade.

In several respects, this painting illustrates the interconnectedness of the eighteenth-century transatlantic world. Copley is an American artist working in London. The action occurs in a Spanish colony during a commercial venture. The person being rescued is an English subject who will become a rich merchant. The boat holds a cross section of races and cultures from Africa, Europe, and the Americas that characterized the world of the plantation economies.

Watson and the Shark is also important in art history for another reason. Through the contrasts of light and dark, Copley set out to achieve a dramatic painting of human beings in combat with powerful natural forces—the sea, the wind, and the shark. This would become a major theme of the late-eighteenth- and early-nineteenth-century artistic and literary movement known as romanticism. *Watson and the Shark* stands as a major forerunner of this new direction of painting and taste.

■ *How is Copley's painting different from traditional history paintings? How does* Watson and the Shark *illustrate the interconnectedness of the eighteenth-century transatlantic economy? Why is this painting important in the history of art?*

Sources: Jules Prown, *John Singleton Copley* (Cambridge, MA: Harvard University Press, 1966); John Wilmerding, *American Art* (New York: Penguin Books, 1976); Theodore Stebbins, Jr., et al., *A New World: Masterpieces of American Painting 1760–1910* (Boston: Museum of Fine Arts, 1983), pp. 210–211; Hugh Honour, *The Image of the Black in Western Art*, Vol. 4, Part I, *From the American Revolution to World War I: Slave and Liberators* (Cambridge, MA: Harvard University Press, 1989).

The Columbian Exchange: Disease, Animals, and Agriculture

The European encounter with the Americas produced remarkable ecological transformations that have shaped the world to the present moment. The same ships that carried Europeans and Africans to the New World also transported animals, plants, and germs that had never before appeared in the Americas. There was a similar transport back to Europe and Africa. Alfred Crosby, the leading historian of the process, has named this cross-continental flow "the Columbian exchange."

Diseases Enter the Americas

With the exception of a few ships that had gone astray or, in the case of the Vikings, that had gone in search of new lands, the American continents had been biologically separated from Europe, Africa, and Asia for tens of thousands of years. In the Americas no native animals could serve as major beasts of burden except for the llama, which could not transport more than about a hundred pounds. Nor did animals constitute a major source of protein for native Americans, whose diets consisted largely of maize, beans, peppers, yams, and potatoes. At the same time, the American continents included areas of vast grassland without grazing animals that would have transformed those plants into animal protein. Moreover, it also appears that native peoples had lived on the long-isolated American continents without experiencing major epidemics.

By the second voyage of Columbus (1493), that picture began to change in remarkable ways. On his return voyage to Hispaniola and other islands of the Caribbean, Columbus brought a number of animals and plants that were previously unknown to the New World. The men on all his voyages and those on subsequent European voyages also carried diseases novel to the Americas.

The diseases thus transported by Europeans ultimately accounted for the conquest of the people of the Americas as much as the advanced European weaponry. Much controversy surrounds the question of the actual size of the populations of Native Americans in the Caribbean islands, Mexico, Peru, and the North Atlantic coast. All accounts present those populations as quite significant, with those of Mexico in particular numbering many millions. Yet in the first two centuries after the encounter, wherever Europeans went either as settlers or as conquerors, extremely large numbers of Native Americans died from diseases they had never before encountered. The most deadly such disease was smallpox, which destroyed millions of people. Beyond the devastation wrought by that disease, bubonic plague, typhoid, typhus, influenza, measles, chicken pox, whooping cough, malaria, and diphtheria produced deadly results in more localized epidemics. For example, an unknown disease, but quite possibly typhus, caused major losses among the Native Americans of New England between approximately 1616 and 1619.

Native Americans appear to have been highly susceptible to these diseases because, with no earlier exposure, they lacked immunity. Wherever such outbreaks are recorded, Europeans either contracted or died from them at a much lower rate than the Native Americans. These diseases would continue to victimize Native Americans at a higher rate than Americans of European descent through the end of the nineteenth century when smallpox and measles still killed large numbers of the Plains Indian peoples of North America.

Although many historical and medical questions still surround the subject, it appears almost certain that syphilis, which became a rampant venereal disease in Europe at the close of the fifteenth century and eventually spread around the globe, originated in the New World. It seems to have been an

Within one year of Columbus's encounter with the Americas, the event had been captured in a woodcut published in Giuliano Dati's Narrative of Columbus *(1493). Columbus's several voyages, and those of later Europeans as well, introduced not only European warfare but began a vast ecological exchange of plants, animals, and diseases between the Old and New Worlds.* The Granger Collection

entirely new disease, spawned through a mutation when the causal agent for yaws migrated from the Americas to new climatic settings in Europe. Until the discovery of penicillin in the 1940s, syphilis remained a major concern of public health throughout the world.

Animals and Agriculture

The introduction of European livestock to the Americas quite simply revolutionized the agriculture of two continents. The most important new animals were pigs, cattle, horses, goats, and sheep. Once transported to the New World, these animals multiplied at unprecedented rates. The place where this first occurred was in the islands of the Caribbean, during the first forty years of Spanish settlement and exploitation. This situation established the foundation for the later Spanish conquest of both Mexico and Peru by providing the Spanish with strong breeds of animals, especially horses, acclimated to the Americas when they set out to conquer the mainland of South America.

The horse became first the animal of the conquest and then the animal of colonial Latin American culture. Native Americans had no experience with such large animals who would obey the will of a human rider. The mounted Spanish horseman struck fear into these people, and for good reason. After the conquest, however, the Americas from Mexico southward became the largest horse-breeding region of the world, with ranches raising thousands of animals. Horses became relatively cheap, and even Native Americans could acquire them. By the nineteenth century, the possession of horses would allow the Plains Indians of North America to resist the advance of their white conquerors.

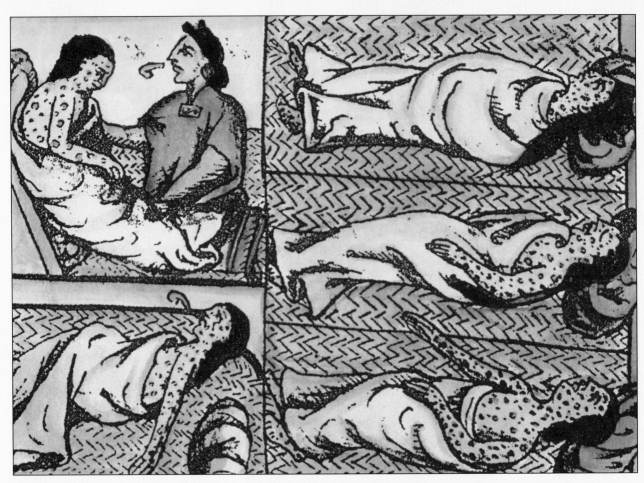

Nothing so destroyed the life of the Native Americans whom the Spanish encountered as the introduction of smallpox. With no immune defenses to this new disease, millions of Native Americans died of smallpox during the sixteenth and seventeenth centuries. The Granger Collection.

The flourishing of pigs, cattle, and sheep allowed a vast economic exploitation of the Americas. These animals produced enormous quantities of hides and wool. Their presence in such large numbers also meant the Americas from the sixteenth century through the present would support a diet more plentiful in animal protein than anywhere else in the world.

Europeans also brought their own plants to the New World, including peaches, oranges, grapes, melons, bananas, rice, onions, radishes, and various green vegetables. Socially, for three centuries the most significant of these was sugarcane, whose cultivation created the major demand for slavery throughout the transatlantic plantation economy.

Nutritionally, European wheat would, over the course of time, allow the Americas not only to feed themselves, but also to export large amounts of grain throughout the world. This American production of wheat on the vast plains of the two continents contrasted sharply with the difficulty Europeans faced raising grain in the northern and northeastern parts of the Continent, particularly in Russia.

No significant animals from the Americas, except the turkey, actually came to be raised in Europe. But the Americas did send to Europe a series of plants that eventually changed the European diet: maize, the potato, the sweet potato, the pepper, beans, manioc (tapioca), the peanut, squash, the pumpkin, pineapple, cocoa, and the tomato. All of these, to a greater or lesser degree, eventually entered the diet of Europeans and of European settlers and their descendants in the Americas. Maize and the potato, however, had the most transforming impact. Each of these two crops became a major staple in European farming, as well as the European diet. Both crops grow rapidly, supplying food quickly and steadily if not attacked by disease. Tobacco, we should note, originated in the Americas, too.

Maize was established as a crop in Spain within thirty years of the country's encounter with the New World. A century and a half later it was a commonplace in the Spanish diet, and its cultivation had spread to Italy and France. Maize produced more grain for the seed and farming effort than wheat did. Throughout Europe, maize was associated primarily with fodder for animals. But as early as the eighteenth century, travelers noted the presence of polenta in the peasant diet, and other forms of maize dishes, such as fried mush, spread.

The potato established its European presence more slowly than maize. The Spanish encountered the potato only when Pizarro conquered Peru, where it was a major part of the Native American food supply. It was adopted slowly by Europeans because it needed to be raised in climates more temperate than that of Spain and the Mediterranean. It appears to have become a major peasant food in Scotland, Ireland, and parts of Germany during the eighteenth century. It became more widely cultivated elsewhere in Europe only after new strains of the plant were imported from Chile in the late nineteenth century. In the middle of the seventeenth century, Irish peasants were urged to cultivate the potato as a major source of cheap nutrition that could grow in quantity on a small plot. The food shortages arising from the wars of Louis XIV and then during the eighteenth century led farmers in northern Europe to adopt the potato for similar reasons. It was nutrient insurance against failure of the grain harvest. There is good reason to believe the cultivation of the potato was one of the major causes of the population increase in eighteenth- and nineteenth-century Europe. It was the quintessential food of the poor.

Many tragedies arose from the encounter between the people of the Americas and those of Europe, as well as the forging of new nations and civilizations in the Americas. But one of the last chapters of those tragedies to arise as a direct fallout of the Columbian exchange three centuries earlier was the Irish famine of the 1840s. Irish peasants had become almost wholly dependent on the potato as a source of food. In the middle of the 1840s, an American parasite infected the Irish potato crop. The result of the failure of the crop was the death of hundreds of thousands of Irish peasants and the migration of still more hundreds of thousands to the Americas and elsewhere in the world.

■ *Define the Columbian exchange. What was the impact of European diseases on the Americas? Why was the impact so profound? Why could so many European crops grow well in the Americas? What was the cultural impact of animals taken from Europe to the Americas? How did food from the Americas change the diet of Europe and then later, as Europeans immigrated, the diet of the entire world?*

PART 4
1700–1850

	POLITICS AND GOVERNMENT	SOCIETY AND ECONOMY	RELIGION AND CULTURE
1700–1789	1713 Treaty of Utrecht	1715–1763 Colonial rivalry in the Caribbean	1721 Montesquieu, *Persian Letters*
	1713–1740 Frederick William I builds Prussian military	1733 James Kay's flying shuttle	1733 Voltaire, *Letters on the English*
	1720–1740 Walpole in England, Fleury in France		1738 Voltaire, *Elements of the Philosophy of Newton*
	1739 War of Jenkins's Ear		
	1740 Maria Theresa succeeds to Habsburg throne		
	1740–1748 War of the Austrian Succession		Voltaire
			1739 Wesley begins field preaching
		1750s Agricultural Revolution in Britain	1748 Hume, *Inquiry into Human Nature*
	1756–1763 Seven Years' War	1750–1840 Growth of new cities	1748 Montesquieu, *Spirit of the Laws*
	1767 Legislative Commission in Russia	1763 British establish dominance in India	1750 Rousseau, *Discourse on the Moral Effects of the Arts and Sciences*
	1772 First Partition of Poland	1763–1789 Enlightened absolutist rulers seek to spur economic growth	1751 First volume of Diderot's *Encyclopedia*
	1775–1783 American Revolution	1765 James Hargreaves's spinning jenny	1762 Rousseau, *Social Contract* and *Émile*
	1785 Catherine the Great of Russia issues Charter of Nobility	1769 Richard Arkwright's waterframe	1763 Voltaire, *Treatise on Tolerance*
		1773–1775 Pugachev's Rebellion	1774 Goethe, *Sorrows of Young Werther*
		1780 Gordon riots in London	1776 Smith, *Wealth of Nations*
		1787 Edmund Cartwright's power loom	1779 Lessing, *Nathan the Wise*
		1789–1802 Revolutionary legislation restructures French political and economic life	1781 Joseph II adopts toleration in Austria
1789–1815	1789 Gathering of the Estates General at Versailles; fall of the Bastille; Declaration of the Rights of Man and Citizen		1781 Kant, *Critique of Pure Reason*
			1789 Blake, *Songs of Innocence*
	1791 French monarchy abolished		1790 Civil Constitution of the Clergy; Burke, *Reflections on the Revolution in France*
	1793 Louis XVI executed; Second Partition of Poland		1792 Wollstonecraft, *Vindication of the Rights of Woman*
	1793–1794 Reign of Terror		1793 France proclaims Cult of Reason
	1795 Third Partition of Poland		

ENLIGHTENMENT AND REVOLUTION

1700–1850

	POLITICS AND GOVERNMENT	SOCIETY AND ECONOMY	RELIGION AND CULTURE
1789–1815 (cont.)	**1795** The Directory established in France **1799** Napoleon named First Consul in France **1803** War resumes between Britain and France **1804** Napoleonic Code; Napoleon crowned emperor **1805** Third Coalition formed against France; battles of Trafalgar and Austerlitz **1806** Napoleon establishes the Continental System **1807** Treaty of Tilsit between France and Russia **1808** Spanish resistance to Napoleon stiffens **1812** Napoleon invades Russia; meets defeat **1814** Napoleon abdicates; Congress of Vienna opens; Louis XVIII restored in France	**1794–1824** Wars of independence in Latin America break the colonial system  Napoleon Bonaparte **1810** Abolition of serfdom in Prussia	**1794** France proclaims Cult of the Supreme Being **1798** Wordsworth and Coleridge, *Lyrical Ballads*; Malthus, *Essay on the Principle of Population* **1799** Schleiermacher, *Speeches on Religion to Its Cultured Despisers* **1802** Chateaubriand, *Genius of Christianity* **1802** Napoleon, Concordat with the Papacy **1806** Hegel, *Phenomenology of Mind* **1807** Fichte, *Addresses to the German Nation* **1808** Goethe, *Faust*, Part I **1812** Byron, *Childe Harold's Pilgrimage*
1815–1850	**1815** Napoleon defeated at Waterloo **1819** Carlsbad Decrees in Germanies; Peterloo Massacre and the Six Acts, Britain **1820** Spanish Revolution begins **1821** Greek Revolution begins **1823** France intervenes in Spanish Revolution **1825** Decembrist Revolt in Russia **1829** Catholic Emancipation Act in Great Britain **1830** Revolution in France, Belgium, and Poland; Serbia gains independence **1832** Great Reform Bill in Britain **1848** Revolutions sweep across Europe	**1800–1850** British industrial dominance **1825** Stockton and Darlington Railway opens **1828–1850** First European police departments **1830–1850** Railway building in western Europe **1833** English Factory Act to protect children **1834** German *Zollverein* established **1842** Chadwick, *Report on the Sanitary Condition of the Labouring Population* **1846** Corn Laws repealed in Britain **1847** Ten Hour Act passed in Britain **1848** Serfdom abolished in Austria and Hungary	**1817** Ricardo, *Principles of Political Economy* **1819** Byron, *Don Juan* **1829** Catholic Emancipation Act in Great Britain **1830–1842** Comte, *The Positive Philosophy* **1830** Lyell, *Principles of Geology* **1833** Russia begins "Official Nationality" policy **1835** Strauss, *Life of Jesus* **1840** Villermé, *Catalogue of the Physical and Moral State of Workers* **1843** Kierkegaard, *Fear and Trembling* **1848** Marx and Engels, *Communist Manifesto*

*Philosopher, dramatist, poet, historian, and popularizer of scientific ideas, Voltaire
(1694–1778) was the most famous and influential of the eighteenth-century philosophes.
His sharp satire and criticism of religious institutions opened the way for a more general
critique of the European political and social status quo.* Nicolas de Largillière. Portrait of
Voltaire at age 23, bust length, 1728. Private Collection, Musée de la Ville de Paris, Musée Carnavalet, Paris,
France. Giraudon/Art Resource, N.Y.

CHAPTER 18

THE AGE OF ENLIGHTENMENT:

Eighteenth-Century Thought

*D*URING THE EIGHTEENTH CENTURY, THE *conviction began to spread throughout the literate sectors of European society that economic change and political reform were both possible and desirable. This attitude is now commonplace, but it came into its own only after 1700. It represents one of the primary intellectual inheritances from that age. The movement of people and ideas that fostered such thinking is called the* Enlightenment.

Its leading voices combined confidence in the human mind and human enterprise inspired by the scientific revolution and faith in the power of rational criticism to challenge the intellectual authority of tradition and the Christian past. These writers stood convinced that human beings could comprehend the operation of physical nature and mold it to the ends of material and moral improvement, economic growth, and political reform. They advocated agricultural improvement, commercial society, expanding consumption, and the application of innovative rational methods to traditional social and economic practices. The rationality of the physical universe became a standard against which the customs and traditions of society could be measured and criticized. Such criticism penetrated every corner of contemporary society, politics, and religious opinion. As a result, the spirit of innovation and improvement came to characterize modern Europe and Western society.

Some of the ideas and outlooks of the Enlightenment had a direct impact on rulers in central and eastern Europe. These rulers, whose policies became known by the term enlightened absolutism, *sought to centralize their authority so as to reform their countries. They often attempted to restructure religious institutions and to sponsor economic growth. Although they frequently associated themselves with the Enlightenment, many of their military and foreign policies were in direct opposition to enlightened ideals. Nonetheless, both the Enlightenment writers and these monarchs were forces for modernization in European life.*

KEY TOPICS

- The intellectual and social background of the Enlightenment
- The philosophes of the Enlightenment and their agenda of intellectual and political reform
- Enlightenment writers' attitude toward Islam
- Efforts of "enlightened" monarchs in central and eastern Europe to increase the economic and military strength of their domains
- The partition of Poland by Prussia, Russia, and Austria

The Philosophes

The writers and critics who forged the new attitudes favorable to change, who championed reform, and who flourished in the emerging print culture were the **philosophes.** Not usually philosophers in a formal sense, they sought rather to apply the rules of reason and common sense to nearly all the major institutions and social practices of the day. The most famous of their number included Voltaire, Montesquieu, Diderot, D'Alembert, Rousseau, Hume, Gibbon, Smith, Lessing, and Kant.

A few of these philosophes occupied professorships in universities. Most, however, were free agents who might be found in London coffeehouses, Edinburgh drinking spots, the salons of fashionable Parisian ladies, the country houses of reform-minded nobles, or the courts of the most powerful monarchs on the Continent. In eastern Europe, they were often found in the royal bureaucracies. They were not an organized group; they disagreed on many issues. Their relationship with each other and with lesser figures of the same turn of mind has been compared with that of a family, which, despite quarrels and tensions, preserves a basic unity.[1]

The bulk of the readership of the philosophes was drawn from the prosperous commercial and professional people of the eighteenth-century towns and cities. These people discussed the reformers' writings and ideas in local philosophical societies, Freemason lodges, and clubs. They had enough income and leisure time to buy and read the philosophes' works. Although the writers of the Enlightenment did not consciously champion the goals or causes of the middle class, they did provide an intellectual ferment and a major source of ideas that could be used to undermine existing social practices and political structures. They taught their contemporaries how to pose pointed, critical questions. Moreover, the philosophes generally supported the growth, the expansion of trade, the improvement of agriculture and transport, and the invention of new manufacturing machinery that were transforming the society and the economy of the eighteenth century and enlarging the business and commercial classes.

The chief bond among the philosophes was their common desire to reform religion, political thought, society, government, and the economy for the sake of human liberty. As Peter Gay once suggested, this goal included "freedom from arbitrary power, freedom of speech, freedom of trade, freedom to realize

---

[1]Peter Gay, *The Enlightenment: An Interpretation*, Vol. 1 (New York: Knopf, 1967), p. 4.

This eighteenth-century engraving shows a dinner party of philosophes. Voltaire is in the center with his hand raised. Next to Voltaire on the right is Diderot. Musée de la Ville de Paris, Musée Carnavalet, Paris, France. Giraudon/Art Resource, N.Y.

IMMANUEL KANT DEFINES ENLIGHTENMENT

Immanuel Kant was one of the most important German philosophers associated with the Enlightenment. His work is more fully discussed in Chapter 20. The passage here is from one of his more accessible articles, written in 1784 for a broad audience. He equates Enlightenment with the courage of the individual to use his or her reason. He indicates that this is difficult because so many people have come by habit to depend on others for guidance. He discusses the freedom the use of reason requires.

■ *What were some of the authorities Kant saw the liberated intellect having the courage to question? Why does Kant believe intellectual liberation requires effort and the rejection of laziness and cowardice? Why does Kant link enlightenment with freedom?*

Enlightenment is man's emergence from his self-imposed nonage. Nonage is the inability to use one's own understanding without another's guidance. This nonage is self-imposed if its causes lie not in lack of understanding but in indecision and lack of courage to use one's own mind without another's guidance. Dare to know! (*Sapere aude*) "Have the courage to use your own understanding," is therefore the motto of the enlightenment.

Laziness and cowardice are the reasons why such a large part of mankind gladly remain minors all their lives, long after nature has freed them from external guidance. They are the reasons why it is so easy for others to set themselves up as guardians. It is so comfortable to be a minor. If I have a book that thinks for me, a pastor who acts as my conscience, a physician who prescribes my diet, and so on— then I have no need to exert myself. I have no need to think, if only I can pay; others will take care of that disagreeable business for me. . . .

Thus it is very difficult for the individual to work himself out of the nonage which has become almost second nature to him. He has even grown to like it and is at first really incapable of using his own understanding, because he has never been permitted to try it. Dogmas and formulas, these mechanical tools designed for reasonable use—or rather abuse—of his natural gifts, are the fetters of an everlasting nonage. The man who casts them off would make an uncertain leap over the narrowest ditch, because he is not used to such movement. That is why there are only a few men who walk firmly, and who have emerged from nonage by cultivating their own minds.

It is more nearly possible, however, for the public to enlighten itself; indeed, if it is only given freedom, enlightenment is almost inevitable. There will always be a few independent thinkers, even among the self-appointed guardians of the multitude. Once such men have thrown off the yoke of nonage, they will spread about them the spirit of a reasonable appreciation of man's value and of his duty to think for himself. . . .

This enlightenment requires nothing but freedom—and the most innocent of all that may be called "freedom": freedom to make public use of one's reason in all matters.

Immanuel Kant, "What Is Enlightenment?" trans. by Peter Gay, in *Introduction to Contemporary Civilization in the West*, 2nd ed., Vol. 2 (New York: Columbia University Press, 1954), pp. 1071–1072.

one's talents, freedom of aesthetic response, freedom, in a word, of moral man to make his way in the world."[2] Though challenged over the last three centuries, no other single set of ideas has done so much to shape the modern world. (See "Immanuel Kant Defines Enlightenment.")

[2]Gay, p. 3.

VOLTAIRE—FIRST AMONG THE PHILOSOPHES

By far the most influential of the philosophes was François-Marie Arouet, known to posterity as Voltaire (1694–1778). During the 1720s, Voltaire had offended the French authorities by certain of his writings. He was arrested and briefly imprisoned. Later he went to England, visiting its best literary circles, observing its tolerant intellectual and religious climate, relishing the freedom he felt in its moderate political atmosphere, and admiring its science and economic prosperity. In 1733, he published *Letters on the English*, which appeared in French the next year. The book praised the virtues of the English and indirectly criticized the abuses of French society. In 1738, he published *Elements of the Philosophy of Newton*, which popularized the thought of Isaac Newton. Both works demonstrated that Voltaire had moved beyond the poetry and plays he had written previously.

Thereafter, Voltaire lived part of the time in France and part near Geneva, just across the French border, where the royal authorities could not bother him. His essays, histories, plays, stories, and letters made him the literary dictator of Europe. He turned the bitter venom of his satire and sarcasm against one evil after another in French and European life. His most famous satire is *Candide* (1759), in which he attacked war, religious persecution, and what he considered unwarranted optimism about the human condition. Like most of the philosophes, Voltaire believed human society could and should be improved. But he was never certain that reform, if achieved, would be permanent. The optimism often associated with the Enlightenment was actually a guarded hopefulness rather than a glib certainty. Pessimism was an undercurrent in most of the works of the period. As d'Alembert wrote, "Barbarism lasts for centuries; it seems that it is our natural element; reason and good taste are only passing."[3]

Formative Influences on the Enlightenment

The Newtonian worldview, the stability and commercial prosperity of Great Britain after 1688, the need for administrative and economic reform in France after the wars of Louis XIV, and the consolidation of what is known as a *print culture* were the chief factors that fostered the ideas of the Enlightenment and the call for reform throughout Europe.

IDEAS OF NEWTON AND LOCKE

Isaac Newton (1642–1727) and John Locke (1632–1704) were the major intellectual forerunners of the Enlightenment. Newton's formulation of the law of universal gravitation exemplified the power of the human mind. By example and in his writing,

he encouraged Europeans to approach the study of nature directly and to avoid metaphysics and supernaturalism. Newton had always insisted on empirical support for his general laws and constantly used empirical experience to check his rational speculations. This emphasis on concrete experience became a key feature of Enlightenment thought. (See "Art & the West: Joseph Wright, an Experiment on a Bird in the Air-Pump," p. 622.)

Newton also seemed to have revealed a pattern of rationality in the physical world. During the eighteenth century, thinkers began to apply this insight to society. If nature was rational, they reasoned, society, too, should be organized rationally.

As explained in Chapter 14, Newton's success in physics inspired his countryman John Locke to explain human psychology in terms of experience. In *An Essay Concerning Human Understanding* (1690), Locke argued that all humans enter the world a **tabula rasa**, or blank page. Personality is the product of the sensations that impinge on an individual from the external world throughout his or her life. Thus experience, and only experience, shapes character. The implication of this theory was that human nature is changeable and can be molded by modifying the surrounding physical and social environment. Locke's was a reformer's psychology. It suggested the possibility of improving the human condition. Locke's psychology also, in effect, rejected the Christian doctrine that human beings are permanently flawed by sin. Human beings need not wait for the grace of God or other divine aid to better their lives. They could take charge of their own destiny.

THE EXAMPLE OF BRITISH TOLERATION AND STABILITY

Newton's physics and Locke's psychology provided the theoretical basis for a reformist approach to society. The domestic stability of Great Britain after the Revolution of 1688 furnished a living example of a society in which, to many contemporaries, enlightened reforms appeared to function for the benefit of all. England permitted religious toleration to all except Unitarians and Roman Catholics, and even they were not actually persecuted. Relative freedom of the press and free speech prevailed. The authority of the monarchy was limited, and political sovereignty resided in Parliament. The courts protected citizens from arbitrary government action. The army was small. Furthermore, the domestic economic life of Great Britain displayed far less regulation than that of France or other continental nations. In the view of reformist observers on the Continent, these liberal policies had produced not

[3]Jean Le Rond d'Alembert, *Preliminary Discourse to the Encyclopedia of Diderot*, trans. by Richard N. Schwab (Indianapolis: ITT Bobbs-Merrill Educational Publishing, 1985), p. 103.

disorder and instability, but prosperity, stability, and a loyal citizenry. This view may have been idealized, but England was nonetheless significantly freer than any other European nation at the time. Many of the philosophes contrasted what they regarded as the wise, progressive features of English life with the absence of religious toleration, the extensive literary censorship, the possibility of arbitrary arrest, the overregulation of the economy, and the influence of aristocratic military values in French political and social life.

THE EMERGENCE OF A PRINT CULTURE

The Enlightenment was the first major intellectual movement of European history to flourish in a *print culture*, that is, a culture in which books, journals, newspapers, and pamphlets had achieved a status of their own. Although printed books and pamphlets played a significant role during the Reformation and Counter-Reformation, the powerful messages of those movements were spread mostly by preaching. During the eighteenth century, the volume of printed material—books, journals, magazines, and daily newspapers—increased sharply throughout Europe, most notably in Britain. Prose came to be valued as highly as poetry, and the novel emerged as a distinct genre. The printed word had become the chief vehicle for the communication of ideas and would remain so until the electronic revolution of our own day.

A growing concern with everyday life and material concerns—with secular as opposed to religious issues—accompanied this expansion of printed forms. Toward the end of the seventeenth century, half the books published in Paris were religious; by the 1780s, only about 10 percent were.

Books were not inexpensive in this era, but they, and the ideas they conveyed, circulated in a variety of ways to reach a broad public. Private and public libraries grew in number, allowing single copies to reach many readers. Authors might also publish the same material in different formats. The English essayist, critic, and dictionary author Samuel Johnson (1709–1784), for example, published as books collections of essays that had first appeared in newspapers or journals.

Familiarity with books and secular ideas came increasingly to be expected within aristocratic and middle-class society. Popular publications, such as *The Spectator*, begun in 1711 by Joseph Addison (1672–1719) and Richard Steele (1672–1729), fostered the value of polite conversation and the reading of books. Coffeehouses became centers for the discussion of writing and ideas (see "Encountering the Past: Coffeehouses and Enlightenment"). The lodges of Freemasons, the meeting places for members of a movement that began in Britain and spread to the Continent, provided another site for the consideration of secular ideas in secular books.

The expanding market for printed matter allowed writers to earn a living from their work for the first time, making authorship an occupation. Parisian ladies sought out popular writers for their fashionable salons. Some writers, notably Alexander Pope (1688–1744) and Voltaire, grew wealthy, providing an example for their aspiring young colleagues. In a challenge to older aristocratic values,

Printing shops were the productive centers for the book trade and newspaper publishing that spread the ideas of the Enlightenment.
The Granger Collection

Coffeehouses and Enlightenment

The ideas of the Enlightenment not only spread through books and journals. They took on a life of their own in public discussions in what was a new popular institution of European social life—the coffeehouse.

Coffee, originally imported into Europe from the Ottoman Empire, is the chief Turkish contribution to the Western diet. Coffeehouses had long existed in the Muslim world, encouraged by the Islamic prohibition on alcoholic drink. The first European coffeehouse appeared in Venice in the 1640s, and the first coffeehouse in Vienna opened its doors in 1683 with coffee left behind when the Turks abandoned their siege of the city.

By the middle of the eighteenth century, thousands of coffeehouses dotted European cities and towns. Customers were attracted to them in part because the coffeehouses did not serve alcoholic beverages, which made unruly behavior less likely than in taverns. (The practice of tipping began in the coffeehouses of London. The word *tips* originated as an acronym for "to insure prompt service.")

Throughout Europe, the coffeehouse provided a social space for the open, spontaneous discussion of events, politics, literature, and ideas (but only for men; respectable women did not enter coffeehouses). By furnishing copies of newspapers and other journals, the proprietors of coffeehouses linked their customers to the growing print culture just as today Internet cafés link customers to the World Wide Web. In London coffeehouses, members of the Royal Society and other men associated with the new science mixed with merchants and bankers. Some London coffeehouse proprietors invited learned persons to lecture, usually for a fee, on Newtonian physics, the mechanical philosophy, ethics, and the relationship of science and religion. One historian has described these lecturers as "the philosophical brotherhood of the coffeehouses."[1]

In France the philosophes, such as Voltaire, Rousseau, and Diderot, looked to the café as a place to meet other writers. By 1743 a German commented, "A coffeehouse is like a political stock exchange, where the most gallant and wittiest heads of every estate come together. They engage in wide-ranging and edifying talk, issue well-founded judgments on matters concerning the political and the scholarly world, converse sagaciously about the most secret news from all courts and states, and unveil the most hidden truths."[2]

One irony, however, should be noted about the eighteenth-century European coffeehouses. Although they provided one of the chief locations for the public discussion of the ideas of the Enlightenment, which fostered greater liberty of thought in Europe, the coffee and sugar consumed in these establishments were cultivated by slave labor on plantations in the Caribbean and Brazil. The coffeehouse was one of many institutions of European life that was connected to the transatlantic plantation slave economy.

■ *How did coffeehouses help spread the ideas of the Enlightenment? How was the consumption of coffee related to the transatlantic slave trade?*

Business, science, religion, and politics were discussed in London coffeehouses such as this. Permission of the Trustees of the British Museum

[1]Larry Stewart, *The Rise of Public Science: Rhetoric, Technology, and Natural Philosophy in Newtonian Britain, 1660–1750* (Cambridge: Cambridge University Press, 1992), p. 145.

[2]Quoted in James Van Horn Melton, *The Rise of the Public in Enlightenment Europe* (Cambridge: Cambridge University Press, 2001), p. 243.

status for authors in this new print culture was based on merit and commercial competition, not heredity and patronage.

A division, however, soon emerged between high and low literary culture. Successful authors of the Enlightenment addressed themselves to monarchs, nobles, the upper middle classes, and professional groups and were read and accepted in these upper levels of society. Other authors found social and economic disappointment. They lived marginally, writing professionally for whatever newspaper or journal would pay for their pages. Many of these lesser writers grew resentful, blaming a corrupt society for their lack of success. From their anger, they often espoused radical ideas or carried Enlightenment ideas to radical extremes, transmitting them in this embittered form to their often lower class audience. The new print culture thus circulated the ideas of the Enlightenment to virtually all literate groups in society.

An expanding literate public and the growing influence of secular printed materials created a new and increasingly influential social force called *public opinion*. This force—the collective effect on political and social life of views circulated in print and discussed in the home, the workplace, and centers of leisure—seems not to have existed before the middle of the eighteenth century. Books and newspapers could have thousands of readers, who in effect supported the writers whose works they bought, discussing their ideas and circulating them widely. The writers, in turn, had to answer only to their readers. The result changed the cultural and political climate in Europe. In 1775, a new member of the French Academy declared,

A tribunal has arisen independent of all powers and that all powers respect, that appreciates all talents, that pronounces on all people of merit. And in an enlightened century, in a century in which each citizen can speak to the entire nation by way of print, those who have a talent for instructing men and a gift for moving them—in a word, men of letters—are, amid the public dispersed, what the orators of Rome and Athens were in the middle of the public assembled.[4]

Governments could no longer operate wholly in secret or with disregard to the larger public sphere. They, as well as their critics, had to explain and discuss their views and policies openly.

Continental European governments sensed the political power of the new print culture. They regulated the book trade, censored books and newspapers, confiscated offending titles, and imprisoned offending authors. The eventual expansion of freedom of the press represented also an expansion of the print culture—with its independent readers, authors, and publishers—and the challenge it posed to traditional intellectual, social, and political authorities.

The *Encyclopedia*

The midcentury witnessed the publication of the *Encyclopedia*, one of the greatest monuments of the Enlightenment and its most monumental undertaking in the realm of print culture. Under the heroic leadership of Denis Diderot (1713–1784) and Jean Le Rond d'Alembert (1717–1783), the first volume appeared in 1751. Eventually, numbering seventeen volumes of text and eleven of plates (illustrations), the project was completed in 1772.

The *Encyclopedia*, in part a collective plea for freedom of expression, reached fruition only after many attempts to censor it and to halt its publication. It was the product of the collective effort of more than a hundred authors, and its editors had at one time or another solicited articles from all the major French philosophes. It included the most advanced critical ideas of the time on religion, government, and philosophy. To avoid official censure, these ideas often had to be hidden in obscure articles or under the cover of irony. The *Encyclopedia* also included important articles and illustrations on manufacturing, canal building, ship construction, and improved agriculture, making it an important source of knowledge about eighteenth-century social and economic life. (See "The *Encyclopedia* Praises Mechanical Arts and Artisans.")

Between 14,000 and 16,000 copies of various editions of the *Encyclopedia* were sold before 1789. The project had been designed to secularize learning and to undermine intellectual assumptions that lingered from the Middle Ages and the Reformation. The articles on politics, ethics, and society ignored divine law and concentrated on humanity and its immediate well-being. The Encyclopedists looked to antiquity rather than to the Christian centuries for their intellectual and ethical models. For them, the future welfare of humankind lay not in pleasing God or following divine commandments, but rather in harnessing the power and resources of the earth and in living at peace with one's fellow human beings. The good life lay here and now and was to be achieved through the application of reason to human relationships. With the publication of the *Encyclopedia*, Enlightenment

[4]Chrétien-Guillaume Malesherbes, as quoted in Roger Chartier, *The Cultural Origins of the French Revolution*, trans. by Lydia G. Cochran (Durham, NC: Duke University Press, 1991), pp. 30–31.

THE *ENCYCLOPEDIA* PRAISES MECHANICAL ARTS AND ARTISANS

The leading intellectuals and men of letters of the day wrote the articles of the Encyclopedia. *Yet the concrete reality of contemporaneous economic life in towns and the countryside fill its pages. Two of the most remarkable features of the* Encyclopedia *are the vast quantity of information it included in numerous articles about the mechanical arts and, in these articles, engravings that portrayed eighteenth-century French artisans in their workplace. The editors of the* Encyclopedia *believed disseminating such information was necessary to aid the spirit of improvement and to promote economic growth. In the "Preliminary Discourse," which served as a general introduction to the* Encyclopedia, *d'Alembert explained the importance of the mechanical arts and the way the authors had explored these arts and the workshops where they were practiced.*

■ *How does d'Alembert defend the importance of the mechanical arts? Why does he think they have not always received proper attention and appreciation? How did the authors of the* Encyclopedia *familiarize themselves with such work? What kind of conversation might have occurred between one of those authors and a skilled artisan operating his machinery?*

The mechanical arts, which are dependent upon manual operation and are subjugated . . . to a sort of routine, have been left to those among men whom prejudices have placed in the lowest class. Poverty has forced these men to turn to such work more often than taste and genius have attracted them to it. Subsequently it became a reason for holding them in contempt. . . . However, the advantage that the liberal arts have over the mechanical arts . . . is sufficiently counterbalanced by the quite superior usefulness which the latter for the most part have for us. It is this very usefulness which reduced them perforce to purely mechanical operations in order to make them accessible to a larger number of men. But while justly respecting great geniuses for their enlightenment, society ought not to degrade the hands by which it is saved. . . .

Too much has been written on the sciences; not enough has been written well on the mechanical arts. . . . Thus everything impelled us to go directly to the workers.

We approached the most capable of them. . . . We took the trouble of going into their shops, of questioning them, of writing at their dictation, of developing their thoughts and of drawing therefrom the terms peculiar to their professions, of setting up tables of these terms and of working out definitions for them, of conversing with those from whom we obtained memoranda, and (an almost indispensable precaution) of correcting through long and frequent conversations with others what some of them imperfectly, obscurely, and sometimes unreliably had explained. There are some artisans who are also men of letters, and we would be able to cite them here; but their numbers are very small. Most of those who engage in the mechanical arts have embraced them only by necessity and work only by instinct. . . .

But there are some trades so unusual and some operations so subtle that unless one does the work oneself, unless one operates a machine with one's own hands, and sees the work being created under one's own eyes, it is difficult to speak of it with precision. Thus several times we had to get possession of the machines, to construct them, and to put a hand to the work. It was necessary to become apprentices, so to speak, and to manufacture some poor object ourselves in order to learn how to teach others the way good specimens are made.

From Jean Le Rond d'Alembert, *Preliminary Discourse to the Encyclopedia of Diderot,* trans. by Richard N. Schwab (Indianapolis: ITT Bobbs-Merrill Educational Publishing, 1985), pp. 41–42, 122–123.

thought became more fully diffused over the Continent, penetrating German and Russian intellectual and political circles.

The Enlightenment and Religion

For many, but not all, philosophes of the eighteenth century, ecclesiastical institutions were the chief impediment to human improvement and happiness. Voltaire's cry, "Crush the Infamous Thing," summed up the attitude of a number of philosophes toward the church and Christianity. Almost all varieties of Christianity, but especially Roman Catholicism, felt their criticism as also did both Judaism and Islam.

The critical philosophes complained that the churches hindered the pursuit of a rational life and the scientific study of humanity and nature. The clergy taught that humans were basically depraved, becoming worthy only through divine grace. According to the doctrine of original sin—either Protestant or Catholic—meaningful improvement in human nature on earth was impossible. Religion thus turned attention away from this world to the world to come. For example, the philosophes argued that the Calvinist doctrine of predestination denied that virtuous behavior in this life could affect the fate of a person's soul after death. Mired in conflicts over obscure doctrines, the churches promoted intolerance and bigotry, inciting torture, war, and other forms of human suffering.

With this attack, the philosophes were challenging not only a set of ideas, but also some of Europe's most powerful institutions. The churches were deeply enmeshed in the power structure of the Old Regime. They owned large amounts of land and collected tithes from peasants before any secular authority collected its taxes. Most clergy were legally exempt from taxes and made only annual voluntary grants to the government. The upper clergy in most countries were relatives of aristocrats. Clerics were actively involved in politics, serving in the British House of Lords and advising princes on the Continent. In Protestant countries, the leading local landowner usually appointed the parish clergyman. In Britain and the Continent, membership in the state church conferred political and social advantages. Those who did not belong were often excluded from political life, the universities, and the professions. Clergy frequently provided intellectual justification for the social and political status quo, and they were active agents of religious and literary censorship.

DEISM

The philosophes, although critical of many religious institutions and frequently anticlerical, did not oppose all religion. In Scotland, for example, the enlightened historian William Robertson (1721–1793) was the head of the Scottish Kirk. In England, Anglican clergymen did much to popularize the thought of Newton. What the philosophes sought, however, was religion without fanaticism and intolerance, a religious life that would largely substitute human reason for the authority of churches. The Newtonian worldview had convinced many writers that nature was rational. Therefore, the God who had created nature must also be rational, and the religion through which that God was worshiped should be rational. Most of them believed the life of religion and of reason could be combined, giving rise to a movement known as **deism.**

The title of one of the earliest deist works, *Christianity Not Mysterious* (1696) by John Toland (1670–1722), indicates the general tenor of this religious outlook. Toland and later deist writers promoted religion as a natural and rational, rather than a supernatural and mystical, phenomenon. In this respect they differed from Newton and Locke, both of whom regarded themselves as distinctly Christian. Newton believed God could interfere with the natural order, whereas the deists regarded God as a kind of divine watchmaker who had created the mechanism of nature, set it in motion, and then departed. Most of the deist writers were also strongly anticlerical and were for that reason regarded as radical.

There were two major points in the deists' creed. The first was a belief in the existence of God, which they thought could be empirically justified by the contemplation of nature. Joseph Addison's poem on the spacious firmament (1712) illustrates this idea:

The spacious firmament on high,
With all the blue ethereal sky,
And spangled heav'n, a shining frame,
Their great Original proclaim:
Th' unwearied Sun, from day to day,
Does his Creator's power display,
And publishes to every land
The work of an Almighty hand.

Because nature provided evidence of a rational God, that deity must also favor rational morality. So the second point in the deists' creed was a belief in life after death, when rewards and punishments would be meted out according to the virtue of the lives people led on this earth.

Deism was empirical, tolerant, reasonable, and capable of encouraging virtuous living. Voltaire wrote,

The great name of Deist, which is not sufficiently revered, is the only name one ought to take. The only gospel one ought to read is the great book of Nature, written by the hand of God and sealed with his seal. The only religion that ought to be professed is the religion of worshiping God and being a good man.[5]

Deists hoped that wide acceptance of their faith would end rivalry among the various Christian sects and with it religious fanaticism, conflict, and persecution. They also felt deism would remove the need for priests and ministers, who, in their view, were often responsible for fomenting religious differences and denominational hatred. Deistic thought led some contemporaries to believe God had revealed himself in different ways and that many religions might embody divine truth.

TOLERATION

According to the philosophes, religious toleration was a primary social condition for the virtuous life. Again Voltaire took the polemical lead in championing this cause. In 1762, the Roman Catholic political authorities in Toulouse ordered the execution of a Huguenot named Jean Calas. He stood accused of having murdered his son to prevent him from converting to Roman Catholicism. Calas was viciously tortured and publicly strangled without ever confessing his guilt. The confession would not have saved his life, but it would have given the Catholics good propaganda to use against Protestants.

Voltaire learned of the case only after Calas's death. He made the dead man's cause his own. In 1763, he published his *Treatise on Tolerance* and hounded the authorities for a new investigation. Finally, in 1765, the judicial decision against the unfortunate man was reversed. For Voltaire, the case illustrated the fruits of religious fanaticism and the need for rational reform of judicial processes. (See "Voltaire Attacks Religious Fanaticism.") Somewhat later in the century, the German playwright and critic Gotthold Lessing (1729–1781) wrote *Nathan the Wise* (1779), a plea for toleration not only of different Christian sects, but also of religious faiths other than Christianity.

The premise behind all of these calls for toleration was, in effect, that life on earth and human relationships should not be subordinated to religion. Secular values and considerations were more important than religious ones.

RADICAL ENLIGHTENMENT CRITICISM OF CHRISTIANITY

Some philosophes went beyond the formulation of a rational religious alternative to Christianity and the advocacy of toleration to attack the churches and the clergy with great vehemence. Voltaire repeatedly questioned the truthfulness of priests and the morality of the Bible. In his *Philosophical Dictionary* (1764), he humorously pointed out inconsistencies in biblical narratives and immoral acts of the biblical heroes. The Scottish philosopher David Hume (1711–1776), in "Of Miracles," a chapter in his *Inquiry into Human Nature* (1748), argued that no empirical evidence supported the belief in divine miracles central to much of Christianity. For Hume, the greatest miracle was that people believed in miracles. In *The Decline and Fall of the Roman Empire* (1776), Edward Gibbon (1737–1794), the English historian, explained the rise of Christianity in terms of natural causes rather than the influence of miracles and piety.

A few philosophes went further. Baron d'Holbach (1723–1789) and Julien Offray de La Mettrie (1709–1751) embraced positions very near to atheism and materialism. Theirs was distinctly a minority position, however. Most of the philosophes sought not the abolition of religion, but its transformation into a humane force that would encourage virtuous living. In the words of the title of a work by the German philosopher Immanuel Kant, they sought to pursue *Religion within the Limits of Reason Alone* (1793).

JEWISH THINKERS IN THE AGE OF ENLIGHTENMENT

Despite their emphasis on toleration, the philosophes' criticisms of traditional religion often reflected an implicit contempt not only for Christianity but also, and sometimes more vehemently, for Judaism and, as we see later, for Islam as well. Their attack on the veracity of biblical miracles and biblical history undermined the authority of the Hebrew scriptures as well as the Christian. They often aimed their satirical barbs at personalities from the Hebrew scriptures. Some philosophes characterized Judaism as a more primitive faith than Christianity and one from which philosophical rationalism provided a path of escape. The Enlightenment view of religion thus served in some ways to further stigmatize Jews and Judaism in the eyes of non-Jewish Europeans.

Enlightenment values also, however, allowed certain Jewish intellectuals to rethink the relationship of their communities to wider European culture from which they had largely lived apart.

---

[5]Quoted in J. H. Randall, *The Making of the Modern Mind*, rev. ed. (New York: Houghton Mifflin, 1940), p. 292.

VOLTAIRE ATTACKS RELIGIOUS FANATICISM

The chief complaint of the philosophes against Christianity was that it bred a fanaticism that led people to commit crimes in the name of religion. In this passage from Voltaire's Philosophical Dictionary (1764), he directly reminds his readers of the intolerance of the Reformation era and indirectly refers to examples of contemporary religious excesses. He argues that the philosophical spirit can overcome fanaticism and foster toleration and more humane religious behavior. Shocking many of his contemporaries, he praises the virtues of Confucianism over those of Christianity.

■ *What concrete examples of religious fanaticism might Voltaire have had in mind? Why does Voltaire contend that neither religion nor laws can contain religious fanaticism? Why does Voltaire admire the Chinese?*

Fanaticism is to superstition what delirium is to fever and rage to anger. The man visited by ecstasies and visions, who takes dreams for realities and his fancies for prophecies, is an enthusiast; the man who supports his madness with murder is a fanatic. . . .

The most detestable example of fanaticism was that of the burghers of Paris who on St. Bartholomew's Night [1572] went about assassinating and butchering all their fellow citizens who did not go to mass, throwing them out of windows, cutting them in pieces.

Once fanaticism has corrupted a mind, the malady is almost incurable. . . .

The only remedy for this epidemic malady is the philosophical spirit which, spread gradually, at last tames men's habits and prevents the disease from starting; for once the disease has made any progress, one must flee and wait for the air to clear itself. Laws and religion are not strong enough against the spiritual pest; religion, far from being healthy food for infected brains, turns to poison in them. . . .

Even the law is impotent against these attacks of rage; it is like reading a court decree to a raving maniac. These fellows are certain that the holy spirit with which they are filled is above the law, that their enthusiasm is the only law they must obey.

What can we say to a man who tells you that he would rather obey God than men, and that therefore he is sure to go to heaven for butchering you?

Ordinarily fanatics are guided by rascals, who put the dagger into their hands; these latter resemble that Old Man of the Mountain who is supposed to have made imbeciles taste the joys of paradise and who promised them an eternity of the pleasures of which he had given them a foretaste, on condition that they assassinated all those he would name to them. There is only one religion in the world that has never been sullied by fanaticism, that of the Chinese men of letters. The schools of philosophy were not only free from this pest, they were its remedy; for the effect of philosophy is to make the soul tranquil, and fanaticism is incompatible with tranquility. If our holy religion has so often been corrupted by this infernal delirium, it is the madness of men which is at fault.

From Voltaire, *Philosophical Dictionary*, trans. by P. Gay (New York: Basic Books, 1962), pp. 267–269.

Two major Jewish writers—one a few decades before the opening of the Enlightenment and one toward the close—entered the larger debate over religion and the place of Jews in European life. These were Baruch Spinoza (1632–1677), who lived in the Netherlands, and Moses Mendelssohn (1729–1786), who lived in Germany. Spinoza set the example for a secularized version of Judaism, and Mendelssohn established the main outlines of an assimilationist position. Although their approaches to the problem displayed certain similarities, there were also important differences.

Spinoza, the son of a Jewish merchant of Amsterdam, was deeply influenced by the new science of the mid–seventeenth century. Like his contemporaries, Hobbes and Descartes, he looked to the power of human reason to reconceptualize traditional thought. In that regard his thinking reflected the age of scientific revolution and looked toward the later Enlightenment.

The Dutch Jewish philosopher Baruch Spinoza was deeply influenced by the new science of the mid–seventeenth century. In his writings, Spinoza argued for rationality over traditional spiritual beliefs. Library of Congress

In his *Ethics*, the most famous of his works, Spinoza so closely identified God and nature, or the spiritual and material worlds, that contemporaries condemned him. Many thought he drew God and nature too intimately into a single divine substance, leaving little room for the possibility of a distinctly divine revelation to humankind in scripture. Both Christians and Jews also believed Spinoza's near pantheistic position meant human beings might not be personally responsible for their actions and that there could be no personal, individual immortality of the human soul after death. During his lifetime the controversial character of his writings led both Jews and Protestants to criticize him as an atheist. At the age of twenty-four, he was excommunicated by his own synagogue and thereafter lived apart from the Amsterdam Jewish community.

In his *Theologico-Political Treatise* (1670), Spinoza directly anticipated much of the religious criticism of the Enlightenment and its attacks on the power of superstition in human life. Spinoza described the origins of religion in thoroughly naturalistic terms. He believed the Hebrew Bible provided Jews with divine legislation but not with specially revealed theological knowledge. In this respect, he was calling on both Jews and Christians to use their own reason in religious matters and to read the Bible like other ancient books. Spinoza's extensive rational and historical criticism of the biblical narratives disturbed Christian and Jewish contemporaries who saw him as a writer seeking to lead people away from all religion. He actually argued, however, that the formally organized religious institutions of both Christianity and Judaism led people away from the original teaching of scripture and encouraged them to persecute those who disagreed with the leaders of their respective churches and synagogues.

Because of Spinoza's excommunication from his synagogue, the later philosophes viewed him as a martyr for rationality against superstition. He also symbolized a Jew who, through the use of his critical reason, had separated himself from traditional Jewish religion and practices and attempted to enter the mainstream society. In that regard, he left Judaism to pursue a secular existence with little or no regard for his original faith. Consequently, his life and his writings, as one commentator has stated, "made it possible for defenders of the Enlightenment to advocate toleration of Jews while simultaneously holding Judaism in contempt."[6] This stance of championing toleration while condemning Judaism itself would later characterize the outlook of many non-Jewish Europeans to the assimilation of Jews into European civic life. It was, however, an outlook that could not without much modification be welcomed by Jewish communities themselves.

Moses Mendelsohn, the leading Jewish philosopher of the eighteenth century and a person known as the "Jewish Socrates," writing almost a century later also advocated the entry of Jews into modern European life. In contrast to Spinoza, however, Mendelsohn argued for the possibility of loyalty to Judaism combined with adherence to rational, Enlightenment values. Mendelsohn could hold this position in part because of the influence of Lessing's arguments for toleration. Indeed, Mendelsohn had been the person on whose life Lessing had modeled the chief character of *Nathan the Wise*.

Mendelsohn's most influential work was *Jerusalem; or, On Ecclesiastical Power and Judaism* (1783) in which he argued both for advancing extensive religious toleration and for maintaining the religious distinction of Jewish communities. Mendelsohn urged that religious diversity within a nation did not harm loyalty to the government; therefore, governments should be religiously neutral and Jews should enjoy the same civil rights as other subjects. Then in the spirit of the deists, he

---

[6]Steven B. Smith, *Spinoza, Liberalism, and the Question of Jewish Identity* (New Haven, CT: Yale University Press, 1997), p. 166.

presented Judaism as one of many religious paths revealed by God. Jewish law and practice were intended for the moral benefit of Jewish communities; other religions similarly served other people. Consequently, various communities should be permitted to practice their religious faith alongside other religious groups.

Unlike Spinoza, Mendelsohn wished to advocate religious toleration while genuinely sustaining the traditional religious practices and faith of Judaism. Nevertheless, Mendelsohn believed Jewish communities should not have the right to excommunicate their members over differences in theological opinions, but should tolerate within themselves a wide spectrum of outlooks. In this respect, Mendelsohn set forth a far more extensive vision of religious toleration than John Locke almost a century earlier, who had contended that numerous religious communities should be tolerated but that each should retain the right of excommunication (see Chapter 14). Mendelsohn advocated broad toleration within the Jewish communities so their members, if they wished, could embrace modern secular ideas without danger of excommunication. He thus sought both toleration of Jews within the broader non-Jewish European society and toleration by Jews of a wider spectrum of opinion within their own communities and congregations. His hope was that the rationalism of the Enlightenment would provide the foundation for both modes of toleration.

ISLAM IN ENLIGHTENMENT THOUGHT

Unlike Judaism, Islam, except in the Balkan Peninsula, had few adherents in eighteenth-century Europe. Although European merchants traded with the Ottoman Empire or with those parts of South Asia where Islam prevailed, most Europeans came to know what little they did know about the Islamic world and Islam as a religion through books—the religious commentaries of Christian missionaries, histories, and the reports of travelers—that with rare exceptions were hostile to Islam and deeply misleading.

Islam continued to be seen as a rival to Christianity. European writers, such as Pascal in his *Pensées* (see Chapter 14), repeated what other Christian critics had said for centuries. They portrayed Islam as a false religion and Muhammed as an impostor and a false prophet because he had not performed miracles. Furthermore, they also attacked Islam as an exceptionally carnal or sexually promiscuous religion because of its teaching that heaven was a place of sensuous delights, its permission for a man to have more than one wife, Muhammed's own polygamy, and the presence of harems in the Islamic world.

Christian authors also ignored the Islamic understanding of the life and mission of Muhammed. They referred to Islam as Muhammedanism, thus implying that Muhammed was divine rather than a human being with whom God had chosen to communicate. For Muslims, the suggestion that Muhammed was divine is blasphemous.

Several European universities did endow professorships for the study of Arabic during the seventeenth century. But these university scholars generally agreed with theological critics that Islam too often embodied religious fanaticism. Even relatively well-informed works based on considerable knowledge of Arabic and Islamic sources, such as Barthélemy d'Herbelot's *Bibliothèque orientale* (*Oriental Library*), a reference book published in 1697, Simon Ockley's *History of the Saracens* (1718), and George Sale's introduction to the first full English translation of the Qur'an (1734) were largely hostile to their subject. All of these books continued to be reprinted and remained influential well into the nineteenth century, demonstrating how little disinterested information was available to Europeans about Islam.

Enlightenment philosophes spoke with two voices regarding Islam. Voltaire indicated his opinion along with that of many of his contemporaries in the title of his 1742 tragedy, *Fanaticism, or Mohammed the Prophet*. Although he sometimes spoke well of the Qur'an, Voltaire declared in a later historical work, "We must suppose that Muhammed, like all enthusiasts, violently impressed by his own ideas, retailed them in good faith, fortified them with fancies, deceived himself in deceiving others, and finally sustained with deceit a doctrine he believed to be good."[7] Thus for Voltaire, Muhammed and Islam in general represented simply one more example of the religious fanaticism he had so often criticized among Christians.

Some Enlightenment writers, however, spoke well of the Islamic faith. The deist John Toland, who opposed prejudice against both Jews and Muslims, contended that Islam derived from early Christian writings and was thus a form of Christianity. These views so offended most of his contemporaries that Toland became known as a "Mohametan" Christian. Edward Gibbon (1737–1794), who blamed Christianity for contributing to the fall of the Roman Empire, wrote with respect of Muhammed's leadership and Islam's success in conquering so vast a territory in the first century of its existence. Other commentators approved of Islam's tolerance and the charitable work of Muslims.

[7]Quoted in Theodore Besterman, *Voltaire* (New York: Harcourt, Brace, & World, 1969), p. 409.

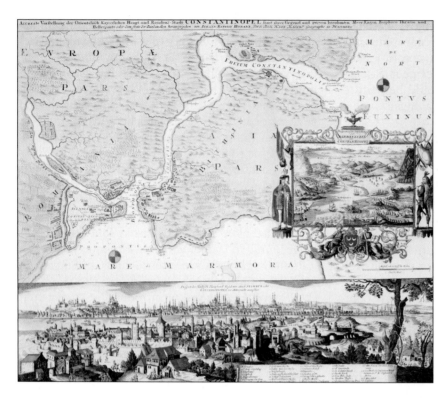

Few Europeans visited the Ottoman Empire. What little they knew about it came from reports of travelers and from illustrations such as this view of Constantinople, the empire's capital. © Historical Picture Archive/ CORBIS

Some philosophes criticized Islam on cultural and political grounds. In *The Persian Letters* (1721), supposedly written by two Muslim Persians visiting Europe, the young Montesquieu used Islamic culture as a foil to criticize his own European society. But by the time he wrote his more influential *Spirit of the Laws* (1748), discussed more fully later in this chapter, Montesquieu associated Islamic society with the passivity that he ascribed to people subject to political despotism. Like other Europeans, Montesquieu believed the excessive influence of Islamic religious leaders prevented the Ottoman Empire from adapting itself to new advances in technology.

One of the most positive commentators on eighteenth-century Islam was a woman. Between 1716 and 1718, Lady Mary Wortley Montagu (1689–1762) lived in Constantinople with her husband, the British ambassador to Turkey. She wrote a series of letters about her experiences there that were published the year after her death. In these *Turkish Embassy Letters*, she praised much about Ottoman society and urged the English to copy the Turkish practice of vaccination against smallpox. Unlike European males, Montagu had access to the private quarters of women in Istanbul. In contrast to the constraints under which English women found themselves, she thought upper-class Turkish women were remarkably free and well treated by their husbands despite having to wear clothing that completely covered them in public. In fact,

Montagu thought the anonymity these coverings bestowed allowed Turkish women to move freely about Istanbul. She also considered the magnificent Ottoman architecture better than anything in western Europe. Montagu repeatedly criticized the misinformation that prevailed in Europe about the Ottoman Empire and declared that many of the hostile comments about Islam and Islamic morality were simply wrong.

Yet the European voices demanding fairness and expressing empathy for Islam were rare throughout the eighteenth century. As one historian has commented, "The basic Christian attitude was still what it had been for a millennium: a rejection of the claim of Muslims that Muhammad was a prophet and the Qur'an the word of God, mingled with a memory of periods of fear and conflict, and also, a few thinkers and scholars apart, with legends, usually hostile and often contemptuous."[8]

Nor were Muslims very curious about the Christian West. Only a handful of people from the Ottoman Empire visited western Europe in the eighteenth century, and no Islamic writers showed much interest in contemporary European authors. The Ulama, the Islamic religious establishment, reinforced these attitudes. They taught that God's revelations to Muhammad meant Islam had

[8]A. Hourani, *Islam in European Thought* (Cambridge: Cambridge University Press, 1991), p. 136.

superceded Christianity as a religion and therefore there was little to be learned from the Christian culture of Europe.

The Enlightenment and Society

Although the philosophes wrote much on religion, humanity was the center of their interest. As one writer in the *Encyclopedia* observed, "Man is the unique point to which we must refer everything, if we wish to interest and please amongst considerations the most arid and details the most dry."[9] The philosophes believed the application of human reason to society would reveal laws in human relationships similar to those found in physical nature. At the same time, the use of the word *man* in this passage was not simply an accident of language. Most philosophes were thinking primarily of men, not women, when they framed their reformist ideas. With a few exceptions, as we see later in the chapter, they had little interest in expanding women's intellectual and social opportunities.

Although the term did not appear until later, the idea of *social science* originated with the Enlightenment. Philosophes hoped to end human cruelty by discovering social laws and making people aware of them. These concerns are most evident in the philosophes' work on law and prisons.

BECCARIA AND REFORM OF CRIMINAL LAW

In 1764, Cesare Beccaria (1738–1794), an Italian philosophe, published *On Crimes and Punishments*, in which he applied critical analysis to the problem of making punishments both effective and just. He wanted the laws of monarchs and legislatures—that is, positive law—to conform with the rational laws of nature. He rigorously and eloquently attacked both torture and capital punishment. He thought the criminal justice system should ensure a speedy trial and certain punishment and the intent of punishment should be to deter further crime. The purpose of laws was not to impose the will of God or some other ideal of perfection; their purpose was to secure the greatest good or happiness for the greatest number of human beings. This utilitarian philosophy based on happiness in this life permeated most Enlightenment writing on practical reforms.

THE PHYSIOCRATS AND ECONOMIC FREEDOM

Economic policy was another area in which the philosophes saw existing legislation and administration preventing the operation of natural social laws. They believed mercantilist legislation (designed to protect a country's trade from external competition) and the regulation of labor by governments and guilds actually hampered the expansion of trade, manufacture, and agriculture. In France, these economic reformers were called the **physiocrats.** Their leading spokespeople were François Quesnay (1694–1774) and Pierre Dupont de Nemours (1739–1817).

The physiocrats believed the primary role of government was to protect property and to permit its owners to use it freely. They particularly felt all economic production depended on sound agriculture. They favored the consolidation of small peasant holdings into larger, more efficient farms. Here, as elsewhere, there was a close relationship between the rationalism of the Enlightenment and the spirit of improvement at work in eighteenth-century European economic life.

ADAM SMITH ON ECONOMIC GROWTH AND SOCIAL PROGRESS

The most important economic work of the Enlightenment was Adam Smith's (1723–1790) *Inquiry into the Nature and Causes of the Wealth of Nations* (1776). Smith, who was for a time a professor at Glasgow, believed economic liberty was the foundation of a natural economic system. As a result, he urged that the mercantile system of England—including the navigation acts, the bounties, most tariffs, special trading monopolies, and the domestic regulation of labor and manufacture—be abolished. These regulations were intended to preserve the wealth of the nation, to capture wealth from other nations, and to maximize the work available for the nation's laborers. Smith argued, however, that they hindered the expansion of wealth and production. The best way to encourage economic growth, he maintained, was to unleash individuals to pursue their own selfish economic interests. As self-interested individuals sought to enrich themselves by meeting the needs of others in the marketplace, the economy would expand. Consumers would find their wants met as manufacturers and merchants competed for their business.

It was a basic assumption of mercantilism that the earth's resources are limited and scarce, so one nation can acquire wealth only at the expense of

---

[9]Quoted in F. L. Baumer, *Main Currents of Western Thought*, 4th ed. (New Haven, CT: Yale University Press, 1978), p. 374.

others. Smith's book challenged this assumption. He saw the resources of nature—water, air, soil, and minerals—as boundless. To him, they demanded exploitation for the enrichment and comfort of humankind. In effect, Smith was saying the nations and peoples of Europe need not be poor.

Smith is usually regarded as the founder of **laissez-faire** economic thought and policy, which favors a limited role for the government in economic life. *The Wealth of Nations* was, however, a complex book. Smith was no simple dogmatist. For example, he did not oppose all government activity touching the economy. The state, he argued, should provide schools, armies, navies, and roads. It should also undertake certain commercial ventures, such as the opening of dangerous new trade routes that were economically desirable, but too expensive or risky for private enterprise.

Within *The Wealth of Nations*, Smith, like other Scottish thinkers of the day, embraced an important theory of human social and economic development, known as the *four-stage theory*. According to this theory, human societies can be classified as hunting and gathering, pastoral or herding, agricultural, and commercial. The hunters and gatherers have little or no settled life. Pastoral societies are groups of nomads who tend their herds and develop some private property. Agricultural or farming societies are settled and have clear-cut property arrangements. Finally, in the commercial state there exist advanced cities, the manufacture of numerous items for wide consumption, extensive trade between cities and the countryside, as well as elaborate forms of property and financial arrangements. Smith and other Scottish writers described the passage of human society through these stages as a movement from barbarism to civilization.

The four-stage theory implicitly evaluated the later stages of economic development and the people dwelling in them as higher, more progressive, and more civilized than the earlier ones. A social theorist using this theory could thus very quickly look at a society and, on the basis of the state of its economic development and organizations, rank it in terms of the stage it had achieved. In point of fact, the commercial stage, the highest rank in the theory, described society as it appeared in northwestern Europe. Thus Smith's theory allowed Europeans to look about the world and always find themselves dwelling at the highest level of human achievement. This outlook served as one of the major justifications in the minds of Europeans for their economic and imperial domination of the world during the next century. They repeatedly portrayed themselves as bringing a higher level of civilization to people elsewhere who, according to

the four-stage theory, lived in lower stages of human social and economic development. Europeans thus imbued with the spirit of the Enlightenment presented themselves as carrying out a civilizing mission to the rest of the world.

Political Thought of the Philosophes

Nowhere was the philosophes' reformist agenda, as well as tensions among themselves, so apparent as in their political thought. Most philosophes were discontented with certain political features of their countries, but they were especially discontented in France. There the corruptness of the royal court, the blundering of the administrative bureaucracy, the less-than-glorious midcentury wars, and the power of the church compounded all problems. Consequently, the most important political thought of the Enlightenment occurred in France. The French philosophes, however, stood quite divided on the proper solution to their country's problems. Their attitudes spanned a wide political spectrum, from aristocratic reform to democracy to absolute monarchy.

MONTESQUIEU AND *SPIRIT OF THE LAWS*

Charles Louis de Secondat, baron de Montesquieu (1689–1755), was a lawyer, a noble of the robe, and a member of a provincial *parlement*. He also belonged to the Bordeaux Academy of Science, before which he presented papers on scientific topics.

Although living comfortably within the bosom of French society, he saw the need for reform. In 1721, as already noted, he published *The Persian Letters* to satirize contemporary institutions. Behind the humor lay the cutting edge of criticism and an exposition of the cruelty and irrationality of much contemporaneous European life. About a decade after this volume appeared, Montesquieu, like Voltaire, visited England and deeply admired English institutions.

In his most enduring work, *Spirit of the Laws* (1748), Montesquieu held up the example of the British constitution as the wisest model for regulating the power of government. With his interest in science, his hope for reform, and his admiration for Britain, he embodied all the major elements of the Enlightenment mind.

Montesquieu's *Spirit of the Laws*, perhaps the single most influential book of the century, exhibits the internal tensions of the Enlightenment. In it, Montesquieu pursued an empirical method, taking illustrative examples from the political experience of both ancient and modern nations. From these, he concluded there could be no single set of political laws that applied to all peoples at all times and in all places. The good political life depended rather on the relationship among many political variables. Whether the best form of government for a country was a monarchy or a republic, for example, depended on that country's size, population, social and religious customs, economic structure, traditions, and climate. Only a careful examination and evaluation of these elements could reveal what mode of government would prove most beneficial to a particular people.

So far as France was concerned, Montesquieu had some definite ideas. He believed in a monarchical government tempered and limited by various sets of intermediary institutions, including the aristocracy, the towns, and the other corporate bodies that enjoyed liberties the monarch had to respect. These corporate bodies might be said to represent various segments of the general population and thus of public opinion. In France, he regarded the aristocratic courts, or *parlements*, as the major example of an intermediary association. Their role was to limit the power of the monarchy and thus to preserve the liberty of its subjects.

In championing these aristocratic bodies and the general role of the aristocracy, Montesquieu was a political conservative. He adopted this conservatism in the hope of achieving reform, however, for he believed the oppressive and inefficient absolutism of the monarchy accounted for the degradation of French life.

One of Montesquieu's most influential ideas was that of the division of power in government. For his model of a government with authority wisely separated among different branches, he took contemporary Great Britain. There, he believed, executive power resided in the king, legislative power in the Parliament, and judicial power in the courts. He thought any two branches could check and balance the power of the other. His perception of the eighteenth-century British constitution was incorrect because he failed to see how patronage and electoral corruption allowed a handful of powerful aristocrats to dominate the government. Moreover, he was also unaware of the emerging cabinet system, which was slowly making the executive power a creature of the Parliament.

Nevertheless, Montesquieu's analysis illustrated his strong sense that monarchs should be subject to constitutional limits on their power and a separate legislature, not the monarch, should formulate laws. For this reason, although he set out to defend the political privileges of the French aristocracy,

Montesquieu's ideas had a profound and still-lasting effect on the constitutional form of liberal democracies for more than two centuries.

ROUSSEAU: A RADICAL CRITIQUE OF MODERN SOCIETY

Jean-Jacques Rousseau (1712–1778) held a view of the exercise and reform of political power that was quite different from Montesquieu's. Rousseau was a strange, isolated genius who never felt particularly comfortable with the other philosophes. His own life was troubled. He could form few close friendships. He sired numerous children, whom he abandoned to foundling hospitals. Yet perhaps more than any other writer of the mid–eighteenth century, he transcended the political thought and values of his own time. Rousseau had a deep antipathy toward the world and the society in which he lived. It seemed to him impossible for human beings living according to the commercial values of his time to achieve moral, virtuous, or sincere lives. In 1750, in his *Discourse on the Moral Effects of the Arts and*

Jean-Jacques Rousseau (1712–1778) raised some of the most profound social and ethical questions of the Enlightenment. This portrait is by Maurice Quentin.
Maurice Quentin de la Tour, Jean-Jacques Rousseau, ca. 1740. Original: Genf, Musée d'Art et d'Histoire. Bildarchiv Preussischer Kulturbesitz

Sciences, he contended that the process of civilization and Enlightenment had corrupted human nature. In 1755, in his *Discourse on the Origin of Inequality,* Rousseau blamed much of the evil in the world on the uneven distribution of property.

In both works, Rousseau brilliantly and directly challenged the social fabric of the day. He drew into question the concepts of material and intellectual progress and the morality of a society in which commerce and industry were regarded as the most important human activities. The other philosophes generally believed life would improve if people could enjoy more of the fruits of the earth or could produce more goods. Rousseau raised the more fundamental question of what constitutes the good life. This question has haunted European social thought ever since the eighteenth century.

Rousseau carried these same concerns into his political thought. His most extensive discussion of politics appeared in *The Social Contract* (1762). Although the book attracted rather little immediate attention, by the end of the century it was widely read in France. Compared with Montesquieu's *Spirit of the Laws, The Social Contract* is a very abstract book. It does not propose specific reforms, but outlines the kind of political structure that Rousseau believed would overcome the evils of contemporary politics and society.

In the tradition of John Locke, most eighteenth-century political thinkers regarded human beings as individuals and society as a collection of individuals pursuing personal, selfish goals. These writers wished to liberate individuals from the undue bonds of government. Rousseau picked up the stick from the other end. His book opens with the declaration, "All men are born free, but everywhere they are in chains."[10] The rest of the volume is a defense of the chains of a properly organized society over its members.

Rousseau suggested that society is more important than its individual members, because they are what they are only by virtue of their relationship to the larger community. Independent human beings living alone can achieve very little. Through their relationship to the larger community, they become moral creatures capable of significant action. The question then becomes, What kind of community allows people to behave morally? In his two previous discourses, Rousseau had explained that the contemporaneous European society was not such a community; it was merely an aggregate of competing individuals whose chief social goal was to preserve selfish independence in spite of all potential social bonds and obligations.

Rousseau envisioned a society in which each person could maintain personal freedom while behaving as a loyal member of the larger community. Drawing on the traditions of Plato and Calvin, he defined freedom as obedience to law. In his case, the law to be obeyed was that created by the general will. In a society with virtuous customs and morals in which citizens have adequate information on important issues, the concept of the general will is normally equivalent to the will of a majority of voting citizens. Democratic participation in decision making would bind the individual citizen to the community. Rousseau believed the general will, thus understood, must always be right and that to obey the general will is to be free. This argument led him to the notorious conclusion that under certain circumstances some people must be forced to be free. Rousseau's politics thus constituted a justification for radical direct democracy and for collective action against individual citizens.

Rousseau had in effect launched an assault on the eighteenth-century cult of the individual and the fruits of selfishness. He stood at odds with the commercial spirit that was transforming the society in which he lived. Rousseau would have disapproved of the main thrust of Adam Smith's *Wealth of Nations,* which he may or may not have read, and would no doubt have preferred a study on the virtue of nations. Smith wanted people to be prosperous; Rousseau wanted them to be good even if being good meant they might remain poor. He saw human beings not as independent individuals, but as creatures enmeshed in necessary social relationships. He believed loyalty to the community should be encouraged. As one device to that end, he suggested a properly governed society should decree a civic religion based on the creed of deism. Such a shared religion, the observance of which he thought should be enforced by repressive legislation, could, he argued, help unify a society.

Rousseau had only a marginal impact on his own time. The other philosophes questioned his critique of material improvement. Aristocrats and royal ministers could hardly be expected to welcome his proposal for radical democracy. Too many people were either making or hoping to make money to appreciate his criticism of commercial values. He proved, however, to be a figure to whom later generations returned. Many leaders in the French Revolution were familiar with his writing, and he influenced many writers in the nineteenth and twentieth centuries who were critical of the general tenor and direction of Western culture. Rousseau hated much about the emerging modern society in

---

[10]Jean-Jacques Rousseau, *The Social Contract and Discourses,* trans. by G. D. H. Cole (New York: Dutton, 1950), p. 3.

Europe, but he contributed much to modernity by exemplifying for later generations the critic who dared to call into question the very foundations of social thought and action.

Women in the Thought and Practice of the Enlightenment

Women, especially in France, helped significantly to promote the careers of the philosophes. In Paris, the salons of women such as Marie-Thérèse Geoffrin (1699–1777), Julie de Lespinasse (1733–1776), and Claudine de Tencin (1689–1749) gave the philosophes access to useful social and political contacts and a receptive environment in which to circulate their ideas. Association with a fashionable salon brought philosophes increased social status and added luster and respectability to their ideas. They clearly enjoyed the opportunity to be the center of attention that a salon provided, and their presence at them could boost the sales of their works. The women who organized the salons were well connected to major political figures who could help protect the philosophes and secure them pensions. The marquise de Pompadour, the mistress of Louis XV (1721–1764), played a key role in overcoming efforts to censor the *Encyclopedia*. She also helped block the circulation of works attacking the philosophes. Other salon hostesses purchased the writings of the philosophes and distributed them among their friends. Madame de Tencin was responsible for promoting Montesquieu's *Spirit of the Laws* in this way.

Despite this help and support from the learned women of Paris, the philosophes were on the whole not strong feminists. Many urged better and broader education for women. They criticized the education women did receive as overly religious, and they tended to reject ascetic views of sexual relations. But in general, they displayed rather traditional views toward women and advocated no radical changes in the social condition of women.

Montesquieu, for example, illustrates some of these tensions in the views of Enlightenment writers toward women. He maintained in general that the status of women in a society was the result of climate, the political regime, culture, and women's physiological nature. He believed women were not naturally inferior to men and should have a wider role in society. He showed himself well aware of the kinds of personal, emotional, and sexual repression European women endured in his day. He sympathetically observed the value placed on women's appearance and the prejudice women met as they aged. In *The Persian Letters,* he included a long exchange

Major Works of the Enlightenment and Their Publication Dates

1670	Spinoza's *Theologico-Political Treatise*
1677	Spinoza's *Ethics* (published pothumously)
1687	Newton's *Principia Mathematica*
1690	Locke's *Essay Concerning Human Understanding*
1696	Toland's *Christianity Not Mysterious*
1721	Montesquieu's *Persian Letters*
1733	Voltaire's *Letters on the English*
1738	Voltaire's *Elements of the Philosophy of Newton*
1748	Montesquieu's *Spirit of the Laws*
1748	Hume's *Inquiry into Human Nature,* with the chapter "Of Miracles"
1750	Rousseau's *Discourse on the Moral Effects of the Arts and Sciences*
1751	First volume of the *Encyclopedia,* edited by Diderot
1755	Rousseau's *Discourse on the Origin of Inequality*
1759	Voltaire's *Candide*
1762	Rousseau's *Social Contract* and *Emile*
1763	Voltaire's *Treatise on Tolerance*
1764	Voltaire's *Philosophical Dictionary*
1764	Beccaria's *On Crimes and Punishments*
1776	Gibbon's *Decline and Fall of the Roman Empire*
1776	Smith's *Wealth of Nations*
1779	Lessing's *Nathan the Wise*
1783	Mendelsohn's *Jerusalem; or, On Ecclesiastical Power and Judaism*
1792	Wollstonecraft's *Vindication of the Rights of Woman*
1793	Kant's *Religion within the Limits of Reason Alone*

about the repression of women in a Persian harem, condemning by implication the restrictions on women in European society. Yet there were limits to Montesquieu's willingness to consider social change in regard to the role of women in European life. Although in the *Spirit of the Laws* he indicated a belief in the equality of the sexes, he still retained a traditional view of marriage and family and expected men to dominate those institutions. Furthermore, although he supported the right of women to divorce and opposed laws directly oppressive of women, he upheld the ideal of female chastity.

The views about women expressed in the *Encyclopedia* were less generous than those of Montesquieu. It suggested some ways to improve

The salon of Madame. Marie Thérèse Geoffrin (1699–1777) was one of the most important gathering spots for Enlightenment writers during the middle of the eighteenth century. Well-connected women such as Madame Geoffrin were instrumental in helping the philosophes they patronized to bring their ideas to the attention of influential people in French society and politics. Giraudon/Art Resource, N.Y.

women's lives, but in general, it did not include the condition of women as a focus of reform. The editors, Diderot and d'Alembert, recruited men almost exclusively as contributors and evidently saw no need to include many articles by women. Most of the articles that dealt with women specifically or discussed women in connection with other subjects often emphasized their physical weakness and inferiority, usually attributed to menstruation or childbearing. Contributors disagreed on the social equality of women. Some favored it, others opposed it, and still others were indifferent. The articles conveyed a general sense that women were reared to be frivolous and unconcerned with important issues. The Encyclopedists discussed women primarily in a family context—as daughters, wives, and mothers—and presented motherhood as their most important occupation. And on sexual behavior, the Encyclopedists upheld an unquestioned double standard.

In contrast to the articles, however, illustrations in the *Encyclopedia* showed women deeply involved in the economic activities of the day. The illustrations also showed the activities of lower-class and working-class women, about whom the articles had little to say.

One of the most surprising and influential analyses of the position of women came from Jean-Jacques Rousseau. This most radical of all Enlightenment political theorists urged a very traditional and conservative role for women. In his novel *Emile* (1762) (discussed again in Chapter 20), he set forth a radical version of the view that men and women occupy separate spheres. He declared that women should be educated for a position subordinate to

men, emphasizing especially women's function in bearing and rearing children. In his vision, there was little else for women to do but make themselves pleasing to men. He portrayed them as weaker and inferior to men in virtually all respects, except perhaps for their capacity for feeling and giving love. He excluded them from political life. The world of citizenship, political action, and civic virtue was to be populated by men. Women were assigned the domestic sphere alone. (See "Rousseau Argues for Separate Spheres for Men and Women.") Many of these attitudes were not new—some have roots as ancient as Roman law—but Rousseau's powerful presentation and the influence of his other writings gave them new life in the late eighteenth century. Rousseau deeply influenced many leaders of the French Revolution, who, as we see in the next chapter, often incorporated his view on gender roles in the policies they implemented.

Paradoxically, in spite of these views and in spite of his own ill treatment of the woman who bore his many children, Rousseau achieved a vast following among women in the eighteenth century. He is credited with persuading thousands of upper-class women to breast-feed their own children rather than putting them out to wet nurses. One explanation for this influence is that his writings, although they did not advocate liberating women or expanding their social or economic roles, did stress the importance of their emotions and subjective feelings. He portrayed the domestic life and the role of wife and mother as a noble and fulfilling vocation, giving middle- and upper-class women a sense that their daily occupations had

ROUSSEAU ARGUES FOR SEPARATE SPHERES FOR MEN AND WOMEN

• •

Rousseau published Emile, *a novel about education, in 1762. In it, he made one of the strongest and most influential arguments of the eighteenth century for distinct social roles for men and women. Furthermore, he portrayed women as fundamentally subordinate to men. In the next document, Mary Wollstonecraft, a contemporary, presents a rebuttal.*

■ *How does Rousseau move from the physical differences between men and women to an argument for distinct social roles and social spheres? What would be the proper kinds of social activities for women in Rousseau's vision? What kind of education would he think appropriate for women?*

There is no parity between the two sexes in regard to the consequences of sex. The male is male only at certain moments. The female is female her whole life or at least during her whole youth. Everything constantly recalls her sex to her; and, to fulfill its functions well, she needs a constitution which corresponds to it. She needs care during her pregnancy; she needs rest at the time of childbirth; she needs a soft and sedentary life to suckle her children; she needs patience and gentleness, a zeal and an affection that nothing can rebuff in order to raise her children. She serves as the link between them and their father; she alone makes him love them and gives him the confidence to call them his own. How much tenderness and care is required to maintain the union of the whole family! And, finally, all this must come not from virtues but from tastes, or else the human species would soon be extinguished.

The strictness of the relative duties of the two sexes is not and cannot be the same. When woman complains on this score about unjust man-made inequality, she is wrong. This inequality is not a human institution—or, at least, it is the work not of prejudice but of reason. It is up to the sex that nature has charged with the bearing of children to be responsible for them to the other sex. Doubtless it is not permitted to any one to violate his faith, and every unfaithful husband who deprives his wife of the only reward of the austere duties of her sex is an unjust and barbarous man. But the unfaithful woman does more; she dissolves the family and breaks all the bonds of nature. . . .

Once it is demonstrated that man and woman are not and ought not be constituted in the same way in either character or temperament, it follows that they ought not to have the same education. In following nature's directions, man and woman ought to act in concert, but they ought not to do the same things. The goal of their labors is common, but their labors themselves are different, and consequently so are the tastes directing them. . . .

The good constitution of children initially depends on that of their mothers. The first education of men depends on the care of women. Men's morals, their passions, their tastes, their pleasures, their very happiness also depend on women. Thus the whole education of women ought to relate to men. To please men, to be useful to them, to make herself loved and honored by them, to raise them when young, to care for them when grown, to counsel them, to console them, to make their lives agreeable and sweet—these are the duties of women at all times, and they ought to be taught from childhood. So long as one does not return to this principle, one will deviate from the goal, and all the precepts taught to women will be of no use for their happiness or for ours.

purpose. He assigned them a degree of influence in the domestic sphere that they could not have competing with men outside it.

In 1792, in A *Vindication of the Rights of Woman,* Mary Wollstonecraft (1759–1797) brought Rousseau before the judgment of the rational Enlightenment ideal of progressive knowledge. The immediate incentive for this essay was her opposition to certain policies of the French Revolution, unfavorable to women, which were inspired by Rousseau. Wollstonecraft (who, like so many women of her day, died of puerperal fever shortly after

MARY WOLLSTONECRAFT CRITICIZES ROUSSEAU'S VIEW OF WOMEN

Mary Wollstonecraft published A Vindication of the Rights of Woman *in 1792, thirty years after Rousseau's* Emile *had appeared. In this pioneering feminist work, she criticizes and rejects Rousseau's argument for distinct and separate spheres for men and women. She portrays that argument as defending the continued bondage of women to men and as hindering the wider education of the entire human race.*

■ *What specific criticisms does Wollstonecraft direct against Rousseau's views? Why does Wollstonecraft put so much emphasis on a new kind of education for women?*

The most perfect education . . . is such an exercise of the understanding as is best calculated to strengthen the body and form the heart. Or, in other words, to enable the individual to attain such habits of virtue as will render it independent. In fact, it is a farce to call any being virtuous whose virtues do not result from the exercise of its own reason. This was Rousseau's opinion respecting men: I extend it to women. . . .

I may be accused of arrogance; still I must declare what I firmly believe, that all the writers who have written on the subject of female education and manners from Rousseau to Dr. Gregory [a Scottish physician], have contributed to render women more artificial, weak characters, than they would otherwise have been; and, consequently, more useless members of society. . . .

Strengthen the female mind by enlarging it, and there will be an end to blind obedience; but, as blind obedience is ever sought for by power, tyrants and sensualists are in the right when they endeavour to keep women in the dark, because the former only wants slaves, and the latter a play-thing. The sensualist, indeed, has been the most dangerous of tyrants, and women have been duped by their lovers, as princes by their ministers, whilst dreaming that they reigned over them. . . .

Rousseau declares that a woman should never, for a moment, feel herself independent, that she should be governed by fear to exercise her natural cunning, and made a coquettish slave in order to render her a more alluring object of desire, a sweeter companion to man, whenever he chooses to relax himself. He carries the arguments, which he pretends to draw

childbirth) accused Rousseau and others after him who upheld traditional roles for women of attempting to narrow women's vision and limit their experience. She argued that to confine women to the separate domestic sphere because of supposed limitations of their physiological nature was to make them the sensual slaves of men. Confined in this separate sphere, they were the victims of male tyranny, their obedience was blind, and they could never achieve their own moral or intellectual identity. Denying good education to women would impede the progress of all humanity. (See "Mary Wollstonecraft Criticizes Rousseau's View of Women.") With these arguments, Wollstonecraft was demanding for women the kind of liberty that male writers of the Enlightenment had been championing for men for more than a century. In doing so, she placed herself among the philosophes and broadened the agenda of the Enlightenment to include the rights of women as well as those of men.

Enlightened Absolutism

Most of the philosophes favored neither Montesquieu's reformed and revived aristocracy nor Rousseau's democracy as a solution to contemporary political problems. Like other thoughtful people of the day in other stations and occupations, they looked to the existing monarchies. Voltaire was a very strong monarchist. In 1759, he published a *History of the Russian Empire under Peter the Great,* which declared, "Peter was born, and Russia was formed."[11] Voltaire and other philosophes, such as Diderot, who visited Catherine II of Russia, and the physiocrats, some of whom were ministers to the French kings, did not wish to limit the power of monarchs. Rather, they sought to redirect that power toward the rationalization of economic and political

[11]Quoted in Larry Wolff, *Inventing Eastern Europe: The Map of Civilization on the Mind of the Enlightenment* (Palo Alto, CA: Stanford University Press, 1994), p. 200.

from the indications of nature, still further, and insinuates that truth and fortitude, the cornerstones of all human virtue, should be cultivated with certain restrictions, because, with respect to the female character, obedience is the grand lesson which ought to be impressed with unrelenting rigour.

What nonsense! when will a great man arise with sufficient strength of mind to put away the fumes which pride and sensuality have thus spread over the subject! If women are by nature inferior to men, their virtues must be the same in quality, if not in degree, or virtue is a relative idea; consequently, their conduct should be founded on the same principles, and have the same aim.

Connected with man as daughters, wives, and mothers, their moral character may be estimated by their manner of fulfilling those simple duties; but the end, the grand end of their exertions should be to unfold their own faculties and acquire the dignity of conscious virtue. . . .

But avoiding . . . any direct comparison of the two sexes collectively, or frankly acknowledging the inferiority of women, according to the present appearance of things, I shall only insist that men have increased that inferiority till women are almost sunk below the standard of rational creatures. Let their faculties have room to unfold, and their virtues to gain strength, and then determine where the whole sex must stand in the intellectual scale. . . .

I . . . will venture to assert, that till women are more rationally educated, the progress of human virtue and improvement in knowledge must receive continual checks. . . .

The mother, who wishes to give true dignity of character to her daughter, must, regardless of the sneers of ignorance, proceed on a plan diametrically opposite to that which Rousseau has recommended with all the deluding charms of eloquence and philosophical sophistry: for his eloquence renders absurdities plausible, and his dogmatic conclusions puzzle, without convincing, those who have not ability to refute them.

From Mary Wollstonecraft, *A Vindication of the Rights of Woman*, ed. by Carol H. Poston (New York: W.W. Norton, 1975), pp. 21, 22, 24–26, 35, 40, 41.

---

structures and the liberation of intellectual life. Most philosophes were not opposed to power if they could find a way of using it for their own purposes or if they could profit in one way or another from their personal relationships to strong monarchs.

During the last third of the century, it seemed to some observers that several European rulers had actually embraced many of the reforms set forth by the philosophes. *Enlightened absolutism* is the term used to describe this phenomenon. It indicates monarchical government dedicated to the rational strengthening of the central absolutist administration at the cost of other lesser centers of political power. The monarchs most closely associated with it are Frederick II of Prussia, Joseph II of Austria, and Catherine II of Russia. Each had complicated relationships to the community of enlightened writers.

Frederick II corresponded with the philosophes, provided Voltaire with a place at his court for a time, and even wrote history and political tracts. Catherine II, adept at what would later be called public relations, consciously sought to create the image of being enlightened. She read and cited the works of the philosophes, provided financial subsidies to Diderot, and corresponded extensively with Voltaire, lavishing compliments on him, all in the hope that she would receive favorable comments from them, as she indeed did. Joseph II continued numerous initiatives begun by his mother, Maria Theresa. He imposed a series of religious, legal, and social reforms that contemporaries believed he had derived from suggestions of the philosophes.

The relationship between these rulers and the writers of the Enlightenment was, however, more complicated than these appearances suggest. The humanitarian and liberating zeal of the Enlightenment writers was only part of what motivated the policies of the rulers. Frederick II, Joseph II, and Catherine II were also determined that their nations would play major diplomatic and military roles in Europe. In no small measure, they adopted Enlightenment policies favoring the rational economic and social integration

Mary Wollstonecraft insisted that women possessed reason just as men did and thus should be treated as the equals of men. Bettmann/Corbis

retaining Silesia, which he had seized from Austria in 1740, and worked to promote it as a manufacturing district. Like his Hohenzollern forebears, he continued to import workers from outside Prussia. He directed new attention to Prussian agriculture. Under state supervision, swamps were drained, new crops introduced, and peasants encouraged and sometimes compelled to migrate where they were needed. For the first time in Prussia, potatoes and turnips came into general production. Frederick also established a land-mortgage credit association to help landowners raise money for agricultural improvements.

The impetus for these economic policies came from the state. The monarchy and its bureaucracy were the engine for change. Most Prussians, however, did not prosper under Frederick's reign. The burden of taxation continued to fall disproportionately on peasants and townspeople.

Frederick's noneconomic policies met with somewhat more success. Continuing the Hohenzollern policy of toleration, he allowed Catholics and Jews to settle in his predominantly Lutheran country, and he protected the Catholics living in Silesia. This policy permitted the state to benefit from the economic contribution of foreign workers. Frederick, however, virtually always appointed Protestants to major positions in the government and army.

Frederick also ordered a new codification of Prussian law, completed after his death. His objective was to rationalize the existing legal system, making it more efficient, eliminating regional peculiarities, and reducing aristocratic influence. Frederick shared this concern for legal reform with the other enlightened monarchs, who saw it as a means of extending and strengthening royal power.

Reflecting an important change in the European view of the ruler, Frederick liked to describe himself as "the first servant of the State." The impersonal state was beginning to replace the personal monarchy. Kings might come and go, but the apparatus of government—the bureaucracy, the armies, the laws, the courts, and the combination of power, service, and protection that compelled citizens' loyalty—remained. The state as an entity separate from the personality of the ruler came into its own after the French Revolution, but it was born in the monarchies of the Old Regime.

of their realms because these policies also increased their military strength. As explained in Chapter 17, all the states of Europe had emerged from the Seven Years' War knowing they would need stronger armies for future wars and increased revenues to finance those armies. The search for new revenues and internal political support was one of the incentives prompting the "enlightened" reforms of the monarchs of Russia, Prussia, and Austria. Consequently, they and their advisers used rationality to pursue many goals admired by most philosophes, but also to further what some among the philosophes considered irrational militarism. The flattery of monarchs could bend the opinions of a philosophe. For example, Voltaire, who had written against war, could praise the military expansion of Catherine's Russia because it appeared in his mind to bring civilization to peoples he regarded as uncivilized and because he enjoyed being known as a literary confidant of the empress.

FREDERICK THE GREAT OF PRUSSIA

Frederick II, the Great (r. 1740–1786), sought the recovery and consolidation of Prussia in the wake of its suffering and near defeat in the midcentury wars. He succeeded, at great military and financial cost, in

JOSEPH II OF AUSTRIA

No eighteenth-century ruler so embodied rational, impersonal force as the emperor Joseph II of Austria. He was the son of Maria Theresa and co-ruler with her from 1765 to 1780. During the next ten years he ruled alone. He was an austere and humorless person. During much of his life, he slept on straw and ate little but beef. He prided himself on a narrow, passionless rationality, which he sought to impose by his own will on the various Habsburg domains. Despite his eccentricities and the coldness of his personality, Joseph II sincerely wished to improve the lot of his people. He was much less a political opportunist and cynic than either Frederick the Great of Prussia or Catherine the Great of Russia. The ultimate result of his well-intentioned efforts was a series of aristocratic and peasant rebellions extending from Hungary to the Austrian Netherlands.

Centralization of Authority As explained in Chapter 15, of all the rising states of the eighteenth century, Austria was the most diverse in its people and problems. Robert Palmer likened it to "a vast holding company."[12] The Habsburgs never succeeded in creating either a unified administrative structure or a strong aristocratic loyalty. To preserve the monarchy during the War of the Austrian Succession (1740–1748), Maria Theresa had guaranteed the aristocracy considerable independence, especially in Hungary.

During and after the conflict, however, Maria Theresa took steps to strengthen the power of the crown outside of Hungary, building more of a bureaucracy than had previous Habsburg rulers. In Austria and Bohemia, through major administrative reorganization, she imposed a much more efficient system of tax collection that extracted funds even from the clergy and the nobles. She also established several central councils to deal with governmental problems. To assure her government a sufficient supply of educated officials, she sought to bring all educational institutions into the service of the crown. She also expanded primary education on the local level.

Maria Theresa was concerned about the welfare of the peasants and serfs. She brought them some assistance by extending the authority of the royal bureaucracy over local nobles and decreeing limits on the amount of labor, or *robot*, landowners could demand from peasants. Her concern was not particularly humanitarian; rather, it arose from her desire to assure a good pool from which to draw military recruits. In all these policies and in her general desire to stimulate prosperity and military strength by royal initiative, Maria Theresa anticipated the policies of her son.

Joseph II was more determined than his mother, and his projected reforms were more wide ranging. He aimed to extend the borders of his territories in the direction of Poland, Bavaria, and the Ottoman Empire. His greatest ambition, however, was to increase the authority of the Habsburg emperor over his various

realms. He sought to overcome the pluralism of the Habsburg holdings by imposing central authority in areas of political and social life in which Maria Theresa had wisely chosen not to exert authority.

In particular, Joseph sought to reduce Hungarian autonomy. To avoid having to guarantee Hungary's existing privileges or extend new ones at the time of his coronation, he refused to have himself crowned king of Hungary and even had the Crown of Saint Stephen sent to the Imperial Treasury in Vienna. He reorganized local government in Hungary to increase the authority of his own officials. He also required the use of German in all governmental matters. The Magyar nobility resisted these measures, and in 1790 Joseph had to rescind most of them.

Ecclesiastical Policies Another target of Joseph's assertion of royal absolutism was the church. From the reign of Charles V in the sixteenth century to that of Maria Theresa, the Habsburgs had been the most important dynastic champion of Roman Catholicism. Maria Theresa was devout, but she had not allowed the church to limit her authority. Although she had attempted to discourage certain of the more extreme modes of Roman Catholic popular religious piety, such as public flagellation, she adamantly opposed toleration. (See "Maria Theresa and Joseph II of Austria Debate Toleration.")

Joseph II was also a practicing Catholic, but from the standpoint of both Enlightenment and pragmatic politics, he favored a policy of toleration. In October 1781, Joseph issued a toleration patent or decree that extended freedom of worship to Lutherans, Calvinists, and the Greek Orthodox. They were permitted to have their own places of worship, to sponsor schools, to enter skilled trades, and to hold academic appointments and positions in the public service. From 1781 through 1789, Joseph issued a series of patents and other enactments that relieved the Jews in his realms of certain taxes and signs of personal degradation. He also extended to them the right of private worship. Although these actions benefited the Jews, they did not grant them full equality with other Habsburg subjects.

Joseph also sought to bring the various institutions of the Roman Catholic Church directly under royal control. He forbade direct communication between the bishops of his realms and the pope. Viewing religious orders as unproductive, he dissolved more than six hundred monasteries and confiscated their lands. He excepted, however, certain orders that ran schools or hospitals. He dissolved the traditional Roman Catholic seminaries, which instilled in priests too great a loyalty to the papacy and too little concern for their future parishioners. In their place, he sponsored eight general seminaries whose training

[12]Robert R. Palmer, *The Age of Democratic Revolution*, Vol. 1 (Princeton, NJ: Princeton University Press, 1959), p. 103.

MARIA THERESA AND JOSEPH II OF AUSTRIA DEBATE TOLERATION

In 1765, Joseph, the eldest son of the Empress Maria Theresa, had become co-regent with his mother. He began to believe some measure of religious toleration should be introduced into the Habsburg realms. Maria Theresa, whose opinions on many political issues were quite advanced, adamantly refused to consider adopting a policy of toleration. This exchange of letters sets forth their sharply differing positions. The toleration of Protestants that is in dispute related only to Lutherans and Calvinists. Maria Theresa died in 1780; the next year Joseph issued an edict of toleration.

■ *How does Joseph define toleration, and why does Maria Theresa believe it is the same as religious indifference? Why does Maria Theresa fear that toleration will bring about political as well as religious turmoil? Why does Maria Theresa think that Joseph's belief in toleration has come from Joseph's acquaintance with wicked books?*

JOSEPH TO MARIA THERESA, JULY 20, 1777

It is only the word "toleration" which has caused the misunderstanding. You have taken it in quite a different meaning [from mine expressed in an earlier letter]. God preserve me from thinking it a matter of indifference whether the citizens turn Protestant or remain Catholic, still less, whether they cleave to, or at least observe, the cult which they have inherited from their fathers! I would give all I possess if all the Protestants of your states would go over to Catholicism.

The word "toleration," as I understand it, means only that I would employ any persons, without distinction of religion, in purely temporal matters, allow them to own property, practice trades, be citizens, if they were qualified and if this would be of advantage to the State and its industry. Those who, unfortunately, adhere to a false faith, are far further from being converted if they remain in their own country than if they migrate into another, in which they can hear and see the convincing truths of the Catholic faith. Similarly, the undisturbed practice of their religion makes them far better subjects and causes them to avoid irreligion, which is a far greater danger to our Catholics than if one lets them see others practice their religion unimpeded.

MARIA THERESA TO JOSEPH, LATE JULY 1777

Without a dominant religion? Toleration, indifference are precisely the true means of undermining everything, taking away every foundation; we others will then be the greatest losers. . . . He is no friend of humanity, as the popular phrase is, who allows everyone his own thoughts. I am speaking only in the political sense, not as a Christian; nothing is so necessary and salutary as religion. Will you allow everyone to fashion his own religion as he pleases? No fixed cult, no subordination to the Church—what will then become of us? The result will not be quiet and contentment; its outcome will be the rule of the stronger and more unhappy times like those which we have already seen. A manifesto by you to this effect can produce the utmost distress and make you responsible for many thousands of souls. And what are my own sufferings, when I see you entangled in opinions so erroneous? What is at stake is not only the welfare of the State but your own salvation. . . . Turning your eyes and ears everywhere, mingling your spirit of contradiction with the simultaneous desire to create something, you are ruining yourself and dragging the Monarchy down with you into the abyss. . . . I only wish to live so long as I can hope to descend to my ancestors with the consolation that my son will be as great, as religious as his forebears, that he will return from his erroneous views, from those wicked books whose authors parade their cleverness at the expense of all that is most holy and most worthy of respect in the world, who want to introduce an imaginary freedom which can never exist and which degenerates into license and into complete revolution.

As quoted in C. A. Macartney, ed., *The Habsburg and Hohenzollern Dynasties in the Seventeenth and Eighteenth Centuries* (New York: Walker, 1970), pp. 151–153. Reprinted by permission of Walker and Co.

emphasized parish duties. He also issued decrees creating new parishes in areas with a shortage of priests, funding them with money from the confiscated monasteries. In effect, Joseph's policies made Roman Catholic priests the employees of the state, ending the influence of the Roman Catholic Church as an independent institution in Habsburg lands. In many respects, the ecclesiastical policies of Joseph II, known as *Josephinism*, prefigured those of the French Revolution.

Economic and Agrarian Reform Like Frederick of Prussia, Joseph sought to improve the economic life of his domains. He abolished many internal tariffs and encouraged road building and the improvement of river transport. He went on personal inspection tours of farms and manufacturing districts. Joseph also reconstructed the judicial system to make laws more uniform and rational and to lessen the influence of local landlords. National courts with power over the landlord courts were established. All of these improvements were expected to bring new unity to the state and more taxes into the imperial coffers in Vienna.

Joseph's policies toward serfdom and the land were a far-reaching extension of those Maria Theresa had initiated. Over the course of his reign, he introduced a series of reforms that touched the very heart of the rural social structure. He did not seek to abolish the authority of landlords over their peasants, but he did seek to make that authority more moderate and subject to the oversight of royal officials. He abolished serfdom as a legally sanctioned state of servitude. He granted peasants a wide array of personal freedoms, including the right to marry, to engage in skilled work, and to have their children trained in skilled work without the landlord's permission.

Joseph reformed the procedures of the manorial courts and opened avenues of appeal to royal officials. He also encouraged landlords to change land leases so it would be easier for peasants to inherit them or to transfer them to other peasants. His goal in all of these efforts to reduce traditional burdens on peasants was to make them more productive and industrious farmers.

Near the end of his reign, Joseph proposed a new and daring system of land taxation. He decreed in 1789 that all proprietors of the land were to be taxed regardless of social status. No longer were the peasants alone to bear the burden of taxation. He abolished *robot* and commuted it into a monetary tax, only part of which was to go to the landlord, the rest reverting to the state. Resistant nobles blocked the implementation of this decree, and after Joseph died in 1790 it did not go into effect. This and other of Joseph's earlier measures, however, brought turmoil throughout the Habsburg realms. Peasants revolted over disagreements about the interpretation of their newly granted rights. The nobles of the various realms protested the taxation scheme. The Hungarian Magyars resisted Joseph's centralization measures and forced him to rescind them.

On Joseph's death, the crown went to his brother Leopold II (r. 1790–1792). Although sympathetic to Joseph's goals, Leopold found himself forced to repeal many of the most controversial decrees, such as that on taxation. In other areas, Leopold thought his brother's policies simply wrong. For example, he returned much political and administrative power to local nobles because he thought it expedient for them to have a voice in government. Still, he did not repudiate his brother's policies wholesale. He retained, in particular, Joseph's religious policies and maintained political centralization to the extent he thought possible.

CATHERINE THE GREAT OF RUSSIA

Joseph II never grasped the practical necessity of forging political constituencies to support his policies. Catherine II (r. 1762–1796), who had been born a German princess, but who became empress of Russia, understood only too well the fragility of the Romanov dynasty's base of power.

Russia from Peter the Great Through Catherine the Great	
1725	Death of Peter the Great
1725–1727	Catherine I
1727–1730	Peter II
1730–1741	Anna
1740–1741	Ivan VI
1741–1762	Elizabeth
1762	Peter III
1762	Catherine II (the Great) becomes empress
1767	Legislative commission summoned
1769	War with Turkey begins
1773–1775	Pugachev's Rebellion
1772	First Partition of Poland
1774	Treaty of Kuchuk-Kainardji ends war with Turkey
1775	Reorganization of local government
1783	Russia annexes the Crimea
1785	Catherine issues the Charter of the Nobility
1793	Second Partition of Poland
1795	Third Partition of Poland
1796	Death of Catherine the Great

Catherine the Great ascended to the Russian throne after the murder of her husband. She tried initially to enact major reforms, but she never intended to abandon absolutism. She assured nobles of their rights and by the end of her reign had imposed press censorship.
The Granger Collection

After the death of Peter the Great in 1725, the court nobles and the army repeatedly determined the Russian succession. As a result, the crown fell primarily into the hands of people with little talent. Peter's wife, Catherine I, ruled for two years (1725–1727) and was succeeded for three years by Peter's grandson, Peter II. In 1730, the crown devolved on Anna, a niece of Peter the Great. During 1740 and 1741, a child named Ivan VI, who was less than a year old, was the nominal ruler. Finally, in 1741, Peter the Great's daughter Elizabeth came to the throne. She held the title of empress until 1762, but her reign was not notable for new political departures or sound administration. Her court was a shambles of political and romantic intrigue. Much of the power possessed by the tsar at the opening of the century had vanished.

At her death in 1762, Elizabeth was succeeded by Peter III, one of her nephews. He was a weak ruler whom many contemporaries considered mad. He immediately exempted the nobles from compulsory military service and then rapidly made peace with Frederick the Great, for whom he held unbounded admiration. That decision probably saved Prussia from military defeat in the Seven Years' War. The one positive feature of this unbalanced creature's life was his marriage in 1745 to a young German princess born in Anhalt Zerbst. This was the future Catherine the Great.

For almost twenty years, Catherine lived in misery and frequent danger at the court of Elizabeth. During that time, she befriended important nobles and read widely in the books of the philosophes. She was a shrewd person whose experience in a court crawling with rumors, intrigue, and conspiracy had taught her how to survive. She exhibited neither love nor fidelity toward her demented husband. A few months after his accession as tsar, Peter was deposed and murdered with Catherine's approval, if not her aid, and she was immediately proclaimed empress.

Catherine's familiarity with the Enlightenment and the general culture of western Europe convinced her Russia was very backward and that it must make major reforms if it was to remain a great power. She understood that any major reform must have a wide base of political and social support, especially since she had assumed the throne through a palace coup. In 1767, she summoned a legislative commission to advise her on revisions in the law and government of Russia. There were more than five hundred delegates, drawn from all sectors of Russian life. Before the commission convened, Catherine issued a set of instructions, partly written by herself. They contained many ideas drawn from the political writings of the philosophes. The commission considered the instructions as well as other ideas and complaints raised by its members.

The revision of Russian law, however, did not occur for more than half a century. In 1768, Catherine dismissed the commission before several of its key committees had reported. Yet the meeting had not been useless, for a vast amount of information had been gathered about the conditions of local administration and economic life throughout the realm. The inconclusive debates and the absence of programs from the delegates themselves suggested that most Russians saw no alternative to an autocratic monarchy. For her part, Catherine had no intention of departing from absolutism.

Limited Administrative Reform Catherine proceeded to carry out limited reforms on her own authority. She gave strong support to the rights and local power of the nobility. In 1775, she reorganized local government to solve problems brought to light by the legislative commission. She put most local offices in the hands of nobles rather than creating a royal bureaucracy. In 1785, Catherine issued the

Charter of the Nobility, which guaranteed nobles many rights and privileges. In part, the empress had no choice but to favor the nobles. They had the capacity to topple her from the throne. There were too few educated subjects in her realm to establish an independent bureaucracy, and the treasury could not afford an army strictly loyal to the crown. So Catherine wisely made a virtue of necessity. She strengthened the stability of her crown by making convenient friends with her nobles.

Economic Growth   Part of Catherine's program was to continue the economic development begun under Peter the Great. She attempted to suppress internal barriers to trade. Exports of grain, flax, furs, and naval stores grew dramatically. She also favored the expansion of the small Russian urban middle class that was so vital to trade. And through all of these departures Catherine tried to maintain ties of friendship and correspondence with the philosophes. She knew that if she treated them kindly, they would be sufficiently flattered to give her a progressive reputation throughout Europe.

Territorial Expansion   Catherine's limited administrative reforms and her policy of economic growth had a counterpart in the diplomatic sphere. The Russian drive for warm-water ports continued. (See Map 18–1.) This goal required warfare with the Turks. In 1769, as a result of a minor Russian incursion, the Ottoman Empire declared war on Russia. The Russians responded in a series of strikingly successful military moves.

During 1769 and 1770, the Russian fleet sailed all the way from the Baltic Sea into the eastern Mediterranean. The Russian army won several major victories that by 1771 gave Russia control of Ottoman provinces on the Danube River and the Crimean coast of the Black Sea. The conflict dragged on until 1774, when it was closed by the Treaty of Kuchuk-Kainardji. The treaty gave Russia a direct outlet on the Black Sea, free navigation rights in its waters, and free access through the Bosporus. The province of the Crimea became an independent state, which Catherine painlessly annexed in 1783. Finally, under this treaty Catherine as empress of Russia was made the protector of the orthodox Christians living in the Ottoman Empire. In the future this would cause conflict with France whose monarch had previously been recognized as the protector of Roman Catholic Christians in the empire.

THE PARTITION OF POLAND

The Russian military successes obviously brought Catherine much domestic political support, but they made the other states of eastern Europe uneasy.

MAP 18–1   EXPANSION OF RUSSIA, 1689–1796   *The overriding territorial aim of Peter the Great in the first quarter of the eighteenth century, and of Catherine the Great in the latter half, was to secure year-round navigable outlets to the sea for the vast Russian Empire—hence Peter's push to the Baltic Sea and Catherine's to the Black Sea. Catherine also managed to acquire large areas of Poland through the partitions of that country.*

These anxieties were overcome by an extraordinary division of Polish territory known as the First Partition of Poland.

The Russian victories along the Danube River were most unwelcome to Austria, which also harbored ambitions of territorial expansion in that direction. At the same time, the Ottoman Empire was pressing Prussia for aid against Russia. Frederick the Great made a proposal to Russia and Austria that would give each something it wanted, prevent conflict among the powers, and save appearances.

After long, complicated secret negotiations, the three powers agreed Russia would abandon the conquered Danubian provinces. In compensation, Russia received a large portion of Polish territory with almost 2 million inhabitants. As a reward for remaining neutral, Prussia annexed most of the territory between East Prussia and Prussia proper. This land allowed Frederick to unite two previously separate sections of his realm. Finally, Austria took Galicia, with its important salt mines, and other Polish territory with more than 2.5 million inhabitants. (See Map 18–2.)

In September 1772, the helpless Polish aristocracy, paying the price for maintaining internal liberties at the expense of developing a strong central government, ratified this seizure of nearly one-third of Polish territory. The loss was not necessarily fatal to Poland's continued existence, and it inspired a revival of national feeling. Real attempts were made

to adjust the Polish political structures to the realities of the time. These proved, however, to be too little and too late. The political and military strength of Poland could not match that of its stronger, more ambitious neighbors. The partition of Poland clearly demonstrated that any nation that had not established a strong monarchy, bureaucracy, and army could no longer compete within the European state system. It also demonstrated that the major powers in eastern Europe were prepared to settle their own rivalries at the expense of such a weak state. If such territory from a weaker state had not been available, the tendency of the international rivalries would have been to warfare.

Russia and Prussia partitioned Poland again in 1793, and Russia, Prussia, and Austria partitioned it a third time in 1795, removing it from the map of Europe for more than a century. Each time, the great powers contended they were saving themselves, and by implication the rest of Europe, from Polish anarchy. The fact of the matter was that Poland's political weakness left it vulnerable to plunderous aggression. The partitions of 1793 and 1795 took place in the shadow of the French Revolution, which left the absolute monarchies of eastern Europe concerned for their own stability. As a result, they reacted harshly even to minor attempts at reform by the Polish nobles, fearing they might infect their own domains.

THE END OF THE EIGHTEENTH CENTURY IN CENTRAL AND EASTERN EUROPE

During the last two decades of the eighteenth century, all three regimes based on enlightened absolutism became more conservative and politically repressive. In Prussia and Austria, the innovations of the rulers stirred resistance among the nobility. In Russia, fear of peasant unrest was the chief factor.

Frederick the Great of Prussia grew remote during his old age, leaving the aristocracy to fill important military and administrative posts. A reaction to Enlightenment ideas also set in among Prussian Lutheran writers.

In Austria, Joseph II's plans to restructure society and administration in his realms provoked growing frustration and political unrest, with the nobility calling for an end to innovation. In response, Joseph turned increasingly to censorship and his secret police.

Russia faced a peasant uprising, the Pugachev Rebellion, between 1773 and 1775, and Catherine the Great never fully recovered from the fears of social and political upheaval that it raised. Once the French Revolution broke out in 1789, the Russian empress censored books based on Enlightenment

MAP 18–2 PARTITIONS OF POLAND, 1772, 1793, AND 1795 *The callous eradication of Poland from the map displayed eighteenth-century power politics at its most extreme. Poland, without strong central governmental institutions, fell victim to those states in central and eastern Europe that had developed such institutions.*

ALEXANDER RADISHCHEV ATTACKS RUSSIAN CENSORSHIP

Alexander Radishchev (1749–1802) was an enlightened Russian landowner who published A Journey from Saint Petersburg to Moscow *in 1790. The book criticized many aspects of Russian political and social life, including the treatment of serfs. Shortly after its publication, Catherine the Great, fearing the kind of unrest associated with the French Revolution might spread to Russia, had Radishchev arrested. He was tried and sentenced to death, but Catherine commuted the sentence to a period of Siberian exile. All but eighteen copies of his book were destroyed. It was not published in Russia again until 1905. These passages criticizing censorship illustrate how a writer filled with the ideas of the Enlightenment could question some of the fundamental ways in which an enlightened absolutist ruler, such as Catherine, governed.*

■ *How does Radishchev satirize censorship and the censors? Why does he contend that public opinion rather than the government will act as an adequate censor? Would work censored by public opinion be truly free from censorship? Why might Catherine the Great or other enlightened absolutist rulers have feared opinions like these?*

Having recognized the usefulness of printing, the government has made it open to all; having further recognized that control of thought might invalidate its good intention in granting freedom to set up presses, it turned over the censorship or inspection of printed works to the Department of Public Morals. Its duty in this matter can only be the prohibition of the sale of objectionable works. But even this censorship is superfluous. A single stupid official in the Department of Public Morals may do the greatest harm to enlightenment and may for years hold back the progress of reason: he may prohibit a useful discovery, a new idea, and may rob everyone of something great. Here is an example on a small scale. A translation of a novel is brought to the Department of Public Morals for its imprimatur. The translator, following the author in speaking of love, calls it "the tricky god." The censor in uniform and in the fullness of piety strikes out the expression saying, "It is improper to call a divinity tricky." He who does not understand should not interfere. . . .

Let anyone print anything that enters his head. If anyone finds himself insulted in print, let him get his redress at law. I am not speaking in jest. Words are not always deeds, thoughts are not crimes. These are the rules in the Instruction for a New Code of Laws. But an offense in words or in print is always an offense. Under the law no one is allowed to libel another, and everyone has the right to bring suit. But if one tells the truth about another, that cannot, according to the law, be considered a libel. What harm can there be if books are printed without a police stamp? Not only will there be no harm; there will be an advantage, an advantage from the first to the last, from the least to the greatest, from the Tsar to the last citizen. . . .

I will close with this: the censorship of what is printed belongs properly to society, which gives the author a laurel wreath or uses his sheets for wrapping paper. Just so, it is the public that gives its approval to a theatrical production, and not the director of the theater. Similarly the Censor can give neither glory nor dishonor to the publication of a work. The curtain rises, and everyone eagerly watches the performance. If they like it, they applaud; if not, they stamp and hiss. Leave what is stupid to the judgment of public opinion, stupidity will find a thousand censors. The most vigilant policy cannot check worthless ideas as well as a disgusted public. They will be heard just once; they will die, never to rise again. But once we have recognized the uselessness of the censorship, or, rather, its harmfulness in the realm of knowledge, we must also recognize the vast and boundless usefulness of freedom of the press.

From Alexander Radishchev, *A Journey from Saint Petersburg to Moscow* (Cambridge, MA: Harvard University Press, 1958), pp. 9–19. Copyright © 1958 by the President and Fellows of Harvard College. Reprinted by permission of Harvard University Press. As quoted in Thomas Riha, ed., *Readings in Russian Civilization*, 2nd rev. ed., Vol. 2 (Chicago: University of Chicago Press, 1969), pp. 269–271.

thought and sent offensive authors into Siberian exile. (See "Alexander Radishchev Attacks Russian Censorship.")

By the close of the century, fear of, and hostility to, change permeated the ruling classes of central and eastern Europe. This reaction had begun before 1789, but the events in France bolstered and sustained it for almost half a century. Paradoxically, nowhere did the humanity and liberalism of the Enlightenment encounter greater rejection than in those states that had been governed by "enlightened" rulers.

IN PERSPECTIVE

The writers of the Enlightenment, known as philosophes, charted a major new path in modern European and Western thought. They operated within a print culture that made public opinion into a distinct cultural force. Admiring Newton and the achievements of physical science, they tried to apply reason and the principles of science to the cause of social reform. They believed also that passions and feelings are essential parts of human nature. Throughout their writings they championed reasonable moderation in social life. More than any other previous group of Western thinkers, they strongly opposed the authority of the established churches and especially of Roman Catholicism. Most of them championed some form of religious toleration. They also sought to achieve a science of society that could discover how to maximize human productivity and material happiness. The great dissenter among them was Rousseau, who also wished to reform society, but in the name of virtue rather than material happiness.

The political influence of these writers went in several directions. The founding fathers of the American republic looked to them for political guidance, as did moderate liberal reformers throughout Europe, especially within royal bureaucracies. The autocratic rulers of eastern Europe consulted the philosophes in the hope that Enlightenment ideas might allow them to rule more efficiently. The revolutionaries in France would honor them. This diverse assortment of followers illustrates the diverse character of the philosophes themselves. It also shows that Enlightenment thought cannot be reduced to a single formula. Rather, it should be seen as an outlook that championed change and reform, giving central place to humans and their welfare on earth rather than to God and the hereafter.

REVIEW QUESTIONS

1. How did the Enlightenment change basic Western attitudes toward reform, faith, and reason? What were the major formative influences on the philosophes? How important were Voltaire and the *Encyclopedia* in the success of the Enlightenment?

2. Why did the philosophes consider organized religion to be their greatest enemy? Discuss the basic tenets of deism. How did Jewish writers contribute to Enlightenment thinking about religion? What are the similarities and differences between the Enlightenment evaluation of Islam and its evaluations of Christianity and Judaism?

3. What were the attitudes of the philosophes toward women? What was Rousseau's view of women? What were the separate spheres he imagined men and women occupying? What were Mary Wollstonecraft's criticisms of Rousseau's view?

4. Compare the arguments of the mercantilists with those of Adam Smith in his book *The Wealth of Nations*. How did both sides view the earth's resources? Why might Smith be regarded as an advocate of the consumer? How did his theory of history work to the detriment of less economically advanced non-European peoples?

5. Discuss the political views of Montesquieu and Rousseau. Was Montesquieu's view of England accurate? Was Rousseau a child of the Enlightenment or its enemy? Which did Rousseau value more, the individual or society?

6. Were the enlightened monarchs true believers in the ideal of the philosophes, or was their enlightenment a mere veneer? Were they really absolute in power? What motivated their reforms? What does the partition of Poland indicate about the spirit of enlightened absolutism?

SUGGESTED READINGS

D. BEALES, *Joseph II: In the Shadow of Maria Theresa, 1741–1780* (1987). The best treatment in English of the early political life of Joseph II.

D. D. BIEN, *The Calas Affair: Persecution, Toleration, and Heresy in Eighteenth-Century Toulouse* (1960). The standard treatment of the famous case.

R. CHARTIER, *The Cultural Origins of the French Revolution* (1991). A wide-ranging discussion of the emergence of the public sphere and the role of books and the book trade during the Enlightenment.

R. Darnton, *The Forbidden Best-Sellers of Pre-Revolutionary France* (1995). An exploration of what books the French read and the efforts of the government to control the book trade.

T. S. Dock, *Women in the Encyclopédie: A Compendium* (1983). An analysis of the articles from the *Encyclopedia* that deal with women.

P. Gay, *The Enlightenment: An Interpretation*, 2 vols. (1966, 1969). A classic.

P. Gay, *Voltaire's Politics* (1988). An important discussion.

D. Goodman, *The Republic of Letters: A Cultural History of the French Enlightenment* (1994). Concentrates on the role of salons.

M. C. Jacob, *Living the Enlightenment: Freemasonry and Politics in Eighteenth-Century Europe* (1991). The best treatment in English of Freemasonry.

J. B. Landes, *Women and the Public Sphere in the Age of the French Revolution* (1988). An extended essay on the role of women in public life during the eighteenth century.

J. P. Ledonne, *The Russian Empire and the World, 1700–1917* (1996). An exploration of the major determinants in Russian expansion from the eighteenth to the early twentieth century.

D. MacMahon, *Enemies of the Enlightenment: The French Counter-Enlightenment and the Making of Modernity* (2001). A very fine exploration of French writers critical of the philosophes.

I. De Madariaga, *Russia in the Age of Catherine the Great* (1981). The best discussion in English.

J. M. McManners, *Death and the Enlightenment: Changing Attitudes to Death among Christians and Unbelievers in Eighteenth-Century France* (1982). Explores a wide spectrum of religious beliefs.

M. A. Meyer, *The Origins of the Modern Jew: Jewish Identity and European Culture in Germany, 1749–1824* (1967). Remains a clear introduction.

D. Outram, *The Enlightenment* (1995). An excellent brief introduction.

P. A. Rahe, D. Carrithers, and M. A. Mocher, *Montesquieu's Science of Politics: Essays on "The Spirit of the Laws"* (2001). An expansive collection of essays on Montesquieu and his relationship to other major thinkers.

P. Riley, *The Cambridge Companion to Rousseau* (2001). Excellent accessible essays by major scholars.

E. Rothchild, *Economic Sentiments: Adam Smith, Condorcet, and the Enlightenment* (2001). A sensitive account of Smith's thought and its relationship to the social questions of the day.

R. B. Sher, *Church and University in the Scottish Enlightenment: The Moderate Literati of Edinburgh* (1985). Examines the role of religious moderates in aiding the goals of the Enlightenment.

J. N. Shklar, *Men and Citizens, a Study of Rousseau's Social Theory* (1969). Remains a thoughtful and provocative overview of Rousseau's political thought.

S. B. Smith, *Spinoza, Liberalism, and the Question of Jewish Identity* (1997). A brilliant work.

D. Spadafora, *The Idea of Progress in Eighteenth-Century Britain* (1990). A major study that covers many aspects of the Enlightenment in Britain.

J. Starobinski, *Jean-Jacques Rousseau: Transparency and Obstruction* (1971). A classic analysis of Rousseau.

R. E. Sullivan, *John Toland and the Deist Controversy: A Study in Adaptation* (1982). An important and informative discussion.

M. S. Trouille, *Sexual Politics in the Enlightenment: Women Writers Read Rousseau* (1997). Narrates the very different reactions to Rousseau from his women readers.

A. M. Wilson, *Diderot* (1972). A splendid biography of the person behind the *Encyclopedia* and other major Enlighte1nment publications.

L. Wolff, *Inventing Eastern Europe: The Map of Civilization on the Mind of the Enlightenment* (1994). A remarkable study of the manner in which Enlightenment writers recast the understanding of this part of the Continent.

J. Yolton (ed.), *The Blackwell Companion to the Enlightenment* (1995). An excellent collection of essays.

DOCUMENTS CD-ROM

The Enlightenment

18.1 John Locke: Chapter I from *Essay Concerning Human Understanding*

18.2 David Hume: *Of the Dignity or Meanness of Human Nature*

18.3 Charles Montesquieu: Book 4 from *The Spirit of the Laws*

18.4 The *Encyclopédie*

18.5 A Doctor Criticizes Midwives

18.7 Adam Smith: Division of Labor

Joseph Wright, *An Experiment on a Bird in the Air-Pump*: Science in the Drawing Room

Joseph Wright of Derby, *An Experiment on a Bird in the Air-Pump* (1768).   National Gallery, London, UK. The Bridgeman Art Library.

The air-pump, devised by the pioneering English natural philosopher Robert Boyle in the 1650s, stood for over a century as a major symbol of the new experimental science championed by the Royal Society of London. The instrument permitted air to be pumped out of a spherical glass jar to create a vacuum for the purpose of demonstrating the qualities of air and air pressure. The early air-pumps often functioned quite poorly because air would seep in through leaky seals, invading the vacuum. By the middle of the eighteenth century, however, many provincial English scientific societies possessed effective models such as the one portrayed in Joseph Wright's *An Experiment on a Bird in the Air-Pump* (1768).

Wright, who lived near Derby in an early industrial region of England, was a close friend of manufacturers and other persons interested in science, several of whom belonged to the Lunar Society. In this dramatically lit painting, Wright portrays the excited interest of fashionable upper-class audiences in experimental science. At the same time, though, he suggests genuine apprehension about the practice of science.

Wright presents the central figure, who is operating the pump, as a natural philosopher about to demonstrate his superior knowledge and scientific skill through an experiment meant to indicate the necessity of air for the life of an animal. The experimenter holds the life and death of the bird in his hands as he moves to turn the switch that will create the vacuum. One figure observes the experiment with a sense of amazement; another looks on with an expression of stoic acceptance. The man speaking to the young women, one of whom appears fearful and the other cautiously curious, may be explaining the need to place rationality above feelings in the pursuit of knowledge. Sacrificing the bird would advance the progress of science.

In his depiction of women (including one more interested in her male companion than in the experiment), Wright seems to be suggesting the commonly held view of the day that women may approach science and experiments as observers, but may lack the intellectual qualities required for active participation in the experimental method.

In art historical terms, Wright, an English artist, has taken a genre of painting known as the *conversation piece* and made a scientific experiment the center of attention. Wright has also made another important substitution of a scientific subject for a more traditional one. The painting dramatically contrasts light and dark, a technique originally devised to highlight elements in paintings of religious scenes. Here the drama of the light highlights a secular scientific experiment on a natural subject that, especially in England, many people believed might lead to a new understanding of the divine. Thus Wright could see the reverence once reserved for religious subjects now being evoked by a scientific one.

His painting, though coming a century after the first air-pump experiments, demonstrates the manner in which, by the mid–eighteenth century, experimental science had established its cultural presence within polite society and its ability to foster civil conversation in place of political and religious disputes. Rather than discussing the Bible or politics, this group is observing a scientific experiment that will provide them with the opportunity for polite and presumably noncontroversial conversation, or at least conversation that will not lead to destructive quarrels.

Although, as an artist, Wright explored the challenges of painting light, the setting of this experiment would also seem to suggest that even in the eighteenth century he and others saw science as an uncertain and possibly temporary light surrounded by darkness and potential superstition.

■ *How does Wright's* An Experiment on a Bird in the Air-Pump *show both fascination and apprehension about science? What common perception about women in this age does the work illustrate? As an artistic conversation piece, how does Wright's painting challenge tradition?*

Sources: David H. Solkin, *Painting for Money: The Visual Arts and the Public Sphere in Eighteenth-Century England* (New Haven, CT: Yale University Press, 1993); Steven Shapin and Simon Schaffer, *Leviathan and the Air-Pump: Hobbes, Boyle, and the Experimental Life* (Princeton, NJ: Princeton University Press, 1985).

Civic equality was one of the hallmarks of the revolutionary era. This figure of Equality holds in her hand a copy of the Declaration of the Rights of Man and Citizen. Corbis

CHAPTER 19

THE FRENCH REVOLUTION

*I*N THE SPRING OF 1789, *the long-festering conflict between the French monarchy and the aristocracy erupted into a new political crisis. This dispute, unlike earlier ones, quickly outgrew the issues of its origins and produced the wider disruption known as the French Revolution. Before the turmoil settled, small-town provincial lawyers and Parisian street orators exercised more influence over the fate of the Continent than did aristocrats, royal ministers, or monarchs. Armies commanded by people of low birth and filled by conscripted village youths defeated forces composed of professional soldiers led by officers of noble birth. The very existence of the Roman Catholic faith in France was challenged. Politically and socially, neither France nor Europe would ever be the same after these events.*

KEY TOPICS

- The financial crisis that impelled the French monarchy to call the Estates General
- The transformation of the Estates General into the National Assembly, the Declaration of the Rights of Man and Citizen, and the reconstruction of the political and ecclesiastical institutions of France
- The second revolution, the end of the monarchy, and the turn to more radical reforms
- The war between France and the rest of Europe
- The Reign of Terror, the Thermidorian Reaction, and the establishment of the Directory

The Crisis of the French Monarchy

Although the French Revolution was a turning point in modern European history, it grew out of the tensions and problems that characterized practically all late-eighteenth-century states. From the close of the Seven Years' War (1763) until the opening of the French Revolution in 1789, the monarchies of both western and eastern Europe found themselves lacking adequate revenues and had become major agents of institutional and political change. In every case they provoked aristocratic, and sometimes popular, resistance and resentment. George III of Britain fought for years with Parliament and lost the colonies of North America in the process. Frederick II of Prussia succeeded with his program of reform only because he accepted new aristocratic influence over the bureaucracy and the army. Catherine II of Russia had to come to terms with Russia's nobility. At his death in 1790, Joseph II of Austria, who did not consult with the nobility of his domains, left those domains in turmoil. In France also, the royal drive for adequate fiscal resources also led to aristocratic resistance. In France, however, neither the monarchy nor the aristocracy could control the social and political forces their quarrel unleashed.

The French monarchy emerged from the Seven Years' War (1756–1763) defeated, deeply in debt, and unable thereafter to put its finances on a sound basis. French support of the American revolt against Great Britain further deepened the financial difficulties of the government. On the eve of the revolution, the interest and payments on the royal debt amounted to just over one-half of the entire budget. Given the economic vitality of the nation, the debt was neither overly large nor disproportionate to the debts of other European powers. The problem lay with the inability of the royal government to tap the wealth of the French nation through taxes to service and repay the debt. Paradoxically, France was a rich nation with an impoverished government.

THE MONARCHY SEEKS NEW TAXES

The debt was symptomatic of the failure of the late-eighteenth-century French monarchy to come to terms with the resurgent social and political power of aristocratic institutions and, in particular, the *parlements*. For twenty-five years after the Seven Years' War, there was a standoff between them as one royal minister after another attempted to devise new tax schemes that would tap the wealth of the nobility, only to be confronted by the opposition of both the *Parlement* of Paris and provincial *parlements*. Both Louis XV (r. 1715–1774) and Louis XVI (r. 1774–1792) lacked the character and the resolution to carry the dispute to a successful conclusion. The moral and political corruption of their courts and the indecision of Louis XVI meant the monarchy could not rally the French public to its side. In place of a consistent policy for dealing with the growing debt and aristocratic resistance to change, the monarchy hesitated, retreated, and even lied.

In 1770, Louis XV appointed René Maupeou (1714–1792) as chancellor. The new minister was determined to break the *parlements* and increase taxes on the nobility. He abolished the *parlements* and exiled their members to different parts of the country. He then began an ambitious program to make the administration more efficient. What ultimately doomed Maupeou's policy was less the resistance of the nobility than the death of Louis XV in 1774. His successor, Louis XVI, in an attempt to regain what he conceived to be popular support, restored all the *parlements* and confirmed their old powers.

Throughout these and later disputes, the *parlements*, which were completely dominated by the aristocracy, defended their cause in the language of liberty and reform against an intrusive and arbitrary monarchy. Here they drew on the ideas and arguments of many Enlightenment writers, such as Montesquieu and the physiocrats, discussed in Chapter 18. The French nobility was seeking nothing less than to roll back more than a century of monarchical absolutism in order to give themselves a genuine role in government, which they had lost under the reign of Louis XIV (r. 1643–1715).

The fiscal crisis gave them the lever of influence they had long lacked.

France's successful intervention on behalf of the American colonists against the British only worsened the financial problems of the monarchy. By 1781, as a result of the aid to America, its debt was larger and its sources of revenues were unchanged. The new director-general of finances, Jacques Necker (1732–1804), a Swiss banker, then produced a public report that suggested the situation was not so bad as had been feared. He argued that if the expenditures for the American war were removed, the budget was in surplus. Necker's report also revealed that a large portion of royal expenditures went to pensions for aristocrats and other royal court favorites. This revelation angered court aristocratic circles, and Necker soon left office. His financial sleight of hand, nonetheless, made it more difficult for later government officials to claim a real need to raise new taxes.

CALONNE'S REFORM PLAN AND THE ASSEMBLY OF NOTABLES

The monarchy hobbled along until 1786. By this time, Charles Alexandre de Calonne (1734–1802) was the minister of finance. Calonne proposed to encourage internal trade, to lower some taxes, such as the *gabelle* on salt, and to transform peasants' services to money payments. More important, Calonne urged the introduction of a new land tax that would require payments from all landowners regardless of their social status. If this tax had been imposed, the monarchy could have abandoned other indirect taxes. The government would also have had less need to seek additional taxes that required approval from the aristocratically dominated *parlements*. Calonne also intended to establish new local assemblies to approve land taxes; in these assemblies the voting power would have depended on the amount of land owned rather than on the social status of the owner. All these proposals would have undermined both the political and the social power of the French aristocracy.

Calonne's policies and the country's fiscal crisis made a new clash with the nobility unavoidable, and the monarchy had very little room to maneuver. The creditors were at the door; the treasury was nearly empty. In 1787, Calonne met with an Assembly of Notables drawn from the upper ranks of the aristocracy and the church to seek support for his plan. The assembly adamantly refused any such action; rather, it demanded that the aristocracy be allowed a greater share in the direct government of the kingdom. The notables called for the reappointment of Necker, who they believed had left the country in sound fiscal condition. Finally, they claimed they had no right to consent to new taxes and that such a right was vested only in the medieval institution of the Estates General of France, which had not met since 1614. The notables believed that calling the Estates General, which had been traditionally organized to allow aristocratic and church dominance, would produce a victory for the nobility over the monarchy.

DEADLOCK AND THE CALLING OF THE ESTATES GENERAL

Again, Louis XVI backed off. He dismissed Calonne and replaced him with Etienne Charles Loménie de Brienne (1727–1794), archbishop of Toulouse and the chief opponent of Calonne at the Assembly of Notables. Once in office, Brienne found, to his astonishment, that the situation was as bad as his predecessor had asserted. Brienne himself now sought to reform the land tax. The *Parlement* of Paris, however, took the new position that it lacked authority to authorize the tax and said only the Estates General could do so. Shortly thereafter, Brienne appealed to the Assembly of the Clergy to approve a large subsidy to allow funding of that part of the debt then coming due for payment. The clergy, like the *Parlement* dominated by aristocrats, not only refused the subsidy, but also reduced its existing contribution, or *don gratuit*, to the government.

As these unfruitful negotiations were taking place at the center of political life, local aristocratic *parlements* and estates in the provinces were making their own demands. They wanted a restoration of the privileges they had enjoyed during the early seventeenth century, before Richelieu and Louis XIV had crushed their independence. Consequently, in July 1788, the king, through Brienne, agreed to convoke the Estates General the next year. Brienne resigned and Necker replaced him. The institutions of the aristocracy—and to a lesser degree, of the church—had brought the French monarchy to its knees. In the country of its origin, royal absolutism had been defeated and some kind of political reform was at hand.

The Revolution of 1789

The year 1789 proved to be one of the most remarkable in the history of both France and Europe. The French aristocracy had forced Louis XVI to call the Estates General into session. Yet the aristocrats' triumph was brief. From the moment the monarch

This late-eighteenth-century cartoon satirizes the French social structure. It shows a poor man in chains, who represents the vast majority of the population, supporting an aristocrat, a bishop, and a noble of the robe. The aristocrat is claiming feudal rights, the bishop holds papers associating the church with religious persecution and clerical privileges, and the noble of the robe holds a document listing the rights of the noble-dominated parlements. Corbis

summoned the Estates General, the political situation in France changed drastically. Social and political forces that neither the nobles nor the king could control were immediately unleashed.

From that calling of the Estates General to the present, historians have heatedly debated the meaning of the event and the turmoil that followed over the next decade. Many historians long believed the calling and gathering of the Estates General unleashed a clash between the bourgeoisie and the aristocracy that had been building in the decades before 1789. More recently, other historians have countered that the two groups actually had much in common by 1789 and that many members of both the bourgeoisie and the aristocracy resented and opposed the clumsy absolutism of the late-eighteenth-century monarchy. This second group of historians contends the fundamental issue of 1789 was the determination of various social groups to reorganize the French government to assure the future political influence of all forms of wealth.

As this complicated process was being worked out, the argument goes, distrust arose between the aristocracy and increasingly radical middle-class leaders. The latter then turned to the tradespeople of Paris, building alliances with them to achieve their goals. That alliance radicalized the revolution. When, in the mid-1790s, revolutionary policies and actions became too radical, aristocratic and middle-class leaders once again cooperated to reassert the security of all forms of private wealth and property. According to this view, conflict did exist among different social groups during the years of the revolution, but its causes were immediate, not hidden in the depths of French economic and social development.

Other historians also look to the influence of immediate rather than long-term causes. They believe the faltering of the monarchy and the confusion following the calling, election, and organization of the Estates General created a political vacuum. Various leaders and social groups, often using the political vocabulary of the Enlightenment, stepped into that

Well-meaning but weak and vacillating, Louis XVI (r. 1774–1792) stumbled from concession to concession until he finally lost all power to save his throne. Joseph Siffred Duplessis, *Louis XVI.* Versailles, France. Giraudon/Art Resource, N.Y.

vacuum, challenging each other for dominance. The precedent for such public debate had been set during the years of conflict between the monarchy and the *parlements* when the latter had begun to challenge the former as the true representative of the nation. These debates and conflicts over the language, and hence values, of political life and activity had been made possible by the emergence of the new print culture with its reading public and numerous channels for the circulation of books, pamphlets, and newspapers. Emerging from this culture were a large number of often-unemployed authors who were resentful of their situation and ready to use their skills to radicalize the discussion. The result was a political debate wider than any before in European history. The events of the era represented a continuing effort to dominate public opinion about the future course of the nation. The French Revolution, according to this view, thus illustrates the character of a new political culture created by changes in the technology and distribution of print communication.

Yet another group of historians maintains that the events of 1789 through 1795 are only one chapter in a longer-term political reorganization of France following the paralysis of monarchical government, a process that was not concluded until the establishment of the Third Republic in the 1870s. According to this interpretation, the core accomplishment of the revolution of the 1790s was to lay the foundations for a republic that could assure both individual liberty and the safety of property. It was not until the last quarter of the nineteenth century, however, that such a republic actually came into existence.

To some extent, how convincing we find each of these interpretations depends on which years or even months of the revolution we examine. The various interpretations are not, in any case, always mutually exclusive. Certainly, the weakness and ultimate collapse of the monarchy influenced events more than was once acknowledged. All sides did indeed make use of the new formats and institutions of the print culture. Individual leaders shifted their positions and alliances quite frequently, sometimes out of principle, more often for political expediency. Furthermore, the actual political situation differed from city to city and from region to region. The controversial and divisive religious policies of the revolutionary government itself were often determining factors in the attitudes that French citizens assumed toward the revolution. What does seem clear is that much of the earlier consensus—that the revolution arose almost entirely from conflict between the aristocracy and bourgeoisie—no longer stands, except with many qualifications. The interpretive situation is now much more complicated, and a new consensus has yet to emerge.

THE ESTATES GENERAL BECOMES THE NATIONAL ASSEMBLY

Conflict between the French monarchy and the aristocracy had caused the calling of the Estates General. But almost immediately after it was called, the three groups, or estates, represented within it clashed with each other. The First Estate was the clergy, the Second Estate the nobility, and the **Third Estate** theoretically everyone else in the kingdom, although its representatives were drawn primarily from wealthy members of the commercial and professional middle classes. All the representatives in the Estates General were men. During the widespread public discussions preceding the meeting of the Estates General, representatives of the Third Estate made it clear they would not permit the monarchy and the aristocracy to decide the future of the nation.

A comment by the Abbé Siéyès (1748–1836) in a pamphlet published in 1789 captures the spirit of the Third Estate's representatives: "What is the Third Estate? Everything. What has it been in the political order up to the present? Nothing. What does it ask? To become something."[1] (See "Abbé Siéyès Presents the Cause of the Third Estate.")

Debate over Organization and Voting Before the Estates General gathered, a public debate over its proper organization drew the lines of basic disagreement. The aristocracy made two moves to limit the influence of the Third Estate. First, they demanded an equal number of representatives for each estate. Second, in September 1788, the *Parlement* of Paris ruled that voting in the Estates General should be conducted by order rather than by head—that is, each estate, or order, in the Estates General, rather than each member, should have one vote. This procedure would in all likelihood have ensured the aristocratically dominated First and Second Estates could always outvote the Third by a vote of two estates to one estate. Both moves raised doubt about the aristocracy's previously declared concern for French liberty and revealed it as a group hoping to

maintain its privileges no matter what government reforms might be enacted. Spokespeople for the Third Estate denounced the arrogant claims of the aristocracy. Although the aristocracy and the Third Estate shared many economic interests and goals, and some intermarriage had occurred throughout the country between nobles and the elite of the Third Estate, a fundamental social distance separated the members of the two orders. There were far more examples of enormous wealth and military experience among the nobility than among the Third Estate; the latter also had experienced various forms of political and social discrimination from the nobility. The resistance of the nobility to voting by head simply confirmed the suspicions and resentments of the members of the Third Estate, who were overwhelmingly lawyers of substantial, but not enormous, economic means.

Doubling the Third The royal council eventually decided the cause of the monarchy and fiscal reform would best be served by a strengthening of the Third Estate. In December 1788, the council announced the Third Estate would elect twice as many representatives as either the nobles or the clergy. This so-called doubling of the Third Estate meant it could easily dominate the Estates General if voting proceeded by head rather than by order. It was correctly assumed that liberal nobles and clergy would support the Third Estate, confirming that, despite social differences, these groups shared important interests and reform goals. The method of voting had not yet been decided when the Estates General gathered at Versailles in May 1789.

The *Cahiers de Doléances* When the representatives came to the royal palace, they brought with them *cahiers de doléances,* or lists of grievances, registered by the local electors, to be presented to the king. Many of these lists have survived and provide considerable information about the state of the country on the eve of the revolution. The documents recorded criticisms of government waste, indirect taxes, church taxes and corruption, and the hunting rights of the aristocracy. They included calls for periodic meetings of the Estates General, more equitable taxes, more local control of administration, unified weights and measures to facilitate trade and commerce, and a free press. The overwhelming demand of the *cahiers* was for equality of rights among the king's subjects.

The Third Estate Creates the National Assembly These complaints and demands could not, however, be discussed until the questions of organization and

---

[1]Quoted in Leo Gershoy, *The French Revolution and Napoleon* (New York: Appleton-Century-Crofts, 1964), p. 102.

ABBÉ SIÉYÈS PRESENTS THE CAUSE OF THE THIRD ESTATE

Among the many pamphlets that appeared after the calling of the Estates General, one of the most famous was What Is the Third Estate? *by Abbé Emmanuel Siéyès. In this pamphlet Siéyès contrasted the vital contributions of the Third Estate to the nation with its exclusion from political and social privilege. He presents an image of the Third Estate in direct conflict with the aristocracy rather than with the monarchy. On the basis of this pamphlet many later observers and historians argued that the revolution was a conflict between the middle class and the aristocracy. The social structure of France, however, and the interactions of those two groups was much more complicated than Siéyès suggests. Both groups were discontented with monarchical government.*

■ *How does Siéyès define the Third Estate? What injustices does he claim it suffers? What are the complaints that he makes on behalf of the Third Estate against the aristocracy? Why does Siéyès make a distinction between the court and the monarchy?*

Who, then would dare to say that the third estate has not within itself all that is necessary to constitute a complete nation? It is the strong and robust man whose one arm remains enchained. If the privileged order were abolished, the nation would be not something less but something more. Thus, what is the third estate? Everything; but an everything shackled and oppressed. . . .

The third estate must be understood to mean the mass of the citizens belonging to the common order. Legalized privilege in any form deviates from the common order, constitutes an exception to the common law, and, consequently, does not appertain to the third estate at all. We repeat, a common law and a common representation are what constitute ONE nation. It is only too true that one is NOTHING in France when one has only the protection of the common law; if one does not possess some privilege, one must resign oneself to enduring contempt, injury, and vexations of every sort. . . .

But here we have to consider the order of the third estate less in its civil status than in its relation

with the constitution. Let us examine its position in the Estates General.

Who have been its so-called representatives? The ennobled or those privileged for a period of years. These false deputies have not even been always freely elected by the people. . . .

Add to this appalling truth that, in one manner or another, all branches of the executive power also have fallen to the case which furnishes the Church, the robe, and the Sword. A sort of spirit of brotherhood causes the nobles to prefer themselves . . . to the rest of the nation. Usurpation is complete; in truth they reign. . . .

[I]t is a great error to believe that France is subject to a monarchical regime. . . .

[I]t is the court, and not the monarch, that has reigned. It is the court that makes and unmakes, appoints and discharges ministers, creates and dispenses positions, etc. And what is the court if not the head of this immense aristocracy which overruns all parts of France; which though its members attains all and everywhere does whatever is essential in all parts of the commonwealth?

From John Hall Stewart, *A Documentary Survey of the French Revolution*, (c) 1951. Reprinted by permission of Prentice Hall, Inc., Upper Saddle River, NJ.

voting had been decided. From the beginning, the Third Estate, whose members consisted largely of local officials, professionals, and other persons of property, refused to sit as a separate order as the king desired. For several weeks there was a standoff. Then, on June 1, the Third Estate invited the clergy and the nobles to join them in organizing a new leg-

islative body. A few members of the lower clergy did so. On June 17, that body declared itself the National Assembly, and on June 19 by a narrow margin the Second Estate voted to join the assembly.

The Tennis Court Oath   On June 20, finding themselves accidentally locked out of their usual meeting

Louis XVI presided over the opening of the Estates General, which met at Versailles on May 5, 1789. On this occasion each estate—clergy, nobility, and commoners—sat as a separate group. Convocation of the Estates General at Versailles. Bibliotheque Nationale, Paris, France. Giraudon/Art Resource, N.Y.

place, the National Assembly moved to a nearby tennis court. There its members took an oath to continue to sit until they had given France a constitution. This was the famous Tennis Court Oath. Louis XVI unsuccessfully ordered the National Assembly to desist from its actions. Shortly thereafter, however, a large group of clergy and a significant group of nobles joined the assembly.

On June 27, the king capitulated and formally requested the First and Second Estates to meet with the National Assembly, where voting would occur by head rather than by order. The Third Estate because of the doubling of the third had twice as many members as either of the other estates that joined them. Had nothing further occurred, the government of France would have been transformed. Henceforth, the monarchy could govern only in cooperation with the National Assembly, and the National Assembly would not be a legislative body organized according to privileged orders. The National Assembly, which renamed itself the National Constituent Assembly, was composed of a majority of members drawn from all three orders, who shared liberal goals for the administrative, constitutional, and economic reform of the country. The revolution in France against government by privileged hereditary orders, however, soon extended beyond events occurring at Versailles.

FALL OF THE BASTILLE

Two new forces soon intruded on the scene. The first was Louis XVI himself, who attempted to regain the political initiative by mustering royal troops near Versailles and Paris. It appeared that he might, following the advice of Queen Marie Antoinette (1755–1793), his brothers, and the most conservative nobles, be contemplating disruption of the National Constituent Assembly. On July 11, without consulting assembly leaders, Louis abruptly dismissed Necker, his minister of finance. These actions marked the beginning of a steady, but consistently poorly executed, royal attempt to

This painting of the Tennis Court Oath, June 20, is by Jacques-Louis David (1748–1825). In the center foreground are members of different estates joining hands in cooperation as equals. The presiding officer is Jean-Sylvain Bailly, soon to become mayor of Paris.
Jacques-Louis David, *Oath of the Tennis Court*. Chateau, Versailles, France. Giraudon/Art Resource, N.Y.

undermine the assembly and halt the revolution. Most of the National Constituent Assembly wished to establish some form of constitutional monarchy, but from the start Louis's refusal to cooperate thwarted that effort. The king fatally decided to throw his lot in with the conservative aristocracy against the emerging forces of reform drawn from across the social and political spectrum.

The second new factor to impose itself on the events at Versailles was the populace of Paris. The mustering of royal troops created anxiety in the city, where throughout the winter and spring of 1789 there had been several bread riots. The Parisians who had elected their representatives to the Third Estate had continued to meet after the elections. By June they were organizing a citizen militia and collecting arms. They regarded the dismissal of Necker as the opening of a royal offensive against the National Constituent Assembly and the city.

On July 14, somewhat more than eight hundred people, most of them small shopkeepers, tradespeople, artisans, and wage earners, marched to the Bastille in search of weapons for the militia. This great fortress, with ten-foot-thick walls, had once held political prisoners. Through miscalculations and ineptitude on the part of the governor of the fortress, the troops in the Bastille fired into the crowd, killing ninety-eight people and wounding many others. Thereafter, the crowd stormed the fortress and eventually gained entrance. They released the seven prisoners inside, none of whom was there for political reasons, and killed several troops and the governor.

On July 15, the militia of Paris, by then called the National Guard, offered its command to the Marquis de Lafayette (1757–1834). This hero of the American Revolution gave the guard a new insignia: the red and blue stripes of Paris, separated by the white stripe of the king. The emblem became the

On July 14, 1789, crowds stormed the Bastille, a prison in Paris. This event, whose only practical effect was to free a few prisoners, marked the first time the populace of Paris redirected the course of the revolution. France, 18th c., *Siege of the Bastille, 14 July, 1789.* Musée de la Ville de Paris, Musée Carnavalet, Paris, France. Giraudon/Art Resource, N.Y.

revolutionary *cockade* (badge) and eventually the flag of revolutionary France.

The attack on the Bastille marked the first of many crucial *journées*, days on which the populace of Paris redirected the course of the revolution. The fall of the fortress signaled the National Constituent Assembly alone would not decide the political future of the nation. As the news of the taking of the Bastille spread, similar disturbances took place in provincial cities. A few days later, Louis XVI again bowed to the force of events and personally visited Paris, where he wore the revolutionary cockade and recognized the organized electors as the legitimate government of the city. The king also recognized the National Guard. The citizens of Paris were, for the time being, satisfied.

They also had established themselves as an independent political force with which other political groups might ally for their own purposes.

THE "GREAT FEAR" AND THE NIGHT OF AUGUST 4

Simultaneous with the popular urban disturbances, a movement known as the "Great Fear" swept across much of the French countryside. Rumors had spread that royal troops would be sent into the rural districts. The result was an intensification of the peasant disturbances that had begun during the spring. The Great Fear saw the burning of châteaux, the destruction of records and documents, and the refusal to pay feudal dues. The peasants were determined to take possession of food supplies and land that they considered rightfully theirs. They were reclaiming rights and property they had lost through the aristocratic resurgence of the last quarter century, as well as venting their general anger against the injustices of rural life.

On the night of August 4, 1789, aristocrats in the National Constituent Assembly attempted to halt the spreading disorder in the countryside. By prearrangement, several liberal nobles and clerics rose in the assembly and renounced their feudal rights, dues, and tithes. In a scene of great emotion, hunting and fishing rights, judicial authority, and special exemptions were surrendered. These nobles gave up what they had already lost and what they could not have regained without civil war in the rural areas. Later they would also, in many cases, receive compensation for their losses. Nonetheless,

after the night of August 4, all French citizens were subject to the same and equal laws. That dramatic session of the assembly paved the way for the legal and social reconstruction of the nation. Without those renunciations, the constructive work of the National Constituent Assembly would have been much more difficult. (See "The National Assembly Decrees Civic Equality in France.")

Both the attack on the Bastille and the Great Fear displayed characteristics of the rural and urban riots that had occurred often in eighteenth-century France. Louis XVI first thought the turmoil over the Bastille was simply another bread riot. Indeed, the popular disturbances were only partly related to the events at Versailles. A deep economic downturn had struck France in 1787 and continued into 1788. The harvests for both years had been poor, and food prices in 1789 were higher than at any time since 1703. Wages had not kept

THE NATIONAL ASSEMBLY DECREES CIVIC EQUALITY IN FRANCE

These famous decrees of August 4, 1789, in effect created civic equality in France. The special privileges previously possessed or controlled by the nobility were removed.

■ *What institutions and privileges are included in "the feudal regime"? How do these decrees recognize that the abolition of some privileges and former tax arrangements will require new kinds of taxes and government financing to support religious, educational, and other institutions?*

1. The National Assembly completely abolishes the feudal regime. It decrees that, among the rights and dues . . . all those originating in real or personal serfdom, personal servitude, and those which represent them, are abolished without indemnification; all others are declared redeemable, and that the price and mode of redemption shall be fixed by the National Assembly. . . .
2. The exclusive right to maintain pigeon-houses and dove-cotes is abolished. . . .
3. The exclusive right to hunt and to maintain unenclosed warrens is likewise abolished. . . .
4. All manorial courts are suppressed without indemnification.
5. Tithes of every description and the dues which have been substituted for them . . . are

abolished, on condition, however, that some other method be devised to provide for the expenses of divine worship, the support of the officiating clergy, the relief of the poor, repairs and rebuilding of churches and parsonages, and for all establishments, seminaries, schools, academies, asylums, communities, and other institutions, for the maintenance of which they are actually devoted. . . .
6. The sale of judicial and municipal offices shall be suppressed forthwith. . . .
7. Pecuniary privileges, personal or real, in the payment of taxes are abolished forever. . . .
8. All citizens, without distinction of birth, are eligible to any office or dignity, whether ecclesiastical, civil or military. . . .

From Frank Maloy Anderson, ed. and trans., *The Constitutions and Other Select Documents Illustrative of the History of France, 1789–1907,* 2nd. ed., rev. and enl. (Minneapolis: H.W. Wilson, 1908), pp. 11–13.

up with the rise in prices. Throughout the winter of 1788–1789, an unusually cold one, many people suffered from hunger. Several cities had experienced wage and food riots. These economic problems helped the revolution reach the vast proportions it did.

The political, social, and economic grievances of many sections of the country became combined. The National Constituent Assembly could look to the popular forces as a source of strength against the king and the conservative aristocrats. When the various elements of the assembly later fell into quarrels among themselves, the resulting factions appealed for support to the politically sophisticated and well-organized shopkeeping and artisan classes. They, in turn, would demand a price for their cooperation.

THE DECLARATION OF THE RIGHTS OF MAN AND CITIZEN

In late August 1789, the National Constituent Assembly decided that before writing a new constitution, it should set forth a statement of broad political principles. On August 27, the assembly issued the Declaration of the Rights of Man and Citizen. This declaration drew on much of the political language of the Enlightenment and was also influenced by the Declaration of Rights adopted by Virginia in America in June 1776.

The French declaration proclaimed that all men were "born and remain free and equal in rights." The natural rights so proclaimed were "liberty, property, security, and resistance to oppression." Governments existed to protect those rights. All political sovereignty resided in the nation and its representatives. All citizens were to be equal before the law and were to be "equally admissible to all public dignities, offices, and employments, according to their capacity, and with no other distinction than that of their virtues and talents." There were to be due process of law and presumption of innocence until proof of guilt. Freedom of religion was affirmed. Taxation was to be apportioned equally according to capacity to pay. Property constituted "an inviolable and sacred right."[2]

Although these statements were rather abstract, almost all of them were directed against specific abuses of the old aristocratic and absolutist regime. If any two principles of the future governed the declaration, they were civic equality and protection of property. The Declaration of the Rights of Man and Citizen has often been considered the death certificate of the Old Regime.

It was not accidental that the Declaration of the Rights of Man and Citizen specifically applied to men and not to women. As discussed in Chapter 18, much of the political language of the Enlightenment, and especially that associated with Rousseau, separated men and women into distinct gender spheres. According to this view, which influenced the legislation of the revolutionary era, men were suited for citizenship, women for motherhood and the domestic life. Nonetheless, in the charged atmosphere of the summer of 1789, many politically active and informed Frenchwomen hoped the guarantees of the declaration would be extended to them. Their issues of particular concern related to property, inheritance, family, and divorce. Some people saw in the declaration a framework within which women might eventually enjoy the rights and protection of citizenship.

THE PARISIAN WOMEN'S MARCH ON VERSAILLES

Louis XVI stalled before ratifying both the declaration and the aristocratic renunciation of feudalism. The longer he hesitated, the stronger grew suspicions that he might again try to resort to the use of troops. Moreover, bread continued to be scarce. On October 5, a crowd of as many as 7,000 Parisian women armed with pikes, guns, swords, and knives marched to Versailles demanding more bread. They milled about the palace, and many stayed the night. Intimidated by these Parisian women, the king agreed to sanction the decrees of the assembly. The next day he and his family appeared on a balcony before the crowd. The Parisians, however, were deeply suspicious of the monarch and believed he must be kept under the watchful eye of the people. They demanded that Louis and his family return to Paris. The monarch had no real choice in the matter. On October 6, 1789, his carriage followed the crowd into the city, where he and his family settled in the palace of the Tuileries.

The march of the women of Paris was the first example of a popular insurrection employing the language of popular sovereignty directed against the monarch. The National Constituent Assembly also soon moved into Paris. Thereafter, both Paris and France remained relatively stable and peaceful until the summer of 1792. (See "Art &

[2]Quoted in Georges Lefebvre, *The Coming of the French Revolution*, trans. by R. R. Palmer (Princeton, NJ: Princeton University Press, 1967), pp. 221–223.

The women of Paris marched to Versailles on October 5, 1789. The following day the royal family was forced to return to Paris with them. Henceforth, the French government would function under the constant threat of mob violence. France, 18th c., *To Versailles, to Versailles*. The women of Paris going to Versailles, 7 October, 1789. Musée de la Ville de Paris, Musée Carnavalet, Paris, France. Giraudon/Art Resource, N.Y.

the West: Jacques-Louis David Champions Republican Values," p. 664.)

The Reconstruction of France

Once established in Paris, the National Constituent Assembly set about reorganizing France. In government, it pursued a policy of constitutional monarchy; in administration, rationalism; in economics, unregulated freedom; and in religion, anticlericalism. Throughout its proceedings the assembly was determined to protect property in all its forms. In those policies, the aristocracy and the middle-class elite stood united. The assembly also sought to limit the impact on national life of the unpropertied elements of the nation and even of possessors of small amounts of property. Although championing civic equality before the law, the assembly spurned social equality and extensive democracy. In all these ways, the assembly charted a general course that, to a greater or lesser degree, nineteenth-century liberals across Europe would follow.

POLITICAL REORGANIZATION

The Constitution of 1791, the product of the National Constituent Assembly's deliberations, established a constitutional monarchy. The major political authority of the nation would be a unicameral Legislative Assembly, in which all laws would originate. The monarch was allowed a suspensive veto that could delay, but not halt, legislation. Powers of war and peace were vested in the assembly.

Active and Passive Citizens The constitution provided for an elaborate system of indirect elections intended to thwart direct popular pressure on the government. The citizens of France were divided into active and passive categories. Only active citizens—that is, men paying annual taxes equal to three days of local labor wages—could vote. They chose electors, who then in turn voted for the members of the legislature. At the level of electors or members, still further property qualifications were imposed. Only about 50,000 citizens of a population of about 25 million could qualify as electors or members of the Legislative Assembly. Women could neither vote nor hold office.

These constitutional arrangements effectively transferred political power from aristocratic wealth to all forms of propertied wealth in the nation. Political authority would no longer be achieved through hereditary privilege or through purchase of titles, but through the accumulation of land and commercial property. These new political arrangements based on property rather than birth recognized the new complexities of French society that had developed over the past century and allowed more social and economic interests to have a voice in the governing of the nation.

Olympe de Gouges's Declaration of the Rights of Woman The laws that excluded women from both voting and holding office did not pass unnoticed. In 1791, Olympe de Gouges (d. 1793), a butcher's daughter from Montauban who became a major revolutionary radical in Paris, composed a Declaration of the Rights of Woman, which she ironically addressed to Queen Marie Antoinette. Much of the document reprinted the Declaration of the Rights of Man and Citizen, adding the word *woman* to the various original clauses. That strategy demanded that women be regarded as citizens and not merely as daughters, sisters, wives, and mothers of citizens. Olympe de Gouges further outlined rights that would permit women to own property and require men to recognize the paternity of their children. She called for equality of the sexes in marriage and improved education for women. She declared, "Women, wake up; the *tocsin* of reason is being heard throughout the whole universe; discover your rights."[3] Her declaration illustrated how the simple listing of rights in the Declaration of the Rights of Man and Citizen created a structure of universal civic expectations even for those it did not cover. The National Assembly had established a set of values against which it could itself be measured. It provided criteria for liberty, and those to whom it had not extended full liberties could demand to know why and could claim the revolution was incomplete until they enjoyed those freedoms.

Departments Replace Provinces In reconstructing the local and judicial administration, the National Constituent Assembly applied the rational spirit of

the Enlightenment. It abolished the ancient French provinces, such as Burgundy and Brittany, and established in their place eighty-three departments, or *départements*, of generally equal size named after rivers, mountains, and other geographical features. (See Map 19-1.) The departments in turn were subdivided into districts, cantons, and communes. Most local elections were also indirect. The departmental reconstruction proved to be a permanent achievement of the assembly. The departments exist to the present day.

All the ancient judicial courts, including the seigneurial courts and the *parlements*, were also abolished. Uniform courts with elected judges and prosecutors were organized in their place. Procedures were simplified, and the most degrading punishments were removed from the books.

ECONOMIC POLICY

In economic matters, the National Constituent Assembly continued the policies formerly advocated by Louis XVI's reformist ministers. It suppressed the guilds and liberated the grain trade. The assembly established the metric system to provide the nation with uniform weights and measures. (See "Encountering the Past: The Metric System.")

Workers' Organizations Forbidden The new policies of economic freedom and uniformity disappointed both peasants and urban workers caught in the cycle of inflation. By decrees in 1789, the assembly placed the burden of proof on the peasants to rid themselves of the residual feudal dues for which compensation was to be paid. On June 14, 1791, the assembly crushed the attempts of urban workers to protect their wages by enacting the Chapelier Law, which forbade workers' associations. Peasants and workers were henceforth to be left to the freedom and mercy of the marketplace. (See "The Revolutionary Government Forbids Workers' Organizations.")

Confiscation of Church Lands While these various reforms were being put into effect, the original financial crisis that had occasioned the calling of the Estates General persisted. The assembly did not repudiate the royal debt, because it was owed to the bankers, the merchants, and the commercial traders of the Third Estate. The National Constituent Assembly had suppressed many of the old, hated indirect taxes and had substituted new land taxes, but these proved insufficient. Moreover, there were not enough officials to collect them. The continuing financial problem led the assembly to take what

[3]Quoted in Sara E. Melzer and Leslie W. Rabine, eds., *Rebel Daughters: Women and the French Revolution* (New York: Oxford University Press, 1992), p. 88.

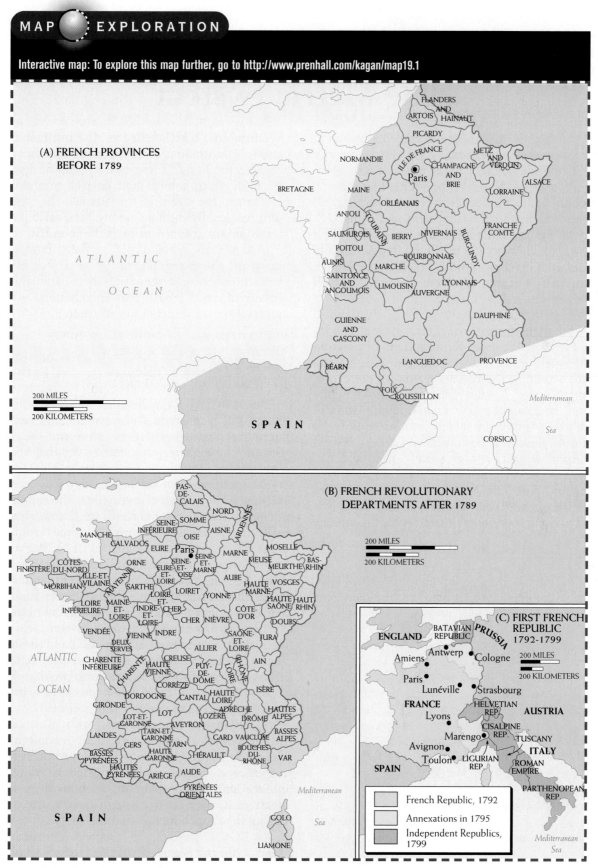

(A) FRENCH PROVINCES BEFORE 1789

FLANDERS AND HAINAUT
ARTOIS
PICARDY
NORMANDIE
ILE DE FRANCE
METZ AND VERDUN
CHAMPAGNE AND BRIE
ALSACE
Paris
LORRAINE
BRETAGNE
MAINE
ORLÉANAIS
FRANCHE COMTÉ
ANJOU
TOURAINE
SAUMUROIS
BERRY
NIVERNAIS
BURGUNDY
POITOU
BOURBONNAIS
AUNIS
MARCHE
SAINTONGE AND ANGOUMOIS
LIMOUSIN
AUVERGNE
LYONNAIS
GUIENNE AND GASCONY
DAUPHINÉ
BÉARN
LANGUEDOC
PROVENCE
FOIX
ROUSSILLON

ATLANTIC OCEAN

200 MILES
200 KILOMETERS

SPAIN

Mediterranean Sea

CORSICA

(B) FRENCH REVOLUTIONARY DEPARTMENTS AFTER 1789

PAS-DE-CALAIS
NORD
SEINE INFÉRIEURE
SOMME
AISNE
ARDENNES
MANCHE
CALVADOS
OISE
EURE
Paris
MARNE
MOSELLE
MEUSE
MEURTHE
BAS-RHIN
CÔTES-DU-NORD
FINISTÈRE
ORNE
SEINE-ET-OISE
SEINE-ET-MARNE
ILLE-ET-VILAINE
MAYENNE
SARTHE
EURE-ET-LOIRE
AUBE
VOSGES
HAUT RHIN
MORBIHAN
LOIRE-ET-CHER
LOIRET
YONNE
HAUTE MARNE
LOIRE INFÉRIEURE
MAINE-ET-LOIRE
INDRE-ET-CHER
CHER
NIÈVRE
CÔTE-D'OR
HAUTE SAÔNE
VENDÉE
VIENNE
INDRE
DOUBS
DEUX-SERVES
ALLIER
SAÔNE-ET-LOIRE
JURA
CHARENTE INFÉRIEURE
CREUSE
PUY-DE-DÔME
RHÔNE
AIN
CHARENTE
HAUTE VIENNE
DORDOGNE
CORRÈZE
CANTAL
HAUTE LOIRE
ISÈRE
GIRONDE
LOT
LOZÈRE
ADRÈCHE
DRÔME
HAUTES ALPES
LOT-ET-GARONNE
AVEYRON
LANDES
TARN-ET-GARONNE
GARD
VAUCLUSE
BASSES ALPES
GERS
HAUTE GARONNE
TARN
HÉRAULT
BOUCHES-DU-RHÔNE
VAR
BASSES PYRÉNÉES
HAUTES PYRÉNÉES
ARIÈGE
AUDE
PYRÉNÉES ORIENTALES

ATLANTIC OCEAN

200 MILES
200 KILOMETERS

SPAIN

Mediterranean Sea

GOLO
LIAMONE

(C) FIRST FRENCH REPUBLIC 1792–1799

ENGLAND
BATAVIAN REPUBLIC
PRUSSIA
Amiens
Antwerp
Cologne
Paris
Lunéville
Strasbourg
FRANCE
HELVETIAN REP.
AUSTRIA
Lyons
CISALPINE REP.
TUSCANY
Avignon
Marengo
ITALY
Toulon
LIGURIAN REP.
ROMAN EMPIRE
SPAIN
PARTHENOPEAN REP.

200 MILES
200 KILOMETERS

Mediterranean Sea

French Republic, 1792
Annexations in 1795
Independent Republics, 1799

MAP 19–1   FRENCH PROVINCES AND THE REPUBLIC   *In 1789, the National Constituent Assembly redrew the map of France. The ancient provinces (A) were replaced with a larger number of new, smaller departments (B). This redrawing of the map was part of the assembly's effort to impose greater administrative rationality in France. The borders of the republic (C) changed as the French army conquered new territory.*

The Metric System

Much about the era of the French Revolution seems alien to us today. One French regime followed another in the midst of confusion, violence, and bloodshed. Yet one thing that the revolutionaries did still touches the lives of virtually all Europeans living on the Continent and if the U.S. Congress and the European Community have their way will touch everyone in the United States and the United Kingdom as well. In 1795, the French revolutionary government decreed a new standard for weights and measures—the metric system.

Inspired by the rationalism of the eighteenth-century Enlightenment, the metric system was intended to bring the order and simplicity of a system based on ten to the chaos of different weights and measures used in the various regions of prerevolutionary France. For its adherents, the republic marked the dawn of a new era in human history in which the triumph of science would replace the reign of superstition and obscurity. A new system of uniform weights and measures would also further one of the revolutionaries' political goals: centralization. With one set of weights and measures in use throughout the country, France would be closer to becoming a single "indivisible" republic.

Jean-Baptiste Delambre (1749–1822) was one of the French astronomers whose measurements of the arch of meridians formed the basis for establishing the length of the meter. Mary Evans Picture Library Ltd.

Astronomy, which relied on the rational application of mathematics to measure the heavens, provided the basis for the new system of distance or length. Astronomers had devised methods for measuring the arch of meridians—the highest point reached by the sun—around the earth. So the revolutionary authorities took the meridian in the latitude of Paris, which is 45°, as their standard for measuring the meter. The meter was to be one ten-millionth of one quarter of that meridian. All other measurements of length were then defined as decimal fractions or multiples of the meter.

1 centimeter (cm) = 10 millimeters (mm)
1 decimeter (dm) = 10 centimeters
1 meter = 100 centimeters
1 kilometer (km) = 1,000 meters

The standard for measuring weights was the gram, which constituted the weight of a cube of pure water measuring 0.01 meter on each side. Each measure of weight was defined as a decimal fraction or multiple of a gram. So a kilogram is 1,000 grams.

The metric system was soon adopted by working scientists, but in their everyday lives the population of France clung to their old and familiar weights and measures. Change, however "rational," did not come easily and was resisted. In 1812, Napoleon, bowing to popular sentiment, brought back the old units, but in 1840, the French government reimposed the metric system. Thereafter, rationality—and convenience—triumphed, and by the close of the nineteenth century, the metric system was used throughout continental Europe and had been introduced into Latin America. In the twentieth century it was adopted throughout Asia and Africa.

Today, much of the English-speaking world remains the great exception. Despite efforts by scientists, engineers, and doctors, who all use the metric system in their work, many people in the United States and Britain still prefer to measure in inches, feet, yards, and miles and to weigh in ounces and pounds. Perhaps without even being aware of it, they are rejecting a system introduced during the French Revolution.

■ *Why did the French revolutionary government introduce the metric system? Why may it be said to reflect the ideas of the Enlightenment? Why has most of the world come to accept this system?*

THE REVOLUTIONARY GOVERNMENT FORBIDS WORKERS' ORGANIZATIONS

The Chapelier Law of June 14, 1791, was one of the most important pieces of revolutionary legislation. It abolished the kinds of labor organizations that had protected skilled workers under the Old Regime. The principles of this legislation prevented effective labor organization in France for well over half a century.

■ *Why are workers' organizations declared to be contrary to the principles of liberty? Why were guilds seen as one of the undesirable elements of the Old Regime? What are the coercive powers that are to be brought to bear against workers' organizations? In light of this legislation, what courses of actions were left open to workers as they confronted the operation of the market economy?*

1. Since the abolition of all kinds of corporations of citizens of the same occupation and profession is one of the fundamental bases of the French Constitution, reestablishment thereof under any pretext or form whatsoever is forbidden.
2. Citizens of the same occupation or profession, entrepreneurs, those who maintain open shop, workers, and journeymen of any craft whatsoever may not, when they are together, name either president, secretaries, or trustees, keep accounts, pass decrees or resolutions, or draft regulations concerning their alleged common interests. . . .
4. If, contrary to the principles of liberty and the Constitution, some citizens associated in the same professions, arts, and crafts hold deliberations or make agreements among themselves tending to refuse by mutual consent or to grant only at a determined price the assistance of their industry or their labor, such deliberations and agreements, whether accompanied by oath

or not, are declared unconstitutional, in contempt of liberty and the Declaration of the Rights of Man, and noneffective; administrative and municipal bodies shall be required so to declare them. . . .

8. All assemblies composed of artisans, workers, journeymen, day laborers, or those incited by them against the free exercise of industry and labor appertaining to every kind of person and under all circumstances arranged by private contract, or against the action of police and the execution of judgments rendered in such connection, as well as against public bids and auctions of divers enterprises, shall be considered as seditious assemblies, and as such shall be dispersed by the depositories of the public force, upon legal requisitions made thereupon, and shall be punished according to all the rigor of the laws concerning authors, instigators, and leaders of the said assemblies, and all those who have committed assaults and acts of violence.

From John Hall Stewart, *A Documentary Survey of the French Revolution*, © 1951. Reprinted by permission of Prentice Hall, Inc., Upper Saddle River, NJ.

may well have been, for the future of French life and society, its most decisive action. The assembly decided to finance the debt by confiscating and then selling the land and property of the Roman Catholic Church in France. The results were further inflation, religious schism, and civil war. In effect, the National Constituent Assembly had opened a new chapter in the relations of church and state in Europe.

The *Assignats* Having chosen to plunder the land of the church, the assembly authorized the issuance of **assignats,** or government bonds, in De-

cember 1789. Their value was guaranteed by the revenue to be generated from the sale of church property. Initially, a limit was set on the quantity of *assignats* to be issued. The bonds, however, proved so acceptable to the public that they began to circulate as currency. The assembly decided to issue an ever-larger number of them to liquidate the national debt and to create a large body of new property owners with a direct stake in the revolution. Within a few months, however, the value of the *assignats* began to fall and inflation increased, putting new stress on the lives of the urban poor.

THE CIVIL CONSTITUTION OF THE CLERGY

The confiscation of church lands required an ecclesiastical reconstruction. In July 1790, the National Constituent Assembly issued the Civil Constitution of the Clergy, which transformed the Roman Catholic Church in France into a branch of the secular state. This legislation reduced the number of bishoprics from 135 to 83 and brought the borders of the dioceses into conformity with those of the new departments. It also provided for the election of priests and bishops, who henceforth became salaried employees of the state. The assembly consulted neither the pope nor the French clergy about these broad changes. The king approved the measure only with the greatest reluctance.

The Civil Constitution of the Clergy was the major blunder of the National Constituent Assembly. It created embittered relations between the French church and state that have persisted to the present day. The measure immediately created immense opposition within the French church, even from bishops who had long championed Gallican liberties over papal domination. In the face of this resistance, the assembly unwisely ruled that all clergy must take an oath to support the Civil Constitution. Only seven bishops and about half the clergy did so. In reprisal, the assembly designated those clergy who had not taken the oath as "refractory" and removed them from their clerical functions.

Further reaction was swift. Refractory priests attempted to celebrate mass. In February 1791, the pope condemned not only the Civil Constitution of the Clergy, but also the Declaration of the Rights of Man and Citizen. That condemnation marked the opening of a Roman Catholic offensive against liberalism and the revolution that continued throughout the nineteenth century. Within France itself, the pope's action created a crisis of conscience and political loyalty for all sincere Catholics. Religious devotion and revolutionary loyalty became incompatible for many people. French citizens were divided between those who supported the constitutional priests and those who resorted to the refractory clergy. Louis XVI and his family favored the refractory clergy.

COUNTERREVOLUTIONARY ACTIVITY

The revolution had other enemies besides the pope and the devout Catholics. As it became clear that the old political and social order was undergoing fundamental and probably permanent change, many aristocrats left France. Known as the **émigrés,** they settled in countries near the French border, where they sought to foment counterrevolution. Among the most important of their number was the king's younger brother, the count of Artois (1757–1836). In the summer of 1791, his agents and the queen persuaded Louis XVI to attempt to flee the country.

Flight to Varennes On the night of June 20, 1791, Louis and his immediate family, disguised as servants, left Paris. They traveled as far as Varennes on their way to Metz. At Varennes the king was recognized, and his flight was halted. On June 24, a company of soldiers escorted the royal family back to Paris. The leaders of the National Constituent

The assignats *were government bonds that were backed by confiscated church lands. They circulated as money. When the government printed too many of them, inflation resulted and their value fell.* Bildarchiv Preussischer Kulturbesitz

Assembly, determined to save the constitutional monarchy, announced the king had been abducted from the capital. Such a convenient public fiction could not cloak the realities that the chief counterrevolutionary in France now sat on the throne and the constitutional monarchy might not last long.

Declaration of Pillnitz Two months later, on August 27, 1791, under pressure from a group of émigrés, Emperor Leopold II of Austria, who was the brother of Marie Antoinette, and Frederick William II (r. 1786–1797), the king of Prussia, issued the Declaration of Pillnitz. The two monarchs promised to intervene in France to protect the royal family and to preserve the monarchy if the other major European powers agreed. This provision rendered the declaration meaningless because, at the time, Great Britain would not have given its consent. The declaration was not, however, so read in France, where the revolutionaries saw the nation surrounded by aristocratic and monarchical foes.

The National Constituent Assembly drew to a close in September 1791. Its task of reconstructing the government and the administration of France had been completed. One of its last acts was the passage of a measure that forbade any of its own members to sit in the Legislative Assembly then being elected. The new body met on October 1 and had to confront the immense problems that had emerged during the earlier part of the year. Within the Legislative Assembly, major political divisions also soon developed over the future course of the nation and the revolution. Those groups whose members had been assigned to passive citizenship began to demand full political participation in the nation.

By the autumn of 1791, the government of France had been transformed into a constitutional monarchy. Virtually all the other administrative and religious structures of the nation had also

In June 1791, Louis XVI and his family attempted to flee France. They were recognized in the town of Varennes, where their flight was halted and they were returned to Paris. This ended any realistic hope for a constitutional monarchy. Corbis

been reformed. The situation both inside and outside France, however, remained unstable. Louis XVI had reluctantly accepted the constitution on July 14, 1790. French aristocrats resented their loss of position and plotted to overthrow the new order. In the west of France, peasants resisted the revolutionary changes, especially as they affected the church. In Paris, many groups of workers believed the revolution had not gone far enough. Furthermore, during these same months, women's groups in Paris began to organize both to support the revolution and to demand a wider civic role and civic protection for women. Radical members of the new Legislative Assembly also believed the revolution should go further. The major foreign powers saw the French Revolution as dangerous to their own domestic political order. By the spring of 1792, all these unstable elements had begun to overturn the first revolutionary settlement and led to a second series of revolutionary changes far more radical and democratically extensive than the first.

The End of the Monarchy: A Second Revolution

EMERGENCE OF THE JACOBINS

The issues raised by the Civil Constitution of the Clergy and Louis XVI's uncertain trustworthiness undermined the unity of the newly organized nation. Factionalism plagued the Legislative Assembly throughout its short life (1791–1792). Ever since the original gathering of the Estates General, deputies from the Third Estate had organized themselves into clubs composed of politically like-minded persons. The most famous and best organized of these clubs were the **Jacobins,** whose name derived from the fact that Dominican friars were called Jacobins and the group met in a Dominican monastery in Paris. The Jacobins had also established a network of local clubs throughout the provinces. They had been the most advanced political group in the National Constituent Assembly and had pressed for a republic rather than a constitutional monarchy. Their political language and rhetoric were drawn from the most radical thought of the Enlightenment. That thought and language became all the more effective because the events of 1789 to 1791 had destroyed the old political framework, and the old monarchical political vocabulary was less and less relevant. The political language and rhetoric of a republic filled that vacuum and for a time supplied the political values of the day. The events of the summer of 1791 led to the reassertion of demands for establishing a republic.

In the Legislative Assembly, a group of Jacobins known as the *Girondists* (because many of them came from the department of the Gironde) assumed leadership.[4] They were determined to oppose the forces of counterrevolution. They passed one measure ordering the émigrés to return or suffer loss of property and another requiring the refractory clergy to support the Civil Constitution or lose their state pensions. The king vetoed both acts.

Furthermore, on April 20, 1792, the Girondists led the Legislative Assembly in declaring war on Austria, by this time governed by Francis II (r. 1792–1835) and allied to Prussia. The Girondists believed the pursuit of the war would preserve the revolution from domestic enemies and bring the most advanced revolutionaries to power. Paradoxically, Louis XVI and other monarchists also favored the war. They thought the conflict would strengthen the executive power (the monarchy). The king also entertained the hope that foreign armies might defeat French forces and restore the Old Regime. Both sides were playing dangerously foolish politics.

The war radicalized the revolution and led to what is usually called the second revolution, which overthrew the constitutional monarchy and established a republic. Both the country and the revolution seemed in danger. As early as March 1791, a group of women led by Pauline Léon had petitioned the Legislative Assembly for the right to bear arms and to fight for the protection of the revolution. (See "French Women Petition to Bear Arms.") Even before that, Léon had led an effort to allow women to serve in the National Guard. These demands to serve, voiced in the universal language of citizenship, illustrated how the words and rhetoric of the revolution could be used to challenge traditional social roles and the concept of separate social spheres for men and women. Furthermore, the pressure of war raised the possibility that the military needs of the nation could not be met if the ideal of separate spheres was honored. Once the war began, some Frenchwomen did enlist in the army and served with distinction.

Initially, the war effort went quite poorly. In July 1792, the duke of Brunswick, commander of

---

[4]The Girondists are also frequently called the Brissotins after Jacques-Pierre Brissot (1754–1793), their chief spokesperson in early 1792.

the Prussian forces, issued a manifesto promising the destruction of Paris if harm came to the French royal family. This statement stiffened support for the war and increased the already significant distrust of the king.

Late in July, under radical working-class pressure, the government of Paris passed from the elected council to a committee, or *commune*, of representatives from the sections (municipal wards) of the city. On August 10, 1792, a large Parisian crowd invaded the Tuileries palace and forced Louis XVI and Marie Antoinette to take refuge in the Legislative Assembly itself. The crowd fought with the royal Swiss guards. When Louis was finally able to call off the troops, several hundred of them and many Parisian citizens lay dead. The monarchy itself was also a casualty of that melee. Thereafter the royal family was imprisoned in comfortable quarters, but the king was allowed to perform none of his political functions. The recently established constitutional monarchy no longer had a monarch.

THE CONVENTION AND THE ROLE OF THE *SANS-CULOTTES*

The September Massacres Early in September, the Parisian crowd again made its will felt. During the first week of the month, in what are known as the September Massacres, the Paris Commune summarily executed or murdered about 1,200 people who were in the city jails. Many of these people were aristocrats or priests, but the majority were simply common criminals. The crowd had assumed the prisoners were all counterrevolutionaries.

The Paris Commune then compelled the Legislative Assembly to call for the election by universal male suffrage of a new assembly to write a democratic constitution. That body, called the **Convention** after its American counterpart of 1787, met on September 21, 1792. The previous day, the French army had halted the Prussian advance at the Battle of Valmy in eastern France. The victory of democratic forces at home had been confirmed by victory on the battlefield. As its first act, the Convention

On August 10, 1792, the Swiss Guards of Louis XVI fought Parisians who attacked the Tuileries Palace. Several hundred troops and citizens were killed, and Louis XVI and his family were forced to take refuge with the Legislative Assembly. After this event, the monarch virtually ceased to influence events in France. Jean Duplessi-Bertaux, *The Siege of the Palais des Tuileries, August 10, 1792.* Chateau, Versailles, France. Giraudon/Art Resource, N.Y.

FRENCH WOMEN PETITION TO BEAR ARMS

The issue of women serving in the revolutionary French military appeared early in the revolution. In March 1792, Pauline Léon presented a petition to the National Assembly on behalf of more than three hundred Parisian women asking the right to bear arms and train for military service for the revolution. Similar requests were made during the next two years. Some women did serve in the military, but in 1793 legislation specifically forbade women from participating in military service. The ground for that refusal was the argument that women belonged in the domestic sphere and military service would lead them to abandon family duties.

■ Citoyenne *is the feminine form of the French word for citizen. How does this petition seek to challenge the concept of citizenship in the Declaration of the Rights of Man and Citizen? How do these petitioners relate their demand to bear arms to their role as women in French society? How do the petitioners relate their demands to the use of all national resources against the enemies of the revolution?*

Patriotic women come before you to claim the right which any individual has to defend his life and liberty. . . .

We are *citoyennes* [female citizens], and we cannot be indifferent to the fate of the fatherland. . . .

Yes, Gentlemen, we need arms, and we come to ask your permission to procure them. May our weakness be no obstacle; courage and intrepidity will supplant it, and the love of the fatherland and hatred of tyrants will allow us to brave all dangers with ease. . . .

No, Gentlemen, We will [use arms] only to defend ourselves the same as you; you cannot refuse us, and society cannot deny the right nature gives us, unless you pretend the Declaration of Rights does not apply to women and that they should let their throats be cut like lambs, without the right to defend themselves. For can you believe the tyrants would spare us? . . . Why then not terrorize aristocracy and tyranny with all the resources of civic effort and the pure zeal, zeal which cold men can well call fanaticism and exaggeration, but which is

declared France a republic—that is, a nation governed by an elected assembly without a monarch.

Goals of the *Sans-culottes* The second revolution had been the work of Jacobins more radical than the Girondists and of the people of Paris known as the **sans-culottes.** The name of this group means "without breeches" and derived from the long trousers that, as working people, they wore instead of aristocratic knee breeches. The *sans-culottes* were shopkeepers, artisans, wage earners, and, in a few cases, factory workers. The persistent food shortages and the revolutionary inflation had made their difficult lives even more burdensome. The politics of the Old Regime had ignored them, and the policies of the National Constituent Assembly had left them victims of unregulated economic liberty. The government, however, required their labor and their lives if the war was to succeed. From the summer of 1792 until the summer of 1794, their attitudes, desires, and ideals were the primary factors in the in-

ternal development of the revolution. (See "A Pamphleteer Describes a *Sans-culotte*.")

The *sans-culottes* generally knew what they wanted. The Parisian tradespeople and artisans sought immediate relief from food shortages and rising prices through price controls. They believed all people have a right to subsistence and profoundly resented most forms of social inequality. This attitude made them intensely hostile to the aristocracy and the original leaders of the revolution of 1789, who they believed simply wanted to share political power, social prestige, and economic security with the aristocracy. The *sans-culottes'* hatred of inequality did not take them so far as to demand the abolition of property. Rather, they advocated a community of small property owners who would also participate in the political nation.

In politics they were antimonarchical, strongly republican, and suspicious even of representative government. They believed the people should

only the natural result of a heart burning with love for the public weal? . . .

If, for reasons we cannot guess, you refuse our just demands, these women you have raised to the ranks of *citoyennes* by granting that to their husbands, these women who have sampled the promises of liberty, who have conceived the hope of placing free men in the world, and who have sworn to live free or die—such women, I say, will never consent to concede the day to slaves; they will die first. They will uphold their oath, and a dagger aimed at their breasts will deliver them from the misfortunes of slavery! They will die, regretting not life, but the uselessness of their death; regretting moreover, not having been able to drench their hands in the impure blood of the enemies of the fatherland and to avenge some of their own!

But, Gentlemen, let us cast our eyes away from these cruel extremes. Whatever the rages and plots of aristocrats, they will not succeed in vanquishing a whole people of united brothers armed to defend their rights. We also demand only the honor of sharing their exhaustion and glorious labors and of making tyrants see that women also have blood to shed for the service of the fatherland in danger.

Gentlemen, here is what we hope to obtain from your justice and equity:

1. Permission to procure pikes, pistols, and sabres (even muskets for those who are strong enough to use them), within police regulations.
2. Permission to assemble on festival days and Sundays on the Champ de la Fédération, or in other suitable places, to practice maneuvers with these arms.
3. Permission to name the former French Guards to command us, always in conformity with the rules which the mayor's wisdom prescribes for good order and public calm.

Excerpts from Léon, "Petition to the National Assembly on Woman's Rights to Bear Arms" in *Women in Revolutionary Paris 1789–1795*, edited and translated by Darline Gay Levy, Harriet Branson Applewhite, and Mary Durham Johnson. Copyright © 1979, by the Board of Trustees of the University of Illinois. Used with permission of the University of Illinois Press.

make the decisions of government to as great an extent as possible. In Paris, where their influence was most important, the *sans-culottes* had gained their political experience in meetings of the Paris sections. Those gatherings exemplified direct community democracy and were not unlike a New England town meeting. The economic hardship of their lives made them impatient to see their demands met.

The Policies of the Jacobins The goals of the *sans-culottes* were not wholly compatible with those of the Jacobins, republicans who sought representative government. Jacobin hatred of the aristocracy and hereditary privilege did not extend to a general suspicion of wealth. Basically, the Jacobins favored an unregulated economy. From the time of Louis XVI's flight to Varennes onward, however, the more extreme Jacobins began to cooperate with leaders of the Parisian *sans-culottes* and the Paris Commune for the overthrow of the monarchy. Once the Convention began its deliberations, these Jacobins, known as the *Mountain* because of their seats high in the assembly hall, worked with the *sans-culottes* to carry the revolution forward and to win the war. This willingness to cooperate with the forces of the popular revolution separated the Mountain from the Girondists, who were also members of the Jacobin Club.

Execution of Louis XVI By the spring of 1793, several issues had brought the Mountain and its *sans-culottes* allies to domination of the Convention and the revolution. In December 1792, Louis XVI was put on trial as mere "Citizen Capet," the family name of extremely distant forebears of the royal family. The Girondists looked for some way to spare his life, but the Mountain defeated the effort. Louis was convicted, by a very narrow majority, of conspiring against the liberty of the people and the security of the state. He was condemned to death and was beheaded on January 21, 1793.

A PAMPHLETEER DESCRIBES A *SANS-CULOTTE*

This document is a 1793 description of a **sans-culotte** *written either by one or by a sympathizer. It describes the* **sans-culotte** *as a hardworking, useful, patriotic citizen who bravely sacrifices himself to the war effort. It contrasts those virtues with the lazy and unproductive luxury of the noble and the personally self-interested plottings of the politician.*

■ *What social resentments appear in this description? How could these resentments be used to create solidarity among the* **sans-culottes** *to defend the revolution? How does this document relate civic virtue to work? Do you see any relationship between the social views expressed in the document and the abolition of workers' organizations in a previous document? Where does this document suggest that the* **sans-culotte** *may need to confront enemies of the republic?*

A *sans-culotte* you rogues? He is someone who always goes on foot, who has no millions as you would all like to have, no chateaux, no valets to serve him, and who lives simply with his wife and children, if he has any, on a fourth or fifth story.

He is useful, because he knows how to work in the field, to forge iron, to use a saw, to use a file, to roof a house, to make shoes, and to shed his last drop of blood for the safety of the Republic.

And because he works, you are sure not to meet his person in the Café de Chartres, or in the gaming houses where others conspire and game; nor at the National theatre . . . nor in the literary clubs. . . .

In the evening he goes to his section, not powdered or perfumed, or smartly booted in the hope of catching the eye of the citizenesses in the galleries, but ready to support good proposals with all his might, and to crush those which come from the abominable faction of politicians.

Finally, a *sans-culotte* always has his sabre sharp, to cut off the ears of all enemies of the Revolution; sometimes he even goes out with his pike; but at the first sound of the drum he is ready to leave for the Vendée, for the army of the Alps or for the army of the North. . . .

From "Reply to an Impertinent Question: What Is a Sans-culotte?" April 1793. Reprinted in Walter Markov and Albert Soboul, eds., *Die Sansculotten von Paris*, and republished trans. by Clive Emsley in Merryn Williams, ed., *Revolutions: 1775–1830* (Baltimore: Penguin Books, in association with the Open University, 1971), pp. 100–101.

The next month, the Convention declared war on Great Britain, Holland, and Spain. Soon thereafter, the Prussians renewed their offensive and drove the French out of Belgium. To make matters worse, General Dumouriez (1739–1823), the Girondist victor of Valmy, deserted to the enemy. Finally, in March 1793, a royalist revolt led by aristocratic officers and priests erupted in the Vendée in western France and roused much popular support. Thus the revolution found itself at war with most of Europe and much of the French nation. The Girondists had led the country into the war, but had proved themselves incapable either of winning it or of suppressing the enemies of the revolution at home. The Mountain stood ready to take up the task. Every major European power was now hostile to the revolution.

Europe at War with the Revolution

Initially, the rest of Europe had been ambivalent toward the revolutionary events in France. Those people who favored political reform regarded the revolution as wisely and rationally reorganizing a corrupt and inefficient government. The major foreign governments thought that the revolution meant France would cease to be an important factor in European affairs for several years.

EDMUND BURKE ATTACKS THE REVOLUTION

In 1790, however, the Irish-born writer and British statesman Edmund Burke (1729–1799) argued a different position in *Reflections on the Revolution in France*. Burke regarded the reconstruction of French administration as the application of a blind rationalism that ignored the historical realities of political development and the complexities of social relations. He also forecast further turmoil as people without political experience tried to govern France. As the revolutionaries proceeded to attack the church, the monarchy, and finally the rest of Europe, Burke's ideas came to have many admirers. His *Reflections* and later works became the handbook of European conservatives for decades. (See "Burke Denounces the Extreme Measures of the French Revolution.")

By the outbreak of the war with Austria in April 1792, the other European monarchies recognized the danger of both the ideas and the aggression of revolutionary France. The ideals of the Rights of Man and Citizen were highly exportable and applicable to the rest of Europe. In response, one government after another turned to repressive domestic policies.

SUPPRESSION OF REFORM IN BRITAIN

In Great Britain, William Pitt the Younger (1759–1806), the prime minister, who had unsuccessfully supported moderate reform of Parliament during the 1780s, turned against both reform and popular movements. The government suppressed the London Corresponding Society, founded in 1792 as a working-class reform group. In Birmingham, the government sponsored mob action to drive Joseph Priestley (1733–1804), a famous chemist and a radical political thinker, out of the country. In early 1793, Pitt secured parliamentary approval for acts suspending *habeas corpus* and making it possible to commit treason in writing. With less success, Pitt attempted to curb freedom of the press. All political groups who dared oppose the government faced being associated with sedition.

WAR WITH EUROPE

The French invasion of the Austrian Netherlands and the revolutionary reorganization of that territory roused the rest of Europe to the point of active hostility. In November 1792, the Convention declared it would aid all peoples who wished to cast off the burdens of aristocratic and monarchical oppression. The Convention had also proclaimed the Scheldt River in the Netherlands open to the commerce of all nations and thus had violated a treaty that Great Britain had made with Austria and Holland. The British were on the point of declaring war on France over this issue

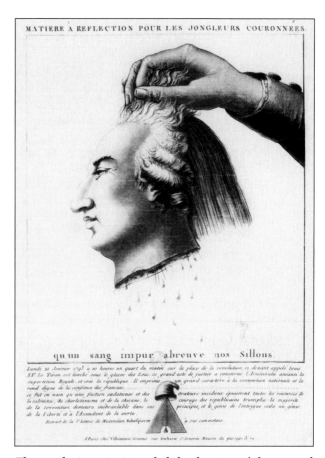

The revolutionaries intended the drawing of the severed head of Louis XVI as a warning to the other crowned heads of Europe. Cliche Bibliotheque nationale de France—Paris.

when the Convention issued its own declaration of hostilities in February 1793.

By April 1793, when the Jacobins began to direct the French government, the nation was at war with Austria, Prussia, Great Britain, Spain, Sardinia, and Holland. The governments of those nations, allied in what is known as the First Coalition, were attempting to protect their social structures, political systems, and economic interests against the aggression of the revolution.

The Reign of Terror

The outbreak of war in the winter and spring of 1793 brought new, radical political actions within France as the revolutionary government mobilized both itself and the nation for the conflict. Throughout the nation, there was the sense that a

BURKE DENOUNCES THE EXTREME MEASURES OF THE FRENCH REVOLUTION

Edmund Burke was undoubtedly the most important and articulate foreign critic of the French Revolution. His first critique, Reflections on the Revolution in France, *appeared in 1790. He continued to attack the revolution in later years. In 1796, he composed* Letters on a Regicide Peace, *which opposed a peace treaty between Great Britain and revolutionary France. In that work, he summarized what he regarded as the most fundamental evils of the revolutionary government: the execution of the king, the confiscation of property of the church and nobles, and the policy of de-Christianization.*

■ *To which of the major events in the French Revolution does Burke make reference? Why, by 1796, would Burke and others have attached so much importance to the religious policies of the revolution? Did Burke exaggerate the evils of the revolution? Who might have been persuaded by Burke's condemnation?*

A government of the nature of that set up at our very door has never been hitherto seen, or even imagined in Europe. . . . France, since her revolution, is under the sway of a sect, whose leaders have deliberately, at one stroke, demolished the whole body of that jurisprudence which France had pretty nearly in common with other civilized countries. . . .

Its foundation is laid in regicide, in Jacobinism, and in atheism, and it has joined to those principles a body of systematic manners, which secures their operation. . . .

I call a commonwealth regicide, which lays it down as a fixed law of nature, and a fundamental right of man, that all government, not being a democracy, is an usurpation. That all kings, as such, are usurpers; and for being kings may and ought to be put to death, with their wives, families, and adherents. That commonwealth which acts uniformly upon those principles . . .—this I call regicide by establishment.

Jacobinism is the revolt of the enterprising talents of a country against its property. When private men form themselves into associations for the purpose of destroying the pre-existing laws and institutions of their country; when they secure to themselves an army, by dividing amongst the people of no property the estates of the ancient and lawful proprietors, when a state recognizes those acts; when it does not make confiscations for crimes, but makes crimes for confiscations; when

it has its principal strength, and all its resources, in such a violation of property . . .—I call this Jacobinism by establishment.

I call it atheism by establishment, when any state, as such, shall not acknowledge the existence of God as a moral governor of the world; . . .—when it shall abolish the Christian religion by a regular decree;—when it shall persecute with a cold, unrelenting, steady cruelty, by every mode of confiscation, imprisonment, exile, and death, all its ministers;—when it shall generally shut up or pull down churches; when the few buildings which remain of this kind shall be opened only for the purpose of making a profane apotheosis of monsters, whose vices and crimes have no parallel amongst men. . . . When, in the place of that religion of social benevolence, and of individual self-denial, in mockery of all religion, they institute impious, blasphemous, indecent theatric rites, in honour of their vitiated, perverted reason, and erect altars to the personification of their own corrupted and bloody republic; . . . when wearied out with incessant martyrdom, and the cries of a people hungering and thirsting for religion, they permit it, only as a tolerated evil—I call this atheism by establishment.

When to these establishments of regicide, of Jacobinism, and of atheism, you add the correspondent system of manners, no doubt can be left on the mind of a thinking man concerning their determined hostility to the human race.

From *The Works of the Right Honourable Edmund Burke* (London: Henry G. Bohn, 1856), 5: 206–208.

new kind of war had erupted. In this war the major issue was not protection of national borders as such, but rather the defense of the bold new republican political and social order that had emerged during the past four years. The French people understood that the achievements of the revolution were in danger. To protect those achievements the government took extraordinary actions that touched almost every aspect of national life. In the course of this government mobilization thousands of people from all walks of life including both peasants and the king and queen were arbitrarily arrested and in many cases executed. These actions came to be known as the **Reign of Terror.**

THE REPUBLIC DEFENDED

To mobilize for war, the revolutionary government organized a collective executive in the form of powerful committees. These in turn sought to organize all French national life on a wartime footing. The result was an immense military effort dedicated to both the protection and the advancement of revolutionary ideals. Ironically, this war effort brought the suppression of many liberties within France itself and led ultimately to a destructive search for internal enemies of the revolution.

The Committee of Public Safety In April 1793, the Convention established a Committee of General Security and a Committee of Public Safety to carry out the executive duties of the government. The latter committee became more important and eventually enjoyed almost dictatorial power. The most prominent leaders of the Committee of Public Safety were Jacques Danton (1759–1794), who had provided heroic leadership in September 1792; Maximilien Robespierre (1758–1794), who became for a time the single most powerful member of the committee; and Lazare Carnot (1753–1823), who was in charge of the military. All of these men and the other figures on the committee were strong republicans who had opposed the weak policies of the Girondists. They conceived of their task as saving the revolution from mortal enemies at home and abroad. They enjoyed a working political relationship with the *sans-culottes* of Paris, but this was an alliance of expediency on the part of the committee.

The *Levée en Masse* The major problem for the Convention was to wage the war and at the same time to secure domestic support for the effort. In early June 1793, the Parisian *sans-culottes* invaded the Convention and successfully demanded the expulsion of the Girondist members. That action further radicalized the Convention and gave the Mountain complete control. On June 22, the Convention approved a fully democratic constitution, but delayed its implementation until the conclusion of the war. In point of fact, it was never implemented. On August 23, Carnot began a mobilization for victory by issuing a ***levée en masse,*** a military requisition on the entire population, conscripting males into the army and directing economic production to military purposes. (See "The French Convention Calls Up the Entire Nation.") On September 17, a ceiling on prices was established in accord with *sans-culotte* demands. During these same months, the armies of the revolution also successfully crushed many of the counterrevolutionary disturbances in the provinces.

Never before had Europe seen a nation organized in this way, nor one defended by a citizen army. Other events within France astounded Europeans even more. The Reign of Terror had begun. Those months of quasi-judicial executions and murders stretching from the autumn of 1793 to the midsummer of 1794 are probably the most famous or infamous period of the revolution. They can be understood only in the context of the war on one hand and the revolutionary expectations of the Convention and the *sans-culottes* on the other.

THE "REPUBLIC OF VIRTUE" AND ROBESPIERRE'S JUSTIFICATION OF TERROR

The presence of armies closing in on the nation made it easy to dispense with legal due process. The people who sat in the Convention and composed the Committee of Public Safety, however, did not see their actions simply in terms of expediency made necessary by war. They also believed they had created something new in world history, a "republic of virtue." In this republic, civic virtue, the sacrifice of one's self and one's interest for the good of the republic, would flourish in place of selfish aristocratic and monarchical corruption. The republic of virtue manifested itself in many ways: in the renaming of streets from the egalitarian vocabulary of the revolution; in republican dress copied from that of the *sans-culottes* or the Roman Republic; in the absence of powdered wigs; in the suppression of plays that were insufficiently republican; and in a general attack against crimes, such as prostitution, that were supposedly characteristic of aristocratic society. But the core value of the republic of virtue was the upholding of the public over the private good. It was in the name of the public

THE FRENCH CONVENTION CALLS UP THE ENTIRE NATION

This proclamation of the levée en masse, *August 23, 1793, marked the first time in European history that all citizens of a nation were called to contribute to a war effort. The decree set the entire nation on a wartime footing under the centralized direction of the Committee of Public Safety.*

■ *How did this declaration put the entire nation on a wartime footing? How does this remarkable call to patriotism and opposition to the enemies of the revolution turn extraordinary power over to the revolutionary government? How could the government believe it would receive the wartime support of the workers whose organizations it had forbidden? (See the document "The Revolutionary Government Forbids Workers' Organizations," earlier in this chapter.)*

1. From this moment until that in which the enemy shall have been driven from the soil of the Republic, all Frenchmen are in permanent requisition for the service of the armies.

   The young men shall go to battle; the married men shall forge arms and transport provisions; the women shall make tents and clothing and shall serve in the hospitals; the children shall turn old linen into lint; the aged shall betake themselves to the public places in order to arouse the courage of the warriors and preach the hatred of kings and the unity of the Republic.

2. The national buildings shall be converted into barracks, the public places into workshops for arms, the soil of the cellars shall be washed in order to extract therefrom the saltpetre.

3. The arms of the regulation calibre shall be reserved exclusively for those who shall march against the enemy; the service of the interior shall be performed with hunting pieces and side arms.

4. The saddle horses are put in requisition to complete the cavalry corps; the draught-horses, other than those employed in agriculture, shall convey the artillery and the provisions.

5. The Committee of Public Safety is charged to take all the necessary measures to set up without delay an extraordinary manufacture of arms of every sort which corresponds with the ardor and energy of the French people. . . .

6. The levy shall be general. . . .

Frank Maloy Anderson, ed. and trans., *The Constitutions and Other Select Documents Illustrative of the History of France, 1789–1907*, 2nd ed., rev. and enl. (Minneapolis: H.W. Wilson, 1908), pp. 184–185.

good that the Committee of Public Safety carried out the policies of the terror.

The person who embodied this republic of virtue defended by terror was Maximilien de Robespierre (1758–1794), who emerged as the leading figure on the Committee of Public Safety. This utterly selfless revolutionary figure has remained controversial from his day to the present. From the beginning of the revolution, he had favored a republic. The Jacobin Club provided his primary forum and base of power. A shrewd and sensitive politician, Robespierre had opposed the war in 1792 because he feared it might aid the monarchy. He depended largely on the support of the *sans-culottes* of Paris, but he continued to dress as he had before the revolution. For him, the republic of virtue meant wholehearted support of republican government and the renunciation of selfish gains from political life. As he once told the Convention,

If the mainspring of popular government in peacetime is virtue, amid revolution it is at the same time virtue and terror: virtue, without which terror is fatal; terror, without which virtue is impotent. Terror is nothing but prompt, severe, inflexible justice; it is therefore an emanation of virtue.[5]

Robespierre and those who supported his policies were among the first of a succession of secular ideologues of the left and the right who, in the

[5]Quoted in Richard T. Bienvenu, *The Ninth of Thermidor: The Fall of Robespierre* (New York: Oxford University Press, 1968), p. 38.

Maximilien Robespierre (1758–1794) emerged as the most powerful revolutionary figure in 1793 and 1794, dominating the Committee of Public Safety. He considered the Terror essential for the success of the revolution. Giraudon/Art Resource, N.Y.

name of humanity, would bring so much suffering to Europe in the following two centuries. The policies associated with terror in the name of republic virtue included the exclusion of women from active political life, the de-Christianization of France, and the use of revolutionary tribunals to dispense justice to alleged enemies of the republic.

REPRESSION OF THE SOCIETY OF REVOLUTIONARY REPUBLICAN WOMEN

Revolutionary women established their own distinct institutions during these months. In May 1793, Pauline Léon and Claire Lacombe founded the Society of Revolutionary Republican Women. Their purpose was to fight the internal enemies of the revolution. They saw themselves as militant citizens. Initially, the Jacobin leaders welcomed the organization. Its members and other women filled the galleries of the Convention to hear the debates and cheer their favorite speakers. The society became increasingly radical, however. Its members sought stricter controls on the price of food and other commodities, worked to ferret out food hoarders, and brawled with working market women thought to be insufficiently revolutionary. The women of the society also demanded the right to wear the revolutionary cockade usually worn only by male citizens. By October 1793, the Jacobins in the Convention had begun to fear the turmoil the society was causing and banned all women's clubs and societies. The debates over these decrees show that the Jacobins believed the society opposed many of their economic policies, but the deputies used the Rousseauian language of separate spheres for men and women to justify their exclusion of women from active political life.

There were other examples of repression of women in 1793. Olympe de Gouges, author of the Declaration of the Rights of Woman, opposed the

THE PARIS JACOBIN CLUB ALERTS THE NATION TO INTERNAL ENEMIES OF THE REVOLUTION

By early 1793, the revolutionary groups in Paris stood sharply divided amongst themselves. The Girondists (also known as Brissotins), who had led the nation into war, faced military reversals. General Dumouriez, a former revolutionary commander, had changed sides and was leading an army against France. At this point, on April 5, the radical Jacobin Club of Paris sent a circular to its provincial clubs, painting a dire picture of the fate of the revolution. While Dumouriez was marching against Paris, they accused members of the government and its administrators of conspiring to betray the revolution. The circular suggested that some people were cooperating with England in the war against France. The Jacobins also portrayed as counterrevolutionaries all those political figures who had opposed the execution of Louis XVI. The Paris Jacobins then called on their allies in the provinces to defend the revolution and to take vengeance against its internal enemies. The distortion of the motives of political enemies, the appeal to a possible reversal of the revolution, and the accusations of internal conspiracy served to justify the demand for justice against enemies of the revolution. The accusations embodied in this circular and the fears it sought to arouse represented the kind of thinking that informed the suspension of legal rights and due process associated with the Reign of Terror.

■ *How did the Jacobins use the war to call for actions against their own domestic political enemies? What real and imagined forces did they see threatening the revolution? How did this circular constitute a smear campaign by one group of revolutionaries against other groups? What actions did the Jacobins seek?*

Friends, we are betrayed! To arms! To arms! The terrible hour is at hand when the defenders of the *Patrie* must vanquish or bury themselves under the bloody ruins of the Republic. Frenchmen, never was your liberty in such great peril! At last our enemies have put the finishing touch to their foul perfidy, and to complete it their accomplice Dumouriez is marching on Paris. . . .

But Brothers, not all your dangers are to be found there!...You must be convinced of a grievous truth! Your greatest enemies are in your midst, they direct your operations. O Vengeance !!! . . .

Yes, brothers and friends, yes, it is in the Senate that parricidal hands tear at your vitals! Yes, the counter-revolution is in the Government . . ., in the National Convention! It is there, at the center of your security and your hope, that criminal delegates hold the threads of the web that they have woven with the horde of despots who come to butcher us! . . . It is there that a sacrilegious cabal is directed by the English court . . . and others. . . .

Let us rise! Yes, let us rise! Let us arrest all the enemies of our revolution, and all suspected persons. Let us exterminate, without pity, all conspirators, unless we wish to be exterminated ourselves. . . .

Let the departments, the districts, the municipalities, and all the popular societies unite and concur in protesting to the Convention, by dispatching thereto a veritable rain of petitions manifesting the formal wish for the immediate recall of all unfaithful members who have betrayed their duty by not wishing the death of the tyrant, and, above all, against those who have led astray so many of their colleagues. Such delegates are traitors, royalists, or fatuous men. The Republic condemns the friends of kings! . . .

Let us all unite equally to demand that the thunder of indictments be loosed against generals who are traitors to the Republic, against prevaricating ministers, against postal administrators, and against all unfaithful agents of the government. Therein lies our most salutary means of defence; but let us repel the traitors and tyrants.

The center of their conspiracy is here: it is in Paris that our perfidious enemies wish to consummate their crime. Paris, the cradle, the bulwark of liberty, is, without doubt, the place where they have sworn to annihilate the holy cause of humanity under the corpses of patriots.

From A *Documentary Survey of the French Revolution* by John Hall Stewart, © 1951. Reprinted by permission of Prentice-Hall, Inc., Upper Saddle River, NJ 07458.

Terror and accused certain Jacobins of corruption. She was tried and guillotined in November 1793. The same year, women were formally excluded from serving in the French army. They were also excluded from the galleries of the Convention. In a very real sense, the exclusion of women from public political life was a part of the establishment of the Jacobin republic of virtue, because in such a republic men would be active citizens in the military and political sphere and women would be active in the domestic sphere.

DE-CHRISTIANIZATION

The most dramatic departure of the republic of virtue, and one that illustrates the imposition of political values that would justify the Terror, was an attempt by the Convention to de-Christianize France. In November 1793, the Convention proclaimed a new calendar dating from the first day of the French Republic. There were twelve months of thirty days each, with names associated with the seasons and climate. Every tenth day, rather than every seventh, was a holiday. Many of the most important events of the next few years became known by their dates on the revolutionary calendar.[6] In November 1793, the Convention decreed the Cathedral of Notre Dame to be a "Temple of Reason." The legislature then sent trusted members, known as deputies on mission, into the provinces to enforce de-Christianization by closing churches, persecuting clergy and believers, and occasionally forcing priests to marry. This religious policy roused much opposition and deeply separated the French provinces from the revolutionary government in Paris. Robespierre personally opposed de-Christianization because he was convinced it would prove a political blunder alienating people from loyalty to the republic.

REVOLUTIONARY TRIBUNALS

The Reign of Terror manifested itself through a series of revolutionary tribunals established by the Convention during the summer of 1793. The mandate of these tribunals was to try the enemies of the republic, but the definition of "enemy" was uncertain and shifted as the months passed. It included those who might aid other European powers, those who endangered republican virtue, and, finally, good republicans who opposed the policies of the dominant faction of the government. In a very real sense, the Terror of the revolutionary tribunals systematized and channeled the popular resentment that had manifested itself in the September Massacres of 1792. Those whom the tribunals condemned in Paris were beheaded on the guillotine. Other modes of execution were used in the provinces.

The first victims of the Terror were Marie Antoinette, other members of the royal family, and some aristocrats, who were executed in October 1793. They were followed by certain Girondist politicians who had been prominent in the Legislative Assembly. These executions took place in the same weeks that the Convention had moved against the Society of Revolutionary Republican Women, whom it had also seen as endangering Jacobin control.

By the early months of 1794, the Terror had moved to the provinces, where the deputies on mission presided over the summary execution of thousands of people, most of whom were peasants, who had allegedly supported internal opposition to the revolution. One of the most infamous incidents occurred in Nantes, where several hundred people were simply tied to rafts and drowned in the river. The victims of the Terror were now coming from every social class, including the *sans-culottes*.

THE END OF THE TERROR

Revolutionaries Turn against Themselves In Paris during the late winter of 1794, Robespierre began to orchestrate the Terror against republican political figures of the left and right. On March 24, he secured the execution of certain extreme *sans-culottes* leaders known as the *enragés*. They had wanted further measures regulating prices, securing social equality, and pressing de-Christianization. Robespierre then turned against more conservative republicans, including Danton. They were accused of being insufficiently militant on the war, profiting monetarily from the revolution, and rejecting any link between politics and moral virtue. Danton was executed during the first week in April. In this fashion, Robespierre exterminated the leadership from both groups that might have threatened his position. Finally, on June 10, he secured passage of the Law of 22 Prairial, which permitted the revolutionary tribunal to convict suspects without hearing substantial evidence. The number of executions was growing steadily.

---

[6]From summer to spring, the months of the revolutionary calendar were Messidor, Thermidor, Fructidor, Vendémiaire, Brumaire, Frimaire, Nivose, Pluviose, Ventose, Germinal, Floreal, and Prairial.

On the way to her execution in 1793, Marie Antoinette was sketched from life by Jacques-Louis David as she passed his window. Jacques-Louis David, *Marie-Antoinette Taken to Her Execution.* Drawing. Bibliothèque Nationale, Paris, France. Giraudon/Art Resource, N.Y.

Fall of Robespierre In May 1794, at the height of his power, Robespierre, considering the worship of "Reason" too abstract for most citizens, abolished it and established the "Cult of the Supreme Being." This deistic cult reflected Rousseau's vision of a civic religion that would induce morality among citizens. Robespierre, however, did not long preside over his new religion. (See "The Convention Establishes the Worship of the Supreme Being.")

On July 26, Robespierre made an ill-tempered speech in the Convention, declaring that other leaders of the government were conspiring against himself and the revolution. Usually, such accusations against unnamed persons had preceded his earlier attacks. On July 27—the Ninth of Thermidor—members of the Convention, by prearrangement, shouted him down when he rose to make another speech. That night Robespierre was arrested, and the next day he was executed. The revolutionary *sans-culottes* of Paris would not save him because he had deprived them of their chief leaders. The other Jacobins turned against him because,

after Danton's death, they feared becoming the next victims. Robespierre had destroyed rivals for leadership without creating supporters for himself. In that regard, he was the selfless creator of his own destruction.

The fall of Robespierre might simply have been one more shift in the turbulent politics of the revolution. Instincts of self-preservation rather than major policy differences motivated those who brought about his demise. They had generally supported the Terror and the executions. Yet within a short time, the Reign of Terror, which ultimately claimed more than 25,000 victims, came to a close. The largest number of executions had involved peasants and *sans-culottes* who had joined rebellions against the revolutionary government. By the late summer of 1794, those provincial uprisings had been crushed, and the war against foreign enemies was also going well. These successes, combined with the feeling in Paris that the revolution had consumed enough of its own children, brought the Terror to an end.

...ENTION ESTABLISHES THE WORSHIP OF THE SUPREME BEING

...7, 1794, the Convention passed an extraordinary piece of revolutionary leg-
...t established the worship of the Supreme Being as a state cult. Although
...ew on the religious ideas of deism, the point of the legislation was to pro-
...ious basis for the new secular French state. Pay particular attention to
...hich outlines the political and civic values that the Cult of the Supreme
...pposed to nurture.

...this declaration reflect the ideas of the Enlightenment? Why has it been
...lishing a civil religion? What personal and social values was this reli-
...to nurture?

...rench people recognize the existence of the Supreme Being and the immortality of the soul.

2. They recognize that the worship worthy of the Supreme Being is the observance of the duties of man.

3. They place in the forefront of such duties de-testation of bad faith and tyranny, punishment of tyrants and traitors, succoring of unfortu-nates, respect of weak persons, defence of the oppressed, doing to others all the good that one can, and being just towards everyone.

4. Festivals shall be instituted to remind man of the concept of the Divinity and of the dignity of his being.

5. They shall take their names from the glorious events of our Revolution, or from the virtues most dear and most useful to man, or from the greatest benefits of nature. . . .

6. On the days of *décade* [the name given to a particular day in each month of the revolution-ary calendar] it shall celebrate the following festivals:
    To the Supreme Being and to nature; to the human race; to the French people; to the bene-factors of humanity; to the martyrs of liberty; to liberty and equality; to the Republic; to the liberty of the world; to the love of the *Patrie* [Fatherland]; to the hatred of tyrants and trai-tors; to truth; to justice; to modesty; to glory and immortality; to friendship; to frugality; to courage; to good faith; to heroism; to disinter-estedness; to stoicism; to love; to conjugal love; to paternal love; to maternal tenderness; to filial piety; to infancy; to youth; to man-hood; to old age; to misfortune; to agriculture; to industry; to our forefathers; to posterity; to happiness.

The Thermidorian Reaction

This tempering of the revolution, called the **Thermidorian Reaction,** began in July 1794. It con-sisted of the destruction of the machinery of terror and the institution of a new constitutional regime. It was the result of a widespread feeling that the revolution had become too radical. In particular, it displayed a weariness of the Terror and a fear the *sans-culottes* were exerting far too much political influence.

The influence of generally wealthy middle-class and professional people soon replaced that of the *sans-culottes*. Within days and weeks of Robespierre's execution, the Convention allowed the Girondists who had been in prison or hiding to return to their seats. There was a general amnesty for political prisoners. The Convention restruc-tured the Committee of Public Safety, giving it much less power, and also repealed the notorious Law of 22 Prairial. Some, though by no means all, of the people responsible for the Terror were re-moved from public life. Leaders of the Paris Com-mune and certain deputies on mission were executed. The Paris Commune itself was out-lawed. The Paris Jacobin Club was closed, and Ja-cobin clubs in the provinces were forbidden to correspond with each other.

The Festival of the Supreme Being, which took place in June 1794, inaugurated Robespierre's new civic religion. Its climax occurred when a statue of Atheism was burned and another statue of Wisdom rose from the ashes. Pierre-Antoine Demachy, *Festival of the Supreme Being at the Champ de Mars on June 8, 1794.* Musée de la Ville de Paris, Musée Carnavalet, Paris, France. Giraudon/Art Resource, N.Y.

The executions of former terrorists marked the beginning of "the white terror." Throughout the country, people who had been involved in the Reign of Terror were attacked and often murdered. Jacobins were executed with little more due process than they had extended to their victims a few months earlier. The Convention itself approved some of these trials. In other cases, gangs of youths who had aristocratic connections or who had avoided serving in the army roamed the streets, beating known Jacobins. In Lyons, Toulon, and Marseilles, these "bands of Jesus" dragged suspected terrorists from prisons and murdered them much as alleged royalists had been murdered during the September Massacres of 1792.

The republic of virtue gave way, if not to one of vice, at least to one of frivolous pleasures. The dress of the *sans-culottes* and the Roman Republic disappeared among the middle class and the aristocracy. New plays appeared in the theaters, and prostitutes again roamed the streets of Paris. Families of victims of the Reign of Terror gave parties in which they appeared with shaved necks, like the victims of the guillotine, and with red ribbons tied about them. Although the Convention continued to favor the Cult of the Supreme Being, it allowed Catholic services to be held. Many refractory priests returned to the country. One of the unanticipated results of the Thermidorian Reaction was a genuine revival of Catholic worship.

The Thermidorian Reaction also saw the repeal of legislation that had been passed in 1792 making divorce more equitable for women. As this suggests, the reaction did not result in any extension of women's rights or improvement in women's education. The Thermidorians and their successors had seen enough attempts at political and social change. They sought to return family life to its status before the outbreak of the revolution. Political authorities and the church articulated a firm determination to reestablish separate spheres for men and women and to reinforce traditional gender roles. As a result, Frenchwomen may have had somewhat less freedom after 1795 than before 1789.

ESTABLISHMENT OF THE DIRECTORY

The Thermidorian Reaction involved further political reconstruction. The fully democratic constitution of 1793, which had never gone into effect, was abandoned. In its place, the Convention issued the Constitution of the Year III, which reflected the Thermidorian determination to reject both constitutional monarchy and democracy. The new document provided for a legislature of two houses. Members of the upper body, or Council of Elders, were to be men over forty years of age who were either husbands or widowers. The lower Council of Five Hundred was to consist of men of at least thirty who were either married or single. The executive body was to be a five-person Directory chosen by the Elders from a list submitted by the Council of Five Hundred. Property qualifications limited the franchise, except for soldiers, who, though without property, were permitted to vote.

The term *Thermidor* has come to be associated with political reaction. If the French Revolution had originated in political conflicts characteristic of the eighteenth century, by 1795 it had become something very different. A political structure and a society based on rank and birth had given way to a political system based on civic equality and social status based on property ownership. People who had never been allowed direct, formal access to political power had, to different degrees, been granted it. Their entrance into political life had given rise to questions of property distribution and economic regulations that could not again be ignored. Representation had been established as a principle of politics. Henceforth, the question before France and eventually before all of Europe would be which new groups would be permitted representation. In the *levée en masse*, the French had demonstrated to Europe the power of the secular ideal of nationhood.

The post-Thermidorian course of the French Revolution did not void these stunning changes in the political and social contours of Europe. What triumphed in the Constitution of the Year III was the revolution of the holders of property. For this reason the French Revolution has often been considered a victory of the bourgeoisie, or middle class. The property that won the day, however, was not industrial wealth, but the wealth stemming from commerce, the professions, and land. The largest new propertied class to emerge from the revolutionary turmoil was the peasantry, who, as a result of the destruction of aristocratic privileges, now owned their land. And unlike peasants liberated from traditional landholding in other parts of Europe during the next century, French peasants had to pay no monetary compensation.

REMOVAL OF THE SANS-CULOTTES FROM POLITICAL LIFE

The most decisively reactionary element in the Thermidorian Reaction and the new constitution was the removal of the *sans-culottes* from political life. With the war effort succeeding, the Convention severed its ties with the *sans-culottes*. True to their belief in an unregulated economy, the Thermidorians repealed the ceiling on prices. As a result, the winter of 1794–1795 brought the worst food shortages of the period. There were many food riots, which the Convention put down with force to prove that the era of the *sans-culottes journées* had come to a close. Royalist agents, who aimed to restore the monarchy, tried to take advantage of their discontent. On October 5, 1795—13 Vendémiaire—the sections of Paris led by the royalists rose up against the Convention. The government turned the artillery against the royalist rebels. A general named Napoleon Bonaparte (1769–1821) commanded the cannon, and with a "whiff of grapeshot" he dispersed the crowd.

By treaties of Basel in March and June 1795, the Convention concluded peace with Prussia and Spain. The legislators, however, feared a resurgence of both radical democrats and royalists in the upcoming elections for the Council of Five Hundred. Consequently, the Convention ruled that at least two-thirds of the new legislature must have been members of the older body. The Thermidorians did not even trust the property owners as voters.

The newly established Directory again faced social unrest. During the spring of 1796 in Paris, Gracchus Babeuf (1760–1797) led the Conspiracy of Equals. He and his followers called for more radical democracy and for more equality of property. They declared at one point, "The aim of the French Revolution is to destroy inequality and to re-establish the general welfare. . . . The Revolution is not complete, because the rich monopolize all the property and govern exclusively, while the poor toil like slaves, languish in misery, and count for nothing in the state."[7] In a sense, they were correct. The Directory fully intended to resist any further social changes in France that might endanger property. Babeuf was arrested and the next year tried and executed. This minor plot

---

[7]Quoted in John Hall Stewart, *A Documentary Survey of the French Revolution* (New York: Macmillan, 1966), pp. 656–657.

The French Revolution

1787	
February–May	Unsuccessful negotiations with the Assembly of Notables
1788	
August 8	Louis XVI summons the Estates General
December 27	Approval of doubling of the Third Estate membership
1789	
May 5	The Estates General opens at Versailles
June 17	The Third Estate declares itself the National Assembly
June 20	The National Assembly takes the Tennis Court Oath
July 14	Fall of the Bastille in the city of Paris
Late July	The Great Fear spreads in the countryside
August 4	The nobles surrender their feudal rights at a meeting of the National Constituent Assembly
August 27	Declaration of the Rights of Man and Citizen
October 5–6	Parisian women march to Versailles and force Louis XVI and his family to return to Paris
1790	
July 12	Civil Constitution of the Clergy adopted
July 14	A new political constitution is accepted by the king
1791	
June 14	Chapelier Law
June 20–24	Louis XVI and his family attempt to flee France and are stopped at Varennes
August 27	The Declaration of Pillnitz
October 1	The Legislative Assembly meets
1792	
April 20	France declares war on Austria
August 10	The Tuileries palace is stormed, and Louis XVI takes refuge with the Legislative Assembly

September 2–7	The September Massacres
September 20	France wins the Battle of Valmy
September 21	The Convention meets, and the monarchy is abolished
1793	
January 21	King Louis XVI is executed
February 1	France declares war on Great Britain
March	Counterrevolution breaks out in the Vendée
April	The Committee of Public Safety is formed
June 22	The Constitution of 1793 is adopted, but not implemented
July	Robespierre enters the Committee of Public Safety
August 23	*Levée en masse* proclaimed
September 17	Maximum prices set on food and other commodities
October 16	Queen Marie Antoinette is executed
October 30	Women's societies and clubs banned
November 10	The Cult of Reason is proclaimed; the revolutionary calendar, beginning on September 22, 1792, is adopted
1794	
March 24	Execution of the leaders of the *sans-culottes* known as the *enragés*
April 6	Execution of Danton
May 7	Cult of the Supreme Being proclaimed
June 8	Robespierre leads the celebration of the Festival of the Supreme Being
June 10	The Law of 22 Prairial is adopted
July 27	The Ninth of Thermidor and the fall of Robespierre
July 28	Robespierre is executed
1795	
August 22	The Constitution of the Year III is adopted, establishing the Directory
1796	
May 10	Babeuf's Conspiracy of Equals
1799	
November 9	End of the Directory by Napoleon's (8 Brumaire) coup d'état

became famous many decades later, when European socialists attempted to find their historical roots in the French Revolution.

The suppression of the *sans-culottes*, the narrow franchise of the constitution, the rule of the two-thirds, and the Catholic royalist revival presented the Directory with problems that it never succeeded in overcoming. It lacked any broad base of meaningful political support. It particularly required active loyalty because France remained at war with Austria and Great Britain. Consequently, the Directory came to depend on the power of the army, rather than on constitutional processes, for governing the country. All the soldiers could vote. Moreover, within the army, created and sustained by the revolution, were officers who were eager for power and ambitious for political conquest. The results of the instability of the Directory and the growing role of the army held profound consequences not only for France but for the entire Western world.

IN PERSPECTIVE

The French Revolution is the central political event of modern European history. It unleashed political and social forces that shaped events in Europe and much of the rest of the world for the next two centuries. The revolution began with a clash between the monarchy and the nobility. Once the Estates General gathered, however, discontent could not be contained within the traditional boundaries of eighteenth-century political life. The Third Estate, in all of its diversity, demanded real influence in government. Initially, that meant the participation of middle-class members of the Estates General, but quite soon the people of Paris and the peasants of the countryside made their demands known. Thereafter, popular nationalism exerted itself on French political life and the destiny of Europe.

Revolutionary legislation and popular uprisings in Paris, the countryside, and other cities transformed the social as well as the political life of the nation. Nobles surrendered traditional social privileges. The church saw its property confiscated and its operations brought under state control. For a time, there was an attempt to de-Christianize the nation. Vast amounts of landed property changed hands, and France became a nation of peasant landowners. Urban workers lost much of the protection they had enjoyed under the guilds and became much more subject to the forces of the marketplace.

Great violence accompanied many of the revolutionary changes. The Reign of Terror took the lives of thousands. France also found itself at war with virtually all of the rest of Europe. Resentment, fear, and a new desire for stability brought the Terror to an end. That desire for stability, combined with a determination to defeat the foreign enemies of the revolution and to carry it abroad, would in turn work to the advantage of the army. Eventually, Napoleon Bonaparte would claim leadership in the name of stability and national glory.

Gracchus Babeuf was executed in 1797 for leading the "Conspiracy of Equals," a radical plot to overthrow the Directory and redistribute property among all French citizens. © Michael Nicholson/Corbis

REVIEW QUESTIONS

1. It has been said that France was a rich nation with an impoverished government. Explain this statement. How did the financial weaknesses of the French monarchy lay the foundations of the revolution of 1789?

2. Discuss the role of Louis XVI in the French Revolution. What were some of his most serious mistakes? Had he been a more able ruler, could the French Revolution have been avoided? Might a constitutional monarchy have succeeded? Or did the revolution ultimately have little to do with the competence of the monarch?

3. How was the Estates General transformed into the National Assembly? How does the Declaration of the Rights of Man and Citizen reflect the social and political values of the eighteenth-century Enlightenment? What were the chief ways in which France and its government were reorganized in the early years of the revolution? Why has the Civil Constitution of the Clergy been called the greatest blunder of the National Assembly?

4. Why were some political factions dissatisfied with the constitutional settlement of 1791? What was the revolution of 1792 and why did it occur? Who were the *sans-culottes*, and how did they become a factor in the politics of the period? How influential were they during the Terror in particular? Why did the *sans-culottes* and the Jacobins cooperate at first? Why did that cooperation end?

5. Why did France go to war with Austria in 1792? What were the benefits and drawbacks for France of fighting an external war while in the midst of a domestic political revolution? What were the causes of the Terror? How did the rest of Europe react to the French Revolution and the Terror?

6. A motto of the French Revolution was "equality, liberty, and fraternity." How did the revolution both support and violate this motto? Did French women benefit from the revolution? Did French peasants benefit from it?

SUGGESTED READINGS

K. M. BAKER, *Inventing the French Revolution: Essays on French Political Culture in the Eighteenth Century* (1990). Influential essays on political thought before and during the revolution.

K. M. BAKER AND C. LUCAS (EDS.), *The French Revolution and the Creation of Modern Political Culture*, 3 vols. (1987). A splendid collection of important original articles on all aspects of politics during the revolution.

T. C. W. BLANNING (ED.), *The Rise and Fall of the French Revolution* (1996). A wide-ranging collection of essays illustrating the recent interpretive debates.

J. R. CENSER AND L. HUNT, *Liberty, Equality, Fraternity: Exploring the French Revolution* (2001). A major survey with numerous douments available through a CD-ROM disk.

R. COBB, *The People's Armies* (1987). The best treatment in English of the revolutionary army.

W. DOYLE, *The French Revolution* (2001). A solid brief introduction.

K. EPSTEIN, *The Genesis of German Conservatism* (1966). Remains a major study of antiliberal forces in Germany before and during the revolution.

F. FURET, *Revolutionary France, 1770–1880* (1988). An important survey by a historian who argues the revolution must be seen in the perspective of an entire century.

C. HESSE, *Publishing and Cultural Politics in Revolutionary Paris* (1991). Probes the world of print culture during the French Revolution.

P. HIGONNET, *Goodness beyond Virtue: Jacobins During the French Revolution* (1998). An outstanding work that clearly relates political values to political actions.

E. KENNEDY, *A Cultural History of the French Revolution* (1989). An important examination of the role of the arts, schools, clubs, and intellectual institutions.

M. KENNEDY, *The Jacobin Clubs in the French Revolution: The First Years* (1982). A careful scrutiny of the organizations chiefly responsible for the radicalizing of the revolution.

M. KENNEDY, *The Jacobin Clubs in the French Revolution: The Middle Years* (1988). A continuation of the previously listed study.

G. LEFEBVRE, *The French Revolution*, 2 vols. (1962–1964). The leading study of the scholar noted for his subtle class interpretation of the revolution.

D. G. LEVY, H. B. APPLEWHITE, AND M. D. JOHNSON (EDS. AND TRANS.), *Women in Revolutionary Paris, 1789–1795* (1979). A remarkable collection of documents on the subject.

S. E. MELZER AND L. W. RABINE (EDS.), *Rebel Daughters: Women and the French Revolution* (1992). A collection of essays exploring various aspects of the role and image of women in the French Revolution.

C. C. O'BRIEN, *The Great Melody: A Thematic Biography of Edmund Burke* (1992). The best recent biography.

M. OZOUF, *Festivals and the French Revolution* (1988). A pioneering study of the role of public festivals in the revolution.

R. R. PALMER, *The Age of Democratic Revolution: A Political History of Europe and America, 1760–1800*, 2 vols. (1959, 1964). Still an impressive survey of the political turmoil in the transatlantic world.

C. PROCTOR, *Women, Equality, and the French Revolution* (1990). An examination of how the ideas of the Enlightenment and the attitudes of revolutionaries affected the legal status of women.

W. J. SEWELL, JR., *A Rhetoric of Bourgeois Revolution: The Abbé Siéyès and What Is the Third Estate* (1994). An important study of the political thought of Siéyès.

T. TACKETT, *Becoming a Revolutionary: The Deputies of the French National Assembly and the Emergence of a Revolutionary Culture (1789–1790)* (1996). The best study of the early months of the revolution.

T. TACKETT, *Religion, Revolution, and Regional Culture in Eighteenth-Century France: The Ecclesiastical Oath of 1791* (1986). The most important study of this topic.

D. K. Van Kley, *The Religious Origins of the French Revolution: From Calvin to the Civil Constitution, 1560–1791* (1996). Examines the manner in which debates within French Catholicism influenced the coming of the revolution.

M. Walzer (ed.), *Regicide and Revolution: Speeches at the Trial of Louis XVI* (1974). An important and exceedingly interesting collection of documents with a useful introduction.

DOCUMENTS CD-ROM

The French Revolution

19.1 The Declaration of the Rights of Man and Citizen
19.2 "Declaration of the Rights of Women and the Female Citizen"
19.3 Petition of Women of the Third Estate
19.4 Robespierre: Justification of Terror
19.5 Louis XVI: *A Royal Reform Proposal, 1787*
19.6 Edmund Burke: *The Moral Imagination*

Jacques-Louis David Champions Republican Values: *Lictors Bringing to Brutus the Bodies of His Sons*

Jacques-Louis David (1748–1825) was the foremost French painter of the late eighteenth and early nineteenth centuries. Much of his art is associated with the movement called *neoclassicism,* which constituted a return to themes and topics drawn from antiquity and the copying in painting, sculpture, and architecture of major elements of classical models. Figures in such paintings rarely suggest movement and often seem to stand in a kind of tableau illustrating a moral theme. These paintings were didactic rather than emotional or playful. They usually pertained in some manner to public life or public morals, rather than to family life or daily routine. David was strongly critical of the Old Regime and used ancient republican themes in his paintings to point to the corruption of the current monarchical government.

David began the painting of *Lictors Bringing to Brutus the Bodies of His Sons* in 1789, before the revolutionary events of that year, but completed it only after the National Assembly had proclaimed itself. The work, which covers a very large canvas, though painted in literally the last days of Old-Regime France, conveys many of the political values and implies a social critique associated with the French Revolution itself.

The painting illustrates a famous incident in the history of republican Rome. Brutus, not to be confused with the later Brutus associated with the assassination of Julius Ceasar, had been instrumental in banishing the last king of Rome. He then became one of the two consuls of the newly formed Roman Republic. Shortly thereafter, his two sons, Titus and Tiberius, became involved in an effort to restore the exiled king, who was a relative of their mother. Once the conspiracy was uncovered, Brutus, in his capacity as Consul, ordered and witnessed the execution of his sons who had betrayed the republic. This story, which formed the background for a famous play by Voltaire earlier in the century, embodied the concept of selfless republican patriotism as a virtue higher than ties to family. During the French revolution itself, Brutus assumed the status of a kind of cult figure who had opposed tyrannical kings.

David portrays the moment when the Lictors return the bodies of the two sons to Brutus's household. The painting has been described as "an interrogation of the idea of civic virtue" through its portrayal of the differing reactions of the parents.[8] David clearly illustrates the concept of separate spheres for men and women, which he may well have derived from Rousseau, a champion of the virtue of the ancient republics. The painting is sharply divided into an active male sphere on the left and a passive female sphere on the right. The male portion of the painting includes the world of politics, civic action, and republican virtue based on the rational values of law symbolized by the document in Brutus's hand.

The female portion of the painting depicts the mother and sisters of the executed sons, as well as a nurse, in various states of emotional distress, illustrating their presumed incapacity to place civic virtue above private family feelings. The basket, wool, and shears on the table, which form a still life within this large history painting, represent the domestic sphere of the daily routine of women. Moreover, their mother, according to Livy, had led the sons into the royalist conspiracy. It has been suggested that a royalist fleur-de-lis appears in the cloth in the basket.

Brutus appears alone, separated from his family and from all other human emotions except dedication to the Roman Republic itself. The presence of the statue portraying the legend of Romulus and Remus suckled by the wolf symbolizes the manner in which the Roman Republic, at its origin, stood

---

[8]Thomas Crow, *Emulation: Making Artists for Revolutionary France* (New Haven, CT: Yale University Press, 1995), p. 108.

Jacques-Louis David (1748–1825), *Lictors Bringing to Brutus the Bodies of His Sons.*
1789.   Oil on canvas, 323 × 422 cm. Inv. 3693. Louvre, Paris, France. Copyright Erich Lessing/Art Resource, N.Y.

distinct from family life. Through this symbolism, David suggests that family loyalties and female influence stand in opposition to republican virtue. Indeed, loyalty to abstract political principles separated from human sympathies mark the years of the Terror, when revolutionary leaders often appealed directly to the experience of the ancient republics.

David himself was one of the great political survivors of the revolutionary era. He painted many of its events, became a strong Jacobin, was imprisoned for a time, and then emerged into public life to portray most of the major events of Napoleon's career. Under the restoration, he spent the end of his life in exile.

Robert Rosenblum and H. W. Janson, *Nineteenth-Century Art* (Englewood Cliffs, NJ and New York: Prentice Hall: Harry N. Abrams, 1984), pp. 24–50; Albert Boime, *Art in an Age of Revolution, 1750–1800* (Chicago: University of Chicago Press, 1987, pp. 417–421); Norman Bryson, *Looking at the Overlooked: Four Essays on Still Life Painting* (Cambridge, MA: Harvard University Press, 1900), pp. 156–158; and Thomas Crow, *Emulation: Making Artists for Revolutionary France* (New Haven, CT: Yale University Press, 1995).

■ *What were the features of the neoclassical movement and how does David's* Lictors *reflect them? How does the subject of this painting foreshadow the French Revolution? What is David saying in this painting about women and their role in society and the state?*

665

This portrait of Napoleon on his throne by Jean Ingres (1780–1867) shows him in the
splendor of an imperial monarch who embodies the total power of the state. Erich Lessing/
Art Resource, N.Y.

CHAPTER 20

THE AGE OF NAPOLEON AND THE TRIUMPH OF ROMANTICISM

*B*Y THE LATE 1790S, THE *French people, especially property owners, who now included the peasants, longed for stability. The Directory was not providing it. Only the army was able to take charge of the nation as a symbol of both order and the popular values of the revolution. The most politically astute general was Napoleon Bonaparte, who had been a radical during the early revolution, a victorious commander in Italy, and a supporter of the repression of revolutionary disturbances after Thermidor.*

Once in power, Napoleon consolidated many of the achievements of the revolution. He also repudiated much of it by establishing an empire. Thereafter, his ambitions drew France into wars of conquest and liberation throughout the Continent. For over a decade Europe was at war, with only brief periods of armed truce. In leading the French armies across the Continent, Napoleon spread many of the ideas and institutions of the revolution and overturned much of the old political and social order. He also provoked popular nationalism in opposition to his conquest. This new force and the great alliances that arose against France eventually defeated Napoleon.

Throughout these Napoleonic years, new ideas and sensibilities, known by the term romanticism, *grew across Europe. Many of the ideas had originated in the eighteenth century, but they flourished in the turmoil of the French Revolution and the Napoleonic Wars. The revolution spurred the imagination of poets, painters, and philosophers. Some romantic ideas, such as nationalism, supported the revolution; others, such as the emphasis on history and religion, opposed its values.*

KEY TOPICS

- Napoleon's rise, his coronation as emperor, and his administrative reforms
- Napoleon's conquests, the creation of a French Empire, and Britain's enduring resistance
- The invasion of Russia and Napoleon's decline
- The reestablishment of a European order at the Congress of Vienna
- Romanticism and the reaction to the Enlightenment
- Islam and Romanticism

The Rise of Napoleon Bonaparte

The chief danger to the Directory came from the royalists, who hoped to restore the Bourbon monarchy by legal means. Many of the émigrés had returned to France. Their plans for a restoration drew support from devout Catholics and from those citizens disgusted by the excesses of the revolution. Monarchy seemed to promise stability. The spring elections of 1797 replaced most incumbents with constitutional monarchists and their sympathizers, thus giving them a majority.

To preserve the republic and prevent a peaceful restoration of the Bourbons, the antimonarchist Directory staged a coup d'état on 18 Fructidor (September 4, 1797). They put their own supporters into the legislative seats won by their opponents. They then imposed censorship and exiled some of their enemies. At the request of the Directors, Napoleon Bonaparte, the general in charge of the Italian campaign, had sent one of his subordinates to Paris to guarantee the success of the coup. In 1797, as in 1795, the army and Bonaparte had saved the day for the government installed in the wake of the Thermidorian Reaction.

Napoleon Bonaparte was born in 1769 to a poor family of lesser nobles at Ajaccio, Corsica. Because France had annexed Corsica in 1768, he went to French schools and in 1785 obtained a commission as a French artillery officer. He favored the revolution and was a fiery Jacobin. In 1793, he played a leading role in recovering the port of Toulon from the British. As a reward for his service, he was appointed a brigadier general. During the Thermidorian Reaction his defense of the new regime on 13 Vendémiaire won him a command in Italy.

EARLY MILITARY VICTORIES

By 1795, French arms and diplomacy had shattered the enemy coalition, but France's annexation of Belgium guaranteed continued fighting with Britain and Austria. The attack on Italy aimed to deprive Austria of Lombardy. In a series of lightning victories, Bonaparte crushed the Austrian and Sardinian armies. On his own initiative, and against the wishes of the government in Paris, he concluded the Treaty of Campo Formio in October 1797. The treaty took Austria out of the war and crowned Napoleon's campaign with success. Before long, France dominated all of Italy and Switzerland.

In November 1797, the triumphant Bonaparte returned to Paris as a hero and to confront France's only remaining enemy, Britain. He judged it impossible to cross the channel and invade England at that time. Instead, he chose to attack British interests through the eastern Mediterranean by capturing Egypt from the Ottoman Empire. By this strategy, he hoped to drive the British fleet from the Mediterranean, cut off British communications with India, damage British trade, and threaten the British Empire.

Napoleon overran Egypt, but the invasion was a failure. Admiral Horatio Nelson (1758–1805) destroyed the French fleet at Abukir on August 1, 1798. The French army was cut off from France. To make matters worse, the situation in Europe was deteriorating. The invasion of Egypt had alarmed Russia, which had its own ambitions in the Near East. The Russians, the Austrians, and the Ottomans joined Britain to form the Second Coalition. In 1799, the Russian and Austrian armies defeated the French in Italy and Switzerland and threatened to invade France.

Napoleon's venture into Egypt in 1798 and 1799 marked the first major west European assault on the Ottoman Empire. It occurred less than a quarter century after Russia under Catherine the Great had taken control of the Crimea in the Treaty of Kuchuk-Kainardji. (See Chapter 18.) Significantly British, not Ottoman forces, drove the French out of Egypt. As we see in Chapter 23, after Napoleon's invasion the Ottoman Empire came to understand it must undertake reforms if it was to resist other European encroachments.

THE CONSTITUTION OF THE YEAR VIII

Economic troubles and the dangerous international situation eroded the Directory's fragile support. One of the Directors, the Abbé Siéyès (1748–1836), proposed a new constitution. The author of the pamphlet *What Is the Third Estate?* (1789) wanted an executive body independent of the whims of electoral politics, a government based on the principle of "confidence from below, power from above." The change would require another coup d'état with military support. News of France's misfortunes had reached Napoleon in Egypt. Without orders and leaving his army behind, he returned to France in October 1799 to popular acclaim. Soon he joined Siéyès. On 19 Brumaire (November 10, 1799), his troops ensured the success of the coup.

Siéyès appears to have thought that Napoleon could be used and then dismissed, but he misjudged his man. The proposed constitution divided executive authority among three consuls. Bonaparte quickly pushed it and Siéyès aside, and in December 1799, he issued the Constitution of the Year VIII. Behind a screen of universal male suffrage that suggested democratic principles, a complicated system of checks and balances that appealed to republican theory, and a Council of State that evoked memories of Louis XIV, the new constitution established the rule of one man—the First Consul, Bonaparte. To find an appropriate historical analogy, we must go back to Caesar, Augustus, and the Greek tyrants. The career of Bonaparte, however, pointed forward to the dictators of the twentieth century. He was the first modern political figure to use the rhetoric of revolution and nationalism, to back it with military force, and to combine those elements into a mighty weapon of imperial expansion in the service of his own power.

The Consulate in France (1799–1804)

Establishing the **Consulate** in effect ended the revolution in France. The leading elements of the Third Estate—that is, officials, landowners, doctors, lawyers, and financiers—had achieved most of their goals by 1799. They had abolished hereditary privilege, and the careers thus opened to talent allowed them to achieve wealth, status, and security for their property. The peasants were also satisfied. They had gained the land they had always wanted and had destroyed oppressive feudal privileges. The newly established dominant classes had little or no desire to share their new privileges with the lower social orders. Bonaparte seemed just the person to give them security. When he submitted his constitution to the voters in a plebiscite, they overwhelmingly approved it. (See "Napoleon Describes Conditions Leading to the Consulate.")

SUPPRESSING FOREIGN ENEMIES AND DOMESTIC OPPOSITION

Bonaparte justified the public's confidence by making peace with France's enemies. Russia had already left the Second Coalition. A campaign in Italy brought another victory over Austria at Marengo in 1800. The Treaty of Luneville early in 1801 took Austria out of the war. Britain was now alone and, in 1802, concluded the Treaty of Amiens, which brought peace to Europe.

In this early-nineteenth-century cartoon, England, personified by a caricature of William Pitt, and France, personified by a caricature of Napoleon, are carving out their areas of interest around the globe. Bildarchiv Preussischer Kulturbesitz

NAPOLEON DESCRIBES CONDITIONS LEADING TO THE CONSULATE

In late 1799 various political groups in France became convinced that the constitution that had established the Directory could not allow France to achieve military victory. They also feared domestic unrest and new outbreaks of the radicalism that had characterized the French Revolution during the mid-1790s. With the aid of such groups Napoleon Bonaparte seized power in Paris in November 1799. Thereafter, under various political arrangements he governed France until 1814. He later gave his own version of the situation that brought him to power.

■ *What are the factors that Napoleon outlines as having created a situation in which the government of France required change? In his narration how does he justify the use of military force? How does he portray himself as a savior of political order and liberty?*

On my return to Paris I found division among all authorities, and agreement upon only one point, namely, that the Constitution was half destroyed and was unable to save liberty.

All parties came to me, confided to me their designs, disclosed their secrets, and requested my support; I refused to be a man of a party.

The Council of elders summoned me; I answered its appeal. A plan of general restoration had been devised by men whom the nation has been accustomed to regard as defenders of liberty, equality, and property; this plan required an examination, calm, free, exempt from all influence and all fear. Accordingly, the Council of Elders resolved upon the removal of the Legislative Body to Saint-Cloud; it gave me the responsibility of disposing the force necessary for its independence. I believed it my duty to my fellow citizens, to the soldiers perishing in our armies, to the national glory acquired at the cost of their blood, to accept the command. . . .

I presented myself to the Council of Five Hundred, alone, unarmed, my head uncovered, just as the Elders had received and applauded me; I came to remind the majority of its wishes, and to assure it of its power.

The stilettos which menaced the deputies were instantly raised against their liberator; twenty assassins threw themselves upon me and aimed at my breast. The grenadiers of the Legislative Body whom I had left at the door of the hall ran forward, placed themselves between the assassins and myself. One of these brave grenadiers had his clothes pieced by a stiletto. They bore me out.

At the same moment cries of "Outlaw" were raised against the defender of the law. It was the fierce cry of assassins against the power destined to repress them.

They crowded around the president, uttering threats, arms in their hands; they commanded him to outlaw me. I was informed of this; I ordered him to be rescued from their fury, and six grenadiers of the Legislative Body secured him. Immediately afterwards some grenadiers of the Legislative Body charged into the hall and cleared it.

The factions, intimidated, dispersed and fled. . . .

Frenchmen, you will doubtless recognize in this conduct the zeal of a soldier of liberty, a citizen devoted to the Republic. Conservative, tutelary, and liberal ideas have been restored to their rights through the dispersal of the rebels who oppressed the Councils. . . .

From *A Documentary Survey of the French Revolution* by Stewart, John Hall, © 1951. Reprinted by permission of Prentice-Hall, Inc., Upper Saddle River, N.J.

Bonaparte also restored peace and order at home. He used generosity, flattery, and bribery to win over enemies. He issued a general amnesty and employed men from all political factions. He required only that they be loyal to him. Some of the highest offices were occupied by men who had been radicals during the Reign of Terror, or who had fled the Terror and favored constitutional monarchy, or who had been high officials under Louis XVI.

Bonaparte was ruthless in suppressing opposition, however. He established a highly centralized administration in which prefects responsible to the government in Paris managed all departments. He employed secret police. He stamped out the royalist rebellion in the west and made the rule of Paris effective in Brittany and the Vendée for the first time in years.

Napoleon also used and invented opportunities to destroy his enemies. When a plot on his life surfaced in 1804, he used it as an excuse to attack the Jacobins, though it was the work of the royalists. Also in 1804, he violated the sovereignty of the German state of Baden to seize the Bourbon duke of Enghien (1772–1804). The duke was accused of participation in a royalist plot and shot, though Bonaparte knew him to be innocent. The action was a flagrant violation of international law and of due process. Charles Maurice de Talleyrand-Périgord (1754–1838), Bonaparte's foreign minister, later termed the act "worse than a crime—a blunder" because it provoked foreign opposition. But it was popular with the former Jacobins, for it seemed to preclude the possibility of a Bourbon restoration. The executioner of a Bourbon was not likely to restore the royal family. The execution also seems to have put an end to royalist plots.

CONCORDAT WITH THE ROMAN CATHOLIC CHURCH

A major obstacle to internal peace was the steady hostility of French Catholics. Refractory clergy continued to advocate counterrevolution. In 1801, to the shock and dismay of his anticlerical supporters, Napoleon concluded a concordat with Pope Pius VII (r. 1800–1823). The settlement gave Napoleon what he most wanted. The agreement required both the refractory clergy and those who had accepted the revolution to resign. Their replacements received their spiritual investiture from the pope, but the state named the bishops and paid their salaries and the salary of one priest in each parish. In return, the church gave up its claims on its confiscated property.

The concordat declared, "Catholicism is the religion of the great majority of French citizens." This was merely a statement of fact and fell far short of what the pope had wanted: religious dominance for the Roman Catholic Church. The clergy had to swear an oath of loyalty to the state. The Organic Articles of 1802, which were actually distinct from the concordat, established the supremacy of state over church. Similar laws were applied to the Protestant and Jewish communities as well, reducing still further the privileged position of the Catholic Church. (See "Napoleon Makes Peace with the Papacy.")

THE NAPOLEONIC CODE

In 1802, a plebiscite ratified Napoleon as consul for life, and he soon produced another constitution that granted him what amounted to full power. He thereafter set about reforming and codifying French law. The result was the Civil Code of 1804, usually known as the Napoleonic Code.

The Napoleonic Code safeguarded all forms of property and tried to secure French society against internal challenges. All the privileges based on birth that had been overthrown during the revolution remained abolished. Employment of salaried officials chosen on the basis of merit replaced the purchase of offices.

The conservative attitudes toward labor and women that had emerged during the revolution also received full support. Workers' organizations remained forbidden, and workers had fewer rights than their employers. Fathers were granted extensive control over their children and husbands over their wives. However, primogeniture remained abolished, and property was distributed among all children, males and females. But married women could dispose of their own property only with the consent of their husbands. Divorce remained more difficult for women than for men. Before this code, French law had differed from region to region. That confused set of laws had given women opportunities to protect their interests. The universality of the Napoleonic Code ended that.

ESTABLISHING A DYNASTY

In 1804, Bonaparte seized on a bomb attack on his life to make himself emperor. He argued that establishing a dynasty would make the new regime secure and make further attempts on his life useless. Another new constitution was promulgated in which Napoleon Bonaparte was called Emperor of the French, instead of First Consul of the Republic. This constitution was also overwhelmingly ratified in a plebiscite.

To conclude the drama, Napoleon invited the pope to Notre Dame to take part in the coronation. At the last minute, however, the pope agreed that Napoleon should crown himself. The emperor would not allow anyone to think his power and authority depended on the the church. Henceforth, he was called Napoleon I.

Napoleon's Empire (1804–1814)

Between his coronation as emperor and his final defeat at Waterloo (1815), Napoleon conquered most of Europe. France's victories changed the

NAPOLEON MAKES PEACE WITH THE PAPACY

In 1801, Napoleon concluded a concordat with Pope Pius VII. This document was the cornerstone of Napoleonic religious policy. The concordat, announced on April 8, 1802, allowed the Roman Catholic Church to function freely in France only within the limits of church support for the government as indicated in the oath included in Article 6.

■ *Why was it to Napoleon's political advantage to make this agreement with the papacy? What privileges or advantages does the church achieve in the document? Would the highest loyalty of a bishop who took the oath in Article 6 reside with the church or the French state?*

The Government of the French Republic recognizes that the Roman, catholic and apostolic religion is the religion of the great majority of French citizens.

His Holiness likewise recognizes that this same religion has derived and in this moment again expects the greatest benefit and grandeur from the establishment of the catholic worship in France and from the personal profession of it which the consuls of the Republic make.

In consequence, after this mutual recognition, as well for the benefit of religion as for the maintenance of internal tranquility, they have agreed as follows:

1. The catholic, apostolic and Roman religion shall be freely exercised in France: its worship shall be public, and in conformity with the police regulations which the government shall deem necessary for the public tranquility. . . .

4. The First Consul of the Republic shall make appointments, within the three months which shall follow the publication of the bull of His Holiness, to the archbishoprics and bishoprics of the new circumscription. His Holiness shall confer the canonical institution, following the forms established in relation to France before the change of government. . . .

6. Before entering upon their functions, the bishops shall take directly, at the hands of the First Consul, the oath of fidelity which was in use before the change of government, expressed in the following terms:

"I swear and promise to God, upon the holy scriptures, to remain in obedience and fidelity to the government established by the constitution of the French Republic. I also promise not to have any intercourse, nor to assist by any counsel, nor to support any league, either within or without, which is inimical to the public tranquility; and if, within my diocese or elsewhere, I learn that anything to the prejudice of the state is being contrived, I will make it known to the government."

From Maloy Anderson, ed. and trans., *The Constitutions and Other Select Documents Illustrative of the History of France, 1789–1907*, 2nd ed., rev. and enl. (Minneapolis: H.W. Wilson, 1908), pp. 296–297.

map of the Continent. The wars put an end to the Old Regime and its feudal trappings throughout western Europe and forced the eastern European states to reorganize themselves to resist Napoleon's armies.

Everywhere, Napoleon's advance unleashed the powerful force of nationalism, discussed more fully in Chapter 21. His weapon was the militarily mobilized French nation, one of the achievements of the revolution. Napoleon could put 700,000 men under arms at one time, risk 100,000 troops in a single battle, endure heavy losses, and fight again. He could conscript citizen soldiers in unprecedented numbers, thanks to their loyalty to the nation and to

him. No single enemy could match such resources. Even coalitions were unsuccessful, until Napoleon finally made mistakes that led to his own defeat.

CONQUERING AN EMPIRE

The Peace of Amiens (1802) between France and Great Britain was merely a truce. Napoleon's unlimited ambitions shattered any hope that it might last. He sent an army to restore the rebellious colony of Haiti to French rule. This move aroused British fears that he was planning a new French empire in America, because Spain had restored Louisiana to France in 1800. More serious were his

The coronation of Napoleon, December 2, 1804, as painted by Jacques-Louis David. Having first crowned himself, the emperor is shown about to place the crown on the head of Josephine. Napoleon instructed David to paint Pope Pius VII with his hand raised in blessing.   Giraudon/Art Resource, N.Y.

interventions in the Dutch Republic, Italy, and Switzerland and his reorganization of Germany. The Treaty of Campo Formio had required a redistribution of territories along the Rhine River, and the petty princes of the region engaged in a scramble to enlarge their holdings. Among the results were the reduction of Austrian influence and the emergence of fewer but larger German states in the west, all dependent on Napoleon.

British Naval Supremacy   The British found these developments alarming enough to justify an ultimatum. When Napoleon ignored it, Britain declared war in May 1803. William Pitt the Younger returned to office as prime minister in 1804 and began to construct the Third Coalition. By August 1805, he had persuaded Russia and Austria to move once more against French aggression. A great naval victory soon raised the fortunes of the allies. On October 21, 1805, the British admiral Horatio, Lord Nelson, destroyed the combined French and Spanish fleets at the Battle of Trafalgar just off the

Spanish coast. Nelson died in the battle, but the British lost no ships. The victory of Trafalgar put an end to all French hope of invading Britain and guaranteed British control of the sea for the rest of the war. (See "Encountering the Past: Sailors and Canned Food.")

Napoleonic Victories in Central Europe   On land the story was different. Even before Trafalgar, Napoleon had marched to the Danube River to attack his continental enemies. In mid-October he forced an Austrian army to surrender at Ulm and occupied Vienna. On December 2, 1805, in perhaps his greatest victory, Napoleon defeated the combined Austrian and Russian forces at Austerlitz. The Treaty of Pressburg that followed won major concessions from Austria. The Austrians withdrew from Italy and left Napoleon in control of everything north of Rome. He was recognized as king of Italy.

Napoleon also made extensive political changes in Germany. In July 1806, he organized the Confederation of the Rhine, which included most of the

Sailors and Canned Food

In 1803, during the Napoleonic wars, the French navy undertook a secret experiment—provisioning a few of their naval vessels involved in long overseas voyages or blockades with food preserved by the then novel process of canning. The results were excellent; the crews thrived; and the French government ordered more canned goods.

Until the discovery of canning, the chief methods for preserving food were drying, salting, pickling, smoking, fermenting, and condensing. Most of these techniques are still used, but they strongly alter the taste of food and destroy some of its nutritive value. Although vitamins were unknown in the eighteenth century, military authorities did know that something in fresh fruit and vegetables kept their men healthy. In the 1790s, the French government offered a reward to anyone who could invent a method of preserving food that would make it both nearer in taste and texture to fresh products and more nourishing for sailors and soldiers who often suffered from scurvy and malnutrition from their rations of dried bread and salted meat. The desired food would allow naval vessels to stay at sea longer without having to put into port for fresh food and armies to campaign without having to live off the land.

Nicholas Appert, a French chef, was determined to produce preserved food that would be both tasty and healthful. In 1795, he established what amounted to a small food preservation laboratory on the outskirts of Paris. He eventually discovered that if he filled glass jars with fresh vegetables, fruit, soups, or meat, added water or a sauce, sealed the jars with tight stoppers, and then cooked them in a hot water bath, the result was a tasty preserved food that lasted indefinitely as long as the jars remained sealed. Although Appert did not know it, one reason the food remained unspoiled was that his process killed any microbes in it.

Although many fine French foods are still canned in jars, the process quickly took a new turn in Great Britain where the navy as well as food producers were interested in it. Appert published a book on his method in 1810, and by 1813 an English company began canning in tins, which were less expensive and more durable than glass jars. Soon other canning companies appeared in Europe, including those that produced canned sardines.

Not only navies but merchant ships discovered they could nourish their crews with canned foods. By midcentury, canned goods had entered the diet of millions of people, particularly in western Europe and North America. By the end of the century, canned goods had become what they remain today—part of everyday life around the world. The basic process used in canning is still that devised by Appert in the 1790s.

■ *What advantages did canning have over other methods of preserving food? Why was the military interested in it? How did canning become a part of everyday life?*

Source: Sue Shephard, *Pickled, Potted, and Canned: How the Art and Science of Food Processing Changed the World* (New York: Simon & Schuster, 2000).

Nicholas Appert (1749–1841) invented canning as a way of preserving food nutritiously. Canned food could be transported over long distances without spoiling.
Private Collection/Bridgeman Art Library

Napoleon's victory at the battle of Austerlitz is considered his most brilliant. A French army of 73,000 crushed an Austro-Russian army of 86,000 under the command of the tsar and the emperor of Austria. Giraudon/Art Resource, N.Y.

western German princes. Their withdrawal from the Holy Roman Empire led Francis II to dissolve that ancient political body and henceforth to call himself Emperor Francis I of Austria.

Prussia, which had remained neutral up to this point, was now provoked into war against France. Napoleon's forces quickly crushed the famous Prussian army at Jena and Auerstädt on October 14, 1806. Two weeks later, Napoleon was in Berlin. There, on November 21, he issued the Berlin Decrees, forbidding his allies from importing British goods. On June 13, 1807, Napoleon defeated the Russians at Friedland and occupied East Prussia. The French emperor was master of all Germany.

Treaty of Tilsit Unable to fight another battle and unwilling to retreat into Russia, Tsar Alexander I (r. 1801–1825) was ready to make peace. He and Napoleon met on a raft in the Niemen River while the two armies and the nervous king of Prussia watched from the bank. On July 7, 1807, they signed

the Treaty of Tilsit, which confirmed France's gains. Moreover, the treaty reduced Prussia to half its previous size. Only the support of Alexander saved it from extinction. Prussia openly and Russia secretly became allies of Napoleon.

Napoleon organized conquered Europe much like the domain of a Corsican family. The great French Empire was ruled directly by the head of the clan, Napoleon. On its borders lay several satellite states carved out as the portions of the several family members. His stepson ruled Italy for him, and three of his brothers and his brother-in-law were made kings of other conquered states. Napoleon denied a kingdom only to his brother Lucien, of whose wife he disapproved. The French emperor expected his relatives to take orders without question. When they failed to do so, he rebuked and even punished them. This establishment of the Napoleonic family as the collective sovereigns of Europe was unpopular and provoked political opposition that needed only encouragement and assistance to flare up into serious resistance. (See "Napoleon Advises His Brother to Rule Constitutionally.")

THE CONTINENTAL SYSTEM

After the Treaty of Tilsit, such assistance could come only from Britain, and Napoleon knew he must defeat the British before he could feel safe. Unable to compete with the British navy, he continued the economic warfare begun by the Berlin Decrees. He planned to cut off all British trade with the European continent and thus to cripple British commercial and financial power. He hoped to cause domestic unrest and drive Britain from the war. The Milan Decree of 1807 went further and attempted to stop neutral nations from trading with Britain.

Despite initial drops in exports and domestic unrest, the British economy survived. British control of the seas assured access to the growing markets of North and South America and of the eastern Mediterranean. At the same time, the Continental System badly hurt the European economies. (See Map 20–1.) Napoleon rejected advice to turn his empire into a free-trade area. Such a policy would have been both popular and helpful. Instead, his tariff policies favored France, increased the resentment of foreign merchants, and made them less willing to enforce the system and more ready to engage in smuggling. It was in part to prevent smuggling that Napoleon invaded Spain in 1808. The resulting peninsular campaign in Spain and Portugal helped bring on his ruin.

Napoleon and the Continental System

1806	Napoleon establishes the Continental System, prohibiting all trade with England
1807	The peace conference at Tilsit results in Russia joining the Continental System and becoming an ally of Napoleon
1809 and 1810	Napoleon at the peak of his power
1810	Russia withdraws from the Continental System and resumes relations with Britain; Napoleon plans to crush Russia militarily
1812	Napoleon invades Russia; the Russians adopt a scorched-earth policy and burn Moscow; the thwarted Napoleon deserts his dwindling army and rushes back to Paris

European Response to the Empire

Wherever Napoleon ruled, the Napoleonic Code was imposed, and hereditary social distinctions were abolished. Feudal privileges disappeared, and the peasants were freed from serfdom and manorial dues. In the towns, the guilds and the local oligarchies that had been dominant for centuries were dissolved or deprived of their power. The established churches lost their traditional independence and were made subordinate to the state. Church monopoly of religion was replaced by general toleration. Despite these reforms, however, it was always clear that Napoleon's policies were intended first for his own glory and that of France. The Continental System demonstrated that France, rather than Europe generally, was to be enriched by Napoleon's rule. Consequently, before long, the conquered states and peoples grew restive.

GERMAN NATIONALISM AND PRUSSIAN REFORM

The German response to Napoleon's success was particularly interesting and important. There had never been a unified German state. The great German writers of the Enlightenment, such as Immanuel Kant and Gotthold Lessing, were neither deeply politically engaged nor nationalistic.

At the beginning of the nineteenth century, the romantic movement had begun to take hold. One of its basic features in Germany was the emergence of nationalism, which went through two distinct stages there. Initially, nationalistic writers emphasized the unique and admirable qualities of German culture, which, they argued, arose from the peculiar history of the German people. Such cultural nationalism prevailed until Napoleon's humiliation of Prussia at Jena in 1806.

At that point many German intellectuals began to urge resistance to Napoleon on the basis of German nationalism. The French conquest endangered the independence and achievements of all German-speaking people. Many nationalists were also critical of the German princes, who ruled selfishly and inefficiently and who seemed ever ready to lick the boots of Napoleon. Only a people united through its language and culture could resist the French onslaught. No less important in forging a German national sentiment was the example of France itself, which had attained greatness by enlisting the active support of the entire people in the patriotic cause. Henceforth, many Germans sought to solve their internal political problems by attempting to

NAPOLEON ADVISES HIS BROTHER TO RULE CONSTITUTIONALLY

As Napoleon swept through Europe, he set his relatives on the thrones of various conquered kingdoms and then imposed written constitutions on them. In this letter of November 1807, Napoleon sent his brother Jerome (1784–1860) a constitution for the Kingdom of Westphalia in Germany. The letter provides a good description of how Napoleon spread the political ideas and institutions of the French Revolution across Europe. Napoleon ignored, however, the possibility of nationalistic resentment that French conquest aroused, even when that conquest brought more liberal political institutions. Such nationalism would be one of the causes of his downfall.

■ *What are the benefits that Napoleon believes his conquest and subsequent rule by his brother will bring to their new subjects? How does he believe that these, rather than military victory, will achieve new loyalty? How does Napoleon suggest playing off the resentment of the upper classes to consolidate power? What is the relationship between having a written constitution such as Napoleon is sending his brother and the power of public opinion that he mentions toward the close of the letter?*

I enclose the constitution for your Kingdom. You must faithfully observe it. I am concerned for the happiness of your subjects, not only as it affects your reputation, and my own, but also for its influence on the whole European situation.

Don't listen to those who say that your subjects are so accustomed to slavery that they will feel no gratitude for the benefits you give them. There is more intelligence in the Kingdom of Westphalia than they would have you believe; and your throne will never be firmly established except upon the trust and affection of the common people. What German opinion impatiently demands is that men of no rank, but of marked ability, shall have an equal claim upon your favour and your employment, and that every trace of serfdom, or of a feudal hierarchy between the sovereign and the lowest class of his subjects shall be done away with. The benefits of the Code Napoleon, public trial, and the introduction of juries, will be the leading features of your Government. And to tell you the truth, I count more upon their effects, for the extension and consolidation of your rule, than upon the most resounding victories. I want your subjects to enjoy a degree of liberty, equality, and prosperity hitherto unknown to the German people. . . . Such a method of government will be a stronger barrier between you and Prussia than the Elbe, the fortresses, and the protection of France. What people will want to return under the arbitrary Prussian rule, once it has tasted the benefits of a wise and liberal administration? In Germany, as in France, Italy, and Spain, people long for equality and liberalism. I have been managing the affairs of Europe long enough now to know that the burden of the privileged classes was resented everywhere. Rule constitutionally. Even if reason, and the enlightenment of the age, were not sufficient cause, it would be good policy for one in your position; and you will find that the backing of public opinion gives you a great natural advantage over the absolute kings who are your neighbors.

From J. M. Thompson, ed., *Napoleon's Letters* (London: Dent, 1954), pp. 190–191, as quoted in Maurice Hutt, ed., *Napoleon* (Englewood Cliffs, NJ: Prentice-Hall, 1972), p. 34.

establish a unified German state, reformed to harness the energies of the entire people.

After Tilsit, only Prussia could arouse such patriotic feelings. Elsewhere German rulers were either under Napoleon's thumb or actively collaborating with him. Defeated, humiliated, and diminished, Prussia continued to resist, however feebly. To Prussia fled German nationalists from other states, calling for reforms and unification that were, in fact, feared and hated by Frederick William III (r. 1797–1840) and the Junker nobility. Reforms came about despite such opposition because the defeat at Jena had made clear the necessity of new departures for the Prussian state.

The Prussian administrative and social reforms were the work of Baron vom Stein (1757–1831) and Count von Hardenberg (1750–1822). Neither of these reformers intended to reduce the autocratic

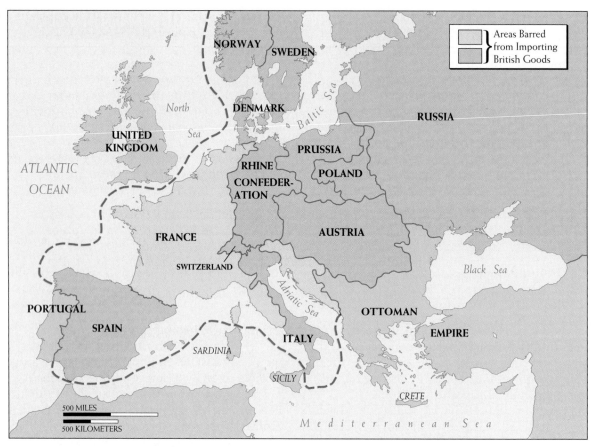

MAP 20–1 THE CONTINENTAL SYSTEM, 1806–1810 *Napoleon hoped to cut off all British trade with the European continent and thereby drive the British from the war.*

power of the Prussian monarch or to put an end to the dominance of the Junkers, who formed the bulwark of the state and of the army officer corps. Rather, they aimed at fighting French power with their own version of the French weapons. As Hardenberg declared,

Our objective, our guiding principle, must be a revolution in the better sense, a revolution leading directly to the great goal, the elevation of humanity through the wisdom of those in authority. . . . Democratic rules of conduct in a monarchical administration, such is the formula . . . which will conform most comfortably with the spirit of the age.[1]

Although the reforms came from the top, they wrought important changes in Prussian society.

Stein's reforms broke the Junker monopoly of landholding. Serfdom was abolished. The power of the Prussian Junkers, however, did not permit the total end of the system in Prussia, as was occurring in the western principalities of Germany. In Prussia,

peasants remaining on the land were forced to continue manorial labor, although they were free to leave the land if they chose. They could obtain the ownership of the land they worked only if they forfeited a third of it to the lord. The result was that Junker holdings grew larger. Some peasants went to the cities to find work, others became agricultural laborers, and some did actually become small freeholding farmers. In Prussia and elsewhere, serfdom had ended, but new social problems had been created as a landless labor force was enlarged by the population explosion.

Military reforms sought to increase the supply of soldiers and to improve their quality. Jena had shown that an army of free patriots commanded by officers chosen on merit rather than by birth could defeat an army of serfs and mercenaries commanded by incompetent nobles. To remedy the situation, the Prussian reformers abolished inhumane military punishments, sought to inspire patriotic feelings in the soldiers, opened the officer corps to commoners, gave promotions on the basis of merit, and organized war colleges that developed new theories of strategy and tactics.

---

[1]Quoted in Geoffrey Brunn, *Europe and the French Imperium* (New York: Harper & Row, 1938), p. 174.

These reforms soon enabled Prussia to regain its former power. Because Napoleon strictly limited the size of the Prussian army to 42,000 men, however, universal conscription could not be introduced until 1813. Before that date, the Prussians evaded the limit by training one group each year, putting them into the reserves, and then training a new group the same size. Prussia could thus boast an army of 270,000 by 1814.

THE WARS OF LIBERATION

Spain In Spain more than elsewhere in Europe, national resistance to France had deep social roots. Spain had achieved political unity as early as the sixteenth century. The Spanish peasants were devoted to the ruling dynasty and especially to the Roman Catholic Church. France and Spain had been allies since 1796. In 1807, however, a French army came into the Iberian Peninsula to force Portugal to abandon its traditional alliance with Britain. The army stayed in Spain to protect lines of supply and communication. When a revolt broke out in Madrid in 1808, Napoleon used it as a pretext to depose the Spanish Bourbons and to place his brother Joseph (1768–1844) on the Spanish throne. Attacks on the privileges of the church increased public outrage. Many members of the upper classes were prepared to collaborate with Napoleon, but the peasants, urged on by the lower clergy and the monks, rose in a general rebellion. (See "Art & the West: Francisco Goya Memorializes a Night of Executions," p. 702.)

In Spain, Napoleon faced a new kind of warfare. Guerrilla bands cut lines of communication, killed stragglers, destroyed isolated units, and then disappeared into the mountains. The British landed an army under Sir Arthur Wellesley (1769–1852), later the duke of Wellington, to support the Spanish insurgents. Thus began the long peninsular campaign that would drain French strength from elsewhere in Europe and play a critical role in Napoleon's eventual defeat. (See "A Commander Recalls an Incident in Spain.")

Austria The French troubles in Spain encouraged the Austrians to renew the war in 1809. Since their defeat at Austerlitz, they had sought a war of revenge. The Austrians counted on Napoleon's distraction in Spain, French war weariness, and aid from other German princes. Napoleon was fully in command in France, however, and the German princes did not move. The French army marched swiftly into Austria and won the Battle of Wagram. The resulting Peace of Schönbrunn deprived Austria of much territory and 3.5 million subjects.

Another spoil of victory was the Austrian archduchess Marie Louise (1791–1847), daughter of the emperor. Napoleon's wife, Josephine de Beauharnais (1763–1814), was forty-six and had borne him no children. His dynastic ambitions, as well as the desire for a marriage matching his new position as master of Europe, led him to divorce his wife and to marry the eighteen-year-old Austrian princess. Napoleon had also considered marrying the sister of Tsar Alexander, but had received a polite rebuff.

THE INVASION OF RUSSIA

The failure of Napoleon's marriage negotiations with Russia emphasized the shakiness of the Franco-Russian alliance concluded at Tilsit. The alliance was unpopular with Russian nobles because of the

Napoleon's second wife, Marie Louise (1791–1847), bore him a son. It was clear that Napoleon hoped to establish a new imperial dynasty in France. This portrait is by J. B. Isabey. Marie Louise (1791–1847) and the King of Rome (1811–1873) (oil on canvas) by Francois Pascal Simon Gerard, Baron (1770–1837). Chateau de Versailles, France/Bridgeman Art Library, London/Giraudon

A COMMANDER RECALLS AN INCIDENT IN SPAIN

William Napier was a British officer during the Napoleonic Wars and later a distinguished leader in the British army. In the passage that follows, he describes his experiences in a battle that took place in 1811 during which he had difficulty leading his troops into battle and received a serious injury himself.

■ *What were Napier's expectations of his men? Of his officers? How does he explain the difficulties his troops had in responding to his orders? How does he indicate his contempt for bad officers and yet a certain understanding that in war a person's character may display different faces?*

I arrived [with two companies] just in time to save Captain Dobbs, 52nd, and two men who were cut off from their regiment. The French were gathering fast about us, we could scarcely retreat, and Dobbs agreed with me that boldness would be our best chance; so we called upon the men to follow, and, jumping over a wall which had given us cover, charged the enemy with a shout which sent the nearest back. . . .

Only the two men of the 52nd followed us, and we four arrived unsupported at a second wall, close to a considerable body of French, who rallied and began to close upon us. Their fire was very violent, but the wall gave cover. I was, however, stung by the backwardness of my men, and told Dobbs I would save him or lose my life by bringing up the two companies; he entreated me not, saying I could not make two paces from the wall and live. Yet I did go back to the first wall, escaped the fire, and, reproaching the men gave them the word again, and returned to Dobbs, who was now upon the point of being taken; but again I returned alone! The soldiers had indeed crossed the wall in their front, but kept edging away to the right to avoid the heavy fire. Being now maddened by this second failure, I made another attempt, but I had not made ten paces when a shot struck my spine, and the enemy very ungenerously continued to fire at me when I was down. I escaped death by dragging myself by my hands—for my lower extremities were paralyzed—towards a small heap of stones which was in the midst of the field, and thus covering my head and shoulders. . . . However, Captain Lloyd and my company, and some of the 52nd, came up at that moment, and the French were driven away.

The excuses for the soldiers were—1st That I had not made allowance for their exertions in climbing from the ravine up the hill-side with their heavy packs, and they were very much blown. 2nd Their own captains had not been with them for a long time, and they were commanded by two lieutenants, remarkable for their harsh, vulgar, tyrannical dispositions, and very dull bad officers withall; and one of them exhibited on this occasion such miserable cowardice as would be incredible if I had not witnessed it. I am sure he ordered the men not to advance, and I saw him leading them the second time to the right. This man was lying down with his face on the ground; I called to him, reproached him, bad him remember his uniform; nothing would stir him; until losing all patience I threw a large stone at his head. This made him get up, but when he got over the wall he was wild, his eyes staring and his hand spread out. He was a duellist, and had wounded one of the officers some time before. I would have broken him, but before I recovered my wound sufficiently to join, he had received a cannon-shot in the leg, and died at the old, desolate, melancholy mill below Sabugal. Everything combined to render death appalling, yet he showed no signs of weakness. Such is human nature, and so hard it is to form correct opinions of character!

Quoted in H. A. Bruce, *Life of Sir William Napier* (London: John Murray, 1864), 1:55–57.

liberal politics of France and because the Continental System prohibited timber sales to Britain. Only French aid in gaining Constantinople could justify the alliance in their eyes, but Napoleon gave them no help against the Ottoman Empire. The organization of the Grand Duchy of Warsaw as a Napoleonic satellite on the Russian doorstep and its enlargement in 1809 after the Battle of Wagram angered Alexander. Napoleon's annexation of Holland in violation of the Treaty of Tilsit, his recognition of the French marshal Bernadotte (1763–1844) as the future King Charles XIV of Sweden, and his marriage to an Austrian princess further disturbed the tsar. At the end of 1810, Russia withdrew from the Continental System and began to prepare for war. (See Map 20–2.)

Napoleon was determined to end the Russian military threat. He amassed an army of more than 600,000 men, including a core of Frenchmen and more than 400,000 other soldiers drawn from the rest of his empire. He intended the usual short campaign crowned by a decisive battle, but the Russians disappointed him by retreating before his advance. His vast superiority in numbers—the Russians had only about 160,000 troops—made it foolish for them to risk a battle. Instead they followed a "scorched-earth" policy, destroying all food and supplies as they retreated. The so-called Grand Army of Napoleon could not live off the country, and the expanse of Russia made supply lines too long to maintain. Terrible rains, fierce heat, shortages of food and water, and the courage of the Russian rear guard eroded the morale of Napoleon's army. Napoleon's advisers urged him to abandon the venture, but he feared an unsuccessful campaign would undermine his position in the empire and in France. He pinned his faith on the Russians' unwillingness to abandon Moscow without a fight.

In September 1812, Russian public opinion forced the army to give Napoleon the battle he wanted despite the canny Russian general Kutuzov's (1745–1813) wish to avoid the fight and to let the Russian winter defeat the invader. At Borodino, not far west of Moscow, the bloodiest battle of the Napoleonic era cost the French 30,000 casualties and the Russians almost twice as many. Yet the Russian army was not destroyed. Napoleon won nothing substantial, and the battle was regarded as a defeat for him.

Fires set by the Russians soon engulfed Moscow and left Napoleon far from home with a badly diminished army lacking adequate supplies as winter came to a vast and unfriendly country. After capturing the burned city, Napoleon addressed several peace offers to Alexander, but the tsar ignored them. By October, what was left of the Grand Army was forced to retreat. By December, Napoleon realized the Russian fiasco would encourage plots against him at home. He returned to Paris, leaving the remnants of his army to struggle westward. Perhaps only as many as 100,000 of the original army of more than 600,000 lived to tell the tale of their terrible ordeal.

EUROPEAN COALITION

Even as the news of the disaster reached the West, the final defeat of Napoleon was far from certain. He was able to put down his opponents in Paris and

raise another 350,000 men. Neither the Prussians nor the Austrians were eager to risk another bout with Napoleon, and even the Russians hesitated. The Austrian foreign minister, Prince Klemens von Metternich (1773–1859), would have been glad to make a negotiated peace that would leave Napoleon on the throne of a shrunken and chastened France rather than see Europe dominated by Russia. Napoleon might have won a reasonable settlement by negotiation had he been willing to make concessions that would have split his jealous opponents. He would not consider that solution, however. As he explained to Metternich,

> Your sovereigns born on the throne can let themselves be beaten twenty times and return to their capitals. I cannot do this because I am an upstart soldier. My domination will not survive the day when I cease to be strong, and therefore feared.[2]

In 1813, patriotic pressure and national ambition brought together the last and most powerful coalition against Napoleon. The Russians drove westward, and Prussia and then Austria joined them. All were assisted by vast amounts of British money. From the west, Wellington marched his peninsular army into France. Napoleon's new army was inexperienced and poorly equipped. His generals had lost confidence and were tired. The emperor himself was worn out and sick. Still, he waged a skillful campaign in central Europe and defeated the allies at Dresden. In October, however, he was decisively defeated by the combined armies of the enemy at Leipzig in what the Germans called the Battle of the Nations. At the end of March 1814, the allied army marched into Paris. A few days later, Napoleon abdicated and went into exile on the island of Elba, off the coast of northern Italy. (See "A German Writer Describes the War of Liberation.")

The Congress of Vienna and the European Settlement

Fear of Napoleon and hostility to his ambitions had held the victorious coalition together. As soon as he was removed, the allies pursued their separate ambitions. The key person in achieving eventual agreement among them was Robert Stewart, Viscount Castlereagh (1769–1822), the British foreign secretary. Even before the victorious armies had entered Paris, he brought about the signing of the Treaty of Chaumont on March 9, 1814. It provided for the restoration of the Bourbons to the French throne

[2]Quoted in Felix Markham, *Napoleon and the Awakening of Europe* (New York: Macmillan, 1965), pp. 115–116.

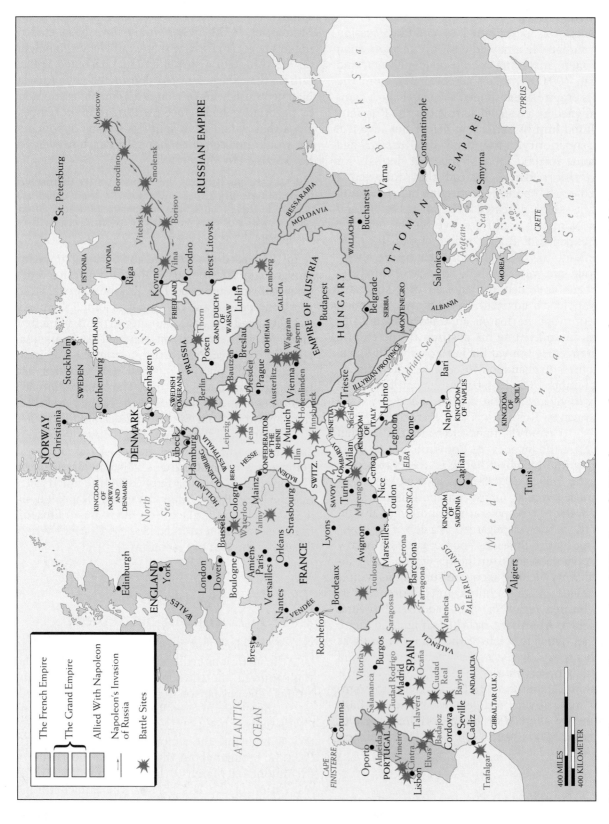

MAP 20–2 NAPOLEONIC EUROPE IN LATE 1812 *By mid-1812, the areas shown in peach were incorporated into France, and most of the rest of Europe was directly controlled by or allied with Napoleon. But Russia had withdrawn from the failing Continental System, and the decline of Napoleon was about to begin.*

A GERMAN WRITER DESCRIBES THE WAR OF LIBERATION

The German resistance to Napoleon as his army retreated from Moscow was the first time in modern German history that people from virtually all German-speaking lands cooperated together. The memory of that action became one of the defining moments in the emergence of a sense of German nationhood. Ernest Moritz Arndt (1769–1860) described the excitement and enthusiasm of that moment. This passage was frequently reprinted in German history textbooks for more than a century.

■ *Why does Arndt claim each of these various groups wanted war? This passage portrays a vast number of German-speaking people resisting Napoleon, but how also does it serve to project the possibility of a united nation that did not yet actually exist? What qualities of action in this passage are similar or dissimilar to the* levée en masse *declared during the French Revolution and reprinted in Chapter 19? Is it possible that Arndt wished to portray the actions of Germans as resembling or equaling the national spirit of the French during the revolution?*

Fired with enthusiasm, the people rose, "with God for King and Fatherland." Among the Prussians there was only one voice, one feeling, one anger and one love, to save the Fatherland and to free Germany. The Prussians wanted war; war and death they wanted; peace they feared because they could hope for no honorable peace from Napoleon. War, war, sounded the cry from the Carpathians to the Baltic, from the Niemen to the Elbe. War! cried the nobleman and landed proprietor who had become impoverished. War! that peasant who was driving his last horse to death. . . . War! the citizen who was growing exhausted from quartering soldiers and paying taxes. War! the widow who was sending her only son to the front. War! the young girl who, with tears of pride and pain, was leaving her betrothed. Youths who were hardly able to bear arms, men with gray hair, officers who on account of wounds and mutilations had long ago been honorably discharged, rich landed proprietors and officials, fathers of large families and managers of extensive businesses—all were unwilling to remain behind. Even young women, under all sorts of disguises, rushed to arms; all wanted to drill, arm themselves and fight and die for the Fatherland. . . .

The most beautiful thing about all this holy zeal and happy confusion was that all differences of position, class, and age were forgotten . . . that the one great feeling for the Fatherland, its freedom and honor, swallowed all other feelings, caused all other considerations and relationships to be forgotten.

Ernst Moritz Arndt, *Das preussische Volk und Heer* (1813), quoted in P. Jennrich, K. Krause, and W. Viernow, eds., *Geschichte für Mittelschulen* (Halle on Saale, 1941), pp. 111–112, as quoted and translated in Louis L. Snyder, ed., *Documents of German History* (New Brunswick, NJ: Rutgers University Press, 1958), pp. 148–149. Reprinted with permission from Rutgers University Press.

and the contraction of France to its frontiers of 1792. Even more important was the agreement by Britain, Austria, Russia, and Prussia to form a Quadruple Alliance for twenty years to preserve whatever settlement they agreed on. Remaining problems—and there were many—and final details were left for a conference to be held at Vienna.

TERRITORIAL ADJUSTMENTS

The Congress of Vienna assembled in September 1814, but did not conclude its work until November 1815. Although a glittering array of heads of state attended the gathering, the four great powers conducted the important work of the conference. The only full session of the congress met to ratify the arrangements made by the big four. The easiest problem facing the great powers was France. All the victors agreed that no single state should be allowed to dominate Europe, and all were determined to see that France should be prevented from doing so again. The restoration of the French Bourbon monarchy, which was temporarily popular, and a nonvindictive boundary settlement were designed to keep France calm and satisfied.

The powers also built up a series of states to serve as barriers to any new French expansion. They established the kingdom of the Netherlands,

Napoleonic Europe	
1797	Napoleon concludes the Treaty of Campo Formio
1798	Nelson defeats the French navy in the harbor of Abukir in Egypt
1799	Consulate established in France
1801	Concordat between France and the papacy
1802	Treaty of Amiens
1803	War renewed between France and Britain
1804	Execution of Duke of Enghien
1804	Napoleonic Civil Code issued
1804	Napoleon crowned as emperor
1805 (October 21)	Nelson defeats French fleet at Trafalgar
1805 (December 2)	Austerlitz
1806	Jena
1806	Continental System established by Berlin Decrees
1807	Friedland
1807	Treaty of Tilsit
1808	Beginning of Spanish resistance to Napoleonic domination
1809	Wagram
1809	Napoleon marries Archduchess Marie Louise of Austria
1812	Invasion of Russia and French defeat at Borodino
1813	Leipzig (Battle of the Nations)
1814	Treaty of Chaumont (March) establishes Quadruple Alliance
1814 (September)	Congress of Vienna convenes
1815 (March 1)	Napoleon returns from Elba
1815 (June 18)	Waterloo
1815 (September 26)	Holy Alliance formed at Congress of Vienna
1815 (November 20)	Quadruple Alliance renewed at Congress of Vienna
1821	Napoleon dies on Saint Helena

including Belgium, in the north and added Genoa to Piedmont in the south. Prussia, whose power was increased by accessions in eastern Europe, was given important new territories along the Rhine River to deter French aggression in the west. Austria was given full control of northern Italy

to prevent a repetition of Napoleon's conquests there. As for the rest of Germany, most of Napoleon's arrangements were left untouched. The venerable Holy Roman Empire, which had been dissolved in 1806, was not revived. (See Map 20–3.) In all these areas, the congress established the rule of legitimate monarchs and rejected any hint of the republican and democratic politics that had flowed from the French Revolution.

On these matters agreement was not difficult, but the settlement of eastern Europe sharply divided the victors. Alexander I of Russia wanted all of Poland under his rule. Prussia was willing to give it to him in return for all of Saxony. Austria, however, was unwilling to surrender its share of Poland or to see Prussian power grow or Russia penetrate deeper into central Europe. The Polish-Saxon question almost caused a new war among the victors. But defeated France provided a way out. The wily Talleyrand, now representing France at Vienna, suggested the weight of France added to that of Britain and Austria might bring Alexander to his senses. When news of a secret treaty among the three leaked out, the tsar agreed to become ruler of a smaller Poland, and Prussia settled for only part of Saxony. Thereafter, France was included as a fifth great power in all deliberations.

THE HUNDRED DAYS AND THE QUADRUPLE ALLIANCE

Unity among the victors was further restored by Napoleon's return from Elba on March 1, 1815. The French army was still loyal to the former emperor, and many of the French people thought their fortunes might be safer under his rule than under that of the restored Bourbons. The coalition seemed to be dissolving in Vienna. Napoleon seized the opportunity, escaped to France, and was soon restored to power. He promised a liberal constitution and a peaceful foreign policy. The allies were not convinced. They declared Napoleon an outlaw (a new device under international law) and sent their armies to crush him. Wellington, with the crucial help of the Prussians under Field Marshal von Blücher (1742–1819), defeated Napoleon at Waterloo in Belgium on June 18, 1815. Napoleon again abdicated and was sent into exile on Saint Helena, a tiny Atlantic island off the coast of Africa, where he died in 1821.

The Hundred Days, as the period of Napoleon's return is called, frightened the great powers and made the peace settlement harsher for France. In addition to some minor territorial adjustments, the victors imposed a war indemnity and an army of occupation on France. Alexander proposed a Holy

Alliance, whereby the monarchs promised to act together in accordance with Christian principles. Austria and Prussia signed; but Castlereagh thought it absurd and England abstained. The tsar, who was then embracing mysticism, believed his proposal a valuable tool for international relations. The Holy Alliance soon became a symbol of extreme political reaction.

The Quadruple Alliance among England, Austria, Prussia, and Russia was renewed on November 20, 1815. Henceforth, it was as much a coalition for the maintenance of peace as for the pursuit of victory over France. A coalition with such a purpose had never existed in European diplomacy before. It represented an important new departure in European affairs. Unlike in eighteenth-century diplomacy, certain powers were determined to prevent war. The statesmen at Vienna had seen the armies of the French Revolution and Napoleon overturning the political and social order of much of the continent. Their nations had experienced unprecedented destruction and been driven to raise enormous military forces. They knew war affected not just professional armies and navies, but entire civilian populations. They were determined to prevent any more such upheaval and destruction.

Consequently, the chief aims of the Congress of Vienna were to prevent a recurrence of the Napoleonic nightmare and to arrange a lasting peace. The leaders of Europe had learned the purpose of a treaty should be to secure not victory, but peace. The diplomats aimed to establish a framework for stability, not to punish France. Through the Vienna Settlement, the great powers framed international relations so the major powers would respect that settlement and not use military force to change it.

The Congress of Vienna achieved its goals. France accepted the new situation without undue resentment, in part because it was recognized as a great power in the new international order. The victorious powers settled difficult problems reasonably. They established a new legal framework whereby treaties were made between states rather than between monarchs. The treaties remained in place when a monarch died. Furthermore, during the quarter century of warfare, European leaders had come to calculate the nature of political and economic power in new ways that went beyond the simple vision of gaining a favorable balance of trade that had caused so many eighteenth-century wars. They took into account their natural resources and economies, their systems of education, and the possibility that general growth in agriculture, commerce, and industry would benefit all states and not one at the expense of others.

MAP 20–3   THE GERMAN STATES AFTER 1815   *As noted, the German states were also recognized.*

The congress has been criticized for failing to recognize and provide for the great forces that would stir the nineteenth century—nationalism and democracy. Such criticism is inappropriate, however. At the time there were relatively few nationalist pressures; the general desire was for peace. The settlement, like all such agreements, was aimed at solving past ills, and in that it succeeded. The statesmen would have had to have been more than human to have anticipated future problems or to have yielded to forces of which they disapproved and that they believed threatened international peace and stability. It was virtually unprecedented to produce an international settlement that remained essentially intact for almost half a century and prevented general war for a hundred years. (See Map 20–4.)

The Romantic Movement

The years of the French Revolution and the conquests of Napoleon saw the emergence of a new and important intellectual movement throughout Europe. **Romanticism,** in its various manifestations, was a reaction against much of the thought of the Enlightenment. Romantic writers and artists saw the imagination or some such intuitive intellectual

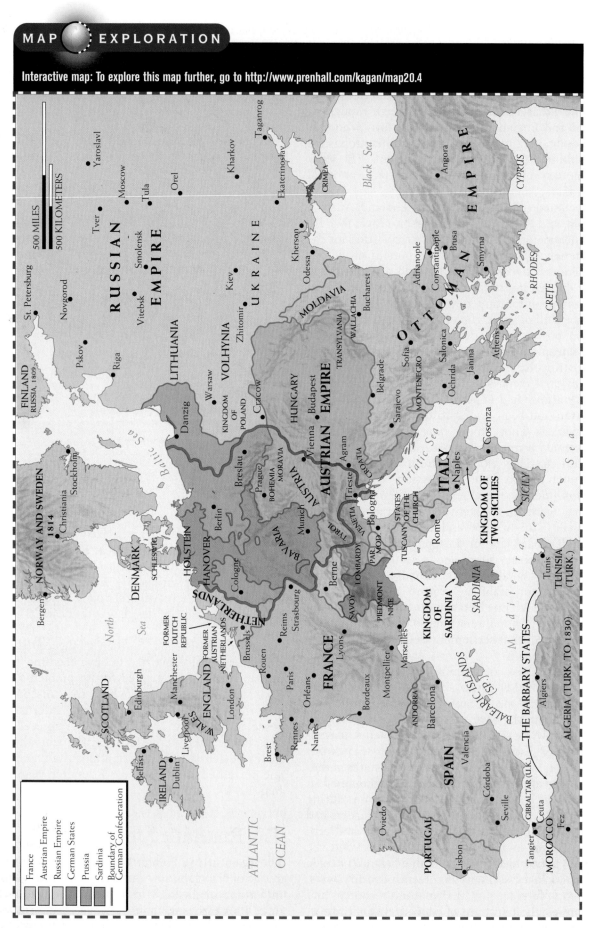
MAP 20–4 EUROPE 1815, AFTER THE CONGRESS OF VIENNA *The Congress of Vienna achieved the post-Napoleonic territorial adjustments shown on the map. The most notable arrangements dealt with areas along France's borders (the Netherlands, Prussia, Switzerland, and Piedmont) and in Poland and northern Italy.*

faculty supplementing reason as a means of perceiving and understanding the world. Many of them urged a revival of Christianity, such as had permeated Europe during the Middle Ages. And unlike the philosophes, the romantics liked the art, literature, and architecture of medieval times. They were also deeply interested in folklore, folk songs, and fairy tales. The romantics were fascinated by dreams, hallucinations, sleepwalking, and other phenomena that suggested the existence of a world beyond that of empirical observation, sensory data, and discursive reasoning.

Romantic Questioning of the Supremacy of Reason

The romantic movement had roots in the individualism of the Renaissance, Protestant devotion and personal piety, sentimental novels of the eighteenth century, and dramatic German poetry of the **Sturm and Drang** movement. However, two writers who were also closely related to the Enlightenment actually provided the immediate intellectual foundations for romanticism: Jean-Jacques Rousseau and Immanuel Kant raised questions about the sufficiency of the rationalism so dear to the philosophes.

ROUSSEAU AND EDUCATION

We already pointed out in Chapter 18 that Jean-Jacques Rousseau, though sharing in the reformist spirit of the Enlightenment, opposed many of its other facets. What romantic writers especially drew from Rousseau was his conviction that society and material prosperity had corrupted human nature.

Rousseau set forth his view on the individual's development toward the good and happy life not corrupted by society in his novel *Emile* (1762), a work for a long time far more influential than *The Social Contract*. (See Chapter 18.) In *Emile*, Rousseau stressed the difference between children and adults. He distinguished the stages of human maturation and urged that children be raised with maximum individual freedom. Each child should be allowed to grow freely, like a plant, and to learn by trial and error what reality is and how best to deal with it. The parent or teacher would help most by providing the basic necessities of life and warding off what was manifestly harmful. Beyond that, the adult should stay completely out of the way, like a gardener who waters and weeds a garden but otherwise lets nature take its course. As noted in Chapter 18, Rousseau thought that, because of their physical differences, men and women would naturally grow into social roles with different spheres of activity.

Arthur Wellesley, the duke of Wellington, first led troops against Napoleon in Spain and later defeated him at the Battle of Waterloo, June 18, 1815. Unlike his great naval contemporary, Nelson, he survived to become an elder statesman of Britain. Bildarchiv Preussischer Kulturbesitz

Rousseau also thought the child's sentiments, as well as its reason, should be permitted to flourish. To romantic writers, this concept of human development vindicated the rights of nature over those of artificial society. They thought such a form of open education would eventually lead to a natural society. In its fully developed form, this view of life led the romantics to value the uniqueness of each individual and to explore childhood in great detail. Like Rousseau, the romantics saw humankind, nature, and society as organically interrelated.

KANT AND REASON

Immanuel Kant (1724–1804) wrote the two greatest philosophical works of the late eighteenth century: *The Critique of Pure Reason* (1781) and *The Critique of Practical Reason* (1788). He sought to accept the rationalism of the Enlightenment and still to preserve a belief in human freedom, immortality, and the existence of God. Against Locke and other philosophers who saw knowledge rooted in sensory experience alone, Kant argued for the subjective character of human knowledge. For Kant, the human mind does not simply reflect the world around it like

LE CONGRÈS.

In this political cartoon of the Congress of Vienna, Tallyrand simply watches which way the wind is blowing, Castlereagh hesitates, while the monarchs of Russia, Prussia, and Austria form the dance of the Holy Alliance. The king of Saxony holds on to his crown and the republic of Geneva pays homage to the kingdom of Sardinia. Bildarchiv Preussischer Kulturbesitz

a passive mirror; rather, the mind actively imposes on the world of sensory experience "forms of sensibility" and "categories of understanding." The mind itself generates these categories. In other words, the human mind perceives the world as it does because of its own internal mental categories. This meant that human perceptions are as much the product of the mind's own activity as of sensory experience.

Kant found the sphere of reality that was accessible to pure reason to be limited. He believed, however, that beyond the phenomenal world of sensory experience, over which "pure reason" was master, there existed what he called the "noumenal" world. This world is a sphere of moral and aesthetic reality known by "practical reason" and conscience. Kant thought all human beings possess an innate sense of moral duty or an awareness of what he called a **categorical imperative.** This term referrs to an inner command to act in every situation as one would have all other people always act in the same situation. Kant regarded the existence of this imperative of conscience as incontrovertible proof of humankind's natural freedom. On the basis of humankind's moral sense, Kant postulated the existence of God, eternal life, and future rewards and punishments. He believed these transcendental truths could not

be proved by discursive reasoning. Still, he was convinced they were realities to which every reasonable person could attest.

To many romantic writers, Kantian philosophy constituted a decisive refutation of the narrow rationality of the Enlightenment. Whether they called it "practical reason," "fancy," "imagination," "intuition," or simply "feeling," the romantics believed in the presence of a special power in the human mind that could penetrate beyond the limits of largely passive human understanding as set forth by Hobbes, Locke, and Hume. Most of them also believed poets and artists possess these powers in abundance. Other romantic writers appealed to the limits of human reason to set forth new religious ideas or political thought that was often at odds with Enlightenment writers.

Romantic Literature

The term *romantic* appeared in English and French literature as early as the seventeenth century. Neoclassical writers then used the word to describe literature they considered unreal, sentimental, or excessively fanciful. In the eighteenth

In A Philosopher in a Moonlit Churchyard, *the British artist Philip James de Loutherbourg captured many of the themes of the romantic movement. The painting suggests a sense of history, a love of Gothic architecture, a sense of the importance of religion, and a belief that the world is essentially mysterious.*   Philip James de Loutherbourg (RA) (1740–1812), *A Philosopher in a Moonlit Churchyard,* signed and dated 1790. Oil on canvas, 34 × 27 inches (86.3 × 68.5 cm). B1974.3.4 *Yale Center for British Art, Paul Mellon Collection.*

century, the English writer Thomas Warton (1728–1790) associated romantic literature with medieval romances. In Germany, a major center of the romantic literary movement, Johann Gottfried Herder (1744–1803) used the terms *romantic* and *Gothic* interchangeably. In both England and Germany, the term came to be applied to all literature that did not observe classical forms and rules and gave free play to the imagination.

As an alternative to such dependence on the classical forms, August Wilhelm von Schlegel (1767–1845) praised the "romantic" literature of Dante, Petrarch, Boccaccio, Shakespeare, the Arthurian legends, Cervantes, and Calderón. According to Schlegel, romantic literature was to classical literature what the organic and living were to the merely mechanical. He set forth his views in *Lectures on Dramatic Art and Literature* (1809–1811).

The romantic movement had peaked in Germany and England before it became a major force in France under the leadership of Madame de Staël (1766–1817) and Victor Hugo (1802–1885). (See "Madame de Staël Describes the New Romantic Literature of Germany.") So influential was the classical tradition in France that not until 1816 did a French writer openly declare himself a romantic. That was Henri Beyle (1783–1842), who wrote under the pseudonym Stendhal. He praised Shakespeare and criticized his own countryman, the seventeenth-century classical dramatist Jean Racine (1639–1699).

The English Romantic Writers

The English romantics believed poetry was enhanced by freely following the creative impulses of the mind. In this belief, they directly opposed Lockean psychology, which regarded the mind as a passive receptor and poetry as a mechanical exercise of "wit" following prescribed rules. For Samuel Taylor Coleridge (1772–1834), the artist's imagination was God at work in the mind. As Coleridge expressed his views, the imagination was "a repetition in the finite mind of the eternal act of creation in the infinite I AM." So conceived of, poetry could not be considered idle play. Rather, it was the highest of human acts, humankind's self-fulfillment in a transcendental world.

MADAME DE STAËL DESCRIBES THE NEW ROMANTIC LITERATURE OF GERMANY

Anne-Louise-Germaine de Staël, known generally as Madame de Staël, was the daughter of Jacques Necker, the finance minister of Louis XVI. In the years following the French Revolution, she was the friend of major French political liberals and a firm critic of Napoleonic absolutism. More important for European literary life, Madame de Staël visited Germany, read widely in the emerging German romantic literature, and introduced it to both French- and English-speaking Europe. Her book Concerning Germany *(1813) constituted a broad exploration of contemporary German culture. In the passage that follows, she gives a strong endorsement to the new literature then emerging in Germany. She points to the novelty of this romantic poetry and then relates it to a new appreciation of Christianity and the Middle Ages. The Christian features she associates with the poetry represent one strain among many of the religious revival that followed upon the de-Christianizing religious policies of the French Revolution.*

■ *How does Madam de Staël characterize the new romantic school of poetry? Why does she contrast it with the literature that had its roots in ancient Greece and Rome? Why does she believe the new literature will continue to grow? What is the relationship of the Middle Ages to the new poetry and other examples of the fine arts touched by romantic sensibilities?*

The word *romantic* has been lately introduced in Germany, to designate that kind of poetry which is derived from the songs of the Troubadours; that which owes its birth to the union of chivalry and Christianity. If we do not admit that the empire of literature has been divided between paganism and Christianity, the north and the south, antiquity and the middle ages, chivalry and the institutions of Greece and Rome, we shall never succeed in forming a philosophical judgment of ancient and of modern taste.

Some French critics have asserted that German literature is still in its infancy; this opinion is entirely false: men who are best skilled in the knowledge of languages, and the works of the ancients, are certainly not ignorant of the defects and advantages attached to the species of literature which they either adopt or reject; but their character, their habits, and their modes of reasoning, have led them to prefer that which is founded on the recollection of chivalry, on the wonders of the middle ages, to that which has for its basis the mythology of the Greeks. The literature of romance is alone capable of further improvement, because, being

rooted in our own soil, that alone can continue to grow and acquire fresh life: it expresses our religion; it recalls our history; its origin is ancient, although not of classical antiquity. Classic poetry, before it comes home to us, must pass through our recollections of paganism; that of the Germans is the Christian era of the fine arts; it employs our personal impressions to excite strong and vivid emotions; the genius by which it is inspired addresses itself immediately to our hearts; of all phantoms at once the most powerful and the most terrible. . . .

The new school maintains the same system in the fine arts as in literature, and affirms that Christianity is the source of all modern genius; the writers of this school also characterize, in a new manner, all that in Gothic architecture agrees with the religious sentiments of Christians. It does not follow however from this, that the moderns can and ought to construct Gothic churches; . . . it is only of consequence to us, in the present silence of genius, to lay aside the contempt which has been thrown on all the conceptions of the middle ages.

From Madame De Staël, *Concerning Germany* (London, John Murray, 1814) as quoted in Howard E. Hugo, ed., *The Romantic Reader* (New York: Viking, 1957), pp. 64–66.

Coleridge was the master of Gothic poems of the supernatural, such as "The Rime of the Ancient Mariner," which relates the story of a sailor cursed for killing an albatross. The poem treats the subject as a crime against nature and God and raises the issues of guilt, punishment, and the redemptive possibilities of humility and penance. At the end of the poem, the mariner discovers the unity and beauty of all things. Having repented, he is delivered from his awful curse, which has been symbolized by the dead albatross hung around his neck:

O happy living things! no tongue
Their beauty might declare:
A spring of love gushed from my heart,
And I blessed them unaware . . .
The self-same moment I could pray;
And from my neck so free
The Albatross fell off, and sank
Like lead into the sea.

Wordsworth William Wordsworth (1770–1850) was Coleridge's closest friend. Together they published *Lyrical Ballads* in 1798 as a manifesto of a new poetry that rejected the rules of eighteenth-century criticism. Among Wordsworth's most important later poems is his "Ode on Intimations of Immortality" (1803), written in part to console Coleridge, who was suffering a deep personal crisis. Its subject is the loss of poetic vision, something Wordsworth also felt then in himself. Nature, which he had worshipped, no longer spoke freely to him, and he feared it might never speak to him again:

There was a time when meadow, grove, and
   stream,
The earth, and every common sight,
To me did seem
Appareled in celestial light,
The glory and the freshness of a dream.
It is not now as it hath been of yore—
Turn whereso'er I may,
By night or day,
The things which I have seen I now can
see no more.

He had lost what he believed all human beings lose in the necessary process of maturation: their childlike vision and closeness to spiritual reality. For both Wordsworth and Coleridge, childhood was the bright period of creative imagination. Wordsworth held a theory of the soul's preexistence in a celestial state before its creation. The child, being closer in time to its eternal origin and undistracted by worldly experience, recollects the supernatural world

Madame de Staël (1766–1817) was a prolific writer. Here she is portrayed as Corinne, the heroine of one of her own novels. Louise Elizabeth Vigee-LeBrun (1755–1842), *Mme de Stael as Corinne Playing a Lyre.* Coppet, Chateau. Copyright Giraudon/Art Resource, N.Y.

much more easily. Aging and urban living corrupt and deaden the imagination, making one's inner feelings and the beauty of nature less important. In his book-length poem *The Prelude* (1850), Wordsworth presented a long autobiographical account of the growth of the poet's mind.

Lord Byron A true rebel among the romantic poets was Lord Byron (1788–1824). In Britain, even most of the other romantic writers distrusted and disliked him. He had little sympathy for their views of the imagination. Outside England, however, Byron was regarded as the embodiment of the new person of the French Revolution. He rejected the old traditions (he was divorced and famous for his paramours) and championed the cause of personal liberty. Byron was outrageously skeptical and mocking, even of his own beliefs. In *Childe Harold's Pilgrimage* (1812), he created a brooding, melancholy romantic hero. In *Don Juan* (1819), he wrote with ribald humor, acknowledged nature's cruelty as well as its beauty, and even expressed admiration for urban life.

THE GERMAN ROMANTIC WRITERS

Much romantic poetry was also written on the Continent, but almost all major German romantics wrote at least one novel. Romantic novels often were highly sentimental and borrowed material from medieval romances. The characters of romantic novels were treated as symbols of the larger truth of life. Purely realistic description was avoided. The first German romantic novel was Ludwig Tieck's (1773–1853) *William Lovell* (1793–1795). It contrasts the young Lovell, whose life is built on love and imagination, with those who live by cold reason alone and who thus become an easy prey to unbelief, misanthropy, and egoism. As the novel rambles to its conclusion, Lovell is ruined by a mixture of philosophy, materialism, and skepticism, administered to him by two women he naively loves.

Schlegel Friedrich Schlegel (1767–1845) wrote a progressive early romantic novel, *Lucinde* (1799), which attacked contemporaneous prejudices against women as capable of being little more than lovers and domestics. Schlegel's novel reveals the ability of the romantics to become involved in the social issues of their day. He depicted Lucinde as the perfect friend and companion, as well as the unsurpassed lover, of the hero. Like other early romantic novels, the work shocked contemporary morals by frankly discussing sexual activity and by describing Lucinde as equal to the male hero.

Publication Dates of Major Romantic Works

• •

1762 Rousseau's *Emile*
1774 Goethe's *Sorrows of Young Werther*
1781 Kant's *Critique of Pure Reason**
1788 Kant's *Critique of Practical Reason**
1789 Blake's *Songs of Innocence*
1794 Blake's *Songs of Experience*
1798 Wordsworth and Coleridge's *Lyrical Ballads*
1799 Schlegel's *Lucinde*
1799 Schleiermacher's *Speeches on Religion to Its Cultured Despisers*
1802 Chateaubriand's *Genius of Christianity*
1806 Hegel's *Phenomenology of Mind*
1808 Goethe's *Faust*, Part I
1812 Byron's *Childe Harold's Pilgrimage*
1819 Byron's *Don Juan*
1825 Scott's *Tales of the Crusaders*
1841 Carlyle's *On Heroes and Hero-Worship*

*Kant's books were not themselves part of the romantic movement, but they were fundamental to later romantic writers.

Goethe Towering above all of these German writers stood Johann Wolfgang von Goethe (1749–1832). Perhaps the greatest German writer of modern times, Goethe defies any easy classification. Part of his literary production fits into the romantic mold, and part of it was a condemnation of romantic excesses. The book that made his early reputation was *The Sorrows of Young Werther*, published in 1774. This novel, like many in the eighteenth century, is a series of letters. The hero falls in love with Lotte, who is married to another man. The letters explore their relationship with the sentimentalism that was characteristic of the age. Eventually Werther and Lotte part, but in his grief, Werther takes his own life. This novel became popular throughout Europe. Romantic authors admired its emphasis on feeling and on living outside the bounds of polite society.

Goethe's greatest masterpiece was *Faust*, a long dramatic poem. Part I, published in 1808, tells the story of Faust, who makes a pact with the devil—he will exchange his soul for greater knowledge than other human beings possess. As the story progresses, Faust seduces a young woman named Gretchen. She dies, but is received into heaven as the grief-stricken Faust realizes he must continue to live.

In Part II, completed in 1832, Faust is taken through a series of adventures involving witches and mythological characters. At the conclusion, however, he dedicates his life, or what remains of it, to the improvement of humankind. He feels this is a goal that will allow him to overcome the restless striving that induced him to make the pact with the devil. That new knowledge breaks the pact. Faust dies and is received by angels.

Religion in the Romantic Period

During the Middle Ages, the foundation of religion had been the church. The Reformation leaders had appealed to the authority of the Bible. Then, later Enlightenment writers had attempted to derive religion from the rational nature revealed by Newtonian physics. Romantic religious thinkers, in contrast, appealed to the inner emotions of humankind for the foundation of religion. Their forerunners were the mystics of Western Christianity. One of the first great examples of a religion characterized by romantic impulses—Methodism—arose in England.

METHODISM

Methodism originated in the middle of the eighteenth century as a revolt against deism and rationalism in the Church of England. The Methodist

Johann Wolfgang von Goethe (1749–1832), perhaps the greatest German writer of modern times, is portrayed here in the garb of a pilgrim against a romantic background of classical ruins in the fields outside Rome. Tischbein, Johann Heinr. Wilh. 1751–1821. *Goethe in der romischen Campagna.* Stadelisches Kunstinstitut, Frankfurt/Artothek

revival formed an important part of the background of English romanticism. The leader of the Methodist movement was John Wesley (1703–1791). His education and religious development had been carefully supervised by his mother, Susannah Wesley, who bore eighteen other children.

While at Oxford, Wesley organized a religious group known as the Holy Club. He soon left England for missionary work in Georgia in America, where he arrived in 1735. While he was crossing the Atlantic, a group of German Moravians on the ship had deeply impressed him with their unshakable faith and confidence during a storm. Wesley, who had despaired of his life, concluded they knew far better than he the meaning of justification by faith. When he returned to England in 1738, Wesley began to worship with Moravians in London. There, in 1739, he underwent a conversion experience that he described in the words, "My heart felt strangely warmed." From that point on, he felt assured of his own salvation.

Wesley discovered he could not preach his version of Christian conversion and practical piety in Anglican church pulpits. Therefore, late in 1739, he began to preach in the open fields near the cities and towns of western England. Thousands of humble people responded to his message of repentance and good works. Soon he and his brother Charles (1707–1788), who became famous for his hymns, began to organize Methodist societies. By the late

eighteenth century, the Methodists had become a separate church. They ordained their own clergy and sent missionaries to America, where they eventually achieved their greatest success and most widespread influence.

Methodism stressed inward, heartfelt religion and the possibility of Christian perfection in this life. John Wesley described Christianity as "an inward principle . . . the image of God impressed on a created spirit, a fountain of peace and love springing up into everlasting life."[3] True Christians were those who were "saved in this world from all sin, from all unrighteousness . . . and now in such a sense perfect as not to commit sin and . . . freed from evil thoughts and evil tempers."[4]

Many people, weary of the dry rationalism that derived from deism, found Wesley's ideal relevant to their own lives. The Methodist preachers emphasized the role of enthusiastic emotional experience as part of Christian conversion. After Wesley, religious revivals became highly emotional in style and content.

[3]Quoted in Albert C. Outler, ed., *John Wesley: A Representative Collection of His Writings* (New York: Oxford University Press, 1964), p. 220.
[4]Ibid.

John Wesley (1703–1791) was the founder of Methodism. He emphasized the role of emotional experience in Christian conversion. Corbis

New Directions in Continental Religion

Similar religious developments based on feeling appeared on the Continent. After the Thermidorian Reaction, a strong Roman Catholic revival took place in France. Its followers disapproved of both the religious policy of the revolution and the anticlericalism of the Enlightenment. The most important book to express these sentiments was *The Genius of Christianity* (1802) by Viscount François René de Chateaubriand (1768–1848). In this work, which became known as the "bible of romanticism," Chateaubriand argued that the essence of religion is "passion." The foundation of faith in the church was the emotion that its teachings and sacraments inspired in the heart of the Christian.

Against the Newtonian view of the world and of a rational God, the romantics found God immanent in nature. No one stated the romantic religious ideal more eloquently or with greater impact on the modern world than Friedrich Schleiermacher (1768–1834). In 1799, he published *Speeches on Religion to Its Cultured Despisers*. It was a response to Lutheran orthodoxy, on the one hand, and to Enlightenment rationalism, on the other. The advocates of both were the "cultured despisers" of real,

or heartfelt, religion. According to Schleiermacher, religion was neither dogma nor a system of ethics. It was an intuition or feeling of absolute dependence on an infinite reality. Religious institutions, doctrines, and moral activity expressed that primal religious feeling only in a secondary, or indirect, way.

Although Schleiermacher considered Christianity the "religion of religions," he also believed every world religion was unique in its expression of the primal intuition of the infinite in the finite. He thus turned against the universal natural religion of the Enlightenment, which he termed "a name applied to loose, unconnected impulses," and defended the meaningfulness of the numerous world religions. Every such religion was seen to be a unique version of the emotional experience of dependence on an infinite being. In so arguing, Schleiermacher interpreted the religions of the world in the same way that other romantic writers interpreted the variety of unique peoples and cultures.

Romantic Views of Nationalism and History

A distinctive feature of romanticism, especially in Germany, was its glorification of both the individual person and individual cultures. Behind these views lay the philosophy of German idealism, which understood the world as the creation of subjective egos. J. G. Fichte (1762–1814), an important German philosopher and nationalist, identified the individual ego with the Absolute that underlies all existing things. According to him and similar philosophers, the world is truly the creation of humankind. The world is as it is because especially strong persons conceive of it in a particular way and impose their wills on the world and other people. Napoleon served as the contemporary example of such a great person. This philosophy has ever since served to justify the glorification of great persons and their actions in overriding all opposition to their will and desires.

Herder and Culture

In addition to this philosophy, the influence of new historical studies lay behind the German glorification of individual cultures. German romantic writers went in search of their own past in reaction to the copying of French manners in eighteenth-century Germany, the impact of the French Revolution, and the imperialism of Napoleon. An early leader in this effort was Johann Gottfried Herder (1744–1803). Herder had early resented the French cultural

The philosopher J. G. Fichte (1762–1814), shown here in the uniform of a Berlin home guard. Fichte glorified the role of the great individual in history. Bildarchiv Preussischer Kulturbesitz

preponderance in Germany. In 1778, he published an influential essay entitled "On the Knowing and Feelings of the Human Soul." In it, he vigorously rejected the mechanical explanation of nature so popular with Enlightenment writers. He saw human beings and societies as developing organically, like plants, over time. Human beings were different at different times and places.

Herder revived German folk culture by urging the collection and preservation of distinctive German songs and sayings. His most important followers in this work were the Grimm brothers, Jakob (1785–1863) and Wilhelm (1786–1859), famous for their collection of fairy tales. Believing each language and culture were the unique expression of a people, Herder opposed both the concept and the use of a "common" language, such as French, and "universal" institutions, such as those imposed on

Europe by Napoleon. These, he believed, were forms of tyranny over the individuality of a people. Herder's writings led to a broad revival of interest in history and philosophy. Although initially directed toward the identification of German origins, such work soon expanded to embrace other world cultures as well. Eventually the ability of the romantic imagination to be at home in any age or culture spurred the study of non-Western religion, comparative literature, and philology.

HEGEL AND HISTORY

The most important philosopher of history in the romantic period was the German, Georg Wilhelm Friedrich Hegel (1770–1831). He is one of the most complicated and significant philosophers in the history of Western civilization.

Hegel believed ideas develop in an evolutionary fashion that involves conflict. At any given time, a predominant set of ideas, which he termed the **thesis,** holds sway. The thesis is challenged by other conflicting ideas, which Hegel termed the **antithesis.** As these patterns of thought clash, a **synthesis** emerges that eventually becomes the new thesis. Then the process begins all over again. Periods of world history receive their character from the patterns of thought predominating during them. (See "Hegel Explains the Role of Great Men in History.")

Several important philosophical conclusions followed from this analysis. One of the most significant was the belief that all periods of history have been of almost equal value because each was, by definition, necessary to the achievements of those that came later. Also, all cultures are valuable because each contributes to the necessary clash of values and ideas that allows humankind to develop. Hegel discussed these concepts in *The Phenomenology of Mind* (1806), *Lectures on the Philosophy of History* (1822–1831), and other works, many of which were published only after his death. During his lifetime, his ideas became widely known through his university lectures at Berlin.

ISLAM, THE MIDDLE EAST, AND ROMANTICISM

The new religious, literary, and historical sensibilities of the romantic period modified the European understanding of both Islam and the Arab world

This colored lithograph of G. W. F. Hegel shows him attired in robes of a university professor. Hegel was the most important philosopher of history in the romantic period.
Bildarchiv Preussischer Kulturbesitz

HEGEL EXPLAINS THE ROLE OF GREAT MEN IN HISTORY

Hegel believed that behind the development of human history from one period to the next lay the mind and purpose of what he termed the World-Spirit, *a concept somewhat resembling the Christian God. Hegel thought particular heroes from the past (such as Caesar) and in the present (such as Napoleon) were the unconscious instruments of that spirit. In this passage from his lectures on the philosophy of history, Hegel explained how these heroes could change history. All these concepts are characteristic of the romantic belief that human beings and human history are always intimately connected with larger, spiritual forces at work in the world. The passage also reflects the widespread belief of the time that the world of civic or political action pertained to men and that of the domestic sphere belonged to women.*

■ *How might the career of Napoleon have inspired this passage? What are the antidemocratic implications of this passage? In this passage, do great men make history or do historical developments make great men? Why do you think Hegel does not associate this power of shaping history with women as well as men? In that regard, note how he relates history with political developments rather than with those of the private social sphere.*

Such are all great historical men—whose own particular aims involve those large issues which are the will of the World-Spirit. They may be called Heroes, inasmuch as they have derived their purposes and their vocation, not from the calm, regular course of things, sanctioned by the existing order, but from a concealed fount—one which has not attained to phenomenal, present existence—from that inner Spirit, still hidden beneath the surface, which, impinging on the outer world as on a shell, bursts it in pieces, because it is another kernel than that which belonged to the shell in question. They are men, therefore, who appear to draw the impulse of their life from themselves; and whose deeds have produced a condition of things and a complex of historical relations which appear to be only their interest, and their work.

Such individuals had no consciousness of the general Idea they were unfolding, while prosecuting those aims of theirs; on the contrary, they were practical, political men. But at the same time they were thinking men, who had an insight into the requirements of the time—what was ripe for development. This was the very Truth for their age, for their world; the species next in order, so to speak, and which was already formed in the womb of time. It was theirs to know this nascent principle; the necessary, directly sequent step in progress, which their world was to take; to make this their aim, and to expend their energy in promoting it. World-historical men—the Heroes of an epoch—must, therefore, be recognized as its clear-sighted ones; their deeds, their words are the best of that time.

From G. W. F. Hegel, *The Philosophy of History*, trans. by J. Sibree (New York: Dover, 1956), pp. 30–31. Reprinted by permission.

while at the same time preserving long-standing attitudes.

The energized Christianity associated with Methodist-like forms of Protestantism, on the one hand, and Chateaubriand's emotional Roman Catholicism, on the other, renewed the traditional sense of necessary conflict between Christianity and Islam. Chateaubriand wrote a travelogue of his journey from Paris to Jerusalem in 1811. A decade later when he was a member of the French parliament, he invoked the concept of a crusade against

the Muslim world in a speech on the danger posed by the Barbary pirates of North Africa.

Indeed, the medieval crusades against Islam fired the romantic imagination. Romantic artists, poets, and novelists throughout Europe saw the Middle Ages as a better period than their own times. Nostalgic European artists painted from a Western standpoint the great moments of the medieval crusades including the devastating destruction of Jerusalem. Stories from those conflicts filled historical novels such as *Tales of the Crusaders* (1825) by Sir Walter Scott. Although they presented heroic images of Muslim warriors, these paintings and novels ignored the havoc that the crusaders had visited on Middle Eastern Muslims, Jews, and Christians.

The general nineteenth-century association of nationalistic aspirations with romanticism also cast the Ottoman Empire and with it Islam in an unfavorable political light. Romantic poets and intellectuals championed the cause of the Greek Revolution (see Chapter 21) and revived older charges of Ottoman despotism.

By contrast, other romantic sensibilities induced Europeans to see the Muslim world in a more positive fashion. The romantic emphasis on the value of literature drawn from different cultures and ages allowed many nineteenth-century European readers to enjoy the stories from *The Thousand and One Nights*, which first appeared in English in 1778 from a French translation. As poets across Europe rejected classicism in literature in favor of folk tales and fairy tales, they saw the *Arabian Nights* as mysterious and exotic. In 1859, Edward FitzGerald (1809–1883) published his highly popular translation of the *Rubáiyát of Omar Khayyám* of Nishapur, a Persian poet of the twelfth century.

Herder's and Hegel's concepts of history gave both the Arab peoples and Islam distinct roles in history. For Herder, Arab culture was one of the numerous communities that composed the human race and manifested the human spirit. Muhammad, while giving voice to the ancient spirit of the Arab people, had drawn them from a polytheistic faith to a great monotheistic vision. For Hegel, Islam represented an important stage of the development of the world spirit. However, Hegel believed Islam had fulfilled its role in history and no longer had any significant part to play. These outlooks, which penetrated much nineteenth-century intellectual life, made it easy for Europeans to believe that Islam could for all practical purposes be ignored or reduced in their thinking to a spent historical force.

The British historian and social commentator Thomas Carlyle (1795–1881) attributed new, positive qualities to Muhammad himself. Carlyle disliked the Enlightenment's disparagement of religion and spiritual values. He was also drawn to German theories of history. In his book *On Heroes and Hero-Worship* (1841), Carlyle presented Muhammad as the embodiment of the hero as prophet. He repudiated the traditional Christian and general Enlightenment view of Muhammad as an impostor. (See Chapter 18.) To Carlyle, Muhammad was straightforward and sincere. Carlyle's understanding of religion was similar to Schleiermacher's and thus in his pages Muhammad appeared as one of the people in history who had experienced God subjectively and thus had come to discern and communicate a sense of the divine. Although friendly to Muhammad from an historical standpoint, Carlyle nonetheless saw him as one of many great religious figures and not as the last of the prophets through whom God had spoken.

But the person whose actions in the long run did perhaps most to reshape the idea of both Islam and the Middle East in the European imagination was Napoleon himself. With his Egyptian expedition of 1798, the first European military invasion of the Near East since the Crusades, the modern study of the Arab world became an important activity within French intellectual life. For his invasion of Egypt to succeed, Napoleon believed he must make it clear he had no intention of destroying Islam, but rather sought to liberate Egypt from the military clique that governed the country in the name of the Ottoman Empire. To that end, he took with him many scholars of Arabic and Islamic culture whom he urged to converse with the most educated people they could meet. Napoleon personally met with the local ulema and had all of his speeches and proclamations translated into classical Arabic. Egyptian scholars were much impressed by such cultural sensitivity and by the serious efforts of the French scholars to learn Arabic and study the Qur'an. (When the French sought to levy new taxes, however, the Egyptians' enthusiasm waned.)

It was on this expedition that the famous Rosetta Stone was discovered. Now housed in the British Museum, it eventually led to the decipherment of ancient Egypt's hieroglyphic writing. Napoleon's scholars also published a twenty-three volume *Description of Egypt* (1809–1828), which concentrated largely on ancient Egypt. Their approach suggested the history of the Ottoman Empire needed to be related first to the larger context of Egyptian history and that Islam, although enormously important, was only part of a larger cultural story. The implication was that if Egypt and Islam were to be understood, it would be through European—if not necessarily Christian—categories of thought.

Two cultural effects in the West of Napoleon's invasion were an increase in the number of European visitors to the Middle East and a demand for architecture based on ancient Egyptian models. Perhaps the most famous example of this fad is the Washington Monument in Washington, D.C., which is modeled after ancient Egyptian obelisks.

When Napoleon invaded Egypt in 1799, he met stiff resistance. On July 25, however, the French won a decisive victory. This painting of that battle by Baron Antoine Gros (1771–1835) emphasizes French heroism and Muslim defeat. Such an outlook was typical of European views of Arabs and the Islamic world. Antoine Jean Gros (1771–1835). Detail, "Battle of Aboukir, July 25, 1799," c. 1806. Oil on canvas. Chateau, Versailles, France. © Giraudon/Art Resource, N.Y.

In the Middle East itself, Napoleon's invasion demonstrated for the first time the military and technological superiority of Europe. Eventually, the political leaders of Egypt and of other regions of the Ottoman Empire would undertake reforms in hope of being able to imitate European technology, armies, and administration.

In Perspective

Romantic ideas made a major contribution to the emergence of nationalism, which proved to be one of the strongest motivating forces of the nineteenth and twentieth centuries. The writers of the Enlightenment had generally championed a cosmopolitan outlook on the world. By contrast, the romantic thinkers emphasized the individuality and worth of each separate people and culture. A people or a nation was defined by a common language, history, and customs and by the possession of a historical homeland. This cultural nationalism gradually became transformed into a political creed. It came to be widely believed that every people, ethnic group, or nation should constitute a separate political entity and that only when it so existed could the nation be secure in its own character.

France under the revolutionary government and Napoleon had demonstrated the power of nationhood. Other peoples came to desire similar strength and confidence. Napoleon's toppling of ancient political structures, such as the Holy Roman Empire, proved the need for new political organization in Europe. By 1815, these were the aspirations of only a few Europeans, but as time passed, such yearnings came to be shared by peoples from Ireland to Ukraine. The Congress of Vienna could ignore such feelings, but for the rest of the nineteenth century, as we see in subsequent chapters, statesmen had to confront the growing power these feelings unleashed.

REVIEW QUESTIONS

1. How did Napoleon rise to power? What groups supported him? What were his major domestic achievements? Did his rule fulfill or betray the French Revolution?

2. What regions made up Napoleon's realm, and what was the status of each region within it? Did his administration show foresight, or was the empire a burden he could not afford?

3. Why did Napoleon decide to invade Russia? Why did the operation fail? Can Napoleon be considered a military genius? Why or why not?

4. What were the results of the Congress of Vienna, and why were they significant?

5. Compare the role of feelings for romantic writers with the role of reason for Enlightenment writers. What questions did Rousseau and Kant raise about reason? Why was poetry important

to romantic writers? How did the romantic concept of religion differ from Reformation Protestantism and Enlightenment deism? How did romantic ideas and sensibilities modify European ideas of Islam and the Middle East? What were the cultural results of Napoleon's invasion of Egypt?

SUGGESTED READINGS

M. H. ABRAMS, *The Mirror and the Lamp: Romantic Theory and the Critical Tradition* (1958). Remains a standard text on romantic literary theory that looks at English romanticism in the context of German romantic idealism.

R. ASPREY, *The Rise of Naopoleon Bonaparte and the Reign of Napoleon Bonaparte* (2001). An extensive two-volume narrative.

E. BEHLER, *German Romantic Literary Theory* (1993). A clear introduction to a difficult subject.

F. C. BEISER, *Enlightenment, Revolution, and Romanticism: The Genesis of Modern German Political Thought, 1790–1800* (1992). The best recent study of the subject.

G. E. BENTLEY, *The Stranger from Paradise: A Biography of William Blake* (2001). Now the standard work.

J. F. BERNARD, *Talleyrand: A Biography* (1973). A useful account.

N. BOYLE, *Goethe* (2001). A challenging two-volume biography.

A. BROOKNER, *Romanticism and Its Discontents* (2001). Exploration of French romanticism by a leading novelist.

M. BROERS, *Europe under Napoleon 1799–1815* (2002). Examines the subject from the standpoint of those Napoleon conquered.

D. B. BROWN, *Romanticism* (2001). A well-illustrated overview.

D. G. CHANDLER, *The Campaigns of Napoleon* (1966). A good military study.

T. CHAPMAN, *Congress of Vienna: Origins, Processes, and Results* (1998). A clear introduction to the major issues.

A. D. CULLER, *The Victorian Mirror of History* (1985). Studies in the writing of the nineteenth century with emphasis on romantic influences.

J. ENGELL, *The Creative Imagination: Enlightenment to Romanticism* (1981). An important book on the role of the imagination in romantic literary theory.

M. GLOVER, *The Peninsular War, 1807–1814: A Concise Military History* (1974). An interesting account of the military campaign that so drained Napoleon's resources in western Europe.

F. W. J. HEMMINGS, *Culture and Society in France: 1789–1848* (1987). Discusses French romantic literature, theater, and art.

H. HONOUR, *Romanticism* (1979). The best introduction to the subject in terms of the fine arts.

P. JOHNSON, *Napoleon* (2002). A brief, thoughtful essay.

H. KISSINGER, *A World Restored: Metternich, Castlereagh and the Problems of Peace, 1812–1822* (1957). A provocative study by an author who became an American secretary of state.

S. KÖRNER, *Kant* (1955). Remains the best brief, clear introduction.

G. LEFEBVRE, *Napoleon*, 2 vols., trans. by H. Stockhold (1969). The fullest and finest biography of the man.

J. LUSVASS, *Napoleon on the Art of War* (2001). A collection of Napoleon's own writings on the subject.

J. J. MCGANN AND J. SODERHOLM (EDS.), *Byron and Romanticism* (2002). Essays on the poet who most embodied romantic qualities to the people of his time.

R. MUIR, *Tactics and the Experience of Battle in the Age of Napoleon* (1998). A splendid account of the experience of troops in battle.

H. NICOLSON, *The Congress of Vienna* (1946). Remains a good, readable account.

T. PINKARD, *Hegel: A Biography* (2000). A long but accessible study.

R. PORTER AND M. TEICH (EDS.), *Romanticism in National Context* (1988). Essays on the phenomenon of romanticism in the major European nations.

B. M. G. REARDON, *Religion in the Age of Romanticism: Studies in Early Nineteenth-Century Thought* (1985). The best introduction to this important subject.

P. W. SCHROEDER, *The Transformation of European Politics, 1763–1848* (1994). A major synthesis of the diplomatic history of the period, emphasizing the new departures of the Congress of Vienna.

S. B. SMITH, *Hegel's Critique of Liberalism: Rights in Context* (1989). An excellent introduction to Hegelian political thought.

A. WALICKI, *Philosophy and Romantic Nationalism: The Case of Poland* (1982). Examines how philosophy influenced the character of Polish nationalism.

I. WOLOCH, *Napoleon and His Collaborators: The Making of a Dictatorship* (2001). A key study by one of the major scholars of the subject.

B. YACK, *The Longing for Total Revolution: Philosophic Sources of Social Discontent from Rousseau to Marx and Nietzsche* (1986). A major exploration of the political philosophy associated with romanticism.

DOCUMENTS CD-ROM

NAPOLEON AND THE BIRTH OF ROMANTICISM

Francisco Goya Memorializes a Night of Executions: *The Third of May, 1808*

Goya y Lucientes, Francisco de Goya. *The Third of May, 1808.* 1814–1815. *Los fusilamientos del 3 de Mayo 1808.* Oil painting on canvas. 8'6" × 11'4" Museo del Prado, Madrid, Spain. Scala/Art Resource, N.Y.

Napoleon had begun to send troops into Spain in 1807 after the king of Spain had agreed to aid France against Portugal, which was assisting Britain. By early 1808, Spain had essentially become an occupied nation. On May 2, riots took place in Madrid between French troops, including many soldiers Napoleon had recruited in Egypt, and Spanish civilians. The Spaniards were attempting to prevent the departure of members of the Spanish royal family whom they considered French prisoners. In response to the riots, the French marshall Joachim Murat ordered numerous executions, especially of artisans and clergy, during the night of May 2 and 3. The events of these two days marked the opening of five years of the Spanish effort to free their country from French rule.

After the restoration of the Spanish monarchy, Francisco Goya (1745–1828) depicted the savagery of those executions in the most memorable war painting of the Napoleonic era, *The Third of May, 1808*. Because the executions had taken place at night, and the French chose their victims at random, Goya portrays a mechanical process of execution. One group has already been shot; another is being killed; and a third group, some of whom are covering their eyes, will be next. None of these people were necessarily heroes of the insurgency of the previous day. They were ordinary people being executed by troops of a nation that considered itself the champion of popular sovereignty. Goya's painting is one of the first works of art to illustrate victims of modern ideological wars.

In portraying these modern political executions, Goya recalled the traditional portrayal of Christian martyrdom—the pose of the central figure suggests a crucifixion. But more important, he drew on popular political prints of military firing squads, such as Paul Revere's famous print of the Boston Massacre. The painting thus presents the French as both infidels violating Christian Spaniards and as a mechanical killing force picking out hapless civilians, as if in prophesy of the summary executions of civilians in modern warfare.

Goya's painting also illustrates two forces of modern warfare confronting each other: the professional soldier and the guerrilla (a term coined during this era). The guerrilla is a civilian who must fight with what he finds. By contrast, the soldiers in this painting appear well disciplined and have modern rifles. They carry out the executions by the light of the large technologically advanced gas or oil lanterns with which Napoleon equipped his troops.

The Napoleonic conquest of Europe awakened the force of nationalism as ordinary people in the conquered nations resisted French domination. In *The Third of May*, Goya succeeds in making ordinary people, rather than elite officers, the symbolic heroes of the national war of liberation. But once the French were defeated and the royal family restored to the Spanish throne, the interpretation of the May 1808 events became more complicated.

In fact, Goya prepared this painting to please the royal family upon its return to Madrid in 1815. The conservative monarchy could not tolerate the insurgency as a popular uprising. It had to be seen as loyal humble citizens protecting the monarchy and the church against Napoleon and an infidel France. The victims portrayed in his painting thus appeared in 1815 to be less martyrs for liberty than defenders of the evicted royal family.

■ *Why is Goya's treatment of war in* The Third of May *a landmark work of art? How does Goya portray ordinary people in the painting, and why did the restored Spanish monarchy find this disturbing? What forces of modern war does the painting highlight?*

Sources: Alfonso E. Perez Sanchez and Eleanor A. Sayre, *Goya and the Spirit of Enlightenment* (Boston: Museum of Fine Arts, 1989); Albert Boime, *Art in an Age of Bonapartism, 1800–1815* (Chicago: University of Chicago Press, 1990), pp. 210–212, 297–300; Janis A. Tomlinson, *Goya in the Twilight of Enlightenment* (New Haven: Yale University Press, 1992), pp. 131–149; Robert Rosenblum and H. W. Janson, *19th-Century Art* (Englewood Cliffs, NJ: Prentice-Hall, Inc. and New York: Harry N. Abrams, Inc., 1984), pp. 55–56.

In 1830, Revolution again erupted in France as well as elsewhere on the Continent. Eugène Delacroix's Liberty Leading the People was the most famous image recalling that event. Note how he portrays persons from different social classes and occupations joining the revolution led by the figure of Liberty. Eugène Delacroix, *Liberty Leading the People,* oil on canvas (1830), 260 × 325 cm, RF 129. Louvre, Département des Peintures, Paris, France. © Photograph by Erich Lessing. Art Resource, N.Y.

THE CONSERVATIVE ORDER AND THE CHALLENGES OF REFORM (1815–1832)

*T*HE CLOSE OF THE CONGRESS *of Vienna was followed by a decade in which conservative political forces controlled virtually all of Europe. In the international arena, these forces sought to maintain peace and to prevent the outbreak of war that would unleash destruction and disorder. They did so through unprecedented forms of cooperation and mutual consultation. Domestically, they sought to maintain the authority of monarchies and aristocracies after the turmoil wrought by the French Revolution and Napoleon. Two sets of critics challenged this conservative order: Nationalists wished to redraw the map of Europe according to the boundaries of nationalities or ethnic groups. Liberals sought moderate political reform and freer economic markets. The goals of nationalists and liberals threatened the dominance of landed aristocracies and the rule of monarchs who governed by virtue of dynastic inheritance rather than nationality. Still another challenge to the status quo came from the efforts of Europe's Latin American colonies to gain independence.*

For the first fifteen years after the Congress of Vienna, the forces of conservatism were successful, except for their failure to retain control of Latin America. In the late 1820s, however, the conservatives faced stronger challenges. Thereafter, certain major liberal goals were achieved when a revolution occurred in France in 1830 and a sweeping reform bill passed through the British Parliament in 1832. During the same period, however, Russia and other countries in eastern and central Europe continued to resist political and social change.

The Challenges of Nationalism and Liberalism

Conservative Governments: The Domestic Political Order

The Conservative International Order

The Wars of Independence in Latin America

The Conservative Order Shaken in Europe

In Perspective

KEY TOPICS

- The challenges of nationalism and liberalism to the conservative order in the early nineteenth century
- The domestic and international politics of the conservative order from the Congress of Vienna through the 1820s
- The wars of Independence in Latin America
- The revolutions of 1830 on the Continent and the passage of the Great Reform Bill in Britain

The Challenges of Nationalism and Liberalism

Observers have frequently regarded the nineteenth century as the great age of isms. Throughout the Western world, secular ideologies began to take hold of the learned and popular imaginations in opposition to the political and social status quo. These included nationalism, liberalism, republicanism, socialism, and communism. A noted historian has called all such words "trouble-breeding and usually thought-obscuring terms."[1] They are just that if we use them as an excuse to avoid thinking or if we fail to see the variety of opinions concealed beneath each of them.

THE EMERGENCE OF NATIONALISM

Nationalism proved to be the single most powerful European political ideology of the nineteenth and early twentieth centuries. It has reasserted itself in present-day Europe following the collapse of communist governments in eastern Europe and in the former Soviet Union. As a political outlook, nationalism was and is based on the relatively modern concept that a nation is composed of people who are joined together by the bonds of a common language, as well as common customs, culture, and history, and who, because of those bonds, should be administered by the same government. That is to say, nationalists in the past and the present contend that political and ethnic boundaries should coincide. Political units had not been so defined or governed earlier in European history. The idea came into its own during the late eighteenth and the early nineteenth centuries.

Opposition to the Vienna Settlement Early-nineteenth-century nationalism directly opposed the principle upheld at the Congress of Vienna that

legitimate monarchies or dynasties, rather than ethnicity, provide the basis for political unity. Nationalists naturally protested multinational states such as the Austrian and Russian empires. They also objected to peoples of the same ethnic group, such as Germans and Italians, dwelling in political units smaller than that of the ethnic nation. Consequently, nationalists challenged both the domestic and the international order of the Vienna settlement.

Behind the concept of nationalism usually, though not always, lay the idea of popular sovereignty, since the qualities of peoples rather than their rulers determine a national character. But this aspect of nationalism frequently led to confusion or conflict because of the presence of minorities. Within many territories in which one national group has predominated, there have also existed significant minority ethnic enclaves that the majority has had every intention of governing with or without their consent. In some cases, a nationalistically conscious group would dominate in one section of a country, but people of the same ethnicity in another region would not have nationalistic aspirations. The former might then attempt to impose their aspirations on the latter.

Creating Nations In fact, it was nationalists who actually created nations in the nineteenth century. During the first half of the century, a particular, usually small, group of nationalistically minded writers or other intellectual elites, using the printed word, spread a nationalistic concept of the nation. These groups were frequently historians who chronicled a people's past or writers and literary scholars who established a national literature by collecting and publishing earlier writings in the people's language. In effect, they gave a people a sense of their past and a literature of their own. As time passed, schoolteachers, by imparting a nation's official language and history, played an important role in spreading nationalistic ideas. These small groups of early nationalists established the cultural beliefs and political expectations on which the later mass-supported nationalism of the second half of the century would grow.

The language to be used in the schools and in government offices was always a point of contention for nationalists. In France and Italy, official versions of the national language were imposed in the schools and replaced local dialects. In parts of Scandinavia and eastern Europe, nationalists attempted to resurrect from earlier times what they regarded as purer versions of the national language. Often, these resurrected languages were virtually invented by modern scholars or linguists. This process of establishing national languages led to far

[1]Arthur O. Lovejoy, *The Great Chain of Being: A Study in the History of an Idea* (New York: Harper Torchbooks, 1963), p. 6.

more linguistic uniformity in European nations than had existed prior to the nineteenth century. Yet even in 1850, perhaps less than half of the inhabitants of France spoke official French.

Language could become such an effective cornerstone in the foundation of nationalism thanks in large measure to the emergence of the print culture discussed in Chapter 18. The presence of large numbers of printed books, journals, magazines, and newspapers "fixed" language in a more permanent fashion than did the spoken word. This uniform language found in printed works could overcome regional spoken dialects and establish itself as dominant. In most countries, spoken and written proficiency in the official printed language became a path to social and political advancement. The growth of a uniform language helped persuade people who had not thought of themselves as constituting a nation that they did so.

Meaning of Nationhood   Nationalists used a whole variety of arguments and metaphors to express what they meant by *nationhood*. Some argued that gathering, for example, Italians into a unified Italy or Germans into a unified Germany, thus eliminating the petty dynastic states that governed those regions, would promote economic and administrative efficiency. Adopting a tenet from political liberalism, certain nationalist writers suggested that nations determining their own destinies resembled individuals exploiting personal talents to determine their own careers. Some nationalists claimed that nations, like biological species in the natural world, were distinct creations of God. Other nationalists claimed a place for their nations in the divine order of things. (See "Mazzini Defines Nationality.") Throughout the nineteenth century, for example, Polish nationalists portrayed Poland as the suffering Christ among nations, thus implicitly suggesting that Poland, like Christ, would experience resurrection and a new life.

A significant difficulty for nationalism was, and is, determining which ethnic groups could be considered nations, with claims to territory and political autonomy. In theory, any of them could, but in reality, nationhood came to be associated with groups that were large enough to support a viable economy, that had a significant cultural history, that possessed a cultural elite that could nourish and spread the national language, and that had the capacity to conquer other peoples or to establish and protect their own independence. Throughout the century many smaller ethnic groups claimed to fulfill these criteria, but could not effectively achieve either independence or recognition. They could and did, however, create domestic unrest within the political units they inhabited.

Regions of Nationalistic Pressure   During the nineteenth century, nationalists challenged the political status quo in six major areas of Europe. England had brought Ireland under direct rule in 1800, allowing the Irish to elect members to the British Parliament in Westminster. Irish nationalists, however, wanted independence or at least larger measures of self-government. The "Irish problem," as it was called, would haunt British politics for the next two centuries. German nationalists sought political unity for all German-speaking peoples, challenging the multinational structure of the Austrian Empire and pitting Prussia and Austria against each other. Italian nationalists sought to unify Italian-speaking peoples on the Italian peninsula and to drive out the Austrians. Polish nationalists, targeting primarily their Russian rulers, struggled to restore Poland as an independent nation. In eastern Europe, a host of national groups, including Hungarians, Czechs, Slovenes, and others, sought either independence or formal recognition within the Austrian Empire. Finally, in southeastern Europe on the Balkan peninsula and eastward, national groups, including Serbs, Greeks, Albanians, Romanians, and Bulgarians, sought independence from Ottoman and Russian control. Although there were never disturbances in all six areas at one time, any one of them could erupt into turmoil. In each area, nationalist activity ebbed and flowed. The dominant governments often thought they needed only to repress the activity or ride it out until stability returned. Over the course of the century, however, nationalists changed the political map and political culture of Europe.

EARLY-NINETEENTH-CENTURY POLITICAL LIBERALISM

The word *liberal*, as applied to political activity, entered the European and American vocabulary during the nineteenth century. Its meaning has varied over time. Nineteenth-century European conservatives often regarded as *liberal* almost anyone or anything that challenged their own political, social, or religious values. For twenty-first-century Americans, the word *liberal* carries with it meanings and connotations that have little or nothing to do with its significance to nineteenth-century Europeans. European conservatives of the last century saw liberals as more radical than they actually were; present-day Americans often think of nineteenth-century liberals as more conservative than they were.

Political Goals   Nineteenth-century liberals derived their political ideas from the writers of the Enlightenment, the example of English liberties, and the so-called principles of 1789 embodied in the

MAZZINI DEFINES NATIONALITY

No political force in the nineteenth and twentieth centuries was stronger than nationalism. It eventually replaced dynastic political loyalty with loyalty based on ethnic considerations. It received new standing after World War I when the concept of the self-determination of nations became one of the cornerstones of the Paris Peace Treaties. Still later, former European colonies embraced this powerful idea. In the passage that follows, written in 1835, the Italian nationalist and patriot Giuseppe Mazzini (1805–1872) explains his understanding of the concept. Note how he combines a generally democratic view of politics with a religious concept of the divine destiny of nations. As nationalism actually realized itself in various parts of Europe and the rest of the world, it was not always associated with democratic governments.

■ *What are the specific qualities of a people that Mazzini associates with nationalism? How and why does Mazzini relate nationalism to divine purposes? How does this view of nationality relate to the goals of liberal freedoms? How might these ideals of nationalism lead to international or domestic conflict?*

The essential characteristics of a nationality are common ideas, common principles and a common purpose. A nation is an association of those who are brought together by language, by given geographical conditions or by the role assigned them by history, who acknowledge the same principles and who march together to the conquest of a single definite goal under the rule of a uniform body of law.

The life of a nation consists in harmonious activity (that is, the employment of all individual abilities and energies comprised within the association) towards this single goal. . . .

But nationality means even more than this. Nationality also consists in the share of mankind's labors which God assigns to a people. This mission is the task which a people must perform to the end that the Divine Idea shall be realized in this world; it is the work which gives a people its rights as a member of Mankind; it is the baptismal rite which endows a people with its own character and its rank in the brotherhood of nations. . . .

Nationality depends for its very existence upon its sacredness within and beyond its borders.

If nationality is to be inviolable for all, friends and foes alike, it must be regarded inside a country as holy, like a religion, and outside a country as a grave mission. It is necessary too that the ideas arising within a country grow steadily, as part of the general law of Humanity which is the source of all nationality. It is necessary that these ideas be shown to other lands in their beauty and purity, free from any alien mixture, from any slavish fears, from any skeptical hesitancy, strong and active, embracing in their evolution every aspect and manifestation of the life of the nation. These ideas, a necessary component in the order of universal destiny, must retain their originality even as they enter harmoniously into mankind's general progress.

The people must be the basis of nationality; its logically derived and vigorously applied principles its means; the strength of all its strength; the improvement of the life of all and the happiness of the greatest possible number its results; and the accomplishment of the task assigned to it by God its goal. This is what we mean by nationality.

From Herbert H. Rowen, ed., *From Absolutism to Revolution, 1648–1848*, 2nd ed. © 1969. Reprinted by permission of Prentice-Hall, Inc., Upper Saddle River, NJ, pp. 277, 280.

French Declaration of the Rights of Man and Citizen. They sought to establish a political framework of legal equality, religious toleration, and freedom of the press. Their general goal was a political structure that would limit the arbitrary power of government against the persons and property of individual citizens. They generally believed the legitimacy of

government emanated from the freely given consent of the governed. The popular basis of such government was to be expressed through elected representative, or parliamentary, bodies. Most important, free government required state or crown ministers to be responsible to the representatives rather than to the monarch. Liberals sought to achieve these political arrangements through the device of written constitutions. Their desire was to see constitutionalism and constitutional governments installed across the Continent.

These goals may seem very limited, and they were. Responsible constitutional government, however, existed nowhere in Europe in 1815. Even in Great Britain, the cabinet ministers were at least as responsible to the monarch as to the House of Commons. Conservatives were suspicious of written constitutions, associating them with the French Revolution and Napoleonic regimes. They also were certain that not all necessary political wisdom could be reduced to writing.

Those who espoused liberal political structures often were educated, relatively wealthy people, usually associated with the professions or commercial life, who were excluded in one manner or another from the existing political processes. Because of their wealth and education, they felt their exclusion was unjustified. Liberals were often academics, members of the learned professions, and people involved in the rapidly expanding commercial and manufacturing segments of the economy. They believed in, and were products of, a career open to talent. The monarchical and aristocratic regimes, as restored after the Congress of Vienna, often failed both to recognize their new status sufficiently and to provide for their economic and professional interests.

Although liberals wanted broader political participation, they did not advocate democracy. What they wanted was to extend representation to the propertied classes. Second only to their hostility to the privileged aristocracies was their general contempt for the lower, unpropertied classes. Liberals transformed the eighteenth-century concept of aristocratic liberty into a new concept of privilege based on wealth and property rather than birth. As the French liberal theorist Benjamin Constant (1767–1830) wrote in 1814,

Those whom poverty keeps in eternal dependence are no more enlightened on public affairs than children, nor are they more interested than foreigners in national prosperity, of which they do not understand the basis and of which they enjoy the advantages only indirectly. Property alone, by giving sufficient leisure, renders a man capable of exercising his political rights.[2]

By the middle of the century, this widely shared attitude meant that throughout Europe liberals had separated themselves from both the rural and the urban working class, a division that was to have important consequences.

Economic Goals The economic goals of nineteenth-century liberals also served to divide them from working people. The manufacturers of Great Britain, the landed and manufacturing middle class of France, and the commercial interests of Germany and Italy, following the Enlightenment ideas of Adam Smith, sought the removal of the economic restraints associated with mercantilism or the regulated economies of enlightened absolutists. They wanted to manufacture and sell goods freely. To that end, they favored the removal of international tariffs and internal barriers to trade. Economic liberals opposed the old paternalistic legislation that established wages and labor practices by government regulation or by guild privileges. They saw labor as simply one more commodity to be bought and sold freely.

Liberals wanted an economic structure in which people were at liberty to use whatever talents and property they possessed to enrich themselves. Such a structure, they contended, would produce more goods and services for everyone at lower prices and provide the basis for material progress.

Because the social and political circumstances of various countries differed, the specific programs of liberals also differed. In Great Britain, the monarchy was already limited and most individual liberties had been secured. With reform, Parliament could provide more nearly representative government. Links between land, commerce, and industry were in place. France likewise had many structures favored by liberals. The Napoleonic Code gave them a modern legal system. They could justify calls for greater rights by appealing to the widely accepted "principles of 1789." As in England, representatives of the different economic interests had worked together. The problem for liberals in both countries was to protect civil liberties, define the respective powers of the monarch and the elected representative body, and expand the electorate moderately while avoiding democracy.

The complex political situation in German-speaking Europe was different from that in France or Britain, and German liberalism differed accordingly from its French and British counterparts. Monarchs and aristocrats offered stiffer resistance to liberal ideas, leaving German liberals less access to direct political influence. A distinct social divide separated the aristocratic landowning classes, which filled the bureaucracies and officer corps, from the small middle-class commercial and industrial interests. Little or no precedent existed for middle-class participation in the government or the military and no strong tradition of civil or individual liberty. From the time of Martin Luther through Kant and Hegel, freedom in Germany had meant conformity to a higher moral law rather than participation in politics.

---

[2]Quoted in Frederick B. Artz, *Reaction and Revolution, 1814–1832* (New York: Harper, 1934), p. 94.

Most German liberals favored a united Germany and looked either to Austria or to Prussia as the instrument of unification. As a result, they were more tolerant of strong state and monarchical power than other liberals were. They believed a freer social and political order would emerge once unification had been achieved. Unfortunately, the monarchies in Austria and Prussia refused to cooperate with these dreams of unification, leaving German liberals frustrated and forcing them to be satisfied with more modest achievements such as the lowering of internal trade barriers.

Relationship of Nationalism to Liberalism Nationalism was not necessarily or even logically linked to liberalism. Indeed, many aspects of nationalism were directly opposed to liberal political values. Some nationalists wished their own particular ethnic group to dominate minority national or ethnic groups within a particular region. This was true of the Hungarian Magyars, who sought political control over non-Magyar peoples living within the historical boundaries of Hungary. Nationalists also often defined their own national group in opposition to other national groups whom they might regard as cultural inferiors or as historical enemies. This darker side of nationalism would emerge starkly in the second half of the nineteenth century and would destructively poison European political life early and late in the twentieth century. Furthermore, conservative nationalists might seek political autonomy for their own ethnic group, but would have no intention of establishing liberal political institutions thereafter.

Nonetheless, although liberalism and nationalism were not identical, they were often compatible. By espousing the cause of representative government, civil liberties, and economic freedom, nationalist groups in one country could gain the support of liberals elsewhere in Europe who might not otherwise share their nationalist interests. Many nationalists in Germany, Italy, and much of the Austrian Empire adopted this tactic. Some nationalists took other symbolic steps to arouse sympathy. Nationalists in Greece, for example, made Athens their capital because they believed it would associate their struggle for independence with ancient Athenian democracy, which English and French liberals revered.

Conservative Governments: The Domestic Political Order

Despite the challenges of liberalism and nationalism, the domestic political order established by the restored conservative institutions of Europe, particularly in Great Britain and eastern Europe, showed remarkable staying power. Not until World War I did their power and pervasive influence come to an end.

CONSERVATIVE OUTLOOKS

The major pillars of nineteenth-century **conservatism** were legitimate monarchies, landed aristocracies, and established churches. The institutions themselves were ancient, but the self-conscious alliance of throne, land, and altar was new. Throughout the eighteenth century, these groups had engaged in frequent conflict. Only the upheavals of the French Revolution and the Napoleonic era transformed them into natural, if sometimes reluctant, allies. In that regard, conservatism as an articulated outlook and set of cooperating institutions was as new a feature on the political landscape as nationalism and liberalism.

The more theoretical political and religious ideas of the conservative classes were associated with thinkers such as Edmund Burke (see Chapter 19) and Friedrich Hegel (see Chapter 20). Conservatives shared other, less formal attitudes forged by the revolutionary experience. The execution of Louis XVI at the hands of a radical democratic government convinced most monarchs they could trust only aristocratic governments or governments of aristocrats in alliance with the wealthiest middle-class and professional people. The European aristocracies believed their property and influence would rarely be safe under any form of genuinely representative government. All conservatives spurned the idea of a written constitution unless they were permitted to promulgate the document themselves. Even then, some could not be reconciled to the concept.

The churches were equally apprehensive of popular movements, except their own revivals. The ecclesiastical leaders throughout the Continent regarded themselves as entrusted with the educational task of supporting the social and political status quo. They also feared and hated most of the ideas associated with the Enlightenment, because those rational concepts and reformist writings enshrined the critical spirit and undermined revealed religion.

Conservative aristocrats retained their former arrogance, but not their former privileges or their old confidence. They saw themselves as surrounded by enemies and as standing permanently on the defensive against the forces of liberalism, nationalism, and popular sovereignty. They knew they could be toppled by political groups that hated them. They understood that revolution in one country could spill over into another.

All of the nations of Europe in the years immediately after 1815 confronted problems arising directly from their entering an era of peace after a quarter century of armed conflict. The war effort, with its loss of life and property and its necessity of organizing people and resources, had distracted attention from other problems. The wartime footing had allowed all the belligerent governments to exercise firm control over their populations. War had fueled economies and had furnished vast areas of employment in armies, navies, military industries, and the demands the military made on agriculture to feed the troops. The onset of peace meant citizens could raise new political issues and that economies were no longer geared to supplying military needs. Soldiers and sailors came home and required employment as civilians. The vast demands of the military effort on industries subsided and caused unemployment. The young were no longer growing up in a climate of war and could turn their minds to other issues. For all of these reasons, the conservative statesmen who led every major government in 1815 confronted new pressures that would cause various degrees of domestic unrest and would lead them to use differing degrees of repressive action.

LIBERALISM AND NATIONALISM RESISTED IN AUSTRIA AND THE GERMANIES

The early-nineteenth-century statesman who more than any other epitomized conservatism was the Austrian prince Metternich (1773–1859). This devoted servant of the Habsburg emperor had been, along with Britain's Viscount Castlereagh (1769–1822), the chief architect of the Vienna settlement. It was he who seemed to exercise chief control over the forces of the European reaction.

Dynastic Integrity of the Habsburg Empire   The Austrian government could make no serious compromises with the new political forces in Europe. To no other country were the programs of liberalism and nationalism potentially more dangerous. Germans and Hungarians, as well as Poles, Czechs, Slovaks, Slovenes, Italians, and other ethnic groups, peopled the Habsburg domains. Through puppet governments Austria also dominated those parts of the Italian peninsula that it did not rule directly.

So far as Metternich and other Austrian officials were concerned, the recognition of the political rights and aspirations of any of the various national groups would mean the probable dissolution of the empire. If Austria permitted representative government, Metternich feared the national groups would fight their battles internally at the probable cost of Austrian international influence.

Pursuit of dynastic integrity required Austrian domination of the newly formed German Confederation to prevent the formation of a German national state that might absorb the heart of the empire

Prince Klemens von Metternich (1773–1859) epitomized nineteenth-century conservatism.   Sir Thomas Lawrence (1769–1830), *Clemens Lothar Wenzel, Prince Metternich (1773–1859),* OM 905 WC 206. The Royal Collection © 2003 Her Majesty Queen Elizabeth II.

and exclude the other realms governed by the Habsburgs. The Congress of Vienna had created the German Confederation to replace the defunct Holy Roman Empire. It consisted of thirty-nine states under Austrian leadership. Each state remained more or less autonomous, but Austria was determined to prevent any movement toward constitutionalism in as many of them as possible.

Defeat of Prussian Reform   An important victory for this holding policy came in Prussia in the years immediately after the Congress of Vienna. In 1815, Frederick William III (r. 1797–1840), caught up in the exhilaration that followed the War of Liberation, as Germans called the last part of their conflict with Napoleon, had promised some mode of constitutional government. After stalling on keeping his pledge, he formally reneged on it in 1817. Instead, he created a new Council of State, which, although it improved administrative efficiency, was not constitutionally based.

In 1819, the king moved further from reform. After a major disagreement over the organization of the army, his chief reform-minded ministers resigned, to be replaced with hardened conservatives. On their advice, in 1823, Frederick William III established eight provincial estates, or diets. These bodies were dominated by the Junkers and exercised only an advisory function. The old bonds linking monarchy, army, and landholders in Prussia had been reestablished. The members of this alliance would oppose the threats posed by the aspirations of German nationalists to the conservative social and political order. (See "Encountering the Past: Dueling in Germany.")

Student Nationalism and the Carlsbad Decrees Three southern German states—Baden, Bavaria, and Württemberg—had received constitutions after 1815 as their monarchs tried to secure wider political support. None of these constitutions, however, recognized popular sovereignty, and all defined political rights as the gift of the monarch. In the minds and hearts of many young Germans, however, nationalist and liberal expectations fostered by the defeat of the French armies remained alive.

The most important of these groups was composed of university students who had grown up during the days of the reforms of Stein and Hardenberg and the initial circulation of the writings of early German nationalists. Many of them or their friends had fought Napoleon. When they went to the universities, they continued to dream of a united Germany. They formed *Burschenschaften*, or student associations. Like student groups today, these clubs served numerous social functions, one of which was to sever old provincial loyalties and replace them with loyalty to the concept of a united German state. It should also be noted that these clubs were often anti-Semitic.

In 1817, in Jena, one such student club organized a large celebration for the fourth anniversary of the Battle of Leipzig and the tercentenary of Luther's Ninety-five Theses. There were bonfires, songs, and processions as more than five hundred people gathered for the festivities. The event made German rulers uneasy, for it was known some republicans were involved with the student clubs.

Two years later, in March 1819, a young man named Karl Sand (d. 1820), a *Burschenschaft* member, assassinated the conservative dramatist August von Kotzebue (1761–1819). Sand, who was tried and publicly executed, became a martyr in the eyes of some nationalists. Although the assassin had acted alone, Metternich decided to use the incident to suppress the student clubs and other potential institutions of liberalism.

In July 1819, Metternich persuaded representatives of the major German states to issue the Carlsbad Decrees, which dissolved the *Burschenschaften*. The decrees also provided for university inspectors and press censors. (See "The German Confederation

Issues the Carlsbad Decrees.") The next year the German Confederation promulgated the Final Act, which limited the subjects that might be discussed in the constitutional chambers of Bavaria, Württemberg, and Baden. The measure also asserted the right of the monarchs to resist demands of constitutionalists. For many years thereafter, the secret police of the various German states harassed potential dissidents. In the opinion of the princes, these included almost anyone who sought even moderate social or political change.

POSTWAR REPRESSION IN GREAT BRITAIN

The years 1819 and 1820 marked a high tide for conservative influence and repression in western as well as eastern Europe. After 1815, Great Britain experienced two years of poor harvests. At the same time, discharged sailors and soldiers and out-of-work industrial workers swelled the ranks of the unemployed.

Lord Liverpool's Ministry and Popular Unrest The Tory ministry of Lord Liverpool (1770–1828) was unprepared for these problems of postwar dislocation. Instead, it sought to protect the interests of the landed and other wealthy classes. In 1815, Parliament passed a Corn Law to maintain high prices for domestically produced grain through import duties on foreign grain. The next year, Parliament abolished the income tax paid by the wealthy and replaced it with excise or sales taxes on consumer goods paid by both the wealthy and the poor. These laws continued a legislative trend that marked the abandonment by the British ruling class of its traditional role of paternalistic protector of the poor. In 1799, Parliament had passed the Combination Acts, outlawing workers' organizations or unions. During the war, wage protection had been removed. And many in the taxpaying classes called for the abolition of the Poor Law that provided public relief for the destitute and unemployed.

In light of these policies and the postwar economic downturn, it is hardly surprising that the lower social orders began to doubt the wisdom of their rulers and to call for a reform of the political system. Mass meetings calling for the reform of Parliament were held. Reform clubs were organized. Radical newspapers, such as William Cobbett's *Political Registrar*, demanded political change. In the hungry, restive agricultural and industrial workers, the government could see only images of continental *sans-culottes* crowds ready to hang aristocrats from the nearest lamppost. Government ministers regarded radical leaders, such as Cobbett (1763–1835), Major John Cartwright (1740–1824), and Henry "Orator" Hunt (1773–1835), as demagogues who were seducing the people away from allegiance to their natural leaders.

THE GERMAN CONFEDERATION ISSUES THE CARLSBAD DECREES

In 1819, the German Confederation, fearful of nationalistic student activism, issued the Carlsbad Decrees under the guidance of Prince Metternich. These decrees limited the activities of German students, faculty, and publishers.

■ *By what devices did the government attempt to replace the university discipline of students with government discipline? What kind of actions by faculty and students do these decrees forbid or discourage? How was the censorship of newspapers to work?*

REGARDING UNIVERSITY LIFE

1. There shall be appointed for each university a special representative of the ruler of each state, the said representatives to have appropriate instructions and extended powers, and they shall have their place of residence where the university is located. . . .

This representative shall enforce strictly the existing laws and disciplinary regulations; he shall observe with care the attitude shown by the university instructors in their public lectures and registered courses; and he shall, without directly interfering in scientific matters or in teaching methods, give a beneficial direction to the teaching, keeping in view the future attitude of the students. Finally, he shall give . . . attention to everything that may promote morality . . . among the students. . . .

2. The confederated governments mutually pledge themselves to eliminate from the universities or any other public educational institutions all instructors who shall have obviously proved their unfitness for the important work entrusted to them by openly deviating from their duties, or by going beyond the boundaries of their functions, or by abusing their legitimate influence over young minds, or by presenting harmful ideas hostile to public order or subverting existing governmental instructions. . . .

Any instructor who has been removed in this manner becomes ineligible for a position in any other public institution of learning in another state of the Confederation.

3. The laws that have for some time been directed against secret and unauthorized societies in the universities shall be strictly enforced. . . . The special representatives of the government are enjoined to exert great care in watching these organizations.

The governments mutually agree that all individuals who shall be shown to have maintained their membership in secret or unauthorized associations, or shall have taken membership in such associations, shall not be eligible for any public office.

4. No student who shall have been expelled from any university by virtue of a decision of the university senate ratified or initiated by the special representative . . ., shall be admitted by any other university. . . .

REGARDING THE PRESS

1. As long as this edict remains in force, no publication which appears daily, or as a serial not exceeding twenty sheets of printed matter, shall be printed in any state of the Confederation without the prior knowledge and approval of the state officials. . . .

4. Each state of the Confederation is responsible, not only to the state against which the offense is directly committed but to the entire Confederation, for any publication printed within the limits of its jurisdiction, in which the honor or security of other states is impinged upon or their constitution or administration attacked. . . .

7. When a newspaper or periodical is suppressed by a decision of the Diet, the editor of such publication may not within five years edit a similar publication in any state of the Confederation.

Quoted from P. A. G. von Meyer, *Corpus juris confoederationis Germanicae,* 2nd ed., Vol. 2 (Frankfort on Main, 1833), pp. 138 ff., as quoted and translated in Louis L. Snyder, ed., *Documents of German History* (New Brunswick, NJ: Rutgers University Press, 1958), pp. 158–160.

Dueling in Germany

Dueling was an aristocratic custom. Until the late eighteenth century, noblemen defended their honor by fighting duels that often left at least one of the participants badly injured or even dead. Governments disliked the custom, and dueling had become illegal across most of western Europe by the mid-1800s. The rise of liberal political and social values also made dueling increasingly unacceptable in modern societies.

But deadly dueling persisted in Germany where it remained technically against the law but socially acceptable. In Germany the conservative military and aristocratic elites dominated the nation well into the twentieth century. German officers saw dueling as essential to military honor and a symbol of their privileged status. If civilian courts attempted to interfere with military dueling, German monarchs would frequently protect the duelists, thus indicating the military was not subject to civilian law. Instead, officers who felt themselves to have been insulted took their disputes to military courts of honor, which would either settle the dispute or order the officers to fight a duel. An officer who then failed might be shunned by his fellow officers or expelled from the military. Even officers in the German reserves, who only served for part of each year and retained their middle-class civilian occupations, were expected to abide by this military code of honor.

Military-aristocratic values so dominated nineteenth-century Germany that dueling spread among middle-class civilians. For many civil servants and professional men, fighting a duel became a way to rise in society and a mark of social standing. It distinguished them from the rest of the middle classes and made them feel socially privileged like the warrior aristocracy. An 1896 book on correct dueling practice made this clear: "In general those may be considered gentlemen who, be it through birth, through self-acquired social position, or as a result of completed studies, raises himself above the level of the common honorable man and by dint of one of the aforementioned can be treated as an equal with the officer."[1]

The German universities, which selected their students mostly from the upper middle classes and the aristocracy, also functioned as schools for dueling with small socially exclusive dueling clubs for students. The pistol was the weapon of choice for duelists outside the university, and the student dueling corps fought with sabers. Again, these student duels were technically illegal, but rarely prosecuted unless one of the students was killed, which seldom happened Most student saber duels resulted only in bloody and painful facial wounds that left highly visible scars. The duelists, usually defending the honor of their club, had to prove they could receive wounds without showing fear and medical treatment without showing pain. By the 1890s, student dueling was considered a form of character building, and a dueling scar on a man's cheek had become a mark of honor.

German dueling all but vanished after World War I and the military collapse of the German Empire in 1918, but so long as dueling persisted, it embodied the power of military and aristocratic values in German society and political life.

■ *What explains the popularity of dueling in imperial Germany? What role did dueling play in the German universities? How was dueling related to German middle-class men's desire for upward social mobility?*

Sources: Ute Frevert, *Men of Honour: A Social and Cultural History of the Duel* (Cambridge: Polity Press, 1995); Kevin McAleer, *Dueling: The Cult of Honor in Fin-de-Siècle Germany* (Princeton: Princeton University Press, 1994); Robert A. Nye, *Masculinity and Male Codes of Honor in Modern France* (New York: Oxford University Press, 1993).

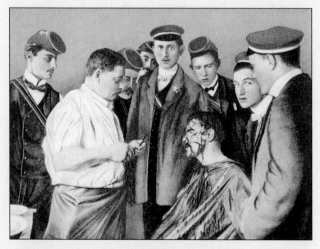

While fellow dueling-club members look on, a German student slashed in a duel is treated by a surgeon. Mary Evans Picture Library, Ltd.

[1]Quoted in Kevin McAleer, *Dueling: The Cult of Honor in Fin-de-Siècle Germany* (Princeton: Princeton University Press, 1994), p. 200.

In May 1820, Karl Sand, a German student and a member of a Burschenschaft, was executed for his murder of the conservative playwright August von Kotzebue the previous year. In the eyes of many young German nationalists, Sand was a political martyr.
Bildarchiv Preussischer Kulturbesitz

The government's answer to the discontent was repression. In December 1816, an unruly mass meeting took place at Spa Fields near London. This disturbance provided Parliament an excuse to pass the Coercion Act of March 1817. These measures temporarily suspended habeas corpus and extended existing laws against seditious gatherings.

"Peterloo" and the Six Acts This initial repression, in combination with improved harvests, brought calm for a time to the political landscape. By 1819, however, the people were restive again. In the industrial north, many well-organized mass meetings were held to demand the reform of Parliament. The radical reform campaign culminated on August 16, 1819, with a meeting in Manchester at Saint Peter's Fields. Royal troops and the local militia were on hand to ensure order. As the speeches were about to begin, a local magistrate ordered the militia to move into the audience. The result was panic and death. At least eleven people in the crowd were killed; scores were injured. The event became known as the Peterloo Massacre, a phrase that drew a contemptuous comparison with the victory at Waterloo.

Peterloo had been the act of the local Manchester officials, whom the Liverpool ministry felt it must support. The cabinet also decided to act once and for all to end these troubles. Most of the radical leaders were arrested and taken out of circulation. In December 1819, a few months after the German Carlsbad Decrees, Parliament passed a series of laws called the Six Acts, which (1) forbade large unauthorized, public meetings, (2) raised the fines for seditious libel, (3) speeded up the trials of political

agitators, (4) increased newspaper taxes, (5) prohibited the training of armed groups, and (6) allowed local officials to search homes in certain disturbed counties. In effect, the Six Acts attempted to remove the instruments of agitation from the hands of radical leaders and to provide the authorities with new powers.

Two months after the passage of the Six Acts, the Cato Street Conspiracy was unearthed. Under the guidance of a possibly demented figure named Thistlewood, a group of extreme radicals had plotted to blow up the entire British cabinet. The plot was foiled. The leaders were arrested and tried, and four of them were executed. Although little more than a half-baked plot, the conspiracy helped further discredit the movement for parliamentary reform.

BOURBON RESTORATION IN FRANCE

The abdication of Napoleon in 1814 opened the way for a restoration of Bourbon rule in the homeland of the great revolution. The new king was the former count of Provence and a brother of Louis XVI. The son of the executed monarch had died in prison. Royalists had regarded the dead boy as Louis XVII, and so his uncle became Louis XVIII (r. 1814–1824). This fat, awkward man had become a political realist during his more than twenty years of exile. He understood he could not govern if he attempted to turn back the clock. France had undergone too many irreversible changes. Consequently, Louis XVIII agreed to become a constitutional monarch, but under a constitution of his own making.

The Charter The constitution of the French restoration was the Charter. It provided for a hereditary

The French Bourbons were restored to the throne in 1815 but would rule only until 1830. This picture shows Louis XVIII, seated, second from left, and his brother, the count of Artois, who would become Charles X, standing on the left. Notice the bust of Henry IV in the background, placed there to associate the restored rulers with their popular late-sixteenth-early-seventeenth-century forebear.
Bildarchiv Preussischer Kulturbesitz

monarchy and a bicameral legislature. The monarch appointed the upper house; the lower house, the Chamber of Deputies, was elected according to a very narrow franchise with a high property qualification. The Charter guaranteed most of the rights enumerated by the Declaration of the Rights of Man and Citizen. There was to be religious toleration, but Roman Catholicism was designated as the official religion of the nation. Most important for thousands of French people at all social levels who had profited from the revolution, the Charter promised not to challenge the property rights of the current owners of land that had been confiscated from aristocrats and the church. With this provision, Louis XVIII hoped to reconcile to his regime those who had benefited from the revolution.

Ultraroyalism This moderate spirit did not penetrate deeply into the ranks of royalist supporters whose families had suffered at the hands of the revolution. Rallying around the count of Artois (1757–1836), those people who were more royalist than the monarch now demanded their revenge. In the months after Napoleon's final defeat at Waterloo, royalists in the south and west carried out a White Terror against former revolutionaries and supporters of the deposed emperor. The king could do little or nothing to halt this bloodbath. Similar extreme royalist sentiment could be found in the Chamber of Deputies. The ultraroyalist majority elected in 1816 proved so dangerously reactionary that the king soon dissolved the chamber. The majority returned by the second election was more moderate. Several years of political give-and-take followed, with the king making mild accommodations to liberals.

In February 1820, however, the duke of Berri, son of Artois and heir to the throne after his father, was murdered by a lone assassin. The ultraroyalists persuaded Louis XVIII that the murder was the result of his ministers' cooperation with liberal politicians, and the king responded with repressive measures. Electoral laws were revised to give wealthy electors two votes. Press censorship was imposed, and people suspected of dangerous political activity were made subject to easy arrest. By 1821, the government placed secondary education under the control of the Roman Catholic bishops.

All these actions revealed the basic contradiction of the French restoration. By the early 1820s, the veneer of constitutionalism had worn away. Liberals were being driven out of politics and into a near-illegal status.

The Conservative International Order

At the Congress of Vienna, the major powers—Russia, Austria, Prussia, and Great Britain—had agreed to consult with each other from time to time on matters affecting Europe as a whole. Such consultation was one of the new departures in international relations achieved by the Congress. The vehicle for this consultation was a series of postwar congresses, or conferences. Later, as differences arose among the powers, the consultations became more informal. This new arrangement for resolving mutual foreign policy issues was known as the *Concert of Europe*. It prevented one nation from taking a major action in international affairs without the assent of the others. The initial goal of the Concert of Europe was to maintain the balance of power against new French aggression and against the military might of Russia. The Concert continued to function, however, on large and small issues until the third quarter of the century. Its goal—a novel one in European affairs—was to maintain the peace. In that respect, although the great powers sought to maintain conservative domestic governments, they were making genuinely new departures in regulating their international relations.

THE CONGRESS SYSTEM

In the years immediately following the Congress of Vienna, the new congress system of mutual cooperation and consultation functioned well. The first congress took place in 1818 at Aix-la-Chapelle. As a result of this gathering, the four major powers removed their troops from France, which had paid its war reparations, and readmitted that nation to good standing among European nations. Despite unanimity on these decisions, the conference was not without friction. Tsar Alexander I (r. 1801–1825) suggested that the Quadruple Alliance (see Chapter 20) agree to uphold the borders and the existing governments of all European countries. Castlereagh, representing Britain, flatly rejected the proposal. He contended the Quadruple Alliance was intended only to prevent future French aggression. These disagreements appeared somewhat academic until a series of revolutions began in southern Europe in 1820.

THE SPANISH REVOLUTION OF 1820

When the Bourbon Ferdinand VII of Spain (r. 1814–1833) was placed on his throne following Napoleon's downfall, he had promised to govern according to a written constitution. Once securely in power, however, he ignored his pledge, dissolved the *Cortés* (the parliament), and ruled alone. In 1820, a group of army officers who were about to be sent to suppress revolution in Spain's Latin American colonies rebelled. In March, Ferdinand once again announced he would abide by the provisions of the constitution. For the time being, the revolution had succeeded.

Almost at the same time, in July 1820, revolution erupted in Naples, where the king of the Two Sicilies quickly accepted a constitution. There were other, lesser revolts in Italy, but none of them succeeded.

These events frightened the ever-nervous Metternich. Italian disturbances were especially troubling to him. Austria hoped to dominate the peninsula to provide a buffer against the spread of revolution on its own southern flank. The other powers were divided on the best course of action. Britain opposed joint intervention in either Italy or Spain. Metternich turned to Prussia and Russia, the other members of the Holy Alliance formed in 1815, for support. The three eastern powers, along with unofficial delegations from Britain and France, met at the Congress of Troppau in late October 1820. Led by

The Period of Political Reaction	
1814	French monarchy restored
1815	Russia, Austria, Prussia form Holy Alliance
1815	Russia, Austria, Prussia, and Britain renew Quadruple Alliance
1818	Congress of Aix-la-Chapelle
1819 (July)	Carlsbad Decrees
1819 (August 16)	Peterloo Massacre
1819 (December)	Great Britain passes Six Acts
1820 (January)	Spanish revolution
1820 (October)	Congress of Troppau
1821 (January)	Congress of Laibach
1821 (February)	Greek revolution
1822	Congress of Verona
1823	France helps crush Spanish revolution

Tsar Alexander, the members of the Holy Alliance issued the Protocol of Troppau. This declaration asserted that stable governments might intervene to restore order in countries experiencing revolution. Yet even Russia hesitated to authorize Austrian intervention in Italian affairs. That decision was finally reached in January 1821 at the Congress of Laibach. Shortly thereafter, Austrian troops marched into Naples and restored the king of the Two Sicilies to nonconstitutional government. From then on, Metternich attempted to foster policies that would improve the efficient administration of the various Italian governments so as to give them more direct local support.

The final postwar congress took place in October 1822 at Verona. Its primary purpose was to resolve the situation in Spain. Once again, Britain balked at joint action. Shortly before the meeting, Castlereagh had committed suicide. George Canning (1770–1827), the new foreign minister, was much less sympathetic to Metternich's goals. At Verona, Britain, in effect, withdrew from continental affairs. Austria, Prussia, and Russia agreed to support French intervention in Spain. In April 1823, the French army crossed the Pyrenees, and within a few months it brutally suppressed the Spanish revolution and established its temporary occupation of the country, which ended in 1827.

What did not happen in Spain, however, was as important for the new international order as what did happen. The intervention had not been used as an excuse to aggrandize French power or territory. The same had been true of all the interventions under the congress system. Despite the conservative intention of the various interventions from the standpoint of domestic politics, they did not represent decisions taken by the great powers to achieve territorial conquest. Rather, they sought the maintenance of the international order established at Vienna. Such a situation stood in sharp contrast to the various alliances to invade or confiscate territory that had been forged among the European powers during the eighteenth century and the wars of the French Revolution and Napoleon. It was just this new mode of international restraint through formal and informal consultation that prevented war until the middle of the century and a general European conflict until 1914. As one historian has commented, "The statesmen of the Vienna generation . . . did not so much fear war because they thought it would bring revolution as because they had learned from bitter experience that war was revolution."[3]

There was a second diplomatic result of the Congress of Verona and the Spanish intervention. George Canning was much more interested in the fate of British commerce and trade than Castlereagh had been. Thus Canning sought to prevent the politics of European reaction from being extended to Spain's colonies in Latin America, which were then in revolt (discussed later). He intended to exploit these South American revolutions to break the old Spanish trading monopoly with its colonies and gain access for Britain to Latin American trade. To that end, the British foreign minister supported the American Monroe Doctrine in 1823, prohibiting further colonization and intervention by European powers in the Americas. Britain soon recognized the Spanish colonies as independent states. Through the rest of the century, British commercial interests dominated Latin America. In this fashion, Canning may be said to have brought the War of Jenkins's Ear (1739) to a successful conclusion.

REVOLT AGAINST OTTOMAN RULE IN THE BALKANS

The Greek Revolution of 1821 While the powers were plotting conservative interventions in Italy and Spain, a third Mediterranean revolt erupted, in Greece. The Greek revolution became one of the most famous of the century because it attracted the support and participation of many illustrious literary figures. Liberals throughout Europe, who were seeing their own hopes crushed at home, imagined the ancient Greek democracy was being reborn. Lord Byron went to fight in Greece and died in 1824 (of cholera) in the cause of Greek liberty. Philhellenic ("pro-Greek") societies were founded in nearly every major country. The struggle was posed in the eighteenth-century Enlightenment terms of Western liberal Greek freedom against the Asian oriental despotism of the Ottoman Empire.

As discussed in Chapter 15, the Ottoman Empire had not changed its fundamental political or economic structures during the eighteenth century even as the major European states grew in wealth and power. The consequent weakness and instability of the empire troubled European diplomacy throughout the nineteenth century, raising what was known as "the Eastern Question": What should the European powers do about Ottoman inability to assure political and administrative stability in its possessions in and around the eastern Mediterranean? Most of the major powers had a keen interest in those territories. Russia and Austria coveted land in the Balkans. France and Britain were concerned with the empire's commerce and with control of key naval positions in the eastern Mediterranean. Also at issue was the treatment of the Christian inhabitants of the empire and access to the Christian shrines in the Holy Land. The goals of the great powers often conflicted with the desire for independence of the many national groups in the Ottoman Empire. But because the powers had little desire to strengthen the empire, they were often more sympathetic to nationalistic aspirations there than elsewhere in Europe.

These conflicting interests, as well as mutual distrust, prevented any direct intervention in Greek affairs for several years. Eventually, however, Britain, France, and Russia concluded an independent Greece would benefit their strategic interests and would not threaten their domestic security. In 1827, they signed the Treaty of London, demanding Turkish recognition of Greek independence, and sent a joint fleet to support the Greek revolt. In 1828, Russia sent troops into the Ottoman holdings in what is today Romania, ultimately gaining control of that territory in 1829 with the Treaty of Adrianople. The treaty also stipulated the Turks would allow Britain, France, and Russia to decide the future of Greece. In 1830, a second Treaty of London declared Greece an independent kingdom. Two years later, Otto I (r. 1832–1862), the son of the king of Bavaria, was chosen to be the first king of the new Greek kingdom.

Serbian Independence The year 1830 also saw the establishment of a second independent state on the Balkan peninsula. Since the late eighteenth century, Serbia had sought independence from the Ottoman Empire. During the Napoleonic wars, its fate had been linked to Russian policy and Russian relations with the Ottoman Empire. Between 1804 and 1813, a remarkable leader, Karageorge (1762–1817), had led a guerrilla war against the Ottoman authorities.

---

[3]Paul W. Schroeder, *The Transformation of European Politics, 1763–1848* (Oxford: Clarendon Press, 1994), p. 802.

This ultimately unsuccessful revolution helped build national self-identity and attracted the interest of the great powers.

In 1815 and 1816, a new leader, Milos (1780–1860), succeeded in negotiating greater administrative autonomy for some Serbian territory, but most Serbs lived outside the borders of this new entity. In 1830, the Ottoman sultan formally granted independence to Serbia, and by the late 1830s the major powers had also extended it their recognition. The political structure of the new nation, however, remained in doubt for many years.

In 1833, Milos, now a hereditary prince, pressured the Ottoman authorities to extend the borders of Serbia, which they did. These new boundaries persisted until 1878. Serbian leaders continued to seek additional territory, however, creating tensions with Austria. The status of minorities, particularly Muslims, within Serbian territory, also created tensions.

In the mid-1820s, Russia became Serbia's formal protector, despite the Austrian territory that separated them. In 1856, Serbia came under the collective protection of the great powers, but the special relationship between Russia and Serbia would continue until the First World War and would play a decisive role in the outbreak of that conflict.

The Wars of Independence in Latin America

The wars of the French Revolution and, more particularly, those of Napoleon sparked movements for independence from European domination throughout Latin America. In less than two decades, between 1804 and 1824, France was driven from Haiti, Portugal lost control of Brazil, and Spain was forced to withdraw from all of its American empire except Cuba and Puerto Rico. Three centuries of Iberian colonial government over the South American continent came to an end. (See Map 21–1.)

Haiti achieved independence in 1804, following a slave revolt led by Toussaint L'Ouverture (1746–1803) and Jean-Jacques Dessalines (1758–1806) that began in 1794. Haiti's revolution, which involved the popular uprising of a repressed social group, proved to be the great exception in the Latin American drive for liberty from European masters. Generally speaking, on the South American continent it was the Creole elite—merchants, landowners, and professional people of Spanish descent—that led the movements against Spain and Portugal. Very few Native Americans, blacks, mestizos, mulattos, or slaves became involved in or benefited from the end of Iberian rule. Indeed, the example of the Haitian slave revolt haunted the Creoles, as did the revolts

George Gordon, Lord Byron (1788–1824), is shown here dressed as an Albanian. The famous English poet died in Greece trying to aid the Greek Revolution. Greek independence was a defining cause for European liberals in the 1820s. The Granger Collection

of Indians in the Andes in 1780 and 1781. The Creoles were determined that any drive for political independence from Spain and Portugal should not cause social disruption or the loss of their existing social and economic privileges. In this respect, the Creole revolutionaries were not unlike American revolutionaries in the southern colonies, who wanted to reject British rule but keep their slaves, or French revolutionaries, who wanted to depose the king but not to extend liberty to the French working class.

Creole Discontent Creole discontent with Spanish colonial government had many sources. (The Brazilian situation will be discussed separately.) Latin American merchants wanted to trade more freely within the region and with North American and European markets. They wanted commercial regulations that would benefit them rather than Spain. They had also experienced increases in taxation by the Spanish crown.

Creoles were deeply resentful of Spanish policies favoring *peninsulares*—whites born in Spain—for political patronage, including appointments in the colonial government, church, and army. The Creoles believed the *peninsulares* improperly secured all the best positions. Seen in this light, the royal patronage system represented another device with which Spain

Interactive map: To explore this map further, go to http://www.prenhall.com/kagan/map21.1

MAP 21–1 LATIN AMERICA IN 1830. *By 1830, Latin America had been liberated from European government. This map shows the initial borders of the states of the region, with the dates of their independence. The United Provinces of La Plata formed the nucleus of what later became Argentina.*

extracted wealth and income from America for its own people rather than its colonial subjects.

Creole leaders had read the Enlightenment philosophes and regarded their reforms as potentially beneficial to the region. They were also well aware of the events and the political philosophy of the American Revolution. Something more than reform programs and revolutionary example, however, was required to transform Creole discontent into revolt against the Spanish government. That transforming event occurred in Europe when Napoleon toppled the Portuguese monarchy in 1807 and the Spanish government in 1808 and then placed his own brother on the thrones of both countries. The Portuguese royal family fled to Brazil and established its government there. But the Bourbon monarchy of Spain stood, for the time being, wholly vanquished. That situation created an imperial political vacuum throughout Spanish Latin America and provided both the opportunity and the necessity for action by Creole leaders.

The Creole elite feared a liberal Napoleonic monarchy in Spain would attempt to impose reforms in Latin America that would harm their economic and social interests. They also feared a Spanish monarchy controlled by France would try to drain the region of the wealth and resources needed for Napoleon's wars. To protect their interests and to seize the opportunity to take over direction of their own political destiny, between 1808 and 1810 various Creole *juntas*, or political committees, claimed the right to govern different regions of Latin America. Many of them quite insincerely declared they were ruling in the name of the deposed Spanish monarch Ferdinand VII. After the establishment of these local juntas, the Spanish would not again directly govern the Continent; following ten years of politically and economically exhausting warfare, they were required to make Latin American independence permanent. The establishment of the juntas also ended the privileges of the *peninsulares*, whose welfare had always depended on the favors of the Spanish crown, and made positions in the government and army more easily available to Creoles.

San Martín in Rio de la Plata The vast size of Latin America, its geographical barriers, its distinct regional differences, and the absence of an even marginally integrated economy meant there would be several different paths to independence. The first region to assert itself was the Rio de la Plata, or modern Argentina. The center of revolt was Buenos Aires, whose citizens, as early as 1806, had fought off a British invasion against the Spanish commercial monopoly and thus had learned they could look to themselves rather than Spain for effective political

Toussaint L'Ouverture (1746–1803) began the revolt that led to Haitian independence in 1804. Corbis

and military action. In 1810, the junta in Buenos Aires not only thrust off Spanish authority, but also sent forces into both Paraguay and Uruguay in the cause of liberation from Spain and control by their own region. The armies were defeated, but Spanish control was nonetheless lost in the two areas. Paraguay asserted its own independence. Uruguay was eventually absorbed by Brazil.

The Buenos Aires government was not discouraged by these early defeats and remained determined to liberate Peru, the greatest stronghold of royalist power and loyalty on the continent. By 1814, José de San Martín (1778–1850) had become the leading general of the Río de la Plata forces. He organized a disciplined army and led his forces in a daring march over the Andes Mountains. By early 1817, he had occupied Santiago in Chile, where the Chilean independence leader Bernardo O'Higgins (1778–1842) was established as supreme dictator. From Santiago, San Martín oversaw the construction and organization of a naval force that, in 1820, he employed to carry his army by sea to an assault on Peru. The next year, San Martín drove royalist forces from Lima and took for himself the title of Protector of Peru.

Simon Bolívar's Liberation of Venezuela While the army of San Martín had been liberating the southern portion of the continent, Simón Bolívar (1783–1830) had been pursuing a similar task in the north. Bolívar had been involved in the organization of a liberating junta in Caracas, Venezuela, in 1810. He was a firm advocate of both independence and republican modes of government. Between 1811 and 1814, civil war broke out throughout Venezuela as both royalists, on one hand, and slaves and *llaneros* (Venezuelan cowboys), on the other, challenged the authority of the republican government. Bolívar had to go into exile first in Colombia and then in Jamaica. In 1816, with help from Haiti, he launched a new invasion against Venezuela. He first captured Bogotá, capital of New Granada (including modern Colombia, Ecuador, Venezuela and Panama), to secure a base for attack on Venezuela. The tactic worked. By the summer of 1821, Bolívar's forces had captured Caracas and he had been named president.

A year later, in July 1822, the armies of Bolívar and San Martín joined as they moved to liberate Quito. At a famous meeting of the two liberators in Guayaquil, a sharp disagreement occurred about the future political structure of Latin America. San Martín believed monarchies were required; Bolívar maintained his republicanism. Not long after the meeting, San Martín quietly retired from public life and went into exile in Europe. Meanwhile, Bolívar purposefully allowed the political situation in Peru to fall into confusion, and in 1823 he sent in troops to establish his control. On December 9, 1824, at the Battle of Ayacucho, the Spanish royalist forces suffered a major defeat at the hands of the liberating army. This battle marked the conclusion of the Spanish effort to retain their American empire.

Independence in New Spain The drive for independence in New Spain, which included present-day Mexico as well as Texas, California, and the rest of the southwest United States, illustrates better than that in any other region the socially conservative outcome of the Latin American colonial revolutions. As elsewhere, a local governing junta was organized. Before it had undertaken any significant measures, however, a Creole priest, Miguel Hidalgo y Costilla (1753–1811), issued a call for rebellion to the Indians in his parish. They and other repressed groups of black and mestizo urban and rural workers responded. Father Hidalgo set forth a program of social change, including hints of changes in landholding. Soon he stood at the head of a loosely organized group of 80,000 followers, who captured several major cities and then marched on Mexico City. Hidalgo's forces and the royalist army that opposed them committed many atrocities. In July 1811, the revolutionary priest was captured and executed. Leadership of his movement then fell to José María Morelos y Pavón (1765–1815), a mestizo priest. Far more radical than Hidalgo, he called for an end to forced labor and for substantial land reforms. He was executed in 1815, ending five years of popular uprising.

The uprising and its demand for fundamental social reforms united all conservative political groups in Mexico, both Creole and Spanish. These groups were unwilling to undertake any kind of reform that might cause loss of their privileges. In 1820, however, they found their recently achieved security challenged from an unexpected source. As already explained, the revolution in Spain had forced Ferdinand VII to accept a liberal constitution. Conservative Mexicans feared the new liberal monarchy would attempt to impose liberal reforms on Mexico.

Simon Bolivar (1783–1830) won Venezuelan independence from Spain with a decisive victory at Carabobo on June 24, 1821. South American Pictures

Dom Pedro I, the son of King John VI of Portugal (r. 1816–1826) was crowned emperor of an independent Brazil in 1822. Although Pedro abdicated in 1831 and returned to Portugal, his son Pedro II succeeded him as emperor and reigned until Brazil became a republic in 1889.
The Bridgeman Art Library

Therefore, for the most conservative of reasons, they rallied behind a former royalist general, Augustín de Iturbide (1783–1824), who declared Mexico independent of Spain in 1821. Shortly thereafter, Iturbide was declared emperor. His own regime did not last long, but an independent Mexico, governed by persons determined to resist any significant social reform, had been created.

Brazilian Independence Brazilian independence, in contrast to that of Spanish Latin America, came relatively simply and peacefully. As already noted, the Portuguese royal family, along with several thousand government officials and members of the court, took refuge in Brazil in 1807. Their arrival immediately transformed Rio de Janeiro into a court city. The prince regent João addressed many of the local complaints, equivalent to those of the Spanish Creoles, by, for example, taking measures that expanded trade. In 1815, he made Brazil a kingdom, which meant it was no longer to be regarded merely as a colony of Portugal. This change was in many respects long overdue, since Brazil was far larger and more prosperous than Portugal itself. Then, in 1820, a revolution occurred in Portugal, and its leaders demanded João's return to Lisbon. They also demanded the return of Brazil to colonial status. João, who had become João VI in 1816 (r. 1816–1826), returned to Portugal, but left his son Dom Pedro as regent in Brazil and encouraged him to be sympathetic to the political aspirations of the Brazilians. In September 1822, Dom Pedro embraced the cause of Brazilian independence against the recolonizing efforts of Portugal. By the end of the year, he had become emperor of an independent Brazil, which maintained an imperial form of government until 1889. Thus, in

contrast to virtually all other nations of Latin America, Brazil achieved independence in a way that left no real dispute as to where the center of political authority lay.

Two other factors aided the peaceful transition to independence in Brazil. First, the political leaders of Brazil were frightened by the destruction that had been unleashed in the Spanish American Empire by the wars of independence. They wanted to avoid that experience. Second, the political and social elite in Brazil had every intention of preserving slavery. The wars of independence elsewhere had generally led to the abolition of slavery or moved the independent states closer to abolition. Any attempt to gain independence from Portugal through warfare might have caused social as well as political turmoil that would open the slavery question.

Consequences of Latin American Independence
The era of the wars of independence left Latin America liberated from direct colonial control but economically exhausted and politically unstable. Only Brazil prospered immediately. Independence there had come peacefully and resulted in the establishment of a clearly recognized political authority prepared to pursue policies desired by the economic elite. In contrast to Brazil, the new republics of the former Spanish Empire felt weak and vulnerable. Because the wars of independence had been largely civil wars, disaffected populations threatened all the new governments. Economic life contracted, and in 1830 overall production was lower than it had been in 1800. Mines had fallen into disrepair or had been flooded. Livestock had been confiscated or destroyed. There were few institutions to foster interregional trade or address the difficult terrain that impeded it.

The disruption of old trade patterns reduced overseas trade. Funds for investment were scarce. Many wealthy *peninsulares* returned to Spain or went to Cuba. Consequently, Latin American governments and businesses looked to Britain for protection and for markets and capital investment.

The Conservative Order Shaken in Europe

During the first half of the 1820s, the institutions of the restored conservative order had in general successfully resisted the forces of liberalism. The two exceptions to this success, the Greek Revolution and the Latin American wars of independence, both occurred on the periphery of the European world. Beginning in the middle of the 1820s, however, the conservative governments of Russia, France, and Great Britain faced new stirrings of political discontent. (See Map 21–2.) In Russia the result was suppression, in France revolution, and in Britain, accommodation.

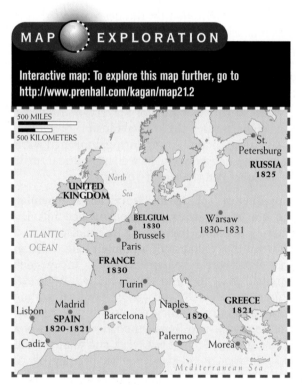

MAP 21–2   CENTERS OF REVOLUTION, 1820–1831
The conservative order imposed by the great powers in post-Napoleonic Europe was challenged by various uprisings and revolutions, beginning in 1820–1821 in Spain, Naples, and Greece and spreading to Russia, Poland, France, and Belgium later in the decade.

RUSSIA: THE DECEMBRIST REVOLT OF 1825

Tsar Alexander I had come to the Russian throne in 1801 after a palace coup against his father, Tsar Paul (r. 1796–1801). After a brief flirtation with Enlightenment ideas, Alexander turned permanently away from reform. Both at home and abroad, he took the lead in suppressing liberalism and nationalism. There would be no significant challenge to tsarist autocracy until his death.

Unrest in the Army As Russian forces drove Napoleon's army across Europe and then occupied defeated France, many Russian officers were exposed to the ideas of the French Revolution and the Enlightenment. Some of them, realizing how economically backward and politically stifled their own nation remained, developed reformist sympathies. Unable to express themselves openly because of Alexander's repressive policies, they formed secret societies. One of these, the Southern Society, was led by an officer named Pestel. It advocated representative government and the abolition of serfdom. Pestel himself even favored limited independence for Poland and democracy. Another secret society, the Northern Society, was more moderate. It favored constitutional monarchy and the abolition of serfdom, but wanted protection for the interests of the aristocracy. Both societies were very small and often in conflict with each other. They agreed only that Russia's government must change. Sometime during 1825, they apparently decided to carry out a coup d'état in 1826.

Dynastic Crisis In late November 1825, Tsar Alexander I died unexpectedly. His death created two crises. The first was dynastic. Alexander had no direct heir. His brother Constantine, the next in line to the throne and at the time the commander of Russian forces in occupied Poland, had married a woman who was not of royal blood. He had thus excluded himself from the throne and was more than willing to renounce any claim to it. Through a series of secret instructions made public only after his death, Alexander had named his younger brother, Nicholas (r. 1825–1855), as the new tsar.

Once Alexander was dead, the legality of these instructions became uncertain. Constantine acknowledged Nicholas as tsar, and Nicholas acknowledged Constantine. This family muddle continued for about three weeks, during which, to the astonishment of all Europe, Russia actually had no ruler. Then, during the early days of December, the army command reported to Nicholas the existence of a conspiracy among certain officers. Able to wait no longer for the working out of legal niceties, Nicholas had himself declared tsar, much to the delight of the by-now-exasperated Constantine.

The second crisis then proceeded to unfold. Several junior officers had indeed plotted to rally the troops under their command to the cause of reform. On December 26, 1825, the army was to take the oath of allegiance to Nicholas, who was less popular than Constantine and regarded as more conservative. Nearly all regiments took the oath. But the Moscow regiment, whose chief officers, surprisingly, were not secret society members, marched into the Senate Square in Saint Petersburg and refused to swear allegiance. Instead, they called for a constitution and the installation of Constantine as tsar. Attempts to settle the situation peacefully failed. Late in the afternoon, Nicholas ordered the cavalry and the artillery to attack the insurgents. More than sixty people were killed. Early in 1826, Nicholas himself presided over the commission that investigated the Decembrist Revolt and the secret army societies. Five of the plotters were executed and more than a hundred others were exiled to Siberia.

Although the Decembrist Revolt failed completely, it was the first rebellion in modern Russian history whose instigators had had specific political goals. They wanted constitutional government and the abolition of serfdom. As the century passed, the Decembrists, in their political martyrdom, came to symbolize the yearnings of all the never very numerous Russian liberals.

The Autocracy of Nicholas I Although Nicholas was neither an ignorant nor a bigoted reactionary, he came to symbolize the most extreme form of nineteenth-century autocracy. He knew economic growth and social improvement in Russia required reform, but he was quite simply afraid of change. In 1842, he told his State Council, "There is no doubt that serfdom, in its present form, is a flagrant evil which everyone realizes, yet to attempt to remedy it now would be, of course, an evil more disastrous."[4] To remove serfdom would necessarily, in his view, have undermined the nobles' support of the tsar. So Nicholas turned his back on this and practically all other reforms. Literary and political censorship and a widespread system of secret police flourished throughout his reign. There was little attempt to forge even an efficient and honest administration. The only significant reform of his rule was a codification of Russian law, published in 1833.

Official Nationality In place of reform, Nicholas and his closest advisers embraced a program called Official Nationality. Presiding over this program was Count S. S. Uvarov, minister of education from 1833 to 1849. Its slogan, published repeatedly in government documents, newspapers, journals, and schoolbooks, was "Orthodoxy, Autocracy, and Nationalism." The Russian Orthodox faith was to provide the basis for morality, education, and intellectual life. The church, which, since the days of Peter the Great, had been an arm of the secular government, controlled the schools and universities. Young Russians were taught to accept their place in life and to spurn social mobility.

The program of autocracy championed the unrestrained power of the tsar as the only authority that could hold the vast expanse of Russia and its peoples together. Political writers stressed that only under the autocracy of Peter the Great, Catherine the Great, and Alexander I had Russia prospered and exerted a major influence on world affairs.

Through the glorification of Russian nationality, Russians were urged to see their religion, language, and customs as a source of perennial wisdom that separated them from the moral corruption and political turmoil of the West. One result of this program was to leave serious Russian intellectuals profoundly alienated from the tsarist government.

Revolt and Repression in Poland Nicholas I was also extremely conservative in foreign affairs, as became apparent in Poland in the 1830s. That nation, which had been partitioned in the late eighteenth century and ceased to exist as an independent state, remained under Russian domination after the Congress of Vienna, but was granted a constitutional government. Under this arrangement, the tsar was Poland's ruler. Both Alexander and Nicholas delegated their brother, the Grand Duke Constantine (1779–1831), to run Poland's government. Although both tsars frequently infringed on the constitution and quarreled with the Polish diet, this arrangement held through the 1820s. Nevertheless, Polish nationalists continued to agitate for change.

In late November 1830, after news of the French and Belgian revolutions of that summer had reached Poland, a small insurrection of soldiers and students broke out in Warsaw. Disturbances soon spread throughout the rest of the country. On December 18, the Polish diet declared the revolution a nationalist movement. Early the next month, the diet voted to depose Nicholas as ruler of Poland. The tsar reacted by sending troops into the country and firmly suppressing the revolt. In February 1832, Nicholas issued the Organic Statute, declaring Poland to be an integral part of the Russian Empire. (See "Russia Reasserts Its Authority in Poland.") Although this statute guaranteed certain Polish liberties, the guarantees were systematically ignored.

---

[4]Quoted in Michael T. Florinsky, *Russia: A History and an Interpretation*, Vol. 2 (New York: Macmillan, 1953), p. 755.

When the Moscow regiment refused to swear allegiance to Nicholas, he ordered the cavalry and artillery to attack them. Although a total failure, the Decembrist Revolt came to symbolize the yearnings of all Russian liberals in the nineteenth century for a constitutional government. The Insurrection of the Decembrists at Senate Square, St. Petersburg on 26th December, 1825 (w/c on paper) by Russian School (19th century). Private Collection/Bridgeman Art Library, London/Novosti

The Polish uprising had confirmed all the tsar's worst fears. Henceforth Russia and Nicholas became the gendarme of Europe, ever ready to provide troops to suppress liberal and nationalist movements.

REVOLUTION IN FRANCE (1830)

The Polish revolt was the most distant of several disturbances that flowed from the overthrow of the Bourbon dynasty in France during July 1830. When Louis XVIII had died in 1824, his brother, the count of Artois, the leader of the ultraroyalist faction at the time of the restoration, succeeded him as Charles X (r. 1824–1830). The new king was a firm believer in rule by divine right.

The Reactionary Policies of Charles X Charles X's first action was to have the Chamber of Deputies in 1824 and 1825 indemnify aristocrats who had lost their lands in the revolution. He did this by lowering the interest rates on government bonds to create a fund to pay an annual sum to the survivors of the émigrés who had forfeited land. Middle-class bondholders, who lost income, naturally resented this measure. Charles also restored the rule of primogen-

iture, whereby only the eldest son of an aristocrat inherited the family domains. And, in support of the Roman Catholic Church, he enacted a law that punished sacrilege with imprisonment or death. Liberals disapproved of all of these measures.

In the elections of 1827, the liberals gained enough seats in the Chamber of Deputies to compel conciliatory actions from the king. He appointed a less conservative ministry. Laws against the press and those allowing the government to dominate education were eased. The liberals, however, wanted a genuinely constitutional regime and remained unsatisfied. In 1829, the king decided his policy of accommodation had failed. He replaced his moderate ministry with an ultraroyalist ministry headed by the Prince de Polignac (1780–1847). The opposition, in desperation, opened negotiations with the liberal Orléanist branch of the royal family.

The July Revolution In 1830, Charles X called for new elections, in which the liberals scored a stunning victory. Instead of accommodating the new Chamber of Deputies, the king and his ministers decided to attempt a royalist seizure of power. In June and July

RUSSIA REASSERTS ITS AUTHORITY IN POLAND

As a result of the three eighteenth-century partitions by Russia, Prussia, and Austria, an independent Poland had disappeared from the map of Europe. Russia governed the largest portion of the partitioned Polish lands. During 1830, Poland rebelled against Russian administration. The revolt failed after several months. Tsar Nicholas I then imposed even more direct and repressive control over Poland. This action constituted a direct rejection of the principle of nationalism, and Polish independence would become one of the major nationalist causes of the nineteenth century. An independent Poland emerged only as a result of the Paris Peace Settlement following World War I.

■ *In what variety of specific ways does this proclamation attempt to offend and repress Polish nationalism? What rights are given to the Poles? What evidence is there of any institutions being established to protect those rights? Is there anything in the proclamation aimed at gaining the support of some parts of the Polish population? Compare this proclamation with the values espoused by Mazzini's vision of nationalism.*

Now that an end has been put by force of arms to the rebellion in Poland, and that the nation, led away by agitators, has returned to its duty, and is restored to tranquillity, we deem it right to carry into execution our plan with regard to the introduction of the new order of things, whereby the tranquillity and union of the two nations, which Providence has entrusted to our care, may be forever guarded against new attempts. . . . The kingdom of Poland, again subject to our sceptre, will regain tranquillity, and again flourish in the bosom of peace, restored to it under the auspices of a vigilant government. Hence we consider it one of our most sacred duties to watch with paternal care over the welfare of our faithful subjects, and to use every means in our power to prevent the recurrence of similar catastrophes, by taking from the ill-disposed the power of disturbing public tranquillity. . . .

Art. 1. The kingdom of Poland is forever to be reunited to the Russian empire and form an inseparable part of that empire. . . .

Art. 2. The Crown of the kingdom of Poland is hereditary in our person and in our heirs and successors, agreeably to the order of succession to the throne prescribed by all the Russians.

Art. 3. The Coronation of the Emperors of all the Russians and Kings of Poland shall be one and the same ceremonial which shall take place at Moscow, in the presence of a deputation from the kingdom of Poland, which shall assist at that solemnity with the deputies from the other parts of the empire. . . .

Art. 5. The freedom of worship is guaranteed. . . . The Roman Catholic religion, being that of the majority of our Polish subjects, shall be the object of especial protection of the Government. . . .

Art. 7. The protection of the laws is assured to all the inhabitants without distinction of rank or class. . . .

Art. 13. Publication of sentiments by means of the press shall be subjected to restrictions which will protect religion, the inviolability of superior authority, the interests of morals, and personal considerations. . . .

Art. 14. The kingdom of Poland shall proportionably contribute to the general expenditure and to the wants of the empire. . . .

Art. 20. Our army in the empire and in the kingdom shall compose one in common, without distinction of Russian or Polish troops. . . .

Art. 21. Those of our subjects of the empire of Russia, who are established in the kingdom of Poland, who possess or shall possess, real property in that country, shall enjoy all the rights of natives. It shall be the same with those of our subjects in the kingdom of Poland, who shall establish themselves, and shall possess property, in the other provinces of the empire.

Published in Joseph Hordynaki, *History of the Late Polish Revolution and the Events of the Campaign* (Boston: Printed for Subscribers, 1833), pp. 424–428, as quoted in Alfred J. Bannan and Achilles Edelenyi, *Documentary History of Eastern Europe* (New York: Twayne Publishers, 1970), pp. 133–137.

Polish rebels marching against their Russian occupiers in 1830. Russia crushed the revolt and instituted sweeping repression in Poland. Archives Charmet/Bridgeman Art Library.

1830, Polignac had sent a naval expedition against Algeria, which was nominally under Ottoman rule but had in fact become a pirate state whose ships preyed on the merchant vessels of all nations. Reports of its victory and the founding of a French Empire in North Africa reached Paris on July 9. Taking advantage of the euphoria created by this victory, Charles issued the Four Ordinances on July 25, 1830, staging what amounted to a royal coup d'état. These ordinances restricted freedom of the press, dissolved the recently elected Chamber of Deputies, restricted the franchise to the wealthiest people in the country, and called for new elections under the new royalist franchise.

The Four Ordinances provoked swift and decisive popular political reactions. Liberal newspapers called on the nation to reject the monarch's actions. The laboring populace of Paris, burdened since 1827 by an economic downturn, took to the streets and erected barricades. The king called out troops, and more than 1,800 people died during the ensuing battles in the city. But the army was not able to gain control of Paris

On August 2, Charles X abdicated and left France for exile in England. The Chamber of Deputies named a new ministry composed of constitutional monarchists. In an act that finally ended the rule of the Bourbon dynasty, it also proclaimed Louis Philippe (r. 1830–1848), the duke d'Orléans, the new king.

In the Revolution of 1830, the liberals of the Chamber of Deputies had filled a power vacuum created by the popular Paris uprising and the failure of effective royal action. Had Charles X provided himself with sufficient troops in Paris, the outcome could

have been quite different. Moreover, had the liberals, who favored constitutional monarchy, not acted quickly, the workers and shopkeepers of Paris might have attempted to form a republic. By seizing the moment, the middle class, the bureaucrats, and the moderate aristocratic liberals overthrew the restoration monarchy and still avoided a republic. These liberals feared a new popular revolution such as had swept France in 1792. They had no desire for another *sans-culottes* republic. A fundamental political and social tension thus underlay the new monarchy. The revolution had succeeded thanks to a temporary alliance between hard-pressed laborers and the prosperous middle class, but these two groups soon realized their basic goals had been quite different.

Monarchy under Louis Philippe Politically, the July Monarchy, as it was called, was more liberal than the restoration government. Louis Philippe was called the "king of the French" rather than "king of France." The tricolor flag of the revolution replaced the white flag of the Bourbons. The new constitution was regarded as a right of the people rather than as a concession of the monarch. Catholicism became the religion of a majority of the people rather than "the official religion." The new government was strongly anticlerical. Censorship was abolished. The franchise became somewhat wider, but remained, on the whole, restricted. The king had to cooperate with the Chamber of Deputies; he could not dispense with laws on his own authority.

Socially, however, the Revolution of 1830 proved conservative. The hereditary peerage was abolished in 1831, but the everyday economic, political, and social influence of the landed oligarchy continued. Money was the path to power and influence in the government. There was much corruption.

Most important, the liberal monarchy displayed little or no sympathy for the lower and working classes. In 1830, the workers of Paris had called for the protection of jobs, better wages, and the preservation of the traditional crafts, rather than for the usual goals of political liberalism. The government of Louis Philippe ignored their demands and their plight. The laboring classes of Paris and the provincial cities seemed just one more possible source of disorder. In late 1831, troops suppressed a workers' revolt in Lyons. In July 1832, an uprising occurred in Paris during the funeral of a popular Napoleonic general. Again the government called out troops, and more than eight hundred people were killed or wounded. In 1834, a very large strike of silk workers in Lyons was crushed. Such discontent might be smothered for a time, but without attention to the social and economic conditions creating it, new turmoil would eventually erupt.

The new French government of 1830 was only too happy to retain the control of the city of Algiers that Charles X had achieved less than a month before his overthrow and to expand French control beyond the coastal regions. The occupation of Algeria gave French merchants in Marseilles new economic ties to North Africa. Moreover, the French quickly dismantled the structures of Ottoman government that had survived in Algeria and set out to conquer and administer the interior of the country, which was larger than France itself and where Ottoman rule had never penetrated. By the middle of the century, the French had extended their rule after constant warfare against Muslim tribesmen as far as the northern Sahara desert. France now had a vast new empire, and French citizens and other Europeans also began to settle in Algeria in large numbers, especially in the cities. In the second half of the nineteenth century, the French government came to regard Algeria, despite its overwhelmingly Muslim population, as not a colony but an integral part of France itself. This was to have serious repercussions after World War II when a pro-independence movement developed among Muslim Algerians.

BELGIUM BECOMES INDEPENDENT (1830)

The July Revolution in Paris sent sparks to other political tinder on the Continent. The revolutionary fires first lighted in neighboring Belgium. The former Austrian Netherlands, Belgium had been merged with the kingdom of Holland in 1815. The two countries differed in language, religion, and economy, however, and the Belgian upper classes never reconciled themselves to Dutch rule.

On August 25, 1830, disturbances broke out in Brussels following the performance of an opera about a rebellion in Naples against Spanish rule. To end the rioting, the municipal authorities and people from the propertied classes formed a provisional national government. When compromise between the Belgians and the Dutch failed, William of Holland (r. 1815–1840) sent troops and ships against Belgium. By November 10, 1830, the Dutch had been defeated. A national congress then wrote a liberal Belgian constitution, which was promulgated in 1831.

Although the major powers saw the revolution in Belgium as upsetting the boundaries established by the Congress of Vienna, they were not inclined to intervene to reverse it. Russia was preoccupied with the Polish revolt. Prussia and the other German states were suppressing small uprisings in their own domains. The Austrians were busy putting down disturbances in Italy. France under Louis Philippe favored an independent Belgium and hoped to dominate it. Britain felt it could tolerate a liberal Belgium, as long as it was free of foreign domination.

In December 1830, Lord Palmerston (1784–1865), the British foreign minister, gathered representatives of the powers in London and persuaded them to recognize Belgium as an independent and neutral state. In July 1831, Leopold of Saxe-Coburg (r. 1831–1865) became king of the Belgians. Belgian neutrality was guaranteed by the Convention of 1839 and remained an article of faith in European international relations for almost a century.

Both Belgium and Serbia gained independence in 1830, and ironically, diplomatic crises involving both nations led to World War I. The assassination of an Austrian archduke by a Serbian

On July 5, 1830 French forces captured Algiers, which France would continue to rule until 1962. Note how this drawing contrasts the power and modernity of the French conquerors with the almost medieval appearance of the Algerian defenses. Getty Images, Inc.

nationalist in Sarajevo in 1914 triggered the war, and Germany's violation of Belgian neutrality brought Britain into it.

THE GREAT REFORM BILL IN BRITAIN (1832)

In Great Britain, the revolutionary year of 1830 saw the election of a House of Commons that debated the first major bill to reform Parliament. The death of George IV (r. 1820–1830) and the accession of William IV (r. 1830–1837) required the calling of a parliamentary election, held in the summer of 1830. Historians once believed the July revolution in France influenced voting in Britain, but close analysis of the time and character of individual county and borough elections has shown otherwise. The passage of the Great Reform Bill, which became law in 1832, was the result of a series of events very different from those that occurred on the Continent. In Britain, the forces of conservatism and reform made accommodations with each other.

Political and Economic Reform Several factors contributed to this spirit of accommodation. First, the commercial and industrial class was larger in Britain than in other countries. No matter what group might

Events Associated with Liberal Reform and Revolution

1824	Charles X becomes king of France
1825	Decembrist Revolt in Russia
1828	Repeal of restrictions against British Protestant nonconformists
1829	Catholic Emancipation Act passed in Great Britain; Ottoman Sultan grants independence to Serbia
1830 (July 9)	News of French colonial conquest in Algeria reaches Paris
1830 (July 25)	Charles X issues the Four Ordinances
1830 (August 2)	Charles X abdicates; Louis Philippe proclaimed king
1830 (August 25)	Belgian revolution
1830 (November 29)	Polish revolution
1832	Organic Statute makes Poland an integral part of Russian Empire
1832	Great Reform Bill passed in Great Britain

control the government, British prosperity required attention to their economic interests. Second, Britain's liberal Whig aristocrats, who regarded themselves as the protectors of constitutional liberty, represented a long tradition in favor of moderate reforms that would make revolutionary changes unnecessary. Early Whig sympathy for the French Revolution reduced their influence. After 1815, however, they reentered the political arena. Finally, British law, tradition, and public opinion all showed a strong respect for civil liberties.

In 1820, the year after the passage of the notorious Six Acts, Lord Liverpool shrewdly moved to change his cabinet. The new members continued to favor generally conservative policies, but they also believed the government had to accommodate itself to the changing social and economic life of the nation. They favored policies of greater economic freedom and repealed the earlier Combination Acts that had prohibited labor organizations.

Catholic Emancipation Act Economic considerations had generally led to the British moderate reforms. English determination to maintain the union with Ireland brought about another key reform. England's relationship to Ireland was similar to that of Russia to Poland or Austria to its several national groups. In 1800, fearful that Irish nationalists might again rebel as they had in 1798 and perhaps turn Ireland into a base for a French invasion, William Pitt the Younger had persuaded Parliament to pass the Act of Union between Ireland and England. Ireland now sent a hundred members to the House of Commons. Only Protestant Irishmen, however, could be elected to represent their overwhelmingly Roman Catholic nation.

During the 1820s, under the leadership of Daniel O'Connell (1775–1847), Irish nationalists organized the Catholic Association to agitate for Catholic emancipation. In 1828, O'Connell secured his own election to Parliament, where he could not legally take his seat. The British ministry of the duke of Wellington realized that henceforth an entirely Catholic delegation might be elected from Ireland. If they were not seated, civil war might erupt across the Irish Sea. Consequently, in 1829, Wellington and Robert Peel steered the Catholic Emancipation Act through Parliament. Roman Catholics could now become members of Parliament. This measure, together with the repeal in 1828 of restrictions against Protestant nonconformists, ended the Anglican monopoly on British political life.

Catholic emancipation was a liberal measure passed for the conservative purpose of preserving order in Ireland. It included a provision raising the franchise in Ireland so that only the wealthier Irish could vote. Nonetheless, this measure alienated many of Wellington's Anglican Tory supporters in the House of Commons. The election of 1830 returned many supporters of parliamentary reform to Parliament. Even some Tories supported reform, because they thought Catholic emancipation could have been passed only by a corrupt House of Commons. The Tories, consequently, were badly divided, and the Wellington ministry soon fell. King William IV then turned to the leader of the Whigs, Earl Grey (1764–1845), to form a government.

Legislating Change The Whig ministry soon presented the House of Commons with a major reform bill that had two broad goals. The first was to abolish "rotten boroughs," or boroughs that had very few voters, and to replace them with representatives for the previously unrepresented manufacturing districts and cities. Second, the number of voters in England and Wales was to be increased by about 50

percent through a series of new franchises. In 1831, the House of Commons narrowly defeated the bill. Grey called for a new election, in which a majority in favor of the bill was returned. The House of Commons passed the reform bill, but the House of Lords rejected it. Mass meetings were held throughout the country. Riots broke out in several cities. Finally, William IV agreed to create enough new peers to give a third reform bill a majority in the House of Lords. Under this pressure, the House of Lords yielded, and in 1832 the measure became law.

The **Great Reform Bill** expanded the size of the English electorate, but it was not a democratic measure. It increased the number of voters by more than 200,000, or almost 50 percent, but it kept a property qualification for the franchise. (Gender was also a qualification. No thought was given to enfranchising women.) Some members of the working class actually lost the right to vote because of the abolition of

THOMAS BABINGTON MACAULAY DEFENDS THE GREAT REFORM BILL

Macaulay (1800–1859) was a member of the House of Commons, which passed the Great Reform Bill in 1831, only to have it rejected by the House of Lords before another measure was successfully enacted in 1832. His speeches in support of the bill reflect his views on the need for Parliament to give balanced representation to major elements in the population without embracing democracy. His arguments had wide appeal.

■ *Who does Macaulay think should be represented in Parliament? Why does he oppose universal suffrage? Why does he regard the Reform Bill as "a measure of conservation"? Why would Metternich have seen little or nothing conservative about the measure?*

[T]he principle of the ministers] is plain, rational, and consistent. It is this,—to admit the middle class to a large and direct share in the Representation, without any violent shock to the institutions of our country. . . . I hold it to be clearly expedient, that in a country like this, the right of suffrage should depend on a pecuniary qualification. Every argument . . . which would induce me to oppose Universal Suffrage, induces me to support the measure which is now before us. I oppose Universal Suffrage, because I think that it would produce a destructive revolution. I support this measure, because I am sure that it is our best security against a revolution. . . . I . . . do entertain great apprehension for the fate of my country. I do in my conscience believe, that unless this measure, or some similar measure, be speedily adopted, great and terrible calamities will befall us. Entertaining this

opinion, I think myself bound to state it, not as a threat, but as a reason. I support this measure as a means of Reform: But I support it still more as a measure of conservation. That we may exclude those whom it is necessary to exclude, we must admit those whom it may be safe to admit. . . . All history is full of revolutions, produced by causes similar to those which are now operating in England. A portion of the community which had been of no account, expands and becomes strong. It demands a place in the system, suited, not to its former weakness, but to its present power. If this is granted, all is well. If this is refused, then comes the struggle between the young energy of one class, and the ancient privileges of another. . . . Such . . . is the struggle which the middle classes in England are maintaining against an aristocracy of mere locality.

From *Hansard's Parliamentary Debates*, 3rd series, Vol. 2, pp. 1191–1197.

certain old franchise rights. New urban boroughs were created to allow the growing cities to have a voice in the House of Commons. Yet the passage of the reform act did not, as was once thought, constitute the triumph of middle-class interests in England: For every new urban electoral district, a new rural district was also drawn, and the aristocracy was expected to dominate rural elections. What the bill permitted was a wider variety of property to be represented in the House of Commons. (See "Thomas Babington Macaulay Defends the Great Reform Bill.")

The success of the reform bill was to reconcile previously unrepresented property owners and economic interests to the political institutions of the country. The act laid the groundwork for further orderly reforms of the church, municipal government, and commercial policy. By admitting into the political forum people who sought change and giving them access to the legislative process, it made revolution in Britain unnecessary. In this manner, Great Britain maintained its traditional institutions of government while allowing an increasingly diverse group of people to influence them. (See "Art & the West: John Constable's Harmonious Landscapes in Unstable Times," p. 734.)

In Perspective

Through the Congress System the major powers had responded to pressures on the Vienna Settlement without going to war against each other or allowing any state or group of states to annex territory. In the fifteen years between the conclusion of the Congress of Vienna and the Revolution of 1830 in France, no revolutionary disturbance had succeeded in Europe except for the Greek revolt that broke out in 1821. In Russia, the Decembrist Revolt of 1825 failed almost before it had begun. The only truly successful revolutionary activity during these years occurred in Latin America, where wars of independence ended Spain's and Portugal's centuries-old colonial domination.

Nonetheless, during the 1820s, liberal political ideas and some liberal political figures began to make inroads into the otherwise conservative domestic order. In 1830, revolution and reform again began to move across Europe. The French rejected the restored Bourbon monarchy and established a more liberal monarchy. Belgium also achieved independence with a liberal government. Perhaps most important, Great Britain moved slowly toward a more liberal position. During the 1820s, Great Britain had become unenthusiastic about a

political role that placed it in opposition to all change. For its own commercial reasons, it favored independence for Latin America. Popular pressures at home led the British aristocratic leadership to enact a moderate reform bill in 1832. Thereafter, Britain would be viewed as the leading liberal state in Europe and one that would support nationalistic causes.

REVIEW QUESTIONS

1. Define nationalism. What were the goals of nationalists? What were the difficulties they confronted in realizing those goals? Why was nationalism a special threat to the Austrian Empire? What areas saw significant nationalist movements between 1815 and 1830? Which were successful and which unsuccessful?

2. What were the tenets of liberalism? Who were the liberals, and how did liberalism affect the political developments of the early nineteenth century? What relationship does liberalism have to nationalism?

3. What difficulties did the conservatives in Austria, Prussia, and Russia face after the Napoleonic wars? How did they respond on both national and international levels? What were the aims of the Concert of Europe? How did international relations after the Congress of Vienna differ from the international relations of the eighteenth century?

4. What political changes took place in Latin America in the twenty years between 1804 and 1824? What were the main reasons for Creole discontent with Spanish rule, and to what extent were the Creole leaders influenced by Enlightenment political philosophy? Who were some of the primary leaders of Latin American independence, and why were they successful?

5. Describe the constitution of the restored monarchy in France. Was the government truly constitutional? What did Charles X hope to accomplish? How much support did he have? What were the causes of the Revolution of 1830? What did this Revolution achieve and at what cost?

6. Before 1820, Britain appeared to be moving down the same reactionary road as the other major powers. What factors led to a different outcome in Britain? What was the purpose of the Great Reform Bill? What did it achieve? Would you call it a "revolutionary" document?

7. By approximately 1830 how had European political ambitions and the ideas of liberalism and nationalism begun to undermine the control of the Ottoman Empire over Greece, Serbia, and Algeria?

SUGGESTED READINGS

B. ANDERSON, *Imagined Communities*, rev. ed. (1991). An influential and controversial discussion of nationalism.

C. I. ARCHER, C. M. MACLACHLAN, AND W. H. BEEZLEY (EDS.), *The Wars of Independence in Spanish America* (2000). Broad selection of essays based on most recent scholarship.

N. M. ATHANASSOGLOU-KALLMYER, *French Images from the Greek War of Independence, 1821–1830: Art and Politics under the Restoration* (2000). Explores both the Greek War of Independence and French politics.

M. BERDAHL, *The Politics of the Prussian Nobility: The Development of a Conservative Ideology, 1770–1848* (1988). A major examination of German conservative outlooks.

A. BRIGGS, *The Making of Modern England* (1959). Classic survey of English history during the first half of the nineteenth century.

M. BROCK, *The Great Reform Act* (1974). The standard work.

G. A. CRAIG, *The Politics of the Prussian Army, 1640–1945* (1955). Remains a splendid study of the conservative political influence of the army on Prussian development.

M. F. CROSS AND D. WILLIAMS, (EDS.), *French Experience from Republic to Monarchy, 1792–1824: New Dawns in Politics, Knowledge and Culture* (2000). Essays examining various institutions of French culture from the revolution through the restoration.

D. DAKIN, *The Struggle for Greek Independence* (1973). An excellent explanation of the intricacies of the Greek independence question.

E. J. EVANS, *Britain Before the Reform Act: Politics and Society, 1815–1832* (1995). A survey.

W. FORTESCUE, *Revolution and Counter-Revolution in France, 1815–1852* (2002). A helpful brief survey.

E. GELLNER, *Nations and Nationalism* (1983). A major theoretical work.

L. GREENFELD, *Nationalism: Five Roads to Modernity* (1992). A major comparative study.

E. J. HOBSBAWM, *Nations and Nationalism since 1780: Programme, Myth, Reality*, rev. ed. (1992). The best recent introduction to the subject.

B. JELAVICH, *Russia's Balkan Entanglements, 1899–1914* (1991). Now the standard discussion of this topic.

C. JELAVICH AND B. JELAVICH, *The Establishment of the Balkan National States, 1804–1920* (1977). A standard, clear introduction.

S. KROEN, *Politics and Theater: The Crisis of Legitimacy in Restoration France, 1815–1830* (2000). Examines how French theater reacted to the climate of changing political regimes.

M. B. LEVINGER, *Enlightened Nationalism: The Transformation of Prussian Political Culture, 1806–1848* (2002). A major work based on the most recent scholarship.

W. B. LINCOLN, *Nicholas I: Emperor and Autocrat of All the Russians* (1978). A serious scholarly treatment.

J. LYNCH, *The Spanish American Revolutions, 1808–1826* (1973). An excellent one-volume treatment.

C. A. MACARTNEY, *The Habsburg Empire, 1790–1918* (1971). An outstanding survey.

P. MANENT, *An Intellectual History of Liberalism* (1994). A penetrating, succinct study.

A. PALMER, *Alexander I: Tsar of War and Peace* (1974). An interesting biography that captures much of the mysterious personality of this ruler.

P. PILBEAM, *The 1830 Revolution in France* (1991). An account that emphasizes the Restoration's accommodation to various interest groups.

D. H. PINKNEY, *The French Revolution of 1830* (1972). The standard narrative account.

M. RAEFF, *The Decembrist Movement* (1966). An examination of the unsuccessful uprising, with documents.

N. V. RIASANOVSKY, *Nicholas I and Official Nationality in Russia, 1825–1855* (1959). A lucid discussion of the conservative ideology that made Russia the major opponent of liberalism.

W. D. D. RUBINSTEIN, *Britain's Century: A Political and Social History, 1815–1905* (1999). Based on the most recent scholarship.

J. SHEEHAN, *German History, 1770–1866* (1989). A very long work that is now the best available survey of the subject.

A. B. ULAM, *Russia's Failed Revolutionaries* (1981). Contains a useful discussion of the Decembrists as a background for other nineteenth-century Russian revolutionary activity.

I. WOLOCH, *The New Regime: Transformations of the French Civic Order, 1789–1820s* (1994). An important overview of just what had and had not changed in France after the quarter century of revolution and war.

DOCUMENTS CD-ROM

REACTION, REFORM, AND REVOLT

21.1 "Sentiments of a Nation": A Mexican Call for Independence

21.2 Thomas MacAulay: *A Radical War-Song*

21.3 Alexis de Tocqueville: *The New Social Morality*

21.4 Simon Bolívar's Political Ideas

John Constable's Harmonious Landscapes in Unstable Times

John Constable (1776–1837) was an English artist whose political views were as conservative as Jacques-Louis David's were radical (see "Art & the West," Chapter 19). The differences in their political outlooks and between the two eras in which they painted are evident in *Salisbury Cathedral, from the Meadows* (1831), one of Constable's many portrayals of the Gothic cathedral with the highest spire in England. His paintings are associated with romanticism because of his interest in nature, local history, and the Middle Ages and because of the very free application of paint. He paid enormous attention to clouds, of which he made many small studies, preparing for his larger paintings. The aim of painting, he wrote, was, "To give 'to one brief moment caught from fleeting time,' a lasting and sober existence, and to render permanent many of those splendid but evanescent Exhibitions, which are ever occurring in the changes of external Nature."[5]

In *Salisbury Cathedral, from the Meadows*, Constable created a landscape that suggests his politically conservative outlook. He was deeply concerned with portraying a landed order that was stable and unchallenged by either political turmoil or industrial development. Although the clouds and sky in the painting depict a severe storm, there is a powerful orderliness present in the works of both nature and humankind. The trees clearly have withstood the storm as they have done so for many years. The cathedral likewise has stood for centuries. Arching over the entire scene and giving it a sacramental nature is the rainbow, suggesting a divine presence.

Constable did not paint idealized classical landscapes, nor did he portray classical heroes dedicated to an abstract higher political good. His landscapes reproduced scenes of English rural and village life with great faithfulness to their appearance. People in Constable's paintings always are working, often at ordinary tasks. They seem to be an integral part of the natural order, suggesting no discontent with their lot. Constable and others of his era tended to look to rural life as the contemporary embodiment of what they regarded as the social stability of the Middle Ages. These artists and thinkers projected on that era a sense of organic stability and religious reverence they saw absent from their own society.

In fact, though, social disruption and the potential for political upheaval marked the rural areas that Constable portrayed. The enclosures and early mechanization of farming had driven many people off the land, and many of the rural poor endured enormous suffering. During the Napoleonic Wars dairy farmers turned their land to grain raising, but after the war they could not reconvert the land efficiently enough to compete with Dutch dairy products. Wartime profits created wealthy farmers who separated themselves from the lives of their laborers. During the 1820s and 1830s, rural riots broke out in East Anglia, the region of England Constable knew best. In his paintings, he idealized a rural landscape and rustic society that had already largely disappeared. Moreover, Constable associated his vision of a staid, orderly landed society with various kinds of "natural" authority, such as family, community itself, and God. In the face of the radical politicalization of the countryside, his paintings depoliticized the landscape. People and nature stand in harmony, with their work part of the natural order.

Like many English conservatives of his day, Constable saw the church and the constitution as intimately related. Religious institutions served to withstand political radicalism. In private letters Constable associated liberal reformers with the devil, leading some scholars to suggest the lightning striking the back roof of the cathedral symbolizes those evil forces and the rainbow indicates the ongoing presence of the divine order of nature and society. Part of this argument is based on the fact that Constable would most certainly have known from his observations of

[5]Quoted in Ann Bermingham, *Landscape and Ideology: The English Rustic Tradition, 1740–1860* (Berkeley: University of California Press, 1986), p. 151.

John Constable (1776–1837), *Salisbury Cathedral, from the Meadows*, 1831.   Oil on canvas,
151.8 × 189.9. © The National Gallery, London.

weather that what he painted could never have occurred. Other commentators believe the dark, boding qualities of this scene, with the rainbow suggesting hope, reflect Constable's inner sadness and turmoil over the death of his wife.

■ *Why is Constable's* Salisbury Cathedral *typical of the romantic movement? How does the painting illustrate the artist's political conservatism?*

How does Constable use nature to highlight his political leanings?

Sources: Ann Bermingham, *Landscape and Ideology: The English Rustic Tradition, 1740–1860* (Berkeley: University of California Press, 1986); Michael Rosenthal, *Constable: The Painter and His Landscape* (New Haven, CT: Yale University Press, 1983); John Barrell, *The Darker Side of Landscape* (Cambridge, UK: Cambridge University Press, 1980).

The Abolition of Slavery in the Transatlantic Economy

One of the most important developments during the age of Enlightenment and revolution was the opening of a crusade to abolish chattel slavery in the transatlantic economy. The antislavery movement constituted the greatest and most extensive achievement of liberal reformers during the eighteenth and nineteenth centuries. Indeed, it marked the first time in the history of the world that a society actually tried to abolish slavery. This achievement came as the result of the impact of Christian ethics, Enlightenment ideals, slave revolts, revolutionary wars in America and Europe, civil war in the United States, and economic dislocation in the slave economies themselves. In 1750, almost no one seriously questioned the existence of slavery, but by 1888 the institution no longer existed in the transatlantic economy.

Chattel slavery—the ownership of one human being by another—had existed in the West as well as elsewhere in the world since ancient times and had received intellectual and religious justification throughout the history of the West. Both Plato and Aristotle provided arguments for slavery based on the assertion that persons in bondage were intended by nature to be slaves. Christian writers similarly accommodated themselves to the institution. They contended that the most harmful form of slavery was the enslavement of the soul to sin rather than the enslavement of the physical body. They also argued that genuine freedom was realized through one's relationship to God and that problems relating to the injustices of inequality would be solved in the hereafter. Christian scholastic thinkers in the Middle Ages had portrayed slavery as part of the natural and necessary hierarchy of the universe.

Slavery Spreads to the Americas

Although a vast slave trade existed throughout the Mediterranean world through the end of the Middle Ages, slavery was no longer a dominant institution on the European continent or within the European economy. The European encounter with America at the end of the fifteenth century radically transformed that situation. The American continent and the West Indies presented opportunities for achieving great wealth, but a major labor shortage existed in these regions. Eventually slavery provided the means to resolve this labor shortage.

The establishment and maintenance of slavery in the transatlantic economy drew Europeans and Americans into various relationships with Africa. About the same time as the encounter with America, Europeans made contact with areas of West Africa where slavery already existed. This region became the chief source of slaves imported into the Americas. Four centuries later, during the antislavery movement, Europeans would seek to change the African economy by ending its dependence on the slave trade. Those efforts led to the penetration of Africa by European traders, missionaries, and finally colonial forces and administrators.

Although at one time or another slaves labored throughout the Americas, the system of slavery became primarily identified with the plantation economy stretching from Maryland south to Brazil, where tropical products, initially primarily sugar, were produced by slave labor. This plantation economy existed from approximately the late sixteenth through the late nineteenth century. The slaves on whose labor this economy was based included Native Americans enslaved within both the Spanish Empire and North America, and Africans forcibly imported into the Americas. Consequently, the slaves were virtually always of a different race from their masters. Race itself soon became part of the justification for the social hierarchy of the plantation world. In and of itself, the fact of slavery in the Americas was not unusual to the Western experience or to that of other societies in Africa or Asia. Slavery had existed at most times and places in human history. Far more unusual in the history of the West and for that matter in the experience of all other societies that had held and continued to hold slaves was the emergence after 1760 of an international movement to abolish chattel slavery in the transatlantic economy.

The Crusade Against Slavery

The eighteenth-century crusade against slavery originated in a profound change in the religious and intellectual outlooks on slavery among small but influential groups in both America and Europe. The entire thrust of Enlightenment reasoning to the extent that it challenged or questioned the wisdom of existing institutions gnawed away at the older defenses of slavery, most particularly the concept of an unchanging social hierarchy. Although some writers associated with the Enlightenment, including John Locke, were reluctant to question slavery and even defended it, the general Enlightenment rhetoric of equality stood in sharp contrast to the radical inequality of slavery. Montesquieu sharply satirized slavery in *The Spirit of the Laws* (1748). Similarly, the emphasis of Adam Smith in *The Wealth of Nations* (1776) on free labor and efficiency of free markets undermined defenses of slavery.

Within much eighteenth-century literature, there emerged a tendency to idealize primitive peoples living in cultures very different from those of Europe. Previously such peoples had been regarded as backward and rebellious. Now numerous writers portrayed them as embodying a lost human virtue. This expanding body of literature transformed the way many people thought about slavery and allowed some Europeans to look on African slaves in the Americas as having been betrayed and robbed of an original innocence. Additionally, much eighteenth-century European ethical thinking, as well as later romantic poetry, emphasized empathy and feeling. In such a climate, attitudes toward slavery were transformed. Once considered to be the natural and deserved result of some deficiency in slaves themselves, slavery now grew to be regarded as undeserved and unacceptable. The same kind of ethical thinking led reformers to believe that by working against slavery, for virtually the first time defined as an unmitigated evil, they would realize their own highest ethical character.

Religious movements became the single most important cultural force to foster the antislavery crusade. The evangelical religious revival associated with Methodism and with other forms of Protestant preaching emphasized the conversion experience and the change of heart as a sign of having received salvation. In 1774, John Wesley, the founder of Methodism, attacked slaveholding in *Thoughts on Slavery*. Turning against slaveholding and slave trading by plantation owners and slave

After 1807, the British Royal Navy patrolled the West African coast attempting to intercept slave-trading ships. In 1846, the British ship HMS Albatross *captured a Spanish slave ship, the* Albanoz, *and freed the slaves. A British officer depicted the appalling conditions in the slavehold in this watercolor.*   The Granger Collection, New York

traders served to illustrate one clear example of such a change of heart. Some slaveholders and slave traders feared they might be endangering their own salvation by their association with the institution. John Newton, a former slave trader who underwent an evangelical conversion, wrote the hymn "Amazing Grace."

The initial religious protest against slavery originated among English Quakers, a radical Protestant religious group founded by George Fox in the seventeenth century. By the early eighteenth century, it had solidified itself into a small but relatively wealthy sect in England. Members of Quaker congregations at that time actually owned slaves in the West Indies and participated in the transatlantic slave trade. During the Seven Years' War (1756–1763), however, many Quakers experienced economic hardship. Furthermore, the war created other difficulties for the English population as a whole. Certain Quakers decided the presence of the evil of slavery in the world explained these troubles. They then sought to remove this evil from their own lives and that of their congregations and began to take action against the whole system of slavery that characterized the transatlantic economy.

Just as the slave system was a transatlantic affair, so was the crusade against it. Quakers in both Philadelphia and England soon moved against the institution. The most influential of the early antislavery writers was Anthony Benezet, a Philadelphia Quaker, whose most important publications were *Some Considerations on the Keeping of Negroes* (1754) and *A Short Account of That Part of Africa Inhabited by the Negroes* (1762). The latter work emphasized the manner in which the slave trade degraded African society itself. Benezet also drew heavily on Montesquieu. This may not be surprising because Enlightenment writers often admired the English Quakers as exemplifying a religion of tolerance and reason.

By the earliest stages of the American Revolution a small group of reformers, normally spearheaded by Quakers, had established an antislavery network. They published pamphlets, sermons, and books on the subject. The Society for the Relief of Free Negroes Illegally Held in Bondage, the first antislavery society in the world, was founded in Philadelphia in 1775 and when reorganized in 1784 as the Pennsylvania Abolition Society, Benjamin Franklin became its president. In 1787, the Committee for the Abolition of the Slave Trade was organized in England. In France, the Société des Amis des Noirs was founded in 1778.

The turmoil of the American Revolution and the founding of the American republic gave these groups the occasion for some of their earliest successes. Emancipation gradually, but nonetheless steadily, spread among the northern states. In 1787, the Continental Congress forbade the presence of slavery in the newly organized Northwest Territory north of the Ohio River. What is important so far as the crusade against slavery is concerned is the disappearance of slavery in approximately half of the new nation and the commitment not to extend it to an important new territory. Despite these American developments, Great Britain became and remained the center for the antislavery movement. In 1772, a decision by the chief justice affirmed that slaves brought into Great Britain could not forcibly be removed. The decision, though of less immediate importance than some thought at the time, gave further impetus to the small but growing group of antislavery reformers.

During the early 1780s, the antislavery reformers in Great Britain decided to work toward ending the slave trade rather than the institution of slavery. The horrors of the slave trade caught the public's attention in 1783 when the captain of the slave ship *Zong* threw more than 130 slaves overboard in order to collect insurance. For the reformers, attacking the trade rather than the institution appeared a less radical and a more achievable reform. To many, the slave trade appeared a more obvious crime than the holding of slaves, which seemed a more nearly passive act. Furthermore, attacking slavery itself involved serious issues of property rights that might alienate potential supporters of the abolition of the slave trade. The antislavery groups also believed that if the trade was ended, planters would have to treat their remaining slaves more humanely.

By the end of the 1780s, the English Quakers were joined by evangelical Christians from the Church of England to form the Society for the Abolition of the Slave Trade. The most famous of the

The slave revolt on the French Island of St. Domingue achieved the largest emancipation of slaves in the eighteenth century. In this print, Toussaint-L'Ouverture leads the revolt. Corbis

new leaders was William Wilberforce who, for the rest of his life, fought the slave trade. Year after year, he introduced a bill to abolish the slave trade. Finally, in 1807 he saw it passed.

Slave Revolts

While the British reformers worked for the abolition of the slave trade, slaves themselves in certain areas took matters into their own hands. The largest emancipation of slaves to occur in the eighteenth century came on the island of Saint Domingue (Haiti), France's wealthiest colony, as a result of the slave revolt of 1794 led by Toussaint L'Ouverture and Jean-Jacques Dessalines. The revolt in Haiti and Haiti's eventual independence in 1804 stood as a warning to slave owners throughout the West Indies. There would be other slave revolts such as those in Virginia led by Gabriel Prosser in 1800 and by Nat Turner in 1831, in South Carolina led by Denmark Vesey in 1822, in British-controlled Demarra in 1823 and 1824 and in Jamaica in 1831. Each of these was brutally suppressed.

Economic Pressures

Through the conclusion of the Seven Years' War, the West Indies interest group had been one of the most powerful in the British Parliament. During the second half of the eighteenth century and beyond, new and different economic interest groups began to displace the influence of that group. Within the West Indies themselves the planters were experiencing soil exhaustion and new competition from newly tilled islands controlled by France and other new islands opened for sugar cultivation. Some older plantations were being abandoned while others operated with low profitability. Now with the new islands under cultivation there was a glut of sugar on the market, and as a consequence the price was falling.

Under these conditions some British West Indies planters, for reasons that had nothing to do with religion or humanitarianism, began to favor curtailing the slave trade. Without new slaves, French planters would lack the labor they needed to exploit their islands. During the Napoleonic Wars, the British captured a number of the valuable French islands. In order to protect the planters on the older British West Indies islands, in 1805 the British cabinet issued Orders in Council, which forbade the importation of slaves into the newly acquired French islands. By 1807, the abolition sentiment was strong enough for Parliament to pass Wilberforce's measure prohibiting slave trading from any British port.

The suppression of this trade through the navy became one of the fundamental pillars of nineteenth-century British foreign policy. Throughout the rest of the Napoleonic era the British attempted to draw allies into a policy of forbidding the slave trade. They also attempted unsuccessfully to incorporate the abolition of the slave trade into the settlement of the Congress of Vienna. In addition, the British navy maintained squadrons of ships around the coast of West Africa to halt slave traders. Although the French and Americans also patrolled the West African coast, neither was deeply committed to ending the slave trade. Nonetheless, in 1824 the American Congress had made slave trading a capital offense.

The French invasion of Spain in 1808, as discussed in Chapter 21, provided the spark for the Latin American wars of independence. The leaders of these movements had been influenced by the liberal ideas of the Enlightenment and were thus generally predisposed to disapprove of slavery. The political groups seeking independence from Spain also sought the support of slaves by promises of emancipation. Furthermore, the newly independent nations needed good relations with Britain to support their economies, and consequently most of them very quickly freed their slaves to gain such support. The actual freeing of slaves was gradual and often came some years after the emancipation legislation. Despite the gradual nature of this abolition, slavery would disappear by approximately the middle of the century from all of the newly independent nations of Latin America. The great exception was Brazil.

Abolishing Slavery in the New World

British reformers gradually recognized that the abolition of the slave trade had not actually improved the lot of slaves. In 1823, they adopted as a new goal the gradual emancipation of slaves. The chief voices calling for this change were those of William Wilberforce and Thomas Clarkson, who were active in founding the Abolition Society. The savagery with which West Indian planters put down slave revolts in 1823 and 1824 and again in 1831 strengthened the resolve of the antislavery reformers. By 1830, the reformers had abandoned the goal of gradual abolition and demanded the complete abolition of slavery. In 1833, after the passage of the Reform Bill in Great Britain, they achieved that goal when Parliament abolished the right of British subjects to hold slaves. In the British West Indies, 750,000 slaves were freed within a few years.

The other old colonial powers in the New World tended to be much slower in their own abolition of slavery. Portugal did little or nothing about slavery in Brazil, and when that nation became independent of Portugal, its new government continued slavery. Portugal ended slavery elsewhere in its American possessions in 1836; the Swedes, in 1847; the Danes, in 1848; but the Dutch not until 1863. France had witnessed a significant antislavery movement throughout the first half of the century, but slavery was not abolished in its West Indian possessions until the revolution of 1848.

During the first thirty years of the nineteenth century, the institution of slavery revived and achieved strong new footholds in the transatlantic world. These areas were the lower south of the United States for the cultivation of cotton, Brazil for the cultivation of coffee, and Cuba for the cultivation of sugar. World demand for those products made the slave system economically viable in these regions. Consequently, despite the drive to emancipation, which had succeeded in the northern states of the United States, slavery persisted in much of the Caribbean and in most of Latin America.

An antislavery movement had existed in the United States since the end of the eighteenth century, but it took on a new life in the early 1830s. The British abolition of slavery in the West Indies served as an inspiration to a new generation of American antislavery leaders, the most famous of whom was William Lloyd Garrison. He and other American abolitionists raised the question of slavery throughout the 1830s and 1840s. It was, however, the disposition of lands the United States had acquired in the Mexican War of 1847 that placed slavery at the heart of American political debate. For over a decade the question of slavery sharply divided Americans. The election of Lincoln in 1860 brought those sectional tensions to a head, and the American Civil War erupted in the spring of 1861. In 1863, Lincoln issued the Emancipation Proclamation, which declared the end of slavery in regions of the states in rebellion and unoccupied by Union forces. The passage of the Thirteenth Amendment to the American Constitution in 1865 abolished slavery in the United States.

The end of slavery in the United Sates left both Cuba, the most important remaining possession of the Spanish Empire in the Americas, and Brazil with slave economies. In 1868, an insurgency against Spanish colonial policy broke out in Cuba and lasted for ten years. This war disrupted much of the Cuban economy and saw some planters move toward using free labor. The Spanish forces attacked other planters by freeing their slaves. In 1870, the Spanish government passed a measure for gradual emancipation of slaves in both Cuba and Puerto Rico. In subsequent years, the sugar economy collapsed, making slavery unprofitable. Abolitionist agitation grew in Spain, and slavery was abolished in its New World colonies in 1886.

Brazil, under British pressure, had effectively ended the slave trade in 1850, but the question of the abolition of slavery was postponed for many years. In 1871, as a result of abolitionist agitation and because the Emperor Pedro II opposed slavery, a law providing for an extremely gradual abolition of slavery was passed. During the next two decades, abolitionist sentiment grew, and public figures from across the political spectrum voiced opposition to slavery. In 1888, Isabel Christiana, then regent while her father Pedro II was in Europe for medical treatment, signed a law abolishing slavery in Brazil without any form of compensation to the slave owners.

The abolition of slavery in Brazil ended a system of forced labor that had characterized the transatlantic economy for almost four hundred years. Wherever slavery had existed, however, its presence left and would continue to leave long-term consequences for the realization of equality and social justice. The end of slavery consequently did not end the problems that slavery created in the transatlantic world.

Africa and the End of Slavery

The transatlantic slave trade itself had adversely affected the life of Africa both through the vast loss of population over the centuries as well as through the undermining of African society through the internal slave trade. Similarly, the crusade against transatlantic slavery had drawn Europeans much more deeply into the affairs of the African continent. The various efforts by antislavery groups began to impact Africa in the first half of the nineteenth century. Their goal was to transform the African economy by substituting new peaceful trade in tropical goods for the slave trade. The reformers hoped to spread both free trade and Christianity into Africa. "Christianity and civilization" and "Christianity and commerce" were popular slogans of the day. Missionaries and traders saw themselves as natural allies in the cause.

The first effort in this direction was the resettlement of black slaves or children of black slaves into Africa. In 1787, the British established a colony of poor free blacks from Britain in Sierra Leone. The effort went badly, but a few years later former slaves once owned by British loyalists in America were settled there. Then former slaves from the Caribbean were brought to Sierra Leone. The colony became relatively successful only after 1807, when the British navy landed slaves rescued from captured slave trading ships. Sierra Leone, though quite small, became a place on the coast of West Africa where Christianity and commerce rather than the slave trade flourished. The French established a smaller experiment at Libreville in Gabon. The most famous and lasting attempt to resettle former black slaves in Africa was the establishment of Liberia by the efforts of the American Colonization Society after 1817. Liberia became an independent republic in 1847. All of these efforts to move former slaves back to Africa had only modest success, but they did affect the life of West Africa.

Other antislavery reformers were less interested in establishing outposts for the settlement of former slaves than in transforming the African economy itself. In 1841, the African Civilization Society under the leadership of Thomas Fowell Buxton sent a group of paddle-steamer ships up the Niger River in the hope of creating the basis for new trade with Africa. The goal was to establish free trade between Britain and Africa in which the manufactured goods of the former, most particularly textiles, would be exchanged for tropical agricultural goods produced by Africans. The expedition failed because most of its members died of disease. Yet the impulse to penetrate Africa for purposes of spreading trade and Christianity would continue for the rest of the century.

The antislavery movement marked the first of the intrusions of the European powers well beyond the coast of West Africa into the heart of the continent. After the American Civil War finally halted any large-scale demand for slaves from Africa, the antislavery reformers began to focus on ending the slave trade in East Africa and the Indian Ocean. This drive against slavery and the slave trade in Africa itself became one of the rationales for European interference in Africa during the second half of the century and served as one of the foundations for the establishment of the late-century colonial empires.

The crusade against slavery in the transatlantic economy eventually touched most of the world. It radically transformed the economies and societies of both North and South America. It led to a transformation of the African economy and eventually to a significant European presence in the life of African societies. Efforts to eradicate slavery, particularly the efforts by British reformers, caused the spread of the reform movement into Asia. Slavery was not abolished throughout the world, and antislavery societies still exist, though they receive little publicity. But the abolition of slavery in the transatlantic world stands as one of the most permanent achievements of the forces of eighteenth-century Enlightenment and revolution.

■ *What were the justifications of slavery prior to the eighteenth century? What religious and intellectual developments led some Europeans and some Americans to question and criticize the institution of slavery? Why did antislavery reformers first concentrate on the abolition of the slave trade? How did both slavery and antislavery lead Americans and Europeans to become involved with Africa? How did that involvement change between approximately 1600 and 1870?*

The Great Exhibition held in London in 1851 to celebrate progress in industry and commerce was housed in a vast structure made of iron and glass known as the Crystal Palace. Although the 1840s had been a decade of widespread political and economic unrest in much of Europe, thousands of people from around the world visited the Crystal Palace and marveled at its exhibits. *London's Crystal Palace during the International Exhibition of 1851.* Victoria and Albert Museum, London, Great Britain. Art Resource/N.Y.

CHAPTER 22

ECONOMIC ADVANCE AND SOCIAL UNREST (1830–1850)

*B*Y 1830, E*UROPE WAS HEADED* toward an industrial society. Only Great Britain had already attained that status, but the pounding of new machinery and the grinding of railway engines soon began to echo across much of the Continent. Yet what characterized the second quarter of the century was not the triumph of industrialism but the final protests of those economic groups who opposed it. Intellectually, the period saw the formulation of the major creeds supporting and criticizing the newly emerging society.

These were years of uncertainty for almost everyone. Even the most confident entrepreneurs knew the trade cycle could bankrupt them for weeks. For the industrial workers and the artisans, unemployment became a haunting and recurring problem. For the peasants, the question was sufficiency of food. It was a period of self-conscious transition that culminated in 1848 with a continent-wide outbreak of revolution. People knew one mode of life was passing, but no one knew what would replace it.

KEY TOPICS

- The development of industrialism and its effects on the organization of labor and the family
- The changing role of women in industrial society
- The establishment of police forces and reform of prisons
- Early developments in European socialism
- The revolutions of 1848

Toward an Industrial Society

BRITAIN'S INDUSTRIAL LEADERSHIP

The Industrial Revolution had begun in eighteenth-century Great Britain with the advances in textile production described in Chapter 16. Natural resources, adequate capital, native technological skills, a growing food supply, a social structure that allowed considerable mobility, and strong foreign and domestic demand for goods had given Britain an edge in achieving a vast new capacity for production in manufacturing. British factories and recently invented machines allowed producers to furnish customers with a greater number of products whose quality was higher and whose prices were lower than those of any competitors. Also, the French Revolution and the wars of Napoleon had finally destroyed the French Atlantic trade and had disrupted continental economic life for two decades. The Latin American wars of independence opened the markets of South America to British goods. In North America, both the United States and Canada demanded British products. Through its control of India, Britain commanded the markets of southern Asia.

The British textile industry was a vast worldwide economic network. For much of its raw cotton the industry depended on the labor of American slaves, although Britain itself had been trying to end the slave trade since 1807. In turn, the finished textiles were shipped all over the world along sea-lanes protected by the British navy. The wealth that Britain gained through textile production and its other industries of ironmaking, shipbuilding, china production, and the manufacture of other finished goods was invested all over the world, but especially in the United States and Latin America. This enormous activity provided the economic foundation for British dominance of the world scene in the nineteenth century.

Despite their economic lag, the continental nations were beginning to make material progress. By the 1830s, in Belgium, France, and Germany, the number of steam engines in use was growing steadily. Exploitation of the coalfields of the Ruhr and the Saar basins had begun. Coke was replacing charcoal in iron and steel production.

Industrial areas on the Continent were generally less concentrated than in Britain, and large manufacturing districts, such as the British Midlands, did not yet exist there. Major pockets of production, such as Lyons, Rouen, Liège, and Lille, did exist in western Europe, but most continental manufacturing still took place in the countryside. New machines were integrated into the existing domestic system. The extreme slowness of continental imitation of the British example meant that at midcentury peasants and urban artisans remained more important politically than industrial factory workers.

POPULATION AND MIGRATION

While the process of industrialization spread, the population of Europe continued to grow on the base of the eighteenth-century population explosion. The number of people in France rose from 32.5 million in 1831 to 35.8 million in 1851. The population of Germany rose from 26.5 million to 33.5 million during approximately the same period. That of Britain grew from 16.3 million to 20.8 million. More and more of the people of Europe lived in cities. By midcentury, one-half of the population of England and Wales and one-quarter of the population of France and Germany had become town dwellers. Eastern Europe, by contrast, remained overwhelmingly rural, with little industrial manufacturing.

The sheer numbers of human beings put considerable pressure on the physical resources of the cities. Migration from the countryside meant that existing housing, water, sewers, food supplies, and lighting were completely inadequate. Slums with indescribable filth grew, and disease, especially cholera, ravaged the population. Crime increased and became a way of life for those who could make a living in no other manner. Human misery and degradation in many early-nineteenth-century cities seemed to have no bounds.

The situation in the countryside was scarcely better. During the first half of the century, the productive use of the land remained the basic fact of life for most Europeans. The enclosures of the late eighteenth century, the land redistribution of the French Revolution, and the emancipation of serfs in Prussia and later in Austria (1848) and Russia (1861) commercialized landholding. Liberal reformers had hoped the legal revolution in ownership would transform peasants into progressive, industrious farmers. Instead, most peasants had become conservative landholders without enough land to make agricultural innovations or, often, even to support themselves.

It is important to note the differing dates of rural emancipation across Europe. In England, France, and the Low Countries, persons living in the countryside could move freely between country and town. In Germany, eastern Europe, and Russia, such migration was difficult until after emancipation of the serfs. Even when emancipation did occur, as throughout Germany early in the century, it did not make migration simple. So from Germany eastward, the pace of industrialization was much slower in part because of the absence of a fluid market for free labor moving to the cities.

The specter of poor harvests still haunted Europe. The worst such experience of the century was the Irish famine of 1845 to 1847. Perhaps as many as half a million Irish peasants with no land or small plots simply starved when disease blighted the potato crop. Hundreds of thousands emigrated. (See "Encountering the Past: The Potato and the Great Hunger in Ireland.") By midcentury, the revolution in landholding had led to greater agricultural production. It also resulted in a vast uprooting of people from the countryside into cities and from Europe into the rest of the world. The countryside thus provided many of the workers for the new factories, as well as people with few economic skills who slowly emigrated to cities in hope of finding work.

RAILWAYS

Industrial advance itself had also contributed to this migration. The 1830s and 1840s were the great age of railway building. The Stockton and Darlington Line opened in England in 1825. By 1830, another major line had been built between Manchester and Liverpool and had several hundred passengers a day. Belgium had undertaken railway construction by 1835. The first French line opened in 1832, but serious construction came only in the 1840s. Germany entered the railway age in 1835. At midcentury, Britain had 9,797 kilometers of railway, France 2,915, and Germany 5,856 (Map 22–1).

The railroads, plus canals and improved regular roads, meant people could leave the place of their birth more easily than ever before. The improvement in transportation also allowed cheaper and more rapid passage of raw materials and finished products.

Railways epitomized the character of the industrial economy during the second quarter of the century. They represented investment in capital goods rather than in consumer goods. Consequently, there was a shortage of consumer goods at cheap prices. This favoring of capital over consumer production was one

Cities all across the Continent grew during the first half of the nineteenth century. Some developed with little planning into bewildering places. Others—as this Berlin street scene suggests—developed in ways more congenial to their residents, with neighborhoods that continued to combine workshops, stores, and residences. Bildarchiv Preussischer Kulturbesitz

reason the working class often found itself able to purchase so little for its wages. The railways in and of themselves also brought about still more industrialization. Embodying the most dramatic application of the steam engine, they created a sharply increased demand for iron and steel and then for a more skilled labor force. The new iron and steel capacity soon permitted the construction of ironclad ships and iron machinery rather than ships and machinery made of wood. These great capital industries led to the formation of vast industrial fortunes that would be invested in still newer enterprises. Industrialism had begun to grow on itself. (See "Art & the West": J. M. W. Turner, *Rain, Steam, and Speed*, p. 776.)

The Labor Force

The composition and experience of the early-nineteenth-century labor force was varied. No single description could include all the factory workers, urban artisans, domestic craftspeople, household

MAP **EXPLORATION**

Interactive map: To explore this map further, go to http://www.prenhall.com/kagan/map22.1

MAP 22–1   EUROPEAN RAILROADS IN 1850   *At mid-century Britain had the most extensive rail network, and the most industrialized economy, in Europe, but rail lines were expanding rapidly in France, the German states, and Austria. Southern and eastern Europe had few railways, and the Ottoman Empire had none.*

servants, miners, countryside peddlers, farmworkers, or railroad navvies. The work force was composed of some persons who were reasonably well off, enjoying steady employment and decent wages. It also numbered the "laboring poor," who held jobs, but who earned little more than subsistence wages. Then there were others, such as the women and children who worked naked in the mines of Wales, whose conditions of life shocked all of Europe when a parliamentary report in the early 1840s publicized them. Furthermore, the conditions of workers varied from decade to decade and from industry to industry within any particular decade.

Although historians have traditionally emphasized the role and experience of industrial factory workers, only the textile-manufacturing industry became thoroughly mechanized and moved into the factory setting during the first half of the century. Far more of the nonrural, nonagricultural work force consisted of skilled artisans living in cities or small towns. They were attempting to maintain the value of their skills and control over their trades in the face of changing features of production. All these working people faced possible unemployment, with little or no provision for their security. During their lives, they confronted the dissolution of many of the traditional social ties of custom and community.

PROLETARIANIZATION OF FACTORY WORKERS AND URBAN ARTISANS

During the nineteenth century, both artisans and factory workers underwent a process of *proletarianization.* This term is used to indicate the entry of workers into a wage economy and their gradual loss of significant ownership of the means of production, such as tools and equipment, and of control over the conduct of their own trades. The process occurred rapidly wherever the factory system arose. The factory owner provided the financial capital to construct the factory, to purchase the machinery, and to secure the raw materials. The factory workers contributed

The Potato and the Great Hunger in Ireland

Any agricultural economy that depends on a single product stands in a precarious position. If that economy also depends on a single source of food, the people it supports also stand on the edge of catastrophe—they have nothing to fall back on if their single source of food fails. That kind of catastrophe occurred in Ireland, which was under British rule, in the 1840s when the potato crop failed.

During the eighteenth century, almost half of the Irish population came to depend on the potato, which had been brought to Europe from South America in the seventeenth century, as virtually their only food. On less than one acre of land, a single Irish peasant could raise enough potatoes to feed ten other people for a year and pay his rent (few Irish peasants owned their own land).

Before the 1840s, there had been isolated potato crop failures in parts of Ireland, but never a general failure. Then in 1845, a new, mysterious blight, caused by a fungus, struck potato crops across Ireland. The potato vines withered in the fields, and potatoes in storage became moldy and inedible. Half the crop was lost. The Irish with modest aid from the British government survived this first blight, but in 1846 it reappeared and destroyed the entire crop. The crop of 1847 was better, but the blight came again in 1848.

This series of Irish potato crop failures was the worst natural disaster to strike nineteenth-century Europe. Because there were no potatoes, Irish tenants could not pay the rent on their land. Landlords drove starving tenants off their farms. Disease spread, and tens of thousands died.

In 1846, as a response to the Irish famine, the English government repealed the tariffs on imported grain known as the Corn Laws and enacted a program of public works to employ the dispossessed. But the help was inadequate. Most economists and politicians believed government aid caused more harm than good, and the government was reluctant to provide charity. The 1847 Irish Poor Relief Act required anyone who occupied more than one-quarter acre of land to enter a government-run workhouse before receiving poor relief. But the workhouses were overwhelmed by the disaster.

To escape the famine, soon known as The Great Hunger, many of the Irish poor emigrated, primarily to the United States and Britain itself. Much of Ireland became depopulated. The census of 1841 counted 8,197,000 people in Ireland; ten years later, death and emigration had cut the population by more than 1.5 million. By 1901, more waves of emigration had reduced it to 4,459,000. The population had still not recovered to prefamine levels at the dawn of the twenty-first century: In 2000, the combined population of the Irish Republic and British-ruled Northern Ireland was only 5,460,000. Alone among the nations of Europe, Ireland has fewer inhabitants today than it did in the nineteenth century.

■ *Why was the failure of the potato crop such a disaster for Ireland? What effect did the famine have on the Irish population?*

R. N. Salaman, *The History and Social Influence of the Potato* (Cambridge: Cambridge University Press, 1985); Cecil Woodham-Smith, *The Great Hunger: Ireland 1845–1849* (New York: Harper & Row, 1962).

So many people starved in the Irish Famine that the workhouses could not shelter them all. Private Collection/Bridgeman Art Library.

George Stephenson (1781–1848) invented the locomotive in 1814, but the "Rocket," his improved design shown here, did not win out over other competitors until 1829. In the following two decades the spread of railways transformed the economy of Western Europe. Mary Evans Picture Library Ltd.

their labor for a wage. The process could also occur outside the factory setting if a new invention, such as a mechanical printing press, could do the work of several artisans within a workshop setting. (See "Andrew Ure Praises the Factory System.")

Factory workers also submitted to various kinds of factory discipline that was virtually always unpopular and difficult to impose. This discipline meant the demands for smooth operation of the machinery largely determined working conditions. Closing of factory gates to late workers, fines for such lateness, dismissal for drunkenness, and public scolding of faulty laborers were attempts to create human discipline that would match the regularity of the cables, wheels, and pistons. The factory worker had no direct say about the quality of the product or its price.

For all the difficulties of factory conditions, however, the economic situation was often better than for the textile workers who resisted the factory mode of production. In particular, English hand-loom weavers, who continued to work in their homes, experienced decades of declining trade and growing poverty in their unsuccessful competition with power looms.

Urban artisans in the nineteenth century experienced proletarianization more slowly than factory workers, and machinery had little to do with the process. The emergence of factories in and of itself did not harm urban artisans. Many even prospered from the development. For example, the construction and maintenance of the new machines generated major demand for metalworkers, who consequently prospered. The actual erection of factories and the expansion of cities benefited all craftspeople in the building trades, such as carpenters,

roofers, joiners, and masons. The lower prices for machine-made textiles aided artisans involved in the making of clothing, such as tailors and hatters, by reducing the costs of their raw materials. Where the urban artisans encountered difficulty and where they found their skills and livelihood threatened was in the organization of production.

In the eighteenth century, a European town or city workplace had usually consisted of a few artisans laboring for a master. They labored first as apprentices and then as journeymen, according to established guild regulations and practices. The master owned the workshop and the larger equipment, and the apprentices and journeymen owned their tools. The journeyman could expect to become a master. This guild system had allowed considerable worker control over labor recruitment and training, the pace of production, the quality of the product, and its price.

In the nineteenth century, it became increasingly difficult for artisans to continue to exercise corporate or guild direction and control over their trades. The legislation of the French Revolution had outlawed such organizations in France. Across Europe, political and economic liberals disapproved of labor and guild organizations and attempted to ban them.

Other destructive forces were also at work. The masters often found themselves under increased competitive pressure from larger, more heavily capitalized establishments or from the introduction of machine production into a previously craft-dominated industry. In many workshops masters began to follow a practice, known in France as *confection*, whereby goods, such as shoes, clothing, and furniture, were produced in standard sizes and styles rather than by special orders for individual customers.

ANDREW URE PRAISES THE FACTORY SYSTEM

The factory was itself as much an invention of the Industrial Revolution as were the new machines the factory often housed. The factory required a new organization of labor. It also made possible the production of vast new quantities of manufactured goods. Andrew Ure (1778–1857), a generally uncritical observer of the factory system, explains the changes brought about by the new sites of production.

■ *What does Ure understand to be new about the factory system? Why does he emphasize the willingness of workers to be employed in factories? How does he portray the factory system as creating the possibility of new abundance?*

The term Factory, in technology, designates the combined operation of many orders of work-people, adult and young, in tending with assiduous skill a system of productive machines continuously impelled by a central power. This definition includes such organizations as cotton-mills, flax-mills, silk-mills, woolen-mills, and certain engineering works. . . . I conceive that this title, in its strictest sense, involves the idea of a vast automaton, composed of various mechanical and intellectual organs, acting in uninterrupted concert for the production of a common object, all of them being subordinated to a self-regulated moving force. . . .

In its precise acceptation, the Factory system is of recent origin, and may claim England for its birthplace. . . .

When the first water-frames for spinning cotton were erected at Cromford, in the romantic valley of the Derwent, about sixty years ago, mankind were little aware of the mighty revolution which the new system of labor was destined by Providence to achieve, not only in the structure of British society, but in the fortunes of the world at large.

Arkwright alone had the sagacity to discern, and the boldness to predict in glowing language, how vastly productive human industry would become, when no longer proportioned in its results to muscular effort, which is by its nature fitful and capricious, but when made to consist in the task of guiding the work of mechanical fingers and arms, regularly impelled with great velocity by some indefatigable physical power. . . .

In my recent tour, continued during several months, through the manufacturing districts, I have seen tens of thousands of old, young, and middle-aged of both sexes, many of them too feeble to get their daily bread by any of the former modes of industry, earning abundant food, raiment, and domestic accommodation, without perspiring at a single pore, screened meanwhile from the summer's sun and the winter's frost, in apartments more airy and salubrious than those of the metropolis, in which our legislative and fashionable aristocracies assemble. In those spacious halls the benignant power of steam summons around him his myriads of willing menials, and assigns to each the regulated task, substituting for painful muscular effort on their part, the energies of his own gigantic arm, and demanding in return only attention and dexterity to correct such little aberrations as casually occur in his workmanship. . . . Such is the factory system, replete with prodigies in mechanics and political economy, which promises, in its future growth, to become the great minister of civilization to the terraqueous globe, enabling this country, as its heart, to diffuse along with its commerce, the life-blood of science and religion to myriads of people still lying "in the region and shadow of death."

Andrew Ure, *The Philosophy of Manufactures; or, An Exposition of the Scientific, Moral, and Commercial Economy of the Factory System* (London, 1835), pp. 13 ff., as quoted in Mack Walker, ed., *Metternich's Europe* (New York: Walker and Company, 1968), pp. 275–276, 278–279.

This practice increased the division of labor in the workshop. Each artisan produced a smaller part of the more-or-less uniform final product. Thus less skill was required of each artisan, and the particular skills possessed by a worker became less valuable. Masters also tried to increase production and reduce costs by lowering the wages paid for piecework. Those attempts often led to work stoppages or strikes. Migrants from the countryside or small towns into the cities created, in some cases, a surplus of relatively unskilled workers. They were willing to work for lower wages or under less favorable and protected conditions than traditional artisans. This situation made it much more difficult for urban journeymen ever to hope to become masters with their own workshops in which they would be in charge. Increasingly, these artisans became lifetime wage laborers whose skills were simply bought and sold in the marketplace.

WORKING-CLASS POLITICAL ACTION: THE EXAMPLE OF BRITISH CHARTISM

By the middle of the century, such artisans, proud of their skills and frustrated in their social expectations, became the most radical political element in the European working class. From at least the 1830s onward, these artisans took the lead in one country after another in attempting to formulate new ways of protecting their social and economic interests.

By the late 1830s, significant numbers of people in the British working class linked the solution of their economic plight to a program of political reform known as **Chartism.** In 1836, William Lovett (1800–1877) and other London radical artisans formed the London Working Men's Association. In 1838, the group issued the Charter, demanding six specific reforms. The Six Points of the Charter included universal male suffrage, annual election of the House of Commons, the secret ballot, equal electoral districts, the abolition of property qualifications for members of the House of Commons, and payment of salaries to members of the House of Commons.

For more than ten years, the Chartists, who were never tightly organized, agitated for their reforms. On three occasions the Charter was presented to Parliament, which refused to pass it. Petitions with millions of signatures were presented to the House of Commons. Strikes were called. The Chartists published a newspaper, the *Northern Star*. Feargus O'Connor (1794–1855), the most important Chartist leader, made speeches across Britain. Despite this vast activity, Chartism as a national movement failed. Its ranks were split between those who favored violence and those who wanted to use peaceful tactics. On the local level, however, the Chartists scored several successes and controlled the city councils in Leeds and Sheffield.

As prosperity returned after the depression of the late 1830s and early 1840s, many working people abandoned the movement. Chartists' demonstrations in 1848 fizzled. Nevertheless, Chartism was the first large-scale European working-class political movement. It had specific goals and largely working-class leadership. Eventually, several of the Six Points were enacted into law. Continental working-class observers saw in Chartism the kind of mass movement that workers must eventually adopt if they were to improve their situation.

Family Structures and the Industrial Revolution

It is more difficult to generalize about the European working-class family structure in the age of early industrialism than under the Old Regime. Industrialism developed at such different rates across the Continent, and the impact of industrialism cannot be separated from that of migration and urbanization. Furthermore, industrialism did not touch all families directly; the structures and customs of many peasant families changed little for much of the nineteenth century.

Much more is known about the relationships of the new industry to the family in Great Britain than elsewhere. Many of the British developments foreshadowed those in other countries as the factory system spread.

In the 1830s and 1840s, the Chartists circulated petitions throughout Britain demanding political reform. Here the petitions are being taken to Parliament in a vast ceremonious procession. Museum of London

THE FAMILY IN THE EARLY FACTORY SYSTEM

Contrary to the opinion historians and other observers once held, the adoption of new machinery and factory production did not destroy the working-class family. Before the late-eighteenth-century revolution in textile production in England, the individual family involved in textiles was the chief unit of production. The earliest textile-related inventions, such as the spinning jenny, did not change that situation. As noted in Chapter 16, the new machine was initially simply brought into the home to spin the thread. It was the mechanization of weaving that led to the major change. The father who became a machine weaver was then employed in a factory. His work was thus separated from his home. Although one should not underestimate the changes and pressures in family life that occurred when the father left for the factory, the structure of early English factories allowed the father to preserve certain of his traditional family roles as they had existed before the factory system.

In the domestic system of the family economy, the father and mother had worked with their children in textile production as a family unit. They had trained and disciplined the children within the home setting. Their home life and their economic life were largely the same. Moreover, in the home setting, the wife who worked as a spinner might have earned as much or even more income than her husband. Early factory owners and supervisors permitted the father to employ his wife and children as his assistants. Thus parental training and discipline could be transferred from the home into the early factory. In some cases, in both Britain and France, whole families would move near a new factory so the family as a unit could work there. Those accommodations to family life nonetheless did not relieve any family members of having to face the new work discipline of the factory setting. Moroever, as we discuss later, women assisting their husbands in the factory often undertook less skilled work than they had pursued in their homes.

A major shift in this family and factory structure began in the mid-1820s in England and had been more or less completed by the mid-1830s. As spinning and weaving were put under one roof, the size of factories and of the machinery became larger. These newer machines required fewer skilled operators, but many relatively unskilled attendants. This relatively unskilled machine tending became the work of unmarried women and of children. Factory owners found these workers would accept lower wages and were less likely than adult men to try to form worker or union organizations.

Factory wages for the more skilled adult males, however, became sufficiently high to allow some fathers to remove their children from the factory and to send them to school. The children who were left working in the factories as assistants were often the children of the economically depressed hand-loom weavers. The wives of the skilled operatives also usually no longer worked in the factories. So the original links of the family in the British textile factory that had existed for well over a quarter century largely disappeared. Men were supervising women and children who did not belong to their families.

Concern for Child Labor It was at this point in the 1830s that workers became concerned about the plight of child laborers because parents were no longer exercising discipline over their own children in the factories. The English Factory Act of 1833 forbade the employment of children under age nine, limited the workday of children aged nine to thirteen to nine hours, and required that these children be given two hours of education a day, paid for by the factory owner. The effect was further to divide work and home life. The workday for adults and older teenagers remained twelve hours. Younger children often worked in relays of four or six hours. Consequently, the parental link was thoroughly broken. The education requirement began the process of removing nurturing and training from the home and family to a school, where a teacher rather than the parents was in charge of education.

After passage of the English Factory Act, many of the British working class demanded shorter workdays for adults. They desired to reunite, in some manner, the workday of adults with that of their children or at least to allow adults to spend more time with their children. In 1847, Parliament mandated a ten-hour workday. By present standards, this was long. At that time, however, it allowed parents and children more hours together as a domestic unit, since their relationship as a work or production unit had ceased wherever the factory system prevailed. By the middle of the 1840s, in the lives of industrial workers, the roles of men as breadwinners and as fathers and husbands had become distinct in the British textile industry. Furthermore, the concerns raised by reformers about the working conditions of women in factories and in mines arose in part from the relatively new view that the place of women was in the home rather than in either an industrial or even agrarian workplace.

Changing Economic Role for the Family What occurred in Britain presents a general pattern for what would happen elsewhere with the spread of industrial capitalism and public education. The European family was passing from being the chief unit of both production and consumption to becoming the chief unit of consumption alone. This development did not mean the end of the family as an economic unit. Parents and children, however, now came to depend on sharing wages often derived from several sources, rather than on sharing work in the home or factory.

Ultimately, the wage economy meant that families were less closely bound together than in the past. Because wages could be sent over long distances to parents, children might now move farther away from home. Once they moved far away, the economic link was, in time, often broken. In contrast, when a family settled in an industrial city, the wage economy might, in that or the next generation, actually discourage children from leaving home as early as they had in the past. Children could find wage employment in the same city and then live at home until they had accumulated enough savings to marry and begin their own household. That situation meant children often remained with their parents longer than in the past.

Women in the Early Industrial Revolution

As we noted in Chapter 16, the industrial economy ultimately produced an immense impact on the home and family life of women. First, it eventually took most productive work out of the home and allowed many families to live on the wages of the male spouse. That transformation prepared the way for a new concept of gender-determined roles in the home and in domestic life generally. Women came to be associated with domestic duties, such as housekeeping, food preparation, child rearing and nurturing, and household management, or with very poorly paid, largely unskilled cottage industries. Men came to be associated almost exclusively with supporting the family. Children were raised to conform to these expected gender patterns. Previously, this domestic division of labor into separate male and female spheres had prevailed only among the relatively small middle class and the gentry. During the nineteenth century, that division came to characterize the working class as well.

OPPORTUNITIES AND EXPLOITATION IN EMPLOYMENT

Because the early Industrial Revolution had begun in textile production, women and their labor were deeply involved from the start. Although both spinning and weaving were still domestic industries, women usually worked in all stages of production. Hand spinning was virtually always a woman's task. At first, when spinning was moved into factories and involved large machines, women often were displaced by men. Furthermore, the higher wages commanded by male cotton-factory workers allowed many married women not to work or to work only to supplement their husbands' wages.

Women in Factories With the next generation of machines in the 1820s, however, unmarried women rapidly became employed in the factories, where they often constituted the majority of workers. But their new jobs often demanded fewer skills than those they had previously exercised in the home production of textiles. Women's factory work also required fewer skills than most work done by men. Tending a machine required less skill than actually spinning or weaving or acting as forewoman. There was thus a certain paradox in the impact of the factory on women: Many new jobs were opened to them, but the level of skills was lowered. The supervisors of women were almost invariably men.

Moreover, almost always, the women in the factories were young single women or widows. Upon marriage or perhaps after the birth of the first child, young women usually found their husbands earned enough money for them to leave the factory. Or they found themselves unwanted by the factory owners, who disliked employing married women because of the likelihood of pregnancy, the influence of their husbands, and the duties of child rearing. Widows might return to factory work because they lacked their husbands' former income.

Work on the Land and in the Home In Britain and elsewhere by midcentury, industrial factory work still accounted for less than half of all employment for women. The largest group of employed women in France continued to work on the land. In England, they were domestic servants. Throughout western Europe, domestic cottage industries, such as lace making, glove making, garment making, and other kinds of needlework, employed a vast number of women. In almost all such cases, their conditions of labor were harsh, whether they worked in their homes or in sweatshops. It cannot be overemphasized that all work by women commanded low wages and involved low skills. They had virtually no effective modes of protecting themselves from exploitation. The charwoman, a common sight across the Continent, symbolized the plight of working women.

The low wages of female workers in all areas of employment sometimes led to their becoming prostitutes to supplement their wage income. This situation prevailed across Europe throughout the century. In 1844, Louise Aston (1814–1871), a German political radical, portrayed this situation in a poem looking at the experience of a Silesian weaver as she confronts a factory owner on whom her family depends to purchase the cloth they have woven:

The factory owner has come,
And he says to me: "My darling child,
I know your people
Are living in misery and sorrow;
So if you want to lie with me
For three or four nights,
See this shiny gold coin!
It's yours immediately."[1]

Such sexual exploitation of women was hardly new to European society, but the particular pressures of the transformation of the economy from one of skilled artisans to that of unskilled factory workers made many women especially vulnerable. (See "Women Industrial Workers Explain Their Economic Situation.")

CHANGING EXPECTATIONS IN WORKING-CLASS MARRIAGE

Moving to cities and entering the wage economy gave women wider opportunities for marriage. Cohabitation before marriage was not uncommon. Parents had less to do with arranging marriages than in the past. (See "A Young Middle-Class French-woman Writes to Her Father about Marriage.") Marriage now usually meant a woman would leave the work force to live on her husband's earnings. If all went well, that arrangement might improve her situation. If the husband became ill or died, however, or if he deserted his wife, she would have to reenter the market for unskilled labor at an advanced age.

Despite these changes, many of the traditional practices associated with the family economy survived into the industrial era. As a young woman came of age, both family needs and her desire to marry still directed what she would do with her life. The most likely early occupation for a young woman was domestic service. A girl born in the country normally migrated to a nearby town or city for such employment, often living initially with a relative. As in the past, she would try to earn enough in wages to give her a dowry, so she might marry and set up her own household. If she became a factory worker, she would probably live in a supervised dormitory. These dormitories helped attract young women into their employ by convincing parents their daughters would be safe.

As textile production became increasingly automated in the nineteenth century, textile factories required fewer skilled workers and more unskilled attendants. To fill these unskilled positions, factory owners turned increasingly to unmarried women and widows, who worked for lower wages than men and were less likely to form labor organizations.   Bildarchiv Preussischer Kulturbesitz

The life of young women in the cities was more precarious than earlier. There were fewer family and community ties. There were also perhaps more available young men. These men, who worked for wages rather than in the older apprenticeship structures, were more mobile, so relationships between men and women often were more fleeting. In any case, illegitimate births increased; fewer women who became pregnant before marriage found the father willing to marry them.

Marriage in the wage industrial economy was also different in certain respects from marriage in earlier times. It still involved the starting of a separate household, but the structure of gender relationships within the household was different. Marriage was less an economic partnership. The husband's wages might well be able to support the entire family. The wage economy and the industrialization separating workplace from home made it difficult for women to combine domestic duties with work. When married women worked, it was usually in the nonindustrial sector of the economy. More often than not, it was the children rather than the wife

[1]As quoted in Lia Secci, "German Women Writers and the Revolution of 1848," in John C. Fout, ed., *German Women in the Nineteenth Century: A Social History* (New York: Holmes & Meier, 1984), p. 162.

WOMEN INDUSTRIAL WORKERS EXPLAIN THEIR ECONOMIC SITUATION

In 1832, there was much discussion in the British press about factory legislation. Most of that discussion was concerned with the employment of children, but the Examiner *newspaper made the suggestion that any factory laws should not only address the problem of child labor, but also, in time, eliminate women from employment in factories. That article provoked the following remarkable letter to the editor, composed by or on behalf of women factory workers, which eloquently stated the real necessity of such employment for women and the unattractive alternatives.*

■ *What are the reasons these women enumerate to prove the necessity of their holding manufacturing jobs? What changes in production methods have led women from the home to the factory? How does the situation of these women relate to the possibility of their marrying? Compare the plight of these English working-class women with that of the French middle-class woman in the next document.*

Sir,

Living as we do, in the densely populated manufacturing districts of Lancashire, and most of us belonging to that class of females who earn their bread either directly or indirectly by manufactories, we have looked with no little anxiety for your opinion on the Factory Bill. . . . You are for doing away with our services in manufactories altogether. So much the better, if you had pointed out any other more eligible and practical employment for the surplus female labour, that will want other channels for a subsistence. If our competition were withdrawn, and short hours substituted, we have no doubt but the effects would be as you have stated, "not to lower wages, as the male branch of the family would be enabled to earn as much as the whole had done," but for the thousands of females who are employed in manufactories, who have no legitimate claim on any male relative for employment or support, and who have, through a variety of circumstance, been early thrown on their own resources for a livelihood, what is to become of them?

In this neighbourhood, hand-loom has been almost totally superseded by power-loom weaving, and no inconsiderable number of females, who must depend on their own exertions, or their parishes for support, have been forced, of necessity into the manufactories, from their total inability to earn a livelihood at home.

It is a lamentable fact, that, in these parts of the country, there is scarcely any other mode of employment for female industry, if we except servitude and dressmaking. Of the former of these, there is no chance of employment for one-twentieth of the candidates that would rush into the field, to say nothing of lowering the wages of our sisters of the same craft; and of the latter, galling as some of the hardships of manufactories are (of which the indelicacy of mixing with the men is not the least), yet there are few women who have been so employed, that would change conditions with the ill-used genteel little slaves, who have to lose sleep and health, in catering to the whims and frivolities of the butter-flies of fashion.

We see no way of escape from starvation, but to accept the very tempting offers of the newspapers, held out as baits to us, fairly to ship ourselves off to Van Dieman's Land [Tasmania] on the very delicate errand of husband hunting, and having safely arrived at the "Land of Goshen," jump ashore, with a "Who wants me?" . . .

The Female Operatives of Todmorden

From *The Examiner*, February 26, 1832, as quoted in Ivy Pinchbeck, *Women Workers and the Industrial Revolution, 1750–1850* (New York: Augustus M. Kelley, 1969), pp. 199–200.

who were sent to work. This may help explain the increase in the number of births within marriages, as children in the wage economy usually were an economic asset. Married women worked outside the home only when family needs, illness, or the death of a spouse forced them to do so.

In the home, working-class women were by no means idle. Their domestic duties were an essential factor in the family wage economy. If work took place elsewhere, someone had to be directly in charge of maintaining the home front. Homemaking came to the fore when a life at home had to be

A YOUNG MIDDLE-CLASS FRENCHWOMAN WRITES TO HER FATHER ABOUT MARRIAGE

Stéphanie Jullien was a young middle-class woman whose father wished her to marry a man who was courting her. She had already rejected one suitor, and her father was greatly concerned about her future. In this letter, she explains to her father the matters that disturb her and make her wish to delay her decision. Ultimately, she did marry the man in question, and the marriage appears to have been happy.

■ *How does Stéphanie Jullien distinguish between the vocational and social opportunities available to a woman and those to a man? What are her expectations of a relationship with a husband? What does the letter also tell you about her sense of her relationship to her father? Compare this letter with the preceding letter by English working-class women. What problems do the women share? How are their lives different? What does a comparison of the two letters tell you about the difference in class experience in the early nineteenth century?*

You men have a thousand occupations to distract you: society, business, politics, and work absorb you, exhaust you, upset you. . . . As for us women who, as you have said to me from time to time, have only the roses in life, we feel more profoundly in our solitude and in our idleness the sufferings that you can slough off. I don't want to make a comparison here between the destiny of man and the destiny of woman: each sex has its own lot, its own troubles, its own pleasures. I only want to explain to you that excess of moroseness of which you complain and of which I am the first to suffer. . . . I am not able to do anything for myself and for those around me. I am depriving my brothers in order to have a dowry. I am not even able to live alone, being obliged to take from others, not only in order to live but also in order to be protected, since social convention does not allow me to have independence. And yet the world finds me guilty of being the only person that I am at liberty to be; not having useful or productive work to do, not having any calling except marriage, and not being able to look by myself for someone who will suit me, I am full of cares and anxieties. . . .

I am asking for more time [before responding to a marriage proposal]. It is not too much to want to see and know a man for ten months, even a year when it is a matter of passing one's life with him. There is no objection to make, you say. But the most serious and the most important presents itself: I do not love him. Don't think I am talking about a romantic and impossible passion or an ideal love, neither of which I ever hope to know. I am talking of a feeling that makes one want to see someone, that makes his absence painful and his return desirable, that makes one interested in what another is doing, that makes one want another's happiness almost in spite of oneself, that makes, finally, the duties of a woman toward her husband pleasures and not efforts. It is a feeling without which marriage would be hell, a feeling that cannot be born out of esteem, and which to me, however, seems to be the very basis of conjugal happiness. I can't feel these emotions immediately. . . . Let me have some time. I want to love, not out of any sense of duty, but for myself and for the happiness of the one to whom I attach my life, who will suffer if he only encounters coldness in me, when he brings me love and devotion.

From the Jullien Family Papers, 39 AP 4, Archives Nationales, Paris, trans. by Barbara Corrado Pope, as quoted in Erna Olafson Hellerstein, Leslie Parker Hume, and Karen M. Offen, eds., *Victorian Women: A Documentary Account of Women's Lives in Nineteenth-Century England, France, and the United States* (Stanford, CA: Stanford University Press, 1981), pp. 247–248.

organized separately from the place of work. Wives were concerned primarily with food and cooking, but they often also were in charge of the family's finances. The role of the mother expanded when the children still living at home became wage earners. She was now providing home support for her entire wage-earning family. She created the environment to which the family members returned after work. The longer period of home life of working children may also have increased and strengthened familial bonds of affection between those children and their hardworking homebound mothers. In all these respects, the culture of the working-class marriage and family tended to imitate the family patterns of the middle and upper classes, whose members had often accepted the view of separate gender spheres set forth by Rousseau and popularized in hundreds of novels, journals, and newspapers.

Problems of Crime and Order

Throughout the nineteenth century, the political and economic elite in Europe were profoundly concerned about social order. The revolutions of the late eighteenth and early nineteenth centuries made them fearful of future disorder and threats to life and property. The processes of industrialization and urbanization also contributed to this problem of order. Thousands of Europeans migrated from the countryside to the towns and cities. There, they often encountered poverty or unemployment and general social frustration and disappointment. Cities became places associated with criminal activity, especially crimes against property, such as theft and arson. Throughout the first sixty years of the nineteenth century, crime appears to have increased slowly but steadily before more or less reaching a plateau.

Historians and social scientists are divided about the reasons for this rise in the crime rate. So little is known about crime in rural settings that comparisons with the cities are difficult. There are also many problems with crime statistics in the nineteenth century. No two nations kept them in the same manner. Different legal codes and systems of judicial administration were in effect in different areas of the Continent, thus giving somewhat different legal definitions of criminal activity. The result has been confusion, difficult research, and tentative conclusions.

NEW POLICE FORCES

From the propertied elite classes, two major views about containing crime and criminals emerged during the nineteenth century: prison reform and better systems of police. The result of these efforts was the triumph in Europe of the idea of a policed society. This concept means the presence of a paid, professionally trained group of law-enforcement officers charged with keeping order, protecting property and lives, investigating crime, and apprehending offenders. These officers are distinct from the army and are charged specifically with domestic security. It is to them that the civilian population normally turns for law enforcement. One of the key features of the theory of a policed society is that crime may be prevented by the visible presence of law-enforcement officers. These police forces, at least in theory, did not perform a political role, although in many countries that distinction was often ignored. Police forces also became one of the major areas of municipal government employment.

Such professional police forces did not really exist until the early nineteenth century. They differed from one country to another in both authority and organization, but their creation proved to be one of the main keys to the emergence of an orderly European society. The prefect of Paris set forth the chief principles that lay behind the founding of all of these new police units when he announced in 1828 that "Safety by day and night, free traffic movement, clean streets, the supervision of and precaution against accidents, the maintenance of order in public places, the seeking out of offences and their perpetrators. . . . The municipal police is a parental police."[2]

Professional police forces appeared in Paris in 1828. The same year, the British Parliament passed legislation sponsored by Sir Robert Peel (1788–1850) that placed police on London streets. They were soon known as *bobbies*, after the sponsor of the legislation. Similar police departments were deployed in Berlin after the Revolution of 1848. All of these forces were distinguished by an easily recognizable uniform. Police on the Continent were armed; those in Britain were not.

Although citizens sometimes viewed police with a certain suspicion, by the end of the century, most Europeans held friendly views toward police and regarded them as their protectors. Persons from the upper and middle classes felt their property to be more secure. Persons from the working class also frequently turned to the police to protect their lives and property and to aid them in other ways in emergencies. Of course, such was not the attitude toward political or secret police, who were hated and dreaded wherever governments created them.

PRISON REFORM

Before the nineteenth century, European prisons were local jails or state prisons, such as the Bastille. Governments also sent criminals to prison ships, called *hulks*. Some Mediterranean nations sentenced prisoners to naval galleys, where, chained to their benches, they rowed until they died or were eventually released. In prisons, inmates lived under wretched conditions. Men, women, and children were housed together. Persons guilty of minor offenses were left in the same room with those guilty of the most serious offenses.

Beginning in the late eighteenth century, the British government used the penalty of **transportation**

[2]Quoted in Clive Emsley, *Policing and Its Context, 1750–1870* (London: Macmillan, 1983), p. 58.

for persons convicted of the most serious offenses. Transportation to the colony of New South Wales in Australia was regarded as an alternative to capital punishment and was used by the British until the middle of the nineteenth century, when the colonies began to object. Thereafter, the British government established public works prisons in Britain to house long-term prisoners.

By the close of the eighteenth century and in the early decades of the nineteenth century, reformers, such as John Howard (1726–1790) and Elizabeth Fry (1780–1845) in England and Charles Lucas (1803–1889) in France, exposed the horrendous conditions in prisons and demanded change. Reform came slowly because of the expense of constructing new prisons and a general lack of sympathy for criminals.

In the 1840s, however, both the French and the English undertook several bold efforts at prison reform. These efforts would appear to indicate a shift in opinion whereby crime was seen not as an assault on order or on authority but as a mark of a character fault in the criminal. Thereafter, part of the goal of imprisonment was to rehabilitate or transform the prisoner during the period of incarceration. The result of this change was the creation of exceedingly repressive prison systems designed according to the most advanced scientific modes of understanding criminals and criminal reform.

Europeans used various prison models originally established in the United States. All these experiments depended on separating prisoners from each other. One was known as the *Auburn system* after Auburn Prison in New York State. According to it, prisoners were separated during the night but could associate while working during the day. The other was the *Philadelphia system*, in which prisoners were kept rigorously separated at all times.

The chief characteristics of these systems were an individual cell for each prisoner and long periods of separation and silence among prisoners. The most famous example of this kind of prison in Europe was Pentonville Prison near London. There, each prisoner occupied a separate cell and was never allowed to speak to or see another prisoner. Each prisoner wore a mask when in the prison yard; in the chapel, each had a separate stall. The point of the system was to turn the prisoner's mind in on itself to a mode of contemplation that would reform criminal tendencies. As time passed, the system became more relaxed because the intense isolation often led to mental collapse.

In France, imprisonment became more repressive as the century passed. The French constructed prisons similar to Pentonville in the 1840s. In 1875, the French also adopted a firm general policy of isolation of inmates in prison. Sixty prisons based on

London policeman. Professional police forces did not exist before the early nineteenth century. The London police force was created in 1828. Peter Newark's Pictures

this principle were constructed by 1908. Prisoners were supposed to be trained in some kind of trade or skill while in prison so they could reemerge as reformed citizens.

The vast increase in repeat offenses led the French government in 1885 to declare transportation the penalty for repeated serious crimes. It did this long after the British had abandoned the practice. The French sent serious repeat offenders to places such as the infamous Devil's Island off the coast of South America, literally to purge the nation of its worst criminals and to ensure they would never return.

All of these attempts to create a police force and to reform prisons illustrate the new post–French Revolution concern about order and stability on the part of European political and social elites. On the whole, by the end of the century, an orderly society had been established, and the new police and prisons had no small role in that development.

Classical Economics

Economists whose thought derived largely from Adam Smith's *Wealth of Nations* (1776) dominated private and public discussions of industrial and

In many prisons, treadmills like these were the only source of exercise available to English prisoners.
Bildarchiv Preussischer Kulturbesitz

commercial policy. Their ideas are often associated with the phrase *laissez-faire*. Although they thought the government should perform many important functions, the classical economists favored economic growth through competitive free enterprise. They conceived of society as consisting of atomistic individuals whose competitive efforts met the demands of consumers in the marketplace. They believed most economic decisions should be made through the mechanism of the marketplace. They distrusted government action, believing it to be mischievous and corrupt. The government should maintain a sound currency, enforce contracts, protect property, impose low tariffs and taxes, and leave the remainder of economic life to private initiative. The economists naturally assumed the state would maintain enough armed forces and naval power to protect the nation's economic structure and foreign trade. The emphasis on thrift, competition, and personal industriousness voiced by the political economists appealed to the middle classes.

MALTHUS ON POPULATION

The classical economists suggested complicated and pessimistic ideas about the working class. Thomas Malthus (1766–1834) and David Ricardo (1772–1823), probably the most influential of all these writers, suggested, in effect, that the condition of the working class could not be improved. In 1798, Malthus published the first edition of his *Essay on the Principle of Population*. His ideas have haunted the world ever since. He contended that population

must eventually outstrip the food supply. Although the human population grows geometrically, the food supply can expand only arithmetically. There was little hope of averting the disaster, in Malthus's opinion, except through late marriage, chastity, and contraception, the last of which he considered a vice. It took three-quarters of a century for contraception to become a socially acceptable method of containing the population explosion.

Malthus contended that the immediate plight of the working class could only become worse. If wages were raised, the workers would simply produce more children, who would, in turn, consume both the extra wages and more food. Later in his life, Malthus suggested, in a more optimistic vein, that if the working class could be persuaded to adopt a higher standard of living, their increased wages might be spent on consumer goods rather than on begetting more children.

RICARDO ON WAGES

In his *Principles of Political Economy* (1817), David Ricardo transformed the concepts of Malthus into the "iron law of wages." If wages were raised, more children would be produced. They, in turn, would enter the labor market, thus expanding the number of workers and lowering wages. As wages fell, working people would produce fewer children. Wages would then rise, and the process would start all over again. Consequently, in the long run, wages would always tend toward a minimum level. These arguments simply supported employers in their natural reluctance to raise wages and also provided strong theoretical support for opposition to labor unions. The ideas of the economists were spread to the public during the 1830s through journals, newspapers, and even short stories, such as Harriet Martineau's (1802–1876) series entitled *Illustrations of Political Economy*.

GOVERNMENT POLICIES BASED ON CLASSICAL ECONOMICS

The working classes of France and Great Britain, needless to say, resented the attitudes of the economists, but the governments embraced them. Louis Philippe (1773–1850) and his minister François Guizot (1787–1874) told the French to go forth and enrich themselves. People who simply displayed sufficient energy need not be poor. A number of the French middle class did just that. The July Monarchy (1830–1848) saw the construction of major capital-intensive projects, such as roads, canals, and railways. Little, however, was done about the poverty in the cities and the countryside.

In Germany, the middle classes made less headway. After the Napoleonic wars, however, the Prussian reformers had seen the desirability of abolishing internal tariffs that impeded economic growth. In 1834, all the major German states, except Austria, formed the **Zollverein,** or free trading union. Classical economics had less influence in Germany because of the tradition dating from the enlightened absolutism of state direction of economic development. The German economist Friedrich List (1789–1846) argued for this approach to economic growth during the second quarter of the century.

Britain was the home of the major classical economists, and their policies were widely accepted. The utilitarian thought of Jeremy Bentham (1748–1832) increased their influence. Although **utilitarianism** did not originate with him, Bentham sought to create codes of scientific law that were founded on the principle of utility, that is, the greatest happiness for the greatest number. In his *Fragment on Government* (1776) and *The Principles of Morals and Legislation* (1789), Bentham explained the application of the principle of utility would overcome the special interests of privileged groups who prevented rational government. He regarded the existing legal and judicial systems as burdened by traditional practices that harmed the very people the law should serve. The application of reason and utility would remove the legal clutter that prevented justice from being realized. He believed the principle of utility could be applied to other areas of government administration.

Bentham gathered round him political disciples who combined his ideas with those of classical economics. In 1834, the reformed House of Commons

Major Works of Economic and Political Commentary
1776 Adam Smith, *The Wealth of Nations*
1798 Thomas Malthus, *Essay on the Principle of Population*
1817 David Ricardo, *Principles of Political Economy*
1830s Harriet Martineau, *Illustrations of Political Economy*
1839 Louis Blanc, *The Organization of Labor*
1845 Friedrich Engels, *The Condition of the Working Class in England*
1848 Karl Marx and Friedrich Engels, *The Communist Manifesto*

passed a new Poor Law that had been prepared by followers of Bentham. This measure established a Poor Law Commission that set out to make poverty the most undesirable of all social situations. Government poor relief was to be disbursed only in workhouses. Life in the workhouse was consciously designed to be more unpleasant than life outside. Husbands and wives were separated, the food was bad, and the enforced work was distasteful. The social stigma of the workhouse was even worse. The law and its administration presupposed that people would not work because they were lazy. The laboring class, not unjustly, regarded the workhouses as new "bastilles."

The second British monument to applied classical economics was the repeal of the Corn Laws in 1846. The Anti-Corn Law League, organized by manufacturers, had sought this goal for more than six years. The league wanted to abolish the tariffs protecting the domestic price of grain. That change would lead to lower food prices, which would then allow lower wages at no real cost to the workers. In turn, the prices on British manufactured goods could also be lowered to strengthen their competitive position in the world market.

The actual reason for Sir Robert Peel's repeal of the Corn Laws in 1846 was the Irish famine. Peel had to open British ports to foreign grain in order to feed the starving Irish. He realized the Corn Laws could not be reimposed. Peel accompanied the abolition measure with a program for government aid to modernize British agriculture and to make it more efficient. The repeal of the Corn Laws was the culmination of the lowering of British tariffs that had begun during the 1820s. The repeal marked the opening of an era of free trade that continued until late in the century.

Jeremy Bentham (1748–1832) was the father of English utilitarianism. He began his career by demanding the reform of English law and ended it by demanding the radical reform of Parliament. Portrait of Jeremy Bentham (1748–1832). British jurist and philosopher. Painting by Henry W. Pickengild (1829). National Portrait Gallery, London.

Early Socialism

During the twentieth century, the socialist movement, in the form of either communist or social democratic political parties, constituted one of the major political forces in Europe. Less than 150 years ago, the advocates of socialism lacked any meaningful political following, and their doctrines appeared blurred and confused to most of their contemporaries. It is important to understand their early ideas and then to see, as we shall in later chapters, how those ideas, which for many years appeared on the margins of European political life, came to assume great importance in the late nineteenth century.

The early socialists generally applauded the new productive capacity of industrialism. They denied, however, that the free market could adequately produce and distribute goods the way the classical economists claimed. In the capitalist order, the socialists saw primarily mismanagement, low wages, maldistribution of goods, and suffering arising from the unregulated industrial system. Moreover, the socialists thought human society should be organized as a community, rather than merely as a conglomerate of atomistic, selfish individuals.

UTOPIAN SOCIALISM

Among the earliest people to define the social question were a group of writers called the **utopian socialists** by their later critics. They were considered utopian because their ideas were often visionary and because they frequently advocated the creation of ideal communities. They were called socialists because they questioned the structures and values of the existing capitalistic framework. In some cases, they actually deserved neither description. A significant factor in the experience of almost all these groups was the discussion, and sometimes the practice, of radical ideas in regard to sexuality and the family. People who might have been sympathetic to their economic concerns were profoundly unsympathetic to their views on free love and open family relationships.

Saint-Simonianism   Count Claude Henri de Saint-Simon (1760–1825) was the earliest of the socialist pioneers. As a young liberal French aristocrat, he had fought in the American Revolution. Later he welcomed the French Revolution, during which he made and lost a fortune. By the time of Napoleon's ascendancy, he had turned to a career of writing and social criticism.

Above all else, Saint-Simon believed modern society would require rational management. Private wealth, property, and enterprise should be subject to an administration other than that of its owners. His ideal government would have consisted of a large board of directors organizing and coordinating the activity of individuals and groups to achieve social harmony. In a sense, he was the ideological father of technocracy. Not the *redistribution* of wealth, but its *management* by experts, would alleviate the poverty and social dislocation of the age.

When Saint-Simon died in 1825, he had persuaded only a handful of people his ideas were correct. Nonetheless, Saint-Simonian societies were always centers for lively discussion of advanced social ideals. Some of the earliest debates in France over feminism took place within those societies. During the late 1820s and 1830s, the Saint-Simonians became well known for advocating sexuality outside marriage. Interestingly enough, several of Saint-Simon's disciples became leaders in the French railway industry during the 1850s.

Owenism   The major British contributor to the early socialist tradition was Robert Owen (1771–1858), a self-made cotton manufacturer. In his early twenties, Owen became a partner in one of the largest cotton factories in Britain at New Lanark, Scotland. Owen was a firm believer in the environmentalist psychology of the Enlightenment. If human beings were placed in the correct surroundings, they and their character could be improved. Moreover, Owen saw no incompatibility between creating a humane industrial environment and making a good profit.

At New Lanark, he put his ideas into practice. Workers were provided with good quarters. Recreational possibilities abounded, and the children received an education. There were several churches, although Owen himself was a notorious freethinker on matters of religion and sex. In the factory itself, various rewards were given for good work. His plant made a fine profit. Visitors flocked from all over Europe to see what Owen had accomplished through enlightened management.

In numerous articles and pamphlets, as well as in letters to influential people, Owen pleaded for a reorganization of industry based on his own successful model. He envisioned a series of communities shaped like parallelograms in which factory workers and farmworkers might live together and produce their goods in cooperation. During the 1820s, Owen sold his New Lanark factory and then went to the United States, where he established the community of New Harmony, Indiana. When quarrels among the members led to the community's failure, he refused to give up his reformist causes. He returned to Britain, where he became the moving force behind the organization of the Grand National Union, an attempt to draw all British trade unions into a single body. It collapsed with other labor organizations during the early 1830s.

Fourierism Charles Fourier (1772–1837) was the French intellectual counterpart of Owen. He was a commercial salesperson who never succeeded in attracting the same kind of public attention as Owen. He wrote his books and articles and waited at home each day at noon, hoping to meet a patron who would undertake his program. No one ever arrived to meet him. Fourier believed the industrial order ignored the passionate side of human nature. Social discipline ignored all the pleasures that human beings naturally seek.

Fourier advocated the construction of communities, called *phalanxes*, in which liberated living would replace the boredom and dullness of industrial existence. Agrarian rather than industrial production would predominate in these communities. Sexual activity would be relatively free, and marriage was to be reserved only for later life. Fourier also urged that no person be required to perform the same kind of work for the entire day. People would be both happier and more productive if they moved from one task to another. Through his emphasis on the problem of boredom, Fourier isolated one of the key difficulties of modern economic life.

Saint-Simon, Owen, and Fourier expected some existing government to carry out their ideas. They failed to confront the political difficulties of their envisioned social transformations. Other figures paid more attention to the politics of the situation. In 1839, Louis Blanc (1811–1882) published *The Organization of Labor*. Like other socialist writers, this Frenchman demanded an end to competition, but he did not seek a wholly new society. He called for political reform that would give the vote to the working class. Once so empowered, workers could use the vote to turn the political processes to their own economic advantage. A state controlled by a working-class electorate would finance workshops to employ the poor. In time, such workshops might replace private enterprise, and industry would be organized to ensure jobs. Blanc recognized the power of the state to improve life and the conditions of labor. The state itself could become the great employer of labor.

ANARCHISM

Other writers and activists of the 1840s, however, rejected both industry and the dominance of government. These were the **anarchists.** They are usually included in the socialist tradition, although they do not exactly fit in there. Some favored programs of violence and terrorism; others were peaceful. Auguste Blanqui (1805–1881) was a major spokesperson for terror. He spent most of his adult life in jail. Seeking the abolition of both capitalism and the state, Blanqui urged the development of a professional revolutionary vanguard to attack capitalist society. His ideas for the new society were vague, but in his call for professional revolutionaries, he foreshadowed Lenin.

Pierre-Joseph Proudhon (1809–1865) represented the other strain of anarchism. In his most famous work, *What Is Property?* (1840), Proudhon attacked the banking system, which rarely extended credit to small-property owners or the poor. He wanted credit expanded to allow such people to engage in economic enterprise that would not involve unfair or unearned profits. Society should be organized on the basis of mutualism, which amounted to a system of small businesses and other cooperative enterprises among which there would be peaceful cooperation and exchanges of goods based on mutual recognition of the labor required in each area of production. With such a social system, the state as the protector of property would be unnecessary. Later in the century anarchists would favor a wide variety of cooperative businesses whose point was to favor the community good over that of the individual as well as to afford an essential fairness in exchange. Proudhon's ideas later influenced the French labor movement, which was generally less directly political in its activities than the movements in Britain and Germany.

MARXISM

Too often, the history of European socialism is regarded as a linear development leading naturally or necessarily to the late-century triumph of **Marxism** within the major socialist political parties. Nothing could be further from the truth. Marxist socialist ideas did eventually triumph over much, though not all, of Europe, but only through competition with other socialist formulas and largely as a result of the political situation in Germany during the last quarter of the century. At midcentury, the ideas of Karl Marx were simply one more contribution to a heady mixture of concepts and programs criticizing the emerging industrial capitalist society. Marxism differed from its competitors in its claims to scientific accuracy, its rejection of reform, and its call for revolution, though the character of that revolution was not well defined. Furthermore, Marx set the emergence of the industrial work force into the context of a world historical development from which he drew sweeping political conclusions. With the collapse of the Soviet Union and of the communist governments in Eastern Europe in the last quarter of the twentieth century, it is difficult for many people to recapture the power that Marx's political and social vision exerted over Europe and then many other parts of the world for more than a hundred years.

Karl Marx (1818–1883) was born in the Rhineland. His family was Jewish, but his father had converted to Lutheranism, and Judaism played no role in his education. Marx's middle-class parents sent him to the University of Berlin, where he became deeply involved in Hegelian philosophy and radical politics. During 1842 and 1843, he edited the radical *Rhineland Gazette* (*Rheinische Zeitung*). Soon the German authorities drove him from his native land. He lived as an exile in Paris, then in Brussels, and finally, after 1849, in London.

Partnership with Engels In 1844, Marx met Friedrich Engels (1820–1895), another young middle-class German, whose father owned a textile factory in Manchester, England. The next year Engels published *The Condition of the Working Class in England*, which presented a devastating picture of industrial life. The two men became fast friends. Late in 1847, they were asked to write a pamphlet for a newly organized and ultimately short-lived secret Communist League. *The Communist Manifesto*, published in German, appeared early in 1848. Marx, Engels, and the league had adopted the name *communist* because the term was much more self-consciously radical than socialist. Communism implied the outright abolition of private property, rather than some less extensive rearrangement of society. A work of fewer than fifty pages, the *Manifesto* would become the most influential political document of modern European and possibly world history, but that development lay in the future. At the time, it was simply one more political tract. Moreover, neither Marx nor his thought had any effect on the revolutionary events of 1848.

Sources of Marx's Ideas The major ideas of the *Manifesto* and of Marx's later work, including *Capital* (vol. 1, 1867), were derived from German Hegelianism, French socialism, and British classical economics. Marx applied to concrete historical, social, and economic developments Hegel's abstract philosophical concept that thought develops from the clash of thesis and antithesis into a new

Karl Marx's socialist philosophy eventually triumphed over most alternative versions of socialism in Europe, but his monumental work became subject to varying interpretations, criticisms, and revisions that continue to this day. Bildarchiv Preussischer Kulturbesitz

intellectual synthesis. For Marx, the conflict between dominant and subordinate social groups generated conditions that led to the emergence of a new dominant social group. These new social relationships, in turn, generated new discontent, conflict, and development.

The French socialists provided Marx with a portrayal of the problems of capitalist society and had raised the issue of property redistribution. Both Hegel and Saint-Simon led Marx to see society and economic conditions as developing through historical stages. The classical economists had produced the analytical tools for an empirical, scientific examination of industrial capitalist society.

Using the intellectual tools provided by Hegel, the French socialists, and the British classical economists, Marx fashioned a philosophy that gave a very special role or function to the new industrial work force as the single most important driving force of contemporary history. Marx later explained to a friend,

What I did that was new was to prove: (1) that the existence of classes is bound up with particular historical phases in the development of production; (2) that the class struggle necessarily leads to the dictatorship of the proletariat; (3) that this dictatorship itself only constitutes the transition to the abolition of all classes and to a classless society.[3]

In the *Communist Manifesto* and his numerous other writings, Marx equated the fate of the proletariat—that is, the new industrial labor force—with the fate of humanity itself. According to Marx, as the proletariat came to liberate itself from its bondage to the capitalist mode of industrial production, such liberation would eventually amount to the liberation of all humanity. It was this utopian vision of human emancipation, no matter how the actual later development of the European and world economy failed to conform to Marx's predictions, that drew many people from Europe and elsewhere to embrace much of his thought and to base their political actions on their understanding of his philosophy. But besides this wider vision, the details of Marx's argument were important as well for later nineteenth-century and twentieth-century European political life.

Revolution through Class Conflict In the *Communist Manifesto*, Marx and Engels contended that human history must be understood rationally and as a whole. History is the record of humankind's coming to grips with physical nature

to produce the goods necessary for survival. That basic productive process determines the structures, values, and ideas of a society. Historically, the organization of the means of production has always involved conflict between the classes that owned and controlled the means of production and the classes that worked for them. That necessary conflict has provided the engine for historical development; it is not an accidental by-product of mismanagement or bad intentions. Thus piecemeal reforms cannot eliminate the social and economic evils inherent in the very structures of production. A radical social transformation is required. The development of capitalism will make such a revolution inevitable.

In Marx's and Engels's eyes, the class conflict that had characterized previous Western history had become simplified during the early nineteenth century into a struggle between the bourgeoisie and the proletariat, or between the middle class associated with industry and commerce on the one hand and the workers on the other. The character of capitalism itself ensured the sharpening of the struggle. Capitalist production and competition would steadily increase the size of the unpropertied proletariat. Large-scale mechanical production crushed both traditional and smaller industrial producers into the ranks of the proletariat. As the business structures grew larger and larger, the competitive pressures would squeeze out smaller middle-class units. Competition among the few remaining giant concerns would lead to more intense suffering for the proletariat. The process also meant the proletariat itself would continue to expand to include more and more people. As this ever-expanding body of workers suffered increasingly from the competition among the ever-enlarging firms, Marx contended, they would eventually begin to foment revolution. Finally, they would overthrow the few remaining owners of the means of production. For a time, the workers would organize the means of production through a dictatorship of the proletariat. This would eventually give way to a propertyless and classless communist society.

This proletarian revolution was inevitable, according to Marx and Engels. The structure of capitalism required competition and consolidation of enterprise. Although the class conflict involved in the contemporary process resembled that of the past, it differed in one major respect: The struggle between the capitalistic bourgeoisie and the industrial proletariat would culminate in a wholly new society that would be free of class conflict. The victorious proletariat, by its very nature, could not be a new oppressor class: "The proletarian movement is the self-conscious, independent movement of the immense majority, in the interest of the immense

[3]Albert Fried and Ronald Sanders, eds., *Socialist Thought: A Documentary History* (Garden City, NY: Anchor Doubleday, 1964), p. 295.

majority."[4] The result of the proletarian victory would be "an association, in which the free development of each is the condition for the free development of all."[5] The victory of the proletariat over the bourgeoisie would represent the culmination of human history. For the first time in human history, one group of people would not be oppressing another.

The economic environment of the 1840s had conditioned Marx's analysis. The decade had seen much unemployment and deprivation. During the later part of the century, however, capitalism did not collapse as he had predicted, nor did the middle class become proletarianized. Rather, more and more people came to benefit from the industrial system. Nonetheless, within a generation Marxism had captured the imagination of many socialists, especially in Germany, and large segments of the working class. Marxist doctrines appeared to be based on the empirical evidence of hard economic fact. This scientific claim of Marxism helped spread the ideology as science became more influential during the second half of the century. But at its core, the attraction of the ideology was its utopian vision of ultimate human liberation, no matter how illiberal or authoritarian the governments were that embraced that vision in the twentieth century.

1848: Year of Revolutions

In 1848, a series of liberal and nationalistic revolutions erupted across the Continent (Map 22–2). No single factor caused this general revolutionary groundswell; rather, similar conditions existed in several countries. Severe food shortages had prevailed since 1846. Grain and potato harvests had been poor. The famine in Ireland was simply the worst example of a more widespread situation. The commercial and industrial economy was also depressed. Unemployment was widespread. All systems of poor relief were overburdened. These difficulties, added to the wretched living conditions in the cities, heightened the sense of frustration and discontent of the urban artisan and laboring classes.

The dynamic force for change in 1848 originated, however, not with the working classes, but with the political liberals, who were generally drawn from the middle classes. Throughout the Continent, liberals were pushing for their program of more representative government, civil liberty, and unregulated economic life. The repeal of the English Corn Laws and the example of peaceful agitation by the Anti-Corn

Law League encouraged them. The liberals on the Continent wanted to pursue similar peaceful tactics. To put additional pressure on their governments, however, they began to appeal for the support of the urban working classes. The goals of the latter were improved working and economic conditions, rather than a liberal framework of government. Moreover, the tactics of the working classes were frequently violent rather than peaceful. The temporary alliance of liberals and workers in several states overthrew or severely shook the old order; then the allies began to fight each other.

Finally, outside France, nationalism was an important common factor in the uprisings. Germans, Hungarians, Italians, Czechs, and smaller national groups in eastern Europe sought to create national states that would reorganize or replace existing political entities. The Austrian Empire, as usual, was the state most profoundly endangered by nationalism. At the same time, however, various national groups clashed with each other during these revolutions.

The immediate results of the 1848 revolutions were stunning. Never in a single year had Europe known so many major uprisings. The French monarchy fell, and many other thrones were badly shaken. Yet the revolutions proved a false spring for progressive Europeans. Without exception, the revolutions failed to establish genuinely liberal or national states. The conservative order proved stronger and more resilient than anyone had expected. Moreover, the liberal middle-class political activists in each country discovered they could no longer push for political reform without also raising the social question. The liberals refused to follow political revolution with social reform and thus isolated themselves from the working classes. Once separated from potential mass support, the liberal revolutions became an easy prey to the armies of the reactionary classes.

FRANCE: THE SECOND REPUBLIC AND LOUIS NAPOLEON

As had happened twice before, the revolutionary tinder first blazed in Paris. The liberal political opponents of the corrupt regime of Louis Philippe and his minister Guizot had organized a series of political banquets. These occasions were used to criticize the government and to demand further middle-class admission to the political process. The poor harvests of 1846 and 1847 and the resulting high food prices and unemployment brought working-class support to the liberal campaign. On February 21, 1848, the government forbade further banquets. A large one had been scheduled for the next day. On February 22, disgruntled Parisian workers paraded

---

[4]Robert C. Tucker, ed., *The Marx-Engels Reader* (New York: W.W. Norton, 1972), p. 353.

[5]Ibid.

MAP 22–2 CENTERS OF REVOLUTION
IN 1848–1849 *The revolution that
toppled the July Monarchy in Paris
in February 1848 soon spread to
Austria and many of the German
and Italian states. Yet by the end of
1849, most of these uprisings had
been suppressed.*

through the streets demanding reform and Guizot's
ouster. The next morning the crowds grew, and by
afternoon Guizot had resigned. The crowds had
erected barricades, and numerous clashes had occurred between the citizenry and the municipal
guard. On February 24, 1848, Louis Philippe abdicated and fled to England.

The National Assembly and Paris Workers The
liberal opposition, led by the poet Alphonse de
Lamartine (1790–1869), organized a provisional government. The liberals intended to call an election
for an assembly that would write a republican constitution. The various working-class groups in Paris,
however, had other ideas: They wanted a social as

well as a political revolution. Led by Louis Blanc,
they demanded representation in the cabinet. Blanc
and two other radical leaders were made ministers.
Under their pressure, the provisional government
organized national workshops to provide work and
relief for thousands of unemployed workers.

On Sunday, April 23, an election based on universal male suffrage chose the new National Assembly.
The result was a legislature dominated by moderates
and conservatives. In the French provinces, much resentment had been expressed against the Paris radicals. The church and the local notables still
exercised considerable influence. Small landowning
peasants feared possible confiscation of their holdings by Parisian socialists. The new conservative

During the February days of the French Revolution of 1848, crowds in Paris burned the throne of Louis Philippe. Bildarchiv Preussischer Kulturbesitz

National Assembly had little sympathy for the expensive national workshops, which they incorrectly perceived to be socialistic.

Throughout May, government troops and the Parisian crowd of unemployed workers and artisans clashed. As a result, the assembly closed the workshops to new entrants and planned the removal of many enrolled workers. By late June, barricades again appeared in Paris. On June 24, under orders from the government, General Cavaignac (1802–1857), with troops drawn largely from the conservative countryside, moved to destroy the barricades and to quell potential disturbances. During the next two days, more than four hundred people were killed. Thereafter, troops hunted down another 3,000 persons in street fighting. The drive for social revolution had ended.

Emergence of Louis Napoleon The so-called June Days confirmed the political predominance of conservative property holders in French life. They wanted a state that was safe for small property. This search

for social order received further confirmation late in 1848. The victor in the presidential election was Louis Napoleon Bonaparte (1808–1873), a nephew of the great emperor. For most of his life, he had been an adventurer living outside France. Twice he had attempted to lead a coup against the July Monarchy. The disorder of 1848 gave him a new opportunity to enter French political life. After the corruption of Louis Philippe and the turmoil of the early months of the Second Republic, the voters turned to the name of Bonaparte as a source of stability and greatness.

The election of the "Little Napoleon" doomed the Second Republic. Louis Napoleon was dedicated to his own fame rather than to republican institutions. He was the first of the modern dictators who, by playing on unstable politics and social insecurity, greatly changed European life. He constantly quarreled with the National Assembly and claimed that he, rather than they, represented the will of the nation. In 1851, the assembly refused to amend the constitution to allow the president to run for reelection. Consequently, on December 2, 1851, the anniversary

The Revolutionary Crisis of 1848 to 1851

1848

February 22–24	Revolution in Paris forces the abdication of Louis Philippe
February 26	National workshops established in Paris
March 3	Kossuth attacks the Habsburg domination of Hungary
March 13	Revolution in Vienna
March 15	The Habsburg emperor accepts the Hungarian March Revolution Laws in Berlin
March 18	Frederick William IV of Prussia promises a constitution; revolution in Milan
March 19	Frederick William IV is forced to salute the corpses of slain revolutionaries in Berlin
March 22	Piedmont declares war on Austria
April 23	Election of the French National Assembly
May 15	Worker protests in Paris lead the National Assembly to close the national workshops
May 17	Habsburg emperor Ferdinand flees from Vienna to Innsbruck
May 18	The Frankfurt Assembly gathers to prepare a German constitution
June 2	Pan-Slavic Congress gathers in Prague
June 17	A Czech revolution in Prague is suppressed
June 23–26	A workers' insurrection in Paris is suppressed by the troops of the National Assembly
July 24	Austria defeats Piedmont
September 17	General Jellachich invades Hungary
October 31	Vienna falls to the bombardment of General Windischgraetz

November 15	Papal minister Rossi is assassinated in Rome
November 16	Revolution in Rome
November 25	Pope Pius IX flees Rome
December 2	Habsburg Emperor Ferdinand abdicates and Francis Joseph becomes emperor
December 10	Louis Napoleon is elected president of the Second French Republic

1849

January 5	General Windischgraetz occupies Budapest
February 2	The Roman Republic is proclaimed
March 12	War is resumed between Piedmont and Austria
March 23	Piedmont is defeated, and Charles Albert abdicates the crown of Piedmont in favor of Victor Emmanuel II
March 27	The Frankfurt Parliament completes a constitution for Germany
March 28	The Frankfurt Parliament elects Frederick William IV of Prussia to be emperor of Germany
April 21	Frederick William IV of Prussia rejects the crown offered by the Frankfurt Parliament
June 18	The remaining members of the Frankfurt Parliament are dispersed by troops
July 3	Collapse of the Roman Republic after invasion by French troops
August 9–13	The Hungarian forces are defeated by Austria, aided by Russian troops

1851

December 2	Coup d'état of Louis Napoleon

of the great Napoleon's victory at Austerlitz, Louis Napoleon personally seized power. Troops dispersed the assembly, and the president called for new elections. More than 200 people died resisting the coup, and more than 26,000 persons were arrested throughout the country. Almost 10,000 persons who opposed the coup were transported to Algeria.

Yet, in the plebiscite of December 21, 1851, more than 7.5 million voters supported the actions of Louis Napoleon and approved a new constitution that consolidated his power. Only about 600,000 citizens dared to vote against him. A year later, in

December 1852, an empire was proclaimed, and Louis Napoleon became Emperor Napoleon III. Again a plebiscite approved the action. For the second time in just over fifty years, France had turned from republicanism to Caesarism. (See "Karl Marx Ponders the Revolutionary History of France and Louis Napoleon's Coup.")

Frenchwomen in 1848   The years between the February Revolution of 1848 and the Napoleonic coup of 1852 saw major feminist activity on the part of Frenchwomen. Especially in Paris, women seized

KARL MARX PONDERS THE REVOLUTIONARY HISTORY OF FRANCE AND LOUIS NAPOLEON'S COUP

Besides being a major political philosopher, Karl Marx was a gifted newspaper journalist noted for his biting sarcasm and wit. In late 1851 and early 1852, he contributed to a German-language journal published in New York City a series of articles on the recent coup of Louis Napoleon. Marx used the articles in part to outline his understanding of the constraints within which human beings could function as historical actors. He saw them as repeatedly attempting to interpret their present historical actions in terms of those of the past. He emphasized how the events in France from 1848 through 1851 had appeared to some people to repeat those of the French Revolution of the late eighteenth century. The attraction of Louis Napoleon caricatured the attraction of his much greater uncle. Marx, however, went beyond commenting on events in France to suggest that the future social revolution of the nineteenth century he hoped to foster must be different than previous revolutions in France and must seek different goals and look to different actors.

■ *What constraints does Marx say limit human beings as historical actors? Why do people attempt to depict their actions as repetitions of earlier eras? Why does Marx write so contemptuously of Louis Napoleon? Why does he believe the social revolution of the nineteenth century must be different from revolutions of the past?*

Hegel remarks somewhere that all facts and personages of great importance in world history occur, as it were twice. He forgot to add: the first time as tragedy, the second as farce. . . .

Men make their own history, but they do not make it just as they please; they do not make it under circumstances chosen by themselves, but under circumstances directly encountered, given and transmitted from the past. The tradition of all the dead generations weighs like a nightmare on the brain of the living. And just when they seem engaged in revolutionizing themselves and things, in creating something that has never yet existed, precisely in such periods of revolutionary crisis they anxiously conjure up the spirits of the past to their service and borrow from them names, battle-cries and costumes in order to present the new scene of world history in this time-honored disguise and this borrowed language. Thus Luther donned the mask of the apostle Paul, the revolution of 1789 to 1814 draped itself alternately as the Roman Republic and the Roman Empire, and the revolution of 1848 knew nothing better to do than to parody, now 1789, now the revolutionary tradition of 1793 to 1795. In like

manner a beginner who has learnt a new language always translates it back into his mother tongue, but he has assimilated the spirit of the new language and can freely express himself in it only when he finds his way into it without recalling the old and forgets his native tongue in the use of the new. . . .

The French, so long as they were engaged in revolution, could not get rid of the memory of Napoleon. . . . They hankered to return from the perils of revolution to the fleshpots of Egypt, and December 2, 1851 was the answer. They have not only a caricature of the old Napoleon, they have the old Napoleon himself, caricatured as he must appear in the middle of the nineteenth century.

The social revolution of the nineteenth century cannot draw its poetry from the past, but only from the future. It cannot begin with itself before it has stripped off all superstition about the past. Earlier revolutions required recollections of past world history in order to dull themselves to their own content. In order to arrive at its own content, the revolution of the nineteenth century must let the dead bury their dead.

From Karl Marx, *The Eighteenth Brumaire of Louis Napoleon*, in Karl Marx, *Selected Writings*, ed. by Lawrence H. Simon © 1994 International Publishers Co., pp. 188–189, 190. Reprinted by permission of International Publishers Co.

the opportunity of the collapse of the July Monarchy to voice demands for reform of their social conditions. They joined the wide variety of political clubs that emerged in the wake of the revolution. Some of these clubs particularly emphasized women's rights. Some women even tried unsuccessfully to vote in the various elections of 1848. Both middle-class and working-class women were involved in these activities. The most radical group of women called themselves the Vesuvians, after the volcano in Italy. They claimed it was time for the demands of women to come forth like pent-up lava. They demanded full domestic household equality between men and women, the right of women to serve in the military, and similarity in dress for both sexes. They also conducted street demonstrations. The radical character of their demands and actions lost them the support of more moderate women.

Certain Parisian women quickly attempted to use for their own cause the liberal freedoms that suddenly had become available. They organized the *Voix des femmes (The Women's Voice)*, a daily newspaper that addressed issues of concern to women. The newspaper insisted that improving the lot of men would not necessarily improve the condition of women. They soon organized a society with the same name as the newspaper. Many of the women involved in the newspaper and society had earlier been involved in Saint-Simonian or Fourierist groups. Members of the *Voix des femmes* group were relatively conservative feminists. They cooperated with male political groups, and they urged the integrity of the family and fidelity in marriage. They furthermore warmly embraced the maternal role for women, but tried to use that social function to raise the importance of women in society. Because motherhood and child rearing are so important to a society, they argued, women must receive better education, the right to work, economic security, equal civil rights, property rights, and the right to vote. The provisional government made no move to enact these rights, although some members of the assembly supported the women's groups. The emphasis on family and motherhood represented in part a defensive strategy to prevent conservative women and men from accusing the advocates of women's rights of seeking to destroy the family and traditional marriage.

The fate of French feminists in 1848 was similar to that of the radical workers. They were thoroughly defeated and their efforts wholly frustrated. Once the elections were held that spring, the new government expressed no sympathy for their causes. The closing of the national workshops adversely affected women workers as well as men and blocked one outlet that women had used to make their needs

known. The conservative crackdown on political clubs closed another arena in which women had participated. Women were soon specifically forbidden to participate in political clubs either by themselves or with men. These repressive actions repeated what had happened to politically active Frenchwomen and their organizations in 1793.

At this point, women associated with the *Voix des femmes* attempted to organize workers' groups to improve the economic situation for working-class women. Two leaders of this effort, Jeanne Deroin (d. 1894) and Pauline Roland (1805–1852), were arrested, tried, and imprisoned for these activities. The former eventually went into exile from France; the latter was sent off to Algeria during the repression after the coup of Louis Napoleon. By 1852, the entire feminist movement that had sprung up in 1848 had been thoroughly eradicated.

THE HABSBURG EMPIRE: NATIONALISM RESISTED

The events of February 1848 in Paris immediately reverberated throughout the Habsburg domains. The empire was susceptible to revolutionary challenge on every score. Its government rejected liberal institutions. Its borders cut across national lines. Its society perpetuated serfdom. During the 1840s, even Metternich had urged reform, but none was forthcoming. In 1848, the regime confronted major rebellions in Vienna, Prague, Hungary, and Italy. It was also intimately concerned about the disturbances that broke out in Germany.

The Vienna Uprising The Habsburg troubles began on March 3, 1848, when Louis Kossuth (1802–1894), a Magyar nationalist and member of the Hungarian diet, attacked Austrian domination of Hungary, called for the independence of Hungary, and demanded a responsible ministry under the Habsburg dynasty. Ten days later, inspired by Kossuth's speeches, students led a series of major disturbances in Vienna. The army failed to restore order. Metternich resigned and fled the country. The feebleminded Emperor Ferdinand (r. 1835–1848) promised a moderately liberal constitution. Unsatisfied, the radical students then formed democratic clubs to press the revolution further. On May 17, the emperor and the imperial court fled to Innsbruck. The government of Vienna at this point lay in the hands of a committee of more than two hundred persons concerned primarily with alleviating the economic plight of Viennese workers.

What the Habsburg government actually most feared was not the urban rebellions but a potential uprising of the serfs in the countryside. Already

there had been isolated instances of serfs invading manor houses and burning records. Consequently, almost immediately after the Vienna uprising, the imperial government had emancipated the serfs in much of Austria. The Hungarian diet also abolished serfdom in March 1848. These actions smothered the most serious potential threat to order in the empire. The emancipated serfs now had little reason to support the revolutionary movement in the cities. These emancipations were one of the most important permanent results of the Revolutions of 1848.

The Magyar Revolt   The Vienna revolt had further encouraged the Hungarians. The Magyar leaders of the Hungarian March Revolution were primarily liberals supported by nobles who wanted their aristocratic liberties guaranteed against the central government in Vienna. The Hungarian diet passed the March Laws, a series of laws that ensured equality of religion, jury trials, the election of a lower chamber, a relatively free press, and payment of taxes by the nobility. Emperor Ferdinand approved these measures because in the spring of 1848 he could do little else.

The Magyars also hoped to establish a separate Hungarian state within the Habsburg domains. They would retain considerable local autonomy while Ferdinand remained their emperor. As part of this scheme for a partially independent state, the Hungarians attempted to annex Transylvania, Croatia, and other eastern territories of the Habsburg Empire. That policy of annexation would have brought Romanians, Croatians, and Serbs under Magyar government. These national groups resisted

the drive toward Magyarization, the most important element of which was the imposition on them of the Hungarian language. The national groups now being repressed by the Hungarians believed they had a better chance of maintaining their national or ethnic identity, their languages, and their economic self-interest under Habsburg control. In late March, the Vienna government sent Count Joseph Jellachich (1801–1859) to aid the national groups who were rebelling against the rebellious Hungarians. By early September 1848, he was leading an invasion force against Hungary with the strong support of the national groups who were resisting Magyarization. These events in Hungary represented a prime example of the clash between liberalism and nationalism. The state that the Hungarian March Laws would have governed was liberal in political structure, but it would not have allowed autonomy to the non-Magyar peoples within its borders.

Czech Nationalism   In the middle of March 1848, with Vienna and Budapest in revolt, Czech nationalists demanded that Bohemia and Moravia be permitted to constitute an autonomous Slavic state within the empire similar to that just constituted in Hungary. Conflict immediately developed, however, between the Czechs and the Germans living in these regions. The Czechs summoned a congress of Slavs, including Poles, Ruthenians, Czechs, Slovaks, Croats, Slovenes, and Serbs, which met in Prague during early June. Under the leadership of Francis Palacky (1798–1876), this first Pan-Slavic Congress issued a manifesto calling for the national equality of Slavs within the Habsburg Empire. The manifesto

Louis Kossuth, a Magyar nationalist, seeking to raise troops to fight for Hungarian independence during the revolutionary disturbances of 1848.
Bildarchiv Preussischer Kulturbesitz

also protested the repression of all Slavic peoples under Habsburg, Hungarian, German, and Ottoman domination. The document raised the vision of a vast east European Slavic nation or federation of Slavic states that would extend from Poland south and eastward through Ukraine and within which Russian interests would surely dominate. (See "The Pan-Slavic Congress Calls for the Liberation of Slavic Nationalities.") Although such a state never came into being, the prospect of a unified Slavic people freed from Ottoman and Habsburg control was an important political factor in later European history. Pan-Slavism would become a tool that Russia would use in attempts to gain the support of nationalist minorities in eastern Europe and the Balkans and to bring pressure against both the Habsburg Empire and Germany.

On June 12, the day the Pan-Slavic Congress closed, a radical insurrection broke out in Prague. General Prince Alfred Windischgraetz (1787–1862), whose wife had been killed by a stray bullet, moved his troops against the uprising. The local middle class was happy to see the radicals suppressed, as they were by June 17. The Germans in the area approved the smothering of Czech nationalism. The policy of "divide and conquer" had succeeded.

Rebellion in Northern Italy While repelling the Hungarian and Czech bids for autonomy, the Habsburg government also faced war in northern Italy. A revolution against Habsburg domination began in Milan on March 18. Five days later, the Austrian commander General Count Joseph Wenzel Radetzky (1766–1858) retreated from the city. King Charles Albert of Piedmont (r. 1831–1849), who wanted to

expand the influence of his kingdom in Lombardy (the province of which Milan is the capital), aided the rebels. The Austrian forces fared badly until July, when Radetzky, reinforced by new troops, defeated Piedmont and suppressed the revolution. For the time being, Austria had held its position in northern Italy.

Vienna and Hungary remained to be recaptured. In midsummer, the emperor returned to the capital. A newly elected assembly was trying to write a constitution, and within the city the radicals continued to press for further concessions. The imperial government decided to reassert its control. When a new insurrection occurred in October, the imperial army bombarded Vienna and crushed the revolt. On December 2, Emperor Ferdinand, now clearly too feeble to govern, abdicated in favor of his young nephew Francis Joseph (r. 1848–1916). Real power now lay with Prince Felix Schwarzenberg (1800–1852), who intended to use the army with full force.

On January 5, 1849, troops occupied Budapest. By March the triumphant Austrian forces had imposed military rule over Hungary, and the new emperor repudiated the recent constitution. The Magyar nobles attempted one last revolt. In August, Austrian troops, reinforced by 200,000 soldiers happily furnished by Tsar Nicholas I of Russia (r. 1825–1855), finally crushed the Hungarian revolt. Croatians and other nationalities that had resisted Magyarization welcomed the collapse of the revolt. The imperial Habsburg government had survived its gravest internal challenge because of the divisions among its enemies and its own willingness to use military force with a vengeance.

ITALY: REPUBLICANISM DEFEATED

The brief Piedmont-Austrian war of 1848 marked only the first stage of the Italian revolution. Many Italians hoped King Charles Albert of Piedmont would drive Austria from the peninsula and thus prepare the way for Italian unification. The defeat of Piedmont was a sharp disappointment to them. Liberal and nationalist hopes then shifted to the pope. Pius IX (r. 1846–1878) had a liberal reputation. He had reformed the administration of the Papal States. Nationalists believed some form of a united Italian state might emerge under the leadership of this pontiff.

In Rome, however, as in other cities, political radicalism was on the rise. On November 15, 1848, a democratic radical assassinated Count Pelligrino Rossi (r. 1787–1848), the liberal minister of the Papal States. The next day, popular demonstrations forced the pope to appoint a radical ministry. Shortly thereafter, Pius IX fled to Naples for refuge. In February 1849, the radicals proclaimed the Roman Republic. Republican nationalists from all over Italy, including Giuseppe Mazzini (1805–1872) and Giuseppe Garibaldi (1807–1882), two of the most prominent, flocked to Rome. They hoped to use the new republic as a base of operations to unite the rest of Italy under a republican government.

In March 1849, radicals in Piedmont forced Charles Albert to renew the patriotic war against Austria. After the almost immediate defeat of Piedmont at the Battle of Novara, the king abdicated in favor of his son, Victor Emmanuel II (r. 1849–1878). The defeat meant the Roman Republic must defend itself alone. The troops that attacked Rome and restored the pope came from France. The French wanted to prevent the rise of a strong, unified state on their southern border. Moreover, protection of the pope was good domestic politics for the French Republic and its president, Louis Napoleon. In early June 1849, 10,000 French soldiers laid siege to Rome. By the end of the month, the Roman Republic had dissolved. Garibaldi attempted to lead an army north against Austria, but he was defeated. On July 3, Rome fell to the French forces, which stayed there to protect the pope until 1870.

Pius IX returned, having renounced his previous liberalism. He became one of the arch conservatives of the next quarter century. Leadership toward Italian unification would have to come from another direction.

GERMANY: LIBERALISM FRUSTRATED

The revolutionary contagion had also spread rapidly through numerous states of Germany. Württemberg, Saxony, Hanover, and Bavaria all experienced insurrections calling for liberal government and greater German unity. The major revolution, however, occurred in Prussia.

Revolution in Prussia By March 15, 1848, large popular disturbances had erupted in Berlin. Frederick William IV (r. 1840–1861), believing the trouble stemmed from foreign conspirators, refused to turn his troops on the Berliners. He even announced certain limited reforms. Nevertheless, on March 18, several citizens were killed when troops cleared a square near the palace.

The monarch was still hesitant to use his troops forcefully, and there was much confusion in the government. The king also called for a Prussian constituent assembly to write a constitution. The next day, as angry Berliners crowded around the palace, Frederick William IV appeared on the balcony to salute the corpses of his slain subjects. He made further concessions and implied that henceforth Prussia would aid the movement toward German unification. For all practical purposes, the Prussian monarchy had capitulated.

Frederick William IV appointed a cabinet headed by David Hansemann (1790–1864), a widely respected moderate liberal. The Prussian constituent assembly, however, proved to be radical and democratic. As time passed, the king and his conservative supporters decided they would ignore the assembly. The liberal ministry resigned and was replaced by a conservative one. In April 1849, the assembly was dissolved, and the monarch proclaimed his own constitution. One of its key elements was a system of three-class voting. All adult males were allowed to vote. They voted, however, according to three classes arranged by ability to pay taxes. Thus the largest taxpayers, who constituted only about 5 percent of the population, elected one-third of the Prussian Parliament. This system prevailed in Prussia until 1918. In the finally revised Prussian constitution of 1850, the ministry was responsible to the king alone. Moreover, the Prussian army and officer corps swore loyalty directly to the monarch.

The Frankfurt Parliament While Prussia was moving from revolution to reaction, other events were unfolding in Germany as a whole. On May 18, 1848, representatives from all the German states gathered in Saint Paul's Church in Frankfurt to revise the organization of the German Confederation. The Frankfurt Parliament intended to write a moderately liberal constitution for a united Germany. The liberal character of the Frankfurt Parliament alienated both German conservatives and the German working class. The offense to the conservatives was simply the challenge to the existing political order. The Frankfurt Parliament lost the support of the

THE PAN-SLAVIC CONGRESS CALLS FOR THE LIBERATION OF SLAVIC NATIONALITIES

The first Pan-Slavic Congress met in Prague in June 1848. It called for the reorganization of the Austrian Empire and the political reorganization of most of the rest of eastern Europe. Its calls for changes in the national standing of the various Slavic peoples would have touched the Russian, Austrian, and Ottoman empires, as well as some of the then disunited states of Germany. The national aspirations voiced in the manifesto of the Congress would affect Europe from that time to the present. Note that the authors recognize that the principle of nationality, as adapted to the political life of Slavic peoples, is relatively new in 1848.

■ *How did the authors of the manifesto apply the individual freedoms associated with the French Revolution to the fate of individual nations? What are the specific areas of Europe that these demands would have changed? What potential national or ethnic differences among the Slavic peoples does the manifesto ignore or gloss over?*

The Slavic Congress in Prague is something unheard-of, in Europe as well as among the Slavs themselves. For the first time since our appearance in history, we, the scattered members of a great race, have gathered in great numbers from distant lands in order to become reacquainted as brothers and to deliberate our affairs peacefully. We have understood one another not only through our beautiful language, spoken by eighty millions, but also through the consonance of our hearts and the similarity of our spiritual qualities. . . .

It is not only in behalf of the individual within the state that we raise our voices and make known our demands. The nation, with all its intellectual merit, is as sacred to us as are the rights of an individual under natural law. . . .

In the belief that the powerful spiritual stream of today demands new political forms and that the state must be re-established upon altered principles, if not within new boundaries, we have suggested to the Austrian Emperor, under whose constitutional government we, the majority [of Slavic peoples] live, that he transform his imperial state into a union of equal nations. . . .

We raise our voices vigorously in behalf of our unfortunate brothers, the Poles, who were robbed of their national identity by insidious force. We call upon the governments to rectify this curse and these old onerous and hereditary sins in their administrative policy, and we trust in the compassion of all Europe. . . . We demand that the Hungarian Ministry abolish without delay the use of inhuman and coercive means toward the Slavic races in Hungary, namely the Serbs, Croats, Slovaks, and Ruthenians, and that they promptly be completely assured of their national rights. Finally, we hope that the inconsiderate policies of the Porte will no longer hinder our Slavic brothers in Turkey from strongly claiming their nationality and developing it in a natural way. If, therefore, we formally express our opposition to such despicable deeds, we do so in the confidence that we are working for the good of freedom. Freedom makes the peoples who hitherto have ruled more just and makes them understand that injustice and arrogance bring disgrace not to those who must endure it but to those who act in such a manner.

industrial workers and artisans by refusing to restore the protection once afforded by the guilds. The liberals were too attached to the concept of a free labor market to offer meaningful legislation to workers. This failure marked the beginning of a profound split between German liberals and the German working class. For the rest of the century, German conservatives would be able to play on that division.

As if to demonstrate its disaffection from workers, in September 1848 the Frankfurt Parliament called in troops of the German Confederation to suppress a radical insurrection in the city. The liberals in the parliament wanted nothing to do with workers who erected barricades and threatened the safety of property.

The Frankfurt Parliament also floundered on the issue of unification. Members differed over whether to include Austria in the projected united Germany. The "large German [**grossdeutsch**] solution" favored inclusion, whereas the "small German [**kleindeutsch**] solution" advocated exclusion. The latter formula prevailed because Austria rejected the whole notion of German unification, which raised too many other nationality problems within the Habsburg domains. Consequently, the Frankfurt Parliament looked to Prussian rather than Austrian leadership.

On March 27, 1849, the parliament produced its constitution. Shortly thereafter, its delegates offered the crown of a united Germany to Frederick William IV of Prussia. He rejected the offer, asserting that kings ruled by the grace of God rather than by the permission of man-made constitutions. On his refusal, the Frankfurt Parliament began to dissolve. Not long afterward, troops drove off the remaining members.

German liberals never fully recovered from this defeat. The Frankfurt Parliament had alienated the artisans and the working class without gaining any compensating support from the conservatives. The liberals had proved themselves to be awkward, hesitant, unrealistic, and ultimately dependent on the armies of the monarchies. They had failed to unite Germany or to confront effectively the realities of political power in the German states. The various revolutions did achieve an extension of the franchise in some of the German states and the establishment of conservative constitutions. The gains were not negligible, but they were a far cry from the hopes of March 1848.

In Perspective

The first half of the nineteenth century witnessed enormous, unprecedented social change in Europe. The foundations of the industrial economy were laid. Virtually no existing institution was untouched by that emerging economy. Railways crossed the Continent. New consumer goods were available. Family patterns changed, as did the social and economic expectations of women. The crowding of cities presented new social and political problems. Issues of social order came to the fore with the new concern about crime and the establishment of police forces. An urban working class became one of the chief facts of both political and social life. The ebb and flow of the business cycle caused increased economic anxiety for workers and property owners alike.

While all these fundamental social changes took place, Europe was also experiencing continuing political strife. The turmoil of 1848 through 1850 ended the era of liberal revolution that had begun in 1789. Liberals and nationalists had discovered that rational argument and small insurrections would not achieve their goals. The political initiative passed for a time to the conservative political groups. Henceforth, nationalists were less romantic and more hardheaded. Railways, commerce, guns, soldiers, and devious diplomacy, rather than language and cultural heritage, became the future weapons of national unification. The working class also adopted new tactics and a new organization. The era of the riot and urban insurrection was ending; in the future, workers would turn to trade unions and political parties to achieve their political and social goals.

Perhaps most important after 1848, the European middle class ceased to be revolutionary. It became increasingly concerned about protecting its property against radical political and social movements associated with socialism and, increasingly, as the century passed, with Marxism. The middle class remained politically liberal only so long as liberalism seemed to promise economic stability and social security for its own style of life.

REVIEW QUESTIONS

1. What inventions were particularly important in the development of industrialism? What changes did industrialism make in society? Why were the years covered in this chapter so difficult for artisans? What is meant by "the proletarianization of workers"?

2. In what ways did the industrial economy change the working-class family? What roles and duties did various family members assume? Most specifically, how did the role of women change in the new industrial era?

3. What were the goals of the working class in the new industrial society, and how did they differ from middle-class goals? How do you explain the separation of working-class and middle-class goals?

4. How did police change in the nineteenth century, and why were new systems of enforcement instituted? In what ways were prisons improved, and how do you account for the reform movement that led to the improvements?

5. How would you define socialism? What were the chief ideas of the early socialists? How did the ideas of Karl Marx differ from those of earlier writers?

6. What factors, old and new, led to the widespread outbreak of revolutions in 1848? Were the causes in the various countries essentially the same, or did each have its own particular set of circumstances? Why did these revolutions fail throughout Europe? What roles did liberals and nationalists play in the revolutions? Why did they sometimes clash?

SUGGESTED READINGS

B. S. Anderson and J. P. Zinsser, *A History of Their Own: Women in Europe from Prehistory to the Present*, vol. 2 (1988). A wide-ranging survey.

D. S. Barnes, *The Making of a Social Disease: Tuberculosis in Nineteenth-Century France* (1995). An in-depth examination of one of the most prevalent lethal diseases of its day.

I. Berlin, *Karl Marx: His Life and Environment*, 4th ed. (1996). A classic introduction.

P. Brock, *The Slovak National Awakening* (1976). A standard work.

E. D. Brose, *The Politics of Technological Change in Prussia: Out of the Shadow of Antiquity, 1809–1848* (1993). Examines the roles of the various social groups in the economic growth and industrialization of Prussia.

R. B. Carlisle, *The Proffered Crown: Saint-Simonianism and the Doctrine of Hope* (1987). The best treatment of the broad social doctrines of Saint-Simonianism.

J. Coffin, *The Politics of Women's Work* (1996). Examines the subject in France.

I. Deak, *The Lawful Revolution: Louis Kossuth and the Hungarians, 1848–1849* (1979). The most significant study of the topic in English.

J. F. C. Harrison, *Quest for the New Moral World: Robert Owen and the Owenites in Britain and America* (1969). The standard work.

G. Himmelfarb, *The Idea of Poverty: England in the Early Industrial Age* (1984). A major work covering the subject from the time of Adam Smith through 1850.

M. Ignatieff, *A Just Measure of Pain: The Penitentiary in the Industrial Revolution, 1750–1850* (1978). An important treatment of early English penal thought and practice.

D. I. Kertzer and M. Barbagli (eds.), *Family Life in the Long Nineteenth Century, 1789–1913: The History of the European Family* (2002). Wide-ranging collection of essays.

K. Kolakowski, *Main Currents of Marxism: Its Rise, Growth, and Dissolution*, 3 vols. (1978). An important and comprehensive survey.

D. Landes, *The Unbound Prometheus: Technological Change and Industrial Development in Western Europe from 1750 to the Present* (1969). Classic one-volume treatment of technological development in a broad social and economic context.

F. Manuel, *The Prophets of Paris* (1962). Remains a stimulating treatment of French utopian socialism and social reform.

J. M. Merriman, *The Agony of the Republic: The Repression of the Left in Revolutionary France, 1848–1851* (1978). Study of how the Second French Republic and popular support for it were suppressed.

H. Perkin, *The Origins of Modern English Society, 1780–1880* (1969). A provocative attempt to look at the society as a whole.

D. H. Pinkney, *Decisive Years in France, 1840–47* (1986). A detailed and careful examination of the years leading up to the Revolution of 1848.

J. D. Randers-Pehrson, *Germans and the Revolution of 1848–1849* (2001). An exhaustive treatment of the subject.

P. Robertson, *An Experience of Women: Pattern and Change in Nineteenth-Century Europe* (1982). A useful survey.

W. H. Sewell, Jr., *Work and Revolution in France: The Language of Labor from the Old Regime to 1848* (1980). A fine analysis of French artisans.

D. Sorkin, *The Transformation of German Jewry, 1780–1840* (1987). An examination of the decades of Jewish emancipation in Germany.

J. Sperber, *The European Revolution, 1841–1851* (1993). An excellent synthesis.

D. Thompson, *The Chartists: Popular Politics in the Industrial Revolution* (1984). An important study.

E. P. Thompson, *The Making of the English Working Class* (1964). A classic work.

L. A. Tilly and J. W. Scott, *Women, Work, and Family* (1978). A useful and sensitive survey.

D. Winch, *Riches and Poverty: An Intellectual History of Political Economy in Britain, 1750–1834* (1996). A superb survey from Adam Smith through Thomas Malthus.

DOCUMENTS CD-ROM

Reaction, Reform and Revolt

21.5 Karl Marx and Friedrich Engels: *The Communist Manifesto*

21.6 Michael Harrington, from *Socialism: Past and Future*

21.7 Anarchism: Michael Bakunin

Industrialization

22.1 Extolling the Virtues of the Manufacturer

22.2 Child Labor Inquiry

22.6 Improving the Poor?

J. M. W. Turner, *Rain, Steam, and Speed—The Great Western Railway*

Joseph Mallord William Turner, *Rain, Steam, and Speed—The Great Western Railway*, 1844. Oil on canvas, 90.8 × 121.9. © The National Gallery, London.

During the first half of the nineteenth century, Britain was the center of the new industrial economy. The railway, first in Britain, then across the world, was the most powerful transforming technology of the age. It embodied the industrial power and social shock of the early Industrial Revolution. Both the building of the railways and their daily operation tore across the physical and social structures of traditional rural life. The Great Western Railway shown here in Joseph Mallord William Turner's *Rain, Steam, and Speed—The Great Western Railway*, extended from London to the West Country of England and was the largest railway system yet constructed.

Turner's painting introduced the railway into the realm of high art. Turner (1775–1851) was an English artist who used the techniques of romantic painting to portray subjects as distinct as Hannibal crossing the Alps, warships, and, as in this work, the recently invented steam locomotive. Turner's ability to produce profound effects on his viewers from images filled with light and color rather than through precise linear portrayals, later influenced the French impressionists, who themselves often painted scenes depicting railways. Turner was thus one of the pioneers in the movement that was revolutionizing Western art in the nineteenth century at the same time that technology was revolutionizing the economy and society.

Turner had begun as a painter of watercolors, and many of his paintings give a watercolor-like sense of transparency and of light emerging through the art itself. His paintings thus often appear as almost ethereal visions. One British newspaper could not decide whether *Rain, Steam, and Speed* represented "dazzling unrealities . . . or realities seized upon at a moment's glance."[1]

[1]*The Times*, May 8, 1844, quoted in Martin Butlin and Evelyn Joll, *The Paintings of J. M. W. Turner*, rev. ed. (New Haven, CT: Yale University Press, 1984), p. 257.

Despite the luminous quality of Turner's paintings, he sought to portray as much as possible from real life. In *Rain, Steam, and Speed*, the new technology is part of the natural world. The engine is made from iron. Its movement embodies speed itself as it passes through the rain and fog. Yet the bridges in the painting suggest a new human-constructed infrastructure.

Turner also was convinced that individual human beings loomed small before the forces of nature, history, and technology. For this reason, he is known as a painter of the sublime—that is, of subjects that aroused strong emotions like fear, dread, and awe and raise questions about our control over our lives. In *Rain, Steam, and Speed*, a farmer plows a field on the right while a much slower boat glides in the river on the left as the train seems to barrel ahead directly into the viewer. The farmer and the boat suggest the technologies of an earlier age that must yield to iron and steam. The steam locomotive, the chief symbol of the new technology of the day, thus surpasses animals, bypasses earlier technology, and moves boldly from the clouds of the past into a new era in human history.

■ *Why is Turner considered a pioneer of impressionism? Why is Turner known as a painter of the "sublime," and how does his painting reflect this? How does* Rain, Steam, and Speed *illustrate advances in nineteenth-century technology?*

Sources: Michael Freeman, *Railways and the Victorian Imagination* (New Haven, CT: Yale University Press, 1999); Gerard Finley, *Angel in the Sun: Turner's Vision of History* (Montreal, and Kingston, ON: McGill-Queen's University Press, 1999); Martin Butlin and Evelyn Joll, *The Paintings of J. M. W. Turner*, rev. ed. (New Haven, CT: Yale University Press, 1984).

PART 5

1850–1939

	POLITICS AND GOVERNMENT	SOCIETY AND ECONOMY	RELIGION AND CULTURE
1850–1890	1851 Louis Napoleon seizes power in France	1850–1910 Height of European outward migration	1850–1880 Jewish emancipation in much of Europe
	1854–1856 Crimean War	1853–1870 Haussmann redesigns Paris	1853–1854 Gobineau, *Essay on the Inequality of the Human Races*
	1861 Proclamation of the Kingdom of Italy	1857 Bessemer steelmaking process	1857 Flaubert, *Madame Bovary*
	1862 Bismarck becomes prime minister of Prussia	1861 Serfdom abolished in Russia	1859 Darwin, *On the Origin of Species*
	1864 First International founded		
	1867 Austro-Hungarian Dual Monarchy founded		
	1868 Gladstone becomes British prime minister		
	1869 Suez Canal completed		

Charles Darwin

	POLITICS AND GOVERNMENT	SOCIETY AND ECONOMY	RELIGION AND CULTURE
	1870 Franco-Prussian War; French Republic proclaimed	1870 Education Act and first Irish Land Act, Britain	1864 Plus IX, *Syllabus of Errors*
	1871 German Empire proclaimed; Paris Commune		1867 Mill, *The Subjection of Women*
	1874 Disraeli becomes British prime minister		1869 Disestablishment of the Irish Church
	1875 Britain gains control of Suez	1875 Public Health and Artisan Dwelling Acts, Britain	1871 Darwin, *The Descent of Man*; Religious tests abolished at Oxford and Cambridge
	1880s Britain establishes Protectorate in Egypt		1872 Nietzsche, *The Birth of Tragedy*
	1881 People's Will assassinates Alexander II; Three Emperors' League is renewed	1881 Second Irish Land Act	1873–1876 Bismarck's *Kulturkampf*
			1879 Ibsen, *A Doll's House*
	1882 Italy, Germany, Austria form Triple alliance		1880s Growing anti-Semitism in Europe
	1884–1885 Germany forms African protectorates		1880 Zola, *Nana*
	1888 William II becomes German emperor	1886 Daimler invents internal combustion engine	1883 Mach, *The Science of Mechanics*
1890–1918	1894 Dreyfus convicted in France; Nicholas II becomes tsar of Russia	1890s Oil begins to have impact on world economy	1883 Nietzsche, *Thus Spake Zarathustra*
		1894 Union of German Women's Organizations founded	1892 Ibsen, *The Master Builder*
	1898 Germany begins to build a battleship navy	1895 Diesel engine invented	1893 Shaw, *Mrs. Warren's Profession*
	1902 British Labour Party formed	1897 German and Czech language equality in Austrian Empire; Russia mandates eleven-and-a-half hour workday	1896 Herzl, *The Jewish State*
	1903 Bolshevik-Menshevik split		1899 Bernstein, *Evolutionary Socialism*
	1904 Britain and France in Entente Cordiale	1901 National Council of French Women founded	1900 Freud, *The Interpretation of Dreams*; Key, *The Century of the Child*
			1902 Lenin, *What Is to Be Done?*

TOWARD THE MODERN WORLD

1850–1939

POLITICS AND GOVERNMENT	SOCIETY AND ECONOMY	RELIGION AND CULTURE

1890–1918 (cont.)

POLITICS AND GOVERNMENT

1905   Revolution in Saint Petersburg suppressed; first Moroccan Crisis

1906   Dreyfus conviction set aside

1908–1909   Bosnian crisis

1911   Second Moroccan crisis

1912   Third Irish Home Rule Bill passed

1912–1913   First and Second Balkan Wars

1914–1918   World War I

1917   Russian Revolution; Bolsheviks seize power

SOCIETY AND ECONOMY

1903   Third Irish Land Act; British Women's Social and Political Union founded; Wright brothers fly the first airplane

1906   Land redemption payments canceled for Russian peasants

1907   Women vote on national issues in Norway

1918   Vote granted to some British women

RELIGION AND CULTURE

1903   Shaw, *Man and Superman*

1905   Weber, *The Protestant Ethic and the Spirit of Capitalism*; Termination of the Napoleonic Concordat in France

1907   Bergson, *Creative Evolution*

1908   Sorel, *Reflections on Violence*

1910   Pope Pius X requires anti-Modernist oath

1914   Joyce, *Portrait of the Artist as a Young Man*

1918–1939

POLITICS AND GOVERNMENT

1919   Paris Peace Conference; Weimar constitution proclaimed in Germany

1922   Mussolini takes power in Italy

1923   France invades the Ruhr; Hitler's Beer Hall *Putsch*; first Labour government in Britain

1924   Death of Lenin

1925   Locarno Agreements

1931   National Government formed in Great Britain

1933   Hitler appointed chancellor of Germany

1935   Nuremburg Laws; Italy invades Ethiopia

1936   Popular Front in France; purge trials in the Soviet Union; Spanish Civil War begins

1938   Munich Conference; *Kristallnacht* in Germany

1939   Germany invades Poland, starts World War II

SOCIETY AND ECONOMY

1920s   Worldwide commodity crisis

1921   Soviet Union begins New Economic Policy

1922   French Senate rejects vote for women

1923   Rampant inflation in Germany

1926   General strike in Great Britain

1928   Britain extends full franchise to women

1928–1933   First Five-Year Plan and agricultural collectivization in the Soviet Union

1929   Wall Street crash

1932   Lausanne Conference ends German reparations

mid-1930s   Nazis stimulate German economy through public works and defense spending

RELIGION AND CULTURE

1919   Barth, *Commentary on the Epistle to the Romans*

1920   Keynes, *Economic Consequences of the Peace*

1922   Joyce, *Ulysses*

1924   Hitler, *Mein Kampf*

1925   Woolf, *Mrs. Dalloway*

1927   Heidegger, *Being and Time*; Mann, *Buddenbrooks*

1927   Woolf, *To the Lighthouse*; Mann, *Magic Mountain*

1929   Woolf, *A Room of One's Own*

1936   Keynes, *General Theory of Employment, Interest, and Money*

1937   Orwell, *Road to Wigan Pier*

1938   Sartre, *Nausea*

The proclamation of the German Empire in the Hall of Mirrors at Versailles, January 18, 1871, after the defeat of France in the Franco-Prussian War. Kaiser Wilhelm I is standing at the top of the steps under the flags. Bismarck is in the center in a white uniform.
Bildarchiv Preussischer Kulturbesitz. Original Friedrichsruh, Bismarck-Museum.

CHAPTER 23

THE AGE OF NATION-STATES

*T*HE REVOLUTIONS OF 1848 HAD *collapsed in defeat for both liberalism and nationalism. In the 1850s, conservative regimes were entrenched across the Continent. Yet only a quarter century later, many of the major goals of early-nineteenth-century liberals and nationalists had been reached. Italy and Germany were each united under constitutional monarchies. The Habsburg emperor accepted constitutional government and recognized the liberties of the Magyars of Hungary. In Russia, the tsar emancipated the serfs. France was a republic. Liberalism and even democracy flourished in Great Britain. The Ottoman Empire also undertook major reforms.*

Paradoxically, most of these developments occurred under conservative leadership. Events within European international affairs compelled some governments to pursue new policies at home as well as abroad. They had to find novel methods of maintaining the loyalty of their subjects. Some conservative leaders preferred to carry out a popular policy on their own terms, so that they, rather than the liberals, would receive credit. Other leaders acted as they did because they had no choice.

KEY TOPICS

- Reforms in the Ottoman Empire
- The unification of Italy and Germany
- The shift from empire to republic in France
- The emergence of a dual monarchy in Austria-Hungary
- Reforms in Russia, including the emancipation of the serfs
- The emergence of Great Britain as the exemplary liberal state and its confrontation with Irish nationalists

The Crimean War (1853–1856)

As has so often been true in modern European history, the impetus for change originated in war. The Crimean War (1853–1856) was rooted in the long-standing desire of Russia to extend its influence over the Ottoman Empire. Two disputes led to the conflict. First, as noted in Chapter 18, the Russians had since the time of Catherine the Great been given protective oversight of Orthodox Christians in the Empire, and France had similar oversight of Roman Catholics. In 1851, yielding to French pressure, the Ottoman sultan had assigned care of certain holy places in Palestine to Roman Catholics. This decision angered the Russians. Second, Russia wanted to extend its control over the Ottoman provinces of Moldavia and Walachia (now in Romania). In the summer of 1853, the Russians used their right to protect Orthodox Christians in the Ottoman Empire as the pretext to occupy the two provinces. Shortly thereafter, the Ottoman Empire declared war on Russia.

Of far more significance to the great powers than the protection of Christian sites in Palestine was the fate of the weak Ottoman Empire. The Russian government envisioned the eventual breakup of the empire and hoped to extend its influence at the cost of that Ottoman demise. Both France and Britain, though recognizing the difficulties of the Ottoman government and using it to their own advantage when the opportunity presented itself, opposed Russian expansion in the eastern Mediterranean, where they had extensive naval and commercial interests. Napoleon III also thought an activist foreign policy would shore up domestic support for his regime.

On March 28, 1854, France and Britain declared war on Russia in alliance with the Ottomans. Much to the disappointment of Tsar Nicholas I, Austria and Prussia remained neutral. The Austrians had their own ambitions in the Balkans, and, for the moment, Prussia followed Austrian leadership.

Both sides conducted the conflict ineptly, a fact that became widely known in western Europe because the Crimean War was the first to be covered by war correspondents and photographers. The ill-equipped and poorly commanded armies became bogged down along the Crimean coast of the Black Sea. In September 1855, after a long siege, the Russian fortress of Sevastopol finally fell to the French and British. (See "Art & the West: Elizabeth Thompson, Lady Butler," p. 812.)

Peace Settlement and Long-Term Results   In March 1856, a conference in Paris concluded the Treaty of Paris. This treaty required Russia to surrender territory near the mouth of the Danube River, to recognize the neutrality of the Black Sea, and to renounce its claims of protection over orthodox Christians in the Ottoman Empire. Even before the conference, Austria had forced Russia to withdraw from Moldavia and Walachia. The image of an invincible Russia that had prevailed across Europe since the close of the Napoleonic wars was shattered.

Also shattered was the Concert of Europe (see Chapter 21) as a means of dealing with international relations on the Continent. Following the successful repression of the 1848 uprisings, the great powers feared revolution less than they had earlier in the century, and consequently they displayed much less reverence for the Vienna settlement. As historian Gordon Craig put it, "After 1856 there were more powers willing to fight to overthrow the existing order than there were to take up arms to defend it."[1] Consequently, for about twenty-five years after the Crimean War, European affairs were unstable, producing a period of adventurism in foreign policy. But while these events reshaped western Europe, the Ottoman Empire over whose fate the Crimean War had been fought undertook a series of reforms. These need to be considered before we return to events in Europe.

Reforms in the Ottoman Empire

The short-lived Napoleonic invasion of the Ottoman province of Egypt in 1798–1799 (see Chapter 20) had sparked a drive for change in the Ottoman Empire. In 1839, under pressure from imperial bureaucrats who had studied in Europe, the sultan issued a decree, called the *Hatt-i Sharif of Gülhane,*

---

[1]*The New Cambridge Modern History*, Vol. 10 (Cambridge, UK: Cambridge University Press, 1967), p. 273.

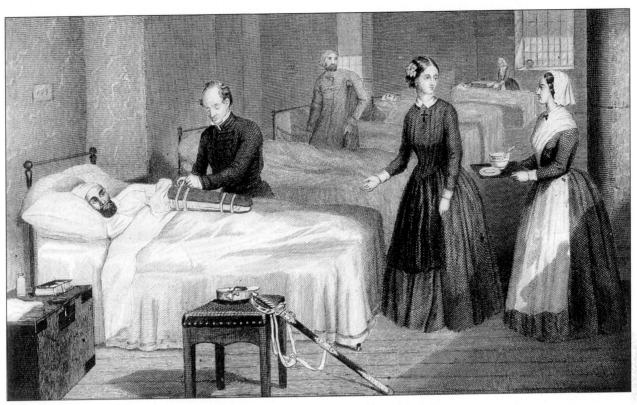

During the Crimean War, Florence Nightingale of Great Britain organized nursing care for the wounded. Corbis

that attempted to reorganize the empire's administration and military along European lines. This decree opened what became known as the *Tanzimat* (meaning reorganization) era of the Ottoman Empire, lasting from 1839 to 1876. The reforms, which were drawn up by administrative councils and not issued arbitrarily by the sultan, liberalized the economy, ended the practice of tax farming, and sought to eliminate corruption. The *Hatt-i Sharif* was particularly remarkable for extending civic equality to Ottoman subjects regardless of their religion. Muslims, Christians, and Jews were now equal before the law. The empire also made it much easier for Muslims to enter into commercial agreements with non-Muslims, both within the empire and from abroad.

Another reform decree, called the *Hatti-i Hümayun*, was promulgated in 1856 at the close of the Crimean War. Under the influence of Britain and France, it spelled out the rights of non-Muslims more explicitly, giving them equal obligations with Muslims for military service and equal opportunity for state employment and admission to state schools. The decree also abolished torture and allowed foreigners to acquire some forms of property. In time, printing presses and Western-oriented schools appeared in the empire mainly via Christian missionaries, many of whom were Americans. For

the first time in its long history, the Ottoman Empire actually sought to copy European legal and military institutions and the secular values flowing from liberalism.

The imperial government took these steps in the hope of eliciting the loyalty of Christian subjects at a time when nationalism was making increasing inroads among them. In effect, during this reform era the Ottoman government broke down the millet system (see Chapter 15) and sought to define all its citizens as Ottoman subjects rather than as members of particular religious communities.

However, it proved difficult to put these reforms into practice. In some regions of the empire, especially Egypt and Tunis, local rulers were virtually independent of Istanbul. They carried out their own modernizing reforms, often working closely with European powers. In the capital itself, power struggles developed among courtiers, European-oriented administrators and army officers, merchants who prospered from the changes, and the ulema, which sought to maintain the rule of Islamic law. Because of these tensions, as well as growing nationalism in various regions, the Ottoman Empire failed to achieve genuine political strength and stability. Many Ottomans questioned the wisdom of Tanzimat and warned that abandoning long-standing

Islamic institutions in favor of the rapid adoption of European ones would lead to disaster.

The inability of the Ottoman Empire to master its own destiny was demonstrated by the Balkan wars of the late 1870s, which resulted in either the independence of, or Russian or Austrian dominance over, most of the empire's European holdings. (See Chapter 26.) The response to those foreign policy defeats was greater efforts to modernize the army and the economy and to build railways and telegraphs. In 1876, reformers persuaded the sultan to proclaim an Ottoman constitution on the grounds that European political arrangements as well as technology accounted for European strength. The constitution called for a parliament consisting of an elected chamber of deputies and an appointed senate (these met for the first time in 1877) but left the sultan's power mostly intact. Nonetheless, a new sultan soon rejected even these limited steps toward constitutionalism and dismissed the parliament. In 1908, military officers carried out a revolution against the authority though not the person of the sultan. Another group of reformist officers, known as the *Young Turks,* came to the fore with another program to modernize the empire. They were still in charge when World War I broke out, and their decision to enter the war on the side of the Central Powers in November 1914 led to the empire's defeat and collapse. (See Chapter 26.)

One of the underlying themes of all of these attempts at reform and modernization from 1839 to 1914 was the increasing secularization of the government, which sought less to question the Islamic foundations of society than to reduce the influence of the Muslim religious authorities on the state.

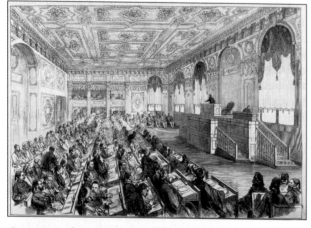

Ottoman reformers established a parliament in 1877, but the sultan retained most political authority. Illustrated London News of April 14, 1877. Mary Evans Picture Library Ltd.

Italian Unification

Nationalists had long wanted to unite the small, absolutist principalities of the Italian peninsula into a single state. During the first half of the century, however, opinion differed about how to achieve Italian unification.

ROMANTIC REPUBLICANS

One approach to the issue was *romantic republicanism.* After the Congress of Vienna, secret republican societies were founded throughout Italy, the most famous of which was the **Carbonari** ("charcoal burners"). They were ineffective.

Following the failure of nationalist uprisings in 1831, the leadership of romantic republican nationalism passed to Giuseppe Mazzini (1805–1872). He became the most important nationalist leader in Europe and brought new fervor to the cause. He once declared, "Nationality is the role assigned by God to a people in the work of humanity. It is its mission, its task on earth, to the end that God's thought may be realized in the world."[2] In 1831, he founded the Young Italy Society to drive Austria from the peninsula and establish an Italian republic.

During the 1830s and 1840s, Mazzini and his fellow republican Giuseppe Garibaldi (1807–1882) led insurrections. Both were deeply involved in the ill-fated Roman Republic of 1849. Throughout the 1850s, they continued to conduct what amounted to guerrilla warfare. Because both men spent much time in exile, they became well known across the Continent and in the United States.

Republican nationalism frightened moderate Italians, who wanted to rid themselves of Austrian domination but not establish a republic. For a time, these people had looked to the papacy to sponsor unification. That solution became impossible after the experience of Pius IX with the Roman Republic in 1849. Consequently, at midcentury, "Italy" remained a geographical expression rather than a political entity.

Yet by 1860, the Italian peninsula was transformed into a nation-state under a constitutional monarchy. The process was carried out not by romantic republican nationalists, but by Count Camillo Cavour (1810–1861), the moderately liberal prime minister of Piedmont. His method was force of arms tied to secret diplomacy. The spirit of Machiavelli must have smiled over the enterprise.

[2]Quoted in William L. Langer, *Political and Social Upheaval, 1832–1852* (New York: Harper Torchbooks, 1969), p. 115.

CAVOUR'S POLICY

Piedmont (officially styled the Kingdom of Sardinia), in northwestern Italy, was the most independent state on the peninsula. The Congress of Vienna had restored the kingdom as a buffer between French and Austrian ambitions. As we have seen, during 1848 and 1849, King Charles Albert of Piedmont, after having promulgated a conservative constitution, twice unsuccessfully fought Austria. Following the second defeat, he abdicated in favor of his son, Victor Emmanuel II (r. 1849–1878). In 1852, the new monarch chose Count Camillo Cavour as his prime minister.

A cunning statesman, Cavour had begun political life as a strong conservative, but had gradually moved toward a moderately liberal position. He had made a fortune by investing in railroads, reforming agriculture on his own estates, and editing a newspaper. He was deeply imbued with the ideas of the Enlightenment, classical economics, and utilitarianism. Cavour was a nationalist of a new breed who had no respect for Mazzini's ideals. A strong monarchist, Cavour rejected republicanism. It was economic and material progress rather than romantic ideals that required a large, unified state on the Italian peninsula.

Cavour believed that if Italians proved themselves to be efficient and economically progressive, the great powers might decide that Italy could govern itself. He joined the Piedmontese Cabinet in 1850 and became premier two years later. He worked for free trade, railway construction, expansion of credit, and agricultural improvement. He felt that such material and economic bonds, rather than fuzzy romantic yearnings, must unite the Italians. Cavour also recognized the need to capture the loyalties of those Italians who believed in other varieties of nationalism. He thus fostered the Nationalist Society, which established chapters in other Italian states to press for unification under the leadership of Piedmont. Finally, the prime minister believed Italy could be unified only with the aid of France. The recent accession of Napoleon III in France seemed to open the way for such aid.

French Sympathies Cavour used the Crimean War to bring Italy into European politics. In 1855, Piedmont joined the conflict on the side of France and Britain and sent 10,000 troops to the front. This small but significant participation in the war allowed Cavour to raise the Italian question at the Paris conference. He left Paris with no diplomatic reward, but his intelligence and political capacity had impressed everyone. Cavour also gained the sympathy of Napoleon III. During the rest of the decade, he achieved further international re-

Count Camillo Cavour (1810–1861) used an opportunistic alliance with France against Austria and military interventions in the Papal States and southern Italy to secure Italian unification under King Victor Emmanuel II of Piedmont, rather than as the republic that Mazzini and Garibaldi had advocated. © Archivo Iconografico, S.A./Corbis

spectability for Piedmont by opposing various plots of Mazzini, who was still attempting to lead nationalist uprisings. By 1858, Cavour represented a moderate liberal alternative to both republicanism and reactionary absolutism in Italy.

Cavour continued to bide his time. Then, in January 1858, an Italian named Orsini attempted to assassinate Napoleon III. The incident made the French emperor, who had once belonged to a nationalist group, newly concerned about the Italian issue. He saw himself continuing his more famous uncle's liberation of the peninsula. He also saw Piedmont as a potential ally against Austria. In July 1858, Cavour and Napoleon III met at Plombières in southern France. Riding alone in a carriage, with the emperor at the reins, the two men plotted to provoke a war in Italy that would permit them to defeat Austria. A formal treaty in December 1858 confirmed the agreement. France was to receive French-speaking Nice and Savoy from Piedmont for its aid.

War with Austria In early 1859, tension grew between Austria and Piedmont as Piedmont mobilized its army. On April 22, Austria demanded that Piedmont demobilize. That demand allowed Piedmont to claim that Austria was provoking a war. France intervened to aid its ally. On June 4, the Austrians were defeated at Magenta, and on June 24 at Solferino. Meanwhile, revolutions had broken out in Tuscany, Modena, Parma, and the Romagna provinces of the Papal States.

With the Austrians in retreat and the new revolutionary regimes calling for union with Piedmont, Napoleon III feared too extensive a Piedmontese victory. On July 11, he independently concluded a peace with Austria at Villafranca. Piedmont received Lombardy, but Venetia remained under Austrian control. Cavour felt betrayed by France, but the war had driven Austria from most of northern Italy. Later that summer, Parma, Modena, Tuscany, and the Romagna voted to unite with Piedmont. (See Map 23–1.)

Garibaldi's Campaign At this point, the forces of romantic republican nationalism compelled Cavour to pursue the complete unification of northern and southern Italy. In May 1860, Garibaldi landed in Sicily with more than 1,000 troops, who had been outfitted in the north. He captured Palermo and prepared to attack the mainland. By September he controlled the city and kingdom of Naples, probably the most corrupt example of Italian absolutism. For more than two decades Garibaldi had hoped to form a republican Italy, but Cavour forestalled him. He rushed Piedmontese troops south to confront Garibaldi. On the way, they conquered the rest of the Papal States except the area around Rome,

which was protected for the pope by French troops. Garibaldi's nationalism won out over his republicanism, and he accepted Piedmontese domination. In late 1860, Naples and Sicily voted to join the Italian kingdom.

THE NEW ITALIAN STATE

In March 1861, Victor Emmanuel II was proclaimed king of Italy. Three months later Cavour died. The new state more than ever needed his skills, because Italy had, in effect, been more nearly conquered than united by Piedmont. The republicans resented the treatment of Garibaldi. The clericals resented the conquest of the Papal States. In the south, armed resistance against the imposition of Piedmontese-style administration continued until 1866. The economies of north and south Italy were incompatible. The south was rural, poor, and backward. The north was industrializing, and its economy was increasingly linked to that of the rest of Europe. The social structures of the two regions reflected those differences, with large landholders and peasants dominant in the south and an urban working class emerging in the north.

The political framework of the united Italy could not overcome these problems. The constitution, which was that promulgated for Piedmont in 1848, provided for a conservative constitutional monarchy. Parliament consisted of two houses: a senate appointed by the king and a chamber of deputies elected on a narrow franchise. Ministers were

Giuseppe Garibaldi represented the forces of romantic Italian nationalism. The landing of his Redshirts on Sicily and their subsequent invasion of southern Italy in 1860 forced Cavour to unite the entire peninsula sooner than he had intended. Bildarchiv Preussischer Kulturbesitz

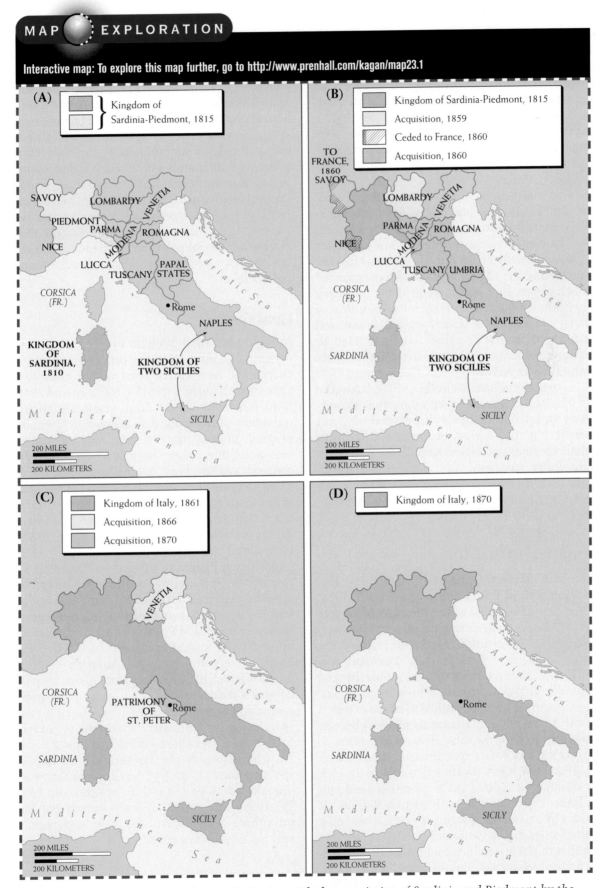

MAP EXPLORATION

Interactive map: To explore this map further, go to http://www.prenhall.com/kagan/map23.1

(A)

Kingdom of Sardinia-Piedmont, 1815

SAVOY
LOMBARDY
VENETIA
PIEDMONT
PARMA
MODENA
ROMAGNA
NICE
LUCCA
TUSCANY
PAPAL STATES
Adriatic Sea
CORSICA (FR.)
•Rome
NAPLES
KINGDOM OF SARDINIA, 1810
KINGDOM OF TWO SICILIES
Mediterranean Sea
SICILY
200 MILES
200 KILOMETERS

(B)

Kingdom of Sardinia-Piedmont, 1815
Acquisition, 1859
Ceded to France, 1860
Acquisition, 1860

TO FRANCE, 1860 SAVOY
LOMBARDY
VENETIA
PARMA
MODENA
ROMAGNA
NICE
LUCCA
TUSCANY
UMBRIA
Adriatic Sea
CORSICA (FR.)
•Rome
SARDINIA
NAPLES
KINGDOM OF TWO SICILIES
Mediterranean Sea
SICILY
200 MILES
200 KILOMETERS

(C)

Kingdom of Italy, 1861
Acquisition, 1866
Acquisition, 1870

VENETIA
Adriatic Sea
CORSICA (FR.)
PATRIMONY OF ST. PETER
•Rome
SARDINIA
Mediterranean Sea
SICILY
200 MILES
200 KILOMETERS

(D)

Kingdom of Italy, 1870

Adriatic Sea
CORSICA (FR.)
•Rome
SARDINIA
Mediterranean Sea
SICILY
200 MILES
200 KILOMETERS

MAP 23–1   THE UNIFICATION OF ITALY   *Beginning with the association of Sardinia and Piedmont by the Congress of Vienna in 1815, unification was achieved through the expansion of Piedmont between 1859 and 1870. Both Cavour's statesmanship and the campaigns of ardent nationalists played large roles.*

responsible to the monarch, not to Parliament. These arrangements did not foster vigorous parliamentary life. Political leaders often simply avoided major problems. In place of efficient, progressive government, such as Cavour had brought to Piedmont, a system called *transformismo* developed. Political opponents were "transformed" into government supporters through bribery, favors, or a seat in the cabinet. Italian politics became a byword for corruption.

Nor was unification complete. Many Italians believed other territories should be added to their nation. The most important of these were Venetia and Rome. The former was gained in 1866 in return for Italy's alliance with Prussia in the Austro-Prussian War. Rome and the papacy continued to be guarded by French troops, first sent there in 1849, until they were withdrawn during the Franco-Prussian War of 1870. The Italian state then annexed Rome and made it the capital. The papacy confined itself to the Vatican and remained hostile to the Italian state until the Lateran Accord of 1929. (See Chapter 27.)

By 1870, only the small province of Trent and the city of Trieste, both ruled by Austria, remained outside Italy. In and of themselves, these areas were not important, but they fueled the continued hostility of Italian nationalists toward Austria. The desire to liberate **Italia irredenta,** or "unredeemed Italy," was one reason for the Italian support of the Allies against Austria and Germany during World War I.

German Unification

German unification was the most important political development in Europe between 1848 and 1914. (See Map 23–2.) It transformed the balance of economic, military, and international power. Moreover, the method of its creation largely determined the character of the new German state. Germany was united by the conservative army, the monarchy, and the prime minister of Prussia, who wanted to outflank Prussian liberals. A unified Germany, which two generations of German liberals had sought, was actually achieved for the most illiberal of reasons.

During the 1850s, German unification seemed remote. The major states continued to trade with each other through the *Zollverein* (tariff union), and railways linked their economies. Frederick William IV of Prussia had given up thoughts of unification under Prussian leadership. Austria continued to oppose any union that might lessen its influence. Liberal nationalists had not recovered from the humiliating experiences of 1848 and 1849. What quickly modified this situation was a series of domestic political changes and problems within Prussia.

In 1858, Frederick William IV was adjudged insane, and his brother William assumed the regency. William I (r. 1861–1888), who became king in his own right in 1861, was less idealistic than his brother and more of a Prussian patriot. In the usual Hohenzollern tradition, his first concern was to strengthen the Prussian army. In 1860, his war minister and chief of staff proposed to enlarge the army, to increase the number of officers, and to extend the period of conscription from two to three years. The Prussian Parliament, created by the Constitution of 1850, refused to approve the necessary taxes. The liberals, who dominated the body, sought to avoid placing additional power in the hands of the monarchy. For two years, monarch and Parliament were deadlocked.

BISMARCK

In September 1862, William I turned for help to the person who, more than any other single individual, shaped the next thirty years of European history: Otto von Bismarck (1815–1898). Bismarck came from Junker (noble landlord) stock. He attended a university and displayed an interest in German unification. During the 1840s, he was elected to the provincial diet, where he was so reactionary as to disturb even the king. Yet he had made his mark. From 1851 to 1859, Bismarck served as the Prussian minister to the Frankfurt diet of the German Confederation. Later he became Prussian ambassador to Russia and was ambassador to France when William I appointed him prime minister.

Although Bismarck entered public life as a reactionary, he had mellowed into a conservative. He opposed parliamentary government, but not a constitutionalism that provided for a strong monarch. He understood that Prussia—and later, Germany—must have a strong industrial base. His years in Frankfurt arguing with his Austrian counterpart had hardened his Prussian patriotism. In politics, he was a pragmatist who put more trust in power and action than in ideas. As he declared in his first speech as prime minister, "Germany is not looking to Prussia's liberalism but to her power. . . . The great questions of the day will not be decided by speeches and majority decisions—that was the mistake of 1848–1849—but by iron and blood."[3] Yet this same minister, after having led Prussia into three wars, spent the next nineteen years seeking to preserve peace.

---

[3]Quoted in Otto Pflanze, *Bismarck and the Development of Germany: The Period of Unification: 1815–1871* (Princeton, NJ: Princeton University Press, 1963), p. 177.

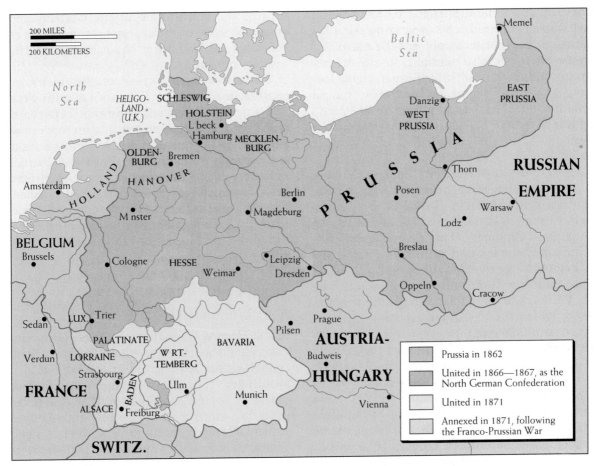

MAP 23–2   THE UNIFICATION OF GERMANY   *Under Bismarck's leadership, and with the strong support of its royal house, Prussia used diplomatic and military means, on both the German and international stages, to forcibly unify the German states into a strong national entity.*

Upon becoming prime minister in 1862, Bismarck immediately moved against the liberal Parliament. He contended that even without new financial levies, the Prussian constitution permitted the government to carry out its functions on the basis of previously granted taxes. Therefore, taxes could be collected and spent despite the parliamentary refusal to vote them. The army and most of the bureaucracy supported this interpretation of the constitution. In 1863, however, new elections sustained the liberal majority in the Parliament. Bismarck had to find some way to attract popular support away from the liberals and toward the monarchy and the army. He therefore set about uniting Germany through the conservative institutions of Prussia.

The Danish War (1864)   Bismarck pursued a *kleindeutsch*, or small German, solution to unification. Austria was to be excluded from a united German state. This goal required complex diplomacy. The Schleswig-Holstein problem gave Bismarck the handle for his policy. These two northern duchies had long been ruled by the kings of Denmark without being part of Denmark itself. Their populations were a mixture of Germans and Danes. Holstein, where Germans predominated, belonged to the German Confederation. In 1863, the Danish Parliament moved to incorporate both duchies into Denmark. The smaller states of the German Confederation proposed an all-German war to halt this move. Bismarck wanted Prussia to act alone or only in cooperation with Austria. Together, the two large states easily defeated Denmark in 1864.

The Danish defeat increased Bismarck's personal prestige, and over the next two years he maneuvered Austria into war with Prussia. In August 1865, the two powers negotiated the Convention of Gastein, which put Austria in charge of Holstein and Prussia in charge of Schleswig. Bismarck then moved to mend other diplomatic fences. He had gained Russian sympathy by supporting the 1863 suppression of a Polish revolt, and he persuaded Napoleon III to promise neutrality in an Austro-Prussian conflict. In April 1866, Bismarck concluded a treaty with Italy promising that Italy would get Venetia if it attacked Austria in support of Prussia when war broke out. Now Bismarck had to provoke his war.

The Austro-Prussian War (1866) Constant Austro-Prussian tension had arisen over the administration of Schleswig and Holstein. Bismarck ordered the Prussian forces to be as obnoxious as possible to the Austrians. On June 1, 1866, Austria appealed to the German Confederation to intervene in the dispute. Bismarck claimed that this violated the 1864 alliance and the Convention of Gastein. The Seven Weeks' War, which resulted in the summer of 1866, led to the decisive defeat of Austria at Königgrätz in Bohemia.

The Treaty of Prague, which ended the conflict on August 23, was lenient toward Austria, which only lost Venetia, ceded to Napoleon III, who in turn ceded it to Italy. Austria refused to give Venetia directly to Italy because the Austrians had crushed the Italians during the war. The Habsburgs were permanently excluded from German affairs. Prussia had thus established itself as the only major power among the German states.

The North German Confederation In 1867, Hanover, Hesse, Nassau, and the city of Frankfurt, which had all supported Austria during the war, were annexed by Prussia, and their rulers were deposed. Under Prussian leadership, all Germany north of the Main River now formed a federation known as the North German Confederation. Each state retained its own local government, but all military forces were under federal control. The president of the federation was the king of Prussia, represented by his chancellor, Bismarck. A legislature consisted of two houses: a federal council, or **Bundesrat**, composed of members appointed by the governments of the states, and a lower house, or **Reichstag**, chosen by universal male suffrage.

Bismarck had little fear of this broad franchise, because he sensed the peasants would vote for conservatives. Moreover, the *Reichstag* had little real power, because the ministers were responsible only to the monarch. The *Reichstag* could not even originate legislation. All laws had to be proposed by the chancellor. The legislature did have the right to approve military budgets, but these were usually submitted to cover several years at a time. The constitution of the confederation, which after 1871 became the constitution of the German Empire, possessed some of the appearances, but none of the substance, of liberalism. Germany was in effect a military monarchy.

The spectacular success of Bismarck's policy overwhelmed the liberal opposition in the Prussian Parliament. The liberals were split between those who prized liberalism and those who supported unification. In the end, nationalism proved more attractive. In 1866, the Prussian Parliament retroactively approved the military budget that had been disputed earlier. Bismarck had crushed the Prussian liberals by making the monarchy and the army the most popular institutions in the country. The drive toward unification had achieved his domestic political goal.

THE FRANCO-PRUSSIAN WAR AND THE GERMAN EMPIRE (1870–1871)

Bismarck now wanted to complete unification by bringing the states of southern Germany into the confederation. Spain gave him the excuse. In 1868, a military coup deposed the corrupt Bourbon queen of Spain, Isabella II (r. 1833–1868). To replace her, the Spaniards chose Prince Leopold of Hohenzollern-Sigmaringen, a Catholic cousin of William I of Prussia. On June 19, 1870, Leopold accepted the Spanish crown with Prussian blessings. Bismarck knew that France would object strongly to a Hohenzollern Spain.

On July 2, the Spanish government announced Leopold's acceptance, and the French reacted as expected. France sent its ambassador Count Vincent Benedetti (1817–1900) to consult with William I, who was vacationing at Bad Ems. They discussed the matter at several meetings. On July 12, Leopold's father renounced his son's candidacy for the Spanish throne, fearing the issue would cause war between Prussia and France. William was relieved that conflict had been avoided and he had not had to order Leopold to renounce the Spanish throne.

There the matter might have rested had it not been for the impetuosity of the French and the guile of Bismarck. On July 13, the French government instructed Benedetti to ask William for assurances he would tolerate no future Spanish candidacy for Leopold. The king refused, but said he might take the question under further consideration. Later that day he sent Bismarck, who was in Berlin, a telegram reporting the substance of the meeting. The chancellor, who desperately wanted a war with France to complete unification, had been disappointed by the peaceful resolution of the controversy. The king's telegram gave him a new opportunity to incite a war. Bismarck released an edited version of the dispatch. The revised Ems telegram made it appear that William had insulted the French ambassador. The idea was to goad France into declaring war.

The French government fell for Bismarck's bait and declared war on July 19. Napoleon III was sick and not eager for war, but his government believed victory over the North German Confederation would give the empire renewed popular support. Once the conflict erupted, the southern German states, honoring treaties of 1866, joined Prussia against France, whose defeat was not long in coming. On September 1, at the Battle of Sedan, the Germans not only beat the French army but also captured Napoleon III. By late September, Paris was besieged; it finally capitulated on January 28, 1871.

Ten days earlier, in the Hall of Mirrors at the Palace of Versailles, the German Empire had been proclaimed. The German princes requested William to accept the title of German emperor. The princes remained heads of their respective states within the new federation. From the peace settlement with France, Germany annexed Alsace and part of Lorraine. (See "Heinrich von Treitschke Demands the Annexation of Alsace and Lorraine.")

Both the fact and the manner of German unification produced long-range effects in Europe. A powerful new state had been created in north central Europe. It was rich in natural resources and talented citizens. Militarily and economically, the German Empire would be far stronger than Prussia had been alone. The unification of Germany was also a blow to European liberalism, because the new state was a conservative creation. Conservative politics was now backed not by a weak Austria or an economically retrograde Russia, but by the strongest state on the Continent.

The two nations most immediately affected by German and Italian unification were France and Austria. The emergence of the two new unified states revealed French and Habsburg weakness. Each had to change. France returned to republican government, and the Habsburgs came to terms with their Magyar subjects.

France: From Liberal Empire to the Third Republic

Historians divide the reign of Napoleon III (r. 1851–1870) into the years of the authoritarian empire and those of the liberal empire. The year of division is 1860. Initially, after the coup in December 1851, Napoleon III had controlled the legislature, strictly censored the press, and harassed political dissidents. His support came from

---

German and Italian Unification

1854	Crimean War opens
1855	Cavour leads Piedmont into the war on the side of France and England
1856	Treaty of Paris concludes the Crimean War
1858	(January 14) Attempt to assassinate Napoleon III
1858	(July 20) Secret conference between Napoleon III and Cavour at Plombières
1859	War of Piedmont and France against Austria
1860	Garibaldi lands his forces in Sicily and invades southern Italy
1861	(March 17) Proclamation of the Kingdom of Italy
1861	(June 6) Death of Cavour
1862	Bismarck becomes prime minister of Prussia
1864	Danish-Prussian War
1865	Convention of Gastein
1866	Austro-Prussian War
1866	Venetia ceded to Italy
1867	North German Confederation formed
1870	(June 19–July 12) Crisis over Hohenzollern candidacy for the Spanish throne
1870	(July 13) Bismarck publishes the edited Ems dispatch
1870	(July 19) France declares war on Prussia
1870	(September 1) France defeated at Sedan and Napoleon III captured
1870	(September 4) French Republic proclaimed
1870	(October 2) Italian state annexes Rome
1871	(January 18) Proclamation of the German Empire at Versailles
1871	(March 28–May 28) Paris Commune
1871	(May 23) Treaty of Frankfurt ratified between France and Germany

---

the army, property owners, the French Catholic Church, and businesspeople. They approved the security he ensured for property, his protection of the pope, and his economic program. French victory in the Crimean War had confirmed the emperor's popularity.

From the late 1850s onward, Napoleon III began to modify his policy. In 1860, he concluded a free-trade treaty with Britain and permitted freer debate in the legislature. By the late 1860s, he had relaxed the press laws and permitted labor unions. In 1870, he allowed the leaders of the moderates in the legislature to form a ministry, and he also agreed to a liberal constitution that made the ministers responsible to the legislature.

HEINRICH VON TREITSCHKE DEMANDS THE ANNEXATION OF ALSACE AND LORRAINE

The Franco-Prussian War witnessed outbursts of extreme nationalistic rhetoric on both sides. One such voice was that of the German historian Heinrich von Treitschke (1834–1896). In a newspaper article, he demanded the annexation of Alsace and Lorraine from France. He did so even though the population of Alsace wished to remain part of France and German was not the dominant language in the region. He appealed to an earlier time when the region had been German in language and culture, and he asserted a policy that "might makes right" to assure German domination. Read this passage in conjunction with Lord Acton's condemnation of nationalism. (See "Lord Acton Condemns Nationalism," p. 800.)

■ *On what grounds does Treitschke base the German claim to Alsace and Lorraine? Why does he contend it is proper to ignore the wishes of the people involved? What, if any, political morality informs his views?*

The sense of justice to Germany demands the lessening of France. . . .

What is demanded by justice is, at the same time, absolutely necessary for our security. . . .

Every State must seek the guarantees of its own security in itself alone. . . .

In view of our obligation to secure the peace of the world, who will venture to object that the people of Alsace and Lorraine do not want to belong to us? The doctrine of the right of all the branches of the German race to decide on their own destinies, the plausible solution of demagogues without a fatherland, shiver to pieces in presence of the sacred necessity of these great days. These territories are ours by the right of the sword, and we shall dispose of them in virtue of a higher right—the right of the German nation, which will not permit its lost children to remain strangers to the German Empire. We Germans, who know Germany and France, know better than these unfortunates themselves what is good for the people of Alsace. . . . Against their will we shall restore them to their true selves. We have seen with joyful wonder the undying power of the moral forces of history, manifested far too frequently in the immense changes of these days, to place much confidence in the value

Napoleon III's liberal concessions sought to shore up domestic support to compensate for his failures in foreign policy. By 1860, he had lost control of the diplomacy of Italian unification. Between 1861 and 1867, he had supported a disastrous military expedition against Mexico led by Archduke Maximilian of Austria that ended in defeat and Maximilian's execution. In 1866, France had watched passively while Bismarck and Prussia reorganized German affairs. The war of 1870 against Germany had been the French government's last and most disastrous attempt to shore up its foreign policy and secure domestic popularity.

The Second Empire, but not the war, came to an inglorious end with the Battle of Sedan in September 1870. The emperor was captured and then allowed to go to England, where he died in 1873. Shortly after news of Sedan reached Paris, a republic was proclaimed and a government of national defense established. Paris itself was soon under Prussian siege, and the government moved to Bordeaux. Paris finally surrendered in January 1871, but France had been ready to sue for peace long before.

THE PARIS COMMUNE

The division between the provinces and Paris became sharper after the fighting with Germany stopped. Monarchists dominated the new National Assembly elected in February. For the time being, the assembly gave executive power to Adolphe Thiers (1797–1877), who had been active in French politics since 1830. He negotiated a settlement with Prussia (the Treaty of Frankfurt) whereby parts of France remained occupied by Prussian troops until a large indemnity had been paid. France also lost Alsace and part of Lorraine. The treaty was officially ratified on May 23.

Many Parisians, having suffered during the siege, resented what they regarded as a betrayal by the

of a mere popular disinclination. The spirit of a nation lays hold, not only of the generation which live beside it, but of those who are before and behind it. We appeal from the mistaken wishes of the men who are there to-day to the wishes of those who were there before them. We appeal to all those strong German men who once stamped the seal of our German nature on the language and manners, the art and the social life of the Upper Rhine. Before the nineteenth century closes the world will recognize that . . . we were only obeying the dictates of national honor when we made little account of the preferences of the people who live in Alsace to-day. . . .

At all times the subjection of a German race to France has been an unhealthy thing; to-day it is an offence against the reason of History—a vassalship of free men to half-educated barbarians. . . .

There is no perfect identity between the political and national frontier of any European country. Not one of the great Powers, and Germany no more than the rest of them, can ever subscribe to the principle that "language alone decides the formation of States." It would be impossible to carry that principle into effect. . . .

The German territory which we demand is ours by nature and by history. . . . In the tempests of the great Revolution the people of Alsace, like all the citizens of France, learned to forget their past. . . .

Most assuredly, the task of reuniting there the broken links between the ages is one of the heaviest that has ever been imposed upon the political forces of our nation. . . .

The people of Alsace are already beginning to doubt the invincibility of their nation, and at all events to divine the mighty growth of the German Empire. Perverse obstinancy, and a thousand French intrigues creeping in the dark, will make every step on the newly conquered soil difficult for us: but our ultimate success is certain, for on our side fights what is stronger than the lying artifices of the stranger—nature herself and the voice of common blood.

From Heinrich von Treitschke, "What We Demand from France" (1870), in Heinrich von Treitschke, *Germany, France, Russia and Islam* (New York: G. P. Putnam's Sons, 1915), pp. 100, 102, 106, 109, 120, 122, 134–135, 153, 158.

monarchist National Assembly sitting at Versailles. The Parisians elected a new municipal government, called the *Paris Commune*, which was formally proclaimed on March 28, 1871. The Commune intended to administer Paris separately from the rest of France. (See "The Paris Commune Is Proclaimed.") Radicals and socialists of all stripes participated in the Commune. In April, the National Assembly surrounded Paris with an army. On May 8, this army bombarded the city. On May 21, it broke through the city's defenses. During the next seven days, the troops killed about 20,000 inhabitants while the communards shot scores of hostages.

The Paris Commune became a legend throughout Europe. Marxists regarded it as a genuine proletarian government that the French bourgeoisie had suppressed. This interpretation is mistaken. The Commune, though of shifting composition, was dominated by petty bourgeois members. The socialism of the Commune had its roots in Blanqui's and Proudhon's anarchism rather than in Marx's concept of class conflict. The Commune wanted not a worker's state, but a nation of relatively independent, radically democratic enclaves. Its suppression thus represented not only the protection of property, but also the triumph of the centralized nation-state. Just as the armies of Piedmont and Prussia had united the small states of Italy and Germany, the army of the French National Assembly destroyed the particularistic political tendencies of Paris and, by implication, those of any other French community.

THE THIRD REPUBLIC

The National Assembly backed into a republican form of government against its will. Its monarchist majority was divided in loyalty between the House of Bourbon and the House of Orléans. They could have surmounted this problem, because the Bourbon claimant, the count of Chambord, had no children

THE PARIS COMMUNE IS PROCLAIMED

In September 1870, the French Republic was proclaimed, and shortly thereafter a National Assembly was elected. Paris, which had held out against Prussia longer than any other part of France, was hostile to the National Assembly. On March 18, 1871, a revolt against the assembly occurred in Paris. The National Guard of Paris sought to organize the city as a separate part of France. What follows is an excerpt of the proclamation of March 28 of Paris as an autonomous commune separate from the rest of France. The rebellious Parisians wanted all of France to be organized into a federation of politically autonomous communes. This communal concept was directly opposed to that of the large national state. Two months after the proclamation, the troops of the assembly crushed the Commune.

■ *How does this document interpret the French defeat at the hands of Prussia as a punishment? How does the declaration portray the proclamation of the Commune as a continuation of the French Revolution? What are the specific political goals and values of the Commune, according to this declaration?*

By its revolution of the 18th March, and the spontaneous and courageous efforts of the National Guard, Paris has regained its autonomy. . . . On the eve of the sanguinary and disastrous defeat suffered by France as the punishment it has to undergo for the seventy years of the Empire, and the monarchical, clerical, parliamentary, legal and conciliatory reaction, our country again rises, revives, begins a new life, and retakes the tradition of the Communes of old and of the French Revolution. This tradition, which gave victory to France, and earned the respect and sympathy of past generations, will bring independence, wealth, peaceful glory and brotherly love among nations in the future.

Never was there so solemn an hour. The Revolution which our fathers commenced and we are finishing . . . is going on without bloodshed, by the might of the popular will. . . . To secure the triumph of the Communal idea . . . it is necessary to determine its general principles, and to draw up . . . the programme to be realized. . . .

The Commune is the foundation of all political states, exactly as the family is the embryo of human society. It must have autonomy; that is to say, self-administration and self-government, agreeing with its particular genius, traditions, and wants; preserving, in its political, moral, national, and special groups its entire liberty, its own character, and its complete sovereignty, like a citizen of a free town.

To secure the greatest economic development, the national and territorial independence, and security, association is indispensable; that is to say, a federation of all communes, constituting a united nation.

The autonomy of the Commune guarantees liberty to its citizens; and the federation of all the communes increases, by the reciprocity, power, wealth, markets, and resources of each member, the profit of all. It was the Communal idea . . . which triumphed on the 18th of March, 1871. It implies, as a political form, the Republic, which is alone compatible with liberty and popular sovereignty.

From G. A. Kertesz, ed., *Documents in the Political History of the European Continent, 1815–1939* (Oxford, U. K.: Clarendon Press, 1968), pp. 312–313.

and agreed to accept the Orléanist heir as his successor. Chambord refused to become king, however, if France retained the revolutionary tricolor flag. Even the conservative monarchists would not return to the white flag of the Bourbons, which symbolized extreme political reaction.

While the monarchists quarreled among themselves, events marched on. By September 1873, the indemnity had been paid, and the Prussian occupa-

tion troops had withdrawn. Thiers was ousted from office because he had displayed clear republican sentiments. The monarchists wanted a more sympathetic executive. They elected as president a conservative army officer, Marshal MacMahon (1808–1893), who was expected to prepare for a monarchist restoration. In 1875, the National Assembly, still monarchist in sentiment, but unable to find a king, decided to regularize the political system. It adopted a law that provided for a Chamber of Deputies elected by universal male suffrage, a Senate chosen indirectly, and a president elected by the two legislative houses. This rather simple republican system had resulted from the bickering and frustration of the monarchists.

After numerous quarrels with the Chamber of Deputies, MacMahon resigned in 1879. His departure meant that dedicated republicans controlled the national government despite lingering opposition from the church, wealthy families, and a part of the army.

The political structure of the Third Republic proved much stronger than many citizens suspected at the time. It survived challenges from persons such as General Georges Boulanger (1837–1891), who would have imposed stronger executive authority. It also survived several scandals, such as those involving sales of awards of the Legion of Honor and widespread corruption of politicians by a company that tried to construct a canal in Panama, which made its politics appear increasingly sleazy to conservatives. The institutions of the republic, however, allowed new ministers to replace those whose corruption was exposed.

THE DREYFUS AFFAIR

The greatest trauma of the Third Republic occurred over what became known as the *Dreyfus affair*. On December 22, 1894, a French military court found Captain Alfred Dreyfus (1859–1935) guilty of passing secret information to the German army. The evidence against him was flimsy and was later revealed to have been forged. Someone in the officer corps had been passing documents to the Germans, and it suited the army investigators to accuse Dreyfus, who was Jewish. After Dreyfus had been sent to Devil's Island, a notorious prison in French Guiana, however, secrets continued to flow to the German army. In 1896, a new head of French counterintelligence reexamined the Dreyfus file and found evidence of forgery. A different officer was implicated, but a military court acquitted him of all charges.

By then the affair had provoked near-hysterical public debate. The army, the French Catholic Church, political conservatives, and vehemently anti-Semitic newspapers contended that Dreyfus was guilty. Such anti-Dreyfus opinion was dominant at the beginning of the affair. In 1898, however, the novelist Emile Zola published a newspaper article entitled *"J'accuse"* ("I accuse"), in which he contended that the army had consciously denied due process to Dreyfus and had plotted to suppress or forge evidence. Zola was convicted of libel and received a one-year prison sentence, which he avoided by fleeing to England.

Mass graves were dug for thousands of Parisians killed or executed during the fighting that marked the suppression of the Paris Commune in 1871. Mass grave at the Pere Lachaise cemetery. Commune of Paris, June 25, 1871. Snark/Art Resource. Print. Bibliotheque Nationale, Paris, France.

Zola was only one of numerous liberals, radicals, and socialists who had begun to demand a new trial for Dreyfus. Although these forces of the political left had come to Dreyfus's support rather slowly, they soon realized his cause could aid their own public image. They portrayed the conservative institutions of the nation as having denied Dreyfus the rights belonging to any citizen of the republic. They also claimed, and properly so, that Dreyfus had been singled out, so the guilty persons, who were still in the army, could be protected. In August 1898, further evidence of forged material came to light. The officer responsible for those forgeries committed suicide in jail, but a new military trial again convicted Dreyfus. The president of France immediately pardoned him, however, and eventually, in 1906, a civilian court set aside the results of both military trials.

The Dreyfus case divided France as no issue had done since the Paris Commune. By its conclusion, the conservatives were on the defensive. They had allowed themselves to persecute an innocent person and to manufacture false evidence against him to protect themselves from disclosure. They had also embraced violent anti-Semitism. On the political left, radicals, republicans, and socialists developed an informal alliance, which outlived the fight over the Dreyfus case itself. These groups realized that republican institutions must be supported if the political left was to achieve its goals. Nonetheless, the political, religious, and racial divisions and suspicions growing out of the Dreyfus affair continued to divide the Third Republic until France's defeat by Germany in 1940.

Major Dates in the History of the Third French Republic

1870	Defeat by Prussia and proclamation of republic
1871	Paris Commune
1873	Prussian occupation troops depart
1873	Marshal MacMahon elected president
1875	Major political institutions of Third Republic organized
1894	Captain Dreyfus convicted
1906	Dreyfus's conviction set aside

The Habsburg Empire

After 1848, the Habsburg Empire was a problem both to itself and for the rest of Europe. An ungenerous critic remarked that a standing army of soldiers, a kneeling army of priests, and a crawling army of informers supported the empire. In the age of national states, liberal institutions, and industrialism, the Habsburg domains remained primarily dynastic, absolutist, and agrarian. The Habsburg response to the revolts of 1848–1849 had been to reassert absolutism. Francis Joseph, who reigned from 1848 until 1916,

was honest and hardworking, but unimaginative. He reacted to events, but rarely commanded them.

During the 1850s, his ministers attempted to impose a centralized administration on the empire. The system amounted to a military and bureaucratic regime dominated by German-speaking Austrians. The Vienna government abolished internal tariffs in the empire. It divided Hungary, which had been so revolutionary in 1848, into military districts. The Roman Catholic Church acquired control of education. National groups, such as the Croats and Slovaks, who had supported the empire against the Hungarians, received no rewards for their loyalty. Although this system provoked resentment, it eventually floundered because of setbacks in foreign affairs.

Austrian refusal to support Russia during the Crimean War meant the new tsar would no longer help preserve Habsburg rule in Hungary, as Nicholas I had done in 1849. An important external prop of Habsburg power for the past half century thus disappeared. The Austrian defeat in 1859 at the hands of France and Piedmont and the subsequent loss of territory in Italy confirmed the necessity for a new domestic policy. For seven years the emperor, the civil servants, the aristocrats, and the politicians tried to construct a viable system of government.

The prosecution of Captain Alfred Dreyfus, who is shown here standing on the right at his military trial, provoked the most serious crisis of the Third Republic. © Bettman/Corbis

FORMATION OF THE DUAL MONARCHY

In 1860, Francis Joseph issued the October Diploma, which created a federation among the states and provinces of the empire. There were to be local diets dominated by the landed classes and a single imperial parliament. The Magyar nobility of Hungary, however, rejected the plan.

Consequently, in 1861, the emperor issued the February Patent, which set up an entirely different form of government. It established a bicameral imperial parliament, or *Reichsrat*, with an upper chamber appointed by the emperor and an indirectly elected lower chamber. Again the Magyars refused to cooperate in a system designed to give political dominance in the empire to German-speaking Austrians. The Magyars sent no delegates to the legislature. Nevertheless, for six years, the February Patent governed the empire, and it prevailed in Austria proper until World War I. Ministers were responsible to the emperor, not the *Reichsrat*, and civil liberties were not guaranteed. Armies could be levied and taxes raised without parliamentary consent. When the *Reichsrat* was not in session, the emperor could simply rule by decree.

Meanwhile, secret negotiations between the emperor and the Magyars produced no concrete result until the Prussian defeat of Austria in the summer of 1866 and the consequent exclusion of Austria from German affairs. Francis Joseph now had to come to terms with the Magyars. The subsequent **Ausgleich,** or Compromise, of 1867 transformed the Habsburg Empire into a dual monarchy known as Austria-Hungary. (See "The Austrian Prime Minister Explains the Dual Monarchy.")

Francis Joseph was crowned king of Hungary in Budapest in 1867. Except for the common monarch, Austria and Hungary became almost wholly separate states. They shared ministers of foreign affairs,

Major Dates in the Late-Nineteenth-Century Habsburg Empire	
1848	Francis Joseph becomes emperor
1860	October Diploma
1861	February Patent
1866	Defeat by Prussia
1867	Compromise between emperor and Hungary, establishing the Dual Monarchy
1897	Ordinances giving equality of language between Germans and Czechs in Austria
1907	Universal male suffrage introduced for Austria

defense, and finance, but the other ministers were different for each state. There were also separate parliaments. Each year, sixty parliamentary delegates from each state met to discuss mutual interests. Every ten years, Austria and Hungary renegotiated their trade relationship. By this cumbersome machinery, unique in European history, the Magyars were reconciled to Habsburg rule. They had achieved the free hand they had long wanted in Hungary.

UNREST OF NATIONALITIES

The Compromise of 1867 had introduced two different principles of political legitimacy into the two sections of the Habsburg Empire. In Hungary, political loyalty was based on nationality because Hungary had been recognized as a distinct part of the monarchy on the basis of nationalism. In effect, Hungary was a Magyar nation under the Habsburg emperor. In the rest of the Habsburg domains, the principle of legitimacy meant dynastic loyalty to

The coronation of Francis Joseph of Hungary in 1867 is depicted in this painting. The so-called Ausgleich, *or Compromise, of 1867 transformed the Habsburg Empire into a dual monarchy in which Austria and Hungary became almost separate states except for defense and foreign affairs.*
Bildarchiv der Oesterreichische Nationalbibliothek

THE AUSTRIAN PRIME MINISTER EXPLAINS THE DUAL MONARCHY

The multinational character of the Austrian Empire had long been a source of internal weakness and political discontent. After the defeat of Austria by Prussia in 1866, the Austrian government attempted to regain the loyalty of the Hungarians by making Hungary a separate kingdom within a dual monarchy, known thereafter as Austria-Hungary.

■ *How does the Austrian prime minister define the problems of nationality within the empire? Why does he distinguish Hungary from the other national groups that seek independence or association with another nation? What are the principles he claims lie behind the establishment of the dual monarchy?*

The dangers which Austria has to face are of a twofold nature. The first is presented by the tendency of her liberal-minded German population to gravitate toward that larger portion of the German-speaking people. . . . the second is the diversity of language and race in the empire. Of Austria's large Slav population, the Poles have a natural craving for independence after having enjoyed and heroically fought for it for centuries; while the other nationalities are likely at a moment of dangerous crisis to develop pro-Russian tendencies.

Now my object is to carry out a bloodless revolution—to show the various elements of this great empire that it is to the benefit of each of them to act in harmony with its neighbor. . . . But to this I have made one exception. Hungary is an ancient monarchy, more ancient as such than Austria proper. . . . I have endeavoured to give Hungary not

a new position with regard to the Austrian empire, but to secure her in the one which she has occupied. The Emperor of Austria is King of Hungary; my idea was that he should revive in his person the Constitution of which he and his ancestors have been the heads. The leading principles of my plan are . . . the resuscitation of an old monarchy and an old Constitution; not the separation of one part of the empire from the other, but the drawing together of the two component parts by the recognition of their joint positions, the maintenance of their mutual obligations, their community in questions affecting the entire empire, and their proportional pecuniary responsibility for the liabilities of the whole State. It is no plan of separation that I have carried out: on the contrary, it is one of close union, not by the creation of a new power, but by the recognition of an old one. . . .

From *Memoirs of Friedrich Ferdinand Count von Beust*, Vol. 1, ed. by Baron Henry de Worms (London: Remington, 1887), pp. xx–xxvi.

the emperor. Many of the other nationalities wished to achieve the same type of settlement that the Hungarians had won, or to govern themselves, or to unite with fellow nationals who lived outside the empire. (See Map 23–3.)

Many of those other national groups—including the Czechs, the Ruthenians, the Romanians, and the Croatians—opposed the Compromise of 1867 that, in effect, had permitted the German-speaking Austrians and the Hungarian Magyars to dominate all other nationalities within the empire. The most vocal critics were the Czechs of Bohemia. They favored a policy of "trialism," or triple monarchy, in which the Czechs would be given a position similar to that of the Hungarians. In 1871, Francis Joseph was willing to accept this concept. The Magyars,

however, vetoed it lest they be forced to make similar concessions to their own subject nationalities. Furthermore, the Germans of Bohemia were afraid the Czech language would be imposed on them.

For more than twenty years, the Czechs were placated by generous patronage and posts in the bureaucracy. By the 1890s, however, Czech nationalism again became more strident. In 1897, Francis Joseph gave the Czechs and the Germans equality of language in various localities. Thereafter, the Germans in the Austrian *Reichsrat* opposed these measures by disrupting Parliament. The Czechs replied in kind. By the turn of the century, this obstructionism, which included the playing of musical instruments in the *Reichsrat*, had paralyzed parliamentary life. The emperor ruled by imperial decree

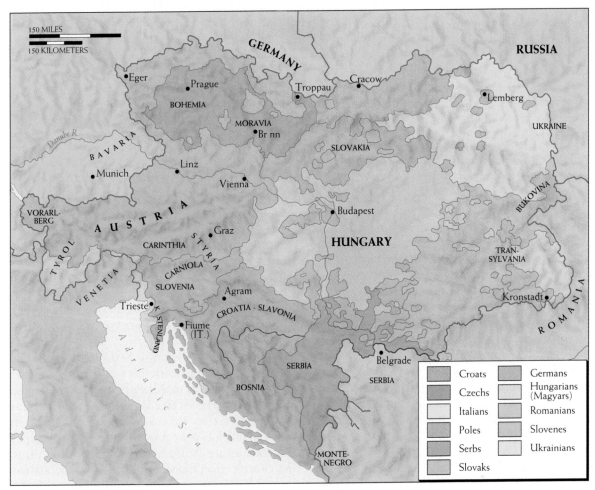

MAP 23–3 NATIONALITIES WITHIN THE HABSBURG EMPIRE *The patchwork appearance reflects the unusual problem of the numerous ethnic groups that the Habsburgs could not,
of course, meld into a modern national state. Only the Magyars were recognized in
1867, leaving nationalist Czechs, Slovaks, and the others chronically dissatisfied.*

through the bureaucracy. In 1907, Francis Joseph introduced universal male suffrage in Austria (but not
in Hungary), but this action did not eliminate the
chaos in the *Reichsrat.* In effect, by 1914 constitutionalism was a dead letter in Austria. It flourished
in Hungary, but only because the Magyars relentlessly exercised political supremacy over all other
competing national groups except Croatia, which
was permitted considerable autonomy.

There is reason to believe nationalism became
stronger during the last quarter of the nineteenth
century. Language became the single most important factor in defining a nation. The expansion of
education made this possible. In all countries where
nationalistic groups prospered, their membership
was dominated by intellectuals, students, and educated members of the middle class, all of whom
were literate in the literary version of particular national languages. Furthermore, during these same
years, as we see in Chapter 25, racial thinking be-

came important in Europe. Racial thought maintained there was a genetic basis for ethnic and cultural groups that had hitherto been generally
defined by a common history and culture. Once language and race became the ways to define an ethnic
or national group, the lines between such groups became much more sharply drawn. (See "Lord Acton
Condemns Nationalism.")

The unrest of the various nationalities within the
Habsburg Empire not only caused internal political
difficulties; it also became a major source of political instability for all of central and eastern Europe.
Each of the nationality problems normally had ramifications for both foreign and domestic policy. Both
the Croats and the Poles wanted an independent
state in union with their fellow nationals who lived
outside the empire—and in the case of the Poles,
with fellow nationals in the Russian Empire. Other
national groups, such as Ukrainians, Romanians,
Italians, and Bosnians, saw themselves as potentially

LORD ACTON CONDEMNS NATIONALISM

Lord Acton (1834–1902) was a major nineteenth-century English historian and commentator on contemporary religious and political events. In all his writings, he was deeply concerned with the character and preservation of liberty. His was one of the earliest voices to warn against the political dangers of nationalism.

■ *Why does Acton see the principle of nationality as dangerous to liberty? Why does he see nationalism as a threat to minority groups? Why does he see nationalism as a threat to democracy?*

The greatest adversary of the rights of nationality is the modern theory of nationality. By making the State and the nation commensurate with each other in theory, it reduces practically to a subject condition all other nationalities that may be within the boundary. It cannot admit them to an equality with the ruling nation which constitutes the State, because the State would then cease to be national, which would be a contradiction of the principle of its existence. According, therefore, to the degree of humanity and civilization in that dominant body which claims all the rights of the community, the inferior races are exterminated, or reduced to servitude, or outlawed, or put in a condition of dependence.

If we take the establishment of liberty for the realization of moral duties to be the end of civil society, we must conclude that those states are substantially the most perfect which, like the British and Austrian Empires, include various distinct nationalities without oppressing them. Those in which no mixture of races has occurred are imperfect; and those in which its effects have disappeared are decrepit. A State which is incompetent to satisfy different races condemns itself; a State which labors to neutralize, to absorb, or to expel them, destroys its own vitality; a State which does not include them is destitute of the chief basis of self-government. The theory of nationality, therefore, is a retrograde step in history. . . .

[N]ationality does not aim either at liberty or prosperity, both of which it sacrifices to the imperative necessity of making the nation the mold and measure of the State. Its course will be marked with material as well as moral ruin, in order that a new invention may prevail over the works of God and the interests of mankind. There is no principle of change, no phrase of political speculation conceivable, more comprehensive, more subversive, or more arbitrary than this. It is a confutation of democracy, because it sets limits to the exercise of the popular will, and substitutes for it a higher principle.

From John Emerich Edward Dalbert-Acton, *First Baron Acton, Essays in the History of Liberty*, ed. by J. Rufus Fears (Indianapolis: Liberty Classics, 1985), pp. 431–433.

linked to Russia, Romania, Serbia, Italy, or a yet-to-be established south Slavic, or Yugoslav, state. Many of these nationalities looked to Russia to protect their interests or influence the government in Vienna. The Romanians were also concerned about the Romanian minority in Hungary. Serbia sought to expand its borders to include Serbs who lived within Habsburg or Ottoman territory. Out of these Balkan tensions emerged much of the turmoil that would spark the First World War. Many of the same ethnic tensions account for warfare in the former Yugoslavia.

The dominant German population of Austria proper was generally loyal to the emperor. A part of it, however, yearned to join the new German Empire. These Austro-Germans often hated the non-German national groups of the empire, and many of them were anti-Semites. Such attitudes would influence the young Adolf Hitler.

For the next century of European and even world history, the significance of this nationalist unrest within the late-nineteenth-century Austrian Empire and its neighbors can hardly be overestimated. Nationality problems touched all four of the great central and eastern European empires—the German, the Russian, the Austrian, and the Ottoman. The first three had large Polish populations, and Russia, Austria, and the Ottomans had many minority groups. Each nationality regarded its own aspirations and discontents as more important than the larger good or even survival of the empires that they inhabited. The weakness of the Ottoman Empire allowed both Austria and Russia to compete in the Balkans for influence and thus further inflame nationalistic resentments. Such nationalistic stirrings affected the fate of all four empires from the 1860s through the outbreak of World War I. The government of each of those empires would be overturned during the war, and the Habsburg monarchy and the Ottoman Empire would disappear. Those same unresolved problems of central and eastern European nationalism would then lead directly to World War II. They continue to fester today.

Russia: Emancipation and Revolutionary Stirrings

Russia changed remarkably during the last half of the nineteenth century. The government finally both addressed the long-standing problem of serfdom and undertook a broad range of administrative reforms. During the same period, however, radical revolutionary groups began to organize. These groups tried to draw the peasants into revolutionary activity and assassinated government officials, including the tsar. The government's response was renewed repression.

REFORMS OF ALEXANDER II

Russia's defeat in the Crimean War and its humiliation in the Treaty of Paris compelled the government to reconsider its domestic policies. Nicholas I had died in 1855 during the conflict. Because of extensive travel in Russia and an early introduction to government, his son Alexander II (r. 1855–1881) was familiar with the chief difficulties facing the nation. The debacle of the war had made reform both necessary and possible. Alexander II took advantage of this turn of events to institute the most extensive restructuring of Russian society and administration since Peter the Great. Like Peter, Alexander imposed his reforms from the top.

Abolition of Serfdom In every area of economic and public life, a profound cultural gap separated Russia from the rest of Europe. Nowhere was this more apparent than in the survival of serfdom. In Russia, the institution had changed very little since the eighteenth century, although every other nation on the Continent had abandoned it. Russian landowners still had a free hand with their serfs, and

the serfs had little recourse against the landlords. In March 1856, at the conclusion of the Crimean War, Alexander II announced his intention to abolish serfdom. He had decided that only its abolition would permit Russia to maintain its status as a great power.

Serfdom was economically inefficient. There was always the threat of revolt, and the serfs forced into the army had performed poorly in the Crimean War. Moreover, nineteenth-century moral opinion condemned serfdom. Only Russia, Brazil, and certain portions of the United States among the Western nations retained such forms of involuntary servitude. For five years, government commissions wrestled over how to implement the tsar's desire. Finally, in February 1861, against opposition from the nobility and the landlords, Alexander II ended serfdom.

The actual emancipation law was a disappointment, however, because freedom was not accompanied by land. Serfs immediately received the personal right to marry without their landlord's permission, as well as the rights to purchase and sell property freely, to engage in court actions, and to pursue trades. What they did not receive was free title to their land. They had to pay the landlords over a period of forty-nine years for allotments of land that were frequently too small to support them. They were also charged interest during this period. The serfs made the payments to the government, which had already reimbursed the landlords for their losses. The serfs would not receive title to the land until the debt was paid.

The procedures were so complicated and the results so limited that many serfs believed real emancipation was still to come. The redemption payments led to almost unending difficulty. Poor harvests made it impossible for many peasants to keep up with the payments, and they fell increasingly behind in their debt. The situation was not remedied until 1906, when, during the widespread revolutionary unrest following the Japanese defeat of Russia in 1905, the government grudgingly completed the process of emancipation by canceling the remaining debts.

Reform of Local Government and the Judicial System The abolition of serfdom required the reorganization of local government and the judicial system. The authority of village communes replaced that of the landlord over the peasant. The village elders settled family quarrels, imposed fines, issued internal passports, and collected taxes. Often, also, it was the village commune rather than individual peasants who owned the land. The nobility were permitted a larger role in local administration through a system of provincial and county *zemstvos*, or councils, organized in 1864. These councils were to oversee local matters, such as bridge and road repair, education, and agricultural improvement. Because the councils received inadequate funds, however, local governments were never vitalized.

The flagrant inequities and abuses of the preemancipation judicial system could not continue. In 1864, Alexander II promulgated a new statute on the judiciary. For the first time, western European legal principles were introduced into Russia. These included equality before the law, impartial hearings, uniform procedures, judicial independence, and trial by jury. The new system was far from perfect. The judges were not genuinely independent, and the tsar could increase as well as reduce sentences. Certain offenses, such as those involving the press, were not tried before a jury. Nonetheless, the new courts were both more efficient and less corrupt than the old system.

Military Reform The government also reformed the army. Russia possessed the largest military force on the Continent, but it had floundered badly in the Crimean War. The usual period of service for a soldier was twenty-five years. Villages had to provide quotas of serfs to serve in the army. Often, recruiters simply seized serfs from their families. Once in the army, recruits rarely saw their homes again. Life in the army was harsh, even by the brutal standards of most midcentury armies. In the 1860s, the army lowered the period of service to fifteen years and relaxed discipline slightly. In 1874, the enlistment period was lowered to six years of active duty and nine years in the reserves. All males were subject to military service after the age of twenty.

Repression in Poland Alexander's reforms became more measured shortly after the Polish Rebellion of 1863. As in 1830, Polish nationalists attempted to overthrow Russian dominance. Once again the Russian army suppressed the rebellion. Alexander II then moved to Russify Poland. In 1864, he emancipated the Polish serfs to punish the politically restive Polish nobility. Russian law, language, and administration were imposed on all areas of Polish life. Henceforth, until the close of World War I, Poland was treated as merely another Russian province.

As the Polish suppression demonstrated, Alexander II was a reformer only within the limits of his own autocracy. His changes in Russian life failed to create new loyalty to, or gratitude for, the government among his subjects. The serfs felt their emancipation had been inadequate. The nobles and the wealthier educated segments of Russian society resented the tsar's persistent refusal to allow them a meaningful role in government and policy making. Consequently, although Alexander II became known as the Tsar Liberator, he was never popular. He could be indecisive and closed minded. These characteristics became more pronounced after 1866, when an attempt was made on his life. Thereafter, Russia increasingly became a police state. This new repression fueled the activity of radical groups within Russia. Their actions, in turn, made the autocracy more reactionary.

REVOLUTIONARIES

The tsarist regime had long had its critics. One of the most prominent was Alexander Herzen (1812–1870), who lived in exile. From London, he published a newspaper called *The Bell*, in which he set forth reformist positions. The initial reforms of Alexander II had raised great hopes among Russian students and intellectuals, but they soon became discontented with the limited character of the reforms. Drawing on the ideas of Herzen and other radicals, these students formed a revolutionary movement known as *populism*. They sought a social revolution based on the communal life of the Russian peasants. The chief radical society was called *Land and Freedom*.

In the early 1870s, hundreds of young Russians, including both men and women, took their revolutionary message into the countryside. They intended to live with the peasants, to gain their trust, and to teach them about the peasant's role in

Major Dates in Late-Nineteenth-Century Russia
1855   Alexander II becomes tsar
1856   Defeat in Crimean War
1861   Serfdom abolished
1863   Suppression of Polish rebellion
1864   Reorganization of local government
1864   Reform of judicial system
1874   Military enlistment period reduced
1878   Attempted assassination of military governor of Saint Petersburg
1879   Land and Freedom splits
1881   The People's Will assassinates Alexander II
1881   Alexander III becomes tsar
1894   Nicholas II becomes tsar

the coming revolution. The bewildered and distrustful peasants turned most of the youths over to the police. In the winter of 1877–1878, almost two hundred students were tried. Most were acquitted or given light sentences, because they had been held for months in preventive detention and because the court believed a display of mercy might lessen public sympathy for the young revolutionaries. The court even suggested the tsar might wish to pardon those students given heavier sentences. The tsar refused and let it become known he favored heavy penalties for all persons involved in revolutionary activity.

Thereafter, the revolutionaries decided the tsarist regime must be attacked directly. They adopted a policy of terrorism. In January 1878, Vera Zasulich (1849–1919) attempted to assassinate the military governor of Saint Petersburg. A jury acquitted her because the governor she had shot had a reputation for brutality. Some people also believed Zasulich had a personal rather than a political grievance against her victim. Nonetheless, the verdict further encouraged the terrorists.

In 1879, Land and Freedom split into two groups. One advocated educating the peasants, and it soon dissolved. The other, known as *The People's Will*, was dedicated to the overthrow of the autocracy. Its members decided to assassinate the tsar himself. (See "The People's Will Issues a Revolutionary Manifesto.") Several attempts failed, but on March 1, 1881, a bomb hurled by a member of The People's Will killed Alexander II. Four men and two women were sentenced to death for the deed. All of them had been willing to die for their cause. The emergence of such dedicated revolutionary opposition was as much a part of the reign of Alexander II as were his reforms. The limited character of those reforms convinced many Russians that the autocracy could never truly redirect Russian society.

The reign of Alexander III (r. 1881–1894) strengthened that pessimism. He possessed all the autocratic and repressive characteristics of his grandfather, Nicholas I, and none of the better qualities of his father, Alexander II. Some slight improvements were made to conditions in Russian

Tsar Alexander II (r. 1855–1881) was assassinated on March 1, 1881. The assassins first threw a bomb that wounded several Imperial guards. When the tsar stopped his carriage to see the wounded, the assassins threw a second bomb, killing him. Bildarchiv Preussischer Kulturbesitz

THE PEOPLE'S WILL ISSUES A REVOLUTIONARY MANIFESTO

In the late 1870s, an extreme revolutionary movement appeared in Russia calling it-self The People's Will. It advocated the overthrow of the tsarist government and the election of an Organizing Assembly to form a government based on popular representation. It directly embraced terrorism as a path toward its goal of the Russian people governing themselves. Members of this group assassinated Alexander II in 1881.

■ *Which of the group's seven demands might be associated with liberalism, and which go beyond liberalism in their radical intent? Why does the group believe it must engage in terrorism as well as propaganda? Would there have been any reforms or steps toward reform that the Russian government might have taken which might have satisfied this group or dissuaded them from terrorist action?*

Although we are ready to submit wholly to the popular will, we regard it as none the less our duty, as a party, to appear before the people with our program. . . . It is as follows:

1. Perpetual popular representation . . . having full power to act in all national questions.

2. General local self-government, secured by the election of all officers, and the economic independence of the people.

3. The self-controlled village commune as the economic and administrative unit.

4. Ownership of the land by the people.

5. A system of measures having for their object the turning over to the laborers of all mining works and factories.

6. Complete freedom of conscience, speech, association, public meeting, and electioneering activity.

7. The substitution of a territorial militia for the army. . . .

In view of the stated aim of the party its operations may be classified as follows:

1. Propaganda and agitation. Our propaganda has for its object the popularization, in all social classes, of the idea of a political and popular revolution as a means of social reform, as well as popularization of the party's own program. Its essential features are criticism of the existing order of things, and a statement and explanation of revolutionary methods. The aim of agitation should be to incite the people to protest as generally as possible against the present state of affairs, to demand such reforms as are in harmony with the party's purposes, and, especially, to demand the summoning of an Organizing Assembly. . . .

2. Destructive and terroristic activity. Terroristic activity consists in the destruction of the most harmful persons in the Government, the protection of the party from spies, and the punishment of official lawlessness and violence in all the more prominent and important cases in which such lawlessness and violence are manifested. The aim of such activity is to break down the prestige of Governmental power, to furnish continuous proof of the possibility of carrying on a contest with the Government, to raise in that way the revolutionary spirit of the people and inspire belief in the practicability of revolution, and, finally, to form a body suited and accustomed to warfare.

Quoted in George Kennan, *Siberia and the Exile System*, Vol. 2 (New York: The Century Co., 1891), pp. 495–499.

factories, but Alexander III sought primarily to roll back his father's reforms. He favored the centralized bureaucracy over the *zemstvos*. He strengthened the secret police and increased censorship of the press. In effect, he confirmed all the evils that the revolutionaries saw as inherent in autocratic government. His son, Nicholas II (r. 1894–1917), would discover that autocracy could not survive the pressures of the twentieth century.

Great Britain: Toward Democracy

While the continental nations became unified and struggled toward internal political restructuring, Great Britain continued to symbolize the confident liberal state. Britain was not without its difficulties and domestic conflicts, but it seemed able to deal with these through existing political institutions.

The general prosperity of the third quarter of the century mitigated the social hostility of the 1840s. All classes shared a belief in competition and individualism. Even the leaders of trade unions during these years asked mainly to receive more of the fruits of prosperity and to have their social respectability acknowledged. Parliament itself remained an institution through which new groups and interests were absorbed into the existing political processes. In short, the British did not have to create new liberal institutions and then learn how to live within them. (See "Encountering the Past: The Arrival of Penny Postage.")

THE SECOND REFORM ACT (1867)

By the early 1860s, most observers realized the franchise would again have to be expanded. The prosperity and social respectability of the working class convinced many politicians that the workers deserved the vote. Organizations such as the Reform League, led by John Bright (1811–1889), were agitating for parliamentary action. In 1866, Lord Russell's Liberal ministry introduced a reform bill that was defeated by a coalition of traditional Conservatives and antidemocratic Liberals. Russell resigned, and the Conservative Lord Derby (1799–1869) replaced him. A surprise then occurred.

The Conservative ministry, led in the House of Commons by Benjamin Disraeli (1804–1881), introduced its own reform bill in 1867. As the debate proceeded, Disraeli accepted one amendment after another and expanded the electorate well beyond the limits proposed earlier by the Liberals. When the final measure was passed, the number of voters had been increased from approximately 1,430,000 to 2,470,000. Britain had taken a major step toward democracy. Large numbers of male working-class voters had been admitted to the electorate.

Disraeli hoped that by sponsoring the measure, the Conservatives would receive the gratitude of the new voters. Because reform was inevitable, it was best for the Conservatives to enjoy the credit for it. Disraeli thought that eventually significant portions of the working class would support Conservative candidates who were responsive to social issues. He also thought the growing suburban middle class would become more conservative. In the long run, his intuition proved correct. The Conservative Party dominated British politics in the twentieth century.

The immediate election of 1868, however, dashed Disraeli's hopes. William Gladstone (1809–1898) became the new prime minister. Gladstone had begun political life in 1833 as a strong Tory, but over the next thirty-five years he became steadily more liberal. He had supported Robert Peel, free trade, repeal of the Corn Laws, and efficient administration. As chancellor of the exchequer (finance minister) during the 1850s and early 1860s, he had lowered taxes and government expenditures. He had also championed Italian nationalism. Yet he had continued to oppose a new reform bill until the early 1860s. In 1866, he had been Russell's spokesperson in the House of Commons for the unsuccessful Liberal reform bill.

A House of Commons debate. William Ewart Gladstone, standing on the right, is attacking Benjamin Disraeli, who sits with legs crossed and arms folded. Gladstone served in the British Parliament from the 1830s through the 1890s. Four times the Liberal Party prime minister, he was responsible for guiding major reforms through Parliament. Disraeli, regarded as the founder of modern British conservatism, served as prime minister from 1874 to 1880. Mary Evans Picture Library Ltd.

The Arrival of Penny Postage

While the armies of the great powers were redrawing the map of Europe during the middle of the nineteenth century, new forms of administration were drawing people closer together. One of the most important of these innovations was the development of postal systems for delivering mail inexpensively. The British government took the lead.

Sending letters and newspapers through the mail had become increasingly expensive, and the British postal service ran large deficits. Other countries had similar problems. At that time the weight of the item to be mailed and the distance over which it had to be carried determined how much it cost to mail it. Furthermore, the person receiving the letter or packet, not the sender, had to pay the postage. Many officials had the privilege of franking their letters and thus paying nothing. The system encouraged resentment and schemes to avoid paying postage. Some people could not afford the postage on letters sent to them. Others put symbols on the outside of a letter, so the recipient could refuse to accept the letter but still "get the message."

Rowland Hill (1795–1879), an English reformer, proposed a simple new procedure in 1837. The price of postage would be lowered, would be uniform for most letters and newspapers regardless of distance, and would be prepaid by the sender. Franking by government officials would also end.

In 1840, the system, known as the Uniform Penny Post, began. Within two years the volume of British mail grew from approximately 75 million items to 196.5 million and by 1849 to 329 million. The reduced cost of postage meant almost everyone could afford to send letters and postcards. It also led to a huge increase in the size of the government work force. In Britain and most countries, the number of postal workers was soon rivaled only by the number of soldiers and sailors.

Hill had also suggested a small, self-adhesive stamp be attached to a letter to indicate the postage had been paid. The first such stamp bore only the words POSTAGE ONE PENNY. It paid for letters up to one-half ounce. A two-penny stamp was used for letters that weighed an ounce.

Other nations soon issued their own stamps. It soon became as important for governments to prevent the forging of postage stamps as currency. Consequently, stamps were printed from engraved steel plates to which small changes were made from time to time. Those changes, introduced to prevent fraud or to commemorate famous people and events, together with the sheer number of national postal systems with their own stamps, gave rise to the hobby of stamp collecting.

The rise of the modern postal system also fostered international cooperation. A treaty signed in Berne, Switzerland, in 1874 established what became the Universal Postal Union, which is still functioning. It mandates that the postage paid in the sender's nation assures delivery of a letter or package anywhere in the world.

■ *What changes did Rowland Hill introduce into the British postal service? How did those changes affect the quantity of mail and the size of the government work force?*

M.J. Daunton, "Rowland Hill and the Penny Post," *History Today*, August 1985; "Post, and Postal Service," *Encyclopedia Britannica*, 11th ed.

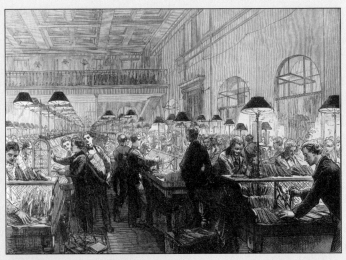

With the new British postal system, the volume of mail vastly increased as did the number of postal workers involved in sorting and delivering it. Mary Evans Picture Library Ltd.

GLADSTONE'S GREAT MINISTRY (1868–1874)

Gladstone's ministry of 1868 to 1874 witnessed the culmination of classical British liberalism. Those institutions that remained the preserve of the aristocracy and the Anglican church were opened to people from other classes and religious denominations. In 1870, competitive examinations for the civil service replaced patronage. In 1871, the purchase of officers' commissions in the army was abolished. The same year, Anglican religious requirements for the faculties of Oxford and Cambridge universities were removed. The Ballot Act of 1872 introduced voting by secret ballot.

The most momentous measure of Gladstone's first ministry was the Education Act of 1870. For the first time in British history, the government assumed the responsibility for establishing and running elementary schools. Previously, British education had been a task relegated to the religious denominations, which received small amounts of state support for the purpose. Henceforth, the government would establish schools where the efforts of religious denominations to establish them had proved inadequate.

These reforms were typically liberal. They sought to remove abuses without destroying institutions and to permit all able citizens to compete on the grounds of ability and merit. They tried to avoid the potential danger to a democratic state of an illiterate citizenry. These reforms also constituted a mode of state building, because they created new bonds of loyalty to the nation by abolishing many sources of discontent.

DISRAELI IN OFFICE (1874–1880)

The liberal policy of creating popular support for the nation by extending political liberties and reforming abuses had its conservative counterpart in concern for social reform. Disraeli succeeded Gladstone as prime minister in 1874, when the election produced sharp divisions among Liberal Party voters over religion, education, and the sale of alcohol.

The two men differed on most issues. Whereas Gladstone looked to individualism, free trade, and competition to solve social problems, Disraeli believed in paternalistic legislation to protect the weak and alleviate class antagonisms.

Disraeli talked a better line than he produced. He had few specific programs or ideas. The significant social legislation of his ministry stemmed primarily from the efforts of his home secretary, Richard Cross (1823–1914). The Public Health Act of 1875

consolidated previous legislation on sanitation and reaffirmed the duty of the state to interfere with private property on matters of health and physical well-being. Through the Artisan Dwelling Act of 1875, the government became actively involved in providing housing for the working class. That same year, in an important symbolic gesture, the Conservative majority in Parliament gave new protection to British trade unions and allowed them to raise picket lines. The Gladstone ministry, although recognizing the legality of unions, had refused such protection.

THE IRISH QUESTION

In 1880, a second Gladstone ministry took office after an agricultural depression and an unpopular foreign policy undermined the Conservative government. In 1884, with Conservative cooperation, a third reform act gave the vote to most male farmworkers. The major issue of the decade, however, was Ireland. From the late 1860s onward, Irish nationalists had sought to achieve **home rule** for Ireland, by which they meant Irish control of local government.

Major Dates in Late-Nineteenth-Century Britain

1867	Second Reform Act
1868	Gladstone becomes prime minister
1869	Disestablishment of Church of Ireland
1870	Education Act and first Irish Land Act
1871	Purchase of army officers' commissions abolished
1871	Religious tests abolished at Oxford and Cambridge
1872	Ballot Act
1874	Disraeli becomes prime minister
1875	Public Health Act and Artisan Dwelling Act
1880	Beginning of Gladstone's second ministry
1881	Second Irish Land Act and Irish Coercion Act
1884	Third Reform Act
1885	Gladstone announces support of Irish home rule
1886	Home Rule Bill defeated and Lord Salisbury becomes the Conservative prime minister
1892	Gladstone begins his third ministry; second Irish Home Rule Bill defeated
1903	Third Irish Land Act
1912	Third Irish Home Rule Bill passed
1914	Provisions of Irish Home Rule Bill suspended because of the outbreak of World War I

PARNELL CALLS FOR HOME RULE FOR IRELAND

Since 1800, Ireland had been governed as part of Great Britain, sending representatives to the British Parliament in Westminster. Throughout the century, there had been tension and violent conflict between the Irish and their English governors. Agitation for home rule whereby the Irish would directly control many of their own affairs reached a peak in the 1880s. Charles Stewart Parnell was the chief leader for the cause of Irish nationalism during that decade. His program at the time was home rule for Ireland, by which he meant Irish administration of Irish domestic affairs in the context of a continuing ill-defined union with England. In 1885, he made a speech in which he outlined the resentments the Irish had felt toward the English since the Act of Union of 1800. He also drew direct parallels between the relationship of Ireland to England and that of Hungary to Austria. Compare his remarks with those of the Austrian prime minister explaining the dual monarchy in the document, "The Austrian Prime Minister Explains the Dual Monarchy," p. 798. The efforts toward achieving home rule failed during the nineteenth century.

■ *How does Parnell say the Act of Union affected Irish sentiment toward England? What parallel does he draw with Hungary and Austria? Why might Parnell be regarded as a moderate nationalist?*

It is not possible for human intelligence to forecast the future in the matter; but we can point to this—we can point to the fact that under 85 years of parliamentary connection with England, Ireland has become intensely disloyal and intensely disaffected; that notwithstanding the Whig policy of so-called conciliation, alternative conciliation and coercion . . . that disaffection has broadened, deepened and intensified from day to day. Am I not, then, entitled to assume that one of the roots of this disaffection and feeling of disloyalty is the assumption by England of the management of our affairs. It is admitted that the present system can't go on, and what are you going to put in its place? My advice to English statesmen considering this question would be this—trust the Irish people altogether or trust them not at all. . . . Whatever chance the English rulers may have of drawing to themselves the affection of the Irish people lies in destroying the abominable system of legislative union between the two countries by conceding fully and freely to Ireland their right to manage her own affairs. It is impossible for us to give guarantees, but we can point to the past; we can show that the record of English rule is a constant series of steps from bad to worse, that the condition of English power is more insecure and more unstable at the present moment than it has ever been. We can point to the example of other countries; of Austria and of Hungary—to the fact that Hungary having been conceded self-government became one of the strongest factors in the Austrian empire. We can show the powers that have been freely conceded in the colonies [such as Canada and Australia have led to loyalty] . . . I am confident that the English statesman who is great enough . . . to carry out these teachings . . . to give Ireland full legislative liberty, full power to manage her own domestic concerns will be regarded in the future by his countrymen as one who has removed the greatest peril to the English empire—a peril, I firmly believe, which if not removed will find some day . . . an opportunity of revenging itself to the destruction of the British empire for the misfortunes, the oppressions, and the misgovernment of our country.

From Charles Stewart Parnell, "Speech at Wicklow," October 5, 1885, as quoted in Raymond Phineas Stearns, *Pageant of Europe: Sources and Selections from the Renaissance to the Present Day* (New York: Harcourt, Brace and Company, 1948), pp. 634–635.

During his first ministry, Gladstone had addressed the Irish question through two major pieces of legislation. In 1869, he had disestablished the Church of Ireland, the Irish branch of the Anglican church. Henceforth, Irish Roman Catholics would not pay taxes to support the hated Protestant church, to which few of the Irish belonged. Second, in 1870, the Liberal ministry sponsored a land act that provided compensation to those Irish tenants who were evicted and loans for those who wished to purchase their land. Throughout the 1870s, the Irish question continued to fester. Land remained the center of the agitation. Today, Irish economic development seems more complicated, and who owned the land seems less important than the methods of management and cultivation. Nevertheless, the organization of the Irish Land League in the late 1870s led to intense agitation and intimidation of landlords, who were often English. The leader of the Irish movement for a just land settlement and for home rule was Charles Stewart Parnell (1846–1891). In 1881, the second Gladstone ministry passed another Irish land act that strengthened tenant rights. It was accompanied, however, by a Coercion Act to restore law and order to Ireland.

By 1885, Parnell had organized eighty-five Irish members of the House of Commons into a tightly disciplined party that often voted as a bloc. They frequently disrupted Parliament to gain attention for the cause of home rule. They bargained with the two English political parties. In the election of 1885, the Irish Party emerged holding the balance of power between the English Liberals and Conservatives. (See "Parnell Calls for Home Rule for Ireland.") Irish support could decide which party took office. In December 1885, Gladstone announced his support of home rule for Ireland. Parnell gave his votes to a Liberal ministry. The home rule issue then split the Liberal Party. In 1886, a group known as the Liberal Unionists joined with the Conservatives to defeat home rule. Gladstone called for a new election, but the Liberals were defeated. They remained divided, and Ireland remained firmly under English administration.

The new Conservative ministry of Lord Salisbury (1830–1903) attempted to reconcile the Irish through public works and administrative reform. The policy, which was tied to further coercion, had only marginal success. In 1892, Gladstone returned to power. A second Home Rule Bill passed the House of Commons but was defeated in the House of Lords. There the Irish question stood until after the turn of the century. The Conservatives sponsored a land act in 1903 that carried out the final transfer of land to tenant ownership. Ireland became a country of small farms. In 1912, a Liberal ministry passed the third Home Rule Bill. Under the provisions of the House of Lords Act of 1911, which curbed the power of the Lords, the bill had to pass the Commons three times over the Lords' veto to become law. The third passage occurred in the summer of 1914, but the implementation of home rule was suspended for the duration of World War I.

The Irish question affected British politics in a manner not unlike that of the Austrian nationalities problem. Normal British domestic issues could not be resolved because of the political divisions created by Ireland. The split of the Liberal Party proved especially harmful to the cause of further social and political reform. People who could agree about reform could not agree about Ireland, and the Irish problem seemed more important. Because the two traditional parties failed to deal with the social questions by the turn of the century, a newly organized Labour Party began to fill the vacuum.

In Perspective

Between 1850 and 1875, the major contours of the political systems that would dominate Europe until World War I had been drawn. Those systems and political arrangements solved, so far as such matters can be solved, many of the political problems that had troubled Europeans during the first half of the nineteenth century. On the whole, the concept of the nation-state had triumphed. Support for governments no longer stemmed from loyalty to dynasties, but from citizen participation. Moreover, the unity of nations was now based on ethnic, cultural, linguistic, and historical bonds. The parliamentary governments of western Europe were different from the autocracies of eastern Europe, but both political systems had been compelled to recognize the force of nationalism and the larger role of citizens in political affairs. Only Russia failed to make such concessions. In Russia the only concession to popular opinion had been the emancipation of the serfs.

Future discontent would arise primarily from the demands of labor to enter the political processes and the unsatisfied aspirations of subject nationalities. Those two sources of unrest would trouble Europe for the next forty years and would eventually undermine the political structures created during the late nineteenth century.

REVIEW QUESTIONS

1. Why did the Ottoman Empire attempt to reform itself between 1839 and 1914? How successful were these efforts?

2. Why was it so difficult to unify Italy? What groups wanted unification? Why did Cavour succeed? What did Garibaldi contribute to Italian unification?

3. How and why did Bismarck unify Germany? Why had earlier attempts failed? How did German unification affect the rest of Europe?

4. What events led to the establishment of the Third Republic? How were foreign and domestic policies intertwined during the Second Empire? What were the objectives of the Paris Commune? How did the Dreyfus affair affect the Third Republic?

5. What problems did Austria share with other eastern European empires? Were they solved? Why did the Habsburgs agree to the Compromise of 1867? Was it a success?

6. What reforms did Alexander II institute in Russia? Did they solve Russia's domestic problems? Why did the abolition of serfdom not satisfy the peasants?

7. How did the policies of the British Liberal and Conservative parties differ between 1860 and 1890? Why was home rule such a divisive issue in British politics?

SUGGESTED READINGS

M. BENTLEY, *Politics without Democracy, 1815–1914* (1984). A well-informed survey of British development.

D. BLACKBOURN, *The Long Nineteenth Century: A History of Germany, 1780–1918* (1998). An outstanding survey based on up-to-date scholarship.

R. BLAKE, *Disraeli* (1967). Remains the best biography of the man.

J. BLUM, *Lord and Peasant in Russia from the Ninth to the Nineteenth Century* (1961). A clear discussion of emancipation in the later chapters.

A. BUCHOLZ, *Moltke and the German Wars, 1864–1871* (2001). Examines the manner in which Prussian leaders invented many aspects of modern warfare.

M. CUNNINGHAM, *Mexico and the Foreign Policy of Napoleon III* (2001). Explores one of the most controversial subjects in French foreign policy.

R. B. EDGERTON, *Death or Glory: The Legacy of the Crimean War* (2000). Multifaceted study of a badly mismanaged war that transformed many aspects of European domestic politics.

S. ELWITT, *The Making of the Third Republic: Class and Politics in France, 1868–1884* (1975). An excellent introduction.

S. ELWITT, *The Third Republic Defended: Bourgeois Reform in France, 1880–1914* (1986). A study that continues the survey of the previously listed volume.

R. A. KANN, *The Multinational Empire*, 2 vols. (1950). The basic treatment of the nationality problem of Austria-Hungary.

R. KEE, *The Green Flag: A History of Irish Nationalism* (2001). A vast survey.

D. LANGEWIESCHE, *Liberalism in Germany* (1999). A broad survey that is particularly good on the problems unification caused for German Liberals.

D. C. LIEVAN, *The Russian Empire and Its Rivals* (2001). Explores the imperial side of Russian government.

R. R. LOCKE, *French Legitimists and the Politics of Moral Order in the Early Third Republic* (1974). An excellent study of the social and intellectual roots of monarchist support.

H. C. G. MATTHEW, *Gladstone, 1809–1898* (1998). A superb biography.

A. J. MAY, *The Habsburg Monarchy, 1867–1914* (1951). Narrates in considerable detail and with much sympathy the fate of the dual monarchy.

J. F. McMILLAN, *Napoleon III* (1991). The best recent biography.

N. M. NAIMARK, *Terrorists and Social Democrats: The Russian Revolutionary Movement under Alexander III* (1983). Useful discussion of a complicated subject.

C. C. O'BRIEN, *Parnell and His Party* (1957). An excellent treatment of the Irish question.

J. P. PARRY, *The Rise and Fall of Liberal Government in Victorian Britain* (1994). An outstanding study.

O. PFLANZE, *Bismarck and the Development of Germany*, 3 vols. (1990). A major biography and history of Germany for the period.

A. PLESSIS, *The Rise and Fall of the Second Empire, 1852–1871* (1985). A useful survey of France under Napoleon III.

J. RIDLEY, *Garibaldi* (2001). An extensive biography of a remarkable personality.

A. SKED, *Decline and Fall of the Habsburg Empire 1815–1918* (2001). A major, accessible survey of a difficult subject.

D. M. SMITH, *Cavour* (1984). An excellent biography.

F. VENTURI, *The Roots of Revolution* (trans., 1960). A major treatment of late-nineteenth-century revolutionary movements.

H. U. WEHLER, *The German Empire, 1871–1918* (1985). An important, controversial work.

D. WETZEL, *A Duel of Giants: Bismarck, Napoleon III, and the Origins of the Franco-Prussian War* (2001). Broad study based on most recent scholarship.

C. B. WOODHAM-SMITH, *The Reason Why* (1953). A classic account of the Crimean War and the charge of the Light Brigade.

T. ZELDIN, *France: 1848–1945*, 2 vols. (1973, 1977). Emphasizes the social developments.

DOCUMENTS CD-ROM

INDUSTRIALIZATION

22.3   Women Miners
22.4   A Factory Girl: Countering the Stereotypes
22.5   A View from Downstairs: A Servant's Life

Elizabeth Thompson, Lady Butler, *Roll Call after an Engagement, Crimea* (1874)

Lady Elizabeth Thompson Butler, *The Roll Call: Calling the Roll after an Engagement, Crimea.* (Unframed). The Royal Collection © 2003, Her Majesty Queen Elizabeth II. Photo by SC.

The most famous and prolific nineteenth-century painter of military scenes was a woman, Elizabeth Thompson, later Lady Butler (1850–1933). Her wealthy father believed women should receive a first-rate education and saw to it that his daughter had excellent artistic training. By the time she was in her mid-twenties, she had begun to paint battle scenes. Although hers was not a military family and she herself had never witnessed a battle, Thompson was fascinated by the army and realized there was a good market for such paintings among the military and the patriotic Victorian middle classes.

Thompson exhibited *Roll Call after an Engagement, Crimea* in 1874. The painting was purchased by Queen Victoria and earned Thompson an international reputation. She completed this work almost twenty years after the Crimean War (1853–1856), but the British people had not forgotten the enormous suffering that the ill-equipped and poorly led British troops had been forced to endure during that conflict. The painting depicts the cold winter climate in which the soldiers were fighting, their wounds, and what appears to be one comrade who has died as the roll is being called. The men stand with remarkable dignity in the face of hardship, pain, and loss as the sun rises after a night battle. The scene highlights Thompson's gift for portraying ordinary soldiers rather than aristocratic officers.

Roll Call was so successful, newspapers of the day wrote that Thompson had earned women artists the respect they deserved by demonstrating their capacity to treat subjects of the highest seriousness.

Thompson painted military engagements throughout her career and became enormously famous for a series of works illustrating the Battle of Waterloo. But during her long, productive life, she also depicted battles from the British colonial wars, the Boer War (1899–1902), and World War I.

In 1877, Thompson married William Butler (1838–1910), an Irish officer who was later knighted and became a general in the British Army. Although her marriage gave her firsthand knowledge of military life—she always got the details of uniforms right—both she and her husband favored home rule for Ireland, a stand that may have hurt her popularity with some sections of the British public later in her career.

Prints of Lady Butler's battle scenes were reproduced in vast numbers and hung on the walls of barracks, offices, clubs, schools, and homes. She was easily the British Army's favorite painter. Yet despite her reputation, the Royal Academy of Art refused to elect Thompson as a member because she was a woman.

■ *Why did Thompson's* Roll Call *earn her international fame? Why did she specialize in military painting, and how did critics react to a woman artist who painted battles and soldiers? How did Thompson's political opinions and sex affect her career?*

Whitney Chadwick, *Women, Art, and Society*, 3rd ed. (London: Thames and Hudson, 2002), pp. 196–199; Matthew Lalumia, "Lady Elizabeth Thompson Butler in the 1870s," *Woman's Art Journal*, 4 (1983): 9–14.

In the late nineteenth century, the European middle classes exercised unprecedented influence on social and cultural life. In paintings such as Gustave Caillebotte's (1848–1894) Paris Street on a Rainy Day, they stroll with confidence and authority. Note that this painting does not show any of the workers who were challenging the middle class by joining trade unions and socialist parties during these years. Gustave Caillebotte (French 1848–1894). Paris Street, "Place de L'Europe on a Rainy Day," 1876–1877. Oil on canvas. 212.2 × 276.2 cm. Charles H. & Mary F. S. Worcester Collection, 1964.336/photograph © 1996, The Art Institute of Chicago. All rights reserved.

CHAPTER 24

THE BUILDING OF EUROPEAN SUPREMACY:

Society and Politics to World War I

*T*HE GROWTH OF INDUSTRIALISM BETWEEN 1860 and 1914 increased Europe's productive capacity to unprecedented and unparalleled levels. New steel mills, railways, shipyards, and chemical plants reflected an expanding supply of capital goods in the second half of the nineteenth century. By the first decade of the twentieth century, the age of the automobile, the airplane, the bicycle, the refrigerated ship, the telephone, the radio, the typewriter, and the electric lightbulb had dawned. The world's economies, based on the gold standard, became increasingly interdependent. European manufactured goods and financial capital flowed into markets all over the globe. In turn, Europeans imported foreign raw materials and foodstuffs. Within Europe itself, the eastern and southern European countries tended to import finished goods from the west and the north and to export agricultural products.

During this half century, European political, economic, and social life assumed many of its current characteristics. Nation-states with large electorates, political parties, and centralized bureaucracies emerged. Business adopted large-scale corporate structures, and the labor force organized itself into trade unions. Increasing numbers of white-collar workers appeared. Urban life came to predominate throughout western Europe. Socialism became a major ingredient in the political life of all nations. The foundations of the welfare state and of vast military establishments were laid. Taxation increased accordingly.

Europe had also quietly become dependent on the resources and markets of the rest of the world. Changes in the weather conditions in Kansas, Argentina, or New Zealand might now affect the European economy. Before World War I, however, Europe's industrial, military, and financial supremacy concealed that dependency. Many Europeans assumed their supremacy to be natural and permanent, but the twentieth century would reveal it to have been temporary.

KEY TOPICS

- The transformation of European life by the Second Industrial Revolution
- Urban sanitation, housing reform, and the redesign of cities
- The condition of women in late-nineteenth-century Europe and the rise of political feminism
- The emancipation of the Jews
- The development of labor politics and socialism in Europe to the outbreak of World War I
- Industrialization and political unrest in Russia

Population Trends and Migration

The proportion of Europeans in the world's total population was apparently greater around 1900—estimated at about 20 percent—than ever before or since. The number of Europeans had risen from approximately 266 million in 1850 to 401 million in 1900 and 447 million in 1910. Thereafter, birth and death rates declined or stabilized in Europe and other developed regions, and population growth began to slow in those areas but not elsewhere. The result has been the demographic differential between the developed and undeveloped world—stable or slowly growing populations in developed countries and large, rapidly growing populations in undeveloped regions—that contributes to the world's present food and resource crisis.

Europe's peoples were on the move in the latter half of the century as never before. The midcentury emancipation of peasants lessened the authority of landlords and made legal movement and migration easier. Railways, steamships, and better roads increased mobility. Cheap land and better wages accompanied economic development in Europe, North America, Latin America, and Australia, enticing people to move. Europeans left their continent in record numbers. Between 1846 and 1932, more than 50 million Europeans left their homelands. The major areas to benefit from this movement were the United States, Canada, Australia, South Africa, Brazil, and Argentina. At midcentury, most of the emigrants were from Great Britain (especially Ireland), Germany, and Scandinavia. After 1885, migration from southern and eastern Europe rose. This exodus helped relieve the social and population pressures on the Continent. The outward movement of peoples, in conjunction with Europe's economic and technological superiority, contributed heavily to the

Europeanization of the world. Not since the sixteenth century had European civilization had such an impact on other cultures.

The Second Industrial Revolution

During the third quarter of the nineteenth century, the gap that had long existed between British and continental economic development closed (Map 24–1). The basic heavy industries of Belgium, France, and Germany underwent major expansion. In particular, the growth of all areas of German industry was stunning. German steel production surpassed that of Britain in 1893 and was nearly twice that of Britain by the outbreak of World War I. This emergence of an industrial Germany was the major fact of European economic and political life at the turn of the century.

NEW INDUSTRIES

Initially, the economic expansion of the third quarter of the century involved the spread of industries similar to those pioneered earlier in Great Britain. In particular, the expansion of railway systems on the Continent spurred economic growth. Thereafter, however, wholly new industries emerged. It is this latter development that is usually termed the **Second Industrial Revolution.** The first Industrial

Major Dates of the Second Industrial Revolution	
1856–1870	Passage of laws permitting joint stock companies: 1856, Britain; 1863, France; 1870, Prussia
1857	Bessemer process for making steel
1873	Beginning of major economic downturn
1876	Alexander Graham Bell invents the telephone
1879	Edison perfects the electric lightbulb
1881	First electric power plant in Britain
1886	Daimler invents the internal combustion engine
1887	Daimler's first automobile
1895	Diesel engine invented
1895	Wireless telegraphy invented
1890s	Decade of first major impact of petroleum
1903	Wright brothers make first successful airplane flight
1909	Ford manufactures the Model T

Revolution was associated with textiles, steam, and iron; by contrast, the second was associated with steel, chemicals, electricity, and oil.

In the 1850s, Henry Bessemer (1830–1898), an English engineer, discovered a new process, named after him, for manufacturing steel cheaply in large quantities. In 1860, Great Britain, Belgium, France, and Germany had produced 125,000 tons of steel. By 1913, the figure had risen to over 32 million tons.

The chemical industry also came of age during this period. The Solway process of alkali production replaced the older Leblanc process, allowing the recovery of more chemical by-products. The new process permitted increased production of sulfuric acid and laundry soap. New dyestuffs and plastics were also developed. Formal scientific research played an important role in this growth of the chemical industry, marking the beginning of a direct link between science and industrial development. As in so many other aspects of the Second Industrial Revolution, Germany was a leader in forging this link, fostering scientific research and education.

The most significant change for industry and, eventually, for everyday life involved the application of electrical energy to production. Electricity was the most versatile and transportable source of power ever discovered. It could be delivered almost anywhere to run either large or small machinery, making the locations of factories more flexible and factory construction more efficient. The first major public power plant was constructed in 1881 in Great Britain. Soon electric poles, lines, and generating stations dotted the European landscape. Homes began to use electric lights. Streetcar and subway systems were electrified.

The internal combustion engine was invented in 1886. When the German engineer Gottlieb Daimler (1834–1900) put it on four wheels and obtained a French patent in 1887, the automobile was born. France initially took the lead in auto manufacturing, but for many years the car remained a novelty item that only the wealthy could afford. It was the American, Henry Ford (1863–1947), who later made the automobile accessible to large numbers of people.

The automobile and new industrial and chemical uses for petroleum had, by the turn of the century, created the first significant demand for oil. Then as now, Europe depended on imported supplies. The major oil companies were Standard Oil of the United States, British Shell Oil, and Royal Dutch Petroleum.

ECONOMIC DIFFICULTIES

Despite the multiplication of new industries, the second half of the nineteenth century was not a period of uninterrupted or smooth economic growth.

During the second half of the nineteenth century, millions of immigrants left Europe in hopes of bettering their lives in the Americas and in European colonies.
UPI/Lewis W. Hine/Corbis

Both industry and agriculture generally prospered from 1850 to 1873, but in the last quarter of the century economic advance was slower. Bad weather and foreign competition put grave pressures on European agriculture. Although these problems for agriculture lowered consumer food prices, they also put a drag on the economy. Many of the emigrants who left Europe during these years came from the countryside or from the least industrialized parts of Europe.

Several large banks failed in 1873, and the rate of capital investment slowed. Some industries then entered a two-decade-long period of stagnation that many contemporaries regarded as a depression. Overall, however, the general standard of living in the industrialized nations improved in the second half of the nineteenth century. Both prices and wages, as well as profits, fell, so real wages generally held firm and even rose in some countries. Yet many workers still lived and labored in abysmal conditions. There were pockets of *unemployment* (a word that was coined during this period), and strikes and other forms of labor unrest were common.

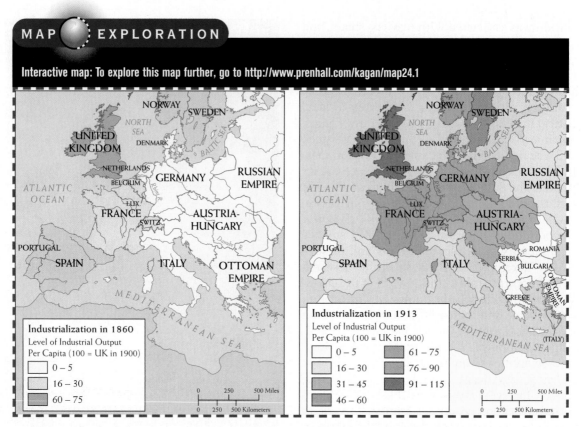

Interactive map: To explore this map further, go to http://www.prenhall.com/kagan/map24.1

MAP 24–1 EUROPEAN INDUSTRIALIZATION, 1860–1913 *In 1860 Britain was far more industrialized than other European countries. But in the following half century, industrial output rose significantly, if unevenly, across much of Western Europe, especially in the new German Empire. The Balkan states and the Ottoman Empire, however, remained economically backward.*

The economic difficulties fed the growth of trade unions and socialist political parties.

The new industries produced consumer goods, and expansion in consumer demand brought the economy out of stagnation by the end of the century. (See "Encountering the Past: Bicycles: Transportation, Freedom, and Sport.") Lower food prices eventually allowed all classes to spend a marginally larger amount of their income on consumer goods. Urbanization naturally created larger markets. People living in cities simply saw more things they wanted to buy than they would have seen in the countryside. New forms of retailing and marketing appeared—department stores, chain stores, packaging techniques, mail-order catalogs, and advertising—simultaneously stimulating and feeding consumer demand. Overseas imperialism also opened new markets for European consumer goods.

The Middle Classes in Ascendancy

The sixty years before World War I were the age of the middle classes. The London Great Exhibition of 1851 held in the Crystal Palace had displayed the

products and the new material life they had forged. Thereafter, the middle classes became the arbiter of consumer taste. After the revolutions of 1848, the middle classes ceased to be a revolutionary group. Once the question of social equality and equality of property had been raised, large and small property owners across the Continent moved to protect what they possessed against demands from socialists and other working-class groups.

SOCIAL DISTINCTIONS WITHIN THE MIDDLE CLASSES

The middle classes, never perfectly homogeneous, grew increasingly diverse. Their most prosperous members—the owners and managers of great businesses and banks—lived in splendor that rivaled, and sometimes exceeded, that of the aristocracy. Some, such as W. H. Smith (1825–1891), the owner of railway newsstands in England, were made members of the House of Lords. The Krupp family of Germany were pillars of the state and received visits from the German emperor and his court.

Only a few hundred families gained such wealth. Beneath them were the comfortable small entrepreneurs and professional people, whose incomes

Bicycles: Transportation, Freedom, and Sport

Before the car, there was the bicycle. Bicycles were the first mass-produced, affordable machines for individual travel, and between 1880 and 1900, they took Europe and North America by storm. For the first time in history, individual men and, significantly, women had a machine that gave them the freedom to travel on their own for work or pleasure. Bicycles had an immense impact on Western society.

The first functioning bicycles had been invented in Germany about 1817, but they were clumsy and dangerous. Made of wood, these machines lacked pedals and tires. They had to be pushed along the ground, and their riders could not control their speed. It took another eighty years for the modern bicycle to take shape. Pedals were introduced in the 1860s. Metal frames, solid rubber tires, and chain drives, which increased speed, appeared in the 1870s. In the 1880s, the ride became much smoother when John Boyd Dunlop, an Irish physician, invented the pneumatic tire and in France the Michelin brothers introduced the inner tube. (Before then, the ride was so rough that bicycles were sometimes called "boneshakers.") By the 1890s, the "safety bicycle" with its now familiar triangular frame and chain drive attached to the pedal and back wheel was being mass produced across Europe and North America, and men and women of the working class could afford them. By 1900, male workers of modest means across Europe were riding bicycles to work.

By increasing individual mobility, the bicycle made it easier to get to work, to hold a job farther from home, and to move about one's city or town or reach the countryside. New clothing designs, especially "bloomers," which were trousers worn under skirts, permitted women to bicycle while maintaining modesty. In the 1890s, feminists like Marie Pognon in France and Susan B. Anthony in the United States hailed the "egalitarian and leveling bicycle" for the freedom it gave women.

By 1914, there were millions of cyclists across the transatlantic world. Europeans and Americans organized cycling clubs with distinctive uniforms. Some of these clubs, such as the English Clarion Cycling Clubs, the French Union Sportive du Parti Socialiste, and the German *Solidaritet*, used cycling trips to spread pamphlets and newspapers for left-wing causes. Other groups cycled for pleasure. The kinds of touring clubs now associated with automobiles were first organized for cyclists, as were many of the early European travel guides such as the *Guides Michelin*, which first appeared in 1900. Then as now, Michelin made tires and stood to sell more of them the more people toured the countryside.

Bicycle racing quickly became a competitive sport. The most famous professional racer in the world was Marshall Walter "Major" Taylor, an African American who raced in both the United States and Europe. Paris and other French cities built velodromes for indoor cycle racing, which was one of the official sports of the first modern Olympics in 1896. In 1903, *L'Auto*, a French sports paper, organized the first Tour de France race to increase its circulation. Six riders raced a 2,500 km-course over 19 days.

■ *Why did bicycles become so popular in Europe in the late nineteenth century? What advantages did bicycles bring to women?*

Eugen Weber, *France: Fin de Siècle* (Cambridge, MA: Harvard University Press, 1986), pp. 103–104, 195–206; Will and Terra Hanger, "Bicycles," *History Magazine*, October/November 2001.

The bicycle helped liberate women's lives, but as this poster suggests, it also was associated with glamour and fashion. © Archivo Iconografico, S.A./Corbis

permitted private homes, large quantities of furniture, pianos, pictures, books, journals, education for their children, and vacations. Also in this group were the shopkeepers, schoolteachers, librarians, and others who had either a bit of property or a skill derived from education that provided respectable nonmanual employment.

Finally, there was a wholly new element—"white-collar workers"—who formed the lower middle class, or **petite bourgeoisie.** They included secretaries, retail clerks, and lower-level bureaucrats in business and government. They often had working-class origins and might even belong to unions, but they had middle-class aspirations and consciously sought to distance themselves from a lower-class lifestyle. They pursued educational opportunities and chances for even the slightest career advancement for themselves and, especially, for their children. Many of them spent a large part of their disposable income on consumer goods, such as stylish clothing and furniture, that were distinctively middle class in appearance.

Significant tensions and social anxieties marked relations among the various middle-class groups. Small shopkeepers resented the power of the great capitalists, with their department stores and mail-order catalogs. There is some evidence that the professions were becoming overcrowded. People who had only recently attained a middle-class lifestyle feared losing it in bad economic times. Nonetheless, the decades immediately before World War I saw the middle classes setting the values and goals for most of the society.

Late-Nineteenth-Century Urban Life

Europe became more urbanized than ever in the latter half of the nineteenth century as migration to the cities continued. Between 1850 and 1911, urban dwellers rose from 25 to 44 percent of the population in France and from 30 to 60 percent of the population in Germany. Other western European countries experienced similar increases.

The rural migrants to the cities were largely uprooted from traditional social ties. They often faced poor housing, social anonymity, and, because they rarely possessed the right kinds of skills, unemployment. People from different ethnic backgrounds found themselves in proximity to one another and had difficulty mixing socially. Competition for jobs generated new varieties of political and social discontent, such as the anti-Semitism directed at the thousands of Russian Jews who had migrated to western Europe. Indeed, much of the political anti-Semitism of the latter part of the century had its roots in the problems generated by urban migration.

THE REDESIGN OF CITIES

The inward urban migration placed new social and economic demands on already strained city resources and gradually produced significant transformations in the patterns of urban living. National and municipal governments redesigned the central portions of many major European cities during the second half of the century. Previously, the central

The Eiffel Tower, shown under construction in this painting, was to become a symbol of the newly redesigned Paris and its steel structure a symbol of French industrial strength. Liaison Agency, Inc.

urban areas had been places where many people from all social classes both lived and worked. From the middle of the century onward, planners transformed these districts into areas where businesses, government offices, large retail stores, and theaters were located, but where fewer people resided. Commerce, trade, government, and leisure activities now dominated central cities.

The New Paris The most famous and extensive transformation of a major city occurred in Paris. Like so many other European cities, Paris had expanded from the Middle Ages onward with little or no design or planning. Great public buildings and squalid hovels stood near each other. The Seine River was little more than an open sewer. The streets were narrow, crooked, and crowded. It was impossible to cross easily from one part of the city to another either on foot or by carriage. In 1850, a fully accurate map of the city did not even exist. Of more concern to the government of Napoleon III (r. 1852–1870), the city's streets had for sixty years provided battlegrounds for urban insurrections that had toppled French governments on numerous occasions, most recently in 1848.

Napoleon III personally determined that Paris must be redesigned. He appointed Georges Haussmann (1809–1891), who, as prefect of the Seine from 1853 to 1870, oversaw a vast urban reconstruction program. Whole districts were destroyed to open the way for the broad boulevards and streets that became the hallmark of modern Paris. Much, though by no means all, of the purpose of this street planning was political. The wide vistas not only were beautiful, but they also allowed for the quick deployment of troops to put down riots. The eradication of the many small streets and alleys removed areas where barricades could be, and had been, erected.

The project was also political in another sense. In addition to the new boulevards, parks such as the Bois de Boulogne and major public buildings such as the Paris Opera were also constructed or completed. These projects, along with the demolition and street building, created thousands of public jobs. Many other laborers found employment in the private construction that accompanied the public works.

Further rebuilding and redesign occurred under the Third Republic after the destruction that accompanied the suppression of the Commune. Many department stores, office complexes, and largely middle-class apartment buildings were constructed. By the late 1870s, mechanical trams were operating in Paris. After much debate, construction of a subway system (the *métro*) began in 1895, long after that of London (1863). New railway stations

Growth of Major European Cities (figures in thousands)			
	1850	**1880**	**1910**
Berlin	419	1,122	2,071
Birmingham	233	437	840
Frankfurt	65	137	415
London	2,685	4,470	7,256
Madrid	281	398	600
Moscow	365	748	1,533
Paris	1,053	2,269	2,888
Rome	175	300	542
Saint Petersburg	485	877	1,962
Vienna	444	1,104	2,031
Warsaw	160	339	872

were also erected near the close of the century. This transport linked the refurbished central city to the suburbs.

In 1889, the Eiffel Tower was built, originally as a temporary structure for the international trade exposition of that year. Not all the new structures of Paris bespoke the impact of middle-class commerce and the reign of iron and steel, however. Between 1873 and 1914, the French Roman Catholic Church oversaw the construction of the Basilica of the Sacred Heart high atop Montmartre as an act of national penance for the sins that had led to French defeat in the Franco-Prussian War (1870–1871). Those two landmarks—the Eiffel Tower and the Basilica of the Sacred Heart—visibly symbolized the social and political divisions between liberals and conservatives in the Third Republic.

Development of Suburbs Commercial development, railway construction, and the clearing of slums displaced many city dwellers and raised urban land values and rents. Consequently, both the middle classes and the working class began to seek housing elsewhere. The middle classes looked for neighborhoods removed from urban congestion. The working class looked for affordable housing. The result, in virtually all countries, was the development of suburbs surrounding the city proper. These suburbs housed families whose breadwinners worked in the central city or in a factory located within the city limits. European suburbs, unlike those that developed in the United States, often consisted of apartment buildings or private houses built closely together with small lawns and gardens.

The expansion of railways with cheap workday fares and the introduction of mechanical and, later, electric tramways, as well as subways, allowed tens of thousands of workers from all classes to move daily between the city and the outlying suburbs. For hundreds of thousands of Europeans, home and work became more physically separated than ever before.

URBAN SANITATION

The efforts of governments and of the increasingly conservative middle classes to maintain public order after 1848 led to a growing concern with the problems of public health and housing for the poor. A widespread feeling arose that only when the health and housing of the working class were improved would middle-class health also be secure and the political order stable.

Impact of Cholera Concerns with health and housing first manifested themselves as a result of the great cholera epidemics of the 1830s and 1840s. Unlike many other common deadly diseases of the day that touched only the poor, cholera struck all classes, impelling the middle class to demand a solution. Before the development of the bacterial theory of disease late in the century, physicians and sanitary reformers believed cholera and other diseases were spread through infection from miasmas in the air. These miasmas, the presence of which was marked by their foul odors, were believed to arise from filth. The way to get rid of the dangerous, foul-smelling air was to clean up the cities.

During the 1840s, many physicians and some government officials began to publicize the dangers posed by the unsanitary conditions associated with overcrowding in cities and with businesses such as basement slaughterhouses. In 1840, Louis René Villermé published his *Tableau de l'état physique et moral des ouvriers* (*Catalog of the Physical and Moral State of Workers*). In 1842, Edwin Chadwick's (1800–1890) *Report on the Sanitary Condition of the Labouring Population* shocked the English public. In Germany, Rudolf Virchow (1821–1902) published similar findings. These and various other private and public-commission reports closely linked the issues

Major Dates Relating to Sanitation Reform
• •
1830s and 1840s   Cholera epidemics
1840   Villermé's *Catalog of the Physical and Moral State of Workers*
1842   Chadwick's *Report on the Sanitary Condition of the Labouring Population*
1848   British Public Health Act
1851   French Melun Act

of wretched living conditions and public health. They also demonstrated that sanitary reform would remove the dangers. The reports, incidentally, now provide some of the best information available about working-class living conditions in the middle of the nineteenth century. (See "A French Physician Describes a Working-Class Slum in Lille Before the Public Health Movement.")

New Water and Sewer Systems The proposed solution to the health hazard was cleanliness, to be achieved through new water and sewer systems. These facilities were constructed slowly, beginning usually in capital cities and then much later in provincial cities. Some major urban areas did not have good water systems until after the turn of the century. Nonetheless, the building of such systems was one of the major health and engineering achievements of the second half of the nineteenth century. The sewer system of Paris was a famous part of Haussmann's rebuilding program. In London, the construction of the Albert Embankment along the Thames involved not only large sewers discharging into the river, but gas mains and water pipes as well; all were encased in thick walls of concrete, one of the new building materials of the day, and granite. Wherever these sanitary facilities were installed, the mortality rate dropped considerably.

Expanded Government Involvement in Public Health The concern with public health led to an expansion of governmental power on various levels. In Britain the Public Health Act of 1848, in France the Melun Act of 1851, and various laws in the still-disunited German states, as well as later legislation, introduced new restraints on private life and enterprise. This legislation allowed medical officers and building inspectors to enter homes and other structures in the name of public health. Private property could be condemned for posing health hazards. Private land could be excavated for the construction of the sewers and water mains required to protect the public. New building regulations put restraints on the activities of private contractors.

Full acceptance at the close of the century of the bacterial theory of disease associated with the discoveries of Louis Pasteur (1822–1895) in France, Robert Koch (1843–1910) in Germany, and Joseph Lister (1827–1912) in Britain made cleanliness an even more prominent public concern. Throughout Europe, issues related to the maintenance of public health and the physical well-being of national populations repeatedly opened the way for new modes of government intervention in the lives of citizens.

A FRENCH PHYSICIAN DESCRIBES A WORKING-CLASS SLUM IN LILLE BEFORE THE PUBLIC HEALTH MOVEMENT

It is difficult to conceive of the world before the sanitation movement. The work of medical doctors frequently carried them into working-class areas of industrial cities rarely visited by other members of the middle class. Louis Villermé was such a French physician. He wrote extensive descriptions of the slums and the general living conditions of industrial workers. The passage here, published in 1840, describes a particularly notorious section of Lille, a major cotton-manufacturing town in northern France.

■ *What does this physician find most disturbing about the scene he describes? How is his description possibly designed to call forth sympathy and concern from a middle-class reader? How might the conditions described have led the poor of France toward socialism or radical politics? How would addressing the problems described have led to a larger role for government?*

The poorest live in the cellars and attics. These cellars . . . open onto the streets or courtyards, and one enters them by a stairway which is very often at once the door and the window. . . . Commonly the height of the ceiling is six or six and a half feet at the highest point, and they are only ten to fourteen or fifteen feet wide.

It is in these somber and sad dwellings that a large number of workers eat, sleep, and even work. The light of day comes an hour later for them than for others, and the night an hour earlier.

Their furnishings normally consist, along with the tools of their profession, of a sort of cupboard or a plank on which to deposit food, a stove . . . a few pots, a little table, two or three poor chairs, and a dirty pallet of which the only pieces are a straw mattress and scraps of a blanket. . . .

In their obscure cellars, in their rooms, which one would take for cellars, the air is never renewed, it is infected; the walls are plastered with garbage. . . . If a bed exists, it is a few dirty, greasy planks; it is damp and putrescent straw; it is a coarse cloth whose color and fabric are hidden by a layer of grime; it is a blanket that resembles a sieve. . . . The furniture is dislocated, worm-eaten, covered with filth. Utensils are thrown in disorder all over the dwelling. The windows, always closed, are covered by paper and glass, but so black, so smoke-encrusted, that the light is unable to penetrate . . . everywhere are piles of garbage, of ashes, of debris from vegetables picked up from the streets, of rotten straw; of animal nests of all sorts; thus, the air is unbreathable. One is exhausted, in these hovels, by a stale, nauseating, somewhat piquante odor, odor of filth, odor of garbage. . . .

And the poor themselves, what are they like in the middle of such a slum? Their clothing is in shreds, without substance, consumed, covered, no less than their hair, which knows no comb, with dust from the workshops. And their skin? . . . It is painted, it is hidden, if you wish, by indistinguishable deposits of diverse exudations.

From Louis René Villermé, *Tableau de l'état physique et moral des ouvriers employés dans les manufactures de coton, de laine et de soie* (Paris, 1840), as quoted and trans. in William H. Sewell, Jr., *Work and Revolution in France: The Language of Labor from the Old Regime to 1848* (Cambridge, UK.: Cambridge University Press, 1980), p. 224.

HOUSING REFORM AND MIDDLE-CLASS VALUES

The information about working-class living conditions brought to light by the sanitary reformers also led to heated debates over the housing problem. The wretched dwellings of the poor were themselves a cause of poor sanitation and thus became a newly perceived health hazard. Furthermore, middle-class reformers and bureaucrats found themselves shocked by the domestic arrangements of the poor, whose large families might live in a single room lacking all forms of personal privacy. A single toilet facility might serve a whole block of tenements. After the revolutions of 1848, the overcrowding in housing and the social discontent that it generated were also seen to pose a political danger.

Middle-class reformers thus turned to housing reform to solve the medical, moral, and political dangers posed by slums. Proper, decent housing would foster a good home life, in turn leading to a healthy, moral, and politically stable population. As A. V. Huber, one of the early German housing reformers, declared,

Certainly it would not be too much to say that the home is the communal embodiment of family life. Thus the purity of the dwelling is almost as important for the family as is the cleanliness of the body for the individual. Good or bad housing is a question of life and death if ever there was one.[1]

Later advocates of housing reform, such as Jules Simon in France, saw good housing as leading to good family life and, ultimately, to strong patriotic feeling. It was widely believed that providing the poor and the working class with adequate, respectable, cheap housing would alleviate social and political discontent. It was also believed the personal saving and investment required for owning a home would lead the working class to adopt the thrifty habits of the middle classes.

Private philanthropy made the first attack on the housing problem. Companies operating on low profit margins or making low-interest loans encouraged housing for the poor. Firms such as the German Krupp armaments concern, seeking to ensure a contented, healthy, and stable work force, constructed model housing projects and industrial communities.

By the mid-1880s, the migration into cities had made housing a political issue. Legislation in England in 1885 lowered the interest rates for the construction of cheap housing, and soon thereafter government authorities began public housing projects. In Germany, action on housing came later in the century through the initiative of local municipalities. In 1894, France made inexpensive credit available for constructing housing for the poor. None of these governments, however, adopted wide-scale housing experiments.

Nonetheless, by 1914, the housing problem had been fully recognized if not adequately addressed. The goal of housing reform across western Europe came to be to provide homes for the members of the working class that would allow them to enjoy a family life more or less like that of the middle class. Such a home would be in the form of a detached house or some kind of affordable city apartment with several rooms, a private entrance, and separate toilet facilities.

---

[1]Quoted in Nicholas Bullock and James Read, *The Movement for Housing Reform in Germany and France, 1840–1914* (Cambridge, U. K.: Cambridge University Press, 1985), p. 42.

Varieties of Late-Nineteenth-Century Women's Experiences

Late-nineteenth-century women and men led lives that reflected their social rank. Yet, within each rank, the experience of women was distinct from that of men. Women remained, generally speaking, in positions of economic dependence and legal inferiority, whatever their social class.

SOCIAL DISABILITIES CONFRONTED BY ALL WOMEN

At the middle of the nineteenth century, virtually all European women faced social and legal disabilities in three areas: property rights, family law, and education. By the close of the century, there had been some improvement in each area.

Women and Property Until the last quarter of the century in most European countries, married women could not own property in their own names, no matter what their social class. For all practical purposes, upon marriage, women lost to their husbands' control any property they owned or that they might inherit or earn by their own labor. Their legal identities were subsumed in their husbands' identities, and they had no independent standing before the law. The courts saw the theft of a woman's purse as a theft of her husband's property. Because European society was based on private property and wage earning, these disabilities put married women at a great disadvantage, limiting their freedom to work, to save, and to move from one location to another.

Reform of women's property rights came very slowly. By 1882, Great Britain had passed the Married Woman's Property Act, which allowed married women to own property in their own right. In France, however, a married woman could not even open a savings account in her own name until 1895, and not until 1907 were married women granted possession of the wages they earned. In 1900, Germany allowed women to take jobs without their husbands' permission, but except for her wages, a German husband retained control of most of his wife's property. Similar laws prevailed elsewhere in Europe.

Family Law Virtually all European family law also worked to the disadvantage of women. Legal codes actually required wives to "give obedience" to their husbands. The Napoleonic Code and the remnants of Roman law still in effect made women legal minors throughout Europe. Divorce was difficult everywhere for most of the century. In England before

1857, divorce required an act of Parliament. Thereafter, divorce could be procured, with difficulty, through the Court of Matrimonial Causes. Most nations did not permit divorce by mutual consent. French law forbade divorce between 1816 and 1884. Thereafter, the chief recognized legal cause for divorce was cruelty and injury, which had to be proven in court. In Great Britain, adultery was the usual cause for divorce, but to obtain a divorce, a woman had to prove her husband's adultery plus other offenses, whereas a man only had to prove his wife's adultery. In Germany, only adultery or serious maltreatment were recognized as reasons for divorce. Across Europe, some version of the double standard prevailed whereby extramarital sexual relations of husbands were tolerated to a greater degree than those of wives. Everywhere, divorce required legal hearings and the presentation of legal proof, making the process expensive and all the more difficult for women who did not control their own property.

The authority of husbands also extended to children. A husband could take children away from their mother and give them to someone else for rearing. Only the husband, in most countries, could permit his daughter to marry. In some countries, he could virtually force his daughter to marry the man of his choice. In cases of divorce and separation, the husband normally assumed authority over children, no matter how he had treated them previously.

The issues surrounding the sexual and reproductive rights of women that have been so widely debated recently could hardly be discussed in the nineteenth century. Until well into the twentieth century, both contraception and abortion were illegal. The law surrounding rape normally worked to the disadvantage of women. Wherever they turned with their problems—whether to physicians or lawyers—women confronted an official or legal world almost wholly populated and controlled by men.

Educational Barriers Throughout the nineteenth century, women had less access to education than men had and what was available to them was inferior to that available to men. Not surprisingly, the percentage of illiterate women exceeded that of men. Most women were educated only enough for the domestic careers they were expected to follow.

University and professional education remained reserved for men until at least the third quarter of the century. The University of Zurich first opened its doors to women in the 1860s. The University of London admitted women for degrees in 1878. Women's colleges were founded at Cambridge during the last quarter of the century. Women could

take Oxford and Cambridge university examinations, but were not awarded degrees at Oxford until 1920 and at Cambridge until 1921. Women could not attend Sorbonne lectures until 1880. Just before the turn of the century, universities and medical schools in the Austrian Empire allowed women to matriculate, but Prussian universities did not admit women until after 1900. Russian women did not attend universities before 1914, but other institutions that awarded degrees were open to them. Italian universities proved themselves more open to both women students and women instructors than similar institutions elsewhere in Europe. In many countries, there were frequently more foreign than native women attending university classes. This was especially the case in Zurich, where many Russian women studied for medical degrees. Many of the American women who founded or taught in the first women's colleges in the United States studied at European universities.

The absence of a system of private or public secondary education for women prevented most of them from gaining the qualifications they needed to enter a university whether or not the university prohibited them. Considerable evidence suggests that educated, professional men feared their professions would be overcrowded if they admitted women. Women who attended universities and medical schools, like the young Russian women who studied medicine at Zurich, were sometimes labeled political radicals.

By the turn of the century, some men in the educated elites feared the challenge educated women posed to traditional gender roles in the home and workplace. Restricting women's access to secondary and university education helped bar them from social and economic advancement. Women would benefit only marginally from the expansion of professional employment that occurred during the late nineteenth and early twentieth centuries. Some women did enter the professions, most particularly medicine, but their number remained few. Most nations refused to allow women to become lawyers until after World War I.

Schoolteaching at the elementary level, which had come to be seen as a "female job" because of its association with the nurturing of children, became a professional haven for women. Trained at institutions designed particularly for elementary schoolteachers, usually known as normal schools, women schoolteachers at the elementary level were regarded as educated, but not as university educated. Secondary education remained largely the province of men.

The few women who pioneered in the professions and on government commissions and school boards or who dispersed birth control information

Women only gradually gained access to secondary and university education during the second half of the nineteenth century and the early twentieth century. Young women on their way to school, the subject of this 1880 English painting, would thus have been a new sight when it was painted. Sir George Clausen (RA) (1852–1944), *Schoolgirls, Haverstock Hill*, signed and dated 1880, oil on canvas, 20-1/2 × 30-3/8 inches (52 × 77.2 cm), Yale Center for British Art/ Paul Mellon Collection B1985.10.1

faced grave social obstacles, personal humiliation, and often outright bigotry. These women and their male supporters were challenging that clear separation into male and female spheres that had emerged in middle-class European social life during the nineteenth century. Women themselves were often hesitant to support feminist causes or expanded opportunities for females because they had been so thoroughly acculturated into the recently stereotyped roles. Many women, as well as men, saw a real conflict between family responsibilities and feminism.

NEW EMPLOYMENT PATTERNS FOR WOMEN

During the decades of the Second Industrial Revolution, two major developments affected the economic lives of women. The first was a significant expansion in the variety of jobs available outside the better paying learned professions. The second was a significant withdrawal of married women from the work force. These two seemingly contradictory developments require some explanation.

Availability of New Jobs The expansion of governmental bureaucracies, the emergence of corporations and other large-scale businesses, and the vast growth of retail stores opened many new employment opportunities for women. The need for elementary school teachers, usually women, grew as governments adopted compulsory education laws. Technological inventions and innovations, such as the typewriter and, eventually, the telephone exchange, also fostered female employment. Women by the thousands became secretaries and clerks for governments and for private businesses. Still more thousands became shop assistants.

Although these jobs did open new and often somewhat better employment opportunities for women, they nonetheless required low-level skills and involved minimal training. They were occupied primarily by unmarried women or widows. Women were rarely to be found in more prominent positions.

Women working in the London Central Telephone Exchange. The invention of the telephone opened new employment opportunities for women. Mary Evans Picture Library

Employers continued to pay women low wages, because they assumed, although they often knew better, that a woman did not need to live on what she herself earned, but could expect additional financial support from her father or her husband. Consequently, a woman who did need to support herself independently could seldom find a job that paid an adequate income—or a position that paid as well as one held by a man who was supporting himself independently.

Withdrawal from the Labor Force Most of the women filling the new service positions were young and unmarried. Upon marriage, or certainly after the birth of her first child, a woman normally withdrew from the labor force. Either she did not work or she worked at some occupation that could be pursued in the home. This pattern was not new, but it had become significantly more common by the end of the nineteenth century. The kinds of industrial occupations that women had filled in the middle of the nineteenth century, especially textile and garment making, were shrinking. There were thus fewer opportunities for employment in those industries for either married or unmarried women. Employers in offices and retail stores preferred young unmarried women whose family responsibilities would not interfere with their work. The decline in the number of children being born also meant that fewer married women were needed to look after other women's children.

The real wages paid to male workers increased during this period, so families had a somewhat reduced need for a second income. Also, thanks to improving health conditions, men lived longer than before, so wives were less likely to be thrust into the work force by the death of their husbands. The smaller size of families also lowered the need for supplementary wages. Working children stayed at home longer and continued to contribute to the family's wage pool.

Finally, the cultural dominance of the middle class established a pattern of social expectations, especially for wives. The more prosperous a working-class family became, the less involved in employment its women were supposed to be. Indeed, the less income-producing work a wife did, the more prosperous and stable the family was considered.

Yet behind these generalities stands the enormous variety of social and economic experiences late-nineteenth-century women actually encountered. As might be expected, the chief determinant of these individual experiences was social class.

WORKING-CLASS WOMEN

Although the textile industry and garment making were much less dominant than earlier in the century, they continued to employ many women. The German clothing-making trade illustrates the kind of vulnerable economic situation that women could encounter as a result of their limited skills and the way the trade was organized. The system of manufacturing mass-made clothes of uniform sizes in Germany was designed to require minimal capital investment by manufacturers and to protect them from risk. A major manufacturer would arrange for the production of clothing through what was called a *putting-out system*. The manufacturer would purchase the material and then put it out for tailoring.

The clothing was produced not in a factory, but usually in numerous, independently owned, small sweatshops or by workers in their homes.

In Berlin in 1896, more than 80,000 garment workers, mostly women, were so employed. When business was good and demand strong, employment for these women was high. As the seasons shifted or business became poor, however, less and less work was put out, idling many of them. In effect, the workers who actually sewed the clothing carried much of the risk of the enterprise. Some women did work in factories, but they, too, were subject to lay-offs. Furthermore, women in the clothing trade were nearly always in positions less skilled than those of the male tailors or the middlemen who owned the workshops.

The expectation of separate social and economic spheres for men and women and the definition of women's chief work as pertaining to the home contributed mightily to the exploitation of women workers outside the home. Because their wages were regarded merely as supplementing their husbands' wages, they became particularly vulnerable to the kind of economic exploitation that characterized the German putting-out system for clothing production and similar systems elsewhere. Women were nearly always treated as casual workers everywhere in Europe.

POVERTY AND PROSTITUTION

A major, but little recognized, social fact of most nineteenth-century cities was the presence of a surplus of working women who did not fit the stereotype of wife or daughter supplementing a family's income. There were almost always many more women seeking employment than there were jobs. The economic vulnerability of women and the consequent poverty many of them faced were among the chief causes of prostitution. In any major late-nineteenth-century European city, there were thousands of prostitutes. (See "Art & the West: Edouard Manet, *A Bar at the Folies-Bergère,*" p. 850.)

Prostitution was, of course, not new. It had always been one way for very poor women to find some income. In the late nineteenth century, however, it was closely related to the difficulty encountered by indigent women who were trying to make their way in an overcrowded female labor force. On the Continent, prostitution was generally legalized and was subject to governmental and municipal regulations passed by male legislatures and councils and enforced by male police and physicians. In Great Britain, prostitution received only minimal regulation.

Many myths and misunderstandings have surrounded the subject of prostitution. The most recent studies of the subject in England emphasize that most prostitutes were active on the streets for a very few years, generally from their late teens to about age twenty-five. They often were very poor women who had recently migrated from nearby rural areas. Others were born in the towns where they became prostitutes. Certain cities—those with large army garrisons or naval ports or those, like London, with large transient populations—attracted many prostitutes. Far fewer prostitutes worked in manufacturing towns, where there were more opportunities for steady employment and community life was more stable.

Women who became prostitutes usually came from families of unskilled workers and had minimal skills and education themselves. Many had been servants. They also often were from broken homes or were orphaned. Contrary to many sensational late-century newspaper accounts, there were few child prostitutes. Furthermore, rarely were women seduced into prostitution by middle-class employers or middle-class clients, although working-class women were always potentially subject to such pressure. The customers of poor working-class prostitutes were primarily working-class men.

WOMEN OF THE MIDDLE CLASS

A vast social gap separated poor working-class women from their middle-class counterparts. As their fathers' and husbands' incomes permitted, middle-class women participated in the vast expansion of consumerism and domestic comfort that marked the end of the nineteenth century and the early twentieth century. They filled their homes with manufactured items, including clothing, china, furniture, carpets, drapery, wallpaper, and prints. They enjoyed all the improvements of sanitation and electricity. They could command the services of numerous domestic servants. They moved into the fashionable new houses being constructed in the rapidly expanding suburbs.

The Cult of Domesticity For the middle classes, the distinction between work and family, defined by gender, had become complete and constituted the model for all other social groups. Middle-class women, if at all possible, did not work. More than any other women, they became limited to the roles of wife and mother. As a result, they might enjoy great domestic luxury and comfort, but their lives, talents, ambitions, and opportunities for applying their intelligence were markedly circumscribed.

Middle-class women became, in large measure, the product of a particular understanding of social life. Home life was to be very different from the life of business and the marketplace. The home was to be a private place of refuge, a view set forth in scores of women's journals across Europe.

As studies of the lives of middle-class women in northern France have suggested, this image of the middle-class home and of the role of women in the home is quite different from the one that had existed earlier in the nineteenth century. During the first half of the century, the spouse of a middle-class husband might very well contribute directly to the business, handling accounts or correspondence. These women also frequently had little to do with rearing their children, leaving that task first to nurses and later to governesses. The reasons for the change over the course of the century are not certain, but it appears that men began to insist on doing business with other men. Magazines and books directed toward women began to praise motherhood, domesticity, religion, and charity as the proper work of women in accordance with the concept of separate spheres. (See "The Virtues of a French Middle-Class Lady Praised.")

For middle-class Frenchwomen, as well as for middle-class women elsewhere, the home came to be seen as the center of virtue, children, and the proper life. Marriages were usually arranged for some kind of family economic benefit. Romantic marriage was viewed as a danger to social stability. Most middle-class women in northern France married by the age of twenty-one. Children were expected to follow very soon after marriage, and the first child was often born within the first year. The rearing and nurturing of her children was a woman's chief task. She would receive no experience or training for any role other than that of dutiful daughter, wife, and mother.

Within the home, a middle-class woman performed major roles. She was largely in charge of the household. She oversaw virtually all domestic management and child care. She was in charge of the home as a unit of consumption, which is why so much advertising was directed toward women. All this domestic activity, however, occurred within the limits of the approved middle-class lifestyle that set strict limits on a woman's initiative. In her conspicuous position within the home and family, a woman symbolized first her father's and then her husband's worldly success.

Religious and Charitable Activities The cult of domesticity in France and elsewhere assigned firm religious duties to women, which the Roman Catholic Church strongly supported. Women were

Department stores, such as Bon Marche in Paris, sold wide selections of consumer goods under one roof. These modern stores increased the economic pressure on small traditional merchants who specialized in selling only one kind of good.   Mary Evans Picture Library Ltd.

expected to attend mass frequently and assure the religious instruction of their children. They were charged with observing meatless Fridays and with participating in religious observances. Prayer was a major part of their lives and daily rituals. They internalized those portions of the Christian religion that stressed meekness and passivity. In other countries as well, religion and religious activities became part of the expected work of women. For this reason, women were regarded by political liberals as especially susceptible to the influence of priests. This close association between religion and a strict domestic life for women was one of the reasons for later tension between feminism and religious authorities.

Another important role for middle-class women was the administration of charity. Women were judged especially qualified for this work because of their presumed innate spirituality and their capacity to instill domestic and personal discipline. Middle-class women were often in charge of clubs for poor youth, societies to protect poor young women, schools for infants, and societies for visiting the poor. Women were supposed to be particularly interested in the problems of poor women, their families,

THE VIRTUES OF A FRENCH MIDDLE-CLASS LADY PRAISED

One of the chief social roles assigned to middle-class Frenchwomen was that of charitable activity. This obituary of Madame. Emile Delesalle from a Roman Catholic Church paper of the late nineteenth century describes the work of that woman among the poor. It is a very revealing document because it clearly shows the class divisions that existed in the giving of charity. Also through the kinds of virtues it praises, it gave instruction to its women readers. Note the emphasis on home life, spirituality, and the instruction of children in charitable acts.

■ *What assumptions about the character of women allowed writers to see charity as a particularly good occupation for women? What middle-class attitudes toward the poor are displayed in this passage? How did the assignment of charity work to women lead to their being excluded from other kinds of work and the learned professions?*

The poor were the object of her affectionate interest, especially the shameful poor, the fallen people. She sought them out and helped them with perfect discretion which doubled the value of her benevolent interest. To those whom she could approach without fear of bruising their dignity, she brought, along with alms to assure their existence, consolation of the most serious sort—she raised their courage and their hopes. To others, each Sunday, she opened all the doors of her home, above all when her children were still young. In making them distribute these alms with her, she hoped to initiate them early into practices of charity.

In the last years of her life, the St. Gabriel Orphanage gained her interest. Not only did she accomplish a great deal with her generosity, but she also took on the task of maintaining the clothes of her dear orphans in good order and in good repair. When she appeared in the courtyard of the establishment at recreation time, all her protégés surrounded her and lavished her with manifestations of their profound respect and affectionate gratitude.

Quoted in Bonnie G. Smith, *Ladies of the Leisure Class: The Bourgeoises of Northern France in the Nineteenth Century* (Princeton, NJ: Princeton University Press, 1981), pp. 147–148. Copyright © 1981 by Princeton University Press. Reprinted by permission of Princeton University Press.

and their children. Quite often, charity from middle-class women required the poor recipient to demonstrate good character. By the end of the century, middle-class women seeking to expand their spheres of activity became social workers for the church, for private charities, or for the government. These vocations were a natural extension of the roles socially assigned to them.

Sexuality and Family Size   The world of the middle-class wife and her family is now understood to have been much more complicated than was once thought. Neither wives nor their families all conformed to the stereotypes. Recent studies have suggested that the middle classes of the nineteenth century enjoyed sexual relations within marriage far more than was once thought. Diaries, letters, and even early medical and sociological sex surveys indicate that sexual enjoyment rather than sexual repression was fundamental to middle-class marriages. Much of the inhibition about sexuality stemmed from the dangers of childbirth rather than from any dislike or disapproval of sex itself.

One of the major changes in this regard during the second half of the century was the acceptance of a small family size among the middle classes. The birthrate in France dropped throughout the nineteenth century. It began to fall in England steadily from the 1870s onward. During the last decades of the century, various new contraceptive devices became available, which middle-class couples used. One of the chief reasons for the apparently conscious decision of couples to limit their family size was to maintain a relatively high level of material consumption. Children had become much more expensive to rear, and at the same time, more material comforts had become available. Fewer children probably meant more attention for each of them, possibly bringing mothers and their children emotionally closer.

Family was central to the middle-class conception of a stable and respectable social life. This portrait of the Bellelli family is by Edgar Degas. Notice that the husband and father sits at his desk, suggesting his association with business and the world outside their home, whereas the wife and mother stands with their children, suggesting her domestic role.
Edgar Degas (1834–1917), "The Bellelli Family." Musee d'Orsay, Paris, France. © Giraudon/Art Resource, N.Y.

THE RISE OF POLITICAL FEMINISM

Plainly, liberal society and its values had neither automatically nor inevitably improved the lot of women. In particular, it did not give women the vote or access to political activity. Male liberals feared that granting the vote to women would benefit political conservatives, because women were thought to be unduly controlled by Roman Catholic priests. A similar apprehension existed about the alleged influence of the Anglican clergy over women in England. Consequently, anticlerical liberals often had difficulty working with feminists.

Obstacles to Achieving Equality But women also were often reluctant to support feminist causes. Political issues relating to gender were only one of several priorities for many women. Some were very sensitive to their class and economic interests.

Others subordinated feminist political issues to national unity and patriotism. Still others would not support particular feminist organizations because of differences over tactics. The various social and tactical differences among women led quite often to sharp divisions within the feminists' own ranks. Except in England, it was often difficult for working-class and middle-class women to cooperate. Roman Catholic feminists were uncomfortable with radical secularist feminists. And there were other disagreements about which goals for improvement in women's legal and social conditions were most important.

Although liberal society and law presented women with many obstacles, they also provided feminists with many of their intellectual and political tools. As early as 1792 in Britain, Mary Wollstonecraft (1759–1797), in *The Vindication of the Rights of Woman*, had applied the revolutionary

The creator of this poster cleverly reveals the hypocrisy and absurdity of denying the vote to women. The Bridgeman Art Library International

doctrines of the rights of man to the predicament of the members of her own sex. (See Chapter 18.) John Stuart Mill (1806–1873), together with his wife, Harriet Taylor (1804–1858), had applied the logic of

Major Dates in Late-Nineteenth-Century and Early-Twentieth-Century Women's History	
1857	Revised English divorce law
1865	University of Zurich admits women for degrees
1869	John Stuart Mill's *The Subjection of Women*
1878	University of London admits women as candidates for degrees
1882	English Married Woman's Property Act
1894	Union of German Women's Organizations founded
1901	National Council of French Women founded
1903	British Women's Social and Political Union founded
1907	Norway permits women to vote on national issues
1910	British suffragettes adopt radical tactics
1918	Vote extended to some British women
1919	Weimar constitution allows German women to vote
1920–1921	Oxford and Cambridge Universities award degrees to women
1922	French Senate defeats bill extending vote to women
1928	Britain extends vote to women on same basis as men

liberal freedom to the position of women in *The Subjection of Women* (1869). The arguments for utility and efficiency so dear to middle-class liberals could be used to expose the human and social waste implicit in the inferior role assigned to women.

Furthermore, the socialist criticism of capitalist society often, though by no means always, included a harsh indictment of the social and economic position to which women had been relegated. The earliest statements of feminism arose from critics of the existing order and were often associated with people who had unorthodox opinions about sexuality, family life, and property. This hardened resistance to the feminist message, especially on the Continent.

These difficulties prevented continental feminists from raising the kind of massive public support or mounting the large demonstrations that feminists in Great Britain and the United States could. Everywhere in Europe, however, including Britain, the feminist cause was badly divided over both goals and tactics. (See "An English Feminist Defends the Cause of the Female Franchise.")

Votes for Women in Britain Europe's most advanced women's movement was in Great Britain. There, Millicent Fawcett (1847–1929) led the moderate National Union of Women's Suffrage Societies. She believed Parliament would grant women the vote only if it were convinced they would be respectable and responsible in their political activity. In 1908, the National Union could rally almost half a million women in London. Fawcett's husband was a former Liberal Party cabinet minister and economist. Her tactics were those of English liberals.

AN ENGLISH FEMINIST DEFENDS THE CAUSE OF THE FEMALE FRANCHISE

Frances Power Cobbe (1822–1904) wrote widely on many religious and social issues of the second half of the century. She had been a feminist since early adulthood. In this letter to a British feminist magazine in 1884, she explains why women should seek the vote.

■ *What motives does Cobbe assign to the pursuit of the right to vote? Why does she emphasize the issue of "womanliness" as one that must not be allowed to undermine the cause of women? What is Cobbe's attitude toward violence? Why would later British advocates of votes for women turn to violent tactics?*

If I may presume to offer an old woman's counsel to the younger workers in our cause, it would be that they should adopt the point of view—that it is before all things our duty to obtain the franchise. If we undertake the work in this spirit, and with the object of using the power it confers, whenever we gain it, for the promotion of justice and mercy and the kingdom of God upon earth, we shall carry on all our agitation in a corresponding manner, firmly and bravely, and also calmly and with generous good temper. And when our opponents come to understand that this is the motive underlying our efforts, they, on their part, will cease to feel bitterly and scornfully toward us, even when they think we are altogether mistaken. . . .

The idea that the possession of political rights will destroy "womanliness," absurd as it may seem to us, is very deeply rooted in the minds of men; and when they oppose our demands, it is only just to give them credit for doing so on grounds which we should recognize as valid, if their premises were true. It is not so much that our opponents (at least the better part of them) despise women, as that they really prize what women now are in the home and in society so highly that they cannot bear to risk losing it by any serious change in their condition. These fears are futile and faithless, but there is nothing in them to affront us. To remove them, we must not use violent words, for every such violent word confirms their fears; but, on the contrary, show the world that while the revolutions wrought by men have been full of bitterness and rancor and stormy passions, if not of bloodshed, we women will at least strive to accomplish our great emancipation calmly and by persuasion and reason.

From letter to the *Woman's Tribune*, May 1, 1884, quoted in Frances Power Cobbe, *Life of Frances Power Cobbe by Herself*, Vol. 2 (Boston: Houghton Mifflin, 1894), pp. 532–533.

Emmeline Pankhurst (1858–1928) led a different and much more radical branch of British feminists. Pankhurst's husband, who died near the close of the century, had been active in both labor and Irish nationalist politics. Irish nationalists had developed numerous disruptive political tactics. Early labor politicians had also sometimes had confrontations with police over the right to hold meetings. In 1903, Pankhurst and her daughters, Christabel and Sylvia, founded the Women's Social and Political Union. For several years they and their followers, known derisively as **suffragettes,** lobbied publicly and privately for the extension of the vote to women. By 1910, having failed to move the government, they turned to the violent tactics of arson, breaking windows, and sabotage of postal boxes. They marched en masse on Parliament. The Liberal government of Herbert Asquith imprisoned many of the demonstrators and force-fed those who went on hunger strikes in jail. The government refused to extend the franchise. Only in 1918, and then as a result of their contribution to the war effort, did some British women receive the vote.

Political Feminism on the Continent The contrast between the women's movement in Britain and those in France and Germany shows how advanced the British women's movement was. In France, when Hubertine Auclert (1848–1914) began campaigning for the vote in the 1880s, she stood virtually alone. During the 1890s, several women's organizations emerged. In 1901, the National Council of French Women (CNFF) was organized among upper-middle-class women, but it did not support

Emmeline Pankhurst (1857–1928) was frequently arrested for forcibly advocating votes for British women. Getty Images Inc.—Hulton Archive Photos

the vote for women for several years. French Roman Catholic feminists such as Marie Mauguet (1844–1928) supported the franchise. Almost all French feminists, however, rejected any form of violence. They also were never able to organize mass rallies. The leaders of French feminism believed the vote could be achieved through careful legalism. In 1919, the French Chamber of Deputies passed a bill granting the vote to women, but in 1922, the French Senate defeated the bill. It was not until after World War II that French women received the right to vote.

In Germany, feminist awareness and action were even more underdeveloped. German law actually forbade German women from political activity. Because no group in the German Empire enjoyed extensive political rights, women were not certain they would benefit from demanding them. Any such demand would be regarded as subversive not only of the state, but also of society.

In 1894, the Union of German Women's Organizations (BDFK) was founded. By 1902, it was supporting a call for the right to vote. But it was largely concerned with improving women's social conditions, their access to education, and their right to other protections. The group also tried to gain women's admittance to political or civic activity on the municipal level. Its work usually included education, child welfare, charity, and public health. The German Social Democratic Party supported women's suffrage, but that socialist party was so disdained by the German authorities and German Roman Catholics, that its support served only to make suffrage more suspect in their eyes. Women received the vote in Germany only in 1919, when the constitution of the Weimar Republic was promulgated after German defeat in war and revolution at home.

Throughout Europe in the years before World War I, women demanded rights widely and vocally. The tactics they used and the success they achieved, however, varied from country to country depending on political and class structures. Before World War I, only in Norway (1907) could women vote on national issues.

Jewish Emancipation

The emancipation of European Jews from the narrow life of the ghetto into a world of equal or nearly equal citizenship and social status was a major accomplishment of political liberalism and had an enduring impact on European life. The process of emancipation, slow and never fully completed, began in the late eighteenth century and continued throughout the nineteenth. It moved at different paces in different countries.

DIFFERING DEGREES OF CITIZENSHIP

In 1782, Joseph II, the Habsburg emperor, issued a decree that placed the Jews of his empire under more or less the same laws as Christians. In France, the National Assembly recognized Jews as French citizens in 1789. During the turmoil of the Napoleonic wars, Jewish communities in Italy and Germany were allowed to mix on a generally equal footing with the Christian population. These various steps toward political emancipation were always somewhat uncertain and were frequently limited or partially repealed with changes in rulers or governments. Certain freedoms were granted, only to be partially withdrawn later. Even in countries that had advanced Jews some political rights, they could not own land and could be subject to special discriminatory taxes. Nonetheless, during the first half of the century, European Jews in western Europe, and to a much lesser extent in central and eastern Europe, began to gain significant rights that brought them equal or more nearly equal citizenship.

In Russia, and in Poland under Russian rule, the traditional modes of prejudice and discrimination continued unabated until World War I. Jews were treated as aliens under Russian rule. The government undermined Jewish community life, limited the publication of Jewish books, restricted areas where Jews might live, required internal passports from Jews, banned Jews from many forms of state service, and excluded Jews from many institutions of higher education. The police and others were allowed to conduct *pogroms*—organized riots—against Jewish neighborhoods and villages.

The era of Jewish emancipation allowed European Jews more freedom and a wider recognition of their faith and culture. This painting by G. E. Opitz portrays the dedication of a new synagogue in Alsace in 1820. Jewish Museum, N.Y./Art Resource, N.Y.

BROADENED OPPORTUNITIES

After the revolutions of 1848, European Jews saw a general improvement in their situation that lasted for several decades. In Germany, Italy, the Low Countries, and Scandinavia, Jews attained full rights of citizenship. After 1858, Jews in Great Britain could sit in Parliament. Austria-Hungary extended full legal rights to Jews in 1867. Indeed, from about 1850 to 1880, relatively little organized or overt prejudice was expressed against Jews. They entered the professions and other occupations once closed to them. They participated fully in the literary and cultural life of their nations. They were active in the arts and music. They became leaders in science and education. Jews intermarried freely with non-Jews as legal secular prohibitions against such marriages were repealed during the last quarter of the century.

Outside of Russia, Jewish political figures entered cabinets and served in the highest offices of the state. Politically, they often were aligned with liberal parties because these groups had championed equal rights. Later in the century, especially in eastern Europe, many Jews became associated with socialist parties.

The prejudice that had been associated with Christian religious attitudes toward Jews seemed for a time to have dissipated, although it still appeared in Russia and other parts of eastern Europe. Hundreds of thousands of European Jews migrated from these regions to western Europe and the United States. Almost anywhere in Europe, Jews might encounter prejudice on a personal level. But in western Europe, including England, France, Italy, Germany, and the Low Countries, Jews felt fairly secure from the legalized persecution and discrimination that had so haunted them in the past.

That newfound security began to erode during the last two decades of the nineteenth century. Anti-Semitic voices began to be heard in the 1870s, attributing the economic stagnation of the decade to Jewish bankers and financial interests. In the 1880s, organized **anti-Semitism** erupted in Germany, as it did in France at the time of the Dreyfus affair. As we will see in the next chapter, these developments gave rise to the birth of Zionism, initially a minority movement within the Jewish community. Most Jewish leaders believed the attacks on Jewish life were merely temporary recurrences of older forms of prejudice; they felt their communities would remain safe under the liberal legal protections that had been extended during the century. That analysis would be proved disastrously wrong in the 1930s and 1940s.

Labor, Socialism, and Politics to World War I

The late-century industrial expansion wrought further changes in the life of the labor force. In all industrializing continental countries, the numbers of the urban proletariat rose. The proportion of artisans and highly skilled workers declined, and for the first time factory wage earners predominated. The number of people engaged in unskilled work associated with shipping, transportation, and building also grew considerably.

Workers still had to look to themselves to improve their lot. After 1848, however, European workers stopped rioting in the streets to voice their grievances. They also stopped trying to revive the paternal guilds and similar institutions of the past. After midcentury, workers turned to new institutions and ideologies. Chief among these were trade unions, democratic political parties, and socialism.

TRADE UNIONISM

Trade unionism came of age as governments extended legal protections to unions during the second half of the century. Unions became fully legal in Great Britain in 1871 and were allowed to picket in 1875. In France, Napoleon III at first used troops against strikes, but as his political power waned, he allowed weak labor associations in 1868. The Third French Republic fully legalized unions in 1884. In Germany, unions were permitted to function with little disturbance after 1890. Union participation in the political process was at first marginal. As long as the representatives of the traditional governing classes looked after labor interests, members of the working class rarely sought office themselves.

Unions directed their midcentury organizational efforts toward skilled workers and the immediate improvement of wages and working conditions. By the close of the century, industrial unions for unskilled workers were being organized. With thousands of workers, these large unions met intense opposition from employers. They frequently had to engage in long strikes to convince employers to accept their demands. Europe suffered a rash of strikes in the prewar decade as unions sought to keep wages in line with inflation. Despite union advances, however, and the growth of union membership (in 1910 to approximately 3 million in Britain, 2 million in Germany, and 977,000 in France), most of Europe's labor force was never unionized in this period. What the unions did represent for workers was a new collective form of association for confronting economic difficulties and improving security.

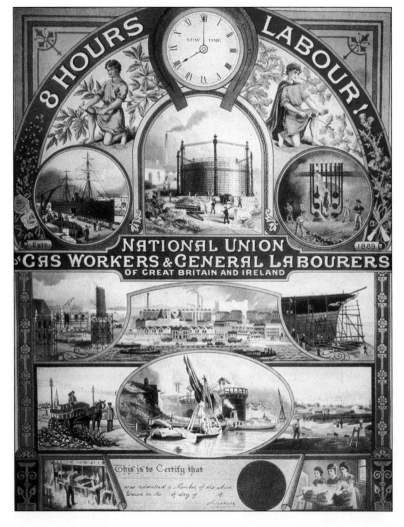

Trade unions continued to grow in late-century Great Britain. The effort to curb the unions eventually led to the formation of the Labour Party. The British unions often had quite elaborate membership certificates, such as this one for the National Union of Gas Workers and General Labourers of Great Britain and Ireland.
The Granger Collection

DEMOCRACY AND POLITICAL PARTIES

Except for Russia, all the major European states adopted broad-based, if not perfectly democratic, electoral systems in the late nineteenth century. Great Britain passed its second voting reform act in 1867 and its third in 1884. Bismarck brought universal male suffrage to the German Empire in 1871. The French Chamber of Deputies was democratically elected. Universal male suffrage was adopted in Switzerland in 1879, in Spain in 1890, in Belgium in 1893, in the Netherlands in 1896, and in Norway in 1898. Italy finally fell into line in 1912. The broadened franchise meant politicians could no longer ignore workers and discontented groups could now voice their grievances and advocate their programs within the institutions of government rather than from the outside.

The advent of democracy brought organized mass political parties like those already in existence in the United States to Europe for the first time. In the liberal European states with narrow electoral bases, most voters had been people of property who knew what they had at stake in politics. Organization had been minimal. The expansion of the electorate brought into the political process many people whose level of political consciousness, awareness, and interest was quite low. This electorate had to be organized and taught the nature of power and influence in the liberal democratic state.

The organized political party—with its workers, newspapers, offices, social life, and discipline—was the vehicle that mobilized the new voters. The largest single group in these mass electorates was the working class. The democratization of politics presented the socialists with opportunities and required the traditional ruling classes to vie with the socialists for the support of the new voters.

During these years, socialism as a political ideology and plan of action opposed nationalism. The problems of class were supposed to be transnational, and socialism was supposed to unite the working classes across national borders. European socialists, however, badly underestimated the emotional drawing power of nationalism. Many workers had both socialist and nationalist sympathies, which were rarely in conflict with each other. When the outbreak of war in 1914 did bring them into conflict, however, nationalist feelings prevailed.

The major question for late-century socialist parties throughout Europe was whether the improvement of the lot of the working class would come about through revolution or democratic reform. This question sharply divided all socialist parties and most especially those whose leadership adhered to the intellectual legacy of Karl Marx.

KARL MARX AND THE FIRST INTERNATIONAL

Karl Marx himself made considerable accommodation to the new practical realities that developed during the third quarter of the century. Although he continued to predict the disintegration of capitalism, his practical, public political activity reflected a somewhat different approach.

In 1864, a group of British and French trade unionists founded the International Working Men's Association. Known as the First International, its membership encompassed a vast array of radical political types, including socialists, anarchists, and Polish nationalists. In the inaugural address for the International, Marx supported and approved efforts by workers and trade unions to reform the conditions of labor within the existing political and economic processes. In his private writings he often criticized such reformist activity, but these writings were not made public until near the end of the century, years after his death.

The violence involved in the rise and suppression of the Paris Commune (see Chapter 23), which Marx had declared a genuine proletarian uprising, cast a pall over socialism throughout Europe. British trade unionists, who received legal protections in 1871, wanted no connection with the events in Paris. The French authorities used the uprising to suppress socialist activity. Under these pressures, the First International held its last European congress in 1873. It soon transferred its offices to the United States, where it was dissolved in 1876.

The short-lived First International had a disproportionately great impact on the future of European socialism. Throughout the late 1860s, the organization had gathered statistics, kept labor groups informed of mutual problems, provided a forum for the debate of socialist doctrine, and extravagantly proclaimed its own influence over contemporary events. From these debates and activities, Marxism emerged as the single most important strand of socialism. Marx and his supporters defeated or drove out anarchists and advocates of other forms of socialism. The apparently scientific character of Marxism made it attractive, science being more influential than at any previous time in European history. German socialists, who were to establish the most powerful socialist party in Europe, were deeply impressed by Marx's thought and were the chief vehicle for preserving and developing it. The full development of German socialism also, however, involved the influence of non-Marxist socialists in Great Britain.

GREAT BRITAIN: FABIANISM AND EARLY WELFARE PROGRAMS

Neither Marxism nor any other form of socialism made significant progress in Great Britain, the most advanced industrial society of the day. There trade unions grew steadily, and their members normally supported Liberal Party candidates. The "new unionism" of the late 1880s and the 1890s organized the dockworkers, the gas workers, and similar unskilled groups. In 1892, Keir Hardie became the first independent working man to be elected to Parliament, but the small socialist Independent Labour Party founded a year later remained ineffective. Until 1901, general political activity on the part of labor remained quite limited. In that year, however, the House of Lords, through the Taff Vale decision, removed the legal protection previously accorded union funds. The Trades Union Congress responded by launching the Labour Party. In the election of 1906, the fledgling party sent twenty-nine members to Parliament. Their goals as trade unionists, however, did not yet include socialism. In this same period, the British labor movement became more militant. In scores of strikes before the war, workers fought for wages to meet the rising cost of living. The government took a larger role than ever before in mediating these strikes, which in 1911 and 1912 involved the railways, the docks, and the mines.

British socialism itself remained primarily the preserve of non-Marxist intellectuals. The **Fabian** Society, founded in 1884, was Britain's most influential socialist group. The society took its name from Q. Fabius Maximus, the Roman general whose tactics against Hannibal involved avoiding direct conflict that might lead to defeat. The name reflected the society's gradualist approach to major social reform. Its leading members were Sidney Webb (1859–1947) and Beatrice Webb (1858–1943), H. G. Wells (1866–1946), Graham Wallas (1858–1932), and George Bernard Shaw (1856–1950). Many Fabians were civil servants who believed the problems of industry, the expansion of ownership, and state direction of production could be achieved gradually, peacefully, and democratically. They sought to educate the country about the rational wisdom of socialism. They were particularly interested in modes of collective ownership on the municipal level, the so-called gas-and-water socialism.

The British government and the major political parties responded slowly to these various pressures. In 1903, Joseph Chamberlain (1836–1914) launched his unsuccessful campaign to match foreign tariffs and to finance social reform through higher import duties. The campaign badly split the Conservative

Party. After 1906, the Liberal Party, led by Sir Henry Campbell-Bannerman (1836–1908) and, after 1908, by Herbert Asquith (1852–1928), pursued a two-pronged policy. Fearful of losing seats in Parliament to the new Labour Party, they restored the former protection of the unions. Then, after 1909, with Chancellor of the Exchequer David Lloyd George (1863–1945) as its guiding light, the Liberal ministry undertook a broad program of social legislation that included the establishment of labor exchanges, the regulation of certain trades, such as tailoring and lace making, and the passage of the National Insurance Act of 1911, which provided unemployment benefits and health care.

The financing of these programs brought the House of Commons into conflict with the Conservative-dominated House of Lords. The result was the Parliament Act of 1911, which allowed the Commons to override the legislative veto of the upper chamber. The new taxes and social programs meant that in Britain, the home of nineteenth-century liberalism, the state was taking on an expanded role in the life of its citizens. The early welfare legislation was only marginally satisfactory to labor, many of whose members still thought they could gain more from the direct action of strikes.

FRANCE: "OPPORTUNISM" REJECTED

At the turn of the century, Jean Jaurès (1859–1914) and Jules Guesde (1845–1922) led the two major factions of French socialists. Jaurès believed socialists should cooperate with middle-class Radical ministries to ensure the enactment of needed social legislation. Guesde opposed this policy, arguing that socialists could not, with integrity, support a bourgeois cabinet they were theoretically dedicated to overthrow. The government's response to the Dreyfus affair brought the quarrel to a head. In 1899, seeking to unite all supporters of Dreyfus, Prime Minister René Waldeck-Rousseau (1846–1904) appointed the socialist Alexander Millerand (1859–1943) to the cabinet.

The Second International had been founded in 1889 in a new effort to unify the various national socialist parties and trade unions. By 1904, the Amsterdam Congress of the Second International debated the issue of *opportunism*, as such cabinet participation by socialists was termed. The Congress condemned opportunism in France and ordered French socialists to form a single party. Jaurès accepted the decision. Thereafter French socialists began to work together, and by 1914 the recently united Socialist Party had become the second largest group in the Chamber of Deputies. But Socialist Party members would not again serve in a French cabinet until the Popular Front Government of 1936.

The French labor movement, with deep roots in anarchism, was uninterested in either politics or socialism. French workers usually voted socialist, but the unions themselves, unlike those in Great Britain, avoided active political participation. The Confédération Générale du Travail, founded in 1895, regarded itself as a rival to the socialist parties. Its leaders sought to improve the workers' conditions through direct action. They embraced the doctrines of syndicalism, which had been most persuasively expounded by Georges Sorel (1847–1922) in *Reflections on Violence* (1908). This book enshrined the general strike as a device for generating worker unity and power. The strike tactic often conflicted with the socialist belief in aiding labor through state action. Strikes were common between 1905 and 1914, and the middle-class Radical ministry used troops to suppress them on more than one occasion.

GERMANY: SOCIAL DEMOCRATS AND REVISIONISM

The negative judgment rendered by the Second International against French socialist participation in bourgeois ministries reflected a policy of permanent hostility to nonsocialist governments previously adopted by the German Social Democratic Party, or SPD. The organizational success of this party, more than any other single factor, kept Marxist socialism alive during the late nineteenth and early twentieth centuries.

The SDP had been founded in 1875. Its origins lay in the labor agitation of Ferdinand Lasalle (1825–1864), who sought worker participation in German politics. Wilhelm Liebknecht (1826–1900) and August Bebel (1840–1913), who were Marxists and opposed reformist politics, soon joined the party. Thus, from its founding, the SPD was divided between those who advocated reform and those who advocated revolution.

Bismarck's Repression of the SPD Twelve years of persecution under Bismarck forged the character of the SPD. The so-called Iron Chancellor believed socialism would undermine German politics and society. He used an assassination attempt on William I in 1878, in which the socialists were not involved, to steer several antisocialist laws through the *Reichstag*. The measures suppressed the organization, meetings, newspapers, and other public activities of the SPD. Thereafter, to remain a socialist meant to remove oneself from the mainstream of respectable German life and possibly to lose one's

job. The antisocialist legislation proved politically counterproductive. From the early 1880s onward, the SPD steadily polled more and more votes in elections to the *Reichstag.*

As simple repression failed to isolate German workers from socialist loyalties, Bismarck undertook a program of social welfare legislation. In 1883, the German Empire adopted a health insurance measure. The next year saw the enactment of accident insurance legislation. Finally, in 1889, Bismarck sponsored a plan for old age and disability pensions. These programs, to which both workers and employers contributed, represented a paternalistic, conservative alternative to socialism. The state itself would organize a system of social security that did not require any change in the system of property holding or politics. Germany became the first major industrial nation to enjoy this kind of welfare program.

The Erfurt Program After forcing Bismarck's resignation, Emperor William II (r. 1888–1918) allowed the antisocialist legislation to expire, hoping to build new political support among the working class. Even under the repressive laws, members of the SPD could sit in the *Reichstag*. With the repressive measures lifted, the party needed to decide what attitude to assume toward the German Empire.

The answer came in the Erfurt Program of 1891, formulated under the political guidance of Bebel and the ideological tutelage of Karl Kautsky (1854–1938). In good Marxist fashion, the program declared the imminent doom of capitalism and the necessity of socialist ownership of the means of production. The party intended to pursue these goals through legal political participation rather than by revolutionary activity. Kautsky argued that because capitalism by its very nature must collapse, the immediate task for socialists was to work for the improvement of workers' lives rather than for the revolution, which was inevitable. So, although in theory the SPD was vehemently hostile to the German Empire, in practice the party functioned within its institutions. The SPD members of the *Reichstag* maintained clear political consciences by refusing to enter the cabinet (to which they were not invited anyway) and by refraining for many years from voting in favor of the military budget.

The Debate over Revisionism The dilemma of the SPD, however, generated the most important challenge within the socialist movement to the orthodox Marxist analysis of capitalism and the socialist revolution. The author of this socialist heresy, Eduard Bernstein (1850–1932), had spent over a decade of his life in Great Britain and was familiar with the

Fabians. Bernstein questioned whether Marx and his later orthodox followers, such as Kautsky, had been correct in their pessimistic appraisal of capitalism and the necessity of revolution. In *Evolutionary Socialism* (1899), Bernstein pointed to conditions that did not meet orthodox Marxists' expectations. The standard of living was on the rise in Europe. Ownership of capitalist industry was becoming more widespread through stockholding. The middle class was not falling into the ranks of the proletariat and was not identifying its problems with those of the workers. The inner contradictions of capitalism as expounded by Marx had simply not developed. Moreover, the extension of the franchise to the working class meant that parliamentary methods might achieve revolutionary social change. For Bernstein, social reform through democratic institutions replaced revolution as the path to a humane socialist society. (See "Eduard Bernstein Criticizes Orthodox Marxism.")

Bernstein's doctrines, known as **Revisionism,** generated heated debate among German socialists, who finally condemned them. His critics argued that evolution toward social democracy might be possible in liberal, parliamentary Britain, but not in authoritarian, militaristic Germany, with its basically powerless *Reichstag*. Nonetheless, while still calling for revolution, the SPD pursued a course of action similar to that advocated by Bernstein. Its trade union members, prospering within the German economy, did not want revolution. Its grassroots members wanted to consider themselves patriotic Germans as well as good socialists. Its leaders feared any actions that might renew the persecution they had experienced under Bismarck.

Consequently, the SPD worked for electoral gains, expansion of its membership, and short-term political and social reform. It prospered and became one of the most important institutions of imperial Germany. Even some middle-class Germans voted for it as a way to oppose the illiberal institutions of the empire. And in August 1914, after long debate among themselves, the SPD members of the *Reichstag* abandoned their former practice and unanimously voted for the war credits that would finance Germany's participation in World War I.

RUSSIA: INDUSTRIAL DEVELOPMENT AND THE BIRTH OF BOLSHEVISM

During the last decade of the nineteenth century, Russia entered the industrial age and confronted many of the problems that the more advanced nations of the Continent had experienced fifty or seventy-five years earlier. Unlike those other countries, Russia had to deal with major political discontent and economic development simultaneously. Russian socialism reflected that peculiar situation.

Witte's Program for Industrial Growth Alexander III (r. 1881–1894) and, after him, Nicholas II (r. 1894–1917) were determined that Russia should become an industrial power. Only by doing so, they believed, could the country maintain its European military position and diplomatic role. It was Sergei Witte (1849–1915) who led Russia into the industrial age. After a career in railways and other private business, he was appointed finance minister in 1892. Witte, who pursued a policy of planned economic development, protective tariffs, high taxes, the gold standard, and efficiency, epitomized the nineteenth-century modernizer. He established strong financial relationships with the French money market, which later led to diplomatic cooperation between Russia and France.

Witte favored heavy industries. Between 1890 and 1904, the Russian railway system grew from 30,596 to 59,616 kilometers. The 5,000-mile Trans-Siberian Railroad was almost completed. Coal output more than tripled during the same period. There was a vast increase in pig-iron production, from 928,000 tons in 1890 to 4,641,000 tons in 1913. During the same period, steel production rose from 378,000 to 4,918,000 tons. Textile manufacturing continued to expand and was still the single largest industry. The factory system began to be used more extensively throughout the country.

Industrialism brought considerable social discontent to Russia, as it had elsewhere. Landowners felt that foreign capitalists were earning too much of the profit. The peasants saw their grain exports and tax payments finance development that did not measurably improve their lives. A small, but significant, industrial proletariat emerged. At the turn of the century, there were approximately 3 million factory workers in Russia. Their working and living conditions were poor by any standard. They enjoyed little state protection, and trade unions were illegal. In 1897, Witte did enact a measure providing for an 11.5-hour workday. But needless to say, discontent and strikes continued.

Similar social and economic problems arose in the countryside. Russian agriculture had not prospered after the emancipation of the serfs in 1861. The peasants remained burdened with redemption payments, local taxes, excessive national taxes, and falling grain prices. Free peasants owned their land communally through the *mir*, or village. They farmed the land inefficiently through strip farming or the tilling of small plots. Many free peasants with too little land to support their families had to work on larger noble estates or for more prosperous

EDUARD BERNSTEIN CRITICIZES ORTHODOX MARXISM

Eduard Bernstein was responsible for the emergence of Revisionism within the German Social Democratic Party. He was a dedicated socialist who recognized the Communist Manifesto *(1848) had not predicted the actual future of the European working classes. He believed there would be no sudden collapse or catastrophe in the capitalist system and that socialists should change their tactics to work to achieve political rights and pursue reform instead of revolution.*

■ *According to Bernstein, what specific predictions in the* Communist Manifesto *failed to materialize? Why is the advance of democracy important to his argument? Why does he see the extension of political rights to German workers as so important?*

I set myself against the notion that we have to expect shortly a collapse of the bourgeois economy, and that social democracy should be induced by the prospect of such an imminent, great, social catastrophe to adapt its tactics to that assumption. . . .

The adherents of this theory of a catastrophe, base it especially on the conclusion of the *Communist Manifesto.* This is a mistake in every respect. . . .

Social conditions have not developed to such an acute opposition of things and classes as is depicted in the *Manifesto.* . . . The number of members of the possessing classes is to-day not smaller but larger. The enormous increase of social wealth is not accompanied by a decreasing number of large capitalists but by an increasing number of capitalists of all degrees. . . .

In all advanced countries we see the privileges of the capitalist bourgeoisie yielding step by step to democratic organizations. . . . Factory legislation, the democratizing of local government, and the extension of its area of work, the freeing of trade unions and systems of co-operative trading from legal restrictions, the consideration of standard conditions of labour in the work undertaken by public authorities—all these characterize this phase of the evolution. . . .

The conquest of political power by the working classes, the expropriation of capitalists, are not ends in themselves but only means for the accomplishment of certain aims and endeavours. As such they are demands in the program of social democracy. . . . Nothing can be said beforehand as to the circumstances of their accomplishment; we can only fight for their realization. But the conquest of political power necessitates the possession of political rights; and the most important problem of tactics which German social democracy has at the present time to solve, appears to me to be to devise the best ways for the extension of the political and economic rights of the German working classes.

From Eduard Bernstein, *Evolutionary Socialism: A Criticism and Affirmation, 1899* (New York: Schocken Books, 1961), pp. xxiv–xxvi, xxix–xxx.

peasant farmers, known as **kulaks.** Between 1860 and 1914, the population of European Russia rose from about 50 million to around 103 million people. Land hunger and discontent spread among the peasants and sparked frequent uprisings in the countryside.

New political developments accompanied economic changes. The membership and intellectual roots of the Social Revolutionary Party, founded in 1901, reached back to the Populists of the 1870s. The new party opposed industrialism and looked to the communal life of rural Russia as a model for the future. In 1903, the Constitutional Democratic Party, or Cadets, was formed. This liberal party drew its members from those who participated in local councils called **zemstvos.** Modeling themselves on the liberal parties of western Europe, the Cadets wanted a parliamentary regime with ministries responsible to a parliament, civil liberties, and economic progress.

Lenin's Early Thought and Career The situation of Russian socialists differed radically from that of socialists in other major European countries. Russia had no representative institutions and only a small working class. The compromises and accommodations achieved elsewhere were meaningless in Russia, where socialists believed that in both theory

In this photograph taken in 1895, Lenin sits at the table among a group of other young Russian radicals from Saint Petersburg. Corbis

and practice they must be revolutionary. The repressive policies of the tsarist regime required the Russian Social Democratic Party, founded in 1898, to function in exile. The party members greatly admired the German Social Democratic Party and adopted its Marxist ideology.

The leading late-nineteenth-century Russian Marxist was Gregory Plekhanov (1857–1918), who wrote from exile in Switzerland. At the turn of the century, his chief disciple was Vladimir Ilyich Ulyanov (1870–1924), who later took the name of Lenin. The future leader of the communist revolution was the son of a high bureaucrat. His older brother, while a student in Saint Petersburg, had become involved in radical politics; arrested for participating in a plot against Alexander III, he was executed in 1887. In 1893, Lenin moved to Saint Petersburg, where he studied law. Soon he, too, was drawn to the revolutionary groups among the factory workers. He was arrested in 1895 and exiled to Siberia. In 1900, after his release, Lenin left Russia for the West. He spent most of the next seventeen years in Switzerland.

In Switzerland, Lenin became deeply involved in the disputes of the exiled Russian Social Democrats. They all considered themselves Marxists, but they differed on what a Marxist revolution meant for primarily rural Russia and on how to structure their own party. Unlike the backward-looking Social Revolutionaries, the Social Democrats were modernizers who favored further industrial development. The majority believed Russia must develop a large proletariat before the revolution could come. They also hoped to build a mass political party like the German SPD.

Lenin dissented from both positions. In *What Is to Be Done?* (1902), he condemned any accommodations, such as those practiced by the German SPD. He also criticized trade unionism that settled for short-term gains rather than true revolutionary change for the working class. Lenin further rejected the concept of a mass democratic party composed of workers. He declared that revolutionary consciousness would not arise spontaneously from the working class. Rather, "people who make revolutionary activity their profession" must carry that consciousness to the workers.[2] Only a small, tightly organized, elite party could possess the proper dedication to revolution and prove able to resist penetration by police spies. The guiding principle of that party should be "the strictest secrecy, the strictest selection of members, and the training of professional revolutionaries."[3] Within the context of turn-of-the-century European socialist debates, Lenin thus rejected both Kautsky's view that revolution was inevitable and Bernstein's view that it would arrive democratically. Lenin substituted the small, professional, nondemocratic revolutionary party for Marx's proletariat as the instrument of revolutionary change. (See "Lenin Argues for the Necessity of a Secret and Elite Party of Professional Revolutionaries.")

In 1903, at the London Congress of the Russian Social Democratic Party, Lenin forced a split in the party ranks. During much of the congress, he and

[2]Quoted in Albert Fried and Ronald Sanders, eds., *Socialist Thought: A Documentary History* (Garden City, NY: Anchor Doubleday, 1964), p. 459.

[3]Fried and Sanders, p. 468.

LENIN ARGUES FOR THE NECESSITY OF A SECRET AND ELITE PARTY OF PROFESSIONAL REVOLUTIONARIES

Social democratic parties in western Europe had mass memberships and generally democratic structures of organization. In this passage from What Is to Be Done? *(1902), Lenin explains why the autocratic political conditions of Russia demanded a different kind of organization for the Russian Social Democratic Party. Lenin's ideas became the guiding principles of Bolshevik organization.*

■ *What does Lenin mean by "professional revolutionaries"? Why are such revolutionaries especially needed in Russia? How does Lenin reconcile his antidemocratic views to the goal of aiding the working class?*

I assert that it is far more difficult [for government police] to unearth a dozen wise men than a hundred fools. This position I will defend, no matter how much you instigate the masses against me for my "anti-democratic" views, etc. As I have stated repeatedly, by "wise men," in connection with organization, I mean professional revolutionaries, irrespective of whether they have developed from among students or working men. I assert: (1) that no revolutionary movement can endure without a stable organization of leaders maintaining continuity; (2) that the broader the popular mass drawn spontaneously into the struggle, which forms the basis of the movement and participates in it, the more urgent the need for such an organization, and the more solid this organization must be . . .; (3) that

such an organization must consist chiefly of people professionally engaged in revolutionary activity; (4) that in an autocratic state [such as Russia], the more we confine the membership of such an organization to people who are professionally engaged in revolutionary activity and who have been professionally trained in the art of combating the political police, the more difficult will it be to unearth the organization; and (5) the greater will be the number of people from the working class and from other social classes who will be able to join the movement and perform active work in it. . . .

The only serious organization principle for the active workers of our movement should be the strictest secrecy, the strictest selection of members, and the training of professional revolutionaries.

From Albert Fried and Ronald Sanders, eds., *Socialist Thought: A Documentary History* (Garden City, NY: Anchor Doubleday, 1964), pp. 460, 468.

---

his followers lost many votes on questions put before the body, but near the close they mustered a slim majority. Thereafter Lenin's faction assumed the name **Bolsheviks,** meaning "majority," and the other, more moderate, democratic revolutionary faction came to be known as the **Mensheviks,** or "minority." There was, of course, a considerable public relations advantage to the name *Bolshevik.* (In 1912, the Bolsheviks organized separately.)

A fundamental organizational difference had existed between what in 1903 were the two chief factions of the Russian Social Democratic Party. The Mensheviks wanted a party with a large mass membership, similar to the German SDP and other west European socialist parties, which would function democratically. The Bolsheviks intended the party to consist of elite professional revolutionaries who would provide centralized leadership for the

working class. Lenin believed a mass party functioning in a democratic fashion would seek only to reform workers' wages, hours, and living conditions, whereas he was intent on a revolution that would transform Russia.

In 1905, Lenin complemented his organizational theory with a program for revolution in Russia. In *Two Tactics of Social Democracy in the Bourgeois-Democratic Revolution*, he urged the socialist revolution to unite the proletariat and the peasantry. Lenin grasped better than any other revolutionary the profound discontent in the Russian countryside. He believed the tsarist government probably could not suppress an alliance of workers and peasants in rebellion.

Lenin's two principles—an elite party and a dual social revolution—guided later Bolshevik activity. The Bolsheviks ultimately seized power in

Major Dates in the Development of Socialism

1864	International Working Men's Association (the First International) founded
1875	German Social Democratic Party founded
1876	First International dissolved
1878	German antisocialist laws passed
1884	British Fabian Society founded
1889	Second International founded
1891	German antisocialist laws permitted to expire
1891	German Social Democratic Party's Erfurt Program
1895	French Confédération Générale du Travail founded
1899	Eduard Bernstein's *Evolutionary Socialism*
1902	Formation of the British Labour party
1902	Lenin's *What Is to Be Done?*
1903	Bolshevik-Menshevik split
1904	"Opportunism" debated at the Amsterdam Congress of the Second International

November 1917, transforming the political landscape of the modern world. But they did so only after the turmoil of World War I had undermined support for the tsar and only after other political forces had toppled the tsarist government earlier in 1917. Prior to World War I, the Bolsheviks constituted the odd man out in European socialist politics; they exerted no significant prewar influence on members of other socialist groups, who, in general, ignored them. For their part, the Bolsheviks responded by scorning the west European socialist parties that worked within their nations' political systems. Between 1900 and the outbreak of World War I, the government of Nicholas II managed to confront political upheaval more or less successfully.

The Revolution of 1905 and Its Aftermath The quarrels among the exiled Russian socialists and Lenin's doctrines had no immediate influence on events in Russia. Industrialization proceeded and continued to stir resentment in many sectors. In 1903, Nicholas II dismissed Witte, hoping to quell the criticism. The next year Russia went to war against Japan, partly in hopes the conflict would rally public opinion to the tsar. Instead, the Russians lost the war and the government faced an internal political crisis. The Japanese captured Port Arthur early in 1905. A few days later, on January 22, a priest named Father Gapon led several hundred workers to present a petition to the tsar for the improvement of industrial conditions. As the petitioners approached the Winter Palace in Saint Petersburg, the tsar's troops opened fire, killing approximately 40 people and wounding hundreds of others. As word of this massacre spread and large crowds gathered elsewhere in the city preparing to march on the tsar's Winter Palace, the military shot more people. The final death toll is estimated at approximately 200 killed and 800 wounded, though at the time rumors made the numbers much larger. The day, soon known as Bloody Sunday, marked a

On Bloody Sunday, January 22, 1905, troops of Tsar Nicholas II fired on a peaceful procession of workers who sought to present a petition at the Winter Palace in Saint Petersburg. After this event, there was little chance of reconciliation between the tsarist government and the Russian working class.
Bildarchiv Preussischer Kulturbesitz

TWO EXAMPLES OF RUSSIAN SOCIAL AND POLITICAL PROTEST: 1906

The Revolution of 1905 in Russia and the calling of a Duma unleashed more open, public political activity than ever before in Russian history. It was a time of enormous expectations for both social and political reform. Following are two political manifestos of the day. The first is a call for the union organization of Plumbers' Apprentices. The second is the introduction to a much longer document outlining the goals of the Women's Progressive Party. In both selections, observe the strident rhetoric of protest that then gives way to statements of goals which combine the political ideas of the French Revolution and the language of reform rather than outright revolution. Such was characteristic of many of the Russian political groups of 1905 and 1906, who believed such programs of advanced reform could solve the nation's problems. In the Russian context, these were radical proposals, but they were, of course, moderate compared to the Bolshevik revolution that erupted in 1917.

■ *To what conditions of employment do the advocates of the plumbers' union appeal to gain members? How much do their complaints relate to working conditions and how much to their economic situation? About what specific legal and social disabilities does the Women's Progressive Party protest? What political values and outlooks do the union and the party share? How do they differ?*

A. PROCLAMATION OF THE UNION OF PLUMBERS' APPRENTICES, JANUARY 1906

Comrade Plumbers!

Your condition is unbearably onerous. Your wages, compared to the inflation of prices, are so insignificant that every worker is doomed to slow death by starvation. . . . You work in stifling, disgustingly filthy shops, in stinking manholes, underground and in water, out in the frost (where your feet even freeze in your boots)—wherever there are dirty, harmful places, where your weak strength is quickly drained and you are overcome by every kind of disease, which quickly carries you to a premature death . . . the slightest caprice of the proprietor or foreman—and you workers are mercilessly thrown into the street, into famine, into the cold in penury. . . . But there is a way out of this terrible condition. Though powerless as individuals, you can make yourself into a great power by joining together in a union of plumber-workers. This union sets as its goal the organization and defense of the proletariat in order to form a unified family of workers, aimed at one and the same goal: the pursuit, for each Russian worker, of the right of man and citizen, and a striving for final victory of living human labor over a soulless capitalism.

B. PROGRAM OF THE WOMEN'S PROGRESSIVE PARTY, 30 JANUARY 1906

Women are the most rightless, dispossessed part of the population. They find themselves in subordination to men and in complete dependence upon their will. They are deprived of their human personality and enslaved by the existing laws and their economic dependence on the ruling sex. Because of their subordination, economic dependence and lack of rights, women cannot develop all their spiritual abilities and render active assistance to the perfection of mankind (in spiritual and physical respects) and improvement of the social order. Because lack of political rights is one of the main causes of the enslavement of women, the Women's Progressive Party makes its immediate goal the attainment of complete political equality of women with men.

The Women's Progressive Party regards it as necessary to struggle with all the shortcomings of contemporary life and to realize general human ideals: truth, equality, fraternity, freedom, justice and humanitarianism. It holds that realization of these ideals is only possible through a peaceful, evolutionary path.

Major Dates in Turn-of-the-Century Russian History

1892	Witte appointed finance minister
1895	Lenin arrested and sent to Siberia
1897	11.5-hour workday established
1898	Russian Social Democratic Party founded
1900	Lenin leaves Russia for western Europe
1901	Social Revolutionary Party founded
1903	Constitutional Democratic Party (Cadets) founded
1903	Bolshevik-Menshevik split
1903	Witte dismissed
1904	Russo-Japanese War begins
1905 (January)	Japan defeats Russia
1905 (January 22)	Revolution breaks out in Saint Petersburg after Bloody Sunday massacre
1905 (October 20)	General strike
1905 (October 26)	October Manifesto establishes constitutional government
1906 (May 10)	Meeting of first Duma
1906 (June)	Stolypin appointed prime minister
1906 (July 21)	Dissolution of first Duma
1906 (November)	Land redemption payments canceled for peasants
1907 (March 5– June 16)	Second Duma seated and dismissed
1907	Franchise changed and a third Duma elected, which sits until 1912
1911	Stolypin assassinated by a Social Revolutionary
1912	Fourth Duma elected
1914	World War I breaks out

turning point when vast numbers of ordinary Russians came to believe they could no longer trust the tsar or his government.

During the next ten months, revolutionary disturbances spread throughout Russia. Sailors mutinied, peasants revolted, and property was attacked. The uncle of Nicholas II was assassinated. Liberal leaders of the Constitutional Democratic Party from the *zemstvos* demanded political reform. University students went on strike. Social Revolutionaries and Social Democrats agitated among urban working groups. In early October 1905, strikes broke out in Saint Petersburg, and for all practical purposes,

worker groups, called **soviets,** controlled the city. Nicholas II recalled Witte and issued the October Manifesto, which promised Russia constitutional government.

Early in 1906, Nicholas II announced the election of a representative body, the **Duma,** with two chambers. He reserved to himself, however, ministerial appointments, financial policy, and military and foreign affairs. The April elections returned a highly radical group of representatives. (See "Two Examples of Russian Social and Political Protest: 1906.") The tsar then replaced Witte with P. A. Stolypin (1862–1911), who had little sympathy for parliamentary government. Stolypin persuaded Nicholas to dissolve the Duma. A second assembly was elected in February 1907. Again, cooperation proved impossible, and the tsar dissolved that Duma in June. A third Duma, elected in late 1907 on the basis of a more conservative franchise, proved sufficiently pliable for the tsar and his minister. Thus, within two years of the 1905 Revolution, Nicholas II had recaptured much of the ground he had conceded.

Stolypin set about repressing rebellion, removing some causes of the revolt, and rallying property owners behind the tsarist regime. Early in 1907, special field courts-martial condemned almost 700 rebellious peasants to death. Before undertaking this repression, Stolypin, in November 1906, had canceled any redemptive payments that the peasants still owed the government from the emancipation of the serfs in 1861. He took this step to encourage peasants to assume individual proprietorship of their landholdings and to abandon the communal system associated with the *mirs*. Stolypin believed farmers would be more productive working for themselves. Combined with a program to instruct peasants on how to farm more efficiently, this policy improved agricultural production. However, many small-proprietor peasants sold their land and joined the industrial labor force.

The moderate liberals who sat in the Duma approved of the new land measures. They liked the idea of competition and individual property ownership. The Constitutional Democrats wanted a more genuinely parliamentary mode of government, but they compromised out of fear of new revolutionary disturbances. Hatred of Stolypin was still widespread, however, among the country's older conservative groups, and industrial workers remained antagonistic to the tsar. In 1911, Stolypin was assassinated by a Social Revolutionary, who may have been a police agent in the pay of conservatives. Nicholas II found no worthy successor. His government simply muddled along.

Meanwhile, at court, the monk Grigory Efimovich Rasputin (1871?–1916) came into ascendancy because of his alleged power to heal the tsar's hemophilic son, the heir to the throne. The undue influence of this strange, uncouth man, as well as continued social discontent and conservative resistance to any further liberal reforms, undermined the position of the tsar and his government after 1911. Once again, as in 1904, he and his ministers thought that some bold move in foreign policy might bring the regime the popular support it desperately needed.

IN PERSPECTIVE

From 1860 through 1914 two apparently contradictory developments emerged in European social life. On one hand, the lifestyle of the urban middle classes became the model to which much of society aspired. The characteristics of this lifestyle included a relatively small family living in its own house or large apartment, servants, and a wife who did not earn an income. The middle classes in general benefited from the many material comforts that the Second Industrial Revolution generated.

During the same period, the forces of socialism and labor unions assumed a new and major role in European political life. Their leaders demanded greater social justice and a fairer distribution of the vast quantities of consumer goods being produced in Europe. Some socialists sought in one way or another to work within existing political systems. Others—most particularly, those in Russia—advocated revolution. The growth in wealth and the availability of new goods and services magnified the injustices suffered by the poor and the contrast between them and the middle classes, contributing to the stridency of the demands of labor and the socialists. In Russia, the strains of the early stages of industrialization intensified social unrest. These strains, compounded by a humiliating defeat in a war against Japan, triggered the unsuccessful revolution of 1905.

The working class, however, was not alone in seeking change. Women, for the first time in European history, began in significant ways to demand a political role and to protest the gender inequalities embedded in law and family life. They were beginning to enter the professions in small numbers and were taking a significant role in the service economy, such as the new telephone companies. These changes, as much as the demands of socialists, would in time raise questions about the adequacy of the much admired late-nineteenth-century middle-class lifestyle.

REVIEW QUESTIONS

1. How was European society transformed by the Second Industrial Revolution? What new industries developed, and which do you think had the greatest impact in the twentieth century? How do you account for European economic difficulties in the second half of the nineteenth century?

2. How would you describe living conditions in European cities during the late nineteenth century? Why were European cities redesigned during this period? In what ways were they redesigned? Why were housing and health key issues for urban reform? Be specific in your examples.

3. What was the status of European women in the second half of the nineteenth century? Why did they grow discontented with their lot? What factors led to change? To what extent had they improved their position by 1914? What tactics did they use in effecting change? Was the emancipation of women inevitable? How did women approach their situation differently from country to country?

4. What were the major characteristics of Jewish emancipation in the nineteenth century?

5. What was the status of the proletariat in 1860? Had it improved by 1914? What caused the growth in trade unions and organized mass political parties? Why were the debates over "opportunism" and "revisionism" important to the western European socialist parties?

6. What were the benefits and drawbacks of industrialization for Russia? Were the tsars wise to attempt to modernize their country, or should they have left it as it was? How did Lenin's view of socialism differ from that of the socialists in western Europe?

SUGGESTED READINGS

J. ALBISETTI, *Schooling German Girls and Women: Secondary and Higher Education in the Nineteenth Century* (1988). Contains much information on the subject beyond Germany.

H. ANDERSON, *Utopian Feminism: Women's Movements in Fin-de-Siècle Vienna* (1992). Examines movements to improve the status of women in the Austrian Empire.

M. ARONSON, *Troubled Waters: The Origins of the 1881 Anti-Jewish Pogroms in Russia* (1990). The best discussion of this subject.

A. ASCHER AND P. A. STOLYPIN, *The Search for Stability in Late Imperial Russia* (2000). A broad-ranging biography based on extensive research.

P. BIRNBAUM, *Jewish Destinies: Citizenship, State, and Community in Modern France* (2000). Explores the subject from the French Revolution to the present.

T. W. CLYMAN AND J. VOWLES, *Russia through Women's Eyes: Autobiographies from Tsarist Russia* (1996). A splendid collection of relatively brief memoirs.

G. CROSSICK AND S. JAUMAIN (EDS.), *Cathedrals of Consumption: The European Department Store, 1850–1939* (1999). Essays on the institutionalization of a new mode of distribution of consumer goods.

J. FRANKEL AND S. ZIPPERSTEIN, *Assimilation and Community: The Jews in Nineteenth-Century Europe* (1992). A major collection of essays that ranges widely over the Continent.

P. GAY, *The Dilemma of Democratic Socialism: Eduard Bernstein's Challenge to Marx* (1952). Remains a clear presentation of the problems raised by Bernstein's revisionism.

A. GEIFMAN, *Thou Shalt Kill: Revolutionary Terrorism in Russia, 1894–1917* (1993). An examination of political violence in late imperial Russia.

R. F. HAMILTON, *Marxism, Revisionism, and Leninism: Explication, Assessment, and Commentary* (2000). A contribution from the perspective of a historically minded sociologist.

J. HARSIN, *Policing Prostitution in Nineteenth-Century Paris* (1985). A major study of this very significant subject in French social history.

S. C. HAUSE, *Women's Suffrage and Social Politics in the French Third Republic* (1984). A wide-ranging examination of the question.

P. HILDEN, *Working Women and Socialist Politics in France, 1880–1914* (1986). A study that traces both cooperation and tension between socialism and feminism in the French working class.

G. HIMMELFARB, *Poverty and Compassion: The Moral Imagination of the Late Victorians* (1991). The best examination of late Victorian social thought.

E. HOBSBAWM, *The Age of Empire, 1875–1914* (1987). A stimulating survey that covers cultural as well as political developments.

S. S. HOLTON, *Feminism and Democracy: Women's Suffrage and Reform Politics in Britain, 1900–1918* (1986). An excellent treatment of the subject.

T. HOPPEN, *The Mid-Victorian Generation, 1846–1886* (1998). The most extensive treatment of the subject.

M. MALIA, *Russia under Western Eyes: From the Bronze Horseman to the Lenin Mausoleum* (2000). A brilliant work recording the manner in which intellectuals in western Europe understood Russia.

W. O. MCCAGG, JR., *A History of Habsburg Jews, 1670–1918* (1989). An excellent examination of the political and economic life of the Jews under Habsburg rule.

G. L. MOSSE, *German Jews Beyond Judaism* (1985). Sensitive essays exploring the relationship of Jews to German culture in the nineteenth and early twentieth centuries.

P. G. NORD, *The Republican Moment: Struggles for Democracy in Nineteenth-Century France* (1996). A major new examination of nineteenth-century French political culture.

D. H. PINKNEY, *Napoleon III and the Rebuilding of Paris* (1958). A classic study.

E. D. RAPPAPORT, *Shopping for Pleasure: Women in the Making of London's West End* (2001). A study of the rise of department stores in London.

H. ROGGER, *Jewish Policies and Right-Wing Politics in Imperial Russia* (1986). A very learned examination of Russian anti-Semitism.

M. L. ROZENBLIT, *The Jews of Vienna, 1867–1914: Assimilation and Identity* (1983). Covers the cultural, economic, and political life of Viennese Jews.

J. SCOTT, *Only Paradoxes to Offer: French Feminists and the Rights of Man* (1997). A series of case studies from the French Revolution to the end of the nineteenth century.

R. SERVICE, *Lenin: A Biography* (2002). Based on new sources and will no doubt become the standard biography.

B. G. SMITH, *Ladies of the Leisure Class: The Bourgeoises of Northern France in the Nineteenth Century* (1981). Emphasizes the importance of the reproductive role of women.

G. P. STEENSON, *Not One Man! Not One Penny!: German Social Democracy, 1863–1914* (1999). An extensive survey.

N. STONE, *Europe Transformed* (1984). A sweeping survey that emphasizes the difficulties of late-nineteenth-century liberalism.

R. STUART, *Marxism at Work: Ideology, Class, and French Socialism During the Third Republic* (1992). The most extensive examination of French Marxism during this period.

A. THORPE, *A History of the British Labour Party* (2001). A survey from its inception to the present.

J. TOSH, *A Man's Place: Masculinity and the Middle-Class Home in Victorian England* (1999). A pioneering work.

J. R. WALKOWITZ, *Prostitution and Victorian Society: Women, Class, and the State* (1980). A work of great insight and sensitivity.

DOCUMENTS CD-ROM

Nineteenth-Century Society

23.1 The Church Weighs In: *Rerum Novarum*
23.2 Women Without Power Change the System
23.3 Sex in Society

23.4 John Stuart Mill: from *The Subjection of Women*
23.5 Bernard Shaw: Act III from *Mrs. Warren's Profession*
23.6 Gertrude Himmelfarb: from *Poverty and Compassion*

Édouard Manet,
A Bar at the Folies-Bergère: Painting Modern Life

The decade of the 1870s witnessed enormous political turmoil in France. It also witnessed the flowering of new painting dedicated to depicting contemporary society. In the mid–nineteenth century, primarily in Paris, European painting began to change in ways that would dominate art for the next century and a half. Two major characteristics marked this new art. First, instead of portraying religious, mythological, and overtly political themes, painters began to depict modern life itself, focusing on the social life and leisured activities of the urban middle and lower middle class. Second, many of these artists were fascinated with light, color, and the representation of momentary, largely yet unfocused, visual experience. Contemporaries called these paintings impressionistic and considered them curious and artistically shocking when they were first displayed in Paris.

Édouard Manet (1832–1883) was probably the most influential painter of the second half of the nineteenth century. He did not consider himself an impressionist, but by the time of his early death in 1883, Manet had begun to adopt many of the techniques of the impressionists, particularly their use of bright colors. *A Bar at the Folies-Bergère* was Manet's last major work. From the time it was first displayed in 1882, its technique and its meaning have been controversial.

The new paintings of modern life by Manet and the impressionists, including Claude Monet, Camille Pissaro, Pierre-Auguste Renoir, and Edgar Degas, recorded the middle- and lower-middle classes of Paris attending cafés, dance halls, concerts, picnics, horse races, boating excursions, and beach parties. The backdrop for these works was Paris as it had been reconstructed under Napoleon III into a city of wide boulevards and many places for middle-class leisure. The sites often included in these paintings allowed people from different classes to mix socially while pursuing a leisure activity. One such meeting place was the Folies-Bergère, a café/concert hall where patrons could enjoy a wide variety of popular entertainment, including singers, musicians, dancers, gymnasts, and animal shows. Paris had many such establishments, but the Folies-Bergère was one of the largest and most expensive.

In *A Bar at the Folies-Bergère*, Manet has painted a young barmaid standing behind a table holding liquor and wine bottles and in front of a very large mirror that reflects the activity occurring in front of her. (Manet actually painted this picture in his studio with a woman who worked as a barmaid posing as his model.) The table, together with its bottles, fruit, vase, and flowers, constitutes a formal still-life composition, but unlike traditional still lifes, this one shows objects of commercial consumption in a setting where leisure itself is commercially consumed. The mirror reflects the table and its contents, the music hall itself with the legs of a trapeze artist appearing in the top left corner, the audience for the performance, the back of the barmaid, and a man she is serving. Manet took great pains to paint the interior light of the hall, which appears to be coming from the newly invented electric lightbulbs.

The mirror in *A Bar at the Folies-Bergère* has provoked enormous comment. Nothing reflected in the mirror exactly relates to the objects in the foreground. The reflected barmaid is leaning; the woman before the mirror is not. The painting seems to demand that we visualize the male figure whom we see only by reflection. Indeed, a contemporary cartoonist published a drawing of the painting with the male patron standing in front of the table with his back to the viewer. Many art historians believe Manet intended this painting as a comment on late-nineteenth-century urban life—a time of uncertain class relations and growing fears that prosperity would be destroyed by an economic downturn or war. The problem of the reflections in the mirror and their uncertain relationship to the real world may indicate that absence of security in social life.

Édouard Manet (1832–1883), *A Bar at the Folies-Bergère*, 1882.   Oil on canvas, 96 × 130 cm.
Signed, dated. Courtauld gift 1932. Courtauld Institute of Galleries, London.

One of the great questions of the painting is the meaning and expression of the barmaid. The hubbub and restlessness of the reflected audience and the noise and excitement of the performance music do not register on her face. One art historian has called her a "disconcerting figure because her matter-of-fact, cool glance seems to lack expression."[4] The barmaid's expression may suggest the anonymity of so many social encounters in modern urban life. Because it was commonly assumed in Paris that many barmaids and shop girls needed to supplement their meager wages through prostitution, some scholars have also suggested that the woman in this painting, like the liquor and the fruit, is simply another object of commerce. Does the slightly foreboding reflected male image suggest that possibility? Or is the barmaid simply an attractive young woman, hired to encourage the sale of alcohol?

■ *What major characteristics began to dominate European painting in the mid–nineteenth century? How is Manet's* A Bar at the Folies-Bergère *reflective of French middle-class life of the period? Why are the mirror and the barmaid so significant in the painting?*

Sources: T. J. Clark, *The Painting of Modern Life: Paris in the Art of Manet and His Followers* (Princeton, NJ: Princeton University Press, 1984); Anne Coffin Hanson, *Manet and the Modern Tradition* (New Haven, CT: Yale University Press, 1977); Robert L. Herbert, *Impressionism: Art, Leisure, and Parisian Society* (New Haven, CT: Yale University Press, 1988); Bradford R. Collins, ed., *Twelve Views of Manet's Bar* (Princeton, NJ: Princeton University Press, 1996).

[4]Robert L. Herbert, *Impressionism: Art, Leisure, and Parisian Society* (New Haven, CT: Yale University Press, 1988), p. 80.

The German physicist Albert Einstein's theory of relativity, published in 1905, set the fundamental theory of physics in a new direction. His work was part of a multifaceted series of intellectual developments that changed and challenged much Western thought not only in science but also in literature, politics, and philosophy, redirecting Western thinking in ways that were often quite different from those of the Enlightenment.
Corbis

CHAPTER 25

THE BIRTH OF MODERN EUROPEAN THOUGHT

*D*URING THE SAME PERIOD THAT *the modern nation-state developed and the Second Industrial Revolution laid the foundations for modern life, the ideas that marked European thought for much of the twentieth century took shape. Like previous intellectual changes, these arose from earlier patterns of thought. The Enlightenment provided late-nineteenth-century Europeans with a heritage of rationalism, toleration, cosmopolitanism, and appreciation of science. Romanticism led them to value feelings, imagination, national identity, and the autonomy of the artistic experience.*

By 1900, these strands of thought had become woven into a new fabric. Many of the traditional intellectual signposts were disappearing. Christianity had experienced the most severe intellectual attack in its history. The picture of the physical world prevailing since Newton had undergone major modification. Darwin and Freud had challenged the special place that Western thinkers had assigned to humankind. Writers began to question rationality. The humanitarian ideals of liberalism and socialism gave way to aggressive nationalism. European intellectuals were more daring than ever before, but they were also probably less certain and optimistic.

KEY TOPICS

- The dominance of science in the thought of the second half of the nineteenth century
- The conflict between church and state over education
- Islam and late-nineteenth-century European thought
- The effect of modernism, psychoanalysis, and the revolution in physics on intellectual life
- Racism and the resurgence of anti-Semitism
- Late-nineteenth- and early-twentieth-century developments in feminism

The New Reading Public

The social context of intellectual life changed in the latter nineteenth century. For the first time in Europe, a mass reading public came into existence as more people than ever before became drawn into the world of print culture. In 1850, about half the population of western Europe and a much higher proportion of Russians were illiterate. That situation changed during the next half century.

ADVANCES IN PRIMARY EDUCATION

Literacy on the Continent improved steadily from the 1860s onward as governments financed education. Hungary provided elementary education in 1868, Britain in 1870, Switzerland in 1874, Italy in 1877, and France between 1878 and 1881. The already advanced education system of Prussia was extended throughout the German Empire after 1871. By 1900, in Britain, France, Belgium, the Netherlands, Germany, and Scandinavia, approximately 85 percent or more of the people could read, but Italy, Spain, Russia, Austria-Hungary, and the Balkans still had illiteracy rates of between 30 and 60 percent.

The new primary education in the basic skills of reading, writing, and elementary arithmetic reflected and generated social change. Both liberals and conservatives regarded such minimal training as necessary for orderly political behavior by the newly enfranchised voters. They also hoped that literacy would create a more productive labor force. This side of the educational crusade embodied the Enlightenment faith that right knowledge would lead to right action.

Literacy and its extension, however, soon became forces in their own right. The schoolteaching profession grew rapidly in numbers and prestige and, as noted in Chapter 24, became a major area for the employment of women. Those people who learned to read soon discovered that much of the education that led to better jobs and political influence was still open only to those who could afford it. Having created systems of primary education, the major nations had to give further attention to secondary education by the time of World War I. In another generation, the question would become one of democratic university instruction.

READING MATERIAL FOR THE MASS AUDIENCE

The expanding literate population created a vast market for new reading material. The number of newspapers, books, magazines, mail-order catalogs, and libraries grew rapidly. Cheap mass-circulation newspapers, such as *Le Petit Journal* of Paris and the *Daily Mail* and *Daily Express* of London, enjoyed their first heyday. Such newspapers carried advertising that alerted readers to the new consumer products available through the Second Industrial Revolution. Other publishers produced newspapers with specialized political or religious viewpoints. The number of monthly and quarterly journals for families, women, and freethinking intellectuals increased. Probably more people with different ideas could get into print in the late nineteenth century than ever before in European history. And more people could read their ideas than ever before.

Because many of the new readers were only marginally literate and still ignorant about many subjects, the books and journals catering to them often were mediocre. The cheap newspapers prospered on stories of sensational crimes and political scandal and on pages of advertising. Religious journals depended on denominational rivalry. A brisk market existed for pornography. Newspapers with editorials on the front page became major factors in the emerging mass politics. The news could be managed, but in central Europe more often by the government censor than by the publisher.

Critics pointed to the low level of public taste, but the new education, the new readers, and the myriad new books and journals permitted a popularization of knowledge that has become a hallmark of our world. The new literacy was the intellectual parallel of the railroad and the steamship. People could leave their original intellectual surroundings because literacy is not an end in itself, but leads to other skills and other knowledge. (See "Encountering the Past: The Birth of Science Fiction.")

Public education became widespread in Europe during the second half of the nineteenth century and women came to dominate the profession of schoolteaching, especially at the elementary level. This 1905 photograph shows English schoolchildren going through morning drills. Corbis

Science at Midcentury

In about 1850, Voltaire would have felt at home in a general discussion of scientific concepts. The basic Newtonian picture of physical nature that he had popularized still prevailed. Scientists continued to believe that nature operates as a vast machine according to mechanical principles. At midcentury, learned persons regarded the physical world as rational, mechanical, and dependable. Its laws could be ascertained objectively through experiment and observation. Scientific theory purportedly described physical nature as it really existed. Moreover, by 1850, science had a strong institutional life in French and German universities and in new professional societies. The word *scientist* had been invented in the early 1830s by William Whewell of Cambridge University and was in common use by the end of the century.

COMTE, POSITIVISM, AND THE PRESTIGE OF SCIENCE

During the early nineteenth century, science had continued to establish itself as the model for all human knowledge. The French philosopher Auguste Comte (1798–1857), a late child of the Enlightenment and a onetime follower of Saint-

Simon, developed **positivism,** a philosophy of human intellectual development that culminated in science. In *The Positive Philosophy* (1830–1842), Comte argued that human thought had developed in three stages. In the first, or theological, stage, physical nature was explained in terms of the action of divinities or spirits. In the second, or metaphysical, stage, abstract principles were regarded as the operative agencies of nature. In the final, or positive stage, explanations of nature became matters of exact description of phenomena, without recourse to an unobservable operative principle.

Physical science had, in Comte's view, entered the positive stage, and similar thinking should penetrate other areas of analysis. In particular, Comte believed that positive laws of social behavior could be discovered in the same fashion as laws of physical nature. He is thus generally regarded as the father of sociology. Works like Comte's helped convince learned Europeans that all knowledge must resemble scientific knowledge.

From the middle of the nineteenth century onward, the links of science to the technology of the Second Industrial Revolution made the general European public aware of science and technology as never before. The British Fabian socialist Beatrice Webb (1858–1943) recalled this situation from her youth:

The Birth of Science Fiction

During the Renaissance many European writers composed works about fantasy voyages to distant lands. In the seventeenth century, authors published some two hundred accounts of trips to the moon. Throughout the nineteenth century, other authors told tales of fantastic voyages into space or beneath the earth.

However, the real father of today's works of popular science fiction was Jules Verne (1828–1905). His *Five Weeks in a Balloon* (1863), a tale of a balloon trip across Africa, sold so well that a French publisher immediately gave Verne a contract to write two such stories each year for serialization in a magazine. So influential was Verne's image of the future that the United States named its first atomic submarine the *Nautilus* after the vessel commanded by the mysterious Captain Nemo in Verne's *Twenty Thousand Leagues under the Sea* (1870).

Verne prided himself on his scientific veracity. He also located his stories in his own age so readers felt they were experiencing a contemporary adventure.

Toward the turn of the century, science fiction found another master in the English novelist H. G. Wells (1866–1946), who in 1895 published *The Time Machine* in which the characters travel through time. Wells's first success was rapidly followed by *The Island of Dr. Moreau* (1896) about a mad surgeon's inhuman experiments on animals, and *The War of the Worlds* (1898) about a Martian invasion of the earth. Wells invented many of the devices, such as new stars appearing near the solar system, Martians and other planetary creatures unfriendly to humans, machinery that goes astray, and strange diseases, that would become the stock in trade for later science fiction writers.

Verne, Wells, and their many imitators, published their stories in cheap illustrated magazines with mass circulations. Consequently, science fiction immediately entered popular culture. Throughout the twentieth century popular movies and television series were made based on the stories of both Verne and Wells. In 1938, when Orson Welles (1915–1985) broadcast Wells's *War of the Worlds* over the radio, many Americans actually believed Martians had landed in New Jersey. The works of Verne and Wells continue to influence the writing of science fiction.

■ *Why is Jules Verne considered the father of modern science fiction? What enduring plot devices did H. G. Wells introduce? Why did science fiction become so popular?*

P. Nichols and J. Clute, *The Encyclopedia of Science Fiction* (New York: St. Martin's Press, 1995); Dieter Wuckel and Bruce Cassidy, *The Illustrated History of Science Fiction* (New York: Ungar, 1986); David Kyle, *A Pictorial History of Science Fiction* (London: Hamlyn, 1976).

Captain Nemo's submarine confronts a giant octopus in Verne's Twenty Thousand Leagues under the Sea. Bettman/Corbis

Who will deny that the men of science were the leading British intellectuals of that period; that it was they who stood out as men of genius with international reputations; that it was they who were the self-confident militants of the period; that it was they who were routing the theologians, confounding the mystics, imposing their theories on philosophers, their inventions on capitalists, and their discoveries on medical men; whilst they were at the same time snubbing the artists, ignoring the poets, and even casting doubts on the capacity of the politicians?[1]

Her remarks would have applied in every industrialized nation in Europe. Writers spoke of a religion of science that would explain all nature without resorting to supernaturalism. Popularizers, such as Thomas Henry Huxley (1825–1895) in Britain and Ernst Haeckel (1834–1919) in Germany, worked for government support of scientific research and for the inclusion of science in the schools and universities.

DARWIN'S THEORY OF NATURAL SELECTION

In 1859, Charles Darwin (1809–1882) published *On the Origin of Species*, which carried the mechanical interpretation of physical nature into the world of living things. The book was one of the seminal works of Western thought and earned Darwin the honor of being regarded as the "Newton of biology." Both Darwin and his book have been much misunderstood. He did not originate the concept of evolution, which had been discussed widely before he wrote. What he and Alfred Russel Wallace (1823–1913) did, working independently, was to formulate the principle of natural selection, which explained how species had changed or evolved over time. Earlier writers had believed evolution might occur; Darwin and Wallace explained how it could occur.

Drawing on Malthus, the two scientists contended that more living organisms come into existence than can survive in their environment. Those organisms with a marginal advantage in the struggle for existence live long enough to propagate. This principle of survival of the fittest Darwin called **natural selection.** It was naturalistic and mechanistic, requiring no guiding mind behind the development in organic nature. What neither Darwin nor anyone else in his day could explain was the origin of those chance variations that provided some living things with the marginal chance for survival. Only after 1900, when the work on heredity of the Austrian monk, Gregor Mendel

(1822–1884), received public attention, did the mystery of those variations begin to be unraveled.

Darwin and Wallace's theory represented the triumph of naturalistic explanation, which removed the idea of purpose from organic nature. Eyes were not made for seeing according to the rational wisdom and purpose of God, but had developed mechanistically over time. Thus the theory of evolution through natural selection not only contradicted the biblical narrative of the Creation, but also undermined both the deistic argument for the existence of God from the design of the universe and the whole concept of fixity in nature or the universe at large. The world was a realm of flux. The idea that physical and organic nature might be constantly changing allowed people to believe that society, values, customs, and beliefs should also change.

Darwin's theories about the evolution of humankind from the higher primates aroused enormous controversy. This caricature shows him with a monkey's body holding a mirror to an apelike creature. National History Museum, London. UK/Bridgeman Art Library.

DARWIN DEFENDS A MECHANISTIC VIEW OF NATURE

In the closing paragraphs of On the Origin of Species *(1859), Charles Darwin contrasted the view of nature he championed with that of his opponents. He argued that an interpretation of organic nature based on mechanistic laws was actually nobler than an interpretation based on divine creation. In the second edition, however, Darwin added the term* Creator *to these paragraphs.*

■ *Why does Darwin believe a mechanistic creation suggests no less dignity than creation by God? How does the insertion of the term* Creator *change this passage? What is the grandeur that Darwin finds in his view of life?*

Authors of the highest eminence seem to be fully satisfied with the view that each species has been independently created. To my mind it accords better with what we know of the laws impressed on matter by the Creator, that the production and extinction of the past and present inhabitants of the world should have been due to secondary causes, like those determining the birth and death of the individual. When I view all beings not as special creations, but as the lineal descendants of some few beings which lived long before the first bed of the Cambrian [geological] system was deposited, they seem to me to become ennobled. . . .

It is interesting to contemplate a tangled bank, clothed with many plants of many kinds, with birds singing on the bushes, with various insects flitting about, and with worms crawling through the damp earth, and to reflect that these elaborately constructed forms, so different from each other, and dependent upon each other in so complex a manner, have all been produced by laws acting around us. These laws, taken in the largest sense, being Growth with Reproduction; Inheritance which is almost implied by reproduction; Variability from the indirect and direct action of the conditions of life, and from use and disuse: a Ratio of Increase so high as to lead to a Struggle for Life, and as a consequence to Natural Selection, entailing Divergence of Character and the Extinction of less-improved forms. Thus, from the war of nature, from famine and death, the most exalted object which we are capable of conceiving, namely the production of the higher animals, directly follows. There is grandeur in this view of life, with its several powers, having been originally breathed by the Creator into a few forms or into one; and that, whilst this planet has gone cycling on according to the fixed law of gravity, from so simple a beginning endless forms most beautiful and most wonderful have been, and are being evolved.

Charles Darwin, *On the Origin of Species and the Descent of Man* (New York: Modern Library, n.d.), pp. 373–374.

In 1871, in *The Descent of Man*, Darwin applied the principle of evolution by natural selection to human beings. Darwin was hardly the first person to treat human beings as animals, but he contended that humankind's moral nature and religious sentiments, as well as its physical frame, had developed naturalistically largely in response to the requirements of survival. Neither the origin nor the character of humankind, in Darwin's view, required the existence of a god for their explanation. Not since Copernicus had removed the earth from the center of the universe had the pride of Western human beings received so sharp a blow. (See "Darwin Defends a Mechanistic View of Nature.")

Darwin's theory of evolution by natural selection was controversial from the moment *On the Origin of Species* appeared. It encountered criticism from both the religious and the scientific communities. By the end of the century, scientists widely accepted the concept of evolution but not yet Darwin's mechanism of natural selection. The acceptance of the latter really dates from the 1920s and 1930s, when Darwin's theory was combined with modern genetics.

SCIENCE AND ETHICS

One area in which science came to have a new significance was social thought and ethics. Philosophers applied the concept of the struggle for survival to human social relationships. The phrase "survival of the fittest" predated Darwin and reflected the competitive outlook of classical economics. Darwin's use of the phrase gave it the prestige associated with advanced science.

The most famous advocate of evolutionary ethics was Herbert Spencer (1820–1903), a British philosopher. Spencer, a strong individualist, believed human society progresses through competition. If the weak receive too much protection, the rest of humankind is the loser. In Spencer's work, struggle against one's fellow human beings became a kind of ethical imperative. The concept could be applied to justify the avoidance of aiding the poor and the working class or to justify the domination of colonial peoples or to advocate aggressive competition among nations. Evolutionary ethics and similar concepts, all of which are usually termed **social Darwinism,** often came close to saying that might makes right.

One of the chief opponents of such thinking was Thomas Henry Huxley, the great defender of Darwin. In 1893, Huxley declared that the physical process of evolution was at odds with human ethical development. The struggle in nature only showed how human beings should not behave. (See "T. H. Huxley Criticizes Evolutionary Ethics.")

Christianity and the Church under Siege

The nineteenth century was one of the most difficult periods in the history of the organized Christian churches. Many European intellectuals left the faith. The secular, liberal nation-states attacked the influence of the church. The expansion of population and the growth of cities challenged its organizational capacity. Yet during all of this turmoil, the Protestant and Catholic churches remained popular.

INTELLECTUAL SKEPTICISM

The intellectual attack on Christianity challenged its historical credibility, its scientific accuracy, and its morality. The philosophes of the Enlightenment had delighted in pointing out contradictions in the Bible. The historical scholarship of the nineteenth century brought new issues to the fore.

History In 1835, David Friedrich Strauss (1808–1874) published *The Life of Jesus,* in which he questioned whether the Bible provides any genuine historical evidence about Jesus. Strauss contended the story of Jesus is a myth that arose from the particular social and intellectual conditions of first-century Palestine. Jesus' character and life represent the aspirations of the people of that time and place, rather than events that actually occurred. Other authors also published skeptical examinations of the life of Jesus.

During the second half of the century, scholars such as Julius Wellhausen (1844–1918) in Germany, Ernst Renan (1823–1892) in France, and William Robertson Smith (1847–1894) in Great Britain contended that human authors had written and revised the books of the Bible with the problems of Jewish society and politics in mind. The Bible was not an inspired book, but had, like the Homeric epics, been written by normal human beings in a primitive society. This questioning of the historical validity of the Bible caused more literate men and women to lose faith in Christianity than any other single cause.

Science Science also undermined Christianity. This blow was particularly cruel because many eighteenth-century writers had led Christians to believe the scientific examination of nature buttressed their faith. William Paley's (1743–1805) *Natural Theology* (1802) and books by numerous scientists had enshrined that belief. The geology of Charles Lyell (1797–1875) suggested the earth is much older than the biblical records contend. By looking to natural causes to explain floods, mountains, and valleys, Lyell removed the miraculous hand of God from the physical development of the earth. Darwin's theory cast doubt on the Creation. His ideas and those of other writers suggested that the moral nature of humankind can be explained without appeal to God. Finally, anthropologists, psychologists, and sociologists proposed that religious sentiments are just one more set of natural phenomena.

Morality Other intellectuals questioned the morality of Christianity. The issue of immoral biblical stories was again raised. The morality of the Old Testament God, his cruelty and unpredictability, did not fit well with the tolerant, rational values of liberals. They also wondered about the morality of the New Testament God, who would sacrifice for his own satisfaction the only perfect being ever to walk the earth. Many of the clergy began to wonder if they could preach doctrines they felt to be immoral.

From another direction, writers like Friedrich Nietzsche (1844–1900) in Germany portrayed Christianity as a religion that glorified weakness rather than the strength life required. Christianity demanded a useless and debilitating sacrifice of the flesh and spirit, rather than heroic living and daring. Nietzsche once observed, "War and courage

T. H. HUXLEY CRITICIZES EVOLUTIONARY ETHICS

T. H. Huxley (1825–1895) was a British scientist who had been among Darwin's strongest defenders. He was also an outspoken advocate for the advancement of science in the late nineteenth century. Huxley, however, became a major critic of social Darwinism, which attempted to deduce ethical principles from evolutionary processes involving struggle in nature. Drawing a strong distinction between the cosmic process of evolution and the social process of ethical development, he argued in Evolution and Ethics *(1893) that human ethical progress occurs through combating the cosmic process.*

■ *What does Huxley mean by the "cosmic process"? Why does he equate "social progress" with the "ethical process"? In this passage, does Huxley present human society as part of nature or as something that may be separate from nature?*

Men in society are undoubtedly subject to the cosmic process. As among other animals, multiplication goes on without cessation, and involves severe competition for the means of support. The struggle for existence tends to eliminate those less fitted to adapt themselves to the circumstances of their existence. The strongest, the most self-assertive, tend to tread down the weaker. But the influence of the cosmic process on the evolution of society is the greater the more rudimentary its civilization. Social progress means a checking of the cosmic process at every step and the substitution for it of another, which may be called the ethical process; the end of which is not the survival of those who may happen to be the fittest, in respect of the whole of the conditions which obtain, but of those who are ethically the best.

As I have already urged, the practice of that which is ethically best—what we call goodness or virtue—involves a course of conduct which, in all respects, is opposed to that which leads to success in the cosmic struggle for existence. In place of ruthless self-assertion it demands self-restraint; in place of thrusting aside, or treading down, all competitors, it requires that the individual shall not merely respect, but shall help his fellows; its influence is directed, not so much to the survival of the fittest, as to the fitting of as many as possible to survive. It repudiates the gladiatorial theory of existence.

It is from neglect of these plain considerations that the fanatical individualism of our time attempts to apply the analogy of cosmic nature to society. . . .

Let us understand, once for all, that the ethical progress of society depends, not on imitating the cosmic process, still less in running away from it, but in combating it.

From T. H. Huxley, *Evolution and Ethics* (London: Macmillan & Co., 1893), as quoted in Franklin L. Baumer, *Main Currents of Western Thought: Readings in Western European Intellectual History from the Middle Ages to the Present*, 3rd ed., rev. (New York: Alfred A. Knopf, 1970), pp. 561–562.

have accomplished more great things than love of neighbor."[2]

These skeptical currents created a climate in which Christianity lost much of its intellectual respectability. Fewer educated people joined the clergy. Many found they could live with little or no reference to Christianity. The secularism of everyday life proved as harmful to the faith as the direct attacks. This situation was especially prevalent in the cities, which were growing faster than the capacity of the churches to meet the challenge. Whole generations of the urban poor grew up with little or no experience of the church as an institution or of Christianity as a religious faith.

CONFLICT BETWEEN CHURCH AND STATE

The secular state of the nineteenth century clashed with both the Protestant and the Roman Catholic churches. Liberals disliked the dogma and

[2]Walter Kaufmann, ed. and trans., *The Portable Nietzsche* (New York: Viking, 1967), p. 159.

the political privileges of the established churches. National states were often suspicious of the supranational character of the Roman Catholic Church. The primary area of conflict between the state and the churches, however, was education. Previously, most education in Europe had taken place in church schools. The churches feared that future generations would emerge from the new state-financed schools without any religious teaching. From 1870 through the turn of the century, religious education was debated in every major country.

Great Britain   In Great Britain, the Education Act of 1870 provided for state-supported schools run by elected school boards, whereas earlier the government had given small grants to religious schools. The new schools were to be built in areas where the religious denominations did not provide satisfactory education. There was rivalry both between the Anglican church and the state and between the Anglican church and the Nonconformist denominations—that is, those Protestant denominations that were not part of the Church of England. All the churches opposed improvements in education because these increased the costs of church schools. In the Education Act of 1902, the government provided state support for both religious and nonreligious schools, but imposed the same educational standards on each.

France   The British conflict was calm compared with that in France, which had a dual system of Catholic and public schools. Under the Falloux Law of 1850, the local priest provided religious education in the public schools. The conservative French Catholic Church and the Third French Republic loathed each other. Between 1878 and 1886, a series of educational laws sponsored by Jules Ferry (1832–1893) replaced religious instruction in the public schools with civic training. The number of public schools was expanded, and members of religious orders could no longer teach in them. After the Dreyfus affair, the French Catholic Church again paid a price for its reactionary politics. The Radical government of Pierre Waldeck-Rousseau (1846–1904), drawn from pro-Dreyfus groups, suppressed the religious orders. In 1905, the Napoleonic Concordat was terminated, and church and state were separated.

Germany and the *Kulturkampf*   The most extreme church-state conflict occurred in Germany during the 1870s. At unification, the German Catholic hierarchy had wanted freedom for the churches guaranteed in the constitution. Bismarck left the matter to the federal states, but he soon felt the Roman

Catholic Church and the Catholic Center Party threatened the unity of the German Empire. In 1870 and 1871, he removed the clergy from overseeing local education in Prussia and set education under state direction. This secularization of education represented the beginning of a concerted attack on the Catholic Church in Germany.

The "May Laws" of 1873, which applied to Prussia, but not to the entire German Empire, required priests to be educated in German schools and universities and to pass state examinations. The state could veto the appointments of priests. The legislation abolished the disciplinary power of the pope and the church over the clergy and transferred it to the state. Many of the clergy refused to obey these laws, and by 1876 Bismarck had either arrested or expelled all Catholic bishops from Prussia.

In the end, Bismarck's ***Kulturkampf*** ("cultural struggle") against the Catholic Church failed. By the end of the 1870s, he abandoned his attack. He had gained state control of education and civil laws governing marriage only at the price of provoking Catholic resentment against the German state. The *Kulturkampf* was probably his greatest blunder.

Areas of Religious Revival

The German Catholic resistance to the intrusions of the secular state illustrates the continuing vitality of Christianity during this period of intellectual and political hardship for the church. In Great Britain, both the Anglican church and the Nonconformist denominations expanded and raised vast sums for new churches and schools. In Ireland, the 1870s saw a Catholic devotional revival. In France, after the defeat by Prussia, priests organized special pilgrimages to shrines for thousands of penitents who believed France had been defeated because of their sins. The cult of the miracle of Lourdes grew during these years. Churches of all denominations gave more attention to the urban poor.

In effect, the last half of the nineteenth century witnessed the final great effort to Christianize Europe. It was well organized, well led, and well financed. It failed only because the population of Europe had outstripped the resources of the churches. The vitality of the churches accounts in part for the intense hostility of their enemies.

The Roman Catholic Church and the Modern World

The most striking feature of Christian religious revival was the resilience of the papacy. The brief hope for a liberal pontificate from Pope Pius IX

Zwischen Berlin und Rom.

The conflict between church and state disrupted German politics during the 1870s. In this contemporary cartoon, Bismarck and Pope Pius IX seek to checkmate each other in a game of chess. Bildarchiv Preussischer Kulturbesitz

(r. 1846–1878) vanished when he fled the turmoil in Rome in November 1848. In the 1860s, embittered by the process of Italian unification, he launched a counteroffensive against liberalism. In 1864, he issued the *Syllabus of Errors*, which set the Catholic Church squarely against contemporary science, philosophy, and politics.

In 1869, the pope summoned the First Vatican Council. The next year, through the political manipulations of the pontiff and against opposition from many bishops, the council promulgated the dogma of **papal infallibility** when speaking officially on matters of faith and morals. No earlier pope had asserted such centralized authority within the church. The First Vatican Council ended in 1870, when Italian troops occupied Rome at the outbreak of the Franco-Prussian War. Thereafter the territory of the papacy was limited to the Vatican City, and the papacy made no formal accommodation to the Italian state until 1929. Pius IX and many other Roman Catholics believed the Catholic Church could only sustain itself in the modern world of nation-states with large electorates by centering the authority of the church in the papacy itself. The spiritual authority of the papacy became a substitute for its lost political and temporal authority.

Pius IX was succeeded by Leo XIII (r. 1878–1903). Leo, who was sixty-eight years old at the time of his election, sought to make accommodations to the modern age and to address its great social questions. He looked to the philosophy of Thomas Aquinas (1225–1274) to reconcile the claims of faith and reason.

Leo's most important pronouncement on public issues was the encyclical *Rerum Novarum* (1891).

In that document, he defended private property, religious education, and religious control of the marriage laws and condemned socialism and Marxism, but he also declared that employers should treat their employees justly, pay them proper wages, and permit them to organize labor unions. The pope supported laws to protect workers and urged that modern society be organized in corporate groups that would include people from various classes who would cooperate according to Christian principles. The corporate society, based on medieval social organization, was to be an alternative to both socialism and competitive capitalism. On the basis of Leo XIII's pronouncements, democratic Catholic political parties and Catholic trade unions were founded throughout Europe. (See "Leo XIII Considers the Social Question in European Politics.")

His successor Pius X (r. 1903 to 1914) hoped to resist modern thought and restore traditional devotional life. Between 1903 and 1907, he condemned Catholic modernism, a movement of modern biblical criticism within the church, and in 1910 he required all priests to take an anti-Modernist oath. The struggle between Catholicism and modern thought was resumed.

ISLAM AND LATE-NINETEENTH-CENTURY EUROPEAN THOUGHT

The few European thinkers who wrote about Islam in the late nineteenth century discussed it using the same scientific and naturalistic scholarly methods they applied to Christianity and Judaism. They interpreted Islam as a historical phenomenon without

LEO XIII CONSIDERS THE SOCIAL QUESTION IN EUROPEAN POLITICS

• •

In his 1891 encyclical Rerum Novarum, *Pope Leo XIII addressed the social question in European politics, providing the Catholic Church's answer to secular calls for social reforms. The pope denied the socialist claim that class conflict is the natural state of affairs. He urged employers to seek just and peaceful relations with workers.*

■ *How does Leo XIII reject the concept of class conflict? What responsibilities does he assign to the rich and to the poor? Are the responsibilities of the two classes equal? What kinds of social reform might emerge from these ideas?*

The great mistake that is made in the matter now under consideration is to possess oneself of the idea that class is naturally hostile to class; that rich and poor are intended by Nature to live at war with one another. So irrational and so false is this view that the exact contrary is the truth. . . . Each requires the other; capital cannot do without labour, nor labour without capital. Mutual agreement results in pleasantness and good order; perpetual conflict necessarily produces confusion and outrage. Now, in preventing such strife as this, and in making it impossible, the efficacy of Christianity is marvelous and manifold. . . . Religion teaches the labouring man and the workman to carry out honestly and well all equitable agreements freely made; never to injure capital, or to outrage the person of an employer; never to employ violence in representing his own cause, or to engage in riot or disorder; and to have nothing to do with men of evil principles, who work upon the people with artful promises and raise hopes which usually end in disaster and in repentance when too late. Religion teaches the rich man and the employer that their work people are not their slaves; that they must respect in every man his dignity as a man and as a Christian; that labour is nothing to be ashamed of, if we listen to right reason and to Christian philosophy, but is an honourable employment, enabling a man to sustain his life in an upright and creditable way; and that it is shameful and inhuman to treat men like chattels to make money by, or to look upon them merely as so much muscle or physical power. Thus, again, Religion teaches that, as among the workman's concerns are Religion herself and things spiritual and mental, the employer is bound to see that he has time for the duties of piety; that he be not exposed to corrupting influences and dangerous occasions; and that he be not led away to neglect his home and family or to squander his wages. Then, again, the employer must never tax his work people beyond their strength, nor employ them in work unsuited to their sex or age. His great and principal obligation is to give every one that which is just.

As quoted in F. S. Nitti, *Catholic Socialism*, trans. by Mary Mackintosh (London: S. Sonnenschein, 1895), p. 409.

---

any reference to the supernatural, and the Qur'an received the same kind of critical historical analysis that was being directed toward the Bible. Islam, like the other great world religions, was seen as a product of a particular culture. In the works of scholars such as the influential French writer Ernest Renan (1823–1892), Islam was, like Judaism, a manifestation of the ancient Semitic mentality, which had given rise to a powerful monotheistic vision. Renan, and sociologists such as Max Weber, also dismissed Islam as a religion and culture incapable of developing science and closed to new ideas.

However, Renan's views were opposed in a French journal by Jamal al-din Al-Afghani (1839–1897), an Egyptian intellectual, who argued that over time Islam, which had arisen six hundred years after Christianity, would eventually produce cultures as modern as those in Europe. Al-Afghani was one of the rare Islamic writers who directly contested a European thinker.

The European racial and cultural outlooks that denigrated nonwhite peoples and their civilizations were also directed toward the Arab world. European authors who championed white racial superiority looked to India and the Aryan civilization that was supposed to have risen there and later influenced northern European life as the source of Europe's cultural superiority.

Christian missionaries reinforced these anti-Islamic attitudes. They blamed Islam for Arab economic backwardness, for mistreating women, and for condoning slavery. They also often came into conflict with Islamic religious authorities. Because the penalty for abjuring Islam is death, the missionaries made few converts among Muslims. So they turned their efforts to founding schools and hospitals, hoping these Christian foundations would eventually lead some Muslims to Christianity. Few Muslims converted, but these institutions did educate young Arabs in Western science and medicine, and many of their students became leaders in the Middle East. Eventually, as missionary families came to live for long periods of time among Arabs, they became more sympathetic to Arab political aspirations.

Within the Islamic world, and especially in the decaying Ottoman Empire, as political leaders continued to champion Western scientific education and technology, they confronted a variety of responses from religious thinkers. Some of these thinkers sought to combine modern thought with Islam. For example, the Salafi, or the salafiyya movement, believed there was no inherent contradiction between science and Islam. They believed Muhammad had wisely and properly addressed the issues of his day, and a reformed Islamic faith could do so again. The Arab world should cease direct imitation of the West and modernize itself on the basis of a pure, restored Islamic faith. The Salafi emphasized a rational reading of the Qur'an and saw Ottoman decline as the result of Muslim religious error. This outlook, which had originally sought to reconcile Islam with the modern world, eventually led many Muslims in the twentieth century to oppose Western influence.

Other Islamic religious leaders simply rejected the West and modern thought. They included the Mahdist movement in Sudan, the Sanussiya in Libya, and the Wahhabi movement in the Arabian peninsula. Such religious-based opposition was strongest in those portions of the Middle East where the European presence was least direct, which is to say outside of Morocco, Algeria, Egypt, and Tunisia, which for all intents and purposes were under the control of Western powers by 1900, and Turkey, where Ottoman leaders had long been deeply involved with the West.

Toward a Twentieth-Century Frame of Mind

The last quarter of the nineteenth century and the first decade of the twentieth century were the crucible of modern Western thought. Philosophers, scientists, psychologists, and artists began to portray physical reality, human nature, and society in ways different from those of the past. Their new concepts challenged the major presuppositions of mid-nineteenth-century science, rationalism, liberalism, and bourgeois morality.

SCIENCE: THE REVOLUTION IN PHYSICS

The changes in the scientific worldview originated within the scientific community itself. By the late 1870s, discontent existed over the excessive realism of midcentury science. It was thought that many scientists believed their mechanistic models, solid atoms, and absolute time and space actually described the real universe.

In 1883, Ernst Mach (1838–1916) published *The Science of Mechanics*, in which he urged that scientists consider their concepts descriptive not of the physical world, but of the sensations experienced by the scientific observer. Scientists could describe only the sensations, not the physical world that underlay those sensations. In line with Mach, the French scientist Henri Poincaré (1854–1912) urged that the theories of scientists be regarded as hypothetical constructs of the human mind rather than as true descriptions of nature. In 1911, Hans Vaihinger (1852–1933) suggested the concepts of science be considered "as if" descriptions of the physical world. By World War I, few scientists believed they could portray the "truth" about physical reality. Rather, they saw themselves as recording the observations of instruments and as offering useful hypothetical or symbolic models of nature.

X Rays and Radiation Discoveries in the laboratory paralleled the philosophical challenge to nineteenth-century science. With those discoveries, the comfortable world of supposedly "complete" nineteenth-century physics vanished forever. In December 1895, Wilhelm Roentgen (1845–1923) published a paper on his discovery of X rays, a form of energy that penetrated various opaque materials. Major steps in the exploration of radioactivity followed within months of the publication of his paper.

In 1896, Henri Becquerel (1852–1908) discovered that uranium emitted a similar form of energy. The next year, J. J. Thomson (1856–1940), at Cambridge University, formulated the theory of the electron. The interior world of the atom had become a new area for human exploration. In 1902, Ernest Rutherford (1871–1937) explained the cause of radiation through the disintegration of the atoms of radioactive materials. Shortly thereafter, he speculated on the immense store of energy present in the atom.

Theories of Quantum Energy, Relativity, and Uncertainty The discovery of radioactivity and discontent with the existing mechanical models led to revolutionary theories in physics. In 1900, Max Planck (1858–1947) pioneered the articulation of the quantum theory of energy, according to which energy is a series of discrete quantities, or packets, rather than a continuous stream. In 1905, Albert Einstein (1879–1955) published his first epoch-making papers on **relativity** in which he contended that time and space exist not separately, but rather as a combined continuum. Moreover, the measurement of time and space depends on the observer as well as on the entities being measured.

In 1927, Werner Heisenberg (1901–1976) set forth his uncertainty principle, according to which the behavior of subatomic particles is a matter of statistical probability rather than of exactly determinable cause and effect. Much that had seemed unquestionable about the physical universe had now become ambiguous.

The mathematical complexity of twentieth-century physics meant science would rarely again be successfully popularized. At the same time, through applied technology and further research in chemistry, physics, and medicine, science affected daily living more than ever before. Scientists from the late nineteenth century onward became the most successful group of Western intellectuals in gaining the financial support of governments and private institutions for the pursuit of their research. They did so by relating the success of science to the economic progress, military security, and the health of their nations. Science, through research, medicine, and technological change, has thus affected modern life more significantly than any other intellectual activity.

Marie Curie (1869–1934) and Pierre Curie (1859–1906) were two of the most important figures in the advance of physics and chemistry. Marie was born in Poland but worked in France for most of her life. She is credited with the discovery of radium, for which she was awarded the Nobel Prize in Chemistry in 1911. Bildarchiv Preussischer Kulturbesitz

LITERATURE: REALISM AND NATURALISM

Between 1850 and 1914, the moral certainties of middle-class Europeans underwent changes no less radical than their concepts of the physical universe. The realist movement in literature portrayed the hypocrisy, brutality, and the dullness that underlay bourgeois life. The **realist** and **naturalist** writers brought scientific objectivity and observation to their work. By using the midcentury cult of science so vital to the middle class, they confronted readers with the harsh realities of life. Realism rejected the romantic idealization of nature, the poor, love, and polite society. Realist novelists portrayed the dark side of life, almost, some people thought, for its own sake.

Earlier writers, including Charles Dickens (1812–1870) and Honoré de Balzac (1799–1850), had portrayed the cruelty of industrial life and of a society based on money. Other authors, such as George Eliot (born Mary Ann Evans, 1819–1880), had paid close attention to the details of her characters. These authors' work had, however, included imagination and artistry. A better morality was possible through Christian or humane values or, for Eliot, through an appreciation of humanity arising from Auguste Comte's thought.

The major figures of late-century realism examined the dreary and unseemly side of life without being certain whether a better life was possible. In good Darwinian fashion, they portrayed human beings as subject to the passions, the materialistic

Mary Anne Evans (1819–1880) wrote influential novels about religious, moral, and political issues. She was deeply influenced by Auguste Comte's positivism.
Hulton Getty Images/Tony Stone Images

determinism, and the pressures of the environment like any other animals. Most of them, however, also saw society itself as perpetuating evil.

Flaubert and Zola   Critics have often considered Gustave Flaubert's (1821–1880) *Madame Bovary* (1857), with its story of colorless provincial life and a woman's hapless search for love in and outside of marriage, as the first genuinely realistic novel. The work portrayed life without heroism, purpose, or even civility.

But the author who turned realism into a movement was Emile Zola (1840–1902). He found artistic inspiration in Claude Bernard's (1813–1878) *Introduction to the Study of Experimental Medicine* (1865). Zola argued that he could write an experimental novel in which he would observe and report the characters and their actions as the scientist might relate a laboratory experiment. He once declared, "I have simply done on living bodies the work of analysis which surgeons perform on corpses."[3] He believed absolute physical and psychological determinism ruled human events in the way it did the physical world.

---

[3]Quoted in George J. Becker, *Documents of Modern Literary Realism* (Princeton, NJ: Princeton University Press, 1963), p. 159.

Between 1871 and 1893, Zola published twenty volumes of novels exploring subjects normally untouched by writers: alcoholism, prostitution, labor strife. He refused to turn his readers' thoughts away from the ugly aspects of life. Nothing in his purview received the light of hope or the aura of romance. Although critics faulted his taste and moralists condemned his subject matter, Zola enjoyed a worldwide following. As noted in Chapter 23, he took a leading role in the defense of Captain Dreyfus.

Ibsen and Shaw   The Norwegian playwright Henrik Ibsen (1828–1906) carried realism into the dramatic presentation of domestic life. He sought to strip away the illusory mask of middle-class morality. His most famous play is *A Doll's House* (1879). Its chief character, Nora, has a narrowminded husband who cannot tolerate independence of character or thought on her part. She finally leaves him, slamming the door behind her. In *Ghosts* (1881), a respectable woman must deal with a son suffering from syphilis inherited from her husband. In *The Master Builder* (1892), an aging architect kills himself while trying to impress a young woman. Ibsen's works were controversial. He had dared to attack sentimentality, the ideal of the female "angel of the house," and the cloak of respectability that hung so insecurely over the middle-class family.

One of Ibsen's greatest champions was the Irish writer George Bernard Shaw (1856–1950), who spent most of his life in England. Shaw defended Ibsen's work and made his own realistic onslaught against romanticism and false respectability. In *Mrs. Warren's Profession* (1893), he dealt with prostitution. In *Arms and the Man* (1894) and *Man and Superman* (1903), he heaped scorn on the romantic ideals of love and war, and in *Androcles and the Lion* (1913), he pilloried Christianity.

Realist writers believed it their duty to portray reality and the commonplace. In dissecting what they considered the "real" world, they helped change the moral perception of the good life. They refused to let public opinion dictate what they wrote about or how they treated their subjects. By presenting their audiences with unmentionable subjects, they sought to remove the veneer of hypocrisy that had forbidden such discussion. They hoped to destroy illusions and compel the public to face reality. That change in itself seemed good. Few of the realist writers who raised these problems posed solutions to them. They often left their readers unable to sustain old values and uncertain about where to find new ones.

MODERNISM

From the 1870s onward throughout Europe, a new multifaceted movement usually called **modernism** touched all the arts. Like realism, modernism was critical of middle-class society and morality. Modernism, however, was not deeply concerned with social issues. What drove the modernists was a concern for the aesthetic or the beautiful. The English essayist Walter Pater (1839–1903) set the tone of the movement when he declared in 1877 that all art "constantly aspires to the condition of music."

Across the spectrum of the arts, modernists tried to break the received forms and to create new forms. To many contemporaries, the new forms seemed formless. Practitioners of the modern believed that each of the arts should and could influence the others. Painters gave their works musical titles, as did James Abbott McNeill Whistler (1834–1903) in *Nocturnes*. Musicians combined material from many sources. In his at first notorious and then famous ballet, *The Rite of Spring* (1913), Igor Stravinsky (1882–1971) combined jazz rhythms, dissonance, and anthropological theory. Pablo Picasso (1881–1973) and other artists associated with cubism constructed paintings that involved viewing objects from a variety of angles at the same time and drew inspiration from primitive masks they saw in Paris museums. In England, practitioners of what was called the New Sculpture mixed various materials in sensuous statues. Other sculptors rejected traditional forms entirely. For these artists, the immediate aesthetic experience of a work of art dominated other concerns. (See "Art & the West: Cubism Changes the Shape of Painting," p. 882.)

Among the chief proponents of modernism in England were the members of the Bloomsbury Group, including authors Virginia Woolf (1882–1941) and Leonard Woolf (1880–1969), artists Vanessa Bell (1879–1961) and Duncan Grant (1885–1978), the historian and literary critic Lytton Strachey (1880–1932), and the economist John Maynard Keynes (1883–1946). These authors challenged the values of their Victorian forebears. In *Eminent Victorians* (1918), Strachey used a series of biographical sketches to heap contempt on his subjects. Grant and Bell looked to the modern artists on the Continent for their models. **Keynesian economics** eventually challenged much of the structure of nineteenth-century economic theory. In both personal practice and theory, the Bloomsbury Group rejected what they regarded as the repressive sexual morality of their parents' generation.

Emile Zola of France was the master of the realistic novel. Emile Zola, 1840–1902. Franzosischer Schriftsteller. Gemalde von Edouard Manet, 1868. Original: Paris, Louvre. Photograph: Lauros-Giraudon. (c) Bildarchiv Preussischer Kulturbesitz, Berlin.

No one charted these changing sensibilities with more eloquence than Virginia Woolf. Her novels, such as *Mrs. Dalloway* (1925) and *To the Lighthouse* (1927), portrayed individuals seeking to make their way in a world with most of the nineteenth-century social and moral certainties removed.

On the Continent, one of the major practitioners of modernism in literature was Marcel Proust (1871–1922). In his seven-volume novel *In Search of Time Past* (*A la Recherche du temps perdu*), published between 1913 and 1927, he adopted a stream-of-consciousness format that allowed him to explore his memories. He would concentrate on a single experience or object and then allow his mind to wander through all the thoughts and memories it evoked. In Germany, Thomas Mann (1875–1955), through a long series of novels, the most famous of which were *Buddenbrooks* (1901) and *The Magic Mountain* (1924), explored both the social experience of middle-class Germans and how they dealt with the intellectual heritage of the nineteenth century. In *Ulysses* (1922), James Joyce (1882–1941), who was born in Ireland, but spent much of his life on the Continent, transformed not only the novel, but also the structure of the paragraph.

Virginia Woolf charted the changing sentiments of a world with most of the nineteenth-century social and moral certainties removed. In A Room of One's Own, *quoted in the document selection on p. 879, she also challenged some of the accepted notions of feminist thought, asking whether women writers should bring to their work any separate qualities they possessed as women, and concluding that men and women writers should strive to share each other's sensibilities.* Hulton Getty/Archive Photos

Modernism in literature arose before World War I and flourished after the war, nourished by the turmoil and social dislocation it created. The war removed many of the old political structures and social expectations. After its appalling violence, readers found themselves much less shocked by upheavals in literary forms and the moral content of novels and poetry.

FRIEDRICH NIETZSCHE AND THE REVOLT AGAINST REASON

During the second half of the century, philosophers began to question the adequacy of rational thinking to address the human situation. No writer better exemplified this new attitude than the German philosopher Friedrich Nietzsche (1844–1900). His books remained unpopular until late in his life, when his brilliance had deteriorated into insanity. He was wholly at odds with the values of the age and attacked Christianity, democracy, nationalism, rationality, science, and progress. He sought less to change values than to probe their sources in the human character. He wanted not only to tear away the masks of respectable life, but to explore how human beings made such masks.

His first important work was *The Birth of Tragedy* (1872) in which he urged that the nonrational aspects of human nature are as important and noble as the rational characteristics. He insisted on the positive function of instinct and ecstasy in human life. To limit human activity to strictly rational behavior was to impoverish human life. In this work, Nietzsche regarded Socrates as one of the major contributors to Western decadence because of the Greek philosopher's appeal for rationality. In Nietzsche's view, the strength for the heroic life and the highest artistic achievement arises from sources beyond rationality.

In later works, such as the prose poem *Thus Spake Zarathustra* (1883), Nietzsche criticized democracy and Christianity. Both would lead only to the mediocrity of sheepish masses. He announced the death of God and proclaimed the coming of the *Overman* (Übermensch), who would embody heroism and greatness. The term was frequently interpreted as some mode of superman or superrace, but such was not Nietzsche's intention.

Dates of Major Works of Fiction
1857 Flaubert, *Madame Bovary*
1877 Zola, *L'Assommoir*
1879 Ibsen, *A Doll's House*
1880 Zola, *Nana*
1881 Ibsen, *Ghosts*
1892 Ibsen, *The Master Builder*
1893 Shaw, *Mrs. Warren's Profession*
1894 Shaw, *Arms and the Man*
1901 Mann, *Buddenbrooks*
1903 Shaw, *Man and Superman*
1913 Shaw, *Androcles and the Lion*
1913 Proust, first volume of *In Search of Time Past*
1922 Joyce, *Ulysses*
1924 Mann, *The Magic Mountain*
1925 Woolf, *Mrs. Dalloway*
1927 Woolf, *To the Lighthouse*

He was critical of contemporary racism and anti-Semitism. He sought a return to the heroism that he associated with Greek life in the Homeric age. He thought the values of Christianity and of bourgeois morality prevented humankind from achieving life on a heroic level.

Two of Nietzsche's most profound works are *Beyond Good and Evil* (1886) and *The Genealogy of Morals* (1887). Both are difficult books. Nietzsche sought to discover not what is good and what is evil, but the social and psychological sources of the judgment of good and evil. He declared, "There are no moral phenomena at all, but only a moral interpretation of phenomena."[4] He dared to raise the question of whether morality itself was valuable: "We need a critique of moral values; the value of these values themselves must first be called in question."[5] In Nietzsche's view, morality was a human convention that had no independent existence. For Nietzsche, this discovery liberated human beings to create life-affirming values instead. Christianity, utilitarianism, and middle-class respectability could, in good conscience, be abandoned. Human beings could create a new moral order that would glorify pride, assertiveness, and strength rather than meekness, humility, and weakness.

In his appeal to feelings and emotions and in his questioning of the adequacy of rationalism, Nietzsche drew on the romantic tradition. The kind of creative impulse that earlier romantics had considered the gift of artists Nietzsche saw as the burden of all human beings. The character of the human situation that this philosophy urged on its contemporaries was that of an ever-changing flux in which nothing but change itself was permanent. Human beings had to forge from their own will and determination the values that were to exist in the world.

THE BIRTH OF PSYCHOANALYSIS

A determination to probe beneath surface or public appearance united the major figures of late-nineteenth-century science, art, and philosophy. They sought to discern the undercurrents, tensions, and complexities that lay beneath the calm surfaces of hard atoms, respectable families, rationality, and social relationships. As a result of their theories and discoveries, educated Europeans could never again view the surface of life with complacency or even much confidence. No intellectual development more exemplified this trend than psychoanalysis through the work of Sigmund Freud (1856–1939).

Marcel Proust's multi-volume In Search of Time Past, *which was published between 1913 and 1927, was one of the most significant modernist novels.*   Corbis

Development of Freud's Early Theories   Freud was born into an Austrian Jewish family that settled in Vienna. He planned to become a lawyer, but soon moved to the study of physiology and medicine. In 1886, he opened his medical practice in Vienna, where he lived until driven out by the Nazis in 1938. Freud conducted all his research and writing from the base of his medical practice. His earliest medical interests had been psychic disorders, to which he sought to apply the critical method of science. In late 1885, he had studied in Paris with Jean-Martin Charcot (1825–1893), who used hypnosis to treat cases of hysteria. In Vienna, he collaborated with another physician, Josef Breuer (1842–1925), and in 1895 they published *Studies in Hysteria.*

In the mid-1890s, Freud abandoned hypnosis and allowed his patients to talk freely and spontaneously about themselves. He found that they associated their particular neurotic symptoms with experiences related to earlier experiences, going back to childhood. He also noted that sexual matters were significant in his patients' problems. For a time, he thought that perhaps sexual incidents during childhood accounted for their illnesses.

By 1897, however, Freud had rejected this view. In its place he formulated a theory of infantile sexuality,

[4]*The Basic Writings of Nietzsche*, ed. and trans. by Walter Kaufman (New York: The Modern Library, 1968), p. 275.

[5]Kaufman, p. 456.

according to which sexual drives and energy already exist in infants and do not simply emerge at puberty. For Freud, human beings are sexual creatures from birth through adulthood. He thus questioned in the most radical manner the concept of childhood innocence. He also portrayed the little-acknowledged matter of sexuality as one of the bases of mental order and disorder.

Freud's Concern with Dreams   During the same decade, Freud also examined the psychic phenomena of dreams. Romantic writers had taken dreams seriously, but few psychologists had examined them scientifically. Freud believed the seemingly irrational content of dreams must have a reasonable, scientific explanation. His research led him to reconsider the general nature of the human mind. He concluded that dreams allow unconscious wishes, desires, and drives that had been excluded from everyday conscious life to enjoy freer play in the mind. "The dream," he wrote, "is the [disguised] fulfillment of a [suppressed, repressed] wish."[6] During the waking hours, the mind represses or censors certain wishes, which are as important to the individual's psychological makeup as conscious thought is. In fact, Freud argued, unconscious drives and desires contribute to conscious behavior. Freud developed these concepts and related them to his idea of infantile sexuality in his most important book, *The Interpretation of Dreams*, published in 1900.

Freud's Later Thought   In later books and essays, Freud developed a new model of the internal organization of the mind as an arena of struggle and conflict among three entities: the id, the superego, and the ego. The **id** consists of amoral, irrational, driving instincts for sexual gratification, aggression, and general physical and sensual pleasure. The **superego** embodies the external moral imperatives and expectations imposed on the personality by society and culture. The **ego** mediates between the impulses of the id and the asceticism of the superego and allows the personality to cope with the inner and outer demands of its existence. Consequently, everyday behavior displays the activity of the personality as its inner drives are partially repressed through the ego's coping with external moral expectations, as interpreted by the superego.

In his acknowledgment of the roles of instinct, will, dreams, and sexuality, Freud reflected the romantic tradition of the nineteenth century. In other respects, however, he was a son of the

Enlightenment. Like the philosophes, he was a realist who wanted human beings to live free of fear and illusions by rationally understanding themselves and their world. He saw the personalities of human beings as being determined by finite physical and mental forces in a finite world. He was hostile to religion and spoke of it as an illusion. Freud, like the writers of the eighteenth century, wished to see civilization and humane behavior prevail. More fully than those predecessors, however, he understood the immense sacrifice of instinctual drives required for rational civilized behavior. It has been a grave misreading of Freud to see him as urging humankind to thrust off all repression. He did indeed believe that excessive repression could lead to mental disorder, but he also believed civilization and the survival of humankind required some repression of sexuality and aggression. Freud thought the sacrifice and struggle were worthwhile, but he was pessimistic about the future of civilization in the West.

Divisions in the Psychoanalytic Movement   By 1910, Freud had gathered around him a small, but able, group of disciples. Several of his early followers soon moved toward theories of which the master disapproved. The most important of these dissenters was Carl Jung (1875–1961), a Swiss whom for many years Freud regarded as his most promising student. Before World War I, the two men, however, had come to a parting of the ways. Jung questioned the primacy of sexual drives in forming personality and in contributing to mental disorder. He also put less faith in reason.

Jung believed the human subconscious contains inherited memories from previous generations. These collective memories, as well as the personal experience of an individual, constitute his or her soul. Jung regarded human beings in the twentieth century as alienated from these useful collective memories. In *Modern Man in Search of a Soul* (1933) and other works, Jung tended toward mysticism and saw positive values in religion. Freud was highly critical of most of Jung's work. If Freud's thought derived primarily from the Enlightenment, Jung's was more dependent on romanticism.

By the 1920s, the psychoanalytic movement had become even more fragmented. Nonetheless, it influenced not only psychology, but also sociology, anthropology, religious studies, and literary theory. In recent years, psychoanalysis has confronted criticism. Whether or not it survives as a model for understanding human behavior, however, it profoundly influenced the intellectual life of the twentieth century.

[6]*The Basic Writings of Sigmund Freud*, trans. by A. A. Brill (New York: The Modern Library, 1938), p. 235.

In 1909 Freud and his then-devoted disciple Carl Jung visited Clark University in Worchester, Massachusetts during Freud's only trip to the United States. Here Freud sits on the right holding a cane. Jung is sitting on the far left. Archives of the History of American Psychology—The University of Akron.

RETREAT FROM RATIONALISM IN POLITICS

Nineteenth-century liberals and socialists agreed that rational analysis could discern the problems of society and prepare solutions. These thinkers felt that, once given the vote, individuals would behave according to their rational political self-interest. Education would improve the human condition. By 1900, these views had come under attack. Political scientists and sociologists painted politics as frequently irrational. Racial theorists questioned whether rationality and education could affect human society at all.

Weber   During this period, however, one major social theorist was impressed by the role of reason in human society. The German sociologist Max Weber (1864–1920) regarded the emergence of rationalism throughout society as the major development of human history. Such rationalization displayed itself in the rise of both scientific knowledge and bureaucratic organization.

Weber saw bureaucratization as the basic feature of modern social life. He used this view to oppose Marx's concept of the development of capitalism as the driving force in modern society. Bureaucratization involved the division of labor as each individual fit into a particular role in much larger organizations. Furthermore, Weber believed that in modern society people derive their own self-images and sense of personal worth from their positions in these organizations.

Weber also contended—again, in contrast to Marx—that noneconomic factors might account for major developments in human history. For example, in his best known essay, *The Protestant Ethic and the Spirit of Capitalism* (1905), Weber traced much of the rational character of capitalist enterprise to the ascetic religious doctrines of Puritanism. The Puritans, in his opinion, had worked for worldly success less for its own sake than to assure themselves that they stood among the elect of God. The theory has generated historical research and debate from its publication to the present.

Theorists of Collective Behavior   In his emphasis on the individual and on the dominant role of rationality, Weber differed from many contemporary social scientists, such as Gustave LeBon (1841–1931), Emile Durkheim (1858–1917), and Georges Sorel (1847–1922) in France, Vilfredo Pareto (1848–1923) in Italy, and Graham Wallas (1858–1932) in England. LeBon was a psychologist who explored the activity of crowds and mobs. He believed that crowds behave irrationally. In *Reflections on Violence* (1908), Sorel argued that people do not pursue rationally perceived goals but are led to action by collectively shared ideals. Durkheim and Wallas became deeply interested in the necessity of shared values and activities in a society. These elements, rather than a logical analysis of the social situation, bind human beings together. Instinct, habit, and affections, instead of reason, direct human social behavior. Besides playing down the function of reason in society, all of these theorists emphasized the role of collective groups in politics rather than that of the individual, formerly championed by liberals.

RACISM

The same tendencies to question or even to deny the constructive activity of reason in human affairs and to sacrifice the individual to the group manifested themselves in theories of race. **Racism** had long existed in Europe. Renaissance explorers had displayed prejudice against nonwhite peoples. Since at least the eighteenth century, biologists and anthropologists had classified human beings according to the color of their skin, their language, and their stage of civilization. After late-eighteenth-century linguistic scholars observed similarities between many of the European languages and Sanskrit, they postulated the existence of an ancient race called the Aryans, who had spoken the original language from which the rest derived. During the romantic period, writers had called the different cultures of Europe races.

The debates over slavery in the European colonies and the United States had given further opportunity for the development of racial theory. In the late nineteenth century, however, race emerged as a single dominant explanation of the history and the character of large groups of people. What transformed racial thinking at the end of the century was its association with the biological sciences. The prestige associated with biology and science in general became transferred to racial thinking, whose advocates now claimed to possess a materialistic, scientific basis for their thought. They came to claim that racial science could support a hierarchy of superior and inferior races within Europe and among the various peoples outside Europe.

Gobineau Count Arthur de Gobineau (1816–1882), a reactionary French diplomat, enunciated the first important theory of race as the major determinant of human history. In his four-volume *Essay on the Inequality of the Human Races* (1853–1854), Gobineau portrayed the troubles of Western civilization as the result of the long degeneration of the original white Aryan race. He claimed it had unwisely intermarried with the inferior yellow and black races, thus diluting the greatness and ability that originally existed in its blood. Gobineau saw no way to reverse this degeneration. (See "Alexis de Tocqueville Forecasts the Danger of Gobineau's Racial Thought.")

Gobineau's essay remained little known for years. However, a growing literature by anthropologists and explorers spread racial thinking. In the wake of Darwin's theory, thinkers applied the concept of survival of the fittest to races and nations. The recognition of the animal nature of humankind made the racial idea all the more persuasive.

Chamberlain At the close of the century, Houston Stewart Chamberlain (1855–1927), an Englishman who settled in Germany, drew together these strands of racial thought into the two volumes of his *Foundations of the Nineteenth Century* (1899). He championed the concept of biological determin-

ism through race, but believed that through genetics the human race could be improved and even that a superior race could be developed. (See "H. S. Chamberlain Exalts the Role of Race.")

Chamberlain was anti-Semitic. He pointed to the Jews as the major enemy of European racial regeneration. Chamberlain's book and the works on which it drew aided the spread of anti-Semitism in European political life. Also in Germany, the writings of Paul de Lagarde (1827–1891) and Julius Langbehn (1851–1907) emphasized the supposed racial and cultural dangers posed by the Jews to German national life.

Late-Century Nationalism Racial thinking was one part of a wider late-century movement toward more aggressive nationalism. Previously, nationalism had in general been a movement among European literary figures and liberals. The former had sought to develop what they regarded as the historically distinct qualities of particular national or ethnic literatures. The liberal nationalists had hoped to redraw the map of Europe to reflect ethnic boundaries. The drive for the unification of Italy and Germany had been major causes, as had been the liberation of Poland from foreign domination. The various national groups of the Habsburg Empire had also sought emancipation from Austrian domination.

From the 1870s onward, however, nationalism became a movement with mass support, well-financed organizations, and political parties. Nationalists often redefined nationality in terms of race and blood. The new nationalism opposed the internationalism of both liberalism and socialism. The ideal of nationality was used to overcome the pluralism of class, religion, and geography. The nation replaced religion for many secularized people. It sometimes became a secular religion in the hands of state schoolteachers, who were replacing the clergy as the instructors of youth. Nationalism of this aggressive racist variety became the most powerful ideology of the early twentieth century and would reemerge after the collapse of communism in the 1990s.

Some Europeans also used racial theory to support harsh, condescending treatment of colonial peoples in the late nineteenth and early twentieth centuries. They were convinced that white Europeans were racially superior to the peoples of color whom they governed and that these peoples would always be inferior to them. Similar racial theory also informed attitudes toward peoples of color in the West itself as was the case with the inferiority ascribed to African Americans and Native Americans in the United States.

ALEXIS DE TOCQUEVILLE FORECASTS THE DANGER OF GOBINEAU'S RACIAL THOUGHT

Alexis de Tocqueville is best known for having written Democracy in America *(2 vols., 1835, 1840). He was also a major historian of the French Revolution, an active politician, and an important commentator on the events and ideas of his time. He knew Arthur de Gobineau and read the first volume of the latter's* Essay on the Inequality of the Human Races *shortly after it was published in 1853. Tocqueville then wrote Gobineau a letter in which he sharply criticized the idea of the racial determination of human actions. Tocqueville also pointed to how dangerous it would be if the idea ever influenced the political life of nations with mass electorates.*

■ *Why does Tocqueville see Gobineau's idea as a kind of materialistic determinism? Why does he think Gobineau's views are wrong? Why does he see political danger in racial thinking?*

Your doctrine is rather a sort of fatalism, of predestination, if you wish, but at any rate, very different from that of St. Augustine, from the Jansenists, and from the Calvinists. . . . You continually speak about races regenerating or degenerating, losing, or acquiring through an infusion of new blood social capacities which they have not previously had. . . . I must frankly say that, to me, this sort of predestination is a close relative of the purest materialism. And be assured that should the masses, whose reasoning always follows the most beaten tracks, accept your doctrines, it would lead them straight from races to individuals and from social capacities to all sorts of potentialities. Whether the element of fatality should be introduced into the material order of things, or whether God willed to make different kinds of men so that He imposed special burdens of race on some, withholding from them a capacity for certain feelings,

for certain thoughts, for certain habits, for certain qualities—all this has nothing to do with my own concern with the practical consequences of these philosophical doctrines. The consequence of both theories is that of a vast limitation, if not a complete abolition, of human liberty. Thus I confess that after having read your book I remain, as before, opposed in the extreme to your doctrines. I believe that they are probably quite false; I know that they are certainly very pernicious. Surely among the different families which compose the human race there exist certain tendencies, certain proper aptitudes resulting from thousands of different causes. But that these tendencies, that these capacities should be insuperable has not only never been proved but no one will ever be able to prove it since to do so one would need to know not only the past but also the future.

From Alexis de Tocqueville to Arthur de Gobineau, 17 November 1853, in Alexis de Tocqueville, *The European Revolution and Correspondence with Gobineau*, edited by J. Lukacs (Gloucester, MA: Peter Smith, 1968), pp. 227–228.

Anti-Semitism and the Birth of Zionism

Political and racial anti-Semitism, which cast such dark shadows across the twentieth century, developed in part from the prevailing atmosphere of racial thought and the retreat from rationality in politics. Religious anti-Semitism dated from at least the Middle Ages. Since the French Revolution, west European Jews had gradually gained entry into civil life. Popular anti-Semitism, however, survived,

with the Jewish community being identified with money and banking interests. During the last third of the century, as finance capitalism changed the economic structure of Europe, many non-Jewish Europeans pressured by the changes became hostile toward the Jewish community.

Anti-Semitic Politics In Vienna, Mayor Karl Lueger (1844–1910) used anti-Semitism as a major attraction for his Christian Socialist Party. In Germany, the ultraconservative Lutheran chaplain

H. S. CHAMBERLAIN EXALTS THE ROLE OF RACE

Houston Stewart Chamberlain's Foundations of the Nineteenth Century *(1899) was one of the most influential late-century works of racial thought. Chamberlain believed that most people in the world are racially mixed and this mixture weakens those human characteristics most needed for physical and moral strength. He also believed people who were assured of their racial purity could act with the most extreme self-confidence and arrogance. Chamberlain's views had a major influence on the Nazi Party in Germany and on others who wished to establish their alleged racial superiority for political purposes.*

■ *What does Chamberlain mean by "Race" in this passage? How, in his view, does race, as opposed to character or environment, determine human nature? How might a nationalist use these ideas?*

Nothing is so convincing as the consciousness of the possession of Race. The man who belongs to a distinct, pure race, never loses the sense of it. The guardian angel of his lineage is ever at his side, supporting him where he loses his foothold, warning him like the Socratic Daemon where he is in danger of going astray, compelling obedience, and forcing him to undertakings which, deeming them impossible, he would never have dared to attempt. Weak and erring like all that is human, a man of this stamp recognises himself, as others recognise him, by the sureness of his character, and by the fact that his actions are marked by a certain simple and peculiar greatness, which finds its explanation in his distinctly typical and super-personal qualities. Race lifts a man above himself; it endows him with extraordinary—I might almost say supernatural—powers, so entirely does it distinguish him from the individual who springs from the chaotic jumble of peoples drawn from all parts of the world: and should this man of pure origin be perchance gifted above his fellows, then the fact of Race strengthens and elevates him on every hand, and he becomes a genius towering over the rest of mankind, not because he has been thrown upon the earth like a flaming meteor by a freak of nature, but because he soars heavenward like some strong and stately tree, nourished by thousands and thousands of roots—no solitary individual, but the living sum of untold souls striving for the same goal.

From Houston Stewart Chamberlain, *Foundations of the Nineteenth Century*, Vol. 1, trans. by John Lees (London: John Lane, 1912), p. 269.

Adolf Stoecker (1835–1909) revived anti-Semitism. The Dreyfus affair in France focused a new hatred toward the Jews.

To this ugly atmosphere, racial thought contributed the belief that no matter to what extent Jews assimilated themselves into the culture of their country, their Jewishness—and thus their alleged danger to society—would remain. For racial thinkers, the problem of race was not in the character, but in the blood of the Jew. An important Jewish response to this new, rabid outbreak of anti-Semitism was the launching in 1896 of the **Zionist** movement to found a separate Jewish state. Its founder was the Austro-Hungarian Theodor Herzl (1860–1904).

Herzl's Response The conviction in 1894 of Captain Dreyfus in France and the election of Karl Lueger in 1895 as mayor of Vienna, as well as personal experiences of discrimination, convinced Herzl that liberal politics and the institutions of the liberal state could not protect the Jews in Europe or ensure that they would be treated justly. In 1896, Herzl published *The Jewish State*, in which he called for a separate state in which all Jews might be assured of those rights and liberties that they should be enjoying in the liberal states of Europe. Furthermore, Herzl followed the tactics of late-century mass democratic politics by directing his appeal particularly to the poor Jews who lived in the ghettos of eastern Europe and the slums of western

Europe. The original call to Zionism thus combined a rejection of the anti-Semitism of Europe and a desire to realize some of the ideals of both liberalism and socialism in a state outside Europe. (See "Herzl Calls for a Jewish State.")

Women and Modern Thought

The ideas that so shook Europe from the publication of *The Origin of Species* through the opening of World War I produced, at best, mixed results for women. Within the often radically new ways of thinking about the world, views of women and their roles in society often remained remarkably unchanged.

ANTIFEMINISM IN LATE-CENTURY THOUGHT

The influence of biology on the thinking of intellectuals during the late nineteenth century and their own interest in the nonrational side of human behavior led many of them to sustain what had become stereotyped views of women. The emphasis on biology, evolution, and reproduction led intellectuals to concentrate on women's mothering role. Their interest in the nonrational led them to reassert the traditional view that feeling and the nurturing instinct are basic to women's nature. Many late-century thinkers and writers of fiction also often displayed real fear and hostility toward women, portraying them as creatures susceptible to overwhelming and often destructive feelings and instincts. A genuinely misogynist strain emerged in late-century fiction and painting.

Much of the biological thought that challenged religious ideas and the accepted wisdom in science actually reinforced the traditional view of women as creatures weaker and less able than men. Darwin himself held such views of women, and he expressed them directly in his scientific writings. Medical thought of the late century similarly sustained these views. Whatever social changes were to be wrought through science, significant changes in the organization of the home and the relationship between men and women were not among them.

This conservative and hostile perception of women manifested itself in several ways within the scientific community. In London in 1860, the Ethnological Society excluded women from its discussions on the grounds that the subject matter of the customs of primitive peoples was unfit for women and that women were amateurs whose presence would lower the level of the discussion. T. H. Huxley, the great defender of Darwin, took the lead in

Theodor Herzl's visions of a Jewish state would eventually lead to the creation of Israel in 1948. BBC Hulton/Corbis

this exclusion, as he had in a previous exclusion of women from meetings of the Geological Society. Male scientists also believed women should not discuss reproduction or other sexual matters. Huxley, in public lectures, claimed to have found scientific evidence of the inferiority of women to men. Karl Vogt (1817–1895), a leading German anthropologist, held similar views about the character of women. Darwin would repeat the ideas of both Huxley and Vogt in his *Descent of Man*. Late-Victorian anthropologists tended likewise to assign women, as well as nonwhite races, an inferior place in the human family. Still, despite their otherwise conservative views on gender, both Darwin and Huxley supported the expansion of education for women.

The position of women in Freud's thought is controversial. Many of his earliest patients, on whose histories he developed his theories, were women. Critics have claimed, nonetheless, that Freud portrayed women as incomplete human beings who might be inevitably destined to unhappy mental lives. He saw the natural destiny of women as motherhood and the rearing of sons as their greatest fulfillment. The first psychoanalysts were trained as medical doctors, and their views of women reflected

HERZL CALLS FOR A JEWISH STATE

In 1896, Theodor Herzl published his pamphlet The Jewish State. *Herzl had lived in France during the turmoil and anti-Semitism associated with the Dreyfus affair. He became convinced that only the establishment of a separate state for Jews would halt the outbreaks of anti-Semitism that characterized late-nineteenth-century European political and cultural life. Following the publication of this pamphlet, Herzl began to organize the Zionist movement among Jews in both eastern and western Europe.*

■ *Why does Herzl define what he calls the Jewish Question as a national question? What objections does he anticipate to the founding of a Jewish state? Why does he believe the founding of a Jewish state will be an effective move against anti-Semitism?*

The idea which I develop in this pamphlet is an age-old one: the establishment of a Jewish State.

The world resounds with outcries against the Jews, and this is what awakens the dormant idea. . . .

I believe I understand anti-Semitism, a highly complex movement. I view it from the standpoint of a Jew, but without hatred or fear. I think I can discern in it the elements of vulgar sport, of common economic rivalry, of inherited prejudice, of religious intolerance—but also of a supposed need for self-defense. To my mind, the Jewish Question is neither a social nor a religious one, even though it may assume these and other guises. It is a national question, and to solve it we must first of all establish it as an international political problem which will have to be settled by the civilized nations of the world in council.

We are a people, one people.

Everywhere we have sincerely endeavored to merge with the national communities surrounding us and to preserve only the faith of our fathers. We are not permitted to do so. . . .

And will some people say that the venture is hopeless, because even if we obtain the land and the sovereignty only the poor people will go along? They are the very ones we need first! Only desperate men make good conquerors.

Will anybody say, Oh yes, if it were possible it would have been done by now?

It was not possible before. It is possible now. As recently as a hundred, even fifty years ago it would have been a dream. Today it is all real. The rich, who have an epicurean acquaintance with all technical advance, know very well what can be done with money. And this is how it will be: Precisely the poor and plain people, who have no idea of the power that man already exercises over the forces of Nature, will have the greatest faith in the new message. For they have never lost their hope of the Promised Land. . . .

Now, all this may seem to be a long-drawn-out affair. Even in the most favorable circumstances it might be many years before the founding of the State is under way. In the meantime, Jews will be ridiculed, offended, abused, whipped, plundered, and slain in a thousand different localities. But no; just as soon as we begin to implement the plan, anti-Semitism will immediately grind to a halt everywhere.

From Theodor Herzl, *The Jewish State* (New York: The Herzl Press, 1970), pp. 27, 33, 109, as quoted in William W. Hallo, David B. Ruderman, and Michael Stanislawski, eds., *Heritage: Civilization and the Jews' Source Reader* (New York: Praeger, 1984), pp. 234–235.

contemporary medical education, which, like much of the scientific establishment, tended to portray women as inferior. Distinguished women psychoanalysts, such as Karen Horney (1885–1952) and Melanie Klein (1882–1960), would later challenge Freud's views on women, and other writers would try to establish a psychoanalytic basis for feminism.

Nonetheless, the psychoanalytic profession would remain dominated by men, as would academic psychology. Because psychology increasingly influenced child rearing and domestic relations law in the twentieth century, it, ironically, gave men a large impact in the one area of social activity that women had dominated.

The social sciences of the late nineteenth and early twentieth centuries similarly reinforced traditional gender roles. Most major theorists believed that women's role in reproduction and child rearing demanded a social position inferior to men. Auguste Comte, whose thought in this area owed much to Rousseau, portrayed women as biologically and intellectually inferior to men. Herbert Spencer, although an advocate for improving women's lot, thought they could never achieve equality with men. Emile Durkheim portrayed women as creatures of feeling and family rather than of intellect. Max Weber favored improvements in the condition of women, but did not really support significant changes in their social roles or in their relationship to men. Virtually all of the early sociologists took a conservative view of marriage, the family, child rearing, and divorce.

New Directions in Feminism

The close of the century witnessed a revival of feminist thought in Europe that would grow in the twentieth century. The role of feminist writers during these years was difficult. Many women's organizations, as seen in Chapter 24, concentrated on achieving the vote for women, but feminist writers and activists raised other questions as well. Women confronted their problems as women in a variety of ways, not just by seeking the vote. Some organizations redefined ways of thinking about women and their relationships to men and society. Few of these groups were large, and their victories were rare. Nonetheless, by the early 1900s, they had defined the issues that would become more fully and successfully explored after World War II.

Sexual Morality and the Family In various nations, middle-class women began to challenge the double standard of sexual morality and the traditional male-dominated family. This often meant challenging laws about prostitution.

Between 1864 and 1886, English prostitutes were subject to the Contagious Diseases Acts. The police in certain cities with naval or military bases could require any woman identified as, or suspected of being, a prostitute to undergo an immediate internal medical examination for venereal disease. Those found to have a disease could be confined for months to locked hospitals (women's hospitals for the treatment of venereal diseases) without legal recourse. The law took no action against their male customers. Indeed, the purpose of the laws was to protect men, presumably sailors and soldiers, and not the women themselves, from infection.

These laws angered English middle-class women who believed the harsh working conditions and the poverty imposed on so many working-class women were the true causes of prostitution. They framed the issue in the context of their own efforts to prove that women are as human and rational as men and thus properly subject to equal treatment. They saw poor women being made victims of the same kind of discrimination that prevented women of their class from entering the universities and professions. The Contagious Diseases Acts assumed that women were inferior to men and treated them as less than rational human beings. The laws literally put women's bodies under the control of male customers, male physicians, and male law-enforcement personnel. They denied to poor women the freedoms that all men enjoyed in English society.

By 1869, the Ladies' National Association for the Repeal of the Contagious Diseases Acts, a distinctly middle-class organization led by Josephine Butler (1828–1906), began actively to oppose those laws. The group achieved the suspension of the acts in 1883 and their repeal in 1886. Government and

Josephine Butler (1828–1906) was an English reformer who campaigned relentlessly to repeal the Contagious Diseases Acts. Getty Images Inc.—Hulton Archive Photos

police regulation of prostitution roused similar movements in other nations, which adopted the English movement as a model. In Vienna during the 1890s, the General Austrian Women's Association, led by Auguste Ficke (1833–1916), combated the legal regulation of prostitution, which would have put women under the control of police authorities. In Germany, women's groups divided between those who would have penalized prostitutes and those who saw them as victims of male society. By the turn of the century, the latter had come to dominate, although tensions between the groups would remain for some time.

The feminist groups that demanded the abolition of laws that punished prostitutes without questioning the behavior of their customers were challenging the double standard and, by extension, the traditional relationship of men and women in marriage. In their view, marriage should be a free union of equals with men and women sharing responsibility for their children. In Germany, the Mothers' Protection League (*Bund für Mutterschutz*) contended that both married and unmarried mothers required the help of the state, including leaves for pregnancy and child care. This radical group emphasized the

need to rethink all sexual morality. In Sweden, Ellen Key (1849–1926), in *The Century of the Child* (1900) and *The Renaissance of Motherhood* (1914), maintained that motherhood is so crucial to society that the government, rather than husbands, should support mothers and their children.

Virtually all turn-of-the-century feminists in one way or another supported wider sexual freedom for women, often claiming it would benefit society as well as improve women's lives. Many of the early advocates of contraception had also been influenced by social Darwinism. They hoped that limiting the number of children would allow more healthy and intelligent children to survive. Such was the outlook of Marie Stopes (1880–1958), an Englishwoman who pioneered contraception clinics in the poor districts of London.

Women Defining Their Own Lives For Josephine Butler and Auguste Ficke, as well as other continental feminists, achieving legal and social equality for women would be one step toward transforming Europe from a male-dominated society to one in which both men and women could control their own destinies. Ficke wrote, "Our final goal is therefore not the acknowledgement of rights, but the elevation of our intellectual and moral level, the development of our personality."[7] Increasingly, feminists would concentrate on freeing and developing women's personalities through better education and government financial support for women engaged in traditional social roles, whether or not they had gained the vote.

Some women also became active within socialist circles. There they argued that the socialist transformation of society should include major reforms for women. Socialist parties usually had all-male leadership. By the close of the century, most male socialist leaders, including Lenin and later Stalin, were intolerant of demands for changes in the family or greater sexual freedom for either men or women. Nonetheless, socialist writings began to include calls for improvements in the economic situation of women that were compatible with more advanced feminist ideals.

It was within literary circles, however, that feminist writers often most clearly articulated the problems that they now understood themselves to face. Distinguished women authors were actually doing, on a more or less equal footing, something that men had always done, leading some to wonder whether simple equality was the main issue. Virginia Woolf's

Publication Dates of Major Nonfiction Works

1830	Lyell, *Principles of Geology*
1830–1842	Comte, *The Positive Philosophy*
1835	Strauss, *The Life of Jesus*
1853–1854	Gobineau, *Essay on the Inequality of the Human Races*
1859	Darwin, *The Origin of Species*
1864	Pius IX, *Syllabus of Errors*
1865	Bernard, *An Introduction to the Study of Experimental Medicine*
1871	Darwin, *The Descent of Man*
1872	Nietzsche, *The Birth of Tragedy*
1883	Mach, *The Science of Mechanics*
1883	Nietzsche, *Thus Spake Zarathustra*
1891	Leo XIII, *Rerum Novarum*
1893	Huxley, *Evolution and Ethics*
1896	Herzl, *The Jewish State*
1899	Chamberlain, *The Foundations of the Nineteenth Century*
1900	Freud, *The Interpretation of Dreams*
1900	Key, *The Century of the Child*
1905	Weber, *The Protestant Ethic and the Spirit of Capitalism*
1908	Sorel, *Reflections on Violence*
1929	Woolf, *A Room of One's Own*
1933	Jung, *Modern Man in Search of a Soul*

[7]Quoted in Harriet Anderson, *Utopian Feminism: Women's Movements in Fin-de-Siècle Vienna* (New Haven, CT: Yale University Press, 1992), p. 13.

VIRGINIA WOOLF URGES WOMEN TO WRITE

In 1928, Virginia Woolf, the English novelist, delivered two papers at women's colleges at Cambridge University that became the basis for A Room of One's Own, *published a year later. There, discussing the difficulty a woman writer confronted in finding women role models, she outlined obstacles that women faced in achieving the education, the time, and the income that would allow them to write. In the passage that follows, which closes her essay, she urges women to begin to write so future women authors would have models. She then presents an image of Shakespeare's sister, who, lacking such models, had not written anything, but who, through the collective efforts of women, might in the future emerge as a great writer because she would have the literary models of the women Woolf addressed to follow and to imitate.*

■ *How does Woolf's fiction of Shakespeare's sister establish a benchmark for women writers? What does Woolf mean by the common life through which women will need to work to become independent writers? Why does she emphasize the need for women to have both income and space if they are to become independent writers?*

A thousand pens are ready to suggest what you should do and what effect you will have. My own suggestion is a little fantastic, I admit; I prefer, therefore, to put it in the form of fiction.

I told you in the course of this paper that Shakespeare had a sister; but do not look for her in Sir Sidney Lee's life of the poet. She died young—alas, she never wrote a word. She lies buried where the omnibuses now stop, opposite the Elephant and Castle [a London intersection]. Now my belief is that this poet who never wrote a word and was buried at the cross-roads still lives. She lives in you and in me, and in many other women who are not here to-night, for they are washing up the dishes and putting the children to bed. But she lives; for great poets do not die; they are continuing presences; they need only the opportunity to walk among us in the flesh. This opportunity, as I think, it is now coming within your power to give her. For my belief is that if we live another century or so—I am talking of the common life which is the real life and not of the little separate lives which we live as individuals—and have five hundred [pounds income]

a year each of us and rooms of our own; if we have the habit of freedom and the courage to write exactly what we think; if we escape a little from the common sitting-room and see human beings not always in their relation to each other but in relation to reality; and the sky, too, and the trees or whatever it may be in themselves; . . . if we face the fact, for it is a fact, that there is no arm to cling to, but that we go alone and that our relation is to the world of reality and not only to the world of men and women, then the opportunity will come and the dead poet who was Shakespeare's sister will put on the body which she has so often laid down. Drawing her life from the lives of the unknown who were her forerunners, as her brother did before her, she will be born. As for her coming without that preparation, without that effort on our part, without that determination that when she is born again she shall find it possible to live and write her poetry, that we cannot expect, for that would be impossible. But I maintain that she would come if we worked for her, and that so to work, even in poverty and obscurity, is worth while.

From Virginia Woolf, *A Room of One's Own* (London: The Hogarth Press, 1974), pp. 170–172.

A Room of One's Own (1929) became one of the fundamental texts of twentieth-century feminist literature. In it, she meditated first on the difficulties that women of both brilliance and social standing encountered in being taken seriously as writers and intellectuals. She concluded that a woman who wishes to write requires both a room of her own, meaning a space not dominated by male institutions, and an adequate independent income. But Woolf was concerned with more than asserting the right of women to participate in intellectual life. Establishing a new stance for feminist writers, she asked whether women, as writers, must imitate men or whether they should bring to their endeavors separate intellectual and psychological qualities they possessed as women. As she had challenged some of the literary conventions of the traditional novel in her fiction, she challenged some of the accepted notions of feminist thought in *A Room of One's Own* and concluded that male and female writers must actually be able to think as both men and women and share the sensibilities of each. In this sense, she sought to open the whole question of gender definition. (See "Virginia Woolf Urges Women to Write.")

By World War I, feminism in Europe, fairly or not, had become associated in the popular imagination with challenges to traditional gender roles and sexual morality and with either socialism or political radicalism. So when extremely conservative political movements arose between the world wars, their leaders often emphasized traditional roles for women and traditional ideas about sexual morality. Lenin and Stalin would follow a similar path in the Soviet political experiment. (See Chapters 27 and 28.)

IN PERSPECTIVE

By the opening of the twentieth century, European thought had achieved contours that seem familiar to us today. Science had revolutionized thinking about nature. Physicists had transformed the traditional views of matter and energy as they probed the mysteries of the atom. Evolutionary biology had revealed that human beings are not distinct from the natural order. Many believed science would provide a new basis for ethics and morality. Christianity had experienced its most severe challenge in modern times from science, history, philosophy, and the secular national states.

Nonreligious thinkers and writers also assailed the primacy of reason. Nietzsche and Freud, in their different ways, questioned whether human beings are rational creatures at all. Weber and other social and political theorists doubted that politics could ever be entirely rational. All these developments challenged the rational values of the Enlightenment. The racial theorists questioned whether mind and character were as important as racial characteristics allegedly carried in the blood. Racial thinking also allowed some Europeans to believe they were inherently superior to non-Europeans, Jews, and ethnic minorities in Europe itself.

Turn-of-the-century feminists demanded equal treatment for women under the law and contended that the relationship between men and women within marriage required rethinking. They set forth much of the feminist agenda for the twentieth century.

REVIEW QUESTIONS

1. Why was science dominant in the second half of the nineteenth century? What were some of the major changes in the scientific outlook between 1850 and 1914? What was positivism? How did Darwin and Wallace's theory of natural selection affect ethics, Christianity, and European views of human nature?

2. Why was Christianity attacked in the late nineteenth century? Why was Leo XIII regarded as a liberal pope? Why was the papacy itself so resilient?

3. Why did Europeans feel superior toward Islam? How did Islamic thinkers respond to the European challenge?

4. How did social conditions of literature change in the late nineteenth century? What was the significance of the explosion of literary matter? How did the realists undermine middle-class morality? How did literary modernism differ from realism?

5. How did Nietzsche and Freud challenge traditional morality?

6. Why were many late-nineteenth-century intellectuals afraid of and hostile to women? How did Freud view the position of women? What social and political issues affected women in the late nineteenth and early twentieth centuries? What new directions did feminism take?

7. What was the character of late-nineteenth-century racism? How did it become associated with anti-Semitism?

SUGGESTED READINGS

M. ADAS, *Machines as the Measure of Men: Science, Technology, and Ideologies of Western Dominance* (1989). The best single volume on racial thinking and technological advances as forming ideologies of European colonial dominance.

C. ALLEN, *The Human Christ: The Search for the Historical Jesus* (1998). A broad survey of the issue for the past two centuries.

S. ASCHHEIM, *The Nietzsche Legacy in Germany 1890–1990* (1992). Examines the influence of Nietzsche.

M. D. Biddis, *Father of Racist Ideology: The Social and Political Thought of Count Gobineau* (1970). Sets the subject in the more general context of nineteenth-century thought.

P. Bowler, *Evolution: The History of an Idea* (1990). An outstanding survey of the subject.

P. Bowler, *Reconciling Science and Religion: The Debate in Early-Twentieth-Century Britain* (2001). A superb survey of the cooperation between religious and scientific writers during the period.

J. Burrow, *The Crisis of Reason: European Thought, 1848–1914* (2000). The best overview available.

F. J. Coppa, *The Modern Papacy since 1789* (1999). A straightforward survey.

K. Dalsimer, *Virginia Woolf: Becoming a Writer* (2002). A psychoanalytic study.

A. Desmond and J. Moore, *Darwin* (1992). A brilliant biography.

J. Efron, *Defenders of the Race: Jewish Doctors and Race Science in Fin-de-Siècle Europe* (1994). How Jewish physicians responded to anti-Semitic racial thought.

P. Gay, *Freud: A Life for Our Time* (1988). The new standard biography.

A. Harrington, *Reenchanted Science: Holism in German Culture from Wilhelm II to Hitler* (1996). A superb analysis of the conflation of science and cultural ideologies.

R. Harris, *Lourdes: Body and Soul in a Secular Age* (1999). The best available discussion of Lourdes in its religious and cultural contexts.

R. Helmstadter (ed.), *Freedom and Religion in the Nineteenth Century* (1997). Major essays on the relationship of church and state.

A. Hourani, *Arab Thought in the Liberal Age 1789–1939* (1967). A classic account, clearly written and accessible to the nonspecialist.

J. Katz, *From Prejudice to Destruction: Anti-Semitism, 1700–1933* (1980). An excellent and far-reaching analysis.

J. Köhler, *Zarathustra's Secret: The Interior Life of Friedrich Nietzsche* (2002). A controversial new biography.

W. Lacqueur, *A History of Zionism* (1989). The most extensive one-volume treatment.

M. Levenson, *The Cambridge Companion to Modernism* (1999). Excellent essays on a wide range of subjects.

G. L. Mosse, *Toward the Final Solution: A History of European Racism* (1978). A sound introduction.

R. Noll, *The Jung Cult: Origins of a Charismatic Movement* (1994). A highly critical account of the origins of Jung's thought in nineteenth-century occult science.

M. R. O'Connell, *Critics on Trial: An Introduction to the Catholic Modernist Crisis* (1994). An extensive, accessible account.

A. Pais, *Subtle Is the Lord: The Science and Life of Albert Einstein* (1983). Remains the most accessible scientific biography.

L. Poliakov, *The Aryan Myth: A History of Racist and Nationalist Ideas in Europe* (1971). Remains the best introduction to the problem.

P. G. J. Pulzer, *The Rise of Political Anti-Semitism in Germany and Austria* (rev. 1989). A sound discussion of anti-Semitism in the world of central European politics.

L. Rainey, *Institutions of Modernism* (1999). A superb exploration of how modernist writers got their books published.

C. E. Schorske, *Fin de Siècle Vienna: Politics and Culture* (1980). Classic essays on the explosively creative intellectual climate of Vienna.

H. W. Smith, *German Nationalism and Religious Conflict: Culture, Ideology, Politics, 1870–1914* (1995). Important exploration of the religious rivalries in the German Empire.

W. Smith, *Politics and the Sciences of Culture in Germany, 1840–1920* (1991). A major survey of the interaction between science and the various social sciences.

F. Stern, *Einstein's German World* (1999). An exploration of German science from the turn of the century to the rise of Hitler.

F. M. Turner, *Contesting Cultural Authority: Essays in Victorian Intellectual Life* (1993). Essays on the relationship between science and religion.

D. Vital, *A People Apart: The Jews in Europe 1789–1939* (1999). A remarkably broad and deeply researched volume.

A. N. Wilson, *God's Funeral* (1999). Explores the thinkers who contributed to religious doubt during the nineteenth and twentieth centuries.

DOCUMENTS CD-ROM

Nineteenth-Century Thought

Cubism Changes the Shape of Painting

Cubism was the single most important new departure in the twentieth-century art of the West. A contemporary critic first coined the term to describe the paintings of Pablo Picasso (1881–1973) and Georges Braque (1882–1963). Cubism emerged in the heady turn-of-the century cultural climate that also fostered the new physics, philosophies that questioned the adequacy of rationality, psychoanalysis, atonality in music, and growing sensitivities to non-Western cultures. Each of these developments in a very real sense led to a refocusing of Western thought just as cubism led to a refocusing of perspective in painting.

For over five hundred years, painting in the West had sought to reproduce the appearance of reality. From the time of the Renaissance, paintings functioned as a kind of window on an artistic depiction of the real world. Even the most advanced art of the nineteenth century, including the Impressionists and post-Impressionists, essentially stood in this tradition, as seen in Manet's *A Bar at the Folies-Bergère.* (See pp. 850–851.)

During the late nineteenth century, artists generally, though not always, working in Paris undertook a number of experiments in both the content and style of painting. In reaction to the impressionists' fascination with light, Paul Cezanne, working largely in isolation, attempted to bring form and solidity back into painting. A new sensitivity also arose in regard to non-Western peoples and their art. Paul Gauguin, for example, produced works portraying peoples living in the South Pacific. Other artists collected African masks or studied such objects in the anthropological museum in Paris. Whereas Cezanne had given artists a new way of looking at and then shaping reality, the art of Africa and of the Pacific gave artists examples of remarkably beautiful works that had no relationship to the long-standing Western artistic tradition.

Beginning in 1907, Picasso and Braque rejected the idea of a painting as constituting a window looking onto the depiction of the real world. Rather, they saw painting as an autonomous realm of art itself with no purpose beyond itself. Braque once commented, "The painter thinks in forms and colors.

The aim is not to reconstitute an anecdotal fact but to constitute a pictorial fact. . . . One does not imitate the appearance; the appearance is the result."[8] Echoing the art of Egypt, medieval primitives, and Africa, Picasso and Braque represented only two dimensions in their painting. They made little or no effort to go beyond the flatness of the surface itself. They attempted to include at one time on a single surface as many different perspectives, angles, or views of the object painted as possible. "Reality" was the construction of their experience of multiple perceptions. The space in the paintings was literally the space of two dimensions filled with geometric shapes as well as geometric voids. The shapes stand dismantled, set in new and usually unexpected positions, communicating a sense of dislocation.

Braque's still life *Violin and Palette* (1909 and 1910) represents the cubist determination to present "a new, completely non-illusionistic and non-imitative method of depicting the visual world."[9] Various shapes seem to flow into other shapes. Portions of the violin and of the palette are recognizable, but as shapes, not as objects in and of themselves. The violin appears at one moment from a host of perspectives, but the violin has interest only in its relationship to the other shapes of color in the painting. As we move to the right of the painting there are no elements that reproduce a recognizable object. The painting exists as its own world and as the construction of the artist. Throughout the painting Braque is quite literally taking apart the violin and other objects so he and the viewer can analyze them. As one commentator explained in 1919 in regard to cubism, "[T]he true picture will constitute an individual object, which will possess an existence of its own apart from the subject that has inspired it."[10] The elements of the palette, the violin, and the notes of a musical score floating on folded paper tents hold interest

[8]Quoted in Max Kozloff, *Cubism/Futurism* (New York: Charterhouse, 1973), p. 11.

[9]Edward F. Fry, *Cubism* (New York: McGraw-Hill, 1966), p. 38.

[10]Maurice Raynal, "Some Intentions of Cubism," 1919, as quoted in Fry, *Cubism*, p. 153.

and meaning in this painting only because they are in the painting, not because they are imitations of a violin, a palette, or a musical score.

At the same time the appearance of elements of these objects in a single painting may indicate Braque's desire to unify the arts. It is known that he was interested in achieving in painting the kind of abstract purity that informed the radically innovative musical compositions of Igor Stravinsky and Arnold Schoenberg. It was also a commonplace modernist outlook that all art aspired to the condition of music. Braque's painting may indicate his aesthetic ambition to carry painting toward the condition of music.

■ *Why was cubism so important in twentieth-century art? How did artists such as Picasso and Braque change the traditional concept of painting? What were their chief aims? How does* Violin and Palette *reflect these aims?*

Sources: Max Kozloff, *Cubism/Futurism* (New York: Charterhouse, 1973); Edward F. Fry, *Cubism* (New York: McGraw-Hill, 1966); Douglas Cooper, *The Cubist Epoch* (New York: Paidon, 1970); Christopher Green, *Cubism and Its Enemies* (New Haven, CT: Yale University Press, 1987); Christine Poggi, *In Defiance of Painting: Cubism, Futurism, and the Invention of Collage* (New Haven, CT: Yale University Press, 1992); Marilyn Stokstad, *Art History* (Englewood Ciffs, NJ: Prentice Hall and New York: Harry N. Abrams, 1999).

Georges Braque, *Violin and Palette* (*Violon et Palette*), 1909–1910. Oil on canvas. 91.7 × 42.8 cm (36 $^1/_8$ × 16 $^7/_8$ inches). Solomon R. Guggenheim Museum, New York, 154.1412. Photography by Lee B. Ewing, © The Solomon R. Guggenheim Foundation, New York. © 2002 Artists Rights Society (ARS), New York/ADAGP, Paris

This recruiting poster was one of many forms of propaganda used in the first years of World War I to encourage enlistment in the armed forces before Britain adopted conscription in 1916, for the first time in its history © Swim Ink/Corbis

CHAPTER 26

IMPERIALISM, ALLIANCES, AND WAR

*D*URING THE SECOND HALF OF *the nineteenth century, and especially after 1870, Europe exercised unprecedented influence and control over the rest of the world. North and South America, as well as Australia and New Zealand, almost became part of the European world as great streams of European immigrants populated them. Until the nineteenth century, Asia (with the significant exception of India) and most of Africa had gone their own ways, having little contact with Europe. But in the latter part of that century, almost all of Africa was divided among a number of European nations. Europe also imposed its economic and political power across Asia. By the next century, European dominance had brought every part of the globe into a single world economy. Events in any corner of the world had significant effects thousands of miles away.*

These developments might have been expected to lead to greater prosperity and good fortune. Instead, they helped foster competition and hostility among the great powers of Europe and bring on a terrible war that undermined Europe's strength and its influence in the world. The peace settlement, proclaimed as "a peace without victors," disillusioned idealists in the West. It treated Germany almost as harshly as Germany would have treated its foes if it had been victorious. Also, the new system failed to provide realistic and effective safeguards against a return to power of a vengeful Germany. The withdrawal of the United States into a disdainful isolation from world affairs destroyed the basis for keeping the peace on which the hopes of Britain and France relied. The frenzy for imperial expansion that seized Europeans in the late nineteenth century had done much to destroy Europe's peace and prosperity and its dominant place in the world.

KEY TOPICS

- The economic, cultural, and strategic factors behind Europe's New Imperialism in the late nineteenth and early twentieth centuries
- The formation of alliances and the search for strategic advantage among Europe's major powers
- The origins and progress of World War I
- The Russian Revolution
- The peace treaties ending World War I

Expansion of European Power and the New Imperialism

The explosive developments in nineteenth-century science, technology, industry, agriculture, transportation, communication, and military weapons provided the chief sources of European power. They made it possible for a few Europeans (or Americans) to impose their will, by force or the threat of force, on other peoples many times their number. Institutional as well as material advantages allowed westerners to have their way. The growth of national states that commanded the loyalty, service, and resources of their inhabitants to a degree previously unknown was a Western phenomenon. It permitted the European nations to deploy their resources more effectively than ever before.

The Europeans also possessed another, less tangible, weapon: They considered their civilization and

way of life to be superior to all others. This gave them a self-confidence that was often unpleasantly arrogant and fostered their expansionist mood.

The expansion of European influence was not anything new. Spain, Portugal, France, Holland, and Britain had controlled territories overseas for centuries, but by the mid–nineteenth century, only Great Britain still had extensive holdings. The first half of the century was generally hostile to colonial expansion. Even the British had been sobered by their loss of the American colonies. The French acquired Algeria and part of Indochina, and the British added territory to their holdings in Canada, India, Australia, and New Zealand. The dominant doctrine of free trade, however, opposed political interference in other lands as economically unprofitable.

Britain ruled the waves and had great commercial advantages as a result of being the first country to experience the Industrial Revolution. Therefore, the British were usually content to trade and invest overseas without annexations. Yet they were prepared to interfere forcefully if a less industrialized country placed barriers in the way of their trade. Still, at midcentury, in Britain as elsewhere, most people opposed further political or military involvement overseas.

In the last third of the century, however, the European states swiftly spread their control over perhaps 10 million square miles and 150 million people—about one-fifth of the world's land area and one-tenth of its population. During this period, European expansion went forward with great speed, and participation in it came to be regarded as necessary for a great power. The movement has been called the **New Imperialism.**

THE NEW IMPERIALISM

The word **imperialism** is now so loosely used that it has almost lost real meaning. It may be useful to offer a definition that might be widely accepted: "the policy of extending a nation's authority by territorial acquisition or by establishing economic and political hegemony over other nations."[1] That definition seems to apply equally well to ancient Egypt and Mesopotamia and to the European performance in the late nineteenth century. But there were new elements in the latter case. Previous imperialisms had taken the form either of seizing land and settling it with the conqueror's people or of establishing trading centers to exploit the resources of the dominated area. The New Imperialism did not completely abandon these devices, but it also introduced new ones.

India was "the jewel in the crown" of the British Empire, its most profitable and valued possession. This engraving from 1875 pictures the Prince of Wales entering the Indian town of Baroda on an elephant. The Granger Collection

---

[1] *American Heritage Dictionary of the English Language,* 3rd ed. (New York: Houghton Mifflin, 1993), p. 681.

The usual pattern of the New Imperialism was for a European nation to invest capital in a "less industrialized" country, to develop its mines and agriculture, to build railroads, bridges, harbors, and telegraph systems, and to employ great numbers of natives in the process. The local economy and culture were thereby transformed. To safeguard its investments, the dominant European state would make favorable arrangements with the local government, either by loaning the rulers money or by intimidating them.

If these arrangements proved inadequate, the dominant power would establish more direct political control. Sometimes this meant full annexation and direct rule as a colony, or it could be a protectorate status, whereby the local ruler became a figurehead controlled by the dominant European state and maintained by its military power. In other instances, the European state established "spheres of influence" in which it received special commercial and legal privileges without direct political involvement.

MOTIVES FOR THE NEW IMPERIALISM: THE ECONOMIC INTERPRETATION

The predominant interpretation of the motives for the New Imperialism has been economic, in the form given by the English radical economist J. A. Hobson (1858–1928) and later adapted by Lenin. As Lenin put it, "Imperialism is the monopoly stage of capitalism,"[2] the last stage of a dying system. Competition inevitably eliminates inefficient capitalists and therefore leads to monopoly. Powerful industrial and financial capitalists soon run out of profitable areas of investment in their own countries and persuade their governments to gain colonies in "less developed" countries. Here they can find higher profits from their investments, new markets for their products, and safe sources of raw materials.

Facts do not support this viewpoint, however. The European powers did invest considerable capital abroad, but not in a way that fit the model of Hobson and Lenin. Britain, for example, made heavier investments abroad before 1875 than during the next two decades. Only a small percentage of British and European investments overseas, moreover, went to their new colonies. Most capital went into other European countries or to older, well-established areas like the United States, Canada, Australia, and New Zealand. Even when investments were made in new areas, they were not necessarily put into colonies held by the investing country.

The facts are equally discouraging for those who emphasize the need for markets and raw materials. Colonies were not usually important markets for the great imperial nations, and all these states were forced to rely on areas that they did not control as sources of vital raw materials. It is not even clear that control of the new colonies was particularly profitable, though Britain, to be sure, benefited greatly from its rule of India. It is also true that some European businesspeople and politicians hoped colonial expansion would cure the great depression of 1873 to 1896.

Nevertheless, as one of the leading students of the subject has said, "No one can determine whether the accounts of empire ultimately closed with a favorable cash balance."[3] That is true of the European imperial nations collectively, but it is certain that for some of them, like Italy and Germany, empire was a losing proposition. Some individuals and companies, of course, made great profits from particular colonial ventures, but such people were able to influence national policy only occasionally. Economic motives certainly played a part, but a full understanding of the New Imperialism requires a search for other motives.

[3]D. K. Fieldhouse, *The Colonial Empires* (New York: Delacorte, 1966), p. 393.

THE DEVILFISH IN EGYPTIAN WATERS.

An American cartoonist in 1888 depicted John Bull (England) as the octopus of imperialism, grabbing land on every continent. The Granger Collection

[2]V. I. Lenin, *Imperialism, the Highest Stage of Capitalism* (New York: International Publishers, 1939), p. 88.

CULTURAL, RELIGIOUS, AND SOCIAL INTERPRETATIONS

Advocates of imperialism gave various justifications for it. Some argued that the advanced European nations had a duty to bring the benefits of their higher culture and superior civilization to more so-called backward peoples. (See "Social Darwinism and Imperialism.") Religious groups demanded that Western governments furnish political and even military support for Christian missionaries. Some politicians and diplomats supported imperialism as a tool of social policy. In Germany, for instance, some people suggested that imperial expansion would deflect public interest away from domestic politics and social reform. Yet Germany acquired few colonies, and such considerations played little, if any, role in its colonial policy.

In Britain, Joseph Chamberlain (1836–1914), the colonial secretary from 1895 to 1903, argued for the empire as a source of profit and economic security that would finance a great program of domestic reform and welfare. These arguments were not important as motives for British imperial expansion, because they were made well after Britain had acquired most of its empire.

Another common and apparently plausible justification for imperialism was that colonies would attract a European country's surplus population. In fact, most European emigrants went to areas not controlled by their countries, chiefly North and South America and Australia.

STRATEGIC AND POLITICAL INTERPRETATIONS: THE SCRAMBLE FOR AFRICA

Strategic and political considerations were more important in bringing on the New Imperialism. The scramble for Africa in the 1880s is one example. (See Maps 26–1 and 26–2.)

SOCIAL DARWINISM AND IMPERIALISM

One of the intellectual foundations of the New Imperialism was the doctrine of social Darwinism, a pseudoscientific application of Darwin's ideas about biology to nations and races. The impact of social Darwinism was substantial. In the selection that follows, an Englishman, Karl Pearson (1857–1936), attempts to connect concepts from evolutionary theory—the struggle for survival and the survival of the fittest—to the development of human societies.

■ *How does the author connect Darwin's ideas to the concept of human progress? Is it reasonable to equate biological species with human societies, races, or nations? How do the author's ideas justify imperial expansion? What arguments can you make against the author's assertions?*

History shows me one way, and one way only, in which a state of civilisation has been produced, namely, the struggle of race with race, and the survival of the physically and mentally fitter race. This dependence of progress on the survival of the fitter race, terribly black as it may seem to some of you, gives the struggle for existence its redeeming features; it is the fiery crucible out of which comes the finer metal. You may hope for a time when the sword shall be turned into the ploughshare, when American and German and English traders shall no longer compete in the markets of the world for raw materials, for their food supply, when the white man and the dark shall share the soil between them, and each till it as he lists. But, believe me, when that day comes mankind will no longer progress; there will be nothing to check the fertility of inferior stock; the relentless law of heredity will not be controlled and guided by natural selection. Man will stagnate. . . . The path of progress is strewn with the wreck of nations; traces are everywhere to be seen of the hecatombs of inferior races, and of victims who found not the narrow way to the greater perfection. Yet these dead peoples are, in very truth, the stepping stones on which mankind has arisen to the higher intellectual and deeper emotional life of today.

From Karl Pearson, *National Life from the Standpoint of Science*, 2nd ed. (Cambridge, UK: Cambridge University Press, 1907), pp. 21, 26–27, 64.

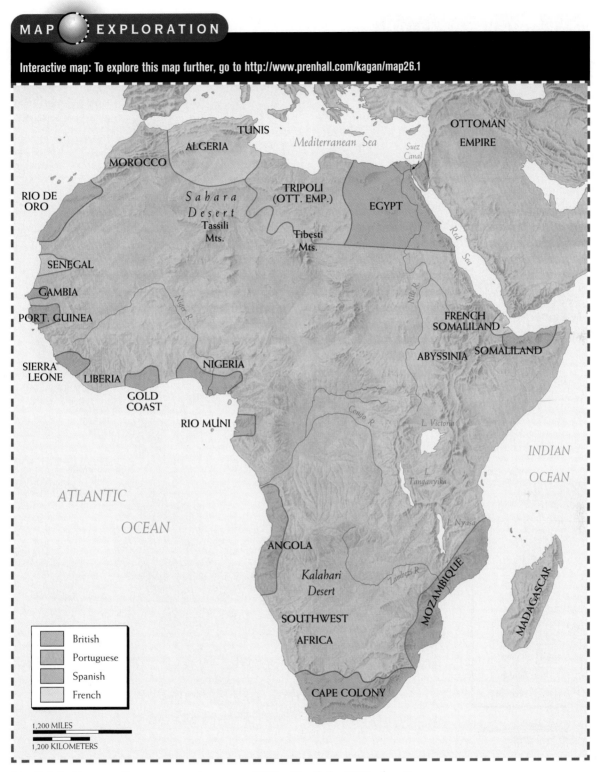

Interactive map: To explore this map further, go to http://www.prenhall.com/kagan/map26.1

MAP 26–1 IMPERIAL EXPANSION IN AFRICA TO 1880 *Until the 1880s, few European countries held colonies in Africa, mostly on its fringes.*

Great Britain Britain was the only great power with extensive overseas holdings on the eve of the scramble. The completion of the Suez Canal in 1869 made Egypt vitally important to the British because it sat astride the shortest route to India. Under Disraeli, Britain purchased a major, but not a controlling, interest in the canal in 1875. When internal troubles threatened Egypt's stability in the 1880s, the British established control. Then, to protect Egypt, they advanced into the Sudan.

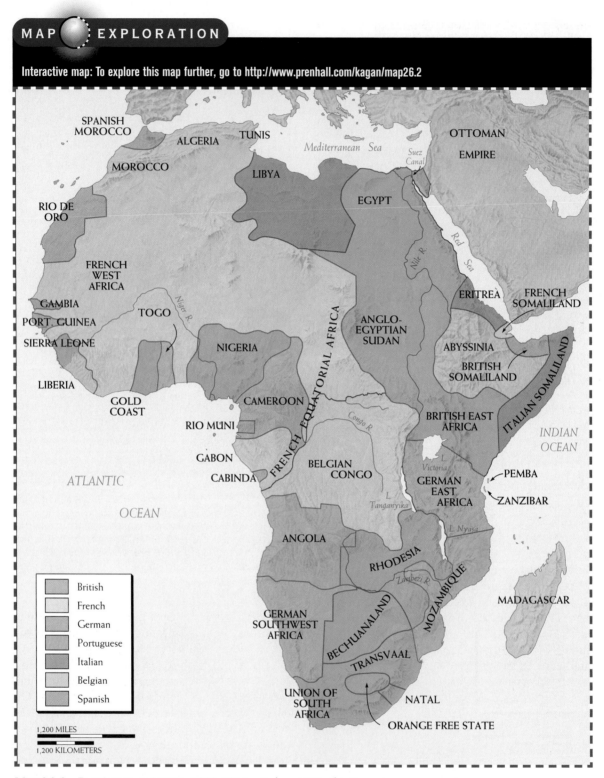

MAP 26–2 PARTITION OF AFRICA, 1880–1914 *Before 1880, the European presence in Africa was largely the remains of early exploration by old imperialists and did not penetrate the heart of the continent. By 1914, the occupying powers included most large European states; only Liberia and Abyssinia remained independent.*

France and Smaller Nations France became involved in North Africa in 1830 by sending an expedition to attack pirates in Algiers. The French gradually extended their control, and thousands of Europeans settled in the country. By the 1880s, France was in full control of Algeria. In 1882, to prevent Tunisia from falling into Italy's hands, France took over that country also. In addition, the French annexed much of West Africa, the Congo, and the island of Madagascar.

Soon smaller states like Belgium, Portugal, Spain, and Italy were acquiring new African colonies or expanding old ones. By the 1890s, their intervention had compelled Britain to expand northward from the Cape of Good Hope into what is now Zimbabwe and Zambia. Britain may have had significant strategic reasons for protecting the Suez and Cape routes to India, but France and the other European nations did not. Their motives were political as well as economic, for they equated political status (Britain was the chief model) with the possession of colonies. They therefore sought colonies to buttress their own importance.

Germany Bismarck appears to have pursued an imperial policy, however briefly, from cold political motives. In 1884 and 1885, Germany declared protectorates over Southwest Africa (Namibia), Togoland, the Cameroons, and East Africa (Tanzania). None of these places was particularly valuable or of intrinsic strategic importance. Bismarck himself had no interest in overseas colonies and once compared them to fine furs worn by impoverished Polish nobles who had no shirts underneath. His concern lay in Germany's exposed position in Europe. On one occasion he said, "My map of Africa lies in Europe. Here is Russia, and there is France, and here in the middle are we. That is my map of Africa."[4] He acquired colonies chiefly to improve Germany's diplomatic position in Europe. He hoped colonial expansion would divert French hostility against Germany. Also, German colonies in Africa could be used as a subtle weapon with which to persuade the British to be reasonable.

THE IRRATIONAL ELEMENT

Germany's annexations started a wild scramble by the other European powers to acquire what was left of Africa. By 1890, almost all the continent had been parceled out. Great powers and small had expanded into areas neither profitable nor strategic for reasons less calculating and rational than Bismarck's.

Le Petit Journal

LA FRANCE VA POUVOIR PORTER LIBREMENT AU MAROC LA CIVILISATION LA RICHESSE ET LA PAIX

France's imperialism always reflected its sense of its unique cultural superiority, and the French liked to think of themselves as benevolently sharing it with the colonial people they ruled. This magazine cover from 1911 shows the symbol of France bringing civilization, peace, and prosperity to Morocco. The Granger Collection

"Empire in the modern period," D. K. Fieldhouse observed, "was the product of European power: its reward was power or the sense of power."[5]

Such motives were not new. They had been well understood by the Athenian spokesman at Melos in 416 B.C.E., whose words were reported by Thucydides: "Of the gods we believe and of men we know clearly that by a necessity of their nature where they have the power they rule."[6]

In Asia, the emergence of Japan as a great power frightened the other powers that were interested in China. (See Map 26–3.) The Russians were building a railroad across Siberia to Vladivostok and were afraid of any threat to Manchuria. Together with France and Germany, they applied diplomatic pressure that forced Japan out of the Liaotung Peninsula

[4]Quoted in J. Remak, *The Origins of World War I, 1871–1914* (New York: Holt, Rinehart & Winston, 1967), p. 5.

[5]Fieldhouse, p. 393.
[6]Thucydides, *The Peloponnesian War*, 5, 105:2.

Expansion of European Power and the New Imperialism	
1869	Suez Canal completed
1875	Britain gains control of Suez
1882	France controls Algeria and Tunisia
1880s	Britain establishes protectorate over Egypt
1884–1885	Germany establishes protectorate over Southwest Africa (Namibia), Togoland, the Cameroons, and East Africa (Tanzania)
1898	Spanish-American War: United States acquires Puerto Rico, Philippines, and Guam, annexes Hawaiian Islands, and establishes protectorate over Cuba
1899	United States proposes Open Door Policy in Far East

in northern China and its harbor, Port Arthur. All pressed feverishly for concessions in China. Fearing that China, its markets, and its investment opportunities would soon be closed to U.S. citizens, the United States proposed the Open Door Policy in 1899. This policy opposed foreign annexations in China and allowed entrepreneurs of all nations to trade there on equal terms. The support of Britain helped win acceptance of the policy by all the powers except Russia.

The United States had only recently emerged as a force in international affairs. After freeing itself of British rule and consolidating its independence during the Napoleonic wars, the Americans had busied themselves with westward expansion on the North American continent until the end of the nineteenth century. The Monroe Doctrine of 1823 had, in effect, made the entire Western Hemisphere an American protectorate. Cuba's attempt to gain independence from Spain was the spark for the new U.S. involvement in international affairs. Sympathy for the Cuban cause, U.S. investments on the island, the desire for Cuban sugar, and concern over the island's strategic importance in the Caribbean all helped persuade the United States to fight Spain.

Victory in the Spanish-American War of 1898 brought the United States an informal protectorate over Cuba and the annexation of Puerto Rico and drove Spain completely out of the Western Hemisphere. The United States forced Spain to sell the Philippine Islands and Guam, and Germany bought the other Spanish islands in the Pacific. The United States and Germany also divided Samoa between them. The remaining Pacific Islands were

taken by France and Britain. Hawaii had been under American influence for some time and was annexed in 1898. This burst of activity after the Spanish-American War made the United States an imperial and Pacific power.

Thus, by the turn of the century, most of the world had come under the control of the industrialized West. The one remaining area of great vulnerability was the Ottoman Empire. Its fate, however, was closely tied up with European developments and must be treated in that context.

Emergence of the German Empire and the Alliance Systems (1873–1890)

Prussia's victories over Austria and France and its creation of a large, powerful German Empire in 1871 revolutionized European diplomacy. A vast new political unit had united the majority of Germans to form a nation of great and growing population, wealth, industrial capacity, and military power. Its sudden appearance created new problems and upset the balance of power that had been forged at the Congress of Vienna. Britain and Russia retained their positions, although the latter had been weakened by the Crimean War.

Austria, however, had been severely weakened, and the forces of nationalism threatened it with disintegration. French power and prestige were badly damaged by the Franco-Prussian War and the German annexation of Alsace-Lorraine. The French were both afraid of their powerful new neighbor and resentful of their defeat, their loss of territory, and the loss of France's traditional position as the dominant western European power.

BISMARCK'S LEADERSHIP (1873–1890)

Until 1890, Bismarck continued to guide German policy. After 1871, he insisted Germany was a satisfied power and wanted no further territorial gains, and he meant it. He wanted to avoid a new war that might undo his achievement. He tried to assuage French resentment by pursuing friendly relations and by supporting French colonial aspirations. He also prepared for the worst. If France could not be conciliated, it must be isolated. Bismarck sought to prevent an alliance between France and any other European power—especially Austria or Russia—that would threaten Germany with a war on two fronts.

War in the Balkans Bismarck's first move was to establish the Three Emperors' League in 1873. The League brought together the three great conservative

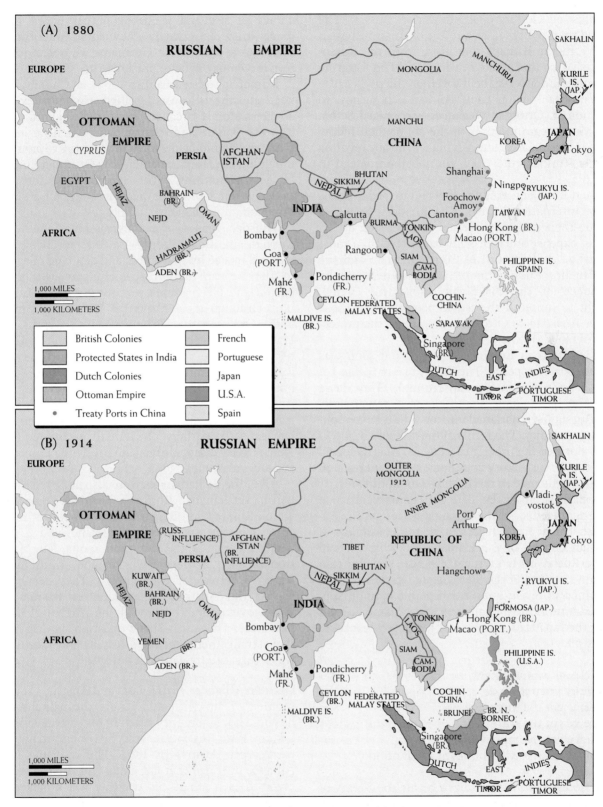

MAP 26–3 ASIA, 1880–1914   *As in Africa, the decades before World War I saw imperialism spread widely and rapidly in Asia. Two new powers, Japan and the United States, joined the British, French, and Dutch in extending control both to islands and to the mainland and in exploiting an enfeebled China.*

empires of Germany, Austria, and Russia. The league soon collapsed as a result of Austro-Russian rivalry in the Balkans that arose from the Russo-Turkish War that broke out in 1875. The tottering Ottoman Empire was held together chiefly because the European powers could not agree about how to partition it. Ottoman weakness encouraged Serbia and Montenegro to come to the aid of their fellow Slavs in Bosnia and Herzegovina when they revolted against Turkish rule. Soon the rebellion spread to Bulgaria.

Then Russia entered the fray and turned it into a major international crisis. The Russians hoped to pursue their traditional policy of expansion at Ottoman expense and especially to achieve their most cherished goal: control of Constantinople and the Dardanelles. Russian intervention also reflected the influence of the Pan-Slavic movement, which sought to unite all the Slavic peoples, even those under Austrian or Ottoman rule, under the protection of Holy Mother Russia.

The Ottoman Empire was weak and soon was forced to sue for peace. The Treaty of San Stefano of March 1878 was a Russian triumph. The Slavic states in the Balkans were freed of Ottoman rule, and Russia itself obtained territory and a large monetary indemnity. The terms of the settlement, however, alarmed the other great powers. Austria feared that the Slavic victory and the powerful increase in Russian influence in the Balkans would threaten its own Balkan provinces. The British were alarmed both by the effect of the Russian victory on the European balance of power and by the possibility of Russian control of the Dardanelles, which would make Russia a Mediterranean power and threaten Britain's control of the Suez Canal. Disraeli was determined to resist, and British public opinion supported him. A music-hall song that became popular gave the language a new word for superpatriotism: *jingoism*.

> We don't want to fight,
> But by jingo if we do,
> We've got the men,
> We've got the ships,
> We've got the money too!
> The Russians will not have Constantinople!

The Congress of Berlin Even before the Treaty of San Stefano, Disraeli sent a fleet to Constantinople. After the magnitude of Russia's appetite was known, Britain and Austria forced Russia to agree to an international conference at which the other great powers would review the provisions of San Stefano. The resulting Congress of Berlin met in June and July 1878 under the presidency of Bismarck. The choice of site and presiding officer was a clear recognition of Germany's new importance and of Bismarck's claim that Germany wanted no new territory and sought to preserve the peace.

Bismarck referred to himself as an "honest broker," and the title was justified. He agreed to the congress simply because he wanted to avoid a war between Russia and Austria into which he feared Germany would be drawn with nothing to gain and much to lose. From the collapsing Ottoman Empire, he wanted nothing. "The Eastern Question," he said, "is not worth the healthy bones of a single Pomeranian musketeer."[7]

The decisions of the congress were a blow to Russian ambitions. Bulgaria, a Russian client, was reduced in size by two-thirds and deprived of access to the Aegean Sea. Austria-Hungary was given Bosnia and Herzegovina to "occupy and administer," although those provinces remained formally under Ottoman rule. Britain received Cyprus, and France was encouraged to occupy Tunisia. These territories were compensation for the gains that Russia was permitted to keep. Germany asked for nothing, but still earned Russian resentment. The Russians believed they had saved Prussia in 1807 from complete dismemberment by Napoleon and had expected a show of German gratitude. They were bitterly disappointed, and the Three Emperors' League was dead.

All of the Balkan states were also annoyed by the Berlin settlement. Romania wanted Bessarabia, which Russia kept; Bulgaria wanted a return to the borders of the Treaty of San Stefano; and Greece wanted a part of the Ottoman spoils. The major trouble spot, however, was in the south Slavic states of Serbia and Montenegro. They deeply resented the Austrian occupation of Bosnia and Herzegovina, as did many of the natives of those provinces. The south Slavic question, no less than the estrangement between Russia and Germany, was a threat to the peace of Europe.

German Alliances with Russia and Austria For the moment, Bismarck could ignore the Balkans, but he could not ignore the breach in his eastern alliance system. With Russia alienated, he concluded a secret treaty with Austria in 1879. The resulting Dual Alliance provided that Germany and Austria would come to each other's aid if either was attacked by Russia. If either was attacked by another country, each promised at least to maintain neutrality.

The treaty was for five years and was renewed regularly until 1918. As the anchor of German policy,

---

[7]Quoted in Hajo Holborn, *A History of Modern Germany, 1840–1945* (New York: Knopf, 1969), p. 239.

it was criticized at the time, and in retrospect, some have considered it an error. It appeared to tie German fortunes to those of the troubled Austro-Hungarian Empire and thus to borrow trouble for Germany. And, by isolating the Russians, it pushed them to seek alliances in the West.

Bismarck was fully aware of these dangers, but discounted them with good reason. He never allowed the alliance to drag Germany into Austria's Balkan quarrels. As he put it, in any alliance there is a horse and a rider, and he meant Germany to be the rider. He made it clear to the Austrians that the alliance was purely defensive and Germany would never be a party to an attack on Russia. "For us," he said, "Balkan questions can never be a motive for war."[8]

Bismarck believed that monarchical, reactionary Russia would not seek an alliance either with republican, revolutionary France or with increasingly democratic Britain. In fact, he expected the news of the Austro-German negotiations to frighten Russia into seeking closer relations with Germany, and he was right. Russian diplomats soon approached him, and by 1881 he had concluded a renewal of the Three Emperors' League on a firmer basis. The three powers promised to maintain friendly neutrality in case any of them was attacked by a fourth power. Other clauses included the right of Austria to annex Bosnia-Herzegovina whenever it wished and the support of all three powers for closing the Dardanelles to all nations in case of war.

The agreement allayed German fears of a Russian-French alliance and Russian fears of a combination of Austria and Britain against it, of Britain's fleet sailing into the Black Sea, and of a hostile combination of Germany and Austria. Most importantly, the agreement aimed to resolve the conflicts in the Balkans between Austria and Russia. Though it did not end such conflicts, it was a significant step toward peace.

The Triple Alliance In 1882, Italy, ambitious for colonial expansion and bothered by the French occupation of Tunisia, asked to join the Dual Alliance. The provisions of its entry were defensive and directed against France. At this point, Bismarck's policy was a complete success. He was allied with three of the great powers and friendly with the other, Great Britain, which held aloof from all alliances. France was isolated and no threat. Bismarck's diplomacy was a great achievement, but an even greater challenge was to maintain this complicated system of secret alliances in the face of the continuing rivalries among Germany's allies. Despite

another Balkan war that broke out in 1885 and again estranged Austria and Russia, he succeeded.

Although the Three Emperors' League lapsed, the Triple Alliance (Germany, Austria, and Italy) was renewed for another five years. To restore German relations with Russia, Bismarck negotiated the Reinsurance Treaty of 1887, in which both powers promised to remain neutral if either was attacked. All seemed smooth, but a change in the German monarchy soon upset Bismarck's arrangements.

In 1888, William II (r. 1888–1918) came to the German throne. He was twenty-nine years old, ambitious, and impetuous. He was imperious by temperament and believed he ruled by divine right. He had suffered an injury at birth that left him with a withered left arm. He compensated for this disability with vigorous exercise, a military bearing and outlook, and an often embarrassingly bombastic rhetoric.

Like many Germans of his generation, William II was filled with a sense of Germany's destiny as the leading power of Europe. He wanted to achieve recognition of at least equality with Britain, the land of his mother and of his grandmother, Queen Victoria. To achieve a "place in the sun," he and his contemporaries wanted a navy and colonies like Britain's. These aims, of course, ran counter to Bismarck's limited continental policy. When William argued for a navy as a defense against a British landing in North Germany, Bismarck replied, "If the British should land on our soil, I should have them arrested." This was only one example of the great distance between the young emperor, or kaiser, and his chancellor. In 1890, William used a disagreement over domestic policy to dismiss Bismarck.

As long as Bismarck held power, Germany was secure, and there was peace among the great European powers. Although he made mistakes and was not always successful, there was much to admire in his understanding and management of international relations in the hard world of reality. He had a clear and limited idea of his nation's goals. He resisted pressures for further expansion with few and insignificant exceptions. He understood and used the full range of diplomatic weapons: appeasement and deterrence, threats and promises, secrecy and openness. He understood the needs and hopes of other countries and, where possible, tried to help them satisfy their needs or used those countries to his own advantage. His system of alliances created a stalemate in the Balkans and ensured German security.

During Bismarck's time, Germany was a force for European peace and increasingly understood to be so. This position would not, of course, have been possible without its great military power. It

[8]Quoted in Remak, p. 14.

Bismarck and the young Kaiser William II meet in 1888. The two disagreed over many issues, and in 1890 William dismissed the aged chancellor. German Information Center

also required, however, the leadership of a statesman who was willing and able to exercise restraint and who understood what his country needed and what was possible.

FORGING OF THE TRIPLE ENTENTE (1890–1907)

Franco-Russian Alliance Almost immediately after Bismarck's retirement, his system of alliances collapsed. His successor was General Leo von Caprivi (1831–1899), who had once asked, "What kind of jackass will dare to be Bismarck's successor?" Caprivi refused the Russian request to renew the Reinsurance Treaty, in part because he felt incompetent to continue Bismarck's complicated policy and in part because he wished to draw Germany closer to Britain. The results were unfortunate as Britain remained aloof and Russia was alienated.

Even Bismarck had assumed that ideological differences would prevent a Franco-Russian alliance.

Political isolation and the need for foreign capital, however, unexpectedly drove the Russians toward France. The French, who were even more isolated, were glad to encourage their investors to pour capital into Russia if it would help produce an alliance and security against Germany. In 1894, a defensive Franco-Russian alliance against Germany was signed.

Britain and Germany Britain now became the key to the international situation. Colonial rivalries pitted the British against the Russians in central Asia and against the French in Africa. Traditionally, Britain had also opposed Russian control of Constantinople and the Dardanelles and French control of the Low Countries. There was no reason to think Britain would soon become friendly to its traditional rivals or abandon its accustomed friendliness toward the Germans.

Yet within a decade of William II's accession, Germany had become the enemy in British minds. Before the turn of the century, popular British thrillers about imaginary wars portrayed the French as the invader; after the turn of the century, the enemy was always Germany. This remarkable transformation has often been attributed to economic rivalry between Germany and Britain, in which Germany made vast strides to challenge and even overtake British production in various materials and markets. Certainly, Germany made such gains and many Britons resented them. Yet the problem was not a serious cause of hostility, and it waned during the first decade of the century. The real problem lay in the foreign and naval policies of the German emperor and his ministers.

William II admired Britain's colonial empire and mighty fleet. At first, Germany tried to win the British over to the Triple Alliance, but when Britain clung to its "splendid isolation," German policy changed. The idea was to demonstrate Germany's worth as an ally by withdrawing support and even making trouble for Britain. This odd manner of gaining an ally reflected the kaiser's confused feelings toward Britain, which mixed dislike and jealousy with admiration. These feelings were shared by many Germans, especially in the intellectual community. Like William, they were eager for Germany to pursue a "world policy" rather than Bismarck's limited one that confined German interests to Europe. They, too, saw England as the barrier to German ambitions. Their influence in the schools, the universities, and the press guaranteed popular approval of actions and statements hostile to Britain.

The Germans began to exert pressure against Britain in Africa by barring British attempts to build a railroad from Capetown to Cairo. They also openly sympathized with the Boers of South Africa in their resistance to British expansion. In 1896, William insulted the British by sending a congratulatory telegram to Paul Kruger (1825–1904), president of the Transvaal, for repulsing a British raid "without having to appeal to friendly powers [i.e., Germany] for assistance."

In 1898, William began to realize his dream of a German navy with the passage of a naval law providing for nineteen battleships. In 1900, a second law doubled that figure. The architect of the new navy was Admiral Alfred von Tirpitz (1849–1930), who openly proclaimed that Germany's naval policy was aimed at Britain. His "risk" theory argued that Germany could build a fleet strong enough, not to defeat the British, but to do enough damage to make the British navy inferior to that of other powers like France or the United States. The theory was, in fact, absurd, because as Germany's fleet became menacing, the British would certainly build enough ships to maintain their advantage, and Britain had greater financial resources than Germany.

The naval policy, therefore, was doomed to failure. Its main achievements were to waste German resources and to begin a great naval race with Britain. Eventually, the threat posed by the German navy so antagonized and alarmed British opinion that the British abandoned their traditional attitudes and policies.

At first, however, Britain was not unduly concerned. The British were embarrassed by the general hostility of world opinion during the Boer War (1899–1902), in which their great empire crushed a rebellion by South African farmers, and their isolation no longer seemed so splendid. The Germans had acted with restraint during the war. Between 1898 and 1901, Joseph Chamberlain, the colonial secretary, made several attempts to conclude an alliance with Germany. The Germans, confident that a British alliance with France or Russia was impossible, refused and expected the British to make greater concessions in the future.

The Entente Cordiale   The first breach in Britain's isolation came in 1902, when it concluded an alliance with Japan to defend British interests in the Far East against Russia. Next, Britain abandoned its traditional antagonism toward France and in 1904 concluded a series of agreements with the French, collectively called the Entente Cordiale. It was not a formal treaty and had no military provisions, but it settled all outstanding colonial differences between the two nations. In particular, Britain gave France a free hand in Morocco in return for French recognition of British control over Egypt. The Entente Cor-

diale was a long step toward aligning the British with Germany's great potential enemy.

Britain's new relationship with France was surprising, but in 1904 hardly anyone believed the British whale and the Russian bear would ever come together. The Russo-Japanese War of 1904–1905 made such a development seem even less likely, because Britain was allied with Russia's enemy. But Britain had behaved with restraint, and the Russians were chastened by their unexpected and humiliating defeat, which also led to the Russian Revolution of 1905. Although the revolution was put down, it weakened Russia and reduced British apprehensions about Russian power. The British were also concerned that Russia might again drift into the German orbit.

The First Moroccan Crisis   At this point, Germany decided to test the new understanding between Britain and France and to press for colonial gains. In March 1905, Emperor William II landed at Tangier, made a speech in favor of Moroccan independence, and by implication asserted Germany's right to participate in Morocco's destiny. This was a challenge to France. Germany's chancellor, Prince Bernhard von Bülow (1849–1929), intended to show France how weak it was and how little support it could expect from Britain. He also hoped to gain significant colonial concessions.

The Germans demanded an international conference to show their power more dramatically. The conference met in 1906 at Algeciras in Spain. Austria sided with its German ally, but Spain, which also had claims in Morocco, Italy, and the United States, voted with Britain and France. The Germans had overplayed their hand, receiving trivial concessions, and the French position in Morocco was confirmed. German bullying had, moreover, driven Britain and France closer together. In the face of the threat of a German attack on France, Sir Edward Grey (1862–1933), the British foreign secretary, without making a firm commitment, authorized conversations between the British and French general staffs. Their agreements became morally binding as the years passed. By 1914, French and British military and naval plans were so mutually dependent that the two countries were effectively, if not formally, allies.

British Agreement with Russia   Britain's fear of Germany's growing naval power, its concern over German ambitions in the Near East (as represented by the German-sponsored plan to build a railroad from Berlin to Baghdad), and its closer relations with France made it desirable for Britain to become more friendly with France's ally, Russia. With French support, in 1907 the British concluded an agreement with Russia much like the Entente Cordiale with France. It settled Russo-British quarrels in central Asia and opened the door for wider cooperation. The Triple Entente, an informal, but powerful, association of Britain, France, and Russia, was now ranged against the Triple Alliance. Italy was an unreliable ally, however, which meant Germany and Austria-Hungary were encircled by two great land powers and Great Britain.

William II and his ministers had turned Bismarck's nightmare of the prospect of a two-front war with France and Russia into a reality. They had made it more horrible by adding Britain to their foes. The equilibrium that Bismarck had worked so hard to achieve was destroyed. Britain would no longer support Austria in restraining Russian ambitions in the Balkans. Germany, increasingly alarmed by a sense of being encircled, was less willing to restrain the Austrians for fear of alienating them, too. In the Dual Alliance of Germany and Austria, it had become less clear who was the horse and who was the rider.

Bismarck's alliance system had been intended to maintain peace, but the new alliance increased the risk of war and made the Balkans a likely spot for it to break out. Bismarck's diplomacy had left France isolated and impotent; the new arrangement associated France with the two greatest powers in Europe besides Germany. The Germans could rely only on Austria, and Austria's troubles made it less likely to provide aid than to need it.

World War I

THE ROAD TO WAR (1908–1914)

The weak Ottoman Empire still controlled the central strip of the Balkan Peninsula running west from Constantinople to the Adriatic. North and south of it were the independent states of Romania, Serbia, and Greece, as well as Bulgaria, technically still part of the empire, but legally autonomous and practically independent. The Austro-Hungarian Empire included Croatia and Slovenia and, since 1878, had "occupied and administered" Bosnia and Herzegovina.

Except for the Greeks and the Romanians, most of the inhabitants of the Balkans spoke variants of the same Slavic language and felt a cultural and historical kinship with one another. For centuries they had been ruled by Austrians, Hungarians, or Turks, and the growing nationalism that characterized late-nineteenth-century Europe made many of them eager for independence. The more radical among them longed for a union of the south Slavic, or

Yugoslav, peoples in a single nation. They looked to independent Serbia as the center of the new nation and hoped to detach all the Slavic provinces (especially Bosnia, which bordered on Serbia) from Austria. Serbia believed its destiny was to unite the Slavs at the expense of Austria, as Piedmont had united the Italians and Prussia the Germans.

In 1908, a group of modernizing reformers called the Young Turks brought about a revolution in the Ottoman Empire. Their actions threatened to revive the life of the empire and to interfere with the plans of the European jackals preparing to pounce on the Ottoman corpse. These events brought on the first of a series of Balkan crises that would eventually lead to war.

The Bosnian Crisis In 1908, the Austrian and Russian governments decided to act quickly before Turkey became strong enough to resist. They struck a bargain in which Russia agreed to support the Austrian annexation of Bosnia and Herzegovina in return for Austrian backing for opening the Dardanelles to Russian warships.

Austria, however, declared the annexation before the Russians could act. The British and French, eager for the favor of the Young Turks, refused to agree to the Russian demand for the opening of the Dardanelles. The Russians were humiliated and furious, but too weak to do anything but protest. Their "little brothers," the Serbs, were frustrated and angered by the Austrian annexation of Bosnia, which they had hoped one day to annex themselves.

Germany had not been warned in advance of Austria's plans and was unhappy because the action threatened their relations with Russia. Germany felt so dependent on the Dual Alliance, however, that it nevertheless assured Austria of its support. Austria had been given a free hand, and to some extent, German policy was being made in Vienna. It was a dangerous precedent. Also, the failure of Britain and France to support Russia strained the Triple Entente. This made it harder for them to oppose Russian interests in the future if they were to keep Russian friendship.

The Second Moroccan Crisis The second Moroccan crisis, in 1911, emphasized the French and British need for mutual support. When France sent an army to Morocco to put down a rebellion, Germany took the opportunity to "protect German interests" there as a means of extorting colonial concessions in the French Congo. To add force to their demands, the Germans sent the gunboat *Panther* to the Moroccan port of Agadir, purportedly to protect German citizens there. Once again, as in 1905, the Germans went too far. The *Panther*'s visit to Agadir provoked a strong reaction in Britain. For some time Anglo-German relations had been growing worse, chiefly because of the intensification of the naval race. In 1907, Germany had built its first dreadnought, a new type of battleship that Britain had launched in 1906. In 1908, Germany had passed still another naval law that accelerated the challenge to British naval supremacy.

These actions frightened and angered the British because they threatened the security of the island kingdom and its empire. The German actions also forced Britain to increase taxes to pay for new armaments just when the Liberal government in Britain was launching its expensive program of social legislation. Negotiations failed to persuade William II and Tirpitz to slow down naval construction.

In this atmosphere, the British heard of the *Panther*'s arrival in Morocco. They wrongly believed the Germans meant to turn Agadir into a naval base on the Atlantic. The crisis passed when France yielded some insignificant bits of the Congo and Germany recognized the French protectorate over Morocco. The main result was to increase British fear and hostility and to draw Britain closer to France. Specific military plans were formulated for a British expeditionary force to defend France in case of German attack, and the British and French navies agreed to cooperate. Without any formal treaty, the German naval construction and the Agadir crisis had turned the Entente Cordiale into a de facto alliance. If Germany attacked France, Britain must defend the French, for its own security was inextricably tied up with that of France.

War in the Balkans The second Moroccan crisis also provoked another crisis in the Balkans. Italy sought to gain colonies and to take its place among the great powers. It wanted Libya, which, though worth little before the discovery of oil in the 1950s, was at least available. Italy feared that the recognition of the French protectorate in Morocco would encourage France also to move into Libya. So, in 1911, Italy attacked the Ottoman Empire to preempt the French, defeated the faltering Turks, and forced Turkey to cede Libya and the Dodecanese Islands in the Aegean. The Italian victory demonstrated Turkish weakness and encouraged the Balkan states to try their luck. In 1912, Bulgaria, Greece, Montenegro, and Serbia jointly attacked the Ottoman Empire and won easily. (See Map 26–4.) After this First Balkan War, the victors fell out among themselves over the division of Macedonia, and in 1913 a Second Balkan War erupted. This time, Turkey and Romania joined the other states against Bulgaria and stripped away much of what the Bulgarians had gained in 1878 and 1912.

After the First Balkan War, the alarmed Austrians were determined to limit Serbian gains and especially to prevent the Serbs from gaining a port on the Adriatic. This policy meant keeping Serbia out of Albania, but the Russians backed the Serbs, and tensions mounted. An international conference sponsored by Britain in early 1913 resolved the matter in Austria's favor and called for an independent kingdom of Albania. Austria, however, felt humiliated by the public airing of Serbian demands, and the Serbs defied the powers and continued to occupy

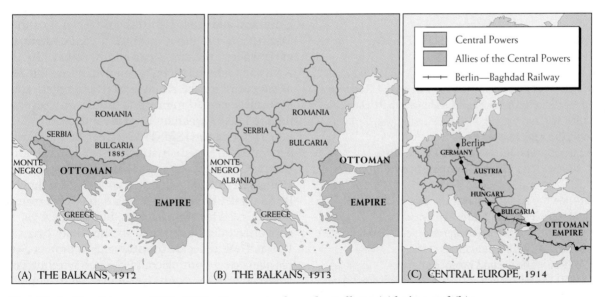

MAP 26–4 THE BALKANS, 1912–1913 *Two maps show the Balkans (a) before and (b) after the two Balkan wars; note the Ottoman retreat. In (c), we see the geographical relationship of the Central Powers and their Bulgarian and Turkish allies.*

parts of Albania. Under Austrian pressure they eventually withdrew, but they returned to Albania in September 1913, after the Second Balkan War. Finally, in mid-October, Austria unilaterally issued an ultimatum, and Serbia again withdrew its forces from Albania.

During this crisis, many people in Austria had wanted an all-out attack on Serbia to remove its threat to the empire once and for all. Those demands had been resisted by Emperor Francis Joseph and the heir to the throne, Archduke Francis Ferdinand. At the same time, Pan-Slavic sentiment in Russia pressed Tsar Nicholas II to take a firm stand, but Russia once again let Austria have its way in its confrontation with Serbia. Throughout the crisis, Britain, France, Italy, and Germany restrained their allies, although each worried about seeming too reluctant to help its friends.

The lessons learned from this crisis of 1913 profoundly influenced behavior in the final crisis in

1914. As in 1908, the Russians had been embarrassed by their passivity; and their allies were more reluctant to restrain them again. The Austrians were embarrassed by the results of accepting an international conference and were determined not to do it again. They had gotten better results from a threat of direct force; they and their German allies did not miss the lesson.

SARAJEVO AND THE OUTBREAK OF WAR (JUNE–AUGUST 1914)

The Assassination On June 28, 1914, a young Bosnian nationalist shot and killed Archduke Francis Ferdinand, heir to the Austrian throne, and his wife as they drove in an open car through the Bosnian capital of Sarajevo. The assassin was a member of a conspiracy hatched by a political terrorist society called Union or Death, better known as the Black Hand. The chief of intelligence of the Serbian army's general staff had helped plan and prepare the crime. Though his role was not actually known at the time, it was generally believed throughout Europe that Serbian officials were involved. The glee of the Serbian press after the assassination lent support to that belief.

The archduke was not popular in Austria, and his funeral evoked few signs of grief. He had been known to favor a form of federal government for Austria that would have raised the status of the Slavs in the empire. This position alienated the conservatives among the Habsburg officials and the Hungarians. It also alarmed radical Yugoslav nationalists, who feared Habsburg reform might end their dream of an independent south Slav state.

Germany and Austria's Response News of the assassination produced outrage and condemnation everywhere in Europe except in Serbia. To those Austrians who had long favored an attack on Serbia as a solution to the empire's Slavic problem, the opportunity seemed irresistible. But it was never easy for the Dual Monarchy to make a decision. Conrad von Hotzendorf (1852–1925), chief of the Austrian general staff, urged an attack, as he had often done before. Count Stefan Tisza (1861–1918), speaking for Hungary, resisted. Count Leopold von Berchtold (1863–1942), the Austro-Hungarian foreign minister, felt the need for strong action, but he knew German support would be required in the likely event that Russia should decide to intervene to protect Serbia. He also knew nothing could be done without Tisza's approval and that only German support could persuade the Hungarians to accept the policy of war. The question of peace or war against Serbia, therefore, had to be answered in Berlin.

The Coming of World War I	
1871	The end of the Franco-Prussian War; creation of the German Empire; German annexation of Alsace-Lorraine
1873	The Three Emperors' League (Germany, Russia, and Austria-Hungary)
1875	The Russo-Turkish War
1878	The Congress of Berlin
1879	The Dual Alliance between Germany and Austria
1881	The Three Emperors' League is renewed
1882	Italy joins Germany and Austria in the Triple Alliance
1888	William II becomes the German emperor
1890	Bismarck is dismissed
1894	The Franco-Russian alliance
1898	Germany begins to build a battleship navy
1899–1902	Boer War
1902	The British alliance with Japan
1904	The Entente Cordiale between Britain and France
1904–1905	The Russo-Japanese War
1905	The first Moroccan crisis
1907	The British agreement with Russia
1908–1909	The Bosnian crisis
1911	The second Moroccan crisis
1911	Italy attacks Turkey
1912–1913	The First and Second Balkan wars
1914	Outbreak of World War I

William II and Chancellor Theobald von Bethmann-Hollweg (1856–1921) readily promised German support for an attack on Serbia. It has often been said that they gave the Austrians a "blank check," but their message was more specific than that. They urged the Austrians to move swiftly while the other powers were still angry at Serbia. They also made the Austrians feel they would view a failure to act as evidence of Austria-Hungary's weakness and uselessness as an ally. (See "The Austrian Ambassador Gets a 'Blank Check' from the Kaiser.") Therefore, the Austrians never wavered in their determination to make war on Serbia. They hoped, with the protection of Germany, to fight Serbia alone, but they were prepared to risk a general European conflict. The Germans also knew they risked a general war, but they too hoped to "localize" the fight between Austria and Serbia.

Some scholars believe Germany had long been plotting war, and some even think a specific plan for war in 1914 was set in motion as early as 1912. The vast body of evidence on the crisis of 1914, however, gives little support to such notions. The German leaders plainly reacted to a crisis they had not foreseen and just as plainly made decisions in response to events. The fundamental decision to support Austria, however, made war difficult, if not impossible, to avoid. That decision was made by the emperor and chancellor without significant consultation with either their military or diplomatic advisers.

William II appears to have reacted violently to the assassination. He was moved by his friendship for the archduke and by outrage at an attack on royalty. A different provocation would probably not have moved him so much. Bethmann-Hollweg was less emotional, but under severe pressure. To resist the decision would have meant flatly opposing the emperor. The powerful military circles favored by William suspected the chancellor of being soft. It would have been difficult for him to take a conciliatory position.

Moreover, Bethmann-Hollweg, like many other Germans, feared for the future. Russia was recovering its strength and would reach a military peak in 1917. The Triple Entente was growing closer and more powerful, and Germany's only reliable ally was Austria. The chancellor recognized the danger of supporting Austria, but he believed it to be even more dangerous to withhold that support. If Austria did not crush Serbia, it would soon collapse before the onslaught of Slavic nationalism defended by Russia. If Germany did not defend its ally, the Austrians might look elsewhere for help. His policy was one of calculated risk.

Unfortunately, the calculations proved to be incorrect. Bethmann-Hollweg hoped the Austrians

Above: The Austrian archduke Francis Ferdinand and his wife in Sarajevo on June 28, 1914. Later in the day the royal couple were assassinated by young revolutionaries trained and supplied in Serbia, igniting the crisis that led to World War I. Below: Moments after the assassination the Austrian police captured one of the assassins.
Brown Brothers

would strike swiftly and present the powers with a fait accompli while the outrage of the assassination was still fresh. And he felt German support would deter Russian involvement. Failing that, he was prepared for a continental war against France and Russia. This policy, though, depended on British neutrality, and the German chancellor convinced himself the British could be persuaded to stand aloof.

The Austrians, however, were slow to act. They did not even deliver their deliberately unacceptable ultimatum to Serbia until July 24, when the general hostility toward Serbia had begun to subside. Serbia further embarrassed the Austrians by returning so soft and conciliatory an answer that even the mercurial German emperor thought it removed all

THE AUSTRIAN AMBASSADOR GETS A "BLANK CHECK" FROM THE KAISER

It was at a meeting at Potsdam on July 5, 1914, that the Austrian ambassador received assurance from the kaiser that Germany would support Austria in the Balkans, even at the risk of war.

■ *Why did the Austrians need to consult the Germans? How did the kaiser's response compare with German policy in recent crises? Was the check "written" by the kaiser really blank? How important for the coming of the war was this meeting?*

After lunch, when I again called attention to the seriousness of the situation, the Kaiser authorised me to inform our gracious Majesty that we might in this case, as in all others, rely upon Germany's full support. He must, as he said before, first hear what the Imperial Chancellor has to say, but he did not doubt in the least that Herr von Bethmann Hollweg would agree with him. Especially as far as our action against Serbia was concerned. But it was his [William II's] opinion that this action must not be delayed. Russia's attitude will no doubt be hostile, but to this he had been for years prepared, and should a war between Austria-Hungary and Russia be unavoidable, we might be convinced that Germany, our old faithful ally, would stand at our side. Russia at the present time was in no way prepared for war, and would think twice before it appealed to arms. But it will certainly set other powers on to the Triple Alliance and add fuel to the fire in the Balkans. He understands perfectly well that His Apostolic Majesty in his well-known love of peace would be reluctant to march into Serbia; but if we had really recognised the necessity of warlike action against Serbia, he [William II] would regret if we did not make use of the present moment, which is all in our favour.

From *Outbreak of the World War: German Documents Collected by Karl Kautsky, Max Montgelas and Walther Schücking* (eds.) (New York: Carnegie Endowment for International Peace, 1924), p. 76.

reason for war. But the Austrians were determined not to turn back. On July 28, they declared war on Serbia, even though the army would not be ready to attack until mid-August.

The Triple Entente's Response The Russians, previously so often forced to back off, responded angrily to the Austrian demands on Serbia. The most conservative elements of the Russian government opposed war, fearing it would lead to revolution, as it had in 1905. But nationalists, Pan-Slavs, and most of the politically conscious classes in general demanded action. The government responded by ordering partial mobilization, against Austria only. This policy was militarily impossible, but its intention was to put diplomatic pressure on Austria to refrain from attacking Serbia.

Mobilization of any kind, however, was a dangerous weapon because it was generally understood to be equivalent to an act of war. It was especially alarming to the German general staff. The possibility that the Russians might start mobilization before the Germans could move would upset the delicate timing of Germany's only battle plan, the **Schlieffen Plan,** which required an attack on France before the Russians were ready to act, and would put Germany in great danger. From this point on, the general staff pressed for German mobilization and war. The pressure of military necessity soon became irresistible.

France and Britain were not eager for war. France's president and prime minister were on their way back from a visit to Russia when the crisis flared on July 24. The Austrians had, in fact, timed their ultimatum precisely so these two men would be at sea when it was delivered to the Serbs. Had they been in Paris, they might have tried to restrain the Russians. The French ambassador to Russia gave the Russians the same assurances, however, that Germany had given its ally. The British worked hard to resolve the crisis by traditional means: a conference of the powers. Austria, still smarting from its humiliation after the London Conference of 1913, would not hear of it. The Germans privately supported the Austrians, but publicly took on a conciliatory tone in the hope of keeping the British neutral.

Soon, however, Bethmann-Hollweg came to realize what he should have known from the first: If Germany attacked France, Britain must fight. Until July 30, his public appeals to Austria for restraint were a sham. Thereafter, he sincerely tried to persuade the Austrians to negotiate and avoid a general war, but it was too late. The Austrians could not turn back without losing their own self-respect and the respect of the Germans.

On July 30, Austria ordered mobilization against Russia. Bethmann-Hollweg resisted the enormous pressure to mobilize, not because he hoped to avoid war, but because he wanted Russia to mobilize against Germany first and appear to be the aggressor. Only in that way could he win the support of the German nation for war, especially the support of pacifist Social Democrats. His luck was good for a change. The news of Russian general mobilization came only minutes before Germany would have mobilized in any case. The Schlieffen Plan went into effect. The Germans occupied Luxembourg on August 1 and invaded Belgium, which resisted, on August 3. The invasion of Belgium violated the treaty of 1839 in which the British had joined the other powers in guaranteeing Belgian neutrality. This factor undermined sentiment in Britain for neutrality and united the nation against Germany, which then invaded France. On August 4, Britain declared war on Germany.

The Great War had begun. As Sir Edward Grey, the British foreign secretary, put it, the lights were going out all over Europe. They would come on again, but Europe would never be the same.

Although debate on the causes of the war continues, the most common opinion today is that German ambitions for a higher place in the international order under the new kaiser William II led to a new challenge to the status quo. Germany adopted a bullying policy resulting in a series of crises that led to the final crisis in July 1914, when Germany supported—indeed, pushed—its only reliable ally Austria into a war against Serbia that touched off the world war. The deeper causes of that war are seen to be Germany's new ambitions to become a world power like Great Britain and to become the dominant power on the European continent. Germany's decision to build a battleship navy aimed at Great Britain and strong enough at least to make the British stand aside and permit this vast change in the balance of power threatened Britain's interests and security. The British became so alarmed at the prospect, they launched an expensive and unwelcome naval race to maintain their superiority at sea and abandoned their cherished

"splendid isolation" and long-standing competitions with their colonial rivals France and Russia. In an unprecedented reversal of policy, they made an alliance with Japan and agreements with France and Russia to form the "Triple Entente," which grew from a set of colonial accords to an informal, but visible, check on German ambitions. This new international configuration alarmed Germany, which complained it was being "encircled" by jealous and hostile forces. The Germans feared the growing power of the country's enemies, and consequently, Germany did not seek any serious attempt at negotiations to ease the tension. Instead, a new arms race ensued, and Germany assumed a rigid stance in the final crisis that ended in war.

STRATEGIES AND STALEMATE: 1914–1917

Throughout Europe, jubilation greeted the outbreak of war. No general war had been fought since Napoleon, and few understood the horrors of modern warfare. The dominant memory was of Bismarck's swift and decisive campaigns, in which the costs and casualties were light and the rewards great. After the repeated crises of recent years and the fears and resentments they had created, war came as a release of tension. The popular press had increased public awareness of, and interest in, foreign affairs and had fanned the flames of patriotism. The prospect of war moved even a rational man of science like Sigmund Freud to say, "My whole libido goes out to Austria-Hungary."[9]

Both sides expected to take the offensive, force a battle on favorable ground, and win a quick victory. The Triple Entente powers—or the Allies, as they called themselves—held superiority in numbers and financial resources, as well as command of the sea. (See figure on p. 904.) Germany and Austria, the Central Powers, had the advantages of possessing internal lines of communication and having launched their attack first.

After 1905, Germany's only war plan was the one developed by Count Alfred von Schlieffen (1833–1913), chief of the German general staff from 1891 to 1906. (See Map 26–5.) It aimed at going around the French defenses by sweeping through Belgium to the Channel and then wheeling to the south and east to envelop the French and crush them against the German fortresses in Lorraine. The secret of success lay in making the right wing of the advancing German army immensely strong and deliberately weakening the left opposite the French frontier.

---

[9]Quoted in Remak, p. 134.

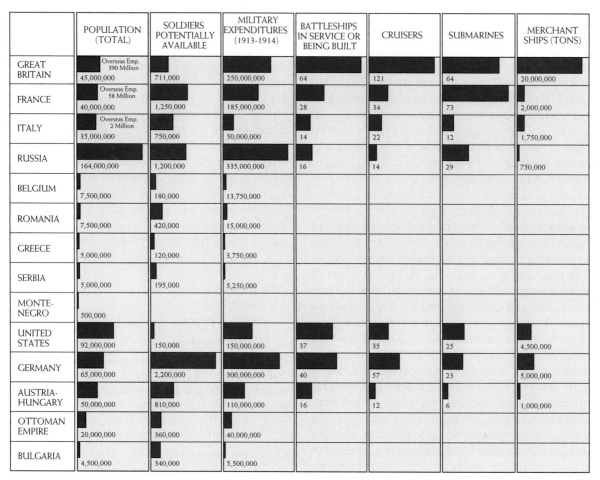

	POPULATION (TOTAL)	SOLDIERS POTENTIALLY AVAILABLE	MILITARY EXPENDITURES (1913-1914)	BATTLESHIPS IN SERVICE OR BEING BUILT	CRUISERS	SUBMARINES	MERCHANT SHIPS (TONS)
GREAT BRITAIN	Overseas Emp. 390 Million / 45,000,000	711,000	250,000,000	64	121	64	20,000,000
FRANCE	Overseas Emp. 58 Million / 40,000,000	1,250,000	185,000,000	28	34	73	2,000,000
ITALY	Overseas Emp. 2 Million / 35,000,000	750,000	50,000,000	14	22	12	1,750,000
RUSSIA	164,000,000	1,200,000	335,000,000	16	14	29	750,000
BELGIUM	7,500,000	180,000	13,750,000				
ROMANIA	7,500,000	420,000	15,000,000				
GREECE	5,000,000	120,000	3,750,000				
SERBIA	5,000,000	195,000	5,250,000				
MONTE-NEGRO	500,000						
UNITED STATES	92,000,000	150,000	150,000,000	37	35	25	4,500,000
GERMANY	65,000,000	2,200,000	300,000,000	40	57	23	5,000,000
AUSTRIA-HUNGARY	50,000,000	810,000	110,000,000	16	12	6	1,000,000
OTTOMAN EMPIRE	20,000,000	360,000	40,000,000				
BULGARIA	4,500,000	340,000	5,500,000				

FIGURE 26–1 *Relative strengths of the combatants in World War I.*

The weakness of the left was meant to draw the French into attacking the wrong place while the war was decided on the German right. As one keen military analyst has explained,

It would be like a revolving door—if a man pressed heavily on one side, the other side would spring round and strike him in the back. Here lay the real subtlety of the plan, not in the mere geographical detour.[10]

In the east, the Germans planned to stand on the defensive against Russia until France had been crushed, a task they thought would take only six weeks.

The apparent risk, besides the violation of Belgian neutrality and the consequent alienation of Britain, lay in weakening the German defenses against a direct attack across the frontier. The strength of German fortresses and the superior firepower of German howitzers made that risk more theoretical than real. The true danger was that the German striking force on the right through Belgium would not be powerful enough to make the swift progress vital to success. Schlieffen is said to have died uttering the words, "It must come to a fight. Only make the right wing strong."

The execution of his plan, however, was left to Helmuth von Moltke (1848–1916), the nephew of Bismarck's most effective general. Despite Schlieffen's warning, Moltke (chief of staff 1906–1914) added divisions to the left wing and even weakened the Russian front for the same purpose. As a result of this hesitant strategy and of theoretical mistakes by German commanders in the field, the Schlieffen Plan failed by a narrow margin.

The War in the West The French had also put their faith in the offensive, but with less reason than the Germans. They badly underestimated the numbers and effectiveness of the German reserves and overestimated the importance of the courage and spirit of their own troops. Courage and spirit could not

[10]B. H. Liddell Hart, *The Real War, 1914–1918* (Boston: Little, Brown, 1964; first published in 1930), p. 47.

win against machine guns and heavy artillery. The French offensive on Germany's western frontier failed totally. This defeat probably was preferable to a partial success, because it released troops for use against the main German army. As a result, the French and the British were able to stop the German advance on Paris at the Battle of the Marne in September 1914. (See Maps 26–6 and 26–7.)

Thereafter, the nature of the war in the west became one of position instead of movement. Both sides dug in behind a wall of trenches protected by barbed wire that stretched from the North Sea to Switzerland. Strategically placed machine-gun nests made assaults difficult and dangerous. Both sides, nonetheless, attempted massive attacks preceded by artillery bombardments of unprecedented and horrible force and duration. Still, the defense was always able to recover and to bring up reserves fast enough to prevent a breakthrough.

Sometimes assaults that cost hundreds of thousands of lives produced advances of only hundreds of yards. The introduction of poison gas to resolve the problem proved ineffective. In 1916, the British introduced the tank, which eventually proved to be the answer to the machine gun. The Allied command was slow to understand this, however, and until the end of the war, defense was supreme. For three years after its establishment, the western front moved only a few miles in either direction. (See "Art & the West: John Singer Sargent, *Gassed*: The Horrors of Modern War," p. 924.)

The War in the East   In the east, the war began auspiciously for the Allies. The Russians advanced into Austrian territory and inflicted heavy casualties, but Russian incompetence and German energy soon reversed the situation. A junior German officer, Erich Ludendorff (1865–1937), under the command of the elderly general Paul von Hindenburg (1847–1934), destroyed or captured an entire Russian army at the Battle of Tannenberg and defeated another one at the Masurian Lakes. In 1915, the Central Powers pressed their advantage in the east and drove into the Baltic states and Russian Poland, inflicting more than 2 million casualties in a single year.

As the battle lines hardened, both sides sought new allies. Turkey (because of its hostility to Russia) and Bulgaria (the enemy of Serbia) joined the Central Powers.

Both sides bid for Italian support with promises of the spoils of victory. Because what the Italians wanted most was held by Austria, the Allies could promise more. In a secret treaty of 1915, they agreed to deliver to Italy after victory most of *Italia irredenta* (i.e., the South Tyrol, Trieste, and

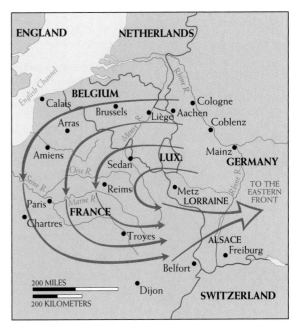

MAP 26–5   THE SCHLIEFFEN PLAN OF 1905   *Germany's grand strategy for quickly winning the war against France in 1914 is shown by the wheeling arrows on the map. In the original plan, the crushing blows at France were to be followed by the release of troops for use against Russia on Germany's eastern front. The plan, however, was not adequately implemented, and the war on the western front became a long contest in place.*

some of the Dalmatian Islands), plus new colonies in Africa and a share of the Turkish Empire. By the spring of 1915, Italy was engaging Austrian armies. The Italian campaign weakened Austria and divided some German troops, but the Italian alliance was generally a disappointment to the Allies and never produced significant results. Romania joined the Allies in 1916 but was quickly defeated and driven from the war.

In the Far East, Japan honored its alliance with Britain and entered the war. The Japanese quickly overran the German colonies in China and the Pacific and used the opportunity to improve their own position against China.

Both sides also appealed to nationalistic sentiment in areas held by the enemy. The Germans supported nationalist movements among the Irish, the Flemings in Belgium, and the Poles and the Ukrainians under Russian rule. They even tried to persuade the Turks to lead a Muslim uprising against the British in Egypt and India and the French in North Africa.

The Allies made the same appeals with greater success. They sponsored movements of national autonomy for the Czechs, the Slovaks, the south Slavs, and the Poles that were under Austrian rule.

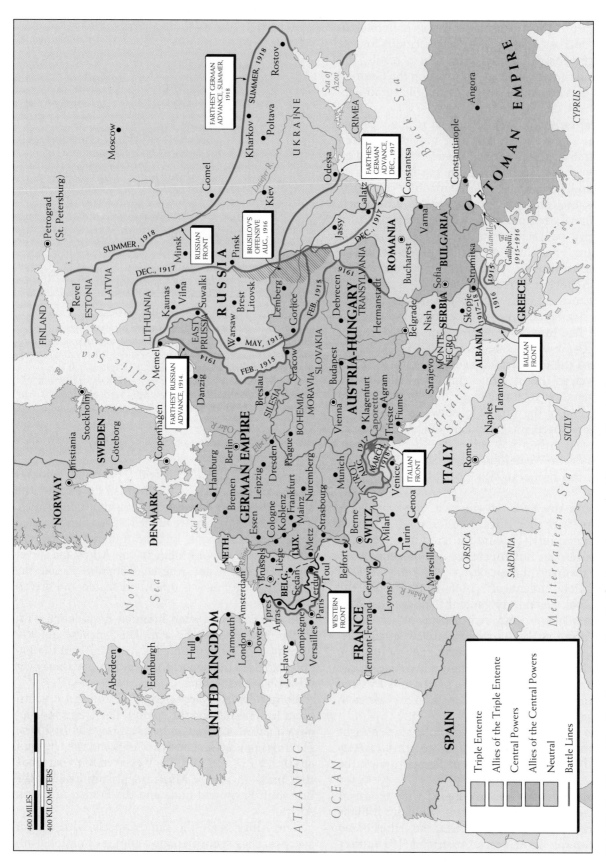

MAP 26–6 WORLD WAR I IN EUROPE *Despite the importance of military action in the Far East, in the Arab world, and at sea, the main theaters of activity in World War I were in the European areas.*

MAP 26–7   THE WESTERN FRONT, 1914–1918   *This map shows the crucial western front in detail.*

and as Turkish resistance continued, the Allied commitment increased. Before the campaign was abandoned, the Allies lost almost 150,000 men and diverted three times that number from more useful occupations.

Return to the West   Both sides turned back to the west in 1916. General Erich von Falkenhayn (1861–1922), who had succeeded Moltke in September 1914, sought success by an attack on the French stronghold of Verdun. His plan was not to take the fortress or to break through the French line, but to inflict enormously heavy casualties on the French, who would have to defend Verdun against superior firepower from several directions. He, too, underestimated the superiority of the defense. The French were able to hold Verdun with comparatively few men and to inflict almost as many casualties as they suffered. The commander of Verdun, Henri Pétain (1856–1951), became a national hero, and "They shall not pass" became a slogan of national defiance.

The Allies tried to end the impasse by launching a major offensive along the River Somme in July. Aided by a Russian attack in the east that drew off some German strength and by an enormous artillery bombardment, they hoped at last to break through. Once again, the defense was superior. Enormous casualties on both sides brought no result. On all fronts, the losses were great and the results meager. The war on land dragged on with no end in sight.

They also favored a movement of Arab independence from Turkey. Guided by Colonel T. E. Lawrence (1888–1935), this last scheme proved especially successful later in the war.

In 1915, the Allies undertook action to break the deadlock on the western front by going around it. The idea came chiefly from Winston Churchill (1874–1965), first lord of the British admiralty. He proposed to attack the Dardanelles and capture Constantinople. This policy would knock Turkey from the war, bring help to the Balkan front, and ease communications with Russia. The plan was daring, but promising, and in its original form, it presented little risk. British naval superiority and the element of surprise would allow the forcing of the straits and the capture of Constantinople by purely naval action. Even if the scheme failed, the fleet could escape with little loss.

The success of Churchill's plan depended on timing, speed, and daring leadership, but all of these were lacking. Worse, the execution of the attack was inept and overly cautious. Troops were landed,

A British machine gun crew in action on the Western Front. Machine guns, barbed wire, and trenches gave great advantages to the defense in the war and helped produce a long stalemate on the Western Front.
© Corbis

British tanks moving toward the Battle of Cambrai in Flanders late in 1917. Tanks were impervious to machine-gun fire. Had they been used in great numbers they might have broken the stalemate in the west. Bildarchiv Preussischer Kulturbesitz

The War at Sea As the war continued, control of the sea became more important. The British ignored the distinction between war supplies (which were contraband according to international law) and food or other peaceful cargo (which was not subject to seizure). They imposed a strict blockade meant to starve out the enemy, regardless of international law. The Germans responded with submarine warfare meant to destroy British shipping and starve the British. They declared the waters around the British Isles a war zone, where even neutral ships would not be safe. Both policies were unwelcome to neutrals, and especially to the United States, which conducted extensive trade in the Atlantic. Yet the sinking of neutral ships by German submarines was both more dramatic and more offensive than the British blockade.

In May 1915, a German submarine torpedoed the British liner *Lusitania*. Among the 1,200 who drowned were 118 Americans. President Woodrow Wilson (1856–1924) warned Germany that a repetition would have grave consequences; the Germans desisted for the time being, rather than further anger the United States. This development gave the

Allies a considerable advantage: Thereafter, the German fleet that had cost so much money and had caused so much trouble played no significant part in the war. The only battle it fought was at Jutland in the spring of 1916. The battle resulted in a standoff and confirmed British domination of the surface of the sea.

America Enters the War In December 1916, President Woodrow Wilson intervened to try to bring about a negotiated peace. Neither side, however, was willing to renounce war aims that its opponent found unacceptable. The war seemed likely to continue until one or both sides reached exhaustion.

Two events early in 1917 changed the situation radically. On February 1, the Germans announced the resumption of unrestricted submarine warfare, which led the United States to break off diplomatic relations. On April 6, the United States declared war on the Central Powers. One of the deterrents to an earlier American intervention had been the presence of autocratic tsarist Russia among the Allies. Wilson could conceive of the war only as an idealistic crusade "to make the world safe for democracy." That problem was resolved in March 1917 by a revolution in Russia that overthrew the tsarist government.

The Russian Revolution

The March Revolution in Russia was neither planned nor led by any political faction. It was the result of the collapse of the monarchy's ability to govern. Although public opinion in Russia had strongly supported the country's entry into the war, the conflict put far too great demands on Russia's resources and the efficiency of the tsarist government.

Nicholas II was weak and incompetent and suspected of being under the domination of his German wife and the insidious peasant faith healer Rasputin, who was assassinated by a group of Russian noblemen in 1916. Military and domestic failures produced massive casualties, widespread hunger, strikes by workers, and disorganization in the army. The peasant discontent that had plagued the countryside before 1914 did not subside during the conflict. In 1916, the tsar adjourned the Duma, Russian's parliament, and proceeded to rule alone. All political factions were discontented.

THE PROVISIONAL GOVERNMENT

In early March 1917, strikes and worker demonstrations erupted in Petrograd, as Saint Petersburg had been renamed. The ill-disciplined troops in the city refused to fire on the demonstrators. (See "The Outbreak of the Russian Revolution.") The tsar abdicated on March 15. The government of Russia fell into the hands of members of the reconvened Duma, who soon formed a provisional government composed chiefly of Constitutional Democrats (Cadets) with Western sympathies.

At the same time, the various socialists, including both Social Revolutionaries and Social Democrats of the Menshevik wing, began to organize the workers into soviets, councils of workers and soldiers. Initially, they allowed the provisional government to function without actually supporting it. As relatively orthodox Marxists, the Mensheviks believed a bourgeois stage of development must come to Russia before the revolution of the proletariat could be achieved. They were willing to work temporarily with the Constitutional Democrats in a liberal regime, but they became estranged when the Cadets failed to control the army or to purge "reactionaries" from the government.

In this climate, the provisional government decided to remain loyal to the existing Russian alliances and to continue the war against Germany.

Major Campaigns and Events of World War I	
August 1914	Germans attack in West
August–September 1914	First Battle of the Marne; Battles of Tannenberg and the Masurian Lakes
April 1915	British land at Gallipoli, start of Dardanelles campaign
May 1915	Germans sink British ship *Lusitania*
February 1916	Germans attack Verdun
May–June 1916	Battle of Jutland
February 1917	Germans declare unrestricted submarine warfare
March 1917	Russian Revolution
April 1917	United States enters war
November 1917	Bolsheviks seize power
March 1918	Treaty of Brest-Litovsk
March 1918	German offensive in the West
November 1918	Armistice

The provisional government thus accepted tsarist foreign policy and associated itself with the source of much domestic suffering and discontent. Its fate was sealed by the collapse of the last Russian offensive in the summer of 1917. Disillusionment with the war, shortages of food and other necessities at home, and the growing demand by the peasants for land reform undermined the government. This occurred even after its leadership had been taken over by the moderate socialist Alexander Kerensky (1881–1970). Moreover, discipline in the army had disintegrated.

LENIN AND THE BOLSHEVIKS

Ever since April, the Bolshevik wing of the Social Democratic Party had been working against the provisional government. The Germans, in their most successful attempt at subversion, had rushed the brilliant Bolshevik leader V. I. Lenin in a sealed train from his exile in Switzerland across Germany to Petrograd. They hoped he would cause trouble for the revolutionary government.

Lenin saw the opportunity to achieve the political alliance of workers and peasants he had discussed before the war. In speech after speech, he hammered away on the theme of peace, bread, and land. The Bolsheviks demanded that all political power go to the soviets, which they controlled. The failure of the summer offensive encouraged them to attempt a coup, but the effort was a failure. Lenin fled to Finland, and his chief collaborator, Leon Trotsky (1879–1940), was imprisoned.

THE OUTBREAK OF THE RUSSIAN REVOLUTION

The great Russian Revolution of 1917 started with a series of ill-organized demonstrations in Petrograd early in March. The nature of these actions and the ineffectuality of the government's response are described in the memoirs of Maurice Paléologue (1859–1944), the French ambassador.

■ *What elements contributing to the success of the March Revolution emerge from this selection? Why might the army have been unreliable? Why did the two ambassadors think a new ministry should be appointed? What were the grievances of the revolutionaries? Why is there no discussion of the leaders of the revolution? What role did the emperor (tsar) play in these events?*

MONDAY, MARCH 12, 1917

At half-past eight this morning, just as I finished dressing, I heard a strange and prolonged din which seemed to come from the Alexander Bridge. I looked out: there was no one on the bridge, which usually presents such a busy scene. But, almost immediately, a disorderly mob carrying red flags appeared at the end which is on the right bank of the Neva, and a regiment came towards it from the opposite side. It looked as if there would be a violent collision, but on the contrary the two bodies coalesced. The army was fraternizing with revolt.

Shortly afterwards, someone came to tell me that the Volhynian regiment of the Guard had mutinied during the night, killed its officers and was parading the city, calling on the people to take part in the revolution and trying to win over the troops who still remain loyal.

At ten o'clock there was a sharp burst of firing and flames could be seen rising somewhere on the Liteïny Prospekt which is quite close to the embassy. Then silence. Accompanied by my military attaché, Lieutenant-Colonel Lavergne, I went out to see what was happening. Frightened inhabitants were scattering through the streets. There was indescribable confusion at the corner of the Liteïny. Soldiers were helping civilians to erect a barricade. Flames mounted from the Law Courts. The gates of the arsenal burst open with a crash. Suddenly the crack of machine-gun fire split the air: it was the regulars who had just taken up position near the Nevsky Prospekt. The revolutionaries replied. I had seen enough to have no doubt as to what was coming.

The failure of a right-wing countercoup gave the Bolsheviks another chance. Trotsky, released from prison, led the powerful Petrograd soviet. Lenin returned in October, insisted to his doubting colleagues that the time was ripe to take power, and by the extraordinary force of his personality persuaded them to act. Trotsky organized the coup that took place on November 6 and concluded with an armed assault on the provisional government. The Bolsheviks, almost as much to their own astonishment as to that of the rest of the world, had come to rule Russia.

THE COMMUNIST DICTATORSHIP

The victors moved to fulfill their promises and to assure their own security. The provisional government had decreed an election for late November to select a Constituent Assembly. The Social Revolutionaries won a large majority over the Bolsheviks.

When the assembly gathered in January, it met for only a day before the Red Army, controlled by the Bolsheviks, dispersed it. (See "Lenin Establishes His Dictatorship.") All other political parties also ceased to function in any meaningful fashion. In November and January, the Bolshevik government issued decrees that nationalized the land and turned it over to its peasant proprietors. Factory workers were put in charge of their plants. Banks were taken from their owners and seized for the state, and the debt of the tsarist government was repudiated. Property of the church reverted to the state.

The Bolshevik government also took Russia out of the war, which they believed benefited only capitalism. They signed an armistice with Germany in December 1917. On March 3, 1918, they accepted the Treaty of Brest-Litovsk, by which Russia yielded Poland, the Baltic states, and the Ukraine. Some territory in the Transcaucasus region went to

Under a hail of bullets I returned to the embassy with Lavergne who had walked calmly and slowly to the hottest corner out of sheer bravado.

About half-past eleven I went to the Ministry for Foreign Affairs, picking up Buchanan [the British ambassador to Russia] on the way.

I told Pokrovski [the Russian foreign minister] everything I had just witnessed.

"So it's even more serious than I thought," he said.

But he preserved unruffled composure, flavoured with a touch of scepticism, when he told me of the steps on which the ministers had decided during the night:

"The sitting of the Duma has been prorogued to April and we have sent a telegram to the Emperor, begging him to return at once. With the exception of M. Protopopov [the Minister of the Interior, in charge of the police], my colleagues and I all thought that a dictatorship should be established without delay; it would be conferred upon some general whose prestige with the army is pretty high, General Russky for example."

I argued that, judging by what I saw this morning, the loyalty of the army was already too heavily shaken for our hopes of salvation to be based on the use of the "strong hand," and that the immediate appointment of a ministry inspiring confidence in the Duma seemed to me more essential than ever, as there is not a moment to lose. I reminded Pokrovski that in 1789, 1830, and 1848, three French dynasties were overthrown because they were too late in realizing the significance and strength of the movement against them. I added that in such a grave crisis the representative of allied France had a right to give the Imperial Government advice on a matter of internal politics.

Buchanan endorsed my opinion.

Pokrovski replied that he personally shared our views, but that the presence of Protopopov in the Council of Ministers paralyzed action of any kind.

I asked him:

"Is there no one who can open the Emperor's eyes to the real situation?"

He heaved a despairing sigh.

"The Emperor is blind!"

Deep grief was writ large on the face of the honest man and good citizen whose uprightness, patriotism and disinterestedness I can never sufficiently extol.

From Maurice Paléologue, *An Ambassador's Memoirs* (London: Doubleday & Company, Inc., and Hutchinson Publishing Group, Ltd., 1924), pp. 221–225.

Turkey. The Bolsheviks also agreed to pay a heavy war indemnity.

These terms were a terribly high price to pay for peace, but Lenin had no choice. Russia was incapable of renewing the war effort, and the Bolsheviks needed time to impose their rule on a devastated and chaotic Russia. Moreover, Lenin believed communist revolutions would soon occur across Europe as a result of the war and the Russian example.

Until 1921, the new Bolshevik government met major domestic resistance. A civil war erupted between the Red Russians, who supported the revolution, and the **White Russians,** who opposed it. In the summer of 1918, the Bolsheviks murdered the tsar and his family. Loyal army officers continued to fight the revolution and eventually received aid from the Allied armies. Under the leadership of Trotsky, however, the Red Army eventually overcame the domestic opposition. By 1921, Lenin and his supporters were in firm control.

The End of World War I

The collapse of Russia and the Treaty of Brest-Litovsk were the zenith of German success. The Germans controlled eastern Europe and its resources, especially food, and by 1918 they were free to concentrate their forces on the western front.

These developments would probably have been decisive had they not been balanced by American intervention. Still, American troops would not arrive in significant numbers for about a year, and both sides tried to win the war in 1917.

An Allied attempt to break through in the west failed disastrously. Losses were heavy and the French army mutinied. The Austrians, supported by the Germans, defeated the Italians at Caporetto and threatened to overrun Italy, until they were checked with the aid of Allied troops. The deadlock continued, but time was running out for the Central Powers.

Petrograd munitions workers demonstrating in 1917.   Ria-Novosti/Eastfoto

GERMANY'S LAST OFFENSIVE

In March 1918, the Germans decided to gamble everything on one last offensive. (In this decision they were persuaded chiefly by Ludendorff, by then quartermaster-general, second in command to Hindenburg, but the real leader of the army.) The German army pushed forward and even reached the Marne again, but got no farther. They had no more reserves, and the entire nation was exhausted. The Allies, in contrast, were bolstered by the arrival of American troops in ever-increasing numbers. They were able to launch a counteroffensive that proved to be irresistible. As the Austrian fronts in the Balkans and Italy collapsed, the German high command knew the end was imminent.

Ludendorff was determined that peace should be made before the German army could be thoroughly defeated in the field and that the responsibility for ending the war should fall on civilians. For some time, he had been the effective ruler of Germany under the aegis of the emperor. He now allowed a new government to be established on democratic principles and

to seek peace immediately. The new government, under Prince Max of Baden, asked for peace on the basis of the **Fourteen Points** that President Wilson had declared as the American war aims. These were idealistic principles, including self-determination for nationalities, open diplomacy, freedom of the seas, disarmament, and the establishment of a league of nations to keep the peace. Wilson insisted he would deal only with a democratic German government because he wanted to be sure he was dealing with the German people and not merely their rulers.

GERMAN REPUBLICAN GOVERNMENT ACCEPTS DEFEAT

The disintegration of the German army forced William II to abdicate on November 9, 1918. The majority branch of the Social Democratic Party proclaimed a republic to prevent the establishment of a soviet government under the control of their radical Leninist wing, which had earlier broken away as the Independent Socialist Party. Two days

LENIN ESTABLISHES HIS DICTATORSHIP

After the Bolshevik coup in October, elections for the Constituent Assembly were held in November. The results gave a majority to the Social Revolutionary Party and embarrassed the Bolsheviks. Using his control of the Red Army, Lenin closed the Constituent Assembly in January 1918, after it had met for only one day, and established the rule of a revolutionary elite and his own dictatorship. Here is the crucial Bolshevik decree.

■ *What reasons does Lenin give for closing the legitimately elected Constituent Assembly? What other reasons might he have had? What were the soviets? Did they have a legitimate claim to the monopoly of political power? Was the dissolution of the assembly a temporary or permanent measure? What defense can be made for the Bolsheviks' action? Is it enough to justify that action?*

The Constituent Assembly, elected on the basis of lists drawn up prior to the October Revolution, was an expression of the old relation of political forces which existed when power was held by the compromisers and the Cadets. When the people at the time voted for the candidates for the Socialist-Revolutionary Party, they were not in a position to choose between the Right Socialist-Revolutionaries, the supporters of the bourgeoisie, and the Left Socialist-Revolutionaries, the supporters of Socialism. Thus the Constituent Assembly, which was to have been the crown of the bourgeois parliamentary republic, could not but become an obstacle in the path of the October Revolution and the Soviet power.

The October Revolution, by giving the power to the Soviets, and through the Soviets to the toiling and exploited classes, aroused the desperate resistance of the exploiters, and in the crushing of this resistance it fully revealed itself as the beginning of the socialist revolution. . . . the majority in the Constituent Assembly which met on January 5 was secured by the party of the Right Socialist-Revolutionaries, the party of Kerensky, Avksentyev, and Chernov. Naturally, this party refused to discuss the absolutely clear, precise, and unambiguous proposal of the supreme organ of Soviet power, the Central Executive Committee of the Soviets, to recognize the program of the Soviet power, to recognize the "Declaration of Rights of the Toiling and Exploited People," to recognize the October Revolution and the Soviet power. . . .

The Right Socialist-Revolutionary and Menshevik parties are in fact waging outside the walls of the Constituent Assembly a most desperate struggle against the Soviet power. . . .

Accordingly, the Central Executive Committee resolves: The Constituent Assembly is hereby dissolved.

Reprinted from *A Documentary History of Communism: Communism in Russia*, Vol. 1, edited by Robert V. Daniels, by permission of University Press of New England; pp. 91–92, "The Dissolution of the Constituent Assembly." Copyright 1984 by the Trustees of the University of Vermont.

later, this republican, socialist-led government signed the armistice that ended the war by accepting German defeat. The German people were, in general, unaware their army had been defeated in the field and was crumbling. No foreign soldier stood on German soil. Many Germans expected a negotiated and mild settlement. The real peace was quite different and embittered the Germans. Many of them came to believe Germany had not been defeated but had been tricked by the enemy and betrayed—even stabbed in the back—by republicans and socialists at home.

The victors rejoiced, but they also had much to mourn. The casualties on all sides came to about 10 million dead and twice as many wounded. The economic and financial resources of the European states were badly strained. The victorious Allies, formerly creditors to the world, became debtors to the new American colossus, itself barely touched by the calamities of war.

The Great War, as contemporaries called it, the First World War to those who lived through its horrible offspring, lasted more than four years, doing terrible damage. Battle casualties alone counted 4 million

Women munitions workers in England. World War I demanded more from the civilian populations than had previous wars, resulting in important social changes. The demands of the munitions industries and a shortage of men (so many of whom were in uniform) brought many women out of traditional roles at home and into factories and other war-related work. Hulton Getty/Archive Photos

dead and 8.3 million wounded among the Central Powers and 5.4 million dead and 7 million wounded from their opponents, and millions of civilians died from the war and causes arising from it. Among the casualties also were the German, Austro-Hungarian, Russian, and Turkish empires. The American intervention in 1917 thrust the United States into European affairs with a vengeance, and the collapse of the Russian autocracy brought the Bolshevik revolution and the reality of a great communist state. Disappointment, resentment, and economic dislocations caused by the war brought various forms of fascism to Italy, Germany, and other countries. The comfortable nineteenth-century assumptions of inevitable progress based on reason, science and technology, individual freedom, democracy, and free enterprise gave way in many places to cynicism, nihilism, dictatorship, statism, official racism, and class warfare. It is widely agreed that the First World War was the

mother of the Second and to most of the horrors of the rest of the century.

These kinds of changes affected the colonial peoples ruled by the European powers, and overseas empires would never again be as secure as they had seemed before the war. Europe was no longer the center of the world, free to interfere when it wished or to ignore the rest of the world if it chose. The memory of that war lived on to shake the nerve of the victorious Western powers as they faced the new conditions of the postwar world.

OTTOMAN EMPIRE: THE CREATION OF THE MODERN NEAR EAST

At the outbreak of World War I in August 1914, the Ottoman Empire was neutral, but many military officers, the so-called Young Turks who had taken control of the Ottoman government in 1909, were pro-German. (See Chapter 23.) After hesitating for three months, the Turks decided to enter the war on the German side in November 1914. This decision ultimately brought about the end of the Ottoman Empire. Early victories gave way to defeat after defeat at the hands of the Russians and the British, the latter assisted by Arabs from the Arabian peninsula and neighboring lands, most notably Hussein (1856–1931), *sherif* (ruler or emir) of Mecca, the city of Muhammad. They drove the Ottomans out of Palestine and advanced deep into Mesopotamia, as far north as the oil fields of Mosul in modern Iraq. By October 30, 1918, Turkey was out of the war. In November, an Allied fleet sailed into the harbor of Constantinople and landed troops who occupied the city. The Ottoman government was helpless.

The peace treaty signed in Paris in 1920 between Turkey and the Allies dismembered the Ottoman Empire, placing large parts of it, particularly the area inhabited by Arabs, under the control of Britain and France. In Mesopotamia the British created the state of Iraq; it and Palestine became British mandates. Syria and Lebanon became French mandates. (**Mandates** were territories that were legally supposed to be administered under the auspices of the League of Nations, but were in effect ruled as colonies.) A Greek invasion of the Turkish homeland in Asia Minor in 1919 provoked a nationalist reaction, bringing the young general Mustafa Kemal (1881–1938), who later took the name Ataturk, meaning "Father of the Turks," to power. He drove the Greeks out of Asia Minor and compelled the victorious powers to make a new arrangement

sealed by the treaty of Lausanne in 1923. Ataturk abolished the Ottoman sultanate and deposed the last caliph. The new Republic of Turkey abandoned most of the old Ottoman Empire but became fully independent of control by the European powers and sovereign in its Anatolian homeland. Under Ataturk and his successors, Turkey, although consisting chiefly of Muslims, became a secular state and a force for stability in the region.

The Arab portions of the old empire, however, were a different story. Divided into a collection of artificial states that had no historical reality, governed or dominated as client regimes by the British and French, they were relatively quiet during the 1920s and 1930s. The weakening of Britain and France during and after the Second World War, however, and their subsequent abandonment of control in the Mideast would create problems in the latter part of the century.

The Settlement at Paris

The representatives of the victorious states gathered at Versailles and other Parisian suburbs in the first half of 1919. Wilson speaking for the United States, David Lloyd George (1863–1945) for Britain, Georges Clemenceau (1841–1929) for France, and Vittorio Emanuele Orlando (1860–1952) for Italy made up the Big Four. Japan also had an important part in the discussions. The diplomats who met in Paris had a far more difficult task than those who had sat at Vienna a century earlier. Both groups attempted to restore

The Allies promoted Arab efforts to secure independence from Turkey in an effort to remove Turkey from the war. Delegates to the peace conference of 1919 in Paris included British colonel T. E. Lawrence, who helped lead the rebellion, and representatives from the Middle Eastern region. Prince Feisal, the third son of King Hussein, stands in the foreground of this picture; Colonel T. E. Lawrence is in the middle row, second from the right; and Brigadier General Nuri Pasha Said of Baghdad is second from the left. Corbis

Ataturk (1881–1938), the father of the Turkish Republic, sought to modernize his country by forcing Turks to adopt western ways, including the Latin alphabet. Here he is shown teaching the alphabet as president in 1928.
Turkish Cultural Office

order to the world after long and costly wars. At the earlier conference, however, Metternich and his associates could confine their thoughts to Europe. France had acknowledged defeat and was willing to take part in and uphold the Vienna settlement. The diplomats at Vienna were not much affected by public opinion; and they could draw the new map of Europe along practical lines determined by the realities of power and softened by compromise.

OBSTACLES FACED BY THE PEACEMAKERS

The negotiators at Paris in 1919 were less fortunate. They represented constitutional, generally democratic governments, and public opinion had become a mighty force. Though there were secret sessions, the conference often worked in the full glare of publicity. Nationalism had become almost a secular religion, and Europe's many ethnic groups could not be relied on to remain quiet while they were distributed on the map at the whim of the

great powers. World War I, moreover, had been transformed by propaganda and especially by the intervention of Woodrow Wilson into a moral crusade to achieve a peace that would be just as well as secure. (See "Encountering the Past: War Propaganda and the Movies.") The Fourteen Points set forth the right of nationalities to self-determination as an absolute value; but in fact, the map of Europe could not be drawn to match ethnic groups perfectly with their homelands. All these elements made compromise difficult.

Wilson's idealism, moreover, came into conflict with the more practical war aims of the victorious powers and with many of the secret treaties that had been made before and during the war. The British and French people had been told that Germany would be made to pay for the war. Russia had been promised control of Constantinople in return for recognition of the French claim to Alsace-Lorraine and British control of Egypt. Romania had been promised Transylvania at the expense of Hungary.

Some of the agreements contradicted others. Italy and Serbia had competing claims to the islands and shore of the Adriatic. During the war, the British had encouraged Arab hopes of an independent Arab state carved out of the Ottoman Empire. Those plans, however, contradicted the Balfour Declaration (1917), in which the British seemed to accept Zionist ideology and to promise the Jews a national home in Palestine. Both of these plans conflicted with an Anglo-French agreement to divide the Near East between themselves.

The continuing national goals of the victors presented further obstacles to an idealistic "peace without victors." France was painfully conscious of its numerical inferiority to Germany and of the low birthrate that would keep it inferior. So France was naturally eager to weaken Germany permanently and preserve French superiority. Italy continued to seek the acquisition of *Italia irredenta*, Britain continued to look to its imperial interests, and Japan pursued its own advantage in Asia. The United States insisted on freedom of the seas, which favored American commerce, and on its right to maintain the Monroe Doctrine.

Finally, the peacemakers of 1919 faced a world still in turmoil. The greatest immediate threat appeared to be the spread of Bolshevism. While Lenin and his colleagues were distracted by civil war, the Allies landed small armies at several places in Russia to help overthrow the Bolshevik regime. The revolution seemed likely to spread as communist governments were established in Bavaria and Hungary. Berlin also experienced a dangerous communist uprising led by the "Spartacus group." The Allies were sufficiently worried by these developments to

War Propaganda and the Movies: Charlie Chaplin

The vast scope of the First World War required mass support from all the people. As the war stretched on and its costs, both human and material, increased, the governments of all the competing nations intensified propaganda campaigns to justify the vast expenditure of lives and resources. Sometimes this took the form of painting the enemy in brutal and lurid colors to provoke hatred, and sometimes it took the form of sympathetic images of patriotism and sacrifice for a noble cause. These efforts, sponsored both by government and private agencies, saturated the lives of everyone—men, women, and even children—while the war lasted.

At first, most of the propaganda came in the form of writing: newspaper articles and pamphlets, justifying the war and demonizing the enemy. Soon, however, verbal efforts gave way to more emotionally powerful visual devices such as posters, cartoons, and caricatures. By the middle of the war, however, the relatively new medium of film became the most powerful weapon of propaganda. Graphically and dramatically movies showed the enemy as either horrible or ridiculous and one's own soldiers and people as brave and noble. Such images could reach the rich and poor, literate and illiterate, young and old with great emotional effect.

Both sides produced films that became enormously popular, but none more so than those done on the Allied side by Charlie Chaplin (1889–1977). Born in England, he came to America as a vaudeville star in 1914 and was already famous when the war broke out. His tragicomic character the tramp, in many variations, had universal appeal. His wartime films had amazing effects: They helped sell great quantities of Liberty Bonds (which the American government used to help pay for its involvement in the war), raised the morale of civilians, and even eased the miseries of shell-shocked soldiers.

Chaplin's 1918 movie *Shoulder Arms* was his greatest wartime success. It gave a comic picture of the difficulties of basic training for American recruits and made the Germans seem like bumbling fools. In the film, Chaplin's character, exhausted by the rigors of drilling, falls asleep. He wakes up at the front, where he deceives the enemy by pretending to be a tree, captures first a German unit and finally the kaiser, all by himself.

The Germans, too, soon learned the propaganda value of films, which were more completely in the hands of the government than those made in the Allied states. The German army made comedies, melodramas, and newsreels and showed them widely both to the troops and the civilian public. The German government thought movies so important that even during the freezing, brutal winter of 1917–1918 when fuel supplies were at a premium it gave movie theaters special priority to use coal and electricity. But there was no German Charlie Chaplin.

■ *What were the purposes of propaganda in the war? What were the advantages of using movies in the war effort?*

Charlie Chaplin in Shoulder Arms. © Sunset Boulevard/ Corbis Sygma

support their suppression by right-wing military forces. They even allowed an army of German volunteers to operate against the Bolsheviks in the Baltic states.

Fear of the spread of communism affected the diplomats at Versailles, but it was far from dominant. The Germans played on such fears to get better terms, but the Allies, especially the French, would not hear of it. Fear of Germany remained the chief concern for France. More traditional and more immediate interests governed the policies of the other Allies.

THE PEACE

The Paris settlement consisted of five separate treaties between the victors and the defeated powers. Formal sessions began on January 18, 1919, and the last treaty was signed on August 10, 1920. (See Map 26–8.) Wilson arrived in Europe to unprecedented popular acclaim. Liberals and idealists expected a new kind of international order achieved in a new and better way, but they were soon disillusioned. "Open covenants openly arrived at" soon

Britain's David Lloyd George, France's Georges Clemenceau, and America's Woodrow Wilson (l. to r.) were the dominant figures at the Paris peace conference in 1919. Corbis

gave way to closed sessions in which Wilson, Clemenceau, and Lloyd George made arrangements that seemed cynical to outsiders.

The notion of "a peace without victors" became a mockery when the Soviet Union (as Russia was now called) and Germany were excluded from the peace conference. The Germans were simply presented with a treaty and compelled to accept it, fully justified in their complaint that the treaty had been dictated, not negotiated. The principle of national self-determination was violated many times, as was unavoidable. Still, the diplomats of the small nations were angered by their exclusion from decisions. The undeserved adulation accorded Wilson on his arrival gradually turned into equally undeserved scorn. He had not abandoned his ideals lightly, but had merely given way to the irresistible force of reality.

The League of Nations Wilson could make unpalatable concessions without abandoning his ideals because he put great faith in a new instrument for peace and justice: the **League of Nations.** Its covenant was an essential part of the peace treaty. The league was to be not an international government, but a body of sovereign states that agreed to pursue common policies and to consult in the common interest, especially when war threatened. The members promised to submit differences among themselves to arbitration, an international court, or the League Council. Refusal to abide by the results would justify league actions in the form of economic sanctions and even military intervention. The league was unlikely to be effective, however, because it had no armed forces at its disposal. Furthermore, any action required the unanimous consent of its council, consisting permanently of Britain, France, Italy, the United States, and Japan, as well as four other states that had temporary seats. The Covenant of the League bound its members to "respect and preserve" the territorial integrity of all its members; this was generally seen as a device to ensure the security of the victorious powers. The exclusion of Germany and the Soviet Union from the League Assembly further undermined its claim to evenhandedness.

Colonies Another provision of the covenant dealt with colonial areas. These were called mandates and were placed under the "tutelage" of one of the great powers under league supervision and encouraged to advance toward independence. This provision had no teeth, and little advance was made. Provisions for disarmament were equally ineffective. Members of the league remained fully sovereign and continued

MAP 26–8 W ORLD W AR I P EACE S ETTLEMENT IN E UROPE AND THE M IDDLE E AST *The map of central and eastern Europe, as well as that of the Middle East, underwent drastic revision after World War I. The enormous territorial losses suffered by Germany, Austria-Hungary, the Ottoman Empire, Bulgaria, and Russia were the other side of the coin represented by gains for France, Italy, Greece, and Romania and by the appearance or reappearance of at least eight new independent states from Finland in the north to Yugoslavia in the south. The mandate system for former Ottoman territories outside Turkey proper laid foundations for several new, mostly Arab, states in the Middle East. In Africa, the mandate system placed the former German colonies under British, French, and South African rule. (See Map 26–2.)*

to pursue their own national interests. Only Wilson put much faith in the league's future ability to produce peace and justice. To get the other states to agree to the league, he approved territorial settlements that violated his own principles.

Germany   In the West, the main territorial issue was the fate of Germany. Although a united Germany was less than fifty years old, no one seems to have thought of undoing Bismarck's work and dividing the country into its component parts. The French would have liked to set the Rhineland up as a separate buffer state, but Lloyd George and Wilson would not permit it. Still, they could not ignore France's need for protection against a resurgent Germany. France received Alsace-Lorraine and the right to work the coal mines of the Saar for fifteen years. Germany west of the Rhine and fifty kilometers east of it was to be a demilitarized zone; Allied troops could stay on the west bank for fifteen years.

In addition to this physical barrier to a new German attack, the treaty provided that Britain and the United States would guarantee aid to France if it were attacked by Germany. Such an attack was made more unlikely by the permanent disarmament of that country. Germany's army was limited to 100,000 men on long-term service, its fleet was reduced to a coastal defense force, and it was forbidden to have warplanes, submarines, tanks, heavy artillery, or poison gas. As long as these provisions were observed, France would be safe.

The East   The settlement in the East reflected the collapse of the great defeated empires that had ruled it for centuries. Germany lost part of Silesia, and East Prussia was cut off from the rest of Germany by a corridor carved out to give the revived state of Poland access to the sea. The Austro-Hungarian Empire disappeared entirely, giving way to five small successor states. Most of its German-speaking people were gathered in the Republic of Austria, cut off from the Germans of Bohemia and forbidden to unite with Germany.

The Magyars were left with the much-reduced kingdom of Hungary. The Czechs of Bohemia and Moravia joined with the Slovaks and Ruthenians to the east to form Czechoslovakia, and this new state included several million unhappy Germans plus Poles and Magyars. The southern Slavs were united in the Kingdom of Serbs, Croats, and Slovenes, or Yugoslavia. Italy gained Trentino and Trieste. Romania was enlarged by receiving Transylvania from Hungary and Bessarabia from Russia. Bulgaria lost territory to Greece, Romania, and Yugoslavia. Russia lost vast territories in the west.

Finland, Estonia, Latvia, and Lithuania became independent states, and most of Poland was carved out of formerly Russian soil.

Reparations   Perhaps the most debated part of the peace settlement dealt with **reparations** for the damage done by Germany during the war. Before the armistice, the Germans promised to pay compensation "for all damages done to the civilian population of the Allies and their property." The Americans judged the amount would be between $15 billion and $25 billion and that Germany would be able to pay that amount. France and Britain, however, worried about repaying their war debts to the United States, were eager to have Germany pay the full cost of the war, including pensions to survivors and dependents.

There was general agreement that Germany could not afford to pay such a huge sum, whatever it might be, and no sum was fixed at the conference. In the meantime, Germany was to pay $5 billion annually until 1921. At that time, a final figure would be set, which Germany would have to pay in thirty years. The French did not regret the outcome. Either Germany would pay and be bled into impotence, or Germany would refuse to pay and French intervention would be warranted.

To justify these huge reparation payments, the Allies inserted the notorious **war guilt clause** (Clause 231) into the treaty:

The Allied and Associated Governments affirm, and Germany accepts, the responsibility of Germany and her allies for causing all the loss and damage to which the Allied and Associated Governments and their nationals have been subjected as a consequence of the war imposed upon them by aggression of Germany and her allies.

The Germans, of course, did not believe they were solely responsible for the war and bitterly resented the charge. They had lost territories containing badly needed natural resources. Yet they were presented with an astronomical and apparently unlimited reparations bill. To add insult to injury, they were required to admit to a war guilt they did not feel.

Finally, to heap insult upon insult, they were required to accept the entire treaty as it was written by the victors, without any opportunity for negotiation. Germany's prime minister Philipp Scheidmann (1865–1939) spoke of the treaty as the imprisonment of the German people and asked, "What hand would not wither that binds itself and us in these fetters?" But there was no choice. The Social Democrats and the Catholic Center Party formed a new government, and their representatives signed the treaty. These parties formed the backbone of the Weimar government that ruled Germany until 1933. They never overcame the stigma of having accepted the Treaty of Versailles.

EVALUATION OF THE PEACE

Few peace settlements have undergone more severe attacks than the one negotiated in Paris in 1919. It was natural that the defeated powers should object to it, but the peace soon came under bitter criticism in the victorious countries as well. Many of the French objected that the treaty tied French security to promises of aid from the unreliable Anglo-Saxon countries. In England and the United States, a wave of bitter criticism arose in liberal quarters because the treaty seemed to violate the idealistic and liberal aims that the Western leaders had professed.

It was not a peace without victors. It did not put an end to imperialism, but attempted to promote the national interests of the winning nations. It violated the principles of national self-determination by leaving significant pockets of minorities outside the borders of their national homelands.

The Economic Consequences of the Peace The most influential economic critic of the treaty was John Maynard Keynes (1883–1946), a brilliant British economist who took part in the peace conference. He resigned in disgust when he saw the direction it was taking. His book, *The Economic Consequences of the Peace* (1920), was a scathing attack, especially on reparations and the other economic aspects of the peace. It was also a skillful assault on the negotiators and particularly on Wilson, who was depicted as a fool and a hypocrite. Keynes argued that the Treaty of Versailles was both immoral and unworkable. He called it a Carthaginian peace, referring to the utter destruction of Carthage by Rome after the Third Punic War. He argued that such a peace would bring economic ruin and war to Europe unless it was repudiated.

Keynes's argument had a great effect on the British, who were already suspicious of France and glad of an excuse to withdraw from continental affairs. The decent and respectable position came to be one that supported revision of the treaty in favor of Germany. Even more important was the book's influence in the United States. It fed the traditional American tendency toward isolationism and gave powerful weapons to Wilson's enemies. Wilson's own political mistakes helped prevent American ratification of the treaty. Thus America was out of the League of Nations and not bound to defend France. Britain, therefore, was also free from its obligation to France. France was left to protect itself without adequate means to do so for long.

Many of the attacks on the Treaty of Versailles are unjustified. It was not a Carthaginian peace. Germany was neither dismembered nor ruined. Reparations could be and were scaled down. Until the great world depression of the 1930s, the Germans recovered a high level of prosperity. Complaints against the peace should also be measured against the peace that the victorious Germans had imposed on Russia at Brest-Litovsk and their plans for a European settlement in case of victory. Both were far more severe than anything enacted at Versailles. The attempt at achieving self-determination for nationalities was less than perfect, but it was the best effort Europe had ever made to do so.

Divisive New Boundaries and Tariff Walls The peace, nevertheless, was unsatisfactory in important ways. The elimination of the Austro-Hungarian Empire, however inevitable, created several serious problems. Economically, it was disastrous, for it separated raw materials from manufacturing areas and producers from their markets by new boundaries and tariff walls. In hard times, this separation created friction and hostility that aggravated other quarrels also created by the peace treaties. Poland contained unhappy German and Ukrainian minorities, and Czechoslovakia was a collection of nationalities that did not find it easy to live together as a nation. Disputes over territories in eastern Europe promoted further tension.

The peace was inadequate on another level as well. It rested on a victory that Germany did not admit. The Germans believed they had been cheated rather than defeated. And the high moral principles proclaimed by the Allies undercut the validity of the peace, for it plainly fell far short of those principles.

Failure to Accept Reality Finally, the great weakness of the peace was its failure to accept reality. Germany and Russia must inevitably play an important part in European affairs, yet they were excluded from the settlement and from the League of Nations. Given the many discontented parties, the peace was not self-enforcing; yet no satisfactory machinery for enforcing it was established. The League of Nations was never a serious force for this purpose. It was left to France, with no guarantee of support from Britain and no hope of help from the United States, to defend the new arrangements. Finland, the Baltic states, Poland, Romania, Czechoslovakia, and Yugoslavia were expected to be a barrier to the westward expansion of Russian communism and to help deter a revival of German power. Most of these states, however, would have to rely on France in case of danger, and France was simply not strong enough to protect them if Germany was to rearm.

The tragedy of the Treaty of Versailles was that it was neither conciliatory enough to remove the desire for change, even at the cost of war, nor harsh enough to make another war impossible. The only hope for a lasting peace was that Germany would remain disarmed while the more obnoxious clauses of the peace treaty were revised. Such a policy required continued attention to the problem, unity among the victors, and farsighted leadership; but none of these was consistently present during the next two decades.

In Perspective

The outburst of European imperialism in the last part of the nineteenth century brought the Western countries into contact with almost all the inhabited areas of the world. They intensified their activity in places where they had already been interested. The growth of industry, increased ease of transportation and communication, and the burgeoning of a world economic system all brought previously remote and isolated places into the orbit of the West.

By the time of the outbreak of the war, European nations had divided Africa among themselves for exploitation in one way or another. The vast subcontinent of India had long been a British colony. The desirable parts of China were under European commercial control. Indochina was under French rule, and the islands of the Pacific had been divided among the powers. Much of the Near East was under the nominal control of the Ottoman Empire, in its death throes and under European influence. The Monroe Doctrine made Latin America a protectorate of the United States. Japan, pushed out of its isolation, had itself become an imperial power at the expense of China and Korea.

But the world created by the New Imperialism did not last long. What began as yet another Balkan war involving the European powers became a general war that profoundly affected much of the rest of the world. As the terrible war of 1914–1918 dragged on, the real motives that had driven the European powers to fight gave way to public affirmations of the principles of nationalism and self-determination. The peoples under colonial rule took the public statements—and promises sometimes made to them in private—seriously and sought to win their independence and nationhood.

Mostly, they were disappointed by the peace settlement. The establishment of the League of Nations and the system of mandates in place of the previous system of open colonial rule changed little. The British Empire grew even larger as it inherited vast territories from the defeated German and the defunct Ottoman empires. The French retained and expanded their holdings in Africa, the Pacific, and the Near East. The Americans added to the islands they controlled in the Pacific. Japanese imperial ambitions were rewarded at the expense of China.

A glance at the new map of the world could give the impression that the old imperial nations, especially Britain and France, were more powerful than ever, but that impression would be superficial and misleading. The great western European powers had paid an enormous price in lives, money, and will for their victory in the war. Colonial peoples pressed for the rights that were proclaimed as universal by the West, but denied to their colonies; and some influential minorities in the countries that ruled those colonies sympathized with colonial aspirations for independence. Tension between colonies and their ruling nations was a cause of serious instability in the world created by the Paris treaties of 1919.

REVIEW QUESTIONS

1. To what areas of the world did Europe extend its power after 1870? How and why did European attitudes toward imperialism change after 1870? What features differentiate the New Imperialism from previous imperialistic movements? What features did they have in common?

2. What role in the world did Bismarck envisage for the new Germany after 1871? How successful was he in carrying out his vision? What was Bismarck's attitude toward colonies? Was he wise to tie Germany to Austria-Hungary?

3. Why and in what stages did Britain abandon its policy of "splendid isolation" at the turn of the century? Were the policies it pursued instead wise ones, or should Britain have followed a different course altogether?

4. How did developments in the Balkans lead to the outbreak of World War I? What was the role of Serbia? Of Austria? Of Russia? What was the aim of German policy in July 1914? Did Germany want a general war?

5. Why did Germany lose World War I? Could Germany have won, or was victory never a possibility? Assess the settlement of Versailles. What were its benefits to Europe, and what were its drawbacks? Was the settlement too harsh or too conciliatory? Could it have secured lasting peace in Europe? How might it have been improved?

6. Why was Lenin successful in establishing Bolshevik rule in Russia? What role did Trotsky play? Was it wise policy for Lenin to take Russia out of the war?

SUGGESTED READINGS

L. ALBERTINI, *The Origins of the War of 1914*, 3 vols. (1952, 1957). Discursive, but invaluable.

M. BALFOUR, *The Kaiser and His Times* (1972). A fine biography of William II.

V. R. BERGHAHN, *Germany and the Approach of War in 1914* (1973). A work similar in spirit to Fischer's 1967 book (see later), but stressing the importance of Germany's naval program.

R. BOSWORTH, *Italy and the Approach of the First World War* (1983). A fine analysis of Italian policy.

L. CECIL, *Wilhelm II, Prince and Emperor, 1859–1900* (1989). The first part of a projected two-volume history of the kaiser.

S. B. FAY, *The Origins of the World War*, 2 vols. (1928). The best and most influential of the revisionist accounts.

N. FERGUSON, *The Pity of War* (1999). An analytic study of important aspects of the First World War with controversial interpretations, especially of why it began and why it ended.

D. K. FIELDHOUSE, *The Colonial Empires: A Comparative Study from the Eighteenth Century* (1966). An excellent study.

F. FISCHER, *Germany's Aims in the First World War* (1967). An influential interpretation that stirred an enormous controversy by emphasizing Germany's role in bringing on the war.

F. FISCHER, *War of Illusions* (1975). A long and diffuse book that tries to connect German responsibility for the war with internal social, economic, and political developments.

I. GEISS, *July 1914* (1967). A valuable collection of documents by a student of Fritz Fischer. The emphasis is on German documents and responsibility.

O. J. HALE, *The Great Illusion, 1900–1914* (1971). A fine survey of the period, especially good on public opinion.

M. B. HAYNE, *The French Foreign Office and the Origins of the First World War* (1993). An examination of the work and the influence on French policy of the professionals in the foreign service.

H. HERWIG, *The First World War: Germany and Austria, 1914–18* (1997). A fine study of the war from the losers' perspective.

J. N. HORNE, *Labour at War: France and Britain, 1914–1918* (1991). An examination of a major issue on the home fronts.

J. JOLL, *The Origins of the First World War* (1984). A brief, but thoughtful, analysis.

J. KEEGAN, *The First World War* (1999). A vivid and readable narrative account.

P. KENNEDY, *The Rise of the Anglo-German Antagonism, 1860–1914* (1980). An unusual and thorough analysis of the political, economic, and cultural roots of important diplomatic developments.

W. L. LANGER, *The Diplomacy of Imperialism* (1935). An excellent study of the diplomatic history of the years 1890 to 1902.

W. L. LANGER, *European Alliances and Alignments*, 2nd ed. (1966). An admirable diplomatic history of the years 1871 to 1890.

D. C. B. LIEVEN, *Russia and the Origins of the First World War* (1983). A good account of the forces that shaped Russian policy.

W. J. MOMMSEN, *Theories of Imperialism* (1980). A study of the debate on the meaning of imperialism.

G. SCHÖLLGEN, *Escape into War? The Foreign Policy of Imperial Germany* (1990). A valuable collection of interpretive essays.

J. STEINBERG, *Yesterday's Deterrent* (1965). An excellent study of Germany's naval policy and its consequences.

Z. STEINER, *Britain and the Origins of the First World War* (1977). A perceptive and informed account of the way British foreign policy was made before the war.

A. J. P. TAYLOR, *The Struggle for Mastery in Europe, 1848–1918* (1954). Clever, but controversial.

L. C. F. TURNER, *Origins of the First World War* (1970). Especially good on the significance of Russia and its military plans.

S. R. WILLIAMSON, JR., *Austria-Hungary and the Origins of the First World War* (1991). A valuable study of a complex subject.

DOCUMENTS CD-ROM

NATIONALISM AND IMPERIALISM

25.1 *Confessions of Faith*, Cecil Rhodes
25.2 Manifesto for the Society for German Colonization
25.3 A White Women's Perspective of Africa
25.4 Black Man's Burden
25.5 Between Ruler and Ruled
25.6 Advocating Change

WORLD WAR I

26.1 Rupert Booke: *The Soldier*
26.2 Siegfried Sassoon: *They*
26.3 Isaac Rosenberg: *Dead Man's Drop*
26.4 Woodrow Wilson: *Speech on the Fourteen Points*
26.5 Anna Eisenmenger, A German Soldier Returns Home: *A Complete Stranger*
26.6 A French Baker's Wife's Role in War
26.7 Non-European's View of the Start of World War I
26.8 Pressing for Peace
26.9 George Clemenceau Presents the French Demands at the Paris Peace Conference

John Singer Sargent, *Gassed:* The Horrors of Modern War

John Singer Sargent, *Gassed*, 1918–1919.   Imperial War Museum, London

Many new weapons were used extensively for the first time in the Great War of 1914–1918, including machine guns, barbed wire, tanks, airplanes, and several kinds of poison gas. The Germans were the first to employ gas as a weapon, firing a nonlethal kind of tear gas at the Russians on the eastern front in January 1915. By April, they had learned how to use the poison gas chlorine against the Allies on the western front. Releasing it from pressurized cylinders, they counted on favorable winds to blow it at the enemy, to kill or disable soldiers, and to permit a breakthrough that was otherwise not possible. In time, they brought other horrible gases into play on both fronts, but the device—which killed, blinded, and permanently disabled many—was not militarily effective. Wind proved an unreliable means of propulsion, and better gas masks further reduced the value of such attacks. The use of poison gas as a weapon and the dreadful character of its effects especially caught the public's imagination as a symbol of the horrors of modern war.

The American painter John Singer Sargent (1856–1925) chose one of these attacks as the subject of a vast painting, 20 feet long by 7.5 feet high, that now hangs in the Imperial War Museum in London. Sargent might be thought an unlikely artist to carry out such an assignment. Born in Florence of American parents, he was trained in Paris in the 1870s. He is best known as the favorite portrait painter of the American and British upper classes. Later in his career, he specialized in watercolor pictures of European landscapes done in the style of the impressionist painters, and even when the war broke out, he continued with the same subjects.

Propaganda was an important part of the war effort on both sides, and artists, too, were called on to do their part. In 1918, the British War Memorials Committee and Britain's prime minister Lloyd George asked Sargent to come to England and paint a very large picture that would show British soldiers and their new American allies cooperating in the fighting. The painter agreed, but changed the subject to a picture of soldiers after a gas attack. He went to France and made sketches on which he based the painting. A friend who traveled with him wrote an account of what they saw:

Gassed cases kept coming in, led along in parties of six just as Sargent depicted them, by an orderly. They sat or lay down on the grass, there may have been several hundred, evidently suffering a great deal, chiefly, I fancy from their eyes which were covered by a piece of lint.

The gas was mustard which causes temporary blindness from swelling the conjunctiva and lids. Sargent was very struck by the scene and immediately made a lot of notes. It was a very fine evening and the sun toward setting.[11]

Gassed has been compared with ancient Greek friezes depicting mythical battles, and there is a clear resemblance, in part because of the shape and size of the canvas and because of the common subject of men at war. There is, however, an important difference in treatment: Whereas the Greek sculptures always portrayed an element of heroism along with death and suffering, Sargent's painting reveals only the horror of battle.

■ *Why was Sargent an unlikely artist to paint* Gassed? *Why did he change the focus of his work? In what ways does* Gassed *resemble a Greek frieze?*

[11]Quotation from Web site of the Imperial War Museum in London, viewed September 1, 1999.

Sources: John Keegan, *The First World War* (New York: Alfred A. Knopf, 1999); Martin Gilbert, *The First World War* (New York: Henry Holt and Co., 1994); Radcliff Carter, *John Singer Sargent* (Abbeville Press, 1982); Web site, Imperial War Museum, London.

Imperialism:
Ancient and Modern

The concept of "empire" does not win favor today, and the word *imperialism*, derived from it, has carried an increasingly pejorative meaning since it was coined in the nineteenth century. Both words imply forcible domination by a nation or a state that exploits an alien people for its own benefit. Although, in our time, the charge of imperialism arises whenever a large and powerful nation influences weaker ones, exertion of influence alone is not imperialism. To be true to historical experience, one nation's actions toward another are imperialistic only if the dominant nation exerts both political and military control over the weaker one. In that sense, the last great empire in the modern world was the conglomeration of republics and ostensibly independent satellite states dominated by Russia prior to the USSR's collapse. But the Russians and the other imperial powers after World War II took no public pride in their domination. In our day, ruling an "empire" or engaging in "imperialism" is generally considered among the worst acts a nation can commit.

Such views are rare, perhaps unique, in the history of civilization. A major source for this opinion is the Christian religious tradition, especially parts of the New Testament that deprecate power and worldly glory and praise humility. But in fact, Christianity was not hostile to power and empire, for it took control of the Roman Empire in the fourth century C.E. and has lived comfortably with "empire" until our own century. The rise of democracy and nationalism in the last two centuries may have been more influential in changing attitudes toward imperialism because these movements exalt the freedom and autonomy of a people. But perhaps the modern disdain for empire building has its principal origins in the extraordinary horror of modern warfare and the historical knowledge that competition for empire has often led to war.

If, however, we are to understand the widespread experience of empire throughout history, we must be alert to the great gap that separates the views of most people throughout history from our current opinions. The earliest empires go back more than

4,000 years to the valleys of the Nile and the Tigris-Euphrates, and empires arose later in China, Japan, India, Iran, and Central and South America, among other areas. Typically, they were led by rulers who were believed to be gods or the representatives of gods, or at least were godlike in their ability to rule over many people. To their own people they brought wealth and prosperity, power, and reflected glory, all considered highly desirable. No one appears to have questioned the propriety of conquering another people and taking their lands, property, and persons to benefit the conquerors. Empire seemed to be part of the order of things—good for the rulers, usually bad for the ruled.

The Greeks: Ambiguities of Power

In most respects, the Greeks resembled other ancient peoples in their attitudes toward power, conquest, empire, and the benefits that came with them. Their Olympian gods held sway over earth, heaven, and the underworld because of victorious wars over other deities, and they gloried in their rule. The heroes in the epic poems that formed the Greek system of values won glory and honor through battle, conquest, and rule over other people. They viewed the world as a place of intense competition in which victory and domination, which brought fame and glory, were the highest goals, whereas defeat and subordination brought ignominy and shame.

When the legendary world of aristocratic heroes gave way to the world of city-states (*poleis*), competition was elevated from contests among individuals, households, and clans to contests and wars among *poleis*. In 416 B.C.E., more than a decade after the death of Pericles (c. 490–429 B.C.E.), Athenian spokesmen explained to some Melian officials their view of international relations: "Of the gods we believe, and of men we know, that by a necessity of their nature they always rule wherever they have the power" (Thucydides 5.105). Although their language was shockingly blunt, it reflected the views of most Greeks.

Yet this was also a dramatic presentation of the morally problematic status of the Athenian Empire. The Athenians' harsh statement would have struck a sympathetic chord among the Greeks. They appreciated power and the security and glory it can bring, but their own historical experience was different from that of other ancient nations. Their culture had been shaped by small autonomous, independent city-states, and they considered freedom natural for people raised in such an environment. Citizens, they believed, should be free in their persons, free to maintain their own constitutions, laws, and customs, and their city-states should be free to conduct their own foreign relations and to compete for power and glory. The free, autonomous *polis*, they thought, was greater than the mightiest powers in the world, and the sixth-century B.C.E. poet Phocylides was prepared to compare it to the great Assyrian Empire: "A little *polis* living orderly in a high place is greater than block-headed Nineveh" (Fragment 5).

When *poleis* fought one another, the victor typically took control of a piece of border land that was usually the source of the dispute. They did not normally enslave the defeated enemy or annex and occupy its land. In these matters, as in many others, the Greeks distinguished themselves from alien peoples who did not speak Greek and were not shaped by the Greek cultural tradition. These people were called barbarians, *barbaroi*, because their speech sounded to the Greeks like "bar bar." Because they had not been raised as people in free communities, but lived as subjects to a ruler, they were, it seemed, slaves by nature. To the Greeks, then, dominating and enslaving such people was perfectly acceptable. Greeks, however, viewed themselves as naturally free, as they demonstrated by creating and living in the free institutions of the *polis*. To rule over such people, to deny them their freedom and autonomy, would be wrong. So the Greeks thought, but they did not always act accordingly. The early Spartans, for instance, had changed the status of the conquered Greeks of Laconia and Messenia to *Helots*, or slaves of the state.

The Greeks shared still another belief that interfered with the comfortable acceptance of great power and empire: They thought any good thing amassed by humans to excess, beyond moderation, eventually led to *hubris*, a condition of wanton violence arising from arrogant pride in one's greatness. Those overcome by hubris were thought to have overstepped the limits established for human beings, to have shown contempt for the gods and, thereby, to have incurred *nemesis*, or divine anger and retribution. The great example to the Greeks of the fifth century of the workings of hubris and nemesis was the fate of Xerxes (r. 486–465 B.C.E.), Great King of the Persian Empire. His power became so great, it filled him with a blind arrogance that led him to try to extend his rule over the Greek mainland and thus brought disaster to himself and his people. When, therefore, the Athenians undertook the leadership of a Greek alliance after the Persian War, and that leadership brought them wealth and power and, in fact, turned into what was frankly acknowledged to be an empire, their response was ambiguous and contradictory. These developments were a source of

The philosopher–emperor Marcus Aurelius was compelled to spend much of his time fighting against tribal invaders on Rome's northern frontiers. This relief from the triumphal arch dedicated to him in Rome (176–180) shows him mounted, on campaign.
Nimatallah/Art Resource

927

pride and gratification, but also of embarrassment and, to some Athenians, shame.

The Macedonian conquest of the Greek city-states in 338 B.C.E. marked a return to an older attitude toward empire. Alexander the Great (r. 340–323 B.C.E.) conquered the vast Persian Empire, itself the successor of empires that had stretched from the Nile to the Indus valley. The death of Alexander led to its division and eventual absorption by the emergent Roman Empire by the second century B.C.E.

The Romans: A Theory of Empire

The Romans had fewer hesitations about the desirability of imperial power than the Greeks. Their culture, which arose from a world of farmers accustomed to hard work, deprivation, and subordination to authority, venerated the military virtues. Roman society valued power, glory, and the responsibilities of leadership, even domination, without embarrassment. In time, the Romans formulated a theory of empire that claimed Roman rule brought great advantages to its subjects: prosperity, justice, the rule of law, and, most valuable of all, peace. In the words of their great epic poet Vergil (70–19 B.C.E.), it was the Roman practice "To humble the arrogant and be sparing to their subjects." These claims had considerable foundation, and the Romans could not have ruled so vast an empire with a relatively small army for more than half a millennium if their subjects had not enjoyed these benefits. Some of the conquered had a different viewpoint, however. As one British chieftain put it in the first century C.E.: "They make a wilderness and call it peace."

Muslims, Mongols, and Ottomans

The rise of Islam in the seventh century C.E. produced a new kind of empire that derived its energy from religious zeal. Bursting out of Arabia, the Muslim armies swiftly gained control of most of the territory held by the old Persian Empire, North Africa, and Spain.

In the twelfth and thirteenth centuries, the great Mongol Empire, at its height, dominated Eurasia from the Pacific to central Europe, ruling Russia for more than two centuries. As in most ancient empires, the Mongols demanded taxes and military service from the conquered. They also imposed their rule over the mighty and long-standing Chinese Empire, parts of India, and much of the Islamic world before their power declined.

Still another great empire that spanned Europe and Asia was that of the Ottomans, a Turkish people, originally from central Asia. In the fourteenth century, they established a kingdom in Anatolia (Asia Minor) and soon conquered the ancient Byzantine Empire, seizing Constantinople in 1453. In the next century, the Ottoman Empire dominated southeastern Europe, the Black Sea, North Africa from Morocco to Egypt, Palestine, Syria and Arabia, Mesopotamia and Iraq, and Kurdistan and Georgia in the Caucasus. As late as 1683, Ottoman armies threatened to take Vienna and push into western Europe. Over the next two centuries, however, Ottoman power declined as the European national states grew stronger. Russia, in particular, inflicted defeats that left Turkey in the late nineteenth century, "the sick man of Europe."

European Expansion

Europe, divided first by feudalism, then by the emergence of multiple nascent national states, had been the victim of Islamic imperial expansion during the Middle Ages, first at the hands of the Arabs, then the Turks. The crusades had produced small and transitory conquests. It was only in the late 1400s that Europeans began the economic and political expansion that culminated in their command of much of the planet by 1900. The first phase of European expansion involved the "discovery," exploration, conquest, exploitation, and settlement of the Americas. It was made possible by important developments in naval and military technology, the dynamism inherent in early commercial and financial capitalism, and the freedom to compete for wealth and power unleashed by the division into separate states.

Spain and Portugal took the lead, founding empires in Central and South America, sometimes conquering existing empires ruled by native peoples. In Central America, the Aztecs exacted labor and taxes from their subject peoples, using some of them as human sacrifices. In the Andes, the Incas ruled a great empire that also required military service and forced labor from its subjects. Both Native American empires were overthrown by Spain, which then established a vast American empire whose resources, especially gold and silver, formed the basis of the great Spanish Empire

The Ottoman Turks began to overrun the Balkans in the mid 1300s. In 1526 Sultan Suleyman the Magnificent destroyed a Hungarian army at the Battle of Mohacs. The Ottoman Empire ruled most of the Balkans until the late nineteenth century. Sultan Suleyman battles the Mohacs. Lokman, The Military Campaigns of Suleyman the Magnificent. Ms. Hunemame. Ottoman dynasty. Topkapi Palace Museum, Istanbul, Turkey. Giraudon/Art Resource, N.Y.

in Europe. Portugal exploited the agricultural and mineral riches of Brazil using slaves imported from Africa.

The seventeenth century saw the establishment of European trading posts and then colonies on the Indian subcontinent and in the East Indies, chiefly by the Dutch, British, and French. In North America, Spain held Mexico, Florida, and California. Of more lasting significance were French and British settlements in Canada and what was to become the United States. The British colonies, especially, represented a special kind of European overseas settlement in which concern for commerce was less important than the acquisition of land for farming.

The wars of the eighteenth century ultimately cleared North America and India of French competition, leaving both as British monopolies and important bases of what would become a worldwide British Empire. The largest and most populous empire in the history of the world, it included colonies of one sort or another on all the inhabited continents; the sun, as the saying went, never set on the British Empire. Whether European colonialism was profitable for the imperial powers is still controversial, but Great Britain certainly benefited more than the others. Unlike most colonial powers, the British imported great quantities of natural resources from their colonies and carried on a high percentage of their trade with them. Even more singular, the British Empire included such self-governing areas as Canada, Australia, New Zealand, and South Africa, ruled by emigrants from Britain who remained loyal to the mother country and were willing to assist it in wartime. The jewel in Britain's imperial crown, as another saying went, was India. With a population of some 300 million, it contained perhaps 80 percent of the empire's subjects and provided much of the imperial profit.

At the height of its power in the mid–nineteenth century, it is remarkable how little money and effort Britain needed to spend to maintain these desired conditions. The cost of its armed services, including its great navy, during these years was only about 2 to 3 percent of its gross national product—a low figure compared with other nations, and incredibly low considering Britain's status as the world's greatest empire. The British army was the smallest among the European powers: By 1880 it numbered fewer than a quarter of a million men, less than half the size of France's and barely a quarter of Russia's.

France returned to its imperial pursuits after its defeat in the Napoleonic Wars, especially in North Africa and Southeast Asia, and in the last quarter of the century, Germany and Italy joined the competition for colonies. The latter part of the century brought the European partition of Africa and the establishment of European economic and political

European imperialism ultimately rested on the willingness to use force. When anti-British agitation mounted in India after World War I, General Reginald Dyer's troops fired on unarmed Indian demonstrators at Amritsar. More than 300 Indians were killed. UPI/Corbis

power throughout Asia. Modernized Japan, too, became a colonial power, modeling itself on the imperialist policies of the European powers. (See Chapter 26.)

By the next century, European dominance had created a single global economy and had made events in any corner of the world significant thousands of miles away. The possession of colonies became part of the definition of a great power, and competition for colonies helped bring on World War I.

Toward Decolonization

The weakening of the European colonial powers in World War II began the process of decolonization. The economic value of most colonies had proved to be much smaller than anticipated, and the colonial powers lacked both the capacity and the incentive to restore their former rule. Nationalist movements in the old colonies, moreover, would make such attempts costly and unpleasant. These movements flourished under the banner of national self-determination, self-government, and independence, ideas that came from and were cherished by the European colonial powers themselves. The example of Nazi Germany, moreover, had discredited theories of racial superiority that had justified much of European imperial rule. For European imperialism the handwriting was on the wall, although some colonial powers held on more fiercely than others. The French, for instance, fought at great cost—but in vain—to retain Algeria and Indochina. By the 1970s, a postcolonial world had emerged, and the concept of empire had become unclean. (See Chapter 31.)

■ *What were the major ancient attitudes toward imperialism? What are the major modern attitudes? How do you account for the differences? What justifications and explanations have modern people used in connection with imperialism? Which do you think are the most important? Do you think ancient and modern reasons for imperialism are fundamentally different?*

Anxiety over the spread of the Bolshevik revolution was a fundamental factor of European politics during the 1920s and 1930s. Images like this Soviet portrait of Lenin as a heroic revolutionary conjured fears among people in the rest of Europe of a political force determined to overturn their social, political, and economic institutions. Gemalde von A. M. Gerassimow, *Lenin as Agitator* /Bildarchiv Preussischer Kulturbesitz

POLITICAL EXPERIMENTS
OF THE 1920S

*E*XPERIMENTATION IN POLITICS AND THE *pursuit of normality in economic life marked the decade following the conclusion of the Paris treaties, also known throughout the period as the Versailles settlement. These treaties, as examined in Chapter 26, established a bold new experiment in European diplomatic relations. The Paris settlement instituted the League of Nations and imposed economic and military terms that fostered friction among all the powers and deep resentment in Germany. Through war and revolution the Habsburg Empire collapsed and was replaced by small successor states, only one of which became a generally successful democracy. In Russia, the Bolsheviks, after seizing control of the government in 1917 and then winning a civil war, reorganized every aspect of life, transforming the state into the Soviet Union. In Italy, the political turmoil and social strains of the postwar era resulted in the emergence of the authoritarian movement known as fascism. In Great Britain, the Labour Party came to power for the first time, and most of Ireland became an independent nation. Germany, after suffering a humiliating military defeat, jettisoned the imperial monarchy and set out on the experiment of the Weimar Republic, which encountered numerous determined and violent opponents. All of those transformations involved considerable domestic violence for at least five years after the close of the war itself.*

Many of these political experiments failed, and the economic and social normality so many Europeans sought proved elusive. By the close of the 1920s, the political path had been paved for the nightmares of brutally authoritarian governments and international aggression that were to mark the 1930s and 1940s. Yet many of the people who had survived the Great War had hoped and worked for a better outcome. Authoritarianism and aggression were not the inescapable destiny of Europe. They emerged from the failure to secure alternative modes of democratic political life and stable international relations and from the inability to achieve long-term economic prosperity.

KEY TOPICS

- Economic and political disorder in the aftermath of World War I
- The Soviet Union's far-reaching political and social experiment
- Mussolini and the fascist seizure of power in Italy
- French determination to enforce the Versailles treaty
- First Labour government and general strike in Britain
- The development of authoritarian governments in all the successor states to the Austrian Empire except Czechoslovakia
- Reparations, inflation, political turmoil, and the rise of nazism in the German Weimar Republic

Political and Economic Factors after the Paris Settlement

NEW GOVERNMENTS

In 1919, experimental political regimes studded the map of Europe. From Ireland to Russia, new governments were seeking to gain the active support of their citizens and to solve the grievous economic problems caused by the war. In the Soviet Union, the Bolsheviks regarded themselves as forging a new kind of civilization, one built on achieving communism. To that end, they constructed a vast authoritarian state apparatus.

The situation was different elsewhere on the Continent. In many, though not all, countries, the turn to liberal democracy resulted in the right to vote being given to women and previously disenfranchised males. For the first time in European history, governments were responsible to mass electorates. Even where the authoritarian, military empires of Germany and Austria-Hungary had held sway, democratically elected parliamentary governments took form. Their goals were more modest and less utopian than those of the Bolsheviks. Yet to pursue parliamentary politics where it had never been meaningfully practiced proved no simple task. The Wilsonian vision of democratic, self-determined nations foundered on the harsh realities of economics, aggressive nationalism, and political conservatism. Too often, nations that had been given democratic parliamentary government lacked both the will and the political skill to make the new system work. Many of the constitutional arrangements, themselves flawed, contained the seeds of their own destruction. Moreover, in many of the new democracies, important sectors of the citizenry believed parliamentary politics was inherently corrupt or feeble. Economics and politics were more intimately connected than ever before. The economic and social anxieties of the electorate, as well as nationalistic ambitions, could, and eventually did, overcome political scruples.

DEMANDS FOR REVISION OF THE PARIS SETTLEMENT

The Paris peace treaties themselves became domestic political issues. Usually, the objections arose from nationalistic concerns and resentments. Germany had been humiliated. The arrangements for reparations led to endless haggling over payments. Various national groups in the successor states of eastern Europe also felt they had been treated unjustly or been denied self-determination. There were important demands for further border adjustments because significant national minorities, particularly German, still resided outside national boundaries, as drawn in Paris. On the other side, the victorious powers, and especially France, often believed the provisions of the treaty were not being adequately enforced. So, throughout the 1920s, calls either to revise or to enforce the Paris treaties contributed to domestic political turmoil across the Continent. Many political figures were willing to fish in these troubled international waters for a large catch of domestic votes.

POSTWAR ECONOMIC PROBLEMS

Along with the move toward political experimentation and the demands for revision of the new international order, there existed a widespread desire to return to the economic prosperity of the prewar years. After 1918, however, it was impossible to restore in the economic realm what American president Warren Harding (1865–1923) would shortly term *normalcy*. During the Great War, Europeans had turned the military and industrial power that they had created during the previous century against themselves. What had been "normal" in economic and social life before 1914 could not be reestablished.

The casualties from the war numbered in the millions. (See Table 27–1.) This represented not only a waste of human life and talent, but also the loss of producers and consumers.

TABLE 27–1	Total Casualties in the First World War		
Country	Dead	Wounded	Total Killed as a Percentage of Population
France	1,398,000	2,000,000	3.4
Belgium	38,000	44,700	0.5
Italy	578,000	947,000	1.6
British Empire	921,000	2,090,000	1.7
Romania	250,000	120,000	3.3
Serbia	278,000	133,000	5.7
Greece	26,000	21,000	0.5
Russia	1,811,000	1,450,000	1.1
Bulgaria	88,000	152,000	1.9
Germany	2,037,000	4,207,000	3.0
Austria-Hungary	1,100,000	3,620,000	1.9
Turkey	804,000	400,000	3.7
United States	114,000	206,000	0.1

Source: Niall Ferguson, The Pity of War *(New York: Basic Books, 1998).*

Another casualty of the conflict was the financial dominance and independence of Europe. In 1914, Europe had been the financial and credit center of the world. By 1918, European states were deep in debt to each other and to the United States. The Bolsheviks had repudiated the debt of the tsarist government, much of which was owed to French creditors. Other nations could not pursue this revolutionary course. The Paris settlement had imposed heavy financial obligations on Germany and its allies. The United States refused to ask reparations from Germany, but demanded repayment of war debts from its own allies.

On one hand, the reparation and debt structure meant no nation was fully in control of its own economic life. On the other hand, the absence of international economic cooperation meant that, more than ever, individual nations felt compelled to pursue or to try to pursue selfish, nationalistic economic aims. It was perhaps the worst of all possible international economic worlds.

The market and trade conditions that had prevailed before 1914 had also changed radically. Much of Europe's transport facilities, mines, and industry had been damaged or destroyed. Russia all but withdrew from the European economic order. The division of eastern and central Europe into a multitude of small states broke up the trade region formerly encompassed by Germany and Austria-Hungary. Most of those new states had weak economies hardly capable of competing in modern economic life.

The new political boundaries separated raw materials from the factories that used them. Railway systems on which finished and unfinished products traveled might now lie under the control of two or more nations. Political and economic nationalism went together. Nations raised new customs barriers where before there had been none.

International trade also followed novel patterns. The United States became less dependent on European production and was now a major competitor. During the war, the belligerents had been forced to sell many of their investments on other continents to finance the conflict. As a consequence, European dominance over the world economy weakened. Slow postwar economic growth or even the decline of economic activity within colonies or former colonies lowered the international demand for European goods. The United States and Japan began to penetrate markets in Latin America and Asia that European producers and traders had dominated.

NEW ROLES FOR GOVERNMENT AND LABOR

The war had given labor new prominence. In every country, the unions had supported the war effort and ensured labor peace for wartime production. In turn, their members had received better wages, and their leaders had been admitted to high political councils. This wartime cooperation of unions and labor leaders with national governments destroyed the internationalism of the prewar labor movement. It also, however, meant that henceforth governments could not ignore the demands of labor. After the war, many wages fell, but rarely to prewar levels. European workers intended to receive their just share of the fruits of their labor. Collective bargaining and union recognition brought on by the war were also there to stay. This improvement in both the status and the influence of labor was one of the most significant changes to flow from World War I. In reaction to it, middle-class European voters became increasingly conservative.

The Soviet Experiment Begins

The consolidation of the Bolshevik revolution in Russia established the most extensive and durable of all the twentieth-century authoritarian governments that came to power in the political turmoil of World War I and its aftermath. The Communist Party of the Soviet Union retained power from 1917 until the end of 1991, and its presence influenced the political history of Europe during this century as did no other single factor. The Communist Party was neither a mass party nor a nationalistic one. Its early membership rarely exceeded 1 percent of the Russian population. For several years after 1917, the party faced widespread domestic opposition, and the communist leaders long felt their hold on the country was insecure. Yet the communists also regarded their government and their revolution not as local events in a national history, but as epoch-making events in the history of the world and the development of humanity. Communism was an exportable commodity that could disrupt the political life of other nations, and throughout the history of the Soviet Union, its leaders sought to export its ideology and doctrines. Fear of communism and a

determination to stop its spread became one of the leading political forces in western Europe and the United States for most of the rest of the century.

WAR COMMUNISM

Within the Soviet Union, the Red Army, under the organizational direction of Leon Trotsky (1879–1940), eventually suppressed internal and foreign military opposition to the new government. The White Russian armies, which fought the Red Army for several years, could not adequately organize themselves, and Allied help was inadequate to defeat the Bolsheviks. The existence of a military threat allowed the Bolsheviks to pursue authoritarian policies rapidly. Within months of the revolution, a new secret police, known as the *Cheka*, appeared. Throughout the civil war, Lenin had declared that the Bolshevik Party, as the vanguard of the revolution, was imposing the dictatorship of the proletariat. Political and economic administration became highly centralized. All major decisions flowed from the top in a nondemocratic manner. Under the economic policy of war communism, the revolutionary government confiscated and then operated the banks, the transport system, and heavy industry. The state also seized grain from the peasants to feed the army and the workers in the cities. The fact of the civil war permitted the Bolsheviks to suppress resistance to this economic policy. Throughout the period of the civil war, the government headed by Lenin carried out extensive repression of all actual or potential sources of opposition. (See "Trotsky Urges the Use of Terror.")

War communism aided the victory of the Red Army. The revolution had survived and triumphed. The policy, however, generated domestic opposition to the Bolsheviks, who in 1920 numbered only about 600,000 members. The alliance of workers

During the civil war in the Soviet Union, hunger and starvation haunted the countryside. Here a group of malnourished children posed for a photograph. Bildarchiv Preussischer Kulturbesitz

TROTSKY URGES THE USE OF TERROR

Leon Trotsky led the Red Army to victory in the brutal and extensive civil war that followed the Bolshevik revolution in 1918. He became a major opponent, and later a victim, of Stalin. In this 1920 discussion, he explains how terror and intimidation must be used to achieve communist revolution. He contends that capitalist society itself came to power through the use of force and that only force will allow the working class to establish its dominance. He argues that there is no real moral argument against the use of terror and violence. In particular, he directs his remarks toward liberals, who thought social change could be achieved by parliamentary means, and against the German Marxist socialists, the Kautskians, who had argued that historical forces would bring about the revolution of the working class without the use of violence. These words of Trotsky help explain the fear of Bolshevism that swept across much of Europe immediately after World War I, a fear right-wing politicians manipulated during the 1920s and 1930s.

■ *How does Trotsky's justification of terror compare with that associated with the Reign of Terror during the French Revolution? How might the circumstances of the Russian civil war have led Trotsky to these views? Do you agree that the communist terror advocated by Trotsky differed from the repressive police policies of the tsars?*

The problem of revolution, as of war, consists in breaking the will of the foe, forcing him to capitulate and to accept the conditions of the conqueror. The will, of course, is a fact of the physical world, but in contradistinction to a meeting, a dispute, or a congress, the revolution carries out its object by means of the employment of material resources—though to a lesser degree than war. The bourgeoisie itself conquered power by means of revolts, and consolidated it by the civil war. In the peace period, it retains power by means of a system of repression. As long as class society, founded on the most deep-rooted antagonisms, continues to exist, repression remains a necessary means of breaking the will of the opposing side.

Even if, in one country or another, the dictatorship of the proletariat grew up within the external framework of democracy, this would by no means avert the civil war. The question as to who is to rule the country, i.e., of the life or death of the bourgeoisie, will be decided on either side, not by references to the paragraphs of the constitution, but by the employment of all forms of violence. . . .

The question of the form of repression, or of its degree, of course, is not one of "principle." It is a question of expediency. . . .

Terror can be very efficient against a reactionary class which does not want to leave the scene of operations. Intimidation is a powerful weapon of policy, both internationally and internally. A victorious war, generally speaking, destroys only an insignificant part of the conquered army, intimidating the remainder and breaking their will. The revolution works in the same way: it kills individuals, and intimidates thousands. In this sense, the Red Terror is not distinguishable from the armed insurrection, the direct continuation of which it represents. The State terror of a revolutionary class can be condemned "morally" only by a man who, as a principle, rejects (in words) every form of violence whatsoever—consequently, every war and every uprising. For this one has to be merely and simply a hypocritical Quaker.

"But, in that case, in what do your tactics differ from the tactics of Tsarism?" we are asked by the high priests of Liberalism and Kautskianism.

You do not understand this, holy men? We shall explain to you. The terror of Tsarism was directed against the proletariat. The gendarmerie of Tsarism throttled the workers who were fighting for the Socialist order. Our Extraordinary Commissions shoot landlords, capitalists, and generals who are striving to restore the capitalist order. Do you grasp this—distinction? Yes? For us Communists it is quite sufficient.

From Leon Trotsky, *Terrorism and Communism,* 1920; English trans., *Dictatorship vs. Democracy: A Reply to Karl Kautsky* (New York: Workers' Party of America, 1922), pp. 54, 57–59, as quoted in Robert V. Daniels, *A Documentary History of Communism,* rev. ed., Vol. 1 (Hanover, NH, and London: University Press of New England, 1984), pp. 121–122.

and peasants forged by the slogan of "Peace, Bread, and Land" had begun to come apart at the seams. Many Russians were no longer willing to make the sacrifices demanded by the central party bureaucrats. In 1920 and 1921, large strikes occurred in many factories. Discontented peasants resisted the requisition of grain as they had since 1918. In March 1921, the Baltic fleet mutinied at Kronstadt. The Red Army crushed the rebellion with grave loss of life.

THE NEW ECONOMIC POLICY

Under these difficult conditions, Lenin made a strategic retreat. In March 1921, following the Kronstadt mutiny and in the face of continuing peasant resistance to the requisition of grain needed to feed the urban population, he outlined the **New Economic Policy (NEP).** Apart from what he termed "the commanding heights" of banking, heavy industry, transportation, and international commerce, the government would tolerate private enterprise. In particular, peasants could farm for profit. They would pay taxes like other citizens, but they could sell their grain on the open market. The NEP was in line with Lenin's earlier conviction that the Russian peasantry held the key to the success of the revolution.

After 1921, the countryside did become more stable, and a more secure food supply seemed assured for the cities. Similar free enterprise flourished within light industry and domestic retail trade. The implementation of the NEP, however, was not fully successful, because there were virtually no consumer goods for the peasants to purchase with the money they received for their grain. Yet by 1927, industrial production had reached its 1913 level. The revolution seemed to have transformed Russia into a land of small, if frequently discontented, family farmers and owners of small private shops and businesses.

STALIN VERSUS TROTSKY

The NEP had caused disputes within the Politburo, the governing committee of the Communist Party. Some members considered the partial return to capitalism a betrayal of Marxist principles. These frictions increased when Lenin's firm hand disappeared. In 1922, he suffered a stroke and never again dominated party affairs. In 1924, he died.

The resulting power vacuum led to an intense struggle for the leadership of the party. Two factions emerged. One was led by Leon Trotsky, the other by Joseph Stalin (1879–1953), who had become general secretary of the party in 1922. Shortly before his death, Lenin had criticized both men, but was especially harsh toward Stalin. Stalin's power base, however, lay with the party membership and in the day-to-day management of party affairs. Consequently, he was able to withstand the posthumous strictures of Lenin.

Trotsky's Position   The issue between the two factions was power within the party, but the struggle was fought out over the question of Russia's path toward industrialization and the future of the communist revolutionary movement. Trotsky, speaking for what became known as the left wing, urged rapid industrialization financed through the expropriation of farm production. Agriculture should be collectivized, and the peasants should be made to pay for industrialization. Trotsky further argued that the revolution in Russia could succeed only if new revolutions took place elsewhere. Russia needed the skills and wealth of other nations to build its own economy. As Trotsky's influence within the party waned, he also demanded that party members be permitted to criticize the government and the party. Trotsky was, however, a latecomer to the advocacy of open discussion. When he had controlled the Red Army, he had been an unflinching disciplinarian.

Stalin's Rise   Stalin had been born in 1879 into a poor family. Unlike the other early Bolshevik leaders, he had not spent a long period of exile in western Europe and was much less intellectual and internationalist in his outlook. He was also more brutal. During his tenure as commissar of nationalities,

Lenin (l.) and Trotsky worked closely together during the early years of the Bolshevik regime and the Russian Civil War.   Getty Images Inc.—Hulton Archive Photos

Stalin's handling of various recalcitrant national groups within Russia after the revolution had shocked even Lenin, though not enough for Lenin to dismiss him. As the party general secretary, a post that party intellectuals disdained as merely clerical, Stalin amassed power through his command of bureaucratic and administrative methods. He was neither a brilliant writer nor an effective public speaker. He did, however, master the crucial, if dull, details of party structure, including admission to the party and promotion within it. That mastery meant he had the support of the lower levels of the party apparatus when he clashed with other leaders.

During the mid-1920s, a Communist Party faction known as the right wing opposed Trotsky's drive for rapid industrialization. Its chief ideological voice was that of Nikolai Bukharin (1888–1938), the editor of *Pravda* (*Truth*), the official party newspaper. In the face of the uncertain economic recovery, the right wing pressed for the continuation of Lenin's NEP and for relatively slow industrialization. At the time, this position represented a policy based largely on decentralized economic planning and tolerating modest free enterprise and small landholdings. Stalin manipulated these intraparty rivalries.

In the mid-1920s, Stalin expediently supported Bukharin's position on economic development. In 1924, he also enunciated, in opposition to Trotsky, the doctrine of "socialism in one country," which contended that socialism could be achieved in Russia alone. Russian success did not depend on the fate of revolutions elsewhere. Stalin thus nationalized the previously international scope of the Marxist revolution. He cunningly used his control over the Central Committee of the Communist Party to edge out Trotsky and his supporters.

By 1927, Trotsky had been removed from all his offices, expelled from the party, and exiled to Siberia. In 1929, he was forced out of Russia, and eventually he moved to Mexico, where he was murdered in 1940, presumably by one of Stalin's agents. With Trotsky defeated, Stalin was firmly in control of the Soviet state. It remained to be seen where he would take it and what "socialism in one country" would mean in practice.

THE THIRD INTERNATIONAL

The Bolshevik revolution in Russia stunned west European socialists. In the West, prior to the war, as discussed in Chapter 24, social democratic parties had debated among themselves whether they might participate in parliamentary structures. They had regarded the Russian Bolsheviks as eccentric, politically marginal Marxist extremists. The Bolshevik victory consequently required west European social democrats to rethink their position within the world of international socialism. For their part, the Bolsheviks regarded such reformist social democrats as a major enemy. The Bolsheviks intended to establish themselves as the international leaders of Marxism.

To that end, in 1919 the Soviet communists founded the Third International of the European socialist movement, better known as the *Comintern*. The Comintern worked to make the Bolshevik model of socialism, as developed by Lenin, the rule for all socialist parties outside the Soviet Union. In 1920, the Comintern imposed its Twenty-one Conditions on any socialist party that wished to join it. (See "The Third International Issues Conditions of Membership.") These conditions included acknowledging Moscow's leadership, rejecting reformist or revisionist socialism, repudiating previous socialist leaders, and adopting the Communist Party name. In effect, the Comintern sought to destroy democratic socialism, which it accused of having betrayed the working class through reform policies and parliamentary accommodation.

In 1919, the new Soviet government established the Comintern to sponsor and organize communist parties outside the Soviet Union. In this Bolshevik propaganda poster the banner declares, "You have nothing to lose but your chains, but the world will soon be yours." The figures in the foreground represent peoples from around the globe as an indication of the Soviet ambition to spread communism far beyond the borders of the Soviet Union. Museum of the Revolution, Moscow/Bridgeman Art Library, London

THE THIRD INTERNATIONAL ISSUES CONDITIONS OF MEMBERSHIP

After the Russian Revolution, the Russian Communist Party organized the Third Communist International. Any communist party outside the Soviet Union was required to accept these twenty-one conditions, adopted in 1920, to join the International. In effect, this program demanded that all such parties adopt a distinctly revolutionary program. They also needed to cease operating as legal parties within their various countries. By this means, the Soviet Union sought to achieve leadership of the socialist movement throughout Europe. The non-Russian socialist parties quickly split into social democratic parties that remained independent of Moscow and communist parties that adopted the policy imposed by the Russian Communist Party.

■ *What are the major forms of revolutionary agitation that these conditions assume? Why was the Russian Communist Party willing to forgo all alliances with other socialist parties that would not declare and rename themselves communist? How could this document and the organization it established be used by conservative and right-wing political groups elsewhere in Europe?*

1. The daily propaganda and agitation must bear a truly communist character and correspond to the program and all the decisions of the Third International. All the organs of the press that are in the hands of the party must be edited by reliable communists who have proved their loyalty to the cause of the proletarian revolution. . . .

4. The obligation to spread communist ideas includes the particular necessity of persistent, systematic propaganda in the army. . . .

5. It is necessary to carry on systematic and steady agitation in the rural districts. . . .

14. Every party that desires to belong to the Communist International must give every possible support to the Soviet Republics in their struggle against all counterrevolutionary forces. . . .

16. All decisions of the congresses of the Communist International . . . are binding on all parties affiliated to the Communist International. . . .

17. In connection with all this, all parties desiring to join the Communist International must change their names. Every party that wishes to join the Communist International must bear the name: Communist party of such-and-such country. This question as to name is not merely a formal one, but a political one of great importance. The Communist International has declared a decisive war against the entire bourgeois world and all the yellow social democratic parties. Every rank-and-file worker must clearly understand the difference between the communist parties and the old official "social democratic" or "socialist" parties which have betrayed the cause of the working class.

18. Members of the party who reject the conditions and thesis of the Communist International, on principle, must be expelled from the party.

From *The Communist International 1919–1923, Documents*, Vol. 1 by Jane Degras, (London: Frank Cass & Co., 1971), pp. 168–169, 171–172. Reproduced by permission of Frank Cass Pubishers, London.

The decision whether to accept these conditions split every major European socialist party. As a result, separate communist and social democratic parties emerged in many countries. The communist parties modeled themselves after the Soviet party, and Moscow dictated their policies. The social democratic parties attempted to pursue both social reform and liberal parliamentary politics. Throughout the 1920s and early 1930s, the communists and social democrats fought each other more intensely than they fought either capitalism or conservative political parties. Their fierce conflict was one of the fundamental features of the interwar European political landscape.

These policies of the Comintern directly affected the rise of the fascists and the nazis in western Europe. It is difficult to exaggerate the fears that Soviet political rhetoric and Communist Party activity aroused in Europe during the 1920s and 1930s. These fears, often exaggerated, were manipulated by conservative and right-wing political groups. The presence of separate communist parties in western Europe meant that right-wing politicians always had a convenient target they could justly accuse of seeking to overthrow the government and to impose Soviet-style political and economic systems in their respective nations. Furthermore, right-wing politicians also accused the democratic socialist parties of supporting policies that might facilitate a communist takeover. The division of the European political left also meant that right-wing political movements rarely had to confront a united left.

WOMEN AND THE FAMILY IN THE EARLY SOVIET UNION

Communist views toward women and the family assumed the traditional family embodied middle-class capitalist values that were at odds with what was socially good and with the liberty of the proletariat. In the early years of the Russian Revolution, this outlook led to utopian projections of what the life of women and the family would resemble under socialism. The most famous such utopian writer was Alexandra Kollontai (1872–1952). In *Communism and the Family* (1918) and other works, she envisioned a new kind of family that she thought would liberate both women and men. (See "Alexandra Kollontai Demands a New Family Life.") Her views included both the expansion of sexual freedom and the radical sharing of tasks about the home between wives and husbands. She wanted to replace what she regarded as egoistic, exploitative family relationships with families based on love and comradeship. Few people in the Soviet Union, even among the communists, agreed with Kollontai, but her views became well known and were often assumed to reflect those of a wide spectrum of the Soviet leadership and citizenry. At a time when the Soviet Union was isolated from the rest of the world, people on the outside could imagine that Kollontai's visions were the reality of the bold new life being forged there. As we see later in this chapter and in the next, both Italian fascists and German nazis contrasted their own traditionalist views of women with these radical views.

Family Legislation from Reform to Repression Soon after achieving power in late 1917, the Bolsheviks began to issue laws pertaining to women. Divorce became far easier, marriage was no longer a religious ceremony, and legitimate and illegitimate children were given the same rights. Various protections were extended to women in the workplace and within marriage. Abortion was legalized in 1920. All of these measures were enacted to create a socialist society. Women obtained high positions in the Communist Party, and more women voted, but in fact, women had no significant impact on Soviet government.

The dislocations flowing from the civil war, the confiscation of property, shifting economic policies, and the general reordering of Soviet society during the 1920s seriously disrupted Soviet family life. Domestic violence appears to have been common. The birthrate fell while the number of both abortions and abandoned children rose. The new divorce law made it easy for husbands to abandon their wives, and a housing shortage made it difficult for divorced couples to live separately.

In the 1920s and 1930s, and after, women could advance through the party structures into leadership positions there and elsewhere in the economy. Educational opportunities for women were readily available, yet women who worked, even in professional careers, were still expected to do the housework, and there was no significant structure of child care. Typically, women were paid less than men. Throughout the history of the Soviet Union, the culture of economic shortage of consumer goods affected women more than any other group. It was they who most often had to stand in the long lines, cope with an absence of goods, and somehow make their own lives and those of their families hang together.

The Fascist Experiment in Italy

Italy witnessed the first authoritarian political experiment in western Europe that arose in part from fears of the spread of Bolshevism. From the Italian fascist movement of Benito Mussolini (1883–1945) came the general terms *fascist*, and **fascism,** frequently used to describe a number of right-wing dictatorships that arose across Europe between the wars.

Both historians and political scientists disagree about the exact meaning of *fascism* as a political term. Most scholars agree, however, that the government regimes regarded as fascist were antidemocratic, anti-Marxist, antiparliamentary, and frequently anti-Semitic. These governments claimed to hold back the spread of Bolshevism, which, because of Soviet rhetoric and the activity of domestic communist parties, seemed at the time a real threat. They sought to make the world safe for the middle class, small businesses, owners of moderate amounts of property, and small farmers. The fascist regimes rejected the political inheritance of the French Revolution and of nineteenth-century liberalism. Fascist movements were invariably nationalistic

ALEXANDRA KOLLONTAI DEMANDS A NEW FAMILY LIFE

While Lenin sought to consolidate the Bolshevik revolution against internal and external enemies, there existed within the young Soviet Union a vast utopian impulse to change and reform virtually every social institution that had existed before the revolution or that was associated in the communists' minds with capitalist society. Alexandra Kollontai (1872–1952) was a spokesperson of the extreme political left within the early Soviet Union. In communist circles, there had been much speculation on how the end of bourgeois society might change the structure of the family and the position of women. In the passage that follows, written in 1920, Kollontai states one of the most radically idealistic visions of this change. During the years immediately after the revolution, rumors circulated in both Europe and America about sexual and family experimentation in the Soviet Union. Statements such as this one fostered such rumors. Kollontai herself later became a supporter of Stalin and a Soviet diplomat.

■ *Why did Kollontai see the restructuring of the family as essential to the establishment of a new kind of communist society? Would these changes make people loyal to that society? What changes in society does the kind of economic independence she seeks for women presuppose? What might childhood be like if the state, rather than their parents, assumed responsibility for their children?*

There is no escaping the fact: the old type of family has seen its day. It is not the fault of the Communist State, it is the result of the changed conditions of life. The family is ceasing to be a necessity of the State, as it was in the past; on the contrary, it is worse than useless, since it needlessly holds back the female workers from more productive and far more serious work. . . . But on the ruins of the former family we shall soon see a new form rising which will involve altogether different relations between men and women, and which will be a union of affection and comradeship, a union of two equal members of the Communist society, both of them free, both of them independent, both of them workers. No more domestic "servitude" of women. No more inequality within the family. No more fear on the part of the woman lest she remain without support or aid with little ones in her arms if her husband should desert her. The woman in the Communist city no longer depends on her husband but on her work. It is not her husband but her robust arms which will support her. There will be no more anxiety as to the fate of her children. The State of the Workers will assume responsibility for these. Marriage will be purified of all its material elements, of all money calculations, which constitute a hideous blemish on family life in our days. . . .

The woman who is called upon to struggle in the great cause of the liberation of the workers—such a woman should know that in the new State there will be no more room for such petty divisions as were formerly understood: "These are my own children, to them I owe all my maternal solicitude, all my affection; those are your children, my neighbour's children; I am not concerned with them. I have enough to do with my own." Henceforth the worker-mother, who is conscious of her social function, will rise to a point where she no longer differentiates between yours and mine; she must remember that there are henceforth only our children, those of the Communist State, the common possession of all the workers.

The Worker's State has need of a new form of relation between the sexes. The narrow and exclusive affection of the mother for her own children must expand until it embraces all the children of the great proletarian family. In place of the indissoluble marriage based on the servitude of woman, we shall see rise the free union, fortified by the love and mutual respect of the two members of the Workers' State, equal in their rights and in their obligations. In place of the individual and egotistic family there will arise a great universal family of workers, in which all the workers, men and women, will be, above all, workers, comrades.

From Alexandra Kollontai, *Communism and the Family*, as reprinted in Rudolf Schlesinger, ed. and trans., *The Family in the USSR* (London: Routledge and Kegan Paul, 1949), pp. 67–69. Reprinted by permission of Taylor & Francis Books, Ltd.

in response to the feared international expansion of communism.

Fascists believed that normal parliamentary politics and parties sacrificed national honor and greatness to petty disputes. They wanted to overcome the class conflict of Marxism and the party conflict of liberalism by consolidating the various groups and classes within the nation for great national purposes. As Mussolini declared in 1931, "The fascist conception of the state is all-embracing, and outside of the state no human or spiritual values can exist, let alone be desirable."[1] The fascist governments were usually single-party dictatorships characterized by terrorism and police surveillance. In contrast to the Communist Party of the Soviet Union, their base was mass political parties.

THE RISE OF MUSSOLINI

The Italian *Fasci di Combattimento*, or "Bands of Combat," was founded in 1919 in Milan. Its members came largely from Italian war veterans who felt the Paris conference had cheated Italy of the hard-won fruits of victory. They especially resented Italy's failure to gain Fiume (now Rijeka) on the northeast coast of the Adriatic Sea. They also feared the spread of socialism and the effects of inflation.

Their leader, Benito Mussolini, had been born the son of a blacksmith. He had worked as a schoolteacher and a day laborer before becoming active in Italian socialist politics. By 1912, he had become editor of the socialist newspaper *Avanti* (meaning "forward"). In 1914, Mussolini broke with the socialists and supported Italian entry into the war on the side of the Allies. His interventionist position lost him the editorship of *Avanti*. He had in effect moved from championing the proletariat to championing the nation. Nationalism replaced socialism as his ideology for a national revolution that would transform what he and many others regarded as a weak liberal state. He soon established his own paper, *Il Popolo d'Italia* (*The People of Italy*). Later he served in the army and was wounded. In 1919, although of some prewar political stature, Mussolini was simply one of many Italian politicians, and his Fasci organization was just one more small political group in a country full of them. As a politician, Mussolini was an opportunist par excellence. He could change his ideas and principles to suit every new occasion. Action for him was always more important than thought or rational justification. His one real goal was political survival. (See "Mussolini Heaps Contempt on Political Liberalism.")

Postwar Italian Political Turmoil Postwar Italian politics was a muddle. During the conflict, the Italian Parliament had virtually ceased to function, and it allowed ministers to rule by decree. Many Italians, however, were already dissatisfied with the parliamentary system. Italian nationalists—not just Mussolini's followers—felt Italy had not been treated as a great power at the peace conference and had not received the territories it deserved.

The main spokesperson for this discontent was the extreme nationalist writer Gabriele D'Annunzio (1863–1938). In 1919, he seized Fiume with a force of patriotic Italians. He was eventually driven out, but D'Annunzio had shown how a nongovernmental military force could be put to political use. Moreover, the use of force against D'Annunzio embarrassed the Italian government and made it appear less patriotic than the ultranationalists.

Between 1919 and 1921, Italy also experienced considerable internal social turmoil. Many industrial strikes occurred, and workers occupied factories. Peasants seized uncultivated land from large estates. Parliamentary and constitutional government seemed incapable of dealing with this unrest. The Socialist Party had captured a plurality of seats in the Chamber of Deputies in the 1919 election. The sharp division between socialists and communists had not yet emerged, and the Socialist Party included many people who were soon to become communists. A new Catholic Popular Party had also done well in the election. Both appealed to the working and agrarian classes. Neither party, however, would cooperate with the other; parliamentary deadlock resulted. Under these conditions, many Italians honestly, and still others conveniently, believed the social upheaval and political paralysis would lead to a communist revolution.

Early Fascist Organization Initially, Mussolini was uncertain of the direction of the political winds. He first supported the factory occupations and land seizures. Never one to be concerned with consistency, however, he soon reversed himself. He had discovered that many upper-class and middle-class Italians, pressured by inflation and fearing the loss of their property, had no sympathy for the workers or the peasants. They wanted order, rather than some vague social justice that might harm their own interests. Moreover, Mussolini was coming to see any social group pursuing its own goals as undermining great national purposes and national unity. The socialists became easy and obvious targets because they had always espoused internationalism as well as working-class interests.

Consequently, Mussolini and his fascists took direct action in the face of government inaction.

[1]Quoted in Denis Mack Smith, *Italy: A Modern History* (Ann Arbor: University of Michigan Press, 1959), p. 412.

MUSSOLINI HEAPS CONTEMPT ON POLITICAL LIBERALISM

The political tactics of the Italian fascists wholly disregarded the liberal belief in the rule of law and the consent of the governed. In 1923, Mussolini explained why the fascists so hated and repudiated these liberal principles. Note his emphasis on the idea of the twentieth century as a new historical epoch requiring a new kind of politics and his undisguised praise of force in politics.

■ *Who would be some nineteenth-century liberal political leaders included in Mussolini's attack? Why might Mussolini's audience have been receptive to these views? What events or developments within liberal states allowed Mussolini to portray liberalism as so corrupt and powerless?*

Liberalism is not the last word, nor does it represent the definitive formula on the subject of the art of government. . . . Liberalism is the product and the technique of the 19th century. . . . It does not follow that the Liberal scheme of government, good for the 19th century, for a century, that is, dominated by two such phenomena as the growth of capitalism and the strengthening of the sentiment of nationalism, should be adapted to the 20th century, which announces itself already with characteristics sufficiently different from those that marked the preceding century. . . .

I challenge Liberal gentlemen to tell if ever in history there has been a government that was based solely on popular consent and that renounced all use of force whatsoever. A government so constructed there has never been and never will be. Consent is an ever-changing thing like the shifting sand on the sea coast. It can never be permanent: It can never be complete. . . . If it be accepted as an axiom that any system of government whatever creates malcontents, how are you going to prevent this discontent from overflowing and constituting a menace to the stability of the State?

You will prevent it by force. By the assembling of the greatest force possible. By the inexorable use of this force whenever it is necessary. Take away from any government whatsoever force—and by force is meant physical, armed force—and leave it only its immortal principles, and that government will be at the mercy of the first organized group that decides to overthrow it. Fascism now throws these lifeless theories out to rot. . . . The truth evident now to all who are not warped by [liberal] dogmatism is that men have tired of liberty. They have made an orgy of it. Liberty is today no longer the chaste and austere virgin for whom the generations of the first half of the last century fought and died. For the gallant, restless and bitter youth who face the dawn of a new history there are other words that exercise a far greater fascination, and those words are: order, hierarchy, discipline. . . .

Know then, once and for all, that Fascism knows no idols and worships no fetishes. It has already stepped over, and if it be necessary it will turn tranquilly and step again over, the more or less putrescent corpse of the Goddess of Liberty.

Benito Mussolini, "Force and Consent" (1923), as trans. in Jonathan F. Scott and Alexander Baltzly, eds., *Readings in European History since 1814* (New York: F. S. Crofts, 1931), pp. 680–682.

They formed local squads of terrorists who disrupted Socialist Party meetings, beat up socialist leaders, and intimidated socialist supporters. They attacked strikers and farmworkers and protected strikebreakers. Conservative land and factory owners were grateful. The officers and institutions of the law simply ignored the crimes of the fascist squads. By early 1922, the fascists had turned to intimidation through arson, beatings, and murder against local officials in cities such as Ferrara,

Ravenna, and Milan. They controlled the local government in much of northern Italy.

March on Rome In the election of 1921, Italian voters sent Mussolini and thirty-four of his followers to the Chamber of Deputies. Their importance grew as the local fascists gained more direct power. The movement now had hundreds of thousands of supporters. In October 1922, the fascists, dressed in their characteristic black shirts, began a rather

Mussolini greets his blackshirted supporters after their march on Rome in October 1922. Mussolini himself, who had journeyed to Rome by train, is dressed in formal attire to meet King Victor Emmanuel III (r. 1900–1946) who offered him the post of prime minister in a new government. © Copyright 2003/Corbis

haphazard march on Rome, which became known as the Black Shirt March. King Victor Emmanuel III (r. 1900–1946), because of both personal and political concerns, refused to sign a decree that would have authorized the army to stop the marchers. Probably no other single decision so ensured a fascist seizure of power. The cabinet resigned in protest. On October 29, the monarch telegraphed Mussolini in Milan and asked him to become prime minister. The next day, Mussolini arrived in Rome by sleeping car and greeted his followers as head of the government when they entered the city. Although the march on Rome became a famous moment in fascist history, Mussolini would not have achieved authority if he had not made allies within the political system during the months preceding the march.

Technically, Mussolini had come into office by legal means. The monarch had the constitutional authority to appoint the prime minister. Mussolini, however, had no majority or even near majority in the Chamber of Deputies. Behind the legal facade of his coming to power lay months of terrorist disruption and intimidation and the threat of the fascist march itself. The nonfascist politicians, whose ineptitude had prepared the way for Mussolini, believed his ministry, like others since 1919, would be brief. They did not comprehend that he was not a traditional Italian politician.

THE FASCISTS IN POWER

Mussolini had not really expected to be appointed prime minister. He moved cautiously to shore up his support and to consolidate his power. His success was the result of the impotence of his rivals, his own effective use of his office, his power over the masses, and his sheer ruthlessness. On November 23, 1922, the king and Parliament granted Mussolini dictatorial authority for one year to bring order to local and regional government. Wherever possible, Mussolini appointed fascists to office.

Repression of Opposition Late in 1924, under Mussolini's guidance, Parliament changed the election law. Previously, parties had been represented in the Chamber of Deputies in proportion to the popular vote cast for them. According to the new election law, the party that gained the largest popular vote (if they won at least 25 percent) received two-thirds of the seats in the chamber. Coalition government, with all its compromises and hesitant policies, would no longer be necessary. In the election of 1924, the fascists won a great victory and complete control of the Chamber of Deputies. They used that majority to end legitimate parliamentary life. A series of laws passed in 1925 and 1926 permitted Mussolini, in effect, to rule by decree. In 1926, all other political parties were dissolved. By the close of that year, Mussolini had transformed Italy into a single-party dictatorial state.

Their growing dominance over the government had not, however, diverted the fascists from their course of violence and terror. Fascists were put in charge of the police force, and the terrorist squads became a government militia. In late 1924, their thugs murdered Giacomo Matteotti (1885–1924), a leading noncommunist socialist leader and member of Parliament. He had persistently criticized Mussolini and had exposed the criminality of the fascist movement. In protest against the murder, most opposition deputies withdrew from the Chamber of Deputies. That tactic gave Mussolini an even freer hand. The deputies were refused readmission.

Thanks to very effective Fascist Party propaganda, a cult of personality surrounded Mussolini. His skills in oratory and his general intelligence allowed him to hold his own with both large crowds and prominent individuals, foreign as well as Italian. Many respectable Italians tolerated and even admired Mussolini because they believed he had saved them from Bolshevism. Those who did have the courage to oppose him were usually driven into exile, and some, like Matteotti, were murdered.

Accord with the Vatican Mussolini made one important domestic departure that brought him significant political dividends. Through the Lateran Accord of February 1929, the Roman Catholic Church and the Italian state made peace with each other. Ever since the armies of Italian unification had seized papal lands in the 1860s, the church had been hostile to the state. The popes had remained secluded in the Vatican after 1870. The agreement of 1929 recognized the pope as the temporal ruler of Vatican City. The Italian government agreed to pay an indemnity to the papacy for the territory it had confiscated. The state also recognized Catholicism as the religion of the nation, exempted church property from taxes, and allowed church law to govern marriage. The Lateran Accord brought further respectability to Mussolini's authoritarian regime.

MOTHERHOOD FOR THE NATION IN FASCIST ITALY

Fascist policy encouraged Italian women to have more children and to remain in the home to rear them for the good of the Italian state. To that end, the government instituted policies such as maternity leaves, insurance, subsidies to large families, and the dissemination of information about sound child-rearing practices. Other legislation outlawing contraception and abortion and discouraging the publication of information about sexuality and reproduction made it more difficult for women to limit the size of their families. Italian mothers were expected to see that their children attended fascist school programs. Government agencies provided modest benefits to mothers and their children, which tended to make them dependent on the government because Italian wages were low.

Despite the government's emphasis on the home and child rearing and the image of the father as earning a wage to support his family, 25 percent of the Italian work force was women, a percentage of women workers second only to Sweden. The fascist government nonetheless actively discouraged female participation in the work force or sought to keep women in lower skilled jobs. For example, although the fascists opened civil service jobs to women, over the years they made it more difficult for women to compete with male workers. Laws favored the employment of skilled workers when, in Italy as elsewhere in Europe, most women worked in less skilled jobs. Laws that protected women from exploitation also limited their access to the labor market. In 1938, the government forbade both government and private offices from having more than 10 percent women employees. Although most of these exclusions were modified when Italy entered the Second World War, the policies had succeeded in degrading women's work. By 1940, women's participation in the Italian labor force was more part time and low skilled than it had been before the fascists took power. For example, whereas the number of domestic servants declined elsewhere in western Europe during the 1920s and 1930s, it increased in Italy.

Joyless Victors

Compared with events in Russia and Italy, the postwar political development of France and Great Britain seems rather tame. Neither experienced a revolution or a shift to authoritarian government. Yet this surface calm was largely illusory. Both France and Britain were troubled democracies. To neither did victory in war bring the good life in peace.

FRANCE: THE SEARCH FOR SECURITY

At the close of World War I, as after Waterloo, the revolution of 1848, and the defeat of 1871, the French voters elected a doggedly conservative Chamber of Deputies. The preponderance of military officers in blue uniforms among its members led to the nickname of the "Blue Horizon Chamber." The overwhelmingly conservative character of the chamber was registered in 1920 when it defeated Georges

Clemenceau's bid for the presidency. The crucial factor had been, of all things, the alleged leniency of the Paris treaties and Clemenceau's failure to establish a separate Rhineland state. The deputies wanted to achieve future security against Germany and Russian communism. They intended to make as few concessions to domestic social reform as possible. The 1920s were marked by frequent changes of ministries and drift in domestic policy. The political turnstile remained ever active. Between the end of the war and January 1933, France was governed by no fewer than twenty-seven different cabinets.

New Alliances During the first five years after the conclusion of the Paris settlement, France accepted its role as the leading European power. The French plan was to enforce strictly the clauses of the treaty that were meant to keep Germany weak and also to build a system of eastern alliances to replace the prewar alliance with Russia. In 1920 and 1921, three eastern states that had much to lose from revision of the Versailles treaty—Czechoslovakia, Romania, and Yugoslavia—formed the Little Entente. Before long, France made military alliances with these states and with Poland. A border dispute with Czechoslovakia prevented the Poles from joining the Little Entente, but Poland's independence depended on the maintenance of the Paris settlement.

This new system of eastern pacts was the best France could do, but it was far weaker than the old Franco-Russian alliance. Even combined, the new states were no match for the former power of tsarist Russia, and they were neither united nor reliable. Poland and Romania were more concerned about Russia than about Germany, and the main target of the Little Entente was Hungary. If one of these states was threatened by a resurgent Germany, it could not rely on the others to come to its aid.

The formation of this new alliance system heightened the sense of danger and isolation felt by the two excluded powers, Germany and the Soviet Union. In 1922, while the European states were holding an economic conference at Genoa, the Russians and the Germans met at nearby Rapallo and signed a treaty of their own. It established diplomatic and economic relations that proved useful to each of them. Although the treaty contained no secret political or military clauses, other governments suspected that such arrangements did exist. And it is now known that the Germans did help train the Russian army, and their own army got valuable experience in the use of tanks and planes in the Soviet Union. Rapallo confirmed the French in their belief that Germany would not live up to the terms of the Versailles treaty and helped move them to strong action.

Quest for Reparations In early 1923, the Allies, and France in particular, declared Germany to be in technical default on payment of its reparations. Raymond Poincaré (1860–1934), France's powerfully nationalistic prime minister, decided to teach the Germans a lesson and force them to comply. On January 11, 1923, to ensure receipt of the hard-won reparations, the French government ordered its troops to occupy Germany's borderland Ruhr mining and manufacturing district. In response, the German government ordered passive resistance. The policy amounted to calling a general strike in the largest industrial region of Germany.

The French invasion of the German Ruhr began a crisis that brought strikes and rampant inflation in Germany. Here French troops have commandeered a German locomotive during one of the strikes.
UPI/Corbis

Confronted with this tactic, Poincaré sent French civilians to run the German mines and railroads. France prevailed.

The Germans paid, but France's victory was costly. The English were alienated by the French heavy-handedness and took no part in the occupation. They became more suspicious of France and more sympathetic to Germany. The cost of the Ruhr occupation, moreover, vastly increased French as well as German inflation and hurt the French economy. The Ruhr invasion demonstrated how the uncertainties surrounding the Versailles treaty could harm even the nations it was intended to benefit.

In 1924, Poincaré's conservative ministry gave way to a coalition of leftist parties, the so-called *Cartel des Gauches*, led by Edouard Herriot (1872–1957). The new cabinet recognized the Soviet Union and adopted a more conciliatory policy toward Germany. This policy was the work of Aristide Briand (1862–1932), who was foreign minister for the remainder of the decade. He championed the League of Nations and tried to persuade France that its military power did not give it unlimited influence in the foreign affairs of Europe.

Under the leftist coalition, a mild inflation also occurred. It had begun under the conservatives, but picked up intensity in 1925. When the value of the franc fell sharply on the international money market in 1926, Poincaré returned to office as head of a national government of several parties. The value of the franc recovered somewhat, and inflation cooled. For the rest of the 1920s, the conservatives remained in power, and France enjoyed a general prosperity that lasted until 1931, longer than any other nation did.

GREAT BRITAIN: ECONOMIC CONFUSION

World War I profoundly changed British politics if not the political system. In 1918, Parliament expanded the electorate to include all men aged twenty-one and women aged thirty. (In 1928, the age for women voters was also lowered to twenty-one.) The prewar structure of parties and leadership shifted. A coalition cabinet of Liberal, Conservative, and Labour ministers had directed the war effort. The wartime ministerial participation of the Labour Party helped dispel its radical image. For the Liberal Party, however, the conflict brought further division.

Until 1916, Liberal prime minister Herbert Asquith (1852–1928) had presided over the cabinet. As disagreements over war management developed, he was ousted by fellow Liberal David Lloyd George (1863–1945). The party split sharply between followers of the two men. In 1918, against the wishes of both the Labour Party and the Asquith Liberals, Lloyd George decided to maintain the coalition through the tasks of the peace conference and the domestic reconstruction. In December 1918, the wartime coalition, now minus its Labour members, won a stunning victory at the polls. Lloyd George, however, could thereafter remain prime minister only as long as his dominant Conservative partners wished to keep him.

During the election campaign, there had been much talk about creating "a land fit for heroes to live in." It did not happen. Except for the three years immediately after the war, the British economy was depressed throughout the 1920s. There was no genuine postwar recovery. Unemployment never dipped below 10 percent and often hovered near 11 percent. There were never fewer than a million workers unemployed. Government insurance programs to cover unemployed workers, widows, and orphans were expanded. There was no similar meaningful expansion in the number of jobs available. From 1922 onward, accepting the "dole" with little expectation of future employment became a wretched and degrading way of life for scores of thousands of poor British families.

The First Labour Government In October 1922, the Conservatives replaced Lloyd George with Andrew Bonar Law (1858–1923), one of their own. A Liberal would never again be prime minister. Stanley Baldwin (1867–1947) soon replaced Law, who had fallen victim to throat cancer. Baldwin decided to attempt to cure Britain's economic plight by abandoning free trade and imposing protective tariffs. The voters rejected that policy in 1923. In the election, the Conservative Party lost its majority in the House of Commons, but only votes from both Liberal and Labour party members could provide an alternative majority.

Labour had elected the second largest group of members to the Commons. Consequently, in December 1923, King George V (r. 1910–1936) asked Ramsay MacDonald (1866–1937) to form the first Labour ministry in British history. The Liberal Party did not serve in the cabinet, but provided the necessary votes to give Labour a working majority in the House of Commons.

The Labour Party was socialistic in its platform, but democratic and distinctly nonrevolutionary. The party had expanded beyond its early trade-union base. MacDonald himself had opposed World War I and for a time had also broken with the party. His own version of socialism owed little, if anything, to Marx. His program consisted of plans for extensive social reform rather than for the nationalization or public seizure of industry. A sensitive politician, if not a great leader, MacDonald understood the most important task facing his government was proving to the nation that the Labour Party was both respectable and responsible. His nine months in office achieved that goal, if little else of major importance. The establishment of Labour as a viable governing party signaled the permanent demise of the Liberal Party. It has continued to exist, but the bulk of its voters have drifted into either the Conservative or the Labour ranks.

The General Strike of 1926 The Labour government fell in the autumn of 1924 over charges of inadequate prosecution of a communist writer. Stanley Baldwin returned to office, where he remained until 1929. The stagnant economy remained uppermost in the public mind. Business and political leaders continued to believe all would be well if they could restore the prewar conditions of trade. A major element in these conditions had been the gold standard as the basis for international trade. In 1925, the Conservative government returned to the gold standard, abandoned during the war, in hopes of recreating the former monetary stability. The government, however, set the conversion rate for the pound too high against other currencies and thus, in effect, raised the price of British goods to foreign customers.

To make their products competitive on the world market, British management attempted to lower prices by cutting wages. The coal industry was the sector most directly affected by the wage cuts. It was inefficient and poorly managed and had been in trouble since the end of the war.

Labor relations in the coal industry long had been unruly. In 1926, after cuts in wages and a breakdown in negotiations, the coal miners went on strike. Soon thereafter, in May 1926, sympathetic workers in other industries engaged in a general strike lasting nine days. There was much tension but little violence. In the end, the miners and the other unions capitulated. With such high levels of unemployment, organized labor was in a weak position. After the general strike, the Baldwin government attempted to reconcile labor primarily through new housing and reforms in the poor laws. Despite the economic difficulties of these years, the actual standard of living of most British workers, including those receiving government insurance payments, actually improved. (See "Encountering the Past: The Coming of Radio: The BBC.")

Empire World War I also modified Britain's imperial position. The aid given by the dominions, such as Canada and Australia, demonstrated a new independence on their part. Empire was a two-way proposition. The idea of self-determination as applied to Europe filtered into imperial relationships. In India, the Congress Party, led by Mohandas Gandhi (1869–1948), was beginning to attract widespread support. The British started to talk more about eventual self-government for India. Moreover, during the 1920s, the government of India achieved the right to impose tariffs to protect its own industry rather than for the advantage of British manufacturers. British textile producers no longer had totally free access to the vast Indian market.

Ireland A new chapter was written in the unhappy relations between Britain and Ireland during and after the war. In 1914, the Irish Home Rule Bill had passed Parliament, but its implementation was postponed until after the war. As the war dragged on, Irish nationalists determined to wait no longer. On Easter Monday in April 1916, a nationalist uprising occurred in Dublin. It was the only rebellion of a national group to occur against any government engaged in the war. The British suppressed it in less than a week but then made a grave tactical blunder: They executed the Irish nationalist leaders who had been responsible for the uprising. Overnight those rebels became national martyrs. Leadership of the nationalist cause quickly shifted from the Irish Party in Parliament to the extremist **Sinn Fein,** or "Ourselves Alone," movement.

In the election of 1918, the Sinn Fein Party won all but four of the Irish parliamentary seats outside Ulster. They refused to go to the Parliament at Westminster. Instead, they constituted themselves into a *Dail Eireann,* or Irish Parliament. On January 21, 1919, they declared Irish independence. The military wing of Sinn Fein became the Irish Republican Army (IRA). The first president was Eamon De Valera (1882–1975), who had been born in the United States. What amounted to a guerrilla war broke out between the IRA and the British army, with the latter supported by auxiliaries known as the Black and Tans. There was intense bitterness and hatred on both sides.

In late 1921, the two governments began secret negotiations. In the treaty concluded in December 1921, the Irish Free State took its place beside the earlier dominions in the British Commonwealth: Canada, Australia, New Zealand, and South Africa. The six counties of Ulster, or Northern Ireland, were permitted to remain part of what was now called the United Kingdom of Great Britain and Northern Ireland, with provisions for home rule. No sooner had the treaty been signed than a new civil war broke out between Irish moderates and diehards. The moderates supported the treaty; the

The Coming of Radio: The BBC

Radio was the first form of mass electronic communication. Radio, or wireless telegraphy, as it was called at the time, was first developed by the Italian inventor Guglielmo Marconi (1874–1937) in the 1890s. The first company devoted to radio communication was the Marconi Company, organized in Great Britain in 1897. Many other companies soon followed, including General Electric and RCA (the Radio Corporation of America) in the United States. The first American commercial station, KADA, opened in Pittsburgh in 1920, and radio flourished in the United States through advertising and popular programming from thousands of stations.

In Great Britain, the soon to be world-famous British Broadcasting Company (BBC) operated on very different principles. The BBC, founded in 1922, possessed a broadcasting monopoly granted by the British government. There was no advertising; instead, when people bought radios, they also had to purchase a radio license, and the funds generated paid the costs of broadcasting. About a million radios had been sold when the BBC first went on the air; by the end of the 1930s, almost everyone in Britain had access to a radio.

Because it was a monopoly, the management of the BBC could decide what image of Britain they wished to project over the radio waves. Unlike American radio stations, the BBC began with what some might consider an elitist mission: It set out to improve the level of British cultural life, not to broadcast the kind of popular music, dramas, or other programs that might too easily appeal to a mass audience. To preserve a sense of decorum, the early BBC broadcasters often dressed in white tie and tails even though their listeners could obviously not see them. In addition to news, beginning in 1923, the BBC also broadcast classical music and productions of the great plays from British literature and thus made them easily and inexpensively available to a mass audience. Yet even the BBC could not ignore popular taste, and after a few years it began to broadcast light music, sports, and even vaudeville acts.

The BBC also tapped into—some would say helped create—another aspect of popular culture: fascination with the British royal family and the intimate details of their lives. Radio enabled millions of Britons for the first time to hear the voice of their monarch. In 1924, King George V (r. 1910–1936) became the first British sovereign ever to speak to the nation on radio; in 1932, he broadcast the first royal Christmas speech. Thereafter royal speeches on the BBC would become an enduring tradition and the monarchy a mass-market phenomenon.

The BBC in the 1920s and 1930s saw itself as transmitting official polite culture, though of an increasingly broad sort. In this it was not alone. Although the audience for radio was powerfully democratic, most European—and Asian—governments tried to monopolize or at least dominate the airways. But unlike the BBC, which strove to be above politics, the authoritarian governments operating in Europe from the 1920s onward would use their control of radio for their own political purposes. (See "Josef Goebbels Explains How to Use Radio for Political Propaganda" in Chapter 28.)

■ *In what ways was the BBC different from American commercial radio stations? How did the BBC affect the popularity of the British monarchy?*

In 1932 King George V (r. 1910–1936) delivered the first royal Christmas address over the BBC to the British people. Hulton-Deutsch Collection/Corbis

Eamon De Valera inspects troops of the Irish Republican Army during the Irish Civil War.   Archive Photos

diehards wanted to abolish the oath to the British monarch and establish a totally independent republic. The second civil war continued until 1923. De Valera, who supported the diehards, resigned the presidency and organized resistance to the treaty. In 1932, he was again elected president. The next year, the *Dail Eireann* abolished the oath of allegiance to the monarch.

During World War II, the Irish Free State remained neutral. In 1949, it declared itself the wholly independent republic of Eire.

Trials of the Successor States in Eastern Europe

It had been an article of faith among nineteenth-century liberals sympathetic to nationalism that only good could flow from the demise of Austria-Hungary, the restoration of Poland, and the establishment of nation-states throughout eastern Europe. These new states were to embody the principle of national self-determination and to provide a buffer against the westward spread of Bolshevism. They were, however, in trouble from the beginning.

Both France and Great Britain had long experience in liberal democratic government. Their primary challenges during the 1920s lay in responding to economic pressures and allowing new groups, such as the Labour Party, to share political power. In Germany, Poland, Austria, Czechoslovakia, and the other successor states, the challenge for the 1920s was to make new parliamentary governments function in a satisfactory and stable manner. Before the war, the elected parliaments of both Germany and Austria-Hungary had not exercised genuine political power. The question after the war became whether those groups that had previously sat powerless in parliaments could assume both power and responsibility. Another question was how long conservative political groups and institutions, such as the armies, would tolerate or cooperate with the liberal experiments.

ECONOMIC AND ETHNIC PRESSURES

All the new states faced immense postwar economic difficulties. None of them possessed the kind of strong economy that nation-states such as France and Germany had developed in the nineteenth century. Indeed, political independence disrupted the previous economic relationships that each of them had developed as part of one of the prewar empires. None of the new states was financially independent; except for Czechoslovakia, all of them depended on foreign loans to finance economic development. Nationalistic antagonisms often prevented these states from trading with each other, and as a consequence, most became highly dependent on trade with Germany. The successor states of eastern Europe were poor and overwhelmingly rural nations in an industrialized world. The depression hit them especially hard, because they had to import finished goods for which they paid with agricultural exports whose value was falling sharply.

Finally, throughout eastern Europe, the collapse of the old German, Russian, and Austrian empires allowed various ethnic groups—large and small—to pursue nationalistic goals unchecked by any great power or central political authority. The major social and political groups in these countries were generally unwilling to make compromises lest they undermine their nationalist identity and independence. Each state included minority groups that wanted to be independent or to become part of a different nation in the region. Again, except for Czechoslovakia, all of these states succumbed to some form of domestic authoritarian government.

It is important to recognize these interwar economic difficulties and nationalistic pressures, because many of them reemerged in the region in the 1990s. Indeed, to a considerable extent, the breakup of Yugoslavia and Czechoslovakia, the present uncertainties in the former Soviet Union, and the efforts at political reorganization in the rest of the areas dominated by the Soviet Union constitute one more attempt by the peoples of eastern Europe to achieve political and economic stability in the wake of the upheaval in that region caused by the events surrounding World War I.

POLAND: DEMOCRACY TO MILITARY RULE

The nation whose postwar fortunes probably most disappointed liberal Europeans was Poland. For more than a hundred years, the country had been erased from the map. (See Chapter 18.) An independent Poland had been one of Woodrow Wilson's Fourteen Points. When the country was restored in 1919, nationalism proved an insufficient bond to overcome political disagreements stemming from class differences, diverse economic interests, and regionalism. The new Poland had been constructed from portions governed by Germany, Russia, and Austria for over a century. Each of those regions of partitioned Poland had different administrative systems and laws, different economies, and different degrees of experience with electoral institutions. A host of small political parties bedeviled the new Polish Parliament, and the executive was weak. In 1926, Marshal Josef Pilsudski (1857–1935) carried out a military coup. Thereafter, he ruled, in effect, personally until his death, when the government passed into the hands of a group of his military followers.

CZECHOSLOVAKIA: A VIABLE DEMOCRATIC EXPERIMENT

Only one central European successor state escaped the fate of self-imposed authoritarian government. Czechoslovakia possessed a strong industrial base, a substantial middle class, and a tradition of liberal values. During the war, Czechs and Slovaks had cooperated to aid the Allies. They had learned to work together and generally to trust each other. After the war, the new government had broken up large estates in favor of small peasant holdings. In the per-

son of Thomas Masaryk (1850–1937), the nation possessed a gifted leader of immense integrity and fairness. The country had a real chance of becoming a viable modern nation-state.

There were, however, tensions between the Czechs and the Slovaks, who were poorer and more rural. Moreover, Czechoslovakia encountered discontent among its other non-Czech national groups, including Poles, Magyars, and especially the Germans of the Sudetenland, which the Paris settlement had placed within Czech borders. The parliamentary regime might have been able to work through these problems, but extreme German nationalists in the Sudetenland looked to Hitler, who wanted to expand into eastern Europe, for help. In 1938, at Munich, the great powers first divided liberal Czechoslovakia to appease Hitler's aggressive instincts and then watched passively as he occupied much of the country, gave parts to Poland and Hungary, and manipulated a Slovak puppet state.

HUNGARY: TURMOIL AND AUTHORITARIANISM

Hungary was one of the defeated powers of World War I. In that defeat, it achieved its long-desired separation from Austria, but at a high political and economic price. In Hungary during 1919, Bela Kun (1885–1937), a communist, established a short-lived Hungarian Soviet Republic, which received support from the socialists as well. The Allies authorized an invasion by Romanian troops to remove the communist danger. The Hungarian landowners then established Admiral Miklós Horthy (1868–1957) as regent, a position he held until 1944. After the collapse of the Kun government, thousands of Hungarians were either executed or imprisoned. It was in part in reaction to Kun's cooperation with socialists that Lenin ordered the Comintern to reject such cooperation in the future. Kun himself was later murdered by Stalin in purges of the late 1930s.

There was also deep resentment in Hungary over the territory it had lost in the Paris settlement. The largely agrarian Hungarian economy suffered from a general stagnation. During the 1920s, the effective ruler of Hungary was Count Stephen Bethlen (1874–1947). He presided over a government that was parliamentary in form, but aristocratic in character. In 1932, he was succeeded by General Julius Gömbös (1886–1936), who pursued anti-Semitic policies and rigged elections. No matter how the popular vote turned out, the Gömbös party controlled Parliament. After his death in 1936, anti-Semitism lingered in Hungarian politics.

AUSTRIA: POLITICAL TURMOIL AND NAZI CONQUEST

The situation in Austria was little better than that in the other successor states. A quarter of the 8 million Austrians lived in Vienna. Viable economic life was almost impossible, and the Paris settlement forbade union with Germany. Throughout the 1920s, the leftist Social Democrats and the conservative Christian Socialists contended for power. Both groups employed small armies to terrorize their opponents and to impress their followers.

In 1933, the Christian Socialist Engelbert Dollfuss (1892–1934) became chancellor. He tried to steer a course between the Austrian Social Democrats and the German nazis, who had surfaced in Austria. In 1934, he outlawed all political parties except the Christian Socialists, the agrarians, and the paramilitary groups, which composed his own Fatherland Front. He used troops against the Social Democrats, but was shot later that year during an unsuccessful nazi coup. His successor, Kurt von Schuschnigg (1897–1977), presided over Austria until Hitler annexed it in 1938.

SOUTHEASTERN EUROPE: ROYAL DICTATORSHIPS

In southeastern Europe, revision of the arrangements in the Paris settlement was less of an issue. Parliamentary government floundered there nevertheless. Yugoslavia had been founded by the Corfu Agreement of 1917 and was known as the Kingdom of the Serbs, Croats, and Slovenes until 1929. Throughout the interwar period, the Serbs dominated the government and were opposed by the Croats. The two groups clashed violently, but the Serbs had the advantage of having had an independent state with an army prior to World War I, whereas the Croats and Slovenes had been part of the Austro-Hungarian Empire. The Croats generally were Roman Catholic, better educated, and accustomed to reasonably incorrupt government administration. The Serbs were Orthodox, somewhat less well educated, and considered corrupt administrators by the Croats. Furthermore, although each group predominated in certain areas of the country, each had isolated enclaves in other parts of the nation. Bosnia-Herzegovina, in addition to Serbs and Croats, had a significant Muslim population. The Slovenes, Muslims, and other small national groups often played the Serbs and the Croats against each other. All of the political parties except the small Communist Party represented a particular ethnic group rather than the nation of

Admiral Miklos Horthy (1868–1957) was Regent of Hungary from 1920 until his overthrow by the Nazis in 1944. His government was a typical example of the authoritarian regimes that held power in eastern Europe between the wars. Keystone Press Agency

Yugoslavia. The violent clash of nationalities eventually led to a royal dictatorship in 1929 under King Alexander I (r. 1921–1934), himself a Serb. He outlawed political parties and jailed popular politicians. Alexander was assassinated in 1934, but the authoritarian government continued under a regency for his son.

Other royal dictatorships were imposed elsewhere in the Balkans: in Romania by King Carol II (r. 1930–1940) and in Bulgaria by King Boris III (r. 1918–1943). They regarded their own illiberal regimes as preventing the seizure of power by more extreme antiparliamentary movements and as quieting the discontent of the varied nationalities within their borders. In Greece, the parliamentary monarchy floundered amid military coups and calls for a republic. In 1936, General John Metaxas (1871–1941) instituted a dictatorship that, for the time being, ended parliamentary life in Greece.

The Weimar Republic in Germany

The German **Weimar Republic** was born amid the defeat of the imperial army, the revolution of 1918 against the Hohenzollerns, and the hopes of German Liberals and Social Democrats. Its name derived from the city of Weimar, in which its constitution was written and promulgated in August 1919. While the constitution was being debated, the republic, headed by the Social Democrats, accepted the humiliating terms of the Versailles treaty, the part of the Paris settlement that applied to Germany. Although it had signed only under the threat of an Allied invasion, the republic was nevertheless permanently associated with the national disgrace and the economic burdens of the treaty.

Throughout the 1920s, the government of the republic was required to fulfill the economic and military provisions imposed by the Paris settlement. It became all too easy for German nationalists and military figures, whose policies had brought on the tragedy and defeat in the war, to blame the young republic and the socialists for the military defeat and its grievous social and political results. In Germany, more than in other countries, all political groups shared the desire to revise the treaty, though they differed about the means. Some wished to oppose its provisions whenever good tactical opportunities arose; others simply assumed a position of total opposition to the treaty. Because of those revisionist desires, there were different degrees of loyalty among Germans to the political arrangements of the Weimar constitution, which many of them associated with the Paris settlement.

CONSTITUTIONAL FLAWS

The Weimar constitution was in many respects a highly enlightened document. It guaranteed civil liberties and provided for direct election, by universal suffrage, of the *Reichstag* and the president. It also contained, however, certain crucial structural flaws that eventually allowed its liberal institutions to be overthrown. It provided for proportional representation for all elections. This system made it relatively easy for small parties to gain seats in the *Reichstag*. Ministers were technically responsible to the *Reichstag*, but the president appointed and removed the chancellor. Perhaps most important, Article 48 allowed the president to rule by decree in an emergency. The constitution thus permitted a temporary presidential dictatorship.

LACK OF BROAD POPULAR SUPPORT

Beyond the burden of the Paris settlement and these potential constitutional pitfalls, the Weimar Republic did not command the sympathy or loyalty of many Germans. No social revolution had accompanied the new political structure. Many important political figures favored a constitutional monarchy. The schoolteachers, civil servants, and judges of the republic were generally the same people who had served the kaiser and the empire. Before the war, they had distrusted or even hated the Social Democratic Party, which figured so prominently in the establishment and the politics of the republic.

The officer corps was also deeply suspicious of the government and profoundly resentful of the military provisions of the peace settlement. Its leaders and other nationalistic Germans perpetuated the myth that the German army had surrendered on foreign soil only because it had been stabbed in the back by civilians at home. Thus many Germans in significant social and political positions wanted both to revise the peace treaty and to modify the system of government. The early years of the republic only reinforced those sentiments.

Major and minor humiliations, as well as considerable economic instability, impinged on the new government. In March 1920, the right-wing *Kapp Putsch*, or "armed insurrection," erupted in Berlin. Led by a conservative civil servant and supported by army officers, the attempted coup failed. But the *putsch* collapsed only after the government had fled the city and German workers had carried out a general strike. In the same month, strikes took place in the Ruhr. The government sent in troops. Such extremism from both the left and the right would haunt the republic for all its days.

In May 1921, the Allies presented a reparations bill for 132 billion gold marks. The German republican government accepted this preposterous demand only after new Allied threats of occupation. Throughout the early 1920s, there were numerous assassinations or attempted assassinations of important republican leaders. Violence marked the first five years of the republic.

INVASION OF THE RUHR AND INFLATION

Inflation brought on the major crisis of the period. Borrowing to finance the war and the continued postwar deficit spending generated an immense rise in prices. Consequently, the value of German currency fell. By early 1921, the German mark traded against the American dollar at a ratio of 64 to 1, compared with a ratio of 4.2 to 1 in 1914. German bankers contended that the mark could not be stabilized until the reparations issue had been solved. In the meantime, the printing presses kept pouring forth paper money, used to redeem government bonds as they fell due.

The French invasion of the Ruhr in January 1923 and the German response of economic passive resistance produced cataclysmic inflation. The Weimar government subsidized the Ruhr labor force, which had laid down its tools. Unemployment soon spread from the Ruhr to other parts of the country, creating a new drain on the treasury and also reducing tax revenues. By this point, the printing presses had difficulty providing enough paper currency to keep up with the daily rise in prices. In November 1923, an American dollar was worth more than 800 million German marks. Money was literally not worth the paper it was printed on. Stores were unwilling to exchange goods for the worthless currency, and farmers withheld produce from the market.

The social and economic consequences of the great inflation of 1923 were disastrous for many Germans. Middle-class savings, pensions, and insurance policies were wiped out, as were investments in government bonds. Simultaneously, debts and mortgages could easily be paid off. Speculators in land, real estate, and industry made great fortunes. Union contracts generally allowed workers to keep up with rising prices. Farmers who supplied food to the cities did well, as did food stores whose proprietors benefited from the barter that took place. The inflation thus was not a disaster to everyone. To the middle class and the lower middle class, however, the inflation was another trauma coming hard on the heels of the military defeat and the peace treaty. Only when the social and economic upheaval of these months is grasped can the later German desire for order and security at almost any cost be comprehended.

HITLER'S EARLY CAREER

Late in 1923, Adolf Hitler (1889–1945) made his first major appearance on the German political scene. He was born in 1889, the son of a minor Austrian customs official. By 1907, he had gone to Vienna, where his hopes of becoming an artist were soon dashed. He lived for a time off money sent by relatives and later off his Austrian orphan's allowance. He also painted and sold postcards and worked as a day laborer. In Vienna, he became acquainted with Mayor Karl Lueger's (1844–1910) Christian Social Party, which prospered on an anti-Semitic ideology.

Hitler also absorbed much of the rabid German nationalism, racism, and extreme anti-Semitism that flourished in Vienna. He came to hate Marxism,

In 1923, Germany suffered from cataclysmic inflation. Paper money became worthless and children used packets of it as building blocks. Bettmann/Hulton Deutsch/Corbis

which he associated with Jews. During World War I, Hitler fought in the German army and was wounded; he was promoted to the rank of corporal and awarded the Iron Cross for bravery. The war gave him his first sense of purpose.

After the conflict, Hitler settled in Munich and lived there during a postwar year of violent tumult when Social Democrats briefly governed the city. There he became associated with a small nationalistic, anti-Semitic political party, which in 1920 adopted the name of National Socialist German Workers' Party, better known simply as the **Nazis.** The same year, the group began to parade under a red-and-white banner with a black swastika. It issued a platform, or program, known as the Twenty-five Points, which called for the repudiation of the Versailles treaty, the unification of Austria and Germany, the exclusion of Jews from German citizenship, agrarian reform, the prohibition of land speculation, the confiscation of war profits, state administration of the giant cartels, and the replacement of department stores with small retail shops. In the two years after the war, Hitler seems to have firmly adopted and frequently voiced anti-Semitism as a fundamental part of his political outlook.

During a Nazi Party rally in Nuremberg in 1927, Adolf Hitler stops his motorcade to receive the applause of the surrounding crowd. In the late 1920s, the nazi movement was only one of many bringing strife to the Weimar Republic. Heinrich Hoffman/Bildarchiv Preussischer Kulturbesitz

Originally, the Nazis had called for a broad program of nationalization of industry in an attempt to compete directly with the Marxist political parties for the vote of the workers. When the tactic failed, the Nazis redefined the meaning of the word *socialist* in their name to suggest a nationalistic outlook. In 1922, Hitler said,

Whoever is prepared to make the national cause his own to such an extent that he knows no higher ideal than the welfare of his nation; whoever has understood our great national anthem, *Deutschland, Deutschland, Über Alles* ["Germany, Germany, Over All"], to mean that nothing in the wide world surpasses in his eyes this Germany, people and land, land and people—that man is a Socialist.[2]

This definition, of course, had nothing to do with traditional German socialism. The "socialism" that Hitler and the Nazis had in mind was not state ownership of the means of production, but the subordination of all economic enterprise to the welfare of the nation. It often implied protection for small economic enterprises. Increasingly, the Nazis discovered their party appealed to virtually any economic

group that was experiencing pressure and instability. They often tailored their messages to the particular local problems these groups confronted in different parts of Germany. The Nazis found considerable support among war veterans, who faced economic and social displacement in Weimar society.

Soon after the promulgation of the Twenty-five Points, the storm troopers, or **SA** (*Sturmabteilung*), were organized under the leadership of Captain Ernst Roehm (1887–1934). (See "Ernst Roehm Demands a Return to German Military Values.") The SA was a paramilitary organization that initially provided its members with food and uniforms and eventually also paid them. In the mid-1920s, the SA adopted its infamous brown-shirted uniform. The storm troopers were the chief Nazi instrument for terror and intimidation before the party controlled the government. They were a law unto themselves. They attacked socialists and communists. The organization was a means of preserving military discipline and values outside the small army permitted by the Paris settlement. The existence of such a private party army was a sign of the potential for violence in the Weimar Republic. It also represented widespread contempt for the law and the institutions of the republic. In response to Nazi force, both the Social Democrat and the Communist parties organized paramilitary organizations, but in neither size nor discipline could they rival the Nazis. These paramilitary forces greatly weakened the Weimar Republic. (See "Art & the West: George Grosz Satirizes Germany's Social and Political Elite," p. 962.)

The social and economic turmoil following the French occupation of the Ruhr and the German inflation provided the fledgling Nazi Party with an opportunity for direct action against the Weimar Republic, which seemed incapable of giving Germany military or economic security. Because of his immense oratorical skills and organizational abilities, Hitler personally dominated the Nazi Party.

On November 9, 1923, Hitler and a band of followers, accompanied by General Ludendorff, attempted a *putsch* from a beer hall in Munich that was unsuccessful. When the local authorities crushed the uprising, sixteen Nazis were killed. Hitler and Ludendorff were arrested and tried for treason. The general was acquitted. Hitler used the trial to make himself into a national figure. In his defense, he condemned the republic, the Versailles treaty, the Jews, and the weakened condition of his adopted country. He was convicted and sentenced to five years in prison, but was paroled after serving only a few months.

During his time in prison, Hitler dictated **Mein Kampf,** or *My Struggle*, from which he eventually

[2]Quoted in Alan Bullock, *Hitler: A Study in Tyranny*, rev. ed. (New York: Harper & Row, 1962), p. 76.

ERNST ROEHM DEMANDS A RETURN TO GERMAN MILITARY VALUES

Ernst Roehm (1887–1934) was the early nazi leader who headed the SA (Sturmabteilung, or storm troopers). He had fought in the First World War and saw himself primarily as a soldier. In this passage from his autobiography, he emphasizes a soldier's understanding of German nationalism and how National Socialism could contribute to German renewal. Roehm himself was executed in 1934 along with other SA officers when Hitler consolidated his personal power at their expense.

■ *Why would this speech have appealed to the tens of thousands of German World War I veterans? Why does Roehm favor nationalistic and military values over those of peace and prosperity? Why are "politicians" such a convenient target for his attack?*

I am a believer in plain talk and have not hid my heart like a skeleton in the closet.

I must write without fear, with defiance—just as it comes from my soul. . . .

Soldierly comradeship, cemented with blood, can perhaps temporarily relax, but it can never be torn out of the heart, it cannot be exterminated.

Still, all of Germany has not been awakened yet—despite National Socialism. My words shall be a trumpet call to those who are still asleep.

I am not appealing to the hustling and sneaky trader who has made accursed gold his God, but to the warrior who is struggling in the battle of life, who wants to win freedom and with it the kingdom of heaven.

I approve of whatever serves the purpose of German Freedom. I oppose whatever runs counter to it. Europe, aye, the whole world, may go down in flames—what concern is it of ours? Germany must live and be free.

One may call me a bigoted fool—I can't help that. I am opposed to sport in its present form and to its effects. Moreover, I consider it a definite national danger. We cannot rebuild the Fatherland with champions and artificially nurtured "big guns of sport." Only the most careful development which provides physical strength and capability, with spiritual elasticity and ethical backbone, can be of use to the *Volk* community. . . .

The Germans have forgotten how to hate.

Virile hate has been replaced by feminine lamentation. But he who is unable to hate cannot live either. Fanatical love and hate—their fires kindle flames of freedom.

Passionlessness, matter-of-factness, objectivity, are impersonality, are sophistry.

Only passion gives knowledge, creates wisdom.

"Peace and order" is the battle cry of people living on pensions. In the last analysis you cannot govern a state on the basis of the needs of pensioners. . . .

"Irresponsible dreamers" for years and years have called upon the people to rise up against enslavement and oppression. The "responsible politicians" of the new Germany in these same years have sold Germany lock, stock, and barrel. . . .

From time immemorial Germany was not suited to "diplomacy" and "politics." The sword has always determined the greatness of its history. . . .

Only the soldier could lead his people and Fatherland out of wretchedness and shame to freedom and honor.

From Ernst Roehm, *Die Geschichte eines Hochverraters* (Munich: Verlang Frz. Eher Nachf., 1928), pp. 365–367 (7th ed., 1934), as quoted in George L. Mosse, *Nazi Culture: Intellectual, Cultural, and Social Life in the Third Reich* (New York: Grosset & Dunlap, 1966), pp. 101–103.

made a great deal of money. In this book, not taken seriously enough at the time, he outlined key political views from which he never swerved, including a fierce racial anti-Semitism, a powerful opposition to Bolshevism, which he associated with Jews, and a conviction that Germany must expand eastward beyond the borders established at Versailles to achieve greater "living space." Such expansion assumed the recovery of German military might vanquished by the war and the peace. In effect, Hitler transferred the foreign policy goals and racial outlooks previously associated with German overseas imperialism to the politics of central and eastern Europe. The natural targets of implementing these ideas would be Jews, the successor states of eastern Europe, the Soviet Union, and any groups within Germany that

MAP 27–1 GERMANY'S WESTERN FRONTIER *The French-Belgian-German border area between the two world wars was sensitive. Despite efforts to restrain tensions, there were persistent difficulties related to the Ruhr, Rhineland, Saar, and Eupen-Malmédy regions that required strong defenses.*

During the same months of imprisonment, Hitler reached two other decisions. First, it appears that this was the moment when he came to see himself as the leader who could transform Germany from a position of weakness to strength. Second, he decided that he and the party must pursue power by legal means. But as Hitler emerged from his imprisonment, he was still a regional politician (albeit one in the process of transforming himself into a national figure).

THE STRESEMANN YEARS

Elsewhere, the officials of the republic were trying to repair the damage from the inflation. Gustav Stresemann (1878–1929) was primarily responsible for the reconstruction of the republic and for giving it a sense of self-confidence. As chancellor from August to November 1923, Stresemann abandoned the policy of passive resistance in the Ruhr. The country simply could not afford it. Then, with the aid of the banker Hjalmar Schacht (1877–1970), he introduced a new German currency. The rate of exchange was one trillion of the old German marks for one new *Rentenmark*.

Stresemann also moved against challenges from the left and the right. He supported the crushing of both Hitler's abortive *putsch* and smaller communist disturbances. In late November 1923, he resigned as chancellor and became foreign minister, a post he held until his death in 1929. He continued to exercise considerable influence over the affairs of the republic.

In 1924, the Weimar Republic and the Allies agreed to a new system of reparation payments. The Dawes Plan, submitted by the American banker Charles Dawes, lowered the annual payments and allowed them to vary according to the fortunes of the German economy. The last French troops left the Ruhr in 1925. (See Map 27–1.)

The same year, Friedrich Ebert (1871–1925), the Social Democratic president of the republic, died. Field Marshal Paul von Hindenburg (1847–1934), a military hero and a conservative monarchist, was elected as his successor. He governed in strict accordance with the constitution, but his election suggested that German politics had become more conservative. It looked as if conservative Germans had become reconciled to the republic. This conservatism was in line with the prosperity of the later 1920s. The new political and economic stability meant that foreign capital flowed into Germany, and employment rose smartly. In the steel and chemical industries, large combines spread. The prosperity helped broaden the acceptance of, and appreciation for, the republic.

opposed Hitler's vision of national unity and purpose. In the mid-1920s, most observers discounted the likelihood of any German political party's carrying out such policies.

In foreign affairs, Stresemann was conciliatory. He fulfilled the provisions of the Paris settlement, even as he attempted to revise it by diplomacy. He was willing to accept the settlement in the west, but was a determined, if sometimes secret, revisionist in the east. He aimed to recover German-speaking territories lost to Poland and Czechoslovakia and possibly to unite with Austria, chiefly by diplomatic means. The first step, however, was to achieve respectability and economic recovery. That goal required a policy of accommodation and "fulfillment," for the moment at least.

LOCARNO

These developments gave rise to the Locarno Agreements of October 1925. The spirit of conciliation led foreign secretary Austen Chamberlain (1863–1937) for Britain and Aristide Briand for France to accept Stresemann's proposal for a fresh start. France and Germany both accepted the western frontier established at Paris as legitimate. Britain and Italy agreed to intervene against whichever side violated the frontier or if Germany sent troops into the demilitarized Rhineland. Significantly, no such agreement was reached about Germany's eastern frontier. The Germans signed treaties of arbitration with Poland and Czechoslovakia, however, and France strengthened its ties with the Little Entente. France supported German membership in the League of Nations and agreed to withdraw its occupation troops from the Rhineland in 1930, five years earlier than specified at Paris.

Locarno pleased everyone. Germany was satisfied to have achieved respectability and a guarantee against another Ruhr occupation, as well as to have been afforded the possibility of revision in the east. Britain was pleased to be allowed to play a more evenhanded role. Italy was glad to be recognized as a great power. The French were happy, too, because the Germans voluntarily accepted the permanence of their western frontier, also guaranteed by Britain and Italy, while France maintained its allies in the east.

The Locarno Agreements brought a new spirit of hope to Europe. Germany's entry into the League of Nations was greeted with enthusiasm. Chamberlain and Dawes received the Nobel Peace Prize in 1925, and Briand and Stresemann were awarded it in 1926. The spirit of Locarno was carried even further when the leading European states, Japan, and the United States signed the Kellogg-Briand Pact in 1928, renouncing "war as an instrument of national policy."

The joy and optimism were not justified. France had merely recognized its inability to coerce Germany without help. Britain had shown its unwillingness to uphold the Paris settlement in the east.

Major Political Events of the 1920s	
1919 (August)	Constitution of the Weimar Republic promulgated
1920	*Kapp Putsch* in Berlin
1921 (March)	Kronstadt mutiny leads Lenin to initiate his New Economic Policy
1921 (December)	Treaty between Great Britain and the Irish Free State
1922 (April)	Treaty of Rapallo between Germany and the Soviet Union
1922 (October)	Fascist march on Rome leads to Mussolini's assumption of power
1923 (January)	France invades the Ruhr
1923 (November)	Hitler's beer hall *Putsch*
1923 (December)	First Labour government in Britain
1924	Death of Lenin
1925	Locarno Agreements
1926	General strike in Britain
1928	Kellogg-Briand Pact
1929 (January)	Trotsky expelled from the Soviet Union
1929 (February)	Lateran Accord between the Vatican and the Italian state

Austen Chamberlain declared that no British government would ever "risk the bones of a British grenadier" for the Polish corridor. Germany remained unreconciled to the eastern settlement. It continued its clandestine military connections with the Soviet Union, which had begun with the Treaty of Rapallo, and planned to continue to press for revision of the Paris settlement.

In both France and Germany, moreover, the conciliatory politicians represented only a part of the nation. In Germany, especially, most people continued to reject Versailles and regarded Locarno as only an extension of it. When the Dawes Plan ran out in 1929, it was replaced by the Young Plan. Named after the American businessman Owen D. Young (1874–1962), who devised it on behalf of the Allies, this plan lowered German reparation payments, put a limit on how long they had to be made, and removed Germany entirely from outside supervision and control. The intensity of the outcry in Germany against the continuation of any reparations showed how far the Germans were from accepting their situation.

Despite these problems, major war was by no means inevitable. Europe, aided by American loans, was returning to prosperity. German leaders like

Stresemann would unquestionably have continued to press for change, but they would certainly not have resorted to force, much less to a general war. Continued prosperity and diplomatic success might have won the loyalty of the German people to the Weimar Republic and moderate revisionism. But the **Great Depression** of the 1930s brought new forces into play.

IN PERSPECTIVE

At the close of the 1920s, Europe appeared finally to have emerged from the difficulties of the World War I era. The Soviet Union, regarded in the West as a communist menace, was isolated by the other powers and had withdrawn into its own internal power struggles. Elsewhere, the initial resentments over the Versailles peace settlement seemed to have abated. The major powers were cooperating. Democracy was still functioning in Germany. The Labour Party was about to form its second ministry in Britain. France had settled into a less assertive international role. Mussolini's fascism seemed to have little relevance to the rest of the Continent. The successor states had not fulfilled the democratic hopes of the Paris conference, but their troubles were their own.

The European economy seemed finally to be on an even keel. The frightening inflation of the early years of the decade was over, and unemployment had eased. American capital was flowing into the Continent. The reparation payments had been systematized by the Young Plan. Yet this economic and political stability proved illusory and temporary. What brought it to an end was the deepest economic depression in the modern history of the West. As governments and electorates responded to the economic collapse, the search for liberty yielded in more than one instance to a search for security. The political experiments of the 1920s gave way to the political tragedies of the 1930s.

REVIEW QUESTIONS

1. How did the Bolshevik revolution pose a challenge to the rest of Europe? Why did Lenin institute the New Economic Policy? Could the Russian Revolution have succeeded without Lenin? How did the Comintern affect Western socialist parties? How did Stalin overcome Trotsky and establish himself as head of the Soviet state?

2. What was fascism? How and why did the fascists obtain power in Italy? To whom did they appeal? What were the differences between the fascist dictatorship of Mussolini and the communist dictatorship of Stalin? What was the status of women under these regimes?

3. Why were Britain and France "joyless victors" after World War I? What weakness did each have? How did World War I change British politics? How did Ireland win its independence?

4. Why did France find it difficult to achieve security after the Versailles treaty? Was the invasion of the Ruhr wise? Was the Locarno pact a success?

5. Why was Czechoslovakia the only generally viable democracy in eastern Europe? What forces worked to undermine that stability?

6. Was the failure of the Weimar Republic in Germany inevitable? Between 1919 and 1929, what were the republic's greatest strengths and weaknesses? Why did the Versailles Treaty loom so large in domestic German politics? What was the position of the Nazi Party in the late 1920s?

SUGGESTED READINGS

I. T. BEREND, *Decades of Crisis: Central and Eastern Europe before World War II* (2001). The best recent discussion of a remarkably troubled region of the early twentieth century.

R. BESSEL, *Political Violence and the Rise of Nazism: The Storm Troopers in Eastern Germany, 1925–1934* (1984). A study of the uses of violence by the nazis.

R. J. BOSWORTH, *Mussolini* (2002). A major new biography.

A. BULLOCK, *Hitler: A Study in Tyranny*, rev. ed. (1964). Remains a classic biography.

S. F. COHEN, *Bukharin and the Bolshevik Revolution: A Political Biography, 1888–1938* (1973). An interesting examination of Stalin's chief opponent on the communist right.

I. DEUTSCHER, *The Prophet Armed* (1954), *The Prophet Unarmed* (1959), and *The Prophet Outcast* (1963). A major biography of Trotsky.

G. FELDMAN, *The Great Disorder: Politics, Economics, and Society in the Germany Inflation, 1914–1924* (1993). The best work on the subject.

S. FITZPATRICK, *The Russian Revolution, 1917–1932* (1994). A brief introduction.

F. FURET, *The Passing of an Illusion: The Idea of Communism in the Twentieth Century* (1995). A brilliant account of the manner in which communism shaped politics and thought outside the Soviet Union.

H. J. GORDON, *Hitler and the Beer Hall Putsch* (1972). An excellent account of the event and the political situation in the early Weimar Republic.

H. GRUBER, *International Communism in the Era of Lenin: A Documentary History* (1967). An excellent collection of difficult-to-find documents.

B. HAMANN, *Hitler's Vienna: A Dictator's Apprenticeship* (1999). Probing study of the politics and society of Vienna as experienced by the young Hitler.

J. HELD (ED.), *The Columbia History of Eastern Europe in the Twentieth Century* (1992). Individual essays on each of the nations.

B. JELAVICH, *History of the Balkans*, vol. 2 (1983). The standard work.

B. KENT, *The Spoils of War: The Politics, Economics, and Diplomacy of Reparations, 1918–1932* (1993). A comprehensive account of the intricacies of the reparations problem of the 1920s.

I. KERSHAW, *Hitler, 1889–1936: Hubris* (1998). The best treatment of Hitler's early life and rise to power.

B. LINCOLN, *Red Victory: A History of the Russian Civil War* (1989). An excellent narrative account.

R. MCKIBBIN, *Classes and Cultures: England, 1918–1951* (2000). Viewing the era through the lens of class.

R. PIPES, *The Formation of the Soviet Union: Communism and Nationalism, 1917–1923* (1997). Classic study of internal policy with emphasis on Soviet minorities.

R. PIPES, *The Unknown Lenin: From the Secret Archive* (1996). A collection of previously unpublished documents that indicate the repressive character of Lenin's government.

J. F. POLLARD, *The Vatican and Italian Fascism 1929–32: A Study in Conflict* (1985). Provides the background to the Lateran pacts.

D. M. SMITH, *Italy and Its Monarchy* (1989). A major treatment of an important neglected subject.

R. J. SONTAG, *A Broken World, 1919–1939* (1971). An exceptionally thoughtful and well-organized survey.

Z. STERNHELL, *The Birth of Fascist Ideology: From Cultural Rebellion to Political Revolution* (1994). A controversial examination of the roots of Mussolini's ideology.

R. TUCKER, *Stalin as Revolutionary, 1879–1929: A Study in History and Personality* (1973). A useful and readable account of Stalin's rise to power.

J. WINTER, *Sites of Memory, Sites of Mourning: The Great War in European Cultural History* (1995). A distinguished analysis of the impact of the war on European art, literature, and society.

R. WOHL, *The Generation of 1914* (1979). An important work that explores the effect of the war on political and social thought.

DOCUMENTS CD-ROM

SOCIETY AND CULTURE BETWEEN THE WARS

27.1 Werner Heisenberg: Uncertainty
27.5 Neville Chamberlain Defends the Policy of Appeasement

TOTALITARIANISM

28.1 Nadezhda K. Krupskaya: *What a Communist Ought to Be Like*
28.2 Benito Mussolini: from *The Political and Social Doctrine of Fascism*
28.3 Adolf Hitler: from *Mein Kampf*
28.4 Christopher Dawson: Religion and the Totalitarian State
28.5 The Russian Revolution
28.6 Socialist Marriage to Motherhood for the Fatherland

George Grosz Satirizes Germany's Social and Political Elite

George Grosz, *Pillars of Society*, 1926. Bildarchiv Preussischer
Kulturbesitz

The 1920s saw enormous turmoil and social unrest in the Weimar Republic. Anger over the loss of World War I and bitterness about the Versailles Treaty and its punishing attitude toward Germany poisoned the life of the young republic. The forces of political reaction blamed the problems on the socialists and communists, who in turn blamed the conservative classes.

More than any artist of the day, George Grosz (1893–1959) captured the strife and despair that marked Weimar politics and social life. He had criticized the German government's role in the outbreak of the First World War, but enlisted anyway, knowing he would soon be drafted. Grosz believed that ordinary Germans had blindly followed the ruling elite into the war. He hated what he regarded as the hypocrisy of the conservative middle class and representatives of the old German imperial order. Their economic greed and irrational patriotism, Grosz believed, had led Germany into the war. A socialist himself, Grosz joined the Communist Party in 1919.

Pillars of Society (1926) is one of Grosz's most bitter attacks on the German social elite (1926). Although he had become disgusted with what he saw as the hypocrisy of the Communist Party, he still considered the conservative classes the greatest danger to the Weimar Republic. They would lead Germany into new disasters, he believed, just as they had headed the country into the First World War.

Pillars of Society is a savage attack on the German social and political elite. Toward the top of the painting, an elderly officer stands with sword and pistol drawn. Just below him to the left a clergyman preaches patriotism. Grosz was consistently anticlerical, attacking what he saw as the German churches' support for a resurgent Germany and their unwillingness to oppose militarism. The bloated figure on the left with his flag and the pamphlet in his pocket declaring "Socialism at Work" represents German nationalism. The top of his head is sliced and excrement spews out. Even the pacifist with the palm leaf has a nasty aggressive face. The nationalistic papers he is carrying and the chamber pot he wears suggest he is a hypocrite. The most menacing figure in the painting is the Nazi at the bottom with the swastika on his tie. The beer mug in his hand reminds the viewer of Hitler's abortive beer hall *Putsch* in Munich in 1923. Like the officer at the top of the painting, the Nazi carries a sword. This parallel and the mounted soldier rising from the Nazi's head suggests a future alliance between traditional German militarism and the aggressiveness of Nazi ideology and foreign policy that would lead to war and the destruction of the republic. Grosz grasped the danger of the then small and discredited Nazi Party as early as 1926.

By late 1932, the Nazis were on the verge of taking power, and Grosz fled to the United States. His art represented all that the Nazis and Hitler personally despised. In 1937, they organized an infamous exhibition of "degenerate art." Grosz's work was included.

■ *Why did Grosz despise the First World War? How does his painting reflect his despair about the Weimar Republic? In* Pillars of Society, *what is Grosz saying about the social and political elite of Weimar society?*

Sources: Richard Cork, *A Bitter Truth: Avant-Garde Art and the Great War* (New Haven, CT: Yale University Press, 1994); Bärbel Schrader and Jürgen Scheber, *The "Golden" Twenties: Art and Literature in the Weimar Republic* (New Haven, CT: Yale University Press, 1988).

Thousands of German troops listen to a speech by Hitler at a Nuremberg rally in 1936. Corbis

CHAPTER 28

EUROPE AND THE GREAT DEPRESSION OF THE 1930S

*I*N EUROPE, UNLIKE IN THE *United States, the 1920s had not been "roaring." Economically, the 1920s had been a decade of insecurity, of a search for elusive stability, of a short-lived upswing, followed by collapse in finance and production. The Great Depression that began in 1929 was the most severe downturn capitalist economies had ever experienced. High unemployment, low production, financial instability, and shrinking trade arrived and would not depart. Business and political leaders despaired over the failure of the market mechanism to save them. Marxists and, indeed, many other observers thought the final downfall of capitalism was at hand.*

European voters looked for new ways out of the doldrums, and politicians sought to escape the pressures that the depression had brought on them. One result of the fight for economic security was the establishment of the Nazi dictatorship in Germany. Another was the piecemeal construction of what has become known as the mixed economy; that is, governments became directly involved in economic decisions alongside business and labor. In both cases, most of the political and economic guidelines of nineteenth-century liberalism were abandoned. So were decency and civility in political life.

KEY TOPICS

- Financial collapse and depression in Europe
- The emergence of the National Government in Great Britain and the Popular Front in France in response to the political pressures caused by the Depression
- The Nazi seizure of power and the establishment of a police state and racial laws in Germany
- Forced industrialism and agricultural collectivization in the Soviet Union, and purges in the Soviet Communist Party and Soviet army under Stalin

Toward the Great Depression

Three factors combined to bring about the intense severity and the extended length of the Great Depression. First, there was a financial crisis that stemmed directly from the war and the peace settlement. Second, a crisis arose in the production and distribution of goods in the world market. These two problems became intertwined in 1929 and, so far as Europe was concerned, reached the breaking point in 1931. Finally, both difficulties became worse because neither the major western European nations nor the United States offered strong economic leadership or acted responsibly. Without cooperation or leadership in the Atlantic economic community, the economic collapse in finance and production simply lingered and deepened.

THE FINANCIAL TAILSPIN

Most European nations emerged from World War I with inflated currencies. Immediately after the armistice, the unleashed demand for consumer and industrial goods drove up prices. The price and wage increases generally subsided after 1921. Yet the problem of maintaining the value of their national currencies still haunted political leaders—and was intensified after the German financial disaster of 1923. The frightening German example of uncontrolled inflation helped explain the later refusal of most governments to run budget deficits when the depression struck. They feared inflation as a source of social instability and political turmoil the way that European governments since World War II have feared unemployment.

Reparations and War Debts Reparation payments and international war-debt settlement further complicated the picture. Here France and the United States were the stumbling blocks. France had twice paid reparations as a defeated nation, once after 1815 and again after 1871. As a victor, it now intended both to receive reparations and to finance its postwar recovery through them. The 1923 invasion of the Ruhr demonstrated French determination on this question.

The United States was no less determined to be repaid for the wartime loans it had made to its allies. Moreover, the European Allies owed various debts to each other. It soon became apparent that German reparations were to provide the means by which other European nations intended to repay all these debts. Most of the money that the Allies collected from each other eventually went to the United States.

In 1922, Great Britain announced it would insist on payment for its own loans only to the extent that the United States required payments from Britain. The American government, however, would not relent. The reparations and the war debts made normal business, capital investment, and international trade difficult and expensive for the European nations. Governments exercised various controls over credit, trade, and currency. Currency speculation drew funds away from capital investment in productive enterprise. The monetary problems reinforced the general tendency toward high tariff policies. If a nation imported too many goods from abroad, it might have difficulty meeting those costs and the expenses of debt or reparation payments. The financial and money muddle thus discouraged trade and production and, in consequence, hurt employment.

American Investments In 1924, the Dawes Plan reorganized the administration and transfer of reparations, which procedures in turn smoothed the debt repayments to the United States. Thereafter, private American capital flowed into Europe—especially Germany. Much of the money, which provided the basis for Europe's brief prosperity after 1925, was in the form of short-term loans.

In 1928, this lending began to contract as American money was withdrawn from European investments into the booming New York stock market. In the Wall Street crash of October 1929—the result of virtually unregulated financial speculation—huge amounts of money were lost. U.S. banks had made large loans to customers, who then invested the money in the stock market. When stock prices collapsed, the customers could not repay the banks. Consequently, within the United States, all kinds of credit that had been available shrank severely or disappeared, and many banks failed. Thereafter, little

American capital was available for investment in Europe. Furthermore, loans already made to Europeans were not renewed as American banks strove to cover domestic shortages.

The End of Reparations   When the credit to Europe began to run out, a major financial crisis struck the Continent. In May 1931, Kreditanstalt, a major bank in Vienna, collapsed. It was a primary lending institution for much of central and eastern Europe. The German banking system came under severe pressure and was saved only through government guarantees. It became clear, however, that in this crisis Germany would be unable to make its next reparation payment as stipulated in the 1929 Young Plan. In June 1931, as the German difficulties mounted, American president Herbert Hoover (1874–1964) announced a one-year moratorium on all payments of international debts.

The Hoover moratorium was a prelude to the end of reparations. Hoover's action was a sharp blow to the French economy, for which the flow of reparations had continued to be important. The French agreed to the moratorium only reluctantly. They really had little alternative because the German economy had all but collapsed. The Lausanne Conference in the summer of 1932 in effect ended the era of reparations. The next year, the debts owed to the United States were settled either through small token payments or simply through default. Nevertheless, the financial politics of the 1920s had done its damage.

Major Dates of the Economic Crisis	
1923	German inflation following French invasion of Ruhr
1924	Dawes Plan on reparations
1929 (June)	Young Plan on reparations
1929 (October)	Wall Street crash
1931 (May)	Collapse of Kreditanstalt in Vienna
1931 (June)	Hoover announces moratorium on reparations
1932	Lausanne Conference ends reparations

PROBLEMS IN AGRICULTURAL COMMODITIES

In addition to the dramatic financial turmoil and collapse, a less dramatic, but equally fundamental, downturn occurred in production and trade. The 1920s saw the market demand for European goods shrink relative to the Continent's capacity to produce goods. This meant idle factories and fewer jobs. Part of the problem originated within Europe, part outside. In both instances, the difficulty arose from agriculture. Better methods of farming, improved strains of wheat, expanded tillage, and more extensive transport facilities all over the globe vastly increased the world supply of grain. World wheat prices fell to record lows. This development was, of course, initially good for consumers. The collapse in

Crowds gathered on Wall Street in New York on October 29, 1929, the day the stock market crashed. The Great Depression in the United States dried up American capital previously available for investment in Europe.   Brown Brothers

grain prices, however, meant lower incomes for European farmers, especially those of central and eastern Europe.

Also, higher industrial wages raised the cost of the industrial goods used by farmers or peasants. The farmers could not purchase those products. Moreover, farmers began to have difficulty paying off their mortgages and normal annual operational debts. Normally, they borrowed money to plant their fields, expecting to pay the debt when the crops were sold, but the fall in commodity prices made it difficult for the farmers to repay those debts.

Farm problems became especially pressing in eastern Europe. Immediately after the war, the new governments there had undertaken land-reform programs. The democratic franchise in the successor states had opened the way for considerable redistribution of tillable soil. In Romania and Czechoslovakia, large amounts of land changed hands. In Hungary and Poland, it occurred to a lesser extent.

The new small farms, however, proved to be inefficient, and the farmers who worked them were unable to earn sufficient incomes. Protective tariffs often prevented the export of grain among European countries. The credit and cost squeeze on eastern

European farmers and on their counterparts in Germany played a major role in their disillusionment with liberal politics. For example, farmers in Germany were a major source of political support for the Nazis.

Outside Europe, similar problems affected other producers of agricultural commodities. The prices they received for their products plummeted. Government-held reserves of agricultural commodities accumulated to record levels. The glut involved the supplies of wheat, sugar, coffee, rubber, wool, and lard. The people who produced these goods in underdeveloped nations in Asia, Africa, and Latin America could no longer make enough money to buy finished goods from industrial Europe. As world credit collapsed, the economic position of these commodity producers worsened. Commodity production had simply outstripped world demand.

The collapse in agricultural prices and the financial turmoil resulted in stagnation and depression for European industry. European coal, iron, and textiles had depended largely on international markets. Unemployment spread from these industries to those producing finished consumer goods. The persistent unemployment in Great Britain and to a lesser extent in Germany during the 1920s had already meant "soft" domestic markets in those countries. The policies of reduced government spending with which the governments confronted the depression further weakened domestic demand. By the early 1930s, the Great Depression was growing on itself.

DEPRESSION AND GOVERNMENT POLICY

The Great Depression did not mean absolute economic decline. Nor did it mean everyone was out of a job. People with work always well outnumbered those without work. New economic sectors, such as the production of automobiles, radios, and synthetics, and the service industries around them did develop. But the economic downturn made people extremely anxious. People in nearly all walks of life feared their own economic security and lifestyle would suffer next. The depression also frustrated social and economic expectations. People with jobs improved their standard of living or were promoted much more slowly than might have been the case under sound economic conditions. They were working, but in their own eyes they seemed to be going nowhere. Their anxieties created a major source of social discontent.

The governments of the late 1920s and the early 1930s were not well fitted in either structure or ideology to confront these problems. The Keynesian theory of governments' spending the economy out

Throughout Europe, unemployment in the 1930s led to profound social and political discontent as the lives and families of unemployed workers, such as this British miner, collapsed. The Granger Collection

of depression was not yet available. John Maynard Keynes's (1883–1946) *General Theory of Employment, Interest, and Money* was not published until 1936. Before Keynes, orthodox economic policy called for cuts in government spending to prevent inflation. Eventually, the market mechanism was supposed to bring the economy back to prosperity.

Nonetheless, the severity of the depression, plus pressure from the new mass electorates, led governments across Europe to interfere with the economy as never before. Government participation in economic life was not new; we need only recall the mercantilistic policies of the seventeenth and eighteenth centuries and the government encouragement of railway building in the nineteenth century. From the early 1930s onward, however, government involvement increased rapidly. Private economic enterprise became subject to new trade, labor, and currency regulations. The political goals of restoring employment and providing for defense required the state to set economic priorities. As in the past, state intervention generally increased as one moved from west to east across the Continent. These new economic policies usually also involved further political experimentation.

Confronting the Great Depression in the Democracies

The Great Depression ended the business-as-usual attitude that had marked the political life of Great Britain and France during the late 1920s. In Britain, the emergency led to a new coalition government and the abandonment of economic policies considered sacred for a century. The economic stagnation in France proved to be the occasion for a bold political and economic program sponsored by the parties of the left. The relative success of the British venture gave the nation new confidence in the democratic processes; the new departures in France created social and political hostilities that undermined faith in republican institutions.

GREAT BRITAIN: THE NATIONAL GOVERNMENT

In 1929, a second minority Labour government, headed by Ramsay MacDonald, took office. As British unemployment rose to more than 2.5 million workers in 1931, the ministry became divided over what to do. MacDonald wanted to slash the budget, reduce government salaries, and cut unemployment benefits. This was a bleak program for a Labour government. MacDonald's strong desire to make the Labour Party respectable led him to reject more radical programs. Many of the cabinet ministers resisted MacDonald's proposals. They refused to penalize the poor and the unemployed. The prime minister requested the resignations of his entire cabinet and arranged for a meeting with King George V.

Everyone assumed the entire Labour ministry was about to leave office. However, to the surprise of his party and the nation, MacDonald did not resign. At the urging of the king and probably of his own ambition, MacDonald formed a coalition ministry, called the National Government, composed of Labour, Conservative, and Liberal ministers. The bulk of the Labour Party believed their leader had sold them out. In the election of 1931, the National Government received a comfortable majority. After the election, however, MacDonald, who remained prime minister until 1935, was a tool of the Conservatives. They held a majority in their own right in the House of Commons, but the appearance of a coalition was useful for imposing unpleasant programs.

The National Government took three decisive steps to attack the depression. First, to balance the budget, it raised taxes, cut insurance benefits to the unemployed and the elderly, and lowered government salaries. Its leaders argued that the fall in prices that had taken place meant those reductions did not appreciably cut real income. Second, in September 1931, Britain went off the gold standard. The value of the British pound on the international money market fell by about 30 percent. This move stimulated exports. Third, in 1932, Parliament passed the Import Duties Bill, which placed a 10 percent ad valorem tariff (a tax levied in proportion to the value of each imported good) on all imports except those from the empire. These steps were extraordinary. Gold and free trade, the hallmarks of almost a century of British commercial policy, were abandoned.

The policies of the National Government produced results. Great Britain avoided the banking crisis that hit other countries. By 1934, industrial production had expanded beyond the level for 1929. Britain was the first nation to restore that level of production. Of course, the mediocre British industrial performance of the 1920s made the task easier. The government also encouraged lower interest rates, which led to the largest private housing boom in British history. Industries related to housing and home furnishing prospered.

Britain had entered the depression with a stagnant economy and left the era with a stagnant economy. Those people who were employed generally improved their standard of living. Nonetheless, the hard core of unemployment remained. In 1937, the number of jobless had fallen to just below 1.5 million.

Yet the British political system was not fundamentally challenged. There were demonstrations by the unemployed, but social insurance, though hardly generous, did support them. To the employed citizens of the country, the National Government seemed to pursue a policy that avoided the extreme wings of both the Labour and the Conservative parties. When MacDonald retired in 1935, Stanley Baldwin again took office. He was succeeded in 1937 by Neville Chamberlain (1869–1940). The new prime minister is today known for the disastrous Munich agreement, but when he took office, he was considered one of the more progressive thinkers on social issues in the Conservative Party.

One movement in Britain did flirt with the extreme right-wing politics of the Continent. In 1932, Sir Oswald Mosley (1896–1980) founded the British Union of Fascists. He had held a minor position in the second Labour government and was disappointed by its feeble attack on unemployment. Mosley urged a program of direct action through a new corporate structure for the economy. His group wore black shirts and attempted to hold mass meetings. Even at the height of his popularity, he gained only a few thousand adherents. Thereafter his anti-Semitism began to alienate supporters, and by the close of the decade, he was little more than a political oddity.

Depression Years in Great Britain and France	
1929	Second Labour government comes to power in Britain with Ramsay MacDonald as prime minister
1931	Formation of National Government in Britain
1931	British government goes off the gold standard
1932	Oswald Mosley founds British Union of Fascists
1933–1934	Stavisky affair in France
1934 (February 6)	Right-wing riots in Paris
1935	Stanley Baldwin becomes British prime minister
1936 (June 5)	Popular Front government in France under Blum
1936 (June 8)	Labor accord in France
1937	Neville Chamberlain becomes British prime minister
1938	Popular Front replaced by Radical ministry in France

FRANCE: THE POPULAR FRONT

The unfolding of the Great Depression in France was the reverse of that in Britain. It came later and lasted longer. Only in 1931 did the economic slide begin to affect the French economy. Even then, unemployment did not become a major problem. Rarely were more than half a million French workers without jobs. One industry after another, however, lowered wages. The government raised tariffs to protect French goods and especially French agriculture. (Ever since that time, French farmers have enjoyed unusual protection by the government.) These measures helped maintain the home market, but did little to overcome industrial stagnation. Relations between labor and management were tense. (See "Art & the West: René Magritte, *The Human Condition*," p. 993.)

The first political fallout of the depression was the election of another Radical coalition government in 1932. Fearful of contributing to inflation as they had after 1924, the Radicals pursued a generally deflationary policy. In the same year that the new ministry took office, reparation payments on which the French economy depended stopped. As the economic crisis tightened, parliamentary and political life became difficult.

Right-Wing Violence Outside the Chamber of Deputies, politics grew ugly. Various right-wing groups with authoritarian tendencies became active. These leagues included the Action Française, founded before World War I in the wake of the Dreyfus affair, and the Croix de Feu, or "Cross of Fire," composed of army veterans. These and similar groups had a total of more than 2 million members. Some of them wanted a monarchy; others favored what would have amounted to military rule. They were hostile to parliamentary government, socialism, and communism. They wanted what they regarded as the greater good and glory of France to be set above the petty machinations of political parties. They thus resembled the fascists and the Nazis.

The activities and propaganda of the right-wing leagues weakened loyalty to republican government and made French political life more bitter. They also led to an incident of extraordinary havoc that produced important long-range political consequences.

This incident grew out of the Stavisky affair, the last of those curious scandals that punctuated the political fortunes of the Third Republic. Serge Stavisky (d. 1934) was a small-time gangster who appears to have had good connections within the government. In 1933, he became involved in a fraudulent bond scheme. When finally tracked down by the police, he committed suicide in January 1934.

The official handling of the matter suggested a political cover-up. It was alleged that people in high places wished to halt the investigation. To the right wing, the Stavisky incident symbolized all the seaminess, immorality, and corruption of republican politics.

On February 6, 1934, a large demonstration of the right-wing leagues took place in Paris. The exact purpose and circumstances of the rally remain uncertain, but the crowd tried to storm the Chamber of Deputies. Violence erupted between right and left political groups and between them and the police. Fourteen demonstrators were killed; scores of others were injured. It was the largest disturbance in Paris since the Commune of 1871.

After this clash, the Radical ministry of Edouard Daladier (1884–1970) was replaced by a government composed of all living former premiers. The Chamber of Deputies permitted the ministry to deal with economic matters by decree. The major result of the right-wing demonstrations, however, was that the parties of the left, Radicals, Socialists, and Communists, began to realize that a right-wing coup might be possible in France.

Socialist-Communist Cooperation Between 1934 and 1936, the French left began to make peace within its own ranks. This was not easy. French Socialists, led by Léon Blum (1872–1950), had been the major target of the French communists since the split over joining the Comintern in 1920. Only Stalin's fear of Hitler as a danger to the Soviet Union made this new cooperation possible. Despite deep suspicions on all sides, what became known as the **Popular Front,** a coalition of all left-wing parties, had been established by July 1935. Its purpose was to preserve the republic and press for social reform.

The election of 1936 gave the Popular Front a majority in the Chamber of Deputies. The Socialists were the largest single party for the first time in French history. They organized the cabinet as they had long promised they would do when they constituted the majority party of a coalition. Léon Blum became premier on June 5, 1936.

From the early 1920s, this Jewish intellectual and humanitarian had opposed the communist version of socialism. Cast as the successor to Jean Jaurès (1859–1914), who had been assassinated in 1914, Blum pursued socialism through a democratic, parliamentary government.

Blum's Government During May 1936, before the Popular Front came to power, strikes had begun to spread throughout French industry. Immediately after assuming office on June 6, the Blum government faced further spontaneous work stoppages involving over half a million workers who had occupied factories in sit-down strikes. These were the most extensive labor disturbances in the history of the Third Republic. They aroused new fears in the conservative business community, already frightened by the election of the Popular Front.

Blum acted swiftly to bring together representatives of labor and management. On June 8, he announced the conclusion of an accord that reorganized labor-management relations in France. Wages were immediately raised between 7 and 15 percent. Employers were required to recognize unions and to bargain collectively with them. Workers were given annual paid two-week vacations. The forty-hour week was established throughout French industry. Blum hoped to overcome labor hostility to French society, to establish a foundation for justice in labor-management relations, and to increase domestic consumer demand.

Blum followed his labor policy with other bold departures. He raised the salaries of civil servants and instituted a program of public works. Government loans were extended to small industry. Spending on armaments was increased, and some armament industries were nationalized. A National Wheat Board was set up to manage the production and sale of grain. Initially, Blum had promised to resist devaluation of the franc. By the autumn of 1936, however, international monetary pressure forced him to devalue. He did so again in the spring of 1937. The devaluations came too late to help French exports.

These moves enraged the conservative banking and general business communities. In March 1937,

Leon Blum (1872–1950) led the Popular Front to victory in the French elections of 1936. These demonstrators are carrying his portrait at a rally in Paris. UPI/Corbis

they brought enough influence to bear on the ministry to cause Blum to halt the program of reform. It was not taken up again. Blum's Popular Front colleagues considered the pause in reform an unnecessary compromise. In June 1937, Blum resigned. The Popular Front ministry itself held on until April 1938, when it was replaced by a Radical ministry under Daladier. Not until 1939 did French industrial production reach the level of 1929.

By the close of the 1930s, citizens from all walks of life had begun to wonder whether the republic was worth preserving. The left remained divided. Businesspeople found the republic inefficient and too subject to socialist pressures. The right wing hated the republic in principle. When the time came in 1940 to defend the republic, too many French citizens had lost faith in it.

Germany: The Nazi Seizure of Power

The most remarkable political event caused by the uncertainty and turmoil of the Great Depression was the coming to power of the National Socialists (Nazis) in Germany. By the late 1920s, the Nazis were a major presence in the Weimar Republic, but were not yet real contenders for political dominance. The financial crisis, economic stress, and social anxiety associated with the onset of the depression rapidly changed that situation. All the fragility of the Weimar constitution stood exposed, and the path opened for the most momentous and far-reaching event of the decade: the Nazi seizure of power.

DEPRESSION AND POLITICAL DEADLOCK

The outflow of foreign—especially American—capital from Germany beginning in 1928 undermined the brief economic prosperity of the Weimar Republic. The resulting economic crisis brought parliamentary government to an end. In 1928, a coalition of center parties and the Social Democrats governed. All went well until the depression struck. Then the coalition partners disagreed on economic policy. The Social Democrats refused to reduce social and unemployment insurance. The more conservative parties, remembering the inflation of 1923, insisted on a balanced budget. The coalition dissolved in March 1930.

To resolve the parliamentary deadlock, President von Hindenburg appointed Heinrich Brüning (1885–1970) as chancellor. Lacking a majority in the Reichstag, Brüning governed through emergency presidential decrees, as authorized by Article 48 of the constitution. The party divisions prevented the Reichstag from overriding the decrees. The Weimar Republic thus became an authoritarian regime.

German unemployment rose from 2,258,000 in March 1930 to more than 6,000,000 in March 1932. There had been persistent unemployment during the 1920s, but nothing of such magnitude or duration. The economic downturn and the parliamentary deadlock worked to the advantage of the more extreme political parties. In the election of 1928, the Nazis had won only 12 seats in the Reichstag, and the Communists had won 54 seats. After the election of 1930, the Nazis held 107 seats and the Communists 77.

For the Nazis, politics meant the capture of power by terror and intimidation as well as by legal elections. All decency and civility in political life vanished. Thousands of unemployed joined the storm troopers (SA), which had 100,000 members in 1930 and almost 1 million in 1933. The SA freely and viciously attacked Communists and Social Democrats, who also went on fighting each other. The Nazis held mass rallies that resembled religious revivals. They gained powerful supporters and sympathizers in business, military, and newspaper circles. Some intellectuals were also sympathetic. The Nazis transformed this new enthusiasm born of economic despair and nationalistic frustration into impressive electoral results.

HITLER COMES TO POWER

For two years Brüning governed with the confidence of his president, Hindenburg. The economy did not improve, however, and the political situation deteriorated. In 1932, the eighty-three-year-old president stood for reelection. Hitler ran against him and forced a runoff. The Nazi leader got 30.1 percent of the first vote and 36.8 percent in the runoff. Although Hindenburg remained in office, the results of the poll convinced him that Brüning no longer commanded sufficient confidence from conservative German voters.

On May 30, 1932, Hindenburg dismissed Brüning. The next day, Hindenburg appointed Franz von Papen (1878–1969) as chancellor. The new chancellor was one of a small group of extremely conservative advisers on whom the aged Hindenburg had become increasingly dependent. Others included the president's son and several military figures. With the continued paralysis in the Reichstag, their influence over the president virtually amounted to control of the government. Thus only a handful of people made the crucial decisions of the next several months.

Papen and the circle around the president wanted to find some way to use the Nazis without giving effective power to Hitler. The government needed the mass popular support that only the Nazis seemed able to generate. The Hindenburg circle decided to convince Hitler the Nazis could not come to power on their own. Papen removed the ban on Nazi meetings that Brüning had imposed. He also called a Reichstag election for July 1932. The Nazis won 230 seats and polled 37.2 percent of the vote. Hitler demanded to be appointed chancellor. Hindenburg refused. The government called another election in November, partly to wear down the Nazis' financial resources, which it did. The Nazis lost 34 seats, and their popular vote dipped to 33.1 percent. The advisers around Hindenburg still refused to appoint Hitler to office.

In November 1932, Papen resigned, and the next month General Kurt von Schleicher (1882–1934) became chancellor. Fear of civil war between the left and the right mounted. Schleicher tried to build a broad coalition of conservatives and trade unionists. Such a coalition, including groups from the political left, frightened the Hindenburg circle even more than the prospect of Hitler. They did not trust Schleicher, whose motives were never clear. Consequently, they persuaded Hindenburg to name Hitler chancellor. To control Hitler and to see he did little mischief, the Hindenburg circle appointed Papen as vice chancellor and named other traditional conservatives to the cabinet. On January 30, 1933, Adolf Hitler became the chancellor of Germany.

Hitler had come into office by legal means. All the proper legal forms and procedures had been observed. This was important, for it permitted the civil service, the courts, and the other agencies of the government to support him in good conscience. He had forged a rigidly disciplined party structure and had mastered the techniques of mass politics and propaganda. (See "Encountering the Past: Cinema of the Political Left and Right" and "Josef Goebbels Explains How to Use Radio for Political Propaganda") He understood how to touch the raw social and political nerves of the electorate. His support appears to have come from across the social spectrum and not simply from the lower middle class, as was once thought to be the case. Pockets of resistance appeared among Roman Catholic voters in the country and small towns. Otherwise, support for Hitler was particularly strong among groups such as farmers, war veterans, and the young, who had especially suffered from the insecurity of the 1920s and the depression of the early 1930s. Hitler promised them security against communists and socialists, effective government in place of the petty politics of the other parties, and an uncompromising nationalist vision of a strong, restored Germany.

German big business once received much of the blame for the rise of Hitler. There is little evidence, however, that business contributions made any crucial difference to the Nazis' success or failure. Hitler's supporters were frequently suspicious of business and giant capitalism. They wanted a simpler world, one in which small property would be safe from both socialism and big business. These people looked to Hitler and the Nazis rather than to the Social Democrats because the latter, though concerned with social issues, were not sufficiently nationalistic. The Nazis won out over other conservative nationalistic parties because, unlike those conservatives, the Nazis did address the problem of social insecurities.

HITLER'S CONSOLIDATION OF POWER

Once in office, Hitler moved with almost lightning speed to consolidate his control. This process had three facets: the capture of full legal authority, the crushing of alternative political groups, and the purging of rivals within the Nazi Party itself.

Reichstag Fire   On February 27, 1933, a mentally ill Dutch communist set fire to the Reichstag building in Berlin. The Nazis quickly claimed the fire was part of an immediate communist threat to the government. To the public, it was plausible the communists might attempt some action against the state now that the Nazis were in power. Under Article 48, Hitler issued an emergency decree suspending civil liberties and proceeded to arrest communists or alleged communists. This decree was not revoked for as long as Hitler ruled Germany.

The Enabling Act   In early March, another Reichstag election took place. The Nazis still received only 43.9 percent of the vote and won 288 seats. The arrest and removal of all communist deputies, however, and the political fear aroused by the fire enabled Hitler to control the Reichstag. On March 23, 1933, the Reichstag passed an Enabling Act that permitted Hitler to rule by decree. Thereafter, there were no legal limits on his exercise of power. The Weimar constitution was never formally repealed or amended; it had simply been supplanted by the February Emergency Decree and the March Enabling Act.

Perhaps better than anyone else, Hitler understood that he and his party had not inevitably come to power, so in a series of complex moves, Hitler outlawed or undermined any German institution that might have served as a rallying point for opposition. In early May 1933, the Nazi Party, rather than any government agency, seized the offices, banks, and newspapers of the free trade unions and

Cinema of the Political Left and Right

Before the invention of television, the cinema was the most powerful cultural vehicle for political regimes to project their power. Film directors of genius were drawn to the authoritarian governments of both the left and the right, and the films they made for these regimes, especially those of Soviet Russia and Nazi Germany, still impress moviegoers.

During the 1920s, the Soviet Union promoted the cinema as a propaganda tool. The greatest Soviet film director was Sergei Eisenstein (1898–1948). His most famous film, *The Battleship Potemkin*, which critics regard as one of the most important films of all time, depicts a mutiny on a warship during the Russian revolution of 1905. In *Potemkin*, Eisenstein portrayed the working class itself as the hero of both the film and, true to Marxist doctrine, of history itself.

As Stalin gained more and more power from the mid-1920s onward, he imposed rigid censorship on the arts. To work in the Soviet Union, Eisenstein had to make films that pleased Stalin. And this he did. However, such was Eisenstein's genius that he also made two movies that many film scholars consider masterpieces: *Alexander Nevsky*, which depicts the victory of a medieval Russian prince over invading Germans, and *Ivan the Terrible*, which some see in its depiction of the sixteenth-century despotic tsar whom Stalin admired as Eisenstein's surrender to Stalin and others as a portrayal of tyranny.

Leni Riefenstahl, (b. 1902) was by the early 1930s the most skilled documentary filmmaker in Germany and perhaps the world, an extraordinary accomplishment for a woman in a field dominated by men. Adolf Hitler asked her to make a documentary extolling the Third Reich after the Nazis took power in 1933. The results were *Triumph of the Will* (1934), about a Nazi Party rally, and *Olympia* (1938), about the Olympic Games held in Berlin in 1936. Both films display innovative, dramatically effective cinematic techniques and also the skilled political theatricality of the Nazi regime. These films dazzled audiences and are still shown in film classes as major works of twentieth-century cinematic art. Yet despite her artistry, Riefenstahl became marked, no matter how much she protested that she was a "pure" artist, as a producer of Nazi propaganda films. No American film studio would distribute her films to U.S. audiences.

After the defeat of Germany in 1945, Riefenstahl was imprisoned by the allies under their de-Nazification program before being released in 1949. Thereafter, she attempted to rescue her career as a filmmaker, but the Nazi taint proved indelible. Instead, she became a noted photographer, especially of underwater photography. To this day, Riefenstahl defends her films for the Third Reich as art, not propaganda.

■ *Why were the Soviet and Nazi regimes so interested in the cinema? How did Leni Riefenstahl's films of Hitler and Nazi rallies affect her later career?*

Leni Riefenstahl filming the 1936 Olympic Games in Berlin with Hitler on the reviewing stand. © Bettmann/Corbis

The Reichstag fire in 1933 provided Hitler with an excuse to consolidate his power. Bildarchiv Preussischer Kulturbesitz

arrested their leaders. In late June and early July, all other German political parties were outlawed. By July 14, 1933, the National Socialists were the only legal party in Germany. During the same months, the Nazis moved against the governments of the individual federal states in Germany. By the close of 1933, all major institutions of potential opposition had been eliminated.

Internal Nazi Party Purges The final element in Hitler's consolidation of power involved the Nazi Party itself. By late 1933 the SA, or storm troopers, consisted of approximately 1 million active members and a larger number of reserves. The commander of this party army was Ernst Roehm (1887–1934), a possible rival to Hitler himself. The German army officer corps, on whom Hitler depended to rebuild the national army, were jealous of the SA leadership. So, to protect his own position and to shore up support with the regular army, on June 30,

1934, Hitler personally ordered the murder of key SA officers, including Roehm. Between June 30 and July 2, more than a hundred persons were killed, including former chancellor General Kurt von Schleicher and his wife. The German army, the only institution that might have prevented the murders, did nothing.

A month later, on August 2, 1934, President Hindenburg died. Thereafter, Hitler combined the offices of chancellor and president and became head of state as well as the head of the government. He was now the sole ruler of Germany and the Nazi Party.

THE POLICE STATE AND ANTI-SEMITISM

Terror and intimidation had been major factors in the Nazi march to office. As Hitler consolidated his power, he oversaw the organization of a police state.

JOSEF GOEBBELS EXPLAINS HOW TO USE RADIO FOR POLITICAL PROPAGANDA

Radio revolutionized communications during the interwar years. It also created an entirely new industry while many other areas of the economy stagnated. Radio, as popular at that time as television is today, also became an important political instrument. Most of the early radio stations were government owned and controlled. Political leaders could address their nations as they never could before. Communication became instant and could enter every home with a radio. Unlike newspapers, radio did not depend upon the literacy of its audience. Shortly after coming into power, Josef Goebbels (1897–1945), who was in charge of Nazi propaganda, discussed the role of radio in the new Nazi order. Note how he urges his listeners, who were broadcasters, never to be boring. All radio broadcasting had to be interesting to audiences so that they would be receptive to its political messages.

■ *Why does Goebbels emphasize the Nazi monopoly on broadcasting? What new attitudes did Goebbels want radio to bring to its audience? What advantages did radio have over newspapers as a propaganda device?*

We make no bones about the fact that the radio belongs to us and to no one else. And we will place the radio in the service of our ideology [*Idee*] and. . .no other ideology will find expression here. . . . The radio must subordinate itself to the goals which the Government of the national revolution has set itself. The Government will give the necessary instructions. . . .

I consider radio to be the most modern and the most crucial instrument that exists for influencing the masses. I also believe—one should not say that out loud—that radio will in the end replace the press. . . .

First, principle: At all costs avoid being boring. I put that before *everything*. . . .So do not think that you have the task of creating the correct attitudes, of indulging in patriotism, of blasting out military music and declaiming patriotic verse—no, that is not what this new orientation is all about. Rather you must help to bring forth a nationalist art and culture which is truly appropriate to the pace of

modern life and to the mood of the times. The correct attitudes must be conveyed but that does not mean they must be boring. And simply because you have the task of taking part in this national enterprise you do not have carte blanche to be boring. You must use your imagination, an imagination which is based on sure foundations and which employs all means and methods to bring to the ears of the masses the new attitude in a way which is modern, up to date, interesting, and appealing; interesting, instructive but not schoolmasterish. Radio must never go down with the proverbial disease—the intention is clear and it puts you off.

I am placing a major responsibility in your hands for you have in your hands the most modern instrument in existence for influencing the masses. By means of this instrument you are the creators of public opinion. If you carry this out well we shall win over the people and if you do it badly in the end the people will once more desert us. . . .

J. Noakes and G. Pridham, eds., *Nazism 1919–1945: Vol. 2, State, Economy and Society, 1933–39, A Documentary Reader,* Exeter Studies in History, No. 8 (Exeter, U.K.: University of Exeter Press, © 1984), p. 386. Reprinted by permission.

SS Organization The chief vehicle of police surveillance was the **SS** (*Schutzstaffel,* or "protective force"), or security units, commanded by Heinrich Himmler (1900–1945). This group had originated in the mid-1920s as a bodyguard for Hitler and had become a more elite paramilitary organization than the much larger SA. In 1933, there were approximately 52,000 members of the SS, which was the

instrument that carried out the blood purges of the party in 1934. By 1936, Himmler had become head of all police matters in Germany and stood second only to Hitler in power and influence.

Attack on Jewish Economic Life The police character of the Nazi regime was all pervasive, but the people who most consistently experienced the terror of the police state were the German Jews. A key plank of the Nazi program was an anti-Semitism based on biological racial theories stemming from late-nineteenth-century thought rather than from religious discrimination. Before World War II, the Nazi attack on the Jews went through three stages of increasing intensity. First, in 1933, shortly after assuming power, the Nazis excluded Jews from the civil service. They also tried to enforce boycotts of Jewish shops and businesses, but these won little public support.

Racial Legislation Then in 1935, a series of measures known as the Nuremberg Laws robbed German Jews of their citizenship. The professions and the major occupations were closed to those defined as Jews. Marriage and sexual intercourse between Jews and non-Jews were prohibited. Legal exclusion and humiliation of the Jews became the order of the day. The definition of who was a Jew in this law was both confusing and complex because the Nazis found they could not produce regulations based on solely a racial concept. The Nazi legal definitions of who was a Jew took into account the number of Jewish parents or grandparents, as well as whether a person practiced the Jewish faith. All persons with at least three Jewish grandparents were defined as Jews, but persons with two Jewish grandparents were accounted Jewish only if practicing the Jewish faith, or if married to a Jew, or if born to a marriage with one Jewish parent, or if born out of wedlock with one Jewish parent.

Kristallnacht The persecution of the Jews increased in 1938. Business careers were forbidden to them. On November 9 and 10, 1938, under Nazi Party orders, thousands of Jewish stores and synagogues were burned or otherwise destroyed on what became known as **Kristallnacht.** (See "An American Diplomat Witnesses *Kristallnacht* in Leipzig.") The Jewish community itself was required to pay for the destruction because the government confiscated the insurance money that was paid to cover the damages. In many other ways, large and petty, German Jews were harassed. This persecution allowed the Nazis to inculcate the rest of the population with the concept of a master race of pure German "Aryans" and also to display their own contempt for civil liberties.

The Final Solution After the war broke out, Hitler decided in 1941 and 1942 to destroy the Jews in Europe. More than 6 million Jews, mostly from eastern Europe, died as a result of that staggering decision, unprecedented in its scope and implementation. (See Chapter 29.)

RACIAL IDEOLOGY AND THE LIVES OF WOMEN

Hitler and other Nazis were less interested in expanding the population as a whole, which was Mussolini's policy, than in producing a population of racially pure Germans. In their role as mothers,

In early November, 1938, the Nazi authorities in Germany increased their persecution of Jews. On what has come to be called Kristallnacht, *Nazis destroyed Jewish businesses and burned synagogues.* Bildarchiv Preussischer Kulturbesitz

AN AMERICAN DIPLOMAT WITNESSES *KRISTALLNACHT* IN LEIPZIG

A key event in the Nazi attack on Jews in Germany occurred on November 9 and 10, 1938, during nights of destructive terror known as Kristallnacht *because of the vast quantity of shattered plate glass from the broken windows of Jewish-owned businesses. David Buffum, the American consul in Leipzig, wrote an extensive report of what happened in that city. In addition to providing the information in the passage that follows, he observed that most German citizens seemed stunned by what had occurred and deeply disapproved of it. But as his observations of the events in the Leipzig Zoo indicate, Germans were intimidated by the Nazi tactics. Buffum also reported that many German Jews came to the American consulate to find aid for emigration or help in locating husbands and sons taken to concentration camps. Both the United States and the nations of western Europe admitted only limited numbers of Jewish refugees from Germany and, later, from Nazi-occupied Europe. Compare the events recorded in this document with the predictions that Alexis de Tocqueville made to Count Arthur de Gobineau about what might happen when racial thinking affected mass politics. (See p. 873.)*

■ *Why did the Nazis claim the destruction of life and property in Leipzig and other German cities arose from spontaneous actions? What steps did the Nazi perpetrators of* Kristallnacht *take to intimidate Jewish citizens? What aid that was available to other German citizens was denied to Jews during these destructive events? How might we account for the failure of other German citizens to oppose the Nazi actions against the Jews?*

At 3 A.M. on 10 November 1938 was unleashed a barrage of Nazi ferocity that has had no equal hitherto in Germany. . . .

Jewish shop windows by the hundreds were systematically and wantonly smashed throughout the entire city at a loss estimated at several millions of marks. . . . According to reliable testimony, the debacle was executed by SS men and Stormtroopers not in uniform, each group having been provided with hammers, axes, crowbars and incendiary bombs.

German women had the special task of preserving racial purity and giving birth to more pure Germans who were healthy in mind and body. According to this view, women were to breed strong sons and daughters for the German nation. Nazi journalists often compared the role of women in childbirth to that of men in battle. Each served the state in particular social and gender roles. In both cases, the good of the nation was more important than that of the individual. (See "Hitler Rejects the Emancipation of Women.")

Nazi racial ideology focused very particularly on women as the carriers and bearers of both the desired and undesired races. Nazi policy favored motherhood only for those whom its adherents regarded as racially fit for motherhood. As early as late 1933, the government raised the issue of what kind of persons were fit to bear children for the nation. This policy disapproved of fostering motherhood among those people condemned by Nazi racism—most particularly the Jews, but also Slavs and Gypsies. During the mass executions of Jews in the Holocaust (see Chapter 29), Jewish women were specifically targeted for death, in part to prevent them from bearing a new generation.

Nazi theorists also discriminated between the healthy and unhealthy, the desirable and undesirable, in the German population itself. The government sought to sterilize undesirables, a policy that led to both the sterilization and death of many women, often because of an alleged mental "degeneracy." Some pregnant women were forced to have abortions. The Nazis' population policy was, in effect, one of selective breeding or antinatalism that profoundly affected the lives of women.

To support motherhood among those whom they believed should have children, the Nazis provided loans to encourage early marriage, tax breaks for families with children, and child allowances. In this respect, Nazi legislation resembled that passed elsewhere in Europe during the decade. The Nazi

Three synagogues in Leipzig were fired simultaneously by incendiary bombs and all sacred objects and records desecrated or destroyed, in most cases hurled through the windows and burned in the streets. . . . All the synagogues were irreparably gutted by flames. . . . One of the largest clothing stores in the heart of the city was destroyed by flames from incendiary bombs, only the charred walls and gutted roof having been left standing. As was the case with the synagogues, no attempts on the part of the fire brigade were made to extinguish the fire. . . . It is extremely difficult to believe, but the owners of the clothing store were actually charged with setting the fire and on that basis were dragged from their beds at 6 A.M. and clapped into prison.

Tactics which closely approached the ghoulish took place at the Jewish cemetery where the temple was fired together with a building occupied by caretakers, tombstones uprooted and graves violated. . . .

Ferocious as was the violation of property, the most hideous phase of the so-called 'spontaneous' action has been the wholesale arrest and transportation to concentration camps of male German Jews between the ages of sixteen and sixty, as well as Jewish men without citizenship. . . . Having demolished dwellings and hurled most of the movable effects onto the streets, the insatiably sadistic perpetrators threw many of the trembling inmates into a small stream that flows through the Zoological Park, commanding horrified spectators to spit at them, defile them with mud and jeer at their plight. The latter incident has been repeatedly corroborated by German witnesses who were nauseated in telling the tale. The slightest manifestation of sympathy evoked a positive fury on the part of the perpetrators, and the crowd was powerless to do anything but turn horror-stricken eyes from the scene of abuse, or leave the vicinity. These tactics were carried out . . . without police intervention and they were applied to men, women, and children.

From *Nazism, 1919–1945: A Documentary Reader, Vol. 2, State, Economy and Society, 1933–39,* edited by J. Noakes and G. Pridham, new edition 2000, pp. 255–256. Reprinted by permission of University of Exeter Press.

subsidies and other family payments were sent to husbands rather than wives, in an effort to make married fatherhood seem preferable to bachelorhood. Furthermore, all of these policies were administered on the premise that only racially and physically desirable children received support.

Although Nazi ideology emphasized motherhood, in 1930 the party vowed to protect the jobs of working women, and the actual number of women working in Germany rose steadily under the Nazi regime. The Nazis recognized that in the midst of the depression many women needed to work, but the party urged them to pursue employment that was "natural" to their character as women. Such employment included agricultural labor, teaching, nursing, social service, and domestic service. The Nazis also intended women to be educators of the young. In that role, whether as mothers or as members of the serving professions, women became special protectors of German cultural values. Through cooking, dress, music, and stories, mothers were to instill a love for the nation in their children. As consumers for the home, women were to support German-owned shops, buy German-made goods, and boycott Jewish merchants.

NAZI ECONOMIC POLICY

Besides consolidating power and pursuing anti-Semitic policies, Hitler still had to confront the Great Depression. German unemployment had helped propel him to power. The Nazis attacked this problem with a success that astonished and frightened Europe. By 1936, while the rest of the European economy remained stagnant, the specter of unemployment and other difficulties associated with the Great Depression no longer haunted Germany.

As far as the economic crisis was concerned, Hitler had become the most effective political leader in Europe. This success was a most important source of the internal strength and support for his tyrannical regime. The Nazi success against the

HITLER REJECTS THE EMANCIPATION OF WOMEN

According to Nazi ideology, women's place was in the home, producing and rearing children and supporting their husbands. In this speech, Hitler urges this view of the role of women. He uses anti-Semitism to discredit those writers who urged the emancipation of women from their traditional roles and occupations. Hitler returns here to the "separate spheres" concept of the relationship of men and women. His traditional view of women was directed against contrary views that were associated with the Soviet experiment during the interwar years. Contrast the Nazi outlook on women and the family with the view expressed by the young Bolshevik Alexandra Kollontai in the document in Chapter 27. Ironically, once World War II began, the Nazi leadership demanded that women leave the home and work in factories to support the war effort.

■ *What are the social tasks Hitler assigns to women? Why does he associate the emancipation of women with Jews and intellectuals? How does he attempt to subordinate the lives of women to the supremacy of the state?*

The slogan "Emancipation of Women" was invented by Jewish intellectuals and its content was formed by the same spirit. In the really good times of German life the German woman had no need to emancipate herself. She possessed exactly what nature had necessarily given her to administer and preserve; just as the man in his good times had no need to fear that he would be ousted from his position in relation to the woman. . . .

If the man's world is said to be the State, his struggle, his readiness to devote his powers to the service of the community, then it may perhaps be said that the woman's is a smaller world. For her world is her husband, her family, her children, and her home. But what would become of the greater world if there were no one to tend and care for the smaller one? How could the greater world survive if there were no one to make the cares of the smaller world the content of their lives? No, the greater world is built on the foundation of this smaller world. This great world cannot survive if the smaller world is not stable. Providence has entrusted to the woman the cares of that world which is her very own, and only on the basis of this smaller world can the man's world be formed and built up. The two worlds are not antagonistic. They complement each other, they belong together just as man and woman belong together.

We do not consider it correct for the woman to interfere in the world of the man, in his main sphere. We consider it natural if these two worlds remain distinct. To the one belongs the strength of feeling, the strength of the soul. To the other belongs the strength of vision, of toughness, of decision, and of the willingness to act. In the one case this strength demands the willingness of the woman to risk her life to preserve this important cell and to multiply it, and in the other case it demands from the man the readiness to safeguard life.

The sacrifices which the man makes in the struggle of his nation, the woman makes in the preservation of that nation in individual cases. What the man gives in courage on the battle field, the woman gives in eternal self-sacrifice, in eternal pain and suffering. Every child that a woman brings into the world is a battle, a battle waged for the existence of her people. . . .

So our women's movement is for us not something which inscribes on its banner as its programme the fight against men, but something which has as its programme the common fight together with men. For the new National Socialist national community acquires a firm basis precisely because we have gained the trust of millions of women as fanatical fellow-combatants, women who have fought for the common life in the service of the common task of preserving life. . . .

Whereas previously the programmes of the liberal, intellectualist women's movements contained many points, the programme of our National Socialist Women's movement has in reality but one single point, and that point is the child, that tiny creature which must be born and grow strong and which alone gives meaning to the whole life-struggle.

From *Nazism, 1919–1945: A Documentary Reader, Vol. 2, State, Economy and Society, 1933–39,* edited by J. Noakes and G. Pridham, new edition 2000, pp. 361–362. Reprinted by permission of University of Exeter Press.

Young women among an enthusiastic crowd extend the Nazi salute at a party rally in 1938. Nazi ideology encouraged women to favor traditional domestic roles over employment in the workplace and to bear many children. The onset of the war, however, forced the government to recruit women workers. Bildarchiv Preussischer Kulturbesitz

Great Depression gave the regime considerable credibility. Behind the direction of both business and labor stood the Nazi terror and police. The Nazi economic experiment proved that, by sacrificing all political and civil liberty, destroying a free trade-union movement, preventing the private exercise of capital, and ignoring consumer satisfaction, full employment to prepare for war and aggression could be achieved.

Nazi economic policies supported private property and private capitalism, but subordinated all significant economic enterprise and decisions about prices and investment to the goals of the state. Hitler reversed the deflationary policy of the cabinets that had preceded him. He instituted a massive program of public works and spending. Many of these projects were related to rearmament. The government built canals, reclaimed land, and constructed an extensive highway system with clear military uses. It also returned unemployed workers to farms if they had originally

come from there. Other laborers were not permitted to change jobs.

In 1935, the renunciation of the military provisions of the Versailles treaty led to open rearmament and expansion of the army with little opposition, as explained in Chapter 29. These measures essentially restored full employment. In 1936, Hitler instructed Hermann Göring (1893–1946), who had headed the air force since 1933, to undertake a four-year plan to prepare the army and the economy for war. The government determined that Germany must be economically self-sufficient. Armaments received top priority. This economic program satisfied both the yearning for social and economic security and the desire for national fulfillment.

With the crushing of the trade unions in 1933, strikes became illegal. There was no genuine collective bargaining. The government handled labor disputes through compulsory arbitration. It also required workers and employers to participate in the Labor Front, an organization intended to

The Volkswagen, which first appeared in 1938, was intended to provide inexpensive transportation for German workers. This advertisement declares that saving five marks a week is all it takes to buy one.
Bildarchiv Preussischer Kulturbesitz

Major Dates in the Nazi Seizure of Power	
1928	National Socialists win 12 seats in the Reichstag
1930	National Socialists win 107 seats in the Reichstag
1930	Brüning appointed chancellor
1932 (April 10)	Hindenburg defeats Hitler for presidency
1932 (May 31)	Von Papen replaces Brüning
1932 (July 31)	National Socialists win 230 seats in the Reichstag
1932 (November 6)	Indecisive Reichstag election; National Socialists lose 34 seats
1932 (November 17)	Von Papen resigns
1932 (December 2)	Von Schleicher appointed chancellor
1933 (January 28)	Von Schleicher resigns
1933 (January 30)	Hitler appointed chancellor
1933 (February 27)	Reichstag fire
1933 (March 5)	National Socialists win 288 seats in the Reichstag
1933 (March 23)	Enabling Act passed
1933 (July 14)	National Socialists declared the only legal party
1934 (June 30)	Murder of SA leadership
1934 (August 2)	Death of Hindenburg
1935	Passage of Nuremberg Laws
1938 (November 9 and 10)	*Kristallnacht* (nights of attacks on Jewish businesses and synagogues)

demonstrate that class conflict had ended. The Labor Front sponsored a "Strength Through Joy" program that provided vacations and other forms of recreation for the labor force.

Italy: Fascist Economics

The fascists had promised to stabilize Italian social and economic life. Discipline was a substitute for economic policy and creativity. During the 1920s, Mussolini undertook vast public works, such as draining the Pontine Marshes near Rome for settlement. The government subsidized the shipping industry and introduced protective tariffs. Mussolini desperately sought to make Italy self-sufficient. He embarked on the "battle of wheat" to prevent foreign grain from appearing in products on Italian tables. Wheat farming in Italy expanded enormously. These policies, however, did not keep the Great Depression from affecting Italy. Production, exports,

and wages fell. Even the increased wheat production backfired. So much poor marginal land that was expensive to cultivate came into production that the domestic price of wheat, and thus of much other food, actually rose.

SYNDICATES

Both before and during the depression, the fascists sought to steer an economic course between socialism and a liberal laissez-faire system. Their policy was known as **corporatism.** It was a planned economy linked to the private ownership of capital and to government arbitration of labor disputes. Major industries were first organized into syndicates representing labor and management. The two groups negotiated labor settlements within this framework and submitted differences to compulsory government arbitration. The fascists contended that class conflict would be avoided if both labor and management looked to the greater goal of productivity for the nation.

Whether this arrangement favored workers or managers is still in dispute. From the mid-1920s, however, Italian labor unions lost the right to strike and to pursue independent economic goals. In that respect, management clearly profited.

CORPORATIONS

After 1930, the industrial syndicates were reorganized into entities called *corporations*. These bodies grouped all industries relating to a major area of production, such as agriculture or metallurgy, from raw materials through finished products and distribution, into one entity. Twenty-two such corporations were established to encompass the whole economy. In 1938, Mussolini abolished the Italian Chamber of Deputies and replaced it with a Chamber of Corporations.

This vast organizational framework did not increase production; instead, bureaucracy and corruption proliferated. The corporate state allowed the government to direct much of the nation's economic life without a formal change in ownership. Consumers and owners could no longer determine what was to be produced. The fascist government gained further direct economic power through the Institute for Industrial Reconstruction, which extended loans to businesses that were in financial difficulty. The loans, in effect, established partial state ownership of those businesses.

How corporatism might have affected the Italian economy in the long run is unknown. In 1935, Italy invaded Ethiopia, and economic life was put on a formal wartime footing. The League of Nations imposed economic sanctions, urging member nations to refrain from purchasing Italian goods. The sanctions had little effect. Thereafter, taxes rose. During 1935, the government imposed a forced loan on the citizenry by requiring property owners to purchase bonds. Wages continued to be depressed. As international tensions increased during the late 1930s, the Italian state assumed more direction over the economy. Fascism had not brought prosperity to Italy; rather, it had brought economic dislocation and a falling standard of living.

The Soviet Union: Central Economic Planning, Collectivization, and Party Purges

While the capitalist economies of western Europe floundered in the Great Depression, the Soviet Union undertook a tremendous industrial advance. As in past eras of Russian economic progress, the direction and impetus came from the top. Stalin far

During the rapid industrialization of the Soviet Union, millions of women did heavy labor in factories. This poster from the 1930s celebrates their work in the chemical industry. Sovfoto/Eastfoto

exceeded his tsarist predecessors in the intensity of state coercion and terror he brought to the task. Russia achieved its stunning economic growth during the 1930s only at the cost of literally millions of human lives and the degradation of still other millions. Stalin's economic policy clearly proved that his earlier rivalry with Trotsky had been a political power struggle rather than one over substantial ideological differences.

THE DECISION FOR RAPID INDUSTRIALIZATION

Through 1927, Lenin's New Economic Policy (NEP), as championed by Bukharin with Stalin's support, had charted Soviet economic development. The government permitted private ownership and enterprise in the countryside to ensure an adequate food supply for the workers in the cities. Although the industrial production level of 1913

STALIN CALLS FOR THE LIQUIDATION OF THE *KULAKS* AS A CLASS

The core of Stalin's agricultural policy undertaken in the late 1920s and early 1930s was the eradication of private farms and their replacement with large collective farms. The greatest obstacle to this policy was the kulaks, *peasants who owned substantial farms. In this remarkable speech of 1929, Stalin first explains why small peasant farming must be replaced with collective farms to achieve an adequate food supply for the cities and the industrial sector of the population. He then calls for the liquidation of the* kulaks *as a class. As might be expected, the* kulaks *resisted collectivization by destroying crops and farm animals. In turn, Communist Party agents killed millions of peasants to achieve collectivization.*

■ *What were the goals of the collectivization of farms in the Soviet Union? How did the* kulaks *stand in the way of collectivization? How does Stalin dehumanize the* kulaks *as people by discussing them entirely as a class and as part of the capitalistic system?*

Can we advance our socialized industry at an accelerated rate as long as we have an agricultural base, such as is provided by small-peasant farming, which is incapable of expanded reproduction, and which, in addition, is the predominant force in our national economy? No, we cannot. . . .

What, then, is the solution? The solution lies in enlarging the agricultural units, in making agriculture capable of accumulation, of expanded reproduction, and in thus transforming the agricultural bases of our national economy.

[T]he socialist way [to enlarge farming units], which is to introduce collective farms and state farms in agriculture, the way which leads to the amalgamation of the small-peasant farms into large collective farms, employing machinery and scientific methods of farming, and capable of developing further, for such agricultural enterprises can achieve expanded reproduction. . . .

The characteristic feature in the work of our Party during the past year is that we, as a Party, as the Soviet power,

had been achieved by 1927, industrial growth had slowed. During 1927, the Party Congress decided to push for rapid industrialization. As implemented through what has been termed "industrialization by political mobilization," this policy, which began in 1928, marked a sharp departure from the NEP.[1]

The drive to rapid industrialization was a major pillar in Stalin's undertaking of "Socialism in One Country." It was to be the path whereby the communist Soviet Union would overtake the productive capacity of capitalist nations and thus protect itself against capitalist enemies. Such a policy required the rapid construction of heavy industries, such as iron, steel, electricity-generating stations, the machine tool industry, and tractor manufacturing. Stalin's organizational vehicle for industrialization was a series of five-year plans, starting in 1928. The State Plan-

ning Commission, or *Gosplan*, oversaw the program, setting goals for production and attempting to organize the economy to meet them. The task of coordinating all facets of production was immensely difficult and complicated. Deliveries of materials from mines or factories had to be assured before the next unit could carry out its part of the plan. Enormous disruption occurred throughout the economy as the *Gosplan* carried out its goals of building power plants and steel mills and increasing the production of mines. Capital projects were consistently favored over consumer production. The number of centralized agencies and ministries involved in planning soared, and they often competed with each other.

The rapid expansion of the industrial base created the first genuinely large factory labor force in what had been Russia. Workers were recruited from the countryside and from the urban unemployed. New cities and new work districts in existing cities arose. More often than not, the workers themselves lived in deplorable conditions. Their lives were

[1] Validmir Andrle, *A Social History of Twentieth-Century Russia* (London: Arnold, 1994), p. 161.

(a) have developed an offensive along the whole front against the capitalist elements in the countryside;

(b) that this offensive, as you know, has brought about and is bringing about very palpable, positive results.

What does this mean? It means that we have passed from the policy of restricting the exploiting proclivities of the *kulaks* to the policy of eliminating the *kulaks* as a class. . . .

Until recently the Party adhered to the policy of restricting the exploiting proclivities of the *kulaks*. . . .

Could we have undertaken such an offensive against the *kulaks* five years or three years ago? Could we then have counted on success in such an offensive? No, we could not. That would have been the most dangerous adventurism. It would have been playing a very dangerous game at offensive. We would certainly have failed, and our failure would have strengthened the position of the *kulaks*. Why? Because we still lacked a wide network of state and collective farms in the rural districts which could be used as strongholds in a determined offensive against the *kulaks*. Because at that time we were not yet able to substitute for the capitalist production of the *kulaks* the socialist production of the collective farms and state farms. . . .

Now we are able to carry on a determined offensive against the *kulaks*, to break their resistance, to eliminate them as a class and substitute for their output the output of the collective farms and state farms. Now, the *kulaks* are being expropriated by the masses of poor and middle peasants themselves, by the masses who are putting solid collectivization into practice. Now, the expropriation of the *kulaks* in the regions of solid collectivization is no longer just an administrative measure. Now, the expropriation of the *kulaks* is an integral part of the formation and development of the collective farms. Consequently it is now ridiculous and foolish to discourse on the expropriation of the *kulaks*. You do not lament the loss of the hair of one who has been beheaded.

From Stalin, "Problems of Agrarian Policy in the USSR," speech at a conference of Marxist students of the agrarian question, December 27, 1929, in *Problems of Leninism*, pp. 391–393, 408–409, 411–412, as quoted in Robert V. Daniels, *A Documentary History of Communism*, rev. ed. (Hanover, NH, and London: University Press of New England, 1984), pp. 224–227.

worse than anything Marx and Engels had decried in the nineteenth century.

The government and the Communist Party undertook a vast program of propaganda to sell the five-year plans to the Russian people and to elicit their cooperation. The government boasted of the sheer size of the plants being constructed and the new town being organized. Such efforts were necessary because most industrial workers were displaced peasants who had no previous factory experience and who often resisted industrial discipline. The party appealed to the idealism of the young in proclaiming its goals of rapidly modernizing the nation. Workers, such as a legendary coal miner named Stakhanov, who exceeded their assigned goals received rewards and publicity.

By the close of the 1930s, the results of the three five-year plans were impressive. The Russian economy grew more rapidly than that of any other nation in the Western world during any similar period. Soviet industrial production rose approximately 400 percent between 1928 and 1940. Industries that had never before existed in Russia challenged their foreign counterparts. New industrial cities had been populated by hundreds of thousands of people. The social and human cost of this effort had, however, been appalling.

THE COLLECTIVIZATION OF AGRICULTURE

The decision to industrialize rapidly devastated Soviet agriculture. Under the NEP, a few farmers, the *kulaks*, had become prosperous. Probably numbering less than 5 percent of the rural population, they and other farmers were discontented because there were few consumer goods to purchase with the cash they received for their crops. They had frequently withheld grain from the market in the 1920s and did so again during 1928 and 1929. Food shortages occurred in the cities, and the government worried about unrest.

AP/Wide World Photos

Stalin used intimidation and propaganda to support his drive to collectivize Soviet agriculture. Communist Party agitators led groups of peasants, such as these shown on the left, to demand the seizure of the farms worked by the better-off and more successful farmers known as kulaks. The poster on the right shows an idealized Soviet collective farm on which tractors owned by the state have replaced peasant labor. In reality, collectivization provoked fierce resistance and caused famines in which millions of peasants died.

The Bridgeman Art Library International Ltd.

During these troubled months, Stalin came to a momentous decision. Agriculture must be collectivized to produce enough grain for food and export, to achieve control over the farm sector of the economy, and to free peasant labor for the factories in the expanding industrial sector.

In 1929, unleashing unprecedented violence in the countryside, Stalin ordered party agents to confiscate any hoarded grain and to carry out a program of **collectivization** of agriculture that was only vaguely defined. As part of this plan, the government decided to eliminate the *kulaks* as a class. (See "Stalin Calls for the Liquidation of the *Kulaks* as a Class.") The definition of a *kulak*, however, soon embraced any peasants, whatever their wealth, who resisted collectivization. In March 1930, Stalin called a brief halt to the process, justifying the slowdown on the grounds of "dizziness from success." After the harvest of that year had been secured, the drive to collectivize the farms was renewed with vehemence, and the costs remained high.

Determined to keep their land, stubborn peasants, often with women in the lead, sabotaged collectivization by slaughtering millions of horses and cattle between 1929 and 1933. Over 2 million peasants were forced from their homes and transported in overcrowded cattle cars to distant areas of the Soviet Union or to prison camps. Even if they survived that ordeal, they then had to patch together some kind of life in Siberia or another inhospitable province, where many of them became industrial workers. Their children were treated as class enemies and potential traitors.

The party also targeted priests of the Russian Orthodox Church. The Soviet Communist Party, atheistic in its ideology, had always opposed religion and the church, but only with collectivization were many priests attacked and churches closed or vandalized. Rabbis, Catholic priests, and mullahs received the same harsh treatment.

Stalin and the Communist Party had won the battle of the grain fields, but they had not solved the problem of producing enough food. That difficulty would plague the Soviet Union until its collapse in 1991 and remains a problem for its successor states.

FLIGHT TO THE SOVIET CITIES

An immediate consequence of Soviet collectivization was a flight of peasants from the land to the cities. Between 1928 and 1932, approximately 12 million peasants left the countryside, a migration unprecedented in European history. Most of them were young males, leaving a disproportionate number of women and elderly people in the villages, where they lived in great poverty.

In the years after the drive toward collectivization, the populations of major cities grew rapidly. Moscow's population almost doubled. Between 1939 and 1980, the proportion of the Soviet population living on the land fell from two-thirds to one-third. Although all of Europe has become more urban in the twentieth century, in the Soviet Union urbanization arose directly from the government-sponsored turmoil in the countryside.

URBAN CONSUMER SHORTAGES

Much of the housing shortage that plagued the Soviet Union for the rest of its history originated in the 1930s. In the new industrial cities, workers lived in barracks. In the older cities, individuals and families had difficulty finding apartments. Those apartments they did find were tiny and several families often had to share kitchens, toilets, and baths. Such cramped quarters led people to value even more what little privacy and few possessions they had, including pots and pans and bits of furniture.

For urban dwellers, in addition to the shortage of housing, the most fundamental fact of everyday life under Stalin and subsequent Soviet leaders was a chronic shortage of the most basic consumer goods, including food, clothing, and particularly shoes. From the end of the NEP through the collapse of the Soviet Union in 1991, city shops had few goods. Throughout the 1930s, Russians consumed less food each year than they had before the revolution, and the famines affected everyone's life. What goods did appear were often sold in stores reserved for party members. A sharp inequality constantly distinguished the small minority of party members and leaders from the general Soviet population. One of the most common experiences of Soviet citizens was standing in line for bread.

Except for certain showplaces in Moscow and Leningrad (formerly and now again Saint Petersburg), Soviet cities generally lacked the kind of urban infrastructure that western European cities had long enjoyed. The transport systems were too small for the rapidly expanding populations. Even

cities as large and important as Stalingrad (today, Volgograd) lacked sewer systems in the mid-1930s. In the new industrial cities, even running water was rare, as were paved streets and electric lighting. Urban crime and disease were widespread.

How did this Soviet society sustain itself? There was much black marketeering, and food was raised on tiny private plots. People bartered with each other and pilfered from the state. This whole informal mode of coping became known as the *blat*. But for much of the century, the Soviet people sustained themselves mainly through the conviction that they were enduring their present troubles to build a greater socialist future. During World War II, this emphasis changed to protecting the fatherland. After the war, the emphasis again fell on a better future, but that future never came.

FOREIGN REACTIONS AND REPERCUSSIONS

Many foreign contemporaries looked at the Soviet economic experiment naïvely. While the capitalist world lay in the throes of the Great Depression, the Soviet economy had grown at a pace never realized in the West. After a trip to Russia, the American writer Lincoln Steffens (1866–1936) reported, "I have seen the future and it works." Beatrice and Sidney Webb, the British Fabian socialists, spoke of "a new civilization" in the Soviet Union. These and similar observers ignored the shortages in consumer goods and the poor housing. More important, they had little idea of the social cost of the Soviet achievement. Millions of human beings had been killed and millions more uprooted. Even with the recent opening of the Soviet archives, the total picture of suffering and human loss during those years will probably never be known; however, the deprivation and sacrifice of Soviet citizens far exceeded anything described by Marx and Engels in relation to nineteenth-century industrialization in western Europe.

The internal difficulties caused by collectivization and industrialization led Stalin to make an important shift in foreign policy. In 1934, he began to fear the nation might be left isolated against future aggression by Nazi Germany. The Soviet Union was not yet strong enough to withstand such an attack. So that year he ordered the Comintern to permit communist parties in other countries to cooperate with noncommunist parties against Nazism and fascism. This reversed the Comintern policy established by Lenin as part of the Twenty-one Conditions in 1919. The new Stalinist policy allowed the formation of the Popular Front Government in France.

THE PURGES

Stalin's decisions to industrialize rapidly, to move against the peasants, and to reverse the Comintern policy aroused internal opposition. Each was a departure from the policies of Lenin. In 1929, Stalin forced Bukharin, the fervent supporter of the NEP and his own former ally, off the Politburo. Little detailed information is known about further opposition, but it seems to have existed among lower-level party followers of Bukharin and other opponents of rapid industrialization. Even at its most extensive, however, such opposition was modest.

In 1933, with turmoil in the countryside and economic dislocation in the industrializing sectors, Stalin and others in the central Soviet bureaucracy began to fear they were losing control of the country and the party apparatus and that effective rivals might emerge. These apprehensions, which were exaggerated, were part of Stalin's own penchant for paranoia and resulted in the **Great Purges,** which remain one of the most mysterious and horrendous political events of the twentieth century. The purges were not understood at the time and have not been fully comprehended since, either inside or outside the former Soviet Union, even with the recent opening of Soviet archives.

On December 1, 1934, Sergei Kirov (1888–1934), the popular party chief of Leningrad and a member of the Politburo, was assassinated. In the wake of the shooting, thousands of people were arrested, and still more were expelled from the party and sent to labor camps. At the time, it was believed that opponents of the regime had murdered Kirov. Complicity in the crime became the normal accusation against those whom Stalin attacked. It has long been thought that Stalin himself authorized

---

Major Dates in Soviet History During the Five-Year Plans and Purges

1927	Decision to move toward rapid industrialization
1928	First five-year plan begins
1929	Beginning of collectivization of agriculture
1929	Expulsion of Bukharin from Politburo affirms Stalin's central position
1930	Stalin's call for moderation in his policy of agricultural collectivization because of "dizziness from success"
1934	Assassination of Kirov
1936–1938	Major purge trials

Kirov's assassination because he was afraid of him. The available documentary evidence does not allow us to know for sure whether Stalin was involved, but he quickly used Kirov's death for his own purposes. Under Stalin, the Soviet Communist Party had already shown it could punish dissent within its ranks. The debates of the 1920s within the party had established a clear precedent for exercising firm discipline, and in the confusion surrounding the implementation of the five-year plans, persons accused of sabotage and disloyalty had been executed. The purges, however, went beyond any of these precedents.

The purges that took place immediately after Kirov's death were just the beginning of a larger and longer process. Between 1936 and 1938, a series of spectacular show trials were held in Moscow. Former high Soviet leaders, including some who had belonged to the Politburo, such as Bukharin, publicly confessed to political crimes and were convicted and executed. It is still not certain why they made their palpably false confessions, although this seems to have been the kind of ritual confession of faults and shortcomings that had characterized previous internal Communist Party life. They had also been interrogated under the most difficult conditions, including torture, and feared for their families' lives. Other lower-level party members were tried in private and shot. Hundreds of thousands of people received no trial at all and were either executed or deported to slave labor camps. The purges touched persons in all areas of party life, as well as their families. Within the party itself, hundreds of thousands of members were expelled, and applicants for membership were removed from the rolls. After the civilian party members had been purged, followed by the purging of major party leaders, the prosecutors turned against the Soviet army, convicting and executing important officers, including heroes of the civil war. The exact number of executions, imprisonments, interrogations, and expulsions is unknown, but ran into the millions.

The rational explanations of the purges probably lie in two directions. First, over the several years of the purges, different portions of the party leadership moved against others. Initially, the central Moscow leadership used the purges to discipline and gain more control over lower levels of the party in the far-flung regions of the Soviet Union. In addition to supporting Stalin's authority, these central bureaucratic groups wanted to eliminate any opposition to their positions or policies. By 1937, however, Stalin seems to have become distrustful of the central party elite, and he began to find enemies within its ranks. Moreover, by that date, local communist groups were allowed to

By the mid-1930s, Stalin's purges had eliminated many leaders and other members from the Soviet Communist Party. This photograph of a meeting of a party congress in 1936 shows a number of the surviving leaders with Stalin, who sits fourth from the right in the front row. To his left is Vyacheslav Molotov, longtime foreign minister. The first person on the left in the front row is Nikita Khruschev, who headed the Soviet Union in the late 1950s and early 1960s. Itar-Tass/Sovfoto/Eastfoto

designate their own victims with little direction from Moscow. Thereafter, a self-destructive cascade of accusations, imprisonments, and executions occurred throughout the party and within its highest levels. The Communist Party leadership at all levels appeared to be consuming itself. This situation has been termed "centrally authorized chaos."[2] (See "A Prosecutor and Victim of the Purges States His Case to the Court.")

Second, no matter how much attention is paid to the tensions and relationships among the different levels and regions of the Communist Party, Stalin's fears for his own power cannot be ignored. He and other leaders who survived the purges selected certain victims and determined the fate of their families. In effect, the purges created a new party structure absolutely subservient and loyal to Stalin. The "old Bolsheviks" of the October Revolution were among his earliest targets. They and others active in the first years of the revolution knew how far Stalin had moved from Lenin's policies. New, younger members replaced the party members who were executed or expelled. The newcomers knew little about old Russia or the ideals of the original Bolsheviks. They had not been loyal to Lenin, Trotsky, or any other Soviet leader except Stalin himself.

[2]J. Arch Getty and Oleg V. Naumov, *The Road to Terror: Stalin and the Self-Destruction of the Bolsheviks, 1932–1939,* trans. by Benjamin Sher (New Haven, CT: Yale University Press, 1999), p. 583.

A PROSECUTOR AND VICTIM OF THE PURGES STATES HIS CASE TO THE COURT

N. I. Yezhov had joined the Communist Party well before the revolution of 1917. He served in the Soviet bureaucracy and had consistently supported Stalin. From 1936 to 1938, he had been the People's Commissar of the USSR for Internal Affairs and had overseen the purging of many people, including Bukharin. Yezhov was arrested in 1939 for reasons he did not understand and was tried early in 1940. The formal charge against him was spying for Poland. He believed he was being brought down by his enemies within the Commissariat for Internal Affairs. He also clearly believed it had been necessary to purge a vast number of enemies of Stalin and the Communist Party. In his statement to the military court, only recently made public from the Soviet archives, he both confessed faults and attempted to defend himself, though he knew he would be convicted. Indeed, Yezhov was found guilty and shot shortly after making this statement. The confessions by victims of the purges made to the courts tended to be long and rambling. The portion quoted gives only a brief sense of such statements.

■ *How does Yezhov indicate his loyalty to the Communist Party and to Stalin? What actions does he boast about? How had he been treated? How can a man who had committed so many injustices against his fellow communists present himself as innocent? What do the personal favors he requests indicate about the purges? What, if any, regrets for his actions does he show?*

At the preliminary investigation I said that I was not a spy, that I was not a terrorist, but they didn't believe me and beat me up horribly. During the 25 years of my party work I have fought honorably against enemies and have exterminated them. . . .

I did not organize any conspiracy against the party and the government. On the contrary, I used everything at my disposal to expose conspiracies. . . .

I purged 14,000 *chekists* [enemies], but my great guilt lies in the fact that I purged so few of them. My practice was as follows: I would hand over the task of interrogating the person under arrest to one or another department head while thinking to myself: "Go on, interrogate him today—tomorrow I will arrest you." All around me were enemies of the people, my enemies. I purged *chekists* everywhere. It was only in Moscow, Leningrad, and the Northern Caucasus that I did not purge them. I thought they were honest, but it turned out, in fact, that I had been harboring under my wings saboteurs, wreckers, spies, and enemies of the people of other stripes. . . .

I understand and honestly declare that the only cause for sparing my life would be for me to admit that I am guilty of the charges brought against me, to repent before the party and to implore it to spare my life. . . .

I'll now finish my final address. I ask the military collegium to grant me the following requests: 1. My fate is obvious. My life, naturally, will not be spared . . . I ask only one thing: shoot me quietly, without putting me through any agony. 2. . . . If my mother is alive, I ask that she be provided for in her old age, and that my daughter be taken care of. 3. I ask that my relatives—nephews—not be subjected to punitive measures because they are not guilty of anything. . . . 5. I request that Stalin be informed that I have never in my political life deceived the party, a fact known to thousands of persons who know my honesty and modesty. I request that Stalin be informed that I am a victim of circumstances and nothing more, yet here enemies I have overlooked may have also had a hand in this. Tell Stalin that I shall die with his name on my lips.

N. I. Yezhov's statement before a secret judicial meeting of the Military Collegium of the Supreme Court of the USSR, February 3, 1940, as quoted in J. Arch Getty and Oleg V. Naumov, *The Road to Terror: Stalin and the Self-Destruction of the Bolsheviks, 1932–1939*, trans, by Benjamin Sher (New Haven, CT: Yale University Press, 1999), pp. 561–562.

IN PERSPECTIVE

By the middle of the 1930s, dictators of the right and the left had established themselves across much of Europe. Political tyranny was hardly new to Europe, but several factors combined to give these rulers unique characteristics. They drew their immediate support from well-organized political parties. Except for the Bolsheviks, these were mass parties. The roots of support for the dictators lay in nationalism, the social and economic frustration of the Great Depression, and political ideologies that promised to transform the social and political order. As long as the new rulers seemed successful, they did not lack support. Many citizens believed these leaders had ended the pettiness of everyday politics.

After coming to power, the dictators possessed a practical monopoly over mass communications. Through armies, police forces, and party discipline, they also monopolized terror and coercive power. They could propagandize large populations and compel people to obey them and their followers. Finally, as a result of the Second Industrial Revolution, they commanded a vast amount of technology and a capacity for immense destruction. Earlier rulers in Europe may have shared the ruthless ambitions of Hitler, Mussolini, and Stalin, but they had lacked the ready implements of physical force to impose their wills.

Mass political support, the monopoly of police and military power, and technological capacity meant the dictators of the 1930s held more extensive sway over their nations than any other group of rulers who had ever governed on the Continent. Soon the issue would become whether they would be able to maintain peace among themselves and with their democratic neighbors.

REVIEW QUESTIONS

1. Why did the Great Depression of the 1930s occur, and why was it more severe and longer lasting than previous depressions?
2. Why did Britain's National Government and France's Popular Front deal with the depression in different ways? Why did the Third Republic have so few supporters?
3. How did the Great Depression affect Germany? Was Hitler's dictatorship inevitable?
4. How did Hitler's economic policies differ from those used in Britain, Italy, and France? Why

did some nations deal with the Great Depression more effectively than others?
5. How and why did Hitler, Mussolini, and Stalin use terror to achieve their goals? What were the particular characteristics of Nazi racial policy? How did this policy in its various guises affect Jewish life?
6. Why did Stalin decide that Russia had to industrialize rapidly? Why did this require the collectivization of agriculture? How did Stalin overcome the obstacles to collectivization? What were the causes of the purges in the Soviet Union?

SUGGESTED READINGS

W. S. ALLEN, *The Nazi Seizure of Power: The Experience of a Single German Town, 1930–1935*, rev. ed. (1984). A classic treatment of Nazism in a microcosmic setting.

M. BURLEIGH AND W. WIPPERMAN, *The Racial State: Germany 1933–1945* (1991). Emphasizes the manner in which racial theory influenced numerous areas of policy.

D. CARROLL, *French Literary Fascism: Nationalism, Anti-Semitism, and the Ideology of Culture* (1995). A study of right-wing political theories in France.

W. CHASE, *Enemies within the Gates?: The Comintern and Stalinist Repression, 1934–1939* (2001). Examines how Soviet policies destroyed the Comintern.

J. COLTON, *Léon Blum: Humanist in Politics* (1966). One of the best biographies of any twentieth-century political figure.

R. CONQUEST, *The Great Terror: Stalin's Purges of the Thirties* (1990). Remains the most useful treatment of the subject to date.

R. CONQUEST, *The Harvest of Sorrow: Soviet Collectivization and the Terror Famine* (1986). A study of how Stalin used starvation against his own people.

I. DEUTSCHER, *Stalin: A Political Biography*, 2nd ed. (1967). A major biography.

B. EICHENGREEN, *Golden Fetters: The Gold Standard and the Great Depression, 1919–1939* (1992). A remarkable study of the role of the gold standard in the economic policies of the interwar years.

B. A. ENGEL AND A. POSADSKAYA-VANDERBECK, *A Revolution of Their Own: Voices of Women in Soviet History* (1998). Long interviews and autobiographical recollections by women who lived through the Soviet era.

S. FITZPATRICK, *Everyday Stalinism, Ordinary Life in Extraordinary Times: Soviet Russia in the 1930s* (1999). A major study based on newly available materials.

S. FITZPATRICK, *Stalin's Peasants: Resistance and Survival in the Russian Village after Collectivization* (1994). An extensive social history.

R. GELLATELY, *Backing Hitler: Consent and Coercion in Nazi Germany* (2001). Controversial study emphasizing widespread support for Hitler.

J. A. GETTY AND O. V. NAUMOV, *The Road to Terror: Stalin and the Self-Destruction of the Bolsheviks, 1933–1939* (1999). A major collection of newly available documents revealing much new information about the purges.

R. F. HAMILTON, *Who Voted for Hitler?* (1982). An important examination of voting patterns.

E. C. HELMREICH, *The German Churches under Hitler: Background, Struggle, and Epilogue* (1979). A useful study.

J. JACKSON, *The Politics of Depression in France, 1932–1936* (1985). A detailed examination of the political struggles prior to the Popular Front.

J. JACKSON, *The Popular Front in France: Defending Democracy, 1934–1938* (1988). An extensive treatment.

I. KERSHAW, *Hitler*, 2 vols. (2000). The best biography now available.

I. KERSHAW, *The Nazi Dictatorship: Problems and Perspectives of Interpretation* (2000). A very accessible analysis.

C. KINDLEBERGER, *The World in Depression, 1929–1939* (1973). An account by a leading economist whose analysis is comprehensible to the layperson.

I. MUELLER, *Hitler's Justice: The Courts of the Third Reich* (1991). An account of how German courts cooperated with the Nazis.

D. J. K. PEUKERT, *Inside Nazi Germany: Conformity, Opposition, and Racism in Everyday Life* (1987). An excellent discussion of life under Nazi rule.

R. PROCTOR, *The Nazi War on Cancer* (2000). A fascinating study.

P. PULZER, *Jews and the German State: The Political History of a Minority, 1848–1933* (1992). A detailed study by a major historian of European minorities.

W. D. SMITH, *The Ideological Origins of Nazi Imperialism* (1986). A study that links Nazi expansionist thought to earlier German foreign policy.

R. SOUCY, *French Fascism: The Second Wave, 1933–1939* (1995). A study of the right-wing leagues.

J. STEPHENSON, *The Nazi Organization of Women* (1981). Examines the attitude and policies of the Nazis toward women.

H. A. TURNER, JR., *German Big Business and the Rise of Hitler* (1985). An important major study of the subject.

H. A. TURNER, JR., *Hitler's Thirty Days to Power* (1996). A narrative of the events leading directly to the Nazi seizure of power.

E. WEBER, *The Hollow Years: France in the 1930s* (1995). Examines France between the wars.

DOCUMENTS CD-ROM

SOCIETY AND CULTURE BETWEEN THE WARS

27.4 The Depression: Germany's Unemployed

TOTALITARIANISM

28.7 Stalin's First Five Year Plan
28.8 Leader of the NAZI Women's Organization

René Magritte, *The Human Condition*: Exploring Illusion and Reality

René Magritte's (1898–1967) *The Human Condition* (1933) seems to be just a picture of a painting, on an easel before a window. But look again. Why does Magritte's painting-within-a-painting match the landscape we can see through the window? Is that landscape also painted, or is the picture on the easel itself a kind of window? And what does this say about being human?

Such questions and enigmatic images are a trademark of Magritte's work. Although Magritte began as an abstract artist, from the mid-1920s until his death he worked in the eerily realist style exemplified by this painting. Magritte's work is "surreal"; it turns straightforward and "realistic" scenes into paradoxes of unresolved meaning. In this, he was influenced by non-artistic sources, from advertising to Sigmund Freud's *The Interpretation of Dreams*. In that work, Freud had argued dreams are a mechanism through which the human unconscious "speaks" desires and fears that are repressed in everyday conscious life. Like other surrealist artists, Magritte was fascinated by dreams. For him, they embody the "surreality" of everyday life.

This painting, as well as other surrealism of the period, indicates that even in the midst of the depression and the rise of authoritarian movements across the Continent, some artists retreated from the engagement with public life seen in the George Grosz painting of Chapter 27 and explored their own inner lives and fantasies. Such an approach to art was easier in western Europe, where unlike Weimar, the democracies were stable even if troubled.

The *Human Condition* could be a dream image. It could also illustrate the nature of dreaming itself: Just as in Magritte's painting, dreams confuse distinctions between image and reality, revealing truths about seemingly straightforward "real" life in the most fantastic forms. Magritte himself opposed any such direct interpretations of his work, however. Instead, he claimed to create "encounters" among diverse images and ideas. In this, he confronted a stumbling block of surrealist theory: For if dreams are a product of the unconscious, how can an artist make a conscious representation of them?

The Human Condition reflects the challenges to accepted scientific truths, from Freud's psychoanalysis to Einstein's general theory of relativity, that shook the intellectual life of the West in the early 1900s. In an era in which previously held absolutes seemed to be falling, Magritte saw uncertainty itself—what is real and what is illusion?—as the condition of being human.

Today, his speculations seem more relevant than ever: "virtual reality" is no longer just the concern of avant-garde artists.

■ *How did Freud's* The Interpretation of Dreams *influence Magritte's* The Human Condition? *Why did Magritte reject straightforward interpretations of his work? How does* The Human Condition *reflect challenges to accepted scientific truths?*

René Magritte (Belgian, 1898–1967), *The Human Condition* (*La Condition Humaine*), 1933. Oil on canvas, 1.000 × .810 × .016. © 2000 Board of Trustees, National Gallery of Art, Washington. Gift of the Collectors Committee. © 2002 C. Herscovici, Brussels/Artists Rights Society (ARS), New York.

PART 6

1939–2000

POLITICS AND GOVERNMENT	SOCIETY AND ECONOMY	RELIGION AND CULTURE

1939–1960

POLITICS AND GOVERNMENT

1939 World War II begins

Jewish children at Auschwitz, Poland

1941 Japan attacks Pearl Harbor, US enters war

1942 Battle of Stalingrad

1944 Normandy invasion

1945 Yalta Conference; Germany surrenders; atomic bombs dropped on Japan; Japan surrenders; United Nations founded

1946 Churchill gives Iron Curtain speech

1947 Truman Doctrine

1948 Communist takeover in Czechoslovakia and Hungary; State of Israel proclaimed

1948–1949 Berlin blockade

1949 NATO founded; East and West Germany emerge as separate states

1950–1953 Korean War

1953 Death of Stalin

1954 French defeat at Dien Bien Phu

1955 Warsaw Pact founded

1956 Khrushchev denounces Stalin; Polish Communist Party crisis; Suez crisis; Soviet invasion of Hungary

SOCIETY AND ECONOMY

1945–1951 Attlee ministry establishes the Welfare State in Great Britain

Churchill, Roosevelt, Stalin at Yalta

1947 Marshall Plan to rebuild Europe instituted

1949 Europe divided into Eastern and Western blocs

1950s and 1960s Increase in agricultural production

1957 European Economic Community founded

RELIGION AND CULTURE

1940 Koestler, *Darkness at Noon*

1942 Lewis, *The Screwtape Letters*

1943 Sartre, *Being and Nothingness*

1947 Camus, *The Plague*; Gramsci, *Letters from Prison*

1949 de Beauvoir, *The Second Sex*; Crossman, *The God That Failed*

1958 Pasternak forbidden to accept Nobel Prize for *Dr. Zhivago*; John XXIII becomes pope

GLOBAL CONFLICT, COLD WAR, AND NEW DIRECTIONS

	POLITICS AND GOVERNMENT	SOCIETY AND ECONOMY	RELIGION AND CULTURE
1960–1980	1960 Khrushchev aborts Paris summit	1960s Rapid growth of student population in universities; migration of workers from eastern and southern to northern and western Europe; migration of non-European workers to northern and western Europe	1960s The Beatles take world by storm
	1961 Berlin Wall erected		
	1962 Cuban Missile Crisis		
	1963 Test Ban Treaty		
	1963–1973 Major US involvement in Vietnam		
	1964–1982 Brezhnev era in Soviet Union		
	1967 Six Days' War between Israel and Arab states		
	1968 Soviet invasion of Czechoslovakia		

The Beatles

			1962–1965 Second Vatican Council
			1963 Solzhenitsyn, *One Day in the Life of Ivan Denisovich*; Robinson, *Honest to God*
	1973 Yom Kippur War between Israel and Egypt	1972 Club of Rome founded	1968 Student rebellion in Paris
	1975 Helsinki Accords	1973–1974 Arab oil embargo	1974 Solzhenitsyn expelled from Soviet Union
	1978 Camp David Accords; Solidarity founded in Poland		1978 John Paul II becomes pope
	1979–1988 Soviet troops in Afghanistan		
1980–2000	1981–1983 Martial law in Poland	1980s and 1990s Internal migration from Eastern to Western Europe; racial and ethnic tensions in Western Europe	
	1985 Gorbachev comes to power in the Soviet Union		1980s Growth of the environmental movement
	1989 Revolutions sweep across Eastern Europe		1990s Expanding influence of Roman Catholic Church in independent eastern Europe
	1990 German reunification; Yugoslavia breaks up		
	1991 Persian Gulf War; civil war in former Yugoslavia; August coup in Moscow; Gorbachev resigns; Soviet Union dissolved		1990s Feminists continue the critical tradition of Western culture
	1992–1999 Ascendancy of Yeltsin in Russia		1990s Era of the Internet opens
	1995 Bosnia recognized as independent		
	1997 Hong Kong returns to China		

Berlin Wall Opens, November, 1989

	1999 NATO military campaign against Serbia	1990s Changes in Eastern Europe and Soviet Union open way for economic growth and new trade relations across Europe	
	2000 Putin elected President of Russia		
	2001 U.S. attacked by terrorists		
	2003 U.S. invades Iraq		

Internet use explodes in China

In this vivid poster, the artist Ben Shahn (1898–1969) memorialized the destruction of Lidice. The Czechoslovakian town was obliterated by the Nazis on June 11, 1942, in vengeance for the resistance by Czechs against their Nazi rulers. The Granger Collection

CHAPTER 29

WORLD WAR II

THE MORE IDEALISTIC SURVIVORS OF World War I, especially in the United States and Great Britain, thought of it as "the war to end all wars" and a war "to make the world safe for democracy." Only thus could they justify the slaughter, expense, and upheaval of that terrible conflict. How appalled they would have been had they known that only twenty years after the peace treaties a second great war would break out, more global than the first. In this war, the democracies would be fighting for their lives against militaristic, nationalistic, authoritarian, and totalitarian states in Europe and Asia, and they would be allied with the communist Soviet Union in the struggle. The defeat of the militarists and dictators would not bring the peace they longed for, but the Cold War, in which the European states would become powers of the second class, subordinate to two new superpowers, partially or fully non-European: the Soviet Union and the United States.

KEY TOPICS

- The origins of World War II
- The course of the war
- Racism and the Holocaust
- The impact of the war on the people of Europe
- Relationships among the victorious allies and the preparations for peace

Again the Road to War (1933–1939)

World War I and the Versailles treaty had only a marginal relationship to the world depression of the 1930s. In Germany, however, where the reparations settlement had contributed to the vast inflation of 1923, economic and social discontent focused on the Versailles settlement as the cause of all ills. Throughout the late 1920s, Adolf Hitler and the Nazi Party had denounced Versailles as the source of all of Germany's troubles. The economic woes of the early 1930s seemed to bear them out. Nationalism and attention to the social question, along with party discipline, had been the sources of Nazi success. They continued to influence Hitler's foreign policy after he became chancellor in January 1933. Moreover, the Nazi destruction of the Weimar constitution and of political opposition meant that Hitler himself totally dominated German foreign policy. Consequently, it is important to know what his goals were and how he planned to achieve them.

HITLER'S GOALS

From the first expression of his goals in a book written in jail, *Mein Kampf (My Struggle)*, to his last days in the underground bunker in Berlin where he killed himself, Hitler's racial theories and goals were at the center of his thought. He meant to go far beyond Germany's 1914 boundaries, which were the limit of the vision of his predecessors. He meant to bring the entire German people—the *Volk*—understood as a racial group, together into a single nation.

The new Germany would include all the Germanic parts of the old Habsburg Empire, including Austria. This virile and growing nation would need more space to live, or **Lebensraum,** which would be taken from the Slavs, who, according to Nazi theory, were a lesser race, fit only for servitude. The new Germany would be purified by the removal of the Jews, another inferior race according to Nazi theory.

The plans required the conquest of Poland and Ukraine as the primary areas for the settlement of Germans and for the provision of badly needed food. Neither *Mein Kampf* nor later statements of policy were blueprints for action. Rather, Hitler was a brilliant improviser who exploited opportunities as they arose. He never lost sight of his goal, however, which would almost certainly require a major war. (See "Hitler Describes His Goals in Foreign Policy.")

Germany Rearms When Hitler came to power, Germany was far too weak to permit a direct approach toward reaching his aims. The first problem he set out to resolve was to shake off the fetters of Versailles and to make Germany a formidable military power. In October 1933, Germany withdrew from an international disarmament conference and also from the League of Nations. Hitler argued that because the other powers had not disarmed as they had promised, it was wrong to keep Germany helpless. These acts alarmed the French, but were merely symbolic. In January 1934, Germany signed a nonaggression pact with Poland that was of greater concern to France, for it undermined France's chief means of containing the Germans. At last, in March 1935, Hitler formally renounced the disarmament provisions of the Versailles treaty with the formation of a German air force, and soon he reinstated conscription, which aimed at an army of half a million men.

The League of Nations Fails Hitler's path was made easier by growing evidence that the League of Nations could not keep the peace and collective security was a myth. In September 1931, Japan occupied Manchuria, provoking an appeal to the League of Nations by China. The league responded by sending out a commission under a British diplomat, the earl of Lytton (1876–1951). The *Lytton Report* condemned the Japanese for resorting to force, but the powers were unwilling to impose sanctions. Japan withdrew from the league and kept control of Manchuria.

When Hitler announced his decision to rearm Germany, the league formally condemned that action, but it took no steps to prevent Germany's rearming. France and Britain opposed German rearmament, but they felt unable to object forcefully because they had not carried out their own promises to disarm. Instead, they met with Mussolini in June 1935 to form the so-called Stresa Front, promising to use force to maintain the status quo in Europe. This show of unity by the three powers was short lived, however. Britain, desperate to maintain superiority at sea, violated the spirit of the Stresa accords and sacrificed French security needs to make a separate

HITLER DESCRIBES HIS GOALS IN FOREIGN POLICY

From his early career, Hitler had certain long-term general views and goals. They were set forth in his Mein Kampf (My Struggle), *which appeared in 1925 and called for consolidation of the German* Volk *(people), more land for the Germans, and contempt for such "races" as Slavs and Jews. Here are some of Hitler's views about land.*

■ *What is the basic principle on which Hitler's policy is founded? How does he justify his plans for expansion? What reasons does he give for hostility to France and Russia? What is the basis for Hitler's claim of a right of every man to own farmland? Was that a practical goal for Germany in the 1930s? Was there any way for Hitler to achieve his goals without a major war?*

The National Socialist movement must strive to eliminate the disproportion between our population and our area—viewing this latter as a source of food as well as a basis for power politics—between our historical past and the hopelessness of our present impotence. . . .

The demand for restoration of the frontiers of 1914 is a political absurdity of such proportions and consequences as to make it seem a crime. Quite aside from the fact that the Reich's frontiers in 1914 were anything but logical. For in reality they were neither complete in the sense of embracing the people of German nationality, nor sensible with regard to geomilitary expediency. . . .

As opposed to this, we National Socialists must hold unflinchingly to our aim in foreign policy, namely, to secure for the German people the land and soil to which they are entitled on this earth. . . .

The soil on which some day German generations of peasants can beget powerful sons will sanction the investment of the sons of today, and will some day acquit the responsible statesmen of blood-guilt and sacrifice of the people, even if they are persecuted by their contemporaries. . . .

Much as all of us today recognize the necessity of a reckoning with France, it would remain ineffectual in the long run if it represented the whole of our aim in foreign policy. It can and will achieve meaning only if it offers the rear cover for an enlargement of our people's living space in Europe. . . .

If we speak of soil in Europe today, we can primarily have in mind only Russia and her vassal border states. . . .

See to it that the strength of our nation is founded, not on colonies, but on the soil of our European homeland. Never regard the Reich as secure unless for centuries to come it can give every scion of our people his own parcel of soil. Never forget that the most sacred right on this earth is a man's right to have earth to till with his own hands, and the most sacred sacrifice the blood that a man sheds for this earth.

Excerpts from *Mein Kampf* by Adolf Hitler, trans. by Ralph Manheim. Copyright © 1943, renewed 1971 by Houghton Mifflin Company, pp. 646, 649, 652, 653, 656. Reprinted by permission of Houghton Mifflin Co. All rights reserved.

naval agreement with Hitler. The pact allowed him to rebuild the German fleet to 35 percent of the British navy. Italy's expansionist ambitions in Africa soon brought it into conflict with the Western powers. Hitler had taken a major step toward his goal without provoking serious opposition.

ITALY ATTACKS ETHIOPIA

In October 1935, Mussolini, using a border incident as an excuse, attacked Ethiopia. This attack made the impotence of the League of Nations and the timidity of the Allies clear. Mussolini's purpose was to avenge a humiliating defeat that the Italians had suffered in Ethiopia in 1896, to begin the restoration of Roman imperial glory, and, perhaps, to distract Italian public opinion from domestic problems.

France and Britain were eager to appease Mussolini in order to offset the growing power of Germany. They were prepared to allow him the substance of conquest if he would only maintain Ethiopia's formal independence. For Mussolini, however, the form was more important than the substance. His attack outraged opinion in the West, and the French and British governments were forced to at least appear to resist.

The League of Nations condemned Italian aggression and, for the first time, voted economic sanctions. It imposed an arms embargo that limited loans and credits to, and imports from, Italy. Britain and France were afraid of alienating Mussolini, however, so they refused to embargo oil, the one economic sanction that could have prevented Italian victory. Even more important, the British fleet allowed Italian troops and munitions to use the Suez Canal. The results of this wavering policy were disastrous. The League of Nations and collective security were totally discredited, and Mussolini was alienated as well. He now turned to Germany, and by November 1, 1936, he could speak publicly of a Rome-Berlin **Axis.**

REMILITARIZATION OF THE RHINELAND

No less important a result of the Ethiopian affair was its effect on Hitler's evaluation of the strength and determination of the Western powers. On March 7, 1936, he took his greatest risk yet, sending a small armed force into the demilitarized Rhineland. This was a breach not only of the Versailles treaty, but of the Locarno Agreements of 1925 as well—agreements Germany had made voluntarily. It also removed a crucial element of French security. France and Britain had every right to resist, and the French especially had a claim to retain the only element of security left to them after the failure of the Allies to guarantee France's defense. Yet neither power did anything but register a feeble protest with the League of Nations. British opinion would not permit support for France, and the French would not act alone. They were paralyzed by internal division and by a military doctrine that concentrated on defense and shunned the offensive. Both countries were further weakened by a growing pacifism.

In retrospect, the Allies lost a great opportunity in the Rhineland to stop Hitler before he became a serious menace. The failure of his gamble, taken against the advice of his generals, might have led to his overthrow; at the least, it would have made German expansion to the east dangerous if not impossible. Nor is there much reason to doubt that the French army could easily have routed the tiny German force in the Rhineland. As the German general Alfred Jodl (1890–1946) said some years later, "The French covering army would have blown us to bits."[1]

A Germany that was rapidly rearming and had a defensible western frontier presented a completely new problem to the Western powers. Their response was the policy of **appeasement,** based on the assumption that Germany had real grievances and that Hitler's goals were limited and ultimately acceptable. They believed the correct policy was to negotiate and make concessions before a crisis could lead to war.

Behind this approach was the universal dread of another war. Memories of the horrors of the last war were still vivid, and the prospect of aerial bombardment made the thought of a new war even more terrifying. A firmer policy, moreover, would have required rapid rearmament. British leaders especially were reluctant to pursue this path because of the expense and the widespread belief that the arms race had been a major cause of the last war. As Germany armed, the French huddled behind their newly constructed defensive wall, the Maginot Line, and the British hoped for the best.

THE SPANISH CIVIL WAR

The new European alignment that found the Western democracies on one side and the fascist states on the other was made clearer by the Spanish Civil War, which broke out in July 1936. (See Map 29–1.) In 1931, the monarchy had collapsed, and Spain became a democratic republic. The new government followed a program of moderate reform that antagonized landowners, the Catholic Church, nationalists, and conservatives without satisfying the demands of peasants, workers, Catalán separatists, or radicals. Elections in February 1936 brought to power a Spanish Popular Front government ranging from republicans of the left to communists and anarchists. The losers, especially the Falangists, the Spanish fascists, would not accept defeat at the polls. In July, General Francisco Franco (1892–1975) led an army from Spanish Morocco against the republic.

Thus began the Spanish Civil War, which lasted almost three years, cost hundreds of thousands of lives, and provided a training ground for World War II. Germany and Italy supported Franco with troops, airplanes, and supplies. The Soviet Union sent equipment and advisers to the republicans. Liberals and leftists from Europe and America volunteered to fight in the republican ranks against fascism.

The civil war, fought on blatantly ideological lines, profoundly affected world politics. It brought Germany and Italy closer together, leading to the Rome-Berlin Axis Pact in 1936. Japan joined the Axis powers that year in the Anti-Comintern Pact, ostensibly directed against international communism, but really a new and powerful diplomatic alliance. Western Europe, especially France, had a

---

[1] Quoted in W. L. Shirer, *The Collapse of the Third Republic* (New York: Simon & Schuster, 1969), p. 281.

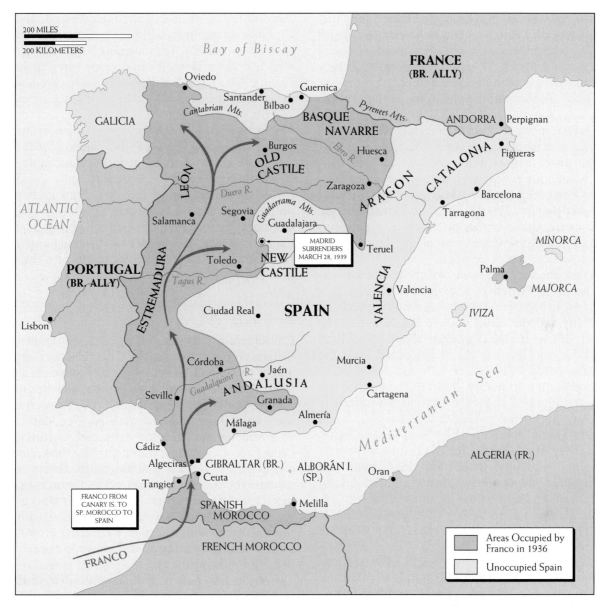

MAP 29–1 THE SPANISH CIVIL WAR, 1936–1939 *The purple area on the map shows the large portion of Spain quickly overrun by Franco's insurgent armies during the first year of the war. In the next two years, progress came more slowly for the fascists as the war became a kind of international rehearsal for the coming World War II. Madrid's fall to Franco in the spring of 1939 had been preceded by that of Barcelona a few weeks earlier.*

great interest in preventing Spain from falling into the hands of a fascist regime closely allied with Germany and Italy. Appeasement reigned, however. Although international law permitted the sale of weapons and munitions to the legitimate republican government, France and Britain forbade the export of war materials to either side, and the United States passed new neutrality legislation to the same end. When Barcelona fell to Franco early in 1939, the fascists had won effective control of Spain. (See "Art & the West: Picasso's *Guernica*," p. 1035.)

AUSTRIA AND CZECHOSLOVAKIA

Hitler made good use of his new friendship with Mussolini. He had always planned to annex his native Austria. In 1934, the Nazi Party in Austria assassinated the prime minister and tried to seize power. Mussolini had not yet allied with Hitler and was suspicious of German intentions. He quickly moved an army to the Austrian border, thus preventing German intervention and causing the coup to fail.

In 1938, the new diplomatic situation encouraged Hitler to try again. He perhaps hoped to achieve his goal by propaganda, bullying, and threats, but Austrian chancellor Kurt von Schuschnigg (1897–1977) refused to be intimidated. Schuschnigg announced a plebiscite for March 13, in which the Austrian people themselves could decide whether to unite with Germany. To forestall the plebiscite, Hitler sent his army into Austria on March 12. To his relief, Mussolini did not object, and Hitler rode to Vienna amid the cheers of his Austrian sympathizers.

The **Anschluss,** or union of Germany and Austria, was another clear violation of Versailles. The treaty, however, was now a dead letter, and the West remained passive. The *Anschluss* had great strategic significance, however, because Germany now surrounded Czechoslovakia, one of the bulwarks of French security, on three sides.

In fact, the very existence of Czechoslovakia was an affront to Hitler. It was democratic and pro-Western; it had been created partly as a check on Germany and was allied both to France and to the Soviet Union. It also contained about 3.5 million Germans who lived in the Sudetenland, near the German border. These Germans had belonged to the dominant nationality group in the old Austro-Hungarian Empire and resented their new minority position. Supported by Hitler and led by Konrad Henlein (1898–1945), the chief Nazi in Czechoslovakia, they made ever-increasing demands for privileges and autonomy within the Czech state. The Czechs made many concessions, but Hitler did not really want to improve the lot of the Sudeten Germans. He wanted to destroy Czechoslovakia. He told Henlein, "We must always demand so much that we can never be satisfied."[2]

As pressure mounted, the Czechs grew nervous. In May 1938, they received false rumors of an imminent attack by Germany and mobilized their army. The French, British, and Russians all warned they would support the Czechs. Hitler, who had not planned an attack at that time, was forced to publicly deny any designs on Czechoslovakia. The humiliation infuriated him, and he planned a military attack on the Czechs. The affair stiffened Czech resistance, but it frightened the French and British. The French, as had become the rule, deferred to British leadership. The British prime minister was Neville Chamberlain (1869–1940), a man committed to the policy of appeasement. He was determined not to allow Britain to go to war again. He pressed the Czechs to make concessions to Germany, but no concession was enough.

On September 12, 1938, Hitler made a provocative speech at the Nuremberg Nazi Party rally. His

rhetoric led to rioting in the Sudetenland, and the Czechs declared martial law. German intervention seemed imminent. Chamberlain, aged sixty-nine, who had never flown before, made three flights to Germany between September 15 and September 29 in an attempt to appease Hitler at Czech expense and thus to avoid war. At Hitler's mountain retreat, Berchtesgaden, on September 15, Chamberlain accepted the separation of the Sudetenland from Czechoslovakia. And he and the French premier, Edouard Daladier (1884–1970), forced the Czechs to agree by threatening to abandon them if they did not. A week later, Chamberlain flew yet again to Germany, only to find that Hitler had raised his demands. He wanted cession of the Sudetenland in three days and immediate occupation by the German army.

MUNICH

Chamberlain returned to England, and France and Britain prepared for war. At Chamberlain's request and at the last moment, Mussolini proposed a conference of Germany, Italy, France, and Britain. It met on September 29 at Munich. Hitler received almost everything he had demanded. (See Map 29–2.) The Sudetenland, the key to Czech security, became part of Germany, thus depriving the Czechs of any chance of self-defense. In return, Hitler agreed to spare the rest of Czechoslovakia. He promised, "I have no more territorial demands to make in Europe." Chamberlain returned to England with the Munich agreement and told a cheering crowd that he had brought "peace with honour. I believe it is peace for our time."

Even in the short run, the appeasement of Hitler at Munich was a failure. Czechoslovakia did not survive. Soon Poland and Hungary tore more territory from it, and the Slovaks demanded a state of their own. Finally, on March 15, 1939, Hitler broke his promise and occupied Prague, putting an end to the Czech state and to illusions that his only goal was to restore Germans to the Reich. Defenders of the appeasers have argued that their policy was justified because it bought valuable time in which the West could prepare for war. But that argument was not made by the appeasers themselves, who thought they were achieving peace, nor does the evidence support it.

If the French and the British had been willing to attack Germany from the west while the Czechs fought in their own defense, their efforts might have been successful. High officers in the German army were opposed to Hitler's risky policies and might have overthrown him. Even failing such developments, a war begun in October 1938 would have

---

[2]Quoted in Alan Bullock, *Hitler, a Study in Tyranny* (New York: Harper & Row, 1962), p. 443.

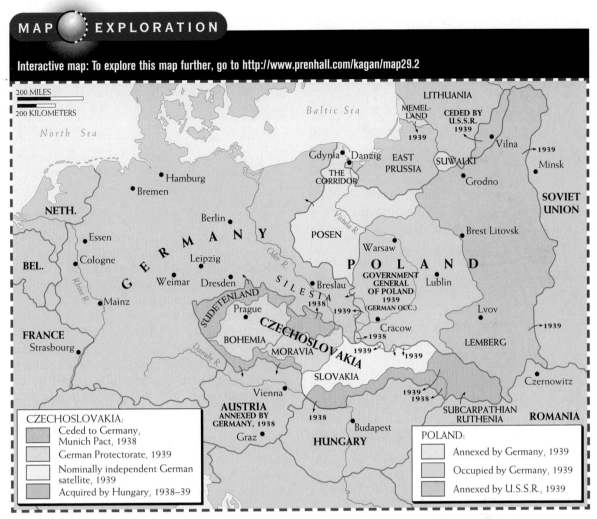

Interactive map: To explore this map further, go to http://www.prenhall.com/kagan/map29.2

MAP 29–2 PARTITIONS OF CZECHOSLOVAKIA AND POLAND, 1938–1939 *The immediate background of World War II is found in the complex international drama unfolding on Germany's eastern frontier in 1938 and 1939. Germany's expansion inevitably meant the victimization of Austria, Czechoslovakia, and Poland. With the failure of the Western powers' appeasement policy and the signing of a German-Soviet pact, the stage for the war was set.*

forced Hitler to fight without the friendly neutrality and material assistance of the Soviet Union—and without the resources of eastern Europe that became available to him as a result of appeasement and Soviet cooperation. If, moreover, the West ever had a chance of concluding an alliance with the Soviet Union against Hitler, the exclusion of the Russians from Munich and the appeasement policy helped destroy it. Munich remains an example of shortsighted policy that helped bring on war in disadvantageous circumstances because of the very fear of war and the failure to prepare for it. (See "Churchill's Response to Munich.")

Hitler's occupation of Prague discredited appeasement in the eyes of the British people. In the summer of 1939, a Gallup Poll showed that three-quarters of

the British public believed it worth a war to stop Hitler. Though Chamberlain himself had not lost all faith in his policy, he felt he had to respond to public opinion, and he responded to excess.

Poland was the next target of German expansion. In the spring of 1939, the Germans put pressure on Poland to restore the formerly German city of Danzig and to allow a railroad and a highway through the Polish Corridor to connect East Prussia with the rest of Germany. When the Poles would not yield, the usual propaganda campaign began, and the pressure mounted. On March 31, Chamberlain announced a Franco-British guarantee of Polish independence. Hitler appears to have expected to fight a war with Poland, but not with the Western allies, for he did not take their guarantee seriously.

As the front page of this British newspaper shows, there was general enthusiasm in Britain for the Munich agreement of September 1938. It did not last. Opinion turned decisively against appeasing Germany when Hitler occupied Prague in March 1939. Getty Images Inc.— Hulton Archive Photos

He had come to hold their leaders in contempt. He knew both countries were unprepared for war and that large segments of their populations were opposed to fighting for Poland.

Moreover, France and Britain had no means of getting effective help to the Poles. The French, still dominated by the defensive mentality of the Maginot Line, had no intention of attacking Germany. The only way to defend Poland was to bring Russia into the alliance against Hitler, but a Russian alliance posed many problems. Each side was profoundly suspicious of the other. The French and the British were hostile to communism, and since Stalin's purge of the Red Army, they were skeptical of the military value of a Russian alliance. Besides, the Russians could not help Poland without being given the right to enter Poland and Romania. Both nations, suspicious of Russian intentions—and with good reason—refused to grant these rights. As a result, Western negotiations for an alliance with Russia made little progress.

THE NAZI-SOVIET PACT

The Russians had at least equally good reason to hesitate. They resented being left out of the Munich agreement. They were annoyed by the low priority that the West gave to negotiations with Russia, compared with the urgency with which they dealt with Hitler. They feared, quite rightly, that the Western powers meant them to bear the burden of the war against Germany. As a result, they opened negotiations with Hitler, and on August 23, 1939, the world was shocked to learn of a Nazi-Soviet nonaggression pact.

The secret provisions of the pact, which were easily guessed and soon carried out, divided Poland between the two powers and allowed Russia to occupy the Baltic states and to take Bessarabia from Romania. The most bitter ideological enemies had become allies. Communist parties in the West changed their line overnight from the ardent advocacy of resistance to Hitler to a policy of peace and quiet. Ideology gave way to political and military reality. The West offered the Russians immediate danger without much prospect of gain. Hitler offered Stalin short-term gain without immediate danger. There could be little doubt about Stalin's decision.

The Nazi-Soviet pact sealed the fate of Poland, and the Franco-British commitment guaranteed a general war. On September 1, 1939, the Germans invaded Poland. Two days later, Britain and France declared war on Germany. World War II had begun.

World War II (1939–1945)

World War II has a better claim to its name than its predecessor, for it was truly global. Fighting took place in Europe and Asia, on the Atlantic and the Pacific Oceans, and in the Northern and Southern Hemispheres. The demand for the fullest exploitation of material and human resources for increased production, the use of blockades, and the intensive bombing of civilian targets made the war of 1939 even more "total"—that is, comprehensive and intense—than that of 1914.

THE GERMAN CONQUEST OF EUROPE

The German attack on Poland produced swift success. The new style of "lightning warfare," or **blitzkrieg,** employed fast-moving, massed armored columns supported by airpower. The Poles had no tanks and few planes, and their defense soon collapsed. The speed of the German victory astonished the Russians, who hastened to collect their share of the booty before Hitler could deprive them of it.

CHURCHILL'S RESPONSE TO MUNICH

In the parliamentary debate that followed the Munich conference at the end of September 1938, Winston Churchill was one of the few critics of what had been accomplished. In the following selections from his speech, he expresses his concerns.

■ *What was decided at Munich? Why were the representatives of Czechoslovakia not at the meeting? Why did Chamberlain think the meeting was successful? Munich was the high point of the policy called appeasement. How would its advocates defend this policy? Churchill was a leading opponent of appeasement. What are his objections to it?*

I will begin by saying what everybody would like to ignore or forget but which must nevertheless be stated, namely, that we have sustained a total and unmitigated defeat, and that France has suffered even more than we have. . . .

We really must not waste time after all this long debate upon the difference between the positions reached at Berchtesgaden, at Godesberg and at Munich. They can be very simply epitomized if the House will permit me to vary the metaphor. One pound was demanded at the pistol's point. When it was given, £2 were demanded at the pistol's point. Finally, the dictator consented to take £1 17s. 6d. and the rest in promises of good will for the future. . . .

All is over. Silent, mournful, abandoned, broken, Czechoslovakia recedes into the darkness. She has suffered in every respect by her association with the Western democracies and with the League of Nations, of which she has always been an obedient servant. . . .

We have been reduced in those five years from a position of security so overwhelming and so unchallengeable that we never cared to think about it. We have been reduced from a position where the very word "war" was considered one which could be used only by persons qualifying for a lunatic asylum. We have been reduced from a position of safety and power—power to do good, power to be generous to a beaten foe, power to make terms with Germany, power to give her proper redress for her grievances, power to stop her arming if we chose, power to take any step in strength or mercy or justice which we thought right—reduced in five years from a position safe and unchallenged to where we stand now. . . .

The responsibility must rest with those who have had the undisputed control of our political affairs. They neither prevented Germany from rearming, nor did they rearm ourselves in time. They quarreled with Italy without saving Ethiopia. They exploited and discredited the vast institution of the League of Nations and they neglected to make alliances and combinations which might have repaired previous errors, and thus they left us in the hour of trial without adequate national defense or effective international security. . . .

We are in the presence of a disaster of the first magnitude which has befallen Great Britain and France. Do not let us blind ourselves to that. It must now be accepted that all the countries of Central and Eastern Europe will make the best terms they can with the triumphant Nazi power. The system of alliances in Central Europe upon which France has relied for her safety has been swept away, and I can see no means by which it can be reconstituted. The road down the Danube Valley to the Black Sea, the road which leads as far as Turkey, has been opened.

From Winston S. Churchill, *Blood, Sweat, and Tears* (New York: G. P. Putnam's Sons, 1941), pp. 55–56, 58, 60–61. Reproduced with permission of Curtis Brown Ltd., on behalf of the Estate of Sir Winston S. Churchill. Copyright Winston S. Churchill.

On September 17, Russia invaded Poland from the east, dividing the country with the Germans. Stalin then forced the encircled Baltic countries to allow the Red Army to occupy them. By 1940, Estonia, Latvia, and Lithuania had become puppet republics within the Union of Soviet Socialist Republics (USSR), or the Soviet Union. In June 1940, the Russians forced Romania to cede Bessarabia. In November 1939, the Russians invaded Finland, but the Finns resisted fiercely for six months. Although they were finally worn down and compelled to yield territory and bases to Russia, the Finns remained independent. Russian expansionism and the poor performance of the Red Army in

---
The Coming of World War II
· · · · · · · · · · · · · · · · · · · ·

1919 (June)	The Versailles treaty
1923 (January)	France occupies the Ruhr
1925 (October)	The Locarno Agreements
1931 (Spring)	Onset of the Great Depression in Europe
1931 (September)	Japan occupies Manchuria
1933 (January)	Hitler comes to power
1933 (October)	Germany withdraws from the League of Nations
1935 (March)	Hitler renounces disarmament, starts an air force, and begins conscription
1935 (October)	Mussolini attacks Ethiopia
1936 (March)	Germany reoccupies and remilitarizes the Rhineland
1936 (July)	Outbreak of the Spanish Civil War
1936 (October)	Formation of the Rome-Berlin Axis
1938 (March)	*Anschluss* with Austria
1938 (September)	The Munich conference and the partition of Czechoslovakia
1939 (March)	Hitler occupies Prague; France and Great Britain guarantee Polish independence
1939 (August)	The Nazi-Soviet pact
1939 (September 1)	Germany invades Poland
1939 (September 3)	Britain and France declare war on Germany

Finland may well have encouraged Hitler to invade the Soviet Union in June 1941, just twenty-two months after the 1939 treaty.

Until the spring of 1940, the western front was quiet. The French remained behind the Maginot Line while Hitler and Stalin swallowed Poland and the Baltic states. Britain rearmed hastily, and the British navy blockaded Germany. Cynics in the West called it the phony war, or *Sitzkrieg*, but Hitler shattered the stillness in the spring of 1940. In April, without warning and with swift success, the Germans invaded Denmark and Norway. Hitler's northern front was secure, and he now had both air and naval bases closer to Britain. A month later, a combined land and air attack struck Belgium, the Netherlands, and Luxembourg. German airpower and armored divisions were irresistible. The Dutch surrendered in a few days; the Belgians, though aided by the French and the British, gave up less than two weeks later.

The British and French armies in Belgium were forced to flee to the English Channel to seek escape on the beaches of Dunkirk. The heroic efforts of hundreds of Britons manning small boats saved more than 200,000 British and 100,000 French soldiers. Casualties, however, were high, and valuable equipment was abandoned.

The Maginot Line ran from Switzerland to the Belgian frontier. Until 1936, the French had expected the Belgians to continue the fortifications along their German border. After Hitler remilitarized the Rhineland without opposition, the Belgians lost faith in their French alliance and proclaimed their neutrality, leaving the Maginot Line exposed on its left flank. Hitler's swift advance through Belgium therefore circumvented France's main line of defense.

The French army, poorly and hesitantly led by aged generals who did not understand how to use tanks and planes, collapsed. Mussolini, eager to claim the spoils of victory when it was clearly safe to do so, invaded southern France on June 10. Less than a week later, the new French government, under the ancient hero of Verdun, Marshal Henri Philippe Pétain (1856–1951), asked for an armistice. In two months Hitler had accomplished what Germany had failed to achieve in four years of bitter fighting in the previous war.

THE BATTLE OF BRITAIN

The fall of France left Britain isolated, and Hitler expected the British to come to terms. He was prepared to allow Britain to retain its empire in return for a free hand for Germany on the Continent. The British had never been willing to accept such an arrangement and had fought the long and difficult war against Napoleon to prevent the domination of the Continent by a single power. If there was any chance the British would consider such terms, it disappeared when Winston Churchill (1874–1965) replaced Chamberlain as prime minister in May 1940.

Churchill had been an early and forceful critic of Hitler, the Nazis, and the policy of appeasement. He was a descendant and biographer of the duke of Marlborough (1650–1722), who had fought to prevent the domination of Europe by Louis XIV in the eighteenth century. Churchill's sense of history, his feeling for British greatness, and his hatred of tyranny and love of freedom made him reject any thought of compromise with Hitler. His skill as a speaker and a writer enabled him to inspire the British people with his own courage and determination and to undertake what seemed a hopeless fight. Hitler and his allies, including the Soviet Union, controlled all of Europe. Japan was having its way in Asia. The United States was neutral, dominated by isolationist sentiment, and determined to avoid involvement outside the Western Hemisphere.

One of Churchill's greatest achievements was establishing a close relationship with the American president Franklin D. Roosevelt (1882–1945). Roosevelt found ways to help the British despite strong political opposition. In 1940 and 1941, before the United States was at war, America sent military supplies, traded badly needed warships for leases on British naval bases, and even convoyed ships across the Atlantic to help the British survive.

As weeks passed and Britain remained defiant, Hitler was forced to contemplate an invasion, and that required control of the air. The first strikes by the German air force (**Luftwaffe**), directed against the airfields and fighter planes in southeastern England, began in August 1940. If these attacks had continued, Germany might soon have gained control of the air and, with it, the chance of a successful invasion.

In early September, however, seeking revenge for some British bombing raids on German cities, the Luftwaffe switched its main attacks to London. For two months, London was bombed every night. Much of the city was destroyed and about 15,000 people were killed. The theories of victory through airpower alone, however, proved false. Casualties were much less than expected, and morale was not shattered. In fact, the bombings united the British people and made them more resolute.

The Royal Air Force (RAF) inflicted heavy losses on the Luftwaffe. Aided by the newly developed radar and an excellent system of communications, the British Spitfire and Hurricane fighter planes destroyed more than twice as many enemy planes as were lost by the RAF. Hitler had lost the Battle of Britain in the air and was forced to abandon his plans for invasion.

THE GERMAN ATTACK ON RUSSIA

The defeat of Russia and the conquest of the Ukraine to provide *Lebensraum,* or "living space," for the German people had always been a major goal for Hitler. Even before the assault on Britain, he had informed his staff of his intention to attack Russia as soon as conditions were favorable. In December 1940, even while the bombing of England continued, he ordered his generals to prepare for an invasion of Russia by May 15, 1941. (See Map 29–3.) He apparently thought a blitzkrieg victory in the east would also destroy any further British hope of resistance.

Operation Barbarossa, the code name for the invasion of Russia, was aimed at destroying Russia before winter could set in. Success depended in part on

Adolf Hitler made his only visit to Paris on June 16, 1940, three days after his troops occupied the city. Hitler, who considered himself an artist, was accompanied by his architect Albert Speer (left) and his favorite sculptor Arno Bekker (right). Getty Images Inc.—Hulton Archive Photos

an early start, but here Hitler's Italian alliance proved costly. Mussolini was jealous of Hitler's success and annoyed by the treatment he had received from the German dictator. His invasion of France was a fiasco, even though the main French forces were being simultaneously crushed by the Germans. Hitler did not allow Mussolini to annex French territory in Europe or North Africa. Mussolini instead launched an attack against the British in Egypt and drove them back some sixty miles. Encouraged by this success, he also invaded Greece from his base in Albania (which he had seized in 1939). His purpose was revealed by his remark to his son-in-law, Count Ciano: "Hitler always faces me with a fait accompli. This time I am going to pay him back in his own coin. He will find out in the newspapers that I have occupied Greece."[3]

In North Africa, however, the British counterattacked and drove the Italians back into Libya. The

[3]Quoted in Gordon Wright, *The Ordeal of Total War, 1939–1945* (New York: Harper & Row, 1968), pp. 35–36.

In August 1941 President Franklin Roosevelt and Prime Minister Winston Churchill met at sea and agreed on a broad program of liberal peace aims, called the Atlantic Charter, in the spirit of Woodrow Wilson's Fourteen Points.   The Granger Collection

Greeks themselves pushed into Albania. In March 1941, the British sent help to the Greeks, and Hitler was forced to divert his attention to the Balkans and Africa. General Erwin Rommel (1891–1944), later to earn the title of "Desert Fox," went to Africa and soon drove the British out of Libya and back into Egypt. In the Balkans, the German army swiftly occupied Yugoslavia and crushed Greek resistance. The price, however, was a delay of six weeks. The diversion caused by Mussolini's vanity proved to be costly the following winter in the Russian campaign.

Operation Barbarossa was launched against Russia on June 22, 1941, and it almost succeeded. Despite their deep suspicion of Germany (and the excuse later offered by apologists for the Soviet Union that the Nazi-Soviet pact was meant to give Russia time to prepare), the Russians were taken quite by surprise. Stalin appears to have panicked. He had not fortified his frontier, nor did he order his troops to withdraw when attacked. In the first two days, 2,000 Russian planes were destroyed on the ground. By November, Hitler had gone further into Russia than Napoleon. The German army stood at the gates of Leningrad, on the outskirts of Moscow, and on the Don River. Of the 4.5 million troops with which the Russians had begun the fighting, they had lost 2.5 million; of their 15,000 tanks, only 700 were left. Moscow was in panic, and a German victory seemed imminent.

Yet the Germans could not deliver the final blow. In August, they delayed their advance while Hitler decided strategy. The German general staff wanted to drive directly for Moscow and take it before winter. This plan probably would have brought victory.

Unlike its status in Napoleon's time, Moscow was the hub of the Russian system of transportation. Hitler, however, diverted a significant part of his forces to the south. By the time he was ready to return to the offensive near Moscow, it was too late. Winter devastated the German army, which was neither dressed nor equipped to face it.

Given precious time, Stalin restored order and built defenses for the city. Even more important, troops arrived from Siberia, where they had been placed to check a possible Japanese attack. In November and December, the Russians counterattacked. The blitzkrieg had turned into a war of attrition, and the Germans began to have nightmares of duplicating Napoleon's retreat.

HITLER'S PLANS FOR EUROPE

Hitler often spoke of the "new order" that he meant to impose after he had established his **Third Reich** (Empire) throughout Europe. The first two German empires were those of Charlemagne in the ninth century and Bismarck in the nineteenth. Hitler predicted that his own would last for a thousand years. If his organization of Germany before the war is a proper guide, he had no single plan of government, but relied frequently on intuition and pragmatism. His organization of conquered Europe had the same patchwork characteristics. Some conquered territory was annexed to Germany, some was not annexed, but administered directly by German officials, and other lands were nominally autonomous, but ruled by puppet governments.

Hitler's regime was probably unmatched in history for carefully planned terror and inhumanity. His plan of giving *Lebensraum* to the Germans was to be accomplished at the expense of people he deemed inferior. Hitler established colonies of Germans in parts of Poland, driving the local people from their land and employing them as cheap labor. He had similar plans on an even greater scale for Russia. The Russians would be driven eastward to central Asia and Siberia; they would be kept in check by frontier colonies of German war veterans. European Russia would be settled by Germans.

Hitler's long-range plans included germanization as well as colonization. In lands inhabited by people racially akin to the Germans, like the Scandinavian countries, the Netherlands, and Switzerland, the natives would be absorbed into the German nation. Such peoples would be reeducated and purged of dissenting elements, but there would be little or no colonization. Hitler even had plans, only slightly realized, of adopting selected people from the lesser races into the master race. One of these plans involved bringing half a million Ukrainian girls

MAP 29–3 AXIS EUROPE, 1941   *On the eve of the German invasion of the Soviet Union, the Germany-Italy Axis bestrode most of western Europe by annexation, occupation, or alliance—from Norway and Finland in the north to Greece in the south and from Poland to France. Britain, the Soviets, a number of insurgent groups, and, finally, America, had before them the long struggle of conquering this Axis "fortress Europe."*

into Germany as servants and finding German husbands for them; about 15,000 were actually sent to Germany.

Hitler regarded the conquered lands as a source of plunder. From eastern Europe, he removed everything useful, including entire industries. In Russia and Poland, the Germans simply confiscated the land itself. In the West, the conquered countries were forced to support the occupying army at a rate several times above the real cost. The Germans used the profits to buy up everything desirable, stripping the conquered peoples of most necessities. The Nazis were frank about their policies. One of Hitler's high officials said, "Whether nations live in prosperity or starve to death interests me only insofar as we need them as slaves for our culture."[4]

[4]Quoted in Wright, p. 117.

JAPAN AND THE UNITED STATES ENTER THE WAR

The American government was very pro-British. The various forms of assistance that Roosevelt gave Britain would have justified a German declaration of war. Hitler, however, held back. The U.S. government might not have overcome isolationist sentiment and entered the war in the Atlantic if war had not been thrust on America in the Pacific.

Since the Japanese conquest of Manchuria in 1931, American policy toward Japan had been suspicious and unfriendly. The outbreak of the war in Europe emboldened the Japanese to accelerate their drive to dominate Asia. They allied themselves with Germany and Italy, made a treaty of neutrality with the Soviet Union, and penetrated Indochina at the expense of defeated France. They also continued their war in China and planned to gain control of Malaya and the East Indies at the expense of beleaguered Britain and the conquered Netherlands. The only barrier to Japanese expansion was the United States.

The Americans had temporized, unwilling to cut off vital supplies of oil and other materials for fear of provoking a Japanese attack on Southeast Asia and Indonesia. The Japanese occupation of Indochina in July 1941 changed that policy, which had already begun to stiffen. The United States froze Japanese assets and cut off oil supplies; the British and Dutch did the same. Japanese plans for expansion could not continue without the conquest of the Indonesian oil fields and Malayan rubber and tin.

In October, a war faction led by General Hideki Tojo (1885–1948) took power in Japan and decided to risk a war rather than yield. On Sunday morning, December 7, 1941, while Japanese representatives were discussing a settlement in Washington, Japan launched an air attack on Pearl Harbor, Hawaii, the chief American naval base in the Pacific. The technique was similar to the one Japan had used against the Russian fleet at Port Arthur in 1904, and it caught the Americans equally by surprise. Much of the American fleet and many airplanes were destroyed; the American capacity to wage war in the Pacific was negated for the time being. The next day, the United States and Britain declared war on Japan. Three days later, Germany and Italy declared war on the United States.

THE TIDE TURNS

The potential power of the United States was enormous, but America was ill prepared for war. Though conscription had been introduced in 1940, the army was tiny, inexperienced, and poorly supplied. American industry was not ready for war. The Japanese swiftly captured Guam, Wake Island, and the Philippine Islands. Also, they attacked Hong Kong, Malaya, Burma, and the Dutch East Indies. By the spring of 1942, they controlled these places and the Southwest Pacific as far as New Guinea. They were poised for an attack on Australia, and it seemed that nothing could stop them.

In 1942, the Germans also advanced deeper into Russia and almost reached the Caspian Sea in their drive for Russia's oil fields. In Africa, too, Axis fortunes were high. Rommel drove the British back into Egypt toward the Suez Canal until he was stopped at El Alamein, only seventy miles from Alexandria. Relations between the democracies and their Soviet ally were not close. German submarine warfare was threatening British supplies. The Allies were being thrown back on every front, and the future looked bleak.

The first good news for the Allied cause in the Pacific came in the spring of 1942. A naval battle in the Coral Sea sank many Japanese ships and gave security to Australia. A month later, the United States defeated the Japanese in a fierce air and naval battle off Midway Island; they thus blunted the chance of another assault on Hawaii and did enough damage to halt the Japanese advance. Soon American marines landed on Guadalcanal in the Solomon Islands and began to reverse the momentum of the war. The war in the Pacific was far from over, but the check to Japan allowed the Allies to concentrate their efforts on Europe.

More than twenty nations located all over the world were opposed to the Axis powers. The main combatants, however, were Great Britain, the Soviet Union, and the United States. The two Western democracies cooperated to an unprecedented degree, but suspicion between them and the Soviet Union continued. The Russians accepted all the aid they could get. Nevertheless, they did not trust their allies, complained of inadequate help, and demanded that the democracies open a "second front" on the mainland of Europe.

In 1942, American preparation and production were inadequate for an invasion of Europe. German submarines made the Atlantic unsafe for crossing by the vast numbers of troops needed for such an invasion. Not until 1944 were conditions right for the invasion, but in the meantime other developments forecast the doom of the Axis. (See "Encountering the Past: Rosie the Riveter and American Women in the War Effort.")

Allied Landings in Africa, Sicily, and Italy In November 1942, an Allied force landed in French North Africa. (See Map 29–4.) Even before that

The successful Japanese attack on the American base at Pearl Harbor in Hawaii on December 7, 1941, together with simultaneous attacks on other Pacific bases, brought the United States into war against the Axis powers. This picture shows the battleships USS West Virginia *and USS* Tennessee *in flames as a small boat rescues a man from the water.* U.S. Army Photograph

landing, after stopping Rommel at El Alamein, British field marshal Bernard Montgomery (1887–1976) had begun a drive to the west. Now, the American general Dwight D. Eisenhower (1890–1969) pushed eastward through Morocco and Algeria. The two armies caught the German army between them in Tunisia and crushed it. The Allies now controlled the Mediterranean and could attack southern Europe.

In July and August 1943, the Allies took Sicily. Mussolini was driven from power, but the Germans occupied Italy. The Allies landed in Italy, and Marshal Pietro Badoglio (1871–1956), the leader of the new Italian government, went over to their side, declaring war on Germany. Churchill had spoken of Italy as the "soft underbelly" of the Axis, but the

Germans there resisted fiercely. Still, the need to defend Italy diverted the Germans' energy and resources and left them vulnerable on other fronts.

Battle of Stalingrad The Russian campaign became especially demanding. In the summer of 1942, the Germans resumed the offensive on all fronts, but were unable to get far except in the south. (See Map 29–5.) Their goal was the oil fields near the Caspian Sea. Stalingrad, on the Volga, was a key point on the flank of the German army in the south. Hitler was determined to take the city and Stalin was equally determined to hold it. The Battle of Stalingrad raged for months with unexampled ferocity. The Russians lost more men in this one battle than the Americans lost in combat during the entire

Rosie the Riveter and American Women in the War Effort

The withdrawal of millions of men from the work force and their induction into the armed forces created a demand for new workers, especially in the burgeoning defense industries. In part, it was filled by millions of women leaving the home to enter the labor force, some of them taking jobs in defense plants doing work usually done only by men. Economic pressures caused by the Great Depression of the 1930s had already brought many more women into the work force than had been common before. Most came from poor families and worked in white-collar jobs to support themselves or to help their families eke out a living. Even so, the heavy burden of housework and the widespread hostility to the idea of women working outside the home kept the vast majority of women at home.

America's entry into the war changed things quickly. The need for vast amounts of equipment to wage the war called for and attracted new groups to seek work in the many enlarged and newly created factories. African Americans from the south came to northern and western cities to seek well-paying jobs, and women, too, came forward in greater numbers than ever before. Prejudices of various kinds had kept them from many opportunities, but the needs of war overcame such prejudice. In October 1942, President Roosevelt made the new situation clear: "In some communities employers dislike to hire women. In others they are reluctant to hire Negroes. We can no longer afford to indulge such prejudice."

Many women already working moved over to jobs in the defense industries; others entered the work force for the first time, lured less by wages than by patriotism. Their brothers and boyfriends were risking their lives for their country and its ideals of freedom and democracy. They were eager to do their part to support them, to be, in the words of a current song, the woman "behind the man behind the gun." Another popular song, "Rosie the Riveter," told of a young woman working in an aircraft factory to provide protection for her boyfriend in the Marines.

Rosie came to be one of the best known symbols of the war effort when she appeared on the cover of the *Saturday Evening Post* as depicted in a painting by Norman Rockwell. With her rivet gun on her lap she stamps on a copy of Hitler's *Mein Kampf*, the hated symbol of the enemy's evil.

■ *How did the war change women's place in American society? What forces did it need to overcome?*

Rosie the Riveter was one of the best known symbols of the U.S. war effort in World War II. The Norman Rockwell Family Trust

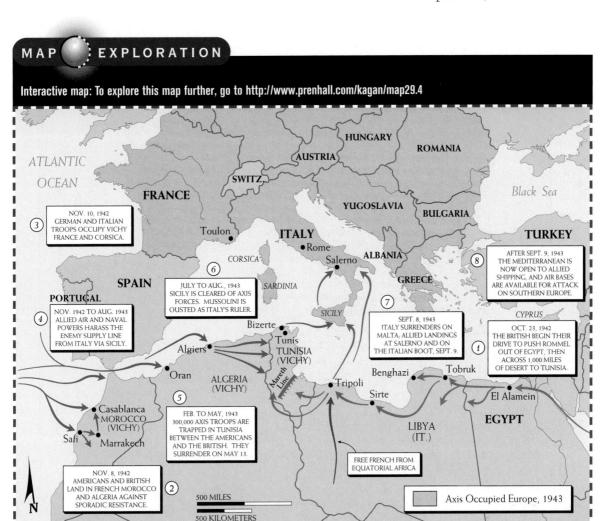

MAP 29–4   NORTH AFRICAN CAMPAIGNS, 1942–1945   *Control of North Africa would give the Allies access to Europe from the south. The map illustrates this theater of the war from Morocco to Egypt and the Suez Canal.*

war, but their heroic defense prevailed. Because Hitler again overruled his generals and would not allow a retreat, an entire German army was lost at Stalingrad.

Stalingrad marked the turning point of the Russian campaign. Thereafter, the Americans provided material help. Even more important, increased production from their own industry, which had been moved to or built up in the safety of the central and eastern regions of the USSR, allowed the Russians to gain and keep the offensive. As the Germans' resources dwindled, the Russians inexorably advanced westward.

Strategic Bombing   In 1943, the Allies also gained ground in production and logistics. The industrial might of the United States began to come into full force, and new technology and tactics greatly reduced the submarine menace.

In the same year, the American and British air forces began a series of massive bombardments of Germany by night and day. The Americans were more committed to the theory of "precision bombing" of military and industrial targets vital to the enemy war effort, so they flew the day missions. The British considered precision bombing impossible and therefore useless. They preferred indiscriminate "area bombing," aimed at destroying the morale of the German people; this kind of bombing could be done at night. Neither kind of bombing had much effect on the war until 1944, when the Americans introduced long-range fighters that could protect the bombers and allow accurate missions by day.

By 1945, the Allies had virtually cleared the skies of German planes and could bomb at will. Concentrated attacks on industrial targets, especially communication centers and oil refineries, did

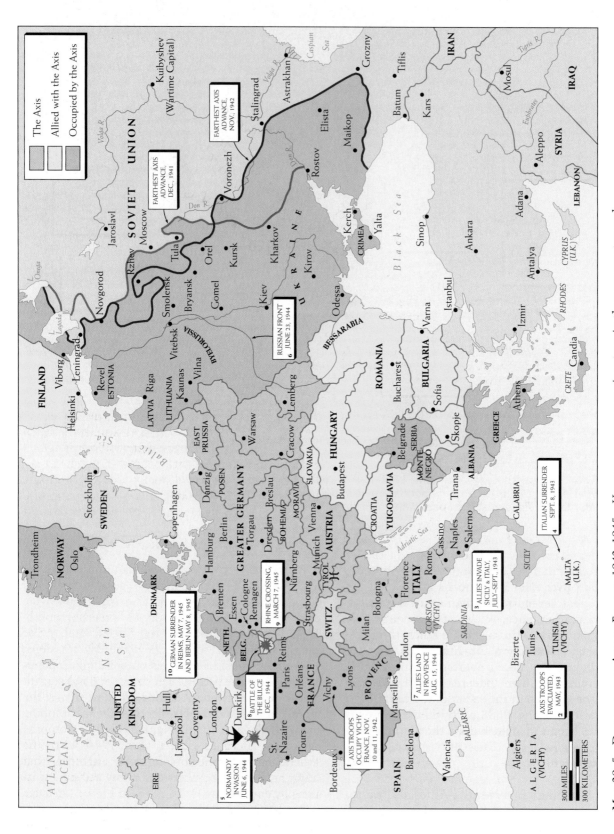

MAP 29–5 DEFEAT OF THE AXIS IN EUROPE, 1942–1945 *Here we see some major steps in the progress toward Allied victory against Axis Europe. From the south through Italy, the west through France, and the east through Russia, the Allies gradually conquered the Continent to bring the war in Europe to a close.*

In the battle of Stalingrad, Russian troops contested every street and building. Although the city was all but destroyed in the fighting and Russian casualties were enormous, the German army in the east never recovered from the defeat it suffered there. Getty Images Inc.—Hulton Archive Photos

extensive damage and helped shorten the war. Terror bombing continued, too, with no useful result. The bombardment of Dresden in February 1945 was especially savage and destructive. It was much debated within the British government and has raised moral questions since. Whatever else it accomplished, the aerial war over Germany did take a heavy toll of the German air force and diverted vital German resources away from other military purposes.

THE DEFEAT OF NAZI GERMANY

On June 6, 1944 ("D-Day"), American, British, and Canadian troops landed in force on the coast of Normandy. The "second front" was opened. General Dwight D. Eisenhower, the commander of the Allied armies, faced a difficult problem. The European coast was heavily fortified. Amphibious assaults, moreover, are especially vulnerable to changes of wind and weather. Success depended on meticulous planning, advance preparation by heavy bombing, and feints to mask the point of attack. The German defense was strong, but the Allies were able to establish a beachhead and then break out of it. In mid-August, the Allies landed in southern France to put more pressure on the enemy. By the beginning of September, France had been liberated.

The Battle of the Bulge All went smoothly until December, when the Germans launched a counterattack in Belgium through the Ardennes Forest. Because the Germans were able to push forward into the Allied line, this was called the Battle of the Bulge. Although the Allies suffered heavy losses, the Bulge was the last gasp for the Germans in the

West. The Allies soon recovered their momentum and pushed eastward. They crossed the Rhine in March 1945, and German resistance rapidly crumbled. This time there could be no doubt the Germans had lost the war on the battlefield.

The Capture of Berlin In the East, the Russians swept forward no less swiftly, despite fierce German resistance. By March 1945, they were near Berlin. Because the Allies insisted on unconditional surrender, the Germans fought on until May. Hitler and his intimates committed suicide in an underground bunker in Berlin on May 1, 1945. The Russians occupied Berlin by agreement with their Western allies. The Third Reich had lasted a dozen years instead of the thousand predicted by Hitler.

FALL OF THE JAPANESE EMPIRE

The war in Europe ended on May 8, 1945, and by then, victory over Japan was also in sight. The original Japanese attack on the United States had been a calculated risk against the odds. Japan was inherently weaker than the United States. The longer the war lasted, the more American superiority in industrial production and population counted.

Americans Recapture the Pacific Islands In 1943, the American forces, still small in number, began a campaign of "island hopping." They did not try to recapture every Pacific island held by the Japanese, but selected major bases and strategic sites along the enemy supply line. (See Map 29–6.) Starting from the Solomon Islands, they moved northeast toward Japan itself. By June 1944, they had reached

Allied troops landed in Normandy on D-Day, June 6, 1944. This photograph, taken two days later, shows long lines of men and equipment moving inland from the beach to re-inforce the troops leading the invasion. Archive Photos

the Mariana Islands, usable as bases for bombing the Japanese in the Philippines, China, and Japan itself.

In October of the same year, the Americans recaptured most of the Philippines and drove the Japanese fleet back into its home waters. In 1945,

Russian soldiers hang the Soviet flag on the ruins of the Reichstag in Berlin. Yevgeeny Khaldei/Getty Images Inc./Hulton Archive Photos

Iwo Jima and Okinawa fell, despite a determined Japanese resistance that included kamikaze attacks, suicide missions in which specially trained pilots deliberately flew their explosive-filled planes into American warships. From these new bases, closer to Japan, the American bombers launched a terrible wave of bombings that destroyed Japanese industry and disabled the Japanese navy. Still the Japanese government, dominated by a military clique, refused to surrender.

Confronted with Japan's determination, the Americans made plans for a frontal assault on the Japanese homeland. They calculated it might cost a million American casualties and even greater losses for the Japanese. At this point, science and technology presented the Americans with another choice.

The Atomic Bomb Since early in the war, a secret program had been in progress. Its staff, made up in significant part of exiles from Hitler's Europe, was working to use atomic energy for military purposes. On August 6, 1945, an American plane dropped an

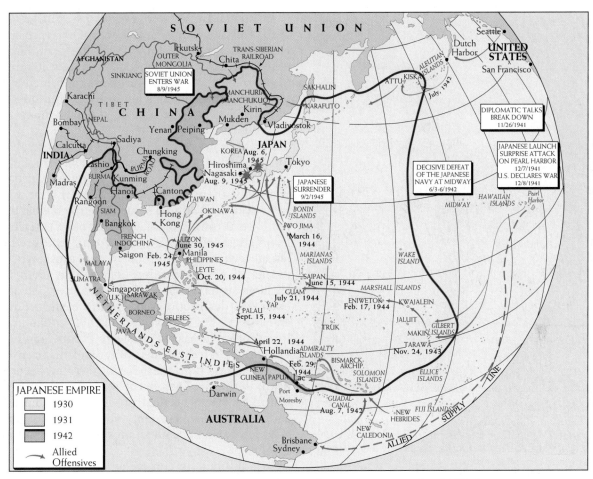

MAP 29–6 WORLD WAR II IN THE PACIFIC   *As in Europe, the Pacific war involved Allied recapture of areas that had been quickly taken earlier by the enemy. The enormous area represented by the map shows the initial expansion of Japanese holdings to cover half the Pacific and its islands, as well as huge sections of eastern Asia, and the long struggle to push the Japanese back to their homeland and defeat them by the summer of 1945.*

atomic bomb on the Japanese city of Hiroshima. The city was destroyed, and more than 70,000 of its 200,000 residents were killed. Two days later, the Soviet Union declared war on Japan and invaded Manchuria. The next day, a second atomic bomb fell, this time on Nagasaki. Even then, the Japanese cabinet was prepared to resist further, to face an invasion rather than give up.

The unprecedented intervention of Emperor Hirohito (r. 1926–1989) finally forced the government to surrender on August 14. Even then, the Japanese set forth the condition that Japan must keep its emperor. Although the Allies had continued to insist on unconditional surrender, President Harry S. Truman (1884–1972), who had come to office on April 12, 1945, on the death of Franklin D. Roosevelt, accepted the condition. Peace was formally signed aboard the USS *Missouri* in Tokyo Bay on September 2, 1945.

Revulsion and horror at the use of atomic bombs, as well as hindsight arising from the Cold War, have

made the decision to use the bomb against Japanese cities controversial. Some have suggested the bombings were unnecessary to win the war and their main purpose was to frighten the Russians into a more cooperative attitude after the war. Others have emphasized the bureaucratic, almost automatic nature of the decision, once it had been decided to develop the bomb. To the decision makers and their contemporaries, however, matters were simpler. The bomb was a way to end the war swiftly and save American lives. The decision to use it was conscious, not automatic, and required no ulterior motive.

THE COST OF WAR

World War II was the most terrible war in history. Military deaths are estimated at some 15 million, and at least as many civilians were killed. If deaths linked indirectly to the war, from disease, hunger, and other causes, are included, the number of victims

Three days after the U.S. dropped the first atomic bomb on Hiroshima, it exploded a second bomb over Nagasaki on August 9, 1945. Despite these terrible blows, Japan still did not surrender for another week. Archive Holdings, Inc./Getty Images, Inc.—Image Bank

might reach as high as 40 million. Most of Europe and significant parts of Asia were devastated. Yet the end of so terrible a war brought little opportunity for relaxation. The dawn of the atomic age and the dramatic end it brought to the war made people conscious that another major war might extinguish humanity. Everything depended on concluding a stable peace, but even as the fighting ended, conflicts among the victors made the prospects of a lasting peace doubtful.

Racism and the Holocaust

The most horrible aspect of the Nazi rule in Europe arose not from military or economic necessity but from the inhumanity and brutality inherent in Hitler's racial doctrines. These were applied to several groups of people in eastern Europe.

Hitler considered the Slavs *Untermenschen*, subhuman creatures like beasts who need not be treated as people. In parts of Poland, the upper and professional classes were entirely removed—jailed, deported, or killed. Schools and churches were closed. The Nazis limited marriage to keep down the Polish birthrate and imposed harsh living conditions.

In Russia, things were even worse. Hitler spoke of his Russian campaign as a war of extermination. Heinrich Himmler (1900–1945), head of Hitler's elite SS formations, planned to eliminate 30 million Slavs to make room for Germans; he formed extermination squads for this purpose. Six million Russian prisoners of war and deported civilians may have died under Nazi rule.

Hitler, however, had envisioned a special fate for the Jews. He meant to make all Europe *Judenrein*, or "free of Jews." For a time, he thought of sending them to the island of Madagascar. Later, he arrived at the "final solution of the Jewish problem"—extermination. The Nazis built extermination camps in Germany and Poland and used the latest technology to achieve the most efficient means of killing millions of men, women, and children simply because they were Jews. The most extensive destruction occurred in eastern Europe and Russia, but the Nazis and their collaborators in occupied areas of western Europe including France, the Netherlands, Italy, and Belgium also deported Jews from those nations to almost certain death in the east. Before the war was over, perhaps 6 million Jews had died in what has come to be called the **Holocaust.** Only about a million European Jews remained alive, most of them in pitiable condition.

It is difficult to comprehend the massive Nazi effort to eradicate the Jews of Europe. The implementation of this destruction took different forms in different regions of the Continent. To explore this central event of twentieth-century European history, we examine the fate of the Polish Jewish community, which before the Second World War was the largest in Europe, consisting of 10 percent of Poland's population.

THE DESTRUCTION OF THE POLISH JEWISH COMMUNITY

A large Jewish community had dwelled within Polish lands for centuries, often in a climate of religious and cultural anti-Semitism. As a result of that anti-Semitism, Polish Jews had long lived in their own villages and later in their own urban neighborhoods. After the late-eighteenth-century partitions of Poland and the Congress of Vienna, most of Poland came under Russian rule. Through the policy of Official Nationalism (see Chapter 21), the nineteenth-century tsars identified loyalty to their government with membership in the Russian Orthodox Church. Other Christian groups, such as Lutherans and Roman Catholics, were often treated with suspicion. Jews were treated worse and were subject to a wide variety of discriminatory legislation. Polish Jews did not experience any of the forms of Jewish emancipation that occurred in western Europe. (See Chapter 24.)

Discrimination against the Jews, if not outright persecution, persisted after Poland was restored after World War I. The new Polish government defined the nation in terms of Polish ethnic nationalism. This policy, no less than tsarist Russian Orthodoxy, defined Jews as outside the Polish nation.

Language, dress, and place of residence as well as religion distinguished Jews from the rest of the Polish population, almost all of whom were Roman Catholics. Hebrew was the Polish Jews' chief written language, and Yiddish their primary spoken language. Many Jews, particularly older ones, wore distinctive dress. They ate food different from that of most Poles. Many Polish Jews also moved to cities, and Jews were regarded as an urban people in a predominantly rural nation. Moreover, Jews were among the poorest people in Poland, often working as self-employed merchants, peddlers, and craftspeople, or in industries, such as textiles, clothing, and paper, that other Poles identified as Jewish dominated. Few Polish Jews belonged to trade unions. These conditions made them vulnerable during the economic turmoil of the 1920s and especially of the 1930s.

Major Campaigns and Events of World War II	
September 1939	Germany and the Soviet Union invade Poland
November 1939	The Soviet Union invades Finland
April 1940	Germany invades Denmark and Norway
May 1940	Germany invades Belgium, the Netherlands, Luxembourg, and France
June 1940	Fall of France
August 1940	Battle of Britain begins
June 1941	Germany invades the Soviet Union
July 1941	Japan takes Indochina
December 1941	Japan attacks Pearl Harbor; United States enters war against Axis powers
June 1942	Battle of Midway Island
November 1942	Battle of Stalingrad begins
July-August 1943	Allies take Sicily, land in Italy
June 1944	Allies land in Normandy
May 1945	Germany surrenders
August 1945	Atomic bombs dropped on Hiroshima and Nagasaki
September 1945	Japan formally surrenders

Initially the Nazis' murder of Jews in Eastern Europe was carried out by roving death squads. Here a German military policeman executes a Jewish mother and her child in eastern Poland in 1941. Yad Vashem Jerusalem

POLISH ANTI-SEMITISM BETWEEN THE WARS

During the interwar years, the Polish government, supported by spokesmen for the Polish Roman Catholic Church, pursued policies that were anti-Semitic. The Polish government nationalized the matches, salt, tobacco, and alcohol industries and then enacted legislation that discriminated against Jews in hiring for those government monopolies. Other laws made it difficult for Jews to observe the Sabbath while keeping their jobs. Regulations requiring businesses to be closed on Sunday meant Jewish shops had to close two days of the week. By the late 1930s, the government required businesses to display their owners' names prominently, which made it easy for people to avoid Jewish shops. Because Jews were excluded from the civil service, they moved into law and medicine, which provoked further resentment.

The path of assimilation into the larger culture that many European Jewish leaders had advocated during the nineteenth century hit a dead end in Poland because Poles generally refused to regard even secular, assimilated Jews as fellow Poles. Nonetheless, many Jews attempted to embrace the social practices, dress, and language of the Polish majority without actually expecting to be considered Polish. In this respect, they saw themselves as moving from a traditional style of life to a more modern and Polish one. Jewish newspapers and other magazines began to be published in Polish. The Polish constitution allowed Jews to participate in political life, but they were divided into different factions and were unable to agree on a single platform to defend Jewish life and culture in Poland. These divisions made the Jews of Poland all the more vulnerable when the Second World War broke out in 1939.

THE NAZI ASSAULT ON THE JEWS OF POLAND

The joint German-Soviet invasion of Poland brought millions of Jews under either German or Soviet authority. By conquering Poland, the Nazi government could carry out the destruction of Jewish communities to an extent far beyond anything possible in Germany itself. From the Nazi standpoint, the destruction of the Polish Jewish community held special importance. Polish Jewry was large and had produced many religious, cultural, and political leaders. It also constituted the single most important source for Jewish emigration beyond eastern Europe. For the Nazis, Poland was the chief breeding ground for world Jewry.

By late autumn of 1939, the Germans had begun to move against Polish Jews. The Nazi government first thought it might herd virtually all the Jews of occupied Europe into the Lublin region of Poland. By early 1940, the Nazis decided to move as many Jews as possible into ghettos, where they would be separated from the rest of the Polish population. The most famous of these ghettos were Lodz and Warsaw, each of which had populations of several hundred thousand. Jews from all over Poland and, eventually, other occupied regions were moved by rail into these ghettos, which were then sealed with police guards and walls. The ghettos were administered by Jewish councils, which were torn between responsibility to their communities and the necessity of responding to German orders. The personal property and businesses of the Jews who were herded into the ghettos were confiscated and sold. Jewish laborers were sent out of the ghettos to work as contract labor while their families remained in the ghettos. By 1941, the Polish Jews had lost their civic standing and property. They had been located in segregated communities within Poland where disease was rampant and the food supply meager. Approximately 20 percent of the population of both the Lodz and Warsaw ghettos died of disease and malnourishment. (See "Oskar Rosenfeld Describes the Food Supply in the Lodz Ghetto.")

The German invasion of the Soviet Union in June 1941 made the situation of Jews in Poland even worse. The advancing German forces killed tens of thousands of Jews in the Soviet Union during 1941 and hundreds of thousands more the next year. Bolsheviks and Jews became conflated in German thinking and propaganda. During the second half of 1941, the Nazi government decided to exterminate the Jews of Europe. From late 1941 through 1944, the Germans transported Jews from the ghettos by rail to death camps in Poland, including Kulmhof, Belzen, Sobibor, Treblinka, Birkenau, and Auschwitz. One or more of the camps were in operation from 1941 to 1944, with Auschwitz being the last closed. In those camps, Jews were systematically killed in gas chambers.

By 1945, approximately 90 percent of the pre-1939 Jewish population of Poland had been destroyed. The tiny minority of Polish Jews who had survived faced bitter anti-Semitism under the postwar Soviet-dominated government. Many immigrated to Israel, leaving only a few thousand Jews within the borders of a nation where they had numbered in the millions and where they had created a rich religious, cultural, and political community. The largest Jewish community in Europe had virtually ceased to exist.

OSKAR ROSENFELD DESCRIBES THE FOOD SUPPLY IN THE LODZ GHETTO

Tens of thousands of Jews were relocated to ghettos in Poland. These were cities sealed off from the rest of the world. Entrances and exits were closely guarded by the German Nazi occupiers. Maintaining the food supply was an enormous challenge for these communities of imprisonment. Oskar Rosenfeld, a professional journalist and one of the inhabitants of Lodz who, along with others, maintained a chronicle of the life of the ghetto, discussed the food supply in the early summer of 1943. Rosenfeld died in 1944, as did most of the people who had lived in the Lodz ghetto.

■ *Why would the cares of everyday life have seemed, as Rosenfeld asserts, more of a burden than the psychological burden of life in the ghetto? What steps had the inhabitants of the ghetto been required to take to look after their own food supply? Why were potatoes more important for nutrition than vegetables? How does this passage suggest what Rosenfeld terms "the nightmare of the ghetto"?*

In general, one can say that people have grown accustomed to living surrounded by barbed wire and tolerate that state as almost natural, as a thing ordained by fate. For, in comparison with the cares of everyday life, the constant psychic constraints seem less burdensome. . . .

Since the offices of food supply are unable to provide the 85,000 inhabitants of the ghetto with the fresh vegetables they need, the gardeners are required to surrender a portion of their produce to the population. . . . In the early morning hours one can see groups of people, with agricultural tools in their hands and on their shoulders, marching through the streets to till the soil—heading out to the vegetable gardens. . . . No such figures were to be seen previously, just as there were no vegetable and potato beds on the grounds of the ghetto. The ghetto has been reconstructed; and as a result, we are supplied with vegetables not only by the [German] Ghetto Administration, but also by our own soil. . . .

During this first week, the month of June was a good friend to the ghetto dwellers. It brought them the most precious food that can be wished for in the ghetto: potatoes. When the carts appeared in the streets—whether horse drawn or in handcarts—passersby halted and stared hopefully at the round fruits of the earth. What do the hungry care whether the potatoes are first or second quality as long as there are potatoes? . . . Suddenly, the potato shipments stopped. Potatoes were replaced by vegetables—spinach, lettuce, red beets, carrots, radishes—too little to fill empty stomachs. And since no more potatoes came in during the second half of June the allocated supplies had already been consumed, hunger and despair loomed in the horizon once again. The end of this month of June is reminiscent of last year's "starvation" June. . . .

The first truckloads of green vegetables are now rolling through the streets, causing renewed hope. Just hold out for a few more weeks, and then there will be potatoes again—the fresh young potatoes, not the sort of which half has to be thrown into the trash as unfit for consumption. This thought can be read on the face in the ghetto. . . . Ultimately, no one escapes the nightmare of the ghetto.

EXPLANATIONS OF THE HOLOCAUST

As interest in the Holocaust has grown since the 1960s, so has debate about its character and meaning. Was it a unique event of unprecedented and unparalleled evil, or was it one specific instance of a more general human wickedness that has found expression throughout history? Are its roots to be found in flaws in human nature as a whole, or are they unique to the experience of the West or, perhaps, to the German people? Some scholars point to the horrible mass murders committed in the twentieth century by communist regimes under Stalin in the Soviet Union and Mao in China, each of which killed many more people than did Hitler, as evidence of the more general character of the phenomenon. Others argue that the Holocaust was unique because

By 1942 the Nazis had begun to industrialize mass murder in death camps set up to exterminate Europe's Jews and others, such as gypsies, whom the Nazis considered racially inferior. These Polish Jews are being forced into a box car that will take them from the Cracow ghetto to one of these death camps where millions perished. United States Holocaust Museum

its goal was the annihilation of a whole people, from infants to the aged, just because of who they were. Some focus on the wickedness personified by Hitler, who was driven by his fixation on the myth of Jewish power and evil.

Perhaps we should think of the problem from the standpoint of two questions: Why were the Jews the main target of Hitler's policy of extermination? How was it possible to carry out such a vast mass murder? Surely, an essential part of an answer to the first question is the persistence of anti-Semitism in Christianity and Western culture, from the Church Fathers to Luther and to the teachings of churches in modern times. Some would combine this religious and historical anti-Semitism with the coming of the Enlightenment and the social sciences, which gave rise to pseudoscientific racial theories that lent a new twist to the old hatred of the Jews. Pseudoscientific racism appears to have been the most powerful influence on Hitler, but it could not have found widespread support without deeply rooted religious and social anti-Semitism.

For example, in at least one instance in Poland local Poles themselves turned against their Jewish neighbors in outbursts of localized anti-Semitic violence. In July 1941, in the town of Jedwabne, in northeastern Poland, non-Jewish townspeople killed approximately 1,600 Jewish inhabitants of the town. This horrendous incident clearly suggests that although most of the atrocities against the Jews were carried out by Nazis, there existed a climate of either indifference or outright support in parts of Poland as well as in other parts of Nazi-occupied Europe.

As to how it was possible to murder 6 million people, part of the answer must lie in the parochial nationalism that arose during and after the French Revolution. For many people, nationalism divided the world into one's fellow nationals and all others. It encouraged, excused, and even justified all sorts of terrible and violent acts performed on behalf of one's homeland. Another part of the answer may derive from the utopian visions also unleashed by some Enlightenment writers, who promised to achieve perfect societies through social engineering, regardless of the human cost. To this were added the scientific and technological advances that gave the modern state new power to command its people, to persuade them to obey by controlling the media of propaganda, and to enforce its will with efficient brutality. All of these permitted the creation of a totalitarian state that, for the first time in history, could conduct mass murder on the scale of the Holocaust. (See "An Observer Describes the Mass Murder of Jews in Ukraine.")

These questions and their possible answers are but suggestions meant to encourage further and deeper thought in what will surely be a continuing debate among scholars and the general public.

World War II was unmatched in cruelty in modern times. When Stalin's armies conquered Poland and entered Germany, they raped, pillaged, and deported millions to the east. The British and American bombing of Germany killed thousands of civilians, and the dropping of atomic bombs on Japan killed and maimed tens of thousands more. The bombings, however, were thought of as acts of war that would help defeat the enemy. Stalin's

Auschwitz in Poland was the most notorious Nazi death camp. Railway lines led up to its gates, so that trains could unload box cars of Jews into a future of almost certain death.   Getty Images Inc.—Hulton Archive Photos

atrocities were not widely known in the West at the time or even today.

The victorious Western allies were shocked by what they saw when they came on the Nazi extermination camps and their pitiful survivors. Little wonder it was that they were convinced the effort to resist the Nazis and all the pain it had cost were well worth it.

The Domestic Fronts

World War II represented an effort at total war by all the belligerents. Never in European or world history had so many men and women and so many resources been devoted to military effort. One result was the carnage that occurred on the battlefields, at sea, and in the air. Another was an unprecedented organization of civilians on the various home fronts. Each domestic effort and experience was different, but few escaped the impact of the conflict. Everywhere there were shortages, propaganda campaigns, and new political developments.

GERMANY: FROM APPARENT VICTORY TO DEFEAT

Hitler had expected to defeat all his enemies by a series of rapid strokes, or blitzkriegs. Such campaigns would have required little change in Germany's society and economy. During the first two years of the war, in fact, Hitler demanded few important sacrifices from the German people. Spending on domestic projects continued, and food was plentiful; the economy as a whole was not on a full wartime footing. Germany's failure to quickly overwhelm the Soviet Union changed everything.

Food could no longer be imported from the east in needed quantities, Germany had to mobilize for total war, and the government demanded major sacrifices from the people.

A great expansion of the army and of military production began in 1942. As minister for armaments and munitions, Albert Speer (1905–1981) directed the economy, and Germany met its military needs instead of making consumer goods. The government sought the cooperation of major German business enterprises to aid the growth of wartime production. Between 1942 and late 1944, the output of military products tripled; as the war went on, more men were drafted from industry into the army, and military production suffered.

As the manufacture of armaments replaced the production of consumer goods, shortages of everyday products became serious. Prices and wages were controlled, but the standard of living of German workers fell. Burdensome food rationing began in April 1942, and shortages were severe until the Nazi government seized more food from the occupied regions of Europe. To preserve their own home front, the Nazis passed on the suffering to their defeated neighbors.

By 1943, there were also serious labor shortages. The Nazis required German teenagers and retired men to work in the factories, and increasing numbers of women joined them. To achieve total mobilization, the Germans closed retail businesses, raised the age of eligibility of women for compulsory service, shifted non-German domestic workers to wartime industry, moved artists and entertainers into military service, closed theaters, and reduced such basic public services as mail and railways. Finally, the Nazis compelled thousands of people from conquered lands to do forced labor in Germany.

AN OBSERVER DESCRIBES THE MASS MURDER OF JEWS IN UKRAINE

After World War II, the victorious powers put some German officers and officials on trial at Nuremberg for crimes they were charged with having committed during the war. The selections that follow, from the testimony of a German construction engineer who witnessed the mass murder of Jews at Dubno in the Ukraine on October 5, 1942, reveal the brutality with which Hitler's attempt at a "final solution of the Jewish problem" was carried out.

■ *Why did the German government commit these atrocities? Why were they directed chiefly at Jews? Was there a cost to Germany in pursuing such a policy? Why did ordinary Germans participate?*

On October 5, 1942, when I visited the building office at Dubno, my foreman told me that in the vicinity of the site, Jews from Dubno had been shot in three large pits, each about 30 metres long and 3 metres deep. About 1,500 persons had been killed daily. All the 5,000 Jews who had still been living in Dubno before the pogrom were to be liquidated. As the shooting had taken place in his presence, he was still much upset.

Thereupon, I drove to the site accompanied by my foreman and saw near it great mounds of earth, about 30 metres long and 2 metres high. Several trucks stood in front of the mounds. Armed Ukrainian militia drove the people off the trucks under the supervision of an S.S. man. The militiamen acted as guards on the trucks and drove them to and from the pit. All these people had the regulation yellow patches on the front and back of their clothes, and thus could be recognized as Jews.

My foreman and I went directly to the pits. Nobody bothered us. Now I heard rifle shots in quick succession from behind one of the earth mounds. The people who had got off the trucks—men, women and children of all ages—had to undress upon the orders of an S.S. man, who carried a riding or dog whip. They had to put down their clothes in fixed places, sorted according to shoes, top clothing and underclothing. I saw a heap of shoes of about 800 to 1,000 pairs, great piles of underlinen and clothing.

Without screaming or weeping, these people undressed, stood around in family groups, kissed each other, said farewells, and waited for a sign from another S.S. man, who stood near the pit, also with a whip in his hand. During the fifteen minutes that I stood near I heard no complaint or plea for mercy. I watched a family of about eight persons, a man and a woman both about fifty with their children of about one, eight and ten, and two grown-up daughters of about twenty to twenty-nine. An old woman with snow-white hair was holding the one-year-old child in her arms and singing to it and tickling it. The child was cooing with delight. The couple were looking on with tears in their eyes. The father was holding the hand of a boy about ten years old and speaking to him softly; the boy was fighting his tears. The father pointed to the sky, stroked his head, and seemed to explain something to him.

At that moment the S.S. man at the pit shouted something to his comrade. The latter counted off about twenty persons and instructed them to go behind the earth mound. Among them was the family which I have mentioned. I well remember a girl, slim and with black hair, who, as she passed close to me pointed to herself and said "23." I walked around the mound and found myself confronted by a tremendous grave. People were closely wedged together and lying on top of each other so that only their heads were visible. Nearly all had blood running over their shoulders from their heads. Some of the people shot were still moving. Some were lifting their arms and turning their heads to show that they were still alive. The pit was already two-thirds full. I estimated that it already contained about 1,000 people.

From the Nuremberg Proceedings, as quoted in Louis L. Snyder, *Documents of German History* (New Brunswick, NJ: Rutgers University Press, 1958), pp. 462–464.

Hitler assigned women a special place in the war effort. The celebration of motherhood continued, with an emphasis on women who were the mothers of important military figures. Films portrayed ordinary women who became especially brave and patriotic during the war and remained faithful to their husbands who were at the front. Women were thereby shown as mothers and wives who sent their sons and husbands off to war. The government pictured other wartime activities of women as the natural fulfillment of their maternal roles. As air-raid wardens, they protected their families; as factory workers in munitions plants, they aided their sons on the front lines. Women working on farms were providing for their soldier sons and husbands; as housewives, they were helping to win the war by conserving food and managing their households frugally. Finally, by their faithful chastity, German women were protecting racial purity. They were not to marry or to engage in sexual relations with men who were not German. The war years also saw an intensification of political propaganda on the domestic front beyond what occurred in other countries. Hitler and other Germans genuinely believed that weak domestic support had led to Germany's defeat in World War I; they were determined this situation would not happen again. Nazi propaganda blamed the outbreak of the war on the British and the Jews and its prolongation on the policies of Germany's opponents. It also stressed the power of Germany and the inferiority of its foes.

Propaganda minister Josef Goebbels (1897–1945) used both radio and films to boost the Nazi cause. Movies of the collapse of Poland, Belgium, Holland, and France were shown in Germany to demonstrate German military might. Throughout the conquered territories, the Nazis used the same mass media to frighten inhabitants about the possible consequences of an Allied victory. Later in the war, the ministry broadcast exaggerated claims of Nazi victories. As the German armies were checked on the battlefield, especially in Russia, propaganda became a substitute for victory. To stiffen German resolve, propaganda now aimed to frighten Germans about the consequences of defeat.

After May 1943, when the Allies began their major bombing offensive over Germany, the German people had much to fear. One German city after another was devastated, but German morale was not undermined. The bombing may even have increased German resistance by seeming to confirm the regime's propaganda about the ruthlessness of Germany's opponents.

World War II increased the power of the Nazi Party in Germany. Every area of the economy and society came under the direct influence or control of the party. The Nazis were determined that they, rather than the traditionally honored German officer corps, would profit from the new authority the war effort was giving to the central government. Throughout the war years, there was virtually no serious opposition to Hitler or his ministers. In 1944, a small group of army officers attempted to assassinate Hitler; the effort failed, and there were few indications of significant popular support for this act.

The war brought great changes to Germany, but what transformed the country most was the experience of vast physical destruction, invasion, and occupation. Hitler and the Nazis had brought Germany to such a complete and disastrous defeat that only a new kind of state with new political structures could emerge.

France: Defeat, Collaboration, and Resistance

The terms of the 1940 armistice between France, under Pétain, and Germany, signed June 22, allowed the Germans to occupy more than half of France, including the Atlantic and English Channel coasts. To prevent the French from continuing the fight from North Africa, and even more to prevent them from turning their fleet over to Britain, Hitler left southern France unoccupied until November 1942. Marshal Pétain set up a dictatorial regime at the resort city of Vichy and followed a policy of close collaboration with the Germans in hopes of preserving as much autonomy as possible.

Some of the collaborators believed the Germans were sure to win the war and wanted to be on the victorious side. A few sympathized with the ideas and plans of the Nazis. Many conservatives regarded the French defeat as a judgment on what they saw as the corrupt, secularized, liberal ways of the Third Republic. Most of the French were not active collaborators but were helpless and demoralized by defeat and the evidence of German power.

Many conservatives and extreme rightists saw in the Vichy government a way to reshape the French national character and to halt the decadence they associated with political and religious liberalism. The Roman Catholic clergy, which had lost power and influence under the Third Republic, gained status under Vichy. The church supported Pétain, and his government restored religious instruction in the state schools and increased financial support for Catholic schools. Vichy adopted the church's views on the importance of family and spiritual values. The government forbade divorce during the first three years of marriage and made subsequent divorce difficult; large families were encouraged and subsidized.

The Vichy regime also encouraged an intense, chauvinistic nationalism. It exploited the long-standing prejudice against foreigners working in France and fostered resentment even against French men and women who were not regarded as genuinely "French." The chief victims were French Jews.

The Vichy regime in France attempted to shore up its rule through nationalistic and anti-Semitic propaganda. This poster contrasts a strong France on the right based on hard work, family, and love of country with a tottering France on the left undermined by communism, speculation, demagogues, internationalism, and laziness and capped with a Star of David.

Anti-Semitism was not new in France, as the Dreyfus affair had demonstrated. Even before Germany undertook Hitler's "final solution" in 1942, the French had begun to remove Jews from positions of influence in government, education, and publishing. In 1941, the Germans began to intern Jews living in occupied France; soon they carried out assassinations and imposed large fines collectively on the Jews of the occupied zone. In the spring of 1942, they began to deport Jews from France—ultimately more than 60,000—to the extermination camps of eastern Europe. The Vichy government had no part in these decisions, but it made no protest, and its own anti-Semitic policies made the whole process easier to carry out.

A few French, most notably General Charles de Gaulle (1890–1969), fled to Britain after the defeat of France. There they organized the French National Committee of Liberation, or "Free French." Until the end of 1942, the Vichy government controlled French North Africa and the navy, but the Free French began operating in central Africa. From London, they broadcast hope and defiance to their compatriots in France. Serious internal resistance to the German occupiers and the Vichy government, however, began to develop only late in 1942. The Germans tried to force young people in occupied France to work in German factories; some of them joined the Resistance, but the number of all the resisters was small. Many were deterred by fear of harsh punishment by the Germans. Some disliked the violence inevitably connected with resistance to a powerful ruthless nation. So long as it appeared the Germans would win the war, moreover, resistance seemed imprudent and futile. For these reasons, the organized Resistance never attracted vast numbers of followers; well under 5 percent of the adult French population appears to have been involved.

By early 1944, the tide of battle had shifted. The Allies seemed sure to win, and the Vichy government would clearly not survive; only then did a large-scale active movement of resistance assert itself. General de Gaulle spoke confidently for Free France from his base in London and urged the French people to resist their conquerors and the German lackeys in the Vichy government. Within France, Resistance groups joined forces to plan for a better day. From Algiers on August 9, 1944, the Committee of National Liberation declared the authority of Vichy illegitimate. Soon French soldiers joined in the liberation of Paris and established a government for Free France. On October 21, 1945, France voted to end the Third Republic and adopted a new constitution as the basis of the Fourth Republic. The French people had experienced defeat, disgrace, deprivation, and suffering in the war. Hostility and bitter quarrels over who had done what during the occupation and under Vichy divided them for decades.

GREAT BRITAIN: ORGANIZATION FOR VICTORY

On May 22, 1940, the British Parliament gave the government emergency powers. Together with others already in effect, this measure allowed the government to institute compulsory military service, food rationing, and various controls over the economy.

To deal with the crisis facing them, all British political parties joined in a national government under Winston Churchill. Churchill and the British war cabinet moved as quickly as possible to mobilize the nation. Perhaps the most pressing immediate need was the production of airplanes to fight the Germans in the Battle of Britain. This effort was led by Lord Beaverbrook (1879–1964), one of Britain's most important newspaper publishers. The demand for more planes and other armaments inspired a massive campaign to reclaim scrap metal. Wrought-iron fences, kitchen pots and pans, and every conceivable kind of scrap metal were collected for the war effort. This was only one successful example of the many ways the civilian population was enthusiastically engaged in the struggle.

By the end of 1941, British production had already surpassed Germany's. To meet the heavy demands on the labor force, factory hours were extended, and many women were brought into the work force. Unemployment disappeared, and the working classes had more money to spend than they had enjoyed for many years. To avoid inflation caused by increased demand for an inadequate supply of consumer goods, savings were encouraged, and taxes were raised to absorb the excess purchasing power.

The "blitz" air attacks of the winter and spring of 1940–1941 were the most immediate and dramatic experience of the war for the British people themselves. The German air raids killed thousands of people and left many others homeless. Once the bombing began, many families removed their children to the countryside. Ironically, the rescue effort improved the standard of living of many of the children, for the government paid for their food and medication. Gas masks were issued to thousands of city dwellers, who were frequently compelled to take shelter from the bombs in the London subways.

After the spring of 1941, Hitler needed most of his air force on the Russian front, but the bombing of Britain continued, killing more than 30,000 people by the end of the war. Terrible as it was, this toll was much smaller than the number of Germans killed by Allied bombing in the war. In England, as in Germany, however, the bombing, far from breaking the people's spirit, may well have made them more determined.

The British made many sacrifices. Transportation facilities were strained simply from carrying enough coal for domestic heating and for running factories. Food and clothing for civilians were scarce, and the government adopted strict rationing to achieve a fair distribution. Every scrap of land was farmed, increasing the productive portion by almost 4 million acres. Gasoline was scarce, and private vehicles almost vanished.

The British established their own propaganda machine to influence the Continent. The British Broadcasting Company (BBC) sent programs to every country in Europe in the local language, to encourage resistance against the Nazis. At home, the government used the radio to unify the nation. Soldiers at the front heard the same programs as their families at home. The most famous program, second only to Churchill's speeches, was *It's That Man Again*, a humorous broadcast filled with imaginary figures that the entire nation came to treasure.

Strangely, for the broad mass of the population, the standard of living improved during the war. The general health of the nation also improved, for reasons that are still not clear. These improvements should not be exaggerated, but they did occur, and many connected them with the active involvement of the government in the economy and in the lives of the citizens. This wartime experience may have contributed to the Labour Party's victory in 1945; many feared a return to Conservative Party rule would also mean a return to the economic problems and unemployment of the 1930s.

Winston Churchill walks through the rubble-strewn streets of London after the city had experienced a night of German bombing. Despite many casualties and widespread devastation, the German bombing of London did not break British morale or prevent the city from functioning. UPI/Corbis

THE SOVIET UNION: "THE GREAT PATRIOTIC WAR"

The war against Germany came as a great surprise to Stalin and the Soviet Union. The German attack violated the 1939 pact with Hitler and put the government of the Soviet Union on the defensive militarily and politically. It showed the failure of Stalin's foreign policy and the ineptness of his preparation for war. He claimed the pact had given the nation an extra year and a half to prepare for war, but this was clearly a lame and implausible excuse in light of the ease of Germany's early victories. Within days, German troops occupied much of the western Soviet Union. The communist government feared that Soviet citizens who had been conquered by the Germans—many of whom were not ethnic Russians—might welcome the conquerors as liberators; these Soviet citizens had been harshly oppressed by the Stalinist regime.

No nation suffered greater loss of life or more extensive physical destruction during World War II than the Soviet Union. Perhaps as many as 16 million people were killed, and vast numbers of Soviet troops were taken prisoner. Hundreds of cities and towns and well over half of the industrial and transportation facilities of the country were devastated. From 1942, thousands of Soviet prisoners worked in German factories as forced labor. The Germans also served their own war effort with grain, mineral resources, and oil confiscated from the Soviet Union.

Stalin conducted the war as virtual chief of the armed forces, and the State Committee for Defense provided strong central coordination. In the decade before the war, Stalin had already made the Soviet Union a highly centralized state; he had tried to manage the entire economy from Moscow through the five-year plans, the collectivization of agriculture, and the purges. The country was thus already on what amounted to a wartime footing long before the conflict erupted. When the war began, millions of citizens entered the army, but the army itself did not grow in influence at the expense of the state and the Communist Party—that is, of Stalin. He was suspicious of the generals, though he had presumably eliminated officers of doubtful loyalty in the purges of the late 1930s. As the war continued, however, the army gained some degree of independence, and eventually the generals were no longer subservient to party commissars. The army thus gained some freedom of action. It was, however, still sharply limited by the power of Stalin and by the nature of Soviet government and society.

Soviet propaganda was different from that of other nations. Because the Soviet government distrusted the loyalty of its citizens, it confiscated radios to prevent the people from listening to German or British propaganda. In cities, the government broadcast to the people over loudspeakers in place of radios. During the war, Soviet propaganda emphasized Russian patriotism rather than traditional Marxist themes that stressed class conflict. The struggle against the Germans was called "The Great Patriotic War."

Great Russian novels of the past were republished; more than half a million copies of Tolstoy's *War and Peace* were printed during the siege of Leningrad (Saint Petersburg). Other authors wrote straightforward propaganda fostering hatred of the Germans. Serge Eisenstein (1898–1948), the great filmmaker (see Encountering the Past, Chapter 28), produced a vast epic entitled *Ivan the Terrible*, which glorified this brutal tsar of the Russian past. Composers, such as Dimitri Shostakovich (1906–1975), produced scores that sought to contribute to the struggle and evoke heroic emotions. The most important of these was Shostakovich's Seventh Symphony, also known as the Leningrad Symphony.

The pressure of war led Stalin to make peace with the Russian Orthodox Church, allowing church leaders to enter the Kremlin. Stalin hoped this new policy would give him more support at home and permit the Soviet Union to be viewed more favorably in eastern Europe, where the Orthodox Church predominated.

Within occupied portions of the western Soviet Union, an active resistance movement arose against the Germans. The swiftness of the German invasion had stranded thousands of Soviet troops behind German lines. Many were shipped to Germany as prisoners of war, but others escaped and carried on guerrilla resistance warfare behind enemy lines. Stalin supported partisan forces in lands held by the enemy for two reasons: He wanted to cause as much difficulty as possible for the Germans, and Soviet-sponsored resistance reminded the peasants in the conquered regions that the Soviet government, with its policies of collectivization, had not disappeared. Stalin feared the peasants' hatred of the communist government might lead them to collaborate with the invaders. When the Soviet army moved westward toward the end of the war, it incorporated the partisans into the regular army.

As its armies reclaimed the occupied areas and then moved across eastern and central Europe, the Soviet Union established itself as a world power second only to the United States. Stalin had entered the war a reluctant belligerent, but he emerged a major victor. In that respect, the war and the extraordinary patriotic effort and sacrifice it generated consolidated the power of Stalin and the party more effectively than the political and social policies of the previous decade.

Preparations for Peace

The split between the Soviet Union and its wartime allies should cause no surprise. As the self-proclaimed center of world communism, the Soviet Union was openly dedicated to the overthrow of the capitalist nations. This message, however, was muted when the occasion demanded. On the other side, the Western allies were no less open about their hostility to communism and its chief purveyor, the Soviet Union. Although they had been friendly to the early stages of the 1917 Russian Revolution, they had intervened to try to overthrow the Bolshevik regime during the civil war resulting from the revolution. The United States did not grant formal recognition to the USSR until 1933. The Western powers' exclusion of the Soviets from the Munich conference and Stalin's pact with Hitler did nothing to improve relations between them during the war.

Nonetheless, the need to cooperate against a common enemy and strenuous propaganda efforts helped improve Western feeling toward the Soviet ally. Still, Stalin remained suspicious and critical of the Western war effort, and Churchill was determined to contain the Soviet advance into Europe. Roosevelt perhaps had been more hopeful that the Allies could continue to work together after the war, but even he was losing faith by 1945. Differences in historical development and ideology, as well as traditional conflicts over political power and influence, soon dashed hopes of a mutually satisfactory peace settlement and continued cooperation to uphold it.

THE ATLANTIC CHARTER

In August 1941, even before the Americans were at war, Roosevelt and Churchill had met on a ship off Newfoundland and agreed to the Atlantic Charter. This broad set of principles in the spirit of Wilson's Fourteen Points provided a theoretical basis for the peace they sought. When Russia and the United States joined Britain in the war, the three powers entered a purely military alliance in January 1942, leaving all political questions aside. The first political conference was the meeting of foreign ministers in Moscow in October 1943. The ministers reaffirmed earlier agreements to fight on until the enemy surrendered unconditionally and to continue cooperating after the war in a united-nations organization.

TEHRAN: AGREEMENT ON A SECOND FRONT

The first meeting of the leaders of the "Big Three" (as the USSR, Britain, and the United States were known) took place at Tehran, the capital of Iran, in 1943. Western promises to open a second front in France the next summer (1944) and Stalin's agreement to join in the war against Japan when Germany was defeated created an atmosphere of goodwill in which to discuss a postwar settlement. Stalin wanted to retain what he had gained in his pact with Hitler and to dismember Germany. Roosevelt and Churchill were conciliatory, but they made no firm commitments.

The most important decision was the one that chose Europe's west coast as the main point of attack instead of the Mediterranean. That meant, in retrospect, that Soviet forces would occupy eastern Europe and control its destiny. At Tehran in 1943, the Western allies did not foresee this clearly, for the Russians were still fighting deep within their own frontiers, and military considerations were still paramount.

Churchill and Stalin By 1944, the situation was different. In August, Soviet armies were before Warsaw, which had revolted against the Germans in expectation of liberation. But the Russians halted, allowing the Polish rebels to be annihilated while they (the Russians) turned south into the Balkans. They gained control of Romania and Hungary, advances that centuries of expansionist tsars had only dreamed of achieving. Alarmed by these developments, Churchill went to Moscow and met with Stalin in October. They agreed to share power in the Balkans on the basis of Soviet predominance in Romania and Bulgaria, Western predominance in Greece, and equality of influence in Yugoslavia and Hungary. These agreements were not enforceable without American approval, and the Americans were known to be hostile to such un-Wilsonian devices as "spheres of influence."

Germany The three powers easily agreed on Germany—its disarmament, de-Nazification, and division into four zones of occupation by France and the Big Three. Churchill, however, began to balk at Stalin's demand for $20 billion in reparations as well as forced labor from all the zones, with Russia to get half of everything. These matters were left to fester and cause dissension in the future.

Eastern Europe The settlement of eastern Europe was an equally thorny problem. Everyone agreed the Soviet Union deserved to have friendly neighboring governments, but the West insisted they also be autonomous and democratic. The Western leaders, particularly Churchill, were not eager to see eastern Europe fall under Russian domination. They were also, especially Roosevelt, committed to democracy and self-determination.

Stalin, however, knew that independent, freely elected governments in Poland and Romania could not be counted on to be friendly to Russia. He had already established a puppet government in Poland in competition with the Polish government-in-exile in London. Under pressure from the Western leaders, however, he agreed to reorganize this government and include some Poles friendly to the West in it. He also signed a Declaration on Liberated Europe, promising self-determination and free democratic elections.

Stalin may have been eager to avoid conflict before the war with Germany was over. He was always afraid the Allies would make a separate peace

Negotiations among the Allies	
August 1941	Churchill and Roosevelt meet off Newfoundland to sign Atlantic Charter
October 1943	American, British, and Soviet foreign ministers meet in Moscow
November 1943	Churchill, Roosevelt, and Stalin meet at Tehran
October 1944	Churchill meets with Stalin in Moscow
February 1945	Churchill, Roosevelt, and Stalin meet at Yalta
July 1945	Attlee, Stalin, and Truman meet at Potsdam

with Germany and betray him. And he probably thought it worth endorsing some hollow principles as the price of continued harmony. In any case, he wasted little time violating these agreements.

YALTA

The next meeting of the Big Three was at Yalta in the Crimea in February 1945. The Western armies had not yet crossed the Rhine, but the Soviet army was within a hundred miles of Berlin. (See Map 29–7.) The war with Japan continued, and no atomic explosion had yet taken place. Roosevelt, faced with a prospective invasion of Japan and heavy losses, was eager to bring the Russians into the Pacific war as soon as possible. As a true Wilsonian, he also suspected Churchill's determination to maintain the British Empire and Britain's colonial advantages. The Americans thought Churchill's plan to set up British spheres of influence in Europe would encourage the Russians to do the same and would lead to friction and war. To encourage Russian participation in the war against Japan, Roosevelt and Churchill made extensive concessions to Russia, ceding the Soviets Sakhalin and the Kurile Islands, and accommodating some of their desires in Korea and in Manchuria.

Again in the tradition of Wilson, Roosevelt laid great stress on a united-nations organization: "Through the United Nations, he hoped to achieve a self-enforcing peace settlement that would not require American troops, as well as an open world without spheres of influence in which American enterprise could work freely."[5] Soviet agreement on these points seemed well worth concessions elsewhere.

POTSDAM

The Big Three met for the last time in the Berlin suburb of Potsdam in July 1945. Much had changed since the previous conference. Germany had been defeated, and news of the successful experimental explosion of an atomic weapon reached the American president during the meetings. The cast of characters was also different: President Truman replaced the deceased Roosevelt, and Clement Attlee (1883–1967), leader of the Labour Party that had defeated Churchill's Conservatives in a general election, replaced Churchill as Britain's spokesperson during the conference. Previous agreements were reaffirmed, but progress on undecided questions was slow.

[5]Robert O. Paxton, *Europe in the Twentieth Century* (New York: Harcourt Brace Jovanovich, 1975), p. 487.

MAP 29–7 YALTA TO THE SURRENDER *"The Big Three"—Roosevelt, Churchill, and Stalin—met at Yalta in the Crimea in February 1945. At the meeting, concessions were made to Stalin concerning the settlement of eastern Europe because Roosevelt was eager to bring the Russians into the Pacific war as soon as possible. This map shows the positions held by the victors when Germany surrendered.*

Russia's western frontier was moved far into what had been Poland and included most of German East Prussia. In compensation, Poland was allowed "temporary administration" over the rest of East Prussia and Germany east of the Oder-Neisse River, a condition that became permanent. In effect, Poland was moved about a hundred miles west, at the expense of Germany, to accommodate the Soviet Union. The Allies agreed that Germany would be divided into occupation zones until the final peace treaty was signed. Germany remained divided until 1990.

A Council of Foreign Ministers was established to draft peace treaties for Germany's allies. Growing disagreements made the job difficult, and Italy, Romania, Hungary, Bulgaria, and Finland did not sign treaties until February 1947. The Russians were dissatisfied with the treaty that the United States made with Japan in 1951 and signed their own agreements with the Japanese in 1956. These disagreements were foreshadowed at Potsdam.

IN PERSPECTIVE

The second great war of the twentieth century (1939–1945) grew out of the unsatisfactory resolution of the first. In retrospect, the two wars appear to some people to be one continuous conflict, a kind of twentieth-century "Thirty Years' War," with the two main periods of fighting separated by an uneasy truce. To others, that point of view oversimplifies and distorts the situation by implying the second war was the inevitable result of the first and its inadequate peace treaties. The latter opinion seems more sound, for, whatever the flaws of the treaties of Paris, the world suffered an even more terrible war than the first because of failures of judgment and will on the part of the victorious democratic powers.

Between the two wars, the United States, which had become the wealthiest and potentially the strongest nation in the world, disarmed almost entirely and withdrew into a shortsighted and foolish isolation. Therefore, it could play no important part in restraining the angry and ambitious dictators who brought on the war. Britain and France refused to face the threat posed by the Axis powers until the most deadly war in history was required to put it down. If the victorious democracies had remained strong, responsible, and realistic, they could easily have remedied whatever injustices or mistakes arose from the treaties without endangering the peace.

The second war itself was so plainly a world war that little need be said to indicate its global character. There is good reason to think that if the Japanese occupation of Manchuria in 1931 was not technically a part of that war, it was a significant precursor. Moreover, there were Italy's attack on the African nation of Ethiopia in 1935, the Italian, German, and Soviet interventions in the Spanish Civil War (1936–1939), and Japan's attack on China in 1937. These acts revealed that aggressive forces were on the march around the globe and the defenders of the world order lacked the will to stop them. The formation of the Axis incorporating Germany, Italy, and Japan guaranteed that when the war came, it would be fought around the world.

There was fighting and suffering in Asia, Africa, the Pacific islands, and Europe, and men and women from all the inhabited continents took part in it. The use of atomic weapons brought the frightful struggle to a close. Still, what are called conventional weapons did almost all the damage; their level of destructiveness threatened the survival of civilization, even without the use of atomic or nuclear devices.

The Second World War ended not with unsatisfactory peace treaties, but with no treaty at all in the European arena, where the war had begun. The world quickly split into two unfriendly camps: the western, led by the United States, and the eastern, led by the Soviet Union. This division, among other things, hastened the liberation of former colonial territories. The bargaining power of the new nations that emerged from them was temporarily increased as the two rival superpowers tried to gain their friendship or allegiance. It became customary to refer to these nations as "the Third World," or "developing countries," with the former Soviet Union and the United States and their respective allies being the first two. The passage of time has shown that the differences among Third World nations are so great as to make the term all but meaningless.

The surprising treatment received by the defeated powers of the Second World War was also largely the result of the emergence of the Cold War. Instead of holding them back, the Western powers installed democratic governments in Italy, West Germany, and Japan, took them into the Western alliances designed to contain communism, and helped them recover economically. Japan and Germany are now among the richest nations in the world, and Italy is more prosperous than it has ever been.

By the last decade of the twentieth century, Japan had become one of the greatest industrial, commercial, and financial powers in the world and a major investor in the American economy. Its manufacturers have offered stiff competition to their counterparts in the United States and western Europe, provoking concern and calls for protective tariffs.

Germany, divided between East and West by the war, never ceased to hope for eventual unification. The startling events of 1989, in which the Soviet Union gave up its hold over eastern Europe, made unification suddenly possible, and it occurred in 1990. One result of this unification has been to open again a question that lay behind the two great wars of the twentieth century: the place of a unified Germany in Europe.

REVIEW QUESTIONS

1. What were Hitler's foreign policy aims? Was he bent on conquest, or did he simply want to return Germany to its 1914 boundaries?

2. Why did Britain and France adopt a policy of appeasement in the 1930s? Did the West buy valuable time to rearm at Munich in 1938?

3. How was Hitler able to defeat France so easily in 1940? Why did the air war against Britain fail? Why did Hitler invade Russia? Could the invasion have succeeded?

4. Why did Japan attack the United States at Pearl Harbor? How important was American intervention in the war? Why did the United States drop atomic bombs on Japan? Was President Truman right to use the bombs?

5. How did experiences on the domestic front in Britain differ from those in Germany and France? What impact did "The Great Patriotic War" have on the people of the Soviet Union?

6. What was Hitler's "final solution" to the Jewish question? Why did he want to eliminate Slavs as well? To what extent can it be said the Holocaust was the defining event of the twentieth century?

SUGGESTED READINGS

A. ADAMTHWAITE, *France and the Coming of the Second World War, 1936–1939* (1977). A careful account making good use of the French archives.

O. BARTOV, *Mirrors of Destruction: War, Genocide, and Modern Identity* (2000). A collection of remarkably penetrating essays.

E. R. BECK, *Under the Bombs: The German Home Front, 1942–1945* (1986). An interesting examination of a generally unstudied subject.

R. S. BOTWINICK, *A History of the Holocaust*, 2nd ed. (2002). A brief but broad and useful account of the causes, character, and results of the Holocaust.

C. BROWNING, *Ordinary Men* (1993). Examines a single Nazi death squad.

A. BULLOCK, *Hitler: A Study in Tyranny*, rev. ed. (1964). A brilliant biography.

M. BURLEIGH AND W. WIPPERMANN, *The Racial State: Germany, 1933–1945* (1991). A powerful examination of how racial policy affected every aspect of Nazi government.

W. S. CHURCHILL, *The Second World War*, 6 vols. (1948–1954). The memoirs of the great British leader.

A. CROZIER, *The Causes of the Second World War* (1997). An examination of what brought on the war.

L. DOBROSZYCKI (ED.), *The Chronicle of the Lodz Ghetto, 1941–1944* (1984). A collection of the official documents of daily life and administration.

R. B. FRANK, *Downfall: The End of the Imperial Japanese Empire* (1998). A thorough, well-documented account of the last months of the Japanese empire and the reasons for its surrender.

J. L. GADDIS, *We Now Know: Rethinking Cold War History* (1998). A fine account of the early years of the Cold War making use of new evidence emerging since the collapse of the Soviet Union.

J. L. GADDIS, P. H. GORDON, AND E. MAY (EDS.), *Cold War Statesmen Confront the Bomb: Nuclear diplomacy since 1945* (1999). A collection of essays discussing the effect of atomic and nuclear weapons on diplomacy since World War II.

M. GILBERT, *The Holocaust: A History of the Jews of Europe during the Second World War* (1985). The best and most comprehensive treatment.

M. HARRISON, *Soviet Planning in Peace and War, 1938–1945* (1985). An examination of the Soviet wartime economy.

C. S. HELLER, *On the Edge of Destruction: Jews of Poland between the Two World Wars* (1994). A probing examination of the subject.

R. HILBERG, *The Destruction of the European Jews*, 3 vols. (1985). Now the classic account of the political and administrative processes that supported the Holocaust.

A. IRIYE, *Pearl Harbor and the Coming of the Pacific War* (1999). Essays on how the Pacific war came about, including a selection of documents.

J. KEEGAN, *The Second World War* (1990). A lively and penetrating account by a master military historian.

W. F. KIMBALL, *Forged in War: Roosevelt, Churchill, and the Second World War* (1998). A study of the collaboration between the two great leaders of the West based on a thorough knowledge of their correspondence.

M. KNOX, *Mussolini Unleashed* (1982). An outstanding study of fascist Italy's policy and strategy in World War II.

S. MARKS, *The Illusion of Peace* (1976). A good discussion of European international relations in the 1920s and early 1930s.

V. MASTNY, *Russia's Road to the Cold War* (1979). Written by an expert on the Soviet Union and eastern Europe.

E. MENDELSOHN, *The Jews of East Central Europe between the World Wars* (1983). An excellent introduction.

W. MURRAY, *The Change in the European Balance of Power 1938–1939* (1984). A brilliant study of the relationship between strategy, foreign policy, economics, and domestic politics in the years before the war.

W. Murray and A. R. Millett, *A War to Be Won: Fighting the Second World War* (2000). A splendid account of the military operations in the war.

D. Ofer and L. J. Weitzman (eds.), *Women in the Holocaust* (1998). A major collection of essays.

R. Overy, *Russia's War: Blood upon the Snow* (1997). An account of Russia's defeat of the German army based on newly available evidence.

R. Overy, *Why the Allies Won* (1997). An analysis of the reasons for the victory of the Allies with special emphasis on technology.

N. Rich, *Hitler's War Aims*, 2 vols. (1973–1974). The best study of the subject in English.

H. Thomas, *The Spanish Civil War*, 3rd ed. (1986). The best account in English.

D. Vital, *A People Apart: The Jews in Europe, 1789–1939* (1999). A major survey with excellent discussions of the interwar.

P. Wandycz, *The Twilight of French Eastern Alliances, 1926–1936* (1988). A well-documented account of the diplomacy of central and eastern Europe in a crucial period.

G. L. Weinberg, *A World at Arms: A Global History of World War II* (1994). A thorough and excellent narrative account.

DOCUMENTS CD-ROM

Society and Culture between the Wars

World War II

ART & THE WEST

Picasso's *Guernica*

Pablo Picasso, *Guernica*, 1937.   Oil on canvas. 11'5" × 25'5 ³/₄". Museo Nacional Centro de Arte Reina Sofia/© 2003 Estate of Pablo Picasso/ Artists Rights Society (ARS), New York.

In July 1936, right-wing rebels based in Spanish Morocco and led by General Francisco Franco landed in Spain and launched an attack on the legitimate government, the Popular Front, a leftist coalition that ranged from moderate republicans to communists and anarchists. The Spanish Civil War that followed divided Europe, with fascist Italy and Nazi Germany assisting Franco, and Soviet Russia aiding the republic. The war was a preview of the horrors that would follow in World War II. Before its end in 1939, the war in Spain took some 500,000 lives.

Pablo Picasso was asked by the government of the republic to paint a mural in the Spanish pavilion for the Paris World's Fair. Soon after he accepted the commission, on April 26, 1937, planes from the German Condor Legion bombed the Basque town of Guernica, killing some 1,000 men, women, and children and destroying about 70 percent of the buildings. Its purpose was simply to create terror.

Picasso seized on Guernica as the subject of his mural. The painting was an enormous success, serving the enemies of Franco, Mussolini, and Hitler as a powerful symbol of their evil. When it was taken to the Metropolitan Museum in New York soon after, it had an enormous impact.

"*Guernica* helped to push a whole segment of Western opinion, including the magazines *Time* and *Newsweek*, over to the Republican side."[1]

The style of *Guernica* is greatly influenced by the surrealists. The painting does not show the attack, but depicts its terrible effects on its victims. It has been called "a stark and surrealistic nightmare. . . . Expressively distorted women, one with her dead child, wail at the carnage. Above a fallen, broken warrior is a screaming horse, symbolizing the suffering republic. To our left is a bull, thought to symbolize either Franco or Spain. An electric light and a woman holding a lantern suggest Picasso's desire to reveal the event in all its horror."[2]

- *Why did Picasso use the town of Guernica as the title of this painting? How did surrealism influence Picasso's* Guernica?

Sources: H. W. Janson and Anthony F. Janson, *History of Art*, rev. 5th ed. (Upper Saddle River, NJ: Prentice Hall, 1997), p. 82; R. O. Paxson, *Europe in the Twentieth Century* (New York: Harcourt, Brace, 1975), pp. 289–398; Paul Johnson, *Modern Times* (New York: Harper & Row, 1983), pp. 321–337; Marilyn Stokstad, *Art History* (New York: Harry N. Abrams, 1999), p. 109.

[1]Paul Johnson, *Modern Times* (New York: Harper & Row, 1983), p. 336.

[2]Marilyn Stokstad, *Art History* (New York: Harry N. Abrams, 1999), p. 1090.

The most important accomplishment of the European Community was the launching on January 1, 1999 of the Euro, a single monetary unit that replaced the national currencies of most of its member nations. In Madrid people crowded around a symbol of the new currency. AP/Wide World Photos

CHAPTER 30

THE COLD WAR ERA AND THE EMERGENCE OF THE NEW EUROPE

*F*ROM THE END OF WORLD *War II in 1945 until the collapse of communist regimes in Eastern Europe between 1989 and 1991, the Soviet Union and the United States—two nuclear-armed superpowers—confronted each other in a simmering conflict known as the* **Cold War.** *While it lasted, this conflict dominated global politics and threatened the peace of Europe, which stood divided between the U.S.-dominated North Atlantic Treaty Organization (NATO) and the Soviet-dominated Warsaw Pact.*

Undertaking an active role in Europe and the rest of the world constituted a major shift in foreign policy for the United States, reflecting its leaders' awareness of the dangers to which the country had been exposed when it retreated from the world scene after World War I. Moving to oppose what it regarded as the expansion of Soviet power and communist influence across the globe, the United States assumed a position of military, political, and economic leadership. This policy of active international leadership prompted the Marshall Plan, the formation of NATO, and military interventions in Korea and Vietnam.

The Cold War rapidly became globalized as regional conflicts outside Europe were drawn into the orbit of the U.S.-Soviet rivalry. As the nations of Europe retreated from empire, the rivalry between the two superpowers expanded into a contest for dominance in the postcolonial world. Superpower intervention aggravated local conflicts on every continent. Southeast Asia in particular became a battleground. In its efforts to limit communism, the United States became embroiled in bitter wars in Korea and Vietnam. The struggle between Israel and the Arab nations likewise became an arena of superpower conflict.

The communist government of the Soviet Union, established in 1917 and consolidated under Stalin, underwent many changes and attempts at redirection after World War II. The turmoil of World War I and Bolshevik victory in the civil war that followed had allowed the Soviet Union to come into existence; the turmoil of World War II permitted it to establish hegemony over Eastern Europe. From the late 1940s through the 1980s, the Soviet Union tried to retain dominance in Eastern Europe and to challenge the United States around the globe.

The Soviet Union pursued two not always compatible foreign policy goals. One was to lead the international communist movement, ideologically dedicated to the overthrow of capitalism throughout the world. Recently opened archives indicate that Marxist-Leninist ideology genuinely shaped Soviet decisions and was not just a language that hid more traditional geopolitical motives. The other goal was to secure its own national interests, which sometimes put it at odds with communist movements elsewhere. Eventually, rivalries emerged between the Soviet Union and other communist nations, notably the People's Republic of China. The leaders of the Soviet Union, meanwhile, failed to build lasting support for their goals, either internally or in their Eastern European dependencies. Nonetheless, the Soviet Union maintained its position as a superpower and its Cold War antagonism to the United States through the early 1980s.

KEY TOPICS

- The origins of the Cold War and the division of Europe into Eastern and Western blocs following World War II

- Decolonization and the conflicts in Korea and Vietnam

- Political and economic developments in Western Europe during the Cold War

- Polish protests against Soviet domination of Eastern Europe

- *Perestroika* and *glasnost* in the Soviet Union

- The collapse of communism in Eastern Europe and the Soviet Union

- The civil war in Yugoslavia

- Europe in the twenty-first century

The Emergence of the Cold War

The tense relationship between the United States and the Soviet Union began in the closing months of World War II. Some scholars attribute the hardening of the atmosphere between the two countries to Harry Truman's assumption of the presidency in April 1945, after the death of the more sympathetic Franklin Roosevelt, and to the American possession of an effective atomic bomb. Evidence suggests, however, that Truman was trying to carry Roosevelt's policies forward and Roosevelt himself had

become distressed by Soviet actions in Eastern Europe. Some have also argued that Truman did not use the atomic bomb to try to keep Russia out of the Pacific. On the contrary, he worked hard to ensure Russian intervention against Japan in 1945. In part, the coldness between the Allies arose from the mutual feeling that each had violated previous agreements. The Russians were plainly asserting permanent control of Poland and Romania under puppet communist governments. The United States, was taking a harder line about German reparation payments to the Soviet Union.

In retrospect, however, and as more information emerges from the previously closed Soviet archives, it appears unlikely that friendlier styles on either side could have avoided a split that arose from basic differences of ideology and interest. The Soviet Union's attempt to extend its control westward into central Europe and the Balkans and southward into the Middle East continued the general thrust of the foreign policy of tsarist Russia. Britain had traditionally tried to restrain Russian expansion into these areas, and the United States inherited that task as Britain's power waned.

The Americans made no attempt to roll back Soviet power where it existed at the close of World War II. (See Map 30–1.) At the time, American military forces were the greatest in U.S. history, American industrial power was unmatched in the world, and atomic weapons were an American monopoly. In less than a year from the war's end, the Americans had reduced their forces in Europe from 3.5 million to half a million. The speed of the withdrawal reflected domestic pressure to "get the boys home," but was also fully in accord with America's peacetime plans and goals, which included support for self-determination, autonomy, and democracy in the political sphere, and free trade, freedom of the seas, no barriers to investment, and an Open Door policy in the economic sphere. Those goals reflected American principles and served American interests well. As the strongest, richest nation in the world—the one with the greatest industrial base and the strongest currency—the United States would benefit handsomely from an international order based on such goals.

Although postwar American hostility to colonial empires created tensions with France and Britain, the main conflict lay with the Soviet Union. The growth in France and Italy of large popular communist parties taking orders from Moscow led the Americans to believe Stalin was engaged in a worldwide plot to subvert capitalism and democracy. From the Soviet perspective, extending the borders of the USSR and dominating the formerly independent successor states of Eastern Europe would provide needed security and compensate for the fearful losses the Soviet people had endured in the war. The Soviets could thus see American resistance to their expansion as a threat to their security and their legitimate aims. They considered American objections to Soviet actions in Poland and other states as an effort to undermine regimes friendly to Russia and to encircle the Soviet Union with hostile neighbors. The Soviets could also use this point of view to justify their own attempts to overthrow regimes friendly to the United States in Western Europe and elsewhere.

Evidence of the new mood of postwar hostility between the former allies was soon apparent. In February 1946, both Stalin and his foreign minister, Vyacheslav Molotov (1890–1986), publicly spoke of the Western democracies as enemies. A month later, Churchill gave a speech in Fulton, Missouri, in which he declared that an "Iron Curtain" had descended on Europe, dividing a free and democratic West from an East under totalitarian rule. He warned against communist subversion and urged Western unity and strength against the new menace. In this atmosphere, difficulties grew.

CONTAINMENT IN AMERICAN FOREIGN POLICY

The resistance of Americans and Western Europeans to what they increasingly perceived as Soviet intransigence and communist plans for subversion and expansion took clearer form in 1947. The American policy became known as one of **containment,** the purpose of which was to resist the extension of Soviet expansion and influence in the expectation that eventually the Soviet Union would collapse from internal pressures and the burdens of its foreign oppression. This strategy, devised by American policymakers in the late 1940s, would direct the broad outlines of American foreign policy for the next four decades, until the Soviet Union did collapse from exactly such pressures. Containment marked a major departure in American foreign policy and transformed the international situation during the second half of the twentieth century. The execution of the policy led the United States to enter overseas alliances, to make formal and informal commitments of support, to undertake enormous military expenditures, and to send large amounts of money abroad. In all these respects, the United States assumed the kind of long-term foreign policy responsibilities that it had not done before in its history. The United States thus became a permanent player in European international relations and in areas of the world where only European nations had been involved earlier in the century.

MAP 30–1 TERRITORIAL CHANGES AFTER WORLD WAR II *The map shows the shifts in territory following the defeat of the Axis. No treaty of peace formally ended the war with Germany.*

The Truman Doctrine Since 1944, civil war had been raging in Greece between the royalist government restored by Britain and insurgents supported by the communist countries, chiefly Yugoslavia. In 1947, Britain informed the United States it could no longer financially support the Greeks. On March 12,

President Truman asked Congress to provide funds to support Greece and Turkey, then under Soviet pressure to yield control of the Dardanelles, and Congress complied. In a speech to Congress that gave these actions much broader significance, the president set forth what came to be called the Truman Doctrine. He advocated a policy of support for "free people who are resisting attempted subjugation by armed minorities or by outside pressures," by implication, anywhere in the world. (See "The Truman Doctrine Declared.")

The Marshall Plan American aid to Greece and Turkey took the form of military equipment and advisers. For Western Europe, where postwar poverty and hunger fueled the menacing growth of communist parties, the Americans devised the European Recovery Program. Named the **Marshall Plan** after George C. Marshall (1880–1959), the secretary of state who introduced it, this program provided broad economic aid to European states on the sole condition that they work together for their mutual benefit. The Soviet Union and its satellites were

THE TRUMAN DOCTRINE DECLARED

In 1947, the British informed the United States they could no longer support the Greeks in their fight against a communist insurrection supported from the outside. On March 12 of that year, President Truman asked Congress for legislation in support of both Greece and Turkey, which were both also in danger. The principle behind that request, which became known as the Truman Doctrine, appears in the selections that follow from Truman's speech to the Congress.

■ *How does Truman relate the goals of the Second World War to the emerging Cold War with the Soviet Union? What are the qualities that Truman associates with free governments, and how were those qualities absent in the Soviet Union and the nations of Eastern Europe under its domination? How does this speech establish guidelines that might be applied to U.S. policy in parts of the world beyond Greece?*

One of the primary objectives of the foreign policy of the United States is the creation of conditions in which we and other nations will be able to work out a way of life free from coercion. This was a fundamental issue in the war with Germany and Japan. Our victory was won over countries which sought to impose their will, and their way of life, upon other nations.

To insure the peaceful development of nations, free from coercion, the United States has taken a leading part in establishing the United Nations. The United Nations is designed to make possible lasting freedom and independence for all its members. We shall not realize our objectives, however, unless we are willing to help free peoples to maintain their free institutions and their national integrity against aggressive movements that seek to impose upon them totalitarian regimes. . . .

At the present moment in world history nearly every nation must choose between alternative ways of life. The choice is too often not a free one.

One way of life is based upon the will of the majority, and is distinguished by free institutions, representative government, free elections, guaranties of individual liberty, freedom of speech and religion, and freedom from political oppression.

The second way of life is based upon the will of a minority forcibly imposed upon the majority. It relies upon terror and oppression, a controlled press and radio, fixed elections, and the suppression of personal freedoms.

I believe that it must be the policy of the United States to support free peoples who are resisting attempted subjugation by armed minorities or by outside pressures.

I believe that we must assist free peoples to work out their own destinies in their own way.

I believe that our help should be primarily through economic and financial aid, which is essential to economic stability and orderly political processes.

From Senate Committee on Foreign Relations, *A Decade of American Foreign Policy: Basic Documents, 1941–1949* (1950), pp. 1235–1237.

President Harry Truman greets Secretary of State George Marshall returning from Europe. Truman and Marshall were the architects of American foreign policy during the early years of the Cold War.
Archive Photos

invited to participate. Finland and Czechoslovakia were willing to do so, and Poland and Hungary showed interest. The Soviets, however, forbade them to take part.

The Marshall Plan restored prosperity to Western Europe and set the stage for Europe's unprecedented postwar economic growth. In addition to the vast program of American economic aid, the strong Christian Democratic movement that dominated the politics of Italy, France, and West Germany worked to keep communist influence at bay outside the Soviet sphere in Eastern Europe.

SOVIET ASSERTION OF DOMINATION OF EASTERN EUROPE

The Soviet determination to control Eastern Europe had both historical and ideological roots. Western European powers had invaded Russia twice in the nineteenth century (under Napoleon and during the Crimean War) and already twice more in the twentieth century. Tsarist Russia had governed most of Poland for over a century and had intervened at the request of the Austrian Empire to put down the Hungarian revolution in 1849. Russia's interests in Turkey and the lands around the Black Sea were similarly long standing. Given this history and the Soviet Union's extraordinary losses in World War II, it is not surprising that Soviet leaders sought to use their Eastern European satellites as a buffer against future invasions.

Stalin may have seen containment as a renewed attempt by the West to isolate and encircle the USSR. In Eastern Europe, the Soviet Union found numerous supporters among those segments of the population who had opposed the various right-wing movements in those countries before the war and who had fought the Nazis during the war. In the autumn of 1947, Stalin called a meeting in Warsaw of all communist parties around the globe. There they organized the Communist Information Bureau (Cominform), a revival of the old Comintern, dedicated to spreading revolutionary communism throughout the world. In Western Europe the establishment of the Cominform officially ended the era of the popular front during which communists had cooperated with noncommunist parties. Communist leaders in the West who favored collaboration and reform were replaced by hard-liners who attempted to sabotage the new structures.

Major Dates of Early Cold War Years

1945	Yalta Conference
1945	Founding of the United Nations
1946	Churchill's Iron Curtain speech
1947	(March) Truman Doctrine regarding Greece and Turkey
1947	(June) Announcement of Marshall Plan
1948	Communist takeover in Czechoslovakia
1948	Communist takeover in Hungary
1948–1949	Berlin blockade
1949	NATO founded
1949	East and West Germany emerge as separate states
1950–1953	Korean conflict
1955	Warsaw Pact founded

THE CHURCH AND THE COMMUNIST PARTY CLASH OVER EDUCATION IN HUNGARY

Throughout eastern Europe, the Roman Catholic church became one of the strongest opponents of the postwar Communist Party governments. It raised issues relating to church schools, free worship, participation in church-sponsored organizations, and the erection of new church buildings. One of the harshest clashes took place in Hungary. Following are two statements that illustrate the opposing positions of the church and the party. Cardinal Mindszenty (1892–1975) was later imprisoned and became one of the most well-known political prisoners in Eastern Europe.

■ *How does Mindszenty relate the position of church-supported schools to the nature and rights of parenthood? How does he compare the actions of the Communist Party to those of Hitler? How does the Minister of Public Worship set party members against the church? How does he attempt to place loyalty to the party above private beliefs? What does the Communist Party fear from religious education and participation in religious activities on the part of its members or their children?*

STATEMENT OF JOSEF CARDINAL MINDSZENTY, MAY 20, 1946

The right of the Church to schools is entirely in concord with the right of parents to educate their children. What is incumbent upon the parents in all questions of natural life is incumbent upon the Church with regard to the supernatural life. Parents are prior to the state, and their rights were always and still are, acknowledged by the Church. The prerogative of parents to educate their children cannot be disputed by the state, since it is the parents who give life to the child. They feed the child and clothe it. The child's life is, as it were, the continuation of theirs. Hence it is their right to demand that their children are educated according to their faith and their religious outlook.

It is their right to withhold their children from schools where their religious convictions are not only disregarded but even made the object of contempt and ridicule. It was this parental right which German parents felt was violated when the Hitler

---

In February 1948, in Prague, Stalin gave a brutal display of his new policy of bringing the governments of Eastern Europe under direct Soviet control. The communists expelled the democratic members of what had been a coalition government and murdered Jan Masaryk (1886–1948), the foreign minister and son of the founder of Czechoslovakia, Thomas Masaryk. President Edvard Beneš (1884–1948) was forced to resign, and Czechoslovakia was brought fully under Soviet rule. There and elsewhere in Eastern Europe, it was clear there would be no multiparty political system.

During the late 1940s, the Soviet Union required the other subject governments in Eastern Europe to impose Stalinist policies, including one-party political systems, close military cooperation with the Soviet Union, the collectivization of agriculture, Communist Party domination of education, and attacks on the churches. (See "The Church and the Communist Party Clash over Education in Hungary.") Longtime Communist Party officials were purged and condemned in show trials like those that had taken place in Moscow during the late 1930s. The catalyst for this harsh tightening probably was the success of Marshal Josip (Broz) Tito (1892–1980), the leader of communist Yugoslavia, in freeing his country from Soviet domination. Stalin wanted to prevent other Eastern European states from following the Yugoslav example.

THE POSTWAR DIVISION OF GERMANY

Soviet actions, especially those in Czechoslovakia, increased the determination of the United States to go ahead with its own arrangements in Germany.

Disagreements over Germany During the war, the Allies had never decided how to treat Germany after its defeat. At first they all agreed it should be dismembered, but they differed on how. By the time

government deprived them of their denominational schools. The children came home from the new schools like little heathens, who smiled derisively or laughed at the prayers of their parents.

You Hungarian parents will likewise feel a violation of your fundamental rights if your children can no longer attend the Catholic schools solely because the dictatorial State closes down our schools by a brutal edict or renders their work impossible.

STATEMENT OF THE HUNGARIAN COMMUNIST MINISTER OF PUBLIC WORSHIP, JUNE 7, 1950

We must start a vast work of enlightenment, and in the first place explain to our party colleagues and also to all workers that any father who sends his child to religion classes places it in the hands of the enemy and entrusts his soul and thinking to the enemies of peace and imperialistic warmongers.

A part of our working people believes that participation of children in religious instruction is a private matter which has nothing to do with the political conviction of their parents. They are wrong. To send children to a reactionary pastor for religious instruction is a political movement against the People's Democracy, whether intentional or not. . . .

In carrying out the basic principles, religion within the party is no private matter, but we must make a difference between plain party members and party officials, and must not in any case make party membership dependent on the fact whether our party members are religious. In the first place, we must expect from our party officials, our leading men, that they do not send their children to religious instruction courses, do not take part in religious ceremonies and train their wives in the spirit of communistic conception.

Also, we must patiently endeavor to enlighten our members, and ensure through training and propaganda that they realize: "In going to Church, taking part in processions, sending our children to religious instruction, we unconsciously further the efforts of clerical reaction."

"The Church and the Communist Party Clash over Education in Hungary" from Colman J. Barry, ed., *Readings in Church History*, pp. 496–498. Copyright © 1965. Reprinted by permission of Christian Classics, Allen, TX.

---

of Yalta, Churchill had come to fear Russian control of Eastern and central Europe and began to oppose dismemberment.

The Allies also differed on economic policy. The Russians swiftly dismantled German industry in the eastern zone, but the Americans acted differently in the western zone. (See Map 30–2.) They concluded that if they followed the Soviet policy, the United States would have to support Germany economically for the foreseeable future. It would also cause chaos and open the way for communism. They preferred, therefore, to try to make Germany self-sufficient, and this meant restoring, rather than destroying, its industrial capacity. To the Soviets, the restoration of a powerful industrial Germany, even in the western zone only, was frightening. The same difference of approach hampered agreement on reparations. The Soviets claimed the right to the industrial equipment in all the zones, and the Americans resisted their demands.

Berlin Blockade   When the Western powers agreed to go forward with a separate constitution for the western sectors of Germany in February 1948, the Soviets walked out of the joint Allied Control Commission. In the summer of that year, the Western powers issued a new currency in their zone. Berlin, though well within the Soviet zone, was governed by all four powers. The Soviets feared the new currency, which was circulating in Berlin at better rates than their own currency. They chose to seal the city off by closing all railroads and highways that led from Berlin to West Germany. Their purpose was to drive the Western powers out of Berlin.

The Western allies responded to the Berlin blockade by airlifting supplies to the city for almost a year. In May 1949, the Russians were forced to reopen access to Berlin. The incident, however, was decisive. It increased tensions and suspicions between the opponents and hastened the separation of Germany into two states. West Germany formally became the German Federal Republic in September

MAP 30–2   OCCUPIED GERMANY AND AUSTRIA   *At the war's end, defeated Germany, including Austria, was occupied by the victorious Allies in the several zones shown here. Austria, by prompt agreement, was reestablished as an independent, neutral state, no longer occupied. The German zones hardened into an "East" Germany (the former Soviet zone) and a "West" Germany (the former British, French, and American zones). Berlin, within the Soviet zone, was similarly divided.*

Located deep within communist East Germany, West Berlin was suddenly cut off from the West when Josef Stalin blockaded all surface traffic in an attempt to take over the war-torn city. Between June 1948 and May 1949, British and U.S. pilots made 272,000 flights, dropping food and fuel to civilians. The Berlin Airlift successfully foiled the blockade, and the Soviet Union reopened access on May 12.

1949, and the eastern region became the German Democratic Republic a month later. Ironically, Germany had been dismembered in a way no one had planned or expected. The two Germanies and the divided city of Berlin, isolated within East Germany, would remain central fixtures in the geopolitics of the Cold War until it ended in 1989.

NATO AND THE WARSAW PACT

Meanwhile, the nations of Western Europe had been coming closer together. The Marshall Plan encouraged international cooperation. In March 1948, Belgium, the Netherlands, Luxembourg, France, and Britain signed the Treaty of Brussels, providing for cooperation in economic and military matters. In April 1949, these nations joined with Italy, Denmark, Norway, Portugal, and Iceland to sign a treaty with Canada and the United States that formed the North Atlantic Treaty Organization (NATO), which committed its members to mutual assistance in case any of them was attacked. The NATO treaty transformed the West into a bloc. A few years later, West Germany, Greece, and Turkey joined the alliance. For the

first time in history, the United States was committed to defend allies outside the Western Hemisphere.

A series of bilateral treaties providing for close ties and mutual assistance in case of attack governed Soviet relations with the states of Eastern Europe. In 1949, these states formed the Council of Mutual Assistance (COMECON) to integrate their economies. Unlike the NATO states, the Eastern alliance system was under direct Soviet domination through local communist parties controlled from Moscow and overawed by the presence of the Red Army. The Warsaw Pact of May 1955, which included Albania, Bulgaria, Czechoslovakia, East Germany, Hungary, Poland, Romania, and the Soviet Union, gave formal recognition to this system. Europe was divided into two unfriendly blocs. The Cold War had taken firm shape in Europe. (See Map 30–3.)

The strategic interests of the United States and the Soviet Union would not, however, permit the Cold War to be limited to the European continent. Major flash points would erupt around the world during the decades that followed, most particularly in the Middle East and in Asia. The establishment of a communist government in Cuba after 1959

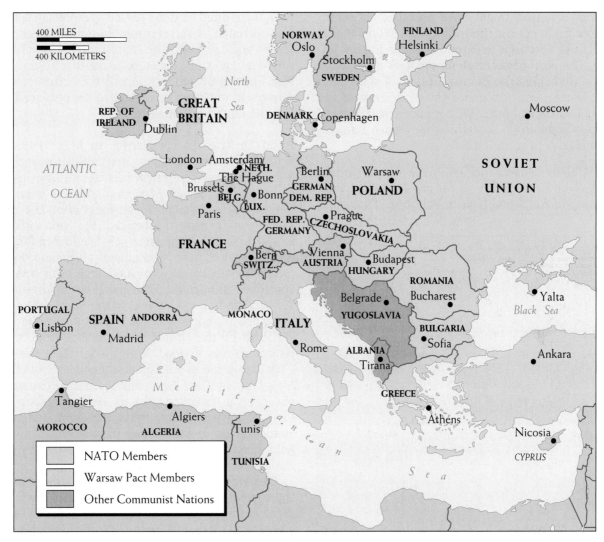

MAP 30–3   MAJOR COLD WAR EUROPEAN ALLIANCE SYSTEMS   *The North Atlantic Treaty Organization, which includes both Canada and the United States, stretched during the Cold War era as far east as Turkey. By contrast, the Warsaw Pact nations were the contiguous communist states of Eastern Europe, with the Soviet Union, of course, as the dominant member.*

would bring the conflict to the American hemisphere as well. In each case, the Cold War rivalry transformed what might otherwise have been regional conflicts into superpower strategic concerns.

THE CREATION OF THE STATE OF ISRAEL

One of the areas of ongoing regional conflict that became a major point of Cold War rivalry was the Middle East. Following World War I, Great Britain had exercised the chief political influence in the region under various postwar mandates. After World War II, both the Zionist movement seeking to establish an independent Jewish state and Arab nationalists seeking to achieve self-determination challenged British authority and influence.

British Balfour Declaration   The modern state of Israel was the achievement of the world Zionist movement, founded in 1897 by Theodor Herzl (see Chapter 25) and later led by Chaim Weizmann (1874–1952). The British Balfour Declaration of 1917 had favored establishing a national home for the Jewish people in Palestine. Between the wars, thousands of Jews, mainly from Europe, immigrated to the area, then governed by Great Britain under a mandate of the League of Nations. During the interwar period, the *Yishuv*, or Jewish community in Palestine, developed its own political parties, press, labor unions, and educational system. There were many conflicts with the Arabs already living in Palestine, who considered the Jewish settlers intruders. The British tried, but failed, to mediate those clashes.

This situation might have prevailed longer in Palestine, except for the outbreak of World War II and Hitler's attempt to exterminate the Jews of Europe. The Nazi persecution united Jews throughout the world behind the Zionist ideal of a Jewish state in Palestine, and it touched the conscience of the United States and other Western powers. It seemed morally right to do something for Jewish refugees from Nazi concentration camps.

The UN Resolution In 1947, the British turned over to the United Nations the problem of the relationship of Arabs and Jews in Palestine. That same year, the United Nations passed a resolution calling for a division of the territory into two states, one Jewish and one Arab. The Arabs in Palestine and the surrounding Arab states resisted this resolution. Not unnaturally, they resented the influx of new settlers. Many Palestinian Arabs were displaced and became refugees themselves.

Israel Declares Independence In May 1948, the British officially withdrew from Palestine and the Yishuv declared the independence of a new Jewish state called *Israel* on May 14. Two days later, the United States, through the personal intervention of President Truman, recognized the new nation, whose first prime minister was David Ben-Gurion (1886–1973). Almost immediately, Lebanon, Syria, Jordan, Egypt, and Iraq invaded Israel. The fighting continued throughout 1948 and 1949. By the end of its war of independence against the Arabs, Israel had expanded its borders beyond the limits originally set forth by the United Nations. (See Map 30–4.) Jerusalem was divided. Jordan controlled the Old City of Jerusalem, but Israel retained control of the New City. By 1949, Israel had secured its existence, but not the acceptance of its Arab neighbors. So long as Egypt, Jordan, Syria, Lebanon, Iraq, and Saudi Arabia, to name those nations closest, withheld diplomatic recognition, the peace was only an armed truce.

The Arab-Israeli conflict would inevitably draw in the superpowers. The dispute directly involved Europe because many of the citizens of Israel had emigrated from there, and Europe, like the United States, was highly dependent on oil from Arab countries. Furthermore, both the United States and the Soviet Union believed they had major strategic and economic interests in the region.

By 1949, the United States had established itself as a firm ally of Israel. Gradually, the Soviet Union began to furnish aid to the Arab nations. The bipolar tensions that had settled over Europe were thus transferred to the Middle East.

THE KOREAN WAR

While early stages of the Cold War took place in Europe and the Arab-Israeli conflict developed in the Middle East, the United States confronted armed aggression in Asia. As part of a UN police action, it intervened militarily in Korea, following the same principle of containment that directed its actions in Europe.

Between 1910 and 1945, Japan, as an Asian colonial power, had occupied and exploited Korea, but at the close of World War II, the Japanese were repelled. The United States and the Soviet Union

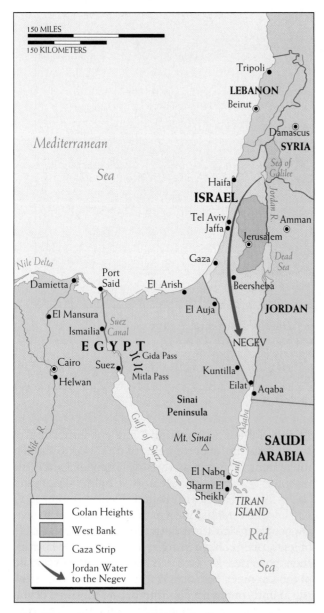

MAP 30–4 ISRAEL AND ITS NEIGHBORS IN 1949 *The territories gained by Israel in 1949 did not secure peace in the region. In fact, the disposition of those lands and the Arab refugees who live there has constituted the core of the region's unresolved problems to the present day.*

divided Korea into two parts along the thirty-eighth parallel of latitude. Korea was supposed to be reunited. By 1948, however, two separate states had been organized: the Democratic People's Republic of Korea in the North, supported by the Soviet Union, and the Republic of Korea in the South, supported by the United States.

In late June 1950, after border clashes, North Korea invaded South Korea across the thirty-eighth parallel. (See Map 30–5.) The United States intervened and was soon supported by a UN mandate. Great Britain, Turkey, Australia, and other countries sent token forces. The Korean police action was technically a UN venture to halt aggression. (It had been made possible when the Soviet ambassador boycotted the United Nations when the key vote was taken.) For the United States, the point of the Korean conflict was to contain the spread and halt the aggression of communism.

Late in 1950, the Chinese, responding to the approach of UN forces near their border, sent troops to support North Korea. The American forces had to retreat. The U.S. policymakers believed the Chinese, who, since 1949, had been under the communist government of Mao Tse-tung (1893–1976), were simply the puppets of the Soviet Union. Accordingly, the Americans viewed the movement of Chinese troops into South Korea as another example of communist pressure against a noncommunist state, similar to what had previously happened in Europe. Today it is clear that tension existed between Moscow and the People's Republic of China, but that was little understood at the time.

On June 16, 1953, the Eisenhower administration concluded an armistice ending the Korean War and restoring the border near the thirty-eighth parallel. American troops, however, have remained stationed in Korea to the present day. The lessons of the Cold War learned in Europe appeared to have been successfully applied to Asia. The American government's faith in containment was confirmed. The Korean conflict transformed the Cold War into a global rivalry that ranged well beyond Europe.

The formation of NATO and the Korean conflict capped the first round of the Cold War. In 1953, Stalin's death and the armistice in Korea fostered hopes that international tensions might ease. In early 1955, Soviet occupation forces left Austria after that nation accepted neutral status. Later that year the leaders of France, Great Britain, the Soviet Union, and the United States held a summit conference in Geneva. Nuclear weapons and the future of divided Germany were the chief items on the agenda. Despite public displays of friendliness, the meeting produced few substantial agreements on major problems, and the rivalry and polemics of the Cold War soon resumed.

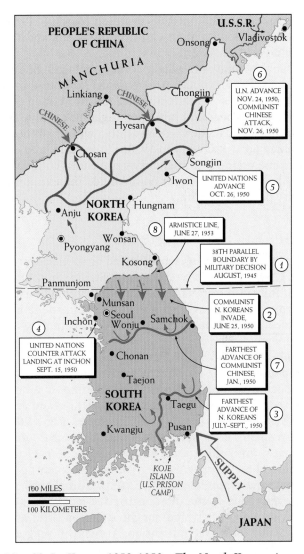

MAP 30–5   KOREA, 1950–1953   *The North Korean invasion of South Korea in 1950 and the bitter three-year war to repulse the invasion and stabilize a firm boundary near the thirty-eighth parallel are outlined here. The war was a dramatic application of the American policy of containment of communism.*

The Khrushchev Era in the Soviet Union

THE LAST YEARS OF STALIN

No other nation had suffered greater losses or more deprivation during World War II than the Soviet Union. Many Russians had hoped the end of the war would signal a reduction in the scope of the police state and a redirection of the economy away from heavy industry to consumer products. They were disappointed. Stalin did little or nothing to modify the character of the regime he had created. If anything, his determination to centralize his authority and a desire to undertake a new wave of internal purges continued until his death on March 6, 1953. (See "Art & the West: Cultural Divisions and the Cold War," p. 1082.)

For a time, no single leader replaced Stalin. Rather, the *presidium* (the renamed Politburo) pursued a policy of collective leadership. Gradually, however, power and influence began to devolve on Nikita Khrushchev (1894–1971), who had been named party secretary in 1953. Three years later, he became premier. Khrushchev's rise ended collective leadership, but he never commanded the extraordinary powers of Stalin.

KHRUSHCHEV'S DOMESTIC POLICIES

The Khrushchev era, which lasted until the autumn of 1964, witnessed a retreat from Stalinism, though not from authoritarianism. Khrushchev sought to reform the Soviet system but to maintain the dominance of the Communist Party. Intellectuals were somewhat freer to express their opinions. Although Boris Pasternak (1890–1960), the author of *Dr. Zhivago* (1957), was not permitted to receive the Nobel prize for literature in 1958, another dissident author, Aleksandr Solzhenitsyn (b. 1918), could publish *One Day in the Life of Ivan Denisovich* (1963). Khrushchev's economic policy also differed somewhat from Stalin's, with modest efforts to meet the demand for more consumer goods and decentralize economic planning. In agriculture, Khrushchev removed many of the more restrictive regulations on private cultivation and sought to expand the area available for wheat cultivation. At first this program led to record grain production, but inappropriate farming techniques soon reduced yields. The Soviet Union had to import vast quantities of grain each year from the United States and other countries.

The Secret Speech of 1956 In February 1956, Khrushchev made an extraordinary departure from expected practice by directly attacking the policies of the Stalin years. At the Twentieth Congress of the

Major Dates of the Early Khrushchev Era

1953	Death of Stalin
1955	Austria established as a neutral state
1955	Geneva summit
1956	(February) Khrushchev's secret speech denouncing Stalin
	(Autumn) Polish crisis
	(October) Suez crisis
	(October) Hungarian uprising
1957	*Sputnik* launched

Communist Party, Khrushchev gave a secret speech (later published outside the Soviet Union) in which he denounced Stalin and his crimes against socialist justice during the purges of the 1930s. The speech caused shock and consternation in party circles, but it also opened the way for genuine, if limited, internal criticism of the Soviet government and for many of the changes in intellectual and economic life cited earlier. Gradually, Khrushchev removed the strongest supporters of Stalinist policies from the presidium. By 1958, all Stalin's former supporters were gone, and none had been executed. (See "Khrushchev Denounces the Crimes of Stalin: The Secret Speech.")

Khrushchev's speech had repercussions well beyond the borders of the Soviet Union. Communist leaders in Eastern Europe took it as a signal that they could govern with greater leeway than before and retreat from Stalinist policies. Indeed, Khrushchev's speech was simply the first of a number of extraordinary events in 1956.

The Three Crises of 1956

THE SUEZ INTERVENTION

In July 1956, Egypt's president Gamal Abdel Nasser (1918–1970), who had seized power in that country in 1952, nationalized the Suez Canal, until then controlled by British and French interests. Egyptian control of the canal threatened the access of Great Britain and France to Persian Gulf oil supplies, essential to their industrial economies. In October 1956, war broke out between Egypt, then receiving arms from the Soviet Union, and the new state of Israel, closely tied to the West. Britain and France seized the opportunity to intervene. Although they justified their actions as a way to separate the combatants, their real motive was to regain control of the canal and reassert their influence in the region. Israel joined with France and Britain. Although this alliance helped Israel fend off Arab guerrilla attacks, it also associated Israel with the former imperial powers.

Although the Suez intervention was a military success, with Israel seizing the Sinai and Britain and France landing troops in the canal zone, it ended in a humiliating diplomatic defeat. The United States refused to support the Anglo-French intervention, and the Soviet Union protested in the most strident terms. The Anglo-French forces had to withdraw, and Egypt retained control of the canal. A UN peacekeeping force separated the armies of Israel and Egypt, and Israel withdrew from the Sinai.

The Suez intervention proved that without the support of the United States the nations of Western Europe could no longer use military force to impose their will on the rest of the world. Also, the United

KHRUSHCHEV DENOUNCES THE CRIMES OF STALIN: THE SECRET SPEECH

In 1956, Khrushchev denounced Stalin in a secret speech to the Party Congress. The New York Times *published a text of that speech, smuggled from Russia.*

■ *What are the specific actions on the part of Stalin that Khrushchev denounced? Why does Khrushchev pay so much attention to Stalin's creation of the concept of an "enemy of the people"? Why does Khrushchev draw a distinction between the actions of Stalin and those of Lenin?*

Stalin acted not through persuasion, explanation, and patient cooperation with people, but by imposing his concepts and demanding absolute submission to his opinion. Whoever opposed this concept or tried to prove his viewpoint and the correctness of his position was doomed to removal from the leading collective [group] and to subsequent moral and physical annihilation. . . .

Stalin originated the concept of "enemy of the people." This term automatically rendered it unnecessary that the ideological errors of a man or men engaged in a controversy be proved; this term made possible the usage of the most cruel repression violating all norms of revolutionary legality, against anyone who in any way disagreed with Stalin, against those who were only suspected of hostile intent, against those who had bad reputations.

This concept "enemy of the people" actually eliminated the possibility of any kind of ideological fight or the making of one's views known on this or that issue, even those of a practical character. In the main, and in actuality, the only proof of guilt used, against all norms of current legal science, was the "confession" of the accused himself; and, as a subsequent probing proved, "confessions" were acquired through physical pressures against the accused. . . .

Lenin used severe methods only in the most necessary cases, when the exploiting classes were still in existence and were vigorously opposing the revolution, when the struggle for survival was decidedly assuming the sharpest forms, even including civil war.

Stalin, on the other hand, used extreme methods and mass repressions at a time when the revolution was already victorious, when the Soviet State was strengthened, when the exploiting classes were already liquidated and Socialist relations were rooted solidly in all phases of national economy, when our party was politically consolidated and had strengthened itself both numerically and ideologically. It is clear that here Stalin showed in a whole series of cases his intolerance, his brutality and his abuse of power. Instead of proving his political correctness and mobilizing the masses, he often chose the path of repression and physical annihilation, not only against actual enemies, but also against individuals who had not committed any crimes against the party and the Soviet Government.

From the *New York Times*, June 5, 1956, pp. 13–16. Copyright © 1956 The New York Times. Reprinted by permission.

States and the Soviet Union showed they would restrain their allies from actions that might result in a wider conflict. But the Arab-Israeli conflict remained unresolved. The Arab states refused to recognize the existence of Israel. The Middle East remained a major flash point.

POLAND'S EFFORTS TOWARD INDEPENDENT ACTION

The autumn of 1956 saw important developments in Eastern Europe, based in large measure on miscalculations about the real meaning of Khruschev's secret speech attacking Stalin.

The Polish Communist Party had been subjected to Stalinist discipline during the late 1940s. One of the communist leaders who had been imprisoned was Wladyslaw Gomulka (1905–1982). Toward the end of 1954, the authorities released him, and he stood ready to reenter a leadership position. The opportunity presented itself in June 1956, when a workers' uprising took place in Poznan, indicating discontent with the highly disciplined communist regime. By October, the hard-line Stalinist leadership of Poland was resigning. Gomulka began to exercise considerable influence and was attending government meetings. The Russians were sufficiently concerned to order troop movements and

These British soldiers during the Suez invasion in 1956 seemed triumphant, but American pressure soon forced the British and French to withdraw from Egypt.
© Hulton-Deutsch Collection/Corbis

send a delegation, including Khrushchev, to Warsaw. In the end, Gomulka emerged as the new communist leader of Poland. The choice of the Polish communists, he also proved acceptable to the Soviets because he was genuinely a communist, promised to continue economic and military cooperation, and, most important to the Soviets, continued Polish membership in the Warsaw Pact. Within those limits, he moved to halt the collectivization of Polish agriculture and to improve the relationship between the communist government and the Polish Roman Catholic Church. This resolution more or less allowed the Polish Communist Party to manage its own affairs, leading another Eastern European country to seek similar autonomy.

UPRISING IN HUNGARY

In late October, as the Polish problem was nearing resolution, Hungarians in Budapest demonstrated in sympathy for the Poles. Hungary's communist government moved to stop the demonstrations, and street fighting erupted. The Hungarian Communist Party then installed a new government headed by former premier Imre Nagy (1896–1958).

Although a communist, Nagy sought greater independence for Hungary. He demanded more than Gomulka had in Poland and appealed to noncommunist groups in Hungary for support. He wanted the Soviets to withdraw their troops and Hungary to become a neutral state. Nagy even called for Hungarian withdrawal from the Warsaw Pact. These demands were wholly unacceptable to the Soviet Union. In early November, Soviet troops invaded

Hungary, deposed Nagy (who was executed in 1958), and installed Janos Kadar (1912–1989) as premier.

The Polish and Hungarian disturbances showed the limits of the Soviet Union's tolerance for independence within its bloc, notwithstanding Khrushchev's criticisms of Stalinism. They also demonstrated that the countries of Eastern Europe would not be permitted to imitate Austrian neutrality. It should also be noted that the Suez intervention had distracted international attention and permitted the Soviet Union freer action within its sphere of influence. Finally, the failure of the United States to support the Hungarian uprising demonstrated the hollowness of American political rhetoric about liberating the captive nations of Eastern Europe.

The events of 1956 in the Middle East and Eastern Europe solidified the position of the United States and the Soviet Union as superpowers. In different ways and to differing degrees, the two superpowers had demonstrated this new political reality to their allies. The nations of Western Europe would be able to make independent policy among themselves within Europe, but were generally curtailed from independent action on the broader international scene. For approximately twenty-five years, the nations of Eastern Europe would be permitted virtually no autonomous actions in either the domestic or the international sphere.

Later Cold War Confrontations

COLLAPSE OF THE 1960 PARIS SUMMIT CONFERENCE

After 1956, the Soviet Union began to talk about "peaceful coexistence" with the United States. With the 1957 launch of *Sputnik*, the Soviet Union appeared to have achieved enormous technological superiority over the West. In 1958, the two countries began negotiations toward limiting the testing of nuclear weapons. The same year, however, the Soviet Union demanded the West grant formal diplomatic recognition to East Germany and then announced the status of West Berlin must be changed and the Allied occupation forces withdrawn. These demands were refused, but they had made Germany, and particularly Berlin, the center of East-West tension. In 1959, matters relaxed sufficiently for several Western leaders to visit Moscow and for Khrushchev to tour the United States. A summit meeting was scheduled for May 1960, and President Eisenhower was to go to Moscow.

Just before the Paris Summit Conference, the Soviet Union shot down an American U-2 aircraft that was flying reconnaissance over Soviet territory. Khrushchev demanded an apology from Eisenhower for this air surveillance. Eisenhower accepted full responsibility for the surveillance policy but refused to apologize publicly. Khrushchev then refused to take part in the summit conference, just as the participants arrived in the French capital. The conference, as well as Eisenhower's proposed trip to the Soviet Union, was thus aborted.

The Soviets did not scuttle the summit meeting on the eve of its opening simply because of the American spy flights. They had long been aware of these flights and had other reasons for protesting them when they did. By 1960, the communist world itself had split between the Soviets and the Chinese. The latter were portraying the Russians as lacking sufficient revolutionary zeal. Destroying the summit was, in part, a way to demonstrate the Soviet Union's hard-line attitude toward the capitalist world.

THE BERLIN WALL

The aborted Paris conference opened the most difficult period of the Cold War. In 1961, the new U.S. president, John F. Kennedy (1917–1963), and Premier Khrushchev met in Vienna. The conference was inconclusive, but the American president left wondering whether the two nations could avoid war.

Throughout 1961, thousands of refugees from East Germany crossed the border into West Berlin. The western sector of the city was the single point in Eastern Europe where persons living under Soviet dominance might escape to a free political climate. This outflow of people embarrassed East Germany and hurt its economy. It also demonstrated the Soviet Union's inability to control events in Eastern Europe.

In August 1961, the East Germans, with the support of the Soviet Union, erected a concrete wall along the border between East and West Berlin, shutting the two parts of the city off from each other. In June 1963, President Kennedy himself appeared in Berlin, making a famous speech in which he declared, *"Ich bin ein Berliner"* ("I am a Berliner"). Despite speeches and symbolic support from the West, the wall halted the flow of refugees and brought the U.S. commitment to West Germany into doubt.

THE CUBAN MISSILE CRISIS

The most dangerous days of the Cold War occurred during the Cuban missile crisis of 1962, which represented another facet of the globalization of the Cold War, on this occasion into the Americas. Cuba lies less than 100 miles from the United States. In 1957, Fidel Castro (b. 1926) launched a communist insurgency in Cuba, which toppled the dictatorship of Flugencio Batista (1901–1973) on New Year's Day of 1959. Thereafter Castro established a communist government, and Cuba became an ally of the Soviet Union. These events caused enormous concern within the United States.

In 1962, the Soviet Union secretly began to place nuclear missiles in Cuba. Now concern turned to confrontation. The American government, under President Kennedy, blockaded Cuba, halted the shipment of new missiles, and demanded the removal of existing installations. After a tense week, during which communications between Washington and Moscow were permeated with admonitions and threats, the Soviets backed down, and the crisis

President John F. Kennedy announcing on television the strategic blockade of Cuba and his warning to the Soviet Union about missile sanctions during the Cuban missile crisis. Hutton Getty/Archive Photos

ended. This adventurism in foreign policy undermined Khrushchev's credibility in the ruling circles of the Soviet Union and caused other non-European communist regimes to question the Soviet Union's commitment to their security and survival. It also increased the influence of the People's Republic of China in communist circles and convinced Soviet military leaders of the need to strengthen their forces, so that they would be as strong as, or stronger than, those of the United States in any future confrontation.

If the Cuban missile crisis had led to war, the United States could have launched missiles over Europe or from European bases into the Soviet Union. The crisis thus threatened Europe directly, but it was the last major Cold War confrontation to do so. In 1963, the United States and the Soviet Union concluded a nuclear test ban treaty. This agreement marked the beginning of a lessening in the overt tensions between the two powers. By 1964, many in the Soviet Communist Party had concluded that Khrushchev had tried to do too much too soon and had done it poorly. On October 16, 1964, Khrushchev was forced to resign. He was replaced by Alexei Kosygin (1904–1980) as premier and Leonid Brezhnev (1906–1982) as party secretary. Brezhnev eventually emerged as the dominant figure.

BREZHNEV AND THE INVASION OF CZECHOSLOVAKIA

In 1968, during what became known as the Prague Spring, the government of Czechoslovakia, under Alexander Dubcek (1921–1992), began to experiment with a more liberal communism. Dubcek expanded freedom of discussion and other intellectual rights at a time when they were being suppressed in the Soviet Union. In the summer of 1968, the Soviet government and its allies in the Warsaw Pact sent troops into Czechoslovakia and installed communist leaders more to its own liking.

Major Dates of Later Cold War Years	
1959	Khrushchev visit to the United States
1960	Failed Paris Summit
1961	Soviet Union erects Berlin Wall
1962	Cuban missile crisis
1963	Test Ban Treaty between Soviet Union and the United States
1964	Khrushchev falls from power
1968	Soviet invasion of Czechoslovakia
1972	Strategic Arms Limitation Treaty

At the time of the invasion, Soviet party chairman Brezhnev, in what came to be termed the Brezhnev Doctrine, declared the right of the Soviet Union to interfere in the domestic politics of other communist countries. Whereas the Truman Doctrine of 1947 had supported democratic governments and offered help to resist further communist penetration in Europe, the Brezhnev Doctrine of 1968 sought to sustain the communist governments of Eastern Europe and prevent any liberalization in the region. No further direct Soviet interventions occurred in Eastern Europe after 1968, yet the invasion of Czechoslovakia showed that any political experimentation involving greater liberalization could trigger Soviet military repression.

Decolonization: The European Retreat from Empire

The transformation of much of Africa and Asia from colonial domains into independent nations was the most remarkable global political event of the second half of the twentieth century. It could hardly have been imagined in 1925. The numbers of people involved alone is revealing of the magnitude of the change. At the founding of the United Nations in 1945, approximately one-third of the population of the world were subject to the government of colonial nations. Since that time, more than eighty of those then non-self-governing territories have been admitted to UN membership. This achievement was the result of the work of numerous leaders throughout the former colonial world and of often complicated political movements. A book devoted primarily to the history of the West can give only a modest account of how decolonization was achieved and how it has changed both the West and the larger world scene.

In 1900, European powers dominated or directly ruled most of Africa and large parts of Asia, and the United States ruled the Philippines. (See Chapter 26.) After World War I, many of the colonial peoples argued unsuccessfully for their independence at the Paris Peace Conference in 1919. The general embrace of the doctrine of the self-determination of nations that had driven European politics since 1919 proved powerful within the European empires because movements of colonial peoples appealed to that very same concept as applicable to their own nations. They also appealed to the ideas associated with the various forms of European socialism as remedies for the social and racial inequalities they experienced as peoples governed by European colonial powers.

In the summer of 1968, Soviet tanks rolled into Czechoslovakia, ending that country's experiment in liberalized communism. This picture shows defiant flag-waving Czechs on a truck rolling past a Soviet tank in the immediate aftermath of the invasion. Archive Photos

Decolonization after 1945 was a direct result of both World War II itself and the rise of indigenous nationalist movements within Africa, Asia, and the Middle East. World War II drew the military forces of the colonial powers back to Europe. The Japanese overran European possessions in East Asia and demonstrated that the European presence there might not be permanent. After the dislocations of the war came the immediate postwar European economic collapse, which left the European colonial powers less able to afford to maintain their military and administrative positions abroad.

The war aims of the Allies had also undermined colonialism. It was difficult to fight against tyranny in Europe while maintaining colonial dominance abroad. The United States, and in particular Franklin Roosevelt, opposed the continuation of the colonial empires. This policy was in part a matter of principle, but it also recognized that both the political and economic interests of the United States were more likely to prosper in a decolonized world. The founding of the United Nations also assured the presence of an international body opposed to colonialism.

The Cold War complicated the process of decolonization. Both the United States and the Soviet Union opposed the old colonial empires. But both also worried about the potential alignment of the new nations and moved to create spheres of influence and, in some cases, alliances. Certain nations, such as India, fiercely pursued policies of neutrality in hopes of receiving aid and support from both sides.

MAJOR AREAS OF COLONIAL WITHDRAWAL

Decolonization was a worldwide event lasting throughout the second half of the twentieth century. It involved such dramatic moments as the Dutch being forced from the East Indies in 1949 to be replaced by the independent nation of Indonesia, the Belgian surrender of the Belgian Congo in 1960, the liberation of Portuguese Mozambique and Angola in 1974 and 1975, and the end of all-white rule in Rhodesia in 1979 and most remarkably in South Africa in 1994.

Each of these events was important, especially to the peoples involved. But the two largest colonial empires were the British and the French. Their retreat from empire produced the most far-reaching repercussions not only in former colonial nations, but in both Europe and the United States. (See Map 30–6.)

INDIA

No anticolonial movement so gripped the imagination of the Western world as that carried out in India under the leadership of Mohandas Gandhi (1869–1948). The British had commenced their rule of India in the middle of the eighteenth century (see Chapter 17), extending and consolidating it throughout the nineteenth. The British administered India by requiring the Indians themselves to pay for British rule. India supplied the raw materials for the British cotton mills. Other British policies pushed many Indians to migrate to other parts of Asia, Africa, and the Caribbean islands. For decades, the

religious, ethnic, linguistic, and political divisions among Indians permitted the British to dominate the country through a divide-and-conquer strategy.

As early as 1885, politically active Hindu Indians founded the Indian National Congress with the goals of modernizing Indian life and liberalizing British policy. Muslims organized the Muslim League in 1887, which for a time cooperated with the National Congress, but eventually sought an independent Muslim nation. After World War I, the Indian nationalist movement grew steadily in strength in part because of British blunders, but more importantly because remarkable leaders pursued effective strategies.

Chief among these leaders was Gandhi, who had studied law in Britain and there began to encounter the ideas of liberal Western thinkers, including the American Henry David Thoreau (1817–1862) from whom he learned the concept of passive resistance. After being called to the bar in London in 1891, he returned briefly to India and then in 1893 went to South Africa where for over twenty years he worked

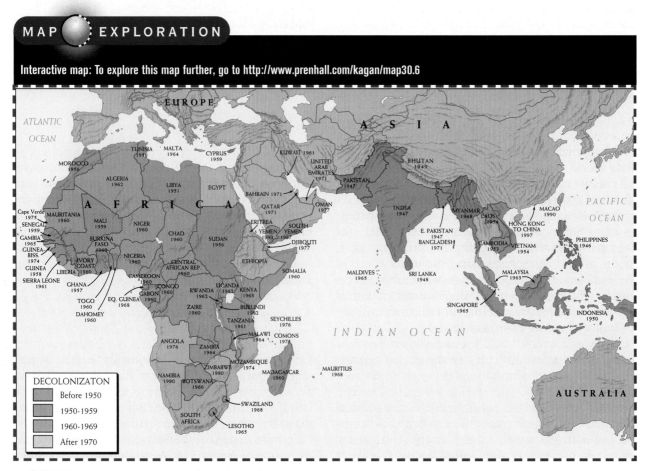

MAP 30–6 DECOLONIZATION IN AFRICA AND ASIA AFTER WORLD WAR II *The map shows when the European possessions in Africa and Asia achieved independence from the late 1940s to the 1970s.*

on behalf of Indian immigrants. During those years he continued to read widely and became convinced of the power of passive resistance. Gandhi returned to India in 1915 and soon distinguished himself as a leader of Indian nationalism by his insistence on religious toleration. From the 1920s to the mid-1940s, he inspired a growing movement of passive resistance to British rule in India. In 1930, he lead a famous march to break the British salt monopoly by collecting salt from the sea. During these years he was repeatedly arrested and jailed by the British authorities. To embarrass the British during these imprisonments and to gain worldwide publicity, he undertook long protest fasts during which he nearly died. In 1942, Gandhi called on the British Government to leave India. In 1947, the British Labor government, weary of the incessant agitation and uncertain of its ability to maintain control in India, decided to do so.

Gandhi became and remains the most famous anticolonial leader of the twentieth century. His career demonstrates how such a leader could repeatedly use ideas taken from the West against colonial regimes. His use of passive resistance became a model for Dr. Martin Luther King, Jr. (1929–1968) during the civil rights movement in the United States during the late 1950s and 1960s. (See "Gandhi Explains His Doctrine of Nonviolence.")

Gandhi and the Congress Party succeeded in forcing the British from India. However, they did not succeed in creating a single nation. Parallel to Gandhi's drive for an India characterized by diverse religions living in mutual toleration, the Muslim League led by Ali Jinnah (1876–1948) sought a distinctly Muslim state. What occurred in 1947 as the British left India was a partition of the country into the states of India and Pakistan. Sectarian warfare and hundreds of thousands of deaths marked the partition. Gandhi himself was assassinated in 1948 by a Hindu extremist. Pakistan was initially a nation of two parts separated geographically by hundreds of miles of Indian territory. In 1971, East Pakistan broke away to become independent Bangladesh. As we see in the next chapter, the founding of Pakistan would be important for the emergence of political Islamism.

The partition of India and Pakistan illustrates an often-neglected factor in the process of decolonization. In many colonial regions, the retreat of the colonial powers opened the way for new or renewed conflicts among different groups within the former colonial empires. For example, since partition India and Pakistan have disputed the ownership of Kashmir in repeated armed clashes. Another example is the conflict over the former Portuguese colony of East Timor whose people have asserted a right to independence against the government of Indonesia, which occupied it after Portugal withdrew in 1975.

Ghandi led India from colonialism to independence. Part of his appeal was the simplicity of his life and dress.   Corbis

FURTHER BRITISH RETREAT FROM EMPIRE

The British surrender of India marked the beginning of a long, steady retreat from empire. Generally speaking, the British accepted the loss of empire as inevitable. British decolonization sought first to maintain whatever links were economically and politically possible without conflict. Indeed, during the 1940s and 1950s, the British undertook various development programs in their remaining Asian and African colonies. These investments paradoxically made both the British government and public more aware of the actual costs of empire and may have led both to accept more easily the end of empire. Second, throughout decolonization the British hoped to oversee the creation of institutions in their former colonies that would assure representative self-government once they had departed.

In 1948, Burma and Sri Lanka (formerly Ceylon) became independent. As already observed, Britain was also forced from the Middle East by the formation of the state of Israel and Arab nationalist movements. During the 1950s, the British tried to

GANDHI EXPLAINS HIS DOCTRINE OF NONVIOLENCE

The most famous device used by Indian nationalists against British colonial rule in India was Gandhi's doctrine of nonviolence. He had come to believe in its power during the years when he resided in South Africa. Nonviolence became the hallmark of his leadership of the drive against British rule when he returned to India. Gandhi wrote this description of the meaning of nonviolence during World War II. Yet even while enunciating its meaning, he refused to associate himself with nonviolence in international relations. This reluctance may have stemmed from his recognition that the war against the Axis powers was a war against Nazi racism and Japanese imperialism, both of which were dangerous for colonial peoples of color.

■ *Why does Gandhi see nonviolence as evidence of strength? How does he refrain from extending nonviolence to external relations? How was Gandhi's doctrine transferable to other political movements, such as the American civil rights movement?*

I do believe that, where there is only a choice between cowardice and violence, I would advise violence. . . .

But I believe that non-violence is infinitely superior to violence, forgiveness is more manly than punishment. . . .

Non-violence is the law of our species as violence is the law of the brute. The spirit lies dormant in the brute, and he knows no law but that of physical might. The dignity of man requires obedience to a higher law—to the strength of the spirit.

I have therefore ventured to place before India the ancient law of self-sacrifice. . . .

Non-violence in its dynamic condition means conscious suffering. It does not mean meek submission to the will of the evil-doer, but it means the pitting of one's whole soul against the will of the tyrant. Working under this law of our being, it is possible for a single individual to defy the whole might of an unjust empire to save his honour, his religion, his soul, and lay the foundation for that empire's fall or its regeneration. . . .

I have not the capacity for preaching universal non-violence to the country. I preach, therefore, non-violence restricted strictly for the purpose of winning our freedom and therefore perhaps for preaching the regulation of international relations by non-violent means. But my incapacity must not be mistaken for that of the doctrine of non-violence. I see it with my intellect in all its effulgence. My heart grasps it. But I have not yet the attainments of preaching universal non-violence with effect. . . .

I do justify entire non-violence, and consider it possible in relation between man and man and nation and nation; but it is not 'a resignation from all fighting against wickedness.' On the contrary, the non-violence of my conception is a more active more real fighting against wickedness than retaliation whose very nature is to increase wickedness. I contemplate a mental, and therefore a moral, opposition to immoralities. I seek entirely to blunt the edge of the tyrant's sword, not by putting up against it a sharper-edged weapon, but by disappointing his expectations that I should be offering physical resistance. . . .

Non-violence, therefore, presupposes ability to strike. It is a conscious deliberate restraint put upon one's desire for vengeance.

M. K. Gandhi, *Non-Violence in Peace and War* (Ahmedabad: Navajivan Publishing House, 1942) as quoted in Ronald Duncan, ed., *Gandhi: Selected Writings* (New York: Harper & Row, 1971), pp. 48, 49, 52–53, 54–55.

prepare colonies for self-government. Ghana (formerly the Gold Coast) and Nigeria—which became self-governing in 1957 and 1960, respectively—were the major examples of planned decolonization. In other areas, such as Malta and Cyprus, the British withdrew under the pressure of militant nationalist movements.

The development of these former colonies in the second half of the twentieth century has followed two distinct paths. The more recent history of the independent states in Africa has, in general, been marked by political instability and poverty. By contrast, Asia has been an area of general political stability and remarkable economic growth, challenging the economies of both the United States and Western Europe.

The Turmoil of French Decolonization

Confronted with national movements in its colonies, Britain generally faced the inevitable and departed. Although there were instances of considerable conflict as in Cyprus and Aden, the process more often than not was relatively peaceful. At no point did the British "make a stand." Moreover, many groups in Britain, including the leadership of the Labour Party, had long been critical of colonialism. Such was not the case with France. Having been defeated by the Nazis and then liberated by the allied forces, France believed it must reassert its position as a great power. This determination led it into two disastrous attempts to maintain its colonial empire, in Algeria and Vietnam. As we will see, the situation in Vietnam because of the intervention of the United States drew French decolonization directly into the tensions of the Cold War.

FRANCE AND ALGERIA

France had conquered Algeria in 1830 as Charles X futilely hoped the invasion would save his monarchy. (See Chapter 21.) In late 1848, the French government made Algeria an integral part of France, establishing three administrative departments that were administered like those in France itself. Over the decades as France consolidated and extended its position in Algeria, French soldiers and thousands of non-Muslim French citizens settled in the country, primarily in the cities and on small farms. By the close of World War I, approximately 20 percent of the population had immigrated from Europe, largely from non-French regions around the Mediterranean. Collectively these immigrants were termed the *pieds noirs* (meaning "black feet," a derogatory term). The voting structure was set up to give the French settlers as large a voice as the majority Arab Muslim population. The further one moved toward the south away from the coast and into the Sahara Desert, the greater the influence of the French military. Algerian Arab Muslims were not given posts in the administration. Shortly after World War I, the French extended the rights of full French citizenship to Algerians who had fought in the war, who were literate, or who owned land, but this meant only a few thousand Algerian Arab Muslims achieved that status.

During World War II, the forces of Free France dominated Algeria after 1942 while the Vichy regime still governed metropolitan France. The Free

Martin Luther King, the foremost American civil rights leader of the 1960s, was deeply influenced by the non-violent doctrines of Gandhi. Here he is shown delivering his famous "I Have a Dream" speech from the steps of the Lincoln Memorial in Washington, D.C., in 1963.
AP/Wide World Photos

French government did little to change the colonial status quo. Moreover, in May 1945, during celebrations of the Allied victory in World War II, a violent clash broke out at Sétif between Muslims and French settlers. Matters rapidly got out of hand, and people on both sides were killed, but the French Algerian government soon repressed the Muslims with considerable loss of life. The Arab Muslims of Algeria saw this incident the same way the Russian working classes viewed Bloody Sunday in 1905. (See Chapter 24.) It robbed the French administration of legitimacy and marked the beginning of conscious Algerian nationalism. Thereafter, many Algerian Arab Muslims believed independence must someday come. To placate Arab opinion, in 1947 the French established a structure for limited political representation of the Muslim population and undertook economic reforms. Not unsurprisingly, these steps proved ineffective.

Algerian nationalists soon founded the National Liberation Front (FLN), which demanded civic equality. In late 1954, insurrections and soon open civil war broke out in Algeria as the FLN undertook highly effective guerrilla warfare. The government of the Fourth French Republic that had been founded in 1945 adamantly declared Algeria was an integral part of France and that no compromise could be made with the insurgents. Thereafter a war lasting until 1962 ground on between the Algerian nationalists and the French. Both sides committed atrocities; hundreds of thousands of Algerian Arab Muslims were killed. The war sharply divided France itself with many French citizens, often of left-wing political opinion, objecting to the attacks on the Algerians, and the French military, still smarting from its surrenders in World War II and in Indochina, determined to fight on. The presence of more than 1 million French and European settlers in Algeria, who saw any settlement with the nationalists as a betrayal, exacerbated the situation. The French government itself became paralyzed and lost control of the army. There was fear of civil war in France itself. In Algeria, violence was spreading.

In the midst of this turmoil, General Charles de Gaulle, who had led the Free French forces during World War II and had briefly governed France immediately after the war, reentered French political life largely at the urging of the military. His condition for taking office was the end of the Fourth French Republic and the promulgation of a new constitution giving strong authority to the president and creating the Fifth French Republic. The voters ratified this, and de Gaulle became president. He then undertook a long strategic retreat from Algeria. The process was neither peaceful nor easy. In 1961, for example, it looked as if a group of officers known as the OAS (Organisation Armée Secrète) would attempt a coup in Paris. There were bombings, murders, and attempts on de Gaulle's life. In 1962, however, de Gaulle held a referendum in Algeria on independence, which passed overwhelmingly. Algeria became independent on July 5, 1962.

Once the FLN took over Algeria under the presidency of Mohammed Ben Bella (b. 1919), however, a second factor came into play in French domestic life. Hundreds of thousands of *pied noirs* settlers fled Algeria for France as did many Muslims who had supported the French and had good cause to fear reprisals (thousands of pro-French Muslims who did not flee were massacred). The emigration of this latter group marked the beginning of a large, and largely unwelcome, Muslim population in France.

FRANCE AND VIETNAM

One of the reasons for the strong French stand against Algerian independence had been the loss of its south Asian empire in Indochina just before the Algerian insurrection broke out in 1954. Whereas the Algerian drive toward independence essentially involved only France and the populations of Algeria, the Indochina problem eventually drew the United States into war in Vietnam.

In its push for empire, France had occupied Indochina (which contained Laos, Cambodia, and Vietnam) between 1857 and 1893. By 1930, Ho Chi Minh (1892–1969) had turned a nationalist movement against French colonial rule into the Indochina Communist Party, which the French for a time succeeded in suppressing. World War II, however, provided new opportunities for Ho Chi Minh and other nationalists as they fought both the Japanese who occupied Indochina in 1941 and the pro-Vichy French colonial administration that collaborated with the Japanese until 1945. The war thus established Ho Chi Minh as a major anticolonial, nationalist leader. He was a communist to be sure, but he had achieved his position in Vietnam during the war without the support of the Chinese communists.

In September 1945, Ho Chi Minh declared the independence of Vietnam under the Viet Minh, a coalition of nationalists that the communists soon

In 1959 Charles De Gaulle as President of the French Republic visited Algiers to great acclaim from its European inhabitants, the colons. By 1962, however, he had sponsored a referendum that led to Algerian independence and the flight of most of the colons. Loomis Dean/TimePix

dominated. By 1947, a full-fledged civil war had erupted in Vietnam. (Cambodia and, to a lesser extent, Laos remained quiescent under pro-French or neutralist monarchies.)

Until 1949, the United States had displayed minimal concern about the Indochina war. The establishment of the Communist People's Republic of China that year dramatically changed the U.S. outlook. The United States now saw the French colonial war against Ho Chi Minh as an integral part of the Cold War conflict. Even though the United States supported the French effort in Vietnam financially, it was not prepared, despite divisions among policymakers, to intervene militarily. In the spring of 1954, during an international conference in Geneva on the future of Vietnam, the French military stronghold of Dien Bien Phu fell to Viet Minh forces after a prolonged siege. France lost the will to continue the struggle, which had become increasingly unpopular with the French people.

By late June, a complicated and generally unsatisfactory peace accord divided Vietnam at the seventeenth parallel of latitude. North of the parallel, centered in Hanoi, the Viet Minh were in charge; below it, centered in Saigon, the French were in charge. This was to be a temporary border. By 1956, elections were to be held to reunify the country. In effect, the conference attempted to transform a military conflict into a political one.

VIETNAM DRAWN INTO THE COLD WAR

Unhappy with these arrangements, the United States in September 1954 formed the Southeast Asia Treaty Organization (SEATO), a collective security agreement that somewhat resembled the European NATO alliance, but without the integration of military forces or inclusion of all states in the region. Its membership consisted of the United States, Great Britain, France, Australia, New Zealand, Thailand, Pakistan, and the Philippines.

By 1955, American policymakers had begun to think about Indochina, and particularly Vietnam, largely in terms of the Korean example. The U.S. government assumed that, like the government of North Korea, the government in North Vietnam was basically a communist puppet. The same year, French troops began to withdraw from South Vietnam. As they left, the various Vietnamese political groups began to fight for power.

The United States stepped into the turmoil in Vietnam with military and economic aid. Among the Vietnamese politicians, it chose to support Ngo Dinh Diem (1901–1963), a strong noncommunist nationalist who had not collaborated with the French. Because the United States had been publicly and deeply

Ho Chi Minh (1892–1969), center, and advisers meet during the war against the French in 1954. Black Star

committed to the French, however, Vietnamese nationalists would view any government it supported with suspicion. In October 1955, Diem established a Republic of Vietnam in the territory for which the Geneva conference had made France responsible. Diem announced that he and his newly established government were not bound by the Geneva agreements and elections would not be held in 1956. The

Major Dates in the Vietnam Conflict	
1945	Ho Chi Minh proclaims Vietnamese independence from French rule
1947–1954	War between France and Vietnam
1950	U.S. financial aid to France
1954	Geneva conference on Southeast Asia opens
1954	French defeat at Dien Bien Phu
1954	Southeast Asia Treaty Organization founded
1955	Diem establishes Republic of Vietnam in the south
1960	Founding of National Liberation Front to overthrow the Diem government
1961	Six hundred American troops and advisers in Vietnam
1963	Diem overthrown and assassinated
1964	Gulf of Tonkin Resolution
1965	Major U.S. troop commitment
1969	Nixon announces policy of Vietnamization
1973	Cease-fire announced
1975	Saigon falls to North Vietnamese troops

American government, which had not signed the Geneva documents, supported his position.

In 1960, the National Liberation Front was founded, with the goals of overthrowing Diem, unifying the country, reforming the economy, and ousting the Americans. It was anticolonial, nationalist, and communist. Its military arm was called the Viet Cong and was aided by the government of North Vietnam. (See Map 30–7.) Diem, a Roman Catholic, also faced mounting criticism from Buddhists and the army. His response to these pressures was further repression and dependence on an ever-smaller group of advisers.

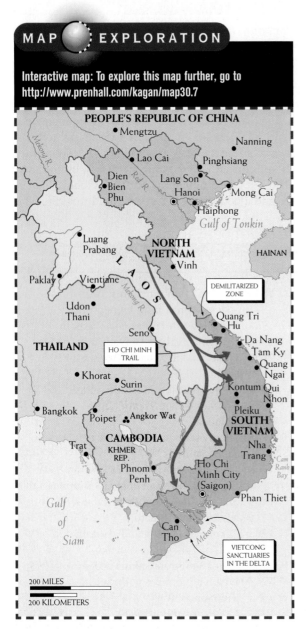

MAP EXPLORATION

Interactive map: To explore this map further, go to http://www.prenhall.com/kagan/map30.7

MAP 30–7 VIETNAM AND ITS NEIGHBORS *This map identifies important locations in the long and complex struggle centered in Vietnam.*

DIRECT U.S. INVOLVEMENT

The Eisenhower and Kennedy administrations continued to support Diem while demanding reforms in his government. The American military presence grew from about 600 people in early 1961 to more than 16,000 troops in late 1963. The political situation in Vietnam became increasingly unstable. On November 1, 1963, Diem was overthrown and murdered in an army coup in which the United States was deeply involved. The United States hoped a new government in South Vietnam would generate popular support. Thereafter, the United States sought to find a leader who could fulfill that hope. It finally settled on Nguyen Van Thieu (1923–2001), who governed South Vietnam from 1966 to 1975.

President Kennedy was assassinated on November 22, 1963. His successor, Lyndon Johnson (1908–1973), vastly expanded the commitment to South Vietnam. In August 1964, after an attack on an American ship in the Gulf of Tonkin, Johnson authorized the first bombing of North Vietnam. In February 1965, major bombing attacks began. They continued, with only brief pauses, until early in 1973. The land war grew until more than 500,000 Americans were stationed in South Vietnam.

In 1969, President Richard Nixon (1913–1994) began a policy known as *Vietnamization*, which involved the gradual withdrawal of American troops from Vietnam while the South Vietnamese army took over the full military effort. Peace negotiations had begun in Paris in the spring of 1968, but a cease-fire was not finally arranged until January 1973. American troops left South Vietnam, and North Vietnam interred its American prisoners of war. In early 1975, an evacuation of South Vietnamese troops from the northern part of their country turned into a rout when they were attacked by the North Vietnamese. On April 30, 1975, Saigon fell to the Viet Cong and the North Vietnamese army.

The U.S. intervention in Vietnam, which grew out of a power vacuum left by French decolonization, affected the entire Western world. For a decade after the Cuban missile crisis, Vietnam largely diverted the attention of the United States from Europe. American prestige suffered, and the U.S. policy in Southeast Asia made many Europeans question the basic wisdom of the American government and its commitment to Western Europe. Many young Europeans and many people in the former colonial world as well as not a few Americans came to regard the United States not as a protector of liberty, but as an ambitious, aggressive, and cruel power trying to keep colonialism alive after the end of the colonial era. Within the United States, the Vietnam conflict produced enormous divisions and debates over American involvement in the rest of the world that persists to the present day.

Western European Political Developments during the Cold War

During the decades spanning the Cold War, the U.S. involvement in Vietnam, and the continuing Soviet domination of Eastern Europe, the nations of Western Europe achieved unprecedented economic prosperity and maintained or inaugurated independent liberal democratic governments. Most of them confronted the problems associated both with decolonization and with maintaining economic growth.

The end of the Second World War saw vast constitutional changes in much of Western Europe, except for Portugal and Spain, which remained dictatorships until the mid-1970s. Either before or during the war, Germany, Italy, and France had experienced authoritarian governments. The construction of stable liberal democratic political frameworks became a major goal of their postwar political leaders, as well as of the United States. All concerned recognized that the earlier political stuctures in those nations had not been able to resist the rise of right-wing antidemocratic movements. It became widely recognized in light of the Great Depression that democracy requires a social and economic base, as well as a political structure. Most Europeans came to feel that government ought to ensure economic prosperity and social security. Success at doing so, they believed, would stave off the kind of turmoil that had brought on tyranny and war and could lead to communism.

CHRISTIAN DEMOCRATIC PARTIES

Except for the British Labour Party, the vehicles of the new postwar politics were not, as might have been expected, the democratic socialist parties. On the whole, those parties did not prosper after the onset of the Cold War. They were opposed by both communists and conservatives. Rather, various Christian democratic parties, usually leading coalition governments, introduced the new policies.

These parties were a major new feature of postwar politics. They were largely Roman Catholic in leadership and membership. Catholic parties had existed in Europe since the late nineteenth century. Until the 1930s, however, they had been conservative and had protected the social, political, and educational interests of the church. They had traditionally opposed communism but proposed

U.S. armed forces patrol in Vietnam. At the war's peak, more than 500,000 American troops were stationed in South Vietnam. The United States struggled in Vietnam for more than a decade, seriously threatening its commitment to Western Europe. C. Simonpietri/Corbis Sygma Photo News

few positive programs of their own. The postwar Christian democratic parties of Germany, France, and Italy, however, were progressive and welcomed non-Catholic members. Democracy, social reform, economic growth, and anticommunism were their hallmarks.

The events of the war years largely determined the political leadership of the postwar decade. On the Continent, those groups and parties, including communist parties, that had been active in the resistance against Nazism and fascism held an initial advantage. After 1947, however, in a policy naturally favored by the United States, communists were systematically excluded from all Western European governments.

The most immediate postwar domestic problems included not only those created by the physical damage of the conflict but often also those that had existed in 1939. The war, however, opened new opportunities for solving those prewar difficulties.

ECONOMIC CONCERNS WITHIN WESTERN EUROPE

Except for France, the economy dominated all other political issues from the end of World War II onward. The most remarkable success story of those years was what became known as the "economic miracle" of West Germany. That nation, under both Christian Democratic and Social Democratic ministries, achieved unprecedented prosperity. In Great Britain, the Labour ministry of Clement Attlee, which governed from 1945 to 1951, introduced the welfare state and nationalized major industries like coal mining and steel. From the 1960s through the 1970s, clashes between unions and business became commonplace. When Margaret Thatcher (b. 1925), the first woman prime minister of Great Britain, took office in 1979, she moved strongly against the unions and pressed for a more nearly free market economy. In 1997, after eighteen years of Conservative government, the Labour Party returned to power, but on a platform of much more limited state intervention. Elsewhere in Europe, parties of the traditional political left also were elected to office, but without exception, at the close of the century they favored retreat from government involvement and government-sponsored welfare programs.

Toward Western European Unification

The unprecedented steps toward economic cooperation and unity that Western European nations have taken during the past five decades are the single most important European success story of the second half of the century. The process arose originally from American encouragement in response to the Soviet domination of Eastern Europe and from the Western European states' own sense that they lacked effective political power.

POSTWAR COOPERATION

The movement toward unity could have occurred in at least three ways: politically, militarily, or economically. Economic cooperation, unlike military and political cooperation, involved little or no immediate loss of sovereignty. Furthermore, it brought material benefits to all the states involved, increasing popular support for their governments. Moreover, the administration of the Marshall Plan and the organization of NATO gave the countries involved new experience in working with each other and demonstrated the productivity and efficiency that resulted from mutual cooperation.

The first effort toward economic cooperation was the formation of the European Coal and Steel Community in 1951 by France, West Germany, Italy, and the Benelux countries (Belgium, the Netherlands, and Luxembourg). The community both benefited from and contributed to the immense growth of material production in Western Europe during this period. Its success reduced the suspicions of government and business groups about coordination and economic integration.

THE EUROPEAN ECONOMIC COMMUNITY

It took more than the prosperity of the European Coal and Steel Community to draw European leaders toward further unity, however. The unsuccessful Suez intervention and the resulting diplomatic isolation of France and Britain persuaded many Europeans that they could only significantly influence the two superpowers or control their own destinies by acting together. So, in 1957, through the Treaty of Rome, the six members of the Coal and Steel Community agreed to form a new organization: the **European Economic Community (EEC).** The members of the Common Market, as the EEC was soon known, envisioned more than a free-trade union: They sought to achieve the eventual elimination of tariffs, a free flow of capital and labor, and similar wage and social benefits in all their countries.

The Common Market achieved stunning success during its early years. By 1968, well ahead of schedule, all tariffs among the six members had been abolished. Trade and labor migration among the members grew steadily. Moreover, nonmember states began to copy the EEC and, later, to seek membership. In 1959, Britain, Denmark, Norway, Sweden, Switzerland, Austria, and Portugal formed the European Free Trade Area. By 1961, however, Great Britain had decided to seek Common Market membership. Twice, in 1963 and 1967, President de Gaulle of France vetoed British membership. He felt Britain was too closely tied to the United States to support the EEC wholeheartedly. Finally, in 1973, Great Britain, Ireland, and Denmark became members. Throughout the late 1970s, however, and into the 1980s, momentum slowed. Norway and Sweden, with relatively strong economies, declined to join. Although in 1982, Spain, Portugal, and Greece applied for membership and were eventually admitted, sharp disagreements and a sense of stagnation within the EEC continued.

THE EUROPEAN UNION

In 1988, the leaders of the EEC reached an important decision. By 1992, the EEC was to be a virtual free-trade zone with no trade barriers or other restrictive trade policies. In 1991, the Treaty of Maastricht made a series of specific proposals leading to a unified EEC currency (the Euro) and a strong central bank. The treaty was submitted to referendums in several European states. Initially, it failed to be adopted in Denmark, and it passed only narrowly in France and Great Britain, making clear that it could not be enforced without wider popular support. When the treaty took effect in November 1993, the EEC was renamed the **European Union.** Throughout the 1990s, the Union grew in influence. Its most notable achievement was the launching in early 1999 of the **Euro,** which has become the common denominator of most West European currencies and became the single circulating currency in most of Western Europe in 2001.

Several major political concerns at present confront the European Union. First, it must decide how to relate to the host of newly independent states in Eastern Europe whose economies and governments are less strong than those of the present members of the union. Second, the profound influence of Germany, now the most populous country of Europe, and of the German economy, Europe's largest, makes many Europeans uneasy. Europeans do not want the further development of the European Union to lead to German economic and political domination. Third, whereas in the past it was primarily the bureaucracy of the European Commission headquartered in Brussels that shaped the policies of the European Union, the political leaders of the member states and the European Parliament, which sits in Strasbourg, will have more influence. Finally, no one knows what the full impact of a common currency and interest rate policies set by a new central bank will be.

The Brezhnev Era in the Soviet Union and Eastern Europe

While Western Europe moved toward unity, democracy, and prosperity during the 1970s and early 1980s, the Soviet Union resisted change both internally and within Eastern Europe. Under Brezhnev, who governed from 1964 to 1982, the Soviet government became markedly more repressive at home, suggesting a return to Stalinist policies. In 1974, the government expelled Aleksandr Solzhenitsyn. It also began to harass Jewish citizens, creating bureaucratic obstacles for those who wanted to emigrate to Israel. This internal repression gave rise to a dissident movement. Certain Soviet citizens dared to criticize the regime in public and to demonstrate against it. They accused the government of violating the human rights provision of the 1975 Helsinki Accords, discussed in the next section. The dissidents included prominent citizens, such as the Nobel Prize–winning physicist Andrei Sakharov (1921–1989). The government responded with further repression, placing some opponents in psychiatric hospitals and others under what amounted to house arrest. During the same period the structures of the Communist Party became both rigidified and corrupt, resulting in the demoralization of younger members moving into the various Soviet bureaucracies.

THE UNITED STATES AND DÉTENTE

Foreign policy under Brezhnev combined attempts to reach an accommodation with the United States with continued efforts to expand Soviet influence and maintain Soviet leadership of the communist movement.

Although the Soviet Union sided with North Vietnam in its war with the United States, Soviet support was restrained. Under President Richard Nixon (1969–1974), the United States began a policy of détente with the Soviet Union, and the two countries concluded agreements on trade and on reducing strategic arms. Despite these agreements, Soviet spending on defense, and particularly on its navy, grew, damaging the consumer sectors of the economy.

During Gerald Ford's presidency (1974–1977), both the United States and the Soviet Union along with other European nations signed the Helsinki Accords. The accords recognized the Soviet sphere of influence in Eastern Europe, but they also recognized the human rights of the signers' citizens, which every government, including the Soviet Union, agreed to protect. President Jimmy Carter (1977–1981), a strong advocate of human rights, sought to induce the Soviet Union to comply with this commitment, a policy that cooled relations between the two countries.

Throughout this period of détente, in addition to its military presence in Eastern Europe, the Soviet Union pursued an activist foreign policy. During the 1970s, it financed Cuban military intervention in Angola, Mozambique, and Ethiopia. Soviet funds also flowed to the Sandinista forces in Nicaragua and to Vietnam, which permitted the Soviets to use naval bases after North Vietnam conquered the south in 1975.

The Soviet Union provided funds and weapons to various Arab governments for use against Israel. Each of these actions represented either Soviet support for what it viewed as its own strategic interests or pressures against those of the United States. Even more important, following its backing down in the Cuban missile crisis, the Soviet government was determined to build up its military forces. By the early 1980s, the Soviet Union possessed the largest armed force in the world and had achieved virtual nuclear parity with the United States.

INVASION OF AFGHANISTAN

It was at this moment of great military strength in 1979 that the Brezhnev government decided to invade Afghanistan, a strategic decision of enormous long-range consequences for the future of the Soviet Union as well as the United States (see Chapter 31). Although the Soviet Union already had a presence in Afghanistan, the Brezhnev government, for reasons that remain unclear, determined to send in troops to ensure its influence in central Asia and to support a client Afghan government.

The invasion brought a sharp response from the United States. The U.S. Senate refused to ratify a second Strategic Arms Limitation agreement that President Carter had signed earlier that year. The United States also embargoed grain shipments to the Soviet Union, boycotted the 1980 Olympic Games in Moscow, and sent aid to the Afghan rebels through various third parties, as did several Islamic nations. The U.S. Central Intelligence Agency also became directly involved with the Afghan forces, some of which were composed of radical Muslims,

The joy shown by these troops reflects the relief with which the Soviet army left Afghanistan in 1989. The Afghan war undermined the morale of the Soviet army and contributed to the collapse of the Soviet Union.
© Reuters NewMedia Inc./Corbis

resisting the Russians. China thoroughly disapproved of the invasion as well and helped the rebels.

Eventually, the Soviet forces bogged down in Afghanistan and could not defeat their guerrilla enemies. The Afghans killed approximately 2,000 Soviet troops a year and inflicted many other casualties. The morale and prestige of the Soviet army plummeted. At first, few Soviets knew about the problems in Afghanistan, but during the 1980s, the military failure became common knowledge in the Soviet Union. Although the Afghan war did not make daily headline news in the Western press, it sapped Soviet strength for ten years and had a demoralizing effect on the Soviet Union not unlike that which the Vietnam conflict had caused in the United States.

COMMUNISM AND SOLIDARITY IN POLAND

Events in Poland commencing in 1980—a time when the Soviet government was becoming increasingly rigidified and involved in Afghanistan—challenged both the authority of the Polish Communist Party and the influence of the Soviet Union.

After the events of late 1956 when the Polish Communist Party had accommodated itself to Soviet domination, Poland was plagued by chronic economic mismanagement and persistent shortages of food and consumer goods for twenty-five years. In 1978, the election of Karol Wojtyla, cardinal archbishop of Kraków, as pope proved important for Polish resistance to communist control and Soviet domination. An outspoken Polish opponent of communism now occupied a position of authority and enormous public visibility well beyond the reach of Soviet communist control. The new pope visited his homeland in 1979 and received a tumultuous welcome.

In July 1980, the Polish government raised meat prices, leading to hundreds of protest strikes across the country. On August 14, workers occupied the Lenin shipyard at Gdansk. The strike soon spread to other shipyards, transport facilities, and factories connected with the shipbuilding industry. The strikers, led by Lech Walesa (b. 1944), refused to negotiate through any of the traditionally government-controlled unions. The Gdansk strike ended on August 31 after the government promised the workers the right to organize an independent union called Solidarity. In September, the head of the Polish Communist Party was replaced, the Polish courts recognized Solidarity as an independent union, and the state-controlled radio broadcast a Roman Catholic mass for the first time in thirty years.

The summer of 1981 saw events that were no less remarkable occur within the Polish Communist

POLAND DECLARES MARTIAL LAW

On December 13, 1981, General Wojciech Jaruzelski, the premier of Poland and the head of the Polish Communist Party, announced the imposition of martial law. The action was taken after months of liberal reform in Poland, led by the independent trade union Solidarity. The government turned to military rule out of fear that the political activity of Solidarity would endanger the rule of the Communist Party in Poland. The reason that was announced for the imposition of martial law was to prevent disorder.

■ *What events in Poland had led to the imposition of martial law? How did Jaruzelski use fear of disorder to justify his action? Why did both the Polish Communist government and the Soviet Union so fear the activities of Solidarity? Are there any indications in this statement that Jaruzelski may have feared a Soviet invasion of Poland if the Polish Communist government did not itself take action?*

Our country is on the edge of the abyss. Achievements of many generations, raised from the ashes, are collapsing into ruin. State structures no longer function. New blows are struck each day at our flickering economy. Living conditions are burdening people more and more.

Through each place of work, in many Polish people's homes, there is a line of painful division. The atmosphere of unending conflict, misunderstanding and hatred sows mental devastation and damages the traditions of tolerance.

Strikes, strike alerts, protest actions have become standard. Even students are dragged into it. . . .

With our aims, it cannot be said that we [the Communist Party government] did not show good will, moderation, patience, and sometimes there was probably too much of it. It cannot be said the Government did not honor the social agreements [made with Solidarity in 1980 at Gdansk]. We even went further. The initiative of the great national understanding was backed by the millions of Poles. It created a chance, an opportunity to deepen the system of democracy of people ruling the country, widening reforms. Those hopes failed.

Around the negotiating table there was no leadership from Solidarity. Words said. . .in Gdansk [strike calls and political demands from Solidarity] showed the real aims of its leadership. These aims are confirmed by everyday practice, growing aggressiveness of the extremists, clearly aiming to take apart the Polish state system.

How long can one wait for a sobering up? How long can a hand reached for accord meet a fist? I say this with a broken heart, with bitterness. It could have been different in our country. It should have been different. But if the current state had lasted longer, it would have led to a catastrophe, to absolute chaos, to poverty and starvation. . . .

I declare that today the army Council of National Salvation has been constituted, and the Council of State obeying the Polish Constitution declared a state of emergency at midnight on the territory of Poland. . . .

From *The New York Times*, December 14, 1981, p. 16.

Party itself. For the first time in any European communist state, secret elections for the party congress were permitted with real choices among the candidates. Poland remained a nation governed by a single party, but for the time being, the party congress permitted real debate within its ranks.

This extraordinary Polish experiment, however, ended abruptly. In 1981, General Wojciech Jaruzelski (b. 1923) became head of the Polish Communist Party, and the army imposed martial law in December. (See "Poland Declares Martial Law.") Several of the leaders of Solidarity were arrested. The Polish military acted to preserve its own position and perhaps to prevent a Soviet invasion similar to the one in Czechoslovakia in 1968. Martial law continued in effect until late in 1983, but the Polish Communist Party continued to fail to solve Poland's major economic problems.

Major Dates of the Brezhnev Era
1974   Solzhenitsyn expelled
1975   Helsinki Accords
1979   Soviet invasion of Afghanistan
1980   U.S. Olympic Games boycott
1981   Martial law declared in Poland in response to Solidarity
1982   Death of Brezhnev

RELATIONS WITH THE REAGAN ADMINISTRATION

Early in the administration of President Ronald Reagan (1981–1989), the United States relaxed its grain embargo and placed less emphasis on human rights. At the same time, however, Reagan intensified Cold War rhetoric, famously describing the Soviet Union as an "evil empire." More important, the Reagan administration increased U.S. military spending, slowed arms limitation negotiations, deployed a major new missile system in Europe, and proposed the Strategic Defense Initiative (dubbed "Star Wars" by the press), involving a high-technology space-based defense against nuclear attack. The Star Wars proposal, although controversial in the United States, was a major issue in later arms control negotiations with the Soviet Union. Star Wars and the Reagan defense spending forced the Soviet Union to increase its own defense spending when it could ill afford to do so and contributed to the economic problems that helped bring about its collapse. Yet even during Reagan's first term (1981–1985), no major transformation of the Soviet Union seemed to be in the offing.

The Collapse of European Communism

The withdrawal of Soviet influence from Eastern Europe and the internal collapse of the Soviet Union are the most important European historical events of the second half of the twentieth century. They had virtually no parallel in modern European history. All of the other major governments that had disappeared in Europe earlier in the century had fallen either as the result of domestic revolution brought on by military defeat, as happened in tsarist Russia, Germany, and Austria after World War I and Italy during World War II, or military defeat followed by military occupation, as was the case with Germany after 1945 and

the Third Republic in France in 1940. By contrast, the Soviet Union essentially imploded from within and then divided into separate successor states. There was no foreign invasion, no military defeat, and no internal revolution. Many of the factors leading to the Soviet collapse remain to be investigated, but a relatively clear narrative of what occurred can be described.

GORBACHEV REDIRECTS THE SOVIET UNION

Although economic stagnation, party corruption, and the lingering Afghan war had long been undermining Soviet authority, what brought those forces to a head and began the dramatic collapse of the Soviet Empire was the accession to power of Mikhail S. Gorbachev (b. 1931) in 1985 after both of Brezhnev's two immediate successors, Yuri Andropov (1914–1984) and Constantin Chernenko (1911–1985), died within thirteen months of each other. In what proved to be the last great attempt to reform the Soviet system, Gorbachev immediately began the most remarkable changes that the Soviet Union had witnessed since the 1920s. These reforms loosed forces that, within seven years, would force him to retire and would end both communist rule and the Soviet Union as it had existed since the Bolshevik revolution of 1917.

In his earlier administrative career, Gorbachev had become impatient with the inefficiencies of the Soviet system and disappointed that the Communist Party had failed to fulfill its socialist promises. He believed that only drastic change could restore the Soviet Union's political and economic health and allow it to achieve its socialist agenda. As a reformer, Gorbachev never repudiated socialism or the intellectual framework of Soviet communism. He hoped to rejuvenate the original Bolshevik vision, which he believed that corruption and political terror had prevented from being realized. However, his reforms unleashed political and social forces that he could not control, and he was ultimately overwhelmed by them.

Economic *Perestroika* Gorbachev's primary goal was to revive the Russian economy in order to raise the country's standard of living. Initially, he and his supporters, most of whom he had appointed himself, challenged traditional party and bureaucractic management of the Soviet government and economy. Under the policy of **perestroika,** or "restructuring," they proposed major economic and political reforms of the various centralized economic ministries, which were reduced in size and importance. During these same years, Gorbachev also confronted labor discontent. A major strike by coal miners occurred in July 1989 in Siberia. Gorbachev had to settle their grievances quickly, because the economy desperately needed their output. He promised them better wages and wider political liberties. By early 1990, in a clear abandonment of traditional Marxist ideology, Gorbachev had begun to advocate private ownership of property and liberalization of the economy toward free market mechanisms. He may have been following Lenin's model of the New Economic Policy of the early 1920s, which had allowed some free markets within the Soviet economy. Despite many organizational changes, the Soviet economy remained stagnated and even declined. The failure of Gorbachev's economic policies affected his political policies. To some extent, he pursued bold political reform because he failed to achieve economic progress.

Glasnost Gorbachev allowed an extraordinary public discussion and criticism of Soviet history and Soviet Communist Party policy. This development was termed ***glasnost,*** or openness. The contributions to Soviet history of such figures from the 1920s as Bukharin, whom Stalin had purged, received official public recognition. Workers were permitted to criticize party officials and the economic plans of the party and the government. Censorship was relaxed and free expression encouraged. Dissidents were released from prison. In the summer of 1988, Gorbachev presided over a party congress that witnessed full debates.

The policy of open discussion allowed national minorities within the Soviet Union to demand political autonomy. Throughout its history, the Soviet Union had remained a vast empire of subject peoples. The tsars had conquered some of those groups, Stalin had incorporated others, such as the Baltic states, into the Soviet Union. *Glasnost* quickly brought to the fore the discontent of all such peoples, no matter how or when they had been subjugated. Gorbachev proved inept in addressing these ethnic complaints. He badly underestimated the unrest that internal national discontent could generate. (See "Encountering the Past: Rock Music and Political Protest".)

Gorbachev soon moved from *glasnost* to *perestroika* in the political arena. In 1988, a new constitution permitted openly contested elections. After real political campaigning—a new experience for the Soviet Union—the Congress of People's Deputies was elected in 1989. One of the new members of the congress was Andrei Sakharov, the dissident physicist who had been persecuted under Brezhnev. After lively debate, the Supreme Soviet, another elected body, although one dominated by the Communist Party, formally elected Gorbachev president in 1989.

***Perestroika* and the Army** The army was perhaps the single most important national institution of the Soviet Union. It had been the institution through which a people with many different national and ethnic loyalties had been given a national identity. As a result of the victory in Word War II, the Soviet Army enjoyed enormous prestige. Throughout the Soviet period, the armed forces had also enjoyed large expenditures of public funds to support them.

By the late 1980s, Gorbachev had concluded that only a significant redeployment of expenditures from military purposes to nonmilitary domestic concerns could stimulate the economic growth that he sought and improve the Soviet standard of living. The political and military structures of the Soviet Union allowed a relatively small group of people to decide to cut the defense budget with little public debate. Gorbachev began to retreat from the Afghan war and reduce expenditures on weaponry. These measures seem to have confused the military leadership and, along with the Afghan war, hurt morale. Furthermore, military spending and manufacture were so large a part of Soviet economic life that any effort to convert more resources to domestic spending caused massive dislocations in what was still a centrally planned economy.

The Soviet military soon faced a new problem. Between 1986 and 1991, the Soviet army was ordered to put down several instances of domestic unrest involving either ethnic groups fighting among themselves (Georgia in 1989 and Azerbaijan, 1990) or national minoritites challenging the central government (in Lithuania, 1990). The greater openness in the press and on television meant the media covered these clashes between the Soviet army and Soviet citizens. Furthermore, in certain cases, the central government let the army take the blame for the incidents even when the army was following the government's orders. Again, morale and military prestige suffered.

Finally, Gorbachev undermined the military just by cutting its size. He carried out this policy, as he had the cuts in defense spending, to convince the West that the Soviet Union was serious about arms reduction in the hope the West would also reduce such spending. Gorbachev forced through reductions in the size of the army at home and, as we discuss in the next section, massive military withdrawals from Eastern Europe. Furthermore,

Rock Music and Political Protest

Rock music, which epitomizes popular culture throughout the Western world, was a form of entertainment that came to have a strident antiestablishment political message. Rock originated in the United States in the 1950s with African-American musicians and working-class and country music singers. By the early 1960s, rock also included folk singers who used their music to champion the civil rights movement and protest the war in Vietnam

European rock groups both embraced and transformed American rock music. The most spectacularly successful European group was the Beatles. Though sporting long hair and attracting the politically active young, the Beatles's lyrics were more laid back than political.

During the 1970s, in both the United States and Europe, punk rock groups with provocative names such as the Sex Pistols, became popular. Punk rock was deeply antiestablishment, but Western society, which was increasingly pluralistic, took punk rock in its stride.

In Eastern Europe and the Soviet Union, however, punk rock was literally revolutionary. There the ever more radical rock music of the 1970s and 1980s became a major vehicle for social and political criticism. In the face of communist cultural conformity, rock stars symbolized daring and personal heroism. Lyrics openly criticized communist governments, as in this example from "Get Out of Control," sung at a rock concert in Leningrad in 1986:

We were watched from the
  days of kindergarten.
Some nice men and kind
  women
Beat us up. They chose the
  most painful places
And treated us like animals on
  the farm.
So we grew up like a disciplined herd.
We sing what they want and
  live how they want

And we look at them downside up, as if we're
  trapped.
We just watch how they hit us
Get out of control!
Get out of control!
And sing what you want
And not just what is allowed
We have a right to yell![1]

This song became popular throughout Eastern Europe. It revealed how alienated the youth of the region had become from the official culture of the communist regimes. Rock music expressed and helped spread the disaffection that contributed to the collapse of communism throughout Eastern Europe at the end of the 1980s.

■ *How did rock music evolve into an antiestablishment form of entertainment? Why was rock considered subversive in the Eastern bloc nations?*

[1]Quoted in Artemy Troitsky, *Back in the USSR: The True Story of Rock in Russia* (Boston: Faber & Faber, 1987), p. 127, as cited in Sabrina P. Ramet (ed.), *Social Currents in Eastern Europe: The Sources and Meaning of the Great Transformation* (Durham, NC: Duke University Press, 1991), p. 239.

The Russian rock group "Dynamic" performs in Moscow in 1987. R. Podemi/TASS/Sovfoto/Eastfoto

some of the Soviet republics began to organize their own national military forces. This development represented movement toward national autonomy and showed disrespect for the Soviet army itself. Finally, there appears to have been resistance against conscription into the army, with various republics failing to fulfill their draft quotas. Again, resistance to conscription indicated the discontent of national groups and their determination to resist central Soviet government policy.

1989: Year of Revolution in Eastern Europe

Solidarity Reemerges in Poland In the early 1980s, Poland's government relaxed martial law, and it eventually released all the Solidarity prisoners, although Jaruzelski remained in control as president. In 1988, new strikes occurred that surprised even the leaders of Solidarity. This time, the communist government could not reimpose control. After consultations between the government and Solidarity, the union was legalized. Lech Walesa again took center stage, as a kind of mediator between the government and the more independent elements of the trade union movement he had founded.

Jaruzelski began some political reforms with the tacit consent of the Soviet Union. He promised free elections to a parliament with increased powers. When elections were held in 1989, the communists lost overwhelmingly to Solidarity candidates. Late in the summer, Jaruzelski, unable to find a communist who could forge a majority coalition in Parliament, turned to Solidarity and appointed the first noncommunist prime minister of Poland since 1945. Gorbachev expressly approved the appointment.

Throughout 1989, as these events unfolded within Poland, one Soviet-dominated state after another in Eastern Europe moved toward independence. Early in the year, the Hungarian government opened its border with Austria, permitting free travel between the two countries. This breach in the Iron Curtain immediately led thousands of East Germans to move into Austria through Hungary. From Austria, they went to West Germany. In May, Janos Kadar, who had been installed after the Soviet intervention in 1956, was stripped of his position as president of the Hungarian Communist Party. Thousands of Hungarians gave an honorary burial to the body of Imre Nagy, whom Kadar had executed in 1958. The Hungarian Communist Party changed its name to the Socialist Party, permitted other opposition political parties to engage, and promised free elections by October.

In the autumn of 1989, popular demonstrations erupted in East German cities. Adding to the

pressure, Gorbachev told the leaders of the East German Communist Party that the Soviet Union would not use force to support them. With startling swiftness, the East German government resigned, making way for a younger generation of communist leaders who remained in office only for a few weeks. In November 1989, in one of the most emotional moments in European history since 1945, the government of East Germany ordered the opening of the Berlin Wall. That week, tens of thousands of East Berliners crossed into West Berlin to celebrate, to visit their families, and to shop with money provided by the West German government. Shortly thereafter, free travel began between East and West Germany. (See Map 30–8.)

Within days of these dramatic events, West Germany and the other Western nations faced the issue of German reunification. Helmut Kohl (b. 1930), the chancellor of West Germany, became the leading force in moving toward full unification. Late in 1989, the European Economic Community accepted, in principle, the unification of Germany. By February 1990, some form of reunification had become a forgone conclusion, accepted by the United States, the Soviet Union, Great Britain, and France.

The opening of the Berlin Wall in November 1989, more than any other event, symbolized the collapse of the communist governments in Eastern Europe. R. Bossu/ Corbis Sygma Photo News

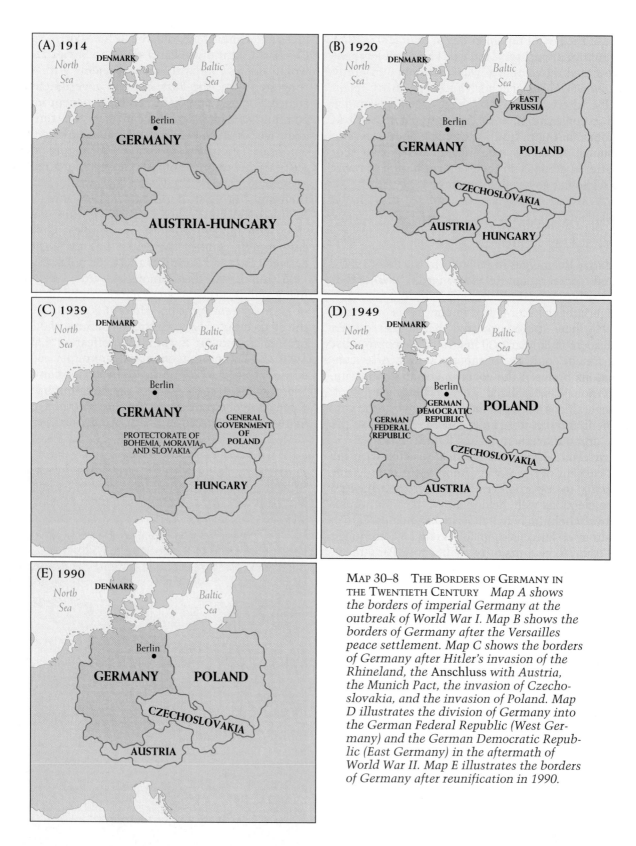

MAP 30–8   THE BORDERS OF GERMANY IN THE TWENTIETH CENTURY   *Map A shows the borders of imperial Germany at the outbreak of World War I. Map B shows the borders of Germany after the Versailles peace settlement. Map C shows the borders of Germany after Hitler's invasion of the Rhineland, the Anschluss with Austria, the Munich Pact, the invasion of Czechoslovakia, and the invasion of Poland. Map D illustrates the division of Germany into the German Federal Republic (West Germany) and the German Democratic Republic (East Germany) in the aftermath of World War II. Map E illustrates the borders of Germany after reunification in 1990.*

Revolution in Czechoslovakia rapidly followed the breach of the Berlin Wall. The popular new Czech leader who led the forces against the party was Václav Havel (b. 1936), a playwright of international standing whom the communist government had frequently imprisoned. In December 1989, the tottering communist government, together with the Soviet Union and other Warsaw Pact states, acknowledged that the invasion of 1968 had been a mistake. Shortly thereafter, Havel's group, known as Civic Forum, forced Gustav Husak (b. 1913), who had been president of Czechoslovakia since 1968, to resign. On December 28, 1989, Alexander Dubcek became chairman of the Parliament, and the next day, Havel was elected president.

The only revolution of 1989 that involved significant violence occurred in Romania. There, in mid-December, the forces of President Nicolae Ceausescu (1918–1989), who had governed without opposition since 1965, fired on crowds protesting conditions in the country. By December 22, Bucharest was in full revolt. Ceausescu and his wife attempted to flee, but were captured, secretly tried, and shot on December 25.

The Soviet Stance on Revolutionary Developments
None of the revolutions of 1989 could have taken place unless the Soviet Union had refused to intervene militarily, in contrast to 1956 and 1968. As events unfolded, it became clear that Gorbachev would not rescue the old-line communist governments and party leaderships in Eastern Europe. In October 1989, he formally renounced the Brezhnev Doctrine. For the first time since the end of World War II, Eastern Europeans could shape their own political destiny without the fear of Soviet military intervention. Once they realized the Soviets would not act, thousands of ordinary citizens took to the streets to denounce Communist Party domination and assert their desire for democracy. The major question facing the Soviet Union became the peaceful withdrawal of its troops from Eastern Europe back home. The haphazard nature of that withdrawal and the general poverty to which those troops returned were another factor undermining the Soviet armed forces.

The peaceful character of most of these revolutions was not inevitable. It may, in part, have resulted from the shock with which much of the world responded to the violent repression of pro-democracy protesters in Beijing's Tiananmen Square by the People's Republic of China in May 1989. The Communist Party officials of Eastern Europe and the Soviet Union clearly decided in 1989 that they could not offend world opinion with a similar attack on democratic demonstrators.

THE COLLAPSE OF THE SOVIET UNION

Gorbachev clearly believed, as his behavior toward Eastern Europe in 1989 showed, that the Soviet Union could no longer afford to support communist governments in that region or intervene to uphold their authority while seeking to restructure its own economy. He also had concluded that the Communist Party in the Soviet Union must restructure itself and its relationship to the Soviet state and society.

Renunciation of Communist Political Monopoly
In early 1990, Gorbachev formally proposed to the Central Committee of the Soviet Communist Party that the party abandon its monopoly of power. (See "Gorbachev Proposes the Soviet Communist Party Abandon Its Monopoly of Power.") After intense debate, the committee adopted his proposal, abandoning the Leninist position that only a single elite party could act as the vanguard of the revolution and forge a new Soviet society. Gorbachev seems not to have wanted wholly to abandon communism and certainly not socialism, but he did want to open the political process to genuine competition. He

The collapse of Communist Party governments in Eastern Europe and the Soviet Union is the most important political event of the closing years of the twentieth century. It was accompanied by the destruction of the public symbols of those governments. Throughout the region, gigantic statues of Communist Party leaders were torn down. Here, Hungarians explore a toppled statue of Lenin.   Corbis Sygma Photo News

Major Events in the Revolutions of 1989			

January 11	Independent parties permitted in Hungary	November 19	Czechoslovak opposition groups organize into Civic Forum and demand resignation of communist leaders responsible for 1968 invasion
April 5	Solidarity legalized in Poland and free elections accepted by government		
May 2	Hungary dismantles barriers along its borders	November 24	Czechoslovak communist leadership resigns
May 8	Janos Kadar removed from office in Hungary	December 1	New Czechoslovak communist leaders denounce 1968 invasion; Soviet Union and Warsaw Pact express regret over 1968 invasion
May 17	Polish government recognizes Roman Catholic Church		
June 4	Solidarity victory in Polish parliamentary elections	December 3	Czechoslovak government announces ministry with noncommunist members
July 25	Solidarity asked to join coalition government	December 16–17	Massacre of civilians in Timisoara, Romania
August 24	Solidarity member appointed premier in Poland	December 22	Ceausescu government overthrown in Romania with many casualties
October 18	Erich Honecker removed from office in East Germany	December 25	Announcement of Ceausescu's execution
October 23	Hungary proclaims itself a republic	December 28	Alexander Dubcek elected chairman of Czechoslovak Parliament
October 25	Gorbachev renounces Brezhnev Doctrine	December 29	Václav Havel elected president of Czechoslovakia
November 9	Berlin Wall opened		
November 17	Large antigovernment demonstration in Czechoslovakia crushed by police		

was determined, however, that the Soviet Union should remain a strong state with a powerful central government.

New Political Forces Gorbachev confronted challenges from three major political forces by 1990. One consisted of those groups—considered conservative in the Soviet context—whose members wanted to preserve the influence of the Communist Party and the Soviet army. The country's economic stagnation and political and social turmoil deeply disturbed them. They still appeared to control significant groups in the economy and society. During late 1990 and early 1991, Gorbachev, who himself seems to have been disturbed by the nation's turmoil, began to appoint members of these factions to key positions in the government. In other words, he seemed to be making a strategic retreat.

Gorbachev initiated these moves because he was now facing opposition from a second group—those who wanted much more extensive and rapid change. Their leading spokesman was Boris Yeltsin (b. 1931). He and his supporters wanted to move quickly to a market economy and a more democratic government.

Like Gorbachev, Yeltsin had risen through the ranks of the Communist Party and had then become disillusioned with its policies. Throughout the late 1980s, he had been critical of Gorbachev. In 1990, he was elected president of the Russian Republic, the largest and most important of the Soviet Union's constituent republics. In the new political climate, that position gave him a firm political base from which to challenge Gorbachev's authority and increase his own.

The third force that came into play from 1989 onward was growing regional unrest in some of the republics of the Soviet Union. These republics had experienced considerable discontent in the past, but it had been repressed by military or Communist Party action. Initially, the greatest unrest came from the three Baltic republics of Estonia, Latvia, and Lithuania, which had been independent states until the eve of World War II. In accord with secret arrangements in the Soviet-German nonaggression pact of 1939, the Soviet Union had occupied them in 1940. That prewar pact with Nazi Germany provided the only seemingly legal basis for the Soviet Union's continued control. In these republics, many local

GORBACHEV PROPOSES THE SOVIET COMMUNIST PARTY ABANDON ITS MONOPOLY OF POWER

On February 5, 1990, President Mikhail Gorbachev proposed to the Central Committee of the Soviet Communist Party that it abandon its position as the single legal party as provided in Article 6 of the Soviet constitution. His proposal followed similar actions by several of the communist parties of Eastern Europe. From the time of Lenin through Brezhnev, the Soviet Communist Party portrayed itself as the sole vanguard of the revolution. Gorbachev argued it should abandon that special role and compete for political power with other political parties. Within two years, the party was no longer in power, Gorbachev had resigned, and the Soviet Union no longer existed.

■ *Why did Gorbachev argue that the Soviet Communist Party must reform itself? To what extent did his speech call for the abandonment of traditional Communist Party goals? How did he think the Soviet Communist Party could function in a pluralistic political system?*

The main thing that now worries Communists and all citizens of the country is the fate of *perestroika*, the fate of the country and the role of the Soviet Communist Party at the current, probably most crucial, stage of revolutionary transformation.

[It is important to understand] . . . that the party will only be able to fulfill the mission of political vanguard if it drastically restructures itself, masters the art of political work in the present conditions and succeeds in cooperating with forces committed to *perestroika*.

The crux of the party's renewal is the need to get rid of everything that tied it to the authoritarian-bureaucratic system, a system that left its mark not only on methods of work and inter-relationships within the party, but also on ideology, ways of thinking and notions of socialism.

The [newly proposed] platform says: our ideal is a humane, democratic socialism, expressing the interests of the working class and all working people; and relying on the great legacy of Marx, Engels and Lenin, the Soviet Communist Party is creatively developing socialist ideals to match present-day realities and with due account for the entire experience of the 20th century.

The platform states clearly what we should abandon. We should abandon the ideological dogmatism that became ingrained during past decades, outdated stereotypes in domestic policy and outmoded views on the world revolutionary process and world development as a whole.

We should abandon everything that led to the isolation of socialist countries from the mainstream of world civilization. We should abandon the understanding of progress as a permanent confrontation with a socially different world. . . .

The party's renewal presupposes a fundamental change in its relations with state and economic bodies and the abandonment of the practice of commanding them and substituting for their functions.

The party in a renewing of society can exist and play its role as vanguard only as a democratically recognized force. This means that its status should not be imposed through constitutional endorsement.

The Soviet Communist Party, it goes without saying, intends to struggle for the status of the ruling party. But it will do so strictly within the framework of the democratic process by giving up any legal and political advantages, offering its program and defending it in discussions, cooperating with other social and political forces, always working amidst the masses, living by their interests and their needs.

From the *New York Times*, February 6, 1990, p. A16.

communist leaders began to see themselves as leaders of their national groups rather than of the party.

During 1989 and 1990, the parliaments of the Baltic republics tried to increase their independence from the Soviet Union, and Lithuania actually declared independence. Gorbachev used military force to resist these moves. Discontent also arose in the Soviet Islamic republics in central Asia. Riots broke out in Azerbaijan and Tajikistan, where the army was used as a police force against Soviet citizens. Throughout 1990 and 1991, Gorbachev sought to negotiate new constitutional arrangements between the republics and the central government. His failure to effect such arrangements may have been the single most important reason for the rapid collapse of the Soviet Union.

The August 1991 Coup The turning point in all of these events came in August 1991, when the conservative forces that Gorbachev had brought into the government attempted a coup. Armed forces occupied Moscow, and Gorbachev himself was placed under house arrest while on vacation in the Crimea. The forces of political and economic reaction—led by people who, at the time, were associated with Gorbachev—had at last tried to seize control. The day of the coup, Boris Yeltsin climbed on a tank in front of the Russian Parliament building to denounce the coup and ask the world for help to maintain the Soviet Union's movement toward democracy.

Within two days, the coup collapsed. Gorbachev returned to Moscow, but in humiliation, having been victimized by the groups to whom he had turned for support. One of the largest public demonstrations in Russian history—perhaps even the largest—celebrated the failure of the coup in Moscow. From that point on, Yeltsin steadily became the dominant political figure in the nation. In the months immediately afterward, the Communist Party, compromised by its participation in the coup, collapsed as a political force. The constitutional arrangements between the central government and the individual republics were revised. On December 25, 1991, the Soviet Union ceased to exist, Gorbachev left office, and the Commonwealth of Independent States came into being. (See Map 30–9.)

THE YELTSIN DECADE

Boris Yeltsin emerged as the strongest leader within the new commonwealth. As president of Russia, he was head of the largest and most powerful of the new states. His popularity was high both in Russia and in the commonwealth in 1992, but within a year he faced serious economic and political problems. The Russian Parliament, most of whom were former communists, opposed Yeltsin personally and his policies of economic and political reform. Relations between the president and Parliament reached an impasse, crippling the government. In September 1993, Yeltsin suspended Parliament, which responded by deposing him. Parliament leaders tried to incite popular uprisings against Yeltsin in Moscow. The military, however, backed Yeltsin, and he surrounded the Parliament building with troops and tanks. On October 4, 1993, after pro-Parliament rioters rampaged through Moscow, Yeltsin ordered the tanks to attack the Parliament building, crushing the opposition.

These actions consolidated Yeltsin's authority. The major Western powers, deeply concerned by the turmoil in Russia, supported him. In December 1993, Russians voted for a new Parliament and approved a new constitution. By 1994, the central government found itself at war in the Islamic province of Chechnya in the Caucasus, a conflict that has continued to the present with the Russian

Following the failure of the coup by hardline Communists in August 1991, Gorbachev and Boris Yeltsin publicly debated the future of the collapsing Soviet Union. The debate marked a key moment in Gorbachev's loss of authority and Yeltsin's popularity. © Peter Turnley/ Corbis

MAP 30–9   THE COMMONWEALTH OF INDEPENDENT STATES   *In December 1991, the Soviet Union broke up into its fifteen constituent republics. Eleven of these are now loosely joined in the Commonwealth of Independent States (CIS). Those not in the new union are Estonia, Latvia, Lithuania, and Georgia.*

government unable to assert its firm control. The ongoing warfare with radical Muslims in Chechnya would make the Russian government sympathetic to the United States in the wake of the attacks of September 11, 2001.

From the mid-1990s, the situation in Russia has remained highly confused and economically stagnant. In 1998, Russia defaulted on its debt payments. Political assassinations occurred. The economic downturn contributed to furthur political unrest. In the face of these problems, Yeltsin resigned the presidency in a dramatic gesture just as the new century opened. His resignation made Vladimir Putin, his premier, the acting president. Putin achieved the presidency on his own in March 2000. The future of Russia remains uncertain. It is possible that Russia for the next decade will resemble

Mexico during the 1920s and 1930s, when in the wake of its own revolution that country experienced almost two decades of uncertain political stability while financing itself through the sale of natural resources to the rest of the world. (See "Aleksandr Solzhenitsyn Ponders the Future of Russian Democracy.")

THE COLLAPSE OF YUGOSLAVIA AND CIVIL WAR

Yugoslavia was created after World War I. Its borders included six major national groups—Serbs, Croats, Slovenes, Montenegrins, Macedonians, and Bosnians (Muslims)—among whom there have been ethnic disputes for centuries. (See Map 30–10.) The Croats and Slovenes are Roman Catholic and use

ALEKSANDR SOLZHENITSYN PONDERS THE FUTURE OF RUSSIAN DEMOCRACY

Aleksandr Solzhenitsyn, the foremost Russian novelist of his generation, was one of the most outspoken critics of the communist government of the Soviet Union. He was expelled from the country in 1974 and lived for many years in the United States. After the collapse of the Soviet Union and of the Soviet communist government, he returned to live in Russia. In recent years, he has been highly critical of the new Russian government. In January 1997, he outlined his criticism in the New York Times.

■ *What are Solzhenitsyn's chief criticisms of the structure of the new Russian government? Why does he not consider it democratic? Why does he emphasize the necessity of establishing structures of local self-government? Why does he believe corruption could undermine democracy in Russia? Have events in Russia since 1997 alleviated those concerns?*

What is known today as "Russian democracy" masks a Government of a completely different sort. *Glasnost*—freedom of the press—is only an instrument of democracy, not democracy itself. And to a great extent freedom of the press is illusory, since the owners of newspapers erect strict taboos against discussion of issues of vital importance, while in the outlying parts of the country newspapers get direct pressure from the province authorities.

Democracy in the unarguable sense of the word means the rule of the people—that is a system in which the people are truly in charge of their daily lives and can influence the course of their own historical fate. There is nothing of the sort in Russia today.

In August 1991, the "councils of people's deputies," though only window dressing under the rule of the Communist Party, were abolished throughout the country. Since then, the united resistance of the President's machine, the Government, State Duma [Parliament], leaders of the political parties and majority of governors has prevented the creation of any agencies of local self-government.

Legislative assemblies do exist at the regional level but are entirely subordinate to the governors, if only because they are paid by the province's executive branches. (The election of governors is only a recent development and far from widespread; most governors were appointed by the President.)

There exists no legal framework or financial means for the creation of local self-government; people will have no choice but to achieve it through social struggle. All that really exists is the government hierarchy, from the President and national Government on down. . . .

The Constitution of 1993, which was passed hastily and not in a manner to inspire confidence, groans under the weight of the President's power. The rights it allocates to the State Duma are exceedingly constrained. . . .

This system of centralized power cannot be called a democracy.

It could be said that throughout the last 10 years of frenetic reorganization our Government has not taken a single step unmarked by ineptitude. Worse, our ruling circles have not shown themselves in the least morally superior to the Communists who preceded them. Russia has been exhausted by crime, by the transfer into private hands of billions of dollars' worth of the nation's wealth. Not a single serious crime has been exposed, nor has there been a single public trial. The investigatory and judicial systems are severely limited in both their actions and their resources.

The destructive course of events over the last decade has come about because the Government, while ineptly imitating foreign models, has completely disregarded the country's creativity and particular character as well as Russia's centuries-old spiritual and social traditions. Only if those paths are freed up can Russia be delivered from its near fatal condition.

MAP 30–10 THE ETHNIC COMPOSITION OF BOSNIA-HERZEGOVINA, CROATIA, AND SERBIA IN THE FORMER YUGOSLAVIA *The rapid changes in Eastern Europe during the close of the 1980s brought to the fore various long-standing ethnic tensions in the former Yugoslavia. This map shows national and ethnic borders and major ethnic enclaves within areas generally dominated by a single ethnic group.*

the Latin alphabet. The Serbs, Montenegrins, and Macedonians are Eastern Orthodox and use the Cyrillic alphabet. The Bosnians are Muslims. Most members of each group reside in a region with which they are associated historically—Serbia, Croatia, Slovenia, Montenegro, Macedonia, and Bosnia-Herzegovina—and these regions constituted individual republics within Yugoslavia. Many Serbs, however, lived outside Serbia proper.

Yugoslavia's first communist leader, Marshal Tito (1892–1980), had acted independently of Stalin in the late 1940s and pursued his own foreign policy. He succeeded in muting ethnic differences by encouraging a cult of personality around himself and by complex political power sharing. After his death, serious economic difficulties undermined the authority of the central government, and Yugoslavia gradually dissolved into civil war.

In the late 1980s, the old ethnic differences came to the fore again in Yugoslav politics. Nationalist leaders—most notably Slobodan Milosevic (b. 1941) in Serbia and Franjo Tudjman (b. 1922) in Croatia—gained increasing authority. The Serbs contended that Serbia did not exercise sufficient influence in Yugoslavia and that Serbs living in

Yugoslavia but outside Serbia encountered systematic discrimination, especially from Croats. Ethnic tension and violence soon resulted. During the summer of 1990, in the wake of the changes in the former Soviet bloc nations, Slovenia and Croatia declared independence from the central Yugoslav government and were soon recognized by several European nations, including, most importantly, Germany. Recognition from the full European community soon followed.

From this point on, violence escalated steadily. Serbia—concerned about Serbs living in Croatia and about the loss of lands and resources there—was determined to maintain a unitary Yugoslav state that it would dominate. Croatia was equally determined to secure independence. Croatian Serbs demanded safeguards against discrimination and violence, providing the Serbian army with a pretext to move against Croatia. By June 1991, full-fledged war had erupted between the two republics. Serbia accused Croatia of reviving fascism; Croatia accused Serbia of maintaining a Stalinist regime. At its core, however, the conflict is ethnic; as such, it highlights the potential for violent ethnic conflict within the former Soviet Union.

The Breakup of Yugoslavia	
June 1991	Slovenia declares independence; Croatia declares independence
September 1991	Macedonia declares independence
April 1992	War erupts in Bosnia and Herzegovina after Muslims and Croats vote for independence
April 1992	Serbia and Montenegro proclaim a new Federal Republic of Yugoslavia
November 1995	Peace agreement reached in Dayton, Ohio
March 1998	War breaks out in Kosovo, a province of Serbia
March 1999	NATO bombing of Serbia begins

The conflict took a new turn in 1992 as Croatian and Serbian forces determined to divide Bosnia-Herzegovina. The Muslims in Bosnia—who had lived alongside Serbs and Croats for generations—soon became crushed between the opposing forces. The Serbs in particular, pursuing a policy called "ethnic cleansing," a euphemism redolent of some of the worst horrors of World War II, have killed or forcibly moved many Bosnian Muslims.

More than any other single event, the unremitting bombardment of Sarajevo, the capital of Bosnia-Herzegovina, brought the violence of the Yugoslav civil war to the attention of the world. The United Nations attempted unsuccessfully to mediate the conflict and imposed sanctions, which had little influence. Early in 1994, however, a shell exploded in the marketplace in Sarajevo, killing dozens of people. Thereafter, NATO forced the Serbs to withdraw their artillery from around Sarajevo.

The events of the civil war came to a head in 1995 when NATO forces carried out strategic air strikes. Later that year, under the leadership of the United States, the leaders of the warring forces completed a peace agreement in Dayton, Ohio. The agreement was of great complexity but recognized an independent Bosnia. The terms of the agreement have been enforced by NATO troops, including those from the United States.

Toward the end of the decade, Serbian aggression against ethnic Albanians in the province of Kosovo again drew NATO into Yugoslavian affairs. For months, through television and other media, the world watched the Serbian military carry out forcible removals of ethnic Albanians from Kosovo

where such Albanians constituted a majority of the population. The tactics closely resembled those previously used in Bosnia. There were many casualties, atrocities, and deaths. Early in 1999, NATO carried out an air campaign whose result was the introduction of NATO forces into Kosovo to restore the ethnic Albanians. This air campaign was the largest military action in Europe since the close of World War II. During the next year a brief revolution overthrew the government of Slobodan Milosevic. The new Yugoslav government turned the former leader over to the International War Crimes Tribunal at the Hague.

IMPLICATIONS OF THE COLLAPSE OF COMMUNISM

The collapse of European communism has closed the era in which Marxism dominated European socialism that began in the 1870s with the German socialists' adoption of Marxist thought. The Bolshevik victory in the Russian Revolution seemed to validate Marxism, and the policies of Lenin and Stalin sought to extend it around the world. Now the Soviet Union and the communist governments of Eastern Europe—heirs to the Bolshevik revolution—have vanished, and the economies they built have collapsed. As a result, Marxist socialism has been discredited, and socialism in general may find itself on the defensive in the future. Other groups—feminists and environmentalists, for example—may now provide the kind of social criticism that had previously flowed from socialism. To play a role in the new era taking shape in Europe, socialists must come to grips with the benefits of markets, economic decentralization, and political democracy.

The collapse of European communism has also profoundly altered international relations within Europe. The demise of the Warsaw Pact has brought the future of NATO to the fore. NATO's primary function had been to deter a Soviet attack on Western Europe. As that danger has disappeared, the purpose of the alliance has become unclear. Many argue that NATO should be kept as an instrument to preserve international order. Its hesitancy to play an effective role in ending the Yugoslav civil war, however, has raised doubts that it could counter the kinds of problems Europe may face in the future. At the same time, NATO's air campaign during the Kosovo crisis, which relied primarily on U.S. aircraft, has led some European leaders to urge the buildup of European armed forces to diminish Europe's dependence on the American military. Much debate also now centers on the possible admission of some Eastern European nations, once members of the Warsaw Pact, into NATO. Poland, the Czech Republic, and Hungary have already joined NATO to protect themselves from any future Russian aggression and to integrate themselves more fully into the Western European economy. In 2002, Russia and NATO entered a new relationship with the founding of a Russia-NATO Council designed to foster future cooperation.

Europe at the Opening of the Global Century

In 1900, the major European nations dominated the entire world. Their wealth in terms of manufacturing, investment banking, and consumer demand profoundly influenced the lives of millions of people on every continent. Their military power, particularly their navies, and their colonial administrators controlled enormous regions of Africa and Asia. Many Europeans were emigrating abroad, especially into the Americas. Wherever Europeans traveled or governed they could expect that people on the other continents would look to Europe as a model for industrial development, accumulation of wealth, and high culture in the arts and sciences. It was the apex of the European era that began at the close of the fifteenth century. In 1900, almost no one could have predicted the enormous human tragedies that would occur in Europe during the next half century or the retreat from world dominance that would mark the European experience during the rest of the twentieth century. Since 1991, and the collapse of the Soviet Union, for the first time in five hundred years no European power can even imagine itself dominating the world. What that new situation will mean for Europeans is not yet clear and probably will not become so for many years.

Consequently, it would be foolish to predict the contours of the new century, let alone the new millennium. Yet some elements of at least the opening years seem more or less clear. Europeans will see themselves more than at any previous time in their history as part of a global economy and global culture in which they will play a major role, but not the dominant role they imagined a hundred years ago. That imperative to placing themselves in the global setting will no doubt continue to spur European economic integration and in all likelihood greater political integration. Language barriers, ethnic prejudices, and the desire of individual nation-state bureaucracies to preserve themselves will make such integration difficult, but it will occur. As

the integration moves forward, the questions of constitutionalism and rule of law will be central to the new vision of the Continent. What many Europeans experienced under fascism, national socialism, and communism was the absence of the rule of law, due process, and respect for the institutions of civil society. It is just those values and institutions that appear to stand in the forefront of European civic thinking and political development today. Their achievement will be as difficult in the new century as in past centuries.

The collapse of communism, as well as the emergence of the European Community, has opened the way for new ways of thinking about Europe as a single community. Europeans, however, have not yet decided if they wish such a community or what price they are willing to pay to achieve it. Beyond that question is the issue of whether the enormous prosperity that forms a geographical line beginning in London, then going through the Benelux countries, France, Germany, and finally into northern Italy, can be expanded into areas of Europe that have been traditionally poorer. Will the East-West tension of the Cold War years be replaced by tensions between prosperous and poor regions? In that respect, the perennial question of the place of Russia in European civilization—a question that has concerned Europeans since the age of Peter the Great—again presents itself.

REVIEW QUESTIONS

1. How did the United States and the Soviet Union come to dominate Europe after 1945? Why were 1956 and 1962 crucial years in the Cold War?

2. How would you define the policy of *containment*? Give some specific examples of how the United States instituted that policy throughout the world from 1945 to 1982.

3. How did Khrushchev's policies and reforms change the Soviet state after the repression of Stalin? Why did many people consider Khrushchev reckless?

4. How did Western Europe move toward political unity after World War II?

5. Why did the nations of Europe give up their empires? How did French decolonization policies differ from Britain's? How did the United States become involved in Vietnam?

6. What internal political pressures did the Soviet Union experience in the 1970s and early 1980s? What steps did the Soviet government take to repress those protests? What role did

Gorbachev's attempted reforms play in the collapse of the Soviet Union?

7. What were the major events in Eastern Europe—particularly Poland—that contributed to the collapse of communism?

8. What are the major economic and political challenges facing Europe as it enters a new century?

SUGGESTED READINGS

F. ANSPRENGER, *The Dissolution of Colonial Empires* (1989). A broad survey.

R. BETTS, *France and Decolonization* (1991). Explores clearly the complexities of the French case.

E. BOTTOME, *The Balance of Terror: Nuclear Weapons and the Illusion of Security, 1945–1985* (1986). An examination of the role of nuclear weapons in the Cold War climate.

A. BROWN, *The Gorbachev Factor* (1996). Reflections by a thoughtful observer.

T. BUCHANAN AND M. CONWAY, *Political Catholicism in Europe, 1918–1965* (1996). Examines the background of Christian democracy.

M. E. CHAMBERLAIN, *Decolonization: The Fall of the European Empires* (1985). A useful treatment.

J. DARWIN, *Britain and Decolonization: The Retreat from Empire in the Postwar World* (1988). An excellent, clear account.

M. ELLMAN AND V. KONTOROVICH, *The Disintegration of the Soviet Economic System* (1992). An overview of the economic strains that the Soviet Union experienced during the 1980s.

H. FEIS, *From Trust to Terror: The Onset of the Cold War, 1945–1950* (1970). A useful general account.

J. L. GADDIS, *The United States and the Origins of the Cold War, 1941–1947* (1992). A major discussion.

M. GLENNY, *The Balkans, 1804–1999: Nationalism, War and the Great Powers* (1999). A lively narrative by a well-informed journalist.

W. F. HANRIEDER, *Germany, America, and Europe: Forty Years of German Foreign Policy* (1989). A major survey.

W. HITCHCOCK, *Struggle for Europe: The Turbulent History of a Divided Continent, 1945–2002* (2003). The best overall narrative now available.

A. HORNE, *A Savage War of Peace: Algeria 1954–1962* (1987). A now somewhat dated classic narrative.

K. H. JARAUSCH, *The Rush to German Unity* (1994). Examines the events and background of the reunification of Germany.

P. JENKINS, *Mrs. Thatcher's Revolution: The Ending of the Socialist Era* (1988). The best work on the subject.

L. JOHNSON, *Central Europe: Enemies and Neighbors and Friends* (1996). Examines the various nations of central Europe with an eye to the recent changes in the region.

T. JUDAH, *The Serbs: History, Myth and the Destruction of Yugoslavia* (1997). A clear overview of a complex event.

J. KEEP, *Last of the Empires: A History of the Soviet Union, 1945–1991* (1995). An outstanding one-volume survey.

M. MANDELBAUM, *The Ideas That Conquered the World: Peace, Democracy, and Free Markets* (2002). An important analysis by a major commentator on international affairs.

R. MANN, *A Grand Delusion: America's Descent into Vietnam* (2001). The best recent narrative.

D. MCKAY, *Rush to Union: Understanding the European Federal Bargain* (1996). Examines the background of the Maastricht treaty.

D. E. MURPHY, S. A. KONDRASHEV, AND G. BAILEY, *Battleground Berlin: CIA vs. KGB in the Cold War* (1997). One of the best of a growing literature on Cold War espionage.

B. NAHAYLO AND V. SWOBODA, *Soviet Disunion: A History of the Nationalities Problem in the USSR* (1990). A discussion of one of the major areas of political difficulty today.

W. E. ODOM, *The Collapse of the Soviet Military* (1999). A study more wide ranging than the title suggests.

B. PAREKH, *Ghandi: A Very Short Introduction* (2001). A very useful introduction to Ghandi's ideas.

S. P. RAMET (ED.), *The Religious Policy in the Soviet Union* (1993). Essays on an important subject that has often received little attention.

J. ROTHSCHILD, *Return to Diversity: A Political History of East Central Europe since World War II* (1989). A clear, well-organized introduction.

H. SIMONIAN, *The Privileged Partnership: Franco-German Relations in the European Community (1969–1984)* (1985). An important examination of the dominant roles of France and Germany.

A. ULAM, *The Communists: The Story of Power and Lost Illusions: 1948–1991* (1992). Narrative of the story of the passage from Soviet Communist strength to collapse.

M. WALKER, *The Cold War and the Making of the Modern World* (1994). A major new survey.

H. WALLACE (ED.), *Policy-Making in the European Union* (1996). A useful introduction to the institutions of European integration.

Cultural Divisions
and the Cold War

Although they may seem like products from different centuries, the Soviet painter Tatjiana Yablonskaya's (b. 1917) sun-strewn *Bread* (1949) and the American Jackson Pollock's (1912–1956) dizzyingly abstract *One* (Number 31, 1950) were painted only one year apart. The stark differences between these two works mirror the cultural divisions of the early Cold War.

Bread, measuring over six feet high and twelve feet wide, is a monumental example of socialist realism. Established as the official doctrine of Soviet art and literature in 1934, socialist realism sought to create optimistic and easily intelligible scenes of a bold socialist future, in which prosperity and solidarity would reign. Manual laborers and prominent historical and political figures were painted in a traditional and often rigid figurative manner. With the spread of Soviet control after World War II, socialist realism became the dominant artistic model throughout Eastern Europe, only waning when Nikita Khrushchev liberalized Soviet cultural policy toward the end of the 1950s.

Although *Bread*'s bountiful harvest, streaming sunlight, and happy workers are typical Soviet realist idealizations—in contrast to the harsh reality of life and food shortages under Stalin—Yablonskaya's painting can also be seen as a tribute to the role of women in Soviet economic life. Between 1928 and 1950, the number of working women in the USSR grew dramatically. By the late 1940s, about half of the USSR's female labor force worked in agricultural occupations.

The looping skeins of paint in *One* (Number 31, 1950) may seem completely different from the kind of "realistic" propaganda visible in *Bread*, but Pollock's painting is in fact a central document of postwar American cultural life. Flinging paint from sticks and brushes onto his floor-bound canvas, Pollock freed his lines from representing any figure or outline. The result, in *One* (Number 31,

Tatjiana Yablonskaya, *Bread*, 1949.   Ria Novosti/Sovfoto/Eastfoto

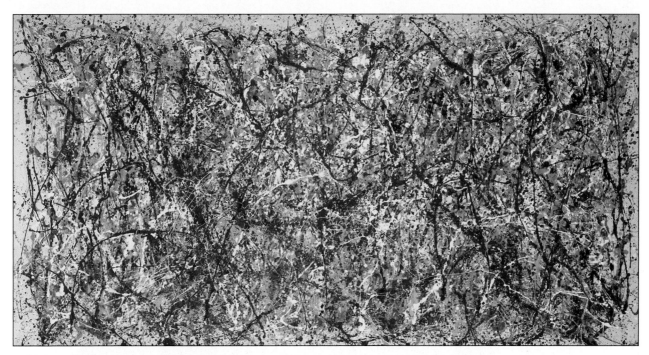

Jackson Pollock, *One* (*Number 31, 1950*).   Oil and enamel on unprimed canvas, 8 feet 10 inches × 17 feet 5⅝ inches (269.5 × 530.8 cm). The Museum of Modern Art, Licensed by Scala–Art Resource, New York. Sidney and Harriet Janis Collection Fund (by exchange). Photograph © 2000 The Museum of Modern Art, New York. 00007.68 © 2000 Pollock-Krasner Foundation/Artists Rights Society (ARS), NY.

1950), which is over 8 feet high and 17 feet wide, is a writing tangle of pure visual energy. In the politically charged atmosphere of the early Cold War, Pollock's exuberant "drip" paintings were seen as the embodiment of American cultural freedom, just as the Wyoming-born Pollock was celebrated as a kind of artist cowboy.

Lurking behind such interpretations was the awareness that the Soviets had forcibly imposed socialist realism on Eastern Europe and the Nazis had persecuted avant-garde artists. As skeptical as many viewers might have been about the merits of abstract art (*Time* magazine, for instance, dismissively called Pollock "Jack the dripper" in 1947), it came to be seen in the West as the antithesis of socialist realist totalitarianism.

Indeed, New York City—not Paris—emerged as the international center of modern art after World War II, a position it still holds today. As the home of growing collections of twentieth-century art and dozens of European avant-garde figures who had fled from the Nazis, New York became a fertile training ground for young artists such as Pollock. And just as American political and economic structures became models for the postwar redevelopment of Western

Europe, so did American cultural developments. By the time Pollock's first posthumous retrospective toured Europe in 1958, much European painting resembled an elegant imitation of his frenetic lines.

Yablonskaya and Pollock together illustrate the two central poles of twentieth-century art: realism and abstraction. Although artistic style is no longer as closely associated with political programs as it once was, these two poles still frame the work of countless artists today.

■ *What were the hallmarks of socialist realism? How does Yablonskaya's* Bread *typify these hallmarks and how does it compliment the role of Soviet women? How was Pollock's* One *related to the Cold War? What different themes in twentieth-century art does the work of Yablonskaya and Pollock illustrate?*

Matthew Cullerne Bown, *Art under Stalin*. (Oxford: Phaidon, 1991); John E. Bowlt, (ed.,) *Russian Art of the Avant-Garde: Theory and Criticism 1902–1934*. (New York: Viking Press, 1976); Alastair McAuley, *Women's Work and Wages in the Soviet Union*. (London: Allen & Unwin, 1981); Francis V. O'Conner, *Jackson Pollock*. (New York: Museum of Modern Art, 1967); Kirk Varnedoe and Pepe Karmel, *Jackson Pollock*. (New York: Museum of Modern Art, 1998).

On September 11, 2001, Al Qaeda terrorists crashed two hijacked airliners into the twin towers of the World Trade Center in New York City. Almost 3,000 people were killed that day including hundreds of firemen and policemen who responded to the emergency.
AP/Wide World Photos

CHAPTER 31

THE WEST AT THE DAWN OF THE TWENTY-FIRST CENTURY

*T*HE COLD WAR DEFINED THE *life of the West during most of the second half of the twentieth century. This was not only a matter of political experiences and military alliances. It affected the lives of millions of Europeans and Americans. The easy travel throughout the world that is possible today and enriches the lives of thousands of American students every year was impossible. Vast areas were closed off. Families were separated by the Iron Curtain. Most of Eastern Europe was simply cut off from the material and technological advances of the second half of the century.*

Yet despite these problems, European society, especially in the West, underwent remarkable changes during the second half of the century as did, of course, the United States. Western Europe enjoyed unprecedented prosperity, peace, and technological advances. This chapter examines some of those changes before turning to the rise of radical political Islamism, which at the time of the publication of this book appears to be the most important new factor affecting the future of Europe and the United States.

KEY TOPICS

- Migration in twentieth-century Europe
- Europe's Muslim minority
- Changing status and role of women in Europe
- New cultural forces and continuing influence of Christianity
- The impact of computer technology
- The rise of political Islam
- War in Afghanistan and Iraq

The Twentieth-Century Movement of Peoples

In the twentieth century, the movement of peoples transformed European society and the character of many European communities. The forced removal of Russian peasants by Soviet communists and the deportations and execution of European Jews by the Nazis were only the most dramatic and now familiar example of this development. The Second World War and the subsequent economic transformation of the Continent brought further extensive migration. The most pervasive trend in this movement of peoples was the continuing shift from the countryside to cities. Today, except for Albania, at least one-third of the population of every European nation lives in large cities. In Western Europe, city dwellers are approximately 75 percent of the population.

But other vast forced movements of peoples were carried out by governments and were little discussed during the Cold War. During the century, millions of Germans, Hungarians, Poles, Ukrainians, Bulgarians, Serbs, Finns, Chechens, Armenians, Greeks, Turks, and Bosnian Muslims were displaced.

This forced displacement transformed parts of Europe. The Soviet government under Stalin literally moved whole nationalities from one area of the country to another and killed many people in the process. The Nazis first displaced the Jews and then sought to exterminate them. Throughout Eastern Europe, cities that once had large Jewish populations and vibrant Jewish religious and cultural life became devoid of a Jewish presence. The displacement of Germans after World War II transformed cities that had been German into places almost wholly populated by Czechs, Poles, or Russians. For example, the present Polish city of Gdansk was once the German city of Danzig, and today's Russian city of Kaliningrad had been the German Königsberg before 1945.

DISPLACEMENT THROUGH WAR

World War II created a vast refugee problem. An estimated 46 million people were displaced in central and Eastern Europe and the Soviet Union alone between 1938 and 1948. Many cities in Germany and in central and Eastern Europe had been bombed or overrun by invading armies. Hundreds of thousands of foreign workers had been moved into Germany to contribute to the war effort. Many more were prisoners of war. Some of these people returned to their homeland willingly; others, particularly Soviet prisoners fearful of being executed by Stalin, had to be forced to go back. Hundreds of thousands of Baltic, Polish, and Yugoslav prisoners found asylum in Western Europe.

Changes in borders after the war also uprooted many people. For example, Poland, Czechoslovakia, and Hungary forcibly expelled millions of ethnic Germans from their territories to Germany. This transfer of over 12 million Germans in effect "solved" the problem of German minorities living outside Germany's national boundaries that had been one of Hitler's excuses for aggression against neighboring countries. In another case of forced migration, hundreds of thousands of Poles were transferred to within Poland's new borders from territory annexed by the Soviet Union. Other minorities, such as Ukrainians in Poland and Italians along the Yugoslav coast, were driven into their ethnic homelands. As one historian has commented, "War, violence and massive social dislocation turned Versailles's dream of national homogeneity into realities."[1]

EXTERNAL AND INTERNAL MIGRATION

Between 1945 and 1960, approximately half a million Europeans left Europe each year. This was the largest outward migration since the 1920s, when around 700,000 persons had left annually. In the second half of the nineteenth century, most immigrants had been from rural areas. After World War II, they often included educated city dwellers. Immediately after the war, some governments encouraged migration because they were afraid that, as in the 1930s, their economies would not be able to provide adequate employment for all their citizens.

Decolonization in the postwar period led many European colonials to return to Europe from overseas. The most dramatic example of this phenomenon was the more than 1 million French colonials

---

[1]Mark Mazower, *Dark Continent: Europe's Twentieth Century* (New York: Knopf, 1999), p. 218.

who moved to France after the end of the Algerian war in 1962 (see Chapter 30). Britons returned from parts of the British Empire, Dutch returned from Indonesia in the late 1940s, Belgians from the Congo in the 1960s, and Portuguese from Mozambique and Angola in the 1970s.

Decolonization also led non-European inhabitants of the former colonies to migrate to Europe. Great Britain, for example, received thousands of immigrants from its former colonies in the Caribbean, Africa, and the Indian subcontinent. France received many immigrants from its empire in Africa, Indochina, and the Arab world. This influx proved to be a long-term source of social tension and conflict. In Britain, racial tensions were high during the 1980s. France faced similar difficulties, which contributed to the emergence of the National Front, an extreme right-wing group led by Jean-Marie Le Pen (b. 1928) that sought to exploit the resentment many working-class voters felt toward North African immigrants. In 2002, Le Pen won enough votes to become one of the two candidates in the run-off election for the French presidency, although he lost overwhelmingly to Jacques Chirac (b. 1932) in the final ballot. Similar pressures have arisen in Germany, Austria, Italy, the Netherlands, and even Denmark. Such tension did not result only from immigration from Africa and Asia; internal European migration—from the Balkans, Turkey, and the former Soviet Union, often of people in search of jobs—also changed the social and economic face of the Continent and led to a backlash. However, the growing Muslim presence in Europe has produced some of the most serious ethnic and political tensions.

THE NEW MUSLIM POPULATION

As recounted earlier in this volume, well into the twentieth century the European relationship with most of the Muslim world was at arm's length or colonialist. Muslims from the Ottoman Empire, the greatest Muslim state, rarely traveled in Europe, and few Europeans traveled in the empire. Europeans encountered Muslims mainly as subjects, in colonies, such as Algeria, Egypt, the Indian subcontinent, sub-Saharan Africa, and the East Indies. In all of these regions from at least the mid–nineteenth century onward, Christian missionaries often clashed with Muslim religious teachers.

At the same time most Europeans, with the exception of a few minority communities in the Balkans and the former Soviet Empire, regarded themselves and their national cultures as either Christian or secular. Indeed, until recently most Europeans paid little attention to Islam.

That indifference began to change in the 1960s and had dissolved by the end of the twentieth century as a sizable Muslim population settled in Europe. This highly diverse immigrant community had become an issue in Europe even before the events of September 11, 2001, discussed later in this chapter.

The immigration of Muslims into Europe and particularly Western Europe arose from two chief sources: European economic growth and decolonization. As the economies of Western Europe began to recover in the quarter century after World War II, a labor shortage developed. To fill this demand, Western Europe imported laborers, many of whom came from Muslim nations. For example, Turkish "guest workers" were invited to move to West Germany—on a temporary basis, it was

When French rule ended in Algeria in 1962, tens of thousands of Algerians, such as these in Oran, left for France. Many of them were Muslims who had sided with the French; others were colons, persons of European descent whose families had lived in Algeria for generations.
© Bettmann/Corbis

presumed—in the 1960s, and Britain welcomed Pakistanis. The aftermath of decolonization and the quest for a better life led Muslims from East Africa and the Indian subcontinent to settle in Great Britain. The Algerian war brought many Muslims from North Africa into France. Today there are approximately 1.3 million Muslims in Great Britain, 3.2 million in Germany, and 4.2 million in France. Smaller but still significant numbers have settled in Italy, Spain, Sweden, Denmark, and the Netherlands, nations that previously had had generally homogeneous populations.

These Muslim immigrant communities share certain social and religious characteristics. Originally, many Muslims came to Europe expecting they would eventually return to their homes, an expectation their host countries shared. Neither the immigrants nor the host nations gave much thought to assimilation. Moreover, except for Great Britain, where all immigrants from the Commonwealth may vote immediately upon settling there, European governments made it difficult for Muslim, or any other, immigrants to take part in civic life. Unlike the United States, few European countries had any experience in dealing with large-scale immigration. The various Muslim communities have therefore generally remained unassimilated and self-contained. This apartness has provided internal community support for Muslim immigrants, but prevented them from fully engaging with the societies in which they live. Many of their children have not learned European languages well, and Muslim women tend to remain strictly confined to their homes.

But the world around these communities has changed. Many of the largely unskilled jobs that the immigrants originally filled have disappeared. Most of the Muslim immigrants to Europe, unlike many who have settled in the United States and Canada, were neither highly skilled nor professionally educated. As a result, they and their adult children who may have grown up in Europe find it difficult to get jobs in the modern service economy. Furthermore, as European economic growth has slowed, European Muslims have become the target of politicians, such as Le Pen in France, who seek to blame the immigrants for a host of problems from crime to unemployment.

The radicalization of parts of the Islamic world has also touched the Muslim communities in Europe. Although Turkish Muslims living in Germany come from a nation that has been secularized since the 1920s and thus tend to be less religiously observant than Pakistani Muslims dwelling in Great Britain, Muslims from both countries have been involved in radical Islamic groups, and some belonged to organizations involved in the September 11, 2001, attack on the United States. By contrast, the French government has exerted more control over its Muslim community.

Nonetheless, European Muslims are not a homogeneous group. They come from different countries, have different class backgrounds, and espouse different Islamic traditions. Many European Muslims and Muslim clerics disagree strongly with each other. Some emphasize a more traditional message; others preach a more radical one that is highly critical of the West. At the same time, these

From the 1960s Turkish "guest workers" emigrated to West Germany to provide much needed labor. Although both Germans and Turks assumed that these workers would eventually return to Turkey, many of them took up permanent residence in Germany.
© Bettmann/Corbis

Muslim communities so often now marked by deep poverty and unemployment have become a major concern for European social workers who disagree among themselves about how their governments should respond to them.

EUROPEAN POPULATION TRENDS

During the past quarter century, the population of Europe measured in terms of the European birthrate has stabilized in a manner that has disturbed many observers. Europeans are having so many fewer children that they are no longer replacing themselves. Whereas in the 1950s European women on average bore 2.1 children, that rate fell to 1.9 in the 1980s and to 1.4 at present. In Mediterranean countries such as Greece, Spain, and Italy, the rate is below 1.4. This situation stands in stark contrast to the increased growth in population that marked the United States during the past decade when the birthrate reached approximately 2.1. If the current rates more or less hold, by the middle of this century the population of the United States will outstrip that of Europe.

There is no consensus on the causes for the decline in the European birthrate. One reason often cited is that of women postponing having children until later in their childbearing years. The barriers raised by governments and public opinion are expected to limit immigration into Europe at a time when it may need new workers.

This falling birthrate means that Europe will face the prospect of an aging population. The energy and drive of youth will shift to the other side of the Atlantic. It is likely that economic innovation will arise from younger populations. The internal European market now larger than the internal American market will become smaller. In contrast to the late nineteenth century (see Chapter 24), there will be fewer Europeans in Europe itself and Europe's share of the world's population will also be much smaller. Part of the strong impact of Europe on the world in the nineteenth and early twentieth centuries was simply a consequence of the size of its population.

The Welfare State

The Great Depression, the rise of authoritarian states in the wake of economic dislocation and unemployment, and World War II, which involved more people in a war effort than ever before, led to a marked change in how many Europeans thought about social welfare. Governments began to spend more on social welfare than they did on the military.

This reallocation of funds was a reaction to the state violence of the first half of the century and was possible because Western Europe was protected after World War II by the NATO defense umbrella primarily staffed and financed by the United States.

The modern European welfare state was broadly similar across the Continent. Before World War II, except in Scandinavia, the two basic models for social legislation were the German and the British. Bismarck had introduced social insurance in Germany during the 1880s to undermine the German Social Democratic Party. In effect, the imperial German government provided workers with social insurance and thus some sense of social security while denying them significant political participation. In early-twentieth-century Britain, where all classes had access to the political system, social insurance was targeted toward the very poor. In both the German and British systems, workers should be insured only against the risks arising from disease, injury on the job, and old age. Unemployment was assumed to be only a short-term problem and often one that workers brought on themselves. People higher up in the social structure could look out for themselves and did not need government help.

After World War II, the concept emerged that social insurance against predictable risks was a social right and should be universally available to all citizens. This concept had been most famously set forth in Britain by William B. Beveridge (1879–1963) in 1942. Paradoxically, making coverage universal, as Beveridge recommended, was attractive to conservatives as well as socialists. If medical care, old age pensions, and other benefits were available to all, they would not be seen as a device for redistributing income from one portion of the population to another.

The first major European nation to begin to create a welfare state was Britain, during the 1945 to 1951 Labour Party ministry of Clement Attlee (1883–1967). The most important element of this early legislation was the creation of the National Health Service. France and Germany did not adopt similar health care legislation until the 1970s, because their governments initially refused to consider making coverage universal.

The spread of welfare legislation (including unemployment insurance) within Western Europe was related to both the Cold War and domestic political and economic policy. The communist states of Eastern Europe were promising their people social security as well as full employment. The capitalist states came to believe they had to provide similar security for their people. But, in fact, the social security of the communist states was often more rhetoric than reality.

Western European attitudes toward the welfare state have reflected what are generally regarded as the three periods that have marked economic life since the end of the war. The first period was one of reconstruction from 1945 through the early 1950s. It was followed by the second period—almost twenty-five years of generally steady and expanding economic growth. The third period brought first an era of inflation in the late 1970s and then one of relatively low growth and high unemployment that persisted throughout the 1990s. During each of the first two periods, a general conviction existed, based on Keynesian economics, that the foundation of economic policy was government involvement in a mixed economy. From the late 1970s, more people came to believe the market should be allowed to regulate itself and that government should be less involved—though not completely withdrawn from—the economy.

The government-furnished welfare services now found across Europe have begun to encounter resistance. The funding on which they are based assumes a growing population and low unemployment. As the proportion of the population consuming the services of the welfare state—the sick, the injured, and the elderly—increases relative to the able-bodied employed population that pays for them, the costs of those services rise. The leveling off of population growth in Europe discussed in the previous section thus imperils the benefits of the welfare state, which Europeans have come to take for granted. Furthermore, during the past two decades, significant levels of unemployment in major Western European nations have increased welfare payments. The low fertility rates across the Continent mean there will be fewer people in the next working generation to support the retired elderly population. Middle-class taxpayers have also become reluctant to support existing systems. The general growth of confidence in the ability of market forces rather than government intervention to sustain social cohesion has also spread in the past twenty-five years and has raised questions about the existing welfare structures. Governments across the Continent, including those normally associated with left-of-center politics, such as the British Labour Party and the German Social Democratic Party, have limited further growth of the welfare state and reduced current benefits. In that respect, Europeans in the next few decades may look at the second half of the twentieth century as the Golden Age of welfare states and may find their own societies dealing with the issues of social welfare differently.

New Patterns in the Work and Expectations of Women

The decades since World War II have witnessed striking changes in the work patterns and social expectations of European women. In all social ranks, women have begun to assume larger economic and political roles. More women have entered the "learned professions," and more are filling major managerial positions than ever before in European history. At the same time, certain more or less traditional patterns continue to describe the position of women in both family and economic life. Despite enormous gains during the second half of the twentieth century, and despite the collapse of those authoritarian governments whose social policies inhibited the advancement of women into the mainstream of society, gender inequality remained a major characteristic of the social life of Europe at the opening of the twenty-first century. (See "Art & the West: The Minimalist Movement: Rachel Whiteread's *House* and *Nameless Library*," p. 1114.)

FEMINISM

Since World War II, European feminism, although less highly organized than American feminism, has set forth a new agenda. The most widely read postwar work on women's issues was undoubtedly Simone de Beauvoir's (1908–1986) *The Second Sex*, published in 1949. In that work, de Beauvoir explored the difference being a woman rather than a man had made in her life. She was part of the French intellectual establishment and thus wrote from a privileged position. Over the years, however, she and other European feminists argued that at all levels, European women experienced distinct social and economic disadvantages. (See "Simone de Beauvoir Urges Economic Freedom for Women.") In the courts, for example, divorce and family laws favored men. European feminists also called attention to the social problems that women faced, including spousal abuse.

In contrast to earlier feminism, recent feminism has been less a political movement pressing for specific rights than a social movement offering a broader critique of European culture. Several new feminist publications appeared during the 1970s, many of which are still published: *Courage, Emma—Magazine by Women for Women*, and *Spare Rib*. A statement in *Spare Rib*, an English magazine, captures the spirit of these publications:

Spare Rib aims to reflect women's lives in all their diverse situations so that they can recognize themselves in its pages. This is done by making the magazine a vehicle

SIMONE DE BEAUVOIR URGES ECONOMIC FREEDOM FOR WOMEN

Simone de Beauvoir was the single most important feminist voice of mid-twentieth-century Europe. In The Second Sex, *published in France in 1949, she explored the experience of women coming of age in a world of ideas, institutions, and social expectations shaped historically by men. Much of the book discusses the psychological strategies that modern European women had developed to deal with their status as "the second sex." Toward the end of her book, de Beauvoir argues strongly that economic freedom and advancement for women are fundamental to their personal fulfillment.*

■ *Why does de Beauvoir argue that the achievement of civic rights must be accompanied by economic freedom for women? Why does the example of the small number of professional women illustrate issues for European women in general? How does she indicate that even professional women must overcome a culture in which the experience of women is fundamentally different from that of men? Do de Beauvoir's comments seem relevant for women at the opening of the twenty-first century? What similarities do you see to the views of Priscilla Wakefield (Chapter 16), Mary Wollstonecraft (Chapter 18), and Virginia Woolf (Chapter 25)?*

According to French law, obedience is no longer included among the duties of a wife, and each woman citizen has the right to vote; but these civil liberties remain theoretical as long as they are unaccompanied by economic freedom. . . . It is through gainful employment that woman has traversed most of the distance that separated her from the male; and nothing else can guarantee her liberty in practice. Once she ceases to be a parasite, the system based on her dependence crumbles; between her and the universe there is no longer any need for a masculine mediator. . . .

When she is productive, active, she regains her transcendence; in her projects she concretely affirms her status as subject; in connection with the aims she pursues, with the money and the rights she takes possession of, she makes trial of and senses her responsibility. . . .

There are . . . a fairly large number of privileged women who find in their professions a means of economic and social autonomy. These come to mind when one considers woman's possibilities and her future . . . [E]ven though they constitute as yet only a minority; they continue to be the subject of debate between feminists and antifeminists. The latter assert that the emancipated women of today succeed in doing nothing of importance in the world and that furthermore they have difficulty in achieving their own inner equilibrium. The former exaggerate the results obtained by professional women and are blind to their inner confusion. There is no good reason . . . to say they are on the wrong road; and still it is certain that they are not tranquilly installed in their new realm: as yet they are only halfway there. The woman who is economically emancipated from man is not for all that in a moral, social, and psychological situation identical with that of man. The way she carried on her profession and her devotion to it depends on the context supplied by the total pattern of her life. For when she begins her adult life she does not have behind her the same past as does a boy; she is not viewed by society in the same way; the universe presents itself to her in a different perspective. The fact of being a woman today poses peculiar problems for an independent human individual.

By Simone de Beauvoir, from *The Second Sex*, trans. by H. M. Parshley. Copyright 1952 and renewed 1980 by Alfred A. Knopf, Inc. Reprinted by permission of Alfred A. Knopf, a division of Random House Inc.

for their writing and their images. Most of all, *Spare Rib* aims to bring women together and support them in taking control of their lives.[2]

[2]Quoted in Bonnie S. Anderson and Judith P. Zinsser, *A History of Their Own: Women in Europe from Prehistory to the Present*, Vol. 2 (New York: Harper Perennial, 1988), p. 412.

This emphasis on women controlling their own lives may be the most important element of recent European feminism. Whereas in the past feminists sought and, in significant measure, gained legal and civil equality with men, they are now pursuing personal independence and issues that are particular

Simone de Beauvoir (1908–1986) and Jean-Paul Sartre (1905–1980) were two leading midcentury French intellectuals. She wrote extensively on the social position, experience, and psychology of women, and he was a major voice in the existentialist movement.
Bildarchiv Preussischer Kulturbesitz

to women. In this sense, feminism is an important manifestation of the critical tradition in Western culture.

MORE MARRIED WOMEN IN THE WORK FORCE

One of the patterns firmly established in 1900 has reversed itself. The number of married women in the work force has risen sharply. Both middle-class and working-class married women have sought jobs outside the home. Because of the low birthrate in the 1930s, few young single women were employed in the years just after World War II. Married women entered the job market to replace them. Some factories changed their work shifts to accommodate the needs of married women. Consumer conveniences and improvements in health care also made it easier for married women to enter the work force by reducing the demands child care made on their time. At the same time, all surveys indicate that the necessity of providing care for their children is the most important difficulty women find in the workplace. This situation is a main reason that women remain overwhelmingly in forms of part-time employment.

In the twentieth century, children were no longer expected to contribute substantially to family income. They now spend years in compulsory education. When families need more income than one worker can provide, both parents work, bringing many married women with children into the work

force. Such financial necessity led many married women back to work. Evidence also suggests that married women began to work to escape the boredom of housework and to find company among other adult workers.

NEW WORK PATTERNS

The work pattern of European women has been far more consistent in the twentieth century than it had been in the nineteenth. Single women enter the work force after their schooling and continue to work after marriage. They may stop working to care for their young children, but they return to work when the children begin school. Several factors created this new pattern, but women's increasing life expectancy is one of the most important.

When women died relatively young, child rearing filled a large proportion of their lives. As a longer life span has shortened that proportion, women throughout the West are seeking ways to lead satisfying lives after their children have grown. Decisions regarding when to have children and how many have also shaped the late-twentieth-century work pattern for women. Many women have begun to choose to limit the number of children they bear or to forgo childbearing and child rearing altogether. The age at which women have decided to bear children has risen, to the early twenties in Eastern Europe and to the late twenties in Western Europe. In urban areas, childbearing is later and the birthrate

Cherie Blair (center), the wife of Prime Minister Tony Blair of Britain, is a lawyer. Like many contemporary European women she has pursued an independent career.
© Corbis

lower than elsewhere. These various personal decisions leave many years free for developing careers and for staying in the work force.

Controversy over abortion has fueled recent public debate and legislation in Europe. Two factors have triggered the debate: the emergence of the European Union and the collapse of communism. From before the formation of the European Union until the Treaty of Maastricht, each nation of Western Europe had its own legislation on the subject. By the 1990s, abortion with various degrees of difficulty of access was legal throughout Western Europe (except Ireland), including the traditionally Roman Catholic Mediterranean countries. The process of working through the details of the European Union provoked debate over abortion as countries with either liberal or conservative policies had to work their way to a common policy. In Eastern Europe before the collapse of communism, abortion was legalized. In the Soviet Union, the 1936 Stalinist prohibition was lifted after his death. With the opening of political life since 1989, abortion has become a matter of new public debate. It also complicated the unification of East and West Germany, because the former had a more liberal policy toward abortion than the latter.

WOMEN IN THE NEW EASTERN EUROPE

Many paradoxes surround the situation of women in Eastern Europe now that communists no longer govern the region. Under communism, women generally enjoyed social equality, as well as a broad spectrum of government-financed benefits. A significant proportion (normally well over 50 percent) of women worked in these societies, both because they could and because they were expected to. There were, however, no significant women's movements because they, like all independent associations, were regarded with suspicion.

The new governments of the region are free, but have so far shown little concern with women's issues. Indeed, the economic difficulties the new governments face may endanger their funding of various health and welfare programs that benefit women and children. For example, a free market economy may limit the extensive maternity benefits to which Eastern European women were previously entitled. Moreover, the high proportion of women in the work force could leave them more vulnerable than men to the region's economic troubles. Women may well find themselves being laid off before men and hired later than men for lower pay.

Transformations in Knowledge and Culture

Knowledge and culture in Europe were rapidly transformed in the twentieth century. Institutions of higher education enrolled an increasingly large and diverse student body, making knowledge more widely available than ever before. Also, movements such as existentialism challenged many traditional intellectual attitudes. Environmental concerns also raised new issues. Throughout this ferment, representatives of the Christian faith tried to keep their religion relevant.

COMMUNISM AND WESTERN EUROPE

Until the final decade of the twentieth century, Western Europe had organized communist parties, as well as groups of intellectuals sympathetic to communism. After the Bolshevik victory in the Russian Revolution and the subsequent civil war, the Western European socialist movement divided into independent democratic socialist parties and Soviet-dominated communist parties that followed the directions of the Third International. Throughout the 1920s and 1930s, those two groups fought each other with only rare moments of cooperation, such as that achieved during the French Popular Front in 1936.

The Intellectuals During the 1930s, as liberal democracies floundered in the face of the Great Depression and as right-wing regimes spread across the Continent, many people saw communism as a

George Orwell (1903–1950), shown here with his son, was an English writer of socialist sympathies who wrote major works opposing Stalin and communist authoritarianism. Felix H. Man/Bildarchiv Preussischer Kulturbesitz

vehicle for protecting humane and even liberal values. Throughout Europe, students in the universities were often affiliated with the Communist Party. They and older intellectuals visited the Soviet Union and praised Stalin's achievements. Some of these intellectuals may not have known of Stalin's terror. Others simply closed their eyes to it, believing humane ends might come from inhumane methods. Still others actually defended Stalinist terror. During the late 1920s and the 1930s, communism became a substitute religion for some Europeans. One group of former communists, writing after World War II, described their attraction toward, and later disillusionment with, communism in a book entitled *The God That Failed* (1949).

Four events proved crucial to the disillusionment of the intellectuals: the great public purge trials of the late 1930s, the Spanish Civil War (1936–1939), the Nazi-Soviet pact of 1939, and the Soviet invasion of Hungary in 1956. Arthur Koestler's (1905–1983) novel *Darkness at Noon* (1940) recorded a former communist's view of the purges. George Orwell (1903–1950), who had never been a communist, but who had sympathized with the party, expressed his disappointment with Stalin's policy in Spain in *Homage to Catalonia* (1938). The Nazi-Soviet pact destroyed the image of Stalin as an opponent of fascism. Other intellectuals, such as the French philosopher Jean-Paul Sartre (1905–1980), continued to believe in the Soviet Union during and after the war, but the Hungarian Revolution cooled their ardor. The invasion of Czechoslovakia in 1968 simply confirmed a general disillusionment with Soviet policies by even left-wing Western European intellectuals.

Yet disillusionment with the Soviet Union or with Stalin did not always mean disillusionment with Marxism or with radical socialist criticisms of European society. Some writers and social critics looked to the establishment of alternative communist governments based on non-Soviet models. During the decade after World War II, Yugoslavia provided such an example. Beginning in the late 1950s, radical students and a few intellectuals found inspiration in the Chinese Revolution. Other groups hoped a European Marxist system would develop. Among the more important contributors to this non-Soviet tradition was the Italian communist Antonio Gramsci (1891–1937), especially in his work *Letters from Prison* (published posthumously in 1947). The thinking of such non-Soviet communists became important to Western European communist parties, such as the Italian Communist party, that hoped to gain office democratically.

Another way to accommodate Marxism within mid-twentieth-century European thought was to redefine the basic message of Marx himself. During the 1930s, many of Marx's previously unprinted essays were published. These books and articles, written before the *Communist Manifesto* of 1848, are abstract and philosophical. They make the "young Marx" appear to belong more nearly to the humanist than to the revolutionary tradition of European thought. Since World War II, works such as *Philosophic Manuscripts* of 1844 and *German Ideology* have been widely read. Today, many people are more familiar with them than with the *Manifesto* or *Capital*. They allowed some people to consider themselves sympathetic to Marxism without also seeing themselves as revolutionaries or supporters of the Soviet Union. With the collapse of the communist governments of Eastern Europe and the Soviet Union, what influence Marxism will continue to have on European intellectual life in the future is unclear.

EXISTENTIALISM

The intellectual movement that perhaps best captured the predicament and mood of mid-twentieth-century European culture was **existentialism.** Like the modern Western mind in general, existentialism, which has been termed the "philosophy of Europe in the twentieth century," was badly divided; most of the philosophers associated with it disagreed with each other on major issues. The movement represented in part a continuation of the revolt against reason that began in the nineteenth century.

Roots in Nietzsche and Kierkegaard Friedrich Nietzsche, discussed in Chapter 25, was a major forerunner of existentialism. Another was the Danish writer Søren Kierkegaard (1813–1855), who received little attention until after World War I. Kierkegaard was a rebel against both Hegelian philosophy and Danish Lutheranism. In works such as *Fear and Trembling* (1843), *Either/Or* (1843), and *Concluding Unscientific Postscript* (1846), he maintained that the truth of Christianity could be grasped only in the lives of those who faced extreme situations, not in creeds, doctrines, and church structures.

Kierkegaard also criticized Hegelian philosophy and, by implication, all modes of academic rational philosophy. Its failure, he felt, was the attempt to contain all of life and human experience within abstract categories. Kierkegaard spurned this faith in the power of mere reason. "The conclusions of passion," he once declared, "are the only reliable ones."[3]

The intellectual and ethical crisis of World War I brought Kierkegaard's thought to the fore and also created new interest in Nietzsche's critique of reason. The war led many people to doubt whether human beings were actually in control of their own destiny. Its destructiveness challenged faith in human rationality and improvement. Indeed, the war's most terrible weapons were the products of rational technology. The pride in rational human achievement that had characterized much nineteenth-century European civilization lay in ruins. The sunny faith in rational human development and advancement had not withstood the extreme experiences of war.

Questioning of Rationalism Existentialist thought thrived in this climate and received further support from the trauma of World War II. The major existential writers included the Germans Martin Heidegger (1889–1976) and Karl Jaspers (1883–1969) and the French Jean-Paul Sartre (1905–1980) and Albert Camus (1913–1960). Their books are often difficult or obscure. Although they frequently disagreed with each other, they all, in one way or another, questioned the primacy of reason and scientific understanding as ways of coming to grips with the human situation. Heidegger, a philosopher deeply compromised by his association with the Nazis, argued, "Thinking only begins at the point where we have come to know that Reason, glorified for centuries, is the most obstinate adversary of thinking."[4]

The romantic writers of the early nineteenth century had also questioned the primacy of reason, but they did so in a much less radical manner than the existentialists. The romantics emphasized the imagination and intuition, but the existentialists dwelled primarily on the extremes of human experience. Death, fear, and anxiety provided their themes. The titles of their works illustrate their sense of foreboding and alienation: *Being and Time* (1927), by Heidegger; *Nausea* (1938) and *Being and Nothingness* (1943), by Sartre; *The Stranger* (1942) and *The Plague* (1947), by Camus. The touchstone of philosophic truth became the experience of the individual under extreme conditions. (See "Sartre Discusses the Character of His Existentialism.")

According to the existentialists, human beings are compelled to formulate their own ethical values and cannot depend on traditional religion, rational philosophy, intuition, or social customs for ethical guidance. The opportunity and need to define values endow humans with a dreadful freedom.

[3]Quoted in Walter Kaufman, ed., *Existentialism from Dostoevsky to Sartre* (Cleveland: World Publishing Company, 1962), p. 18.

[4]Quoted in William Barrett, *Irrational Man* (Garden City, NY: Doubleday, 1962), p. 20.

SARTRE DISCUSSES THE CHARACTER OF HIS EXISTENTIALISM

Jean-Paul Sartre, dramatist, novelist, and philosopher, was the most important French existentialist. In the first paragraph of this 1946 statement, Sartre asserted that all human beings must experience a sense of anguish or the most extreme anxiety when undertaking a major commitment. That anguish arises because, consciously or unconsciously, they are deciding whether all human beings should make the same decision. In the second paragraph, Sartre argued that the existence or nonexistence of God would make no difference in human affairs. What humankind must do is to discover the character of its own situation by itself.

■ *How might the experiences of fascism in Europe and the fall of France to the Nazis have led Sartre to emphasize the need of human beings to choose? Why does Sartre believe existentialism must be related to atheism? Why did Sartre regard existentialism as optimistic?*

The existentialist frankly states that man is in anguish. His meaning is as follows—When a man commits himself to anything, fully realizing that he is not only choosing what he will be, but is thereby at the same time a legislator deciding for the whole of mankind—in such a moment a man cannot escape from the sense of complete and profound responsibility. There are many, indeed, who show no such anxiety. But we affirm that they are merely disguising their anguish or are in flight from it. Certainly, many people think that in what they are doing they commit no one but themselves to anything: and if you ask them, "What would happen if everyone did so?" they shrug their shoulders and reply, "Everyone does not do so." But in truth, one ought always to ask oneself what would happen if everyone did as one is doing; nor can one escape from that disturbing thought except by a kind of self-deception. The man who lies in self-excuse, by saying, "Everyone will not do it" must be ill at ease in his conscience, for the act of lying implies the universal value which it denies. By its very disguise his anguish reveals itself.

Existentialism is nothing else but an attempt to draw the full conclusions from a consistently atheistic position. Its intention is not in the least that of plunging men into despair. And if by despair one means—as the Christians do—any attitude of unbelief, the despair of the existentialist is something different. Existentialism is not atheist in the sense that it would exhaust itself in demonstration of the nonexistence of God. It declares, rather, that even if God existed that would make no difference from its point of view. Not that we believe God does exist, but we think that the real problem is not that of His existence; what man needs is to find himself again and to understand that nothing can save him from himself, not even a valid proof of the existence of God. In this sense existentialism is optimistic. It is a doctrine of action, and it is only by self-deception, by confusing their own despair with ours that Christians can describe us as without hope.

From Jean-Paul Sartre, *Existentialism and Humanism*, trans. by Philip Mairet (London: Methuen), in Walter Kaufman, ed., *Existentialism from Dostoevsky to Sartre* (New York: Meridian Books, 1956), pp. 292, 310–311.

The existentialists were largely protesting against a world in which reason, technology, and politics produced only war and genocide. Their thought reflected the uncertainty of social institutions and ethical values in the era of the two world wars. Since the 1950s, however, their works and ideas have found their way into university curriculums around the world, making them objects of study, if not the source of intellectual ferment they had been. They continue to be discussed in philosophy and literature classes, but their popularity has receded.

European intellectuals were attracted to communism and existentialism before and just after World War II, but in the 1960s, the turmoil over Vietnam and the youth rebellion brought other intellectual and social issues to the fore. Even before the collapse of communism, these had begun to redirect European intellectual interests.

EXPANSION OF THE UNIVERSITY POPULATION AND STUDENT REBELLION

As rapid changes in communications technology vastly expanded access to information, increasing numbers of Europeans received some form of university education. At the turn of the century, only a few thousand people were enrolled in universities in any major European country. By the opening of this century, that figure had risen to hundreds of thousands, although university education is still less common in Europe than in the United States. Higher education is now available to people from a variety of social and economic backgrounds, and, for the first time, it is readily available to women.

One of the most striking and unexpected results of this rising post–World War II population of students and intellectuals was the student rebellion of the 1960s. This development is still not well understood. Student uprisings began in the early 1960s in the United States and assumed major proportions as opposition grew to the war in Vietnam. The student rebellion then spread into Europe and other parts of the world. It was almost always associated with a radical political critique of the United States, although in Eastern Europe resentment was also directed toward the Soviet Union. The movement was generally antimilitarist. In addition to their political concerns, students questioned middle-class values and traditional sexual mores and family life.

The student movement reached its peak in 1968, when students in the United States demonstrated forcibly against U.S. involvement in Vietnam. In the same year, students at the Sorbonne in Paris seriously challenged the government of Charles de Gaulle, and in Czechoslovakia, students were in the forefront of the liberal socialist experiment. These protests failed to have an immediate effect on the policies of the governments at which they were directed. The United States stayed in Vietnam until 1973, de Gaulle remained president of France, and the Soviets suppressed the Czech experiment.

By the early 1970s, the era of student rebellion seemed to have passed. Students remained active in European movements against nuclear weapons and particularly against the placement of American nuclear weapons in Germany and elsewhere in Europe. From the mid-1970s, however, although often maintaining a radical political stance, they generally abandoned the kind of disruptive protests that marked the 1960s.

THE AMERICANIZATION OF EUROPE

During the past half century, through the Marshall Plan, leadership of NATO, the stationing of hundreds of thousands of troops, student exchanges, popular culture, and tourism, the United States has exerted enormous influence on Europe, especially Western Europe. The word *Americanization*, often appearing as a term of criticism in European publications, refers in part to this economic and military influence, but also to concerns about cultural loss. Many Europeans feel that American popular entertainment and business threaten to extinguish some of Europe's unique qualities. Many American firms now have European branches. Large American corporations, such as McDonald's, Starbucks, and the Gap, have outlets in European cities from Dublin to Moscow. American liquor companies and distilleries now sell their goods in Europe. American clothing, such as blue jeans, is now popular in

In 1968 a student rebellion in Paris threatened to bring down the government of Charles De Gaulle. This was only one example of the explosion of student activity that rocked the West in the late 1960s.
© Bettmann/Corbis

Europe. Shopping centers and supermarkets, first pioneered in America, are displacing neighborhood shopping areas. American television programs and movies are readily available. Furthermore, as Europe moves toward greater economic cooperation, English seems to be the most common language of business, technology, and even some academic fields. And American influence, not British, lies behind this trend. (See "Encountering the Past: Toys from Europe.")

A CONSUMER SOCIETY

Although European economies came under pressure during the 1990s and experienced high levels of unemployment, the consumer sector has expanded to an extraordinary degree during most of the last half century.

The consumer orientation of the Western European economy emerged as one of the most important characteristics differentiating it from Eastern Europe. Those differences produced important political results. Throughout the Soviet Union and the nations it dominated in Eastern Europe, economic planning overwhelmingly favored capital investment and military production. Those nations produced inadequate food for their people and few consumer goods. Long lines for staples, such as food and clothing, were common; automobiles were a luxury; housing was inadequate. Consumer goods were shoddy.

By contrast, by the early 1950s, Western Europeans enjoyed an excellent food supply that has continued to improve. And in a sign of the strength of Western Europe's economy, if not the healthfulness of its diet, fast-food outlets have multiplied.

Western Europe has enjoyed a similar expansion of consumer goods and services. Automobile ownership has soared. Refrigerators, washing machines, electric ranges, televisions, microwaves, videocassette recorders, computers, CD players, and other electronic consumer items are taken for granted. Like their American counterparts, Western Europeans now have a whole gamut of products, such as disposable diapers and prepared baby foods, to help them raise children. They take foreign vacations year round, prompting the expansion of ski resorts in the Alps and beach resorts on the Mediterranean.

This vast expansion of consumerism, which, as we noted in Chapter 16, began in the eighteenth century, became a defining characteristic of Western Europe in the late twentieth century. It stood in marked contrast to the consumer shortages in Eastern Europe. Yet through even the limited number of radios, televisions, movies, and videos available to them, people in the East grew increasingly aware of the discrepancy between their lifestyle and that of the West. They saw Western consumerism clearly linked to democratic governments, free societies, and economic policies that favored the free market and limited government planning. Thus the expansion of consumerism in the West, deplored by many intellectuals and moralists, helped generate the discontent that brought down the communist governments of Eastern Europe and the Soviet Union. (See "Václav Havel Reflects on the Future of Europe.")

ENVIRONMENTALISM

After World War II, shortages of consumer goods created a demand that fueled postwar economic reconstruction and growth into the 1950s and 1960s. In those expansive times, there was little room for public debate about the ethics of economic expansion and efficiency and their effects on the environment. Concerns about pollution began to emerge in the 1970s, and by the 1980s, environmentalists had developed real political clout. Among the most important environmental groups were the Club of Rome,

McDonald's restaurants like this one in Moscow are a symbol of American popular culture in Europe. © John Dakers; Eye Ubiquitous/Corbis

Toys from Europe Conquer the United States

Today many Europeans criticize what they often term *Americanization*—the introduction of popular American products and restaurant chains onto the European scene. Yet over the past half century one European toy— LEGO building blocks manufactured in Denmark—has shaped the experience of childhood for many children in the United States and the rest of the world, entering their lives and imaginations no less powerfully than the cartoon figures associated with the American Disney Corporation.

In 1932, in the midst of the depression, Ole Kirk Christiansen opened a small business in Billund, Denmark, that manufactured household goods and wooden toys. The toys sold so well that two years later the firm renamed itself LEGO from the Danish *LEg GOdt* meaning "Play well." The company remained small, producing only wooden toys, until 1947 when it began to make molded plastic toys. It only sold its products in Denmark.

In 1955, LEGO introduced LEGO Bricks—plastic building blocks of the familiar stud-and-tube type—which it sold in sets under the name LEGO System of Play. That system, which the firm patented in 1958, allowed children to combine LEGO Bricks in an almost endless number of ways, limited only by their own imaginations and that of their parents. The company also extended its market, first into Germany and then outside Europe. LEGO first began to sell in the United States in 1961.

Thereafter, the success of LEGO as a toy and as a company grew on itself. The company added many new features to the original concept of interlocking building blocks. For example, the addition of wheels enabled children to use LEGO kits to build their own trucks, trains, and similar mobile toys.

In 1968, the LEGO Company, no doubt following the example of the Disney Corporation in the United States, opened an amusement park in Billund in which the rides were designed to look like huge LEGO toys. By the end of the century, LEGO had opened similar parks in England, the United States, and Germany.

However, the company remained focused on making toys for children. It continued to design new toys, such as plastic figures with human heads to ride in LEGO vehicles, and whole LEGO villages, castles, and pirate ships. By the 1990s, LEGO had become the largest toy manufacturer in Europe and a part of modern culture. Museums featured displays of LEGO products and structures built from LEGO blocks. Contests were held to construct the largest or most unusual LEGO structures. In 1999, *Fortune* magazine included the LEGO brick among the "Products of the Century," and in 2002, LEGO persuaded European and American management consultants that working with LEGO blocks would help business executives think more clearly about corporate planning. But perhaps most astonishing is that over a half century of tumultuous historical change, children around the world have continued to play with these little pieces of plastic.

Children across the world play with LEGO toys.
Tom Prettyman/PhotoEdit

■ *How has LEGO been an example of the European penetration of popular culture throughout the world? Why has the influence of LEGO on children's toys been less controversial than the appearance of American fast-food chains in Europe?*

Source: Factual information derived from the official Lego Company Web site: www.lego.com/eng/info/history.

VÁCLAV HAVEL REFLECTS ON THE FUTURE OF EUROPE

In October 1993, Václav Havel, then president of the Czech Republic, gave a speech in which he outlined many of the problems confronting Europe after the collapse of communism. Havel was addressing the General Assembly of the Council of Europe, so his general theme was European unity. He discussed the danger of resurgent ethnic nationalism and noted nationalism had caused two major wars in Europe in the twentieth century. He was seeking to convince European leaders and nationalist groups to think differently about their interests in the future and to create a European, rather than a particular national, ethos.

■ *What are the values around which Havel believes European nations might integrate and unify themselves? How does he portray special interests as undermining cooperation? What specific dangers does he associate with the appearance of new forms of nationalism?*

All of us—whether from the west, the east, the south, or the north of Europe—can agree that the common basis of any effort to integrate Europe is the wealth of values and ideas we share. Among them are respect for the uniqueness and the freedom for each human being, the principles of a democratic and pluralistic political system, a market economy, and a civic society with the rule of law. All of us respect the principle of unity in diversity and share a determination to foster creative cooperation between the different nations and ethnic, religious, and cultural groups—and the different spheres of civilization—that exist in Europe. . . .

Despite general agreement on the values upon which European integration should stand, this process today, . . . has encountered a number of obstacles. . . .

There are many reasons for this state of affairs, but I feel strongly that they all have one thing in common: the erroneous belief that the great European task before us is a purely technical, a purely administrative, or a purely systematic matter. . . .

To put it more succinctly: Europe today lacks an ethos; it lacks imagination, it lacks generosity, it lacks the ability to see beyond the horizon of its own particular interests, be they partisan or otherwise. . . . Europe does not appear to have achieved a genuine and profound sense of responsibility for itself as a whole, and thus for the future of all those who live in it. . . .

The former Yugoslavia is the first great testing ground for Europe in the era that was initiated by the end of the cold war. . . .

Another one consists in how we deal with the temptation to open the back gate to the demons of nationalist collectivism with an apparently innocent emphasis on minority rights and on the right of minorities to self-determination. At first sight, this emphasis would seem harmless and beyond reproach. But one real consequence could be new unrest and tension, because demands for self-determination inevitably lead to questioning the integrity of the individual states and the inviolability of their present borders, and even the validity of all postwar treaties. Attempts of this kind are dangerous chiefly because they look not to the future, but to the past, for they call in question the very principle of civil society and the indivisible rights of the individual, as well as the certainty that only democracy, individual rights and freedoms, and the civil principle can guarantee the genuinely full development of even that aspect of one's identity represented by membership in a nationality. . . .

If various Western states cannot rid themselves of their desire for a dominant position in their own sphere of interests, if they don't stop trying to outwit history by reducing the idea of Europe to a noble backdrop against which they continue to defend their own petty concerns, and if the post-Communist states do not make radical efforts to exorcise the ghosts their newly won freedom has let loose, then Europe will only with great difficulty be able to respond to the challenge of the present and fulfill the opportunities that lie before it.

From Václav Havel, Address to the General Assembly of the Council of Europe, October 9, 1993, *New York Review of Books*, November 18, 1993, p. 3.

Pollution of waterways poses danger to human health in many parts of Europe and has been one of the conditions giving rise to the European environmental movement. Here, a German factory pours its refuse and chemicals into a river. Such pollution has been a particular problem in the former Soviet bloc nations. Frischmuth/Argos/SABA Press Photos, Inc.

founded in 1972, and the German Greens. The Greens formed a political party in 1979 that immediately became an electoral force. During these same years, concern for environmental issues, such as global warming and the pollution of water and the atmosphere with substances endangering human health, commanded the attention of governments outside Europe and the agencies of the United Nations.

Several developments lay behind this new concern for the environment. The Arab oil embargo of 1973–1974 pressed home two messages to the industrialized West: natural resources are limited, and several critical resources come from foreign countries. By the 1970s, too, the environmental consequences of three decades of economic expansion were becoming increasingly apparent. Fish were dying in the Thames River in England. Industrial pollution was destroying the rivers of Germany and France. Acid rain had begun to kill trees from Sweden to Germany. Finally, long-standing apprehensions about nuclear weapons merged with concerns about their environmental effects, strengthening antinuclear groups and generating opposition to the placement of nuclear weapons in Europe.

The German **Green movement** originated among the radical student groups of the late 1960s. Like them, it was anticapitalist, holding business responsible for pollution. The Greens and other European environmental groups were also strongly antinuclear. Unlike the students of the 1960s, the Greens avoided violence and mass demonstrations, seeking instead to enter the electoral process directly. They elected a few representatives to the West German Parliament and to local offices.

The 1986 disaster at the Chernobyl nuclear reactor in the Soviet Union heightened concern about environmental issues and raised questions that no European government could ignore. The Soviet government had to confront casualties at the site and relocate tens of thousands of people. Clouds of radioactive fallout spread westward across Europe. Environmentalists had always contended that their issues transcended national borders. The Chernobyl fire proved them right.

After Chernobyl, virtually all European governments, East and West, began to respond to environmental concerns. Some observers believe the environment may become a major political issue across the Continent. In Western Europe, environmental groups command a significant share of votes. Economic and political integration opens the possibility of transnational cooperation on environmental matters. As the European Economic Community solidifies, it and its member nations will likely impose environmental regulations on business and industry. The nations of Eastern Europe face the daunting task of cleaning up vast areas polluted by industrial development during the communist era and devising policies that combine environmental protection with economic growth.

The Christian Heritage

In most ways, Christianity in Europe has continued to be as hard pressed during the twentieth century as it had been in the late nineteenth. Material prosperity, political ideologies, environmentalism, gender politics, and simple indifference have replaced religious faith in many people's lives. Still, despite the loss of much of their popular support and former legal privileges, the European Christian churches continue to exercise considerable social and political influence. In Germany, the churches were one of the few major institutions that the Nazis did not wholly subdue. Lutheran clergy, such as Martin Niemöller (1892–1984) and Dietrich Bonhoeffer (1906–1945), were leaders of the opposition to Hitler. After the war, in Poland and elsewhere in Eastern Europe, the Roman Catholic Church opposed communism.

In Western Europe, religious affiliation provided much of the initial basis for the Christian Democratic parties. The churches have also raised critical questions about colonialism, nuclear weapons, human rights, and other issues. Consequently, even in this most secular of ages, Christian churches have influenced state and society.

Neo-Orthodoxy

Liberal theologians of the nineteenth century often softened the concept of sin and portrayed human nature as close to the divine. The horror of World War I destroyed that optimistic faith, leaving many Europeans feeling that evil had stalked the Continent.

The most important Christian response to the experience of World War I appeared in the theology of Karl Barth (1886–1968). In 1919, this Swiss pastor published *A Commentary on the Epistle to the Romans*, which reemphasized the transcendence of God and the dependence of humankind on the divine. Barth portrayed God as wholly other than, and different from, humankind. In a sense, Barth was returning to the Reformation theology of Luther, but the work of Kierkegaard had profoundly influenced his reading of the reformer. Like the Danish writer, Barth regarded the lived experience of men and women as the best testimony to the truth of Luther's theology. Those extreme moments of life described by Kierkegaard provided the basis for a real knowledge of humankind's need for God.

This view challenged outright much nineteenth-century writing about human nature. Barth's theology, which came to be known as neo-Orthodoxy, proved influential throughout the West in the wake of new disasters and suffering.

Liberal Theology

Neo-Orthodoxy did not, however, sweep away liberal theology, which had a strong advocate in Paul Tillich (1886–1965). This German American theologian tended to regard religion as a human, rather than a divine, phenomenon. Whereas Barth saw God as dwelling outside humankind, Tillich believed that evidence of the divine had to be sought in human nature and human culture.

Other liberal theologians, such as Rudolf Bultmann (1884–1976), continued to work on the problems of naturalism and supernaturalism that had troubled earlier writers. Bultmann's major writing took place before World War II, but was popularized thereafter in Anglican bishop John Robinson's *Honest to God* (1963). Another liberal Christian writer from Britain, C. S. Lewis (1878–1963), attracted millions of readers during and after World War II. This layman and scholar of medieval literature often expressed his thoughts on theology in the form of letters and short stories. His most famous work is *The Screwtape Letters* (1942). In recent years, however, European religious thought has produced few major Protestant voices.

Roman Catholic Reform

Among Christian denominations, the most significant postwar changes have been in the Roman Catholic Church. Pope John XXIII (r. 1958–1963) initiated these changes, the most extensive in Catholicism for more than a century and, some would say, since the Council of Trent in the sixteenth century. In 1959, Pope John summoned the Twenty-first Ecumenical Council (the first had been called by Emperor Constantine in the fourth century), which came to be called Vatican II. The council finished its work in 1965 under John's successor, Pope Paul VI (r. 1963–1978). Among many changes in Catholic liturgy, the council required that mass be celebrated in the vernacular languages rather than Latin. It also permitted freer relations with other Christian denominations, fostered a new spirit toward Judaism, and gave more power to bishops. In recognition of the growing importance to the church of the world outside Europe and North America, Pope Paul appointed several cardinals from the former colonial nations, transforming the church into a truly world body.

In contrast to these liberal changes, however, Pope Paul and his successors have firmly upheld the celibacy of priests, maintained the church's prohibition on contraception, and opposed moves to open the priesthood to women. The church's unyielding stand on clerical celibacy has caused many men to leave the priesthood and many men and women to leave religious orders. The laity has widely ignored the prohibition on contraception.

In 1998 Pope John Paul II visited Cuba, where for four decades the government of Fidel Castro had discouraged the open practice of Roman Catholicism. Reuters NewMedia Inc./Corbis

John Paul II, the former Karol Wojtyla, archbishop of Kraków in Poland, was elected in 1978 after the death of John Paul I, whose reign lasted only 34 days. The youngest pope since Pius IX (r. 1846–1878), John Paul II (b.1920) has pursued a three-pronged policy. First, he has maintained traditionalist doctrine, stressing the authority of the papacy and attempting to limit doctrinal and liturgical experimentation.

Second, taking a firm stand against communism, he directly contributed to the spirit of freedom in Eastern Europe that brought down the communist regimes. As a cardinal in Poland, he had clashed with the communist government. After his election, he visited Poland, lending support to Solidarity. His Polish origins undoubtedly helped make him an important factor in the popular resistance to Eastern Europe's communist governments that developed

during the 1980s. In this respect, he opened a new chapter in the relationship between church and state in modern Europe.

Third, Pope John Paul II has encouraged the expansion of the church in the non-Western world, stressing the need for social justice, but limiting the political activity of priests. (See "Pope John Paul II Discusses International Social Justice.") The pope's concern for the expansion of Roman Catholicism beyond Europe and North America has both recognized and encouraged what appears to be a profound transformation in Christianity as a world religion. Whereas in Europe observance of Christianity whether Roman Catholic, Protestant, or Orthodox had declined sharply during the twentieth century, Christianity has grown rapidly and fervently in Africa and Latin America. Observers

POPE JOHN PAUL II DISCUSSES INTERNATIONAL SOCIAL JUSTICE

Pope John Paul II issued his encyclical, The Social Concerns of the Church, *in 1988. In the passages given here, he attempted to set concerns for justice among developed and developing nations into the larger context of Christian moral theology.*

■ *How does the pope relate the fate of the poorest nations to the international system of trade and finance? What evidence is there that the pope did not favor radical social action on the part of Roman Catholic clergy? How does this encyclical illustrate the pope's concerns for non-European parts of the world?*

The Church's social doctrine is not a "third way" between liberal capitalism and Marxist collectivism, nor even a possible alternative to other solutions less radically opposed to one another: rather, it constitutes a category of its own. Nor is it an ideology, but rather the accurate formulation of the results of a careful reflection on the complex realities of human existence, in society and in the international order, in the light of faith and of the Church's tradition. Its main aim is to interpret these realities, determining their conformity with or divergence from the lines of the Gospel teaching on man and his vocation, a vocation which is at once earthly and transcendent; its aim is thus to guide Christian behavior. It therefore belongs to the field, not of ideology, but of theology and particularly moral theology. . . .

The international trade system today frequently discriminates against the products of the young industries of the developing countries and discourages the producers of raw materials. There exists, too, a kind of international division of labor, whereby the low-cost products of certain countries which lack effective labor laws or which are too weak to apply them are sold in other parts of the world at considerable profit for the companies engaged in this form of production, which knows not frontiers. . . .

[H]umanity today is in a new and more difficult phase of its genuine development. It needs a greater degree of international ordering, at the service of the societies, economies and cultures of the whole world. . . .

It is desirable, for example, that nations of the same geographical area should establish forms of cooperation which will make them less dependent on more powerful producers; they should open their frontiers to the products of the area; they should examine how their products might complement one another; they should combine in order to set up those services which each one separately is incapable of providing; they should extend cooperation to the monetary and financial sector. . . .

The Church well knows that no temporal achievement is to be identified with the Kingdom of God, but that all such achievements simply reflect and in a sense anticipate the glory of the Kingdom, the Kingdom which we await at the end of history, when the Lord will come again. But that expectation can never be an excuse for lack of concern for people in their concrete personal situations and in their social, national, and international life, since the former is conditioned by the latter, especially today.

estimate that within a few years, over half of the world's Christians will live in those two continents. Recognizing these changes, John Paul II has created more cardinals from non-Western nations. When his successor is eventually chosen, almost a majority of the college of cardinals will come from outside Europe and North America. These demographic shifts in Christianity will no doubt produce important changes in faith, practice, and organization.

Late-Twentieth-Century Technology: The Arrival of the Computer

During the twentieth century, technology crossed international borders the way popular culture did. As with other areas of European life and society, technology originating in America had an unprecedented impact on the Continent, whether in the guise of the first airplanes or Henry Ford's method of producing affordable automobiles. But it seems certain that no single American technological achievement of the twentieth century will so influence Western life on both sides of the Atlantic, as well as throughout the rest of the world, as the computer.

THE DEMAND FOR CALCULATING MACHINES

Beginning in the seventeenth century, thinkers associated with the scientific revolution—most famously, the French mathematician and philosopher Blaise Pascal (1623–1662)—attempted to construct machines that would carry out mathematical calculations that human beings would find essentially impossible because of the tedium and the amount of time they involved. Starting in the late nineteenth century, the governments of the consolidating nation-states of Europe and of the United States confronted new administrative tasks that involved collecting and organizing vast amounts of data about national censuses, tax collection, economic statistics, and the administration of pensions and welfare legislation. During the same years, private businesses sought calculating machinery to handle and organize growing amounts of economic and business data. Such machines became technologically possible through the development of complex circuitry for electricity, the most versatile mode of energy in human history. Moreover, inventions that were dependent on electricity, including the telephone, the telegraph, underwater cables, and the wireless, created a new communications industry that in and of itself also required the organization of large databases of customer information to deliver their services. By the late 1920s, companies like National Cash Register, Remington Rand, and International Business Machines Corporation had begun to manufacture such business machinery.

EARLY COMPUTER TECHNOLOGY

As has happened so often in history, warfare was the chief catalyst of change. After World War I and during World War II, the major powers developed new weapons that required exact mathematical ballistic calculations to effectively strike targets with bombs delivered by aircraft or long-range guns.

The first machine genuinely recognizable as a modern digital computer was the Electronic Numerical Integrator and Computer (**ENIAC**), built and designed at Moore Laboratories of the University of Pennsylvania and put into use by the U.S. Army in 1946 for ballistics calculation. The ENIAC was an enormous piece of equipment with 40 panels, 1,500 electric relays, and 18,000 vacuum tubes. It also used thousands of punch cards, and a separate tabulator had to print the data from them. Further computer engineering occurred at the Institute for Advanced Research in Princeton, New Jersey, in laboratories at the Massachusetts Institute of Technology, and in other laboratories run by the U.S. government and by private businesses, especially IBM. The other primary site for computer development was British university and government laboratories.

THE DEVELOPMENT OF DESKTOP COMPUTERS

During the 1950s, however, the invention of the transistor revolutionized electronics, permitting a miniaturization of circuitry that made vacuum tubes obsolete and allowed computers to become somewhat smaller. Yet throughout the 1950s and 1960s, computers had to be programmed with difficult computer languages by persons expertly trained to use them.

By the late 1960s, however, two remarkable innovations transformed computing technology. First, direction for the control of the computer became transferred to a bitmap covering the screen of a computer monitor. The mouse, invented in 1964, eased the movement of the cursor around the computer screen. Second, engineers associated with the Intel Corporation—then a California start-up company—invented the microchip, which became the heart of all future computers.

The bitmap on the screen, operated through the mouse, in effect embedded complicated computer language in the machine, hidden from the user, who simply manipulated images on the screen with the mouse. Almost anyone could thus learn to operate computers. At the same time, the tiny microchip, itself a miniature computer or microprocessor, permitted computer technology to abandon the mainframe and move to still smaller computers. At the Xerox Corporation, engineers devised a small computer using a mouse, but the machine never achieved commercial success. By 1982, IBM had produced a small personal computer, but temporarily lost the race for commercialization to a then small company called Apple Computer Corporation. The design features originally developed at Xerox informed the ideas of the Apple engineers, who, in early 1984, produced a

The computer has become an essential tool in advanced countries. Here a group of Hispanic children work with a computer in their school's library. Those societies that can afford to train their populations to use computers have a major advantage over those that cannot. Bob Daemmrich Photography, Inc.

small, highly accessible, commercially successful computer, known as the Macintosh, that would fit on a desktop in the home or office. IBM soon adopted the Apple concept with different engineering and marketing approaches and manufactured a product called the Personal Computer, or PC. By the mid-1980s, for a relatively modest cost (and one that has continued to drop), individuals had available for their own personal use in their offices or homes computers with far more power than the old mainframes. The Apple Macintosh and the IBM PC transformed computers into objects of everyday life and, in doing so, initiated a transformation of everyday life itself. Nonetheless, the chief contemporary users of computers remain governments followed by the telephone industry, followed by banking and finance, automobile operation, and airline reservation systems.

Despite the potential democratizing character of computer technology, the computer revolution has also introduced new concepts of "haves" and "have-nots" to societies around the world. Computers, whatever their possible shortcomings, give their users the ability to do things that nonusers cannot do. Whether in poor school districts in the United States or in poor countries of the former Soviet bloc, students who graduate without computer skills will have difficulty making their way in the world's rapidly computerizing economy. Some commentators also fear that boys are more likely than girls to receive technological training in computers. Nations whose governments and businesses become networked into the world of computers will prosper more fully than those whose access to

computer technology is deficient. In that regard, the possession of computers and the ability to use them will probably determine future economic competition, just as they have determined recent military competition.

The Rise of Radical Political Islamism

On September 11, 2001, Islamic terrorists attacked the United States, crashing hijacked civilian domestic aircraft into the twin towers of the World Trade Center in New York City, the Pentagon in Washington, D. C., and a Pennsylvania field with a vast loss of life and property.

In retrospect, we can see that those attacks were the result of forces that had been affecting not only the United States but the Western world for at least a half century. The end of the Cold War has been succeeded by a new political world in which both the United States and the nations of Europe including the Russian Federation are endangered by terrorist attacks from nongovernmental or non-state-based organizations. These groups are guided by ideologies in the Islamic world that have filled a political and ideological vacuum left by the end of the Cold War.

Radical Islamism is the term used to describe an interpretation of Islam that came to have a significant impact in the Muslim world following decolonization. It is only one—and by no means the most popular—interpretation of Islam. The ideas informing radical Islamism extend back to the 1930s, but for many years had little impact on the politics of the Middle East.

ARAB NATIONALISM

Radical Islamism arose primarily in reaction to the secular Arab nationalism that developed in countries like Egypt and Syria in the 1920s and 1930s. Although the Arab and other Middle Eastern nationalists, like nineteenth-century modernizers in the Ottoman Empire believed the path to independence and strength lay in adopting the technology and imitating the political institutions of the West, advocates of radical Islam wanted to reject Western ideas and create a society based on a rigorist interpretation of Islam and its teachings. (See Chapter 23.)

In the wake of World War II, many of the foremost leaders of Arab nationalism, such as Gamal Abdul Nasser of Egypt (1918–1970), were sympathetic to socialism or the Soviet Union. Because socialism and communism were Western ideologies, left-leaning Arab nationalism was no less Western in its orientation than were nationalists friendly to the United States. Moreover, Soviet communism was overtly atheistic and hence doubly offensive to devout Arab Muslims.

Nationalism forged by nondemocratic Middle Eastern governments, usually traditional monarchies or authoritarian regimes dominated by the military, brought different results to the various Arab nations. Oil made Saudi Arabia wealthy and powerful and the Gulf states, such as Kuwait, rich but not powerful. Other states, such as Jordan, Syria, and Egypt, which lacked oil, remained burdened by large impoverished populations.

Arab governments defining themselves according to the values of nationalism worked out arrangements with local Muslim authorities. For example, the Saudi royal family turned over its educational system to adherents of a rigorist, puritanical form of Islam called *Wahhabism* while modernizing the country's infrastucture. The Egyptian government attempted to play different Islamic groups off against one another. These governments retained the support of prosperous, devout middle-class Muslims while doing little about the plight of the poor. In general, Muslim religious leaders were highly critical of the Soviet Union and its influence in the region.

THE IRANIAN REVOLUTION

The Iranian Revolution of 1979 transformed the Middle East. The Ayatollah Ruhollah Khomeini

(1902–1989) managed to unite both the middle and lower classes of a major Middle Eastern nation against a modernizing government, that had long cooperated with the United States. For the first time, a religiously dominated government defining itself and its mission in distinctly Islamic as well as nationalistic terms took control of a major state. The revolutionary government of Iran was a theocracy, that is, there was no separation of religion and government or in European terms of church and state. The Iranian constitution gave the clergy, acting on behalf of God, the final say in all matters.

The Iranian Revolution challenged the Westernization of Iranian society and in doing so shocked the world. In particular, it challenged the largely secular presuppositions of Arab nationalists in states such as Egypt, Saudi Arabia, and Algeria that had failed to satisfy the needs of their own underclasses. In the mid–twentieth century, Arabs and other Middle Eastern peoples had turned to nationalism in reaction against European colonial powers. Those who grew up under nationalist leadership and still found themselves politically and economically disadvantaged, however, reacted against nationalism. They were deeply attracted to the Iranian Revolution, which many thought would spread throughout the Islamic world.

The Iranian Revolution both embodied and emboldened the forces of what is commonly called Islamic *fundamentalism*, but is more correctly termed Islamic or Muslim *reformism*. This is the belief that a reformed or pure Islam must be established in the contemporary world. Most adherents of this point of view would emphasize personal piety and religious practice. However, a minority wish to see their states strictly governed the way Iran purports to be by Islamic law or the Shari'a. In fact, the Iranian clergy made numerous compromises to the practical demands of everyday government and the oil industry. But the larger public message to the world was that Iran is a strict Islamic state hostile to the West in general and the United States in particular. The Iranian Revolution also opposed the state of Israel on both religious and nationalistic grounds.

After the Iranian Revolution, the conservative Arab governments began to fear the revolution would challenge their own legitimacy. They consequently began to pay much more attention to their own religious authorities and cracked down on radical reformist or fundamentalist Muslims. In Egypt, such actions followed the assassination in 1981 of President Anwar Sadat by a member of the Muslim Brotherhood.

Ayatollah Ruhollah Khomenei led the fundamentalist Iranian Revolution that overthrew the Shah in 1979. He became a symbol of Islamic resistance to Westernization.
© Bettman/Corbis

INVASION OF AFGHANISTAN

The Russian invasion of Afghanistan of 1979 introduced a major new component into this already complicated picture, illustrating the convergence of Cold War and Islamist politics. The Soviet Union sought to impose a communist, and hence both Western and atheist, government in Afghanistan. Certain Muslim religious authorities declared *jihad*, literally meaning "a struggle" but commonly interpreted as a religious war, against the Soviet Union. Thereby the Afghan resistance to the Soviets became simultaneously nationalistic, universalistic, and religious.

Thousands of Muslims, mostly fundamentalist in outlook, arrived in Afghanistan to oust the Soviets and their Afghan puppets. Conservative Arab states

and the United States supported this effort, which succeeded by the late 1980s. The conservative Arab states saw the Afghan war as an opportunity both to resist the expansion of Soviet influence into their sphere and to divert the energies of their own religious extremists. The United States saw the Afghan war as another round in the Cold War. The militant Muslim fundamentalists saw it as a religious struggle against an impious Western power.

DISPERSION OF AFGHAN MUSLIM FIGHTERS

After the Soviets withdrew in ignominy in 1989, a power vacuum in Afghanistan lasted almost a decade. By 1998, however, rigorist Muslims known as the *Taliban* had seized control of the country. They imposed their own version of Islamic law, which involved strict regimentation of women and public executions and mutilations for criminal offenses. The Taliban also allowed groups of Muslim terrorists known as *Al Qaeda*, which means "Base," to establish training camps in their country. The terrorists who attacked the United States on September 11, 2001, came from these camps.

The ideology of these groups had emerged over several decades from different regions of the Islamic world but had been inculcated in Pakistan. The Pakistani government over the years had assigned considerable control over education to Islamic schools, or *madrasas*, that taught reformed Islam, rejection of liberal and nationalist secular values, repudiation of Western civilization and culture, hostility to Israel, and hatred of the United States.

Once the jihad against the Soviet Union had succeeded, radical Muslims largely educated in these Pakistani schools turned their attention to the United States, the other great Western power. The event that brought about this redirection was the Persian Gulf War of 1991. The occasion for that conflict was

the invasion of Kuwait by Iraq, governed by Saddam Hussein. The conservative Arab governments, most importantly Saudi Arabia, not only supported the United States, but permitted it to construct military bases on their territory. Islamic extremists who had fought in Afghanistan, one of whom was Osama Bin Laden, interpreted the establishment of U.S. bases in Saudi Arabia, which was the home of the prophet Muhammed, as a new arrival of Western Crusaders into Muslim territory. The bases added a new grievance to the already long list of radical Muslim complaints against the United States.

The United States became a target because of its secular public morality, its international wealth and power, its military strength, its ongoing support for Israel, and its adherence to the UN sanctions imposed on Iraq after the Gulf War. Certain Muslim religious authorities declared a jihad against the United States, thus transforming opposition to American policies and culture into a religious war. Through the 1990s, a number of terrorists attacks were directed against targets in or associated with the United States. These included the bombing of the World Trade Center in New

In late 2001 the U.S. attacked Afghanistan to topple the Taliban government, which had provided aid and protection to the Al Qaeda terrorist organization.   AP/Wide World Photos

York City in 1993, of U.S. army barracks in Saudi Arabia in 1996, of U.S. embassies in east Africa in 1998, and of the USS *Cole* in the Yemeni port of Aden in 2000. These attacks resulted in considerable loss of life.

A Transformed West

The attacks on the United States on September 11, 2001, transformed and redirected American foreign policy into what the administration of President George W. Bush termed "a war on terrorism." In late 2001, the United States attacked the Taliban government of Afghanistan, rapidly overthrowing it. The defeat of the Taliban destroyed Al Qaeda's Afghan bases but not its leadership, which appears to have survived, although it was dispersed and remains in hiding.

Following the Afghan campaign, the Bush administration set forth a policy of preemptive strikes and intervention against potential enemies of the United States. The administration argued that the danger of weapons of mass destruction developed by governments such as that of Iraq falling into the hands of international terrorist organizations posed so severe a danger to the security of the United States that the nation could not wait to respond to an attack, but must stand prepared to take preemptive action. This argument, which aroused controversy both at home and abroad, marked a major departure from previous United States foreign policy. It is a direct result of the attacks on the United States that occurred on September 11.

Throughout 2002 the Bush administration turned its attention to Saddam Hussein's government in Iraq. Since the defeat of Iraq in 1991 by an international coalition force led by the United States, Saddam Hussein, contrary to widespread expectations, had remained in power and had continued to exercise repressive control over his own

As part of the campaign in 2003 to overthrow Saddam Hussein's regime in Iraq, U.S. forces used missiles and planes to bomb Baghdad, the Iraqi capital. AP/Wide World Photos

people. Throughout the 1990s the Iraqi government had also resisted the work of United Nations inspectors charged with discovering and destroying weapons of mass destruction found in Iraq or facilities capable of manufacturing such weapons. The Iraqi government eventually expelled United Nations inspectors in 1998, and the United Nations was unable to re-insert them for almost five years.

The United States government adopted a policy of regime change in Iraq during the last years of the Clinton administration though it did little to carry out that policy. In the wake of the September 11, 2001, attacks, however, the Bush administration became convinced that the government of Saddam Hussein must be removed and with it any threat from Iraqi weapons of mass destruction. During late 2002 and early 2003 the United States and British governments sought to obtain passage of United Nations Security Council resolutions that would require Iraq to disarm on its own or to face disarmament by military force. The efforts to obtain an effective United Nations Security Council resolution failed primarily because the governments of France and Russia threatened to veto the measure. In the face of United Nations' failure to pass a resolution, the United States, Great Britain, and Australia, backed by a coalition of some fifty other nations, invaded Iraq in late March 2003 and after three weeks of fighting succeeded in removing the government of Saddam Hussein from power. The announced goals of the invasion, in addition to toppling the Iraqi regime, were to destroy Iraq's capacity to manufacture or deploy weapons of mass destruction and to bring consensual government to the Iraqi people.

The invasion of Iraq was undertaken in the face of considerable opposition from France, Germany, and Russia. It also provoked large anti-war demonstrations in the United States and throughout the world. Both the war and the diplomatic difficulties preceding it disrupted the long-standing Atlantic alliance. Moreover, French and German opposition to the war created strains within Europe, and particularly within NATO and the European Union, as many other European governments strongly supported the United States and Great Britain. As a result, the war in Iraq clearly marks a new era in relations between the United States and Europe and between the United States and the rest of the world. As those new relationships emerge, we shall no doubt still see the major themes of this book and of the Western heritage develop in new and still to be determined ways.

In Perspective

The twentieth century was the most destructive in human history. The wars of the first half of the century killed millions of Europeans and disrupted the fabric of European society. The Bolsheviks, Fascists, and National Socialists sought to remake whole societies according to utopian visions that resulted in repression, death, and the uprooting of numerous minority groups.

With the defeat of National Socialism and Fascism, society in Western Europe developed along more peaceful lines with powerful economic and cultural influence coming from the United States. Migration and the economic growth of the second half of the century reshaped the society of many Western nations. Welfare systems provided a network of security. The role and opportunities for women in society expanded. More and more Europeans in both the West and the East attended universities. The Soviet-dominated portions of the Continent lagged badly in terms of political, intellectual, and religious freedom and never produced enough consumer goods.

By the close of the century, Europe, like much of the rest of the world, had entered a new technological revolution through the computer and advances in medical care. Economic growth slowed in the 1990s, but most of Europe outside the former communist-dominated regions continued to enjoy a high standard of living under liberal democratic governments. In the former Soviet Union and its empire, the challenge became how to realize economic growth in some form of market economy without the former centralized state planning.

Now near the middle of the first decade of the twenty-first century, the life of the West in both Europe and the United States stands challenged by radical political Islamism. How this challenge is met may determine the life of the West for the next quarter century and beyond.

REVIEW QUESTIONS

1. How did migration affect twentieth-century European social life? What internal and external forces led to migration?

2. In what specific ways was Europe Americanized in the second half of the twentieth century? How do you explain the trend toward a consumer society?

3. How have women's social and economic roles changed in the second half of the twentieth century? What tensions and difficulties have new work patterns created for women? What changes and problems have women faced amidst the political instability in Eastern Europe?

4. Discuss the changes in the pursuit and diffusion of knowledge in the twentieth century. What has been the effect of the communications revolutions? Of the boom in universities? Has Western intellectual life become more unified or less so? Why?

5. Discuss the contributions of Nietzsche and Kierkegaard to existentialism. How was existentialism a response to the various crises of the twentieth century?

6. Trace the major technological steps in the emergence of the computer. What changes are computers likely to bring in the next decade?

7. Trace the rise of radical political Islamism. How did the Iranian Revolution, the invasion of Afghanistan, and the Persian Gulf War contribute to this movement?

SUGGESTED READINGS

G. AMBROSIUS AND W. H. HUBBARD, *A Social and Economic History of Twentieth-Century Europe* (1989). An excellent one-volume treatment of the subject.

B. S. ANDERSON AND J. P. ZINSSER, *A History of Their Own: Women in Europe from Prehistory to the Present*, vol. 2 (1988). A broad-ranging survey.

R. BERNSTEIN, *Out of the Blue: The Story of September 11, 2001 from Jihad to Ground Zero* (2002). An excellent account by a gifted journalist.

G. BOCK AND P. THANE (eds.), *Maternity and Gender Politics: Women and the Rise of the European Welfare States, 1880s–1950s* (1991). Explores politics relating to population, families, and mothers in the emergence of welfare legislation.

E. BRAMWELL, *Ecology in the 20th Century: A History* (1989). Traces the environmental movement to its late-nineteenth-century origins.

S. COLLINSON, *Beyond Borders: West European Migration Policy and the 21st Century* (1993). An exploration of a major contemporary European social issue.

R. CROSSMAN (ED.), *The God That Failed* (1949). Classic essays by former communist intellectuals.

C. FINK, P. GASERT, AND D. JUNKER, *1968: The World Transformed* (1998). The single best collection of essays on a momentous year.

T. FORESTER (ED.), *The Microelectronics Revolution* (1980). Discusses the basic inventions in electronics that have created the structures for the new computers.

H. H. GOLDSTINE, *The Computer from Pascal to von Neuman* (1972). A clear history of the technological development of the computer.

B. GRAHAM, *Modern Europe: Place, Culture, Identity* (1998). Thoughtful essays on the future of Europe by a group of geographers.

J. HERF, *Divided Memory: The Nazi Past in the Two Germanies* (1997). An exploration of the manner in which writers in East and West Germany interpreted the Nazi years.

H. S. HUGHES, *Sophisticated Rebels: The Political Culture of European Dissent, 1968–1987* (1988). A series of thoughtful essays on recent cultural critics.

P. JENKINS, *The Next Christendom: The Coming of Global Christianity* (2002). A provocative analysis.

T. JUDT, *Past Imperfect: French Intellectuals, 1944–1956* (1992). An important study of French intellectuals and communism.

G. KEPEL, *Jihad: The Trail of Political Islam* (2002). An extensive treatment by a leading French scholar of the subject.

T. K. LANDAUER, *The Trouble with Computers: Usefulness, Usability, and Productivity* (1997). An informed skeptical commentary on the impact of computers.

R. MALTBY (ED.), *Passing Parade: A History of Popular Culture in the Twentieth Century* (1989). A collection of essays on a topic just beginning to receive scholarly attention.

R. MARRUS, *The Unwanted: European Refugees in the 20th Century* (1985). An important work on a disturbing subject.

D. MEYER, *Sex and Power: The Rise of Women in America, Russia, Sweden, and Italy* (1987). A lively, useful survey.

G. MONTEFIORE, *Philosophy in France Today* (1983). A good introduction to one of the major centers of late twentieth-century thought.

N. NAIMARK, *Fires of Hatred: Ethnic Cleansing in Twentieth-Century Europe* (2002). A remarkably sensitive treatment of a tragic subject.

M. POSTER, *Existential Marxism in Postwar France* (1975). An excellent and clear work.

S. STRASSER, C. MCGOVERN, AND M. JUDT, *Getting and Spending: European and American Consumer Societies in the Twentieth Century*

(1998). An extensive collection of comparative essays.

F. THEBAUD (ED.), *A History of Women in the West, Vol. 5: Toward a Cultural Identity in the Twentieth Century* (1994). A collection of wide-ranging essays of the very highest quality.

M. VIORST, *In the Shadow of the Prophet: The Struggle for the Soul of Islam* (2001). Explores the divisions in contemporary Islam.

DOCUMENTS CD-ROM

SOCIETY AND CULTURE BETWEEN THE WARS

27.2   Jean-Paul Sartre: Existentialism

THE COLD WAR AND ITS AFTERMATH

30.5   Stokeley Carmichael: What We Want

The Minimalist Movement: Rachel Whiteread's *House* and *Nameless Library*

The British sculptor Rachel Whiteread (b. 1963) is one of the leading artists of today's Europe. Her work illustrates how European art is breaking out of the modernist contours that were set at the beginning of the twentieth century. On the one hand, Whiteread's art returns to what seem like familiar forms; on the other, it forces us to view these forms in ways that are as new to us as cubism was to the public in its day.

Whiteread's work is associated with the minimalist movement in contemporary art. This movement, which originated in architecture and interior design, seeks to remove from the object being portrayed as many features as possible while still retaining the object's form and the viewer's interest and attention. Minimalist art aims to be as understated as possible. In Whiteread's hands the minimal becomes the austere, and her work often exudes a sense of melancholy and loss.

Whiteread began her career by focusing on objects from everyday life. She would take such an object and make a plaster cast of its interior space. Initially her subjects were small, such as a hot water bottle, a piece of furniture, or the space under a chair. In 1993, however, she made a cast of the interior space of an entire house that was about to be torn down in London. She left the work untitled, but it became known as *House*. It presents interior space as solid but temporary, subject to the passage of time. Like many of Whiteread's subjects, the object that has been molded—in this case the demolished house—no longer exists, and even the sculpture itself will eventually disappear. *House* stood on the site for only two and a half months before being razed, like the actual house itself, as part of an urban redevelopment plan.

Whiteread's most important public work, and one designed to endure, is *Nameless*

Rachel Whiteread's *House*   © Richard Glover/Corbis

Whiteread's *Nameless Library* in Vienna commemorates the thousands of Austrian Jews killed in the Nazi Holocaust. Rachel Whiteread, "Untitled (Library)", 1999. Dental plastere, polystyrene, fiberboard and steel, $112\,^{1}/_{2} \times 210\,^{5}/_{8}$ inches. Hirshhorn Museum and Sculpture Garden, Smithsonian Institution, Joseph H. Hirshhorn Purchase Fund, 2000. Photo: Lee Stalsworth

Library, the Judenplatz Holocaust Memorial in Vienna, which commemorates the deaths of 65,000 Austrian Jews under the Nazis. This memorial, which resembles a vast haunting tomb, is cast in concrete and embodies the outline of books whose spines are turned inward, thus remaining forever unread and as unopenable as are the library's huge concrete doors. Whiteread has said the molded, unopened books, which have been compared to the ghost of a library, symbolize the loss both of Jewish contributions to culture and of Jewish lives in the Holocaust.

In 1997, Rachel Whiteread was elected to the British Royal Academy. Unlike the Victorian painter Lady Elizabeth Thompson Butler, discussed in Chapter 23, who could not be elected because she was a woman, Whiteread felt no need to join and declined. Her refusal may be a measure of the self-confidence and achievement that women artists have attained in the past century.

■ *What were the origins and goals of the minimalist movement? Why is so much of Whiteread's work designed to be temporary? What is the theme of* Nameless Library, *and why was it built in Vienna? What do Whiteread's career and recognition say about the position of women artists in the early twenty-first century?*

James Lingwood, *Rachel Whiteread's House* (London: Phaidon Press, 1995); *Rachel Whiteread: Transient Spaces* (New York: Guggenheim Museum Publications, 2001); L. Denison and C. Houser, *Rachel Whiteread* (New York: Phaidon Press, 2001).

Energy and the Modern World

No single technological factor so determines the social relationships and standard of living of human beings as energy. The more energy a society can command for each of its members, the stronger and more influential it will be. Throughout recorded human history, those societies that have found ways to improve their access to sources of energy, and have then efficiently applied the energy, have dominated both their immediate environments and much of the world beyond. Indeed, the possession of, or the lack of, efficient, inexpensive sources of energy in large measure determines which nations will be wealthy and which will be poor.

Animals, Wind, and Water

For civilization to advance technologically, energy had to be applied to tasks. The earliest source of such energy was animal power, which was used all over the world except among the peoples on the American continent prior to the arrival of the Europeans. Oxen, water buffalo, and horses were the major draft animals. Of these, horses were the most efficient.

Throughout the world until the eighteenth century, however, wind and water furnished most of the energy for machinery. Sailing ships had been used since ancient times for travel, fishing, and the transport of goods. The wind also worked mills that pumped water and ground grain. Waterwheels proved to be highly flexible machines and by the eighteenth century constituted the major sources of mechanical power in Europe and much of the rest of the world. But wind and water were uncertain sources of energy. The wind could cease; drought could dry up streams. Water-powered machinery had to be located near the stream furnishing the water. Consequently, most of the mills employing such machinery were located in the countryside.

Although animals, wind, and water provided energy for relatively complicated machines capable of manufacturing and transporting high-quality goods, the economic and political transformations that have driven the history of the world for the past two and a half centuries could only have occurred through a qualitative as well as quantitative leap in the manner in which human beings commanded energy. The twin sources of this world-transforming energy have been fossil fuels and electricity.

Until the second half of the eighteenth century, fossil fuels—coal, petroleum, and, to a lesser extent, natural gas—contributed only a small portion

Until the eighteenth century, sailing ships were powered by wind alone. In this fourteenth-century manuscript illustration, sailors navigate with the help of an astrolabe. Bibliotheque Nationale, Paris, France/Bridgeman Art Library International

of human energy requirements. Their use as meaningful sources of energy required a series of inventions that allowed the energy of heat to be changed into mechanical energy.

Steam Power and the Age of Coal

Although peoples living near coal deposits had used it as a household fuel for a very long time, only the invention of the steam engine, patented by James Watt in 1769, established a major industrial demand for coal. The steam engine first permitted the pumping of water from coal mines to increase production. But as the industrial uses for the steam engine grew, the invention itself drove the demand for greater quantities of coal as fuel.

Coal-fueled steam power changed the face of human society during the nineteenth century and continues to provide the energy for the most powerful turbogenerators at the dawn of the twenty-first century. Steam-powered machines could be made larger and more flexible than those powered by wind or water, and so long as coal was available, they could run steadily day and night. Steam engines, in contrast to waterwheels, were transportable. Factories could be moved away from streams in the countryside to urban areas where a ready work force existed. And goods produced in factories powered by steam engines could be carried around the world by steam-powered locomotives and ships. Those expanding markets in turn called forth more steam-powered factories and even greater use of coal. Furthermore, steam-powered factories could also produce military weapons that could be placed on steam-powered naval vessels constructed of iron and steel in vast coal-fueled blast furnaces. When Theodore Roosevelt sent the U.S. fleet around the world, it was a testimony to the power of coal and steam as well as to the power of the American navy.

The age of steam was the age of coal. The nations possessing large coal deposits dominated much nineteenth-century economic life as the nations that possess oil reserves dominate much contemporary economic life. For many decades, Great Britain dominated the world's production and delivery of coal, which was transported over the entire world. Its domination was challenged only in the late nineteenth century as the United States and later Russia and China began to produce vast quantities of the fuel. Coal remained the chief fuel for the United States until after World War I and for Western Europe until after World War II. It remains the chief fuel for China.

Coal generated a rising standard of living in Europe and the expansion of European and later American power, but coal also generated a number of social problems. The most shocking conditions of exploited labor occurred in coal mines, where parliamentary reports of the 1840s described and illustrated half-clad women and children drawing coal carts from the depths of the mines to the surface. Throughout the nineteenth and twentieth centuries, thousands of miners died in mining disasters. Work in the mines injured the health of miners, as did the pollution sent into the atmosphere by coal fires from both factories and homes. By the early twentieth century, observers had begun to note the damage to the environment caused by strip mining of coal and the later abandonment of the regions.

The Internal Combustion Engine: The Age of Oil

As with coal, the impact of petroleum, the second major fossil fuel, also depended on the invention of machinery to use it. Originally, the use for oil was limited to kerosene, the fuel used for lighting around much of the world by 1900. It was upon the world demand for lamp oil that John D. Rockefeller founded the Standard Oil Company. The invention of the internal combustion engine in 1882 by Gottlieb Daimler and the diesel engine in 1892 by Rudolf Diesel transformed the demand for oil. Toward the close of the nineteenth century, extensive oil production had begun in the United States, with Russia, Romania, Sumatra, Mexico, Iran, and Venezuela starting to tap their own oil resources before World War I.

Just as the steam engine had spurred the expansion of the coal industry, the internal combustion engine drove the oil industry. Fuel oil would begin to replace coal, not so much because it was cheaper but rather because it was more efficient, easier to store and transport, and cleaner to burn. Initially, fuel oil tended to be used in those countries where it could be produced relatively near the point of use. Until the end of World War II, the United States was the primary world producer and user of oil. As fuel for the internal combustion engine, oil became the driving force of automobiles, locomotives, airplanes, ships, factory machinery, and electric generators. It revolutionized agricultural machinery and world food production, but as a fuel for transportation, it fostered a social transformation over much of the world.

Cancel distance & conquer weather

The woman who drives her own Ford Closed Car is completely independent of road and weather conditions in any season.

It enables her to carry on all those activities of the winter months that necessitate travel to and fro—in or out of town. Her time and energy are conserved; her health is protected, no matter how bitterly cold the day, or how wet and slushy it is underfoot.

A Ford Sedan is always comfortable—warm and snug in winter, and in summer with ventilator and windows open wide, as cool and airy as an open car.

This seasonal comfort is combined with fine looks and Ford dependability; no wonder there is for this car so wide and ever-growing a demand.

FORD MOTOR COMPANY, DETROIT, MICHIGAN

TUDOR SEDAN, $580   FORDOR SEDAN, $660
COUPE, $520   ALL PRICES F. O. B. DETROIT

Ford

CLOSED CARS

Until 1924, Henry Ford had disdained national advertising for his cars. But as General Motors gained a competitive edge by making yearly changes in style and technology, Ford was forced to pay more attention to advertising. This ad was directed at "Mrs. Consumer," combining appeals to both female independence and motherly duties. Ford Motor Company

Starting in the United States and then spreading elsewhere, owning an automobile introduced a new mobility factor into social relationships. People could move easily across long distances to join a new community or to start a new job. Inexpensive gasoline for cars and public transport buses permitted the development of suburbs ever further removed from traditional urban centers. In turn, retailing moved away from city centers to shopping malls. At the same time, wherever the mechanization of farming through improved farm machinery took place, there usually followed a movement of people from farming communities to urban areas.

Electricity Increases the Demand for Oil

The manufacture of automobiles and other forms of transport using the internal combustion or diesel engine was central to all modern industrial life. As those industries expanded, so did the construction of extensive road systems. These in turn created new demands for fuel oil.

But the greatest demand for fuel oil arose from the application of electricity to the needs of everyday life. Electricity proved to be the most flexible and versatile source of energy for the twentieth century, and its generation provided the single greatest source of demand for both coal and oil. Electricity generation would also employ new modes of water power in the forms of hydroelectric generators.

The scientific basis for the production of electric energy was Michael Faraday's study of electromagnetic induction. In 1831, he demonstrated that mechanical energy under the proper conditions could be converted into electric energy. Even more important, the reverse was also true. Electricity could be generated in one location and applied far away wherever electrical lines could be extended. The applications of electrical power have appeared to be restricted only by the limitations of the inventive imagination.

During the second half of the nineteenth century, a whole host of inventors, such as Thomas Alva Edison, worked through the production and application of electrical power to service large regions. Electricity found applications across the spectrum of human society, actions, and enterprises. Access to electricity in the course of the twentieth century became the key factor for an improved standard of living. A fundamental moment in the decision by Japan to modernize during the late nineteenth century was the construction of the Tokyo Electric Light Company in 1888. The extension of electrical lines into the American countryside was one of the major accomplishments of Franklin Roosevelt's New Deal. Electrical power transformed the workplace, but even more strikingly it transformed homes. Without access to electrical power, domestic households could not make use of any of the growing array of labor-saving appliances such as electric washing machines, electric irons, electric stoves, and electric vacuum cleaners. Electric lights brightened whole cities. Electricity replaced both coal and oil as the source of power for many locomotives; it powered public tram systems and opened the way for the telegraph, the telephone, the wireless, the motion picture camera, and television. It planted the seeds for the computer revolution in communication and information. Electricity allowed manufacturing plants and office complexes to be built wherever electric lines could be carried. Indeed, the spread of access to electrical power has been the single best indication of economic advancement for any nation or region.

Yet within this era of ever-expanding electrification, coal and oil—the fundamental fossil fuels— would still provide the underpinnings of the world's energy. In fact, more oil and coal are used to generate electricity than for any other single purpose. Throughout the twentieth century, the demand for these fuels led to the refinement of their production techniques to permit the extraction of coal from ever-deeper seams and the strip mining of it from regions where previously it would have been economically unproductive to do so. The effort to discover, extract, and transport oil would have major consequences for the world's physical and geopolitical environment far into the twentieth century.

Oil and Global Politics in the Twentieth Century

As the century began, the United States was by far the largest producer and exporter of petroleum. Yet by the 1920s, the American government began to worry about running out of oil. So, too, did the British, who depended on imported oil for all of their military and industrial needs. During the 1920s and 1930s, both governments encouraged oil companies to forge agreements for the drilling and export of oil from the Middle East. These arrangements fit into the pattern of formal and informal colonialism that still characterized the interwar period.

After World War II, Western Europe, the Soviet Union, and the nations of the Warsaw Pact began to turn from coal to oil as the basis for economic growth. (Japan followed this course during the 1960s.) By 1947, the United States had begun to import more oil than it produced. These two developments—a new dependence on oil by the industrialized nations and the expanded search for oil by the West—formed the basis for the new role that the nations of the Middle East would play in the world economy as the chief oil exporters. Simultaneously, as the world's industrialized economies were growing dependent on Middle East oil production, nationalistic leaders in that region were denouncing former colonial domination and rejecting relationships with the West and with Israel, a country that received strong political support from the United States and Western Europe. The stage

was thus set for oil to play a new role in the geopolitical conflicts of the Cold War era.

Playing a major role in those conflicts was the Organization of Petroleum Exporting Nations (OPEC), founded in 1960. Regardless of their differences, OPEC members were united in two things: First, they deeply resented former colonial control of their oil supplies, and second, they were determined that their own governments, not foreign oil companies, would control those vital resources. (Mexico had brought its own petroleum industry under state control before World War II.) In 1973, during the Yom Kippur War, OPEC acted, sharply raising oil prices to nations whose governments supported Israel. The action caused severe economic consequences in the West and spurred new efforts to develop local oil reserves in politically safe locations such as in the North Sea. OPEC would attempt similar actions on other occasions, most successfully in 1979. In that year, a revolution in Iran overthrew the government, which had long been supported by the United States. OPEC cut off oil shipments to the West, causing severe dislocations. Concerns about securing oil supplies in the West were again sparked by the Persian Gulf War and other political tensions in the region.

In addition to the political problems associated with Middle East oil production, the industrial world's reliance on oil has had severe environmental consequences. Generally, when the United States dominated oil production, the oil refineries were located near the source of oil production. As the exploitation of oil reserves moved to the Middle East and then later in the century to Alaska and to the North Sea, oil refineries became separated from the drilling locations. Crude oil was shipped to refineries on enormous tankers. More than once, these supertankers have hit shoals or gone aground, causing large oil spills, calamitous to both animals and humans.

The Promise and Danger of Nuclear Energy

Following World War II, nuclear power became a new source for the generation of electrical energy. The power of the atom, first released in the 1940s for military purposes, held the promise of virtually infinite quantities of energy. The world would no longer be dependent on finite supplies of fossil fuel located in politically tense regions of the world. The generation of such energy, however, required

In 1989, when a supertanker spilled 35,000 tons of crude oil into Alaska's Prince William Sound, rescue workers struggled to save the lives of seabirds and animals. Nevertheless, thousands died. Ron Levy/Liaison Agency, Inc.

the most complex sets of machinery ever devised to produce electrical energy. France and Great Britain began to build nuclear reactors in the 1950s with the United States, the Soviet Union, and various other European nations following in the 1960s. Nations outside the West, such as India and Pakistan, looked to the construction of nuclear power stations as a means of moving more rapidly toward the achievements of industrialization and a rising standard of living through extensive electrification. Nations with limited supplies of fossil fuel, such as Japan, hoped nuclear energy would solve their energy supply problem. The oil shock of the mid-1970s brought new enthusiasm to the adoption of nuclear energy, but the economic downturn of the late 1970s and early 1980s slowed the construction of nuclear-generating stations. The construction of breeder reactors, which would produce their own fuel in the process of generating electrical energy,

seemed to promise a world liberated from dependence on a finite supply of fossil fuels. Furthermore, unlike coal and oil, which have many uses besides that of fuel, uranium had no other economic use. The workers in the field of atomic energy were scientists and engineers rather than the kind of industrial labor force that produced coal and oil.

Yet the technology of nuclear energy production proved to be exceedingly dangerous. The atomic reactors produced spent radioactive waste that would remain hazardous for hundreds of years. After many years of warnings of such danger, the Chernobyl nuclear generating plant in the former Soviet Union caused enormous, lasting damage in the spring of 1986. In 1979, the possibility of a similar disaster had occurred at the Three Mile Island plant in Pennsylvania. Both the promise and danger of nuclear power continue to inform the political life of all nations using such power. It is wholly unclear, for example, what will be done with the radioactive spent fuel. Furthermore, the construction of nuclear generating plants has allowed nations that lack atomic weapons to train scientists and other experts who might be able to use that knowledge to develop atomic weapons. Whereas in the United States and Europe the military uses of atomic power came first and were followed by peaceful energy uses, the reverse has been the case in nations such as India and Pakistan. Despite its initial promise, nuclear power has contributed far less to energy production than we originally imagined.

The problem of energy remains with us in the new century. Environmental pollution and all the issues surrounding the nuclear generation of energy will demand increasing attention and expenditure of public funds. Similarly, the political pressures and tensions surrounding the oil supplies of the Middle East will not disappear, as advanced nations seek to secure and protect energy reserves while the nations that possess those reserves seek to secure a rising standard of living for themselves.

■ *Trace the transformation of energy used in the West from wind and water to petroleum. How did coal transform both the industry and the military power of the West? How did inventions, such as the internal combustion engine, change the demands on sources of energy? Why did the rise of electrical power increase the need for petroleum? What opportunities and dangers has nuclear energy posed?*

GLOSSARY

absolutism Term applied to strong centralized continental monarchies that attempted to make royal power dominant over aristocracies and other regional authorities.

Acropolis (ACK-row-po-lis) The religious and civic center of Athens. It is the site of the Parthenon.

Act of Supremacy The declaration by Parliament in 1534 that Henry VIII, not the pope, was the head of the church in England.

agape (AG-a-pay) Meaning "love feast." A common meal that was part of the central ritual of early Christian worship.

agora (AG-o-rah) The Greek marketplace and civic center. It was the heart of the social life of the *polis*.

Agricultural Revolution The innovations in farm production that began in the eighteenth century and led to a scientific and mechanized agriculture.

Albigensians (Al-bi-GEN-see-uns) Thirteenth-century advocates of a dualist religion. They took their name from the city of Albi in southern France. Also called *Cathars.*

Anabaptists Protestants who insisted that only adult baptism conformed to Scripture.

anarchism The theory that government and social institutions are oppressive and unnecessary and society should be based on voluntary cooperation among individuals.

Anschluss (AHN-shluz) Meaning "union." The annexation of Austria by Germany in March 1938.

anti-Semitism Prejudice, hostility, or legal discrimination against Jews.

apostolic primacy The doctrine that the popes are the direct successors to the Apostle Peter and as such heads of the church.

Apostolic Succession The Christian doctrine that the powers given by Jesus to his original disciples have been handed down from bishop to bishop through ordination.

appeasement The Anglo-French policy of making concessions to Germany in the 1930s to avoid a crisis that would lead to war. It assumed that Germany had real grievances and Hitler's aims were limited and ultimately acceptable.

Areopagus The governing council of Athens, originally open only to the nobility. It was named after the hill on which it met.

arete (AH-ray-tay) Manliness, courage, and the excellence appropriate to a hero. It was considered the highest virtue of Homeric society.

Arianism (AIR-ee-an-ism) The belief formulated by Arius of Alexandria (ca. 280–336 C.E.) that Jesus was a created being, neither fully man nor fully God, but something in between. It did away with the doctrine of the Trinity.

aristocratic resurgence Term applied to the eighteenth-century aristocratic efforts to resist the expanding power of European monarchies.

Arminians (are-MIN-ee-ans) A group within the Church of England who rejected Puritanism and the Calvinist doctrine of predestination in favor of free will and an elaborate liturgy.

Asia Minor Modern Turkey. Also called *Anatolia.*

asiento (ah-SEE-ehn-tow) The contract to furnish slaves to the Spanish colonies.

assignants (as-seen-YAHNTS) Government bonds based on the value of confiscated church lands issued during the early French Revolution.

Atomists School of ancient Greek philosophy founded in the fifth century B.C.E. by Leucippus of Miletus and Democritus of Abdera. It held that the world consists of innumerable, tiny, solid, indivisible, and unchangeable particles called *atoms.*

Attica (AT-tick-a) The region of Greece where Athens is located.

Augsburg (AWGS-berg) **Confession** The definitive statement of Lutheran belief made in 1530.

Augustus (AW-gust-us) The title given to Octavian in 27 B.C.E. and borne thereafter by all Roman emperors. It was a semireligious title that implied veneration, majesty, and holiness.

Ausgleich (AWS-glike) Meaning "compromise." The agreement between the Habsburg Emperor and the Hungarians to give Hungary considerable administrative autonomy in 1867. It created the Dual Monarchy, or Austria-Hungary.

autocracy (AW-to-kra-see) Government in which the ruler has absolute power.

Axis The alliance between Nazi Germany and fascist Italy. Also called the *Pact of Steel.*

banalities Exactions that the lord of a manor could make on his tenants.

baroque (bah-ROWK) A style of art marked by heavy and dramatic ornamentation and curved rather than straight lines that flourished between 1550 and 1750. It was especially associated with the Catholic Counter-Reformation.

Beguines (bi-GEENS) Lay sisterhoods not bound by the rules of a religious order.

benefice   Church offices granted by the ruler of a state or the pope to an individual. It also meant *fief* in the Middle Ages.

bishop   Originally a person elected by early Christian congregations to lead them in worship and supervise their funds. In time, bishops became the religious and even political authorities for Christian communities within large geographical areas.

Black Death   The bubonic plague that killed millions of Europeans in the fourteenth century.

blitzkrieg (BLITZ-kreeg)   Meaning "lightning war." The German tactic early in World War II of employing fast-moving, massed armored columns supported by airpower to overwhelm the enemy.

Bolsheviks   Meaning the "majority." Term Lenin applied to his faction of the Russian Social Democratic Party. It became the Communist Party of the Soviet Union after the Russian Revolution.

boyars   The Russian nobility.

Bronze Age   The name given to the earliest civilized era, c. 4000 to 1000 B.C.E. The term reflects the importance of the metal bronze, a mixture of tin and copper, for the peoples of this age for use as weapons and tools.

Bund   A secular Jewish socialist organization of Polish Jews.

Bundesrat (BUHN-dees-raht)   The upper house of the German federal parliament whose members are appointed by the various state governments.

Caesaro-papism (SEE-zer-o-PAY-pi-zim)   The direct involvement of the ruler in religious doctrine and practice as if he were the head of the church as well as the state.

cahiers de doléances (KAH-hee-ay de dough-LAY-ahnce)   Meaning "lists of grievances." Petitions for reforms submitted to the French crown when the Estates General met in 1789.

caliphate (KAH-li-fate)   The true line of succession to Muhammad.

capital goods   Machines and tools used to produce other goods.

Carbonari (car-buh-NAH-ree)   Meaning "charcoal burners." The most famous of the secret republican societies seeking to unify Italy in the 1820s.

categorical imperative   According to Emmanuel Kant (1724–1804), the internal sense of moral duty or awareness possessed by all human beings.

catholic   Meaning "universal." The body of belief held by most Christians enshrined within the church.

Catholic Emancipation   The grant of full political rights to Roman Catholics in Britain in 1829.

censor   Official of the Roman republic charged with conducting the census and compiling the lists of citizens and members of the Senate. They could expel senators for financial or moral reasons. Two censors were elected every five years.

Chartism   The first large-scale European working-class political movement. It sought political reforms that would favor the interests of skilled British workers in the 1830s and 1840s.

chiaroscuro (kyar-eh-SKEW-row)   The use of shading to enhance naturalness in painting and drawing.

civic humanism   Education designed to promote humanist leadership of political and cultural life.

civilization   A form of human culture marked by urbanism, metallurgy, and writing.

classical economics   The theory that economies grow through the free enterprise of individuals competing in a largely self-regulating marketplace with government intervention held to a minimum.

clientage (KLI-ent-age)   The custom in ancient Rome whereby men became supporters of more powerful men in return for legal and physical protection and economic benefits.

Cold War   The ideological and geographical struggle between the United States and its allies and the USSR and its allies that began after World War II and lasted until the dissolution of the USSR in 1989.

collectivization   The bedrock of Stalinist agriculture, which forced Russian peasants to give up their private farms and work as members of collectives, large agricultural units controlled by the state.

coloni (CO-loan-ee)   Farmers or sharecroppers on the estates of wealthy Romans.

Commonwealthmen   British political writers whose radical republican ideas influenced the American revolutionaries.

Concert of Europe   Term applied to the European great powers acting together (in "concert") to resolve international disputes between 1815 and the 1850s.

conciliar theory   The argument that General Councils were superior in authority to the pope and represented the whole body of the faithful.

condottieri (con-da-TEE-AIR-ee)   Military brokers who furnished mercenary forces to the Italian states during the Renaissance.

congregationalist   A congregationalist puts a group or assembly above any one individual and prefers an ecclesiastical polity that allows each congregation to be autonomous, or self-governing.

Congress System   A series of international meetings among the European great powers to promote mutual cooperation between 1818 and 1822.

conquistadores (kahn-KWIS-teh-door-hez)   Meaning "conquerors." The Spanish conquerors of the New World.

conservatism   Support for the established order in church and state. In the nineteenth century, it implied support for legitimate monarchies, landed aristocracies, and established churches. Conservatives favored only gradual, or "organic," change.

Consulate French government dominated by Napoleon from 1799 to 1804.

consuls (CON-suls) The two chief magistrates of the Roman state.

Consumer Revolution The vast increase in both the desire and the possibility of consuming goods and services that began in the early eighteenth century and created the demand for sustaining the Industrial Revolution.

containment The U.S. policy during the Cold War of resisting Soviet expansion and influence in the expectation that the USSR would eventually collapse.

Convention French radical legislative body from 1792 to 1794.

Corn Laws British tariffs on imported grain that protected the price of grain grown within the British Isles.

corporatism The planned economy of fascist Italy that combined private ownership of capital with government direction of Italy's economic life and arbitration of labor disputes. All major areas of production were organized into state-controlled bodies called *corporations*, which were represented in the Chamber of Corporations that replaced the Chamber of Deputies. The state, not consumers and owners, determined what the economy produced.

corvée (cor-VAY) A French labor tax requiring peasants to work on roads, bridges, and canals.

Council of Nicaea (NIGH-see-a) The council of Christian bishops at Nicaea in 325 C.E. that formulated the Nicene Creed, a statement of Christian belief that rejected Arianism in favor of the doctrine that Christ is both fully human and fully divine.

Counter-Reformation The sixteenth-century reform movement in the Roman Catholic Church in reaction to the Protestant Reformation.

coup d'état (COO DAY-ta) The sudden violent overthrow of a government by its own army.

creed A brief statement of faith to which true Christians should adhere.

Creoles (KRAY-ol-ez) Persons of Spanish descent born in the Spanish colonies.

Crusades Religious wars directed by the church against infidels and heretics.

culture The ways of living built up by a group and passed on from one generation to another.

cuneiform (Q-nee-i-form) A writing system invented by the Sumerians that used a wedge-shaped stylus, or pointed tool, to write on wet clay tablets that were then baked or dried (*cuneus* means "wedge" in Latin). The writing was also cut into stone.

Curia (CURE-ee-a) The papal government.

Cynic (SIN-ick) **School** A fourth-century philosophical movement that ridiculed all religious observances and turned away from involvement in the affairs of the *polis*. Its most famous exemplar was Diogenes of Sinope (ca. 400–325 B.C.E.).

deacon Meaning "those who serve." In early Christian congregations, deacons assisted the presbyters, or elders.

deism A belief in a rational God who had created the universe, but then allowed it to function without his interference according to the mechanisms of nature and a belief in rewards and punishments after death for human action.

Delian (DEE-li-an) **League** An alliance of Greek states under the leadership of Athens that was formed in 478–477 B.C.E. to resist the Persians. In time the league was transformed into the Athenian Empire.

deme (DEEM) A small town in Attica or a ward in Athens that became the basic unit of Athenian civic life under the democratic reforms of Clisthenes in 508 B.C.E.

demesne (di-MAIN) The part of a manor that was cultivated directly for the lord of the manor.

divine right of kings The theory that monarchs are appointed by and answerable only to God.

Domesday (DOOMS-day) *Book* A detailed survey of the wealth of England undertaken by William the Conqueror between 1080 and 1086.

domestic system of textile production Method of producing textiles in which agents furnished raw materials to households whose members spun them into thread and then wove cloth, which the agents then sold as finished products.

Donatism The heresy that taught the efficacy of the sacraments depended on the moral character of the clergy who administered them.

Duce (DO-chay) Meaning "leader." Mussolini's title as head of the Fascist Party.

Duma (DOO-ma) The Russian parliament, after the revolution of 1905.

electors German princes who had the right to elect the Holy Roman Emperor, originally numbering seven in 1356, but reaching as many as 10 by 1803 shortly before the dissolution of the Empire following Napoleon's reorganization of the German states.

emigrés (em-ee-GRAYS) French aristocrats who fled France during the Revolution.

empiricism (em-PEER-ih-cism) The use of experiment and observation derived from sensory evidence to construct scientific theory or philosophy of knowledge.

enclosure The consolidation or fencing in of common lands by British landlords to increase production and achieve greater commercial profits. It also involved the reclamation of waste land and the consolidation of strips into block fields.

encomienda (en-co-mee-EN-da) The grant by the Spanish crown to a colonist of the labor of a specific number of Indians for a set period of time.

ENIAC The Electronic Numerical Integrator and Computer. The first genuine modern digital computer, developed in the 1940s.

Enlightenment   The eighteenth-century movement led by the *philosophes* that held that change and reform were both desirable through the application of reason and science.

Epicureans (EP-i-cure-ee-ans)   School of philosophy founded by Epicurus of Athens (342–271 B.C.E.). It sought to liberate people from fear of death and the supernatural by teaching that the gods took no interest in human affairs and that true happiness consisted in pleasure, which was defined as the absence of pain. This could be achieved by attaining *ataraxia*, freedom from trouble, pain, and responsibility by withdrawing from business and public life.

equestrians (EE-quest-ree-ans)   Literally "cavalrymen" or "knights." In the earliest years of the Roman Republic those who could afford to serve as mounted warriors. The equestrians evolved into a social rank of well-to-do businessmen and middle-ranking officials. Many of them supported the Gracchi.

Estates General   The medieval French parliament. It consisted of three separate groups, or "estates": clergy, nobility, and commoners. It last met in 1789 at the outbreak of the French Revolution.

Etruscans (EE-trus-cans)   A people of central Italy who exerted the most powerful external influence on the early Romans. Etruscan kings ruled Rome until 509 B.C.

Eucharist (YOU-ka-rist)   Meaning "thanksgiving." The celebration of the Lord's Supper. Considered the central ritual of worship by most Christians. Also called *Holy Communion.*

Euro   The common currency created by the EEC in the late 1990s.

European Economic Community (EEC)   The economic association formed by France, Germany, Italy, Belgium, the Netherlands, and Luxembourg in 1957. Also known as the *Common Market.*

European Union   The new name given to the EEC in 1993. It included most of the states of Western Europe.

excommunication   Denial by the church of the right to receive the sacraments.

existentialism   The post–World War II Western philosophy that holds human beings are totally responsible for their acts and that this responsibility causes them dread and anguish.

Fabians   British socialists in the late 19th and early 20th century who sought to achieve socialism through gradual, peaceful, and democratic means.

family economy   The basic structure of production and consumption in preindustrial Europe.

fascism   Political movements that tend to be antidemocratic, anti-Marxist, antiparliamentary, and often anti-Semitic. Fascists were invariably nationalists and exhalted the nation over the individual. They supported the interests of the middle class and rejected the ideas of the French Revolution and nineteenth-century liberalism. The first fascist regime was founded by Benito Mussolini (1883–1945) in Italy in the 1920s.

fealty   An oath of loyalty by a vassal to a lord, promising to perform specified services.

feudal (FEW-dull) **society**   The social, political, military, and economic system that prevailed in the Middle Ages and beyond in some parts of Europe.

fief   Land granted to a vassal in exchange for services, usually military.

foederati (FAY-der-ah-tee)   Barbarian tribes enlisted as special allies of the Roman Empire.

folk culture   The distinctive songs, sayings, legends, and crafts of a people.

Fourteen Points   President Woodrow Wilson's (1856–1924) idealistic war aims.

Fronde (FROHND)   A series of rebellions against royal authority in France between 1649 and 1652.

Führer (FYOOR-er)   Meaning "leader." The title taken by Hitler when he became dictator of Germany.

gabelle (gah-BELL)   The royal tax on salt in France.

Gaul (GAWL)   Modern France.

German Confederation   Association of German states established at the Congress of Vienna that replaced the Holy Roman Empire from 1815 to 1866.

ghetto   Separate communities in which Jews were required by law to live.

glasnost (GLAZ-nohst)   Meaning "openness." The policy initiated by Mikhail Gorbachev (MEEK-hail GORE-buh-choff) in the 1980s of permitting open criticism of the policies of the Soviet Communist Party.

Glorious Revolution   The largely peaceful replacement of James II by William and Mary as English monarchs in 1688. It marked the beginning of constitutional monarchy in Britain.

gold standard   A monetary system in which the value of a unit of a nation's currency is related to a fixed amount of gold.

Golden Bull   The agreement in 1356 to establish a seven-member electoral college of German princes to choose the Holy Roman Emperor.

Great Depression   A prolonged worldwide economic downturn that began in 1929 with the collapse of the New York Stock Exchange.

Great Purges   The imprisonment and execution of millions of Soviet citizens by Stalin between 1934 and 1939.

Great Reform Bill (1832)   A limited reform of the British House of Commons and an expansion of the electorate to include a wider variety of the propertied classes. It laid the groundwork for further orderly reforms within the British constitutional system.

Great Schism   The appearance of two and at times three rival popes between 1378 and 1415.

Green movement A political environmentalist movement that began in West Germany in the 1970s and spread to a number of other Western nations.

grossdeutsch (gross-DOYCH) Meaning "great German." The argument that the German-speaking portions of the Habsburg Empire should be included in a united Germany.

guild An association of merchants or craftsmen that offered protection to its members and set rules for their work and products.

hacienda (ha-SEE-hen-da) A large landed estate in Spanish America.

Hegira (HEJ-ear-a) The flight of Muhammad and his followers from Mecca to Medina in 622 C.E. It marks the beginning of the Islamic calendar.

heliocentric (HE-li-o-cen-trick) **theory** The theory, now universally accepted, that the earth and the other planets revolve around the sun. First proposed by Aristarchos of Samos (310–230 B.C.E.). Its opposite, the geocentric theory, which was dominant until the sixteenth century C.E., held that the sun and the planets revolved around the earth.

Helots (HELL-ots) Hereditary Spartan serfs.

heretic (HAIR-i-tick) A person whose beliefs were contrary to those of the Catholic Church.

hieroglyphics (HI-er-o-gli-phicks) The complicated writing script of ancient Egypt. It combined picture writing with pictographs and sound signs. Hieroglyph means "sacred carvings" in Greek.

Holocaust The Nazi extermination of millions of European Jews between 1940 and 1945. Also called the "final solution to the Jewish problem."

Holy Roman Empire The revival of the old Roman Empire, based mainly in Germany and northern Italy, that endured from 870 to 1806.

home rule The advocacy of a large measure of administrative autonomy for Ireland within the British Empire between the 1880s and 1914.

Homo sapiens (HO-mo say-pee-ans) The scientific name for human beings, from the Latin words meaning "Wise man." *Homo sapiens* emerged some 200,000 years ago.

honestiores (HON-est-ee-or-ez) The Roman term formalized from the beginning of the third century C.E. to denote the privileged classes: senators, equestrians, the municipal aristocracy, and soldiers.

hoplite **phalanx** (FAY-lanks) The basic unit of Greek warfare in which infantrymen fought in close order, shield to shield, usually eight ranks deep. The phalanx perfectly suited the farmer-soldier-citizen who was the backbone of the *polis*.

hubris (WHO-bris) Arrogance brought on by excessive wealth or good fortune. The Greeks believed it led to moral blindness and divine vengeance.

Huguenots (HYOU-gu-nots) French Calvinists.

humanism The study of the Latin and Greek classics and of the Church Fathers both for their own sake and to promote a rebirth of ancient norms and values.

humanitas (HEW-man-i-tas) The Roman name for a liberal arts education.

humiliores (HEW-mi-lee-orez) The Roman term formalized at the beginning of the third century C.E. for the lower classes.

Hussites (HUS-Its) Followers of John Huss (d. 1415) who questioned Catholic teachings about the Eucharist.

Iconoclasm (i-KON-o-kla-zoom) A heresy in Eastern Christianity that sought to ban the veneration of sacred images, or icons.

id, ego, superego The three entities in Sigmund Freud's model of the internal organization of the human mind. The id consists of the amoral, irrational instincts for self-gratification. The superego embodies the external morality imposed on the personality by society. The ego mediates between the two and allows the personality to cope with the internal and external demands of its existence.

Iliad (ILL-ee-ad) **and the** *Odyssey* (O-dis-see), **The** Epic poems by Homer about the "Dark Age" heroes of Greece who fought at Troy. The poems were written down in the eighth century B.C.E. after centuries of being sung by bards.

imperator (IM-per-a-tor) Under the Roman Republic, it was the title given to a victorious general. Under Augustus and his successors, it became the title of the ruler of Rome meaning "emperor."

imperialism The extension of a nation's authority over other nations or areas through conquest or political or economic hegemony.

imperium (IM-pear-ee-um) In ancient Rome, the right to issue commands and to enforce them by fines, arrests, and even corporal and capital punishment.

indulgences Remission of the temporal penalty of punishment in purgatory that remained after sins had been forgiven.

Industrial Revolution Mechanization of the European economy that began in Britain in the second half of the eighteenth century.

Inquisition A tribunal created by the Catholic Church in the mid-twelfth century to detect and punish heresy.

insulae (IN-sul-lay) Meaning "islands." The multi-storied apartment buildings of Rome in which most of the inhabitants of the city lived.

intendents (in-TEN-duhnts) Royal officials under the French monarchy who supervised the provincial governments in the name of the king.

Intolerable Acts Measures passed by the British Parliament in 1774 to punish the colony of Massachusetts and strengthen Britain's authority in the colonies. The laws provoked colonial opposition, which led immediately to the American Revolution.

investiture controversy The medieval conflict between the church and lay rulers over who would control bishops and abbots, symbolized by the ceremony of "investing" them with the symbols of their authority.

Ionia (I-o-knee-a) The part of western Asia Minor heavily colonized by the Greeks.

Islam (IZ-lahm) Meaning "submission." The religion founded by the prophet Muhammad.

Italia irredenta (ee-TAHL-ee-a ir-REH-dent-a) Meaning "unredeemed Italy." Italian-speaking areas that had been left under Austrian rule at the time of the unification of Italy.

Jacobins (JACK-uh-bins) The radical republican party during the French Revolution that displaced the Girondins.

Jacquerie (jah-KREE) Revolt of the French peasantry.

Jansenism A seventeenth-century movement within the Catholic Church that taught that human beings were so corrupted by original sin that they could do nothing good nor secure their own salvation without divine grace. (It was opposed to the Jesuits.)

Judah (JEW-da) The southern Israelite kingdom established after the death of Solomon in the tenth century B.C.E.

Julian Calendar The reform of the calendar by Julius Caesar in 46 B.C.E. It remained in use throughout Europe until the sixteenth century and in Russia until the Russian Revolution in 1917.

July Monarchy The French regime set up after the overthrow of the Bourbons in July 1830.

Junkers (YOONG-kerz) The noble landlords of Prussia.

jus gentium (YUZ GEN-tee-um) Meaning "law of peoples." The body of Roman law that dealt with foreigners.

jus naturale (YUZ NAH-tu-rah-lay) Meaning "natural law." The Stoic concept of a world ruled by divine reason.

Ka'ba (KAH-bah) A black meteorite in the city of Mecca that became Islam's holiest shrine.

Keynesian economics The theory of John Maynard Keynes (CANES) (1883–1946) that governments could spend their economies out of a depression by running deficits to encourage employment and stimulate the production and consumption of goods.

kleindeutsch (kline-DOYCH) Meaning "small German." The argument that the German-speaking portions of the Habsburg Empire should be excluded from a united Germany.

Kristallnacht (KRIS-tahl-NAHKT) Meaning "crystal night" because of the broken glass that littered German streets after the looting and destruction of Jewish homes, businesses, and synagogues across Germany on the orders of the Nazi Party in November 1938.

kulaks (koo-LAKS) Prosperous Russian peasant farmers.

Kulturkampf (cool-TOOR-cahmff) Meaning the "battle for culture." The conflict between the Roman Catholic Church and the government of the German Empire in the 1870s.

laissez-faire (lay-ZAY-faire) French phrase meaning "allow to do." In economics the doctrine of minimal government interference in the working of the economy.

latifundia (LAT-ee-fun-dee-a) Large plantations for growing cash crops owned by wealthy Romans.

Latium (LAT-ee-um) The region of Italy in which Rome is located. Its inhabitants were called *Latins*.

League of Nations The association of sovereign states set up after World War I to pursue common policies and avert international aggression.

Lebensraum (LAY-benz-rauhm) Meaning "living space." The Nazi plan to colonize and exploit the Slavic areas of Eastern Europe for the benefit of Germany.

levée en masse (le-VAY en MASS) The French revolutionary conscription (1792) of all males into the army and the harnessing of the economy for war production.

liberal arts The medieval university program that consisted of the *trivium* (TRI-vee-um): grammar, rhetoric, and logic, and the *quadrivium* (qua-DRI-vee-um): arithmetic, geometry, astronomy, and music.

liberalism In the nineteenth century, support for representative government dominated by the propertied classes and minimal government interference in the economy.

Logos (LOW-goz) Divine reason, or fire, which according to the Stoics was the guiding principle in nature. Every human had a spark of this divinity, which returned to the eternal divine spirit after death.

Lollards (LALL-erds) Followers of John Wycliffe (d. 1384) who questioned the supremacy and privileges of the pope and the church hierarchy.

Lower Egypt The Nile delta.

Luftwaffe (LUFT-vaff-uh) The German air force in World War II.

Magna Carta (MAG-nuh CAR-tuh) The "Great Charter" limiting royal power that the English nobility forced King John to sign in 1215.

Magna Graecia (MAG-nah GRAY-see-a) Meaning "Great Greece" in Latin, it was the name given by the Romans to southern Italy and Sicily because there were so many Greek colonies in the region.

Magyars (MAH-jars) The majority ethnic group in Hungary.

Mandates The assigning of the former German colonies and Turkish territories in the Middle East to

Britain, France, Japan, Belgium, Australia, and South Africa as de facto colonies under the vague supervision of the League of Nations with the hope that the territories would someday advance to independence.

mannerism A style of art in the mid to late sixteenth century that permitted artists to express their own "manner" or feelings in contrast to the symmetry and simplicity of the art of the High Renaissance.

manor Village farms owned by a lord.

Marshall Plan The U.S. program named after Secretary of State George C. Marshall of providing economic aid to Europe after World War II.

Marxism The theory of Karl Marx (1818–1883) and Friedrich Engels (FREE-drick ENG-ulz) (1820–1895) that history is the result of class conflict, which will end in the inevitable triumph of the industrial proletariat over the bourgeoisie and the abolition of private property and social class.

Mein Kampf (MINE KAHMFF) Meaning *My Struggle.* Hitler's statement of his political program, published in 1924.

Mensheviks Meaning the "minority." Term Lenin applied to the majority moderate faction of the Russian Social Democratic Party opposed to him and the Bolsheviks.

mercantilism Term used to describe close government control of the economy that sought to maximize exports and accumulate as much precious metals as possible to enable the state to defend its economic and political interests.

Mesopotamia (MEZ-o-po-tay-me-a) Modern Iraq. The land between the Tigris and Euphrates Rivers where the first civilization appeared around 3000 B.C.E.

Messiah (MESS-eye-a) The redeemer whose coming Jews believed would establish the kingdom of God on earth. Christians considered Jesus to be the Messiah (*Christ* means Messiah in Greek).

Methodism An English religious movement begun by John Wesley (1703–1791) that stressed inward, heart-felt religion and the possibility of attaining Christian perfection in this life.

millets Administrative units of the Ottoman Empire that were not geographic but consisted of ethnic or religious minorities to whom particular laws and regulations applied.

Minoans (MIN-o-ans) The Bronze Age civilization that arose in Crete in the third and second millennia B.C.E.

missi dominici (MISS-ee dough-MIN-ee-chee) Meaning "the envoys of the ruler." Royal overseers of the king's law in the Carolingian Empire.

mobilization The placing of a country's military forces on a war footing.

modernism The movement in the arts and literature in the late nineteenth and early twentieth centuries to create new aesthetic forms and to elevate the aesthetic experience of a work of art above the attempt to portray reality as accurately as possible.

moldboard plow A heavy plow introduced in the Middle Ages that cut deep into the soil.

monasticism A movement in the Christian church that arose first in the East in the third and fourth centuries C.E. in which first individual hermits and later organized communities of men and women (monks and nuns) separated themselves from the world to lead lives in imitation of Christ. In the West the Rule of St. Benedict (c. 480–547) became the dominant form of monasticism.

Monophysitism (ma-NO-fiz-it-ism) A Christian heresy that taught that Jesus had only one nature.

monotheism The worship of one universal God.

Mycenaean (MY-cen-a-an) The Bronze Age civilization of mainland Greece that was centered at Mycenae.

"mystery" religions The cults of Isis, Mithra, and Osiris, which promised salvation to those initiated into the secret or "mystery" of their rites. These cults competed with Christianity in the Roman Empire.

nationalism The belief that one is part of a nation, defined as a community with its own language, traditions, customs, and history that distinguish it from other nations and make it the primary focus of a person's loyalty and sense of identity.

natural selection The theory originating with Darwin that organisms evolve through a struggle for existence in which those that have a marginal advantage live long enough to propagate their kind.

naturalism The attempt to portray nature and human life without sentimentality.

Nazis The German Nationalist Socialist Party.

Neolithic (NEE-o-lith-ick) **Revolution** The shift beginning 10,000 years ago from hunter-gatherer societies to settled communities of farmers and artisans. Also called the Age of Agriculture, it witnessed the invention of farming, the domestication of plants and animals, and the development of technologies such as pottery and weaving. The earliest Neolithic societies appeared in the Near East about 8000 B.C.E. "Neolithic" comes from the Greek words for "new stone."

Neoplatonism (KNEE-o-play-ton-ism) A religious philosophy that tried to combine mysticism with classical and rationalist speculation. Its chief formulator was Plotinus (205–270 C.E.).

New Economic Policy (NEP) A limited revival of capitalism, especially in light industry and agriculture, introduced by Lenin in 1921 to repair the damage inflicted on the Russian economy by the Civil War and war communism.

New Imperialism The extension in the late nineteenth and early twentieth centuries of Western political and economic dominance to Asia, the Middle East, and Africa.

nomes Regions or provinces of ancient Egypt governed by officials called *nomarchs*.

oikos (OI-cos) The Greek household, always headed by a male.

Old Believers Those members of the Russian Orthodox Church who refused to accept the reforms of the seventeenth century regarding church texts and ritual.

Old Regime Term applied to the pattern of social, political, and economic relationships and institutions that existed in Europe before the French Revolution.

optimates (OP-tee-ma-tes) Meaning "the best men." Roman politicians who supported the traditional role of the Senate.

orthodox Meaning "holding the right opinions." Applied to the doctrines of the Catholic Church.

Ottoman Empire The imperial Turkish state centered in Constantinople that ruled large parts of the Balkans, North Africa, and the Middle East until 1918.

Paleolithic (PAY-lee-o-lith-ick) **Age, The** The earliest period when stone tools were used, from about 1,000,000 to 10,000 B.C.E. From the Greek meaning "old stone."

Panhellenic (PAN-hell-en-ick) ("all-Greek") The sense of cultural identity that all Greeks felt in common with each other.

Pan-slavism The movement to create a nation or federation that would embrace all the Slavic peoples of Eastern Europe.

papal infallibility The doctrine that the pope is infallible when pronouncing officially in his capacity as head of the church on matters of faith and morals, enumerated by the First Vatican Council in 1870.

Papal States Territory in central Italy ruled by the pope until 1870.

parlements (par-luh-MAHNS) French regional courts dominated by hereditary nobility. The most important was the *Parlement* of Paris, which claimed the right to register royal decrees before they could become law.

parliamentary monarchy The form of limited or constitutional monarchy set up in Britain after the Glorious Revolution of 1689 in which the monarch was subject to the law and ruled by the consent of parliament.

patricians (PA-tri-she-ans) The hereditary upper class of early Republican Rome.

Peloponnesian (PELL-o-po-knees-ee-an) **Wars** The protracted struggle between Athens and Sparta to dominate Greece between 465 and Athens final defeat in 404 B.C.E.

Peloponnesus (PELL-o-po-knee-sus) The southern peninsula of Greece where Sparta was located.

peninsulares (pen-in-SUE-la-rez) Persons born in Spain who settled in the Spanish colonies.

perestroika (pare-ess-TROY-ka) Meaning "restructuring." The attempt in the 1980s to reform the Soviet government and economy.

petite bourgeoisie (peh-TEET BOOSH-schwa-zee) The lower middle class.

pharaoh (FAY-row) The god-kings of ancient Egypt. The term originally meant "great house" or palace.

Pharisees (FAIR-i-sees) The group that was most strict in its adherence to Jewish law.

philosophes (fee-lou-SOPHS) The eighteenth-century writers and critics who forged the new attitudes favorable to change. They sought to apply reason and common sense to the institutions and societies of their day.

Phoenicians (FA-nee-shi-ans) The ancient inhabitants of modern Lebanon. A trading people, they established colonies throughout the Mediterranean.

physiocrats Eighteenth-century French thinkers who attacked the mercantilist regulation of the economy, advocated a limited economic role for government, and believed that all economic production depended on sound agriculture.

Plantation Economy, The The economic system stretching between Chesapeake Bay and Brazil that produced crops, especially sugar, cotton, and tobacco, using slave labor on large estates.

Platonism Philosophy of Plato that posits preexistent Ideal Forms of which all earthly things are imperfect models.

plebeians (PLEB-bee-ans) The hereditary lower class of early Republican Rome.

plenitude of power The teaching that the popes have power over all other bishops of the church.

pogroms (PO-grohms) Organized riots against Jews in the Russian Empire.

polis (PO-lis) (plural, *poleis*) The basic Greek political unit. Usually, but incompletely, translated as "city-state," the Greeks thought of the *polis* as a community of citizens theoretically descended from a common ancestor.

politique Ruler or person in a position of power who puts the success and well-being of his or her state above all else.

polygyny (po-LIJ-eh-nee) The practice of having two or more wives or concubines at the same time.

polytheism (PAH-lee-thee-ism) The worship of many gods

pontifex maximus (PON-ti-feks MAK-suh-muss) Meaning "supreme priest." The chief priest of ancient Rome. The title was later assumed by the popes.

Popular Front A government of all left-wing parties that took power in France in 1936 to enact social and economic reforms.

populares (PO-pew-lar-es) Roman politicians who sought to pursue a political career based on the support of the people rather than just the aristocracy.

positivism The philosophy of Auguste Comte that science is the final, or positive, stage of human intellectual development because it involves exact descriptions of phenomena, without recourse to unobservable operative principles, such as gods or spirits.

Pragmatic Sanction The legal basis negotiated by the Emperor Charles VI (r. 1711–1740) for the Habsburg succession through his daughter Maria Theresa (r. 1740–1780).

predestination The doctrine that God had foreordained all souls to salvation (the "elect") or damnation. It was especially associated with Calvinism.

presbyter (PRESS-bi-ter) Meaning "elder." A person who directed the affairs of early Christian congregations.

Presbyterians Scottish Calvinists and English Protestants who advocated a national church composed of semiautonomous congregations governed by "presbyteries."

proconsulship (PRO-con-sul-ship) In Republican Rome, the extension of a consul's imperium beyond the end of his term of office to allow him to continue to command an army in the field.

Protestant Ethic The theory propounded by Max Weber in 1904 that the religious confidence and self-disciplined activism that were supposedly associated with Protestantism produced an ethic that stimulated the spirit of emergent capitalism.

Ptolemaic (tow-LEM-a-ick) **System** The pre-Copernican explanation of the universe, with the earth at the center of the universe, originated in the ancient world.

Punic (PEW-nick) **Wars** Three wars between Rome and Carthage for dominance of the western Mediterranean that were fought from 264 B.C.E. to 146 B.C.E.

Puritans English Protestants who sought to "purify" the Church of England of any vestiges of Catholicism.

Qur'an (kuh-RAN) Meaning "a reciting." The Islamic bible, which Muslims believe God revealed to the prophet Muhammad.

racism The pseudoscientific theory that biological features of race determine human character and worth.

raison d'état (RAY-suhn day-TAH) Meaning "reason of state." Concept that the interests of the state justify a course of action.

realism The style of art and literature that seeks to depict the physical world and human life with scientific objectivity and detached observation.

Reformation The sixteenth-century religious movement that sought to reform the Roman Catholic Church and led to the establishment of Protestantism.

regular clergy Monks and nuns who belong to religious orders.

Reichstag (RIKES-stahg) The German parliament, which existed in various forms, until 1945.

Reign of Terror The period between the summer of 1793 and the end of July 1794 when the French revolutionary state used extensive executions and violence to defend the Revolution and suppress its alleged internal enemies.

relativity The scientific theory associated with Einstein that time and space exist not separately but as a combined continuum whose measurement depends as much on the observer as on the entities that are being measured.

Renaissance The revival of ancient learning and the supplanting of traditional religious beliefs by new secular and scientific values that began in Italy in the fourteenth and fifteenth centuries.

reparations The requirement incorporated into the Versailles Treaty that Germany should pay for the cost of World War I.

revisionism The advocacy among nineteenth-century German socialists of achieving a humane socialist society through the evolution of democratic institutions, not revolution.

robot (ROW-boht) The amount of labor landowners demanded from peasants in the Habsburg Monarchy before 1848.

Romanitas (row-MAN-ee-tas) Meaning "Romanness." The spread of the Roman way of life and the sense of identifying with Rome across the Roman Empire.

romanticism A reaction in early-nineteenth-century literature, philosophy, and religion against what many considered the excessive rationality and scientific narrowness of the Enlightenment.

SA The Nazi parliamentary forces, or storm troopers.

sans-culottes (SAHN coo-LOTS) Meaning "without kneebreeches." The lower-middle classes and artisans of Paris during the French Revolution.

Schlieffen (SHLEE-fun) **Plan** Germany's plan for achieving a quick victory in the West at the outbreak of World War I by invading France through Belgium and Luxembourg.

Scholasticism Method of study based on logic and dialectic that dominated the medieval schools. It assumed that truth already existed; students had only to organize, elucidate, and defend knowledge learned from authoritative texts, especially those of Aristotle and the Church Fathers.

scientific induction Scientific method in which generalizations are derived from data gained from empirical observations.

scientific revolution The sweeping change in the scientific view of the universe that occurred in the sixteenth and seventeenth centuries. The new scientific concepts and the method of their construction became the standard for assessing the validity of knowledge in the West.

scutage Monetary payments by a vassal to a lord in place of the required military service.

Second Industrial Revolution The emergence of new industries and the spread of industrialization from Britain to other countries, especially Germany and the United States, in the second half of the nineteenth century.

secular clergy Parish clergy who did not belong to a religious order.

seigneur (sane-YOUR) A noble French landlord.

Sejm (SHEM) The legislative assembly of the Polish nobility.

serfs Peasants tied to the land they tilled.

Shi-a (SHE-ah) The minority of Muslims who trace their beliefs from the caliph Ali who was assassinated in 661 C.E.

Sinn Fein (SHIN FAHN) Meaning "ourselves alone." An Irish political movement founded in 1905 that advocated complete political separation from Britain.

social Darwinism The application of Darwin's concept of "the survival of the fittest" to explain evolution in nature to human social relationships.

Sophists (SO-fists) Professional teachers who emerged in Greece in the mid–fifth century B.C.E. who were paid to teach techniques of rhetoric, dialectic, and argumentation.

soviets Workers and soldiers councils formed in Russia during the Revolution.

spinning jenny A machine invented in England by James Hargreaves around 1765 to mass-produce thread.

SS The chief security units of the Nazi state.

Stoics (STOW-icks) A philosophical school founded by Zeno of Citium (335–263 B.C.E.) that taught that umans could only be happy with natural law. Human misery was caused by passion, which was a disease of the soul. The wise sought *apatheia*, freedom from passion.

studia humanitatis (STEW-dee-a hew-MAHN-ee tah-tis) During the Renaissance, a liberal arts program of study that embraced grammar, rhetoric, poetry, history, philosophy, and politics.

Sturm und Drang (SHTURM und DRAHNG) Meaning "storm and stress." A movement in German romantic literature and philosophy that emphasized feeling and emotion.

suffragettes British women who lobbied and agitated for the right to vote in the early twentieth century.

summa (SUE-ma) An authoritative summary in the Middle Ages of all that was allegedly known about a subject.

Sunna (SOON-ah) Meaning "tradition." The dominant Islamic group.

Sunnis Those who follow the "tradition" (sunna) of the Prophet Muhammed. They are the dominant movement within Islam to which the vast majority of Muslims adhere.

symposium (SIM-po-see-um) The carefully organized drinking party that was the center of Greek aristocratic social life. It featured games, songs, poetry, and even philosophical disputation.

syncretism (SIN-cret-ism) The intermingling of different religions to form an amalgam that contained elements from each.

syndicalism French labor movement that sought to improve workers' conditions through direct action, especially general strikes.

Table of Ranks An official hierarchy established by Peter the Great in imperial Russia that equated a person's social position and privileges with his rank in the state bureaucracy or army.

tabula rasa (tah-BOO-lah RAH-sah) Meaning a "blank page." The philosophical belief associated with John Locke that human beings enter the world with totally nformed characters that are completely shaped by experience.

taille (TIE) The direct tax on the French peasantry.

Ten lost tribes The Israelites who were scattered and lost to history when the northern kingdom of Israel fell to the Assyrians in 722 B.C.E.

tertiaries (TER-she-air-ees) Laypeople affiliated with the monastic life who took vows of poverty, chastity, and obedience but remained in the world.

tetrarchy (TET-rar-key) Diocletian's (r. 306–337 C.E.) system for ruling the Roman Empire by four men with power divided territorially.

Thermidorean Reaction The reaction against the radicalism of the French Revolution that began in July 1794. Associated with the end of terror and establishment of the Directory.

thesis, antithesis, and synthesis G. W. F. Hegel's (HAY-gle) (1770–1831) concept of how ideas develop. The *thesis* is a dominant set of ideas. It is challenged by a set of conflicting ideas, the *antithesis*. From the clash of these ideas, a new pattern of thought, the *synthesis*, emerges and eventually becomes the new thesis.

Third Estate The branch of the French Estates General representing all of the kingdom outside the nobility and the clergy.

Third Reich (RIKE) Hitler's regime in Germany, which lasted from 1933 to 1945.

Thirty-Nine Articles (1563) The official statement of the beliefs of the Church of England. They established a moderate form of Protestantism.

three-field system A medieval innovation that increased the amount of land under cultivation by leaving only one-third fallow in a given year.

transportation The British policy from the late eighteenth to the mid–nineteenth centuries of shipping persons convicted of the most serious offenses to Australia as an alternative to capital punishment.

transubstantiation The doctrine that the entire substances of the bread and wine are changed in the Eucharist into the body and blood of Christ.

tribunes (TRIB-unes)   Roman officials who had to be plebeians and were elected by the plebeian assembly to protect plebeians from the arbitrary power of the magistrates.

ulema (oo-LEE-mah)   Meaning "persons with correct knowledge." The Islamic scholarly elite who served a social function similar to the Christian clergy.

Upper Egypt   The part of Egypt that runs from the delta to the Sudanese border.

utilitarianism   The theory associated with Jeremy Bentham (1748–1832) that the principle of utility, defined as the greatest good for the greatest number of people, should be applied to government, the economy, and the judicial system.

utopian socialism   Early-nineteenth-century theories that sought to replace the existing capitalist structure and values with visionary solutions or ideal communities.

vassal   A person granted an estate or cash payments in return for accepting the obligation to render services to a lord.

vernacular   The everyday language spoken by the people as opposed to Latin.

vingtième (VEN-tee-em)   Meaning "one-twentieth." A tax on income in France before the Revolution.

Vulgate   The Latin translation of the Bible by Jerome (348–420 C.E.) that became the standard bible used by the Catholic Church.

Waldensians (wahl-DEN-see-ens)   Medieval heretics who advocated biblical simplicity in reaction to the worldliness of the church.

war communism   The economic policy adopted by the Bolsheviks during the Russian Civil War to seize the banks, heavy industry, railroads, and grain.

war guilt clause   Clause 231 of the Versailles Treaty, which assigned responsibility for World War I solely to Germany.

water frame   A water-powered device invented by Richard Arkwright to produce a more durable cotton fabric. It led to the shift in the production of cotton textiles from households to factories.

Weimar (Why-mar) **Republic**   The German democratic regime that existed between the end of World War I and Hitler's coming to power in 1933.

White Russians   Those Russians who opposed the Bolsheviks (the "Reds") in the Russian Civil War of 1918–1921.

zemstvos (ZEMPST-vohs)   Local governments set up in the Russian Empire in 1864.

Zionism   The movement to create a Jewish state in Palestine (the Biblical Zion).

Zollverein (TZOL-fuh-rine)   A free-trade union established among the major German states in 1834.

INDEX

Italic page numbers refer to illustrations.

H

SINGLE PC LICENSE AGREEMENT AND LIMITED WARRANTY

READ THIS LICENSE CAREFULLY BEFORE OPENING THIS PACKAGE. BY OPENING THIS PACKAGE, YOU ARE AGREEING TO THE TERMS AND CONDITIONS OF THIS LICENSE. IF YOU DO NOT AGREE, DO NOT OPEN THE PACKAGE. PROMPTLY RETURN THE UNOPENED PACKAGE AND ALL ACCOMPANYING ITEMS TO THE PLACE YOU OBTAINED THEM [[FOR A FULL REFUND OF ANY SUMS YOU HAVE PAID FOR THE SOFTWARE]]. *THESE TERMS APPLY TO ALL LICENSED SOFTWARE ON THE DISK EXCEPT THAT THE TERMS FOR USE OF ANY SHAREWARE OR FREEWARE ON THE DISKETTES ARE AS SET FORTH IN THE ELECTRONIC LICENSE LOCATED ON THE DISK:*

1. GRANT OF LICENSE and OWNERSHIP: The enclosed computer programs and data ("Software") are licensed, not sold, to you by Prentice-Hall, Inc. ("We" or the "Company") and in consideration of your purchase or adoption of the accompanying Company textbooks and/or other materials, and your agreement to these terms. We reserve any rights not granted to you. You own only the disk(s) but we and/or our licensors own the Software itself. This license allows you to use and display your copy of the Software on a single computer (i.e., with a single CPU) at a single location for academic use only, so long as you comply with the terms of this Agreement. You may make one copy for back up, or transfer your copy to another CPU, provided that the Software is usable on only one computer.

2. RESTRICTIONS: You may not transfer or distribute the Software or documentation to anyone else. Except for backup, you may not copy the documentation or the Software. You may not network the Software or otherwise use it on more than one computer or computer terminal at the same time. You may not reverse engineer, disassemble, decompile, modify, adapt, translate, or create derivative works based on the Software or the Documentation. You may be held legally responsible for any copying or copyright infringement which is caused by your failure to abide by the terms of these restrictions.

3. TERMINATION: This license is effective until terminated. This license will terminate automatically without notice from the Company if you fail to comply with any provisions or limitations of this license. Upon termination, you shall destroy the Documentation and all copies of the Software. All provisions of this Agreement as to limitation and disclaimer of warranties, limitation of liability, remedies or damages, and our ownership rights shall survive termination.

4. LIMITED WARRANTY AND DISCLAIMER OF WARRANTY: Company warrants that for a period of 60 days from the date you purchase or adopt the accompanying textbook, the Software, when properly installed and used in accordance with the Documentation, will operate in substantial conformity with the description of the Software set forth in the Documentation, and that for a period of 30 days the disk(s) on which the Software is delivered shall be free from defects in materials and workmanship under normal use. The Company does not warrant that the Software will meet your requirements or that the operation of the Software will be uninterrupted or error-free. Your only remedy and the Company's only obligation under these limited warranties is, at the Company's option, return of the disk for a refund of any amounts paid for it by you or replacement of the disk. THIS LIMITED WARRANTY IS THE ONLY WARRANTY PROVIDED BY THE COMPANY AND ITS LICENSORS, AND THE COMPANY AND ITS LICENSORS DISCLAIM ALL OTHER WARRANTIES, EXPRESS OR IMPLIED, INCLUDING WITHOUT LIMITATION, THE IMPLIED WARRANTIES OF MERCHANTABILITY AND FITNESS FOR A PARTICULAR PURPOSE. THE COMPANY DOES NOT WARRANT, GUARANTEE OR MAKE ANY REPRESENTATION REGARDING THE ACCURACY, RELIABILITY, CURRENTNESS, USE, OR RESULTS OF USE, OF THE SOFTWARE.

5. LIMITATION OF REMEDIES AND DAMAGES: IN NO EVENT, SHALL THE COMPANY OR ITS EMPLOYEES, AGENTS, LICENSORS, OR CONTRACTORS BE LIABLE FOR ANY INCIDENTAL, INDIRECT, SPECIAL, OR CONSEQUENTIAL DAMAGES ARISING OUT OF OR IN CONNECTION WITH THIS LICENSE OR THE SOFTWARE, INCLUDING FOR LOSS OF USE, LOSS OF DATA, LOSS OF INCOME OR PROFIT, OR OTHER LOSSES, SUSTAINED AS A RESULT OF INJURY TO ANY PERSON, OR LOSS OF OR DAMAGE TO PROPERTY, OR CLAIMS OF THIRD PARTIES, EVEN IF THE COMPANY OR AN AUTHORIZED REPRESENTATIVE OF THE COMPANY HAS BEEN ADVISED OF THE POSSIBILITY OF SUCH DAMAGES. IN NO EVENT SHALL THE LIABILITY OF THE COMPANY FOR DAMAGES WITH RESPECT TO THE SOFTWARE EXCEED THE AMOUNTS ACTUALLY PAID BY YOU, IF ANY, FOR THE SOFTWARE OR THE ACCOMPANYING TEXTBOOK. BECAUSE SOME JURISDICTIONS DO NOT ALLOW THE LIMITATION OF LIABILITY IN CERTAIN CIRCUMSTANCES, THE ABOVE LIMITATIONS MAY NOT ALWAYS APPLY TO YOU.

6. GENERAL: THIS AGREEMENT SHALL BE CONSTRUED IN ACCORDANCE WITH THE LAWS OF THE UNITED STATES OF AMERICA AND THE STATE OF NEW YORK, APPLICABLE TO CONTRACTS MADE IN NEW YORK, AND SHALL BENEFIT THE COMPANY, ITS AFFILIATES AND ASSIGNEES. HIS AGREEMENT IS THE COMPLETE AND EXCLUSIVE STATEMENT OF THE AGREEMENT BETWEEN YOU AND THE COMPANY AND SUPERSEDES ALL PROPOSALS OR PRIOR AGREEMENTS, ORAL, OR WRITTEN, AND ANY OTHER COMMUNICATIONS BETWEEN YOU AND THE COMPANY OR ANY REPRESENTATIVE OF THE COMPANY RELATING TO THE SUBJECT MATTER OF THIS AGREEMENT. If you are a U.S. Government user, this Software is licensed with "restricted rights" as set forth in subparagraphs (a)-(d) of the Commercial Computer-Restricted Rights clause at FAR 52.227-19 or in subparagraphs (c)(1)(ii) of the Rights in Technical Data and Computer Software clause at DFARS 252.227-7013, and similar clauses, as applicable.

Should you have any questions concerning this agreement or if you wish to contact the Company for any reason, please contact in writing: Legal Department, Prentice Hall, One Lake Street, Upper Saddle River, NJ 07458. If you need assistance with technical difficulties, call: 1-800-677-6337.